Oxford Textbook of Psychopathology

Oxford Textbook of Psychopathology

Third Edition

Edited by

PAUL H. BLANEY, ROBERT F. KRUEGER,
AND THEODORE MILLON

OXFORD
UNIVERSITY PRESS

Oxford University Press is a department of the University of
Oxford. It furthers the University's objective of excellence in research,
scholarship, and education by publishing worldwide.

Oxford   New York
Auckland   Cape Town   Dar es Salaam   Hong Kong   Karachi
Kuala Lumpur   Madrid   Melbourne   Mexico City   Nairobi
New Delhi   Shanghai   Taipei   Toronto

With offices in
Argentina   Austria   Brazil   Chile   Czech Republic   France   Greece
Guatemala   Hungary   Italy   Japan   Poland   Portugal   Singapore
South Korea   Switzerland   Thailand   Turkey   Ukraine   Vietnam

Oxford is a registered trademark of Oxford University Press
in the UK and certain other countries.

Published in the United States of America by
Oxford University Press
198 Madison Avenue, New York, NY 10016

Library of Congress Cataloging-in-Publication Data
Oxford textbook of psychopathology / edited by Paul H. Blaney, Robert F. Krueger,
Theodore Millon. — Third edition.
pages cm
Includes bibliographical references and index.
ISBN 978–0–19–981177–9
1. Psychology, Pathological.   I. Blaney, Paul H.   II. Krueger, Robert F.   III. Millon, Theodore.
RC454.O94 2015
616.89—dc23
2014017943

1 3 5 7 9 8 6 4 2
Printed in the United States of America
on acid-free paper

Contents

Preface

Although this *Textbook* may also serve active professionals by providing them with reviews and updates, it is aimed primarily at graduate students taking an advanced survey course in abnormal psychology. Among texts that might be used in such courses, it has two distinctive aspects. It gives unusually thorough coverage of the personality disorders. And throughout the book the focus is on what is known about the disorders themselves; while assessment and intervention are sometimes mentioned, they are not covered systematically.

We assume that, when studying this book, the reader has *DSM-5* at hand, and that systematic repetition of disorder criteria here would be an unwarranted redundancy.

As with the prior two editions of this *Textbook*, it is the product of an effort to enlist the best possible array of experts on the major emotional disorders, and to charge those individuals with the task of summarizing what future mental health professionals should know. Authors were given considerable latitude; as a result, the reader is exposed to a variety of outlooks and emphases when moving from chapter to chapter.

The roster of chapters shows substantial continuity from prior editions. There are a few changes, related mainly to *DSM-5* innovations and to our decision to add some coverage of developmental psychopathology. Changes within the chapters reflect recent progress in the field, plus (in the case of returning authors) developments in these individuals' thinking. In addition, we specifically asked authors to submit revised chapter manuscripts *after* consulting *DSM-5* as published in May, 2013.

We have departed from standard citation practice by avoiding *DSM* and *ICD* listings in chapter References sections. Thus, though *DSM-5* is mentioned in most chapters, it is found among the references of none of them. Lest there be any uncertainty, *DSM-I* refers to the original version of the *Diagnostic and Statistical Manual of Mental Disorders* (1952), *DSM-II* to the 1968 version, *DSM-III* to the 1980 version, *DSM-III-R* to the 1987 revision, *DSM-IV* to the 1994 version, *DSM-IV-TR* to the 2000 text revision, and *DSM-5* to the edition in current use—all published by the American Psychiatric Association in Washington, DC. Likewise, *ICD* does not appear among chapter references, so mention of *ICD-10* should, for instance, be understood to refer to the *Tenth Revision of the International Classification of Diseases*, published in Geneva in 1992 by the World Health Organization.

Paul H. Blaney   Emory, Virginia
Robert F. Krueger   Minneapolis, Minnesota
Theodore Millon   Port Jervis, New York
August, 2013

About the Editors

Theodore Millon, Ph.D, Sc.D
August 18, 1928–January 29, 2014
Theodore Millon grew up in New York City and earned his B.A. and M.A. degrees from the City College of New York and his Ph.D. from the University of Connecticut. He held faculty appointments at Lehigh University, the University of Illinois, the University of Miami, and Harvard Medical School, and served as Dean and Scientific Director of the Institute for Advanced Studies in Personology and Psychopathology. His classic text *Modern Psychopathology* was published in 1969, and in the ensuing years, his many books included *Disorders of Personality* (1981) and its three revisions, *Toward a New Personology* (1990), *Masters of the Mind* (2004), and *Moderating Severe Personality Disorders* (2007). His enormous impact on the assessment of personality and psychopathology started in 1977 with the Millon Clinical Multiaxial Inventory (MCMI) and continued with the eventual publication of MCMI revisions and with the introduction of related assessment instruments. He was the founding co-editor of the *Journal of Personality Disorders*, the co-founder and president of the International Society for the Study of Personality Disorders, and the American editor of *Psychology & Health: An International Journal*. His many recognitions include an Honorary Doctorate from the Free University of Brussels (1994), and the American Psychological Association's Award

for Distinguished Professional Contributions to Applied Research (2003). His strong influence on the personality disorders aspect of our diagnostic framework started with *DSM-III* and persists today.

Though the foregoing touches only on some of the high points of Dr. Millon's career, it should be obvious that his life was one of great productivity, creativity, and intellectual influence. For a much more textured picture, the reader is referred to Dr. Millon's own reminiscences, as found at http://millon.net/content/tm_bio.htm. There, one learns, for instance, that he spoke only Yiddish until entering first grade, and that he and Maurice Sendak were grade school chums!

P.H.B.

Paul H. Blaney, Ph.D.
Dr. Blaney received his B.A. degree from Eastern Nazarene College, Quincy, MA, and his Ph.D. in clinical psychology from the University of Minnesota. He held faculty positions at the University of Texas at Austin, the University of Miami (where he and Dr. Millon were colleagues), and Emory & Henry College, from which Dr. Blaney retired at the end of the 2013–14 academic year. He served on the editorial boards of a number of journals, including the *Journal of Abnormal Psychology* and the *Journal of Personality and Social Psychology*. While at the University of Miami, he was associate dean of the

College of Arts and Sciences, and from 2000 to 2005 he was dean of faculty of Emory & Henry College.

Robert F. Krueger, Ph.D.

Dr. Krueger is Hathaway Distinguished Professor and Director of Clinical Training in the Department of Psychology at the University of Minnesota. He completed his undergraduate and graduate work at the University of Wisconsin, Madison, and his clinical internship at Brown University. Professor Krueger's major interests lie at the intersection of research on psychopathology, personality disorders, psychometrics, behavior genetics, and neuroscience. He has received a number of major awards, including the University of Minnesota McKnight Land-Grant Professorship, the American Psychological Association's Award for Early Career Contributions, the Award for Early Career Contributions from the International Society for the Study of Individual Differences, and an American Psychological Foundation Theodore Millon Mid-Career Award. He is a Fellow of the American Psychopathological Association (APPA) and the Association for Psychological Science (APS), and he was inducted into the Society for Multivariate Experimental Psychology (SMEP). He is also editor of the *Journal of Personality Disorders.*

Contributors

Amitai Abramovitch
Massachusetts General Hospital & Harvard
  Medical School
Boston, MA
USA

Thomas M. Achenbach
University of Vermont
Burlington, VT
USA

Deepika Anand
Northwestern University
Evanston, IL
USA

Arnoud Arntz
Maastricht University
Maastricht
The Netherlands

Noah Berman
Massachusetts General Hospital & Harvard
  Medical School
Boston, MA
USA

David P. Bernstein
Maastricht University
Maastricht
The Netherlands

Paul H. Blaney
Emory & Henry College
Emory, VA
USA

Roger K. Blashfield
Auburn University
Auburn, AL
USA

Robert F. Bornstein
Adelphi University
Garden City, NY
USA

Theo K. Bouman
University of Groningen
Groningen
The Netherlands

Sandra A. Brown
University of California
San Diego, CA
USA

Amanda Calkins
Massachusetts General Hospital & Harvard
  Medical School
Boston, MA
USA

James M. Cantor
Centre for Addiction and Mental Health &
    University of Toronto
Toronto, Ontario
Canada

Lee Anna Clark
University of Notre Dame
South Bend, IN
USA

Wei-Jean Chung
Adelphi University
Garden City, NY
USA

Jennifer S. Coelho
Simon Fraser University and British Columbia
    Children's Hospital
Vancouver, British Columbia
Canada

Christy A. Denckla
Adelphi University
Garden City, NY
USA

Michelle L. Drapkin
Philadelphia Veterans Affairs Medical Center &
    University of Pennsylvania
Philadelphia, PA
USA

Laura E. Drislane
Florida State University
Tallahassee, FL
USA

Jack D. Edinger
National Jewish Health Center
Denver, CO
USA

Evan W. Good
Villanova University
Villanova, PA
USA

Elisabeth J. Harfmann
University of Kansas
Lawrence, KS
USA

Jill M. Hooley
Harvard University
Cambridge, MA
USA

Rick E. Ingram
University of Kansas
Lawrence, KS
USA

Sheri L. Johnson
University of California Berkeley
and
Center for Advanced Study in the Behavioral
    Sciences at Stanford University
Stanford, CA
USA

Jutta Joormann
Northwestern University
Evanston, IL
USA

Jared W. Keeley
Mississippi State University
Starkville, MS
USA

Ashley D. Kendall
Northwestern University
Evanston, IL
USA

Gun Peggy Knudsen
Norwegian Institute of Public Health
Oslo
Norway

Robert F. Krueger
University of Minnesota
Minneapolis, MN
USA

Jonathan K. Lee
Brown University
Providence, RI
USA

Joelle LeMoult
McMaster University
Hamilton, Ontario
Canada

Mark F. Lenzenweger
The State University of New York at Binghamton
Binghamton, NY
and
Weill Cornell Medical College
New York, NY
USA

Scott O. Lilienfeld
Emory University
Atlanta, GA
USA

Angus MacDonald, III
University of Minnesota
Minneapolis, MN
USA

Julia E. Mackaronis
University of Utah
Salt Lake City, UT
USA

Richard J. McNally
Harvard University
Cambridge, MA
USA

Theodore Millon
Institute for Advanced Studies in Personology
    and Psychopathology
Port Jervis, NY
USA

Charles M. Morin
Université Laval
Québec City, Québec
Canada

Hannah E. Morton
Mississippi State University
Starkville, MS
USA

Mia Nuñez
Northwestern University
Evanston, IL
USA

Shani Ofrat
University of Minnesota
Minneapolis, MN
USA

Jaap Oosterlaan
VU University Amsterdam
Emma Children's Hospital AMC
and
VU Medical Center
Amsterdam
The Netherlands

Christopher J. Patrick
Florida State University
Tallahassee, FL
USA

Kevin Pelphrey
Yale Child Study Center
New Haven, CT
USA

Michael A. Perelman
New York Presbyterian Hospital & Weill Medical
    College of Cornell University
New York, NY
USA

R. O. Pihl
McGill University
Montreal, Quebec
Canada

Aaron L. Pincus
The Pennsylvania State University
University Park, PA
USA

Michael L. Raulin
Youngstown State University
Youngstown, OH
USA

Ted Reichborn-Kjennerud
Norwegian Institute of Public Health
and
University of Oslo
Oslo
Norway

Michael J. Roche
The Pennsylvania State University
University Park, PA
USA

M. Abu Shakra
McGill University
Montreal, Quebec
Canada

Katie L. Sharp
University of Kansas
Lawrence, KS
USA

Jessica R. Skidmore
University of California
San Diego, CA
USA

Howard Steiger
McGill University & Douglas Institute
Montreal, Quebec
Canada

Donald S. Strassberg
University of Utah
Salt Lake City, UT
USA

Katherine S. Sutton
Centre for Addiction and Mental Health
Toronto, Ontario
Canada

Susan R. Tate
VA San Diego Healthcare System & University
   of California
San Diego, CA
USA

Lea Thaler
McGill University & Douglas Institute
Montreal, Quebec
Canada

Laura Travaglini
Columbia University Medical Center
New York, NY
USA

Timothy J. Trull
University of Missouri-Columbia
Columbia, MO
USA

Frederique Van den Eynde
McGill University & Douglas Institute
Montreal, Quebec
Canada

Hanneke van Ewijk
VU University Amsterdam
Amsterdam
The Netherlands

W. Michael Vanderlind
Northwestern University
Evanston, IL
USA

Fred R. Volkmar
Yale Child Study Center
New Haven, CT
USA

Sabine Wilhelm
Massachusetts General Hospital & Harvard
   Medical School
Boston, MA
USA

Christina Williams
University of Kansas
Lawrence, KS
USA

Richard E. Zinbarg
Northwestern University & The Family Institute
   at Northwestern University
Evanston, IL
USA

Part I

FOUNDATIONS

1

A Brief History of Psychopathology

THEODORE MILLON

Efforts to understand and resolve problems of psychopathology can be traced through many centuries in which solutions have taken unanticipated turns and have become enmeshed in obscure beliefs and entangled alliances, all of which have unfolded without the care and watchful eye of scientific methods (Millon, 2004). Psychopathology remains today, however, a relatively young science. Moreover, many current techniques and theories have long histories that connect current thinking to preexisting beliefs and systems of thought, many of which are intertwined in chance associations, primitive customs, and quasi-tribal quests. The path to the present is anything but a simple and straight line; it has come to its current state through an involvement in values and customs of which researchers may be only partly aware. Many are the product of historical accidents and erroneous beliefs that occurred centuries ago when mysticism and charlatanism flourished.

The traditions of psychopathology today are not themselves tight systems of thought in the strict sense of scientific theories; they certainly are neither closed nor completed constructions of ideas that have been worked out in their final details. Rather, they are products of obscure lines of historical development, movements often subject to the misunderstandings of our remote past, when a disaffection with complexities typified life. Nevertheless, interest in ourselves, in our foibles

as well as our achievements, has always been central to humans' curiosity. The origins of interest in the workings of psychopathology were connected in their earliest form to studies of astronomy and spiritual unknowns. Even before human thought had been drafted in written form, humans have asked fundamental questions, such as why we behave, think, act, and feel as we do. Although primitive in their ideas, ancient people were always open to the tragic sources in their lives. Earliest answers, however, were invariably associated with metaphysical spirits and magical spells. Only slowly were more sophisticated and scientific ideas formulated.

It was not until the sixth century B.C. that the actions, thoughts, and feelings of humans were attributed to natural forces, that is, to sources found within ourselves. Philosophers and scientists began to speculate intelligently about a wide range of psychological processes; many of their ideas turned out to be remarkably farsighted. Unfortunately, much of this imaginative and empirical work was forgotten, slowly rediscovered by careful or serendipitous efforts time and again. For example, John Locke in the seventeenth century described a clinical procedure for overcoming unusual fears; the procedure he described is not dissimilar from the systematic desensitization method developed this past century by Joseph Wolpe. Similarly, Gustav Fechner, founder of psychophysics in the mid-nineteenth century, recognized that the human brain was divided into two parallel hemispheres linked by a thin band of connecting fibers, which is now termed the *corpus callosum*. According to his speculations, if the brain were subdivided, it would create two independent realms of consciousness; in the latter part of this past century, Roger Sperry confirmed and elaborated on these speculations, in what has been referred to as split-brain research.

Every historical period has been dominated by certain beliefs that ultimately won out over previously existing conceptions while retaining elements of the old. As the study of mental science progressed, different and frequently insular traditions evolved to answer questions posed by earlier philosophers, physicians, and psychologists (Millon, 2004). Separate disciplines with specialized training procedures developed. Currently, divergent professional groups are involved in the study of the mind (e.g., the neuroscientifically oriented psychiatrist with a clear-eyed focus on biological and physiological processes; the psychoanalytic psychiatrist with an austere yet sensitive attention to unconscious or intrapsychic processes; the personological psychologist with the tools and techniques for appraising, measuring, and integrating the mind; and the academic psychologist with a penchant for empirically investigating the basic processes of behavior and cognition). Each has studied the complex questions generated by mental disorders with a different focus and emphasis. Yet the central issues remain the same. By tracing the history of each of these and other conceptual traditions, humans will learn how different modes of thought today have their roots in chance events, cultural ideologies, and accidental discoveries, as well as in brilliant and creative innovations.

From today's perspective, it seems likely that future developments in the field will reflect recent efforts to encompass and integrate biological, psychological, and sociocultural approaches. No longer will any single and restricted point of view be prominent; each approach will enrich all others as one component of a synergistic whole. Integrating the disparate parts of a clinical science—theory, nosology, diagnosis, and treatment—is the latest phase in the great chain of history that exhibits an evolution in mental science professions from ancient times to the new millennium. Intervening developments, both those that have been successful and those that have not, were genuine efforts

to answer humankind's ceaseless efforts to understand more fully who we are and why we behave the way that we do. The challenge to know who we are is unending owing to the complexity of human functioning. New concepts come to the fore each decade, and questions regarding established principles are constantly raised. Perhaps in this new century humans will bridge the varied aspects of our poignant, yet scientific, understanding of psychopathology, as well as bring the diverse traditions of the past together to form a single, overarching synthesis.

Ancient History

Primitive people and ancient civilizations alike viewed the unusual and strange within a magical and mythological frame of reference. They thought that behavior that could not be understood was controlled by animistic spirits. Although both good and evil spirits were conjectured, the bizarre and often frightening behavior of the mentally disordered led to a prevailing belief that demon spirits must inhabit them. People viewed the possession of evil spirits as a punishment for failing to obey the teachings of the gods and priests. Fears that demons might spread to afflict others often led to cruel and barbaric tortures. These primitive "therapies" of shock, starvation, and surgery have parallels in recent history, although the ancients based them on the more grossly naive conception of demonology.

What has been called the sacred approach in primitive times may be differentiated into three phases, according to Roccatagliata (1973): animistic, mythological, and demonological. These paradigms shared the view that psychopathology was the expression of transcendent magical action brought about by external forces. The *animistic* phase was based on prelogical and emotional reasoning derived from the deep connection between primitive beings and the mysterious forces of nature. From this model events happen because the world is peopled by animated entities driven by obscure and ineffable forces that act on one's mind and soul. The second phase was characterized by *mythological* beliefs; here the animistic conception was transformed so that indistinct and indefinable forces were materialized into myths. Every fact of life was imbued with the powers of a particular entity, and every symptom of a disorder was thought to be caused by a deity who, if appropriately implored, could benevolently cure it. In the third, or *demonological*, phase, the transcendent mythological deities were placed into a formal theological system such as that of Judaism or Christianity. In this latter phase, two competing forces struggled for superiority: one creative and positive, represented by a good parent or God, the other destructive and negative, represented by the willful negation of good in the form of demonic forces. These three conceptions generally followed each other historically, but some overlap did exist, with elements of one appearing in the others.

Many aspects of prehistoric life were not understood by those of the time; magic and supernatural concepts did help early humans create a measure of sense out of life's unfathomable and unpredictable character. For those weighted with life's painful realities and burdensome responsibilities, these beliefs provided a degree of order and a pseudo-logic to fears of the unknown, a repository of unfalsifiable assumptions in which supernatural events and processes filled in answers for that which could not be understood. Ultimately, supernaturalism became the dominant worldview by which the perplexing experiences of life could be objectified and comprehended. Priests and wizards became powerful, capitalizing on the fears and peculiarities of the populace to undo spells, "heal" the physically ill, and "purify" the mentally distressed. To them, spirits that possessed superhuman powers to induce or resolve psychic pathology assuredly touched the eccentric or irrational. Almost all groups permitted healing to fall into the hands of priests and magicians, a situation that still exists today in many societies. In a world populated with imaginary beings, spiritual forces could often calm humans' worst anxieties and expunge the ever-present terrors of life. Despite extensive archaeological analyses, however, knowledge of primitive times is no more than fragmentary. Nevertheless, people today may assume that primitive humans saw a world populated with spirits that were essentially illusions created by their own state of anguish or perplexity.

Many of the contributions of the early Hindus are associated with the name *Susruta*, who lived 100 years before Hippocrates. His works followed the traditional beliefs of his day regarding possible demoniacal possession. Susruta suggested that the passions and strong emotions of the mentally disordered could bring about physical ailments,

best served by psychological help. Anticipating the significance of temperament or innate dispositions, Hindu medicine proposed the existence of three emotional inclinations: wise and enlightened goodness, with its seat in the brain; impetuous passions, the source of the pleasure and pain qualities, with its seat in the chest; and blind crudity of ignorance, the basis of more animalistic instincts, with its seat in the abdomen.

A concern with mental health has long been a part of Indian cultures, which evolved a variety of ways of attempting to understand and negotiate mental disorder and psychological problems. Indians have been involved in constructing explanatory techniques for centuries. In the first formal system of medicine in India, *Ayurveda* (the book of life), physical and mental illnesses were not clearly demarcated. *Caraka Samhita* deals with medical diagnoses and management possibly dating from 600 B.C. and is the foremost text of the ancient Indian medical system. *Caraka* defines *ayu* (life) as a state consisting of *shareera* (body), *indriya* (senses), *satva* (psyche), and *atma* (soul). Soul cannot be destructed and it undergoes reincarnation. The mind is responsible for cognition and it directs the senses, controls the self, reasons, and deliberates. The equilibrium between the self and mind is paramount to good health. *Caraka* uses the term *doshas* to apply to body fluids or humors, *vata*, *pitta*, and *kapha*. The theory of doshas may have developed independently of the Greek humoral theory, or possibly the Hindu system may have traveled to Greece. Various types of food influence the mind, one's personality characteristics, and the interactions between the three doshas. Different personality types leading to mental illness, through either unwholesome diet or moral transgressions, are described in detail. In the Hindu system mental disorders are seen as largely metaphysical, but different appearances of mental disorders (like *unmada*, insanity) are described as results from heredity, imbalanced doshas, temperament, inappropriate diet, and metapsychological factors. *Caraka* also contains many descriptions of possession states regarded as arising from supernatural agents, a belief that is still apparent in many parts of society among the highly religious in India. Religious connotations and references to spiritual enlightenment were only challenged in the early nineteenth century by the emerging Western science–based medicine introduced through British rule. In India, colonial medical institutions became brick-and-mortar symbols of Western intellectual and moral power, with the European doctor being taken as the sole excuse of the empire. Indian magical practices and religious customs have been marginalized to some extent, but a variety of shamans, whose therapeutic efforts combine classical Indian alchemy, medicine, magic, and astrology with beliefs and practices from folk and popular traditions, are still present.

Many of the traditions discussed among the early Greeks and Romans can be traced to ideas generated initially in the *Babylonian Empire*. Babylonians were oriented toward astronomical events; superstitions regarding the stars produced many gods. People often sought help from the gods through magical rites, incantations, prayers, and the special powers of those who were physicians or priests. The Babylonians assigned a demon to each disease; insanity, for example, was caused by the demon *Idta*. Each demon was to be exorcised through special medicines (primarily herbs and plants), confessions, and other methods to help restore a balance between conflicting supernatural forces. As the Babylonians saw it, invariable tensions existed not only among the different gods but also, more importantly, between more or less rational and superstitious explanations of psychic ailments.

In *China*, the first medical book, *Neijing* (*The Canon of Internal Medicine*), was compiled between 300 B.C. and 100 B.C. (Liu, 1981). Organic syndromes, like epileptic seizures (*dian*) and delirium-like states, were also described, but with no clear distinction to the concept of insanity and psychosis (*kuang*). The primary causes of psychiatric illness were suggested to be vicious air, abnormal weather, and emotional stress. A famous doctor, *Zang Zhongjing*, the Hippocrates of China, introduced other concepts and syndromes, such as febrile delirium, globus hystericus, and puerperal psychosis, in his *Jin Kui Yao Lue* (*A Sketchbook in a Golden Box*). Chinese medicine has tended to explain pathology change by means of philosophical concepts, and this framework has undergone little change. It involves the notion of the complementary yin and yang; the five elements gold, wood, water, fire, and earth; and the principle of Tao (i.e., the way), which is considered the ultimate regulator of the universe and the most desirable state of well-being and longevity, achieved by integrating the individual self into

the realm of nature. These ontological principles were described in *The Yellow Emperor's Classic of Internal Medicine* some 20 centuries ago (Liu, 1981). Different personality types were portrayed on the basis of a combination of the five elements—the fiery type, the earthy type, the golden type, and the watery type. Phenomena occurring inside people were understood in phenomena occurring outside in nature. Chinese medicine later became organ oriented. Every visceral organ was believed to have charge of a specific function. The heart was thought to house the mind, the liver to control the spiritual soul, the lung the animal soul, the spleen ideas and intelligence, and the kidney vitality and will. No attention was paid to the brain! For a long time psychiatric symptoms were interspersed with those of physical disease. The dichotomy of mind–body was not a central theme. Mood disturbances and psychiatric symptoms attributed to menstrual irregularities tended to be expressed in somatic terms. In *Chin-Yue's Medical Book* the Chinese word for depression literally meant stagnation, implying an obstruction of vital air circulation in the body (Liu, 1981). Case vignettes of patients deceiving sickness, that is, hysterical neurosis, were presented in the same book explaining symptom formation in people trapped in very difficult situations. In a similar way, sexual impotence was explained by excessive worry. In summary, psychiatric concepts of mental illness in China have undergone basically the same sequence from supernatural, natural, somatic, and psychological stages. Chinese medicine has been relatively less influenced by religious thoughts compared to the extent observed in Europe, where patients in the Middle Ages were declared by the priest to be bewitched and punished. Acupuncture, traditional Chinese medicine, folk herbs, and psychotherapy have been the most commonly used treatment approaches in Chinese medicine.

In *Egypt*, as in other early civilizations, evidence exists that the heart was thought to be the center of mental activity. Egyptians also had difficulty separating prevailing supernatural beliefs from those that could be observed and modified in nature. Astronomical phenomena were the primary objects of worship. Egyptians usually turned "natural" qualities aside in favor of the mystical powers of the gods. Over the course of a century or two, Egyptian philosophers and physicians began studying the brain, ultimately recognizing it as the primary source of mental activity.

In the earliest periods of *Greek* civilization, people considered insanity to be a divine punishment, a sign of guilt for minor or major transgressions. Therapy sought to combat madness by conducting various expiatory rites that removed impurities, the cause of the disorder. Priests mediated the ill person's prayers to the gods so as to assure his or her cure. Thus, with divine help, the person could be purified of the disorder's evil. Albeit slowly, Greek scholars realized that external, but unseen, agents could no longer serve as a logical basis for an explanation of mentally troublesome phenomena. They began to recognize the necessity of understanding how and why mental disorders were expressed in the natural world, and a more tangible and realistic perspective began to emerge. A number of imaginative thinkers led this transition in the fifth and sixth centuries B.C. A central intellectual effort of Greek philosophers was the desire to reduce the vastness of the universe to its fundamental elements. Most proposed that complexities could be simplified to one element—water, air, or fire. Their task was to identify the unit of which all aspects of the universe were composed.

Among the first philosopher-scientists to tackle this task was *Thales (625?–?547 B.C.)*. What little historians know of Thales comes largely from the writings of later Greek philosophers, notably Aristotle and Plato, and the historian Herodotus. According to this nimble-witted Greek, the fundamental unit of the universe was a tangible and identifiable substance: water.

Though Thales was not the prime forerunner of a modern understanding of mental processes, as a radical thinker he redirected attention away from mysticism, recognizing that psychic disorders were natural events that should be approached from a realistic perspective. Equally significant was Thales's view that efforts should be made to uncover underlying principles on which overt phenomena were based. Oriented to find these principles in physical studies and "geometric proportions," he turned to magnetic phenomena, convinced that the essential element of all life was its animating properties. To Thales, action and movement, based on balanced or disarrayed magnetic forces, distinguished human frailty. In this belief, he further derogated the view that external supernatural forces intruded on the psyche; rather, he believed that the source of pathology was inherent within persons themselves.

Paralleling the views of Thales, *Pythagoras (circa 580–circa 500 B.C.)* reasserted the importance of identifying the underlying scientific principles that may account for all forms of behavior. He differed from Thales in that he retrogressively preferred to use ethics and religion as the basis for deriving his principles. More progressively, however, Pythagoras was the first philosopher to claim definitively that the brain was the organ of the human intellect, as well as the source of mental disturbances. He adopted an early notion of biological humors, that is, naturally occurring bodily liquids, as well as positing the concept of emotional temperament to aid in decoding the origins of aberrant passions and behavior. The mathematical principles of balance and ratio served to account for variations in human characterological styles (e.g., degrees of moisture or dryness, proportion of cold or hot). Balances or imbalances among humoral fundamentals would account for whether health or disease was present. Possessing a deep regard for his "universal principles," he applied his ideas to numerous human, ethical, and religious phenomena. Though he believed in immortality and the transmigration of souls, Pythagoras made a serious effort to articulate the inner "equilibrium" of human anatomy and health.

Pythagoras considered mental life as reflecting a harmony between antithetical forces: good–bad, love–hate, single–plural, limited–unlimited. Life was regulated according to his conception of opposing rhythmic movements (e.g., sleep–wakefulness, inspiring–expiring). Mental disorders reflected a disequilibrium of these basic harmonies. To him, the soul could rise from or descend to the body. The more the soul was healthy, in balance, and without psychic symptoms, the more it resembled solar energy. Pythagoras spoke of the soul as composed of three parts: *reason*, which reflected truth; *intelligence*, which synthesized sensory perceptions; and *impulse*, which derived from bodily energies. The rational parts of the soul were centered in the brain; the irrational one, in the heart. Incidentally, Pythagoras coined the term *philosophy*, putting together the words *philo*, meaning "love," and *sophia*, meaning "wisdom."

Also of value during this early period was the work of *Alcmaeon (557–491 B.C.)*, possibly the son or favorite student of Pythagoras. Alcmaeon became a philosopher-physiologist who asserted that the central nervous system was the physical source of mental activity. He asserted that cerebral metabolism was based on the stability of "the humoral fluxes," which, if imbalanced or unstable, would create shifts in cerebral tissue functioning, leading then to various mental disorders. Metabolic fluxes were caused by a disequilibrium between the nervous system's qualities of dry–moist and hot–cold.

Most notable were Alcmaeon's efforts to track the sensory nerves as they ascended to the brain. Through methods of careful dissection, he articulated, as perhaps no one before him had done, the structural anatomy of the body. No less significant was his conviction that the brain, rather than the heart, was the organ of thought. He also anticipated the work of Empedocles and Hippocrates in his belief that health called for a balance among the essential components of life—coolness versus warmth, wetness versus dryness, and so on. The notion of fundamental elements in balance became a central theme of his work. Alcmaeon's "biological model," based on the concept of metabolic harmony called *isonomy*, took the place of the Greeks' early mythological theology and was an extension of the growing secular and democratic spirit of the Greeks' sixth-century-B.C. culture.

Empedocles (circa 490–430 B.C.) adopted the homeostatic model generated in the work of Pythagoras and Alcmaeon. Most significant was his proposal that the basic elements of life (fire, earth, air, and water) interacted with two other "principles" (love versus strife). Empedocles stressed that a balance among the four elements could be complicated by the fact that they might combine in either a complementary or a counteractive way. Love and strife represented human expression of more elementary magnetic processes such as attraction or repulsion. All of the elements/humors could be combined, but Empedocles wondered what the consequences would be if they were organized in different ways. He set out to weave the several threads of his theory and concluded that the force of attraction (love) would likely bring forth a harmonic unity, whereas repulsion (strife) would set the stage for a personal breakdown or social disintegration.

To Empedocles, blood was a perfect representation of an equal mix of water, earth, air, and fire. He therefore suggested that persons with problematic temperaments and mental disorders would exhibit imbalances within their blood. Among his other contributions, Empedocles posited a rudimentary model of an evolutionary theory, one anticipating Darwin's theory by 2,000 years. As he phrased it, "creatures that survive are those whose blood elements are accidentally compounded in a suitable way," whereas a problematic compounding will produce "creatures that will perish and die" (Roccatagliata, 1973). To him, nature created a wide variety of healthful and perishing blood configurations, that is, different ways in which the four elements combined.

Anaxagoras (circa 500–circa 428 B.C.) asserted that a reduction to the basic elements could not explain the universe. He asserted that there were an endless number of qualitatively different elements. It was the organization or arrangement of these diverse elements that was central to the structure of the universe. Anaxagoras's belief that the character of these constituents could not be explained except through the action of human thought was novel, a view similar to one asserted some centuries later by the *phenomenologists* and the *Gestaltists*, who claimed that the structure of objective matter was largely in the interpretive eye of the perceiver.

Later, the philosopher *Democritus (circa 460–circa 370 B.C.)*, following *Leucippus (ca. 445 B.C.)*, proposed that the universe was made of variously shaped atoms, small particles of matter in constant motion, differing in size and form, but always moving and combining into the many complex components that comprise the universe as we know it. This innovative speculation endures to the present time. Extending the theme proposed a century earlier by Anaxagoras, Democritus stressed the view that all truths are relative and subjective. As noted, he asserted that matter was composed of numerous invisible particles called atoms. Each atom was composed of different shapes that combined and were linked in numerous ways, an idea based on pure speculation but one highly innovative and essentially correct to this day. The physical thesis of contemporary times known as the *Heisenberg uncertainty principle* also finds its origins in Democritus's speculation.

A contemporary of Democritus—born the same year—became the great philosopher-physician who set the groundwork for sophisticated clinical medicine for the ensuing centuries. The fertility of this wondrous period of Grecian thought cannot be overestimated, ranging from the brilliant ideas of Democritus and Aristotle to the creative foundations of scientific medicine by Hippocrates.

Hippocrates (circa 460–circa 377 B.C.) (Figure 1.1) was born on the island of Cos, the center of an ancient medical school. He was the son of an Aesculapian priest from whom he acquired his first medical lessons and whose philosophy he would follow in his own future therapeutic efforts. In Hippocrates's work, the inheritor of his father's tradition and of the humoral concepts of Pythagoras and Empedocles, mental disorders progressed from the magical and mythical realm, and the demonological and superstitious therapeutic approaches of an earlier era, to one of careful clinical observation and inductive theorizing. He synthesized the practical and sympathetic elements of the Aesculapian cult with the more "biological" proposals of Pythagoras, blending these elements to elevate mental processes and disequilibria into a clinical science.

The work of Hippocrates highlighted the naturalistic view that the source of all disorders, mental and physical alike, should be sought within the patient and not within spiritual phenomena. For example, the introductory notes to the Hippocratic book on epilepsy state:

It seems to me to be no more divine and no more sacred than other diseases, but like other affections, it springs from natural causes....Those

Figure 1.1 Portrait of Hippocrates.

who first connected this illness with demons and described it as sacred seem to me no different from the conjurers, purificators, mountebanks and charlatans of our day. Such persons are merely concealing, under the cloak of godliness, their perplexity and their inability to afford any assistance....It is not a god which injures the body, but disease. (Hippocrates, 400 B.C.)

As with a number of his progenitors, Hippocrates emphasized that the brain was the primary center of thought, intelligence, and emotions. It is only from within the brain, he asserted, that pleasures, joys, and laughter arise, as well as sorrows, grief, and tears. This very same source makes humans mad or delirious; inspires dread and fear; and brings sleeplessness, inopportune mistakes, aimless anxieties, absentmindedness, and other acts contrary to habitual ways.

Hippocrates's approach was essentially empirical, despite the growing eminence of philosophical thought that characterized his time. As a practical biologist, he stressed the role of the humors of the body, focusing on the use of physical rather than philosophical treatments. Remedies stressed the value of sleep and rest. Central to the medical practices of Hippocrates and his followers was the crucial role given keen observation and fact gathering. Contrary to the thesis of Plato, which addressed abstract hypotheses and so-called self-evident truths, Hippocrates focused his attention on observable symptoms, their treatments, and their eventual outcomes. In this regard, Hippocrates modeled Aristotle's empirical orientation.

Like a number of his forebears, Hippocrates was convinced that dreams could serve as indicators of health or illness. Mental pathology stemmed from a disparity between the content of dreams and the reality of existence. Dream symbolism led him to anticipate later hypotheses concerning the operation of "unconscious forces." Hippocrates also established the tradition of carefully recording personal case histories, detailing the course and outcome of the disorders he observed. These histories have offered surprisingly accurate descriptions of disorders such as depression, phobias, convulsions, and migraines. He provided a logic for differentiating the various mental ailments, not only among those now labeled the *DSM-IV-TR* Axis I syndromes but also among Axis II personality types, the latter construed as abnormalities of temperament.

Hippocrates associated temperament with the "four humors" model, which transformed earth, fire, water, and air into their parallel bodily elements. He characterized individuals in terms of which one of the four elements predominated. Among other clinical syndromes differentiated were delirium, phobia, hysteria, and mania. Lacking precise observations of bodily structure and prevented by taboo from performing dissections, Hippocratic physicians proposed hypothetical explanations of disease. They adhered closely, however, to the first nonsupernatural schema that specified temperament dimensions in accord with the doctrine of bodily humors. Interestingly, history has come full circle in that much of contemporary psychiatry continues to seek answers with reference to inner biochemical and endocrinological processes.

Hippocrates identified four basic temperaments: the *choleric*, the *melancholic*, the *sanguine*, and the *phlegmatic*; these corresponded, respectively, to excesses in yellow bile, black bile, blood, and phlegm. Elaborated on by the Roman *Galen*, centuries later, the choleric temperament was associated with a tendency toward irascibility, the melancholic temperament was characterized by an inclination toward sadness, the sanguine temperament prompted the individual toward optimism, and the phlegmatic temperament was conceived of as an apathetic disposition. Although the doctrine of humors has long been abandoned, it persists in contemporary expressions such as *sanguine* or *good-humored*.

Hippocrates and his Cos associates were among the first to stress the need for a relationship between diagnosis and treatment. The mere description of a clinical disturbance was not sufficient to them, unless there was a clear indication as to the course that therapy should follow. Although naive in conception and execution, Hippocrates's approach to therapy followed logically from his view that disorders were of natural origin. To supplant the prevalent practices of exorcism and punishment, he recommended exercise, tranquility, massage, music, diet, marriage, and bloodletting. He believed these treatments would reestablish the humoral balance. He also employed surgical techniques such as trephining to relieve purported pressure on the brain.

Several themes relevant to the mind and its difficulties characterize *Plato's (circa 428–347 B.C.)* work: (a) powerful emotional forces come to the foreground and overwhelm the everyday behavior that typifies a person's life; (b) conflicts exist among different components of the psyche, recognizing thereby the personal discord that often arises among an individual's rational side, that which is desired, and the surge of emotional feelings; and (c) mental disorders do not result from simple ignorance, but from irrational superstitions and erroneous beliefs. To Plato, all humans were partly animal-like; hence, all humans acted irrationally at times, some more, some less. Evidence for these conclusions could be seen, according to Plato, in dreams in which bizarre events invariably occur and unnatural connections among thoughts and images are dominant.

In his view, therapeutic efforts could modify any and all forms of mental illness. For Plato, the use of educational procedures could dispel ignorance and uncover "truth" through the application of fundamental principles. Specifically, he offered a dialectical model to change a patient's cognitions and belief systems. In this regard, Plato's philosophy provided a methodology for engaging in therapy, essentially the application of rational discussions to modify faulty cognitions (shades of contemporary cognitive therapies).

Plato had many distinguished students; the most eminent was *Aristotle (384–322 B.C.)*. Although he was Plato's student for over 20 years, Aristotle turned sharply away from Plato and toward matters more realistic and tangible than abstract and idealistic. He gave special attention to the need for experimental verification and the use of sensory-based observable data. Aristotle was the first of the major philosophers to take an inductive and empirical approach in his writings. He was interested in the concrete observables of experience as registered through the senses. To him, data should be grounded in empirical observables in order to minimize the risk of subjective misinterpretations. Still, Aristotle believed that thought transcended the sensory realm. As he saw it, imagination could create thoughts of a higher order of abstraction than could sensations themselves.

Aristotle recognized the psychological significance of cognitive processes, dreams, and emotional catharses. For example, it was Aristotle who said that events, objects, and people were linked by their relative similarity to or their relative difference from one another. To Aristotle, things became "associated" if they occurred together; in this he was clearly a forerunner of the associationist school of the eighteenth and nineteenth centuries. Aristotle viewed dreams to be afterimages of the activities of the preceding day. Although he recognized that dreams might fulfill a biological function, he judged the content of dreams to be ideal gauges of potential pathology. He had a specific interest in how physical diagnoses could be deduced from dream content.

Theophrastus (circa 372–circa 287 B.C.), perhaps Aristotle's most important disciple, wrote no fewer than 220 treatises on a variety of different topics. He became best known for a secondary aspect of his career, the writing of personality sketches he called "characters." Each of these portrayals emphasized one or another psychological trait, providing a vignette of various personality "types" (e.g., the flatterers, the garrulous, the penurious, the tactless, the boors, the surly, and so on). Whether these portrayals were penetrating or poignant, Theophrastus (as well as later novelists) was free to write about his subject without the constraints of psychological or scientific caution. Lively and spirited characterizations most assuredly captured the interest of many, but they often misled the reader regarding the true complexities of natural personality patterns.

The *Roman* period spanned roughly a 12-century period, from the seventh century B.C. to the fifth century A.D., when the last of the major Roman emperors was deposed. A mechanistic conception of mental disorders came to the foreground; it was fundamentally materialistic and opposed to all transcendental mythologies, which were regarded as originating from fear and ignorance. The cause of mental disorders was the periodic enlargement or excessive tightening of the pores in the brain. In this corpuscular hypothesis, a derivative of the atomistic notions of Democritus of Greece, the task of the mental healer was to confirm and normalize the diameter of the pores. In certain cases, the mentally ill were seen as apathetic, fearful, and in a depressed mood, which was called a *laxum* state. Others presented an excited, delirious, and aggressive appearance; they were in a *strictum* state. If both sets of these symptoms co-occurred, there was a *mixtum* state.

Aretaeus (30–90 A.D.) was a follower of the vitalist school of thought that adopted the concept of *pneuma*, the natural or animal spirit, the physical embodiment of the soul. He was little known in his time, rarely quoted by fellow Roman scholars, probably owing to the fact that his works were written in the Ionic dialect rather than in Latin or Greek. Further, his vitalistic philosophy, based on the fluidity of the soul's nature and adopted by Galen a century later, rivaled the more atomistic or solidistic corpuscular theory of his contemporary Roman thinkers. Scarcely familiar with the Greek language and its medical philosophies, Aretaeus was a born clinician who was retained as a physician for the ruling Roman classes.

According to Aretaeus, the vicissitudes of the soul served as the basis of psychic disturbances. Specifically, the interconnecting linkages between "solid organs, the humors, and the pneuma" generated all forms of mental aberration. For example, anger and rage stirred the yellow bile, thereby warming the pneuma and increasing brain temperature, and resulted in irritability and excitability. Conversely, fear and oppression stirred black bile, augmenting its concentration in the blood, leading to a cold pneuma and a consequent melancholy.

His descriptions of epilepsy were notably impressive. Aretaeus spoke of its premonitory symptoms such as vertigo and nausea, of the perception of sparks and colors, as well as of harsh noises or nauseating smells. Aretaeus described the origins and characteristics of fanaticism and formulated a primitive psychosomatic hypothesis by stating that emotions could produce problematic effects on humoral metabolism, noting that "the black bile may be stirred by dismay and immoderate anger" (Roccatagliata, 1973). Similarly, he formulated what is spoken of as cyclothymia in describing the alternation of depression with phases of mania. He stated, "Some patients after being melancholic have fits of mania...so that mania is like a variety of melancholy" (Roccatagliata, 1973). In discussing the intermittent character of mania, he recognized its several variants, speaking of one type as arising in subjects "whose personality is characterized by gayness, activity, superficiality, and childishness" (Roccatagliata, 1973). Other types of mania were more expansive in which the patient "feels great and inspired. Still others become insensitive...and spend their lives like brutes" (Roccatagliata, 1973). Perceptive observations by Aretaeus strengthened the notion that mental disorders were exaggerated normal processes. He asserted that a direct connection existed between an individual's normal characteristics of personality and the expression of the symptom disorder he or she displayed when afflicted. His insightful differentiation of disorders according to symptom constellations (i.e., syndromes) was a striking achievement for his day.

Although Hippocrates may have been the first to provide a medical description of depression, it was Aretaeus who presented a complete and modern portrayal of the disorder. Moreover, Aretaeus proposed that melancholia was best attributed to psychological causes, that is, having nothing to do with bile or other bodily humors. As noted, he may have been the first to recognize the covariation between manic behaviors and depressive moods, antedating the views of many clinical observers in the sixteenth and seventeenth centuries.

Aretaeus introduced long-term follow-up studies of patients. He tracked their lifetime course, their periodic disease manifestations, and their return to a more normal pattern of behavior; in this regard he anticipated the writings of Emil Kraepelin, who recognized the course of an illness as a key factor in discriminating a specific disorder from others of comparable appearance. Aretaeus seriously studied the sequence and descriptive characteristics of his patients, contending that a clear demarcation must be made between the personality disposition of a patient and the form in which a symptomatic and transient disorder manifests itself periodically.

Aretaeus also discussed premorbid conditions, viewing them as a form of vulnerability or susceptibility to several clinical syndromes. In his view, persons disposed to mania are characteristically "irritable, violent, easily given to joy, and have a spirit for pleasantry or childish things" (Roccatagliata, 1973). By contrast, those prone to depression and melancholia were seen as characteristically "gloomy and sad often realistic yet prone to unhappiness" (Roccatagliata, 1973). In this matter, Aretaeus elaborated those essentially normal traits that make an individual susceptible to a clinical state.

Claudius Galenus, or *Galen (129–circa 199 A.D.)* (Figure 1.2), was the last major contributor to adopt a psychological perspective in Rome. He preserved much of earlier medical knowledge, yet generated significant new themes of his own.

Galen and his associates set out to synthesize primitive conceptions of disease with then-modern methods of curing the sick. Following the ideas of Hippocrates, he stressed the importance of observation and the systematic evaluation of medical procedures, arguing against untested primitive and philosophical hypotheses in favor of those based on empirical tests.

Figure 1.2 Portrait of Galen.

Galen based his conception of psychic pathology on the physiology of the central nervous system. He viewed clinical symptoms as signs of dysfunctional neurological structures and characterized mental diseases as "a concourse of symptoms," among which a specifically pathognomonic one could be isolated. According to his organic-functional approach, mental symptoms originated from the pathogenic action of a toxic, humoral, vaporous, febrile, or emotional factor that impacted the brain from the body and then altered certain of its psychic functions. Consonant with the beliefs of his time, Galen believed that the activities of the mind were prompted by animal spirits that carried out both voluntary and involuntary actions. Galen divided these spirits (*pneuma*) into two groups: those that controlled sensory perceptions and motility, whose damaging effects would cause neurological symptoms; and those that had a more directive function such as coordinating and organizing imagination, reason, and memory. To him, most psychiatric symptomatology stemmed from alterations of the second group of functions.

In describing catatonic psychosis, Galen suggested a paralysis of the animal spirits in which the imaginative faculty was "blocked or incomplete." As far as the syndrome of hysteria was concerned, his view differed strongly from Hippocrates's uterocentric view of the disease, which reflected the uterus "wandering agitated in the body." Galen asserted, on the basis of his own clinical examinations, that hysterical symptoms, rather than reflecting a wandering uterus, were provoked by the toxic action of vapors that formed in the normal uterus and vagina; they arose from the stagnation of semen, owing to a lack of sufficient sexual intercourse. The disease, therefore, signified a lack of sexual hygiene.

Galen's stature grew over the next millennium, so much so that his views were thought to be sacrosanct. His vast contributions must be considered significant in that no other figure in history was destined to exercise such an extended influence on the course of medicine.

Later in Roman history there emerged an organized church theology known as Christianity, including faith healing, magic, and superstition. Referred to as the *Patristic period*, the Church of Rome's early doctrine became the dominant approach to thought, medicine, and mental healing in the Western world until the seventeenth century. Most of the populace remained illiterate during this period. Education was religious, otherwise inchoate, and of dubious value. The idea of a scientific basis for understanding mental disorders barely appeared on the scene. Faith was the all-powerful guide.

During the first two to three centuries A.D., a distinction was made between two groups of heretics: psychologically normal individuals who doubted the Church's dogma and those whose "peculiar" beliefs arose out of a mental affliction. Nevertheless, both groups were subjected to punishment. Others' implausible or nonsensical behavior ostensibly demonstrated their fervent adherence to Church authorities and their dogma, and such persons were venerated.

Christianity in the third century led physicians to assume a moralistic and judgmental approach to psychic pathology. They proposed that mental cases were definitely the product of mystical events that could not be understood in the natural world. More seriously, they adopted the ancient beliefs that demons often appear under the guise of confused men and that it was the job of physicians to identify and "eliminate" these demons. In this and similar matters, they laid the groundwork for a return to the age of supernaturalism and superstitions; they were nevertheless well thought of until the close of the seventeenth century.

Three major medical figures from the Muslim world of the Middle East around the beginning of the first millennium A.D. are worthy of note: Rhazes, Unhammad, and Avicenna. Each proposed helpful ideas that came to represent a fresh and innovative point of view concerning mental illness.

Rhazes (860–930) wrote textbooks dealing with a wide variety of medical, psychological, philosophical, and religious subjects. In contrast to the predominant religious orientation of Baghdad, Rhazes strongly argued against the notion of a demonological concept of disease and the use of arbitrary authority to determine what is and is not scientific. He attacked the superstitious religious beliefs of his contemporaries and was strongly in favor of building a rational schema for understanding all disorders. Although Rhazes's views were empirically oriented, he nonetheless subscribed to the four elements originally developed by Empedocles and Hippocrates.

Unhammad (870–925) was a contemporary of Rhazes who provided intelligent descriptions of various mental diseases. The observations he compiled of his patients resulted in a nosology that was the most complete classification of mental disorders in its day. Unhammad described nine major categories of mental disorders, which, as he saw it, included 30 different diseases. Among the categories was an excellent description of anxious and ruminative states, which corresponds to present thinking about compulsions and obsessions. Other categories of mental disease were judged to be degenerative in their nature; a few were associated with the involutional period of a person's life. The term used by the Greeks for *mania* was borrowed to describe states of abnormal excitement. Another category, most closely associated with grandiose and paranoid delusions, manifested itself, according to Unhammad, by the mind's tendency to magnify all matters of personal significance, often leading to actions that prove outrageous to society.

A most significant and influential philosopher and physician of the Muslim world was *Avicenna (980–1037),* often referred to as the "Galen of Islam," largely as a consequence of his vast and encyclopedic works called the *Canon of Medicine.* The *Canon* became *the* medical textbook chosen throughout European universities from the tenth through the fifteenth century. Avicenna was regarded not as a highly original writer but as a systematizer who encompassed all knowledge from the past that related to medical events. Similar to Galen, Avicenna noted the important connection between intense emotions and various medical and physiological states, although he fully accepted Hippocrates's humoral explanations of temperament and mental disorder. To his credit as a sophisticated scholar of the brain, Avicenna speculated that intellectual dysfunctions were in large part a result of deficits in the brain's middle ventricle and asserted that the frontal areas of the brain mediated common sense and reasoning.

The Middle Ages

The enlightened ideas of Hippocrates were submerged for centuries following the death of Galen and the fall of the Roman Empire. During the thousand years of the so-called Dark Ages, superstition, demonology, and exorcism returned in full force, intensified by sorcery and witch burning. With few dissenting voices during this period, the naturalism of the Greco-Roman period was all but condemned or distorted by notions of magic. Only in the Middle East did the humane and naturalistic aspects of Hippocratic thought remain free of the primitivism and demonology that had overcome Europe.

Signs for detecting demonic possession became increasingly indiscriminate in the Christian world. During epidemics of famine and pestilence, thousands wandered aimlessly until their haggard appearance and confusion justified the fear that they were cursed. The prevalent turmoil, the fear of one's own contamination, and the frenetic desire to prove one's spiritual purity led widespread segments of the populace to use the roaming destitute and ill as convenient scapegoats. As the terrifying uncertainties of medieval life persisted, fear led to wild mysticism and mass pathology. Entire societies were swept up simultaneously. Epidemic manias of raving, jumping, drinking, and wild dancing were first noted in the tenth century. Referred to as tarantism in Italy, these epidemic manias spread throughout Europe, where they were known as St. Vitus's dance.

Monasteries served during the early Middle Ages as the chief refuge for the mentally ill, providing prayer, incantation, holy water, relic-touching, and mild exorcism as prescriptions for cure. As the turmoil of natural calamity grew more severe, people increasingly equated mental disorders with sin and satanic influence. Although significant advances were made in agriculture, technology, and architecture during the Middle Ages, the interplay between changing theological beliefs and natural catastrophe speeded acceptance of the belief that "madness" and "depravity" were the devil's work. At first, people believed that the devil had seized the mentally ill against their will, and such individuals underwent exorcism. Soon, however, the afflicted were considered willing followers of Satan; classed then as witches, they were flogged, starved, and burned.

Among the major tenets of this medieval mythology was a belief that an international conspiracy, based on satanic forces, was bent on destroying Christianity. The agents of this widespread conspiracy were witches, who worshipped Satan at secret meetings, desecrated Christian symbols and beliefs, and engaged in murder, cannibalism, and sexual orgies. Such ideas of conspiracy existed first and foremost in the imagination of the religious leaders of the day. It was Pope Gregory IX who established the Inquisition in 1233 to root out witches, heretics, and all other agents of Satan. From the fifteenth through the seventeenth century, demonic possession and exorcism became common phenomena among the masses. It was the task of religious authorities to coerce those possessed by demons to admit that they were witches. These individuals could justly be arrested and tortured, especially if they "confessed" to their involvement in these nonexistent satanic conspiracies. "Witch finders" soon became prominent guardians of the faith, prompted by religious authorities that sought to undo the political powers of their ostensive "enemies."

Encouraged by the 1484 *Summis Desiderantes Affectibus*, in which Pope Innocent VIII exhorted the clergy to use all means for detecting and eliminating witchcraft, two inquisitional Dominicans, Jacob Sprenger and Heinrich Kramer, issued their notorious manual, *Malleus Maleficarum* (*The Hammer of Witches*; 1487–1489/1928). Published between 1487 and 1489, this "divinely inspired" text set out to prove the existence of witchcraft, to describe methods of identification, and to specify the procedures of examination and legal sentence. This volume, in effect, represented a joining together of notions of heresy, demon possession, and mental illness. *Maleficarum* reflected the spirit of its time, even though it was published in the early stages of the Renaissance and at the threshold of the Reformation as well. Here, the conflict between paganism and Christianity, between magic and a monotheistic outlook, had not ceased to be a burning issue, in more than one sense of the word. Idols and deities were relegated to the role of fallen angels, but devils and evil demons continued to reside in the world of the human unconscious, a belief that was widely disseminated and embraced.

It was also in the fifteenth century that the medieval period gradually transitioned into what is viewed today as the modern world. Slowly the importance of human emotions and strivings came to be recognized, ultimately replacing the belief that deeper human truths were beyond human capabilities. Psychological processes became increasingly humanized; opportunities to study humans as a biological rather than a purely spiritual organism permitted these processes to be considered a natural rather than a metaphysical science.

The waning of Middle Age supernaturalism and the advent of the liberating Renaissance era exerted numerous effects on the emergence of psychological thought. The Renaissance broke the hold medieval dogma had had on the minds of early clinicians. It also opened new nonphilosophical pathways for purely psychological ventures and inquiries into the general character of human nature as well as into the substantive nature of mental disorders.

An exemplar of pre-Renaissance thinking is *Paracelsus (1493–1541)*, who would have been an extraordinary person in any age but who looms as a strange if not rare blend of mysticism of the past and practicality. As with most thinkers of his day, Paracelsus was a believer in divination from the stars and the healing powers of such preparations as powdered Egyptian mummy. As such, he was both an astrologer and an alchemist. Among his works were efforts to test the effects of various chemical agents to treat several medical conditions. Although he made no lasting discoveries, he was an inventive and creative pioneer. Most notably, he denounced the cruelties of the Inquisition, stating, "there are more superstitions in the Roman Church than in all these poor women and presumed witches" (Millon, 2004). In his rejection of the views of the clergy regarding the sources of mental disorders, Paracelsus (1567/1941) wrote:

In nature there are not only diseases which afflict our body and our health, but many others which deprive us of sound reason, and these

are the most serious. While speaking about the natural diseases and observing to what extent and how seriously they afflict various parts of our body, we must not forget to explain the origin of the diseases which deprive man of reason, as we know from experience that they develop out of man's disposition. The present-day clergy of Europe attribute such diseases to ghostly beings and threefold spirits; we are not inclined to believe them.

Paracelsus was the first physician to abandon the habit of categorizing disorders beginning with the head and then working down step-by-step to the feet. His mental health classification was outlined in a treatise entitled *On the Diseases Which Deprive Men of Health and Reason*. Here, whole families of mental disorders were identified, with those experiencing these disorders referred to as *lunatici, insani, vesani*, and *melancholici*. *Lunatici* suffered from disorders stemming from their reactions to the phases of the moon. *Insani* suffered from disorders identifiable at birth and clearly derived from family heritage. *Vesani* were poisoned or contaminated by food or drink. *Melancholici*, by virtue of their temperament, lost their ability to reason accurately. Paracelsus identified others as *obsessi,* that is, obsessed by the devil, thus dissenting from the view in which a devil obsession lay at the heart of all mental disorders. As he perceived it, numerous sources of mental dysfunction existed, only one of which could be traced to demonic preoccupations, and he saw the majority of these disorders as a problem of defective thought processes rather than as a consequence of supernatural powers.

Physiognomics, the art of interpreting people's psychological characteristics from aspects of their physical characteristics, especially the face, was present in ancient times, reaching its peak of study in the second century A.D. The great thinkers of Greece explored formal efforts to interpret physiognomic characteristics systematically, for example, in Pythagoras's sixth-century-B.C. writings, and later in Aristotle's *Analytica Priora* (Tredennick, 1967) and *Historia Animalium*, in which he wrote (Peck, 1965): "Persons who have a large forehead are sluggish, those who have a small one are fickle; those who have a broad one are excitable, those who have a bulging one, quick tempered."

"Physiognomics" (Hett, 1936), also attributed to Aristotle, but more likely written by his followers, examined parallels between the physiques of humans and animals, to compare different ethnic groups and to investigate the relationship between bodily characteristics and temperamental dispositions. Among the useful signs recorded were the movements, shapes, and colors of the face; the growth of hair; the smoothness of skin; the condition of the flesh; and the general structure of the body. Sluggish movements denoted a soft disposition, quick ones showed a fervent temperament; a deep voice denoted courage, a high one signified cowardice. The writers were wise enough to note that it would be foolish to make one's judgment on the basis of any one of these signs. Centuries later, *Leonardo da Vinci (1452–1519)* made similar physiognomic proposals, in his *Treatise on Painting*, in which he explored relationships between emotional states and overt facial expressions.

A theorist of physiognomy in the late eighteenth century, *Johann Kaspar Lavater (1741–1801)* asserted unequivocally the existence of a relationship between fixed aspects of the body's surface and a person's character. In his well-received book, *Essays on Physiognomy* (1775–1779), published in four lavish volumes, Lavater claimed that physiognomy was truly a science because it offered law-like regularities and depended on empirical observation.

Though similar in many respects to classical approaches in physiognomy, a new "scientific" model known as *phrenology* emerged in the late eighteenth century from the work of *Franz Joseph Gall (1758–1828)*. Both approaches drew inferences about character and personality from external bodily features: physiognomy from facial structure and expression, phrenology from external formations of the skull. Their underlying assumptions, however, were quite different. Physiognomists believed that a person's inner feelings and characteristics were expressed in facial features, voice, and so on. Phrenologists made no assumptions as to the external expression of varied dispositions. Both of these fundamental assumptions were unusual for their time. Phrenologists assumed that different mental functions were located in different regions of the brain and that the skull's external topography reflected the magnitude of these functions. This was a serious attempt to construct a neurological substrate in the brain to undergird a science of character depiction. Although numerous writers, such as

Vesalius, Willis, and Stensen in medieval times (Millon, 2004), had speculated on and explored brain structures as the center of mental functioning, Gall took this view in an original direction. Most early characterologists conceived of the brain as a locale where the immaterial soul might have influenced bodily activities. Gall asserted that the brain *was* the mind, not only in an explicitly material sense but also in that different regions subserved different dispositions.

Gall identified 27 different "organs" in the brain that undergirded separate psychological tendencies. By "reading" the skull, usually by running one's hands over the head, different enlarged organs could be identified. Gall went to prisons and lunatic asylums to read skulls and collect data on correlations between protuberances in certain locations and personality traits.

Gall referred to his studies of brain physiology as *organology* and *crainoscopy*, but the term *phrenology*, which his younger associate Johann Spurzheim coined, came to be its popular designation. Gall sought to employ objective and quantitative methods to deduce the inner structure of the brain. He concluded, quite reasonably, that both the intensity and the character of thoughts and emotions would correlate with variations in the size and shape of the brain or its encasement, the cranium. That this gross expression of personality proved invalid is not surprising when we think of the exceedingly complex structure of neuroanatomy.

The Renaissance

Clergyman and reclusive scholar *Robert Burton (1577–1640)* wrote a single major work of extraordinary insight and sensitivity in 1621, entitled *Anatomy of Melancholy*. Chronically depressed, Burton's introspective accounts of his moods contained a wealth of impressive clinical analyses. He also sought to record the behavior and emotions of others, recognizing patterns similar to his own moodiness and eccentricity. This work, despite rambling irrelevancies and inaccuracies, makes fascinating reading today.

Burton established a limited classification system, one that differentiated melancholy from madness, a distinction akin to recent differentiations of neuroses and psychoses. He outlined the following general categories: (a) diseases emanating from the body, (b) diseases of the head (primarily the brain), (c) madness (mania), and (d) melancholy. Burton further distinguished melancholy of the head, of the body, or of the bowels, and he identified the major sources of melancholy (e.g., excessive love, excessive study, intense preoccupation with religious themes).

His awareness of his own sadness led him to recognize the sources of his own melancholy. He recognized guilt as a major element, despite his exemplary lifestyle. Other causes of melancholy included bodily deterioration and old age; bad diets; sexual excesses; idleness; solitariness; and a consuming preoccupation with imagination, fears, shame, and malice. Burton clearly stated that a wide range of human frailties and life circumstances could engender melancholy.

Burton anticipated what ultimately became the core of modern psychotherapy, that is, engaging a patient in a dialogue with a trusted and sympathetic outsider. Despite the brilliance of his book, Burton's proposals had little effect on the course of mental health study of his time.

Thomas Willis (1621–1675) was the originator of the term *neurology*; he also created the term *psychology* to designate the study of the "corporeal soul." Arguably the most significant founder of what came to be referred to as biological psychiatry, he considered most ailments to be disorders of nerve transmission, rather than diseases of the blood vessels. He is perhaps best known by the circuit of arteries located at the base of the brain, known today as the "circle of Willis."

In 1664, Willis published a book on the history of the brain sciences, entitled *Cerebri Anatome*, which was without equal in the field for many decades thereafter. Willis concerned himself not only with brain functions but also with their behavioral consequences. Willis proposed also that vital and involuntary systems existed in the brain that were mediated not by the higher centers of the brain but by the "cerebellum." The detailed articulation of the functional segments of the brain, grounded in comparative anatomic precision, was enriched by his clinical observations. Drawing ideas from existing theories, his work, both speculative and empirical, stimulated many other neuroanatomists.

Willis reported his observation of a sequence in which "young persons who, lively and spirited, and at times even brilliant in their childhood, passed into obtuseness and hebetude during adolescence"

(1672/1971). Thus, Willis anticipated by two centuries an idea more fully developed by Benjamin Morel, who termed this behavioral course *dementia praecox*. To his credit, Willis rejected the idea of a "wandering womb" that ostensibly led to the syndrome of hysteria. The brain functioned as the center of all mental disturbances to Willis, and the various nerves emanating from the brain served to connect this overarching organ to the rest of the body. Willis, like most others of his time, spoke of processes generated by "animal spirits," that is, the soul, which somehow or other could be sucked out of the brain.

Willis's clinical observations were uncontaminated by formal theories. His accurate inferences were based on repeated observations of patients over time, that is, the long-term course of their difficulties. Included in Willis's classification system were some 14 categories, of which several were primarily neurological. His system, published in *De Anima Brutorum* (1672/1971), specified three major impairments: morosis, mania, and melancholia; each encompassed several subcategories, as well as a number of neurological disorders, such as headache, insomnia, and vertigo.

Thomas Sydenham (1624–1689), a colleague of the philosopher John Locke, held to the view that hypotheses should be set aside in favor of close observation of all forms of natural phenomena, such as various medical diseases. Sydenham did not trust books, believing only what he could see and learn from his own bedside observations of hysterical patients. These observations enabled him to recognize the variations of conversion symptoms among paralyzed and pain patients, as well as to speculate on the operation of intense but unconscious emotions. His description of hysterical phenomena was so comprehensive that little could be added today. Sydenham recognized that hysteria was among the most common of chronic diseases and observed that men exhibited the symptom complex no less so than women did. He averred that hysterical symptoms could simulate almost all forms of truly organic diseases; for example, he noted that a paralysis of the body might be caused not only by stroke but also "from some violent commotion of the mind" (Roccatagliata, 1973). He spoke of hysterical convulsions that resembled epileptic attacks, psychogenic palpitations of the heart, and hysterical pain that might be mistaken for kidney stones. He suggested that differential diagnoses between real biological diseases and those generated by the mind could be made only if the patient's psychological state could be thoroughly known.

In his efforts to formulate a syndromal pattern for numerous disorders, Sydenham extended the range of his observations to include not only the patient's dispositions, emotions, and defenses but also the family context within which they arose. In this way, he sought to determine the overall pathogenesis of certain syndromes, involving both physical and psychological phenomena. What was most informative was Sydenham's recognition that a syndromal picture rarely developed from a single pathogenic agent, be it a humoral imbalance or a systemic disturbance of the body. To Sydenham, multiple influences operated simultaneously on a patient, each of which took a somewhat different turn and produced a somewhat different appearance in the same disease process. He strongly believed in syndrome complexes rather than in a distinct or singular expression of a disorder. As a consequence, and in time, all medical men were trained to consider a wide range of elements, which, together, play a partial role in generating disease. However, Sydenham believed that hypotheses and philosophical systems should be set aside to ensure that pathological phenomena be observed with reliability and accuracy.

Especially notable was Sydenham's belief that nature has its own healing processes. These natural remedies of the body would not invariably solve a problem because they were often delayed or displaced. Included among the healing processes of nature, according to Sydenham, were a variety of well-established "excretions, eruptions, and fevers" (Roccatagliata, 1973). He also emphasized the importance of identifying the antecedent emotional factors that might lead to the development of mental disorders, and he observed the interplay between personal emotions and social pressures.

Born in Germany, *Georg Ernst Stahl (1660–1734)* argued that the then-prevalent theory of animal spirits was essentially incorrect and that the various processes of the mind stemmed from a life-giving force, to which he applied the term *soul*; however, Stahl's soul was not the supernatural phenomenon that characterized ancient and medieval thinking. Instead, it represented the source of energy of all living organisms. Stahl's life force was not notably different from Freud's conception of the libido. It was the sum total of the nonmaterial side of humans and animals that, together with nature, had the power to effect desired cures.

Hence, Stahl's soul was able to perform a variety of functions that would either bring on or stave off various diseases. To him, mental disorders were not the result of physical, mechanical, or supernatural forces but were, in fact, essentially psychogenic. Stahl was appalled by the sharp demarcation of body and mind. He judged this dichotomy to be problematic in understanding the complexity of forces involved in mental diseases. It was his assertion that a synthesis be sought to integrate both physical and mental phenomena.

Psychopathology in the Eighteenth and Nineteenth Centuries

As clinics and hospitals began to record case histories and detail observations, physicians could identify syndromal groupings (i.e., clusters of symptoms) and classify them into disease entities. The success with which botanical taxonomists had systematized their field in the eighteenth century provided additional impetus to the trend toward categorizing symptom clusters into a formal psychiatric taxonomy or nosology. With the waning role of supernaturalism and the advent of liberating thought during the Renaissance, a number of enlightened thinkers of the sixteenth and seventeenth centuries began to explore ideas related to a realistic classification of mental disorders.

A second major trend within biological medicine, the view that mental disorders might result from organic pathology, can be traced to the early writings of Hippocrates, Aretaeus, and Galen. With the advent of valid anatomical, physiological, and biochemical knowledge in the early eighteenth century and the discovery in the nineteenth century of the role played by bacteria and viruses, the disease concept of modern medicine, including the view of mental illness as a disease, was firmly established. Efforts at developing somatic (e.g., electrical, chemical, surgical) treatment methods followed naturally. Although these three stages—diagnostic classification, biological causation, and somatic treatment—rarely proceeded in a smooth or even logical fashion, they characterized psychopathological progress and continue today to guide neuroscientists who follow the medical and biological tradition.

These scientific and medical activities, however, presuppose a classification system (i.e., a taxonomy) that is not only logical but valid.

Unfortunately, physicians classified diseases long before they understood their true nature. Such nosologies have persisted because of widespread or authoritative use; however, they rested most often upon unfounded speculations or, at best, judicious but essentially superficial observations. Criticism of premature nosological schemes is justified, given the frequent slavish adherence to them. On the other hand, there is no reason to overlook the *potential* value of a taxonomy, no less to abolish the utility of a sound classification system, owing to the many important goals it might fulfill.

Perhaps the leading taxonomist of the eighteenth century was *Françoise Boissier de Sauvages (1706–1767)*, who thought that all mental diseases were located in distinct anatomical regions. Beyond this assertion, he believed that the "will" had much to do with not only the generation of mental aberrations but also their ultimate treatment. He believed that physicians had a responsibility to shape or guide individual behaviors, fearing that otherwise there would be no social compact or personal justice. De Sauvages followed the biological taxonomist *Carolus Linnaeus (1707–1778)* in seeking to organize an encyclopedic framework for grouping the many categories of mental disorder. De Sauvages outlined 10 classes, 295 genera, and 24,000 species, spending the better part of his life immersing himself in the large body of medical knowledge that had accumulated from early times. Included in his broad classification were such illnesses as fevers, inflammations, spasms, breathing disturbances, weaknesses, pains, and dementias. Dementias were organized into four types: those of extracerebral origin, disturbances of the instinctual and emotional life, disturbances of the intellectual life, and irregular eccentricities and follies.

De Sauvages completed the three-volume *Nosologie Methodique* late in life, and it was published several years after his death (1771). In this work, de Sauvages made available to others the complete model he had constructed. This model was used as an orderly classification for decades, if not centuries, to come. In this comprehensive volume, de Sauvages organized all forms of mental illness. For example, he grouped the syndrome of melancholia into numerous species (e.g., religious, imaginary, extravagant, vagabonding, enthusiastic, and sorrowful).

The influential Scottish nosologist *William Cullen (1710–1790)* was a notable pioneer of neuropathology who believed that most pathological conditions of the mind should be attributed to diseases of the brain. He did recognize, however, that life experiences could influence the character in which these diseases were expressed. Cullen proposed the term *neuroses* to represent neurologically based diseases. Most obscure mental illnesses were considered to be neuroses, ostensibly to represent diseases of deeply recessed nerves that were inflamed and irritable. As he perceived it, neuroses were affections of sense or motion that stemmed from disharmonies in the nervous system. Within the general category of neuroses, Cullen subcategorized four variants: those representing a diminution of voluntary motion, those representing a diminution of involuntary activity, the regular motions of the muscles or muscle fibers, and disorders of judgment.

Along with Cullen, *Robert Whytt (1714–1766)* played a large role in providing Scottish physicians of his day with a classification system of "neurotic" individuals. Whytt attended to the less severe mental conditions of his time, categorizing them into three broad syndromes: hysteria, hypochondriasis, and nervous exhaustion—the latter referred to subsequently by *George Beard (1839–1883)* as neurasthenia. This classification does not deviate much from the current diagnostic manual. As with Cullen, Whytt's basic theory stated that disturbed motility within the nervous system produced nervous disorders. The selection of the term *neuroses* made good sense, as both Cullen and Whytt assumed that different sensibilities of the nerves could be the foundation on which certain problematic behaviors might be based. This belief continued for at least another century, anticipating ideas that were explored in greater depth first by Charcot and later by Janet and Freud.

John Haslam (1766–1844) provided the first clinical description of various forms of paralysis, most notably that of general paresis. Alert to the epidemic of venereal disease that had spread across Europe in the early nineteenth century, Haslam wrote:

A course of debauchery long persisted would probably terminate in paralysis...[and] frequently induces derangement of mind. Paralytic affections are a much more frequent cause of insanity than has been commonly supposed, and they are also a very common effect of madness; more maniacs die of hemiplegia and apoplexy than from any other disease. (1809, p. 209)

He also recognized that states of excitement and depression alternated in the same individual, an observation recorded by Aretaeus 17 centuries earlier, and Haslam acknowledged the significance of the course of a disease as a factor in classifying mental syndromes. In his 1809 book, *Observations on Madness and Melancholy*, Haslam described a number of cases that would subsequently be classified as *dementia praecox* or schizophrenia. In the following year, he published an innovative text, *Illustrations of Madness*, which presented a detailed examination of an individual with diverse paranoid features.

No less significant was Haslam's sophistication in matters of nomenclature and semantics. In his 1809 text he wrote:

> Mad is therefore not a complex idea, as has been supposed, but a complex term for all the forms and varieties of this disease. Our language has been enriched with other terms expressive of this affliction....Instead of endeavoring to [I Will]discover an infallible definition of madness, which I believe will be found impossible, as it is an attempt to comprise, in a few words, the wide range and mutable character of a Proteus disorder. (1809, pp. 5–6)

Note should be made of the contributions of *Jean Esquirol (1772–1840)*, known best as a humanistic reformer (Millon, 2004). Among Esquirol's diagnostic proposals was the attention he gave to a patient's dispositions and deficits of affect and impulse in his concept of *lypemanie*, by which he meant patients deficient in their capacity to feel or desire. Esquirol (1838) grouped the several variants of mental disorder into five broad classes—*lypemanie, monomanie, manie, dementia*, and *imbecility/idiocy*—which were used in France for over a century. Esquirol also made contributions to the clarification of delusions and hallucinations.

Also notable were the contributions of *Jean-Pierre Falret (1794–1870)*, another reformer, and a student of Esquirol's, who specified several factors instrumental in the formation of delusions: the state of the brain, the character of the patient, the circumstances surrounding onset, and concurrent internal and external sensations.

He also contributed an insightful series of papers that recognized the variable character of mania and melancholy, which he called *forme circulaire de maladie mentale*, consisting of periods of excitation followed by longer periods of weakness. Presenting these as a facet of his 1851 lectures at the Salpêtrière Hospital, he subsequently elaborated on these views in a book published in 1854, ideas proposed almost concurrently by Ballarger, whose work will be touched on later.

A series of classifications in Germany were based on a threefold distinction among the "faculties of the mind"—volition, intellection, and emotion—as well as a number of "morbid" processes such as exaltation and depression. Among the early promoters of this schema was *Johann Christian Heinroth (1773–1843)*, perhaps the first physician to occupy a chair in psychiatry, that at Leipzig University in 1811. He subdivided one of the major categories of mental disorder, *vesania*, into several orders, genera, and species. Designing a complex matrix combining the major faculties on one dimension and the morbid processes on the other, he proposed a classification system that comprised subtypes that became the basis of several variations throughout Germany and England in the ensuing century. Heinroth also composed a theory of mind with a tripartite structure. The basic or undergirding layer was characterized by the animalistic instinctual qualities of human beings; the intermediary layer reflected consciousness, including both intelligence and self-awareness; and the superior layer comprised what would be called conscience (Heinroth, 1818). Akin to later ideas proposed by Freud, he also proposed the notion of conflict when two layers became opposing forces, for example, instinct versus conscience. Heinroth recognized a deep connection between the human qualities of mind and the more vegetative or animal passions that are fundamental to mental disorders, notably those of melancholy and rage. Heinroth also conceived of a term similar to what today is called psychosomatics, in which he took exception to Descartes' contention of a dualism between mind and body. Health reflected harmony between these two components when they acted as a singular entity.

The British alienist *James Cowles Prichard (1786–1848)* is credited with formulating the concept of "moral insanity," signifying a reprehensible defect in character that deserved social condemnation. He included under this label a range of previously diverse mental and emotional conditions. Patients with all these disorders ostensibly shared a common defect in the power to guide themselves in accord with "natural feelings"—that is, a spontaneous and intrinsic sense of rightness, goodness, and responsibility. In his opinion, those afflicted by this disease were swayed, despite their ability intellectually to understand the choices before them, by overpowering "affections" that compelled them to engage in socially repugnant behaviors.

As a major figure in extending the ideas of Esquirol and Falret at the Salpêtrière Hospital, *Felix Voisin (1794–1872)* was also an adherent of the phrenological speculations of Gall and Spurzheim. He stressed the importance of the nervous system as being causally involved in generating a variety of sexual disorders of desire. Placing special attention on the pathologies of nymphomania and satyriasis, especially as they related to hysteria, Voisin articulated a progression in these disorders from their early stages to their more severe forms, contributing to the idea that disease *course* was central to clinical diagnostics. In his major work, *The Analysis of Human Understanding* (1851), Voisin specified three major faculties of human functioning—moral, intellectual, and animal—a division that predated and paralleled Freud's subsequent formulation of the mind's structure of superego, ego, and id. Influenced by Prichard, in his later years Voisin delved briefly into the problems of criminal and forensic pathology, speaking of criminals as a product of lower class origins and of their inevitable moral degeneration.

Another contributor to French thinking of the day was *Paul Briquet (1796–1881)*, who focused primarily on problems of hysteria and its ostensive connection to female maladies. In his extensive monograph, *Traite Clinique et Therapeutique a l'Hysterie* (1859), Briquet took exception to the notion that hysteria was a consequence of sexual incontinence. Briquet specified with great clarity the multiple gastrointestinal and vague sexual and exaggerated complaints that typified the symptoms presented by his "hysterical" patients. He recorded, in contrast to prior beliefs, that married women were no more inclined to hysteria than were unmarried women, that numerous cases appeared before puberty, and, most significantly, that an active sexual life was no assurance that one would not develop such symptoms. Briquet rejected the view that men could not develop

symptoms of hysteria. He noted that painful emotional states, such as sadness and fear, might be elements in precipitating the syndrome. Moreover, he speculated that a variety of untoward developmental and life experiences played a pathogenic role (e.g., parental mistreatment, spousal abuse, unfavorable employment circumstances, or business failures). Recognizing that only a small subset of those subjected to these psychosocial experiences developed the syndrome, Briquet proposed the concept of *predispositions* as pathogenic factors.

Ernst von Feuchtersleben (1806–1849) may have been the first Austrian psychiatrist to gain a distinguished status in European circles during the mid-nineteenth century. His major publication, *The Principles of Medical Psychology* (1847), likely had a significant influence on Freud. A critic of those who supported the mind–body dichotomy, Feuchtersleben considered the mind and the body to be unitary. An exponent of the role of personality qualities in the life of mental patients, Feuchtersleben wrote with great sensitivity on the psychic sources of mental disorders.

In what may have been the first purely psychological description of what is now referred to as the histrionic personality, Feuchtersleben depicted women disposed to hysterical symptoms as being sexually heightened, selfish, and "over-privileged with satiety and boredom." Attributing these traits to the unfortunate nature of female education, he wrote, "It combines everything that can heighten sensibility, weaken spontaneity, give a preponderance to the sexual sphere, and sanction the feelings and impulse that relate to it" (1847, p. 111). Chauvinistic as this judgment may be, he at least recognized and was sensitive to the limitations that Victorian society placed on women in his time.

Though others (such as Thomas Willis) had previously described similar cases, it was particularly influential when the Belgian psychiatrist *Benedict-Augustin Morel (1809–1873)* described the case of a 14-year-old boy who had been a cheerful and good student but had progressively lost his intellectual capacities and increasingly become melancholy and withdrawn. Morel considered such cases to be irremediable and ascribed the deterioration to an arrest in brain development that stemmed from hereditary causes. He named the illness *dementia praecox (demence precoce)* to signify his observation that a degenerative process had begun at an early age and had progressed rapidly. Morel became convinced that so-called degeneration was pervasive in all forms of psychological pathology, especially mental retardation. Speaking of those subjected to hereditary mental disorders, he wrote:

> The degenerate human being, if he is abandoned to himself, falls into a progressive degradation. He becomes...not only incapable of forming part of the chain of transmission of progress in human society, he is the greatest obstacle to this progress through his contact with the healthy portion of the population. (1857, p. 46)

Although his work secured him a niche in the history of psychiatry, Morel's views contributed to the pessimistic attitude regarding mental illness then pervasive in the European public at large, a view that unfortunately would gain a horrendous following a century later in Nazi Germany.

In 1853, *Jules Baillarger (1809–1892)* summarized the results of his work with depressed and suicidal persons. He reported that a large portion of these patients showed a course of extended depression, broken intermittently by periods of irritability, anger, elation, and normality. The terms *la folie circulaire* (Falret, 1854) and *folie à double forme* (Baillarger, 1853) were applied almost simultaneously to signify this syndrome's contrasting and variable character.

Baillarger also contributed his knowledge to a wide range of psychopathological conditions, especially to the syndrome known today as bipolar disorder, notably in his ideas on hallucinations and delusions, neurohistology, epilepsy, and general paralyses. With regard to delusions, he sought to distinguish the perceptual basis of this disorder by recognizing that delusions were based on false interpretations of normal sensations, whereas illusions were distortions at the sensory rather than the ideational level. Similarly, he explored the question of whether hallucinations were sensory or psychological phenomena.

Born and educated in Germany, *Richard von Krafft-Ebing (1840–1902)* was convinced that the Morelian process of degeneration was the primary cause not only of mental disorders but also of criminality and sexual pathology. He wrote: "Madness, when it finally breaks out, represents only the last link in the psychopathic chain of constitutional heredity, or degenerate heredity" (1879, p. 439). He referred to the problem of progressive sexual degeneration as follows: "It is specially frequent for sexual functioning to be...abnormally strong, manifesting itself explosively and seeking satisfaction impulsively, or abnormally early, stirring already in early childhood and leading to masturbation" (1879, p. 424). In his most famous book, entitled *Psychopathia Sexualis* (1882), he spoke of the pervasive pathology of all variants of sexual activity, that is, other than the approved and "proper" behavior of Victorian times.

Krafft-Ebing (1937) proposed the label *masochism* in his catalog of sexual perversions. He asserted that flagellation and physical punishment were necessary elements in the perversion but were less significant than a personal relationship that included enslavement, passivity, and psychological serfdom. Hence, from its first formulations, the concept of masochism included the need to experience not only physical pain but also suffering.

The growth of knowledge in anatomy and physiology in the mid-eighteenth century strengthened the trend toward organically oriented disease classifications. *Wilhelm Griesinger (1817–1868)* (Figure 1.3) asserted the disease concept in his

Figure 1.3 Portrait of Griesinger.

classic text, *Mental Pathology and Therapeutics*, published in 1845. His statement "Mental diseases are brain diseases" shaped the course of German systematic psychiatry for the next 40 years. Griesinger's contention that classifications should be formed on the basis of underlying brain lesions was not weakened by the fact that no relationship had yet been established between brain pathology and mental disorders. In fact, Griesinger's own system of categories—depression, exaltation, and weakness—did not parallel his views regarding brain pathology. He conceived mental disorders, like most medical diseases, to be chronically progressive. Thus, he regarded depression as beginning with a minor level of cerebral irritation, leading next to a chronic and irreversible degeneration, and ending ultimately in pervasive dementia.

Griesinger initiated and assumed the editorship of a new journal, *The Archives for Psychiatry and Nervous Diseases*. In its first volume, he wrote:

Psychiatry has undergone a transformation in its relationship to the rest of medicine....This transformation rests principally on the realization that patients with so-called mental diseases are really individuals with diseases of the nerves and the brain....Psychiatry...must become an integral part of general medicine and accessible to all medical circles. (1868, p. 12)

Although the work of Griesinger and his followers regarding the role of the brain in mental disorders soon dominated continental psychiatry, a different emphasis concerning the basis of classification was developing concurrently. Jean Esquirol had often referred to the importance of age of onset, variable chronicity, and deteriorating course in understanding pathology. This idea was included as a formal part of classification in 1856 when the German psychiatrist *Karl Ludwig Kahlbaum (1828–1899)* developed a classification system that grouped disorders according to their course and outcome. It became the major alternative system to the one Greisinger had proposed. Kraepelin, noting his indebtedness to Kahlbaum's contribution, stated, "identical or remarkably similar symptoms can accompany wholly dissimilar diseases while their inner nature can be revealed only through their progress and termination" (Kraepelin, 1920, p. 116). Kahlbaum wrote of how useless attempts had

been to group disorders on the basis of the similarity of their overt symptomatology, as if such superficial symptom collections could expose something essential concerning the underlying disease. He commented as follows:

It is futile to search for the anatomy of melancholy or mania, because each of these forms occurs under the most varied relationships and combinations with other states, and they are just as little the expression of an inner pathological process as the complex of symptoms we call fever. (1874, p. 2)

In a series of monographs and books published between 1863 and 1874, Kahlbaum not only established the importance of including longitudinal factors in psychiatric diagnosis but also described newly observed disorders that he labeled *hebephrenia* and *catatonia*; he also coined the modern terms *symptom-complex* and *cyclothymia*. Kahlbaum introduced the term *hebephrenia* to represent conditions that began in adolescence, usually starting with a quick succession of erratic moods, followed by a rapid enfeeblement of all functions, and finally progressing to an unalterable psychic decline. The label *catatonia* was introduced to represent "tension insanity" in cases in which the patient displayed no reactivity to sensory impressions, lacked "self-will," and sat mute and physically immobile. These symptoms ostensibly reflected brain structure deterioration. In 1882, Kahlbaum clearly imprinted current thinking on the fixed co-occurrence of mania and melancholia, known today as bipolar disorder. He regarded them as facets of a single disease, which he termed *dysthymia*, and he termed a milder variant of the illness, notable for its frequent periods of normality, as *cyclothymia*.

Henry Maudsley (1835–1918) attempted to redirect the philosophical inclinations typical of British clinicians and sought to anchor the subject more solidly within the biological sciences. He vigorously asserted that mind and body formed a unified organism, "each part of which stirs the furthest components, which then acts upon the rest and is then reacted on by it....Emotions affect every part of the body and [are] rooted in the unity of organic life" (1876, p. 18). In 1876, he wrote, consistent with comparable views by Griesinger in Germany, that "mental disorders are neither more nor less than nervous diseases in which mental symptoms predominate" (1876, p. 41). Despite this view, Maudsley had asserted earlier

> that there is no boundary line between sanity and insanity; and the slightly exaggerated feeling which renders a man "peculiar" in the world differs only in degree from that which places hundreds in an asylum.... Where hereditary predisposition exists, a cause so slight as to be inappreciable to observers is often efficient to produce the disease. (1860, p. 14)

The Japanese first encountered Europeans in the middle of the sixteenth century, but they were highly ambivalent toward the European influences and remained isolated until the latter half of the nineteenth century. Western medicine, including Western psychiatry from Britain and Germany, was introduced, and Japanese psychiatry became strongly organic oriented. The writings of Maudsley (1835–1918), who believed that insanity was a bodily disease, and of Griesinger (1817–1868), whose approach has been described as "psychiatry without psychology," were among the most important influences in Japan. *Shuzo Kure (1865–1932)*, after a visit to Europe, brought back the ideas behind Kraepelin's descriptive psychiatry, as well as the emerging interest in psychoneuroses and psychotherapy. Also introduced was the term *neurasthenia*, in which a wide variety of bodily symptoms were explained as exhaustion of the central nervous system under the influence of physical and social stressors. Kure's pupil *Morita (1874–1938)*, having had personal experiences with neurasthenia, developed a psychogenic theory and treatment of neurosis, subsequently labeled *Morita therapy*, which deserve a closer description as an example of how Western and Eastern thinking met. Morita was influenced by the American neurologist *Silas Weir Mitchell (1829–1914)*, who invented a regimen of bed rest, isolation, rich diet, massage, and electrostimulation for neurasthenia, and by the neuropathologist and psychotherapist *Paul Charles Dubois (1848–1918)*, who believed that the therapist's task was to convince the patient that his or her neurotic feelings, thoughts, and behaviors were irrational. By integrating these ideas of Western scientists with thought from Zen Buddhism, Morita developed Morita therapy, which for a century has been widely used not only in Japan but also in China and in parts of Western societies. Morita's term for

neurosis was *shinkeishitsu*. All individuals are born with *sei no yokubo*, the desire to live, but this drive may be hindered by oversensitivity to oneself and one's limitations. Patients are not regarded as sick persons but as healthy persons who are obsessed by their own anxieties and fears. He described three different kinds of shinkeishitsu: (1) the ordinary type, which resembles what is now labeled somatization disorder; (2) the obsessive/phobic type, or *taijin kyofusho* (TKS), now categorized as agoraphobia, simple phobia, social phobia, and OCD; and (3) the paroxymal neurosis type, with symptoms similar to those seen in agoraphobia or general anxiety disorder. Morita therapy adheres to a strict time schedule, starting with complete isolation in a private familial, homelike room to give a feeling of security for a week, followed by light activities and exchanges of the patient's diary with the therapist. Then comes a stage of work, such as gardening, and finally a stage during which patients turn toward realities regarding their families and society. The goal of treatment is not necessarily the disappearance of symptoms but the ability to function normally and productively despite the symptoms. Morita's concept *arugamama*, meaning "things are as they are," is the mental attitude that patients show toward their symptoms. These ideas of body–mind–nature monism affirming and accepting worldly passion and desires, stressing the practice of daily life, are clearly borrowed from Japanese Shintoism, Zen Buddhism, and oriental psychology, as well as from some of Japan's cultural patterns, such as the meaning of and devotion to work, accepting reality, and persistence. Throughout the nineteenth century, German psychiatrists abandoned what they considered to be the value-laden theories of the French and English alienists of the time. Among this group was *J. A. Koch (1841–1908)*, who proposed replacing the label *moral insanity* with the term *psychopathic inferiority*, under which he included "all mental irregularities whether congenital or acquired which influence a man in his personal life and cause him, even in the most favorable cases, to seem not fully in possession of normal mental capacity" (1891, p. 67). Koch used the term *psychopathic*, a generic label employed to characterize all personality diagnosis until recent decades, to signify his belief that a physical basis existed for these character impairments. Thus, he stated: "They always remain psychopathic in that they are caused by organic states and changes which are beyond the limits of physiological normality. They stem from a congenital or acquired inferiority of brain constitution" (1891, p. 54).

Emergence of Modern Psychiatry

Emil Kraepelin's *(1856–1926)* comprehensive textbooks at the turn of the twentieth century served as one of psychiatry's two major sources of inspiration; the other resulted from Freud's innovative psychoanalytic contributions. As the preeminent German systematist, Kraepelin bridged the diverse views and observations of Greisinger and Kahlbaum in his outstanding texts, revised from a small compendium in 1883 to an imposing four-volume eighth edition in 1915. Kraepelin built a system that integrated Kahlbaum's descriptive and longitudinal approach with Greisinger's somatic disease view. By sifting and sorting prodigious numbers of well-documented hospital records and directly observing the varied characteristics of patients, he sought to bring order between symptom pictures and, most importantly, patterns of onset, course, and outcome. Kraepelin felt that syndromes based on these sequences would be best in leading to accurate identification and distinction among the different conditions and their causes.

Kraepelin (Figure 1.4) was born in Germany in the same year Sigmund Freud was born in Austria. A serious and diligent student, in medical school Kraepelin was exposed to several professors who were instrumental in shaping his thinking and research. Kraepelin became one of the distinguished psychologist Wilhelm Wundt's most competent students; Wundt, however, advised him to pursue medicine rather than psychology, which was then a fledgling science with limited career opportunities. In 1882 Kraepelin began the initial drafts of his first textbook, which later became the standard for educating psychiatrists. In 1891 Kraepelin had achieved sufficient recognition professionally to be invited to the University of Heidelberg. There he kept a card file on every patient, noting clinical symptoms, prior history, and outcome. By this time, Kraepelin had begun to mentor numerous German, British, and American psychiatric researchers.

His first text, a 300-page volume entitled *Compendium of Psychiatry* (1893), was so

Figure 1.4 Portrait of Kraepelin.

successful that it led to several subsequent editions published under the general title *Short Textbook of Psychiatry*. By the sixth edition of what he subsequently called his *Lehrbuch*, or *Textbook of Psychiatry*, completed between 1899 and 1902, Kraepelin was known throughout the Continent and the English-speaking world. In 1904 he became chairman of the Psychiatric Clinic and Laboratory at the University of Munich, a distinguished department where he was able to bring along with him from Heidelberg promising young researchers such as Alois Alzheimer and Franz Nissl, both already known for their excellent neurohistological studies and peculiar work habits. At the time of his death in 1926 at age 70, Kraepelin was actively working on a ninth edition of his textbook, which had expanded to four volumes and more than 3,000 pages.

Kraepelin did not set out initially to create the nosology for which he became so famous. Although he proposed a series of revolutionary ideas concerning the nature of clinical syndromes, it was the astuteness of his observations and the clarity of his writing that proved to be so central to the success of his work. Kraepelin wrote very little about how classification should be organized; that is, he used no formal set of principles to rationalize how a nosology should be structured. Instead, the implicit structure of his books (i.e., their basic table of contents) served as his classification system. Not to be dismissed was the logic that he presented for organizing syndromes on the basis of clinical symptomatology, course, and outcome. Perhaps it was the input of his mentor Wundt's keen observation and analysis of the behavior of his subjects in his research studies that taught Kraepelin to provide such richly descriptive characterization of his own patients. The following paragraphs touch on only a few of his conceptions regarding the major forms of psychoses and the syndromes that are now termed personality disorders.

Kraepelin constantly revised his diagnostic system, elaborating it at times, simplifying it at others. In the sixth edition of 1899, he established the definitive pattern of two modern major disorders: *manic-depressive psychosis* (now known as bipolar disorder) and *dementia praecox* (now known as schizophrenic disorders). Within the manic-depressive group he brought together the excited conditions of mania and the hopeless melancholia of depression, indicating the periodic course through which these moods alternated in the same patient. To be consistent with his disease orientation, he proposed that the cause of this disorder was an irregular metabolic function transmitted by heredity.

In his original treatise, Kraepelin asserted that the diverse symptom complexes of catatonia and hebephrenia, as well as certain paranoid disturbances, displayed a common theme of early deterioration and ultimate incurability. As he conceived them, each of these illnesses was a variation of Morel's concept of dementia praecox. By subsuming the disparate symptoms of these formerly separate syndromes under the common theme of their ostensive early and inexorable mental decline, Kraepelin brought a measure of order and simplicity to what had previously been diagnostic confusion. In line with the traditions of German psychiatry, Kraepelin assumed that a biophysical defect lay at the heart of these new coordinated syndromes. In contrast to his forebears who proposed anatomical lesions, however, he speculated that sexual and metabolic dysfunctions were the probable causal agents. Among the major signs that Kraepelin considered central to these illnesses were progressive and inevitable decline, discrepancies between thought and emotion, negativism and stereotyped behaviors, wandering or unconnected ideas, hallucinations, delusions, and a general mental deterioration.

Despite Kraepelin's rigorous application of the disease concept, in the seventh edition of his text, he recognized that the milder disturbances of neuroses, hysteria, and fright were probably psychogenic. He also separated the "personality" and "temperament" variants of disorders from the clinical state of a disease. He proposed the name *maniacal-depressive insanity* for "the whole domain of periodic and circular insanity," including such diverse disturbances as "the morbid states termed melancholia as well as certain slight colorings of mood, some of them periodic, some of them continuously morbid" (1896, p. 161). Like Kahlbaum, Kraepelin viewed "circular insanity" to be a unitary illness. Moreover, he conceived that every disorder that featured mood disturbances—however regular or irregular and whatever the predominant affect, be it irritability, depression, or mania—was a variant of the same cyclothymic impairment. To Kraepelin, the common denominator for these disturbances was an endogenous metabolic dysfunction that was "to an astonishing degree independent of external influences" (1896, p. 173).

Extending the range of severity of the circular insanities, Kraepelin identified four mild varieties of the cyclothymic disposition: *hypomanic, depressive, irascible,* and *emotionally unstable.* He described the *hypomanic* type as follows:

They acquire, as a rule, but scant education, with gaps and unevenness, as they show no perseverance in their studies, are disinclined to make an effort, and seek all sorts of ways to escape from the constraints of a systematic mental culture. The emotional tone of these patients is persistently elated, carefree, self-confident. Toward others they are overbearing, arbitrary, impatient, insolent, defiant. They mix into everything, overstep their prerogatives, make unauthorized arrangements, as they prove themselves everywhere useless. (1909–1915, Vol. 4, p. 221)

In describing the mild *depressive* type Kraepelin wrote:

There are certain temperaments which may be regarded as rudiments of *manic-depressive* insanity. They may throughout the whole of life exist as peculiar forms of psychic personality, without further development; but they may also become the point of departure for a morbid process which develops under peculiar conditions and runs its course in isolated attacks. Not at all infrequently, moreover, the permanent divergencies are already in themselves so considerable that they also extend into the domain of the morbid without the appearance of more severe, delimited attacks. (1921, p. 118)

Kraepelin considered these personalities to be characterized by an inborn temperamental disposition, one characterized "by a permanent gloomy emotional stress in all experiences in life" (1921, p. 118). According to him, "the morbid picture is usually perceptible already in youth, and may persist without essential change throughout life" (1921, p. 123).

The *irascible* type was ostensibly endowed simultaneously with hypomanic and depressive inclinations. To Kraepelin, "They are easily offended, hot-headed, and on trivial occasions become enraged and give way to boundless outbursts of energy. Ordinarily the patients are, perhaps, serene, self-assertive, ill-controlled; periods, however, intervene in which they are cross and sullen" (1921, p. 222).

The *emotionally unstable* variant presumably also possessed both hypomanic and depressive dispositions but manifested them in an alternating, cyclothymic pattern. He described these patients as follows:

It is seen in those persons who constantly swing back and forth between the two opposite poles of emotion, now shouting with joy to heaven, now grieved to death. Today lively, sparkling, radiant, full of the joy of life, enterprise, they meet us after a while depressed, listless, dejected, only to show again several months later the former liveliness and elasticity. (1921, p. 222)

What Kraepelin termed the *autistic temperament* served as the constitutional soil for the development of dementia praecox, a more severe class of mental disorders. Of particular note was Kraepelin's observation that children of this temperament frequently "exhibited a quiet, shy, retiring disposition, made no friendships, and lived only for themselves" (1921, p. 109). They were disinclined to be open or to become involved with others, were reclusive, and had difficulty adapting to new situations. They showed little interest in what went on about them, often refrained from participating in games and other pleasures, seemed resistant to influence (but in a passive rather than an active way), and were inclined to withdraw increasingly in a world of their own fantasies.

Among the *morbid personalities*, Kraepelin included a wide range of types disposed to criminal activities. As early as 1905 he identified four kinds of persons who had features akin to what we speak of today as antisocial personalities. First were the "morbid liars and swindlers," who were glib and charming but lacked inner morality and a sense of responsibility to others. They made frequent use of aliases, were inclined to be fraudulent con men, and often accumulated heavy debts that were invariably unpaid; this type proves to be descriptively similar to those classified today as "narcissistic" personalities. The second group included "criminals by impulse," individuals who engaged in crimes such as arson, rape, and kleptomania, and were driven by an inability to control their urges; they rarely sought material gains for their criminal actions. The third type, essentially referred to as "professional criminals," included those who were neither impulsive nor undisciplined; in fact, they often appeared well-mannered and socially appropriate, but were inwardly calculating, manipulative, and self-serving. The fourth type, the "morbid vagabonds," consisted of those strongly disposed to wander through life, never taking firm root, lacking both self-confidence and the ability to undertake adult responsibilities.

Although less successful in influencing nosological thinking in the latter half of the nineteenth and early twentieth centuries than Kraepelin, several other distinguished thinkers deserve recognition. *Phillipe Chaslin (1857–1923)* was a great French theorist whose life's work overlapped with Bleuler's in Switzerland, Kraepelin's in Germany, and Freud's in Austria. A philosopher and linguist at heart, he spent the majority of his professional career at the Salpêtrière Hospital in Paris where he wrote on a wide range of topics such as history, linguistics, and mathematics as well as psychiatry. Among his central formulations was the concept of "discordance," a notion he used to describe and explain dementia praecox; Bleuler, who originated the term *schizophrenia* in his 1911 treatise on the subject, stated later that he might have preferred "discordant insanity" as an alternative label, had he known of it earlier.

In his major work, *Elements de Seminologie et de Clinique Mentale*, written in 1912, Chaslin conveyed a series of ideas similar to those formulated concurrently by Freud, but with special reference to psychotic delusions. For example, he wrote:

> Delusional ideas seem to have their source in the emotions of the patient of which they are symbolic representations....One could illustrate the origins of delusions by recollecting the mechanisms of dreaming. Propensities, desires, and feelings from the waking state reappear in dreams in symbolic scenes. (1912, p.178)

Chaslin was concerned, as were many philosophers of the day, with the failure of psychiatric language to adequately represent the nature of the disorders they diagnosed and treated. In describing the difficulties of psychopathological terminology, Chaslin exclaimed:

> I believe that the imprecision of terms is due to the imprecision of our ideas, but I also think that the inexactitude of a language may cause further inexactitude in our ideas....If [the terminology] only helped to combat factual imprecisions, but the opposite is the case; it is often imagined that progress has been made simply because fancy names have been given to old things. (1912, p.18)

Eugen Bleuler (1857–1939) is universally recognized for his description of what is known as *schizophrenia*, the term he coined to replace the historic diagnostic label *dementia praecox*. The term *schizophrenia* is now judged by many to be unfortunate, suggesting a "splitting between segments of the mind." As evidence now indicates, patients diagnosed with schizophrenia do not suffer any form of splitting, but rather are characterized by disordered thinking leading to delusions and hallucinations.

Before the age of 30, Bleuler became director of the Rheinau Mental Hospital. During his 10-year tenure he was known for developing a close, personal, and emotional relationship with each patient. During this period he acquired his deep sensitivity for the most intimate details of his patients' psychological life, a source from which he based his theoretical ideas concerning schizophrenia. In 1898 Bleuler left to head the Burghölzli Mental Hospital, an already distinguished center for the clinical study of mental illness. Bleuler daily spent hours talking with his patients, often in their own unusual dialects, searching to gain an understanding of the psychological meaning of their seemingly senseless verbalizations and delusions. Most importantly, he urged his students and residents to be open-minded and to establish an emotional rapport with their patients, to develop an attitude that would enable them to track the meaning of the words their patients used, as well as the word associations that might give meaning to their utterances. It was in this regard that Bleuler saw the utility of Freud's new free-association methods, and it was also on these grounds that he instilled an interest in his young associate, Carl Jung, in Freud's early psychoanalytic concepts.

Bleuler's studies of "association" led to his theory of schizophrenia, that is, reflecting patients' ostensive inability to connect their thoughts with their feelings, the "loosening" or disintegration in their capacity to associate ideas and emotions, and, hence, the presumed "split" between these two core psychic processes. Following on ideas that were then emerging in the writings of both Freud and Janet, Bleuler asserted that his schizophrenic patients would display secondary symptoms that derived from the primary or fundamental thought/feeling disconnection, symptoms that evidenced themselves in an autistic separation from reality, in repetitive psychic ambivalences, and in verbal behaviors akin to dreaming. Although committed to Kraepelin's view that dementia praecox was primarily an organic disease, Bleuler emphasized the presence of psychological ambivalence and disharmony in this impairment.

The observing of hundreds of patients with dementia praecox in the early 1900s led Bleuler to conclude that it was misleading to compare the type of deterioration they evidenced with that found among patients suffering from metabolic deficiencies or brain degeneration. Moreover, he judged his patients' reactions and thoughts to be qualitatively complex and often highly creative, contrasting markedly with the simple or meandering thinking that Kraepelin observed. Not only did many of his patients display their illness for the first time in adulthood rather than in adolescence, a significant proportion also evidenced *no* progressive deterioration, which Kraepelin considered the sine qua non of the syndrome. To Bleuler, the label *dementia praecox* implied an age of onset and a course of development not supported by the evidence. In Bleuler's view, schizophrenia's primary symptoms were disturbances in the associative link among thoughts, a breach between affect and intellect, ambivalence toward the same objects, and an autistic detachment from reality. The several varieties of patients that displayed these fragmented thoughts, feelings, and actions led Bleuler to term them "the group of schizophrenias."

In what Bleuler termed *Schizoidie* he recognized that some milder temperament dispositions, if left untreated, might ultimately evolve into a clinical schizophrenic state. In 1911 Bleuler described one of the first portrayals that approximate what is now called the avoidant personality. Discussing several of the contrasting routes that often lead to the psychotic schizophrenic syndrome, Bleuler recorded the early schizoidic phase as follows:

There are also cases where the shutting off from the outside world is caused by contrary reasons. Particularly in the beginning of their illness, these patients quite consciously shun any contact with reality because their affects are so powerful that they must avoid everything which might arouse their emotions. The apathy toward the outer world is then a secondary one springing from a hypertrophied sensitivity. (1911/1950, p. 65)

Adolf Meyer (1866–1950), like Bleuler, was born in Switzerland, but he spent most of his professional life in the United States. Meyer introduced the concept of a "constitutionally inferior psychopathic" type into American literature at the turn of the century, shortly after his arrival from Germany. However, Meyer sought to separate psychopathic from psychoneurotic disorders. He was convinced that the etiology of the neuroses was primarily psychogenic, that is, colored less by inherent physical defects or by constitutional inferiorities. Meyer became disillusioned with Kraepelin's approach, particularly the fatalistic view of illness and the strictly deterministic prognosis and outcome for those of a problematic temperament. Meyer turned to a view increasingly shared by psychoanalysts: psychiatric disorders were not fundamentally organic conditions but rather a consequence of environmental factors and life events. Although initially sympathetic to Freud's theories, Meyer soon became critical of the mystical and esoteric nature of psychoanalysis. Despite his break from Freud's metapsychology, Meyer shared a common view regarding the role of life experiences as central to the emergence of all psychiatric disorders.

As early as 1910, Meyer espoused the view that the only way to derive a true understanding of patients would be by studying individuals' total reaction to their organic, psychological, and social experiences. Although Meyer was the most prominent psychiatrist to introduce the Kraepelinian system in this country, he believed that these disorders were not disease entities but "psychobiological reactions" to environmental stress. For example, in 1906 Meyer asserted that dementia praecox was not an organic disease but a maladaptive way of reacting to life's difficulties, fully understandable in terms of the patient's constitutional potentials and life experiences. To him, these maladaptive reactions led to what he called "progressive habit deteriorations," which reflected "inefficient and faulty attempts to avoid difficulties" (1912, p. 98). Meyer regarded symptoms of mental illness as the end product of abortive and self-defeating efforts to establish psychic equilibrium. His psychobiological approach to schizophrenia was the most systematic recognition of his interactive and progressive view of the nature of pathogenesis.

Of note was Meyer's view that schizophrenia could be present in a dilute and nonpsychotic form, that is, without delusions, hallucinations, or deterioration. He considered the classic psychotic symptoms to be advanced signs of a potentially, but not inevitably, evolving habit system that might stabilize at a prepsychotic level. In its nonclinical state, professionals could detect it by a variety of attenuated and soft signs that merely suggested the manifest psychotic disorder. Meyer's proposal of a maladaptive reaction system akin to subclinical schizophrenia was an innovative, but unheeded, notion.

Karl Jaspers (1883–1969) was undoubtedly an influential founding pioneer of phenomenological and existential psychiatry, though, oddly enough, he did not consider himself a phenomenologist. His system of mental illness approached classification in a unique way; that is, it sought to describe the patient's true subjective experience and how he or she faced mental illness, rather than simply describing overt psychological syndromes as observed by the therapist. To this end, Jaspers made distinctions such as that between "feelings" and "sensations"—the former being emotional states of the individual, and the latter being part of the individual's reactions to and perceptions of the environment. The ultimate goal of this system was to orient and enable the therapist to be as sensitive and empathic as possible with the patient. It was Jaspers' contention that the inexhaustibly infinite depth and uniqueness of any single individual, mentally ill or healthfully functioning, could not be completely understood and objectified, but the medical/psychological practitioner had to strive for as close an understanding as possible. It was this existential aspect of humankind that set this system apart from the traditional means of diagnosis and treatment. In contrast with the psychoanalysts, who attempted to probe beneath the surface of patients' verbal reports to uncover their unconscious roots, Jaspers focused on patients' conscious self-description of feelings and experiences, believing that their phenomenological reports were the best source to achieve a true understanding of the world of the abnormal.

Together, Meyer's concept of reaction types, Jasper's existential phenomenology, and Bleuler's focus on cognitive and emotional experience reshaped Kraepelin's original system into a more contemporary psychiatric nosology. Kraepelin's clinical categories were retained as the basic framework, and Meyer's and Bleuler's psychological notions provided guidelines to the patient's inner processes and social reactions.

The Rise and Fall of Psychoanalysis in the Twentieth Century

Many consider *Jean-Martin Charcot (1825–1893)* (Figure 1.5) to be the father of clinical neurology. Charcot was a senior physician at the Bicêtre and later at the deteriorated Salpêtrière women's hospital. There, in 1862, Charcot studied the chronically ill women housed in its decaying wards and recognized that more than half had been incorrectly diagnosed, most having been lumped together in one or two categories indiscriminately. Charcot's first discoveries related to multiple sclerosis (MS), which was unrecognized as a distinct disease in the 1860s. Collaborating with Edme Vulpain, he demonstrated the classic disintegration of the myelin sheath, the anatomical feature of the disorder. Also important was Charcot's recognition of the visual problems typical of those with MS, as well as his patients' tendency to exhibit extreme fluctuations in symptom intensity over time. Another important contribution was his distinction between MS and the "shaking palsy," or what came to be called parkinsonism. Charcot

Figure 1.5 Portrait of Charcot.

identified features of the disorder that Parkinson had overlooked, such as patients' blank stares, motionless and stolid expressions, and periodic and involuntary oscillation of hand movements.

Charcot's work was quickly recognized throughout the Continent, attracting disciples and students from far and wide. Of special note in his later years was an interest in *hysteria*, a label used in his day for patients with clinical signs of pathology that could not be correlated with underlying anatomical or neurological diseases. Hysteria was considered by many to be a catchall, but Charcot made a valiant effort to subdivide the variants of those so categorized. He differentiated subgroups still in use, such as those with defective memories, peculiar or inexplicable losses of sensitivity, motoric seizures that simulated epilepsy, and so on. It was Charcot's contention that all hysterical patients suffered from a "weak" constitution—that is, they possessed neurological vulnerabilities that made them highly susceptible to ordinary life conditions. Charcot asserted that hysterics were readily hypnotized, indeed, that only hysterics could be hypnotized, and that they were readily swayed by the suggestions of others.

Charcot's stature and ideas concerning hysteria attracted numerous students, including the young *Sigmund Freud (1856–1939)*, a neurologist in training from Vienna, who came to study with Charcot during the winter of 1885. So impressed was Freud with Charcot's lectures that he set out to translate the professor's writings for German-reading neurologists. However, Freud progressed in his own direction, disagreeing with Charcot's neurological assertions regarding hysteria.

The concept of the unconscious—inner thoughts and feelings beyond immediate awareness—was brought to the fore through the dramatic methods of an Austrian physician, *Franz Anton Mesmer (1734–1815)*. Borrowing Paracelsus's notion of a physically based planetary magnetism, Mesmer believed that many forms of illness resulted from imbalances of universal magnetic fluids. These imbalances, he concluded, could be restored either by manipulating magnetic devices or by drawing upon invisible magnetic forces that emanated from one person to another.

By the late nineteenth century, both magnetism and hypnotism, a method developed by *James Braid (1795–1860)*, had begun to fall into disrepute as therapeutic procedures. A modest physician working in a rural region near Nancy in France had heard of James Braid's work at a lecture and decided to explore its possibilities in his limited practice. Well-regarded in his local community, *Auguste Ambroise Liebault (1823–1904)* used a simple method of inducing sleep, by suggesting to patients that they look into his eyes while he spoke to them in quiet tones. In the 1866, Liebault published a small book, entitled *Du Sommeil et Des Etates Analogues (Sleep and Analogous States)*, in which he stressed that the power of suggestion was central to successful hypnotism, as well as the primary vehicle of therapeutic efficacy.

Liebault was generally considered to be a simpleton, if not a quack, by his colleagues. Nevertheless, rumors of his therapeutic successes came to the attention of a well-regarded professor of medicine at the Nancy School of Medicine, *Hippolyte-Marie Bernheim (1840–1919)*, a young, Jewish physician who had recently been appointed to this new medical institution. Bernheim had been treating a patient with sciatica for 6 years with minimal success. He referred this patient to Liebault, who used his methods of suggestive sleep and succeeded within 6 months in fully relieving the patient of the disorder. As a result, Bernheim decided to experiment with Liebault's radical hypnotic methods in his own clinic.

As discussed earlier, *Jean Charcot's (1835–1893)* signal importance was in developing methods of clinical neurology. His role in fostering a psychoanalytically oriented psychiatry, by contrast, stems less from the intent or the originality of his work than in the incidental part he played in stimulating the ideas of others, notably Freud and Janet. As noted earlier, Charcot studied the diverse and confusing symptoms of hysteria, at the Salpêtrière hospital in Paris. Because of his neurological orientation, he viewed trances, memory losses, and bodily anesthesia as being diagnostically difficult cases of an underlying nervous system disease. It was not until his associates demonstrated that the symptoms of hysteria could be induced by hypnotic procedures that Charcot reconsidered his views of this puzzling ailment. His inability to differentiate between hypnotized and naturally produced paralyses, as well as the frequently noted migration or disappearance of symptoms and the anatomically impossible location of many of the paralyses he saw, convinced him that hysteria could not be a product of a simple injury or local disease of the nervous system. Despite suggestive evidence to the contrary, Charcot could not abandon his biological perspective. To accommodate his observations, he proposed that hysteria resulted from a wide-ranging and congenital neurological deficiency and that hypnosis merely served as a precipitant that stirred and exposed the inborn defect.

Charcot presented his neurological thesis regarding hysteria and hypnotism at the French Academy of Sciences in the early 1880s. Shortly thereafter, Bernheim offered an alternate view of hypnosis: that it could be employed with a variety of ailments, not only with hysterics; that its effects stemmed from the power of suggestion; and that all humans were susceptible to suggestion in varying degrees. Bernheim elaborated on his views in his book, *Suggestive Therapeutics*, as follows:

We have shown that the phenomena which are present in the hypnotic and waking conditions, are not due to a magnetic fluid, to an emanation from one organism to another, but that the whole explanation lies in suggestion: that is, in the influence exerted by an idea which has been suggested to and received by the mind. The most striking feature in a hypnotized subject is his automatism. The cataleptic condition is the result of suggestion. The subject retains the attitude in which he is placed, and continues the movements communicated to his limbs. He perceives the sensations impressed upon his mind. He believes that the visual images which are suggested, are realities, and refers them to the outer world. (1900, p. 118)

Bernheim advanced the view that hysteria was essentially a psychogenic disorder and applied the term *psychoneurosis* for this and similar puzzling symptom syndromes. His belief that unconscious self-suggestion might underlie the symptoms of many mental disorders played a significant role in influencing subsequent thinking, most notably Freud's. In his psychoneurotic concept, Bernheim sought to parallel the medical tradition of seeking underlying biological causes for the disorder with a comparable notion of underlying psychological causes.

A distinguished Viennese internist, *Josef Breuer (1842–1925)*, whetted Freud's curiosity about both hysteria and hypnosis in discussing a young patient of his, later to become famous under the pseudonym of Anna O. The case of Anna O. was a classical example of hysteria that followed a period when the young woman had nursed her father through a major illness. Breuer employed a hypnotic technique to encourage his patient to voice her experiences and thoughts at the time her symptoms emerged. The memories that Anna O. recalled under hypnosis were accompanied by intense outbursts of emotion that she was unable to vent at the time of her symptoms. Moreover, she developed an intense attachment to Breuer, who became uncomfortable with her affectionate feelings toward him.

Freud traveled to observe Charcot in Paris and later to study with Bernheim in Nancy, where he observed their methods and ideas. On his return from these travels in the latter 1880s, Breuer and Freud continued their discussions with a series of new cases, employing the methods of hypnosis and the stirrings of emotional catharses. This work ultimately led to a series of papers and the publication of a major book, entitled *Studies on Hysteria*, in 1895. In their view, hysterical patients suffered from repressed memories of an emotionally traumatic event that were so distressing that the emotions aroused could not be faced consciously at the time the event occurred. It was Breuer and Freud's contention that the technique for curing hysteria was to unblock the repressed and pent-up emotions that had been "kept secret" in the unconscious.

Concurrent with this work were the studies of *Pierre Janet (1859–1947)*, who might have been considered the most original thinker of psychoanalytic processes had Freud not overshadowed him. Working closely with Charcot, Janet evolved a theory in which neuroses resulted from an inability to integrate co-occurring psychic processes; this thesis foreshadowed and may have led Bleuler to his notion that dementia praecox (schizophrenia) was a split between thought and emotion. Like Freud, Janet observed that his patients could not tolerate painful experiences and undesirable impulses. In his concept of *dissociation*, Janet speculated that intolerable thoughts and feelings might take on an independent existence within the person and manifest themselves in amnesia, multiple personality, hysterical fits, or conversion paralyses. In this formulation, Janet recognized that different systems of thought could become pathologically separated, with one or another part lost to consciousness, strengthening the idea that unconscious processes may persist unmodified within the person.

Returning to the work of Sigmund Freud, he was, perhaps arguably, the most influential psychologist of the early twentieth century. Venerated by some and condemned by others, Freud has been spoken of as one of history's great scientists, as well as a fraudulent cult leader. Numerous historians refer to him as the greatest psychologist of all time. Others are convinced that the unconscious never existed, except in Freud's mind, and that his theories were baseless and aberrational. His most condemning detractors describe him as a neurotic egotist who propounded irrational and fantastic theories. More balanced historians aver that Freud's discoveries merely crystallized previously diffuse ideas of his many predecessors. Personally and professionally, Freud was a man of divergent dispositions, a militant atheist and radical theorist, espousing liberated attitudes toward sexuality but, at the same time, politically conservative, usually somber and unsmiling, impeccably dressed, invariably anxious about finances, clearly suffering in his mid-years from assorted psychosomatic symptoms, and fearfully hesitant about modern contrivances.

Freud devoted his long and fruitful life to the development and elaboration of his theories and techniques. Unlike his contemporary Kraepelin, who sought to classify broad groups of disorders with a common course and symptoms, Freud stressed the brightly etched inner memories, the feverish imaginations, and the unique attributes of each patient. And unlike Janet, his French contemporary, who viewed neuroses as the upshot of an underlying constitutional deficiency, Freud set out to trace the perplexing ambiguities, the afflicted emotional palette, the convoluted psychogenic origins, and the primitive passions that he perceived as the unconscious source of each disorder.

The emphasis Freudian theorists place on early childhood experience represents their contention that disorders of adulthood are a direct product of the continued and insidious operation of past events. To them, knowledge of the past provides information indispensable to understanding adult difficulties. To the question, "What is the basis of adult disorders?" they would answer: "the anxieties of childhood and the progressive sequence of defensive maneuvers that were devised to protect against a recurrence of these feelings." Adult patterns of behavior, therefore, are not a function of random influences according to psychoanalysis but arise from clear-cut antecedent causes. For the most part, these causes persist out of awareness that is kept unconscious owing to their troublesome character, notably the stressful memories and emotions they contain and the primitive nature of the child's youthful defenses. Central also to the analytic viewpoint is the concept of psychic conflict. In this notion, behavior is considered to result from competing desires and their prohibitions, which are expressed overtly, often in disguised form, only through compromise and defensive maneuver. Further, all forms of behavior, emotion, or cognition likely serve multiple needs and goals—that is, they are overdetermined. Behavioral expressions and conscious cognitions emerge as surface manifestations of several hidden forces that reside in the unconscious.

According to Freud, each stage of "psychosexual" development produces a distinctive set of anxieties and defenses resulting from instinct frustration and conflict. Symptoms and character traits arise from the persistence into adulthood of childhood anxieties and defenses. Freud's early disciples, notably *Karl Abraham (1877–1925)* and *Wilhelm Reich (1897–1957)*, differentiated the oral psychosexual period into two phases: the *oral-sucking* phase, in which food is accepted indiscriminately, followed by the *oral-biting* period, in which food is accepted selectively, occasionally rejected, and aggressively chewed. In their view, excessive gratifications, conflicts, or frustrations associated with each of these phases establish different patterns of adult personality. For example, an overly indulgent sucking stage may lead to imperturbable optimism and naive self-assurance. An ungratified sucking period may lead to excessive dependency and gullibility; for example, deprived children may learn to accept anything in order to ensure that they will get something. Frustration experienced at the biting stage might lead to the development of aggressive oral tendencies such as sarcasm and verbal hostility in adulthood. Freud eventually speculated that character classification could be based on his threefold structural distinction of id, ego, and superego. Thus, in 1931 he sought to devise character types in accord with which structure was dominant. First, he proposed an "erotic" type, whose life is governed by the instinctual demands of the id. "Narcissistic" types are so dominated by the ego that neither other persons nor the demands of id or superego can affect them. "Compulsive" types were regulated by the strictness of the superego such that all other functions are dominated. Last, Freud identified a series of mixed types in which two of the three outweighed the third. Freud's compulsive character type has been well represented in the literature, but only in the past 30 years have his proposals for a narcissistic personality disorder gained attention (Millon, 1981; Millon & Davis, 1996).

Alfred Adler (1870–1937), founder of the school of individual psychology, was perhaps the first of Freud's disciples to become an outspoken critic of Freud's views on infantile sexuality. On the basis of his own clinical observations, Adler concluded that superiority and power strivings were more fundamental to pathology than was sexuality. Although many of his patients were not overtly assertive, he observed that their disorders enabled them to dominate others in subtle ways. Phobias and hypochondriases, for example, not only excused patients from disagreeable tasks but also allowed them to manipulate others. Adler hypothesized that these strivings for superiority were a consequence of the inevitable and universal weakness and inferiority in early childhood. In this conception, Adler attempted to formulate a universal drive that would serve as an alternative to Freud's universal sexual strivings. According to Adler, basic feelings of inferiority led to persistent and unconscious compensatory efforts. Among healthier personalities, compensation accounted for strivings at self-improvement and interests in social change and welfare. These compensatory strivings led to a general pattern of behavior that Adler called the style of life.

Although chosen by Freud as his heir apparent, *Carl Gustav Jung (1875–1961)*, too, did not agree with Freud's emphasis on the sexual nature of development and motivation and established his own system of *analytic psychology* in 1920 (Jung, 1920). Jung expanded the notion of libido, Freud's concept for the basic sexual energies, to include all life-propelling forces. The concept of racial memories, known as the collective unconscious, was proposed to suggest that instinctual forces were more than seething animalistic impulses; according to Jung, these forces contained social dispositions as well. These primitive dispositions were often expressed in folklore and mystical beliefs. When no acceptable outlet could be found for them in societal life, they took the form of symptoms such as phobias, delusions, and compulsions. Jung's belief in unconscious social dispositions led also to his formulation of two basic personality types, the *extrovert* and the *introvert*. Despite these and other original contributions, Jung's views had minimal impact on the mainstream of psychoanalytic theory and practice.

Another important psychoanalyst, *Karen Horney (1885–1952)*, contended that the milder personality disorders reflected cultural trends learned within the family; she minimized biological determinants and stressed interpersonal relationships. She believed that anxiety and repressed anger were generated in rejected children and led to feelings of helplessness, hostility, and isolation. As these children matured, they developed an intricate defensive pattern of withdrawal, acquiescence, or aggression as a means of handling their basic anxiety. Horney identified three emergent modes of relating: "moving toward" people, "moving against" people, or "moving away" from them. In her 1945 book, Horney formulated a character type for each of these three solutions: moving toward was found in a "compliant" type; moving against, in an "aggressive" type; and moving away, in a "detached" type. Although Horney felt that adult patterns resulted largely from early experience, she argued, in contrast with Freud, that remedial efforts should focus on its adult form of expression. She averred that the intervening years between childhood and adulthood caused important changes in adaptive behavior. And further, it was important to accept present-day realities, and therapy had to take them into account.

Several major thinkers who had settled from Europe to Great Britain began to formulate what is now referred to as the object-relations approach to psychoanalytic theory, in the 1940s and 1950s. Most inventive of these was *Melanie Klein (1882–1960)*, one of the originators of child psychoanalysis, along with Anna Freud, with whom she vigorously differed and contended for leadership in the British analytic community. Klein's views met with intense opposition in the wider psychoanalytic world, and fierce battles raged within the English analytic society over her inventive concepts. Although a vigorous critic of more orthodox psychoanalytic thought, she believed that to emphasize the very earliest and most primitive stages of development was a natural extension of Freud's original formulations. In the United States, since the mid-1960s, *Otto Kernberg (1928–)* has sought to develop a synthesis of Freud's drive reduction and Klein's object-relations frameworks, an approach that has brought considerable attention to modern analytic thought, as well as generating considerable controversy.

Trends in the Personality Realm

Owing to numerous pragmatic considerations at the time, not the least of which were the advent of effective psychopharmacological medications and the emergence of the sophisticated community mental health movement, the balance of power within American psychiatry shifted in the 1970s slowly but surely away from its early alliance with psychoanalysis. The wider culture had also turned its back on the high repute it formerly had for psychoanalysts; no longer were they seen as wise, generous, and kindly. In a review of what was wrong with psychoanalysis, a number of critics stated that concepts such as infantile sexuality were not so much disproved as incapable of disproof; to them, such concepts should be relegated to the same scientific status as astrology. Others asserted that, just as chemistry had to slough off the fetters of alchemy and the brain sciences to disengage themselves from phrenology, so too psychology and psychiatry had to abandon the pseudo-science of psychoanalysis.

Despite these criticisms, unconscious processes remain a necessary part of the study of humankind's pathological functioning. Although these processes are difficult to formulate according to the tenets of scientific objectivity, their existence cannot be denied or overlooked.

In the middle and latter decades of the twentieth century, several major trends seem to have built a strong foundation for the future course of psychopathologic history. Each of them is briefly mentioned next.

Like intelligence and physique, *personality* is made up of the raw material from which the capacities and functions of each individual may be fashioned, comprising dispositions that are largely assumed to be unchanged throughout most of life. Drawing on Allport's (1937) early definition, personality is the individual's fundamental nature, including his or her susceptibility to experiences, largely dependent on constitutional makeup, yet distinctive and unique.

Kurt Schneider (1887–1967) proposed the best-known European classification of maladaptive personalities. Schneider differed from many of his contemporaries in that he did not view personality characterizations of pathology to be a precursor to other mental disorders but conceived personality as a separate group of entities that covaried with them. Whereas Kraepelin sought to objectify the mental disorders, Schneider's intent was to elucidate more clearly the patient's inner experiences. In the last edition of his text (1950) on psychopathological personalities, Schneider described the following 10 variants as often seen in psychiatric work. *Hyperthymic* personalities reflect a mix of high activity, optimism, and shallowness; they tend to be uncritical, cocksure, impulsive, and undependable. Many such individuals seem unable to concentrate, and those who achieve occasional insights fail to retain them as lasting impressions. The *depressive* personalities have a skeptical view of life, tend to take things seriously, and display little capacity for enjoyment. They are often excessively critical and deprecatory of others; at the same time, they are full of self-reproach and exhibit hypochondriacal anxieties. Schneider grouped *insecure* personalities into two subvarieties, the "sensitives" and the "anankasts" (compulsives). These individuals ruminate excessively over everyday experience but have little capacity for expressing or discharging the feelings these thoughts stir up. Chronically unsure of themselves, they are apt to view life as a series of unfortunate events. They tend to behave in a strict and disciplined manner, holding closely to what is judged as socially correct. *Fanatic*

personalities are expansive individuals inclined to be bitter, combative, and aggressive in promoting their views; they are often querulous and litigious. Among the *attention-seeking* personalities are those with heightened emotional responses who delight in novelty and give evidence of excess enthusiasms, vivid imaginations, and a striving to be in the limelight; showy and capricious, many are boastful and inclined to lie and distort. *Labile* personalities do not evidence a simple chronic emotionality but are characterized by abrupt and volatile mood changes, impulsive urges, sudden dislikes, and a shiftless immaturity. The *explosive* personality is characterized by being impulsively violent, disposed to be fractious, and likely to become combative without warning or provocation. *Affectionless* personalities lack compassion and are often considered callous and cold; they appear distant or indifferent to friends and strangers alike. Historically, these patients correspond to those identified in the literature as exhibiting "moral insanity." The so-called *weak-willed* personalities are not only docile and unassuming but also are easily subjected to seduction by others and readily exploited to no good end; they are inevitably fated to trouble and disillusionment. The last of Schneider's types, the *asthenic* personality, is subject to intense hypochondriacal scrutiny and is so preoccupied with bodily functions that external events fade into the background and appear strange or unreal.

Turning to more recent ideas, *Larry Siever's (1950–)* theoretical model has attempted to link neurotransmitter properties to the various personality disorders. His dimensional model has the major clinical syndromes at one extreme and the milder personality disorders at the other. He proposes four major functional dispositions: *cognitive/perceptual organization, impulsivity/aggression, affective instability*, and *anxiety/inhibition*. For example, his model views schizophrenic disorders as disturbances of a cognitive/perceptual nature, exhibiting themselves in thought disorders, psychotic symptoms, and social isolation; the schizotypal disorder would serve as the prototype among the personality types. He hypothesizes disorders of impulsivity/aggression as resulting in poor impulse control, particularly as evident in aggressive actions. In the more distinct clinical syndromes, Siever suggests the presence of this lack of control in explosive disorders, pathologic gambling, or kleptomania. When this dimension is more pervasive and chronic, as in the personality disorders, the predisposition may be present in persistent self-destructive behaviors, such as in borderline and antisocial personalities. Problems of affective instability are most clearly observed in the intensity and dysregulation of mood disorders. When this inclination is more sustained over time, it may interfere with the development of stable relationships and self-image, as may be manifested in borderline or histrionic personality disorders. Last, the anxiety/inhibition dimension appears to be related to the anxiety clinical syndromes (e.g., social phobia, compulsive rituals); when present at a low threshold over extended periods of development, an avoidant, compulsive, or dependent personality disorder may result.

Aaron Timothy Beck (1921–) has been a prominent and insightful contributor to cognitive therapy, especially as applied to a wide range of the Axis I clinical syndromes. More recently, he and his associates have addressed the subject of personality, articulating "cognitive schemas" that shape the experiences and behaviors of numerous personality disorders. He focused his early research efforts largely on testing psychoanalytic theories of depression, but when his studies failed to support his hypotheses, he explored a more cognitive explanation of the disorder. His inquiries found that most depressed patients had a broad and negative view of themselves and the world at large, as well as their own future. These negative cognitive distortions, Beck reasoned, should be able to be corrected through the application of logic and the rules of evidence by which erroneous beliefs could be reoriented to accord with reality. He eventually applied these cognitive investigations to a broad range of disorders, from anxiety, to substance abuse, to personality. Cognitive approaches to the treatment of mental disorders have become more than merely the mainstream of "talking therapies" today. More than one-third of all therapists speak of themselves as cognitive in orientation; the others employ cognitive techniques periodically.

C. Robert Cloninger (1945–) formulated a recent model anchored to a neurobiological theory of personality dispositions. His elegant model, which seeks to draw upon genetic and neurobiological substrates, proposes a complex theory based on the interrelationship of several trait dispositions. Central to Cloninger's formula are a series of heritable characteristics or functional dispositions, notably: novelty seeking, harm avoidance, and reward dependence. Each of these is associated with different neurobiological systems, respectively, dopaminergic, serotonergic, and noradrenergic.

More specifically, *novelty seeking* is hypothesized to dispose individuals toward exhilaration or excitement in response to novel stimuli, which leads to the pursuit of potential rewards as well as an active avoidance of both monotony and punishment. *Harm avoidance* reflects a disposition to respond strongly to aversive stimuli, leading individuals to inhibit behaviors to avoid punishment, novelty, and frustrations. *Reward dependence* is hypothesized as a tendency to respond to signals of reward (e.g., verbal signals of social approval) and to resist extinction of behaviors previously associated with rewards or relief from punishment. Extending the theme of novelty seeking, for example, individuals with this disposition, but average of the other two dimensions, would be characterized as impulsive, exploratory, excitable, quick-tempered, and extravagant, likely to seek out new interests but inclined to neglect details and to become quickly distracted or bored.

Although *Paul Meehl's (1920–2003)* biologically oriented social learning model is limited to schizophrenia, it is notable both for its elegance and specificity. He hypothesized that only a certain class of people, those with a particular genetic constitution, have any liability to schizophrenia. Meehl suggested that the varied emotional and perceptual-cognitive dysfunctions that people with schizophrenia display are difficult to explain in terms of single-region disorders. The widespread nature of these dysfunctions suggest the operation of a more diffuse integrative neural defect. Although a combination of different neurological disturbances can account for this defect, Meehl opted for an explanation in terms of deficits in synaptic control. More specifically, he believed that the major problem in schizophrenia lay in a malfunctioning of the two-way mutual control system between perceptual-cognitive regions and the limbic motivation center. Meehl's proposal was that integrative neural defects are the only direct phenotypic consequences produced by the genetic disorders; given the label *schizotaxia*, it is all that can properly be spoken of as inherited. The imposition of certain social learning histories on schizotaxic individuals results in a personality organization that Meehl called the *schizotype*. Four core behavior traits, namely anhedonia, cognitive slippage, interpersonal aversiveness, and ambivalence, are not innate. However, Meehl postulated that schizotaxic individuals universally learned them, given any existing social learning regimen, from the best to the worst. If the social environment is favorable and the schizotaxic person has the good fortune of inheriting a low-anxiety readiness, possesses physical vigor, and a general resistance to stress, that person will remain a well-compensated schizotype and may never manifest symptoms of clinical schizophrenia.

In England, two child-oriented analysts, *Michael Balint (1896–1970)* and *John Bowlby (1907–1990)*, contributed to our understanding of developmental vicissitudes. Balint's concept of the "basic fault" spoke of patients whose borderline characteristics appeared to be a consequence of having missed something the first year or two of their early childhood life. In his view, the fault led to one of two extreme reactions: in the "ocnophile" adaptation the infant deals with the experience by clinging excessively to others; and in the "philobat" adaptation children learn to distance themselves from others and rely entirely on themselves. Bowlby stressed "attachment learning," especially that resulting from the loss of a significant early relationship. He speaks of children suffering maternal loss as passing through three phases: protest, despair, and detachment. In the first stage children evidence anger at their loss; in the second, children begin to lose hope that the mother will ever return; and finally, despair turns to disengagement in which children become depressed and unresponsive. Sharing Melanie Klein's object-relations model, Bowlby asserted that the manner in which children deal with affectional deprivation will determine how they will react in later life to problematic relationships with a loved one.

Using a threefold biosocial-learning framework as his original theoretical model in 1969, *Theodore Millon (1928–)* derived "coping patterns" that ultimately corresponded closely to each of the personality disorders published in *DSM-III*. These coping patterns represented complex forms of biologically grounded instrumental behavior, that is, adaptive ways of learning to achieve pleasure (positive reinforcements) and avoid pain (negative reinforcements). These learned strategies reflected what kinds of emotionally anchored reinforcements individuals learned to seek or to avoid (pleasure/pain), where individuals oriented themselves

to obtain them (self/others), and how vigorously they learned to behave to elicit or to escape them (active/passive). Eight basic personality styles, as well as three severe variants and numerous clinical syndromes, were derived by combining the *nature* (positive or pleasure versus negative or pain), the *source* (self versus others), and the *instrumental behaviors* (active versus passive) engaged in to achieve these emotionally divergent reinforcements. Describing psychopathology in terms of these coping behaviors merely cast them in a learning theory conceptual language that paralleled but differed from those conventionally utilized in prior diagnostic systems (Millon, 1969).

In 1990, Millon reconceptualized the theoretical grounding of these psychopathologies. Rather than basing them on learning concepts or neurochemistry, he set them on a foundation of evolutionary theory. Millon deduced that the principles and functional processes of evolution were the most fundamental and universal of nature's phenomena, albeit expressed in nature's realms (physics, biology) at different levels and in different manifest forms (Millon, 1990).

Millon came to believe that the widespread desire among theorists to unify science should not be limited to explicating physics; that is, it should be possible in all fields of nature that have been subdivided by habit, tradition, or pragmatics (e.g., economics, sociology, geology). He believed unification to be a worthy goal even within the newer sciences, such as personology. Efforts to coordinate the separate realms that comprise the field of the mind and, more specifically, that of mental disorders would be particularly useful. Rather than developing independently and being left to stand as autonomous and largely unconnected professional activities and goals, a truly mature mental science, one that would create a synergistic bond among its elements, would embody, five explicit elements:

1. *Universal scientific principles* that are grounded in the ubiquitous laws of nature. Despite their varied forms of expression, these principles may provide an undergirding framework for guiding and constructing narrow-based subject-oriented theories.
2. *Subject-oriented theories*, or explanatory and heuristic conceptual schemas of the mind and mental illness. These theories should be consistent with established

knowledge in both its own and related sciences and should enable reasonably accurate propositions concerning all clinical conditions to be both deduced and understood, enabling thereby the development of a formal classification system.

3. *Classification of personality styles and pathological syndromes*, or a taxonomic nosology that has been derived logically from the theory. The taxonomy should provide a cohesive organization within which its major categories can readily be grouped and differentiated, permitting thereby the development of coordinated assessment instruments.

4. *Personality and clinical assessment instruments*, or tools that are empirically grounded and sufficiently sensitive quantitatively to enable the theory's propositions and hypotheses to be adequately investigated and evaluated. Hence, the clinical categories comprising its nosology should be able to be readily identified (diagnosed) and measured (dimensionalized), thus specifying target areas for interventions.

5. *Integrated therapeutic interventions*, or planful strategies and modalities of treatment. These interventions should accord with the theory and be oriented to modify problematic clinical characteristics, consonant with professional standards and social responsibilities.

The advent of the *DSM-III* in 1980 was a signal advance in classification logic and achievement to numerous psychiatrists. But in recent years, sharp criticisms have been raised against the dominance of the *DSM* as merely a variant of the Kraepelinian system. Many eminent clinicians assert that, except in the organic disorders, classificatory diagnosis is less important than a psychodynamic study of the patient; that is, rather than fitting the symptoms into a classificatory scheme, clinicians should endeavor to understand the sick person in terms of the individual's life experience (American Psychoanalytic Association, 2006). Others have noted that research time is wasted and errors are perpetuated because investigators cling to an outdated classification. *DSM* proponents, in contrast, have argued that the Kraepelinian schema is more valid and practical than existing alternatives.

One of the major problems facing a field as inchoate and amorphous as mental health is its susceptibility to subjective values, cultural biases, and chance events. Were the field a "hard" science, anchored solidly in readily verified empirical fact, progress would presumably derive from advances of a tangible and objective nature. Unfortunately, that is not the case. Nevertheless, the field has endeavored to standardize, as much as possible, the language conventions and classification rules for diagnosing mental disease.

Not until the 1920s was an effort made to develop a relatively uniform nomenclature and classification system for medical disease in the United States. Prior to the first of a series of National Conferences on Nomenclature of Diseases, held in 1928 at the New York Academy of Medicine (New York Academy of Medicine, 1932), each of the major teaching hospitals and university medical centers in the nation developed and promulgated its own terminology and nosology. Although these reflected the idiosyncratic needs of their place of origin, many were transplanted to other settings, not as a function of their special logic or utility but because former staff members and trainees were comfortable with the nomenclature to which they were accustomed and, consequently, recommended its use in their new clinical milieu. Rarely could such transplants be rooted in their entirety, and most were modified to meet the particular needs of their newly adopted setting. These replantings fostered even more diversity in an already variegated babble of medical terms and categories. To say the least, effective communication among clinical centers, no less useful records for epidemiologic statistics and research, was seriously compromised.

Perhaps the only realistic and significant question to be posed in appraising a new taxonomy and nomenclature is not whether they mirror the state of the science perfectly or whether they provide answers to all possible questions professionals within the discipline may ask. Instead, the focus should be on whether they represent advances over preceding nosological systems and whether future practitioners and researchers will employ them with greater clinical accuracy and facility.

That the official American system published in 1980, the *DSM-III*, had been responded to well was evident in both formal questionnaire replies and the number of copies sold. More orders were received in the first 6 months following its publication than all previous editions combined, including its 30-plus reprintings. The *DSM-III* was nevertheless substantially more extensive and thorough than both of its predecessors.

During the development of the fourth edition of the *DSM* proposals to introduce a so-called dimensional system to supplant or supplement the categorical model used in the existing *DSM* were made. The group evaluated several alternative schemas, but none achieved sufficient consensus. Nonetheless, specific modifications regarding the *DSM* criteria were introduced on the basis of a review of numerous published and unpublished statistical analyses. The *DSM-IV* quickly became the standard nosology and soon assumed a life of its own. Clinicians and researchers of all theoretical schools utilized and interpreted it in diverse ways to suit their special purposes and orientations. The rationale that led to the original concepts and terminology formulated by its task force now plays only a small part, as *DSM* users increasingly transform the instrument to fit their own purposes. Few are satisfied with every aspect of the manual, and it is sufficiently broad in scope to permit almost any clinician, theoretician, or researcher to wish to modify one or another segment because of his or her dissatisfactions. In 2000, refinements were made to the *DSM-IV*, published as the *DSM-IV-TR*, to correct several errors and to reflect the data of a number of recent research investigations. Likewise, the American Psychiatric Association (APA) in 2000 established committees to initiate preliminary studies regarding changes proposed for *DSM-5*, which was published in 2013. The coordination of future APA's *DSMs* and the World Health Organization's *Manual of International Statistical Classification of Diseases, Injuries, and Causes of Death* (ICDs) continues as a major goal.

Having participated over two intense 5-year periods as a member of the *DSM-III* and the *DSM-IV* committees, I am considerably more charitable about the purposes and success with which these task forces have met their responsibilities. I have no illusion, however, that the task has been completed. As noted previously:

Classifying mental illness must be an outgrowth of both psychology and medicine. As such, efforts to construct a taxonomy must contend with the goals, concepts, and complications inherent in both disciplines (e.g., context moderators, definitional ambiguities, overlapping symptomatologies, criterion unreliabilities, multidimensional attributes, population heterogeneities, instrument deficits, and ethical constraints). (Millon, 1991, p. 245)

Thus, uncertainty remains today as to whether to conceive of depression as a taxon (category) or an attribute (symptom), whether to view it as a dimension (with quantitative degrees of severity) or as a set of discrete types, or whether to conceive it as a neuroendocrinological disease or as an existential problem of life. Although debates on these issues often degenerate into semantic arguments and theoretic hairsplitting, it is naive to assume that metaphysical verbiage and philosophical word quibbling are all that is involved. Nevertheless, the language used, and the assumptions it reflects, are very much a part of current scientific disagreements.

In addition to reviewing diagnostic history, this chapter illustrates that philosophical issues and scientific modes of analysis must be considered in formulating an understanding of mental illness (see Millon, 1991, 2004). The many alternatives that are yet to be applied will not in themselves achieve clear resolutions to all nosological quandaries. More likely their role will be to unsettle prevailing habits and thereby force progress, if only to challenge cherished beliefs and assumptions.

References

Allport, G. (1937). *Personality: A psychological interpretation*. New York: Holt.

American Psychoanalytic Association. (2006). *Psychodiagnostic manual*. Silver Spring, MD: Author.

Baillarger, J. (1853). De la melancholie avec stupeur. *Annales Medico-Psychologiquies, 5,* 251.

Bernheim, H. (1900). *Suggestive therapeutics: A treatise on the nature and uses of hypnotism* (C. A. Herter, Trans.). New York: Putnam's.

Bleuler, E. (1911/1950). *Dementia praecox oder Gruppe der Schizophrenien*. Leipzig, Germany: Deuticke.

Breuer, J., & Freud, S. (1895). *Studies on hysteria*. Leipzig, Germany: Deuticke.

Briquet, P. (1859). *Traite clinique et therapeutique a l'hysterie*. Paris: Balliere.

Burton, R. (1621). *Anatomy of melancholy, what it is: With all the kindes, avses, symptoms, prognostickes, and severall cvres of it*. Oxford, UK: John James Lichfield for Henry Short Cripps.

Chaslin, P. (1912). *Elements de seminologie et de clinique mentale*. Paris: Asselin et Houzeau.

de Sauvages, F. B. (1771). *Nosologie methodique dans la quelle les maladies sont rangees par classes*. Paris: Herrisant.

Esquirol, J. (1838). *Des maladies mentales* (2 vols.). Paris: Bailliere.

Falret, J. P. (1854). De la folie circulaire. *Bulletin de l'Academie Medicale, 19,* 382–394.

Feuchtersleben, E. von. (1847). *The principles of medical psychology: Being the outlines of a course of lectures.* London: Sydenham Society.

Griesinger, W. (1845). *Mental pathology and therapeutics.* London: New Sydenham Society.

Griesinger, W. (1868). Introductory comments. *Archives for Psychiatry and Nervous Diseases, 1,* 12.

Haslam, J. (1809). *Observations on madness and melancholy.* London: J. Callow.

Haslam, J. (1810). *Illustrations of madness: Exhibiting a singular case of insanity.* London: G. Hayden.

Heinroth, J. C. (1818). *Lehrbuch der Störungen des Seelenlebens.* Leipzig: Thieme.

Hett, W. S. (Ed. & Trans.). (1936). Physiognomics. In *Aristotle: Minor Works.* Cambridge, MA: Harvard University Press.

Hippocrates. (400 B.C.) *On the sacred disease.*

Horney, K. (1945). *Our inner conflicts.* New York: Norton.

Jung, C. J. (1920). *Collected papers on analytical psychology* (C. E. Long, Trans.). London: Bailliere, Tindall & Cox.

Kahlbaum, K. L. (1863). *Die Gruppierung der psychischen Krankenheiten.* Danzig, Germany: A. W. Kafemann.

Kahlbaum, K. L. (1874). *Die Katatonie, oder das Spannungsirresien.* Berlin: Kirschwald.

Kahlbaum, K. L. (1882). *Uber zyklisches Irresein, Irrenfreund.* Berlin: Springer.

Klerman, G.L. (1986). Historical perspectives on contemporary schools of psychopathology. In T. Millon & Klerman, G. (Eds.). *Contemporary directions in psychopathology: Toward the DSM-IV,* (pp. 3–28). New York: Guilford Press.

Koch, J. A. (1891). *Die psychopathischen Minderwertgkeiten.* Ravensburg, Germany: Maier.

Kraepelin, E. (1883). *Compendium of psychiatry.* Leipzig, Germany: Abel.

Kraepelin, E. (1896). *Psychiatrie: Ein Lehrbuch.* (5th ed.). Leipzig, Germany: Barth.

Kraepelin, E. (1899). *Psychiatrie: Ein Lehrbuch.* (6th ed.). Leipzig, Germany: Barth.

Kraepelin, E. (1909–1915). *Psycbiatrie* (8th ed., 4 Vols.). Leipzig, Germany: Barth Verlag.

Kraepelin, E. (1920). *Hundert Jahre Psychiatrie.* Berlin: Springer Verlag.

Kraepelin, E. (1921). *Manic-depressive insanity and paranoia.* Edinburgh: Livingstone.

Krafft-Ebing, R. (1879). *Lehrbuch der Psychiatrie auf klinischer Grundlage.* Stuttgart, Germany: Erike.

Krafft-Ebing, R. (1937). *Psychopathia sexualis.* New York: Physicians and Surgeons Books. (Original work published 1882)

Kramer, H., & Sprenger, J. (1487–1489/1928). *Malleus maleficarum* [The hammer of witches] (Rev. M. Summers, Trans.). London: Rodker.

Lavater, J. C. (1789). *Essays of physiognomy: For the promotion of knowledge and the love of mankind* (T. Holcroft, Trans.). London: Robinson, Paternoster-Row.

Liebault, A. A. (1866). *Du sommeil et des etates analogues consideres surtout au point du une de l'action du moral sur le physique* [Sleep and its analogous states considered from the perspective of the action of the mind upon the body]. Paris: Masson.

Liu, X. (1981). Psychiatry in traditional Chinese medicine. *British Journal of Psychiatry, 138,* 429–433.

Maudsley, H. (1860). *Annual board report at Cheadle Royal Hospital.* Unpublished.

Maudsley, H. (1876). *Physiology and pathology of mind.* New York: Appleton.

Meyer, A. (1906). Fundamental conceptions of dementia praecox. *British Medical Journal, 2,* 757–760.

Meyer, A. (1912). Remarks on habit disorganizations in the essential deteriorations. *Nervous and Mental Disease Monographs, 9,* 95–109.

Millon, T. (1969). *Modern psychopathology: A biosocial approach to maladaptive learning and functioning.* Philadelphia: Saunders.

Millon, T. (1981). *Disorders of personality: DSM–III, Axis II.* New York: Wiley.

Millon, T. (1990). *Toward a new personology: An evolutionary model.* New York: Wiley.

Millon, T. (1991). Classification in psychopathology: Rationale, alternatives, and standards. *Journal of Abnormal Psychology, 100,* 245–261.

Millon, T. (2004). *Masters of the mind: Exploring the story of mental illness from ancient times to the new millennium.* Hoboken, NJ: Wiley.

Millon, T., & Davis, R. D. (1996). *Disorders of personality: DSM–IV and beyond.* New York: Wiley.

Morel, B. A. (1857). *Traite de desgenerescences physiques intellectuelles et morales de l'espece humaine.* Paris: Bailliere.

New York Academy of Medicine. (1932). *Standard classified nomenclature of disease.* New York: Author.

Paracelsus. (1567/1941). In H. Sigerist (Ed.), *Von den Krankheiten, so die Vernufft berauben* (G. Zilboorg, Trans.). Baltimore: Johns Hopkins University Press.

Peck, A. L. (Ed. & Trans.). (1965). *Aristotle: Historia animalium*. Cambridge, MA: Harvard University Press.

Roccatagliata, G. (1973). *Storia de la psichiatria antica*. Milan, Italy: Ulrico Hoepli.

Schneider, K. (1950). *Psychopathic personalities* (9th ed.). London: Cassell. (Original work published 1923).

Tredennick, H. (Ed. & Trans.). (1967). *Aristotle's prior analytics*. Cambridge, MA: Harvard University Press.

Voisin, F. (1851). *The analysis of human understanding*.

Willis, T. (1664/1978). *Cerebri anatome* [The anatomy of the brain and nerves]. Birmingham, AL: Classics of Medicine Library.

Willis, T. (1672/1971). *De anima brutorum* [Two discourses concerning the soul of brutes]. Gainesville, FL: Scholar's Facsimiles & Reprints.

2

Classification

JARED W. KEELEY,

HANNAH E. MORTON,

AND ROGER K. BLASHFIELD

Diagnosis is simple. The clinician meets with the patient and assesses his or her symptoms in an interview. Given the list of symptoms, the clinician then consults the current version of the *DSM* and decides which diagnoses are relevant. However, like most things that appear to be simple, the topic of classification becomes more complicated upon examination. For example, even the name for this topic is more complicated that many readers might think. In popular usage, terms like *diagnosis, classification*, and *taxonomy* are often treated as if they either are synonyms or, at least, are largely interchangeable. However, to those who study this topic, the above three terms have separable meanings.

Diagnostic systems, generally called classifications, are lists of terms for conventionally accepted concepts that are used to describe psychopathology. *Classification*, when the term is used specifically, refers to the activity of forming groups. *Diagnosis*, as this word is used in medicine and the mental health field, is the process by which individuals are assigned to already existing groups. *Taxonomy* is a term usually reserved for the study of how groups are formed. In effect, taxonomy is a meta-level concept that looks at different theoretical ways in which classifications can be organized, studied, and changed.

The classification of mental disorders has a lengthy history. The first description of a specific syndrome is usually ascribed to an Egyptian account of dementia dating to about 3000 B.C. An early classification of mental disorders was found in the Ayurveda, an ancient Indian system of medicine (Menninger, Mayman, & Pruyser, 1963). Ancient Greek and Egyptian writings refer to disorders remarkably similar to concepts of hysteria, paranoia, mania, and melancholia. Since then, numerous classifications have emerged, and enthusiasm for classifying mental disorders has waxed and waned. During the last half of the twentieth century, classification was a prominent theme in the study of psychopathology. Following World War II, American psychiatry saw a need to systematize a single classification system, called the *Diagnostic and Statistical Manual of Mental Disorders* (*DSM*), first published in 1952. At an international level, the classification of mental disorders became part of the *International Classification of Diseases* (*ICD*) in 1948 in its sixth edition (Grob, 1991; Houts, 2000). Currently, *DSM* is in its fifth edition and the 11th edition of *ICD* is slated for publication in 2017.

This productivity has not, however, resolved some of the fundamental problems confronting psychiatric classification. Unresolved issues include the nature of the entities being classified, the definition of what a mental disorder is, the nosological principles for organizing psychiatric classifications, the distinction between normality and pathology, and the validity of many diagnoses. Controversies exist regarding the definition and logical status of some diagnoses and even whether some entities are pathological conditions. For example, heated debates occurred in the 1960s and 1970s over whether homosexuality should be considered a mental disorder. Current debates exist on whether Internet addiction belongs in an official classification. Presently, there is no consensus regarding the taxonomic principles for resolving these controversies.

This chapter provides an overview of some issues associated with the classification of psychopathology. In discussing these issues, the chapter presents an overview of psychiatric classification from a historical perspective so that the reader can understand how these issues have arisen and who have been the central authors involved in discussions of these issues.

Purpose of Classification

Classification involves creating and defining the boundaries of concepts (Sartorius, 1990). Through this process, diagnostic entities are defined (Kendell, 1975) and the boundaries of the discipline are ultimately established. The reason why psychiatric classification has had such an impact is that it has defined the field of psychopathology. For example, should Alzheimer's disease, alcoholism, or oppositional behavior in a child be considered mental disorders? Should they instead be considered medical disorders, or just problems of everyday living? A classification of mental disorders stipulates the range of problems to which mental health professions lay claim.

Classifications serve several purposes with specific goals. The goals of a good classification scheme include (1) providing a *nomenclature* for practitioners; (2) serving as a basis for organizing and *retrieving information*; (3) *describing* the common patterns of symptom presentation; (4) providing the basis for *prediction*; (5) forming the basis for the *development of theories*; and (6) serving *sociopolitical functions*.

The first major function of a classification is the provision of a standard *nomenclature* that facilitates description and communication. A nomenclature is simply a list of names or terms of the categories within a classification system. At its most basic level, a classification of psychopathology

allows clinicians to talk to each other about the "things" in their world—patients and clients who seek the care of mental health professionals. Without a classification system, clinicians would be reduced to talking about clients one after another without any way of grouping these clients into similar types. A classification allows the clinician to have a set of nouns that can be used to provide an overview of the clinician's world when talking to other clinicians, to laypeople, to insurance companies, or to other professionals. Note that this purpose provides a shorthand, and does not imply or require any scientific reality to the concepts.

Second, a classification structures *information retrieval*. Information in a science is organized around its major concepts. Knowing a diagnostic concept helps the clinician to retrieve information about such matters as etiology, treatment, and prognosis. A classification shapes the way information is organized, thereby influencing all aspects of clinical practice and research. In the current world in which information is easily retrieved by electronic searches on the Internet, classificatory concepts are useful devices by which professionals, family members, clients, and interested laypeople can obtain information about the prognosis, treatment, and current research related to various mental disorders.

Third, by providing a nomenclature to describe all levels of psychopathology, a classification establishes the *descriptive basis* for a science of psychopathology. Most sciences have their origins in description. Only when phenomena are systematically organized into categories is a science in the position to transform accounts of individual cases into principles and generalizations. Cases that are diagnosed with a particular disorder should be similar in important ways to other cases with that same diagnosis, and these cases should be different in important ways from cases belonging to other diagnostic categories.

The fourth goal of classification, *prediction*, is the most pragmatic from the perspective of clinicians. What a mental health professional typically wants from a diagnosis is information that is relevant to the most effective treatment of his or her patient. A classification that is useful for prediction is a system in which there is strong evidence that patients with different diagnoses respond differentially to a specific treatment. Classifications are also clinically useful if the categories are associated with different clinical courses, even when the disorders are not treated.

Fifth, by providing systematic descriptions of phenomena, a classification establishes the foundations for the *development of theories*. In the natural sciences, especially biology and chemistry, a satisfactory classification was an important precursor for theoretical progress (Hull, 1988). The systematic classification of species by Linnaeus stimulated important questions about the nature of phenomena or processes that accounted for the system—questions that ultimately led to the theory of evolution. For these reasons, classification occupies a central role in research. For example, the National Institute of Mental Health (NIMH) in the United States has instituted a large-scale project designed to identify common pathological mechanisms that could guide informed understanding of mental disorders (termed the Research Domain Criteria [RDoC] project; NIMH, 2012).

Finally, no classification system exists in a vacuum. Rather, a classificatory system exists in a context of groups and individuals that stand to benefit from the classification. For example, a classification of mental disorders can serve the social purpose of identifying a subset of the population that experts have deemed need treatment. However, the *sociopolitical functions* of a classification are not always so altruistic. The American Psychiatric Association, through its production of the various editions of its classification, has developed a lucrative printing business that serves as a major funding source for the organization. At a more individual level, some authors have argued that the classification of mental disorders serves the objective of maintaining the social power of the majority by marginalizing and stigmatizing those people who fall under the domain of "mental illness" (e.g., Kirk & Kutchins, 1992; Kutchins & Kirk, 1997).

History of Classification

Although attempts to classify psychopathology date to ancient times, our intent is to provide only a brief overview of major developments, especially those occurring in the last century, as a context for understanding modern classifications. Examining previous classifications shows that many current issues have a long history. For example, writers in the eighteenth century, like many contemporary

authorities, believed that the biological sciences had solved the problems of classification and that biological taxonomies could serve as a model for classifying psychopathology. The Edinburgh physician, William Cullen, for example, applied Linnaeus's principles for classifying species to illnesses. The result, published in 1769, was a complex structure involving classes, orders, genera, and species of illness (cited by Kendell, 1990). One class was neurosis (Cullen introduced the concept as a general term for mental disorders) that was subdivided into 4 orders, 27 genera, and over 100 species. Contemporaneous critics, who believed that there were far fewer diagnoses, dismissed Cullen as a "botanical nosologist" (Kendell, 1990). Nonetheless, interest in applying the principles of biological classification to abnormal behavior continues today, as does the debate over the number of diagnoses. "Splitters" seek to divide mental disorders into ever-more narrowly defined categories, whereas "lumpers" maintain that a few broadly defined categories are adequate to represent psychopathology (Havens, 1985). One compromise is to create a hierarchical solution (again, similar to biology) in which there are a relatively small number of higher order groups divided into more specific varieties at lower levels of the hierarchy.

The features used to classify mental disorders varied substantially across eighteenth- and nineteenth-century classifications. Some diagnoses were little more than single symptoms, whereas others were broader descriptions resembling syndromes. Yet other diagnoses were based on speculative, early pre-psychology theories about how the mind worked. As a result, many classifications from the nineteenth century relied heavily on traditional philosophical analyses of the faculties or attempted to organize disorders around poorly articulated views of etiology.

Kraepelin

With the work of Emil Kraepelin, the structure of modern classification began to take shape. Kraepelin was born in 1856, the same year as Freud, an ironic fact considering that they established two very different approaches to conceptualizing psychopathology. Kraepelin was influenced by two traditions (Berrios & Hauser, 1988). The first was the scientific approach to medicine that dominated German medical schools in the late nineteenth century. Many important medical breakthroughs, especially in bacteriology, occurred in Germany during that period. German psychiatrists of the time generally believed that mental disorders were biological and that psychiatry would gradually be replaced by neurology. Kraepelin was also influenced by early work in experimental psychology (Kahn, 1959). During medical training, he worked for a year in the laboratory of Wundt, one of the first experimental psychologists. In early research, Kraepelin applied Wundt's methods to the study of mental disorders.

Kraepelin's reputation was based on his textbooks of psychiatry. Like most textbook authors, Kraepelin organized his volumes with chapters on each of the major groupings of mental disorders. What has become known as Kraepelin's classifications (Menninger et al., 1963) are little more than the table of contents to the nine published editions of his textbooks. In the sixth edition, Kraepelin included two chapters that attracted considerable international attention. One chapter focused on the concept of dementia praecox (now called schizophrenia), which included hebephrenia, catatonia, and paranoia as subtypes—descriptions that remained intact up through *DSM-IV* but were removed in *DSM-5*. The other chapter discussed manic-depressive insanity—a revolutionary idea that combined mania and melancholia, two concepts that had been considered separate entities since the writings of Hippocrates. The two diagnoses, dementia praecox and manic-depressive psychosis, established a fundamental distinction between psychotic and mood disorders that forms a linchpin of contemporary classifications.

The Early Editions of the DSM and ICD

In medicine, the official classification of medical disorders is known as the *Manual of International Statistical Classification of Diseases, Injuries, and Causes of Death* (ICD), published by the World Health Organization. Historically, this classification began at the end of the nineteenth century when a group named the International Statistical Institute commissioned a committee headed by Jacques Bertillon to generate a classification of causes of death. This classification, initially known as *The Bertillon Classification of Causes of Death*, was adopted as an official international classification of medical disorders at a meeting of 26 countries in France in 1900. The name of the classification was slightly modified in the early

1900s to *The International Classification of Causes of Death*. This original version of *ICD* was revised at subsequent conferences held in 1909, 1920, 1929, and 1938.

After World War II, the World Health Organization met to generate a sixth revision of this classification. A decision was made at that point to expand the classification beyond causes of death and to include all diseases regardless of whether those diseases led to death or not (i.e., morbidity as well as mortality). The name of the classification was revised accordingly to the *Manual of International Statistical Classification of Diseases, Injuries, and Causes of Death, Sixth Revision* (ICD-6; 1948). Because it focused on all diseases, *ICD-6* added a section devoted to mental disorders.

Shortly after the publication of *ICD-6*, the American Psychiatric Association published its first official classification of mental disorders (*DSM-I*; 1952). The reason for the creation of this classification was that there were four different classifications of psychopathology in use in the United States during World War II, a situation that American psychiatry found embarrassing. Thus, the United States created its own nomenclature rather than using *ICD-6* (Grob, 1991).

Generally, other countries in the world were like the United States in that, instead of adopting *ICD-6* as the official system, most decided to use locally created classificatory systems whose diagnostic concepts did not have international acceptance. Only five countries adopted the *ICD-6* classification of mental disorders: Finland, New Zealand, Peru, Thailand, and the United Kingdom. To understand why, the World Health Organization asked British psychiatrist Erwin Stengel to review the classifications of mental disorders used in various countries. Stengel's review (1959) was very important because he carefully documented the widespread differences that existed in terminology from country to country (and even within countries). Stengel concluded that the variation in classifications from one country to another meant there was a failure for these systems to become useful nomenclatures. In addition, Stengel documented how different subsections of these classifications were organized according to quite variable beliefs about the etiologies of the disorders being classified. Stengel suggested that the solution was to develop a classification that simply provided operational definitions of mental disorders without reference to etiology. This suggestion led to the eighth revision of the mental disorders section of *ICD*, which was to include a glossary defining the various components of psychopathology to go with the list of diagnoses. Unfortunately, the glossary was not ultimately included. However, at the same time, American psychiatrists did publish a second edition of *DSM* (i.e., *DSM–II*; 1968). *DSM-II*, unlike *ICD-8*, contained short prose definitions of the basic categories in this system.

Criticisms of DSM-I *and* DSM-II

During the 1950s and 1960s, concern about the reliability of psychiatric diagnoses surfaced. Problems with levels of diagnostic agreement had been noted in the 1930s. Masserman and Carmichael (1938), for example, reported that 40% of diagnoses in a series of patients followed up 1 year later required major revision. Ash (1949) compared the diagnoses of three psychiatrists who jointly interviewed 52 individuals applying to work for the Central Intelligence Agency (CIA). These clinicians agreed on the diagnosis for only 20% of the applicants, and in 30% of the cases, all three psychiatrists made a different diagnosis. Beck (1962) reviewed a series of reliability studies and reported that the highest level of interclinician agreement was 42% for *DSM-I*. The problem with reliability was further highlighted by the U.K./U.S. Diagnostic Project, which found major differences in diagnostic practice between Britain and the United States (Cooper et al., 1972; Kendell, Cooper, Gourlay, Sharpe, & Gurland, 1971). These studies suggested that Americans had an overinclusive concept of schizophrenia and tended to apply the diagnosis to any psychotic patient. British psychiatrists, in contrast, were more specific in the use of schizophrenia as a diagnosis.

Diagnostic unreliability creates major problems for clinical practice and research. For example, the results of studies on patients with schizophrenia as diagnosed in Britain cannot generalize to patients diagnosed as having schizophrenia in the United States if these results are based on different applications of the concept of schizophrenia. However, the problem was not confined to schizophrenia. The reliability studies of the 1960s and 1970s were interpreted as indicating that clinicians had problems achieving high levels of agreement for any area of psychopathology. More modern commentators

on this literature have suggested, however, that the criticisms of diagnostic reliability during this era were overstated (Kirk & Kutchins, 1992).

Concurrent with the empirical studies questioning the reliability of psychiatric diagnosis, psychiatry came under considerable attack from the antipsychiatry movement. Much of this criticism focused on the clinical activities of diagnosis and classification. Szasz (1961) went so far as to argue that mental illness was a myth.

By the late 1960s, three major criticisms of psychiatric classification were popular. First, psychiatric diagnosis was widely thought to be unreliable. Second, classification and diagnosis were considered fundamental components of the medical model that was questioned as the basis for understanding mental disorders. This model clashed with other models, particularly those stemming from behavioral and humanistic perspectives that were influential in clinical and counseling psychology. The medical model of illness was viewed as both speculative and as demeaning of patients. Third, widespread concern was expressed, particularly among many sociologists and psychologists, about the labeling and stigmatizing effects of psychiatric diagnoses (Goffman, 1959, 1963; Scheff, 1966, 1975). Labeling theorists tended to view mental illness and other forms of deviant behavior as largely politically defined and reinforced by social factors and agencies. Psychiatric diagnoses were considered to be self-fulfilling prophecies in which patients adopted the behaviors implied by the label. Their arguments were bolstered by philosophers such as Foucault (1988), who condemned psychiatry as little more than an agent of social control.

A demonstration of these issues was contained in a paper published in *Science* by Rosenhan (1973), titled "On Being Sane in Insane Places." In this study, 8 normal persons sought admission to 12 different inpatient units. All accurately reported information about themselves except that they gave false names to avoid a mental hospital record, and they reported hearing an auditory hallucination in which a voice said "thud," "empty," or "hollow." In all instances, the pseudo-patients were admitted. Eleven of these admissions were diagnosed as schizophrenia, the other as mania. On discharge, which occurred on average 20 days later, all received the diagnosis of schizophrenia in remission. Rosenhan concluded that mental health professionals were unable to distinguish between sanity and insanity, an observation that was eagerly seized by the antipsychiatry movement. However, the Rosenhan study was not without its critics. Rosenhan's paper resulted in an explosion of responses that challenged his research and claimed that psychiatric diagnosing is a valid and meaningful process. The majority of the criticisms focused on Rosenhan's flawed methodology and his unfounded interpretations that clinicians are unable to distinguish between those who are sane and those who are insane (Farber, 1975; Millon, 1975; Spitzer, 1975; Weiner, 1975).

The Neo-Kraepelinians

During the 1970s, a small, but effective, group of researchers emerged in North American psychiatry (Compton & Guze, 1995). These individuals influenced both academic psychiatry and practice. The movement, usually referred to as the neo-Kraepelinians (Klerman, 1978), sought to reaffirm psychiatry as a branch of medicine. The neo-Kraepelinians emphasized the importance of diagnosis and classification. The movement was a reaction to the antipsychiatrists and the psychoanalytic dominance of North American psychiatry. Klerman's assumptions of the neo-Kraepelinian positions included emphasizing the medical roots of psychiatry, such that psychiatry provides treatment for people who are sick with mental illness. Klerman further highlighted that the biological aspect of mental illness should be the central focus, and any area of psychopathology that might represent a disease process (e.g., schizophrenia) belonged to psychiatry, whereas other areas could be assigned to ancillary professions such as psychology, social work, and nursing. The neo-Kraepelinians, in the attempt to medicalize psychiatric disorders, emphasized qualitative distinctions between normality and illness, a view criticized by writers such as Szasz, who considered mental disorders to be problems of living that are on a continuum with normal behavior. Furthermore, the position of the neo-Kraepelinians suggested different forms of disorders, which laid the basis for the continued use of a categorical approach to classification.

The neo-Kraepelinians believed that psychiatry should be founded on scientific knowledge. This assumption insisted on a solid empirical foundation to ensure psychiatry as a medical specialty. The neo-Kraepelinians placed additional emphasis

on diagnosis and classification by proposing that diagnosis is the basis for treatment decisions and clinical care—a view that contrasted with that of psychoanalysts, who believed that descriptive classification focused on superficial behavioral aspects of patients' lives (Havens, 1981). Klerman stressed the importance the neo-Kraepelinians placed on improving the reliability and validity of diagnoses through the use of statistical techniques.

Reading these propositions more than 40 years later reveals the extent to which the neo-Kraepelinians felt the need to reaffirm the medical and biological aspects of psychiatry. They felt embattled and surrounded by powerful influences that advocated a very different approach. These propositions now seem curiously dated, perhaps indicating the extent to which the neo-Kraepelinian movement was successful in achieving its objectives. In many ways these propositions are now widely accepted within the profession, although most would probably express these positions less vehemently. Klerman's statements also indicated the importance that the neo-Kraepelinians placed on diagnosis and classification. The way to ensure that their views were adopted was to develop a new classification system. The antipsychiatry movement's concerns about labeling and other negative reactions to psychiatric diagnosis provided an important context that spawned *DSM-III*, but the neo-Kraepelinian movement provided the agenda (Rogler, 1997).

DSM-III *and Its Successors*

DSM-III was the culmination of the neo-Kraepelinian efforts to reestablish psychiatry as a branch of medicine with diagnosis and classification as fundamental components. The classification took over 5 years of extensive committee work and consultation to produce.

DSM-III differed from *DSM-II* in four major ways. First, *DSM-III* adopted more specific and detailed diagnostic criteria, as compared to *DSM-II*, in order to define the various categories of mental disorders. If a patient met the diagnostic criteria, then the patient was said to belong to the category. Before *DSM-III*, most definitions of specific mental disorders were in prose format and implicitly referred to the "essence" of the disorder. Since the publication of *DSM-III*, the use of diagnostic criteria has reflected a shift to a prototype model whereby a category is defined not by a list of necessary and sufficient conditions but rather by a list of characteristics that any individual member may or may not have. Thus, two individuals may qualify for the same diagnosis even though they have few symptoms in common, as long as each of them has enough of the listed symptoms to attain the specified threshold. The more characteristics the individual evidences, the better fit that person is to the category (Cantor, Smith, French, & Mezzich, 1980). The intent of using these diagnostic criteria was to make the diagnostic process more explicit and clear-cut, thus improving reliability. Second, *DSM-III* proposed a multiaxial system of classification. Thus, instead of assigning one diagnosis per patient, as was typical with *DSM-I* and *DSM-II*, clinicians were expected to categorize the patients along five axes: (I) symptom picture, (II) personality style, (III) medical disorder, (IV) environmental stressors, and (V) role impairment. Third, *DSM-III* substantially reorganized the hierarchical arrangement of mental disorder categories. In *DSM-I* and *DSM-II*, the hierarchical system of organization recognized two fundamental dichotomies: (1) organic versus nonorganic disorders and (2) psychotic versus neurotic disorders. *DSM-III* dropped these dichotomies and instead organized mental disorders under 17 major headings, based on the phenomenology of the disorder (e.g., "mood disorder" or "psychotic disorder"). Fourth, *DSM-III* was a much larger document than its predecessors. *DSM-I* contained 108 categories and was 130 pages in length. In contrast, *DSM-III* had 256 categories and was 494 pages long.

By almost any standard, *DSM-III* was an astounding success. Financially, it sold very well. As a result of this success, the American Psychiatric Association developed a publication arm of the organization that began to publish a large number of *DSM*-related books and other psychiatric works. Although explicitly an American classification, *DSM-III* quickly became the most frequently used classification in Europe, overshadowing the competing international classification created by the World Health Organization (*ICD-9*; 1977).

Another way of measuring the success of *DSM-III* is in terms of research. *DSM-III* stimulated a great deal of research, especially regarding the definitions of the categories proposed in this classification. As a result of this research, *DSM-III-R* (1987) was published with the explicit goal of revising the diagnostic criteria for the categories stemming from new research findings. However, like most committee products, the changes from *DSM-III* to *DSM-III-R* were not limited to diagnostic criteria. A number of new categories were introduced, including a group of diagnoses associated with the general category of "sleep disorders." Additionally, many specific categories were revised (e.g., histrionic personality disorder), dropped (e.g., attention deficit disorder without hyperactivity), or added (e.g., premenstrual syndrome had its name changed and was added to an appendix of *DSM-III-R*).

Because of the revolutionary impact of *DSM-III*, the mental disorders section of *ICD-10* was substantially changed relative to earlier *ICDs*. *ICD-9*, published in 1977, had been very similar to *ICD-8*. Hence, *ICD-10* was published in two versions: a clinical version that contained prose descriptions of categories, and a research version that contained diagnostic criteria. However, *ICD-10* did not adopt a multiaxial system.

As work was progressing on *ICD-10*, a decision was made to perform another revision of *DSM-III* that, it was hoped, would make it more similar to *ICD-10*. The result was *DSM-IV*. The committee work that went into the creation of *DSM-IV* was extensive. The American Psychiatric Association even sponsored special research projects that attempted to empirically resolve important debates that had arisen around classificatory issues. One example of such a research project was the 1999 *DSM* Research Planning Conference, sponsored by the American Psychiatric Association and the National Institute of Mental Health. This conference established the research priorities for future *DSM* editions, which included addressing the continued dissatisfaction with the *DSM* nomenclature (Kupfer, First, & Regier, 2002).

DSM-IV was larger than previous *DSMs* in terms of the sheer size of its publication and the number of categories. Interestingly, different commentators have computed different numbers for the total diagnoses in *DSM-IV*, ranging from just under 300 to just under 400 diagnoses (cf. Follette & Houts, 1996; Kutchins & Kirk, 1997; Sarbin, 1997; Stone, 1997). Despite the intent of making *DSM-IV* more like *ICD-10*, *DSM-IV* and *ICD-10* are quite different. In 2000, the American Psychiatric Association published a text revision of *DSM-IV*, titled *DSM-IV-TR*, which updated the prose sections of the manual but left the diagnostic criteria and number of diagnoses the same.

Recently, the current editions of *DSM* and *ICD* have been undergoing yet another revision. *DSM-5* was published in May 2013; *ICD-11* should appear in 2017. The co-chairs of *DSM-5* hoped to make *DSM-5* as revolutionary as *DSM-III* had been. The major changes that they instituted with *DSM-5* were to add diagnostic spectra (e.g., the autism spectrum and the schizophrenia spectrum); to offer dimensional alternatives or enhancements to categorical diagnosis (e.g., the five dimensions for describing personality disorder in Section III titled "Emerging Measures and Models"); to improve the assessment of dysfunction as a result of psychopathology (the adoption of the World Health Organization Disability Assessment Schedule [WHODAS] in place of the Global Assessment of Functioning [GAF], also in Section III); and to drop the multiaxial approach to diagnosis that appeared in *DSM-III* and *DSM-IV* (all diagnoses are now in a single section of the manual instead of spread across five axes; APA, 2012a).

Just as *DSM-III* was partially driven by the attempt to overcome the reliability issues with *DSM-I* and *DSM-II*, one goal of *DSM-5* was to address meta-structure issues that became prominent with *DSM-III-R* and *DSM-IV* (Regier, Kuhl, Narrow, & Kupfer, 2012). Specifically, the arrangement of disorders within the manual could be informed by empirical findings rather than based solely on phenomenological similarity or workgroup arrangement. An example is the dissolution of the childhood disorders grouping of *DSM-IV*, whereby some disorders were placed in a Neurodevelopmental heading (e.g., intellectual disability, ADHD, autism spectrum disorder) and others were placed with similar-appearing "adult" disorders (e.g., reactive attachment disorder in the Trauma- and Stressor-Related Disorders group).

In its final form, *DSM-5* contained 584 diagnostic categories (compared to 357, by our count, in *DSM-IV*). The size of *DSM-5* also grew to 947 pages from 886 pages in *DSM-IV*, while the purchase cost of the manual more than doubled. In contrast, the number of categories with diagnostic criteria was reduced from 201 in *DSM-IV* to 138 in *DSM-5*.

ICD-11, despite undergoing a separate process, has proposed very similar changes to those in *DSM-5*, including similar reorganization and new categories. However, the explicit goal of the creators of *ICD-11* has been to maximize clinical utility for the myriad users of the manual. For instance, the World Health Organization conducted a series of studies of mental health providers (primarily psychiatrists and psychologists) to examine their implicit classifications of mental disorders and used that information to improve the organization of the manual (Reed, 2010; Roberts et al., 2012).

Taxonomic Issues

A number of controversies have arisen around the classification of psychopathology. The purpose of the following list is not to provide a comprehensive overview, but simply to list the issues and controversies that are frequently raised about psychiatric classification.

Classification of Syndromes, Disorders, or Diseases

The terms *syndrome*, *disorder*, and *disease* can (erroneously) be used interchangeably to describe mental health conditions. In fact, these three terms refer to explicitly different assumptions about the nature of the category they describe. At the most basic level of description, a person experiences *symptoms* (self-reported issues) and evidences *signs* (observed by others) of a problem. As mentioned before, if mental health professionals were forced to idiosyncratically describe the unique pattern of symptoms and signs for every patient, their work would be hopelessly stymied by trying to account for each patient. However, symptoms and signs often co-occur. When they co-occur with sufficient frequency, that condition is termed a *syndrome*. Note that the concept of a syndrome does not include any assumptions about the cause of the condition or why those symptoms belong together. It is a purely descriptive notion.

A *disorder*, on the other hand, provides an additional level of description beyond that of a syndrome. A disorder is a pattern of symptoms and signs that includes an implied impact on the functioning of the individual. While some causal factors might be understood for a disorder, its etiology is still unclear or multiply determined. In contrast, a *disease* is a condition where the etiology is known, and the path from the causal agent to the symptoms and signs it causes is clear.

By way of example, a condition known as general paresis was the most common single disorder represented in mental asylums in the mid- to late 1800s. Initial investigations found that certain individuals exhibited similar symptoms: grandiose delusions and excitable behavior. At that point, the concept would properly be termed a syndrome. After further investigation, it became clear that these individuals followed a similar course. The problem began with excitable, grandiose behavior but progressed to degenerative muscle movements, paralysis, and eventually death. Once the course and outcome were known, general paresis was more properly termed a disorder. Many theories were posited about the cause of the disorder, varying from overindulgence in alcohol to inflammation of the meninges. However, eventually the discovery came that it was tertiary syphilis, having migrated from a genital infection through a long dormant phase to the central nervous system. When general paresis was understood as a syphilitic infection, the concept became a disease (Blashfield & Keeley, 2010).

The history of general paresis is important in classification because it was a mental disorder that was understood as a disease and eradicated with proper treatment (i.e., penicillin). Paresis was a major victory for the science of psychiatry, as the majority of asylum patients could be successfully (and simply) treated and sent home. Many individuals believed that all other mental health conditions (especially schizophrenia) would follow similar developments, eventually being "cured" once the proper cause was known. Unfortunately, no other conditions to date have enjoyed the scientific success of general paresis. Rather, nearly all mental health categories are more properly termed disorders, in that their cause and therefore treatment are much more ambiguous.

Classification of Disorders versus Classification of Individuals

On the surface, this controversy appears to be a somewhat simple-minded issue of terminology. Individual patients are diagnosed with various mental disorders. A classification system contains the names of mental disorders that have been recognized or are officially sanctioned as diagnoses by some governing body. What difference does it make whether a classification system is said to classify disorders or individuals?

Interestingly, however, the authors of *DSM-IV-TR* did think that this distinction made a

difference. They adopted an explicit position relative to this issue:

A common misconception is that a classification of mental disorders classifies people, when actually what are being classified are disorders that people have. For this reason, the text of the *DSM-IV* (as did the text of *DSM-III-R*) avoids the use of expressions such as "a schizophrenic" or "an alcoholic" and instead uses the more accurate, but admittedly more cumbersome, "an individual with Schizophrenia" or "an individual with Alcohol Dependence." (*DSM-IV-TR*, p. xxxi)

The reason that *DSM-IV-TR* adopted this position is to try to avoid the problem of stigma. Mental disorders largely refer to undesirable aspects of the human condition. Most of us do not want to be diagnosed with a mental disorder. To call someone "schizophrenic" is to imply that that individual is a member of a diagnostic category that is immutable, unchanging, and destructive both to that person and to the significant others in that person's life. By contrast, the language of "an individual with schizophrenia" implies that the person is not inherently schizophrenic, but that schizophrenia, being a disease of the brain, is something that happens to people, without the occurrence of the disease being their fault. By saying that *DSM* is a classification of disorders, the authors were trying to emphasize the value of beneficence so that no or minimal harm was done by assigning psychiatric diagnoses to individual human beings.

From another perspective, however, to say that *DSMs* classify disorders, not individual human beings, does not align with common sense. Consider, for instance, a zoological classification of animals. A pet cat named Mehitabel is a member of the category known as Felis catus (house cat). In a zoological classification, the focus is on the names and descriptions of the various categories within that classification. But these categories refer to sets (or, more precisely, to populations) of individual animals. When a researcher studies one of these categories of animals, the researcher samples a collection of animals that belong to the category and then studies the characteristics of the animals within that category. From the perspective of formalizing how a zoological classification is structured, the objects of the classification (i.e., the "things" that belong to these categories) are individual organisms (Buck & Hull, 1966; Gregg, 1954; however, contrast with Hull, 1980).

As mentioned at the beginning of this chapter, diagnosis is the process of assigning individuals to categories. Individual clinicians are concerned with the process of how best to characterize the individuals they see. The mental disorder groups characterized in a classification would not exist without individuals who instantiated those symptoms. Admittedly, the population of individuals with mental disorders is much less permanent than species, as many mental disorders are time limited (a person initially does not have the disorder, then does, and goes back to not having it). The conditions that define the presence or absence of the disorder state become crucial to understanding if the classification captures individuals, disorders, or both. Thus, the definition of *mental disorder* has profound consequences for what the classification captures.

Definition of Mental Disorder

The definition of the domain to which *DSM* applies, that is, all mental disorders, is an important aspect of the classification. Neither *DSM-I* nor *DSM-II* provided any definition of a mental disorder. An attempt to define this concept was provided with *DSM-III*, by the head of the task force that created this classification. Robert Spitzer's view about how to define a mental disorder became controversial when he claimed, "mental disorders are a subset of medical disorders" (Spitzer, Sheehy, & Endicott, 1977, p. 4). Many viewed this statement as an attempt to secure exclusive rights to mental disorder treatment for psychiatry, thereby excluding or marginalizing other disciplines such as psychology and social work. However, a psychologist on the *DSM-III* task force, Millon (1983), stated that this sentiment was never the official perspective of those creating *DSM-III*.

One year later, Spitzer and Endicott (1978) made an explicit attempt to define both mental disorder and medical disorder, with the former being a subset of the latter. It is worth reproducing their definitions in toto:

A medical disorder is a relatively distinct condition resulting from an organismic dysfunction which in its fully developed or extreme form is directly and intrinsically associated with distress, disability, or certain other types of disadvantage. The disadvantage may be of physical, perceptual, sexual, or interpersonal nature. Implicitly there is a call for action on the part of the person who has the condition, the medical or its allied professions, and society.

A mental disorder is a medical disorder whose manifestations are primarily signs or symptoms of a psychological (behavioral) nature, or if physical, can be understood only using psychological concepts (p. 18).

Wakefield (1993) argued that Spitzer and Endicott's definition of a mental disorder failed on many levels to successfully operationalize the role of dysfunction inherent to mental disorders. Consequently, Wakefield (1992a, 1992b, 1993) provided an alternative definition of mental disorders, in which he placed dysfunction within an evolutionary framework to better distinguish disorders from nondisorders. Wakefield's approach to mental disorders, termed *harmful dysfunction*, considered mental disorders as "failures of internal mechanisms to perform naturally selected functions" resulting in impairment (Wakefield, 1999, p. 374). Wakefield appreciated the fact that defining a disorder must incorporate both value-based (the harm element) and scientific-based (the dysfunction element) criteria.

Wakefield and others have argued that both values and science are inherent components to the way in which *DSM-III* and its successors have defined individual mental disorders (see Sadler, 2005). Distress, or harm, is included either by definition (feelings of depression, anxiety, etc.) or through the criterion of clinical significance. *Clinical significance* refers to the judgment made by the clinician that the severity of the dysfunction present in the disorder justifies treatment. Spitzer and Wakefield (1999) justified the inclusion of clinical significance in the *DSMs* as a means of limiting false-positive diagnoses, that is, individuals who are symptomatic but do not qualify for a full diagnosis of a disorder. Notice, however, that clinical significance is not an objectively defined concept but rather requires a subjective decision by a clinician regarding when a set of symptoms warrants clinical attention. For a classification system that has argued its strength is objectivity and freedom from clinical bias, the explicit inclusion of subjectivity in the definition of a mental disorder is a problem.

Wakefield's harmful-dysfunction approach has not been without its critics. Lilienfeld and Marino

(1995) criticized Wakefield's evolutionary basis of mental disorders, arguing that mental disorders do not have defined properties and are not necessarily evolutionary dysfunctions. To use a medical example, sickle-cell anemia is evolutionarily functional in malaria-prone regions but typically dysfunctional in malaria-free environments. Similar arguments can be made with specific phobias, such as snake phobias, which could be quite functional when an individual human lives near poisonous snakes; however, a snake phobia is of less functional use for the typical person living in a large city in which snakes are uncommon. Other critics (Fulford, 1999; Richters & Cicchetti, 1993; Sadler & Agich, 1995) have provided analyses and substitutes to Wakefield's harmful-dysfunction concept. For further discussion on the debate centered on Wakefield's harmful-dysfunction approach, we refer the reader to a 1999 special issue of the *Journal of Abnormal Psychology* (Volume 108).

As mentioned briefly in the beginning of this chapter, lack of a consensual definition of mental disorders has important consequences. Definitions establish boundaries, in this case the boundary regarding what is and what is not a mental disorder and, hence, the boundaries of the mental health profession. The current definition posed in *DSM-5* reflects the logic of Wakefield's harmful-dysfunction concept, but it is more lenient regarding the cause of the dysfunction. Further, the *DSM-5* definition includes the phrase "clinically significant disturbance," but the definition does not clarify the meaning of this phrase (p. 20). The WHODAS, in Section III, was included to give clinicians more precision in the measurement of dysfunction.

Dimensions versus Categories

Although the term *classification* traditionally applies to a system of classes or categories, a number of contemporary writers have suggested that dimensional approaches to the classification of psychopathology would be preferable (Widiger & Samuel, 2005; Widiger, Simonsen, Krueger, Livesley, & Verheul, 2005).

The debate about categorical versus dimensional models is an old one. Quantitative approaches to the study of psychopathology instantiated the debate through the adoption of different statistical techniques. Advocates of a dimensional model

were users of factor analysis, a multivariate statistical procedure pioneered in the 1930s by L.L. Thurstone (1934) and his colleagues.

The first known application of a dimensional approach to the classification of psychopathology was performed by a priest and psychiatrist named Thomas Moore. Moore (1930) gathered data on individuals with schizophrenia and subjected his descriptive information to a factor analysis. The result was five factors, which, in retrospect, were quite contemporary in their meaning. Using modern terms, these five factors could be named as follows:

1. Positive symptoms of schizophrenia
2. Negative symptoms of schizophrenia
3. Manic symptoms
4. Depressive symptoms
5. Symptoms of cognitive decline (dementia)

Shortly after World War II, Eysenck (1947), a psychologist in Great Britain, became a strong advocate for a dimensional approach to all psychopathology. He argued for three basic dimensions (Eysenck & Eysenck, 1976) that could be used to organize all descriptive information about mental disorders, which he called:

1. Neuroticism
2. Extroversion
3. Psychoticism

He used *neuroticism* to refer to individuals who were anxious or prone to negative feelings versus those who were emotionally calm and steady. *Extroversion* referred to an individual's proneness to be outgoing versus introverted. His description of *psychoticism* included a variety of other constructs, including constraint, impulsivity, sensation-seeking, and even creativity. Eysenck believed that high levels of the personality trait psychoticism made one prone to schizophrenia or other psychotic disorders. These three dimensions have resurfaced in one form or another in many later models, although the same names are sometimes applied to slightly different constructs.

Eysenck was a protégé of Aubrey Lewis, a leading British psychiatrist of his time. Later, Lewis and Eysenck split over Eysenck's determined advocacy of a dimensional model. Lewis, a physician, believed that a categorical/disease model of psychopathology was more appropriate. Shortly after this split between Eysenck and Lewis in the late 1950s, a related debate appeared in the British literature about whether depression was best viewed from a dimensional perspective or from a categorical model (Kendell, 1968; see Klein, 2010 for a modern discussion of this issue).

After Eysenck, other dimensional models of psychopathology began to appear. Within child psychopathology, Achenbach (1966, 1995) became a proponent of a dimensional model with two constructs: (1) an internalizing dimension and (2) an externalizing dimension. *Internalizing* referred to children who displayed internally expressed emotional problems, like anxiety or depression, whereas *externalizing* referred to children who acted out through disruptive behavior. More recently, Krueger (1999; Krueger, Markon, Patrick, & Iacono, 2005) has shown that this two-dimension approach can be generalized to account for a subset of common *DSM* diagnoses. Under that context, generalized anxiety disorder, major depressive disorder, and other anxiety disorders loaded onto a common factor, while antisocial personality disorder and substance use disorders loaded onto a second factor. However, that organization left many facets of psychopathology unaccounted for (e.g., bipolar disorders, psychotic disorders). Later work investigated a wider range of disorders and found a more complicated structure, but the dimensions of internalizing and externalizing remained (Kotov et al., 2011).

Another subset of psychopathology that has been a focus of dimensional investigation is the personality disorders. A variety of investigators such as Cattell, Guilford, and Goldberg developed dimensional approaches to personality traits in normal human beings. McCrae and Costa (1990) expanded this earlier research into what has become known as the five-factor model (FFM) of personality with five dimensions:

1. Neuroticism
2. Extroversion
3. Agreeableness
4. Openness
5. Conscientiousness

Clark (2007) expressed concern about the application of the FFM to personality disorders because the most commonly used measure of the FFM, known as the NEO-PI-R, was designed to measure normal-range personality.

For example, the construct of openness, as measured in normal-range personality, does not seem to be meaningfully related to pathology, but a separate construct—oddity—does capture behaviors of interest like magical or obsessive thinking (Watson, Clark, & Chmielewski, 2008). In contrast, O'Connor (2002) argued that there was a large overlap between normal and abnormal personality presentations.

Many models of normal and disordered personality were considered by the *DSM-5* workgroup concerned with personality disorders. In the end, the workgroup developed its own distillation of these models, that—when empirically tested—largely resembled the domains of the FFM (Krueger, Derringer, Markon, Watson, & Skodol, 2012). Through an iterative process, they refined a list of 37 initial personality facets into a best-fitting model that contains 25 facets loading onto five higher-order domains (negative affect, detachment, antagonism, disinhibition, and psychoticism). While the structure resembles the FFM, it was intended to represent the more extreme and/or pathological variants of those traits (APA, 2012b).

Although statistical work on the categorical approach to the classification of psychopathology has not been as extensive, a number of studies have appeared. The most notable of these efforts were Maurice Lorr's use of cluster analysis to study individuals with schizophrenia (Lorr, 1966) and Paul Meehl's development of taxometrics—a set of techniques aimed at discerning the latent categorical from dimensional status of specific psychopathological constructs (Meehl, 1995; cf. Schmidt, Kotov, & Joiner, 2004). Interestingly, the majority of taxometric studies have supported dimensional structures for mental disorders rather than categorical, although some have favored distinct groups of disordered individuals (Haslam, Holland, & Kuppens, 2012; Ruscio, Haslam, & Ruscio, 2006).

A new analysis approach termed *factor mixture analysis* (Muthen, 2006; Muthen & Muthen, 2010) creates hybrid dimensional-categorical models, where the taxonicity and dimensionality of a set of measures can be examined simultaneously. This sort of model would represent distinct groups of individuals (taxa) that vary along some latent dimension (i.e., an ordering of the groups). Interestingly, when this sort of hybrid model is employed, some studies find that dimensional structures continue to be favored (Eaton, Krueger,

South, Simms, & Clark, 2011; Eaton et al., 2013; Wright et al., 2013), whereas others find taxons meaningfully differentiated by underlying dimensions (Bernstein et al., 2010; Lenzenweger, Clarkin, Yeomans, Kernberg, & Levy, 2008; Picardi et al., 2012).

Most classifications of psychopathology employ categories because they offer certain advantages. In everyday life, categorical concepts are used because they are familiar and easy to use. In addition, the dominant profession within the mental health field is psychiatry, and psychiatrists have been trained in a tradition associated with medical and biological classification. Both biological and medical classificatory systems are categorical; however, in regard to medical classification, certain portions can be viewed as dimensional (e.g., hypertension).

The tendency to think categorically should not be underestimated. Work in anthropology suggests that hierarchically organized categorical systems are the product of universal cognitive mechanisms that have evolved as adaptive ways of managing information (Atran, 1990; Berlin, 1992). In his study of various indigenous cultures, Berlin (1992) found that these societies had hierarchical organizations for the living things they encounter in their environment, and the structure of these "folk taxonomies" tended to be universal—but not concordant with scientific classifications. Evidence from cognitive and developmental psychologists shows that children seem to learn about the natural world through category formation (Hatano & Inagaki, 1994; Hickling & Gelman, 1995). It is not surprising, therefore, that people, including clinicians, prefer to use concepts that are the products of these cognitive mechanisms that favor categorical concepts (Gelman, 2003; Yoon, 2009).

There are, however, substantial disadvantages to using categories. Categorical diagnoses often result in the loss of some information. Categorical systems also depend on nonarbitrary boundaries or at least on points of rarity between syndromes, such as are seen in the valley between the two modes in a bimodal frequency histogram (Kendell, 1975, 1989).

Haslam (2002) outlined a taxonomy of "kinds of kinds," or a model of category types ranging from true categories to true dimensions. The truest form of a category is what various philosophers have termed a "natural kind" (Kripke, 1980; Putnam, 1982). A natural kind represents a group with a unitary etiology that leads to necessary outcomes and a discrete separation from other psychopathologic syndromes. However, true natural kinds are rare or nonexistent in the realm of psychopathology (Zachar, 2000). It could be that certain groups are qualitatively separate from other entities but lack the underlying "essence" of a natural kind, which Haslam termed "discrete kinds." An example would be the qualitative difference between regular and endogenous depression proposed by some (Schotte, Maes, Cluydts, & Cosyns, 1997). Even though depression exists on a severity dimension, these authors would claim that a qualitative shift occurs at a certain threshold, creating a truly different kind. However, categories of mental disorders are not always well demarcated. When a category does not have a clear boundary, Haslam terms it a "fuzzy kind." A fuzzy kind exists when there is a definable group, but the characteristics of that group blend into other groups. Next, there are phenomena, such as hypertension, that can be thought of existing along a dimension (measured by blood pressure), but for which there are functional reasons to categorically scale the dimension (i.e., a cut point above which the person is seen as needing medical intervention). The choice of the cut point may be debatable, but the presence of a cut point serves a pragmatic purpose. These sorts of groups are termed "practical kinds" (Haslam, 2002; Zachar, 2000). The final entry in Haslam's taxonomy consists of true dimensions, or continua of psychological characteristics that do not justify any cut point.

From this preceding discussion, the selection of the type of theoretical concept to use in classification (i.e., dimensions versus categories) is fundamental to the development of a classification. Jaspers (1963) suggested that different classificatory models might be required for different forms of psychopathology. This idea has merit. Some conditions, especially those traditionally described as organic disorders, are similar to diagnoses in physical medicine. These could probably best be represented using a categorical model in which diagnoses are specified by diagnostic criteria. Other areas of psychopathology, especially the affective disorders and personality disorders, might be better represented using a dimensional framework.

Interestingly, the issue of dimensions versus categories became a focus of significant controversy within *DSM-5*. As noted earlier, the workgroup concerned with the personality disorders proposed a hybrid model whereby some personality disorder categories (those with the most empirical support) would be retained, while also including a dimensional model to describe individuals who did not fit neatly into a category. Within the workgroup, there was not unanimous agreement on the best approach involving dimensions and/or categories. This hybrid structure was a compromise that could capitalize on the benefits of both categories and dimensions. However, the Board of Trustees of the American Psychiatric Association did not accept the proposal, electing to keep the same 10 categorical personality disorders found in *DSM-IV*. Instead, the workgroup proposal was published as a separate chapter in Section III of the manual to foster further research, with the hope of adopting the portions of the model that achieve sufficient empirical support.

DSMs *as Atheoretical*

At the times that *DSM-I* and *DSM-II* were written, the dominant theory in psychiatry was psychoanalysis. However, as the psychoanalytic perspective began to lose favor, a more biological approach began to emerge as the force behind explaining and conceptualizing mental disorders. The committee members of *DSM-III* (headed by Spitzer) were sensitive to this division between the psychoanalytic and biological explanations of mental disorders. Consequently, the determination was made that *DSM-III* would be theory neutral in order for the classification to be more accessible to all mental health professionals. This approach has been preserved throughout the modern *DSMs* and has sparked a number of criticisms on the failure of specifying a theory to guide the classification system (Faust & Miner, 1986; Follette & Houts, 1996; Margolis, 1994). Most writers who have thought about the recent *DSMs* agree that the implicit theoretical model associated with these systems is the biological (medical) approach (Klerman, 1978; Woodruff, Goodwin, & Guze, 1974). According to Follette and Houts (1996), the refusal by the authors of the *DSMs* to postulate a theory of psychopathology explicitly hinders scientific progress within the field and results in definitional problems.

Though the authors of *DSM-III* denied having a theory, Sadler (2005) argued that certain values or assumptions are nonetheless embedded in the structure of the *DSMs* that emerge with their application. Because these six values, as discussed by Sadler, do represent the beginning of a theory of psychopathology, each of them will be discussed next.

The first is the value of empiricism, which is the belief that the contents of the *DSMs* are based on scientific research, complete with testable hypotheses and controlled clinical trials. This empirical advancement discourages the exclusive use of expert opinions and clinical judgment when making nosological decisions, as was seen with *DSM-I* and *DSM-II*.

Second, Sadler discussed how the *DSM* is hyponarrative, a term he coined to describe *DSM*'s lack of storytelling qualities. Narrativity was especially lost during the transition from *DSM-II* to *DSM-III*, when disorder descriptions became symptom listings. Applying *DSM* language to diagnosing an individual loses the richness of the "biographical" explanation of the individual. However, Sadler argued that the role of *DSM* is not to capture necessarily the life story of each patient but to address the signs and symptoms associated with diagnosis. The hyponarrativity of *DSM* leads the clinician to focus exclusively on the symptoms of a patient, rather than on the interactions between the symptoms and the relationships, priorities, aspirations, and daily functioning of the patient. It is these interactions that provide the plot line for the patient's story.

A third assumption of the modern *DSMs* is individualism. As expressed in the *DSM* definition of mental disorder, psychopathology resides within the individual and is not the manifestation of the interactions of the individual with others or with the social forces around that individual. An example of the effect of focusing on individualism as a value can be seen with the removal of homosexuality as a mental disorder. Rationales were put forth for homosexuality not being a mental disorder: the struggles associated with being homosexual were viewed as being society induced and not something inherent within the individual.

Fourth, *DSM* disorders are of a natural essence. In other words, disorders follow a natural order whereby etiologies are multifactorial—including biological, psychological, and sociocultural influences. Sadler stated that this assumption is important to understanding the atheoretical approach of *DSM*, because *DSM* stipulates that multiple theories, not just one all-encompassing explanation, are essential to understanding mental disorders. The inherent pluralism of that approach has many advantages for describing the breadth of psychopathology, but impedes monistic beliefs that a single theory (like evolution in biology) could account for the entire landscape, as might be the agenda of biologically oriented researchers (Ghaemi, 2003).

The fifth value, pragmatism, refers to the use of *DSM* as a means to help individuals with mental disorders. Thus, *DSM*s are designed primarily for clinicians, so their use in research is only secondary. Issues such as *DSM*'s compatibility with *ICD*, its utilization among different mental health professions, and its impact on turf issues surrounding the mental health enterprise all play into the political constraints and limitations that ultimately begin to affect the science and empirical commitment of establishing a classification of mental disorders.

Finally, Sadler described the sixth implicit value of *DSM* as traditionalism. The diagnostic concepts in the *DSM*s have a history. The modern *DSM*s have been built on past *DSM* classifications. Trying to maintain continuity over time is important both for psychiatry and for the other mental health professions. Sadler suggested that the continuity of a classification system results in this system becoming familiar, being valued, and serving as the basis of a long-standing research and clinical infrastructure.

Organization of Recent DSMs by Work Groups

The process used to formulate and revise the *DSM*s warrants comment. A lengthy consultation process with panels of experts and the profession at large was used to ensure the face or content validity of diagnoses and widespread acceptance of the resulting system. The consultation process was partly a scientific exercise designed to produce a classification based on the best available evidence and expertise, and partly a social-political process designed to ensure the acceptability of the resulting product. Because scientific and political objectives often run counter to each other, compromises were necessary.

With *DSM-III*, a task force handled the process and established advisory committees. These committees were composed of experts whose task was to identify and define diagnostic categories in their areas. Each committee also had a panel of consultants to provide additional advice and information. As the process continued, drafts of *DSM-III* were circulated to the profession for review and comment. Finally, field trials were conducted to evaluate the proposals and identify problems.

Although a similar process was used for *DSM-III-R*, *DSM-IV* went a step further. Work groups were established to address specific diagnostic classes, and each group followed a three-stage process. First, comprehensive literature reviews were conducted so that *DSM-IV* reflected current knowledge. Second, existing data sets were reanalyzed to evaluate diagnostic concepts and to provide information on the performance of diagnostic criteria. Third, extensive field trials were conducted to address specific issues.

The *DSM-5* workgroup process appeared to be fairly different from the workgroup process of its predecessors. The workgroups often had broader agenda, and their assignments were not to just one family of disorders. For example, the anxiety disorder workgroup of *DSM-5* had responsibility for the following categories: separation anxiety disorder, body dysmorphic disorder, social phobia, substance-induced obsessive-compulsive disorder, posttraumatic stress disorder, and dissociative amnesia. In addition, from the rationales presented for changes in categories, there appeared to be obvious interaction across the workgroups. For example, substance-induced obsessive-compulsive disorder, as mentioned earlier, involved interaction with the workgroup for substance use disorders. Under the family of schizophrenic disorders, the psychotic disorders workgroup and the personality disorders workgroup integrated their efforts.

There are many laudable features to the process used to revise and develop each edition. Each work group faced a major undertaking that required careful analysis of information as well as consultation with other experts in the field. This division of labor into work groups probably contributed to the acceptance of the resulting classifications. But there were also problems with the process. The initial structure for *DSM-III* was established when the work groups were identified. Each was given a defined area of psychopathology. The separation into committees along major topic areas led to both personal and conceptual conflicts. Psychopathology is not readily divisible into discrete areas. Overlap occurred between various committees, leading to dispute. Once a committee was established with a given mandate, that committee was reluctant to relinquish domains of psychopathology that might have been better classified elsewhere. The superordinate task force was responsible for resolving these disputes and ensuring integration. Inevitably, political processes within and between work groups influenced the solutions adopted. As noted earlier, the *DSM-5* process appears to have attempted to change this political process. How well *DSM-5* succeeded in this goal is yet unclear.

Measurement and Methodological Issues

The final section of this chapter addresses more practical concerns about the classification of mental disorders. While it is good to debate the ontological status of the term *mental disorder* and consider the political forces that impact classification schemes, at some point, practical decisions must be made regarding actual patients. Many of these practical concerns embody decisions about measurement, or how one assesses the nature of the condition. We adopt some of the standard terms of psychological measurement theory, including concepts like reliability and validity, to elucidate issues surrounding psychiatric diagnosis.

Reliability

The reliability of a classification of mental disorders is the degree of diagnostic agreement among users. Reliability is clearly important; diagnoses have little value for communication or prediction if there are high levels of disagreement among clinicians. As Kendell (1975) pointed out, the accuracy of clinical and prognostic decisions based on a diagnosis cannot be greater than the reliability with which the diagnosis is made, and most writers allege that reliability places an upper limit on the validity of a given diagnosis (Spitzer & Fleiss, 1975; Spitzer & Williams, 1980).

There are a variety of factors that influence reliability estimates. For instance, variations in patient characteristics influence clinicians' diagnostic decisions. Farmer and Chapman (2002) found that clinicians were much more consistent

in providing a diagnosis of narcissistic personality disorder to men than to women. Some studies have begun to examine the influence of variables such as race, age, and low socioeconomic status on diagnosis (Abreu, 1999; James & Haley, 1995; Littlewood, 1992). Einfeld and Aman (1995) suggest that reliability in *DSM* diagnoses appears to deteriorate markedly as patient IQ scores decrease. Further, it is important to note that reliability estimates based on well-controlled research studies are likely inflated relative to reliability in day-to-day practice in clinical settings.

History   As noted earlier in this chapter, reliability became a major focus of empirical criticisms of psychiatric diagnosis during the 1950s and 1960s. Generally, the impression from these studies was that psychiatrists and clinical psychologists, when independently diagnosing the same cases, did not agree on the diagnoses that they were assigning to cases. Interestingly, as the methodology of these studies improved, the estimates of reliability generally appeared more positive than in the early, rather hastily designed studies. One study in this series (Ward, Beck, Mendelson, Mock, & Erbaugh, 1962) made the additional conclusion that the reason for this relative lack of diagnostic agreement among clinicians (i.e., poor reliability) was that the definitions of the diagnostic categories in *DSM-I* were too vague. Although the methodology of the Ward et al. study had serious limitations (Blashfield, 1984), this conclusion appealed to the field; and the Ward et al. (1962) paper was often cited prior to the publication of *DSM-III*, when diagnostic criteria were used to improve the precision of defining diagnostic categories.

Another source of variability in early research on reliability was the statistical procedure used to provide reliability estimates. In earlier years, this was a serious problem (Zubin, 1967). By the mid-1970s, a statistic named *kappa* became the standard technique for estimating diagnostic reliability. Kappa corrects for chance levels of agreement between raters and thus is an improvement on a simple percentage of agreement. However, a limitation of this statistic is its instability when the base rate of a diagnosis within a sample is less than 5% (Spitznagel & Helzer, 1985).

Assessing Reliability   It is instructive to compare reliability as applied to psychiatric classification with reliability as applied to psychological tests.

In test theory, *reliability* refers to the consistency of scores obtained with the same test on different occasions or with different sets of equivalent items (Anastasi, 1982). If a test is reliable, parallel scales constructed from an equivalent pool of items will yield the same measurement values. The extent to which this does not occur indicates the extent to which measurement is influenced by error. Traditionally, the reliability of psychological tests is assessed in three ways: (1) test-retest reliability, (2) alternative forms, and (3) internal consistency. A fourth method directly relevant to the clinical enterprise is interrater reliability, or the consistency of different diagnosticians regarding the same patient.

Test-Retest Reliability   The test-retest method assumes that the administration of the same scale at different points in time represents parallel tests. Memory for items is the most common confound with this approach. High test-retest reliability is to be expected only when measuring a variable assumed to be stable; some mental disorders are assumed to follow a relatively stable course (e.g., autism spectrum disorders), but many disorders (e.g., affective disorders) are assumed to fluctuate across time. In a multisite collaborative study of *DSM-IV* disorders, Zanarini et al. (2000) found that test-retest kappa coefficients ranged from .35 to .78 for a variety of clinical disorders and from 0.39 to 1.00 for personality disorders. However, a meta-analysis of diagnostic methods found that concordance between structured diagnostic interviews and standard clinical evaluations varied widely, with some diagnostic areas having relatively good agreement (e.g., eating disorders kappa = .70) and others relatively poor between the two methods (e.g., affective disorders kappa = .14; Rettew, Lynch, Achenbach, Dumenci, & Ivanova, 2009). The field trials for *DSM-5* utilized a methodology that gave a realistic estimate of how reliable diagnoses for these conditions are under natural clinical conditions, versus the stricter standardization present in research protocols (often through structured interviews). As might be expected, test-retest reliabilities were lower, with kappas ranging from zero to .78, with some common diagnoses not faring as well as might be expected (e.g., major depressive disorder = .28; Regier et al., 2013). Generally, the more training and structure provided in the diagnostic assessment, the higher the reliability coefficients will be; however,

one must consider whether the procedure used to obtain a high reliability is feasible for implementation in daily clinical use. With *DSM-III*, obtaining higher reliability was an explicit goal. Now, some have questioned if test-retest reliability should be a goal in and of itself (Kraemer, Kupfer, Clarke, Narrow, & Regier, 2012).

Alternative Forms   The alternative-form method uses equivalent or parallel measures of the same construct. Ideally, different sources of information should converge on the same conclusions. Hilsenroth, Baity, Mooney, and Meyer (2004) examined three sources of information regarding depressive symptoms: in vivo interviews, videotaped interviews, and chart reviews. Clinicians made reliable ratings of depressive symptoms across in vivo interviews and videotaped interviews, but chart reviews were not consistent with either. Diagnostic disagreement can occur when clinicians have different kinds and amounts of information on which to base diagnosis. This problem may arise from differences in clinicians' ability to elicit information, the way patients respond to questions, and the availability of information from other sources. Thus, there are important sources of variance that can contribute to unreliability, including differences in clinical skill, patient responsiveness, and diagnostic setting. The advent of structured interviews has attempted to control for the variability of information received by clinicians in a diagnostic setting. When these interviews are used, especially by well-trained interviewers, diagnostic reliability can be quite good (Farmer & Chapman, 2002; Segal, Hersen, & Van Hasselt, 1994). However, studies comparing diagnostic agreement across different structured interviews administered to the same patients have shown lower than expected concordance, with kappas in the .5 range (Oldham et al., 1992).

Internal Consistency   Internal consistency measures (split-half techniques and coefficient alpha) assume each item on a scale is like a miniature scale. Thus, internal consistency estimates the extent to which the items in a scale are homogeneous. In psychological testing, this estimate of reliability is the most common. Morey (1988) examined the internal consistency of diagnostic criteria for personality disorders and found low correlations among criteria used to diagnose the same disorder. Other studies have found higher estimates of internal consistency, but using logistic regression and calculations of sensitivity and specificity have concluded that some criteria for certain personality disorders could be dropped because they do not form a cohesive diagnosis (Farmer & Chapman, 2002). These criticisms (among others) have led to some of the changes proposed in Section III regarding personality disorder diagnosis in *DSM-5*. However, care should be taken with such conclusions. It is reasonable to posit heterogeneous symptom groupings, for which internal consistency estimates are therefore inappropriate means of measurement, just as test-retest estimates are inappropriate for diagnoses with fluid symptom patterns.

Interrater Reliability   The three forms of reliability just discussed focus on the construct underlying the diagnosis. However, discrepancies can also occur in the application of the diagnosis. Two clinicians, for example, may disagree about what diagnosis is best for the same case. In studies of interrater reliability, two or more clinicians interview each patient either conjointly in a single interview or in separate interviews close together in time. In *DSM-I* and *DSM-II*, consistency among clinicians was low, but with the advent of diagnostic criteria in *DSM-III*, reliability increased. Estimates of interrater reliability fluctuate around values of .75 to .80 or even higher for a variety of mental disorders (Silverman, Saavedra, & Pina, 2001; Zanarini & Frankenburg, 2001) but can be more variable for personality disorders (Farmer & Chapman, 2002; Zanarini & Frankenburg, 2001).

Validity

The main impetus for the development of *DSM-III* was the perceived crisis surrounding diagnostic reliability. Many clinicians purported that a set of criteria could not be valid if it were not first reliable. Although this assumption is not necessarily true (Carey & Gottesman, 1978; Faust & Miner, 1986), the creators of *DSM-III* saw the production of a reliable diagnostic system as their primary task. After establishing reliability, researchers could turn their attention to issues of validity. The introduction of diagnostic criteria and the development of structured interviews based on those criteria greatly improved reliability.

Validity in common usage refers to the truth-value of a statement. However, it is important to note that using *valid* in that sense does not imply that there is only one valid conclusion for a given set of facts; rather, there are many possible valid conclusions based on one's point of view.

History   The concept of validity is often discussed within the context of the classification of psychopathology; but, ironically, like many classificatory concepts themselves, finding a clearly specified, thoughtfully articulated definition of validity has proven elusive. Two major approaches to diagnostic validity have been discussed in the last 50 years. One is a relatively common-sense, medicine-based approach that appeals to psychiatrists. The other, which often is discussed in more abstract, empirical contexts, is the view psychologists have about validity based on their extensive experience with different forms of assessment.

A short paper published by Eli Robins and Samuel Guze of Washington University in 1970 contained the major discussion of validity from the medical perspective. Robins and Guze were leaders of the neo-Kraepelinian group whose views led to *DSM-III*. Robins and Guze discussed validity in the context of five phases of research that would demonstrate that a diagnostic concept represented a disease. These five phases were (1) clinical description (i.e., establishing that the disorder represents a "syndrome" of symptoms that can be empirically shown to co-occur at relatively high rate), (2) laboratory studies (which establish the biological substrate of the disorder), (3) delimitation from other disorders (which would establish that the disorders are relatively, though not perfectly, divided into discrete categories), (4) follow-up studies (which show that the individuals with this disorder have a common course to their symptom patterns), and (5) family studies (which establish the genetic basis of the biological phenomenon associated with the disorder). Robins and Guze believed that their approach to validity not only stemmed from the medical research of Syndenham but also was consistent with the views of validity adopted by German medical researchers of the late nineteenth century when the latter resolved the etiologies of many bacterial-based diseases (e.g., tuberculosis, smallpox, syphilis).

The other approach to the meaning of validity when applied to psychiatric classification has come from the work of psychologists who have drawn on discussions of validity in the context of psychological tests. Joseph Zubin at Columbia University was one of the first to promote the application of a psychological-testing view of validity to psychiatric diagnosis. Zubin (1967) stated that the broad concept of validity should be subdivided into four subsidiary concepts: (1) concurrent validity, (2) predictive validity, (3) construct validity, and (4) content validity.

In the past few years, a new development has occurred in the approach to diagnostic validity. This approach is represented by a concept titled *clinical utility*, which, like the views of Robins and Guze, has a pragmatic emphasis. In the words of First et al. (2004), clinical utility "is the extent to which the *DSM* assists clinical decision makers in fulfilling the various clinical functions of a psychiatric classification system" (p. 947). According to First et al., the clinical functions of a psychiatric classification are to (a) conceptualize diagnostic entities; (b) communicate clinical information to practitioners, patients, and patient families; (c) use diagnostic concepts during intake interviews; (d) choose effective interventions based on empirical evidence; and (e) predict what resources would be needed in the future. Verheul (2005) argued that increased clinical utility (especially regarding communication and clinical decision making) may provide the rationale for shifting from a categorical to dimensional model of personality disorder. Reed (2010) has argued that clinical utility should be the driving force for making classificatory decisions when more convincing scientific information is equivocal or not available.

Issues The psychiatric approach to validity, embodied by the work of Robins and Guze (1970), is based on the medical concept of disease, which has proven elusive in its own right (Nesse, 2001; Scadding, 1980). Many, but not all, references to the concept of disease are making assumptions about essentialism. According to essentialism, a category is defined by some*thing* (an essence) that causes one to be a member of the category. For example, when syphilis was found to be the cause of general paresis, the essence of the disease category became the presence of syphilis in the central nervous system. Thus, a valid category is one that has an identifiable etiological agent. Schizophrenia is valid to the degree some*thing* causes one to be schizophrenic.

Essentialism has proven problematic even in the realm of physical diseases (Nesse, 2001; Scadding, 1996). Even in the most archetypal cases of "disease," for example—a bacterial infection—it is impossible to define the disease category in a way that corresponds to the state of nature and is free of human value assumptions (Smith, 2001). The disease is not the presence of bacteria, as perfectly healthy individuals have the bacteria in their system. Rather, the disease is an interaction effect, which emerges from the presence of the bacteria and an immunological weakness, among other factors. In short, diseases have multiple causes in even the simplest of cases; therefore, to define them as having simple, reified essences is inappropriate at best. The essentialist view of validity has proven even less effective in the case of psychiatric conditions, the causes of which are complex and multiply determined (Zachar, 2000).

In contrast, the psychological approach to validity has been based on psychometric test theory. A psychological test is considered valid to the extent to which its items and resultant scores reflect the construct of interest. For instance, the items on a test should represent the entire domain of the construct, which is generally termed *content validity*. For example, a test of depression should have items that sample all the relevant symptoms and expressions generally considered to be a part of depression. In the same fashion, the diagnostic criteria used to define a mental disorder category should represent the range of behaviors associated with that category.

Second, the test may be considered valid if it meets some predetermined criterion, that is, *criterion validity*. To continue with the example of depression, a test of depression would be criterion valid if it consistently classified people in the same manner as a *DSM-5* diagnosis. The criterion is context dependent. In one context, one might consider a diagnosis from a structured interview (e.g., structured clinical interview for *DSM* disorders [SCID-I]) the "gold standard," whereas in another context, an unstructured interview might be the appropriate criterion.

The third and perhaps most important aspect of validity for psychological tests is *construct validity*—the degree to which the scores on the test measure what they are expected to measure (Cronbach & Meehl, 1955). This definition has several implications. First, raters should respond consistently to items that are meant to tap into the same construct, assuming that the construct is meant to be stable across time and homogenous. In that sense, reliability is an integral part of validity in that a measure's reliability should be consistent with the description of the construct. Second, the items on a test should correlate with each other. In the context of mental disorders, different items, which represent different symptoms, should co-occur (i.e., the construct is a syndrome). The degree to which the items correlate should be consistent with the supposed homogeneity or heterogeneity of the construct. Third, the test score should be related to measures of other constructs in an expected pattern. For example, a test of depression should be negatively correlated with a measure of positive affect. Further, test scores should be related to other measures of the same construct using different measurement methods. This approach is usually evaluated using the classic multitrait-multimethod procedure described by Campbell and Fiske (1959).

A modern statistical procedure termed *structural equation modeling* (SEM) allows researchers to blend investigations of internal and external construct validity. SEM is a correlational and regressional technique that models complex interrelationships in a multivariate format and allows one to test a variety of hypotheses regarding a construct (Campbell-Sills & Brown, 2006). It involves testing reliability and factor structures of measures (internal) as well as the relationships between measures (external). For example, Brown, Chorpita, and Barlow (1998) examined the interrelationships between anxiety and depressive diagnostic constructs. Given the considerable comorbidity between these disorders, they hypothesized that these disorders might be the manifestations of three higher-order constructs: positive affect, negative affect, and autonomic arousal (otherwise known as the tripartite model; Clark, Watson, & Mineka, 1994). Using SEM, Brown et al. tested the relationships among these constructs to see whether they were related in the pattern expected by the tripartite theory. They found that measures of *DSM-IV* disorders loaded in an expected pattern onto their respective latent constructs (e.g., measures of depression correlated with each other, but not necessarily with other disorders). Further, *DSM* disorders were related to the tripartite factors in an expected pattern. Levels of negative affect predicted both depression and the anxiety disorders. Positive affect predicted only depression (in a negative direction) but was unrelated to the anxiety disorders except for social phobia. Panic disorder and generalized anxiety disorder had a significant relationship to autonomic arousal.

Despite developments in psychological testing, substantial theoretical limitation to the psychological-test approach to validation exists in the context of mental disorders. The construct validation approach used in psychology assumes that the construct is already well defined. If the concept of a construct changes, as is inherent in any empirical science, any test purporting to measure that construct must be revalidated. In a strange way, the psychological-test approach puts the cart before the horse, as the structure of the diagnostic construct must be assumed before it can be investigated.

Diagnostic Overlap

Another major problem with *DSM* is the degree of diagnostic overlap that occurs throughout the classification. For example, about 95% of patients meeting the diagnostic criteria for borderline personality disorder meet the criteria for an additional personality disorder (Widiger et al., 1991). This overlap among diagnoses is not unique to personality disorders but occurs across the range of mental disorders. Of those in the general population who meet criteria for a disorder, half meet criteria for two or more other mental disorders (Kessler, Chiu, Demler, & Walters, 2005), a phenomenon termed *comorbidity*.

History In 1984, Boyd and associates published a landmark empirical study that documented a surprisingly high degree of overlap among mental disorders. The sample was taken from a large (nearly 12,000 participants), multisite epidemiological study performed after the publication of *DSM-III*. *DSM-III* included specific exclusionary criteria to prevent the overlap of certain diagnoses. However, Boyd et al. found that if the exclusionary criteria were ignored, instances in which an individual received more than one diagnosis were quite common. For instance, the diagnostic overlap between major depressive disorder and agoraphobia was 15 times what might be expected by chance. Boyd et al. also found that the diagnostic overlap among mental disorders, for which no exclusionary criteria were given in *DSM-III*, was also quite high (e.g., the co-occurrence of schizophrenia and alcohol abuse/dependence was 10 times greater than expected by chance).

Stimulated by the Boyd et al. (1984) finding, the National Institute of Mental Health (NIMH) sponsored a conference in the late 1980s of prominent psychiatrists and psychologists to discuss the implications of this finding, the results of which were later published (Maser & Cloninger, 1990). Later, the NIMH funded a large-scale epidemiological analysis of the occurrence of mental disorders in the United States in two research studies known as the National Comorbidity Survey (Kessler et al., 1994) and the National Comorbidity Survey Replication (Kessler et al., 2005). The results showed that virtually all mental disorders showed a high rate of diagnostic overlap with almost all other mental disorders.

Krueger and Markon (2006) have reviewed the resulting literature on the comorbidity of mental disorders. They noted that this term was rarely used before the mid-1980s when the Boyd et al. study was published, but in the next two decades approximately 8,500 journal articles appeared that had relevance to the concept of comorbidity.

The Meaning of Comorbidity   The issue of diagnostic overlap has been termed comorbidity, although there are those that contend the term is a misnomer (Lilienfeld, Waldman, & Israel, 1994). Feinstein (1970) introduced the term *comorbidity* in the context of medical epidemiology. Later, Lilienfeld (2003) reported that Feinstein had never intended for the term *comorbidity* to refer to all cases of diagnostic overlap, as seems to be its current usage in the literature. In general, one would expect a certain degree of overlap simply by chance. However, when disorders co-occur at greater than chance levels, the overlap begins to have implications for the classification system.

For example, a patient may present with a case of panic disorder and be concurrently depressed. On the other hand, a patient presenting with panic may have a comorbid diagnosis of insomnia. In these cases, it could be that depression and panic are meaningfully correlated; that is, the depression may cause the panic, or vice versa, a third variable could cause both, or some alternative complex causal model could account for the relationship. However, when two co-occurring conditions are not meaningfully related but simply overlap by chance, as could be the case with panic and insomnia, that sort of comorbidity is of decidedly less theoretical interest. Given the base rates of disorders in the population, one would expect a certain number of cases to present with overlap just by chance. Hypothetically, if there were a 10%

chance of having panic disorder and a 15% chance of having insomnia, one would expect a 1.5% (10% 15%) chance of having both conditions in the general population. However, epidemiological work on psychiatric disorders has shown that various mental disorders co-occur at a rate in the population much greater than that expected by chance (Boyd et al., 1984; Kessler et al., 1994, 2005).

When disorders co-occur at greater than chance levels, comorbidity begins to have implications for the classification system. As stated before, the authors of *DSM-III* and beyond have assumed that the categories in the classification are relatively discrete. However, if there is significant covariance between these conditions, that assumption of discreteness is untenable. For example, unipolar affective disorders and anxiety disorders co-occur at a very high rate. This finding has led some authors to contend that these disorders are not discrete conditions, but varied expressions of a single disorder, as discussed in the last section (Brown et al., 1998; Clark & Watson, 1991; Mineka, Watson, & Clark, 1998). If that is the case, the current diagnostic system is not accurately "carving nature at the joints."

However, there are also artifactual reasons why disorders could co-occur at greater than chance levels. For instance, Berksonian bias (Berkson, 1946) states that a person with comorbid disorders has twice the chance of seeking treatment as does a person with a single disorder and so has a greater chance of being included in studies. Similarly, comorbidity rates may be overestimated because of clinical selection bias or because individuals with multiple disorders may be more impaired and thus overrepresented in treatment studies. However, significant rates of comorbidity occur even in community-based samples (e.g., Kessler et al., 2005). Finally, it has been demonstrated that structured interviews generate much higher rates of diagnosis overall, and higher rates of comorbidity specifically, than do unstructured interviews (Verheul & Widiger, 2004; Zimmerman, Rothschild, & Chelminski, 2005). However, such differences in diagnostic method may not be artifactual because structured interviews ensure that the breadth of psychopathology is assessed, whereas unstructured interviews address only salient points, and legitimate disorders may be overlooked.

Recently, increased attention has been paid to developing statistical models of comorbidity (e.g., Borsboom, Cramer, Schmittmann, Epskamp, &

Waldorp, 2011; Krueger & Markon, 2006). Using sophisticated multivariate statistical methods, it is possible to test potential causal models of comorbidity, thereby elucidating the structure of the classification of mental disorders and suggesting changes to the arrangement of the *DSM*. For example, there is increasing support for organizing both childhood and adult disorders along internalizing and externalizing spectra (Krueger, 1999; Krueger et al., 2005). Indeed, this approach led the creators of *DSM-5* to place internalizing groups of disorders (e.g., anxiety, depressive, and somatic disorders) and externalizing disorders (e.g., impulsive, disruptive conduct, and substance use disorders) sequentially next to each other in the organization of the manual.

One approach to understanding comorbidity is that groups of disorders, termed *diagnostic spectra*, are more accurately classified together than as discrete disorders. Criticisms of the structure and organization of previous versions led *DSM-5* workgroups to reconceptualize many sections of the manual. One area of great controversy in the literature regards the external validity of the pervasive developmental disorders (i.e., Kamp-Becker et al., 2010; Klin & Volkmar, 2003). Pervasive Developmental Disorder is a diagnostic group that includes autistic disorder (AD), Asperger's disorder (AS), childhood disintegrative disorder (CDD), Rhett's syndrome, and pervasive developmental disorder–not otherwise specified (PDD-NOS). Since AD was first included in *DSM-III-R* and AS was first included in *DSM-IV*, researchers have questioned the uniqueness of these diagnoses. The distinction between AD and AS was popularized by Wing (1981) when she coined the phrase "Asperger's disorder" to discuss symptoms first described by Hans Asperger (1944). Ironically, Wing (2000) later wrote that she did not intend to imply that AS and AD were distinct disorders. Regardless, varying conceptualizations of these diagnoses have been present since Asperger's 1944 description of what is now called Asperger's disorder and Kanner's 1943 description of autism.

Many researchers have since examined AS and AD to garner additional understanding of the etiology, symptoms, and potential differences in presentation between these diagnoses. Although some studies have proclaimed differences between AD and AS (i.e., Ghaziuddin & Gerstein, 1996; Paul, Orlovski, Marcinko, & Volkmar, 2009; Szatmari et al., 2009), many researchers have concluded that there are no distinguishable or useful differences beyond variations in severity (i.e., Ozonoff, South, & Miller, 2000; Rogers & Ozonoff, 2005; Szatmari et al., 1989). Subsequently, arguments for the combination of AD and AS into one spectrum diagnosis are prevalent (i.e., Miller & Ozonoff, 2000; Via, Radua, Cardoner, Happe, & Mataix-Cols, 2011). The *DSM-5* neurodevelopmental disorders workgroup created a new autism spectrum disorder (ASD) diagnosis that incorporates all individuals who previously held a diagnosis of AS, AD, CDD, or PDD-NOS. Under this "umbrella" there will be a great deal of individualization in symptom presentation and functioning level. The *DSM-5* workgroup has anticipated these variations and states that individuals who meet criteria for ASD should additionally be described on the basis of intellectual level and language ability.

The variation present in this example reflects many areas of psychopathological classification. When differences between two disorders are difficult to identify, it is possible that the disorders may actually be variable presentations of the same, broader diagnosis. Other spectra included in *DSM-5* include a disruptive behavior spectrum of impulse control disorders, conduct disorder, and oppositional defiant disorder; a spectrum of obsessive-compulsive disorders including things like body dysmorphic disorder and trichotillomania; and a psychotic spectrum including schizophrenia, schizoaffective disorder, delusional disorder, and schizotypal personality disorder. When the meta-structure of these disorders has been examined, externalizing and psychotic dimensions seem to emerge, supporting the notion of grouping these disorders (Wright et al., 2013). The relatedness within each of these potential spectra also represents the dimensionality of mental health disorders, in general (discussed earlier). Ultimately, the criteria for a clinical diagnosis are met at a cutoff that splits the dimension between normal functioning and each of the graded severities of the respective disorders (Bernstein et al., 2010).

Conclusion

This chapter starts with the sentence "Diagnosis is simple." Approximately 15,000 words and 190 references later, diagnosis does not seem so simple. This chapter has focused on a taxonomic view of modern psychiatric classification. The organization of this chapter, just by itself, was a complex act of classification into topics, history, discussion of controversies, terminology, and reviews of the writings of others. We could have used quite different organizational principles to structure our chapter. For instance, we could have written the chapter with a chronological structure, moving from one *DSM* edition to another. We could have organized the chapter by professions—what psychiatrists have written about classification, what psychologists have said, what philosophers have written, etc. We could have focused on the prominent individuals in the classification literature: Kraepelin, Menninger, Spitzer, Zubin, Lorr, Frances, Robins, etc. We could have emphasized diagnostic concepts that have been controversial and why: dementia praecox, neurosis, homosexuality, premenstrual syndrome, narcissistic personality disorder, masochistic personality disorder, internet addiction, etc.

Like most "simple" topics, when thought about carefully, diagnosis becomes complex. Our organization of this chapter represented our view of a controversial but important area of concern regarding how knowledge about psychopathology is organized. It is important for the reader of this chapter to note that the problems and dilemmas enumerated here have no easy resolution, if a resolution is even possible. No "perfect" approach to classification exists. Each attempt has its own flaws and limitations. The task of the mental health field is to determine which classificatory scheme best matches the values and goals of the discipline. But perhaps it is even more important to recognize the limitations of the system, because it is all too easy to accept a classification system as "given." We hope this chapter will not only inspire a healthy skepticism regarding the *DSMs* but also help the reader to appreciate the necessity and importance of classification within the mental health field.

Author Note

We would like to thank Danny Burgess for his work on a previous version of this chapter.

References

Abreu, J. M. (1999). Conscious and nonconscious African-American stereotypes: Impact on first impression and diagnostic ratings by therapist. *Journal of Community and Clinical Psychology, 67,* 387–393.

Achenbach, T. M. (1966). The classification of children's psychiatric symptoms: A factor-analytic study. *Psychological Monographs: General and Applied, 80* (7, Whole No. 615).

Achenbach, T. M. (1995). Empirically based assessment and taxonomy: Applications to clinical research. *Psychological Assessment, 7,* 261–274.

American Psychiatric Association. (2012a). Proposed draft revisions to DSM disorders and criteria. Retrieved from http://www.dsm5.org/ProposedRevision/Pages/Default.aspx

American Psychiatric Association. (2012b). Rationale for the proposed changes to the personality disorders classification in DSM-5. Retrieved from http://www.dsm5.org/Documents/Personality%20Disorders/Rationale%20for%20the%20Proposed%20changes%20to%20the%20Personality%20Disorders%20in%20DSM-5%205-1-12.pdf

Anastasi, A. (1982). *Psychological testing* (5th ed.). New York: Macmillan.

Ash, P. (1949). The reliability of psychiatric diagnoses. *Journal of Abnormal and Social Psychology, 44,* 272–276.

Asperger, H. (1944). Die "autistischen Psychopathen" im Kindesalter. *Archiv für Psychiatrie und Nervenkrankheiten, 117,* 76–136. (Reprinted in Autism and Asperger syndrome, by U. Frith, Ed., 1991, Cambridge, UK: Cambridge University Press).

Atran, S. (1990). *Cognitive foundations of natural history: Towards an anthropology of science.* Cambridge, UK: Cambridge University Press.

Beck, A. T. (1962). Reliability of psychiatric diagnoses: A critique of systematic studies. *American Journal of Psychiatry, 119,* 210–216.

Berkson, J. (1946). Limitations of the application of the four-fold table analysis to hospital data. *Biometrics Bulletin, 2,* 47–53.

Berlin, B. (1992). *Ethnobiological classification: Principles of categorization of plants and animals in traditional societies.* Princeton, NJ: Princeton University Press.

Bernstein, A., Stickle, T. R., Zvolensky, M. J., Taylor, S., Abramowitz, J., & Stewart, S. (2010). Dimensional, categorical or dimensional-categories: Testing the latent structure of anxiety sensitivity among adults using factor-mixture modeling. *Behavior Therapy, 41,* 515–529.

Berrios, G. E., & Hauser, R. (1988). The early development of Kraepelin's ideas on classification: A conceptual history. *Psychological Medicine, 18,* 813–821.

Blashfield, R. K. (1984). *The classification of psychopathology: Neo-Kraepelinian and quantitative approaches*. New York: Plenum Press.

Blashfield, R. K., & Keeley, J. (2010). A short history of a psychiatric diagnostic category that turned out to be a disease. In T. Millon, R. Krueger, & E. Simonsen (Eds.). *Contemporary directions in psychopathology* (pp. 324–336). New York: Guilford Press.

Borsboom, D., Cramer, A., Schmittmann, V., Epskamp, S., & Waldorp, L. (2011). The small world of psychopathology. *PLoS One*, 6, e27407.

Boyd, J. H., Burke, J. D., Gruenberg, E., Holzer, C. E., Rae, D. S., George, L. K., et al. (1984). Exclusion criteria of DSM–III: A study of co-occurrence of hierarchy-free syndromes. *Archives of General Psychiatry, 41*, 983–989.

Brown, T. A., Chorpita, B. F., & Barlow, D. H. (1998). Structural relationship among dimensions of the DSM–IV anxiety and mood disorders and dimensions of negative affect, positive affect, and autonomic arousal. *Journal of Abnormal Psychology, 107*, 179–192.

Buck, R., & Hull, D. (1966). The logical structure of the Linnean hierarchy. *Systematic Zoology*, 15, 97–111.

Campbell, D. T., & Fiske, D. W. (1959). Convergent and discriminant validation by the multitrait-multimethod matrix. *Psychological Bulletin, 56*, 81–105.

Campbell-Sills, L., & Brown, T. A. (2006). Research considerations: Latent variable approaches to studying the classification and psychopathology of mental disorders. In F. Andrasik (Ed.), *Comprehensive handbook of personality and psychopathology: Vol. 2. Adult psychopathology* (pp. 21–35). Hoboken, NJ: Wiley.

Cantor, N., Smith, E. E., French, R., & Mezzich, J. (1980). Psychiatric diagnosis as prototype categorization. *Journal of Abnormal Psychology, 89*, 181–193.

Carey G., & Gottesman, I. I. (1978). Reliability and validity in binary ratings. *Archives of General Psychiatry, 35*, 1454–1459.

Clark, L. A. (2007). Assessment and diagnosis of personality disorder: Perennial issues and an emerging reconceptualization. *Annual Review of Psychology, 58*, 227–258.

Clark, L. A., & Watson, D. (1991). Tripartite model of anxiety and depression: Psychometric evidence and taxonomic implications. *Journal of Abnormal Psychology, 100*, 316–336.

Clark, L. A., Watson, D., & Mineka, S. (1994). Temperament, personality, and the mood and anxiety disorders. *Journal of Abnormal Psychology, 103*, 103–116.

Compton, W. M., & Guze, S. B. (1995). The neo-Kraepelinian revolution in psychiatric diagnosis. *European Archives of Psychiatry and Clinical Neuroscience, 245*, 196–201.

Cooper, J. E., Kendell, R. E., Gurland, B. J., Sharpe, L., Copeland, J. R. M., & Simon, R. (1972). *Psychiatric diagnosis in New York and London* [Maudsley Monograph No. 20]. London: Oxford University Press.

Cronbach, L. J., & Meehl, P. E. (1955). Construct validity in psychological tests. *Psychological Bulletin, 52*, 281–302.

Eaton, N. R., Krueger, R. F., Markon, K. E., Keyes, K. M., Skodol, A. E., Wall, M., Hasin, D. S., & Grant, B. F. (2013). The structure and predictive validity of the internalizing disorders. *Journal of Abnormal Psychology, 122*, 86–92.

Eaton, N. R., Krueger, R. F., South, S. C., Simms, L. J., & Clark, L. A. (2011). Contrasting prototypes and dimensions in the classification of personality pathology: Evidence that dimensions, but not prototypes, are robust. *Psychological Medicine, 41*, 1151–1163.

Einfeld, S. L., & Aman, M. (1995). Issues in the taxonomy of psychopathology of mental retardation. *Journal of Autism and Developmental Disorders, 25*, 143–167.

Eysenck, H. J. (1947*). Dimensions of personality*. London: Routledge & Kegan Paul.

Eysenck, H. J., & Eysenck, S. B. (1976). *Psychoticism as a dimension of personality*. London: Hodder & Stoughton.

Farber, I. E. (1975). Sane and insane: Constructions and misconstructions. *Journal of Abnormal Psychology, 84*, 589–620.

Farmer, R. F., & Chapman, A. L. (2002). Evaluation of DSM–IV personality disorder criteria as assessed by the Structured Clinical Interview for DSM–IV Personality Disorders. *Comprehensive Psychiatry, 43*, 285–300.

Faust, D., & Miner, R. A. (1986). The empiricist and his new clothes: *DSM–III* in perspective. *American Journal of Psychiatry, 143*, 962–967.

Feinstein, A. R. (1970). The pre-therapeutic classification of co-morbidity in chronic disease. *Journal of Chronic Diseases, 23*, 455–468.

First, M. B., Pincus, H. A., Levine, J. B., Williams, J. B. W., Ustun, B., & Peele, R. (2004). Clinical utility as a criterion for revising psychiatric diagnoses. *American Journal of Psychiatry, 161*, 946–954.

Follette, W. C., & Houts, A. C. (1996). Models of scientific progress and the role of theory in taxonomy development: A case study of the DSM. *Journal of Consulting and Clinical Psychology, 64*, 1120–1132.

Foucault, M. (1988). *Politics, philosophy, and culture*. London: Routledge.

Fulford, K. W. M. (1999). Nine variations and a coda on the theme of an evolutionary definition of dysfunction. *Journal of Abnormal Psychology, 108*, 412–420.

Gelman, S. (2003). *The essential child: Origins of essentialism in everyday thought*. New York: Oxford University Press.

Ghaemi, S. N. (2003). *The concepts of psychiatry: A pluralistic approach to the mind and mental illness*. Baltimore, MD: Johns Hopkins University Press.

Ghaziuddin, M., & Gerstein, L. (1996). Pedantic speaking style differentiates Asperger syndrome from high-functioning autism. *Journal of Autism and Developmental Disorders, 26*(6), 585–595.

Goffman, E. (1959). The moral career of the mental patient. *Psychiatry, 22*, 123–142.

Goffman, E. (1963). *Stigma*. Englewood Cliffs, NJ: Prentice-Hall.

Gregg, J. R. (1954). *The language of taxonomy*. New York: Columbia University Press.

Grob, G. (1991). Origins of *DSM–I*: A study in appearance and reality. *American Journal of Psychiatry, 148*, 421–431.

Haslam, N. (2002). Kinds of kinds: A conceptual taxonomy of psychiatric categories. *Philosophy, Psychiatry, and Psychology, 9*, 203–217.

Haslam, N., Holland, E., & Kuppens, P. (2012). Categories versus dimensions in personality and psychopathology: A quantitative review of taxometric research. *Psychological Medicine, 42*, 903–920.

Hatano, G., & Inagaki, K. (1994). Young children's naïve theory of biology. *Cognition, 50*, 171–188.

Havens, L. (1981). Twentieth-century psychiatry: A view from the sea. *American Journal of Psychiatry, 138*, 1279–1287.

Havens, L. (1985). Historical perspectives on diagnosis in psychiatry. *Comprehensive Psychiatry, 26*, 326–336.

Hickling, A., & Gelman, S. (1995). How does your garden grow? Evidence of an early conception of plants as biological kinds. *Child Development, 66*, 856–876.

Hilsenroth, M. J., Baity, M. R., Mooney, M. A., & Meyer, G. J. (2004). DSM–IV major depressive episode criteria: An evaluation of reliability and validity across three different rating methods. *International Journal of Psychiatry in Clinical Practice, 8*, 3–10.

Houts, A. (2000). Fifty years of psychiatric nomenclature: Reflections on the 1943 War Department Technical Bulletin, Medical 203. *Journal of Clinical Psychology, 56*, 935–967.

Hull, D. L. (1980). Individuality and selection. *Annual Review of Ecology and Systematics, 11*, 311–332.

Hull, D. L. (1988). *Science as a process*. Chicago: University of Chicago Press.

James, J. W., & Haley, W. E. (1995). Age and health bias in practicing clinical psychologists. *Psychology and Aging, 10*, 610–616.

Jaspers, K. (1963). *General psychopathology* (J. Hoenig & M. W. Hamilton, Trans.). Manchester, UK: University of Manchester Press.

Kahn, E. (1959). The Emil Kraepelin memorial lecture. In B. Pasamanick (Ed.), *Epidemiology of mental disorders* (pp. 1–38). Washington, DC: AAAS.

Kamp-Becker, I., Smidt, J., Ghahreman, M., Heizel-Gutenbrunner, M., Becker, K., & Remschmidt, H. (2010). Categorical and dimensional structure of autism spectrum disorders: The nosologic validity of Asperger syndrome. *Journal of Autism and Developmental Disorders, 40*, 921–929.

Kanner, L. (1943). Autistic disturbances of affective contact. *Nervous Child, 2*(3), 217–250.

Kendell, R.E. (1968). *The classification of depressive illness*. London: Oxford University Press.

Kendell, R. E. (1975). *The role of diagnosis in psychiatry*. Oxford, UK: Blackwell.

Kendell, R. E. (1989). Clinical validity. In L. N. Robins & J. E. Barrett (Eds.), *The validity of psychiatric diagnosis* (pp. 305–321). New York: Raven Press.

Kendell, R. E. (1990). A brief history of psychiatric classification in Britain. In N. Sartorius, A. Jablensky, D. A. Regier, J. D. Burke, Jr., & R. M. A. Hirschfeld (Eds.), *Sources and traditions of psychiatric classification* (pp. 139–151). Toronto: Hogrefe & Huber.

Kendell, R. E., Cooper, J. E., Gourlay, A. J., Sharpe, L., & Gurland, B. J. (1971). Diagnostic criteria of American and British psychiatrists. *Archives of General Psychiatry, 25*, 123–130.

Kessler, R. C., Chiu, W., Demler, O., & Walters, E. E. (2005). Prevalence, severity, and comorbidity of 12-month *DSM–IV* disorders in the National Comorbidity Survey Replication. *Archives of General Psychiatry, 62*, 617–627.

Kessler, R. C., McGonagle, K. A., Zhao, S., Nelson, C. B., Hughes, M., Eschlman, S., et al. (1994). Lifetime and 12-month prevalence of *DSM–III–R* psychiatric disorders in the United States: Results from the National Comorbidity Survey. *Archives of General Psychiatry, 51*, 8–19.

Kirk, S. A., & Kutchins, H. (1992). *The selling of DSM: The rhetoric of science in psychiatry.* Hawthorne, NY: William deGruyter.

Klein, D. (2010). Chronic depression: Diagnosis and classification. *Current Directions in Psychological Science, 19*, 96–100.

Klerman, G. L. (1978). The evolution of a scientific nosology. In J. C. Shershow (Ed.), *Schizophrenia: Science and practice* (pp. 99–121). Cambridge, MA: Harvard University Press.

Klin, A., & Volkmar, F. R. (2003). Asperger syndrome: Diagnosis and external validity. *Child and Adolescent Psychiatric Clinics, 12*, 1–13.

Kotov, R., Ruggero, C. J., Krueger, R. F., Watson, D., Yuan, Q., & Zimmerman, M. (2011). New dimensions in the quantitative classification of mental illness. *Archives of General Psychiatry, 68*, 1003–1011.

Kraemer, H. C., Kupfer, D. J., Clarke, D. E., Narrow, W. E., & Regier, D. A. (2012). *DSM-5*: How reliable is reliable enough? *American Journal of Psychiatry, 169*, 13–15.

Kripke, S. (1980). *Naming and necessity.* Cambridge, MA: Harvard University Press.

Krueger, R. F. (1999). The structure of common mental disorders. *Archives of General Psychiatry, 56*, 921–926.

Krueger, R. F., Derringer, J., Markon, K. E., Watson, D., & Skodol, A. E. (2012). Initial construction of a maladaptive personality trait model and inventory for *DSM-5*. *Psychological Medicine, 42*, 1879–1890.

Krueger, R. F., & Markon, K. E. (2006). Reinterpreting comorbidity: A model-based approach to understanding and classifying psychopathology. *Annual Review of Clinical Psychology, 2*, 111–133.

Krueger, R. F., Markon, K. E., Patrick, C. J., & Iacono, W. G. (2005). Externalizing psychopathology in adulthood: A dimensional-spectrum conceptualization and its implications for *DSM-V*. *Journal of Abnormal Psychology, 114*, 537–550.

Kupfer, D. J., First, M. B., & Regier, D. E. (2002). *A research agenda for DSM-V*. Washington, DC: American Psychiatric Association.

Kutchins, H., & Kirk, S. A. (1997). *Making us crazy.* New York: Free Press.

Lenzenweger, M. F., Clarkin, J. F., Yeomans, F. E., Kernberg, O. F., & Levy, K. N. (2008). Refining the borderline personality disorder phenotype through finite mixture modeling: Implications for classification. *Journal of Personality Disorders, 22*, 313–331.

Lilienfeld, S. O. (2003). Comorbidity between and within childhood externalizing and internalizing disorders: Reflections and directions. *Journal of Abnormal Child Psychology, 31*, 285–291.

Lilienfeld, S. O., & Marino, L. (1995). Mental disorder as a Roschian concept: A critique of Wakefield's "harmful dysfunction" analysis. *Journal of Abnormal Psychology, 104*, 411–420.

Lilienfeld, S. O., Waldman, I. D., & Israel, A. C. (1994). A critical examination of the use of the term and concept of comorbidity in psychopathology research. *Clinical Psychology: Science and Practice, 1*, 71–83.

Littlewood, R. (1992). Psychiatric diagnosis and racial bias: Empirical and interpretive approaches. *Social Science and Medicine, 34*, 141–149.

Lorr, M. (Ed.). (1966). *Explorations in typing psychotics.* New York: Pergamon Press.

Margolis, J. (1994). Taxonomic puzzles. In J. Z. Sadler, O. P. Wiggins, & M. A. Schwartz (Eds.), *Philosophical perspectives on psychiatric diagnostic classification* (pp. 104–128). Baltimore: Johns Hopkins University Press.

Maser, J. D., & Cloninger, C. R. (Eds.). (1990). *Comorbidity of mood and anxiety disorders.* Washington, DC: American Psychiatric Press.

Masserman, J. H., & Carmichael, H. T. (1938). Diagnosis and prognosis in psychiatry. *Journal of Mental Science, 84*, 893–946.

McCrae, R. R., & Costa, P. T. (1990). *Personality in adulthood.* New York: Guilford Press.

Meehl, P. E. (1995). Bootstraps taxometrics: Solving the classification problem in psychopathology. *American Psychologist, 50*, 266–275.

Menninger, K., Mayman, M., & Pruyser, P. (1963). *The vital balance.* New York: Viking Press.

Miller, J. N., & Ozonoff, S. (2000). The external validity of Asperger disorder: Lack of evidence from the domain of neuropsychology. *Journal of Abnormal Psychology, 109*(2), 227–238.

Millon, T. (1975). Reflections on Rosenhan's "On being sane in insane places." *Journal of Abnormal Psychology, 84*, 456–461.

Millon, T. (1983). The *DSM–III*: An insider's perspective. *American Psychologist, 38*, 804–814.

Mineka, S., Watson, D., & Clark, L. A. (1998). Comorbidity of anxiety and unipolar mood disorders. *Annual Review of Psychology, 49*, 377–412.

Moore, T. V. (1930). The empirical determination of certain syndromes underlying praecox and manic-depressive psychoses. *American Journal of Psychiatry, 86,* 719–738.

Morey, L. C. (1988). Personality disorders in the *DSM–III* and *DSM–III–R*: Convergence, coverage and internal consistency. *American Journal of Psychiatry, 145,* 573–577.

Muthen, B. (2006). Should substance use disorders be considered as categorical or dimensional? *Addiction, 101,* 6–16.

Muthen, L. K., & Muthen, B. O. (2010). *Mplus user's guide.* Sixth edition. Los Angeles, CA: Muthen & Muthen.

National Institute of Mental Health. (July, 2012). Research Domain Criteria (RDoC). Retrieved from http://www.nimh.nih.gov/research-funding/rdoc/index.shtml

Nesse, R. (2001). On the difficulty of defining disease: A Darwinian perspective. *Medicine, Health Care, and Philosophy, 4,* 37–46.

O'Connor, B. P. (2002). The search for dimensional structure differences between normality and abnormality: A statistical review of published data on personality and psychopathology. *Journal of Personality and Social Psychology, 83,* 962–982.

Oldham, J. A., Skodol, A. E., Kellman, H. D., Hyler, S. E., Resnick, L., & Davies, M. (1992). Diagnosis of DSM–III–R personality disorders by two structured interviews: Patterns of comorbidity. *American Journal of Psychiatry, 149,* 213–220.

Ozonoff, S., South, M., & Miller, J. N. (2000). *DSM-IV*-defined Asperger syndrome: Cognitive, behavioral and early history differentiation from high-functioning autism. *Autism, 4*(1), 29–46.

Paul, R., Orlovski, S. M., Marcinko, H. C., & Volkmar, F. (2009). Conversational behaviors in youth with high-functioning ASD and Asperger syndrome. *Journal of Autism and Developmental Disorders, 39,* 115–125.

Picardi, A., Viroli, C., Tarsitani, L., Miglio, R., de Girolamo, G., Dell'Acqua, G., & Biondi, M. (2012). Heterogeneity and symptom structure of schizophrenia. *Psychiatry Research, 198,* 386–394.

Putnam, D. (1982). Natural kinds and human artifacts. *Mind, 91,* 418–419.

Reed, G. (2010). Toward *ICD-11*: Improving the clinical utility of WHO's *International Classification of Mental Disorders. Professional Psychology: Research and Practice, 41,* 457–464.

Regier, D. A., Kuhl, E. A., Narrow, W. E., & Kupfer, D. J. (2012). Research planning for the future of psychiatric diagnosis. *European Psychiatry, 27,* 553–556.

Regier, D. A., Narrow, W. E., Clarke, D. E., Kraemer, H. C., Kuramoto, S. J., Kuhl, E. A., & Kupfer, D. J. (2013). *DSM-5* field trials in the United States and Canada, part II: Test-retest reliability of selected categorical diagnoses. *American Journal of Psychiatry, 170,* 59–70.

Rettew, D. C., Lynch, A. D., Achenbach, T. M., Dumenci, L., & Ivanova, M. Y. (2009). Meta-analyses of agreement between diagnoses made from clinical evaluations and standardized diagnostic interviews. *International Journal of Methods in Psychiatric Research, 18,* 169–184.

Richters, J. E., & Cicchetti, D. (1993). Mark Twain meets *DSM-III-R*: Conduct disorder, development, and the concept of harmful dysfunction. *Development and Psychopathology, 5,* 5–29.

Roberts, M., Medina-Mora, M., Reed, G., Keeley, J., Sharan, P., Johnson, D.,…Saxena, S. (2012). A global clinicians' map of mental disorders to improve *ICD-11. International Review of Psychiatry, 24,* 578–590.

Robins, E., & Guze, S. B. (1970). Establishment of diagnostic validity in psychiatric illness: Its application to schizophrenia. *American Journal of Psychiatry, 126,* 983–987.

Rogers, S. J., & Ozonoff, S. (2005). Annotation: what do we know about sensory dysfunction in autism? A critical review of the empirical evidence. *Journal of Child Psychology and Psychiatry, 46*(12), 1255–1268.

Rogler, L. H. (1997). Making sense of historical changes in the *Diagnostic and Statistical Manual of Mental Disorders*: Five propositions. *Journal of Health and Social Behavior, 38,* 9–20.

Rosenhan, D. (1973). On being sane in insane places. *Science, 114,* 316–322.

Ruscio, J., Haslam, N., & Ruscio, A. M. (2006). *Introduction to the taxometric method.* Mahwah, NJ: Erlbaum.

Sadler, J. Z. (2005). *Values and psychiatric diagnosis.* New York: Oxford University Press.

Sadler, J. Z., & Agich, G. (1995). Diseases, functions, values, and psychiatric classification. *Philosophy, Psychiatry, and Psychology, 2,* 219–231.

Sarbin, T. R. (1997). On the futility of psychiatric diagnostic manuals (*DSMs*) and the return of personal agency. *Applied and Preventive Psychology, 6,* 233–243.

Sartorius, N. (1990). Classifications in the field of mental health. *World Health Statistics Quarterly, 43,* 269–272.

Scadding, J. G. (1980). The concepts of disease: A response. *Psychological Medicine, 10,* 425–427.

Scadding, J. G. (1996). Essentialism and nominalism in medicine: Logic of diagnosis in disease terminology. *Lancet, 384,* 594–596.

Scheff, T. J. (1966). *Being mentally ill: A sociological theory.* Chicago: Aldine.

Scheff, T. J. (1975). *Labeling madness.* Englewood Cliffs, NJ: Prentice-Hall.

Schmidt, N. B., Kotov, R., & Joiner, T. E. (2004). *Taxometrics: Towards a new diagnostic scheme for psychopathology.* Washington, DC: American Psychological Association.

Schotte, C., Maes, M., Cluydts, R., & Cosyns, P. (1997). Cluster analytic validation of the *DSM* melancholic depression. The threshold model: Integration of quantitative and qualitative distinctions between unipolar depressive subtypes. *Psychiatric Research, 71,* 181–195.

Segal, D. L., Hersen, M., & Van Hasselt, V. B. (1994). Reliability of the structured clinical interview for *DSM-III-R*: An evaluative review. *Comprehensive Psychiatry, 35,* 316–327.

Silverman, W. K., Saavedra, L. M., & Pina, A. A. (2001). Test-retest reliability of anxiety symptoms and diagnosis with the Anxiety Disorders Interview Schedule for *DSM–IV*: Child and parent versions. *Journal of the American Academy of Child & Adolescent Psychiatry, 40,* 937–944.

Smith, K. (2001). A disease by any other name: Musings on the concept of genetic disease. *Medicine, Health Care, and Philosophy, 4,* 19–30.

Spitzer, R. L. (1975). On pseudoscience in science, logic in remission and psychiatric diagnosis: A critique of Rosenhan's "On being sane in insane places." *Journal of Abnormal Psychology, 84,* 442–452.

Spitzer, R. L., & Endicott, J. (1978). Medical and mental disorder: Proposed definition and criteria. In R. Spitzer & D. Klein (Eds.), *Critical issues in psychiatric diagnosis* (pp. 15–40). New York: Raven Press.

Spitzer, R. L., & Fleiss J. L. (1975). A reanalysis of the reliability of psychiatric diagnosis. *British Journal of Psychiatry, 125,* 341–347.

Spitzer, R., Sheehy, M., & Endicott, J. (1977). *DSM–III*: Guiding principles. In V. Rakoff, H. Stancer, & H. Kedward (Eds.), *Psychiatric diagnosis.* New York: Brunner/Mazel.

Spitzer, R., & Wakefield, J. (1999). *DSM–IV* diagnostic criterion for clinical significance: Does it help solve the false positives problem? *American Journal of Psychiatry, 156,* 1856–1864.

Spitzer, R. L., & Williams, J. B. W. (1980). Classification in psychiatry. In H. I. Kaplan, A. M. Freeman, & B. J. Sadock (Eds.), *Comprehensive textbook of psychiatry III* (pp. 1035–1072). Baltimore: Williams & Wilkins.

Spitznagel, E. L., & Helzer, J. E. (1985). A proposed solution to the base rate problem in the kappa statistic. *Archives of General Psychiatry, 44,* 1069–1077.

Stengel, E. (1959). Classification of mental disorders. *Bulletin of the World Health Organization, 21,* 601–663.

Stone, M. H. (1997). *Healing the mind: A history of psychiatry from antiquity to the present.* New York: Norton.

Szasz, T. S. (1961). *The myth of mental illness.* New York: Hoeber-Harper.

Szatmari, P., Bartolucci, G., & Bremner, R. (1989). Asperger's syndrome and autism: Comparison of early history and outcome. *Developmental Medicine and Child Neurology, 31,* 709–720.

Szatmari, P., Bryson, S., Duku, E., Vaccarella, L., Zwaigenbaum, L., Bennett, T., & Boyle, M. H. (2009). Similar developmental trajectories in autism and Asperger syndrome: From early childhood to adolescence. *The Journal of Child Psychology and Psychiatry, 50*(12), 1459–1467.

Thurstone, L. L. (1934). The vectors of the mind. *Psychological Review, 41,* 1–32.

Verheul, R. (2005). Clinical utility for dimensional models of personality pathology. *Journal of Personality Disorders, 19,* 283–302.

Verheul, R., & Widiger, T. A. (2004). A meta-analysis of the prevalence and usage of the personality disorder not otherwise specified (PDNOS) diagnosis. *Journal of Personality Disorders, 18,* 309–319.

Via, E., Radua, J., Cardoner, N., Happé, F., & Mataix-Cols, D. (2011). Meta-analysis of gray matter abnormalities in autism spectrum disorder: Should Asperger disorder be subsumed under a broader umbrella of autistic spectrum disorder? *Journal of General Psychiatry, 68*(4), 409–418.

Wakefield, J. (1992a). The concept of mental disorder: On the boundary between biological facts and social values. *American Psychologist, 47,* 373–388.

Wakefield, J. (1992b). Disorder as harmful dysfunction: A conceptual critique of *DSM-III-R*'s definition of mental disorder. *Psychological Review, 99,* 232–247.

Wakefield, J. C. (1993). Limits of operationalization: A critique of Spitzer and Endicott's (1978) proposed operational criteria for mental disorder. *Journal of Abnormal Psychology, 102,* 160–172.

Wakefield, J. C. (1999). Evolutionary versus prototype analyses of the concept of disorder. *Journal of Abnormal Psychology, 108,* 374–399.

Ward, C. H., Beck, A. T., Mendelson, M., Mock, J. E. & Erbaugh, J. K. (1962). The psychiatric nomenclature. *Archives of General Psychiatry, 8*, 198–205.

Watson, D., Clark, L. A., & Chmielewski, M. (2008). Structures of personality and their relevance to psychopathology: II. Further articulation of a comprehensive unified trait structure. *Journal of Personality, 76*, 1545–1586.

Weiner, B. (1975). "On being sane in insane places": A process (attributional) analysis and critique. *Journal of Abnormal Psychology, 84*, 433–441.

Widiger, T. A., Frances, A. J., Harris, M., Jacobsberg, L., Fyer, M., & Manning, D. (1991). Comorbidity among the Axis II disorders. In J. Oldham (Ed.), *Personality disorders: New perspectives on diagnostic validity* (pp. 165–194). Washington, DC: American Psychiatric Press.

Widiger, T. A., & Samuel, D. B. (2005). Diagnostic categories or dimensions? A question for the *Diagnostic and Statistical Manual of Mental Disorders—Fifth Edition. Journal of Abnormal Psychology, 114*, 494–504.

Widiger, T. A., Simonsen, E., Krueger, R., Livesley, W., & Verheul, R. (2005). Personality disorder research agenda for the *DSM–V. Journal of Personality Disorders, 19*, 315–338.

Wing, L. (1981). Asperger syndrome: A clinical account. *Psychological Medicine, 11*, 115–130.

Wing, L. (2000). Past and future research on Asperger syndrome. In A. Klin & F. Volkmar (Eds.), *Asperger syndrome* (pp. 418–432). New York: Guilford Press.

Woodruff, R. A., Goodwin, D. W., & Guze, S. B. (1974). *Psychiatric diagnosis*. London: Oxford University Press.

Wright, A. G., Krueger, R. F., Hobbs, M. J., Markon, K. E., Eaton, N. R., & Slade, T. (2013). The structure of psychopathology: Toward an expanded quantitative empirical model. *Journal of Abnormal Psychology, 122*, 281–294.

Yoon, C. K. (2009). *Naming nature*. New York: Norton.

Zachar, P. (2000). Psychiatric disorders are not natural kinds. *Philosophy, Psychiatry, and Psychology, 7*, 167–182.

Zanarini, M. C., & Frankenburg, F. R. (2001). Attainment and maintenance of reliability of Axis I and II disorders over the course of a longitudinal study. *Comprehensive Psychiatry, 42*, 369–374.

Zanarini, M. C., Skodol, A. E., Bender, D., Dolan, R., Sanislow, C., Schaefer, E., et al. (2000). The collaborative longitudinal personality disorders study: II. Reliability of Axis I and Axis II diagnoses. *Journal of Personality Disorders, 14*, 291–299.

Zimmerman, M., Rothschild, L., & Chelminski, I. (2005). The prevalence of *DSM-IV* personality disorders in psychiatric outpatients. *American Journal of Psychiatry, 162*, 1911–1918.

Zubin, J. (1967). Classification of the behavior disorders. *Annual Review of Psychology, 18*, 373–406.

3

Developmental Pathogenesis

THEODORE MILLON

Tracing the developmental background of psychopathology is one of the most difficult but rewarding phases in the study of medical and psychological science. Epidemiologists, who study the incidence, prevalence, and distribution of disease, have evolved a sophisticated vocabulary that partitions the infinitude of potential attributes in a comprehensible way.

The term *etiology* refers to the specific causes of disease, while *pathogenesis* refers to the process by which these causes eventuate in the disease itself. *Vulnerability* is a term that means an underlying susceptibility that reflects the coexistence and interaction of both organismic and environmental factors leading to pathology. While many mental illnesses are believed to be under genetic control, the idea of vulnerability recognizes the role of learning and experience, whether physical or social, in releasing genetic potentials. The words *risk factor* represent anything that increases the probability of developing pathology. The connection between a risk factor and pathology need not, however, be direct. A risk factor simply correlates with the development of pathology, and may not be causally implicated in pathogenesis.

Most people have been conditioned to think of causality in a simple format in which a single event, known as the cause, results in a single effect. Scientists have learned, however, that particular end results usually arise from the interaction of a large number of causes. Furthermore, it is not uncommon for a single cause to play a part in a variety of end results. Each of these individual end results may set off an independent chain of events which will progress through different intricate sequences. Disentangling the varied and intricate pathways to psychopathology is an especially difficult task.

In philosophy, causes are frequently divided into three classes: necessary, sufficient, and contributory. A *necessary* cause is an event which *must* precede another event for it to occur. For example, certain theorists believe that individuals who do not possess a particular genetic defect will not become schizophrenic; they usually contend that this inherent defect must be supplemented by certain detrimental experiences before the schizophrenic pattern will emerge. In this hypothesis, the genetic defect is viewed as a necessary but not a sufficient cause of the pathology.

A *sufficient* condition is one that is adequate *in itself* to cause pathology; no other factor need be associated with it. However, a sufficient condition is neither a necessary nor an exclusive cause of a particular disorder. For example, a neurosyphilitic infection may be sufficient in itself to produce certain forms of psychopathology, but many other causes can result in these disorders as well.

Contributory causes are factors which increase the probability that a disorder will occur, but are neither necessary nor sufficient to do so. These conditions, such as economic deprivation or racial conflict, add to a welter of other factors which, when taken together, shape the course of pathology. Contributory causes usually influence the form in which the pathology is expressed and play relatively limited roles as primary determinants.

In psychopathology, causes are divided traditionally into predisposing and precipitating factors. *Predisposing* factors are contributory conditions that usually are neither necessary nor sufficient to bring about the disorder but that serve as a foundation for its development. They exert an influence over a relatively long time span and set the stage for the emergence of the pathology. Factors such as heredity, socioeconomic status, family atmosphere, and habits learned in response to early traumatic experiences are illustrations of these predispositions.

No hard and fast line can be drawn between predisposing and *precipitating* causes, but a useful distinction may be made between them. Precipitating factors refer to clearly demarcated events that occur shortly before the onset of the manifest pathology. These factors either bring to the surface or hasten the emergence of a pathological disposition; that is, they evoke or trigger the expression of established, but hidden, dispositional factors. The death of a parent, a severe car accident, the sudden breakup of a romantic relationship all illustrate these precipitants.

Some Philosophical and Methodological Problems in Establishing Pathogenesis

A few words of a more-or-less philosophical nature are in order concerning the idea of etiology itself; as in other matters that call for an incisive explication of psychopathological constructs, the reader is directed to the writings of Meehl (1972). In these essays, it is made clear that the nature of etiology is itself a "fuzzy notion" that not only requires the careful separation of its constituent empirical elements but also calls for differentiating its various conceptual meanings. These range from "strong" influences that are both causally necessary and/or sufficient, to progressively weaker levels of specificity, in which causal factors exert consistent though quantitatively marginal differences, to those that are merely coincidental or situationally circumstantial.

The premise that early experience plays a central role in shaping personality attributes is shared by numerous theorists. To say this, however, is not to agree on which specific factors during these developing years are critical in generating particular attributes, nor is it to agree that known formative influences are either necessary or sufficient. Psychoanalytic theorists almost invariably direct their etiological attention to the realm of early childhood experience. Unfortunately, they may differ vigorously among themselves (e.g., Kernberg, Kohut, Erikson) as to which aspects of nascent life are crucial to development.

To be more concrete, there is reason to ask whether etiological analysis is even possible in psychopathology in light of the complex and variable character of developmental influences. Can this most fundamental of scientific activities be achieved given an interactive chain of sequential "causes" comprising inherently inexact data of a highly probabilistic nature in which even the slightest variation in contexts and antecedent conditions, often of a minor or random character, produces highly divergent outcomes? Because this "looseness" in the causal network of variables is unavoidable, are there any grounds for believing that such endeavors could prove more than illusory? Further, will the careful study of individuals reveal repetitive patterns of symptomatic congruence, no less consistency, among the origins of such diverse clinical attributes as overt behavior, intrapsychic functioning, and biophysical disposition? And will etiological commonalities and syndromal coherence prove to be valid phenomena, that is, not merely imposed on observed data by virtue of clinical expectation or theoretical bias (Millon, 1986, 1987, 1990)?

Among other concerns is that the "hard data," the unequivocal evidence from well-designed and well-executed research, are sorely lacking. Consistent findings on causal factors for specific clinical entities would be extremely useful were such knowledge only in hand. Unfortunately, our etiological and pathogenetic database is both scanty and unreliable. As noted, it may continue to be so owing to the obscure, complex, and interwoven nature of influences that shape psychopathological phenomena. The yearning among theorists of all viewpoints for a neat package of etiological attributes simply cannot be reconciled with the convoluted philosophical issues, methodological quandaries, and difficult-to-disentangle subtle and random influences that shape mental disorders. In the main, almost all developmental theses today are, at best, perceptive conjectures that ultimately rest on tenuous empirical grounds, reflecting the views of divergent "schools of thought" positing their favorite hypotheses. These speculative notions should be conceived as questions that call for empirical study and evaluation, rather than be promulgated as the gospel of confirmed fact.

Most empirical studies to date have been of a tenuous or inconclusive nature. Not only are measures of psychopathology inherently inexact, the variables of which interact in ways that are often stochastic or nonlinear, but longitudinal studies are not readily amenable to forms of research design that most investigators find feasible. Psychometric and laboratory methods, case histories, clinical observation, and experimental research all provide hypotheses that *may* unravel the complexities of development, but they often fail to converge on a single, no less definitive set of findings. Given the manifest difficulties in conducting conclusive developmental research, especially needed longitudinal studies, we might ask whether answers to pathogenic questions are even possible.

We should note that there is considerable ambiguity in what is considered to be developmental. Further we may ask, what is it that develops? And when does development end? Additionally, because normality must serve as a necessary reference point whenever pathology is studied, questions such as these become very important. Thus, in the past, development referred to infancy, childhood, and adolescence—the period preceding an organism's physical maturity. More recently, developmental psychologists have adopted a life-span perspective. Development thus now refers to the totality of changes that occur from birth to death. A similar broadening has taken place within psychopathology. The prevailing model today contains axes for both personality and psychosocial functioning, so that pathology, like development, is now considered a property of the entire life span of the organism. Hence, psychopathology development need not be limited to the period that precedes diagnosis.

A most vexing developmental problem is taxonomic. Where diagnostic constructs fail to "carve nature at its joints," efforts to specify their developmental antecedents may be sabotaged at the outset. Rigorous longitudinal studies are of limited value where the taxonomy itself possesses only dubious validity. Unfortunately, most taxonomies in psychopathology have been developed with the goal of providing detailed descriptions of characteristics and functioning in cross section, at a single point in time. For the most part, the various versions of the *DSM-I* (1952) are good examples of cross-sectional taxonomies. Even where diagnostic criteria refer to time, it is usually only to specify the duration that a condition must be present before a particular diagnosis can be assigned. Within 6 months of suffering a natural disaster, for example, an individual will be diagnosed with acute stress disorder. Only after 6 months can posttraumatic stress disorder be assigned. Here, time functions only as an exclusionary or inclusionary condition, and the boundary between the two disorders is essentially arbitrary.

As noted earlier, a taxonomy that fails to "carve nature at its joints" is a great hindrance to the goal of identifying developmental characteristics. Moreover, it is unlikely that any taxonomy of psychopathology can ever be valid without specifying "developmental diagnostic criteria," which allow syndromes with similar cross-sectional presentations to be distinguished. The kinds of confounds to which a cross-sectional, descriptive taxonomy are vulnerable are easily schematized. At a minimum, individuals within a category should be more clinically similar than individuals from different categories. *Similarity* is thus the organizing principle on which all taxonomies are constructed. However, similarity itself is a fuzzy notion. In what way are patients who receive the same diagnosis alike? Individuals with similar presentations do not always have the same disease. Thus, two levels of similarity can be distinguished. First, there is the surface similarity of how things appear (observational, cross-sectional, and descriptive). Second, there is the latent similarity of how things really are—a theoretical, developmental, and explanatory similarity. Taxonomies based on surface characteristics often hide latent distinctions. By crossing these two forms of similarity for any two subjects, we obtain the diagram shown in Figure 3.1, which illustrates the taxonomic dilemma in psychopathology. Starting in the first quadrant, two presentations that appear similar may indeed be similar. In this case, etiologically similar pathways produce manifestly similar results. Second, two presentations that appear similar may in fact require different diagnoses. Despite etiological differences, "convergent causality" results in

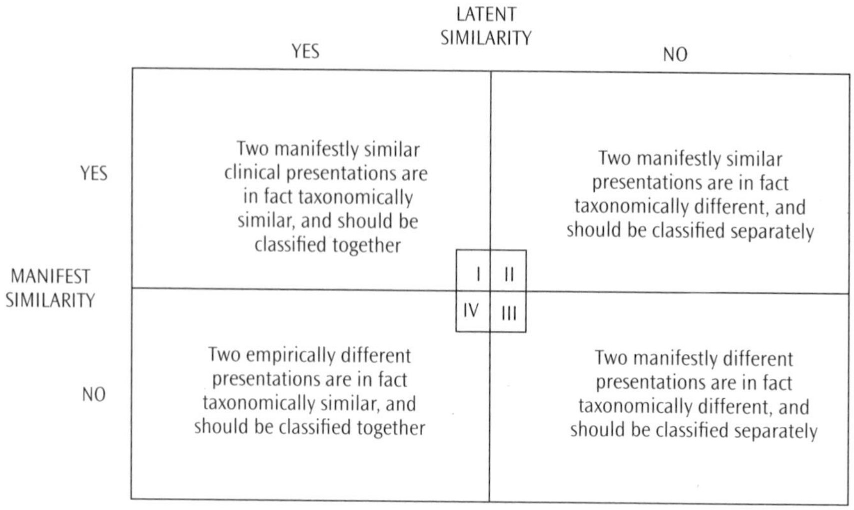

Figure 3.1 Manifest and latent similarity and the taxonomic dilemma.

manifestly similar results that are difficult to tease apart. Third, two presentations that appear different may in fact be different. Once again, what you see is what you get. Differences in classification reflect valid differences in etiology. Fourth, two presentations that appear different may in fact be similar latently. Here, the same disease interacts with individual differences to produce dramatically different presentations, a case of "divergent causality" in development.

A true classification, then, must rest its boundaries where the categorical differences between ostensibly similar persons or conditions actually exist, rather than where they appear to exist. The latent situation, however, is never known with certainty, but is always inferred on the basis of available observational methods and practices. For example, in the second quadrant, several categories should be specified, but only one appears to exist. Here, the covariance of indicators at a manifest level gives the syndrome acceptable internal consistency, providing a further statistical basis for what is in fact a taxonomic illusion. The *DSM-I* criteria for schizophrenia may represent one such category.

Even where a categorical model is appropriate, not all disorders are equally categorical. Some Axis I disorders are likely to be strongly taxonic, while others are only weakly so. Thus, the appropriateness of the categorical model for a given psychopathology is likely to be a matter of degree. *Taxonicity* may be defined as the capacity

of a single given illness or condition to coerce other organismic attributes into a characteristic expression or mold. Mongoloidism, for example, is strongly taxonic. All such subjects share certain physical features and a degree of intellectual deficit. Since the interaction with individual differences is minimized, persons with strongly taxonic conditions follow whatever developmental trajectory is set by their disease. Conversely, weakly taxonic conditions are readily influenced by individual differences, so that diverse outcomes are possible.

The problem of unraveling developmental antecedents in the personality disorders is especially complex. Medical diseases, by contrast, which the clinical syndromes of Axis I more closely resemble, may often be diagnosed with validity even though the exact cause of the condition remains unknown. The developmental course of HIV infection, for example, was known before its cellular mechanisms were uncovered. A history of HIV-related illnesses thus suggests a diagnosis of HIV infection. In contrast, the development of personality and its disorders requires the consideration of at least two additional issues. First, the categorical model may not be appropriate for the personality disorders. Second, theories of normal development, like theories of personality, are typically limited to some circumscribed class of variables.

Arguments pointing to thematic or logical continuities between the character of early experience and later behaviors, no matter how intuitively rational or consonant with established principles they may be, do not provide unequivocal evidence for their causal connections; different, and equally convincing, developmental hypotheses can be and are posited. Each contemporary explication of the origins of most personality disorders is persuasive, yet remains but one among several plausible possibilities. Most theorists favor one cause, a singular experiential event or process—be it the splitting of good and bad introjects, or fears engendered during the individuation-separation phase—that is the sine qua non, for example, of borderline personality development. Unfortunately, causal attributions appear no more advanced today than they were in former times.

Among other troublesome aspects of contemporary proposals are the diverse syndromal consequences attributed to essentially identical causes. Although it is not unreasonable to trace different outcomes to similar antecedents, there is an unusual inclination among theorists to assign the same "early conflict" or "traumatic relationship" to all varieties of psychological ailment. For example, an almost universal experiential ordeal that ostensibly undergirds such varied syndromes as narcissistic and borderline personalities, as well as a host of schizophrenic and psychosomatic conditions, is the splitting or repressing of introjected aggressive impulses engendered by parental hostility, an intrapsychic mechanism requisite to countering the dangers these impulses pose to dependency security, should they achieve consciousness or behavioral expression.

Not only is it unlikely that singular origins would be as ubiquitous as clinicians often posit them, but even if they were, their ultimate psychological impact would differ substantially depending on the configuration of other concurrent or later influences to which individuals were exposed. "Identical" causal factors cannot be assumed to possess the same import, nor can their consequences be traced without reference to the larger context of each individual's life experiences. One need not be a Gestaltist to recognize that the substantive impact of an ostensive process or event, however formidable it may seem in theory—be it explicit parental spitefulness or implicit parental abandonment—will differ markedly as a function of its developmental covariants.

To go one step further, there is good reason, as well as evidence, to believe that the significance of early troubled relationships may inhere less in their singularity or the depth of their impact than in the fact that they are precursors of what is likely to become a recurrent pattern of subsequent parental encounters. It may be sheer recapitulation and consequent cumulative learning that ultimately fashions and deeply embeds the entrenched pattern of distinctive personality attributes we observe. Although early encounters and resolutions may serve as powerful forerunners and substantive templates, the presence of persistent and pervasive clinical symptoms may not take firm root in early childhood, but may stem from simple replication and reinforcement.

The complexities explored in these sections illustrate an important principle: All taxonomies, and all scientific theories, are necessarily simplifications of reality. If it were possible to know the world directly, there would be no distinction between manifest and latent. All knowledge would be tantamount to direct and intuitive mystical knowledge, so that science would need not exist at all. Even given this distinction, however, our scientific mission would be far easier if only psychopathologies did not vary in terms of their degree of taxonicity, in terms of the extent to which they reflect the presumptive disease processes (Axis I) versus pathologies of the entire matrix of the person (Axis II), and finally, in terms of the level of abstraction at which they can be described. But the world is what it is, and the ability of cross-sectional theories and taxonomies to fold its manifest complexities into a finite number of categories that can be understood by a limited cognitive apparatus quickly diminishes when the additional dimension of pathogenic course over time becomes involved.

Systematic Theories of Pathogenesis

From its earliest incarnations, psychology has been concerned with psychopathological development. Sigmund Freud and Jean Piaget had perhaps the greatest impact in these pursuits, but others, such as Charles Darwin and G. Stanley Hall, also offered insights into human development. Even earlier, Jean Jacques Rousseau proposed a theory of development based on the idea that children repeated stages in the history of "the race," suggesting that they should be permitted to mature first like little savages before being expected to act in a civilized manner. With the emergence of evolutionary ideas and embryological studies, the German researcher

Fritz Muller, in the mid-nineteenth century, recorded similarities between the embryos of various species, despite their considerable differences in appearance in adulthood. This led the German biologist Ernst Haeckel, in the late-nineteenth century, to propose that the uniformities in embryological development suggested a biogenic natural law of recapitulation, specifically as stated in the phrase ontogeny recapitulates phylogeny, a theme picked up by G. Stanley Hall, in his theoretical and experimental studies of children and adolescents. Hall actively promoted systematic research on children's educational growth, at the turn of the century at Clark University.

Another major academic of the period was James Mark Baldwin, whose developmental theories were clearly oriented toward the exploration of cognitive maturation, and anticipated many of the themes Jean Piaget later formulated. Piaget's complex sequence of development remained largely intact throughout the last half-century with terms such as *structures, accommodations, assimilation,* and *schemata* still being widely used. Although Piaget may be the most influential thinker in this realm, his ideas may have remained largely unknown, had Lawrence Kohlberg not brought Piaget's ideas to the attention of American psychologists in the mid-twentieth century. Psychologists began doing empirical research to investigate Piaget's theories, with frustratingly inconsistent results. His ideas are by no means settled and are still hotly debated and researched, with cognitive development throughout the life span remaining a major area of research in the broad field of cognitive psychology.

As just noted, the earliest work in developmental theory and research was focused on intellectual and cognitive processes. The expansion of developmental ideas to the realm of psychopathology emerged as a vigorous area of study only in the last half-century, prompted largely by theoretical ideas generated by child psychoanalytic clinicians, such as Anna Freud and Melanie Klein.

Biogenic Hypotheses of Pathogenesis

Although considerable interest in the genetic and biological roots of psychopathology has been a major sphere of research concern during the past century, especially evident as a result of recent advances in the neurosciences, progress has remained rather modest. The role of heredity is usually inferred from evidence based on correlations among traits in members of the same family. Most psychopathologists admit that heredity must play a role in disorder development, but they insist that genetic dispositions are modified substantially by the operation of environmental factors. This view states that heredity operates not as a fixed constant but as a disposition that takes different forms depending on the circumstances of an individual's upbringing. Hereditary theorists may take a more inflexible position, referring to a body of data that implicate genetic factors in a wide range of psychopathologies. Although they are likely to agree that variations in these disorders may be produced by environmental conditions, they are equally likely to assert that these are merely superficial influences that cannot prevent the individual from succumbing to his or her hereditary inclination. The overall evidence seems to suggest that genetic factors serve as predispositions to certain traits, but, with few exceptions, similarly affected individuals display important differences in their symptoms and developmental histories (Livesley, Jang, & Vernon, 2003). Moreover, genetically disposed disorders can be aided by psychological therapies (Millon, 1999; Millon & Grossman, 2007a,b,c), and similar symptomatologies often arise without such genetic dispositions.

A number of biogenic theorists have suggested that the milder pathologies, such as personality disorders, represent undeveloped or minimally expressed defective genes. For example, the schizoid personality may possess a schizophrenic genotype, but in this case the defective gene is weakened by the operation of beneficial modifying genes or favorable environmental experiences (Meehl, 1990). An alternate explanation might be formulated in terms of polygenic action; polygenes have minute, quantitatively similar, and cumulative effects. Thus, a continuum of increasing pathological severity can be accounted for by the cumulative effects of a number of minor genes acting upon the same trait (Millon, 1969).

The idea that psychopathological syndromes comprise well-circumscribed disease entities is an attractive assumption for those who seek a Mendelian or single-gene model of inheritance. Recent thinking forces us to question the validity of this approach to nosology and to the relevance of Mendelian genetic action. Defects in the infinitely complex central nervous system can arise from innumerable genetic anomalies (Plomin,

1990). Moreover, even convinced geneticists make reference to the notion of phenocopies, a concept signifying that characteristics usually traceable to genetic action can be simulated by environmental factors. Thus, overtly identical forms of pathology may arise from either genetic or environmental sources. As a consequence, the clinical picture of a disorder may give no clue to its origins since similar appearances do not necessarily signify similar etiologies. To complicate matters further, different genes vary in their responsiveness to environmental influences; some produce uniform effects under all environmental conditions, whereas others can be entirely suppressed in certain environments (Plomin, DeFries, McClearn, 1990). Moreover, it appears that genes have their effects at particular times of maturation, and that their interaction with environmental conditions is minimal both before and after these periods.

Despite these ambiguities and complications, there can be little question that genetic factors do play some dispositional role in shaping the morphological and biochemical substrate of certain traits. However, these factors are by no means necessary to the development of psychopathology, nor are they likely to be sufficient in themselves to elicit pathological behaviors. They may serve, however, as a physiological base that makes the person susceptible to dysfunction under stress or inclined to learn behaviors that prove socially troublesome.

The general role that neurological lesions and physiochemical imbalances play in producing pathology can be grasped with only a minimal understanding of the structural organization and functional character of the brain. However, it is important that naive misconceptions be avoided. The point to be emphasized is that clinical signs and symptoms cannot be conceived as localized or fixed to one or another sphere of the brain. Rather, they arise from a network of complex interactions and feedbacks (Purves & Lichtman, 1985). We might say that all stimuli, whether generated externally or internally, follow long chains of reverberating circuits that modulate a wide range of activities. Psychological traits and processes must be conceived, therefore, as the product of a widespread and self-regulating pattern of interneuronal activity. If we keep in mind the intricate neural interdependencies underlying these functions, we should avoid falling prey to the error of interpretive simplification.

If these caveats are kept in mind, certain broad hypotheses seem tenable. Possessing more or less of the interactive neurological substrates for a particular function, for example, such as pleasure or pain, can markedly influence the character of experience and the course of learning and development. Quite evidently, the role of neuroanatomical structures in psychopathology is not limited to problems of tissue defect or damage. Natural interindividual differences in structural anatomy and organization can result in a wide continuum of relevant psychological effects (Davidson, 1986; Williams, 1957). If we recognize the network of neural structures that are upset by a specific lesion, and add the tremendous individual differences in brain morphology, the difficulties involved in tracing the role of a neurological disturbance become apparent. If the technical skills required to assess the psychological consequences of a specific brain lesion are difficult, one can only begin to imagine the staggering task of determining the psychological correlates of natural anatomic differences.

Anatomical differences are only part of the story. The highly popular current search for biochemical dysfunctions in psychopathology is equally handicapped by the high degree of natural variability in physiochemical processes among humans. Roger Williams (1973), the eminent biochemist, has made us aware that each individual possesses a distinctive physiochemical pattern that is wholly unlike others and bears no relationship to a hypothetical norm. Such patterns of biological individuality comprise crucial factors that must be built into the equation before we can properly appraise the role of biogenic influences in the development of personality pathology.

The Psychoanalytic Approach to Character Development

The emphasis psychoanalytic theorists place on early childhood experience represents their contention that disorders of adulthood are a direct product of the continued and insidious operation of past events. To them, knowledge of the past provides information indispensable to understanding adult difficulties. To the question, "What is the basis of adult disorders?" they would answer: "the anxieties of childhood and the progressive sequence of defensive maneuvers that were devised to protect against a recurrence of these feelings."

Adult patterns of behavior, therefore, are not a function of random influences according to psychoanalysis, but arise from clear-cut antecedent causes. For the most part, these causes persist out of awareness, that is, kept unconscious owing to their troublesome character, notably the stressful memories and emotions they contain and the primitive nature of the child's youthful defenses.

Sigmund Freud (1925) stressed the importance of early childhood experiences, as it is these experiences that dispose individuals to lifelong patterns of pathological adaptation. In what has been termed the *psychogenetic hypothesis*, early events establish deeply ingrained defensive systems that may lead individuals to react to new situations as if they were duplicates of what occurred in childhood. These anticipatory defensive styles persist throughout life and result in progressive psychopathological maladaptations.

S. Freud's theory of infantile development was that children had immensely complicated emotional lives that were anchored deeply in sexual developmental stages. He did not work directly with children, nor was he particularly disposed to be involved with them, except for his youngest daughter, Anna. Most of his ideas were generated from retrospective reconstructions in the memories of his adult patients.

S. Freud referred to child development as a psychosexual progression, with the primary bodily region of maximal sexual excitation shifting as individuals mature. S. Freud termed this "libidinal" progression of erogenous zones the "psychosexual stages." Thus, in the first year and a half of life, the lips and mouth are the primary locus of libidinal excitation; during this period sucking and eating behavior produce pleasure and gratification. The oral period is followed by a libidinous centering in the anal region, which lasts about a year; it is replaced, in turn, by an erogenous phallic stage, in which the sensory region of the genitals serves as the basis of pleasure. These three pregenital stages are followed by an oedipal phase of familial conflict, partially resolved and followed, in turn, by a latency period, which lasts until puberty, following which the mature genital stage unfolds in preparation for normal adult sexuality.

Evolving the Freudian formulation of a psychosexual stage theory, *Karl Abraham* gradually constructed an "oral character," divided into two variants with appreciably different early experiences. One type was termed the "oral-sucking" or "oral-receptive" character, stemming from an early history of unusual gratification during nurturant feeding and weaning, the other he called "oral pessimists" or "oral-sadistic" characters, whose early experiences were notably frustrating in nature.

It was not until the writings of *Wilhelm Reich* that the concept of psychopathological development appeared in its clearest psychoanalytic formulation. Reich asserted that the neurotic solution of psychosexual conflicts was accomplished by a pervasive restructuring of the individual's defensive style, a set of changes that ultimately crystallizes into what he spoke of as a "total formation" of character. In contrast to his forerunners, Reich claimed that the emergence of specific pathological symptoms was of secondary importance when compared to the total character structuring that evolved as a consequence of these experiences.

Anna Freud left Vienna with her father in 1938 following the German Anschluss in Austria. Throughout her career, Anna set out a systematic program for appraising the developmental lines of childhood maturation. She spelled out three main dimensions of development: the maturation of drives and ego functions, the processes of adaptation to the environment and to the building of object relations, and the organization and integration of problematic experiences and conflicts within the personality structure. She and her colleagues executed numerous research projects, as well as engaged in direct services to children and adolescents.

Erik Erikson constructed a sequence for the development of the ego that paralleled the stages of psychosexual development that S. Freud had formulated. Calling his developmental sequence the "phases of epigenesis," Erikson believed that Freud's focus on psychosexuality was too narrowly conceived. He recognized a broader spectrum of sensorimotor, cognitive, and social capacities in the infant's biological equipment, and proposed the notion of developmental modes, which represented the unfolding of genetically endowed ego capacities. Each of eight stages of ego epigenesis was characterized by a phase-specific task to which solutions must be found. Satisfactory solutions prepared the child to progress to the next phase; unsuccessful solutions led to chronic adaptive difficulties. For example, the oral-sensory stage, or infancy nursing period, determined whether the child would develop trust or mistrust; the struggle over retention and elimination during the anal-muscular stage influenced whether the child would emerge with a sense of autonomy or with shame and doubt; initiative or guilt resulted from the success or failure of sexual assertiveness in the genital-locomotor period, and so on.

Several major thinkers from Great Britain began to formulate new "object-relations" directions for psychoanalytic theory. Most inventive of these was *Melanie Klein*, one of the originators of child psychoanalysis, along with Anna Freud, with whom she vigorously differed and contended for leadership in the British analytic community.

Klein believed that *fantasy* was a major primitive function and ability, a darker, yet implacable wilderness within the infant's psyche. Furthermore, these fantasies exhibited a clear and regular developmental sequence that basically reflected the infant's relationship with his or her mother. The distinctive element of Klein's object-relations theory was the assertion that the mind was composed of pre-formed internal representations of the infant's ultimate external relationships, that is, the infant's "object world." This contrasted with Anna Freud's view that the mind possessed instinctual urges that were "object-seeking" but were not "pre-formed" in their character; in Freud's formulation, objects become part of the mind only secondarily. Klein believed, however, that the mind possessed "pre-wired" fantasies, implying unlearned knowledge that gave shape to and prepared the child for subsequent experiences.

As written previously (Millon, 1969), psychoanalytic arguments pointing to thematic and logical continuities between the character of early experience and later behaviors, no matter how intuitively rational they appear to be, do not provide unequivocal evidence for their causal connections. Different, and equally convincing, developmental hypotheses can be and often are posited.

An Evolutionary Approach to Neurodevelopment

In the text that follows, we will briefly link an evolutionary theory (Millon, 1990) to the maturational sequence of psychopathology.

Maturation refers to the intricate sequence of ontogenetic development in which initially inchoate bodily structures progressively unfold into specific functional units. Early stages of differentiation precede and overlap with more advanced states such that simpler and more diffuse structures interweave and connect into a complex and integrated network of functions displayed ultimately in the adult organism. It was once believed that the course of maturation—from diffusion to differentiation to integration—arose exclusively from inexorable forces within the genes. Maturation was thought to evolve according to a preset timetable that unfolded independently of environmental conditions. This view is no longer tenable. Maturation does follow an orderly progression, but the developmental sequence and level of ultimate neurologically based capacities and dispositions are substantially dependent on environmental stimuli and nutritional supplies. Thus, biological maturation does not progress in a fixed course leading to a predetermined level but is subject to numerous variations that reflect the character of environmental experience.

The belief that the maturing organism requires periodic "psychological nutriments" for proper development has led some to suggest that the organism actively seeks an optimum level of stimulation. Thus, just as the infant cries out in search of food when deprived or wails in response to pain, so too may it engage in behaviors that provide it with psychosensory stimulation requisite to maturation (Butler & Rice, 1963; Murphy, 1947; Rapaport, 1953).

What evidence is there that serious consequences may result from an inadequate supply of early psychological and psychosensory stimulation? Numerous investigators (e.g., Beach & Jaynes, 1954; Killackey, 1990; Melzick, 1965; Rakic, 1985, 1988; Scott, 1968; Thompson & Schaefer, 1961) have shown that an impoverished early environment results in permanent adaptational difficulties. For example, primates reared in isolation tend to be deficient in traits such as emotionality, activity level, social behavior, curiosity, and learning ability. As adult organisms they possess a reduced capacity to cope with their environments, to discriminate essentials, to devise strategies, and manage stress.

Conversely, intense levels of early stimulation also appear to have effects, at least as experimentally demonstrated in lower mammalian species. Several investigators have demonstrated that enriched environments in early life result in measurable changes in brain chemistry and brain weight. Others have found that early stimulation accelerates the maturation of the pituitary–adrenal system, whereas equivalent later stimulation is ineffective. On the behavioral level, enriched environments in animals enhance problem-solving abilities and the capacity to withstand stress. More interesting, however, is the possibility that some kinds of overstimulation may produce detrimental effects. Accordingly, excess stimulation would result in overdevelopment in neurobiological substrates that are disruptive to effective psychological functioning. Just as excess food leads to obesity and physical ill health, so too may excessive psychostimulation of certain neural substrates, such as those subserving emotional reactivity, dispose the organism to be overreactive to social situations.

According to evolutionary theory, in each maturational stage (Millon, 1990; Millon & Grossman, 2005), the individual organism moves through neurodevelopmental periods that have specific functional psychological goals. Within each stage, every individual acquires psychological dispositions that represent a balance or predilection toward one of two survival inclinations; which inclination emerges as dominant over time results from the inextricable and reciprocal interplay of intraorganismic and extraorganismic factors. Thus, during earliest infancy, the primary organismic function is to "continue to exist." Here, evolution has supplied mechanisms that orient the infant toward life-enhancing environments (pleasure) and away from life-threatening ones (pain).

Although four seemingly distinct stages of neurodevelopment will be identified in the following sections, it must be stated at the outset that all four stages and their related processes begin in utero and continue throughout life—that is, they proceed simultaneously and overlap throughout the ontogenetic process. However, there are relatively distinct periods when the organism is especially responsive to neural growth stimulation, hence resulting in normal development, underdevelopment, or overdevelopment.

Neurodevelopmental Stage 1: Sensory Attachment
According to the theory, the first year of life is dominated by sensory processes, functions basic to subsequent development in that they enable the infant to construct some order out of the initial diffusion experienced in the stimulus world, especially that based on distinguishing pleasurable from painful "objects." This period has also been termed that of *attachment* because infants cannot survive on their own (Fox, Kimmerly, & Schafer,

1991) but must "fasten" themselves to others who will protect, nurture, and stimulate them, that is, provide them with experiences of comforting pleasure rather than those discomforting of pain.

Evolution has "provided" mechanisms or substrates that orient the child toward those activities or venues which are life-enhancing and away from those which are potentially life-threatening. Existence during this highly vulnerable stage is quite literally a to-be-or-not-to-be matter.

The theory notes that life-enhancing actions or sensations can be subsumed under the rubric of *pleasure*, while life-threatening actions or sensations can be subsumed under the metaphorical term *pain*. Such a "pleasure–pain polarity" simply recognizes that while the behavioral repertoire of the young child is inchoate its operational orientation is clearly distinct, geared essentially to the maintenance of life itself. The distinction between pleasure and pain becomes central to all subsequent refinements.

According to this neurodevelopmental evolutionary theory, the amount and quality of stimulation to which the neonate is exposed could contribute significantly to infantile normalities, precocities, or retardations, depending on whether levels of stimulation are average or extreme. The nature and patterning of stimulation will lead the infant to experience feelings associated with differing degrees of pleasure–pain, forming a prototype for later-evolving and more distinct emotions such as joy, fear, sadness, and anger.

Separated from the womb, the neonate has lost his or her physical attachment to the mother's body and the protection and nurturance it provided; the infant must turn toward other regions or sources of attachment if the child is to survive and obtain nourishment and stimulation for further development (Bowlby, 1969/1982; Gewirtz, 1963; Hinde, 1982; Lamb, Thompson, Gardner, & Estes, 1985; Ribble, 1943, Spitz, 1965; Sroufe & Fleeson, 1986). Attachment behaviors may be viewed, albeit figuratively, as an attempt to reestablish the unity lost at birth that enhanced and protected life. Whether the infant's world is conceptualized as a buzz or a blank slate, the infant must begin to differentiate venues or objects that further his or her survival aims, supplying nourishment, preservation, and stimulation, from those that diminish, frustrate, or threaten them. These initial relationships, or, "internal representational models" (e.g., Crittenden, 1990), apparently "prepared" by evolution, become the context through which subsequent relationships develop.

A wealth of clinical evidence is available showing that humans deprived of adequate maternal care in infancy display a variety of pathological behaviors. Extensive reviews of the consequences in animals of early "stimulus impoverishment" show that sensory neural fibers atrophy and cannot be regenerated by subsequent stimulation (Beach & Jaynes, 1954; Riesen, 1961). Inadequate stimulation in any major receptor function usually results in decrements in the capacity to utilize these sensory processes in later life. The profound effects of social isolation have been studied thoroughly and show, for example, that deprived monkeys are incapable at maturity of relating to peers, of participating effectively in sexual activity, and of assuming adequate roles as mothers.

Data on the consequences of too much, or "enriched, early sensory stimulation" are few and far between; quite naturally researchers have properly been concerned with the effects of a deficit in, rather than excess, stimulation. A not unreasonable hypothesis, however, is that excess stimulation during the sensory-attachment stage would result in overdevelopments among associated neural structures (Rosenzweig, Krech, Bennett, & Diamond, 1962). These may lead to oversensitivities which might, in turn, result in potentially maladaptive dominance of sensory functions or pleasurable substrates. This is demonstrated most clearly in the "symbiotic child" (Mahler, Pine, & Bergman, 1975), where an abnormal clinging to the mother and a persistent resistance to stimulation from other sources often result in overwhelming feelings of isolation and panic, as when the child is sent to nursery school or "replaced" by a newborn sibling.

Neurodevelopmental Stage 2: Sensorimotor Autonomy
Not until the end of the first year has the infant matured sufficiently to engage in actions independent of parental support. Holding the drinking cup, the first few steps, or a word or two all signify a growing capacity to act autonomously. As the child develops the functions that characterize this stage, he or she begins to comprehend the attitudes and feelings communicated by stimulative sources. No longer is rough parental handling merely excess stimulation, undistinguished from the playful tossing of an affectionate father; the child now discerns the difference between harshness and good-natured roughhousing.

In the sensorimotor-autonomy stage the focus shifts from survival itself to survival within an environment. From an evolutionary perspective, the child in this stage is learning a mode of adaptation, an active tendency to modify his or her ecological niche, versus a passive tendency to accommodate to whatever the environment has provided. The former reflects a disposition toward taking the initiative in shaping the course of life events; the latter a disposition to be unassertive, to react rather than act, to wait for things to happen, and to accept what is given. Whatever alternative is pursued, it is, of course, a matter of degree rather than an all-or-none decision.

Thus, perhaps the most significant aspect of sensorimotor development is that it enables children to begin to take an active stance in doing things for themselves, to influence their environment, to free themselves from external control, to outgrow the dependencies of their first year. Children become aware of their increasing competence and seek new ventures. Needless to say, conflicts and restrictions arise as they assert themselves (Erikson, 1959; White, 1959). These are seen clearly during toilet training, when youngsters often resist submitting to the demands of their parents. A delicate exchange of power and cunning often ensues. Opportunities arise for the child to actively extract promises or deny wishes; in response, parents may mete out punishments, submit meekly, or shift inconsistently. Important precedents for attitudes toward authority, power, and autonomy are generated during this period of parent–child interaction.

A lack of stimulation of sensorimotor capacities can result in retardations in functions necessary to the development of autonomy and initiative, leading children to remain within a passive adaptational mode. This is seen most clearly in children of overprotective parents. Spoon-fed, excused from "chores," restrained from exploration, curtailed in friendships, and protected from "danger"all of these illustrate controls that restrict growing children's opportunities to exercise their sensorimotor skills and develop the means for autonomous behavior. A self-perpetuating cycle often unfolds.

The consequences of excessive enrichment during the sensorimotor-autonomy stage are found most often in children of excessively lax, permissive, or overindulgent parents. Given free rein with minimal restraint, stimulated to explore and manipulate things to their suiting without guidance or control, these children will often become irresponsibly undisciplined in their behaviors. Their active style compels these children to view the entire ecological milieu as a playground or medium to be modified according to their whims. Carried into the wider social context, these behaviors run up against the desires of other children and the restrictions of less permissive adults. Unless the youngsters are extremely adept, they will find that their actively self-centered and free-wheeling tactics fail miserably. For the few who succeed, however, a pattern of egocentrism, unbridled self-expression, and social arrogance may become dominant.

Neurodevelopmental Stage 3: Pubertal-Gender Identity

Somewhere between the 11th and 15th years a rather sweeping series of hormonal changes unsettle the psychic state that had been so carefully constructed in preceding years. These changes reflect the onset of puberty and the instantiation of sexual and gender-related characteristics. Erratic moods, changing self-images, reinterpretations of one's view of others, new urges, hopeful expectancies, and a growing physical and social awkwardness upset the relative equanimity of an earlier age. Disruptive as it may be, this turbulent stage of growth bifurcates and focuses many of the remaining elements of the youngster's biological potential. It is not only a preparatory phase for the forthcoming independence from parental direction, but is when the psychological equivalent of the r- and K-strategies, self (male) and other (female) orientations, begin to diverge and then coalesce into distinct gender roles. Here the male can be prototypically described as more dominant, imperial, and acquisitive, and the female more communal, nurturant, and deferent.

Youngsters must establish a gender identity that incorporates physiological changes and the powerful libidinal feelings with which they are associated. The increase in pubertal libidinal drives requires a reorganization of one's sense of adolescent identity. Developed in a satisfactory manner, the adolescent is enabled to search out relevant extrafamilial love objects. Developing a gender identity is not so much acquiring a means for satisfying libidinal impulses as it is a process of refining the youngster's previously diffused and undifferentiated sense of self.

Without direct tuition from their elders, teenagers will be left to their own devices to master the complexities of a varied world, to control intense aggressive and sexual urges that well up within them, to channel their fantasies and to pursue the goals to which they aspire. They may become victims of their own growth, unable to discipline their impulses or fashion acceptable means for expressing their desires. Scattered and unguided, they cannot get hold of a sense of personal identity, a consistent direction and purpose to their existence. Borderline personality disorders often characterize this pattern of gender diffusion (Millon & Davis, 1996). Their aimlessness and disaffiliation from the mainstream of traditional sociocultural life may be traced, in part, to the failure of experience to provide a coherent set of gender role-models and values around which they can focus their lives and orient themselves toward a meaningful future.

Neurodevelopmental Stage 4: Intracortical Integration

The intracortical-integration stage coordinates with the fourth phase of the evolutionary theory's progression, what is termed the *thinking–feeling polarity* and its functions (Millon, 1990; Millon & Grossman, 2005). The peak period of neurological maturation for these functions generally occurs between the ages of 4 and 18. The amount and kind of intrapsychic and contextual stimulation at these times of rapid growth will have a strong bearing on the degree to which these functions mature. Thinking and feeling are broad and multifaceted constructs with diverse manifestations. While the focus in the first three stages of development was on the child's survival aims, modes of adaptation, and gender identification, here the focus shifts to the individual as a being-in-time.

Initially, the child must acquire abstract capacities that enable the child to transcend the purely concrete reality of the present moment and project the self-as-object into myriad futures contingent upon his or her own style of action or accommodation. Such capacities are both cognitive and emotional, and may have wide-ranging consequences for the personality system if they fail to cohere as integrated structures, as in such severe personality disorders as the borderline.

Progressively more complex arrangements of neural cells become possible as children advance in maturation. Although these higher-order connections begin in early infancy, they do not form into structures capable of rational foresight and adult-level planning until youngsters have fully developed their more basic sensorimotor skills and pubertal maturations. With these capacities as a base, they are able to differentiate and arrange the objects of the physical world. As verbal skills unfold, they learn to symbolize concrete objects; soon they are able to manipulate and coordinate these symbols as well as, if not better than, the tangible events themselves. Free of the need to make direct reference to the concrete world, they are able to recall past events and anticipate future ones. As increasingly complex cortical connections are established, higher conceptual abstractions are formulated. These internal representations of reality, the product of symbolic thought, the construction of events past, present, and future, take over as the primary elements of the representational world. Especially significant at this period is a fusion between the capacities to think and to feel.

When the inner world of symbols is mastered, giving objective reality an order and integration, youngsters are able to create some consistency and continuity in their lives. No longer are they buffeted from one mood or action to another by the swirl of changing events; they now have an internal anchor, a nucleus of cognitions that serves as a base and imposes a sense of sameness and continuity upon an otherwise fluid environment. As they grow in their capacity to organize and integrate their world, one configuration becomes increasingly differentiated and begins to predominate. Accrued from experiences with others and their reactions to the child, an image or representation of self-as-object has taken shape.

The task of integrating a consistent self–other differentiation, as well as consolidating the divergencies of thought and feeling, is not easy in a world of changing events and pluralistic values. From what sources can a genuine balance between reason and emotion be developed? The institutions that interweave to form the complex fabric of society are implicitly designed to shape the assumptive world of its younger members. Family, school, and church transmit implicit values and explicit rules by which the child is guided in behaving and thinking in a manner consonant with those of others. The youngster not only is subject to cultural pressures but requires them to give direction to his or her proliferating capacities and impulses. Without them, potentials may become overly diffuse and scattered; conversely, too much guidance may narrow the child's potentials and restrict their adaptiveness. In either case, the sense of self and other, as well as the relationship of thought and

emotion, are no longer expressed in personally elaborated and multifaceted forms.

The negative consequences of overenrichment at the fourth stage usually occur when parents are controlling and perfectionistic. The overly trained, overly disciplined, and overly integrated youngster is given little opportunity to shape his or her own destiny. Whether by coercion or enticement, children who, too early, are led to control their emergent feelings, to focus their thoughts along narrowly defined paths, and to follow the prescriptions of parental demands have been subverted into adopting the identities of others. Whatever individuality the child may have acquired is drowned in a model of adult orderliness, propriety, and virtue, features most clearly observed among compulsive personality patterns. Such oversocialized and rigid youngsters lack the spontaneity, flexibility, and creativeness we expect of the young; they have been overly trained before their time, too narrow in perspective to respond to the excitement, variety, and challenge of new events. Overenrichment at this stage has fixed them on a restrictive course and has deprived them of the rewards of being themselves.

Miscellaneous Hypotheses Concerning Pathogenic Learning

Attitudes and behaviors may be learned as a consequence of instruction or indoctrination on the part of parents, but most of what is learned accrues from a haphazard series of casual and incidental events to which the child is exposed. Not only is the administration of rewards and punishments meted out most often in a spontaneous and erratic fashion, but the everyday and ordinary activities of parents provide the child with "unintended" models to imitate. Furthermore, children mirror complex behaviors without understanding their significance, as well as without parental intentions of transmitting them. The old saying, "practice what you preach," conveys the essence of this thesis. As noted in the quote, a parent who castigates the child harshly for failing to be kind is likely to create an intrinsically ambivalent learning experience; the contrast between parental manner and their verbalized injunction teaches the conflicted child simultaneously to think "kindly" but to "behave" harshly.

A few words must be stated again on a matter that should be self-evident, but is often overlooked or simplified in presenting pathogenic influences. It relates to our prior notation that most children acquire their ideas and models from *their parent(s)/guardian(s)*, as well as one or more siblings. As a consequence, children are exposed to and frequently learn different and contrasting sets of perceptions, feelings, attitudes, and behaviors, as well as a mixed set of assumptions about themselves and others. In a manner similar to *genetic recombination*, where the child's heredity-based dispositions reflect the contribution of both parents, so too do the child's experiences and learnings reflect the input and interweaving of what he or she has been subjected to by *both* parents. To illustrate, one parent may have been cruel and rejecting, whereas the other may have been kindly and supportive. How this mix will ultimately take psychological form, and which set of these differential experiences will predominate, will be a function of numerous other factors. The point to note, however, is that we should expect that children will be differentially affected by each parent, and that pathogenesis will reflect a complex interaction of these combined experiences. In reading the following, as well as what has already been presented, the reader should be mindful that few experiences are singular in their impact; they are modulated by the interplay of multiple forces, mostly the commingling and consolidation of several sets of influences.

An important source of psychopathology arises from an *insufficiency* of experiences requisite to the learning of adaptive behavior. Thus, general stimulus impoverishment, or minimal social experience, may produce deficits in the acquisition of adaptive behaviors. The sheer lack of skills and competence for mastering the environment is a form of pathological underlearning, which may be as severe as those disorders generated either by stressful experiences or by defective or maladaptive learning.

A few preliminary comments are advisable before detailing the explicit pathogenic sources of learning. The belief that early interpersonal experiences within the family play a decisive role in the development of psychopathology is well accepted among professionals, but reliable and unequivocal data supporting this conviction are difficult to find. The deficits in these data are not due to a shortage of research efforts; rather, they reflect the operation of numerous methodological difficulties that stymies progress. For example, and as

discussed previously, many data depend on retrospective accounts of early experience; these data are notoriously unreliable. Patients interviewed during their illness are prone to give a warped and selective accounting of their relationships with others. Information obtained from relatives often is distorted by feelings of guilt or by a desire to uncover some simple event to which the disorder can be attributed. In general, then, attempts to reconstruct the complex sequence of past events that may have contributed to pathological learning are fraught with almost insurmountable methodological difficulties.

To these procedural complications may be added problems of conceptual semantics and data organization; these complications make comparisons among studies difficult and deter the systematic accumulation of a consistent body of research data. For example, what one investigator calls a "cold and distant" parent, another may refer to as "hostile or indifferent." An "indulgent" mother in one study may be referred to as a "worrier" in another or "overprotective" in a third. Furthermore, descriptive terms such as *cold* and *overprotective* represent gross categories of experience; variations, timing sequences, and other subtleties of interpersonal interaction are lost or blurred when experiences are grouped together into these global categories. The precise element of these experiences that effectively accounts for maladaptive learning remains unclear because of the gross or nonspecific categories into which these experiences are grouped. We must know exactly what aspect of parental "coldness" or "overprotectiveness" is pathogenic. Hopefully, such specifications will be detailed more precisely in future research. Until such time, however, we must be content with the global nature of these categories of psychogenesis.

An atmosphere, a way of handling the daily and routine activities of life, or a style and tone of interpersonal relatedness all come to characterize the family setting within which the child develops. Events, feelings, and ways of communicating are repeated day in and day out. In contrast to the occasional and scattered events of the outside environment, the circumstances of daily family life have an enduring and cumulative effect on the entire fabric of the child's learning. Within this setting the child establishes a basic feeling of security, imitates the ways in which people relate interpersonally, acquires an impression of how others perceive and feel about him or her, develops a sense of self-worth, and learns how to cope with feelings and the stresses of life. The influence of the family environment is preeminent during all of the crucial growth periods in that it alone among all sources exerts a persistent effect on the child.

In what ways can these experiences be differentiated and measured?

Since the ebb and flow of everyday life consists of many inextricably interwoven elements, any subdivision that can be made must reflect some measure of arbitrariness. The reader will not fall prey to the errors of etiological simplification if it is kept in mind that the features discussed next represent only single facets of an ongoing and complex constellation of events.

The most overriding yet most difficult to appraise aspect of learned experience is the extent to which the child develops a feeling of acceptance or rejection by his or her parents. With the exception of cases of blatant abuse or overt deprecation, investigators have extreme difficulty in specifying, no less measuring, the signs of parental neglect, disaffiliation, and disaffection. Despite the methodological difficulties that researchers encounter, the child who is the recipient of rejecting cues has no doubt that he or she is unappreciated, scorned, or deceived. Rejected by parents, the child is likely to anticipate equal devaluation by others (Dodge, Murphy, & Buchsbaum, 1984; Dornbusch, Ritter, Leiderman & Roberts, 1987; Steinberg, Elmen, & Mounts, 1989). As a defense against further pain, the child may learn to avoid others and use indifference as a protective cloak to minimize what is now expected from others. Different strategies may evolve, of course. Thus, some rejected children may imitate parental scorn and ridicule and learn to handle their disturbed feelings by acting in a parallel hostile and vindictive fashion (Cicchetti & Carlson, 1989; Mueller & Silverman, 1989).

Rejection is not the only parental attitude that may result in insidious damage to the child's personality. Attitudes represented by terms such as *seduction, exploitation*, and *deception* contribute their share of damage as well. Children can tolerate substantial punishment and buffeting from their environment if they sense a basic feeling of love and support from their parents; without this, the child's resistance, even to minor stress, is tenuous (Billings & Moos, 1982; Lewinsohn, 1974).

It is not uncommon for children to acquire attitudes and feelings about themselves that are divided or split, partly reflecting the relationship with their mother, and partly with their father, no less also with older siblings or relatives. As we read the background of one or another of our patients, we may find individuals who have experienced two or more of the problematic life histories we describe. Exposed to a single parent, one who was consistent and whose attitudes and feelings were not subverted or countermanded by other adult models, a patient may become a "pure" textbook type. However, for the most part, youngsters develop via the impact of a variety of adult models, resulting in mixed psychological configurations—for example, somewhat narcissistic and somewhat compulsive, or partly dependent and partly avoidant.

Parents disposed to intimidating and ridiculing their offspring, using punitive and repressive measures to control their behavior and thought, may set the stage for a variety of maladaptive patterns (El Sheikh, Cummings, & Goetsch, 1989; Loeber & Stouthamer-Loeber, 1986; Millon & Davis, 1996). If the child submits to pressure and succeeds in fulfilling parental expectations (i.e., learns instrumentally to avoid the negative reinforcement of punishment), he or she is apt to become an overly obedient and circumspect person. Quite typically, these individuals learn not only to keep in check their impulses and contrary thoughts but, through vicarious observation and imitation, to adopt the parental behavior model and begin to be punitive of deviant behavior on the part of others.

Parental methods of control often are irregular, contradictory, and capricious (Maccoby & Martin, 1983; Patterson, 1982). Some degree of variability is inevitable in the course of every child's life, but there are parents who display an extreme inconsistency in their standards and expectations, and an extreme unpredictability in their application of rewards and punishments. Youngsters exposed to such a chaotic and capricious environment cannot learn consistently and cannot devise nonconflictive strategies for adaptive behavior; whatever behavior they display may be countermanded by an unpredictable parental reaction.

Some parents so narrowly restrict the experiences to which their children are exposed that these youngsters fail to learn even the basic rudiments of autonomous behaviors (Baumrind, 1967; Lewis, 1981). Overprotective mothers, worried that their children are too frail or are unable to care for themselves or make sensible judgments on their own, not only succeed in forestalling the growth of normal competencies but, indirectly, give children a feeling that they are inferior and frail. The child, observing his or her actual inadequacies, has verification of the fact that the child is weak, inept, and dependent on others (Millon, 1981; Millon & Davis, 1996; Parker, 1983).

Overly permissive, lax, or undisciplined parents allow children full rein to explore and assert their every whim. These parents fail to control their children and, by their own lack of discipline, provide a model to be imitated that further strengthens the child's irresponsibility. Unconstrained by parental control, and not guided by selective rewards, these youngsters grow up displaying the inconsiderate and often tyrannical characteristics of undisciplined children. Having had their way for so long, they tend to be exploitive, demanding, uncooperative, and antisocially aggressive.

Each family constructs its own style of communication, its own pattern of listening and attending, and its own way of fashioning thoughts and conveying them to others. The styles of interpersonal communication to which the child is exposed serve as a model for attending, organizing, and reacting to the expressions, thoughts, and feelings of others. Unless this framework for learning interpersonal communication is rational and reciprocal, the child will be ill-equipped to function in an effective way with others. Thus, the very symbolic capacities that enable people to transcend their environment so successfully may lend themselves to serious misdirections and confusions; this powerful instrument for facilitating communication with others may serve instead to undermine social relationships. Although illogical ideas, irrational reactions, and irrelevant and bizarre verbalizations often arise as a consequence of extreme stress, its roots can be traced as frequently to the simple exposure to defective styles of family communication (Campbell, 1973; Mash & Johnston, 1982; Morrison, 1980; Tizard & Hodges, 1978).

The effect of amorphous, fragmented, or confusing patterns of family communication has been explored by numerous investigators (Bateson, Jackson, Haley, & Weakland, 1956; Lidz, Cornelison, Terry, & Fleck, 1958; Lu, 1962; Singer & Wynne, 1965). Not only are messages attended to in certain families in a vague erratic or incidental fashion, with a consequent disjunctiveness and loss of focus, but when they are attended to, they frequently convey equivocal or contradictory meanings.

What kinds of teachings lend themselves to the learning of pathological attitudes and behaviors? Just a few will be mentioned here.

The most insidious and destructive of these teachings is training in anxiety. Parents who fret over their own health, who investigate every potential ailment in their child's functioning, and who are preoccupied with failures or the dismal turn of events teach and furnish models for anxiety proneness in their children (Coolidge & Brodie, 1974; Parker, 1983; Waldron, Shrier, Stone, & Tobin, 1975).

Feelings of guilt and shame are generated in the teachings of many homes. A failure to live up to parental expectations, a feeling that one has caused undue sacrifices to be made by one's parents, and the sense that one has transgressed rules and embarrassed the family by virtue of some shortcoming or misbehavior illustrate events that question the individual's self-worth and produce marked feelings of shame and guilt.

The lack of significant adult figures within the family may deprive children of the opportunity to acquire, through imitation, many of the complex patterns of behavior required in adult life (Emery, 1982; Ferri, 1976; Millon, 1981). The most serious deficit usually is the unavailability of a parental model of the same sex (Hetherington, Cox, & Cox, 1982). The frequent absence of fathers in underprivileged homes, or the vocational preoccupations of fathers in well-to-do homes, often produce sons who lack a mature sense of masculine identity; they seem ill-equipped with goals and behaviors by which they can orient their adult lives.

Children subject to persistent parental bickering and nagging not only are exposed to destructive models for imitative learning but are faced with upsetting influences that may eventuate in pathological behaviors (Crockenberg, 1985; Cummings, Pelligrini, Notarius, & Cummings, 1989; Millon, 1981; Rutter & Giller, 1983). The stability of life, so necessary for the acquisition of a consistent pattern of behaving and thinking, is shattered when strife and marked controversy prevail. There is an ever-present apprehension that one parent may be lost through divorce; dissension often leads to the undermining of one parent by the other; an air of mistrust frequently pervades the home, creating suspicions and anxieties. A nasty and cruel competition for the loyalty and affections of children may ensue. Children often become scapegoats in these settings, subject to displaced parental hostilities (Hetherington, 1972). Constantly dragged into the arena of parental strife, the child not only loses a sense of security and stability but may be subjected to capricious hostility and to a set of conflicting and destructive behavior models.

Numerous other features of the family environment, some relating to structural elements (e.g., sex of siblings and presence of "problem" siblings) and some to roles assumed by family members (e.g., domineering or seductive mothers or inadequate or effeminate fathers), can be specified and their likely effects on learning speculated about. A listing of such events and relationships, however, would be too exhaustive for our purposes.

It is a common belief, attributable in large measure to popularizations of psychology in our literature and news media, that most forms of psychopathology can be traced to a single, very severe experience, the hidden residues of which account for the manifest disorder. Freud's early writings gave impetus and support to this notion, but he reversed himself in his later work when he was made aware of the fact that patient reports of early trauma often were imaginative fabrications of their past. Current thinking in the field suggests that most pathological behaviors accrue gradually through repetitive learning experiences.

Despite the primacy that enduring and pervasive experiences play in shaping most pathological patterns, there are occasions when a particularly painful event can shatter the individual's equanimity and leave a deeply embedded attitude that is not readily extinguished. An untimely frightening experience, be it abusive or not, or an especially embarrassing and humiliating social event illustrate conditions that can result in a persistent attitude.

The impact of these events may be particularly severe with young children as they usually are ill-prepared for such events and lack the perspective of prior experience that might serve as a context for moderating their effects (Field, 1985; Garmezy, 1986; Weissman & Paykel, 1974). If a traumatic event is the first exposure for a youngster to a particular class of experiences, the attitude he or she learns in reaction to that event may intrude and color all subsequent events of that kind. Thus, adolescents whose first sexual venture resulted in devastating feelings of guilt, inadequacy, or humiliation may carry such feelings within them long after the event has passed.

Traumatic events persevere in their learned effects for essentially two reasons. First, a high level of neural activation ensues in response to most situations of marked distress or anxiety. This means that many diverse neural associations become connected to the event; the greater the level of neural involvement, the deeper and more pervasive the learned reaction, and the greater the difficulty in extinguishing what was learned. Second, during heightened stress, there often is a decrement in the ability to make accurate discriminations within the environment. As a consequence, the traumatized individual generalizes his or her emotional reaction to a variety of objects and persons who are only incidentally associated with the traumatic source.

Hypotheses Concerning the Continuity of Early Learnings

We are now in a society in which few constants persevere, where values and customs are in conflict, and where the styles of human interaction today are likely to change tomorrow. We see the emergence of a new "unstructured" and "highly fluid" personality style that is commonly diagnosed today as the borderline disorder. In these adults we find a reflection of the contradictory and changing customs and beliefs of contemporary society. This newest pattern of childhood adaptation leaves the person unable to find the "center" of him- or herself. Such persons have learned *not* to demonstrate consistency and continuity in one's behaviors, thoughts, and feelings, much less in one's way of relating to others.

Is the impact of early experience, as we have asserted in previous sections, a consequence of the young child's susceptibilities during "sensitive" maturational stages? That is, are early experiences more significant than later experiences because the developing child is more plastic and impressionable than the fully matured adult? Can other explanations be offered to account for the special status in shaping behavior assigned to early experience?

Among the alternate interpretations offered are the following. Influences common both to children and to adults arise more often in childhood—that is, there is nothing distinctive about childhood other than the *frequency* with which certain experiences occur. Were these events equally frequent in adulthood, there would be no reason to assume that they would affect adults less than they do children. Others state that the difference may be due to the fact that children experience the impact of events more intensely than adults because they have fewer skills to handle challenges and threats. A somewhat similar hypothesis suggests that the importance of childhood experience lies in its *primacy,* that is, the fact that the first event of a set of similar effects will have a more marked impact than later ones. According to this view, an event experienced initially in adulthood will have the same effect on an adult as it does on a child. These theorists note, however, that it is more likely that the first of a series of similar experiences will occur in childhood.

There is little question that the special status of early experience can be ascribed in part to the simple facts of frequency and primacy; events that come first or more often will have a bearing on what comes later and thereby justify our assigning them special impact value. The question remains, however, as to whether frequency and primacy, in themselves, are sufficient to account for the unusual significance attributed to childhood experiences.

Acceptance of the role that these two factors play does not preclude additional hypotheses that assign unusual vulnerabilities or sensitivities to young children. There is no fundamental conflict between these views; each factor—primacy, frequency, and biological sensitivity—may operate conjointly and with undiminished singular effects.

We will concentrate in this section on the notion of continuity in behavior, since we believe that the significance of early experience lies not so much in the intensity of its impact but in its durability and persistence. Experiences in early life are not only ingrained more pervasively and forcefully, but their effects tend to persist and are more difficult to modify than later experiences. For example, early events occur at a presymbolic level and cannot easily be recalled and unlearned. They are reinforced frequently as a function of the child's restricted opportunities to learn alternatives; they tend to be repeated and perpetuated by the child's own behavior. For many reasons, then, a continuity in behavior—a consistent style of feeling, thinking, and relating to the world—once embedded in early life, perseveres into adulthood.

Part of the continuity we observe between childhood and adulthood may be ascribed to the stability of biological constitutional factors, factors described earlier in this chapter. But there are numerous psychological processes that contribute as well to this longitudinal consistency (Caspi, Roberts & Shiner, 2005; Chess & Thomas, 1984; Costa, Terraccino, & McCrae, 2001; Fraley & Roberts, 2005; Kagan, Reznick, & Snidman, 1989; Millon, 1969; Millon & Davis, 1996; Plomin & Dunn, 1986; Roberts & Robins, 2004; Roberts & Wood, 2004; Robins & Rutter, 1990). Because these processes enable us to see more clearly how pathology develops, we cannot afford to take them for granted or merely enumerate them without elaboration.

Broadly speaking, the processes that coalesce to bring about continuity may be grouped into three categories: *resistance to extinction, social reinforcement,* and *self-perpetuation.*

Acquired behaviors and attitudes usually are not fixed or permanent. What has been learned can be modified or eliminated under appropriate conditions, a process referred to as *extinction.* Extinction usually entails exposure to experiences that are similar to the conditions of original learning but which provide opportunities for new learning to occur. Essentially, old habits of behavior change when new learning interferes with, and replaces, what previously had been learned. This progressive weakening of old learnings may be speeded up by special environmental conditions, the details of which are not relevant to our discussion.

What happens if the conditions of original learning cannot be duplicated easily? Are the events of early life experienced in such a manner as to make them difficult to reproduce and, therefore, resistant to extinction? An examination of the conditions of childhood suggests that the answer is yes!

Three interlocking conditions—presymbolic, random and generalized learning—account in large measure for the unusual difficulty of reexperiencing the events of early life and the consequent difficulty of unlearning the feelings, behaviors, and attitudes generated by these events. Biologically speaking, the young child is a primitive organism. The nervous system is incomplete; the child perceives the world from momentary and changing vantage points and is unable to discriminate and identify many of the elements of his or her experience. What the child sees and learns about his or her environment through the infantile perceptual and cognitive systems will never again be experienced in the same manner in later life.

The infant's presymbolic world of fleeting and inarticulate impressions recedes gradually as he or she acquires the ability to identify, discriminate, and symbolize experience. By the time the child is four or five, the child views the world in preformed categories and groups and symbolizes objects and events in a stable way, a way quite different from that of infancy.

Once the growing child's perceptions have taken on discriminative symbolic forms, the child can no longer duplicate the perceptually amorphous, presymbolic, and diffusely inchoate experiences of his or her earlier years. Unable to reproduce these early experiences in subsequent life, the child will not be able to extinguish what he or she learned in response to them; no longer perceiving events as initially sensed, the child cannot supplant his or her early reactions with new ones. These early learnings will persist, therefore, as feelings, attitudes, and expectancies that crop up pervasively in a vague and diffuse way.

Young children lack not only the ability to form a precise image of their environment but the equipment to discern logical relationships among its elements. Their world of objects, people, and events is connected in an unclear and random fashion. They learn to associate objects and events that have no intrinsic relationship; clusters of concurrent but only incidentally connected stimuli are fused erroneously. Thus, when a child experiences fear in response to his or her father's harsh voice, the child may learn to fear not only that voice but the setting, the atmosphere, the pictures, the furniture, and the odors—a whole bevy of incidental objects which by chance was present at that time. Unable to discriminate the precise source in the environment that "caused" the fear, the child connects his or her discomfort randomly to all associated stimuli; now each of them become precipitants for these feelings.

Random associations of early life cannot be duplicated as children develop the capacity for logical thinking and perception. By the time they are four or five, children can discriminate cause-and-effect relationships with considerably accuracy. Early random associations do not "make sense" to them; when they react to one of the precipitants derived from early learning, they are unable to identify what it is in the environment that they are reacting to. They cannot locate the source of their difficulty, since they now think more logically than before.

Young children's discriminations of their environment are crude and gross. As they begin to differentiate the elements of their world, they group and label them into broad and unrefined categories. All men become "daddy"; all four-legged animals are called "doggie"; all foods are "yum yum." When a child learns to fear a particular dog, for example, he or she will learn to fear not only that dog but all strange, mobile four-legged creatures. To the child's primitive perception, all of these animals are one-of-a-kind.

Generalization is inevitable in early learning. It reflects more than the failure of young children to have had sufficient experiences to acquire greater precision; their indiscriminateness represents an intrinsic inability to discriminate events because of their undeveloped cortical capacities. As the undifferentiated mass of early experiences becomes more finely discriminated, learning gets to be more focused, specific, and precise; a 10-year-old will learn to fear bulldogs as a result of an unfortunate run-in with one, but will not necessarily generalize this fear to collies or poodles, since he or she knows and can discern differences among these animals. Generalized learning is difficult to extinguish. The young child's learned reactions are attached to a broader class of objects than called for by his or her specific experiences. To extinguish these broadly generalized reactions in later life, when the child's discriminative capacities are much more precise, will require that he or she be exposed to many and diverse experiences.

Of the many factors that contribute to the persistence of early behavior patterns, few play a more significant role than social and interpersonal relationships. These relationships can be viewed fruitfully from the perspective usually taken by sociologists and social psychologists. To these scientists, the varied cultural and institutional forces of a society promote continuity by maintaining a stable and organized class of experiences to which most individuals of a particular group are repeatedly exposed.

Here our attention will be not on the content of what is learned but on those aspects of relationships that strengthen what has been learned and that lead to their perpetuation. Three such influences will be described: repetitive experiences, reciprocal reinforcement, and social stereotyping.

The typical daily activities in which the young child participates is restricted and repetitive; there is not much variety in the routine experience to which the child is exposed. Day in and day out the child eats the same kind of food, plays with the same toys, remains essentially in the same physical environment, and relates to the same people. This constricted environment, this repeated exposure to a narrow range of family attitudes and training methods, not only builds in deeply etched habits and expectations but prevents the child from new experiences that are so essential to change. Early behaviors may fail to change, therefore, not because they may have jelled permanently but because the same slender band of experiences that helped form them initially continue and persist as influences for many years.

A circular interplay often arises that intensifies the child's initial biological reactivity pattern. Thus, unusually passive, sensitive, or cranky infants frequently elicit feelings on the part of their mothers, which perpetuate their original tendencies. Circular or reciprocal influences may be applied not only to the perpetuation of biological dispositions but also to behavior tendencies that are acquired by learning. Whatever the initial roots may have been—constitutional or learned—certain forms of behaviors provoke or "pull" from others, reactions that result in a repetition of these behaviors (Leary, 1957). For example, a suspicious and defiant child with a chip on his or her shoulder eventually will force others, no matter how tolerant they may have been initially, to counter with perplexity, exasperation, and anger. The child undermines every inclination on the part of others to be nurturant, friendly, and cooperative. Whether the "cause" was the child or the parent, the process has gotten out of hand and will continue its vicious course until some benign influence interferes, or until it deteriorates into pathological form (Gottman & Katz, 1989).

The dominant features of a child's early behavior form a distinct impression on others. Once this early impression is established, people expect that the child will continue to behave in his or her distinctive manner; in time, they develop a fixed and simplified image of "what kind of person the child is." The term *stereotype*, borrowed from social psychology, represents this tendency to simplify and categorize the attributes of others.

People no longer view a child passively and objectively once they have formed a stereotype of him or her; they now are sensitized to those distinctive features they have learned to expect (Farrington, 1977). The stereotype begins to take on a life of its own; it operates as a screen through which the child's behaviors are selectively perceived so as to fit the characteristics attributed to him or her.

The residuals of the past do more than passively contribute their share to the present. By temporal precedence, if nothing else, they guide, shape, or distort the character of current events. Not only are they ever-present, then, but they also operate insidiously to transform new stimulus experiences in line with past. We will elaborate on some of these processes of perpetuation in this section.

Painful memories of the past are kept out of consciousness, a process referred to as *repression*. Similarly, current experiences that may reactivate these repressed memories are judiciously avoided. The individual develops a network of conscious and unconscious protective maneuvers to decrease the likelihood that either of these distressing experiences will occur. As a consequence of these protective efforts, however, the person narrows or constricts his or her world. Repression reduces anxiety by enabling the individual to keep the inner sources of his or her discomfort from awareness, but it also thwarts the person from "unlearning" these feelings or learning new and potentially more constructive ways of coping with them. Likewise, by defensively reducing one's activities to situations that will not reactivate intolerable memories, the individual automatically precludes the possibility of learning to be less anxious than in the past, and diminishes his or her chances for learning new reactions to formerly stressful situations.

As a result of the person's own protective actions, then, the person preserves unaltered his or her memories of the past; in addition, they persist and force the person along paths that prevent their resolution. Moreover, the more vigilant the person's protective maneuvers and the more constrictive his or her boundaries, the more limited will be the competencies for effective functioning and the more the person will be deprived of the positive rewards of life.

Certain processes not only preserve the past but transform the present in line with the past. Cameron (1947) described this process, which he referred to as *reaction-sensitivity*, with insight and clarity. To him, once a person acquires a system of threat expectancies, he or she responds with increasing alertness to similar threatening elements in his or her life situation. For example, persons who develop bodily anxieties often become hypochondriacal, that is, hyperalert to physiological processes that most people experience but ignore.

Beck's notion of cognitive schemas (Beck & Freeman, 1990) may be seen as an extension of the concept of reaction-sensitivity. To him, people acquire anticipatory cognitive attitudes as a consequence of not only threatening but all forms of past experience; these schemas guide, screen, code, and evaluate the stream of new experiences to which the individual is exposed. Thus, a person who has learned to believe that "everyone hates him" will tend to interpret the incidental and entirely innocuous comments of others in line with this premise.

The importance of expectancies, reaction-sensitivities, and language habits lies in the fact that they lead to the distortion of objective realities. Disturbed individuals may transform what most people would have perceived as a beneficent event into one that is humiliating, threatening, and punishing. Instead of interpreting events as they objectively exist, then, the individual selectively distorts them to "fit" his or her expectancies and habits of thought. These expectancies may channel the person's attention and may magnify his or her awareness of irrelevant and insignificant features of the environment; they intrude constantly to obscure and to warp an accurate perception of reality.

This distortion process has an insidiously cumulative and spiraling effect. By misconstruing reality in such ways as to make it corroborate the person's expectancies, the individual, in effect, intensifies his or her misery. Thus, ordinary, even rewarding, events may be perceived as threatening. As a result of this distortion, the person subjectively experiences neutral events "as if" they were, in fact, threatening. In this process, the person creates and accumulates painful experiences for him- or herself where none exists in reality.

We have just described a number of factors that lead individuals to perceive new experiences in a subjective and frequently warped fashion; perceptual and cognitive distortions may be viewed as the defective side of a normal process in which new stimulus conditions are seen as similar to those experienced in the past. This process, though usually described in simpler types of conditions, commonly is referred to as *stimulus generalization*. In the present section, we will turn our attention to another closely related form of generalization,

the tendency to react to new stimuli in a manner similar to the way in which one reacted in the past. We may speak of this process as *behavior generalization*.

The tendency to generalize inappropriate behaviors has especially far-reaching consequences since it often elicits reactions from others that not only perpetuate these behaviors but aggravate the conditions that gave rise to them. Thus, Bateson and Ruesch (1951) have noted that communications between people convey more than a statement; they carry with them some anticipation of what the response will be. Leary (1957), Carson (1969), and Kiesler (1996), along similar lines, suggest that interpersonal behaviors often are designed unconsciously to "pull" a reaction from others. For example, a phrase such as "I think I'm doing poorly" is not merely a message denoting one's personal feelings but a social statement which one normally expects will elicit a reciprocal reaction.

By intruding old behaviors into new situations, individuals will provoke, with unfailing regularity, reactions from others that reinforce their old responses. Almost all forms of generalized behavior set up reciprocal reactions that intensify these behaviors. Docile, ingratiating, or fearful interpersonal actions, for example, draw domineering and manipulative responses; confident and self-assured attitudes elicit admiration and submissiveness. In short, not only is generalization a form of perpetuation itself, but it also creates conditions that promote perpetuation.

Selected Empirical Studies of Pathogenesis

In a seminal article, Alan Sroufe and Michael Rutter (1984), major longitudinal researchers, defined developmental psychopathology as "the study of the origins and course of individual patterns of behaviors maladaptations "(p. 18). Cairns (1990), another long-term investigator, viewed development, both normal and abnormal, as a holistic and synthetic science in which maturational, experiential, and cultural contributions are inseparably linked in ontogeny. Gottlieb's longitudinal research (1992) led him to speak of development as a probabilistic epigenesis in which influences of a genetic and environmental nature are only partially predetermined. And an early developmental researcher, Heinz Werner (1984), referred to an orthogenetic principle in which the developing individual moves from a diffuse and undifferentiated state to an organization of greater articulation and complexity.

A concern facing researchers seeking to carry out extensive and long-term developmental studies is the vast amount of funding required to support and maintain the project. This stumbling block has led investigators to drop their ideas or to narrow them within the confines of available and sustainable funds. Nevertheless, a number of hardy researchers have been reasonably successful in imitating and carrying out studies that provide the profession with a modicum of valid and reliable studies (e.g., Cohen & Leckman, 1993; Costello, 1992; Graham, Rutter, & George, 1973). Extensive meta-analytic reviews have been summarized by numerous authors (e.g., Achenbach, 1995).

Sroufe's (1990) studies led him to conclude that the longer a child continues along a maladaptive ontogenetic pathway, the more difficulty the child will have in attempting to reclaim a normal developmental trajectory. Cicchetti and Cohen (1995), from their research, maintained that developmental psychopathology is inevitably diverse both in process and outcome. Drawing on the general systems theory of von Bertalanffy (1968), they employed the concept of "equifinality" to suggest that diverse or nonlinear epigenesis may lead to the same outcome. In extending the epigenetic notion to that of multifinality, they recognize that the consequences of any event may differ appreciably depending on the context in which it occurs. Rutter (1990) reported further from his investigations that psychic vulnerabilities, risks, and protective factors indicate the operation of multiple and unseen complex factors that may manifest themselves in possible pathological consequences. Recognizing the complicating role of ecological forces, Gould (1980, 1986) noted from his archeological research the difficulty in establishing clear-cut interpretations for the sequences and outcomes of evolutionary anomalies. The embryologist Weiss (1961) recognized early in his investigations that "even the greatest deformity is produced by the same rigorously lawful…interactions that govern normal development" (p. 150). And Norman Garmezy (1971, 1974) illustrated in numerous investigations that most children maintain considerable resilience in the presence of both serious and chronic adversity.

The studies of a number of early research groups (Escalona, 1968; Escalona & Heider, 1959; Escalona & Leitch, 1953; Murphy, 1962; Murphy & Moriarty, 1976; Thomas & Chess, 1977; Thomas, Chess, & Birch, 1963, 1968) have been especially fruitful. Their work has contributed not only to an understanding of development in general but also to the development of psychopathology in particular.

Several behavioral dimensions were found to differentiate the temperament patterns of infants. Children differ in the regularity of their biological functions, including autonomic reactivity, as gauged by initial responses to new situations; sensory alertness to stimuli and adaptability to change; characteristic moods; and intensities of response, distractibility, and persistence (Goldsmith & Gottesman, 1981). Although early patterns were modified only slightly from infancy to childhood, this continuity could not be attributed entirely to the persistence of innate endowments. Subsequent experiences served to reinforce the characteristics that were displayed in early life (Kagan, 1989), according to a number of longitudinal studies. This occurred in great measure because the infant's initial behaviors transformed the environment in ways that intensified and accentuated initial behaviors.

Other researchers have often concluded that disorders may result from experiences that individuals have no part in producing themselves (Jones & Raag, 1989; Zanolli, Saudargas, & Twardosz, 1990). This may be simplification of a complex interaction, according to Sroufe and Waters (1976). As they see it, each infant possesses a biologically based pattern of sensitivities and dispositions that shape the nature of his or her experiences. The interaction of biological dispositions and environmental experience is not a readily disentangled web but an intricate feedback system of criss-crossing influences. Several components of this process are elaborated on here, because of their pertinence to development.

A number of investigators have concluded from their studies that temperament dispositions of the maturing child are important because they strengthen the probability that certain traits will become prepotent (Bates, 1980, 1987). For example, highly active and responsive children relate to and rapidly acquire knowledge about events and persons in their environment. Their zest and energy may lead them to experience personal gratification quickly or, conversely, their lively and exploratory behavior may result in painful frustrations if they run repetitively into insuperable barriers. Unable to fulfill their activity needs, they may strike out in erratic and maladaptive ways. Moreover, temperament also influences the expression of psychological variables such as attachment (Belsky & Rovine, 1987).

Organismic action in passive children may also be shaped by their biological constitution (Thomas, Chess, & Korn, 1982). Ill-disposed to deal with their environment assertively and disinclined to discharge their tensions physically, they may learn to avoid conflicts and step aside when difficulties arise. They may be less likely to develop guilt feelings about misbehavior than active youngsters, who more frequently get into trouble and receive punishment, and who are therefore inclined to develop aggressive feelings toward others. Passive youngsters may also deprive themselves of rewarding experiences, feel "left out of things," and depend on others to protect them from events they feel ill-equipped to handle on their own.

Psychopathology is often seen as a system. A crucial determinant of whether a particular temperament will lead to psychopathology appears to be parental acceptance of the child's individuality (Thomas & Chess, 1977). Parents who accept their child's temperament and then modify their practices accordingly can deter what might otherwise become pathological. On the other hand, if parents experience daily feelings of failure, frustration, anger, and guilt, regardless of the child's disposition, they are likely to contribute to a progressive worsening of the child's adjustment. These comments point once more to the fact that biogenic and psychogenic factors interact in complex ways.

The studies conducted by collaborators noted previously, one associated with the New York Medical College (Thomas, Chess, & Birch, 1963, 1968) and the other with the Menninger Foundation (Escalona, 1968; Escalona & Heider, 1959; Escalona & Leitch, 1953; Murphy, 1962; Murphy & Moriarty, 1976), observed several hundred infants from birth through the early years of adolescence. Rating scales were employed to quantify behavior dimensions such as activity level, rhythmicity, inclinations toward approach or withdrawal, adaptability, intensity of reaction, and quality of mood. It was found that the majority of children displayed a recognizable and distinctive way of behaving from the first few months of life. Some were predictably regular in their schedule, whereas others followed chaotic sequences. Some reached out for everything presented; others avoided anything new. Although any of a number of different dimensions could be used to differentiate children, two dimensions subsumed several characteristics considered significant, if not crucial, to later development. The first of these was labeled the child's "activity pattern." Active children displayed a decisiveness and vigor in their behavior; they related continuously to their environment and insisted that events take place in accord with their desires. In contrast, passive children displayed a receptive orientation; they seemed to be content to wait and see what would be done to meet their needs, accepting matters until their wishes were ultimately fulfilled. The second set of central temperament constellations was organized around what the researchers termed "adaptability." One group of children was characterized by a regularity, a positive approach to new stimuli, and a high degree of flexibility in response to changing conditions. Another group displayed irregularity in their biological functions, exhibited withdrawal reactions to new stimuli, showed minimal flexibility in response to change, and expressed intense and often negative moods.

An approach to pathology development proposed by Buss and Plomin (1975, 1984) was firmly grounded in empirical research. They suggested three fundamental temperaments: activity, emotionality, and sociability. "Activity" referred to total energy output such that active persons are typically busy, in a hurry, constantly moving, and seemingly tireless, whereas passive or lethargic persons display opposite inclinations. "Emotionality" was conceived as equivalent to intensity of reaction; thus, the emotional person is easily aroused, has an excess of affect, and displays strong tempers, violent mood swings, and a high degree of expressiveness. The third dispositional temperament, "sociability," consisted of a need to be with others. Those at the "gregarious" extreme of the sociability dimension find that interaction with others is very gratifying—far more rewarding than nonsocial experiences; they contrast with those at the opposite extreme of the dimension, which Buss and Plomin refer to as "detached." Although all possible permutations of two or three temperaments might be expected theoretically, Buss and Plomin stated that this is not supported in either the research or clinical literature. Low activity or passivity combined with high emotionality appears to underlie agitated depressions. Those high in emotionality and sociability would be inclined to seek the company of others but would perhaps be inhibited by strong anxieties over potential rejection and ridicule. The combination of high sociability and high activity is seen as relating to the classical extrovert pattern, whereas those low in both temperaments are conceived as similar to the introvert.

An excellent follow-up study was carried out by Kagan (1989) with 2-year-old children who evinced extremes in either behavioral restraint or spontaneity in unfamiliar contexts. These children were followed until they were 7 years of age. The majority of the restrained group remained quiet and socially avoidant, whereas those who were spontaneous became talkative and interactive. Group differences in peripheral physiological reactions suggested that inherited variations in arousal thresholds may be associated with selected limbic sites that, in turn, may undergird shyness in childhood and more marked social avoidance in adulthood.

Caspi (Caspi, Roberts, & Shiner, 2005) raised the question of whether individual traits evident in childhood do, in fact, continue or change through development. The longitudinal evidence is "remarkably high" on the basis of their studies. Personality differences remain highly consistent, especially after age 3. Although rank-order stability patterns of traits continue to change, they do so only modestly in adulthood, achieving peak levels of stability some time after 50.

An intriguing paper articulating the relationship of childhood personality differences and their potential psychopathological consequences was written by Rebecca Shiner and Avshalom Caspi (2003). In addition to detailing recent research issues relating to children's personality, they set out a variety of hypotheses linking youthful traits to adult psychopathology.

Data designed to confirm a series of hypotheses proposed by Clark, Watson, and Mineka (1994) call for further investigation. Their hypotheses are worth noting, however. In what they termed *spectrum associations*, the linkage between early personality traits and later disorders may reflect the fact that psychopathological problems are only extreme forms of continuously distributed normal personality traits. Another thesis, referred to as the *vulnerability association*, suggests that personality traits may set into motion processes that lead to psychopathology, a thesis similar to

the early "vicious cycle" notions of Horney (1945) and the "self-perpetuating" ideas of Millon (1969; Millon & Davis, 1996). A third possibility, termed the *resilience association*, states that certain personality traits may protect against the development of psychopathology. A fourth explanatory thesis, labeled the *pathoplastic association*, notes that personality traits may not serve as a direct cause of psychopathology, but may influence the manifest presentation or appearance, as well as the prognosis, of psychopathological disorders. The fifth association between personality and psychopathology they termed *scarring*; it signifies a reversal of the usual linkage in that disorders may influence the character of personality traits and their development.

Detailed and comprehensive as this chapter has been, we must conclude, as did Shiner and Caspi (2003) in their review of the developmental consequences of childhood personality differences, that little of a definitive nature is known about how early individual differences become elaborated into developmental pathogenesis. There are numerous ways in which early trait differences *may* relate to psychopathology, some of which have been elaborated in this chapter, but these can serve only as working hypotheses that should stimulate future studies.

References

Achenbach, T. M. (1995). Developmental issues in assessment, taxonomy, and diagnosis of child and adolescent psychopathology. In D. Cicchetti & D. J. Cohen (Eds.), *Developmental psychopathology: Theory and methods* (Vol 1.) (pp. 57–80). New York: Wiley.

Bates, J. E. (1980). The concept of difficult temperament. *Merrill-Palmer Quarterly, 26*, 299–319.

Bates, J. E. (1987). Temperament in infancy. In J. D. Osofsky (Ed.), *Handbook of infancy* (2nd ed., pp. 1101–1149). New York: Wiley.

Bateson, G., Jackson, D., Haley, J., & Weakland, J. (1956). Toward a theory of schizophrenia. *Behavioral Science, 1*, 251–264.

Bateson, G., & Ruesch, J. (1951). *Communication, the social matrix of psychiatry*. New York: Norton.

Baumrind, D. (1967). Child care practices anteceding three patterns of preschool behavior. *Genetic Psychology Monographs, 75*, 43–83.

Beach, F., & Jaynes, J. (1954). Effects of early experience upon the behavior of animals. *Psychological Bulletin, 51*, 239–262.

Beck, A. T., & Freeman, A. (1990). *Cognitive therapy of personality disorders*. New York: Guilford Press.

Belsky, J., & Rovine, M. (1987). Temperament and attachment security in the strange situation: An empirical rapprochement. *Child Development, 58*, 787–795.

Billings, A. G., & Moos, R. H. (1982). Psychosocial theory and research on depression: An integrative framework and review. *Clinical Psychology Review, 2*, 213–237.

Bowlby, J. (1969/1982). *Attachment and loss: Attachment* (Vol. 1). New York: Basic.

Butler, J. M., & Rice, L. N. (1963). Audience, self-actualization, and drive theory. In J. I. Wepman & R. Heine (Eds.), *Concepts of personality*. Chicago: Aldine.

Buss, A., & Plomin, R. (1975). *A temperament theory of personality development*. New York: Wiley

Buss, A., & Plomin, R. (1984). *Temperament: Early developing personality traits*. Hillsdale, NJ: Erlbaum.

Cairns, R. (1990). Toward a developmental science. *Psychological Science, 1*, 42–44.

Cameron, N. (1947). *The psychology of the behavior disorders: A biosocial interpretation*. Boston: Houghton-Mifflin.

Campbell, S. B. (1973). Mother–infant interaction in reflective, impulsive, and hyperactive children. *Developmental Psychology, 8*, 341–349.

Carson, R. C. (1969). *Interaction concepts of personality*. Chicago: Aldine.

Caspi, A., Roberts, B. W., & Shiner, R. L. (2005). Personality development: Stability and change. *Annual Review of Psychology, 56*, 453–484.

Chess, S., & Thomas, A. (1984). *Origins and evolution of behavior disorders*. New York: Brunner/Mazel.

Cicchetti, D., & Carlson, V. (1989). *Child maltreatment: Theory and research on the causes and consequences of child abuse and neglect*. New York: Cambridge University Press.

Cicchetti, D., & Cohen, D. J. (1995). Perspectives on developmental psychopathology. In D. Cicchetti & D. J. Cohen (eds.), *Developmental psychopathology: Theory and methods* (Vol. 1). New York: Wiley.

Clark, L. A., Watson, D. & Mineka, S. (1994). Temperament, personality, and the mood and anxiety disorders. *Journal of Abnormal Psychology, 103*, 103–116.

Cohen, D. J., & Leckman, J. (1993). Developmental psychopathology and neurobiology of Tourette's syndrome. *Journal of the American Academy of Child & Adolescent Psychiatry, 33*, 2–15.

Coolidge, J. C., & Brodie, R. D. (1974). Observations of mothers of 49 school phobic children. *Journal of the American Academy of Child Psychiatry, 13*, 275–285.

Costa, P. T., Jr., Terracciano, A., & McCrae, R. R. (2001). Gender differences in personality traits across cultures: Robust and surprising findings. *Journal of Personality and Social Psychology, 81*, 322–331.

Costello, C. G. (1992). Conceptual problems in current research on cognitive vulnerability to psychopathology. *Cognitive Therapy and Research, 16*, 379–390.

Cummings, J. S., Pellegrini, D. S., Notarius, C. I., & Cummings, E. M. (1989). Children's responses to angry adults as a function of marital distress and history of interparent hostility. *Child Development, 60*, 1035–1043.

Crittenden, P. M. (1990). Internal representational models of attachment. *Infant Mental Health Journal, 11*(3), 259–277.

Crockenberg, S. (1985). Toddler's reaction to maternal anger. *Merrill-Palmer Quarterly, 31*, 361–373.

Davidson, E. H. (1986). *Gene activity in early development*. Orlando, FL: Academic Press.

Dodge, K., Murphy, R., & Buchsbaum, K. C. (1984). The assessment of intention-cue detection skills in children: Implications for developmental psychopathology. *Child Development, 55*, 163–173.

Dornbusch, S. M., Ritter, P. L. Leiderman, P. H., & Roberts, D. F. (1987). The relation of parenting style to adolescent school performance. *Child Development, 58*, 1244–1257.

El Sheikh, M., Cummings, E. M., & Goetsch, V. (1989). Coping with adult's angry behavior: Behavioral, physiological, and verbal responses in preschoolers. *Developmental Psychology, 25*, 490–498.

Emery, R. E. (1982). Interparental conflict and the children of discord and divorce. *Psychological Bulletin, 92*, 310–330.

Erikson, E. (1959). Growth and crises of the healthy personality. In G. S. Klein (Ed.), *Psychological issues*. New York: International University Press.

Escalona, S. (1968). *Roots of individuality. Normal patterns of development in infancy*. Chicago: Aldine.

Escalona, S., & Heider, G. (1959). *Prediction and outcome*. New York: Basic Books.

Escalona, S., & Leitch, M. (1953). *Early phases of personality development*. Champaign, IL: Child Development.

Farrington, D. P. (1977). The effects of public labeling. *British Journal of Criminology, 17*, 112–125.

Ferri, E. (1976). *Growing up in a one-parent family*. Slough, England: NFER.

Field, T. M. (1985). Affective responses to separation. In T. B. Brazelton & M. W. Yogman (Eds.), *Affective development in infancy*. Norwood, NJ: Ablex.

Fox, N. A., Kimmerly, N. L., & Schafer, W. D. (1991). Attachment to mother/attachment to father: A meta-analysis. *Child Development*, *62*, 210–225.

Fraley, R. C., & Roberts, B. W. (2005). Patterns of continuity: A dynamic model for conceptualizing the stability of individual differences in psychological constructs across the life course. *Psychological Review, 112*(1), 60–74.

Freud, S. (1925). The origin and development of psychoanalysis. In J. S. Van Teslaar (Ed.), *An outline of psychoanalysis*. New York: Modern Library.

Garmezy, N. (1971). Vulnerability research and the issue of primary prevention. *American Journal of Orthopsychiatry, 41*, 101–116.

Garmezy, N. (1974). The study of competence in children at risk for severe psychopathology. In E. J. Anthony & C. Koupernik (Eds.), *The child in his family* (pp. 77–98). New York: Wiley.

Garmezy, N. (1986). Developmental aspects of children's responses to the stress of separation and loss. In M. Rutter, C. E. Izard, & P. B. Read (Eds.), *Depression in young people: Developmental and clinical perspectives* (pp. 297–323). New York: Guilford.

Gewirtz, J. L. (1963). A learning analysis of the effects of normal stimulation upon social and exploratory behavior in the human infant. In B. M. Foss (Ed.), *Determinants of infant behavior II*. New York: Wiley.

Goldsmith, H. H., & Gottesman, I. I. (1981). Origins of variation in behavioral style: A longitudinal study of temperament in young twins. *Child Development, 52*, 91–103.

Gottlieb, G. (1992). *Individual development and evolution: The genesis of novel behavior*. New York: Oxford University Press.

Gottman, J. M., & Katz, L. F. (1989). Effects of marital discord on young children's peer interaction and health. *Developmental Psychology, 25*, 373–381.

Gould, S. (1980). *The panda's thumb*. New York: Norton.

Gould, S. (1986). Evolution and the triumph of homology, or why history matters. *American Scientist, 74*, 60–69.

Graham, P., Rutter, M., & George, S. (1973). Temperamental characteristics as predictors of behavior disorders in children. *American Journal of Orthopsychiatry. 43*, 328–339.

Hetherington, E. M. (1972). Effects of paternal absence on personality development in adolescent daughters. *Developmental Psychology, 7*, 313–326.

Hetherington, E. M., Cox, M., & Cox., C. R. (1982). Effects of divorce on parents and children. In M. Lamb (Ed.), *Nontraditional families* (pp. 223–288). Hillsdale, NJ: Erlbaum.

Hinde, R. A. (1982). Attachment: Some conceptual and biological issues. In J. Stevenson-Hinde & C. P. Parkes (Eds.), *The place of attachment in human behavior* (pp. 60–76). New York: Basic Books.

Horney, K. (1945). *Our inner conflicts; a constructive theory of neurosis*. New York: Norton.

Jones, S. S., & Raag, T. (1989). Smile production in older infants: The importance of a social recipient for the facial signal. *Child Development, 13*, 147–165.

Kagan, J. (1989). Temperamental contribution to social behavior. *American Psychologist, 44*, 668–674.

Kagan, J., Reznick, J. S., & Snidman, N. (1989). Issues in the study of temperament. In G.A. Kohnstamm, J. E. Bates, & M. K. Rothbart (Eds.), *Temperament in childhood* (pp. 133–144). New York: John Wiley.

Kiesler, D. J. (1996). *Contemporary interpersonal theory and research: Personality, psychopathology, and psychotherapy*. New York: Wiley.

Killackey, H. P. (1990). Neocortical expansion: An attempt toward relating phylogeny and ontogeny. *Journal of Cognitive Neuroscience, 2*, 1–17.

Lamb, M. E., Thompson, R. A., & Gardner, W., & Estes, D. (1985). *Infant–mother attachment*. Hillsdale, NJ: Erlbaum.

Leary. T. (1957). *Interpersonal diagnosis of personality*. New York: Ronald Press.

Lewinsohn, P. M. (1974). A behavioral approach to depression. In R. J. Friedman & M. M. Katz (Eds.), *The psychology of depression: Contemporary theory and research* (pp. 157–178). New York: John Wiley & Sons.

Lewis, C. C. (1981). The effects of parental firm control: A reinterpretation of findings. *Psychological Bulletin, 90*, 547–563.

Lidz, T., Cornelison, A., Terry, D., & Fleck, S. (1958). Intrafamilial environment of the schizophrenic patient: VI. The transmission or irrationality. *Archives of Neurology and Psychiatry, 79*, 305–316.

Livesley, W. J., Jang, K. L., & Vernon, P. A. (2003). Genetic basis of personality structure.

In T. Millon & M. Lerner (Eds.), *Handbook of psychology: Volume 5. Personality and social psychology* (pp. 59–85). New York: Wiley.

Loeber, R., & Stouthamer-Loeber, M. (1986). Family factors as correlates and predictors of juvenile conduct problems and delinquency. In M. Toury & N. Morris (Eds.). *Crime and Justice* Vol. 7 (pp. 29–149). Chicago: University of Chicago Press.

Lu, Y. C. (1962) Contradictory parental expectations in schizophrenia: Dependence and responsibility. *Archives of General Psychiatry, 6,* 219–234.

Maccoby, E., & Martin, J. (1983). Socialization in the context of the family: Parent–child interaction. In E. M. Hetherington (Ed.), *Handbook of child psychology, Vol. 4: Socialization, personality, and social development* (pp. 1–101). New York: John Wiley & Sons.

Mahler, M. S., Pine, F., & Bergman, A. (1975). *The psychological birth of the human infant: Symbiosis and individuation.* New York: Basic Books.

Mash, E. J., & Johnston, C. (1982). A comparison of the mother–child interactions of younger and older hyperactive and normal children. *Child Development, 53,* 1371–1381.

Meehl, P. E. (1972). Second-order relevance. *American Psychologist, 27,* 932–940.

Meehl, P. E. (1990). Toward an integrated theory of schizotaxia, schizotypy, and schizophrenia. *Journal of Personality Disorders, 4,* 1–99.

Melzick, R. (1965). Effects of early experience upon behavior: Experimental and conceptual considerations. In P. Hoch & J. Zubin (Eds.), *Psychopathology of perception.* New York: Grune and Stratton.

Millon, T. (1969). *Modern psychopathology: A biosocial approach to maladaptive learning and functioning.* Philadelphia: W.B. Saunders.

Millon, T. (1981). *Disorders of personality: DSM-III, Axis II.* New York: Wiley.

Millon, T. (1986). On the past and future of the DSM-III: Personal recollections and projections. In T. Millon & G. L. Klerman (Eds.) *Contemporary directions in psychopathology: Toward the DSM-IV* (pp. 29–70). New York: Guilford.

Millon, T. (1987). On the nature of taxonomy in psychopathology. In C. G Last, & M. Hersen (Eds.), *Issues in diagnostic research* (pp. 3–85). New York: Plenum Press.

Millon, T. (1990). *Toward a new personology: An evolutionary model.* New York: Wiley-Interscience.

Millon, T. (1999). *Personality-guided therapy.* New York: Wiley.

Millon, T., & Davis, R. (1996). *Disorders of personality: DSM-IV and beyond* (2nd ed.). New York: Wiley.

Millon, T., & Grossman, S. D. (2005). Personology: A theory based on evolutionary concepts. In M. F. Lenzenweger & J. F. Clarkin (Eds.), *Major theories of personality disorder* (2nd ed.) (pp. 332–390). New York: Guilford.

Millon, T., & Grossman, S. (2007a). *Resolving difficult clinical syndromes: A personalized psychotherapy approach.* Hoboken, NJ: Wiley.

Millon, T., & Grossman, S. (2007b). *Overcoming resistant personality disorders: A personalized psychotherapy approach.* Hoboken, NJ: Wiley.

Millon, T., & Grossman, S. (2007c). *Moderating severe personality disorders: A personalized psychotherapy approach.* NJ: Wiley.

Morrison, J. R. (1980). Adult psychiatric disorders in parents of hyperactive children. *American Journal of Psychiatry, 137,* 825–827.

Mueller, E., & Silverman, N. (1989). Peer relations in maltreated children. In D. Cicchetti & V. Carlson (Eds.), *Child maltreatment: Theory and research on the causes and consequences of child abuse and neglect* (pp. 529–578). New York: Cambridge University Press.

Murphy, G. (1947). *Personality: A biosocial approach to origins and structures.* New York: Harper.

Murphy, L. B. (Ed.). (1962). *The widening world of childhood.* New York: Basic Books.

Murphy, L. B., & Moriarty, A. E. (1976). *Vulnerability, coping, and growth.* New Haven, CT: Yale University Press.

Parker, G. (1983). *Parental overprotection: A risk factor in psychosocial development.* New York: Grune & Stratton.

Patterson, G. R. (1982). *Coercive family process.* Eugene, OR: Castalia.

Plomin, R. (1990). The role of inheritance in behavior. *Science, 248,* 183–188.

Plomin, R., DeFries, J. C., & McClearn, G. E. (1990). *Behavioral genetics: A primer* (2nd ed.). New York: W.H. Freeman.

Plomin, R., & Dunn, J. (Eds.) (1986). *The study of temperament: Changes, continuities, and challenge.* Hillsdale, NJ: Erlbaum.

Purves, D., & Lichtman, J. W. (1985). *Principles of neural development.* Sunderland, MA: Sinauer.

Rakic, P. (1985). Limits of neurogenesis in primates. *Science, 227,* 154–156.

Rakic, P. (1988). Specification of cerebral cortical areas. *Science, 241,* 170–176.

Rapaport, D. (1953). Some metapsychological considerations concerning activity and passivity. In M. M. Gill (Ed.), *The collected papers of David Rapaport* (1967, pp. 530–568). New York: Basic Books.

Ribble, M. A. (1943). *The rights of infants.* New York: Columbia University Press.

Riesen, A. H. (1961). Stimulation as a requirement for growth and function in behavioral development. In D. Fiske & S. Maddi (Eds.), *Functions of varied experience* (pp. 57–80). Homewood, IL: Dorsey.

Roberts, B. W., & Robins, R. W. (2004). A longitudinal study of person–environment fit and personality development. *Journal of Personality, 72,* 89–110.

Roberts, B. W., & Wood, D. (2006). Personality development in the context of the neo-socioanalytic model of personality. In D. Mroczek & T. Little (Eds.), *Handbook of personality development* (pp. 11–39). Hillsdale, NJ: Erlbaum.

Robins, L., & Rutter, M. (Eds.) (1990). *Straight and devious pathways from childhood to adulthood.* New York: Cambridge University Press.

Rosenzweig, M. R., Krech, D., Bennett, E. L., & Diamond, M. C. (1962). Effect of environmental complexity and training on brain chemistry and anatomy: A replication and extension. *Journal of Comparative Physiological Psychology, 55,* 429–437.

Rutter, M. (1990). Psychosocial resilience and protective mechanisms. In J. Rolf, A. S. Masten, D. Cicchetti, K. H. Nuechterlein, & S. Weintraug (Eds.), *Risk and protective factors in the development of psychopathology* (pp. 181–214). New York: Cambridge University Press.

Rutter, M., & Giller, H. (1983). *Juvenile delinquency: Trends and perspectives.* Harmondsworth: Penguin.

Scott, J. P. (1968). *Early experience and the organization of behavior.* Belmont, CA: Brooks-Cole.

Shiner, R., & Caspi, A. (2003). Personality differences in childhood and adolescence: Measurement, development, and consequences. *Journal of Child Psychology and Psychiatry, 44,* 2–32.

Singer, M. T., & Wynne, L. C. (1965). Thought disorder and family relations of schizophrenics, III: Methodology using projective techniques. *Archives of General Psychiatry, 12,* 187–212.

Spitz, R. A. (1965). *The first year of life.* New York: International University Press.

Sroufe, L. A. (1990). Considering normal and abnormal together: The essence of developmental psychopathology. *Development and Psychopathology, 2,* 335–347.

Sroufe, L. A., & Fleeson, J. (1986). Attachment and the construction of relationships. In W. Hartup & Z. Rubin. (Eds.), *Relationships and development* (pp. 51–71). Hillsdale, NJ: Erlbaum.

Sroufe, L. A., & Rutter, M. (1984). The domain of developmental psychopathology. *Child Development, 55,* 17–29.

Sroufe, L. A., & Waters, E. (1976). The ontogenesis of smiling and laughter: A perspective on the organization of development in infancy. *Psychological Review, 83,* 173–189.

Steinberg, L., Elmen, J. D., & Mounts, N. S. (1989). Authoritative parenting, psychosocial maturity, and academic success among adolescents. *Child Development, 60,* 1424–1436.

Thomas, A., & Chess, S. (1977). *Temperament and development.* New York: Brunner/Mazel.

Thomas, A., Chess, S., & Birch, H. G. (1963), *Behavioral individuality in early childhood.* New York: New York University Press.

Thomas, A., Chess, S., & Birch, H. G. (1968). *Temperament and behavior disorders in children.* New York: New York University Press.

Thomas, A., Chess, S., & Korn, S. J. (1982). The reality of difficult temperament. *Merrill-Palmer Quarterly, 28,* 1–20.

Thompson, W. R., & Schaefer, T. (1961). Early environmental stimulation. In D. Fiske & S. Maddi (Eds.), *Functions of varied experience* (pp. 81–105). Homewood, IL: Dorsey.

Tizard, B., & Hodges, J. (1978). The effect of early institutional rearing on the development of 8-year-old children. *Journal of Child Psychology and Psychiatry, 19,* 99–118.

von Bertalanffy, L. (1968). *General system theory.* New York: Braziller.

Waldron, S., Shrier, D. K., Stone, B., & Tobin, F. (1975). School phobia and other childhood neuroses: A systematic study of the children and their families. *American Journal of Psychiatry, 132,* 802–808.

Weiss, P. (1961). Deformities as cues to understanding development of form. *Perspective in Biology and Medicine, 4,* 133–151.

Weissman, M. M., & Paykel, E. S. (1974). *The depressed woman: A study of social relationships.* Chicago: University of Chicago Press.

Werner, H. (1984). *Comparative psychology of mental development.* New York: International Universities Press.

White. R. W. (1959). Motivation reconsidered: The concept of competence. *Psychological Review, 66*, 297–323.

Williams, R. J. (1957). Standard human beings versus standard values. *Science, 126*, 453–454.

Williams, R. J. (1973). The biological approach to the study of personality. In T. Millon (Ed.), *Theories of psychopathology and personality* (2nd ed.). Philadelphia: Saunders.

Zanolli, K, Saudargas, R., & Twardosz, S. (1990). Two-year-olds' responses to affectionate and caregiving teacher behavior. *Child Study Journal, 20*, 35–54.

4

Conducting Research in the Field of Psychopathology

MICHAEL L. RAULIN
AND SCOTT O. LILIENFELD

Few things in life are more frightening, puzzling, or intriguing than psychopathology. The human mind is a phenomenal evolutionary achievement, but its proper functioning requires a delicate balance. Upsetting that balance—whether by external stressors that push the organism beyond its limits, by biological aberrations that predispose the organism to respond inappropriately, or by cognitive styles that distort everyday experiences—may result in mental illness.

This chapter examines how researchers study the correlates and causes of psychopathology. We use the plural (causes) because psychological disorders almost certainly have multiple causes (Kendler, 2005). But what is a *cause*? Meehl (1977) described several meanings of causation, four of which are relevant to our discussion.

The strongest meaning of the word *cause*—which Meehl called *specific etiology*—refers to a categorical (all-or-none) variable that is *both necessary and sufficient* for a disorder to emerge. Although rare in psychopathology, such causes occasionally exist in medicine. For example, a single dominant gene is both necessary and sufficient to produce Huntington's disease.

A second and weaker form of causation occurs when a dimensional variable exerts a *threshold effect*. When the threshold is exceeded, the individual is at risk for the disorder. Below this threshold, there is no risk. A variant of this second form

of causation involves a *step function*, in which the individual's risk for the disorder increases sharply once past the threshold. In a step-function model, unlike in a threshold model, the individual's risk for the disorder is low below the threshold, but not zero.

A third and still weaker form of causation involves a variable that is *necessary, but not sufficient*, for a disorder. Included here is the well-known *diathesis-stress* model, in which elevated levels of certain variables create a *diathesis* (i.e., vulnerability) (Zubin & Spring, 1977). This vulnerability is often genetically influenced and is actualized only when the individual encounters a stressor. In diathesis-stress models, both vulnerability factors and stressors are necessary for a disorder to emerge; neither is sufficient. Gottesman (1991), building on Meehl (1962), suggested that schizophrenia fits a diathesis-stress model in which a genetic liability to schizophrenia interacts with psychosocial (e.g., anxiety-provoking events) and/ or biological (e.g., viral exposure in the womb) stressors to produce the disorder.

Finally, a causal factor can be *neither necessary nor sufficient* for psychopathology. General risk factors for psychopathology, such as hyperreactivity to negative emotions (neuroticism), fit this model.

When we talk about causation, we will focus on variables that exert a similar impact across individuals, and we will emphasize research designs that identify such variables. These research designs are called *nomothetic*, which literally means "proposition of the law." Such designs attempt to derive general laws that apply to most or all individuals. Nomothetic studies differ from *idiographic* (the prefix of which has the same root as *idiosyncratic*) studies. Therapists often use idiographic studies to examine the unique pattern of life experiences and personality features that give rise to a client's characteristic pattern of thoughts, feelings, and behaviors.

Basic Research Designs

We will begin by introducing the most common research designs used in psychopathology research.

Case Study Methodology

A *case study* is the detailed examination of a single individual. In general, case studies are better suited to the *context of discovery* rather than to the *context of justification* (Reichenbach, 1938). The context of discovery involves hypothesis generation, whereas the context of justification involves hypothesis testing. Case studies are often helpful for developing hypotheses but poor at testing hypotheses because they lack the controls found in systematic research. For example, imagine that an individual with bipolar disorder reports that her parents were extremely critical of her when she was growing up. That observation is interesting, but we cannot conclude that bipolar disorder is associated with critical parents because this experience might be unique to this individual. Perhaps most people, not just those with bipolar disorder, report that their parents were critical, or perhaps our interviewing method tended to elicit reports of parental criticism. No examination of case studies, no matter how meticulous, will permit psychologists to exclude these and other alternative hypotheses. Moreover, because case studies are limited to small numbers of individuals, generalizing from them to the broader population is ill advised.

Case studies can serve other purposes, such as demonstrating the existence of a rare phenomenon not previously recognized, as in many of the classic case studies in neuropsychology. For example, the case of H. M., whose actual name

(Henry Molaison) was revealed after he died, illustrates the importance of the hippocampus in forming new memories (Scoville & Milner, 1957). H. M. had most of his hippocampus surgically removed in an attempt to control severe seizures; after surgery, H. M was virtually unable to form new memories, although his older memories were intact. He could carry on conversations but within minutes forgot the conversation and the fact that he had had the conversation.

Case studies can also negate a general proposition and thereby function as "existence proofs." For example, many psychologists once believed that individuals with severe mental retardation were incapable of learning, but case studies, and later formal research, demonstrated that to be untrue (e.g., Algozzine & Ysseldyke, 2006).

Quasi-Experimental Designs

Most psychopathology research places investigators in a quandary. They want to determine whether one or more factors (e.g., psychosocial stress, early brain trauma) can cause a disorder. The best design for determining causation is an *experimental design*, in which researchers randomly assign participants to one of two conditions: one that receives the experimental manipulation (experimental group) and one that does not (control group). The researcher manipulates the level of the independent variable to ascertain its effect on the dependent variable(s). However, it is rarely possible to assign participants randomly to conditions in psychopathology research, and it would be unethical even if it were possible. For example, if one wished to study the personality characteristics of individuals with schizophrenia, one could not randomly assign individuals to either a schizophrenic group or a nonschizophrenic group. "Mother Nature" has already assigned these individuals. Similarly, if one wanted to study the effect of trauma on the development of posttraumatic stress disorder (PTSD), it would be unethical to randomly assign participants to either experience or not experience the trauma. Consequently, most research in psychopathology uses *quasi-experimental designs*, which compare two or more groups defined by preexisting characteristics (e.g., depressed versus nondepressed individuals). Such designs are technically correlational studies, and therefore they suffer from all the limitations of such studies. We discuss quasi-experimental designs separately from other correlational studies because psychopathology researchers use them so frequently.

One should not draw causal inferences from quasi-experimental studies. A moment's reflection will reveal why. Because researchers do not randomly assign participants to groups in quasi-experiments, the groups may differ on numerous *potential confounding variables* (also called *nuisance variables* or *extraneous variables*). For example, if researchers compare patients with schizophrenia with a comparison group of individuals without this disorder, it is virtually inevitable that these two groups will differ on variables other than the diagnosis of schizophrenia. For example, the patient group may be lower than the comparison group on socioeconomic status (SES), IQ, hygiene, quality of diet, and a host of other variables, any one of which could affect scores on dependent variables. To address this problem, some investigators have tried to *statistically control* for these potentially relevant variables using analysis of covariance, but this approach is often problematic (Miller & Chapman, 2001). Other investigators use *matching*, equating the quasi-experimental groups on potential confounding variables. Variables are "potentially confounding" if they could affect the dependent variable. Therefore, in the preceding example, the investigator could match schizophrenic and nonschizophrenic groups on variables that might influence scores on personality measures, such as SES, IQ, and gender.

Although matching can be a useful strategy in quasi-experimental designs, it has its limitations. First, even if researchers match on 100 potential confounding variables, the groups might differ on a 101st variable. This unpleasant fact explains why we cannot use quasi-experimental designs to draw definitive causal inferences; it is not possible to rule out every conceivable confounding variable.

A second problem with matching is that it rests on causal assumptions that may be incorrect. Investigators try to match on variables that they assume implicitly to be nuisance variables. However, variables traditionally considered nuisance variables, such as social class, could easily be a critical element in a complex causal chain (Meehl, 1971). If the matching variable is actually a part of the causal chain, matching distorts the picture and may bias interpretations. For example, social class may affect the level of stress and thus increase the risk for developing psychopathology. If so, social class is part of the causal chain, and matching on social class may well remove a factor that contributes to psychopathology. Although matching is a valuable control for nuisance variables, one should never apply it in a cookbook fashion without considering the potential causal theories for a disorder (Miller & Chapman, 2001).

A third problem is that matching on one variable often results in systematic differences between the sample and the population (Chapman & Chapman, 1973). For example, if researchers want to match people with and without schizophrenia on IQ, they would need to select high-scoring patients to match with low-scoring comparison participants, because patients with schizophrenia tend to score lower than controls on almost every task, including IQ tests. The resulting patient group will overrepresent patients with what previous editions of the *DSM* termed paranoid schizophrenia because these patients tend to be brighter and to show less thought disorder than other patients with schizophrenia. Similarly, selecting the low-scoring comparison individuals would produce a sample of participants with a lower SES, less education, and a different upbringing, because IQ is correlated with each of these variables. Therefore, the matching strategy produces unrepresentative patient and comparison samples.

One variation of quasi-experimental designs, called "experiments of nature," can overcome most of these problems. These experiments capitalize on sudden and typically unexpected events that intrude on individuals in a more or less random fashion. For instance, it would be unethical to subject someone to a natural disaster, but when one comes along, it provides an opportunity for research. Technically, such studies are quasi-experiments, because researchers did not randomly assign participants to either experience or not experience these life events. However, if the factors that determine who experiences the event are essentially random, these experiments of nature come close to being true experiments.

Wood, Bootzin, Rosenhan, Nolan-Hoeksema, and Jourden (1992) conducted just such an experiment of nature when they compared the prevalence and content of nightmares among San Francisco and Arizona area college students following the 1989 Loma Prieta earthquake. They found that during the 3 weeks following the earthquake, approximately 40% of the San Francisco students reported earthquake-related nightmares, compared with 5% of Arizona students. Of course, Wood et al. did not randomly assign participants to earthquake and non-earthquake conditions. Consequently, they could not conclusively rule out the possibility that San Francisco students are more prone than Arizona students to earthquake-related nightmares. But the dramatic group difference in the prevalence of these nightmares makes this explanation unlikely. Weems, Pina, and Costa (2007) later used this approach to study the development of PTSD among victims of Hurricane Katrina, and Yamamura (2012) used it to study the impact of technological and natural disasters on the perception of risk of nuclear disasters.

Experimental Designs

Psychopathology researchers often use quasi-experimental designs because they cannot ethically expose participants to events that might trigger psychopathology. Nevertheless, five research paradigms in psychopathology are experimental and thereby allow relatively unambiguous causal conclusions.

The first approach is called an *analogue experiment*, which is an attempt to produce variants of psychopathology in either humans or animals. Imagine that an investigator is interested in the hypothesis that there is an underactivation of the left hemisphere in depression. Rather than study clinically depressed individuals, the investigator uses mood induction procedures to produce mild analogues of depression. For example, the investigator may induce a state called *learned helplessness* (Seligman, 1975) by presenting participants with insoluble puzzles and then examine changes in brain wave activity.

Although useful, analogue experiments have potential pitfalls. In particular, we must assume that the analogue provides an adequate model of the psychopathological condition. If, for example, the mild and transient dysphoria produced by a mood induction procedure differs qualitatively from clinical depression, generalizing from the former to the latter will be misleading (Coyne, 1994).

If it is ethically unacceptable or impractical to create symptoms, an alternative experimental strategy is to try to alleviate them. Such a strategy

provides evidence consistent with the hypothesis that an environmental variable plays a role in the etiology or maintenance of psychopathology, but it also has limitations. Taking two aspirin, for example, may relieve a headache, but this finding does not provide evidence that an aspirin deficiency causes headaches. This simple example highlights the *ex juvantibus* error ("reasoning backward from what helps"). Despite this limitation, treatment outcome can provide crucial data if converging lines of evidence exist. For example, the finding that family therapy reduced both the level of expressed emotion (a construct that includes familial hostility, criticism, and overinvolvement with the affected patient) and the rate of relapse for patients increased the plausibility of the hypothesis that familial expressed emotion (Vaughn & Leff, 1976) contributed to relapse in schizophrenia (e.g., Randolph, Eth, Glynn, & Paz, 1994). Of course, one must still be cautious because other mechanisms may be involved.

A variation of the analogue approach uses *animal models* of psychopathology, which involve attempts to produce a simulated form of a mental disorder in nonhumans (Meadows & Zinbarg, 1991). The learned helplessness model of depression discussed earlier was originally an animal model. Seligman (1975) noticed that exposing animals to uncontrollable aversive stimuli produced persistent apathy, passivity, and loss of appetite, which are common symptoms of human depression. However, researchers who use animal models must be cautious in extrapolating their findings to humans, because humans are likely to be different from other animals on variables potentially relevant to psychopathology (e.g., moral development, abstract thinking, and language). Furthermore, using animals does not sidestep ethical issues, because complex ethical considerations apply to animal studies (Akins & Panicker, 2012). Animal studies may allow researchers to expose animals to more extreme conditions than would be possible with human participants, although researchers disagree on whether doing so is ethical (Carbone, 2004).

Challenge paradigms represent another experimental approach. In the *challenge paradigm*, researchers present participants with stimuli that are thought to trigger a pathological response. Researchers have used biological challenges, such as CO_2 inhalation, with panic patients to see how reliably and under what circumstances the inhalation triggers a panic attack (Barlow, 2002). Of course, challenge paradigms raise ethical concerns; researchers should use them only when their impact is transitory. Nevertheless, clients often cooperate with such studies because they want to help uncover the mechanisms behind their disorder. In the case of panic disorder, challenge paradigms have given us considerable insight into both its biological and its psychological underpinnings (e.g., Gorman, Liebowitz, Fyer, & Stein, 1989; Schmidt, Richey, Maner, & Woolaway-Bickel, 2006).

Finally, researchers interested in the effects of an intervention on a given individual may use *single-subject experimental designs,* in which each participant serves as his or her own control. For example, in an *ABA*, or *reversal*, design, the investigator measures a relevant aspect of the participant's behavior (e.g., nail-biting) at baseline (A) and then again after introducing an intervention (B) (e.g., relaxation training). To ensure that any change in the participant's behavior at B was not due to factors other than the intervention, the researcher withdraws (reverses) the intervention in a second A phase and then often introduces it again in a second B phase. If the participant's behavior improves only when the treatment is present, we can safely conclude that the treatment is effective. This conclusion rests on several assumptions, however. For example, if the treatment has lasting effects, researchers would not expect a return to baseline behavior in the reversal phase (Hartmann & Atkinson, 1973).

Unlike case studies, single-subject experimental designs often permit reasonably strong causal inferences because they involve the systematic manipulation of independent variables. However, like case studies, single-subject experimental designs are idiographic and thus often have limited generalizability. Nevertheless, they can easily be extended to groups of individuals as a way to improve their generalizability (Barlow, Nock, & Hersen, 2009).

Measuring Variables

The study of psychopathology involves the measurement and manipulation of variables. Students often wonder why we need formal procedures to study psychopathology. They often assume that one can identify the causes of mental disorders solely by examining individual clients in depth.

Therefore, we open this section with these two questions:

1. Why can't years of clinical experience provide adequate answers to questions concerning the causes of psychopathology?
2. Do we need formal research studies to obtain these answers?

Why Formal Research is Necessary

We need formal research because the human brain, although remarkably sophisticated, is nonetheless a highly fallible information processor. For example, some social cognition theorists have argued that natural selection "designed" the human brain to extract meaning and order from its environment (Gilovich, 1991; Shermer, 2002). Such a propensity makes good evolutionary sense. Without an innate tendency to organize our complex and often chaotic world into meaningful groupings, humans would soon be overwhelmed. However, this generally adaptive tendency to simplify the world sometimes results in *cognitive illusions*, which are errors in thinking that are nonetheless subjectively compelling (Kahneman, 2011; Piattelli-Palmarini, 1994). For example, we often perceive relationships among variables that are not there. Like visual illusions, cognitive illusions seem real, even after we learn that they are imaginary byproducts of our cognitive apparatus.

Researchers must recognize their propensities toward cognitive illusions and learn to compensate for them. The use of formal research designs is just such a compensatory strategy. Indeed, the failure to use appropriate research designs has often led psychologists to draw faulty inferences. Let's look at two examples.

Example 1. Several authors argued that patients with schizophrenia tend to come from markedly dysfunctional home backgrounds and that such backgrounds contribute to schizophrenia. Yet when Schofield and Balian (1959) compared patients with schizophrenia with a nonpatient comparison group, they found few differences on such life history variables. Indeed, in several cases, individuals in the comparison group exhibited higher levels of adverse environmental variables than did the patients!

One factor that may explain why many clinicians and researchers perceive a strong association between schizophrenia and negative life experiences is the *fallacy of positive instances*. This fallacy, which afflicts everyone, is the error of attending only to data that confirm our hypotheses (Gilovich, 1991). Thus, individuals who expect to observe a relationship between schizophrenia and negative life experiences may pay attention to confirming evidence while ignoring or downplaying disconfirming evidence. The only way to overcome the fallacy of positive instances is to use research designs that force us to attend to all relevant evidence.

Example 2. Many clinicians are convinced of the validity of projective techniques, such as the *Draw-A-Person Test* (DAP). Yet research on the DAP consistently shows that the DAP "signs" posited by many clinicians to be diagnostic of specific personality traits or pathological states are invalid. How can we account for this stunning discrepancy? Chapman and Chapman (1967) hypothesized that individuals, including professionals, are prone to *illusory correlations*—perceived relationships between variables that are, in fact, weak or nonexistent. The Chapmans further suggested that this tendency is especially strong when the variables intuitively "seem" as though they should be associated. They tested this hypothesis by showing undergraduates a series of fabricated DAP protocols containing certain features (e.g., large eyes, big head), along with a description of the personality characteristics of the patient who supposedly produced each drawing (e.g., suspicious, concerned about intelligence). They then asked participants to estimate the extent to which these DAP features co-occurred with certain personality characteristics. Unbeknownst to the participants, there was *no correlation* between the DAP features and the personality characteristics in this stimulus set. Yet participants consistently perceived specific DAP features to be strongly correlated with certain personality features, and these were the same features that clinicians reported using despite research that showed them to be invalid. For example, participants reported that patients who produced DAP protocols with large eyes tended to be suspicious and that patients who produced DAP protocols with large genitals tended to be concerned about their sexuality. The Chapmans found that illusory correlations persisted even when the DAP features and personality characteristics were *negatively* correlated in their stimulus set. Chapman and Chapman (1969) replicated these findings with another commonly used projective measure, the Rorschach. Thus, many clinicians' convictions regarding the validity of projective tests may stem from cognitive propensities to perceive relationships where none exist and from their inattentiveness to disconfirming evidence.

In summary, one major reason why psychopathologists use research designs is *to avoid being fooled.* Sophisticated researchers are aware of their propensities toward cognitive illusions and take pains to ensure that such ubiquitous errors in thinking do not distort their results. For example, researchers routinely score data *blindly* to avoid having their expectations influence the results. The research methods discussed in this chapter, although not infallible, help to protect investigators from their own perceptual and inferential biases. In the Chapman and Chapman studies, a simple cross-tabulation of the DAP characteristics and the clinical concerns would have made it clear that none of these DAP features were predictive of the reported clinical problems.

Reliability and Validity

If researchers could measure psychological variables directly and flawlessly, they could proceed immediately to the interpretation stage. However, we almost never have that luxury. Therefore, we must consider the potential problems introduced by less than perfect measurement.

The term *reliability* refers to the consistency of a measure. There are three types of reliability—*test-retest reliability* (consistency over time), *interrater reliability* (consistency among raters), and *internal consistency reliability* (consistency among the items or observations). Interrater reliability is always relevant; observers should agree on what they see because the laws of nature should apply no matter who tests them. In contrast, the applicability of test-retest reliability and internal consistency depends on the nature of the variable. For example, some variables are theoretically stable over time (e.g., IQ), whereas others are not (e.g., anxiety). Researchers should expect high test-retest reliability only for stable variables. Traditionally, a correlation coefficient is the index of reliability, with 1.00 indicating perfect reliability and 0.00 indicating no reliability.

Researchers may index interrater reliability with either the traditional correlation coefficient (for continuous variables) or percent agreement (for discrete variables). The *kappa coefficient* is preferred over percent agreement, because kappa statistically compensates for the *base rate*—that is, the prevalence of the diagnosis (Cohen, 1960). The more extreme the base rate of a diagnosis (either very high or very low), the easier it is for two raters to agree by chance alone.

The index of interrater reliability should always be based on independent and *blind* ratings, meaning that the raters should not know each other's ratings. The idea is to avoid *criterion contamination*, which refers to the influence of extraneous information, such as the other person's ratings, on one's own ratings. Criterion contamination is also an issue in validity studies. Raters who are unaware of other scores for the participants cannot be influenced by that information. Another principle in interrater reliability is that raters should never know which of their ratings will be checked. Reid (1970) showed that raters produce higher interrater reliabilities when they think they are being evaluated than when they think they are not being evaluated. Therefore, if raters know their ratings will be checked, but not when, they are more motivated to produce careful and precise ratings all of the time.

The *structured diagnostic interview* represents a critical advance in the reliability of psychiatric diagnoses. Spitzer, Endicott, and Robins (1975) spurred the development of structured interviews, as well as the more detailed and descriptive diagnostic criteria first introduced in *DSM-III*, with their analysis of the sources of diagnostic unreliability. Structured interviews reduce a major contributor to diagnostic unreliability—differences in the information available to different diagnosticians. The combination of structured interviews and explicit diagnostic criteria improves diagnostic reliability dramatically (Spitzer et al., 1975). Today, structured diagnostic interviews are the norm in research and increasingly the norm in specialty clinics. One commonly used structured interview is the *Structured Clinical Interview for DSM-5* (SCID; First, Spitzer, Gibbon, & Williams, 2013), which assesses most of the major mental disorders in *DSM-5*.

Validity refers to the extent to which a measure assesses what it purports to assess. Although reliability is necessary for validity, it does not guarantee it. For example, imagine that a researcher claims that the circumference of a person's neck indicates his or her intelligence. Such a measure would be reliable (i.e., repeatable), but it is unlikely to be a valid measure of intelligence.

Psychopathology researchers rarely, if ever, have the luxury of a perfect criterion to judge the validity of their measures. Consequently, their indexes of validity are often intertwined with their theories of what they are measuring. They judge the validity of IQ tests, for example, by observing how well the tests predict criteria that are theoretically related to intelligence. Researchers might validate an IQ test by determining how well it predicts grades in school or performance on a task that they believe requires intellectual skill. This approach to validity is called *criterion-related validity*. In criterion-related validity, researchers must always specify the criterion. For example, an IQ test may be a valid predictor of school grades but have no validity when used to predict happiness. Criterion-related validity may refer to how well a test relates either to a criterion that is already available (*concurrent validity*) or to a criterion that will be available only in the future (*predictive validity*). Also important is *discriminant validity*, which refers to the extent to which a measure *does not relate* to variables that theoretically should not be related. For example, a new measure of schizophrenia should not correlate too highly with an index of a largely unrelated disorder, such as specific phobia. Indeed, large correlations with theoretically unrelated variables can invalidate a measure (Campbell & Fiske, 1959).

Cronbach and Meehl (1955) integrated many of these ideas into an overarching framework called *construct validity*. A *construct* is an attribute that is not directly observable, such as intelligence, extroversion, or schizophrenia. Cronbach and Meehl argued that scientists are often interested in more than just the reliability or validity of measures. Instead, they are concerned about the theoretical concept that the measures are designed to assess and its relationships to specific criteria or other constructs. Validating a construct involves a converging program of research in which researchers systematically test predictions derived from their theory. These predictions are embedded within a *nomological network*, which is an interlocking series of hypotheses derived from one's theoretical understanding of the construct. Researchers can test these predictions with either reliability or validity indexes, depending on the nature of the hypothesized relationship. Furthermore, the theory may predict either strong or weak relationships, so that sometimes researchers expect large validity coefficients and at other times small coefficients. The nomological network of intelligence could include expectations of (a) substantial stability over time (high test-retest reliability); (b) a generalized ability applicable to many different settings, each of which is typically tapped by different items or subtests (high internal consistency reliability); (c) a strong relationship with current academic achievement (high concurrent validity); (d) a strong relationship with future occupational success (high predictive validity); and (e) a weak or absent relationship with most personality traits, such as extroversion (high discriminant validity). We cannot summarize construct validity with a single index (but see Westen & Rosenthal, 2003), but rather we evaluate it by the broad pattern of theoretically relevant observed relationships.

Defining and Refining the Syndrome

A *syndrome* refers to a pattern of signs (objective indicators, such as frequent crying) and symptoms (subjective indicators, such as sad mood) that tend to appear together. How do researchers establish the construct validity of psychopathological syndromes? How can they determine whether their definition of a syndrome is too broad or too narrow, incorporating unrelated disorders or including only a subset of a disorder? Like other constructs, psychiatric diagnoses represent latent attributes that are not directly observable (Morey, 1991). To support the construct validity of their diagnostic criteria for a disorder, researchers must accumulate *indirect* evidence from a variety of sources. Robins and Guze (1970) delineated a comprehensive approach for establishing the construct validity of diagnostic criteria for a psychiatric disorder. They argued that a valid diagnosis should accomplish five things:

1. Describe the clinical syndrome with sufficient clarity to permit high interrater reliability.
2. Predict diagnosed individuals' performance on laboratory tasks (e.g., attentional measures) and psychometric instruments (e.g., personality questionnaires).
3. Predict diagnosed individuals' natural history (i.e., course and outcome).
4. Predict diagnosed individuals' family history of psychiatric syndromes.
5. Differentiate the diagnosis from other superficially similar diagnoses.

In addition, although not mentioned by Robins and Guze, a valid diagnosis should ideally

6. Predict response to treatment.

The Robins and Guze approach is an application of the principle of construct validation to psychiatric diagnoses. Each of these six pieces of information is a component of a nomological network, in which one's predictions concerning the relations between the diagnosis and external variables are embedded (Waldman, Lilienfeld, & Lahey, 1995). The best way to illustrate this approach is to use a specific diagnosis, such as schizophrenia. Research indicates that the diagnosis of schizophrenia (1) can be made reliably and differentiated from other superficially similar diagnoses (e.g., bipolar disorder), (2) predicts performance on laboratory tasks (e.g., smooth pursuit eye tracking) and psychometric instruments (e.g., MMPI-2), (3) is generally, but not invariably, associated with a chronic course and poor outcome, (4) is associated with a family history of schizophrenia and schizophrenia-spectrum disorders (e.g., schizotypal and paranoid personality disorders), (5) differs in its external correlates from other superficially similar conditions (e.g., psychotic mood disorders), and (6) predicts a positive response to medications that block the action of the neurotransmitter dopamine (Gottesman, 1991). Thus, one could argue that the diagnosis of schizophrenia possesses adequate construct validity.

One can also use the Robins and Guze criteria to refine diagnostic criteria. If a revised definition of a syndrome improves the prediction of one or more of these six criteria, this revision is a scientific improvement over previous versions. For example, until the publication of *DSM-III*, schizophrenia was defined more broadly in the United States than in Europe (Gottesman, 1991). This broad definition often included patients that clinicians today would diagnose with bipolar disorder. Differential treatment response between the narrower definition of schizophrenia and bipolar disorder, as well as a differential course, family history, and other criteria, provided convincing evidence to support the narrowing of the diagnostic category of schizophrenia.

One can also apply this approach to the examination of the construct validity of multiple syndromes. If, for example, two syndromes have identical external correlates, such as family history and treatment response, these two syndromes may be manifestations of a single disorder. For example, researchers once distinguished *manic-depression* (manic episodes plus depressive episodes) from *unipolar mania* (manic episodes only). However, subsequent research indicated that mania with associated depression did not differ from mania alone in terms of natural history, family history, response to treatment, and other correlates (Depue & Monroe, 1978). Consequently, the *DSM* regards these two patterns as variations of one syndrome known, perhaps misleadingly, as bipolar disorder.

How should researchers proceed if a proposed diagnosis fails to meet some or all of the Robins and Guze criteria for construct validity? One possible reason for such low construct validity is that the proposed diagnostic criteria are too broad—that is, the people it encompasses are too *heterogeneous*. If that is true, there are several approaches to reduce this heterogeneity. First, the researcher may divide the syndrome into one or more subtypes based on rational or theoretical criteria. For example, numerous researchers have proposed ways of meaningfully subdividing alcohol use disorder (formerly called alcoholism), suggesting, for instance, that alcohol use disorders that appear prior to another psychiatric disorder (primary alcoholism) tend to have an earlier onset and more negative prognosis than alcohol use disorders that appear following another psychiatric disorder (secondary alcoholism) (Goodwin & Guze, 1989). Once proposed, researchers can use the Robins and Guze framework to determine whether subtypes differ in their external correlates.

Researchers may also use statistical techniques to divide the syndrome into narrower, and hopefully more etiologically homogeneous, subtypes. For example, the technique of *factor analysis* allows researchers to ascertain whether one or more underlying dimensions account for the relations among symptoms. For example, factor analyses of measures of schizophrenic symptoms suggested two symptom types—*positive symptoms* (excesses, such as delusions and hallucinations) and *negative symptoms* (deficits, such as flat affect and withdrawal) (Schuldberg, Quinlan, Morganstern, & Glazer, 1990), although other data suggest that a third dimension (disorganization) may also be relevant (Lenzenweger, 2010). Whether positive and negative schizophrenia

represent etiologically distinct conditions will be determined by the application of the Robins and Guze framework.

Another technique used to subdivide syndromes is *cluster analysis*, which can be utilized to sort symptoms (or patients) into different categories. This sorting procedure uses measures of similarity and creates different clusters that are as homogeneous as possible. Although cluster analysis can be useful for generating hypotheses concerning the existence of subtypes that may be nested within a broader diagnosis, this technique often yields quite different results depending on the clustering algorithm used (Meehl & Golden, 1982) or the variables selected (Meehl, 1990). Newer variations that combine the dimensional structure of factor analysis and the similarity analysis of cluster analysis (called *prototypes*) are showing real promise (e.g., Eaton, Krueger, South, Simms, & Clark, 2011).

Meehl and his colleagues pioneered another approach, called *taxometric search procedures*, which are used to examine the mathematical relationships among variables that differentiate one group from another (Waller & Meehl, 1998). Using those mathematical relationships one can determine whether the hypothesized groups are taxonic or continuous. *Taxonic* groups, or taxa, differ in kind (qualitatively) rather than in degree (quantitatively). For example, males and females differ qualitatively in their chromosomal makeup, genitalia, and many variables that affect their behavior. In contrast, geniuses and individuals of average intellect probably differ only quantitatively on the continuous variable of intelligence. Interestingly, some intellectual differences may be taxonic in that most cases of severe retardation result from specific genetic or chromosomal errors (Zigler, 1967).

The heart and soul of statistics in many areas of psychology is the analysis of variance (ANOVA) and its variations, but the ANOVA is ill suited for the task of establishing and refining syndromes. The ANOVA typically treats individual differences as error variance; individual differences are the focus of psychopathology research. Although we adapt the ANOVA for our research by comparing diagnostic groups, within those groups, we are still treating individual differences as error variance. If we rely exclusively and blindly on ANOVA, we will never recognize the kind of data that will lead to a refinement of syndromes. If, however, we carefully examine the variability of responses in our subjects as a routine part of our analysis, we may recognize potential variables that might lead to more refined diagnoses. However, such analyses are exploratory and should not be taken seriously until they have been replicated.

One shortcoming of the Robins and Guze (1970) approach is its exclusive emphasis on *external validation*—that is, the process of ascertaining the construct's associations with correlates that lie "outside" of the construct itself. As Harvey Skinner (1981, 1986; see also Loevinger, 1957) observed, *internal validation*—that is, ascertaining the construct's internal structure—is also a key component of construct validation. Internal validation can help investigators to test hypotheses regarding a construct's homogeneity and factor structure (Waldman et al., 1995). For example, showing that a diagnosis consists of largely independent subtypes would call into question the validity of the diagnosis.

Epidemiological Studies: Gathering Clues to Etiology

Epidemiological research has made major contributions to our understanding of psychopathology and is still in wide use today.

What Is Epidemiology and How Is It Relevant to Psychopathology?

How common is a psychological disorder? What characteristics are associated with the disorder? How often do cases of this disorder arise and disappear? These are the questions addressed by epidemiological methods. Although the term *epidemiology* derives from *epidemic*, epidemiologists concern themselves with far more than the spread of diseases. Epidemiology is the study of (a) the distribution of disorders in a given population and (b) the variables associated with this distribution (Rutter, 1994). Thus, an epidemiological study of antisocial personality disorder (ASPD) would probably focus on the frequency of ASPD in the general population and the factors (e.g., gender, social class, and family history) associated with ASPD.

Research on the rate of a disorder in a population provides a baseline for comparison with the rates in various subpopulations. For example, the

identical co-twins of people with schizophrenia have approximately a 50% chance of developing schizophrenia. However, this 50% figure is meaningful only when compared with the population lifetime prevalence of schizophrenia, which is approximately 1%. Thus, having an identical twin with schizophrenia increases one's risk of schizophrenia nearly 50-fold.

The characteristics that covary with the frequency of a disorder may provide important leads to its etiology. For example, epidemiologists know that ASPD is more common in males than in females, more common among individuals of lower social class, and associated with both a family history of ASPD and criminality. The finding that ASPD is more common in males might suggest that certain biological and/or socialization variables typical of men increase a person's risk for antisocial behavior, such as high testosterone levels (Dabbs & Morris, 1990) or adults' tendency to differentially reinforce physical aggression in boys and girls (Serbin, O'Leary, Kent, & Tonick, 1973).

The strategy of identifying factors associated with the frequency of a disorder has yielded several spectacular successes in medicine. For example, Snow (1855) traced the source of a cholera epidemic in London to a specific water pump by constructing a detailed map of the distribution of affected cases (Tsuang, Tohen, & Murphy, 1988). Later investigators identified the bacterium that produces cholera. Such remarkable success stories have so far eluded epidemiologists investigating psychopathology. For example, although Faris and Dunham's (1939) classic epidemiological study revealed that the rates of schizophrenia in Chicago progressively increased as one moved from the outskirts of the city to its centrally located slums, it did little to uncover the reason for this distribution. Nevertheless, the hope remains that epidemiological research may help to pinpoint risk factors for psychological disorders and ultimately provide clues to their etiology.

Critical Concepts and Terms in Epidemiology

Epidemiology is the study of *who* has *what, where, when,* and *how* (Costello, 1990). Epidemiologists strive to determine which individuals are affected with which disorders, their geographical distribution, the time course of appearance and spread throughout the population, and (ideally) the processes that give rise to them. Answering the question of how is the ultimate goal of epidemiological research.

Several concepts and terms are crucial in epidemiology. *Prevalence* is the percentage of a population afflicted with a disorder during a given period (e.g., 1 month or 1 year). *Point prevalence* is the percentage of a population that is afflicted with a disorder at a single point in time. *Period prevalence* is defined as the percentage of a population afflicted with a disorder during a specified period. *Lifetime prevalence* is the percentage of the population that develops the disorder during their lifetime. The term *base rate* is synonymous with lifetime prevalence. *Incidence*, which is often confused with prevalence, refers to the percentage of *new cases* that arise during a specified period. If in a population of 1 million, 1,000 individuals develop bipolar disorder during a 1-year interval, the 1-year incidence of bipolar disorder is 0.10%. Epidemiologists assess incidence with a longitudinal design by following a sample of unaffected individuals to ascertain what proportion develops the disorder.

Two other important epidemiological terms are the *comparison group* and the *case-control method*, both of which are variants of quasi-experimental designs. Epidemiological researchers often select samples from settings known to have elevated rates of a disorder (e.g., a mental health clinic). This strategy is more efficient than sampling from the general population. For example, we would expect only 1% of a sample from the general population to have a diagnosis of schizophrenia, whereas a sample drawn from a psychiatric hospital might yield 70% or more with that diagnosis. We could then compare the findings from this sample with a sample of individuals without schizophrenia. This latter sample, called a *comparison group*, serves as a baseline with which to compare the rates of various characteristics in the former group. The comparison group is sometimes referred to as a *control group*, although this traditional term is misleading. Unlike a true control group in experimental research, in which random assignment minimizes extraneous group differences, comparison groups often differ from the affected group in many ways. The term *control group* should be reserved for groups that were created through random assignment. Nonetheless, tradition dies hard. The comparison of groups of individuals

with and without a disorder is referred to as the *case-control design*, even though the term *case-comparison design* would be more accurate.

Methods of Sampling

Epidemiological researchers might examine the distribution of disorders in a population, but unless the population is small, it is not feasible to assess everyone. Instead, epidemiologists obtain a *sample* that provides a reasonable approximation to the population. There are at least three ways to do such sampling.

In *random sampling*, every individual in the population has an equal chance of being selected. *Stratified random sampling* is used when researchers want to ensure that one or more subgroups within the population are adequately represented in the sample. For example, if researchers knew that social class affected the dependent variable, they might use a stratified random sample to match precisely the population distribution of social class in their sample. Political polling organizations often use stratified random sampling to obtain representative samples of likely voters. Another use of the stratified random sample is to *oversample* groups with low base rates. Imagine, for example, that researchers were interested in investigating the prevalence of bipolar disorder across different religious groups in the United States. Random sampling might not include sufficient numbers of individuals in certain religious groups (e.g., Hindu, Shinto) to permit a statistically meaningful examination of the rates of bipolar disorder in such groups. Oversampling from these underrepresented groups will provide adequate samples for analysis. If population estimates are needed, researchers can correct statistically for the oversampling. In *cluster sampling*, researchers sample *clusters* of individuals, such as housing projects or hospital wards. They might use either entire clusters or random samples from the available clusters.

Potential Biases in Epidemiological Research

Selection bias can be a major challenge in epidemiological research (Burke & Regier, 1996). Freeman (1979) illustrated this problem in his study of gifted children and their risk for psychopathology. When Freeman sampled children from an association for the families of intellectually gifted children, she found a high rate of psychological disturbance in the children. However, when she sampled gifted children from the general population, she found a low rate. Had she relied exclusively on the former sample, her conclusions would have been misleading. Interestingly, Freeman found that parents who join organizations for gifted children had higher rates of conflict and divorce. It may be that familial dysfunction leads parents to seek out support groups (Rutter, 1994) or, alternatively, that gifted children with psychopathology may increase parental turmoil.

Selection bias is a common problem in psychopathology research. For example, Luchins (1982) argued that the inconsistent findings of cerebral ventricular enlargement in schizophrenia were due to selection bias, with enlarged ventricles found in chronic patients but not in acute patients. As another example, Gorenstein (1982) found frontal lobe deficits in psychopaths, but Hare (1984) did not. In trying to explain this discrepancy, Hare (1984) noted that alcohol abuse was more common in Gorenstein's sample than in his sample and that people who abuse alcohol often show frontal lobe damage.

Using clinical samples can also produce misleadingly high estimates of *comorbidity* (Feinstein, 1985), which is the overlap of two or more diagnoses within an individual (Lilienfeld, Waldman, & Israel, 1994). Comorbidity can result from Berksonian bias (Berkson, 1946), clinical selection bias (Du Fort, Newman, & Bland, 1993), or both. *Berksonian bias* results from the fact that an individual with two disorders can seek treatment for either disorder, and thus is more likely to be in a clinical sample. *Clinical selection bias* results from an increased likelihood of treatment seeking for individuals with one condition because of the presence of another condition. People with alcohol use disorder, for example, may be unlikely to seek treatment unless they are also depressed or anxious. We can think of clinical selection bias as the "straw that breaks the camel's back" effect. People with a single disorder may not be motivated to obtain help until they find themselves unable to cope with an additional disorder. Both biases will produce comorbidity rates that are higher in clinical settings than in the general population.

Virtually no sample in psychopathology research is ever a random sample because researchers are usually restricted to studying the people who live in their geographic area. The National Institute of Mental Health often funds multisite studies to overcome this geographic bias, but unless you are part of such a study, your sample will have regional and other biases. For this reason, psychopathology researchers must describe their samples in sufficient detail to allow other investigators to judge whether differences in the findings from other similar studies might be due to differences in the samples. The variables that are crucial in such descriptions vary, but they usually include standard demographic variables (e.g., age, gender, education, social class), recruitment source (e.g., general population, clinic sample, psychiatric hospital), and characteristics relevant to the disorder (e.g., age of onset, severity of symptoms, comorbid conditions).

Prediction

Epidemiological studies often focus on statistical prediction, such as whether a psychological test predicts a person's diagnosis. In prediction, *sensitivity* refers to how good a test is at correctly identifying those people who have a disorder. *Specificity* refers to how good a test is at correctly identifying those people who do not have a disorder. If a test correctly identifies 70% of people who qualify for a diagnosis of Alzheimer's disease, it has a sensitivity of 70%. If it correctly identifies 90% of the people who *do not* have Alzheimer's disease, it has a specificity of 90% (see Figure 4.1). A sensitivity of 70% means that the diagnostic sign has a *false negative rate* (predicting that the person does not have the disorder when the person does) of 30%. Similarly, a specificity of 90% means that the diagnostic sign has a *false positive rate* (predicting that the person has the disorder when the person does not) of 10%. Ideally, researchers want both high sensitivity and high specificity, but adjusting cutoff scores on a measure to increase sensitivity (i.e., sliding the decision line in Figure 4.1 to the left) will decrease specificity.

Prediction accuracy also interacts with base rates for a disorder in a manner that most people find counterintuitive (Finn & Kamphuis, 1995; Meehl & Rosen, 1955). For example, with 70% sensitivity and 90% specificity of a diagnostic sign, a base rate of 50% for the disorder, and a sample size of 10,000, the test will correctly identify 3,500 of the 5,000 people in a sample who have the disorder and 4,500 of the 5,000 who do not have the disorder. Therefore, when the test

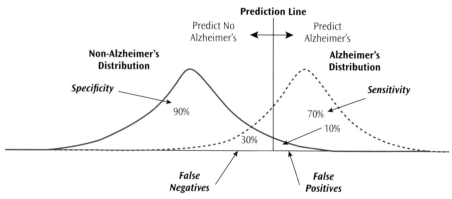

Figure 4.1 Relationship between sensitivity and specificity. The rate of false negatives equals 100% minus sensitivity rate, and a similar relationship exists between specificity and false positives. Moving the prediction line to improve sensitivity will decrease specificity.

predicts that the person has the disorder, it will be correct 87.5% of the time [3,500 / (3,500 + 500)]. Epidemiologists call this figure the *positive predictive value* (sometimes loosely called the "hit rate"), which refers to how often the test is correct when it predicts that the person has the disorder. The numerator in this formula is the number of times that the test predicts the disorder and is correct, and the denominator is the total number of times the test predicts the disorder. However, if the base rate for the disorder drops to 1%, there are only 10 people in the sample of 10,000 with the disorder, and the test will correctly identify 7 of them (70% sensitivity). However, 9,900 people do not have the disorder, and the test will incorrectly identify 10% of them as having the disorder (990). So the positive predictive value when the base rate is 1% is less than 1% [7 / (7 + 990)]. A general principle is that low–base rate disorders or events are extremely difficult to predict unless the test used has very high sensitivity and specificity.

Epidemiological studies are almost never sufficient for establishing specific causal links. Nevertheless, when faced with a field filled with haystacks, it is helpful to know which haystack is likely to hold the needle. Epidemiological studies serve that role well.

Studying Genetic and Environmental Influences

We tend to believe that our family influenced our personality, and we readily point to experiences that have shaped our thinking and attitudes. However, our impressions often leave out one of the most potent family influences—our genetic heritage.

When biological parents raise their offspring, they contribute both genetic and environmental influences to their offspring, which are inseparable in a natural environment. Furthermore, genetic and environmental influences may interact, meaning that individuals with different genetic makeup react differently to an environmental influence. For example, adoptees with a genetic predisposition toward antisocial behavior are more likely to develop antisocial behavior when reared by antisocial parents (Cadoret, Cain, & Crowe, 1983). Moffitt, Caspi, and Rutter (2006) provided a detailed overview of this gene–environment interaction and its implications for psychopathology research.

Modern researchers agree that both genetic and environmental influences contribute to practically every form of psychopathology. However, from the 1940s well into the 1970s, most professionals favored *psychogenic* theories of psychopathology (i.e., having psychological causes), such as the "schizophrenogenic mother" theory (Fromm-Reichman, 1948). These theories were widely accepted, often in the face of contradictory data, because the *Zeitgeist* at the time was to pin the cause of psychopathology on the environment—especially the parents—despite growing evidence of a genetic contribution to many forms of psychopathology. For example, as early as the late 1930s, there was evidence that genes influenced risk for schizophrenia (Kallman, 1938), and by the early 1960s, the data on this point were convincing (Gottesman & Shields, 1972). Yet many people at the time considered Meehl's (1962) suggestion of a genetic diathesis for schizophrenia as revolutionary, and many more thought it implausible.

Behavior genetics is the study of genetic and environmental influences on behavior. The term *behavior genetics* is perhaps unfortunate, because, as you will soon learn, many behavior-genetic designs are the optimal vehicles for demonstrating *environmental* influences (Waldman, 2007). Behavior-genetics research is easier to conduct on animals than humans because of the experimental control that is possible with animals (Plomin, DeFries, & McClearn, 1990). Nevertheless, powerful paradigms allow researchers to probe genetic influences on human behavior. Complete coverage of these approaches is beyond the scope of this chapter; interested readers should consult Plomin, DeFries, Craig, and McGuffin (2002) for more details.

Heritability

Heritability is the extent to which individual differences are attributable to genetic factors. Researchers subdivide genetic factors into additive and nonadditive genetic influences. *Additive genetic influences* involve the direct effects of genes, whereas *nonadditive genetic influences* involve gene interactions, including interactions within genes (*dominance*) and interactions among genes (*epistasis*). The distinction between additive and nonadditive genetic influences has implications for the definition of heritability. The term *broad heritability* refers to both additive and nonadditive genetic effects, and the term *narrow heritability* refers to additive genetic effects only (Loehlin, 1992).

The *heritability index* is the proportion of trait variability that is due to variability in genes. It ranges from 0.00 (no genetic influence) to 1.00 (variability due entirely to genes). Many people assume incorrectly that a high heritability means that environment will have little influence. In fact, high heritability only means that the environment *currently has* little influence, and it says nothing about the influence that the environment *might have*. For example, a recessive gene causes the genetic disorder phenylketonuria (PKU), which involves an enzyme deficiency that leads to severe mental retardation. This form of mental retardation had very high heritability until scientists learned more about the underlying mechanisms and proposed universal screening and the use of a rigid diet to avoid the intake of the destructive enzyme (phenylalanine) in vulnerable infants. Children with PKU who followed this diet no longer developed mental retardation. With the diet available and widely used, the heritability for the PKU mental retardation dropped dramatically, because the environment then had a profound influence on mental functioning, even when the PKU gene was present.

The heritability index is confusing in another sense. Many people believe that it indicates how much genes contribute to a trait. In fact, it indicates how much genes contribute to the *variability* of a trait. For example, you, along with virtually everyone else on earth, have two legs—a feature that is part of the genetic blueprint for the human body. Genes determine such basic physical features, yet the heritability for the number of legs is near zero. Why? Because there is almost no variability in the genes that affect the number of legs. If someone has only one leg, it is probably due to an accident (an environmental event) or toxic effects in utero (another environmental effect). Because there is essentially no variability in the genes that determine how many legs humans have, the heritability is zero, despite the fact that genes are clearly the reason that almost everyone has two legs.

Finally, heritability may be influenced by other nonheritable factors. For example, South and Krueger (2008) found that the influence of a heritable internalizing dimension, which affects disorders such as drug and alcohol abuse and antisocial personality disorder, is moderated by the satisfaction level of one's marriage. Such effects may well influence the heritability of many psychological conditions.

Demonstrating a Genetic Influence

Research on the heritability of disorders typically relies on one of three approaches: family, twin, or adoption paradigms. Each paradigm starts by sampling individuals with specific characteristics (called *probands*), who are selected by both diagnosis and specified nondiagnostic features. For example, in a twin study of panic disorder, probands would (a) have panic disorder and (b) be a twin. Researchers then identify and diagnose the proband's relevant relatives, with the definition of "relevant" depending on the paradigm. In twin studies, it would be the co-twin. The effectiveness of each paradigm rests on the quality of the sampling and on the accuracy of the diagnoses.

Sampling is critical because biased samples can produce misleading results. Random sampling is ideal, although true random sampling is rarely possible. A common strategy is to select all patients meeting the selection criteria admitted for treatment during a specified period. This approach avoids biases that may result from less systematic selection procedures, such as having professionals in the community refer suitable cases. For example, professionals may be more likely to refer a case if they know that there is an unusually high level of pathology in the patient's family. Most sampling approaches have biases. For example, selecting probands from state hospitals overrepresents individuals who lack the resources to live in the community and underrepresents individuals who can afford private treatment. Therefore, one should always detail the sampling procedures to allow other researchers to make informed judgments about potential biases.

Once probands are identified, the next task is to find and diagnose the relevant relatives. There are three approaches for making the diagnosis. The *family history method* uses the secondary reports of cooperative relatives to make the diagnosis. This is the least expensive, but also the least effective and the most biased approach. It tends to produce high false negative rates (not identifying affected family members) but low false positive rates (incorrectly labeling a family member as affected) (Andreasen, Endicott, Spitzer, & Winokur, 1977). The false negatives are probably due to family members not always being good observers of relevant behavior or simply being unaware of the relevant behavior.

The two most widely used diagnostic procedures are the *individual interview approach* (e.g., Gottesman & Shields, 1972) and the *records review approach* (e.g., Kety, Rosenthal, Wender, & Schulsinger, 1968). The most valid procedure, but also the most costly and time-consuming, is to interview each relative individually. When relatives are unavailable for an interview, secondary sources may be used, although analyses are traditionally carried out separately for (a) the primary data, obtained from direct interviews, and (b) the more complete data sets, in which some of the data are obtained from these secondary sources. A less costly approach is to rely on standardized records. Researchers often conduct behavior-genetics studies in countries with socialized medicine, such as Denmark, because these countries maintain extensive standardized medical and psychiatric records. Direct interviews tend to produce higher estimates of psychopathology than a review of hospital records. In general, the more extensive the information available, the more likely researchers will find evidence of pathology. Researchers typically include a comparison group and blindly evaluate all participants. Researchers form comparison groups by identifying participants who are identical to the probands, except for the diagnostic variable, and then finding their relevant family members.

In our review of these research designs, we will use the example of schizophrenia for consistency. However, researchers have used these paradigms to study most psychiatric disorders.

The Family Study Paradigm   This approach begins with probands with schizophrenia and then examines the prevalence of schizophrenia and related conditions (e.g., schizophrenia-spectrum disorders) in biological relatives. The data are organized by the degree of genetic relatedness to the proband. Parents, children, and full siblings (*first-degree relatives*) share, on average, 50% of the proband's genes; grandchildren, grandparents, half-siblings, aunts, and uncles (*second-degree relatives*) share, on average, 25% of the proband's genes; and cousins (*third-degree relatives*) share, on average, 12.5%. If schizophrenia is heritable, the rates of schizophrenia should vary by the degree of genetic relatedness to the schizophrenic proband. Researchers should always include a comparison group (i.e., family members of individuals who do not have schizophrenia) and conduct diagnostic evaluations blindly.

Genetic and environmental influences are confounded in family studies, so finding that psychopathology runs in families does not mean that genes are responsible. However, finding that psychopathology does not run in families all but rules out genetic influences, although it is remotely possible that nonadditive genetic influences exist (Lykken, McGue, Tellegen, & Bouchard, 1992).

The Twin Study Paradigm   Twin studies largely avoid the confounding of environmental and genetic influences by attempting to hold environment constant. This approach begins by identifying probands who (a) have developed schizophrenia and (b) have a twin raised in the same family. The proband's twin is classified as either identical (also called *monozygotic*, or *MZ*) or fraternal (*dizygotic*, or *DZ*). MZ twins share 100% of their genes, whereas DZ twins share 50% of their genes on average. Because environment and sex-linked genes can vary dramatically for men and women, typically only same-sex DZ twins are used (MZ twins are always same sex). When a proband's twin qualifies for a diagnosis of schizophrenia, the two are *concordant*. Researchers evaluate the influence of genes by comparing the concordance rates for the MZ and DZ twins. Because both the MZ and DZ twins are raised together, it is assumed that the environmental influences are approximately equal. Therefore, a difference in concordance rates should be due to the difference in level of shared genes. Some, but not all, researchers advocate correcting the raw concordance rates statistically to take into account the fact that it is twice as easy to sample a concordant twin pair as a nonconcordant pair, because a concordant pair has two potential probands in the population from which the sample is drawn.

A common misconception is that most twin studies use identical twins that have been separated at birth. Researchers have used this approach to study genetic influences (e.g., Johnson et al., 2007), but such twins are rare, and therefore this twin study design is also rare.

Over a dozen studies of schizophrenia used the twin study paradigm. For example, Gottesman and Shields (1972) identified 24 MZ twin pairs and 33 DZ twin pairs from consecutive admissions (1948–1963) at Maudsley Hospital in England. After determining zygosity (MZ vs. DZ), these investigators obtained extensive clinical information on each participant, including case histories, family histories, and personality inventories. They obtained independent and blind diagnoses for each of their participants from expert diagnosticians. They found that MZ twins showed consistently higher concordance than DZ twins, but the real strength of this study was that the data provided potential markers for genetic risk (i.e., schizophrenia-spectrum disorders), and their influence continues to be evident in the current diagnostic manual (*DSM-5*), which, like its predecessors, contains several presumed disorders in the schizophrenia spectrum, such as schizotypal and paranoid personality disorders.

The Adoption Study Paradigm This approach is used to study individuals who were separated from their biological parents at or near birth. For obvious ethical reasons, the separation is not under experimental control. One begins with probands who (a) have developed schizophrenia and (b) were adopted shortly after birth. These individuals have both a genetic heritage, contributed by their biological family, and an environmental heritage, contributed by their adoptive family. By comparing the rates of schizophrenia in both biological and adoptive relatives, one can gauge the relative contribution of genes and environment to the development of the disorder. The comparison group includes individuals who were adopted but never developed schizophrenia.

Kety et al. (1968) conducted an adoption study of schizophrenia using the remarkably complete record system in Denmark. They identified 33 probands, who had developed schizophrenia and were adopted shortly after birth, and a comparison group matched with these probands on a host of potential confounding variables (e.g., social class of adoptive and biological parents, age at adoption). They then obtained the psychiatric records for all biological and adoptive relatives, finding a fivefold elevated risk for schizophrenia in the biological relatives of the proband cases.

Kety et al.'s (1968) approach is known as the *adoptees' relatives approach*, because it begins with adopted schizophrenic probands and non-schizophrenic controls and examines the rates of psychopathology in their relatives. There are other adoption paradigms. For example, Rosenthal et al. (1968) investigated the risk for psychopathology in the adopted-away offspring of patients with schizophrenia, finding a 10-fold higher rate of schizophrenia in these offspring than in the comparison group. This approach is known as the *adoptees' study method*.

Cautionary Notes in Using These Paradigms Although twin and adoption paradigms provide powerful tests of genetic influence, they have limitations. For example, the assumption in twin studies that twins experience the same environment because they grow up together may not always be strictly true, although data suggest that it is usually true (Kendler, 1983). A potential problem with adoption studies is that social service agencies often eliminate potential adoptive parents who show signs of psychopathology, which tends to reduce the level of pathology in the adoptive relatives, although presumably this should affect the proband and comparison samples equally. In addition, adoption agencies often place adoptees with parents who are more similar to the adoptees' biological parents than would be expected by chance. Such *selective placement* can sometimes distort the findings of adoption studies. Researchers can sometimes deal with this problem by measuring the degree of selective placement and correcting for it statistically.

Different designs may yield different estimates of heritability. The heritability estimates derived from twin studies tend to be somewhat higher than estimates derived from adoption studies (Tellegen et al., 1988). One reason is that twin studies provide estimates of broad heritability, whereas adoption studies provide estimates of narrow heritability (Loehlin, 1992). The heritability estimates derived from twin studies may therefore provide the more accurate reflection of total genetic influences.

Finally, psychopathology researchers never control breeding as in animal research. It is unlikely that the random mating assumed by the statistical models actually occurs. Nonrandom mating (called *assortative mating*) distorts estimates of population parameters. Assortative mating may be common in psychopathology; for example, data show that individuals with schizophrenia are more likely to mate with individuals with schizophrenia spectrum disorders than would be expected by chance (Gottesman & Shields, 1982). Despite the limitations, these paradigms have produced reasonably consistent data on genetic influences for many types of psychopathology. The convergence of findings from diverse paradigms offers confidence in the results.

Probing the Nature of Genetic Influences

Population genetics is the study of departures from genetic equilibrium resulting from such factors as selective pressures, mutation, migration, or nonrandom mating. It focuses on population base rates and changes in those base rates over generations. A question of interest to population geneticists is the well-documented negative selection pressure in schizophrenia. Patients with schizophrenia have approximately half as many offspring as do individuals in the general population

(Gottesman, 1991), yet the rate of schizophrenia does not appear to be dropping dramatically from generation to generation. Such data make certain genetic models unlikely (e.g., single dominant-gene models).

Researchers also use genetic paradigms to identify the chromosomal locations for genetic defects. One such approach is the *linkage study*, in which researchers compare the pattern of transmission of a disorder with the pattern of transmission of other genetically determined characteristics for which the specific genes and their locations are known (see Schellenberg et al., 2006, for an example). The Human Genome Project has dramatically increased the number of identified human genes and their locations (DeLisi & Fleischhaker, 2007), making linkage studies much easier and more powerful. However, the small number of genes in the human genome (approximately 20,000) surprised most geneticists (Butler, 2010). They had expected more than four times that number. With so few genes influencing so many phenotypes, it is likely that most traits are due to complex interactions that are far more challenging to identify than single gene or additive gene effects.

The Human Genome Project has opened other avenues of exploration that may prove promising, such as genome-wide association studies (GWAS). These studies use the technology of gene sequencing to search for alleles (gene variations) that are associated with specific disorders. This approach has been used extensively for physical diseases and occasionally psychological disorders (e.g., Fanous et al., 2012). Although in principle a promising approach, early research with traits known to have strong heritability (e.g., height) have produced disappointing results (Maher, 2008), perhaps because of the complex gene interactions that are not easily uncovered by this method. Nevertheless, this is an example of a technological innovation that may provide fertile ground for psychopathology research in the near future.

Environmental Studies

Traditionally, psychopathologists have discussed the environment as if it were a monolithic or uniform entity. However, researchers recognize two types of environmental influences: shared and nonshared. *Shared environmental influences* make individuals within the same family similar to one another, whereas *nonshared environmental influences* make individuals within the same family different from one another. If a father is highly anxious and makes all of his children anxious through his parenting practices, his anxiety would be a shared environmental influence. Alternatively, if a parent severely mistreats one child, but not another child, and the mistreated child becomes more emotionally maladjusted in later life as a result of the parental mistreatment, this would be a nonshared environmental influence. This distinction is critical, because evidence indicates that nonshared, but not shared, environmental influences play a major role in the etiology of most mental disorders and personality traits (Bouchard, Lykken, McGue, Segal, & Tellegen, 1990; Plomin, 1990).

Behavior-Genetic Studies   Behavior-genetic designs can provide a sensitive platform for studying both shared and nonshared environmental influences (Loehlin, 1992). For example, the similarity between adoptive parents and their adopted offspring on a trait can be interpreted, in the absence of selective placement, as an estimate of the influence of shared environment on this trait, because the only factor accounting for their resemblance is environment. The discordance rate of MZ twins can be interpreted as an estimate of nonshared environmental influence. Because MZ twins share 100% of their genes, the only factor accounting for their discordance is environmental. Indeed, the study of MZ twins discordant for schizophrenia has provided a fertile ground for studying potential nonshared environmental influences (e.g., Torrey, Bowler, Taylor, & Gottesman, 1994). However, these estimates of nonshared environment typically include errors of measurement (Loehlin, 1992). Thus, if one's diagnoses of schizophrenia are unreliable, this will decrease the MZ twin concordance rate and increase the estimate of nonshared environmental influence. Note that, although we tend to think of "environment" as one's social environment, it refers to any post-conception influence and might well include differences in diet, medical history, or differences in the womb.

Correlational Studies   Correlational studies can be thought of as extensions of epidemiological studies. In epidemiological studies, one often finds that hypothesized causal variables are associated with increased risk for a disorder. Demonstrating a correlation between a hypothesized causal element and the presence of psychopathology provides evidence consistent with one's hypothesis. Nevertheless, every undergraduate research methods textbook warns, and for good reason, that *correlation does not imply causality*. Variables A and B may be correlated because (1) A causes B, (2) B causes A, (3) or some third variable, C, causes both A and B. Because C could be anything, there is a nearly infinite number of possible causal interpretations of a correlation. Still, it can be tempting to overinterpret a correlation because the favored causal hypothesis seems so plausible. Note that, although a correlation does not necessarily imply causation, causation implies a correlation. Thus, if a variable does not correlate with risk, the hypothesis that this variable is involved in the etiology of the disorder is highly unlikely.

Quasi-experimental designs are a variation of correlational designs. The groups in quasi-experiments are preexisting and not formed through random assignment; instead, they are determined through measurement (e.g., diagnosis). Therefore, clinicians are looking at the correlation between the measurement that determined the group and the measurement of the variables under study.

Longitudinal Studies   Researchers can look for variables that may be part of a disorder's causal chain by using a quasi-experimental design to identify events or traits that reliably precede the onset of the disorder but are not found, or are less likely, in people who do not develop the disorder. There are two types of such studies. In *prospective studies*, researchers follow individuals *longitudinally*, measuring the variables of interest as they occur, and then waiting to see who develops the disorder. In *retrospective studies*, researchers look into the history of people who either did or did not develop the disorder to find variables that differentiate these groups. Retrospective studies are easier to conduct, but they are notoriously prone to memory distortions. For example, how much more likely is it that parents will remember traumatic events in their child's history if that child later develops severe agoraphobia?

We all try to understand our situation by finding things in our past that could explain how the situation developed, and this process, sometimes called "effort after meaning," tends to emphasize some historical events while de-emphasizing others. This is a variation of the illusory correlation phenomenon discussed earlier, and it often distorts retrospective data. However, sometimes we can conduct a retrospective study as if it were prospective. For example, school or medical records are recorded when they occur, but those records may be available years later to inspect in a retrospective study. The advantage of this approach is that it reduces the retrospective bias; the disadvantage is that it is unlikely that the information recorded in such records is optimal for testing the causal hypothesis that the researcher had in mind.

Analogue Studies Manipulating environmental variables is the most direct test of an environmental hypothesis. We have already discussed the *analogue study*, which is an ethically acceptable way to perform this manipulation. For example, several environmental manipulations (e.g., relaxed attention, speeded performance), referred to as *schizomimetic* conditions, produce temporary and mild symptoms of psychosis (see Chapman & Chapman, 1973, for a review). A positive finding in such analogue studies indicates that the variable under study *could* create such symptoms, but not that the symptoms normally develop in this way (McCall, 1977). For example, by providing selective reinforcement and sufficiently powerful incentives, investigators could probably get college students to bark like dogs, but no one would entertain the notion that such data indicate that dogs bark because of selective reinforcement.

Computer Simulations Many investigators have used computer simulations to study neurocognitive processes, and some investigators have used this approach to study psychopathology. For example, Cohen and Servan-Schreiber (1992) used mathematical models in a series of studies of schizophrenic psychopathology. These investigators showed that a single manipulation of their computer models reproduced performance patterns found in people with schizophrenia on three different tasks (Stroop, Continuous Performance Test, and a lexical ambiguity task). They took what neuroscientists know about how the brain is wired (i.e., interconnected), what they know about the role of dopamine in normal brain activity (i.e., a modulatory effect), and the fact that dopamine appears important in schizophrenia, and used that information to simulate several dysfunctions found in schizophrenia by manipulating the single parameter associated with the action of dopamine. Previously, researchers had explained the dysfunctional patterns on these three tasks with different constructs. Cohen and Servan-Schreiber (1992) needed only a single construct. Such parsimonious explanations are highly prized by scientists (Popper, 1959). There have been few computer simulation studies in psychopathology, but as our understanding of cognitive functioning improves, it is likely that these approaches will provide insights into how these processes are disrupted in psychological disorders.

Biological Studies

Biological studies provide invaluable insights into the nature of disorders and their mechanisms. We discuss here three biological approaches: psychophysiological research methods, brain imaging technologies, and neuropsychology.

Psychophysiological Research Methods

Psychophysiology is the study of involuntary physiological responses that may be affected by psychological processes (Lykken, 1982). These responses are somewhat foggy windows into psychological states, because many factors influence these physiological responses. For example, a person's brain is engaged in a host of activities in addition to responding to the researcher's stimuli.

Psychophysiology differs from *physiological psychology* in that the former typically uses behavioral independent variables and physiological dependent variables, whereas the latter typically uses physiological independent variables and behavioral dependent variables (Stern, 1964). For example, psychophysiologists might administer stressful stimuli and monitor skin conductance changes, whereas physiological psychologists might lesion a rat's limbic system and examine changes in aggression.

The fundamental armamentarium of the modern psychophysiologist includes a polygraph, a variety of electrodes and transducers, and one or more computers. A *polygraph* is a multichannel device that records physiological signals, such as heart rate and brain activity. The polygraph amplifies these signals and filters them to eliminate extraneous noise. These signals can be routed to pens, producing the "squiggles" so familiar to psychophysiologists. However, today's researchers are much more likely to send them directly to a computer via an *analogue to digital (A/D) converter*, a device that transforms signals into numerical form. Virtually all psychophysiology laboratories today are automated.

Polygraph signals come from either electrodes or transducers. *Electrodes* are typically small metal disks placed on the person's skin to record electrical signals—either those produced by the person (e.g., the electroencephalograph) or those passed through part of the person's body (e.g., skin conductance). *Transducers* convert changes in temperature, pressure, or other forms of energy to electrical signals. For example, a strain gauge changes its electrical resistance in response to chest motions during respiration (Stern, Ray, & Quigley, 2001).

The polygraph can record such reactions as skin conductance (SC), heart rate (HR), blood pressure (BP), brain waves (electroencephalography [EEG]), muscle activity (electromyography [EMG]), eye movements (electrooculography [EOG]), respiration, and pupillary dilation. We will focus on SC, HR, and EEG because researchers have studied these three variables in many disorders. Because of space constraints, we will not review psychophysiological variables that are relevant primarily to a single disorder. Two such examples are smooth pursuit eye movement dysfunction (SPEM) in schizophrenia (e.g., McDowell & Clementz, 2001) and facial muscle monitoring in depression (e.g., Kring & Sloan, 2007).

Skin Conductance   The eccrine sweat glands, found mostly on our palms and soles, are activated by the sympathetic nervous system and are therefore responsive primarily to psychological stimulation. Consequently, psychologists can use the activity of these glands to measure arousal. They differ from the apocrine glands of the armpits and pubic area, which are primarily responsive to temperature. Because sweat facilitates the flow of electrical current, we can measure the amount of sweating by passing a weak current (≈ 0.5 volts) between electrodes placed on the fingers and measuring changes in conductance (Lykken & Venables, 1971).

There are several skin conductance measures. The *SCL* (skin conductance level) refers to a slow (*tonic*) change in electrodermal activity, which typically reflects the person's state of arousal.

The *SCR* (skin conductance response) refers to a rapid (*phasic*) change in electrodermal activity in response to an external stimulus. Fowles (1980) argued that SCR activity is an indicator of sensitivity to signals of punishment or threat. The *SSCR* (spontaneous skin conductance response) is a phasic response in the absence of identifiable external stimulation. Dawson, Schell, and Filion (1990) argue that the frequency of SSCR fluctuations may be a marker of arousal, anxiety, or both.

Psychopathology researchers use SC measures extensively. For example, some patients with schizophrenia (hyporesponders) exhibit diminished electrodermal reactions, whereas others (hyperresponders) exhibit excessive electrodermal reactions (Katkin & Hastrup, 1982). This finding may help to clarify the etiological heterogeneity of schizophrenia, because hyporesponders are more likely to show a negative symptom pattern, whereas hyperresponders are more likely to show a positive symptom pattern (Cannon, Mednick, & Parnas, 1990). Researchers have also studied SC measures in psychopaths, who typically exhibit smaller SCRs in classical conditioning paradigms involving aversive stimuli (Lykken, 1957) and lower SCLs and fewer SSCRs in anticipation of aversive stimuli (e.g., Lorber, 2004).

Heart Rate   The contraction of the heart's left ventricle (the *systolic* phase) is triggered by a strong electrical impulse. The *diastolic* phase occurs between contractions. The electrical signal triggering the heart contraction is typically measured by placing electrodes on the right arm and the left leg (Stern et al., 2001). This configuration of electrodes, called *Lead II*, is highly sensitive to the electrical innervation of the left ventricle (termed *R spike*) of the *electrocardiogram* (EKG), which precedes contraction by approximately 50 milliseconds (Katkin & Hastrup, 1982). A device known as a *cardiotachometer* calculates the time difference between successive R spikes and converts it to heart rate (HR).

Researchers use HR measures extensively in psychopathology research. For example, criminal and pre-criminal individuals tend to exhibit lower resting HRs than do other individuals (Raine, 1993), and psychopaths tend to exhibit larger HR responses than do nonpsychopaths in anticipation of aversive stimuli (Hare & Quinn, 1971). This latter finding seems to run counter to studies demonstrating lower SCL in psychopaths prior to aversive stimuli, illustrating a phenomenon known as *directional fractionation* (Lacey, 1967), in which different indicators of arousal change in opposite directions. How can we explain this directional fractionation in psychopaths? According to the *intake-rejection hypothesis* (Lacey & Lacey, 1978), HR decreases reflect increased attention (i.e., intake) and HR increases reflect decreased attention (i.e., rejection; for a contrasting view, see Obrist, 1976). Thus, psychopaths' HR increases in anticipation of aversive stimuli may indicate attempts to reduce environmental input, and their low SCLs may indicate that such attempts are successful (Hare, 1978).

EEG   The human brain weighs roughly 3 pounds and contains approximately 100 billion neurons. Neuronal activity creates electrical fields that extend beyond the cells, and we can detect the simultaneous firing of these neurons by placing electrodes on a person's scalp to produce the *EEG*. The EEG record is typically subdivided by frequency: *Delta* waves are 1 to 3 cycles per second (cps); *theta* waves are 4 to 7 cps; *alpha* waves are 8 to 12 cps; and *beta* waves are 13 cps or above. These waves are associated with different states of consciousness. Although it is possible to assess these rhythms by inspecting the raw EEG record, modern psychophysiologists use a *Fourier transformation*, which is a mathematical decomposition of brain waves into their component frequencies (Stern et al., 2001).

Psychophysiologists may examine *resting* EEG activity (brain waves present when the person is not engaged in a task) or *evoked responses* to discrete stimuli (e.g., tones, lights). Evoked responses are almost never observable in the raw EEG record; these small responses are swamped by the other activities of the brain. Researchers measure evoked responses by repeatedly presenting an identical stimulus and then averaging the EEG responses to these presentations. The rationale for this averaging procedure is that the EEG activity that is irrelevant to the stimulus, which is presumably "random," cancels out, whereas the EEG response to the stimulus is the same with each presentation. This averaged EEG signal is known as an *event-related potential* (ERP) and is believed to be a relatively pure measure of the brain's response to a stimulus.

An ERP typically consists of several wave components, which researchers categorize along two parameters: (1) their voltage (positive or negative) and (2) the time lag following the stimulus. An N100 wave component, for example, is a negative voltage occurring approximately 100 milliseconds following stimulus onset. Early ERP components are believed to reflect sensory processing, whereas later ERP components are believed to reflect higher-order cognitive processing (Katkin & Hastrup, 1982).

One ERP component that has received considerable attention in the psychopathology literature is the *P300*. The P300 is most commonly elicited by means of an "oddball" paradigm, in which an aberrant stimulus (e.g., low-frequency tone) is presented periodically, although rarely, amid a large number of identical stimuli (e.g., high-frequency tones). Although controversy persists regarding the P300's functional significance, there is an emerging consensus that it indicates a revision of one's mental model of the environment (Donchin & Coles, 1988; Patrick, Curtin, & Krueger, 2008).

Aberrant resting EEGs are found in several psychological disorders. Patients with schizophrenia, for example, tend to exhibit reduced levels of alpha and increased levels of delta activity in their resting EEGs (Iacono, 1982; Sponheim, Clementz, Iacono, & Beiser, 1994), and psychopaths tend to exhibit elevated levels of theta waves in their resting EEGs (Syndulko, 1978). Because theta waves are often associated with boredom or drowsiness, psychopaths' high levels of theta may reflect low anxiety. Depressed individuals exhibit less left frontal EEG alpha activity than that of nondepressed individuals (Henriques & Davidson, 1991), which may reflect a deficit in biologically based approach systems.

Several ERP components show considerable promise in the study of psychopathology. Begleiter, Porjesz, Bihari, and Kissin (1984), for example, found that sons of alcoholics exhibited lower P300s compared with sons of nonalcoholic parents, although this finding has not been uniformly replicated (e.g., Polich & Bloom, 1988). More recent data suggest that the P300 response may be a nonspecific marker of a host of comorbid conditions that reflect disinhibition (e.g., alcohol use disorder, conduct disorder, and antisocial personality disorder) (Patrick et al., 2006). Jutai and Hare (1983) reported that psychopaths exhibited lower N100s than that of nonpsychopaths in response to video game tones. Because the N100 may reflect selective attention (Coles, Gratton, & Fabiani, 1990), Jutai and Hare have suggested that psychopaths tend to ignore extraneous stimuli when engaged in tasks of immediate interest.

Brain Imaging Technology

It is helpful to document the brain structure and functioning in people suffering from psychopathology. Prior to modern imaging techniques, psychologists had to rely on autopsies or crude imaging techniques. Not surprisingly, few patients consent to a premature autopsy, even in the name of science, and the first imaging technique (the pneumoencephalogram) was painful, risky, and crude. Modern brain imaging technology produces clear images at a reasonable cost and with minimal risk and discomfort.

Observing Brain Structure   *CAT scans* (computerized axial tomography) and *MRIs* (magnetic resonance imaging) produce detailed pictures of the structure of the brain. Both techniques take images from multiple angles, using X-rays in the case of the CAT scan and magnetic properties of certain atoms in the case of the MRI. A mathematical technique converts these multiple images into a three-dimensional (3-D) representation of the brain, a technique so ingenious that it led to a Nobel Prize. Investigators can manipulate this 3-D image to produce detailed images of any section of the brain. Brain imaging techniques have been used to investigate structural abnormalities in individuals with schizophrenia (e.g., Sudath, Christison, Torrey, Casanova, & Weinberger, 1990) and relatives of people with schizophrenia (Boos, Aleman, Cahn, Pol, & Kahn, 2007), and in personality disorders (e.g., Goyer, Konicki, & Schulz, 1994) and drug abuse (Baicy & London, 2007), to name but a few.

Observing Brain Functioning   Detailed pictures of the brain are of little value unless a structural abnormality exists. If the structure is normal, but the functioning is abnormal, procedures that can observe brain functioning are necessary. We have already discussed one measure of brain functioning (the EEG). Two additional measures of brain functioning are the *fMRI* (functional MRI) and the *PET scan* (positron emission tomography). fMRI is used to examine changes in the magnetic properties of brain regions as an indication of the level of activity. PET involves use of harmless radioactive isotopes, which brain tissue absorbs in proportion to its activity level. All of these measures, including the EEG, facilitate investigation of unusual patterns of brain activity. Over- or underactivation of a brain region may suggest deficits in that region or a compensatory response to a deficit in another region. These techniques have been used to investigate dysfunctions in depression (e.g., Kravitz & Newman, 1995), schizophrenia (e.g., Liddle, 1995), and addiction (e.g., Aron & Paulus, 2007), among other conditions. One concern with brain image studies is the high rates of Type I errors (false positives) stemming from the large number of statistical comparisons often conducted (e.g., Vul, Harris, Winkeilman, & Pashler, 2009). As a consequence, independent replication of brain imaging findings is crucial.

In the study of brain functioning, researchers want to maximize both *temporal* and *spatial resolution* (i.e., the sensitivity of the methods to timing and location of a brain action, respectively). The EEG has outstanding temporal resolution (measured in milliseconds), whereas functional imaging techniques have temporal resolutions measured in seconds or even minutes. The strength of functional imaging is its spatial resolution. The best technique depends on the nature of the research question, and combining techniques may provide uniquely informative data (e.g., Pizzagalli et al., 2001).

Neuropsychology

Neuropsychology uses detailed measures of behavior to infer the functional integrity of the brain. For example, right-side weakness and an inability to speak would suggest damage to the posterior left frontal lobe. The proper combination of neuropsychological measures can tap deficits in most regions of the cerebral cortex. Covering even the basics of neuropsychology is impossible in such a brief chapter, but several excellent texts are available (e.g., Lezak, Howieson, Bigler, & Tranel, 2012; Morgan & Ricker, 2008).

Psychopathology researchers have used neuropsychological measures extensively. For example, there are studies of executive function in depression (Elderkin-Thompson, Mintz, Haroon, Lavretsky, & Kumar, 2006), general neurological functioning in recovered alcoholics (Davies et al., 2005), and changes in general neurological functioning during the early stages of schizophrenia (Albus et al., 2006). Neuropsychological measures connect psychopathology researchers to a heavily validated research program on brain functioning, which can take a simple pattern of test score deficits in a disorder and suggest which brain mechanisms likely contributed to that pattern.

High-Risk Research Approaches

Longitudinal designs have a unique advantage in psychopathology research. Following people over time allows us to observe the developmental course of a disorder and to measure the factors that influence that course. However, longitudinal designs are costly and time-consuming. They are efficient when studying processes that virtually all people experience, because each individual provides valuable data. However, few randomly selected individuals develop a specific psychiatric disorder. The base rates for most psychiatric disorders range from 10% to a small fraction of 1%. For disorders such as schizophrenia or bipolar disorder, researchers would need to follow 10,000 initially unaffected individuals for 20+ years to obtain 100 people who develop the disorder.

An alternative is the *high-risk paradigm* (Mednick & Schulsinger, 1968), which uses information about a disorder to select people at elevated risk for the disorder. For example, Mednick and Schulsinger studied offspring of mothers with schizophrenia, because approximately 10% of these offspring will develop schizophrenia—a 10-fold improvement in the yield of a longitudinal study. They called their approach the *genetic high-risk paradigm*, because it relied on selecting participants on the basis of their genetic relationship to an affected individual. In an alternative approach—the *behavioral high-risk paradigm* (e.g., Chapman, Chapman, Raulin, & Edell, 1978)—at-risk individuals are selected on the basis of behavioral characteristics.

Genetic High-Risk Paradigm

The genetic high-risk paradigm traditionally assumes a genetic contribution to a disorder. However, all researchers need to know is that there is an elevated risk in family members, which could be due to genes, shared environment, or both. They select their "at-risk" group on the basis of both their familial relationship to someone with the disorder and their age. Age is important

because most disorders have well-defined *age-of-risk profiles* (the cumulative frequency graph of the age of the first appearance of the disorder). If most people develop a disorder in their 20s, then one wants to select individuals just prior to that period of risk. Selecting older participants will leave out those who have already developed the disorder, and selecting younger participants will increase the time that one must wait to determine which participants develop the disorder. However, if one suspects that critical elements in the causal chain occur well before the development of the disorder, it may be desirable to select a younger sample despite the added cost of following the sample longer. A comparison sample is selected, which is usually matched on variables that might confound the results (e.g., age, sex, social class). Then the researchers evaluate and follow both groups.

The initial evaluation of the at-risk and comparison participants provides a basis for an immediate test of certain hypotheses. Predisposing factors for the disorder should be overrepresented in the at-risk group. The sensitivity of this comparison depends on the proportion of individuals in the at-risk group who truly have an elevated risk of developing the disorder. For example, clinicians know that roughly 10% of the offspring of mothers with schizophrenia will develop schizophrenia. Nevertheless, that figure is probably an underestimate of the number of individuals with an elevated risk for schizophrenia, because it is unlikely that every individual with an elevated risk will actually develop the disorder. As noted earlier, the concordance rate for MZ twins (about 50%) demonstrates that nonshared environmental factors influence risk. Therefore, researchers would expect at least 20% of the offspring of mothers with schizophrenia to possess genetic risk factor(s) for schizophrenia. Actually, the figure is probably higher, because discordant MZ twins presumably share not only the specific genetic risk factor(s) for schizophrenia but also other genetically influenced characteristics—what Meehl (1990) called *polygenic potentiators*—that further increase their risk. Note that the logic of this paradigm does not depend on knowing which individuals in the at-risk group are truly at risk, but only that the at-risk and comparison groups differ in the base rate of the risk factor(s). Identifying groups at differential risk allows us to identify potentially superior selection variables for future studies, a process dubbed *bootstrapping* (Cronbach & Meehl, 1955; Dawes & Meehl, 1966).

Even through researchers can use bootstrapping operations without waiting to see who develops the disorder, the more significant advantages of the design derive from its longitudinal approach. For example, Mednick and Schulsinger (1968) matched their participants in triplets on several potential confounding variables (two at-risk individuals and one comparison individual). So each individual who developed schizophrenia could be compared with both an individual not at risk and a second individual who was at risk but did not succumb to the disorder.

Behavioral High-Risk Paradigm

Identifying at-risk individuals on the basis of their familial relationship to someone with the disorder is one approach, but some disorders have weak genetic or shared familial contributions. Even when there is a strong genetic or shared familial component, the genetic high-risk approach may produce a biased sample. For example, 95% of all individuals who develop schizophrenia do not have a schizophrenic parent (Gottesman & Shields, 1972), and the genetic high-risk approach excludes them. An alternative—the *behavioral high-risk paradigm*—identifies at-risk samples based on behavior or life experiences. For example, Chapman et al. (1978) identified individuals presumed to be at risk for schizophrenia on the basis of characteristics suggested by Meehl (1964) (e.g., anhedonia and body-image aberration). Follow-up studies confirmed that these individuals are at elevated risk for severe psychopathology, although not always schizophrenia (Chapman, Chapman, Kwapil, Eckblad, & Zinser, 1994; Kwapil et al., 2000). Nevertheless, long before the follow-up studies, dozens of construct validation studies suggested that individuals with these traits exhibited characteristics one might expect to find in someone at elevated risk for schizophrenia, such as mild forms of psychotic symptoms (e.g., Chapman et al., 1978), poor social functioning (e.g., Beckfield, 1985), and schizophrenic-like cognitive processing deficits (e.g., Simons, 1981). The behavioral high-risk strategy has also been used successfully to study risk for bipolar disorder (e.g., Klein & Depue, 1984).

Conclusion

In this chapter, we reviewed research methods used to identify the correlates and causes of mental disorders. Two consistent themes guided this chapter. First, psychopathology is almost certainly multiply determined and probably involves a complex interplay of genetic and environmental influences. Second, each methodology has its own advantages and disadvantages. Both of these considerations suggest that the ideal research program in psychopathology incorporates several methodological approaches. By utilizing several approaches, researchers can uncover converging evidence regarding the etiology of a disorder. Because each design is best suited for detecting certain causal factors, it is unlikely that a single design will ever provide a complete picture of the etiology of a disorder. For example, although epidemiological methods are well suited for ascertaining risk factors for psychopathology, they generally provide little information about genetic or environmental contributions. In turn, although behavior-genetic methods are well suited for ascertaining the relative genetic and environmental influences, they generally tell little about how these influences increase risk for a disorder. Psychophysiological, neuropsychological, and brain-imaging studies can provide this information. In addition, because each of the methodological approaches discussed in this chapter has liabilities and potential biases, an exclusive reliance on one approach will often result in misleading conclusions.

Because of these limitations, psychopathology investigators have increasingly turned to hybrid designs that simultaneously incorporate multiple methodologies. For example, high-risk researchers have included measures of psychophysiological and neuropsychological functioning in their investigations. Behavior-genetic researchers have included explicit measures of environmental factors in their studies, including those emphasized by epidemiologists (e.g., social class and education level). Only through a process of painstakingly piecing together evidence from a variety of admittedly imperfect approaches can investigators hope to arrive at a better understanding of the causes of psychopathology.

References

Akins, C. K., & Panicker, S. (2012). Ethics and the regulation of research with nonhuman animals. In H. Cooper, P. M. Camic, D. L. Long, A. T. Panter, D. Rindskopf, & K. J. Sher (Eds.), *APA handbook of research methods in psychology. Volume*

1: *Foundations, planning, measures, and psychometric* (pp. 75–82). Washington, DC: American Psychological Association.

Albus, M., Hubmann, W., Mohr, F., Hecht, S., Hinterberger-Weber, P., Seitz, N., & Kůchenhoff, H. (2006). Neurocognitive functioning in patients with first-episode schizophrenia: Results of a prospective 5-year follow-up study. *European Archives of Psychiatry and Clinical Neuroscience, 256,* 442–451.

Algozzine, B., & Ysseldyke, J. (2006). *Teaching students with mental retardation: A practical guide for every teacher.* Thousand Oaks, CA: Corwin Press.

Andreasen, N. C., Endicott, J., Spitzer, R. L., & Winokur, G. (1977). The family history method using diagnostic criteria: Reliability and validity. *Archives of General Psychiatry, 34,* 1229–1235.

Aron, J. L., & Paulus, M. P. (2007). Location, location: Using functional magnetic resonance imaging to pinpoint brain differences relevant to stimulant use. *Addiction, 102*(Suppl. 1), 33–43.

Baicy, K., & London, E. D. (2007). Corticolimbic dysregulation and chronic methamphetamine abuse. *Addiction, 102*(Suppl. 1), 5–15.

Barlow, D. H. (2002). *Anxiety and its disorders: The nature and treatment of anxiety and panic* (2nd ed.). New York: Guilford Press.

Barlow, D. H., Nock, M., & Hersen, M. (2009). *Single case experimental designs: Strategies for studying behavioral change* (3rd ed.). New York: Pearson/Allyn & Bacon.

Beckfield, D. F. (1985). Interpersonal competence among college men hypothesized to be at risk for schizophrenia. *Journal of Abnormal Psychology, 94,* 397–404.

Begleiter, H., Porjesz, B., Bihari, B., & Kissin, B. (1984). Event-related brain potentials in boys at risk for alcoholism. *Science, 225,* 1493–1496.

Berkson, J. (1946). Limitations of the application of four-fold table analysis to hospital data. *Biometrics, 2,* 247–253.

Boos, H. B., Aleman, A., Cahn, W., Pol, H. H., & Kahn, R. S. (2007). Brain volumes in relatives of patients with schizophrenia: A meta-analysis. *Archives of General Psychiatry, 64,* 297–304.

Bouchard, T. J., Lykken, D. T., McGue, M., Segal, N. L., & Tellegen, A. (1990). Sources of human psychological differences: The Minnesota Study of Twins Reared Apart. *Science, 250,* 223–228.

Burke, J. D., & Regier, D. A. (1996). Epidemiology of mental disorders. In R. E. Hales & S.

C. Yudofsky (Eds.), *The American Psychiatric Press synopsis of psychiatry* (pp. 79–102). Washington, DC: American Psychiatric Association.

Butler, D. (2010). Human genome at ten: Science after the sequence. *Nature, 465,* 1000–1001.

Cadoret, R. J., Cain, C. A., & Crowe, R. R. (1983). Evidence for gene–environment interaction in the development of adolescent antisocial behavior. *Behavior Genetics, 13,* 301–310.

Campbell, D. T., & Fiske, D. W. (1959). Convergent and discriminant validation by the multitrait-multimethod matrix. *Psychological Bulletin, 56,* 81–105.

Cannon, T. D., Mednick, S. A., & Parnas, J. (1990). Two pathways to schizophrenia in children at risk. In L. N. Robins & M. Rutter (Eds.), *Straight and devious pathways from childhood to adulthood* (pp. 328–350). New York: Cambridge University Press.

Carbone, L. (2004). *What animals want: Expertise and advocacy in laboratory animal welfare policy.* New York: Oxford University Press.

Chapman, L. J., & Chapman, J. P. (1967). Genesis of popular but erroneous psychodiagnostic observations. *Journal of Abnormal Psychology, 72,* 193–204.

Chapman, L. J., & Chapman, J. P. (1969). Illusory correlation as an obstacle to the use of valid psychodiagnostic signs. *Journal of Abnormal Psychology, 74,* 271–280.

Chapman, L. J., & Chapman, J. P. (1973). *Disordered thought in schizophrenia.* Englewood Cliffs, NJ: Prentice Hall.

Chapman, L. J., Chapman, J. P., Kwapil, T. R., Eckblad, M., & Zinser, M. C. (1994). Putatively psychosis-prone subjects 10 years later. *Journal of Abnormal Psychology, 103,* 171–183.

Chapman, L. J., Chapman, J. P., Raulin, M. R., & Edell, W. S. (1978). Schizotypy and thought disorder as a high risk approach to schizophrenia. In G. Serban (Ed.), *Cognitive defects in the development of mental illness* (pp. 351–360). New York: Brunner/Mazel.

Cohen, J. A. (1960). A coefficient for agreement for nominal scales. *Educational and Psychological Measurement, 20,* 37–46.

Cohen, J. D., & Servan-Schreiber, D. (1992). Context, cortex, and dopamine: A connectionist approach to behavior and biology in schizophrenia. *Psychological Review, 99,* 45–77.

Coles, M. G. H., Gratton, G., & Fabiani, M. (1990). Event-related brain potentials. In J. T. Cacioppo & L. G. Tassinary (Eds.), *Principles of psychophysiology: Physical, social, and inferential elements* (pp. 413–455). New York: Cambridge University Press.

Costello, E. J. (1990). Child psychiatric epidemiology: Implications for clinical research and practice. In B. B. Lahey & A. E. Kazdin (Eds.), *Advances in clinical child psychology* (Vol. 13, pp. 53–90). New York: Plenum Press.

Coyne, J. C. (1994). Self-reported distress: Analogue or ersatz depression? *Psychological Bulletin, 116*, 20–45.

Cronbach, L. J., & Meehl, P. E. (1955). Construct validity in psychology tests. *Psychological Bulletin, 52*, 281–301.

Dabbs, J. M., & Morris, R. (1990). Testosterone, social class, and antisocial behavior in a sample of 4,462 men. *Psychological Science, 1*, 209–211.

Davies, S. J. C., Pandit, S. A., Feeney, A., Stevenson, B. J., Kervin, R. W., Nutt, D. J.,…Lingford-Hughes, A. (2005). Is there cognitive impairment in clinically "healthy" abstinent alcohol dependence? *Alcohol and Alcoholism, 40*, 498–503.

Dawes, R. M., & Meehl, P. E. (1966). Mixed group validation: A method for determining the validity of diagnostic signs without using criterion groups. *Psychological Bulletin, 66*, 63–67.

Dawson, M. E., Schell, A. M., & Filion, D. L. (1990). The electrodermal system. In J. T. Cacioppo & L. G. Tasinary (Eds.), *Principles of psychophysiology: Physical, social, and inferential elements* (pp. 295–324). New York: Cambridge University Press.

DeLisi, L. E., & Fleischhaker, W. (2007). Schizophrenia research in the era of the genome, 2007. *Current Opinions in Psychiatry, 20*, 109–110.

Depue, R. A., & Monroe, S. M. (1978). The unipolar-bipolar distinction in the depressive disorders. *Psychological Bulletin, 85*, 1001–1029.

Donchin, E., & Coles, M. G. (1988). Is the P300 component a manifestation of context updating? *Behavioral and Brain Sciences, 11*, 357–427.

Du Fort, G. G., Newman, S. C., & Bland, R. C. (1993). Psychiatric comorbidity and treatment seeking: Sources of selection bias in the study of clinical populations. *Journal of Nervous and Mental Disease, 181*, 467–474.

Eaton, N., Krueger, R. F., South, C., Simms, L. J., & Clark, L. A. (2011). Contrasting prototypes and dimensions in the classification of personality pathology: Evidence that dimensions, but not prototypes, are robust. *Psychological Medicine, 41*, 1151–1163.

Elderkin-Thompson, V., Mintz, J., Haroon, E., Lavretsky, H., & Kumar, A. (2006). Executive dysfunction and memory in older patients with major and minor depression. *Archives of Clinical Neuropsychology, 21*, 669–676.

Fanous, A. H. et al. (2012). Genome-wide association study of clinical dimensions of schizophrenia: Polygenic effect on disorganized symptoms. *American Journal of Psychiatry, 169*, 1309–1317.

Faris, R. E. L., & Dunham, H. W. (1939). *Mental disorders in urban areas*. Chicago: University of Chicago Press.

Feinstein, A. R. (1985). *Clinical epidemiology: The architecture of clinical research*. Philadelphia: Saunders.

Finn, S. E., & Kamphuis, J. H. (1995). What a clinician needs to know about base rates. In J. Butcher (Ed.), *Clinical personality assessment: Practical approaches* (pp. 224–235). New York: Oxford University Press.

First, M. B., Spitzer, R. L., Gibbon, M., & Williams, J. B. W. (2013). *Structured clinical interview for DSM-5 Axis I disorders administration booklet*. New York: American Psychiatric Press.

Fowles, D. C. (1980). The three arousal model: Implications of Gray's two-factor learning theory for heart rate, electrodermal activity, and psychopathy. *Psychophysiology, 17*, 87–104.

Freeman, J. (1979). *Gifted children*. Lancaster, UK: Medical Technical Press.

Fromm-Reichman, F. (1948). Notes on the development of treatments of schizophrenics by psychoanalytic psychotherapy. *Psychiatry, 2*, 263–273.

Gilovich, T. (1991). *How we know what isn't so: The fallibility of human reason in everyday life*. New York: Free Press.

Goodwin, D. W., & Guze, S. B. (1989). *Psychiatric diagnosis* (4th ed.). New York: Oxford University Press.

Gorenstein, E. E. (1982). Frontal lobe functions in psychopaths. *Journal of Abnormal Psychology, 91*, 368–379.

Gorman, J. M., Liebowitz, M. R., Fyer, A. J., & Stein, J. (1989). A neuroanatomical hypothesis for panic disorder. *American Journal of Psychiatry, 146*, 148–161.

Gottesman, I. I. (1991). *Schizophrenia genesis: The origins of madness*. New York: Freeman.

Gottesman, I. I., & Shields, J. (1972). *Schizophrenia and genetics: A twin study vantage point*. New York: Academic Press.

Gottesman, I. I., & Shields, J. (1982). *Schizophrenia: The epigenetic puzzle*. New York: Cambridge University Press.

Goyer, P. F., Konicki, P. E., & Schulz, S. C. (1994). Brain imaging in personality disorders. In

K. R. Silk (Ed.), *Biological and neurobehavioral studies of borderline personality disorder. Progress in Psychiatry*, No. 45 (pp. 109–125). Washington, DC: American Psychiatric Press.

Hare, R. D. (1978). Electrodermal and cardiovascular correlates of psychopathy. In R. D. Hare & D. Schalling (Eds.), *Psychopathic behaviour: Approaches to research* (pp. 107–143). Chichester, UK: Wiley.

Hare, R. D. (1984). Performance on psychopaths on cognitive tasks related to frontal lobe function. *Journal of Abnormal Psychology*, *93*, 133–140.

Hare, R. D., & Quinn, M. J. (1971). Psychopathy and autonomic conditioning. *Journal of Abnormal Psychology*, *71*, 223–235.

Hartmann, D. P., & Atkinson, C. (1973). Having your cake and eating it too: A note on some apparent contradictions between therapeutic achievements and design requirements in *N*=1 studies. *Behavior Therapy*, *4*, 589–591.

Henriques, J. B., & Davidson, R. J. (1991). Left frontal hypoactivation in depression. *Journal of Abnormal Psychology*, *100*, 535–545.

Iacono, W. G. (1982). Bilateral electrodermal habituation-dishabituation and resting EEG in remitted schizophrenics. *Journal of Nervous and Mental Disease*, *170*, 91–101.

Johnson, W., Bouchard, T. J., Jr., McGue, M., Segal, N. L., Tellegen, A., Keyes, M., & Gottesman, I. I. (2007). Genetic and environmental influences on the verbal-perceptual-image rotation (VPI) model of the structure of mental abilities in the Minnesota Study of Twins Reared Apart. *Intelligence*, *35*, 542–562.

Jutai, J. W., & Hare, R. D. (1983). Psychopathy and selective attention during performance of a complex perceptual motor task. *Psychophysiology*, *20*, 146–151.

Kahneman, D. (2011). *Thinking, fast and slow*. New York: Farrah, Straus, and Giroux.

Kallman, F. J. (1938). *The genetics of schizophrenia*. New York: Augustin.

Katkin, E. S., & Hastrup, J. L. (1982). Psychophysiological methods in clinical research. In P. C. Kendall & J. N. Butcher (Eds.), *Handbook of research methods in clinical psychology* (pp. 387–425). New York: Wiley.

Kendler, K. S. (1983). Overview: A current perspective on twin studies of schizophrenia. *American Journal of Psychiatry*, *140*, 1413–1425.

Kendler, K.S. (2005). Toward a philosophical structure for psychiatry. *American Journal of Psychiatry*, *162*, 433–440.

Kety, S. S., Rosenthal, D., Wender, P. H., & Schulsinger, F. (1968). The types and prevalence of mental illness in the biological and adoptive families of adopted schizophrenics. In D. Rosenthal & S. S. Kety (Eds.), *The transmission of schizophrenia* (pp. 345–362). Oxford, UK: Pergamon Press.

Klein, D. N., & Depue, R. A. (1984). Continued impairment of persons at risk for bipolar affective disorder: Results of a 19-month follow-up study. *Journal of Abnormal Psychology*, *93*, 345–347.

Kravitz, H. M., & Newman, A. J. (1995). Medical diagnostic procedures for depression: An update from a decade of promise. In E. E. Beckham & W. R. Leber (Eds.), *Handbook of depression* (2nd ed., pp. 280–301). New York: Guilford Press.

Kring, A. M., & Sloan, D. M. (2007). The facial expression coding system (FACES): Development, validation, and utility. *Psychological Assessment*, *19*, 210–224.

Kwapil, T. R., Miller, M. B., Zinser, M. C., Chapman, L. J., Chapman, J., & Eckblad, M. (2000). A longitudinal study of high scorers on the Hypomanic Personality Scale. *Journal of Abnormal Psychology*, *109*, 222–226.

Lacey, B. C., & Lacey, J. I. (1978). Two-way communication between the heart and the brain. *American Psychologist*, *33*, 99–113.

Lacey, J. I. (1967). Somatic response patterning and stress: Some revisions of activation theory. In M. H. Appley & R. Trumbull (Eds.), *Psychological stress: Issues in research* (pp. 14–42). New York: Appleton-Crofts.

Lenzenweger, M. F. (2010). *Schizotypy and schizophrenia: The view from experimental psychopathology*. New York: Guilford Press.

Lezak, M. D., Howieson, D. B., Bigler, E. D., & Tranel, D. (2012). *Neuropsychological assessment* (5th ed.). New York: Oxford University Press.

Liddle, P. F. (1995). Regional cerebral blood flow and subsyndromes of schizophrenia. In J. A. Den Boer, H. Gerrit, M. Westenberg, & H. M. van Praag (Eds.), *Advances in the neurobiology of schizophrenia* (pp. 189–204). Chichester, UK: Wiley.

Lilienfeld, S. O., Waldman, I. D., & Israel, A. C. (1994). A critical examination of the use of the term and concept of comorbidity in psychopathology research. *Clinical Psychology: Science and Practice*, *1*, 71–83.

Loehlin, J. C. (1992). *Genes and environment in personality development*. Newbury Park, CA: Sage.

Loevinger, J. (1957). Objective tests as instruments of psychological theory. *Psychological Reports*, *3*(Monograph Suppl. 9), 635–694.

Lorber, M. F. (2004). Psychophysiology of aggression, psychopathy, and conduct problems: A meta-analysis. *Psychological Bulletin, 130,* 531–552.

Luchins, D. L. (1982). Computerized tomography in schizophrenia: Disparities in the prevalence of abnormalities. *Archives of General Psychiatry, 39,* 859–860.

Lykken, D. T. (1957). A study of anxiety in the sociopathic personality. *Journal of Abnormal Psychology, 55,* 6–10.

Lykken, D. T. (1982). Psychophysiology. In R. J. Corsini (Ed.), *Encyclopedia of psychology* (pp. 175–179). New York: Wiley.

Lykken, D. T., McGue, M., Tellegen, A., & Bouchard, T. J. (1992). Emergenesis: Genetic traits that may not run in families. *American Psychologist, 47,* 1565–1577.

Lykken, D. T., & Venables, P. H. (1971). Direct measurement of skin conductance: A proposal for standardization. *Psychophysiology, 8,* 656–672.

Maher, B. (2008). Personal genomes: The case for missing heritability. *Nature, 456,* 18–21.

McCall, R. B. (1977). Challenges to a science of developmental psychology. *Child Development, 48,* 333–344.

McDowell, J. E., & Clementz, B. A. (2001). Behavioral and brain imaging studies of saccadic performance in schizophrenia. *Biological Psychology, 57,* 5–22.

Meadows, E., & Zinbarg, R. (1991). Animal models of psychopathology: III. Treatment and prevention. *Behavior Therapist, 14,* 225–230.

Mednick, S. A., & Schulsinger, F. (1968). Some powerful characteristics related to breakdown in children with schizophrenic mothers. In D. Rosenthal & S. S. Kety (Eds.), *The transmission of schizophrenia* (pp. 267–291). Oxford, UK: Pergamon Press.

Meehl, P. E. (1962). Schizotaxia, schizotypy, schizophrenia. *American Psychologist, 17,* 827–838.

Meehl, P. E. (1964). *Manual for use with checklist of schizotypic signs.* Minneapolis: University of Minnesota Medical School, Medical Research Unit.

Meehl, P. E. (1971). High school yearbooks: A reply to Schwarz. *Journal of Abnormal Psychology, 77,* 143–148.

Meehl, P. E. (1977). Specific etiology and other forms of strong influence: Some quantitative meanings. *Journal of Medicine and Philosophy, 2,* 33–53.

Meehl, P. E. (1990). Toward an integrated theory of schizotaxia, schizotypy, and schizophrenia. *Journal of Personality Disorders, 4,* 1–99.

Meehl, P. E., & Golden, R. R. (1982). Taxometric methods. In P. C. Kendall & J. N. Butcher (Eds.), *Handbook of research methods in clinical psychology* (pp. 127–181). New York: Wiley.

Meehl, P. E., & Rosen, A. (1955). Antecedent probability and the efficiency of psychometric signs, patterns, or cutting scores. *Psychological Bulletin, 52,* 194–216.

Miller, G. A., & Chapman, J. P. (2001). Misunderstanding analysis of covariance. *Journal of Abnormal Psychology, 110,* 40–48.

Moffitt, T. E., Caspi, A., & Rutter, M. (2006). Measured gene–environment interactions in psychopathology: Concepts, research strategies, and implications for research, intervention, and public understanding of genetics. *Perspectives on Psychological Science, 1,* 5–27.

Morey, L. C. (1991). Classification of mental disorder as a collection of hypothetical constructs. *Journal of Abnormal Psychology, 80,* 289–293.

Morgan, J. E., & Ricker, J. H. (Eds.) (2008). *Textbook of clinical neuropsychology.* New York: Psychology Press.

Obrist, P. A. (1976). The cardiovascular-behavioral interaction: As it appears today. *Psychophysiology, 13,* 95–107.

Patrick, C. J., Bernat, E. M., Malone, S. M., Iacono, W. G., Krueger, R. F., & McGue, M. K. (2006). P300 amplitude as an indicator of externalizing in adolescent males. *Psychophysiology, 43,* 84–92.

Patrick, C. J., Curtin, J. J., & Krueger, R. F. (2008). The externalizing spectrum: Structure and mechanisms. In D. Barch (Ed.), *Handbook of cognitive and affective neuroscience of psychopathology.* New York: Oxford University Press.

Piattelli-Palmarini, M. (1994). *Inevitable illusions: How mistakes in reasoning rule our minds.* New York: Wiley.

Pizzagalli, D., Pascual-Marqui, R. D., Nitschke, J. B., Oakes, T. R., Larson, C. L., Abercrombie,…Davidson, R. J. (2001). Anterior cingulated activity as a predictor of degree of treatment response in major depression: Evidence from brain electrical tomography analysis. *American Journal of Psychiatry, 158,* 405–415.

Plomin, R. (1990). *Nature and nurture.* Pacific Grove, CA: Brooks/Cole.

Plomin, R., DeFries, J. C., Craig, I. W., & McGuffin, P. (Eds.). (2002). *Behavioral genetics in the postgenomic era.* Washington, DC: American Psychological Association.

Plomin, R., DeFries, J. C., & McClearn, G. E. (1990). *Behavioral genetics: A primer* (2nd ed.). New York: Freeman.

Polich, J., & Bloom, F. E. (1988). Event-related brain potentials in individuals at high and low risk for developing alcoholism: Failure to replicate. *Alcoholism: Clinical and Experimental Research, 12,* 368–373.

Popper, K. R. (1959). *The logic of scientific discovery.* New York: Basic Books.

Raine, A. (1993). *The psychopathology of crime.* San Diego: Academic Press.

Randolph, E. T., Eth, S., Glynn, S. M., & Paz, G. G. (1994). Behavioral family management in schizophrenia: Outcome of a clinic based intervention. *British Journal of Psychiatry, 164,* 501–506.

Reichenbach, H. (1938). *Experience and prediction.* Chicago: University of Chicago Press.

Reid, J. B. (1970). Reliability assessment of observation data: A possible methodological problem. *Child Development, 41,* 1143–1150.

Robins, E., & Guze, S. B. (1970). Establishment of diagnostic validity in psychiatric illness: Its application to schizophrenia. *American Journal of Psychiatry, 126,* 983–987.

Rosenthal, D., Wender, P. H., Kety, S. S., Schulsinger, F., Welner, J., & Østergard, L. (1968). Schizophrenics' offspring reared in adoptive homes. In D. Rosenthal & S. S. Kety (Eds.), *The transmission of schizophrenia* (pp. 377–391). Oxford, UK: Pergamon Press.

Rutter, M. (1994). Epidemiologic/longitudinal strategies and causal research in child psychiatry. In J. E. Mezzich, M. R. Jorge, & I. M. Salloum (Eds.), *Psychiatric epidemiology: Assessment concepts and methods* (pp. 139–166). Baltimore: Johns Hopkins University Press.

Schellenberg, G. D., Dawson, G., Sung, Y. J., Estes, A., Munson, J., Rosenthal, E.,…Wijsman, E. M. (2006). Evidence for multiple loci from a genome scan of autism kindreds. *Molecular Psychiatry, 11,* 1049–1060.

Schmidt, N. B., Richey, J. A., Maner, J. K., & Woolaway-Bickel, K. (2006). Differential effects of safety in extinction of anxious responding to a CO2 challenge in patients with panic disorder. *Journal of Abnormal Psychology, 115,* 341–350.

Schofield, W., & Balian, L. (1959). A comparative study of the personal histories of schizophrenia and nonpsychiatric patients. *Journal of Abnormal and Social Psychology, 59,* 216–225.

Schuldberg, D., Quinlan, D. M., Morganstern, H., & Glazer, W. (1990). Positive and negative symptoms in chronic psychiatric outpatients: Reliability, stability, and factor structure. *Psychological Assessment, 2,* 262–268.

Scoville, W. B., & Milner, B. (1957). Loss of recent memory after bilateral hippocampal lesions. *Journal of Neurology, Neurosurgery, and Psychiatry, 20,* 11–21.

Seligman, M. E. P. (1975). *Helplessness: On depression, development, and death.* San Francisco: Freeman.

Serbin, L. A., O'Leary, K. D., Kent, R. N., & Tonick, I. J. (1973). A comparison of teacher response to the preacademic and problem behavior of boys and girls. *Child Development, 44,* 796–804.

Shermer, M. (2002). *Why people believe weird things: Pseudoscience, superstition, and other confusions of our time* (2nd ed.). New York: Freeman.

Simons, R. F. (1981). Electrodermal, electrocordical, heart rate, and eye tracking characteristics of subjects reporting physical anhedonia and body image distortions. *Dissertation Abstracts International, 41*(10-B), 3902–3903.

Skinner, H. A. (1981). Toward the integration of classification theory and methods. *Journal of Abnormal Psychology, 90,* 68–87.

Skinner, H. A. (1986). Construct validation approach to psychiatric classification. In T. Millon & G. L. Klerman (Eds.), *Contemporary directions in psychopathology* (pp. 307–330). New York: Guilford Press.

Snow, J. (1855). *On the mode of communication with cholera* (2nd ed.). London: Churchill.

South, S., & Krueger, R. F. (2008). The moderating effect of marital quality on genetic and environmental contributions to internalizing psychopathology. *Journal of Abnormal Psychology, 117,* 826–837.

Spitzer, R. G., Endicott, J., & Robins, E. (1975). Clinical criteria for diagnosis and *DSM-III. American Journal of Psychiatry, 132,* 1187–1192.

Sponheim, S. R., Clementz, B. A., Iacono, W. G., & Beiser, M. (1994). Resting EEG and first-episode and chronic schizophrenia. *Psychophysiology, 31,* 37–43.

Stern, J. A. (1964). Towards a definition of psychophysiology. *Psychophysiology, 1,* 90–91.

Stern, R. M., Ray, W. J., & Quigley, K. S. (2001). *Psychophysiological recording* (2nd ed.). New York: Oxford University Press.

Sudath, R. L., Christison, G. W., Torrey, E. F., Casanova, M. F., & Weinberger, D. R. (1990). Anatomical abnormalities in the brains of monozygotic twins discordant for schizophrenia. *New England Journal of Medicine, 322,* 789–794.

Syndulko, K. (1978). Electrocortical investigations of sociopathy. In R. D. Hare & D. Schalling (Eds.), *Psychopathic behaviour: Approaches to research* (pp. 145–156). Chichester, UK: Wiley.

Tellegen, A., Lykken, D. T., Bouchard, T. J., Wilcox, K. J., Segal, N. L., & Rich, S. (1988). Personality similarity in twins reared apart and together. *Journal of Personality and Social Psychology, 54,* 1031–1039.

Torrey, E. F., Bowler, A. E., Taylor, E. H., & Gottesman, I. I. (1994). *Schizophrenia and manic- depressive disorder: The biological roots of mental illness as revealed by the landmark of identical twins.* New York: Basic Books.

Tsuang, M. T., Tohen, M., & Murphy, J. M. (1988). Psychiatric epidemiology. In A. M. Nicholi, Jr. (Ed.), *The new Harvard guide to psychiatry* (pp. 761–779). Cambridge, MA: Harvard University Press.

Vaughn, C. E., & Leff, L. P. (1976). The influence of family and social factors on the course of psychiatric illness: A comparison of schizo-phrenic and depressed neurotic patients. *British Journal of Psychiatry, 129,* 125–137.

Vul, E., Harris, C., Winkielman, P., & Pashler, H. (2009). Puzzlingly high correlations in fMRI studies of emotion, personality, and social cognition. *Perspectives on Psychological Science, 4,* 274–290.

Waldman, I. D. (2007). Behavior genetic approaches are integral for understanding the etiology of psychopathology. In S. O. Lilienfeld & W. T. O'Donohue (Eds.), *The great ideas of clinical science: 17 principles that every mental health professional should understand* (pp. 219–242). New York: Routledge.

Waldman, I. D., Lilienfeld, S. O., & Lahey, B. B. (1995). Toward construct validity in the childhood disruptive behavior disorders: Classification and diagnosis in *DSM-IV* and beyond. In T. H. Ollendick & R. J. Prinz (Eds.), *Advances in clinical child psychology* (Vol. 17, pp. 323–363). New York: Plenum Press.

Waller, N. G., & Meehl, P. E. (1998). *Multivariate taxometric procedures: Distinguishing types from continua.* Thousand Oaks, CA: Sage.

Weems, C. F., Pina, A. A., & Costa, N. M. (2007). Predisaster trait anxiety and negative affect predict posttraumatic stress in youths after Hurricane Katrina. *Journal of Consulting and Clinical Psychology, 75,* 154–159.

Westen, D., & Rosenthal, R. (2003). Quantifying construct validity: Two simple measures. *Journal of Personality and Social Psychology, 84,* 608–618.

Wood, J. M., Bootzin, R. R., Rosenhan, D., Nolan-Hoeksema, S., & Jourden, F. (1992). Effects of the 1989 San Francisco earthquake on frequency and content of nightmares. *Journal of Abnormal Psychology, 101,* 219–224.

Yamamura, E. (2012). Experience of technological and natural disasters and their impact on the perceived risk of nuclear accidents after the Fukushima nuclear disaster in Japan 2011: A cross-country analysis. *Journal of Socio-Economics, 41,* 360–363.

Zigler, E. (1967). Familial mental retardation: A continuing dilemma. *Science, 155,* 292–298.

Zubin, J., & Spring, B. (1977). Vulnerability: A new view of schizophrenia. *Journal of Abnormal Psychology, 86,* 103–126.

Part II

MAJOR CLINICAL SYNDROMES

5

Generalized Anxiety Disorder, Panic Disorder, Social Anxiety Disorder, and Specific Phobias

RICHARD E. ZINBARG,

DEEPIKA ANAND,

JONATHAN K. LEE,

ASHLEY D. KENDALL,

AND MIA NUÑEZ

In this chapter, we cover several *DSM-5* anxiety disorders, including generalized anxiety disorder (GAD), panic disorder (PD), social anxiety disorder (SAD[1])—called social phobia in earlier editions of *DSM*—and specific phobias (SP). Whereas obsessive-compulsive disorder (OCD) and post-traumatic stress disorder (PTSD) were classified as anxiety disorders in earlier *DSM* editions, they were moved into new groupings in *DSM-5* and will be covered in later chapters in this volume. There are also two diagnoses (separation anxiety disorder, selective mutism) that were not classified with the other anxiety disorders in earlier *DSM* editions, that were moved into the anxiety disorders grouping in *DSM-5* but will not be covered in this chapter.

We begin by describing the constructs of anxiety and fear, as they are central to defining and differentiating these diagnoses. Following Barlow (2002), *anxiety* is a future-oriented mood state associated with preparation for possible harm, whereas *fear* is an alarm response when danger is perceived to be present. Put differently, fear—or

panic (we use the terms interchangeably)—involves a triggering of the fight-flight-or-freeze (FFF) mechanism when danger is perceived to be present, whereas anxiety involves a priming of (i.e., simultaneous excitatory and inhibitory input to) the FFF mechanism when danger is perceived to be possible at a later point in time (Zinbarg, 1998). Viewed from this perspective, there are both overlapping and distinctive features between anxiety and panic. Anxiety and panic overlap in that they both involve perception of danger and excitatory input to the FFF mechanism. However, they are differentiable in their temporal aspects and in that anxiety involves simultaneous inhibitory input to the FFF mechanism, whereas panic involves purely excitatory input to this mechanism.

DSM-5 distinguishes two types of panic attacks: unexpected and expected. If the individual is aware of a cue or trigger at the time of the attack, then the attack is expected; if not, then the attack is unexpected. Whereas panic attacks of some sort are ubiquitous across the anxiety disorders and even major depression (Craske et al., 2010), panic/fear is not central to the definition of GAD. In contrast, anxiety is central to the definition of each of the anxiety disorders, including PD,

---

1. Note that SAD does *not* refer to seasonal affective disorder in this chapter.

SAD, and SP—the disorders in which fear plays an important role. Thus, for example, the primary distinction between the group of nonclinical panickers—individuals who experience recurrent panic attacks—and those with PD is that those with PD experience anticipatory anxiety about their attacks, whereas those with nonclinical panic do not experience such anxiety (Telch, Lucas, & Nelson, 1989).

The central features of PD in *DSM-5* are (1) recurrent, unexpected panic attacks and (2) persistent worry about having attacks (or about their consequences) or the development of significant, maladaptive behavioral changes designed to avoid having attacks. Note that if all the individual's attacks are of the expected variety, a diagnosis other than PD would be made, perhaps SAD, SP, PTSD, or OCD. A common complication of PD is agoraphobia—the fear and avoidance of situations in which the individual fears having a panic attack and from which it would be difficult to leave or get help in the event of a panic attack. *DSM-5*, however, has reverted to identifying agoraphobia as an independent diagnosis, as it had been in *DSM-III*. Thus, someone with PD who develops fairly extensive agoraphobia receives two *DSM-5* diagnoses (PD and agoraphobia), whereas in *DSM-III-R*, *DSM-IV*, and *DSM-IV-TR* they would have received a single diagnosis (panic disorder with agoraphobia, PDA).

In *DSM-5* the cardinal feature of GAD is excessive, uncontrollable worry about a number of different life circumstances. In addition, this worry must be accompanied by at least three common manifestations of anxiety, such as muscle tension, sleep disturbance, or irritability.

DSM-5 divides SP into five subtypes: animal (fear cued by animals or insects, such as dogs, snakes, or spiders), natural environment (fear cued by an object in the natural environment, such as heights, thunderstorms, or water), blood-injury-injection (fear cued by seeing blood, injury, or receiving an injection), situational (fear cued by specific situations, such as driving, enclosed places, or flying), and other (fear cued by other triggers, such as a fear of falling down, a fear of costumed characters such as clowns, or emetophobia—the fear of vomiting). To receive a *DSM-5* diagnosis of SP, the phobic cue has to almost invariably provoke an immediate fear response, the fear has to be excessive, and the fear must be associated either with some avoidance of

the phobic cue or endurance of exposure to that cue with intense fear. In addition, the fear must be associated with some functional impairment or significant distress about having the fear before one would diagnose a SP. Some individuals are judged by diagnosticians to exhibit excessive fear even though the individuals themselves do not recognize their fear as excessive. Thus, the judgment of excessiveness in *DSM-5* has been made a clinician-judgment rather than a self-judgment (as it had been in *DSM-IV-TR*).

The key feature of SAD is a persistent and marked fear of social situations in which the individual might be judged or evaluated by others. Exposure to the feared social situation(s) has to almost invariably provoke an immediate fear response, and the fear must be associated either with some avoidance of the phobic cue or endurance of exposure to that cue with intense fear or anxiety. In *DSM-IV-TR* an additional criterion was that the individual had to recognize that the fear is excessive, but just as with SP, in *DSM-5* the judgment of excessiveness is now a clinician-judgment.

However, there is some controversy in the field as to whether the different *DSM* anxiety disorder diagnoses truly represent distinct categories. The alternative view is that the different *DSM* anxiety disorders represent inconsequential variations of a broader syndrome that differ solely at the descriptive level in terms of the content of apprehension (Andrews, Stewart, Allen, & Henderson, 1990; Brown & Barlow, 2009; Tyrer, 1990). Even if this alternative view proves to be invalid, theory and empirical evidence in this area suggests a great deal of overlap in the factors and processes involved in the development and maintenance of GAD, PD, SAD, and SP. Thus, we focus primarily on them as a group and their common etiological and maintenance factors, rather than presenting largely redundant analyses of each diagnosis separately.

Epidemiology: Prevalence, Course and Comorbidity

The most recent estimates of lifetime prevalence rates are based on *DSM-IV* criteria from a reanalysis of the National Comorbidity Survey Replication (NCS-R) and the Adolescent Supplement (NCS-A) (Kessler, Petukhova, Sampson, Zaslavsky, & Wittchen, 2012) and of the National Epidemiologic Survey on Alcohol and Related Conditions

(NESARC; Grant & Dawson, 2006). Table 5.1 summarizes many of these results. As can be seen in Table 5.1, these disorders tend to be more prevalent in women (e.g., Kessler et al., 2012).

SP is the most prevalent of the anxiety disorders (Kessler et al., 2012; Stinson et al., 2007). There is some inconsistency in average age of onset, ranging between 5 to 9 (Stinson et al., 2007) and 15 – to 17 years (Kessler et al., 2012). For adults, the mean number of fears reported by an individual is approximately three, with the most common subtypes of SPs being natural environment, situational, animal, and blood-injection injury (Stinson et al., 2007). SP is highly comorbid with PDA, SAD, and GAD (Stinson et al., 2007).

SAD is the second most common of the anxiety disorders covered in this chapter (Grant, Hasin, Blanco, et al., 2005; Kessler et al., 2012). Further, there is some evidence to suggest between-group racial and ethnic differences, with a higher percentage of White Americans being diagnosed than Black/African, Hispanic/Latino, and Asian Americans (Asnaani, Richey, Dimaite, Hinton, &

Hofmann, 2010), but a higher percentage among Native Americans compared with White Americans (Grant, Hasin, Blanco, et al., 2005). The hazard rate for onset of SAD was bimodal, with a first peak at 5 years and a second one at 13 to 15 years according to the NESARC (Grant, Hasin, Blanco, et al., 2005). The most common fears reported are those related to performance-based situations (e.g., public speaking, participating in class, performing in front of others). SAD is highly comorbid with other mood, anxiety, and personality disorders (particulalry avoidant personality disorder; Grant, Hasin, Stinson, Dawson, Chou, et al., 2005). The most common comorbid anxiety disorders are PD, SP, and GAD (Grant, Hasin, Stinson, Dawson, Chou, et al., 2005).

GAD is also fairly common (Grant, Hasin, Stinson, Dawson, Ruan, et al., 2005; Kessler et al., 2012). Although mean age of onset of GAD is reported to be around 30 years of age across epidemiological studies (Grant, Hasin, Stinson, Dawson, Ruan, et al., 2005; Kessler et al., 2012), there exists some evidence to suggest a bimodal

Table 5.1 Epidemiology for SP, SAD, GAD, PD, and PDA, by gender and age cohort

	SP	SAD	GAD	PDA
12-month prevalence (%)	7.1–12.1	2.8–7.4	2–2.1	2.1–2.4
Lifetime prevalence (%)	9.4–15.6	5–10.7	4.1–4.3	3.8–5.1
Lifetime prevalence by age				
Adolescent (13–17) (%)	20	8.6	2.2	2.3
Adult (18–64) (%)	13.8	13	6.2	5.2
Older adult (65+) (%)	6.8	6.3	3.3	2.1
Lifetime prevalence by gender				
Adolescent (13–17)				
Female (%)	23*	11.2*	2.8	2.5
Male (%)	17.7	6.2	1.6	2.1
Adult (18–64)				
Female (%)	17.5*	14.2*	7.7*	7*
Male (%)	9.9	11.8	4.6	3.3
Older adult (65+)				
Female (%)	9.1*	7.1	4.8*	2.5
Male (%)	3.6	5.1	1.3	1.6
Mean age of onset	5–9, 15–17	15	30	28–32
Median years delay to treatment[1]	20	16	9	10
Comorbid diagnoses[2]	3.4	3.5	3.8	4.5
Comorbid personality disorder (%)	38.3	61.0	60.6	44.1–69.4

Note: SP = specific phobia, SAD = social anxiety disorder, GAD = generalized anxiety disorder, PD = panic disorder; PDA = panic disorder with agoraphobia.

[1]Median years delay to treatment are estimated by Wang et al. (2005).

[2]Comorbid diagnoses represent average number of both mental and physical conditions in the National Comorbidity Survey Replication reported by Gadermann et al. (2012).

* Indicates statistically significant gender difference.

distribution in the age of onset, with many individuals with GAD recalling an onset in early childhood (Campbell, Brown, & Grisham, 2003; Hoehn-Saric, Hazlett, & McLeod, 1993). White Americans are more likely to be diagnosed than are Black/African, Hispanic/Latino, and Asian Americans (Asnaani et al., 2010; Grant, Hasin, Stinson, Dawson, Ruan, et al., 2005). Of those with comorbid disorders, 71.4% meet criteria for a mood disorder, and 90% have a comorbid anxiety disorder, with the most common being PD/A and SAD (Grant, Hasin, Stinson, Dawson, Ruan, et al., 2005).

The occurrence of panic attacks (which often do not warrant a diagnosis) is high, with a lifetime prevalence of about 23% (Kessler et al., 2006). PD (with or without agoraphobia), by contrast, is less common (Kessler et al., 2012). Separating PDA from PD without agoraphobia, PDA is less common than PD (Grant et al., 2006). The mean age of onset for PDA was slightly earlier than that for PD without agoraphobia, at 28 versus 32 years according to the NESARC (Grant et al., 2006); however, this estimate is notably higher than the estimate of 23 years provided by the NCS-R/A (which collapsed PD and PDA into one category) (Kessler et al., 2006). Further, individuals with PDA were more likely to seek treatment for the disorder than those with PD without agoraphobia. Individuals with PDA also report higher rates of comorbidity with mood disorders as well as other anxiety disorders, including SAD, SP, and GAD, compared to those with PD without agoraphobia (Grant et al., 2006; Kessler et al., 2006).

Factor Analytic Models of Anxiety Disorders

The Need for Factor Analyses

DSM categorizes anxiety disorders into a single class, separate from other disorder classes (e.g., mood disorders). Within this anxiety disorder category, specific disorders represented a second level of differentiation (e.g., GAD, SP), and subtypes of these disorders a third level of differentiation (e.g., animal and blood-injury-injection SPs). However, this taxonomy was based on shared phenomenological features rather than on empirically observed correlations among these disorders. Therefore, it does not reflect certain empirical findings such as

the high rates of comorbidity of disorders belonging to different classes (e.g., anxiety and mood disorders). Largely inspired by this limitation of DSM, in recent years, much research has been dedicated to analyzing correlational patterns among these disorders and their symptoms with the aim of understanding their latent structure. Whereas in DSM-5 we continue to adopt a rational scheme of classification, our growing knowledge about the factor structure of unipolar depression, anxiety disorders, and their symptoms could pave the way for a more empirically informed classification system. Studies examining the factor structure of anxiety disorders either investigate the covariation patterns of symptom-level data or make use of diagnostic data.

In this section, we review findings that draw from factor analyses of symptoms as well as diagnoses, thus integrating conclusions drawn from both sets of analyses. However, there are several advantages of using symptom-level data. Diagnostic data indicate whether or not individuals meet a specific threshold for obtaining a diagnosis, failing to capture variation in symptom levels above or below this threshold. Therefore, symptom-level data provide more nuanced information about the symptomatology level in an individual. Further, rates of co-occurrence between disorders are subject to changing criteria with each edition of DSM (Watson, 2005). For instance, removing autonomic symptoms from the GAD criteria helped differentiate it from PD but led to greater comorbidity with major depressive disorder (MDD; Brown, Di Nardo, Lehman, & Campbell, 2001).

A Common Negative Affect Factor

Studies examining the structure of depression and anxiety symptoms and disorders have largely converged on certain key principles (Watson, 2005). A vast amount of evidence supports a hierarchical conceptualization, wherein broad latent factors are thought to account for the covariation between disorders. At the broadest level, a Negative Affect (NA) factor is thought to account for the covariation among anxiety disorders (Zinbarg & Barlow, 1996) as well as between anxiety and depressive disorders at the symptom and diagnostic levels. One of the most prominent theories to draw attention to this nonspecific factor was the tripartite model (Clark & Watson, 1991). This model was derived from factor analyses of anxiety and depressive symptom measures. It identified a non-specific general distress factor, marked by symptoms of high NA (e.g., irritability, restlessness, interpersonal sensitivity), as being shared by both anxiety and depression. This factor is thought to be the state manifestation of a temperamental sensitivity to negative stimuli—alternatively referred to as negative emotionality (NE) or neuroticism, resulting in a broad range of negative mood states such as guilt, hostility, anxiety, and sadness (Watson & Clark, 1984). Other factor analytic models have since been proposed that have incorporated this NA factor into a hierarchical structure (e.g., Prenoveau et al., 2010). This nonspecific symptom dimension is consistent with factor-analytic analyses of diagnostic data showing that anxiety and depressive disorders are best grouped into a single category of "internalizing" disorders (Krueger, 1999).

Addressing the Heterogeneity of Anxiety Disorders

In addition to the NA factor, the tripartite model proposed two narrower factors that were meant to differentiate anxiety and depressive disorders. Specifically, low Positive Affect (PA) was thought to be unique to depression. This factor is thought to be the state manifestation of a temperamental sensitivity to positive stimuli, positive emotionality (PE), resulting in positive affective states such as feeling cheerful, lively, and optimistic. Those low in PA experience diminished interest and pleasure in otherwise pleasant activities (e.g., feeling withdrawn from others, feeling slowed down). Hence, NA and PA do *not* represent two ends of a single dimension; rather, they are thought to be two orthogonal dimensions (Watson & Tellegen, 1985). Indeed, there is evidence that PA and NA arise from separate biological systems (e.g., Thayer, 1989; Watson, Wiese, Vaidya, & Tellegen, 1999) and can operate separately from each other (e.g., Gold, MacLeod, Frier, & Deary, 1995).

Within the tripartite model, symptoms characterized by Physiological Hyperarousal (PH) were thought to be unique to anxiety. This factor contains items representing somatic manifestations of anxiety (e.g., feeling dizzy, experiencing shortness of breath). However, this model has certain limitations. It was suggested that a single anxiety-specific factor was not sufficient to account for the heterogeneity among the anxiety disorders (Mineka,

Watson, & Clark, 1998; Zinbarg & Barlow, 1996). In fact, PH was found to relate specifically to PD and PTSD (Brown & McNiff, 2009), rather than to all the anxiety disorders as a group (Brown, Chorpita, & Barlow, 1998). Also, low PA was linked to SAD in addition to depression, suggesting that this factor was not entirely unique to depression (Brown et al., 1998; Chorpita, Plummer, & Moffitt, 2000).

Zinbarg and Barlow (1996) examined the factor structure of anxiety symptom measures and found that in addition to a broad, general factor shared by all anxiety disorders there are *multiple* narrow factors that provide the basis for differentiating the specific anxiety disorders from each other (see later discussion). Taking this and other factor-analytic findings into consideration, Mineka et al. (1998) proposed the integrative hierarchical model. In this model, each disorder consists of a common NA component and a unique component that differentiates it from other disorders. Moreover, not all disorders contain the same level of common factor variance. Particularly, MDD and GAD are characterized by a larger amount of NA variance than other anxiety disorders, such as SP and PD (Kessler, Chiu, Demler, & Walters, 2005; also see Watson, Gamez, & Simms, 2005, for more detail). Also, the specificity of symptoms that differentiate disorders is relative, so that some disorder-specific symptoms could be shared by more than one disorder. This explained the finding that low PA was linked to SAD, in addition to MDD. Also, PH was not common to all anxiety disorders but related more specifically to PD as well as to PTSD.

D. Watson's (2005) Quantitative Structural Model

D. Watson (2005) recognized these important contributions by Mineka et al. (1998) but pointed out that the integrative hierarchical model did not fully explain patterns of comorbidity among anxiety disorders. That is, although the high level of NA in both GAD and MDD explained their co-occurrence, the relatively low levels of NA in disorders like SAD and SP did not explain why these disorders were also highly comorbid with each other (e.g., Krueger, 1999; Vollebergh et al., 2001). Addressing this limitation, D. Watson (2005) formulated an alternative taxonomy of anxiety and mood disorders based on factor-analytic findings—the quantitative structural model. This model retains the broad factor thought to underlie all the internalizing disorders. However, it proposes three subfactors corresponding to subclasses of internalizing disorders—Distress, which underlies MDD, dysthymia, GAD, and PTSD; Fear, which underlies PD, agoraphobia, SAD, and SP; and a third narrow factor underlying the bipolar disorders. Importantly, GAD is classified along with unipolar depression in this model as a disorder of the subfactor Distress rather than as a pure anxiety disorder, whereas the Fear subfactor represents the empirical overlap between SAD, SP, PD, and agoraphobia.

As justification of this empirical classification scheme, D. Watson (2005) cited evidence from factor analyses of diagnostic data in large epidemiological studies. For example, Krueger (1999) conducted confirmatory factor analyses using *DSM-III* diagnoses in the National Comorbidity Survey data. He found that the best-fitting model was a three-factor model with one higher-order Internalizing factor and two highly correlated subfactors labeled Anxious-Misery (MDD, dysthymia, GAD), and Fear (PD, agoraphobia, SAD, and SP). The Anxious-Misery factor was referred to as Distress by D. Watson to signify the large amount of general distress variance characterizing these disorders. This three-factor hierarchical structure with a broad internalizing factor and correlated subfactors of Distress and Fear was replicated by Vollebergh et al. (2001) using *DSM-IV* diagnostic data from the Netherlands Mental Health Survey and Incidence Study (NEMESIS) study, and by Slade and Watson (2006) using *DSM-IV* and *ICD-10* disorders in an Australian epidemiological sample (although this study did not include assessments of SP).

More recently, Eaton et al. (2013) found support for the two-subfactor conceptualization of internalizing disorders using the NESARC data set. In fact, this structure was replicated across two waves of assessments, 3 years apart and for both men and women. Importantly, even though the two subfactors were correlated within a single assessment, Fear at Wave 1 did not significantly predict Distress at Wave 2 (but did predict Fear at Wave 2), and Distress at Wave 1 did not significantly predict Fear at Wave 2 (but did predict Distress at Wave 2). The authors interpreted this result as support for viewing Fear and Distress as two unique pathways toward developing or continuing internalizing disorders.

Other Anxiety-Specific Factors

As mentioned earlier, PH has been found to relate specifically to PD (and PTSD) (Brown et al., 1998; Chorpita et al., 2000). Some researchers have proposed that Anxious Apprehension, a future-oriented mood state, marked by high levels of worry about future negative outcomes, might represent an anxiety-specific factor, separate from PH (Barlow, 1991). Supporting this claim, studies have demonstrated that PH and Anxious Apprehension are separable dimensions, and researchers have hypothesized that Anxious Apprehension is mostly linked to GAD (Nitschke, Heller, Imig, McDonald, & Miller, 2001). However, others have speculated that Anxious Apprehension may instead relate more commonly to all anxiety disorders, as well as to depression, and therefore be thought of as a facet of NA (D. Watson, 1999). More research is needed to clarify the role of Anxious Apprehension as an anxiety-specific dimension.

As noted earlier, Zinbarg and Barlow (1996) obtained a hierarchical factor structure of anxiety symptom measures with a broad, general factor of NA. They also identified six narrow, group factors that they named Generalized Dysphoria, Social Anxiety, Agoraphobia, Fear of Fear, Obsessions and Compulsions, and Simple Fears. Furthermore, they performed discriminant function analyses to examine the relationship between these seven symptom dimensions and *DSM-III-R* diagnoses. They found that the NA factor distinguished each of the anxiety-disordered groups from a no–mental disorder control group, whereas the Fear of Fear, Agoraphobia, Social Anxiety, and Obsessions and Compulsions factors provided the bases for discriminating among the patient groups.

Integrating the Zinbarg and Barlow (1996) hierarchical model with the D. Watson (2005) quantitative structural model, Prenoveau et al. (2010) found good fit for a hierarchical structure of symptoms of anxiety and depression with three levels that differed in terms of the breadth of their loadings. At the narrowest level of the hierarchy, there were five group factors. Four of these related to anxiety: Anxious Arousal, Social Fears, Specific Fears, and Interoceptive/Agoraphobic Fears. Additionally, Narrow Depression emerged as a depression-related, narrow group factor. There were two factors of intermediate breadth that were each loaded on by items that loaded on several of the narrowest factors. That is, the items comprising the narrowest factors are subsets of the items comprising the intermediate factors. The first of the intermediate-breadth factors was labeled Anxious-Misery with loadings from some of the Narrow Depression items (e.g., hopelessness), some Social Fears items (e.g., felt self-conscious), and some items with negative loadings reflecting high PA (e.g., felt really happy). This factor may have captured the overlap between symptoms of social anxiety and low PA reported in several other studies. A second factor of intermediate breadth was labeled Fears, with loadings from the Social Fears, Interoceptive/Agoraphobic Fears, and Specific Fears items. A General Distress factor (loaded on by all of the symptoms) was obtained as the broadest factor.

To summarize, there is consensus that an overarching factor representing high negative affect—sometimes labeled Internalizing or General Distress—is shared by all anxiety disorders and their symptoms. This factor also appears to account for the empirical overlap between anxiety and depression. Beneath this general factor, there is support for two intermediate-level factors—Fear, which underlies the disorders SP, SAD, PD, and agoraphobia, and Distress, which underlies the disorders MDD, dysthymia, and GAD. Finally, there is evidence (primarily from symptom-level data) that we can identify narrow factors that may provide the basis for differentiating individual disorders from each other. However, it should be noted that we have not yet reached consensus about the exact number and nature of these narrow factors.

Etiology and Maintenance Models and Factors

Temperament and Personality

An important pathway to understanding the etiology of anxiety disorders is the link between psychopathology and personality. Findings from such research may reflect a predisposition model, wherein specific personality characteristics play a causal etiological role in developing anxiety disorders. However, they may also result from models in which these characteristics do not play a direct etiological role, but rather simply modify the expression or course of a disorder (pathoplasty

model), result as a consequence of a disorder (scar hypothesis), or represent a continuum such that disorders are extreme manifestations of personality traits. Longitudinal studies that relate premorbid assessments of personality to subsequent onsets of anxiety disorders provide a good design for testing the etiological role of personality characteristics (Clark, Watson, & Mineka, 1994).

Neuroticism The term *neuroses* is historically rooted in the psychoanalytic tradition, referring to a class of mental disorders thought to result from unconscious conflict. However, deviating significantly from this tradition, the term *neuroticism* has subsequently been used to label a set of covarying personality descriptors (such as fretful, moody, insecure, self-critical, and envious)—identified through factor analyses of self-report personality measures—thought to represent a dimension of emotional instability (e.g., Costa & McCrae, 1987; Eysenck, 1970). In fact, neuroticism is closely related to (and often used interchangeably with) the construct of negative emotionality discussed earlier (Watson & Clark, 1984).

Neuroticism is thought to be a partially heritable sensitivity to aversive cues and consequent propensity to experience negative emotions and is hypothesized to be a common diathesis (i.e., risk factor) for all of the anxiety disorders and MDD (e.g., Eysenck, 1967; Gray & McNaughton, 2000; Griffith et al., 2010; Zinbarg & Yoon, 2008). This personality trait has been shown to have robust cross-sectional associations with internalizing disorders, including anxiety (e.g., Bienvenu et al., 2004; Griffith et al., 2010; Rosellini & Brown, 2011; Zinbarg et al., 2010). In addition to this cross-sectional evidence, in a longitudinal study of college students that statistically covaried for baseline symptoms, Jorm et al. (2000) showed that neuroticism predicted anxiety symptoms 3 years later.

One concern with interpreting associations between neuroticism and anxiety is that they may be driven by overlapping items in their measures. Addressing this concern, studies using structural equation modeling have demonstrated that their association extends beyond mere content overlap. For example, Uliaszek et al. (2009) used a hierarchical factor model of neuroticism to evaluate the differential predictive ability of the anxiety facet of neuroticism (which overlaps with anxiety symptoms) and a General Neuroticism factor (GNF) that was common to all neuroticism items. They found that the GNF was associated with a latent Anxiety factor beyond the anxiety facet of neuroticism (Uliaszek et al., 2009). This finding indicates that the association between neuroticism measures and anxiety symptoms cannot be entirely attributed to item overlap.

Some longitudinal studies have found a reciprocal relationship between neuroticism and anxiety, suggesting that anxiety symptoms may increase the level of neuroticism (e.g., Jylhä, Melartin, Rytsälä, & Isometsä, 2009). It remains to be determined, however, how much of this effect can be attributed to item overlap. Additionally, Kendler and Gardner (2011) found that among women, neuroticism influences the temporally stable component of anxiety and depressive symptoms, but it impacts the occasion-specific component of these symptoms only indirectly, by increasing the number of stressful life events. Therefore, more research is needed to rule out the scar and pathoplasty models of association between neuroticism and anxiety.

Behavioral Inhibition Another construct that has been implicated in the etiology of anxiety disorders is behavioral inhibition (BI). This was described by Kagan, Reznick, Clarke, Snidman, and Garcia-Coll (1984) as a specific behavioral response style elicited by novel situations among children as young as 21 months. This response style, observed in about 15–20% of young children, was defined as "an early appearing syndrome characterized by shyness, withdrawal, avoidance, uneasiness, fear of unfamiliar situations, people, objects and events" (Turner, Beidel, & Wolff, 1996). BI was found to be moderately stable from age 21 months to 7.5 years and was linked to physiological correlates (e.g., higher heart rate in response to stressors), thus representing a temperamental construct[2] (see Fox, Henderson, Marshall, Nichols, & Ghera, 2005, for a review).

Rosenbaum and colleagues (1988, 1991) provided early evidence linking BI to the increased risk for developing childhood anxiety disorders. They found a higher incidence of anxiety disorders among parents with behaviorally inhibited children than among those with uninhibited children.

Further, inhibited children themselves had higher rates of anxiety disorders compared to those who were not inhibited (Biederman et al., 1990). More recent evidence has linked BI particularly with risk for developing SAD and avoidant personality disorder among children (Biederman et al., 2001) and SAD among adolescents (Hayward, Killen, Kraemer, & Taylor, 1998). Subsequent studies have shown that this link is strongest among adolescents who showed behavioral inhibition across multiple assessments during their development. For example, Chronis-Tuscano et al. (2009) related BI profiles created via maternal reports of BI at four time points (14 months, 24 months, 4 years, and 7 years of age) prospectively to lifetime SAD assessed at adolescence (with clinically significant distress confirmed to be present after age 7). They found that high BI (across the four assessments in childhood) predicted a fourfold increase in odds of a subsequent SAD diagnosis.

Behavioral inhibition is thought by many to be a developmental precursor to and facet of neuroticism (e.g., Turner et al., 1996; Zinbarg et al., 2010). Indeed, Gray's (1982; Gray & McNaughton, 2000) construct of behavioral inhibition system (BIS) reactivity, which he hypothesized as underlying neuroticism (as described earlier), relates conceptually to Kagan et al.'s (1984) behavioral description of BI in children. Unfortunately, few studies have empirically tested the association between the two. One of the challenges in doing so is that neuroticism has been primarily examined in adults, whereas Kagan's BI model has been rooted in studies using child samples. Future research aimed at integrating these two lines of research is needed to clarify their empirical overlap.

Anxiety Sensitivity (AS) A third trait that has received a lot of attention in etiological theories of anxiety disorders is anxiety sensitivity (AS) (Reiss, Peterson, Gursky, & McNally, 1986). AS represents individual differences in the fear of fear, hypothesized to arise from beliefs that symptoms of anxiety or fear will cause illness, embarrassment, or additional anxiety (Reiss et al., 1986). For example, an individual with high AS may be more likely to misinterpret a pounding heart as an impending heart attack, or worry about the embarrassment caused by increased sweating. These negative beliefs in turn amplify existing anxiety levels, resulting in a cycle that increases risk for panic attacks and anxiety disorders.

---

2. Different theorists define temperament in different ways (see Goldsmith et al., 1987). We define temperament as relatively stable individual differences in emotionality that emerge early in life and have a biological basis.

AS is most commonly assessed using a self-report measure, the Anxiety Sensitivity Index (ASI, Reiss et al., 1986). Using this measure, researchers have shown that AS is associated with anxiety disorders among adults (Olatunji & Wolitzky-Taylor, 2009), children, and adolescents (Noël & Francis, 2011). Several longitudinal studies have also found evidence that AS prospectively predicts panic attacks and other symptoms of panic disorder (e.g., Hayward, Killen, Kraemer, & Taylor, 2000; Li & Zinbarg, 2007; Schmidt, Lerew, & Jackson, 1999; Schmidt, Mitchell, & Richey, 2008). In addition, a 2-year longitudinal study found that AS prospectively predicted the overall incidence of anxiety disorders (including GAD, SAD, SP, and PD) among individuals with no history of Axis I disorders at baseline, while covarying trait-anxiety (Schmidt, Zvolensky, & Maner, 2006). These findings provide strong support for AS as a risk factor for developing anxiety disorders. Among the anxiety disorders, AS has been most extensively linked to an increased vulnerability for developing PD (McNally, 2002).

Much research has focused on the multidimensional structure of AS. Factor-analytic studies using the ASI have found a hierarchical structure with a general factor and three group factors: (a) Physical Concerns involving the fear of physical symptoms, (b) Social Concerns involving the fear of publicly observable symptoms, and (c) Mental Incapacitation Concerns (e.g., Rodriguez, Bruce, Pagano, Spencer, & Keller, 2004; Zinbarg, Barlow, & Brown, 1997; Zinbarg, Mohlman, & Hong, 1999). Studies examining the unique role of these facets in predicting panic have yielded inconsistent results. Schmidt et al. (1999) studied Air Force cadets and found that of the three AS facets, only the facet corresponding to mental incapacitation concerns (AS-Mental) significantly predicted spontaneous panic attacks during a 5-week period, when statistically accounting for trait anxiety and history of panic. Consistent with these findings, Li and Zinbarg (2007) found that the facet corresponding to mental incapacitation concerns, but not the other two facets, uniquely predicted panic onset over a 1-year period among college undergraduates. However, Hayward et al. (2000) reported that only the facet corresponding with physical concerns predicted the onset of four-symptom panic attacks over a 4-year period among high school students. More research is needed to conclusively determine the unique role of these AS facets in predicting anxiety disorders.

An important direction for future research is to examine the relationships between the different personality factors associated with increased risk for anxiety disorders that might be related to neuroticism. It seems likely that these relationships will be best described by a hierarchical structure in which AS and BI measures represent facets of vulnerability toward anxiety disorders that also share some variance with a general neuroticism factor.

Positive Emotionality/Extroversion   Although research on personality risk factors for the anxiety disorders has largely focused on traits related to NA (e.g., neuroticism, BI, and AS, as described earlier), there is increasing interest in the risk associated with low levels of traits related to PA, most notably extroversion. Extroversion is generally considered to be a higher-order dimension that subsumes trait PE along with sociability facets (e.g., Watson & Clark, 1997; but see Smillie, Cooper, Wilt, & Revelle, 2012). To explicitly emphasize both of these facets, we will refer to this higher-order trait as positive emotionality/extroversion (PE/E).

The relative focus on risk factors associated with NA versus PA is attributable in part to early structural models of the emotional disorders. As already mentioned, the tripartite model (Clark & Watson, 1991) posited that high NA is common across the emotional disorders, whereas low PA distinguishes depressive from anxiety disorders. One disconfirmation of the tripartite model predictions was that SAD has also consistently been linked to low PA (e.g., Brown et al., 1998). Thus, the earliest models were updated to account for this discovery (e.g., Mineka et al., 1998), and more attention has since been devoted to the possibility that low PE/E might function as a risk factor for at least some anxiety disorders.

The cross-sectional research linking low PE/E to SAD generally suggests that the magnitude of the inverse association is significant but weaker than that with depression (see Watson & Naragon-Gainey, 2010). Interestingly, there is evidence that the *facets* of PE/E may differentially relate to the symptoms of social anxiety and depression. For example, one study identified four lower-order facets of PE/E: PE, sociability, ascendance, and fun-seeking (Naragon-Gainey, Watson, & Markon, 2009). In this study, it was further found that social anxiety was broadly negatively related to all four facets, whereas depression was strongly related only to low PE, and also more modestly with sociability. One concern with interpreting associations between PE/E—particularly the sociability and ascendance facets—and SAD is that they may be driven by overlapping items in their measures. Thus, an important direction for future research will be to determine the extent to which these associations can be attributed to item overlap.

Less attention has been devoted to the relations between PE/E and the remaining anxiety disorders. However, there is some evidence that low PE/E may be associated—alone and/or in interaction with high neuroticism—with other anxiety disorders. For example, findings from a large meta-analysis revealed that nearly all of the anxiety disorders, with the possible exception of the SPs, were associated with lower PE/E in addition to elevated neuroticism (Kotov, Gamez, Schmidt, & Watson, 2010).

These studies are consistent with the hypothesis that low PE/E may confer risk for the development of the anxiety disorders covered in this chapter, particularly SAD, and perhaps least likely the SPs. However, a number of factors limit the conclusions that can be drawn and highlight directions for future work. The overwhelming majority of available studies are cross-sectional; prospective longitudinal work is sorely needed to determine directionality. At the level of higher-order traits, most studies do not account for the shared variance of trait PE/E with neuroticism, despite evidence that neuroticism is both a strong predictor of psychopathology and a reliable correlate of PE/E (see Kotov et al., 2010). At the lower-order level, more fine-grained analyses are needed to determine if the specific facets of PE/E differentially relate to the different anxiety disorders.

A final consideration pertains to the study not only of low PE/E but also of personality risk factors more broadly: It will be important to distinguish between trait and state variance in putatively "trait" measures to avoid their contamination by the state dimension. Evidence indicates that psychological constructs consist, to varying degrees, of both stability and change (see Roberts & DelVecchio, 2000). Advances in longitudinal analysis (e.g., Cole, Martin, & Steiger, 2005; Kenny & Zautra, 1995; Steyer & Schmitt, 1994) enable isolation of each of these components. Teasing apart traits and states will enhance confidence in the conclusions drawn regarding the associations between traits and disorders, by minimizing the possibility

that it is actually the state dimension—rather than the trait dimension—that is largely responsible for the observed associations with disorders.

Biology

Behavior Genetics   Behavior genetics (BG) studies reveal that anxiety disorders are heritable (see Barlow, 2002, for a review). Multivariate BG studies—that is, BG studies that focus on several disorders simultaneously rather than on a single disorder—have been conducted by Kendler and colleagues (e.g., Hettema, Prescott, Myers, Neale, & Kendler, 2005; Kendler, Prescott, Myers, & Neale, 2003; Kendler et al., 1995). These are particularly interesting because they can potentially answer the question of whether any of the anxiety disorders share a genetic vulnerability or whether they each have unique genetic bases. In general, these studies point to genetic correlational structures that largely correspond to the two subfactors of Internalizing that have emerged from the phenotypic correlational structural patterns of symptoms as described earlier. That is, these studies reported evidence for two genetic factors within the anxiety disorders and MDD. The first is loaded on by MDD and GAD and is characterized as a vulnerability to Anxious-Misery disorders; the second is loaded on by PD and SP and is characterized as a vulnerability to Fear disorders (Kendler et al., 1995, 2003). Interestingly, these two genetic factors were moderately positively correlated, which is consistent with a second-order genetic factor common to all the anxiety disorders and MDD (Kendler et al., 1995, 2003).

The existence of a genetic factor common to all the anxiety disorders and MDD is also consistent with research on the genetic factors associated with neuroticism. Multivariate BG studies of neuroticism and anxiety disorders and MDD have shown that the genetic factor associated with neuroticism overlaps to a substantial degree with the genetic vulnerability to the different anxiety disorders and MDD (e.g., Andrews et al., 1990; Hettema, Neale, Myers, Prescott, & Kendler, 2006; Hettema, Prescott, & Kendler, 2004; Jardine, Martin, & Henderson, 1984). Thus, neuroticism appears to be the phenotype associated with the genetic factors that confer common vulnerability to all the anxiety disorders and MDD.

Whereas BG studies tell us that there is a heritable—and therefore biological—component of the anxiety disorders, studies of molecular genetics, brain lesions, and genetic engineering in animals, and human neuroimaging shed light on the specific biological substrates and genes involved in vulnerability to the anxiety disorders. We turn to some of the major findings of such studies in the next three sections.

Molecular Genetics   Much evidence indicates abnormalities in serotonin (5-HT) systems' functioning in patients with MDD and the anxiety disorders (Hariri & Holmes, 2006). In addition, many of the medications that are effective in treating MDD and the anxiety disorders are known to affect 5-HT systems and transmission (Hariri & Holmes, 2006). That the 5-HT system is also involved in the regulation of various forms of NA, including hostility, anxiety, and fear (Grabe et al., 2005; Schinka, Busch, & Robichauz-Keene, 2004), implies a link between 5-HT systems and neuroticism—the trait discussed earlier that appears to be, or at least to overlap to a great extent with, the inherited diathesis for anxiety disorders and major depression.

One particular polymorphism related to 5-HT systems that has been the focus of a lot of molecular genetics research is the serotonin transporter-linked polymorphism (5-HTTLPR). 5-HTTLPR refers to an insertion/deletion polymorphism in the promoter region of the serotonin transporter gene, *SLC6A4*, that yields a transcriptionally less efficient short (*S*) allele and a relatively more efficient long (*L*) allele (Heils et al., 1996). A number of studies have now tested the associations of the main effect of the 5-HTTLPR gene. For example, evidence supports a gene by environment (G×E) interaction effect in depression where individuals with the *S* allele report greater depression under increasing stress relative to *L/L* homozygotes (Karg, Burmeister, Shedden, & Sen, 2011).

There has not been as much research examining associations of the 5-HTTLPR gene with anxiety disorders as there has been with MDD. In the only study that we are aware of that evaluates genetic risk conferred by the 5-HTTLPR gene for an anxiety disorder, the 5-HTTLPR gene did not significantly moderate the effects of stressful life events on risk for GAD (Kendler, Kuhn, Vittum, Prescott, & Riley, 2005). However, knockout strains of mice lacking the 5-HTTLPR gene, which are produced through genetic engineering, demonstrate evidence of elevated anxiety on

tests sensitive to the effects of anxiolytic medications (for a review see Hariri & Holmes, 2006). Also, meta-analyses have indicated a small but significant association between the 5-HTTLPR gene and "avoidance traits" such as neuroticism (e.g., Munafò, Clark, & Flint, 2005; Schinka et al., 2004). Taken together, these findings suggest that further human studies of the 5-HTTLPR gene and anxiety disorders are warranted.

Although to a lesser extent, there have been some molecular genetics studies implicating a role for genes *other* than the 5-HTTLPR gene in anxiety disorders. For example, motivated by the observation that a GABA receptor is the site of action for the anxiolytic effects of the benzodiazepines and barbiturates, Hettema, An, et al. (2006) studied associations between genes involved in the production of glutamic acid decarboxylase—an enzyme responsible for synthesizing GABA from glutamate—and common genetic risk for anxiety disorders, major depression, and neuroticism. Hettema, An, et al. (2006) found that variations in one of these glutamic acid decarboxylase genes may contribute to susceptibility to anxiety disorders and major depression. Similarly, Thoeringer et al. (2009) found an association between the severity of panic attacks and genetic variation in a polymorphism involved in the production of the GABA transporter. However, Pham et al. (2009) failed to detect associations between GABA receptor genes and common genetic risk for anxiety disorders, major depression, and neuroticism. In addition, the researchers who reported the glutamic acid decarboxylase gene and GABA transporter genes emphasized that their findings needed to be replicated in independent samples. Thus, these findings are very preliminary, but they are also very exciting and suggest that further studies of the glutamic acid decarboxylase gene and GABA transporter gene are warranted.

Animal Lesion Studies   Jeffrey Gray's model of the neuropsychology of anxiety uses as its starting point the behavioral effects of the antianxiety drugs (Gray, 1982; Gray & McNaughton, 2000). Gray synthesized the voluminous literature on the effects of the antianxiety drugs in animals by hypothesizing that antianxiety drugs exert their effects by modulating the output of the behavioral inhibition system (BIS). The BIS is a subsystem of the *conceptual* nervous system. The BIS is described as responding to signals of punishment or signals of frustrative non-reward (but not to punishment or frustrative non-reward itself) and as having three major outputs: an increase in arousal, behavioral inhibition, and negative cognitive bias. By comparing the effects of the antianxiety drugs to the effects of lesions to different regions of the brain, Gray (1982) originally proposed that the septohippocampal system (SHS) constituted the subsystem of the *central* nervous system that is the anatomical substrate of the BIS. Gray and McNaughton (2000) expanded the neuroanatomical seat of anxiety to include the interactions of the SHS system with the amygdala. Gray's model spans multiple levels of analysis, including personality. Thus, according to this model, individual differences in the reactivity of the BIS—that is, the SHS (and its interactions with the amygdala)—underlie the closely related traits of anxiety and neuroticism.

There are two major projections to the SHS—one noradrenergic that originates in the locus coeruleus, and the other serotonergic that originates in the raphe nucleus (Gray, 1982; Gray & McNaughton, 2000). Thus, the recent discoveries described in the field of molecular genetics that link the 5-HTTLPR gene with anxiety (in 5-HTTLPR knockout mice), neuroticism, and MDD are consistent with Gray's model. Indeed, there are several predictions regarding the anxiety disorders and MDD that can be derived from Gray's model, and the evidence to date is largely supportive of each of them (for a review, see Zinbarg & Yoon, 2008).

Human Neuroimaging   A great deal of basic fMRI research on fear in healthy human participants has been conducted. Much of this research was motivated by animal studies, which have reliably identified the amygdala as being a necessary brain structure in the acquisition and expression of conditioned fear (e.g., Davis, 1998; LeDoux, 1995, 2000). Several fMRI studies with healthy human participants have found the amygdala to be involved in human fear conditioning as well (e.g., LaBar, Gatenby, Gore, LeDoux, & Phelps, 1998; Phelps & LeDoux, 2005; Whalen, 1998). Other studies with healthy human participants have extended this research by showing the amygdala to be activated by more subtle fear-related stimuli, such as pictures of fearful facial expressions, even when the fearful expressions have been masked so that the participants are not aware of them (e.g., Phelps & LeDoux, 2005; Whalen, 1998). Though more limited, some basic fMRI research with

healthy humans has focused on areas other than the amygdala that may be involved in anxiety or fear. For example, Somerville, Whalen, and Kelley (2010) conducted an fMRI study with healthy participants that was motivated by the animal research by Davis (1998) implicating the amygdala in fear responses and the bed nucleus of the stria terminalis (BNST) in anxiety. Interestingly, the BNST receives projections from the ventral hippocampus (Lee & Davis, 1997) and thus might be considered part of the SHS. Somerville et al. (2010) found that activity in the BNST correlated with individual differences in trait anxiety levels while participants were engaged in continuous processing of potential signals of threat, much as we would expect if the SHS underlies trait anxiety and neuroticism, as hypothesized by Gray (1982; Gray & McNaughton, 2000).

There have also been several fMRI studies of participants with anxiety disorders. Compared with findings in control participants, greater activation of the amygdala has been found in patients with GAD (McClure et al., 2007; Monk et al., 2008; Nitschke et al., 2009), SAD (Birbaumer et al., 1998; Etkin & Wager, 2007; Evans et al., 2008), PD (van den Heuvel et al., 2005; for a related case study, see Pfleiderer et al., 2007), and SP (Etkin & Wager, 2007). There are also at least two fMRI studies implicating SHS-related structures in anxiety disorders. For instance, Bystritsky et al. (2001) found increased activity relative to controls in the hippocampus and the anterior cingulate—a structure which receives projections from the hippocampus—in patients with PD. Similarly, McClure et al. (2007) found increased activity in the anterior cingulate in patients with GAD compared with that in controls.

Conditioning

J. B. Watson and Rayner (1920) hypothesized that SPs are intense classically conditioned fears that develop when a neutral stimulus is paired with a traumatic event. They demonstrated this process in their famous experiment in which Little Albert, a young boy who did not show fear of a white rat to begin with, acquired an intense fear of rats after hearing a frightening gong paired with the presence of a white rat several times. The gong was said to be a conditioned stimulus (CS) and the fear a conditioned response (CR). Their publication ushered in an era in which conditioning approaches were the dominant empirically grounded theoretical perspective on anxiety disorders.

That era continued until the 1970s, but such approaches have been widely criticized since then (see Mineka, 1985; Rachman, 1978, 1990). Many of these criticisms focused on the apparent inability of conditioning approaches to account for the diversity of factors involved in the origins of anxiety disorders. More recently, however, a resurgence of interest in conditioning approaches has occurred as these approaches have incorporated some of the complexity predicted by contemporary conditioning theory and research. Space limitations prevent us from elucidating all of these complexities, but we will try to provide an introduction to some of them, and the interested reader can find more complete accounts in publications by Mineka and Zinbarg (1996; also see Zinbarg & Mineka, 2007), and Bouton, Mineka, and Barlow (2001).

Vicarious Conditioning   One criticism of early conditioning approaches was that many phobics do not appear to have had any relevant history of classical conditioning. To account for the origins of fears and SPs in these individuals, clinicians have long speculated that vicarious conditioning— that is, simply observing others experiencing a trauma or behaving fearfully—could be sufficient for some fears and SPs to develop. Indeed, some retrospective studies have found evidence consistent with this idea, for PD, SAD, and SP (e.g., Bruch & Heimberg, 1994; Öst & Hugdahl, 1981; see Muris & Mercklebach, 2001). Importantly, Rapee and Melville (1997) extended these findings by including reports from the mothers of individuals with SAD: both the offspring-report and mother-report indicated more social avoidance among the families of patients with SAD than in nonclinical controls.

There is also well-controlled experimental evidence for the role of vicarious conditioning in acquisition of specific fears and SPs that seems likely to be generalizable to other anxiety disorders, including SAD, PD, and GAD. This evidence comes from the work of Mineka and her colleagues on a primate model showing that strong and persistent phobic-like fears can be learned rapidly through observation alone (e.g., Cook, Mineka, Wolkenstein, & Laitsch, 1985). A particularly fascinating finding in this line of research is that this vicarious conditioning also occurred simply through watching videotapes of models behaving fearfully (Cook & Mineka, 1990), suggesting that humans are also susceptible to acquiring fears vicariously through movies and television (as expected from numerous anecdotal observations).

Direct social reinforcement and verbal instruction are also likely to play a role in the acquisition of anxiety disorders. Ehlers (1993) found that patients with PD, individuals with infrequent panic, and patients with anxiety disorders other than PD reported that they received more parental encouragement for sick-role behavior during their childhood experiences of panic-like symptoms (e.g., "Take care of yourself and avoid strenuous activities") than did nonanxious controls. Relatedly, an important study observing parent–child interactions has shown that parents of anxious children may be more likely than other parents to reciprocate their children's proposals of avoidant solutions (Dadds, Barrett, Rapee, & Ryan, 1996). Moreover, when anxious children discuss potentially threatening situations with their parents, such discussions have been found to strengthen the anxious children's avoidant tendencies (Barrett, Rapee, Dadds, & Ryan, 1996).

Selective Associations   A second criticism of early conditioning models of the acquisition of SPs and anxiety disorders is their equipotentiality assumption. That is, early conditioning models predicted that fears, SPs and anxiety would be acquired to any random group of objects and stimuli associated with traumatic outcomes. However, clinical observations show that people are much more likely to have fears of snakes, water, heights, enclosed spaces, elevated heart rate, and other people than they are of bicycles, guns, or cars. This is actually quite remarkable given that, today, the latter objects (not present in our early evolutionary history) are at least as likely to be associated with trauma as the stimuli that commonly trigger anxiety in individuals with anxiety disorders. To explain the nonrandom distribution of phobic objects, Seligman (1971) hypothesized that primates are evolutionarily prepared to rapidly associate certain kinds of objects (such as snakes, spiders, water, heights) with aversive events, as there should have been a selective advantage in the course of evolution for primates who rapidly acquired fears of such objects or situations. The term *prepared fears* refers to those that are not truly inborn or innate but which are very easily acquired and/or especially resistant to extinction.

Öhman and Dimberg (1978) and Öhman, Dimberg, and Öst (1985) subsequently extended Seligman's (1971) preparedness theory to social anxiety by proposing that social anxiety is a byproduct of the evolution of dominance hierarchies. They predicted that social stimuli signaling dominance and intraspecific threat—angry facial expressions—should be prepared CSs for social anxiety.

Preparedness theory has been tested in a series of human conditioning experiments conducted by Öhman and his colleagues. Consistent with predictions, they found superior conditioning using slides of snakes and spiders or of angry faces as fear-relevant (FR) CSs, and mild shock as the unconditioned stimulus (US), compared to what is found using more fear-irrelevant (FI) CSs such as slides of flowers, mushrooms, electric outlets, or neutral or happy faces (e.g., Öhman & Dimberg, 1978; Öhman et al., 1985; Öhman & Mineka, 2001). More recent studies have also shown that with FR-CSs (but not with FI-CSs) conditioning can even occur using subliminal presentations of the CSs (i.e., CSs that cannot be consciously identified; e.g., Esteves, Parra, Dimberg, & Öhman, 1994; Öhman & Soares, 1998). Such results may help explain the irrationality of SPs—that is, a person can claim to "know" rationally that a specific phobic object or social situation is safe and still experience anxiety that is automatically activated in response to subtle nonconsious cues.

Cook and Mineka (e.g., 1989, 1990) conducted an important series of experiments using videotaped model monkeys that demonstrated that observer monkeys can easily acquire fears of FR stimuli (e.g., a toy snake or a toy crocodile) but not of FI stimuli (e.g., flowers or a toy rabbit). Unlike in human preparedness experiments, these observer monkeys had not had any previous exposure to any of the FR or FI stimuli before participating in these experiments. Thus, these monkey experiments strongly support the role of evolutionary factors in the greater conditionability of FR than FI stimuli (Mineka & Öhman, 2002).

Uncontrollability and Unpredictability A third criticism of early conditioning models of the acquisition of SPs and anxiety disorders is that they do not explain why many individuals who do undergo traumatic experiences do not develop an anxiety disorder (e.g., Mineka & Zinbarg, 1996; Rachman, 1990, 2010). That is, many nonphobics retrospectively report having had traumatic experiences in the presence of some potentially phobic object without having acquired a fear or SP (e.g., Poulton & Menzies, 2002). Rachman (1990, 2010) similarly noted that there were very few emotional causalities of the blitzkrieg of London in World War II.

From the perspective of a modern conditioning approach, however, these observations of resilience in the face of trauma can be easily accommodated. For example, several different features of conditioning events themselves can have a strong impact on how much fear is acquired. Far less fear is conditioned, for instance, when the aversive event is escapable than when it is inescapable (e.g., Mineka, Cook, & Miller, 1984).

Perceptions of uncontrollability are a likely source of individual differences not only in the acquisition of SPs but also in the other anxiety disorders. For example, animal research has shown that uncontrollable (but not controllable) electric shock increases social submissiveness (e.g., Williams & Lierle, 1986). In addition, animal studies (e.g., Uhrich, 1938) of repeated social defeat (another uncontrollable stressor) show that it also leads to increased submissiveness not only to the victorious attackers but to any other conspecific behaving in an aggressive manner. Moreover, repeated social defeat in animals produces many of the classic "learned helplessness" effects usually associated with uncontrollable shock, including escape deficits (Hebert, Evenson, Lumley, & Meyerhoff, 1998) and exaggerated-fear CRs (Williams & Scott, 1989). J. L. Williams and colleagues concluded from such findings that the deleterious effects of social defeat are probably mediated by perceptions of uncontrollability. Such research and theorizing suggest that perceptions of uncontrollability are likely to play a role in the etiology of SAD. Indeed, consistent with this prediction, cross-sectional evidence documents a moderate to strong association between generalized perceptions of uncontrollability and SAD (e.g., Kennedy, Lynch, & Schwab, 1998).

Sanderson, Rapee, and Barlow (1989) conducted a fascinating study demonstrating the role of perceptions of controllability in panic attacks experienced by those with PD. Patients with PD underwent a panic provocation procedure involving the breathing of air with higher than normal levels of CO_2. The patients were told that if the experience became too unpleasant, if and when a light in the room came on, they could turn a dial to reduce the amount of CO_2 they were breathing. The patients were then randomly assigned to either a condition in which the light actually came on during the CO_2 inhalation (perceived control) or to a condition in which the light never came on (no perceived control). Eighty percent of the participants in the no-perceived control group reported experiencing a panic attack during the inhalation compared with only 20% in the perceived control group (despite the fact that the only participant in the study who actually attempted to turn the dial to try to reduce the amount of CO_2 inhaled was in the no-perceived control group).

Temperament/Personality and Conditioning   Another part of the explanation of resilience in the face of trauma undoubtedly involves temperamental or personality variables. Theorists ranging from Pavlov (1927) to Eysenck (1967) and Gray (1982; Gray & McNaughton, 2000) have hypothesized that individual differences on variables such as high trait anxiety or neuroticism are related to the speed and strength of conditioning and thus play a role in the origin of anxiety disorders. Indeed, there is considerable experimental evidence demonstrating that individuals high on trait anxiety/neuroticism more rapidly acquire aversive conditioned responses and expectancies than others (e.g., Levey & Martin, 1981; Zinbarg & Mohlman, 1998). There is also evidence from prospective studies, as described earlier, that such traits serve as nonspecific vulnerability factors for the subsequent development of SPs, SAD, and MDD (e.g., Biederman et al., 1990; Hayward et al., 2000; Kendler, Kuhn, & Prescott, 2004; Krueger, Caspi, Moffitt, Silva, & McGee, 1996; Schwartz, Snidman, & Kagan, 1999).

Interoceptive Conditioning   In *interoceptive conditioning*, the CSs are the body's own internal sensations (e.g., Razran, 1961). Bouton, Mineka, and Barlow (2001) proposed that when low-level somatic sensations of anxiety/panic precede and are paired with full-blown panic, the low-level somatic sensations of anxiety/panic come to be CSs that elicit high levels of anxiety and panic. That is, Bouton et al. propose that interoceptive conditioning may contribute to the fear-of-fear vicious cycle described earlier regarding the personality trait of AS. However, the trait of AS is believed to be most directly related to conscious beliefs that can be stated verbally. In contrast, interoceptive

conditioning can contribute to fear of fear even in the absence of conscious awareness of either the somatic sensation that has come to be a CS or the reason the person is afraid of the sensation.

One might object that panic cannot be involved in conditioning of *anxiety* on the grounds that the CR (anxiety) must resemble the unconditioned response (UR) (panic). Indeed, such an understanding of the conditioning process is not uncommon. However, Bouton et al. (2001) noted that although some CRs are very similar to certain components of the UR, other CRs are actually opposite in nature to the UR (although in all cases they serve to "prepare" for an upcoming US and UR). For example, aversive conditioning in rats to a shock US usually involves a CR like freezing rather than the activity burst that constitutes the UR (e.g., Fanselow, 1994). Thus, it is quite possible for anxiety to emerge as a conditioned response even when panic is the unconditioned response. Bouton et al. also noted that interoceptive conditioning has been observed when small increases in blood pressure become associated with larger increases in blood pressure (e.g., Dworkin, 1993). So weak versions of some response can become conditioned by pairing it with a stronger version of the same response— much as when early symptoms of panic, when paired with full-blown panic attacks, come to serve as triggers for full-blown panic attacks.

Bouton et al. also reviewed a great deal of clinical evidence that is consistent with several of the predictions that follow from their interoceptive conditioning model of PD. For example, panics will often be preceded by heightened anxiety if anxiety becomes a CS for panic. Studies using experience sampling and careful monitoring have found this to be the case, rather than panic truly coming from out of the blue as they are often experienced subjectively by patients. Bouton et al. also noted that the initial attacks experienced by patients with PD are generally terrifying, with thoughts of going crazy or dying being common symptoms, and this terror is more than sufficient to allow powerful conditioned responses to develop. Moreover, initial attacks are often perceived as unpredictable and uncontrollable and, as discussed earlier, these perceptions should augment the intensity of the conditioning that results from an initial panic. Consistent with this prediction many patients with PD report that their anxiety about having more panic attacks develops rapidly after the first panic attack.

Summary The origins of anxiety disorders are considerably more complex than was assumed by early conditioning models. However, these complexities are expected from the perspective of contemporary research on conditioning, which reveals a large variety of vulnerability (e.g., temperament) and contextual (e.g., controllability and fear relevance of stimuli) variables that impact the outcome of direct, vicarious, and interoceptive conditioning experiences.

Information-Processing Biases

Attentional Bias Several types of information-processing biases have been identified in anxious populations. Evidence for an attentional bias favoring the processing of threat stimuli has been reliably found for a range of different anxiety disorders (Williams, Watts, MacLeod, & Mathews, 1997). The bias seems to be driven by both a hyperalertness to threatening stimuli (Hirsch et al., 2011) and an impaired ability to direct attention away from such stimuli (Yiend & Mathews, 2001).

This inability to direct attention away from threatening stimuli once attention has been moved there may be an important difference between people with clinical levels of anxiety and people who are highly trait anxious. One paradigm that has been used to test for attentional bias is an emotional Stroop task in which words can be presented either masked (outside of conscious awareness) or unmasked (within conscious awareness). People with anxiety disorder diagnoses show the bias favoring the processing of threat meanings even when words are unmasked (e.g., Mathews & MacLeod, 1985). In contrast, highly trait-anxious people who have not been assessed clinically appear to be able to disengage from the threatening stimuli at later points in the information-processing stream (MacLeod & Rutherford, 1992). Thus, MacLeod and Rutherford (1992) found that when words were masked, highly trait-anxious subjects who were not assessed for anxiety disorders exhibited the attentional bias favoring the processing of threat, whereas low trait-anxious subjects exhibited the opposite bias; that is, the low trait-anxious subjects avoided processing threat. However, when words were unmasked and semantic processing was within conscious awareness, both high and low trait-anxious subjects only attended to relevant threat meanings (words relevant to final exams in this study, which used undergraduates as

subjects) and avoided processing irrelevant threat meanings. MacLeod and Rutherford (1992) concluded that, taken together with the earlier results demonstrating a threat bias with unmasked words in people with anxiety disorders (e.g., Mathews & MacLeod, 1985), this pattern of results suggests that a breakdown in the ability to override the initial, automatic bias favoring the processing of threat may be what discriminates those with anxiety disorders from highly trait-anxious people who have not been assessed for anxiety disorders.

The attentional bias seems to be fairly universal across the different anxiety disorders, though there are differences in the stimuli most likely to be attended to, often such that stimuli that are most self-relevant regarding the nature of a given disorder are more salient. For example, people with SAD are slower than nonanxious controls to color-name social threat words but not physical threat words on an emotional Stroop task (Becker, Rinck, Margraf, & Roth, 2001). In contrast, at least one study found that people with PD attend more to all threatening stimuli than do nonanxious controls (Maidenberg, Chen, Craske, Bohn, & Bystritsky, 1996).

Importantly, recent studies have manipulated the attentional bias using attention bias modification tasks (ABMTs), including some studies that have attempted to induce attention bias and others that have attempted to ameliorate it. Research suggests ABMT manipulations have causal effects on anxiety in the predicted directions (for reviews see Hakamata et al., 2010; Hallion & Ruscio, 2011). That is, inducing attention bias increases anxiety responses to subsequent stressors, whereas ameliorating attentional bias decreases such responses. These results are important for two reasons: they provide evidence that attentional bias favoring the processing of threat plays a causal role in the etiology and/or maintenance of anxiety, and they suggest that ABMTs ameliorating attentional bias can be an effective treatment for anxiety.

Memory Bias and Inhibitory Deficits Evidence regarding a memory bias in anxiety disorders is inconclusive (Craske et al., 2009). Some evidence has been found for an explicit memory bias in PD such that words describing anxiety symptoms were better recalled by people with PD (Becker, Roth, Andrich, & Margraf, 1999). On the other hand, some studies have even shown poorer explicit memory for threat-related information in anxious individuals (Watts, Trezise, & Sharrock, 1986). In the few cases in which superior memory for threat-related stimuli has been demonstrated, the effects could likely be due to increased processing and encoding resulting from the attentional bias (Mathews & MacLeod, 2005).

Interestingly, there is some evidence suggesting that there may be conditions in which anxious patients have difficulty forgetting threat representations when it would be adaptive to do so and that healthy controls can forget them. This is evidenced through use of the retrieval-induced forgetting paradigm, in which practice of words reliably inhibits memory for related, unpracticed words in healthy participants. For instance, a few practice trials at encoding of the word "strawberry" tend to impair recall of the word "apple." People with SAD, however, do not adaptively inhibit as many unpracticed negative social words as do controls (Amir, Coles, Brigidi, & Foa, 2001). State anxiety induced in a psychosocial laboratory stressor also has been shown to prevent adaptive forgetting, or inhibition, to occur (Koessler, Engler, Riether, & Kissler, 2009).

Interpretive Bias   Each day we are confronted with ambiguous information. We might hear a rustling noise outside the bedroom window at night, or be met by a coworker's blank face as we speak at work in the afternoon. Interpretive bias reflects the tendency to resolve such ambiguous information in a particular way.

There is a wealth of evidence from studies using self-report questionnaires that people with clinical and subclinical anxiety of all types interpret ambiguous information that is salient to their emotional concerns in a negative fashion (Mathews & MacLeod, 2005). For example, in one study, when presented with descriptions of ambiguous social situations (e.g., "You have visitors round for a meal and they leave sooner than expected") patients with SAD were more likely than those with other anxiety disorders or healthy controls to draw negative conclusions (Stopa & Clark, 2000).

Of course, it is possible that the findings from these self-report studies reflect a response bias for endorsing negative options, rather than an interpretive bias per se. Study designs that employ *implicit* measures of interpretive bias address this concern. In the first implicit interpretive bias study, MacLeod and Cohen (1993) asked participants to read passages of text, pressing a button in order to view each successive sentence. Although participants were led to believe that the data of interest were their responses to questions about the passages, the critical data were actually the delays between button presses, which provided an index of the comprehension latency for each sentence. Comprehension latency should be inversely related to the degree to which a participant expected the continuation of the preceding text (e.g., Haberlandt & Bingham, 1978). Indeed, MacLeod and Cohen found that participants with high trait anxiety selectively imposed threatening interpretations on ambiguous sentences, whereas participants with low trait anxiety did the opposite. Another set of implicit studies showed that people with elevated social anxiety are more likely than others to interpret neutral faces in a threatening manner (Yoon & Zinbarg, 2007, 2008).

Most recently, interest has turned to interpretive bias modification procedures, in which negative interpretive biases are systematically altered. Although these methods were originally developed to elucidate the causal role of cognitive biases in mental disorders, they have been shown also to have therapeutic benefits (see MacLeod & Mathews, 2012). Findings indicate that a single interpretive bias modification session may reduce symptoms related to anxiety sensitivity (Steinman & Teachman, 2010), chronic worry (Hirsch, Hayes, & Mathews, 2009), or GAD (Hayes, Hirsch, Krebs, & Mathews, 2010). Moreover, extended sessions appear to significantly reduce trait anxiety (Salemink, van den Hout, & Kindt, 2009). There is even evidence that interpretive bias modification is effective with young people, such as adolescents 13–17 years old (Lothmann, Holmes, Chan, & Lau, 2011). Thus, the evidence from interpretive bias modification studies demonstrates that a bias favoring threatening interpretations of ambiguity plays a causal role in the etiology and/or maintenance of anxiety. Future research will benefit from the application of randomized controlled trials to the study of interpretive bias modification, along with modification procedures for cognitive biases more broadly (cf. MacLeod, 2012).

Interpersonal Factors in Etiology and Disorder Maintenance

Attachment   It is well established that adverse events in early life represent a robust risk factor for the development of psychopathology (Kessler et al., 2010; McLaughlin et al., 2012). In addition, interpersonal and systemic variables are gaining increased attention in the anxiety disorders literature as possible etiological and maintenance factors (for a review see Beck, 2010). Indeed, there is emerging evidence that at least some of the anxiety disorders are associated with difficulties in interpersonal relationships (Whisman, 1999; Whisman & Baucom, 2012). Although research in this area is still relatively new, there is a growing body of work highlighting the relevance of attachment, interpersonal functioning, and expressed emotion in the anxiety disorders.

Bowlby (1973) viewed attachment as an evolutionary drive whereby infants develop a relationship to primary caregivers as a survival mechanism. Thus, the development of a secure attachment that is characterized by close proximity with the caregiver and by the perception of safety is hypothesized to allow the infant a secure base from which to explore the world and environment. Conversely, insecure attachment is hypothesized to develop when the caregiver does not provide the conditions of safety and security and is rejecting, inconsistent with attention, or overcontrolling. These early life experiences in attachment are proposed to lead to the development of an *internal working model*, or a cognitive framework that informs how one interacts with others and the world. These internal working models are reflected in attachment styles that are characterized as either secure, insecure-avoidant, or insecure-ambivalent. The development of an insecure attachment style is proposed to represent one pathway to development of anxiety disorders (Colonnesi et al., 2011; Esbjørn, Bender, Reinholdt-Dunne, Munck, & Ollendick, 2012).

One meta-analysis that examined attachment style and childhood anxiety disorders showed a modest relationships ($r = .3$) between insecure attachment style and childhood and adolescent anxiety disorders (Colonnesi et al., 2011), with the strongest relationships being with insecure-avoidant type of attachment. Further, several studies have examined the long-term effects of insecure attachment in anxiety disorders into adulthood. A fairly consistent finding is that adult anxious patients retrospectively report having, as children, had an insecure attachment style with their caregivers (Cassidy, Lichtenstein-Phelps, Sibrava, Thomas, & Borkovec, 2009; Eng & Heimberg, 2006; Eng, Heimberg, Hart, Schneier, & Liebowitz, 2001).

For example, Cassidy and colleagues (2009) examined retrospective reports of attachment style in childhood among treatment-seeking patients with GAD and nonanxious controls to examine the relationship between GAD and attachment. Patients with GAD reported poor attachment with their caregivers that was characterized by increased role-reversal/enmeshment in the caregiving relationship, high maternal rejection, and low maternal love. Further, the more cumulative risk factors one endorsed, the greater the likelihood of a diagnosis of GAD. Similarly, Eng and colleagues (2001) examined the role of adult attachment style in SAD. These researchers found that patients with a diagnosis of SAD fell into either an anxious-attachment cluster, which was associated with greater symptomatology, or a secure-attachment cluster, which was associated with less symptomatology. They also found that social anxiety symptoms mediated the relationship between insecure attachment and depressive symptoms. Taken together, these studies suggest that early development of insecure attachment styles may represent a risk factor for the development of an anxiety disorder and potentially serve a role in maintenance through adulthood through ineffective styles of interpersonal functioning (Snyder et al., 2010).

Interpersonal Problems   Interpersonal pathoplasticity builds on the pathoplasty model to emphasize the role of interpersonal functioning in the expression of psychopathology. *Pathoplasty*, as noted earlier, refers to personality influencing the presentation or course of psychopathology. *Interpersonal pathoplasticity*, then, is a term that has been used to refer to the role of interpersonal functioning in the expression of some forms of psychopathology (Klein, Wonderlich, & Shea, 1993; for a review see Pincus, Lukowitsky, & Wright, 2010). An emphasis on interpersonal theory and psychopathology can be traced back to the work of Harry Stack Sullivan, who viewed the expression of psychopathology and personality as occurring through interpersonal situations and relationships (Evans, 1996; Sullivan, 1953).

Sullivan's ideas were further refined and formalized into a model of interpersonal functioning that could account for the range of interpersonal behavior, referred to as the *interpersonal circumplex model* (IPC; Leary, 1957). The IPC is a two-dimensional circular model for organizing interpersonal behavior around two central axes. Although there is variation in the use of terms to label each axis, in Leary's (1957) original model the poles for each axis are labeled as dominance-submission (agency) on the vertical axis and hostility-affection (communal) on the horizontal axis. All forms of interpersonal behavior are conceptualized as a combination of these two axes, with each quadrant consisting of combinations of each pole. Although a number of variations of circumplex models have been proposed since Leary, they all share in common the central axes (Fournier, Moskowitz, & Zuroff, 2010).

One of the most commonly used circumplex measures is the Inventory of Interpersonal Problems (Alden, Wiggins, & Pincus, 1990; Horowitz, Alden, Wiggins, & Pincus, 2000). Results of several investigations using this measure support the identification of interpersonal subtypes for GAD (Eng & Heimberg, 2006; Przeworski et al., 2011; Salzer et al., 2008; Salzer, Pincus, Winkelbach, Leichsenring, & Leibing, 2011). Although there is some variation in the identification of interpersonal subtypes across studies, intrusiveness (inappropriately self-disclosing, attention seeking, difficulty spending time alone), exploitable (difficulty feeling and expressing anger for fear of offending others, easily taken advantage of by others), cold (inability to express affection toward others, difficulty forgiving others, difficulty making long-term relationships), and nonassertive (difficulty making needs known to others, difficulty being assertive) appear to emerge as four salient interpersonal clusters. Additionally, two studies using the IIP to examine interpersonal problems in SAD found in common a friendly-submissive (i.e., exploitable) interpersonal cluster (Cain, Pincus, & Holtforth, 2010; Kachin, Newman, & Pincus, 2001). The relevance of interpersonal problems in GAD and SAD have clear clinical implications. For example, treatment outcome studies show that interpersonal problems at pretreatment are associated with reduced response to cognitive-behavioral therapy (CBT) for GAD (Borkovec, Newman, Pincus, & Lytle, 2002) and SAD (Cain et al., 2010).

Although an interpersonally based conceptualization of PD has been proposed (Chambless, 2010), empirical research examining interpersonal problems in PD has not applied the IPC model. There does appear to be some evidence that PD is associated with interpersonal difficulties; however, whether interpersonal difficulties represent a salient factor compared with other stressful life events is unclear (Marcaurelle, Bélanger, & Marchand, 2003). The association between interpersonal problems and agoraphobia appears more robust. For example, Goldstein and Chambless (1978) identified a subset of patients with agoraphobia for whom interpersonal problems was the most common antecedent in the development of PD. Similarly, Kleiner and Marshall (1987) found that 84% of agoraphobics recalled experiencing marital/relationship conflicts prior to the onset of the disorder. Further, a notable portion of this sample reported a long history of unassertiveness, dependency, and fear of negative evaluations.

Expressed Emotion   Expressed emotion (EE)—or criticism, hostility, and emotional overinvolvement expressed toward a patient by a family member—has also received increased attention as a possible maintenance factor in anxiety disorders. Criticism may be understood in this context as a remark directed toward the patient by a family member during which the family member expresses disproval or dislike of a specific action the patient does. Hostility may be understood as a more extreme form of criticism intended to devalue or shame the patient. Whereas research on attachment style and interpersonal functioning examines the impact of the patient on the external environment, EE specifically highlights the impact of interpersonal factors on the patient (Hooley, 2004).

Although EE has received considerable attention in the areas of schizophrenia, mood disorders, and eating disorders as a consistent predictor of relapse (Butzlaff & Hooley, 1998), it has only recently been given increased attention in research on anxiety disorders. Emerging research in this area consistently shows that high levels of EE, particularly hostility, are associated with suboptimal treatment response for PDA (Chambless & Steketee, 1999), SAD (Fogler, Tompson, Steketee, & Hofmann, 2007), and GAD (Zinbarg, Lee, & Yoon, 2007). Further, high levels of interpersonal conflict are also associated with increased rates of relapse after treatment (McLeod, 1994). However, not all forms of criticism appear to be detrimental to the patient (Chambless & Steketee, 1999; Zinbarg et al., 2007). That is, while hostile forms of criticism are associated with suboptimal treatment response, criticism presented in a nonhostile manner is associated with improved treatment responses for patients with PD and GAD (and obsessive-compulsive disorder). However, the precise mechanisms of how hostility and nonhostile criticism influence the maintenance and treatment of anxiety still need to be delineated.

Concluding Comments

As documented in this chapter, great progress has been made in the past two decades in understanding the structure, etiology, and maintenance of the anxiety disorders. There is widespread consensus on several points. The anxiety disorders are not entirely independent, rather, there are broad factors shared by several of these disorders (and by the unipolar mood disorders). Further, there is a heritable basis for the anxiety disorders, but learning histories and interpersonal factors also contribute to their etiology and/or maintenance. In addition, there can no longer be any question that information-processing biases play a causal role in the etiology and/or maintenance of anxiety disorders given the results of attention bias modification and interpretive bias modification studies.

Of the various questions raised earlier in this chapter, two appear most fundamental to us. The first is whether the different anxiety disorder diagnoses truly represent distinct categories (or dimensions that differ in fundamental ways) or inconsequential variations of a broader syndrome that differ solely at the descriptive level in terms of the content of apprehension. The second question is whether several of the risk factors discussed earlier (e.g., neuroticism, behavioral inhibition, anxiety sensitivity, information-processing biases, genetic vulnerability) represent distinct pathways and have unique predictive power. Unfortunately, most studies of anxiety disorders focus on a single disorder and a single risk factor at a time. Thus, what the field needs are more studies that include multiple anxiety disorder diagnoses (or dimensions) as outcomes and multiple risk factors. Such designs will enable us to sort out both whether the various anxiety disorders differ at a deeper level than solely in terms of the content of apprehension and whether any of the various risk factors identified to date have unique predictive power.

References

Alden, L. E., Wiggins, J. S., & Pincus, A. L. (1990). Construction of circumplex scales for the Inventory of Interpersonal Problems. *Journal of Personality Assessment, 55,* 521–526.

Amir, N., Coles, M. E., Brigidi, B., & Foa, E. B. (2001). The effect of practice on recall of emotional information in individuals with generalized social phobia. *Journal of Abnormal Psychology, 110,* 76–82.

Andrews, G., Stewart, G., Allen, R., & Henderson, A. S. (1990). The genetics of six neurotic disorders: A twin study. *Journal of Affective Disorders, 19,* 23–29.

Asnaani, A., Richey, J. A., Dimaite, R., Hinton, D. E., & Hofmann, S. G. (2010). A cross-ethnic comparison of lifetime prevalence rates of anxiety disorders. *Journal of Nervous and Mental Disease, 198,* 551–555.

Barlow, D. H. (1991). Disorders of emotion. *Psychological Inquiry, 2,* 58–71.

Barlow, D. H. (2002). *Anxiety and its disorders: The nature and treatment of anxiety and panic* (2nd ed.). New York: Guilford Press.

Barrett, P. M., Rapee, R. M., Dadds, M. R., & Ryan, S. M. (1996). Family enhancement of cognitive style in anxious and aggressive children. *Journal of Abnormal Child Psychology, 24,* 187–203.

Beck, J. G. (2010). *Interpersonal processes in the anxiety disorders: Implications for understanding psychopathology and treatment.* Washington, DC: American Psychological Association.

Becker, E. S., Rinck, M., Margraf, J., & Roth, W. T. (2001). The emotional Stroop effect in anxiety disorders: General emotionality or disorder specificity? *Journal of Anxiety Disorders, 15,* 147–159.

Becker, E. S., Roth, W. T., Andrich, M., & Margraf, J. (1999). Explicit memory in anxiety disorders. *Journal of Abnormal Psychology, 108,* 153–163.

Biederman, J., Hirshfeld-Becker, D. R., Rosenbaum, J. F., He´rot, C., Friedman, D., Snidman, N.,…Faraone, S. V. (2001). Further evidence of association between behavioral inhibition and social anxiety in children. *American Journal of Psychiatry, 158,* 1673–1679.

Biederman, J., Rosenbaum, J. F., Hirshfeld, D. R., Faraone, S. V., Bolduc, E. A., Gersten, M.,…Reznick, J. S. (1990). Psychiatric correlates of behavioral inhibition in young children of parents with and without psychiatric disorders. *Archives of General Psychiatry, 47,* 21–26.

Bienvenu, O. J., Samuels, J. F., Costa, P. T., Reti, I. M., Eaton, W. W., & Nestadt, G. (2004). Anxiety and depressive disorders and the five-factor model of personality: A higher- and lower-order personality trait investigation in a community sample. *Depression and Anxiety, 20,* 92–97.

Birbaumer, N., Grodd, W., Diedrich, O., Klose, U., Erb, M., Lotze, M.,…Flor, H. (1998). fMRI reveals amygdala activation to human faces in social phobics. *Neuroreport, 9,* 1223–1226.

Borkovec, T. D., Newman, M. G., Pincus, A. L., & Lytle, R. (2002). A component analysis of cognitive-behavioral therapy for generalized anxiety disorder and the role of interpersonal problems. *Journal of Consulting and Clinical Psychology, 70,* 288–298.

Bouton, M. E., Mineka, S., & Barlow, D. H. (2001). A modern learning theory perspective on the etiology of panic disorder. *Psychological Review, 108,* 4–32.

Bowlby, J. (1973). *Separation: Anxiety and anger (attachment and loss Vol. II).* New York: Basic Books.

Brown, T. A., & Barlow, D. H. (2009). A proposal for a dimensional classification system based on the shared features of the DSM-IV anxiety and mood disorders: Implications for assessment and treatment. *Psychological Assessment, 21,* 256–271.

Brown, T. A., Chorpita, B. F., & Barlow, D. H. (1998). Structural relationships among dimensions of the DSM-IV anxiety and mood disorders and dimensions of negative affect, positive affect, and autonomic arousal. *Journal of Abnormal Psychology, 107,* 179–192.

Brown, T. A., Di Nardo, P. A., Lehman, C. L., & Campbell, L. A. (2001). Reliability of DSM-IV anxiety and mood disorders: Implications for the classification of emotional disorders. *Journal of Abnormal Psychology, 110,* 49–58.

Brown, T. A., & McNiff, J. (2009). Specificity of autonomic arousal to DSM-IV panic disorder and posttraumatic stress disorder. *Behaviour Research and Therapy, 47,* 487–493.

Bruch, M., & Heimberg, R. (1994). Differences in perceptions of parental and personal characteristics between generalized and nongeneralized social phobics. *Journal of Anxiety Disorders, 8,* 155–168.

Butzlaff, R. L., & Hooley, J. M. (1998). Expressed emotion and psychiatric relapse. *Archives of General Psychiatry, 55,* 547–552.

Bystritsky, A., Pontillo, D., Powers, M., Sabb, F. W., Craske, M. G., & Bookheimer, S. Y. (2001). Functional MRI changes during panic anticipation and imagery exposure. *Neuroreport, 12,* 3953–3957.

Cain, N. M., Pincus, A. L., & Holtforth, M. G. (2010). Interpersonal subtypes in social phobia: Diagnostic and treatment implications. *Journal of Personality Assessment, 92,* 514–527.

Campbell, L. A., Brown, T. A., & Grisham, J. R. (2003). The relevance of age of onset to the psychopathology of generalized anxiety disorder. *Behavior Therapy, 34,* 31–48.

Cassidy, J., Lichtenstein-Phelps, J., Sibrava, N. J., Thomas, C. L., Jr., & Borkovec, T. D. (2009). Generalized anxiety disorder: Connections with self-reported attachment. *Behavior Therapy, 40,* 23–38.

Chambless, D. L. (2010). Interpersonal aspects of panic disorder and agoraphobia. In J. G. Beck (Ed.), *Interpersonal processes in the anxiety disorders: Implications for understanding psychopathology and treatment.* (pp. 209–233). Washington, DC: American Psychological Association.

Chambless, D. L., & Steketee, G. (1999). Expressed emotion and behavior therapy outcome: A prospective study with obsessive-compulsive and agoraphobic outpatients. *Journal of Consulting and Clinical Psychology, 67,* 658–665.

Chorpita, B. F., Plummer, C. M., & Moffitt, C. E. (2000). Relations of tripartite dimensions of emotion to childhood anxiety and mood disorders. *Journal of Abnormal Child Psychology, 28,* 299–310.

Chronis-Tuscano, A., Degnan, K. A., Pine, D. S., Perez-Edgar, K., Henderson, H. A., Diaz, Y.,…Fox, N. A. (2009). Stable early maternal report of behavioral inhibition predicts lifetime social anxiety disorder in adolescence. *Journal of the American Academy of Child & Adolescent Psychiatry, 48,* 928–935.

Clark, L. A., & Watson, D. (1991). Tripartite model of anxiety and depression: Psychometric evidence and taxonomic implications. *Journal of Abnormal Psychology, 100,* 316–336.

Clark, L. A., Watson, D., & Mineka, S. (1994). Temperament, personality, and the mood and anxiety disorders. *Journal of Abnormal Psychology, 103,* 103–116.

Cole, D. A., Martin, N. C., & Steiger, J. H. (2005). Empirical and conceptual problems with longitudinal trait-state models: Introducing a trait-state-occasion model. *Psychological Methods, 10,* 3–20.

Colonnesi, C., Draijer, E. M., Jan J. M. Stams, G., Van der Bruggen, C. O., Bögels, S. M., & Noom, M. J. (2011). The relation between insecure attachment and child anxiety: A meta-analytic review. *Journal of Clinical Child and Adolescent Psychology, 40,* 630–645.

Cook, M., & Mineka, S. (1989). Observational conditioning of fear to fear-relevant versus fear-irrelevant stimuli in rhesus monkeys. *Journal of Abnormal Psychology, 98,* 448–459.

Cook, M., & Mineka, S. (1990). Selective associations in the observational conditioning of fear in monkeys. *Journal of Experimental Psychology: Animal Behavior Processes, 16,* 372–389.

Cook, M., Mineka, S., Wolkenstein, B., & Laitsch, K. (1985). Observational conditioning of snake fear in unrelated rhesus monkeys. *Journal of Abnormal Psychology, 94,* 591–610.

Costa, P. T., & McCrae, R. R. (1987). Neuroticism, somatic complaints, and disease: Is the bark worse than the bite? *Journal of Personality, 55,* 299–316.

Craske, M. G., Kircanski, K., Epstein, A., Wittchen, H.-U., Pine, D. S., Lewis-Fernández, R., & Hinton, D. (2010). Panic disorder: A review of DSM-IV panic disorder and proposals for DSM-V. *Depression and Anxiety, 27,* 93–112.

Craske, M. G., Rauch, S. L., Ursano, R., Prenoveau, J., Pine, D. S., & Zinbarg, R. E. (2009). What is anxiety disorder? *Depression and Anxiety, 26,* 1066–1085.

Dadds, M., Barrett, P., Rapee, R., & Ryan, A. (1996). Family process and child anxiety and aggression: An observational analysis. *Journal of Abnormal Child Psychology, 24,* 715–734.

Davis, M. (1998). Are different parts of the extended amygdala involved in fear versus anxiety? *Biological Psychiatry, 44,* 1239–1247.

Dworkin, B. R. (1993). *Learning and physiological regulation.* Chicago: University of Chicago Press.

Eaton, N. R., Krueger, R. F., Markon, K. E., Keyes, K. M., Skodol, A. E., Wall, M.,…Grant, B. F. (2013). The structure and predictive validity of the internalizing disorders. *Journal of Abnormal Psychology, 122,* 86–92.

Ehlers, A. (1993). Somatic symptoms and panic attacks: A retrospective study of learning experiences. *Behaviour Research and Therapy, 31,* 269–278.

Eng, W., & Heimberg, R. G. (2006). Interpersonal correlates of generalized anxiety disorder: Self versus other perception. *Journal of Anxiety Disorders, 20,* 380–387.

Eng, W., Heimberg, R. G., Hart, T. A., Schneier, F. R., & Liebowitz, M. R. (2001). Attachment in individuals with social anxiety disorder: The relationship among adult attachment styles, social anxiety, and depression. *Emotion, 1,* 365–380.

Esbjørn, B. H., Bender, P. K., Reinholdt-Dunne, M. L., Munck, L. A., & Ollendick, T. H. (2012). The development of anxiety disorders: Considering the contributions of attachment and emotion regulation. *Clinical Child and Family Psychology Review, 15,* 129–143.

Esteves, F., Parra, C., Dimberg, U., & Öhman, A. (1994). Nonconscious associative learning: Pavlovian conditioning of skin conductance responses to masked fear-relevant facial stimuli. *Psychophysiology, 31,* 375–385.

Etkin, A., & Wager, T. D. (2007). Functional neuroimaging of anxiety: A meta-analysis of emotional processing in PTSD, social anxiety disorder, and specific phobia. *American Journal of Psychiatry, 164,* 1476–1488.

Evans, F. B., III. (1996). *Harry Stack Sullivan: Interpersonal theory and psychotherapy.* New York: Routledge.

Evans, K. C., Wright, C. I., Wedig, M. M., Gold, A. L., Pollack, M. H., & Rauch, S. L. (2008). A functional MRI study of amygdala responses to angry schematic faces in social anxiety disorder. *Depression and Anxiety, 25,* 496–505.

Eysenck, H. J. (1967). *The biological basis of personality.* Springfield, IL: Charles C. Thomas.

Eysenck, H. J. (1970). *The structure of human personality* (3rd ed.). London: Methuen.

Fanselow, M. S. (1994). Neural organization of the defensive behavior system responsible for fear. *Psychonomic Bulletin & Review, 1,* 429–438.

Fogler, J., Tompson, M. C., Steketee, G., & Hofmann, S. G. (2007). Influence of expressed emotion and perceived criticism on cognitive-behavioral therapy for social phobia. *Behaviour Research and Therapy, 45,* 235–249.

Fournier, M. A., Moskowitz, D. S., & Zuroff, D. C. (2010). Origins and applications of the interpersonal circumplex. In L. M. Horowitz & S. Strack (Eds.), *Handbook of interpersonal psychology: Theory, research, assessment, and therapeutic interventions* (pp. 57–73). Hoboken, NJ: John Wiley & Sons.

Fox, N. A., Henderson, H. A., Marshall, P. J., Nichols, K. E., & Ghera, M. M. (2005). Behavioral inhibition: Linking biology and behavior within a developmental framework. *Annual Review of Psychology, 56,* 235–262.

Gadermann, A. M., Alonso, J., Vilagut, G., Zaslavsky, A. M., & Kessler, R. C. (2012). Comorbidity and disease burden in the

National Comorbidity Survey Replication (NCS-R). *Depression and Anxiety*, 29, 797–806.

Gold, A. E., MacLeod, K. M., Frier, B. M., & Deary, I. J. (1995). Changes in mood during acute hypoglycemia in healthy participants. *Journal of Personality and Social Psychology*, 68, 498–504.

Goldsmith, H. H., Buss, A. H., Plomin, R., Rothbart, M. K., Thomas, A., Chess, S.,…McCall, R. B. (1987). What is temperament? Four approaches. *Child Development*, 58, 505–529.

Goldstein, A. J., & Chambless, D. L. (1978). A reanalysis of agoraphobia. *Behavior Therapy*, 9, 47–59.

Grabe, H., Lange, M., Wolff, B., Volzke, H., Lucht, M., Freyberger, H.,…Cascorbi, I. (2005). Mental and physical distress is modulated by a polymorphism in the 5-HT transporter gene interacting with social stressors and chronic disease burden. *Molecular Psychiatry*, 10, 220–224.

Grant, B. F., & Dawson, D. A. (2006). Introduction to the National Epidemiologic Survey on Alcohol and Related Conditions. *Alcohol Research & Health*, 29, 74–78.

Grant, B. F., Hasin, D. S., Blanco, C., Stinson, F. S., Chou, S. P., Goldstein, R. B.,…Huang, B. (2005). The epidemiology of social anxiety disorder in the United States: Results from the National Epidemiologic Survey on Alcohol and Related Conditions. *Journal of Clinical Psychiatry*, 66, 1351–1361.

Grant, B. F., Hasin, D. S., Stinson, F. S., Dawson, D. A., Chou, S. P., Ruan, W. J., & Huang, B. (2005). Co-occurrence of 12-month mood and anxiety disorders and personality disorders in the US: Results from the national epidemiologic survey on alcohol and related conditions. *Journal of Psychiatric Research*, 39, 1–9.

Grant, B. F., Hasin, D. S., Stinson, F. S., Dawson, D. A., Goldstein, R. B., Smith, S.,…Saha, T. D. (2006). The epidemiology of DSM-IV panic disorder and agoraphobia in the United States: Results from the National Epidemiologic Survey on Alcohol and Related Conditions. *Journal of Clinical Psychiatry*, 67, 363–374.

Grant, B. F., Hasin, D. S., Stinson, F. S., Dawson, D. A., Ruan, W. J., Goldstein, R. B.,…Huang, B. (2005). Prevalence, correlates, co-morbidity, and comparative disability of DSM-IV generalized anxiety disorder in the USA: Results from the National Epidemiologic Survey on Alcohol and Related Conditions. *Psychological Medicine*, 35, 1747–1759.

Gray, J. A. (1982). *The neuropsychology of anxiety: An enquiry into the functions of the septo-hippocampal system*. New York: Oxford University Press.

Gray, J. A., & McNaughton, N. (2000). *The neuropsychology of anxiety*. Oxford, UK: Oxford University Press.

Griffith, J. W., Zinbarg, R. E., Craske, M. G., Mineka, S., Rose, R. D., Waters, A. M., & Sutton, J. M. (2010). Neuroticism as a common dimension in the internalizing disorders. *Psychological Medicine*, 40, 1125–1136.

Haberlandt, K., & Bingham, G. (1978). Verbs contribute to the coherence of brief narratives: Reading related and unrelated sentence triples. *Journal of Verbal Learning & Verbal Behavior*, 17, 419–425.

Hakamata, Y., Lissek, S., Bar-Haim, Y., Britton, J. C., Fox, N. A., Leibenluft, E.,…Pine, D. S. (2010). Attention bias modification treatment: A meta-analysis toward the establishment of novel treatment for anxiety. *Biological Psychiatry*, 68, 982–990.

Hallion, L. S., & Ruscio, A. M. (2011). A meta-analysis of the effect of cognitive bias modification on anxiety and depression. *Psychological Bulletin*, 137, 940–958.

Hariri, A. R., & Holmes, A. (2006). Genetics of emotional regulation: The role of the serotonin transporter in neural function. *Trends in Cognitive Sciences*, 10, 182–191.

Hayes, S., Hirsch, C. R., Krebs, G., & Mathews, A. (2010). The effects of modifying interpretation bias on worry in generalized anxiety disorder. *Behaviour Research and Therapy*, 48, 171–178.

Hayward, C., Killen, J. D., Kraemer, H. C., & Taylor, C. B. (1998). Linking self-reported childhood behavioral inhibition to adolescent social phobia. *Journal of the American Academy of Child & Adolescent Psychiatry*, 37, 1308–1316.

Hayward, C., Killen, J. D., Kraemer, H. C., & Taylor, C. B. (2000). Predictors of panic attacks in adolescents. *Journal of the American Academy of Child & Adolescent Psychiatry*, 39, 207–214.

Hebert, M. A., Evenson, A. R., Lumley, L. A., & Meyerhoff, J. L. (1998). Effects of acute social defeat on activity in the forced swim test: Parametric studies in DBA/2 mice using a novel measurement device. *Aggressive Behavior*, 24, 257–269.

Heils, A., Teufel, A., Petri, S., Stober, G., Riederer, P., Bengel, D., & Lesch, K. P. (1996). Allelic variation of human serotonin transporter gene expression. *Journal of Neurochemistry*, 66, 2621–2624.

Hettema, J. M., An, S. S., Neale, M. C., Bukszar, J., van den Oord, E. J. C. G., Kendler, K. S., & Chen, X. (2006). Association between glutamic acid decarboxylase genes and anxiety disorders, major depression, and neuroticism. *Molecular Psychiatry, 11,* 752–762.

Hettema, J. M., Neale, M. C., Myers, J. M., Prescott, C. A., & Kendler, K. S. (2006). A population-based twin study of the relationship between neuroticism and internalizing disorders. *American Journal of Psychiatry, 163,* 857–864.

Hettema, J. M., Prescott, C. A., & Kendler, K. S. (2004). Genetic and environmental sources of covariation between generalized anxiety disorder and neuroticism. *American Journal of Psychiatry, 161,* 1581–1587.

Hettema, J. M., Prescott, C. A., Myers, J. M., Neale, M. C., & Kendler, K. S. (2005). The structure of genetic and environmental risk factors for anxiety disorders in men and women. *Archives of General Psychiatry, 62,* 182–189.

Hirsch, C. R., Hayes, S., & Mathews, A. (2009). Looking on the bright side: Accessing benign meanings reduces worry. *Journal of Abnormal Psychology, 118,* 44–54.

Hirsch, C. R., MacLeod, C., Mathews, A., Sandher, O., Siyani, A., & Hayes, S. (2011). The contribution of attentional bias to worry: Distinguishing the roles of selective engagement and disengagement. *Journal of Anxiety Disorders, 25,* 272–277.

Hoehn-Saric, R., Hazlett, R. L., & McLeod, D. R. (1993). Generalized anxiety disorder with early and late onset of anxiety symptoms. *Comprehensive Psychiatry, 34,* 291–298.

Hooley, J. M. (2004). Do psychiatric patients do better clinically if they live with certain kinds of families? *Current Directions in Psychological Science, 13,* 202–205.

Horowitz, L. M., Alden, L. E., Wiggins, J. S., & Pincus, A. L. (2000). *Inventory of Interpersonal Problems Manual.* Menlo Park, CA: Mindgarden.

Jardine, R., Martin, N. G., & Henderson, A. S. (1984). Genetic covariation between neuroticism and the symptoms of anxiety and depression. *Genetic Epidemiology, 1*(2), 89–107.

Jorm, A. F., Christensen, H., Henderson, A. S., Jacomb, P. A., Korten, A. E., & Rodgers, B. (2000). Predicting anxiety and depression from personality: Is there a synergistic effect of neuroticism and extraversion? *Journal of Abnormal Psychology, 109,* 145–149.

Jylhä, P., Melartin, T., Rytsälä, H., & Isometsä, E. (2009). Neuroticism, introversion, and major depressive disorder—traits, states, or scars? *Depression and Anxiety, 26,* 325–334.

Kachin, K. E., Newman, M. G., & Pincus, A. L. (2001). An interpersonal problem approach to the division of social phobia subtypes. *Behavior Therapy, 32,* 479–501.

Kagan, J., Reznick, J. S., Clarke, C., Snidman, N., & Garcia-Coll, C. (1984). Behavioral inhibition to the unfamiliar. *Child Development, 55,* 2212–2225.

Karg, K., Burmeister, M., Shedden, K., & Sen, S. (2011). The serotonin transporter promoter variant (5-HTTLPR), stress, and depression meta-analysis revisited: Evidence of genetic moderation. *Archives of General Psychiatry, 68,* 444–454.

Kendler, K. S., & Gardner, C. O. (2011). A longitudinal etiologic model for symptoms of anxiety and depression in women. *Psychological Medicine, 41,* 2035–2045.

Kendler, K. S., Kuhn, J., & Prescott, C. A. (2004). The interrelationship of neuroticism, sex, and stressful life events in the prediction of episodes of major depression. *American Journal of Psychiatry, 161,* 631–636.

Kendler, K. S., Kuhn, J. W., Vittum, J., Prescott, C. A., & Riley, B. (2005). The interaction of stressful life events and a serotonin transporter polymorphism in the prediction of episodes of major depression. *Archives of General Psychiatry, 62,* 529–535.

Kendler, K. S., Prescott, C. A., Myers, J., & Neale, M. C. (2003). The structure of genetic and environmental risk factors for common psychiatric and substance use disorders in men and women. *Archives of General Psychiatry, 60,* 929–937.

Kendler, K. S., Walters, E. E., Neale, M. C., Kessler, R. C., Heath, A. C., & Eaves, L. J. (1995). The structure of the genetic and environmental risk factors for six major psychiatric disorders in women. *Archives of General Psychiatry, 52,* 374–383.

Kennedy, B. L., Lynch, G. V., & Schwab, J. J. (1998). Assessment of locus of control in patients with anxiety and depressive disorders. *Journal of Clinical Psychology, 54,* 509–515.

Kenny, D. A., & Zautra, A. (1995). The trait-state-error model for multiwave data. *Journal of Consulting and Clinical Psychology, 63,* 52–59.

Kessler, R. C., Chiu, W. T., Demler, O., & Walters, E. E. (2005). Prevalence, severity, and comorbidity of 12-month DSM-IV disorders in the National Comorbidity Survey Replication. *Archives of General Psychiatry, 62,* 617–627.

Kessler, R. C., Chiu, W. T., Jin, R., Ruscio, A. M., Shear, K., & Walters, E. E. (2006). The epidemiology of panic attacks, panic disorder, and agoraphobia in the National Comorbidity Survey Replication. *Archives of General Psychiatry, 63*, 415–424.

Kessler, R. C., McLaughlin, K. A., Green, J. G., Gruber, M. J., Sampson, N. A., Zaslavsky, A. M.,…Williams, D. R. (2010). Childhood adversities and adult psychopathology in the WHO World Mental Health Surveys. *British Journal of Psychiatry, 197*, 378–385.

Kessler, R. C., Petukhova, M., Sampson, N. A., Zaslavsky, A. M., & Wittchen, H. Ä. (2012). Twelve-month and lifetime prevalence and lifetime morbid risk of anxiety and mood disorders in the United States. *International Journal of Methods in Psychiatric Research, 21*, 169–184.

Klein, M. H., Wonderlich, S., & Shea, M. T. (1993). Models of relationships between personalty and depression: Toward a framework for theory and research. In M. Klein, D. Kupfer, & M. T. Shea (Eds.), *Personality and depression: A current view* (pp. 1–54). New York: Guilford Press.

Kleiner, L., & Marshall, W. L. (1987). The role of interpersonal problems in the development of agoraphobia with panic attacks. *Journal of Anxiety Disorders, 1*, 313–323.

Koessler, S., Engler, H., Riether, C., & Kissler, J. (2009). No retrieval-induced forgetting under stress. *Psychological Science, 20*, 1356–1363.

Kotov, R., Gamez, W., Schmidt, F., & Watson, D. (2010). Linking "big" personality traits to anxiety, depressive, and substance use disorders: A meta-analysis. *Psychological Bulletin, 136*, 768–821.

Krueger, R. F. (1999). The structure of common mental disorders. *Archives of General Psychiatry, 56*, 921–926.

Krueger, R. F., Caspi, A., Moffitt, T. E., Silva, P. A., & McGee, R. (1996). Personality traits are differentially linked to mental disorders: A multitrait-multidiagnosis study of an adolescent birth cohort. *Journal of Abnormal Psychology, 105*, 299–312.

LaBar, K. S., Gatenby, J. C., Gore, J. C., LeDoux, J. E., & Phelps, E. A. (1998). Human amygdala activation during conditioned fear acquisition and extinction: A mixed-trial fMRI study. *Neuron, 20*, 937–945.

Leary, T. (1957). *Interpersonal diagnosis of personality: A functional theory and methodology for personality evaluation.* Eugene, OR: Resource Publications.

LeDoux, J. E. (1995). Emotion: Clues from the brain. *Annual Review of Psychology, 46*, 209–235.

LeDoux, J. E. (2000). Emotion circuits in the brain. *Annual Review of Neuroscience, 23*, 155–184.

Lee, Y., & Davis, M. (1997). Role of the septum in the excitatory effect of corticotropin-releasing hormone on the acoustic startle reflex. *Journal of Neuroscience, 17*, 6424–6433.

Levey, A., & Martin, I. (1981). Personality and conditioning. In H. Eysenck (Ed.), *A model for personality* (pp. 123–168). Berlin: Springer-Verlag.

Li, W., & Zinbarg, R. E. (2007). Anxiety sensitivity and panic attacks: A 1-year longitudinal study. *Behavior Modification, 31*, 145–161.

Lothmann, C., Holmes, E. A., Chan, S. W. Y., & Lau, J. Y. F. (2011). Cognitive bias modification training in adolescents: Effects on interpretation biases and mood. *Journal of Child Psychology and Psychiatry, 52*, 24–32.

MacLeod, C. (2012). Cognitive bias modification procedures in age management of mental disorders. *Current Opinion in Psychiatry, 25*, 114–120.

MacLeod, C., & Cohen, I. L. (1993). Anxiety and the interpretation of ambiguity: A text comprehension study. *Journal of Abnormal Psychology, 102*, 238–247.

MacLeod, C., & Mathews, A. (2012). Cognitive bias modification approaches to anxiety. *Annual Review of Clinical Psychology, 8*, 189–217.

MacLeod, C., & Rutherford, E. M. (1992). Anxiety and the selective processing of emotional information: Mediating roles of awareness, trait and state variables, and personal relevance of stimulus materials. *Behaviour Research and Therapy, 30*, 479–491.

Maidenberg, E., Chen, E., Craske, M., Bohn, P., & Bystritsky, A. (1996). Specificity of attentional bias in panic disorder and social phobia. *Journal of Anxiety Disorders, 10*, 529–541.

Marcaurelle, R., Bélanger, C., & Marchand, A. (2003). Marital relationship and the treatment of panic disorder with agoraphobia: A critical review. *Clinical Psychology Review, 23*, 247–276.

Mathews, A., & MacLeod, C. (1985). Selective processing of threat cues in anxiety states. *Behavior Research and Therapy, 23*, 563–569.

Mathews, A., & MacLeod, C. (2005). Cognitive vulnerability to emotional disorders. *Annual Review of Clinical Psychology, 1*, 167–195.

McClure, E. B., Monk, C. S., Nelson, E. E., Parrish, J. M., Adler, J. A., Blair, R. J. R.,…Pine, D. S. (2007). Abnormal attention modulation of fear circuit function in pediatric generalized anxiety disorder. *Archives of General Psychiatry, 64*, 97–106.

McLaughlin, K. A., Green, J. G., Gruber, M. J., Sampson, N. A., Zaslavsky, A. M., & Kessler, R. C. (2012). Childhood adversities and first onset of psychiatric disorders in a national sample of US adolescents. *Journal of the American Medical Association Psychiatry, 69*, 1151–1160.

McLeod, J. D. (1994). Anxiety disorders and marital quality. *Journal of Abnormal Psychology, 103*, 767–776.

McNally, R. J. (2002). Anxiety sensitivity and panic disorder. *Biological Psychiatry, 52*, 938–946.

Mineka, S. (1985). Animal models of anxiety-based disorders: Their usefulness and limitations. In J. Maser & A. Tuma (Eds.), *Anxiety and the anxiety disorders* (pp. 199–244). Hillsdale, NJ: Erlbaum.

Mineka, S., Cook, M., & Miller, S. (1984). Fear conditioned with escapable and inescapable shock: Effects of a feedback stimulus. *Journal of Experimental Psychology: Animal Behavior Processes, 10*, 307–323.

Mineka, S., & Öhman, A. (2002). Phobias and preparedness: The selective, automatic, and encapsulated nature of fear. *Biological Psychiatry, 52*, 927–937.

Mineka, S., Watson, D., & Clark, L. A. (1998). Comorbidity of anxiety and unipolar mood disorders. *Annual Review of Psychology, 49*, 377–412.

Mineka, S., & Zinbarg, R. E. (1996). Conditioning and ethological models of anxiety disorders: Stress-in-dynamic-context models. In D. A. Hope (Ed.), *Perspectives on anxiety, panic, and fear: Current theory and research in motivation* (Vol. 43, pp. 135–210). Lincoln: University of Nebraska Press.

Monk, C. S., Telzer, E. H., Mogg, K., Bradley, B. P., Mai, X., Louro, H. M. C.,...Pine, D. S. (2008). Amygdala and ventrolateral prefrontal cortex activation to masked angry faces in children and adolescents with generalized anxiety disorder. *Archives of General Psychiatry, 65*, 568–576.

Munafò, M. R., Clark, T., & Flint, J. (2005). Does measurement instrument moderate the association between the serotonin transporter gene and anxiety-related personality traits? A meta-analysis. *Molecular Psychiatry, 10*, 415–419.

Muris, P., & Merckelbach, H. (2001). The etiology of childhood specific phobia: A multifactorial model. In M. Vasey & M. Dadds (Eds.), *The developmental psychopathology of anxiety* (pp. 355–385). New York: Oxford University Press.

Naragon-Gainey, K., Watson, D., & Markon, K. E. (2009). Differential relations of depression and social anxiety symptoms to the facets of extraversion/positive emotionality. *Journal of Abnormal Psychology, 118*, 299–310.

Nitschke, J. B., Heller, W., Imig, J. C., McDonald, R. P., & Miller, G. A. (2001). Distinguishing dimensions of anxiety and depression. *Cognitive Therapy and Research, 25*, 1–22.

Nitschke, J. B., Sarinopoulos, I., Oathes, D. J., Johnstone, T., Whalen, P. J., Davidson, R. J., & Kalin, N. H. (2009). Anticipatory activation in the amygdala and anterior cingulate in generalized anxiety disorder and prediction of treatment response. *American Journal of Psychiatry, 166*, 302–310.

Noël, V. A., & Francis, S. E. (2011). A meta-analytic review of the role of child anxiety sensitivity in child anxiety. *Journal of Abnormal Child Psychology, 39*, 721–733.

Öhman, A., & Dimberg, U. (1978). Facial expressions as conditioned stimuli for electrodermal responses: A case of preparedness? *Journal of Personality and Social Psychology, 36*, 1251–1258.

Öhman, A., Dimberg, U., & Öst, L. (1985). Animal and social phobias: Biological constraints on learned fear responses. In S. Reiss & R. R. Bootzin (Eds.), *Theoretical issues in behavior therapy* (pp. 123–178). New York: Academic Press.

Öhman, A., & Mineka, S. (2001). Fears, phobias, and preparedness: Toward an evolved module of fear and fear learning. *Psychological Review, 108*, 483–522.

Öhman, A., & Soares, J. (1998). Emotional conditioning to masked stimuli: Expectancies for aversive outcomes following nonrecognized fear-relevant stimuli. *Journal of Experimental Psychology: General, 127*, 69–82.

Olatunji, B. O., & Wolitzky-Taylor, K. B. (2009). Anxiety sensitivity and the anxiety disorders: A meta-analytic review and synthesis. *Psychological Bulletin, 135*, 974–999.

Öst, L. G., & Hugdahl, K. (1981). Acquisition of phobias and anxiety response patterns in clinical patients. *Behaviour Research and Therapy, 16*, 439–447.

Pavlov, I. P. (1927). *Conditioned reflexes.* London: Oxford University Press.

Pfleiderer, B., Zinkirciran, S., Arolt, V., WHeindel, W., Deckert, J., & Domschke, K. (2007). fMRI amygdala activation during a spontaneous panic attack in a patient with panic disorder. *World Journal of Biological Psychiatry, 8*, 269–272.

Pham, X., Sun, C., Chen, X., van den Oord, E. J. C. G., Neale, M. C., Kendler, K. S., &

Hettema, J. M. (2009). Association study between GABA receptor genes and anxiety spectrum disorders. *Depression and Anxiety*, 26, 998–1003.

Phelps, E. A., & LeDoux, J. E. (2005). Contributions of the amygdala to emotion processing: From animal models to human behavior. *Neuron*, 48, 175–187.

Pincus, A. L., Lukowitsky, M. R., & Wright, A. G. C. (2010). The interpersonal nexus of personality and psychopathology. In T. Millon, R. F. Krueger, & E. Simonsen (Eds.), *Contemporary directions in psychopathology: Scientific foundations of the DSM-V and ICD-11* (pp. 523–552). New York: Guilford Press.

Poulton, R., & Menzies, R. (2002). Non-associative fear acquisition: A review of the evidence from retrospective and longitudinal research. *Behaviour Research and Therapy*, 40, 127–149.

Prenoveau, J. M., Zinbarg, R. E., Craske, M. G., Mineka, S., Griffith, J. W., & Epstein, A. M. (2010). Testing a hierarchical model of anxiety and depression in adolescents: A tri-level model. *Journal of Anxiety Disorders*, 24, 334–344.

Przeworski, A., Newman, M. G., Pincus, A. L., Kasoff, M. B., Yamasaki, A. S., Castonguay, L. G., & Berlin, K. S. (2011). Interpersonal pathoplasticity in individuals with generalized anxiety disorder. *Journal of Abnormal Psychology*, 120, 286–298.

Rachman, S. J. (1978). *Fear and courage*. San Francisco: Freeman.

Rachman, S. J. (1990). *Fear and courage* (2nd ed.). New York: Freeman.

Rachman, S. J. (2010). Courage: A psychological perspective. In C. Pury & S. Lopez (Eds.), *The psychology of courage: Modern research on an ancient virtue*. Washington, DC: American Psychological Association.

Rapee, R. M., & Melville, L. F. (1997). Recall of family factors in social phobia and panic disorder: Comparison of mother and offspring reports. *Depression and Anxiety*, 5, 7–11.

Razran, G. (1961). The observable unconscious and the inferable conscious in current Soviet psychophysiology. *Psychological Review*, 68, 81–147.

Reiss, S., Peterson, R. A., Gursky, D. M., & McNally, R. J. (1986). Anxiety sensitivity, anxiety frequency and the predictions of fearfulness. *Behaviour Research and Therapy*, 24, 1–8.

Roberts, B. W., & DelVecchio, W. F. (2000). The rank-order consistency of personality traits from childhood to old age: A quantitative review of longitudinal studies. *Psychological Bulletin*, 126, 3–25.

Rodriguez, B. F., Bruce, S. E., Pagano, M. E., Spencer, M. A., & Keller, M. B. (2004). Factor structure and stability of the Anxiety Sensitivity Index in a longitudinal study of anxiety disorder patients. *Behaviour Research and Therapy*, 42, 79–91.

Rosellini, A. J., & Brown, T. A. (2011). The NEO Five-Factor Inventory: Latent structure and relationships with dimensions of anxiety and depressive disorders in a large clinical sample. *Assessment*, 18, 27–38.

Rosenbaum, J. F., Biederman, J., Gersten, M., Hirshfeld, D. R., Meninger, S. R., Herman, J. B.,…Snidman, N. (1988). Behavioral inhibition in children of parents with panic disorder and agoraphobia: A controlled study. *Archives of General Psychiatry*, 45, 463–470.

Rosenbaum, J. F., Biederman, J., Hirshfeld, D. R., Bolduc, E. A., Faraone, S. V., Kagan, J.,…Reznick, J. S. (1991). Further evidence of an association between behavioral inhibition and anxiety disorders: Results from a family study of children from a non-clinical sample. *Journal of Psychiatric Research*, 25, 49–65.

Salemink, E., van den Hout, M., & Kindt, M. (2009). Effects of positive interpretive bias modification in highly anxious individuals. *Journal of Anxiety Disorders*, 23, 676–683.

Salzer, S., Pincus, A. L., Hoyer, J., Kreische, R., Leichsenring, F., & Leibing, E. (2008). Interpersonal subtypes within generalized anxiety disorder. *Journal of Personality Assessment*, 90, 292–299.

Salzer, S., Pincus, A. L., Winkelbach, C., Leichsenring, F., & Leibing, E. (2011). Interpersonal subtypes and change of interpersonal problems in the treatment of patients with generalized anxiety disorder: A pilot study. *Psychotherapy*, 48, 304–310.

Sanderson, W. C., Rapee, R. M., & Barlow, D. H. (1989). The influence of an illusion of control on panic attacks induced via inhalation of 5.5% carbon dioxide–enriched air. *Archives of General Psychiatry*, 46, 157–162.

Schinka, J. A., Busch, R. M., & Robichauz-Keene, N. (2004). A meta-analysis of the association between the serotonin transporter gene polymorphism (5-HTTLPR) and trait anxiety. *Molecular Psychiatry*, 9, 197–202.

Schmidt, N. B., Lerew, D. R., & Jackson, R. J. (1999). Prospective evaluation of anxiety sensitivity in the pathogenesis of panic: Replication and extension. *Journal of Abnormal Psychology*, 108, 532–537.

Schmidt, N. B., Mitchell, M. A., & Richey, J. A. (2008). Anxiety sensitivity as an incremental predictor of later anxiety symptoms and syndromes. *Comprehensive Psychiatry, 49,* 407–412.

Schmidt, N. B., Zvolensky, M. J., & Maner, J. K. (2006). Anxiety sensitivity: Prospective prediction of panic attacks and Axis I pathology. *Journal of Psychiatric Research, 40,* 691–699.

Schwartz, C. E., Snidman, N., & Kagan, J. (1999). Adolescent social anxiety as an outcome of inhibited temperament in childhood. *Journal of the American Academy of Child & Adolescent Psychiatry, 38,* 1008–1015.

Seligman, M. E. (1971). Phobias and preparedness. *Behavior Therapy, 2,* 307–320.

Slade, T., & Watson, D. (2006). The structure of common DSM-IV and ICD-10 mental disorders in the Australian general population. *Psychological Medicine, 36,* 1593–1600.

Smillie, L. D., Cooper, A. J., Wilt, J., & Revelle, W. (2012). Do extraverts get more bang for the buck? Refining the affective-reactivity hypothesis of extraversion. *Journal of Personality and Social Psychology, 103,* 306–326.

Snyder, D. K., Zinbarg, R. E., Heyman, R. E., Haynes, S. N., Gasbarrini, M. F., & Uliaszek, M. (2010). Assessing linkages between interpersonal processes and anxiety disorders. In J. G. Beck (Ed.), *Interpersonal processes in the anxiety disorders: Implications for understanding psychopathology and treatment* (pp. 37–67). Washington, DC: American Psychological Association.

Somerville, L. H., Whalen, P. J., & Kelley, W. M. (2010). Human bed nucleus of the stria terminalis indexes hypervigilant threat monitoring. *Biological Psychiatry, 68,* 416–424.

Steinman, S. A., & Teachman, B. A. (2010). Modifying interpretations among individuals high in anxiety sensitivity. *Journal of Anxiety Disorders, 24,* 71–78.

Steyer, R., & Schmitt, T. (1994). The theory of confounding and its application in causal modeling with latent variables. In A. von Eye & C. C. Clogg (Eds.), *Latent variables analysis: Applications for developmental research* (pp. 36–67). Thousand Oaks, CA: Sage.

Stinson, F. S., Dawson, D. A., Chou, S. P., Smith, S., Goldstein, R. B., Ruan, W. J., & Grant, B. F. (2007). The epidmiology of DSM-IV specific phobia in the USA: Result from the National Epidemiologic Survey on Alcohol and Related Conditions. *Psychological Medicine, 37,* 1047–1059.

Stopa, L., & Clark, D. M. (2000). Social phobia and interpretation of social events. *Behaviour Research and Therapy, 38,* 273–283.

Sullivan, H. S. (1953). *The interpersonal theory of psychiatry.* New York: Norton.

Telch, M. J., Lucas, J. A., & Nelson, P. (1989). Nonclinical panic in college students: An investigation of prevalence and symptomatology. *Journal of Abnormal Psychology, 98,* 300–306.

Thayer, R. E. (1989). *The biopsychology of mood and arousal.* New York: Oxford University Press.

Thoeringer, C. K., Ripke, S., Unschuld, P. G., Lucae, S., Ising, M., Bettecken, T.,…Erhardt, A. (2009). The GABA transporter 1 (SLC6A1): A novel candidate gene for anxiety disorders. *Journal of Neural Transmission, 116,* 649–657.

Turner, S. M., Beidel, D. C., & Wolff, P. L. (1996). Is behavioral inhibition related to the anxiety disorders? *Clinical Psychology Review, 16,* 157–172.

Tyrer, P. J. (1990). The division of neurosis: A failed classification. *Journal of the Royal Society of Medicine, 83,* 614–616.

Uhrich, J. (1938). The social hierarchy in albino mice. *Journal of Comparative Psychology, 25,* 373–413.

Uliaszek, A. A., Hauner, K. K. Y., Zinbarg, R. E., Craske, M. G., Mineka, S., Griffith, J. W., & Rose, R. D. (2009). An examination of content overlap and disorder-specific predictions in the associations of neuroticism with anxiety and depression. *Journal of Research in Personality, 43,* 785–794.

van den Heuvel, O. A., Veltman, D. J., Groenewegen, H. J., Witter, M. P., Merkelbach, J., Cath, D. C.,…van Dyck, R. (2005). Disorder-specific neuroanatomical correlates of attentional bias in obsessive-compulsive disorder, panic disorder, and hypochondriasis. *Archives of General Psychiatry, 62,* 922–933.

Vollebergh, W. A. M., Iedema, J., Bijl, R. V., de Graaf, R., Smit, F., & Ormel, J. (2001). The structure and stability of common mental disorders: The NEMESIS Study. *Archives of General Psychiatry, 58,* 597–603.

Wang, P. S., Berglund, P., Olfson, M., Pincus, H. A., Wells, K. B., & Kessler, R. C. (2005). Failure and delay in initial treatment contact after first onset of mental disorders in the National Comorbidity Survey Replication. *Archives of General Psychiatry, 62,* 603–613.

Watson, D. (1999). Dimensions underlying the anxiety disorders: A hierarchical perspective. *Current Opinion in Psychiatry, 12,* 181–186.

Watson, D. (2005). Rethinking the mood and anxiety disorders: A quantitative hierarchical model for DSM-V. *Journal of Abnormal Psychology*, *114*, 522–536.

Watson, D., & Clark, L. A. (1984). Negative affectivity: The disposition to experience aversive emotional states. *Psychological Bulletin*, *96*, 465–490.

Watson, D., & Clark, L. A. (1997). Extraversion and its positive emotional core. In R. Hogan, J. A. Johnson, & S. R. Briggs (Eds.), *Handbook of personality psychology* (pp. 767–793). San Diego, CA: Academic Press.

Watson, D., Gamez, W., & Simms, L. J. (2005). Basic dimensions of temperament and their relation to anxiety and depression: A symptom-based perspective. *Journal of Research in Personality*, *39*, 46–66.

Watson, D., & Naragon-Gainey, K. (2010). On the specificity of positive emotional dysfunction in psychopathology: Evidence from the mood and anxiety disorders and schizophrenia/schizotypy. *Clinical Psychology Review*, *30*, 839–848.

Watson, D., & Tellegen, A. (1985). Toward a consensual structure of mood. *Psychological Bulletin*, *98*, 219–235.

Watson, D., Wiese, D., Vaidya, J., & Tellegen, A. (1999). The two general activation systems of affect: Structural findings, evolutionary considerations, and psychobiological evidence. *Journal of Personality and Social Psychology*, *76*, 820–838.

Watson, J. B., & Rayner, R. (1920). Conditioned emotional reactions. *Journal of Experimental Psychology*, *3*, 1–14.

Watts, F. N., Trezise, L., & Sharrock, R. (1986). Processing of phobic stimuli. *British Journal of Clinical Psychology*, *25*, 253–259.

Whalen, P. J. (1998). Fear, vigilance, and ambiguity: Initial neuroimaging studies of the human amygdala. *Current Directions in Psychological Science*, *7*, 177–188.

Whisman, M. A. (1999). Marital dissatisfaction and psychiatric disorders: Results from the National Comorbidity Survey. *Journal of Abnormal Psychology*, *108*, 701–706.

Whisman, M. A., & Baucom, D. H. (2012). Intimate relationships and psychopathology. *Clinical Child and Family Psychology Review*, *15*, 4–13.

Williams, J. L., & Lierle, D. M. (1986). Effects of stress controllability, immunization, and therapy on the subsequent defeat of colony intruders. *Animal Learning & Behavior*, *14*, 305–314.

Williams, J. L., & Scott, D. K. (1989). Influence of conspecific and predatory stressors and the associated odors on defensive burying and freezing. *Animal Learning & Behavior*, *17*, 383–393.

Williams, J. M. G., Watts, F. N., MacLeod, C., & Mathews, A. (1997). *Cognitive psychology and emotional disorders* (2nd ed.). Chichester, UK: John Wiley and Sons.

Yiend, J., & Mathews, A. (2001). Anxiety and attention to threatening pictures. *Quarterly Journal of Experimental Psychology A: Human Experimental Psychology*, *54A*, 665–681.

Yoon, K. L., & Zinbarg, R. E. (2007). Threat is in the eye of the beholder: Social anxiety and the interpretation of ambiguous facial expressions. *Behaviour Research and Therapy*, *45*, 839–847.

Yoon, K. L., & Zinbarg, R. E. (2008). Interpreting neutral faces as threatening is a default mode for socially anxious individuals. *Journal of Abnormal Psychology*, *117*, 680–685.

Zinbarg, R. E. (1998). Concordance and synchrony in measures of anxiety and panic reconsidered: A hierarchical model of anxiety and panic. *Behavior Therapy*, *29*, 301–323.

Zinbarg, R. E., & Barlow, D. H. (1996). Structure of anxiety and the anxiety disorders: A hierarchical model. *Journal of Abnormal Psychology*, *105*, 181–193.

Zinbarg, R. E., Barlow, D. H., & Brown, T. A. (1997). Hierarchical structure and general factor saturation of the Anxiety Sensitivity Index: Evidence and implications. *Psychological Assessment*, *9*, 277–284.

Zinbarg, R. E., Lee, J. E., & Yoon, K. L. (2007). Dyadic predictors of outcome in a cognitive-behavioral program for patients with generalized anxiety disorder in committed relationships: A "spoonful of sugar" and a dose of non-hostile criticism may help. *Behaviour Research and Therapy*, *45*, 699–713.

Zinbarg, R. E., & Mineka, S. (2007). Is emotion regulation a useful construct that adds to the explanatory power of learning models of anxiety disorders or a new label for old constructs? *American Psychologist*, *62*, 259–261.

Zinbarg, R. E., Mineka, S., Craske, M. G., Griffith, J. W., Sutton, J., Rose, R. D.,…Waters, A. M. (2010). The Northwestern-UCLA Youth Emotion Project: Associations of cognitive vulnerabilities, neuroticism and gender with past diagnoses of emotional disorders in adolescents. *Behaviour Research and Therapy*, *48*, 347–358.

Zinbarg, R. E., & Mohlman, J. (1998). Individual differences in the acquisition of affectively-valenced associations. *Journal of Personality and Social Psychology*, *74*, 1024–1040.

Zinbarg, R. E., Mohlman, J., & Hong, N. N. (1999). Dimensions of anxiety sensitivity. In S. Taylor (Ed.), *Anxiety sensitivity: Theory, research, and treatment of the fear of anxiety* (pp. 83–114). Mahwah, NJ: Lawrence Erlbaum & Associates.

Zinbarg, R. E., & Yoon, K. L. (2008). Reinforcement sensitivity theory and clinical disorders. In P. J. Corr (Ed.), *The reinforcement sensitivity theory of personality* (pp. 360–397). Cambridge, UK: Cambridge University Press.

6

Obsessive-Compulsive and Related Disorders

AMITAI ABRAMOVITCH,

NOAH BERMAN,

AMANDA CALKINS,

AND SABINE WILHELM

Obsessive-compulsive disorder (OCD) is among the five most prevalent mental disorders, with worldwide prevalence rates ranging from 1.5% to 3% (Okasha, 2003; Ruscio, Stein, Chiu, & Kessler, 2010). Indeed, a decade ago, the World Health Organization found OCD to be the 10th most burdensome condition among all medical conditions (Murray & Lopez, 1996). OCD has been discussed for over 300 years (Insel, 1990). However, there have been tremendous advances in our understanding of the disorder in the past three decades, including its cognitive, neuropsychological, and neurobiological mechanisms. *Obsessions* are characterized by recurrent intrusive thoughts, images, and impulses. *Compulsions* are repetitive behaviors or mental rituals, governed by specific rules that the individual feels compelled to perform. These rituals are typically performed to neutralize intrusions. OCD is considered an ego-dystonic disorder as the majority of patients have good insight regarding their obsessions (e.g., most patients will report that they are aware that their hands are in fact clean after washing them a number of times but will feel compelled to continue washing). In fact, one of *DSM-IV* criteria for OCD reads: "At some point during the course of the disorder, the person has recognized that the obsessions or compulsions are excessive or unreasonable" (p. 462).

Since the publication of *DSM-III* in 1980, OCD has been categorized as an anxiety disorder, though it has been part of the "neurotic, stress-related, and somatoform disorders" grouping in the *ICD*. The past two decades have witnessed an increasing interest in the concept of obsessive-compulsive spectrum disorders (OCSD). Phenomenological, pathophysiological, and neurochemical similarities with OCD led researchers to suggest the formation of a new category (OCSD) in *DSM-5*, including OCD as the primary disorder (Phillips, Stein, et al., 2010). Given that the diagnostic grouping to which this chapter is devoted is perhaps the most novel aspect of *DSM-5*, a brief history of the OCSD concept will be presented.

Several disorders have been considered for inclusion in the OCSD category, including body dysmorphic disorder (BDD; Phillips et al., 2007), hoarding disorder (HD; Mataix-Cols et al., 2010), trichotillomania (hair-pulling disorder [HPD] and excoriation (skin picking) disorder (SPD); Stein, Grant, et al., 2010), hypochondriasis (Fallon, Qureshi, Laje, & Klein, 2000), Tourette's syndrome and chronic tic disorders (Ferrao, Miguel, & Stein, 2009), obsessive-compulsive personality disorder (OCPD; Fineberg, Sharma, Sivakumaran, Sahakian, & Chamberlain, 2007), as well as impulse control and eating disorders (Potenza, Koran, & Pallanti, 2009; Storch, Abramowitz, & Goodman, 2008). The formation of a new superordinate OCSD category that is separate from the anxiety disorders has demanded careful examination regarding the validity of the prior conceptualization of OCD as an anxiety disorder (Bartz & Hollander, 2006; Stein, Fineberg, et al., 2010). Stein, Fineberg, and colleagues (2010) outlined the similarities and differences between OCD and other anxiety disorders in their review commissioned by the *DSM-5* Anxiety, Obsessive-Compulsive Spectrum, Posttraumatic, and Dissociative Disorders Work Group. Similarities include pattern of comorbidities (in probands and in families), cognitive and emotional processing, and certain temperamental antecedents, such as behavioral inhibition. However, the authors also observed significant discrepancies concerning both the centrality of anxiety symptoms and the disorder-specific neuronal underpinnings. With regard to the former, the authors concluded that anxiety symptoms do commonly occur in OCD, but they are also observed in other disorders categorized as developmental, psychotic, and affective. In addition, the common denominator among anxiety disorders is the *central* role of anxiety, whereas obsessionality is the central feature in OCD. A second prominent differentiating aspect stems from the different neurobiological pathophysiology associated with OCD compared to that associated with anxiety disorders. Contemporary models for anxiety disorders have focused on amygdala hyperresponsivity and amygdalocortical interactions. Stein, Finerberg, and colleagues (2010) aptly argued that in contrast, the prevailing neurobiological models of OCD have been centered on frontostriatal abnormalities.

Thus, distinctive features in OCD, together with its shared features with several other disorders, supported the formation of a new OCSD category in *DSM-5*. The formation of a new grouping category may appear as a mere technicality and not a significant taxonomical shift. However, formation of a new superordinate category may have several important implications. Grouping disorders together may highlight similarities, as well as subtle but important differences, between disorders in the same group (Phillips, Stein, et al., 2010), which will likely lead to more accurate diagnosis and better treatment outcomes.

The historical development leading to the formation of the OCSD category included extensive investigations and deliberations (for a review, see Phillips, Stein, et al., 2010). In addition, several reviews commissioned by the *DSM-5* Anxiety, Obsessive-Compulsive Spectrum, Posttraumatic,

and Dissociative Disorders Work Group (see special issue in *Depression and Anxiety*, Volume 27, Issue 6), and a meeting of the *DSM-5* Research Planning Conference on Obsessive-Compulsive Spectrum Disorders (Hollander, Kim, & Zohar, 2007; Hollander, Zohar, Sirovatka, & Regier, 2011) resulted in an initial recommendation to include OCD, BDD, trichotillomania, OCPD, and hypochondriasis in the new OCSD category (Phillips, Stein, et al., 2010). This process entailed a careful comparative examination of 11 validators proposed by the Diagnostic Spectra Study Group of the *DSM-5* Task Force (Andrews et al., 2009): (1) shared genetic risk factors; (2) familiality; (3) shared specific environmental risk factors; (4) shared neural substrates; (5) shared biomarkers; (6) shared temperamental antecedents; (7) shared abnormalities of cognitive or emotional processing; (8) symptom similarity; (9) high rates of comorbidity; (10) course of illness; and (11) treatment response. Though accepting the formation of a new OCSD category, the final version of *DSM-5* included OCD, BDD, HPD and SPD, and HD (the latter two as new disorders).

This chapter will focus on the new OCSD category, and will provide comparative examination between each of the five OCSDs and OCD. First, we will focus on OCD by describing its cognitive behavioral formulation and phenomenology, cutting-edge neurobiological and genetic findings, and empirically supported treatments. This will be followed by a detailed validator-based comparative depiction of the newly proposed disorders to be considered for inclusion in this category in the next edition of *DSM* (i.e., the edition that follows *DSM-5*).

Obsessive-Compulsive Disorder

Cognitive-Behavioral Model

Several models, stressing cognitive and behavioral aspects, have been offered to account for psychological mechanisms underlying the etiology of OCD. These models share similar fundamental assumptions, such as an abnormal process of appraisal of intrusive unwanted thoughts (Clark, 2004; Rachman, 1997; Salkovskis, 1999). Patients misinterpret normally occurring intrusive thoughts as overly important and dangerous (Rachman, 1997). As a result of this misinterpretation, the patient will likely feel distressed and attempt to neutralize the threat with a behavioral or mental ritual or with an avoidance behavior. The rituals or avoidance behavior result in a transient reduction in distress, which paradoxically reinforces the likelihood that patients will engage in ritualized (or avoidance) behaviors in the future when confronted with the obsessional phenomena. The rituals (or avoidance behavior) also maintain the false interpretation that intrusive thoughts are dangerous, given that the maladaptive beliefs are never disconfirmed (i.e., the patient does not have the opportunity to learn that his or her feared outcome does not occur when rituals are not completed).

Several additional theories have been discussed to explain the misinterpretation of thoughts. While healthy individuals tend to feel responsible for their actions, individuals with OCD are characterized by an inflated sense of responsibility, defined as the feeling that one has the power to cause or prevent negative outcomes that are perceived as highly probable to the patient (Obsessive Compulsive Cognitions Working Group [OCCWG], 1997, 2003, 2005; Salkovskis et al., 2000). This tendency for "magical thinking" is associated with *thought-action fusion (TAF)*, a prevalent cognitive bias seen in patients with OCD (Shafran & Rachman, 2004) as well as in other disorders. This construct is thought to consist of two components: moral TAF and likelihood TAF. *Moral TAF* represents the phenomenon in which thoughts have an equal moral weight to actions, whereas *likelihood TAF* is a tendency to believe that thoughts increase the probability of real-life events occurring. These cognitive biases, which contribute to the abnormal interpretive process of intrusive thoughts in OCD, are an important cognitive factor in the maintenance of OCD, and are directly targeted in cognitive-behavioral therapy through cognitive restructuring techniques.

Symptom Dimensions

OCD is a symptomatically heterogeneous disorder, one in which different patients are characterized by a variety of symptomatic manifestations. Symptoms related to contamination/washing and checking are the most prevalent in OCD and are seen in more than half the patients (Rasmussen & Eisen, 1988). The gold-standard measure to assess symptom dimensions as well as severity of OCD symptoms is the Yale-Brown Obsessive Compulsive Scale (YBOCS;

Goodman, Price, Rasmussen, Mazure, Delgado, et al., 1989; Goodman, Price, Rasmussen, Mazure, Fleischmann, et al., 1989). Specifically, the YBOCS symptom checklist (YBOCS-CL) includes 74 obsessions and compulsions that are associated with 15 predefined symptoms categories. Several attempts have been made to reduce the number of symptom categories; most studies demonstrate three or four symptom dimensions. A recent meta-analysis conducted by Bloch and colleagues (2008) identified four symptom categories extracted from studies, using the YBOCS checklist: (1) symmetry: symmetry obsessions and repeating, ordering, and counting compulsions; (2) forbidden thoughts: aggression, sexual, religious, and somatic obsessions and checking compulsions, (3) cleaning: cleaning and contamination, and (4) hoarding: hoarding obsessions and compulsions. More recently, a large study examined YBOCS-CL data from 1,224 patients with OCD and found that a five-factor model, including Taboo, Contamination/Cleaning, Doubts, Superstitions/Rituals, and Symmetry/Hoarding, provided the best model fit. In addition, these five factors were found to be heritable (Katerberg et al., 2010).

The heterogeneity of prevailing symptom categories in OCD led researchers to assess neurobiological and neuropsychological correlates of different OCD "subtypes." Indeed, research reported somewhat different neural substrates between OCD patients with primary washing, checking, and hoarding symptoms (Mataix-Cols et al., 2010). In addition, it has been proposed that the extent of set shifting and decision-making impairments may differ among different symptom dimensions (Lawrence et al., 2006).

Neural Substrates

Whereas different neural substrates and different neuropsychological impairments have been associated with symptom dimensions of OCD (Mataix-Cols et al., 2004), the prevailing neurobiological model pertains to a unitary pathophysiology underlying OCD as a syndrome. Neurobiological models implicate the frontostriatal system in OCD, which is found to be hyperactivated in resting state as compared to findings in nonpsychiatric controls (Whiteside, Port, & Abramowitz, 2004).

Alexander, DeLong, and Strick (1986) described a number of frontal-subcortical (frontostriatal) neuroanatomical circuits connecting the prefrontal cortex (PFC), the basal ganglia, and the thalamus. These parallel circuits—initially believed to be segregated entities—are thought to underlie numerous aspects of human cognitive processes and, ultimately, different behaviors. Abnormalities in frontostriatal circuits (originating from various regions of the frontal cortex) are thought to mediate the phenotypic expression of several disorders (Bradshaw & Sheppard, 2000). In OCD, abnormal brain activation has been repeatedly observed in major sites of the frontostriatal system, predominantly in the orbitofrontal (OFC), anterior cingulate cortices (ACC) and in the striatum (Melloni et al., 2012). In fact, these findings are considered among the most robust in the psychiatric literature (Chamberlain, Blackwell, Fineberg, Robbins, & Sahakian, 2005). Notably, the nature of this aberrant hyperactivation is very different from the hypoactivation observed in other disorders (e.g., schizophrenia, ADHD, bipolar disorder, and depression).

The prevailing neurobiological model of OCD argues that resting-state hyperactivation of the frontostriatal system in OCD may reflect several core phenomenological facets of OCD (for a detailed description, see Saxena & Rauch, 2000). For example, Rauch and colleagues (1997) suggeted that this type of activation operates in a circuit that connects the basal parts of the brain (associated with automatic processes) with the frontal parts of the brain (associated with higher-order controlled processes), which exemplifies a global preference for controlled processing in OCD. Others have suggested that this type of hyperactivity represents exaggerated representation of anticipated aversive events (Ursu & Carter, 2009) or a tendency toward executive hypercontrol (Bucci et al., 2004; Ursu, Stenger, Shear, Jones, & Carter, 2003).

Neuropsychological Research

Given the findings regarding aberrant activation in frontal, striatal, and connecting networks, it is expected that performance in cognitive domains will be impaired. The OFC is conceptualized as a crossing point between the limbic system, association cortices, and subcortical regions thought to play an important role in mediating autonomic and motor pathways. In addition, the OFC is thought to have a central role in monitoring and responding to changes in reward value,

including the inhibition of previously learned actions (Menzies et al., 2008). Given the focus of the current neurobiological model on the OFC and striatal connections, it is expected that patients with OCD will perform more poorly than healthy controls on tasks of executive functioning, including tasks assessing response inhibition, planning, organization, task switching, and reward-based decision-making. Indeed, although neuropsychological research in OCD has yielded somewhat divergent results, the majority of studies suggest deficits in these domains. Some researchers have reported reduced performance on tasks of response inhibition, predominantly on the Stop Signal task, Go-No Go tasks, and the Stroop tasks (Abramovitch, Dar, Schweiger, & Hermesh, 2011; Bannon, Gonsalvez, Croft, & Boyce, 2002; Penades et al., 2007; van den Heuvel et al., 2005). However, other researchers have failed to identify impairments on these tasks (Krishna et al., 2011; Rao, Reddy, Kumar, Kandavel, & Chandrashekar, 2008).

Patients with OCD usually perform more poorly than healthy controls on the Tower of London (TOL) task, which is designed to assess planning ability (van den Heuvel, et al., 2005). Additionally, OCD patients' elevated rate of perseverative responses on the Wisconsin Card Sorting Test (Cavedini, Zorzi, Piccinni, Cavallini, & Bellodi, 2010) and impaired performance on the Iowa Gambling Task (Nielen, den Boer, & Smid, 2009) suggest impaired ability to modify one's responses following a reward. Patients with OCD also perform more poorly on tasks that assess task switching (Chamberlain, Fineberg, Blackwell, Robbins, & Sahakian, 2006). Finally, the question of whether patients with OCD have memory impairments is subject to much debate and contrasting results. However, it has been suggested that reduced performance on a nonverbal learning task (predominantly the Rey-Osterrieth Complex Figure Test—ROCF) may be mediated by executive function deficit, hindering effective organization of visual information. This results in poorer quality of information coding and, ultimately, of the retrieval of information (Savage et al., 1999, 2000).

Course of Illness

The average age of onset of OCD is 19.5 years (Ruscio et al., 2010). However, it has been suggested that OCD exhibits a bimodal onset across the life span, with an earlier peak occurring in preadolescence (mean age = 10 years; Geller, 2006). The *DSM* describes OCD as a chronic disorder. Indeed, there is evidence that while waxing and waning occurs across the life span, OCD is usually chronic and persistent. Taken together, results from prospective studies on the course of illness of OCD are rather similar. For example, in a large (*N* = 214) 2-year prospective study, Eisen and colleagues (2010) reported a 2-year full-remission probability of .06 and partial- *or* full-remission probability of .24. Results from a prospective follow-up study of 100 patients with OCD revealed that the probability for partial remission after 5 years was .53, and that being married and having a lower global severity score at intake significantly predicted partial remission (Steketee, Eisen, Dyck, Warshaw, & Rasmussen, 1999).

Treatment

Neurochemical research implicates dysfunctional serotonergic (El Mansari & Blier, 2006) as well the dopaminergic systems (Denys, Zohar, & Westenberg, 2004) in OCD.

Indeed, the most effective pharmacological agents are a specific class of antidepressants called serotonin reuptake inhibitors (SRIs), usually prescribed in relatively high dosages (Fineberg, Brown, Reghunandanan, & Pampaloni, 2012). Individuals with OCD also benefit from dopamine antagonists (i.e., antipsychotic/neuroleptics) as an augmentation agent to SRI treatment (Bloch et al., 2006). The most effective psychological treatment for OCD, recommended by multiple expert consensuses, is cognitive-behavioral therapy (CBT) with a prominent exposure and response prevention (ERP) component (Koran, Hanna, Hollander, Nestadt, & Simpson, 2007). In fact, direct comparisons indicate that ERP may be of equal or better efficacy compared to pharmacological treatment for OCD. For patients who do not respond well to SRIs or ERP alone, a combination of the two is the preferred effective third-line treatment (Koran et al., 2007). In addition, cognitive therapy (CT) for OCD has been developed to more directly challenge maladaptive cognitive processes, such as intolerance of uncertainty (Wilhelm & Steketee, 2006). A significant strength of CT is that it does not require prolonged exposure and response

prevention; rather, this innovative treatment personalizes the patient's maladaptive belief domains and utilizes cognitive restructuring and behavioral experiments to challenge the dysfunctional interpretations. A recent study demonstrated that modular cognitive therapy significantly reduced OCD symptoms (Wilhelm et al., 2009). Finally, for patients who do not respond to any pharmacological and psychological intervention, deep brain stimulation (DBS) procedures have been shown to be effective in at least 50% of cases (McLaughlin & Greenberg, 2011).

Genetics and Familiality

Extensive research on the genetic component of OCD reveals a significant hereditary component. Twin studies show that 35%–65% of symptomatic variance may be attributed to genetic factors. For example, Hudziak and colleagues (2004) examined 4,246 twin pairs and estimated that 45%–61% of OCD symptoms may be attributed to genetics. Taken together, approximately 50% of the symptomatic variance in OCD is attributed to environmental factors. Family studies repeatedly demonstrate that the prevalence of OCD in first-degree relatives of patients with OCD is significantly higher than in the general population. For example, Nestadt and colleagues (2000) compared the prevalence of OCD in first-degree relatives of 80 adults with OCD and 73 controls. The authors found a significantly elevated prevalence rate of OCD in family members of OCD probands (11.7%) compared to the prevalence in families of nonpsychiatric control probands (2.7%).

Comorbidity

Approximately 90% of patients with OCD are diagnosed with at least one additional psychiatric disorder (LaSalle et al., 2004; Ruscio et al., 2010). Major depressive disorder (MDD) is the most prevalent comorbid condition. In fact, the prevalence rate of MDD in OCD is estimated to be 10 times higher than in the general population (Denys, Tenney, van Megen, de Geus, & Westenberg, 2004). In a large U.S. study, LaSalle and colleagues (2004) examined a sample of 334 patients with OCD and found that 66% had comorbid MDD. Comorbid MDD was found to be the most prevalent comorbid condition even in reports that found a lower prevalence rate. For example, one study reported that 39.5% of patients with OCD had comorbid MDD (Tukel, Polat, Ozdemir, Aksut, & Turksoy, 2002).

Anxiety disorders constitute the second most common comorbid group of disorders. In their sample of 420 patients with OCD, Denys and colleagues (2004) found comorbidity rates of 26% for specific phobia, 23% for social phobia, 18% for generalized anxiety disorder, and 14% for panic disorder. Results from the U.S. National Comorbidity Survey revealed comorbidity rates of 42.7% for specific phobia, 43.5% for social phobia, 8.3% for generalized anxiety disorder, and 20% for panic disorder (Ruscio et al., 2010). Other comorbid conditions seen in patients with OCD are bipolar disorder, OCPD, tic disorders, and OCSDs, as detailed in the sections that follow.

Body Dysmorphic Disorder

Formally dysmorphophobia, a term derived from *dysmorfia*, the Greek word for facial ugliness (Phillips, 1991), BDD has been recognized for more than 120 years (Morselli & Jerome, 2001). Nevertheless, up until very recently, BDD did not receive adequate research attention, which may be surprising in light of the high prevalence of the disorder. In fact, large population-based surveys found BDD prevalence rates to be 1.9%–2.5% in females and 1.4%–2.2% in males (Buhlmann et al., 2010; Koran, Abujaoude, Large, & Serpe, 2008; Rief, Buhlmann, Wilhelm, Borkenhagen, & Brahler, 2006).

Historically, BDD was described as a condition in which patients believe they are physically deformed or ugly in a socially noticeable fashion, despite normal appearance (Phillips, 1991). As early as the late nineteenth century, the psychiatrist Enrico Morselli reported symptoms of dysmorphophobia and specifically predicted that the phenomenological picture of this disorder would eventually be conceptualized as part of an obsessive-compulsive spectrum (for a translation of Morselli's 1891 paper, see Morselli & Jerome, 2001). Nevertheless, first appearing in *DSM-III*, and later in *DSM-IV*, BDD was classified as a somatoform disorder, presumably because of early association with hypochondriasis, as well as the perception of patients' complaints as somatic (Phillips, 1991; Phillips,Wilhelm, et al., 2010). Subject to minor changes from *DSM-III*, the

diagnostic criteria for BDD in *DSM-IV-TR* were as follows:

(A) Preoccupation with an imagined defect in appearance. If a slight physical anomaly is present, the person's concern is markedly excessive.
(B) The preoccupation causes clinically significant distress or impairment in social, occupational, or other important areas of functioning.
(C) The preoccupation is not better accounted for by another mental disorder (e.g., dissatisfaction with body shape and size in anorexia nervosa).

In one of the more dramatic changes in *DSM-5*, BDD has been moved to the new category of OCSD, and its diagnostic criteria have been subject to several modifications (Phillips, Wilhelm, et al., 2010). First, criterion A was modified in order to be less offensive and more acceptable to patients, removing terms such as "imagined" and "anomaly." Criterion B, describing disorder-specific symptoms, is an important addition to BDD diagnostic criteria in *DSM-5* that was not attended to in *DSM-IV*. This criterion describes the presence of repetitive behaviors and mental acts. Criterion C remains unchanged and corresponds to Criterion B in *DSM-IV*. Criterion D focuses on ruling out eating disorders. Finally, two specifiers were added to the diagnostic criteria. The first instructs clinicians to specify a muscle dysmorphia form of BDD (predominantly seen in men), where patients believe that their body build is too small or is insufficiently muscular. The addition of the muscle dysmorphia specifier is important, as psychotherapies for muscle dysmorphia may be different from treatment of other forms of BDD (Phillips, Wilhelm, et al., 2010). Another specifier addresses the important issue of insight in BDD, which may be significantly reduced compared to that in OCD (see discussion later in this chapter). Next, the rationale for including BDD as an OCSD will be discussed using the 11 validators previously noted.

Symptom Comparison

BDD and OCD share some central clinical features; in particular, patients with both disorders experience obsessions or preoccupations (Phillips,

Gunderson, Mallya, McElroy, & Carter, 1998). However, patients with BDD are preoccupied primarily with appearance, perceive their appearance as defective, and believe that others view them as deformed and consequently evaluate them negatively (Cororve & Gleaves, 2001). Indeed, with respect to core beliefs, BDD may more closely resemble MDD, in that patients with BDD focus on self-defeating and negative self-worth beliefs (Phillips, Stein, et al., 2010).

Patients with BDD also seek and receive dermatological interventions and cosmetic surgery. The reported prevalence of BDD in cosmetic surgery settings has been reported to range between 6% and 15% and is 12% in dermatology settings (Phillips, Dufresne, Wilkel, & Vittorio, 2000; Sarwer, Wadden, Pertschuk, & Whitaker, 1998; Sarwer, Whitaker, Pertschuk, & Wadden, 1998). Dermatological and cosmetic procedures are generally not effective in treating BDD symptoms; results consistently demonstrate no symptomatic change and at times exacerbation of BDD symptoms (Crerand, Franklin, & Sarwer, 2006). One study, examining 128 patients with BDD who received nonpsychiatric medical and surgical treatment, reported no symptomatic change in 90% of patients (Crerand, Phillips, Menard, & Fay, 2005). Moreover, dissatisfaction with treatment outcomes has often led to complaints against doctors performing these procedures, escalating in extreme cases of physical violence toward them (Phillips & Dufresne, 2000).

One major difference between OCD and BDD is the level of insight. The majority of patients with OCD perceive the content of their obsessional thoughts to be irrational, and intact level of insight has been reported in 66–85% across studies (Catapano et al., 2010). The most severe level of impaired insight, termed "delusional level of insight," has been observed in 2–3% of patients with OCD; in contrast, delusional level of insight is highly prevalent in BDD, estimated to occur in 32–39% of cases (Eisen, Phillips, Coles, & Rasmussen, 2004; Phillips, Pinto, et al., 2012). With regard to specific aspects of insight, appearance-related beliefs of nearly half of patients with BDD are delusional, with delusions of reference (e.g., the belief that others are taking special notice of the patients' perceived defects) seen in two-thirds of patients with BDD (Phillips, McElroy, Keck, Hudson, & Pope, 1994).

Another important difference between OCD and BDD is that suicidal ideation and suicide attempts are significantly higher among individuals with BDD. For example, a large study found that nearly 80% of patients with BDD reported a lifetime history of suicidal ideation and 28% reported a lifetime suicide attempt (Phillips & Menard, 2006). These rates are higher than estimates of suicidality in OCD. In a sample of 582 patients with OCD, 36% had suicidal ideation over their lifetime and 11% reported a lifetime suicide attempt (Torres et al., 2011). Phillips and colleagues (2007) attribute this difference to the prevalent delusional level of insight and the self-defeating perceptions that are often observed in patients with BDD (Phillips, 2007). This may be of tremendous clinical importance in light of the elevated risk of suicide in adolescence, the developmental phase in which BDD usually begins.

In sum, OCD and BDD are similar in that obsessions and compulsions are the core symptoms of both disorders. However, differences include the focus of the obsessions and compulsions, the reduced level of insight, saliency of self-defeating core beliefs, and increased rate of cosmetic procedures and suicidality associated with BDD.

Comorbidity

Approximately one-third of individuals with BDD have a comorbid lifetime diagnosis of OCD, two-thirds have a comorbid lifetime diagnosis of MDD, and nearly 40% have a lifetime history of social phobia (Gunstad & Phillips, 2003). When removal of BDD from the somatoform disorders grouping was considered, various studies examined the comorbidity of BDD with the other somatoform disorders. Results suggested that the comorbidity of BDD with somatoform disorders was lower than the comorbidity with anxiety disorders (Gunstad & Phillips, 2003; Phillips, Menard, Fay, & Weisberg, 2005). Gunstad and Phillips (2003) examined comorbidities in a sample of 293 patients with BDD and found that 64% had lifetime comorbidity with any anxiety disorder, as opposed to 8.5% with a lifetime comorbid somatoform disorder. Notably, BDD-OCD comparative studies revealed a similar pattern of lifetime comorbidities, although a higher prevalence of comorbid MDD and substance abuse were found in BDD (Phillips, Stein, et al., 2010).

Course of Illness

Typically, BDD begins in adolescence, with roughly two-thirds of cases having an onset before age 18. The mean age of onset reported in two large studies was 16 years, with a mode of 13 years (Gunstad & Phillips, 2003; Phillips et al., 2005). BDD's age of onset was found to be similar to (Phillips et al., 2007), and at times earlier than (Frare, Perugi, Ruffolo, & Toni, 2004), that of OCD. As noted earlier, research on pediatric OCD suggests a bimodal distribution of age of onset, with the first peaking in preadolescent childhood and the second in adulthood. This type of bimodality was not observed in BDD.

BDD appears to be a disabling chronic condition. Phillips, Pagano, Menard, and Stout (2006) conducted a 1-year longitudinal study and found that the probabilities of full and partial remission in BDD were .09 and .21, respectively. Notably, while more than 80% of patients in this study received pharmacological, psychological, or combined treatments, approximately 80% of participants met *DSM* criteria for BDD throughout the study. The remission rates reported by the authors are generally similar to the ones reported for OCD and other anxiety disorders. The authors further reported that OCD and MDD symptom improvement predicted BDD remission, suggesting an etiological association with OCD and MDD. Recently, the same group reported the results of a 4-year follow-up that also suggest that BDD is a chronic condition; encouragingly, full remission was found to be .2, and partial remission .55 (Phillips, Menard, Quinn, Didie, & Stout, 2012). Greater severity at intake, longer lifetime duration of BDD, and earlier age of onset were found to be associated with higher risk for chronic BDD.

Familiality

Two studies found that BDD was more prevalent in first-degree relatives of probands with OCD than in first-degree relatives of control probands (Bienvenu et al., 2000, 2012). Another comparative study found that first-degree relatives of BDD and OCD probands did not differ in lifetime prevalence of somatoform disorders (0%), OCD (7% vs. 8%), and MDD (20% vs. 13%), respectively (Phillips et al., 1998). These findings support the categorization of BDD as an OCSD.

Genetic and Environmental Risk Factors

Genetic investigation into BDD is scarce. However, preliminary evidence suggests a possible hereditary component for the main symptomatic construct in BDD, as well as a genetic association with OCD. Recently, a large twin study conducted in England concluded that 44% of the variance of body dysmorphic concerns may be explained by genetic factors (Monzani, Rijsdijk, Anson, et al., 2012; Monzani, Rijsdijk, Iervolino, et al., 2012). Furthermore, the authors reported a significant overlap between obsessive-compulsive symptoms and body dysmorphic concerns (Monzani, Rijsdijk, Iervolino, et al., 2012).

Limited data are available regarding the influence of environmental factors in BDD. There is evidence for a high prevalence of child abuse and neglect in this disorder (Didie et al., 2006). A significantly higher prevalence of childhood sexual and emotional abuse in BDD than in OCD has been reported (Neziroglu, Khemlani-Patel, & Yaryura-Tobias, 2006). In a more recent study, patients with BDD retrospectively reported more experiences of sexual and physical abuse, but not emotional abuse, when compared to nonpsychiatric controls (Buhlmann, Marques, & Wilhelm, 2012). Finally, a recent twin study found that along with genetic factors, individual (but not shared) environmental factors play an important role in the etiology of BDD (Monzani, Rijsdijk, Anson, et al., 2012).

Neural Substrates

A limited number of functional magnetic resonance imaging (fMRI) studies have examined brain activation in BDD during task performance (no research to date has investigated resting-state activation in BDD). In one study, patients with BDD showed increased activation in the lateral prefrontal cortex and lateral temporal lobe while watching pictures of faces, compared to controls (Feusner, Townsend, Bystritsky, & Bookheimer, 2007). Notably, the authors also reported an abnormal increase in activation in the amygdala in response to face stimuli, a finding that is not characteristic of OCD. In a second study (Feusner, Moody, et al., 2010), the authors compared brain activation of BDD patients and controls while participants viewed unaltered photographs of their own face and familiar faces (control stimuli).

Results revealed that, compared to controls, relative hyperactivity was observed in the orbitofrontal cortex and the head of caudate bilaterally in patients with BDD when viewing patients' own faces as compared to viewing the control stimuli. In addition, BDD symptom severity was positively correlated with brain activity in the frontostriatal system and the visual cortex. These findings (i.e., frontostriatal hyperactivation and positive correlation with disorder-specific symptom severity) have been repeatedly observed in patients with OCD (Harrison et al., 2009; Saxena & Rauch, 2000; Whiteside et al., 2004) and thus are in support of the categorization of BDD as an OCSD.

Temperamental Antecedents

Whereas no longitudinal data examining temperamental antecedents from a developmental perspective in BDD are available, cross-sectional findings indicate some striking temperamental similarities between BDD and OCD. Similar to OCD, patients with BDD are characterized by high levels of harm avoidance and general inhibited temperament (Pavan et al., 2006), as well as low levels of extroversion and high levels of neuroticism (Phillips & McElroy, 2000). In addition, one study demonstrated comparable levels of perfectionism in BDD and OCD, which was significantly higher than the degree of perfectionism found in healthy controls (Buhlmann, Etcoff, & Wilhelm, 2008). While there is a need for more research, specifically longitudinal studies, the available cross-sectional data indicate comparable temperamental characteristics between BDD and OCD.

Cognitive and Emotional Processing

Research into neuropsychological functioning in BDD is remarkably limited. However, some neuropsychological impairments have been reported in BDD, predominantly in executive functioning. An early neuropsychological study compared performance on executive function, verbal memory, nonverbal memory, and motor skills tasks in BDD, schizophrenia, and OCD patients as well as in nonpsychiatric controls (Hanes, 1998). The authors reported that, compared to controls, both the OCD and the BDD groups performed poorly on the Stroop and the TOL tests, representing executive function impairments in planning and response inhibition. Notably, the performance

of both groups was found to be equally intact on all other measures. Impaired planning ability in BDD was also observed by Dunai and colleagues (Dunai, Labuschagne, Castle, Kyrios, & Rossell, 2010), who reported impaired performance on a new version of the TOL (i.e., the Stocking of Cambridge test). In addition, compared to an age- and sex-matched control sample, individuals with BDD showed deficient performance on a spatial working memory task, but intact performance on tasks assessing short-term memory, motor speed, and visual memory. In contrast to the intact performance of BDD patients on memory tasks in these two studies, Deckersbach and colleagues (2000) found memory impairments in a sample of BDD patients compared to controls. In this study, the authors administered the Rey-Osterrieth Complex Figure Test (ROCF) and the California Verbal Learning Test (CVLT), assessing nonverbal and verbal memory, respectively. The BDD group scored significantly lower on the ROCF immediate recall, which was partially attributed to deficient organization abilities found for that group. These impairments in short-term delayed nonverbal memory and organization of nonverbal information were accompanied by impaired performance on the verbal learning as well as immediate and delayed verbal memory trials on the CVLT (Deckersbach et al., 2000).

While the results from these three small studies are somewhat inconsistent, there is preliminary evidence for neuropsychological impairments in executive function (i.e., planning, response inhibition, and information organization) and verbal and nonverbal memory in patients with BDD. Although findings from neuropsychological studies in OCD have been inconsistent (Kuelz, Hohagen, & Voderholzer, 2004), there is ample evidence for deficits in executive functions and nonverbal memory in OCD. The latter pattern also has been found to be partially accounted for by deficient organization ability on the ROCF. These impairments may suggest a dysfunctional frontostriatal system, and especially prefrontal regions, that mediate executive functions. Indeed, as noted earlier, current neurobiological models of OCD focus on frontostrial dysfunction, which has been suggested to underlie BDD. Thus, very limited research (a total of 45 patients with BDD) indicates that executive and nonverbal memory impairments in BDD are similar to those observed in OCD. These findings, if further replicated, may suggest that BDD and OCD share a similar fronto-striatal pathophysiology.

However, in contrast to those with OCD, patients with BDD may suffer from an abnormality related to visual perception and processing of faces and emotions. Patients with BDD were found to make significantly more errors matching faces to emotions than did control participants (Feusner, Bystritsky, Hellemann, & Bookheimer, 2010), and more often misidentified emotional expressions as angry compared to controls and OCD patients (Buhlmann, McNally, Etcoff, Tuschen-Caffier, & Wilhelm, 2004). Patients with BDD were also found to rate attractive faces as significantly more attractive than similar assessments made by controls or OCD patients (Buhlmann et al., 2008) and tended to attribute more threatening interpretations to neutral information about appearance compared to interpretations made by controls or OCD patients (Buhlmann et al., 2002). This tendency may be associated with research findings suggesting that two-thirds of patients with BDD experience delusions of reference, where they believe that others take special notice of them (Phillips et al., 1994, 1998). Notably, some of these effects are thought to be associated with disorder-specific traits such as preoccupation with and idealization of body image (Buhlmann et al., 2008). However, as a whole, emotional processing and perceptual and interpretive biases have been associated with increased anxiety that may be related to perfectionism, intolerance of ambiguity, and the tendency to be more detail-oriented, as evidenced by a longer response time for patients with BDD for processing inverted faces (Feusner, Moller, et al., 2010). Thus, the evidence for BDD's shared interpretation biases with anxiety disorders in general and OCD in particular are in support of the inclusion of BDD as an OCSD.

Treatment Response

As with OCD, SRI monotherapy has been demonstrated to be effective for treating BDD (National Collaborating Centre for Mental Health, 2006; Hollander et al., 1999; Ipser, Sander, & Stein, 2009). Another interesting similarity between BDD and OCD is that high SRI dosages are needed to achieve significant treatment response (Phillips & Hollander, 2008). However, neuroleptic augmentation for SRIs, which is effective for OCD (Bloch et al., 2006), was not found to be more effective than placebo in BDD. These findings have been demonstrated in a placebo-controlled study of pimozide augmentation for fluoxetine in BDD (Phillips, 2005b) and in a small study examining olanzapine augmentation to fluoxetine in six patients with BDD (Phillips, 2005a). These findings are somewhat surprising, and more research in this area is needed.

The efficacy of ERP-based individual or group CBT for BDD has been demonstrated in case studies, case series, and two studies using wait-list control groups (for a review, see Ipser et al., 2009). Wilhelm Phillips, Fama, Greenberg, and Steketee (2011) reported that 10 out of 12 patients responded favorably to treatment. Although the sample was small, the results are impressive given that the definition for response to treatment was based primarily on a 30% or greater reduction in symptoms. Moreover, the authors reported that patients were able to maintain their treatment gains after 6 months (Wilhelm et al., 2011). These more encouraging results suggest that when applying appropriate treatment (such as the newer CBT protocols administered in the study cited earlier), better treatment outcomes may be achieved. Of note, although the elements of CBT for BDD are similar to those used in the treatment of OCD and social phobia, the impaired insight associated with BDD may necessitate more intense forms of cognitive restructuring (Phillips, Stein, et al., 2010).

Hoarding Disorder

Hoarding behavior has been described in multiple mental disorders, such as dementia, schizophrenia, and autism (Pertusa et al., 2010; Steketee, Frost, & Kyrios, 2003). Hoarding has been frequently linked with OCD in the literature. In *DSM-IV*, hoarding is listed as one of the eight diagnostic criteria for OCPD. In *DSM-5*, hoarding disorder (HD) is, for the first time, a separate disorder, within OCSD. HD is characterized by a persistent difficulty in discarding or parting with possessions, regardless of their actual value, which results in the accumulation of a large number of possessions that fill up and clutter active living areas of the home or workplace to the extent that their intended use is no longer possible.

An initial field trial of these criteria found that *DSM-5* HD criteria are valid, reliable, and perceived as acceptable and useful by individuals with hoarding problems as well as by clinicians (Mataix-Cols, Billottia, Fernández de la Cruza, & Nordsletten, 2012). Additionally, the criteria appear to be sufficiently conservative and unlikely to overpathologize normative collecting behavior (Mataix-Cols et al., 2012). These criteria need to be further evaluated in clinical samples; however, these criteria have high sensitivity and specificity when used by professionals in the hoarding field (Mataix-Cols, Fernández de la Cruza, Nakaoa, & Pertusa, 2011). Although we do not yet have prevalence rates of HD using the finalized diagnostic criteria, a series of recent epidemiological studies have been conducted using reliable and valid psychometric instruments very similar to the diagnostic criteria (Frost, Steketee, & Grisham, 2004; Tolin, Frost, & Steketee, 2010). The prevalence of clinically significant hoarding is estimated to range between 2% and 5.8% of the general population and 10% and 20% of patients in anxiety disorder or OCD clinics (Iervolino et al., 2009; Pertusa et al., 2010; Samuels et al., 2008; Timpano, Schmidt, Wheaton, Wendland, & Murphy, 2011; Tolin, Meunier, Frost, & Steketee, 2011). Thus, hoarding symptoms appear to be very common. Given HD's inclusion in *DSM-5* in the OCSDs, this section will review the current evidence, which supports this decision, based on the validators used in *DSM-5* field trials.

Symptom Comparison

Although 20–40% of patients with OCD have symptoms of hoarding, in less than 5% are those symptoms at clinically significant levels (Mataix-Cols & Pertusa, 2012; Stein, Carey, et al., 2008). Despite this overlap, hoarding appears to be a distinct entity from OCD based on factor, cluster, and meta-analytic studies in large samples of OCD (Stein & Lochner, 2006).

A significant difference between OCD and HD is that thoughts related to hoarding are not experienced as intrusive or unpleasant but rather as ego-syntonic, and the distress comes from the clutter and/or interference in role obligations rather than the collection of the items (Phillips, Stein, et al., 2010). Another difference is that the thoughts associated with hoarding are not repetitive like those in OCD (Abramowitz & Deacon, 2006; Steketee et al., 2003). Similarly, the primary aim of compulsions in OCD is to avoid, reduce, or neutralize anxiety. Individuals with clinical levels

of hoarding avoid discarding items and end up storing them as a way to avoid the experience of loss, or to avoid making a difficult decision or error in what items to discard, rather than as a way to avoid anxiety (Phillips, Stein, et al., 2010; Steketee et al., 2003). Thus, hoarding behavior is driven by a variety of negative emotions, including guilt, sadness, anger, and distress (Kyrios, Frost, & Steketee, 2004; Phillips, Stein, et al., 2010). In addition to negative emotions, patients with hoarding also report that collecting items is associated with positive emotions (e.g., safety, comfort, joy; Kyrios et al., 2004). Another symptom presentation difference is that unlike in OCD, compulsive hoarding symptoms worsen as patients get older and may be exacerbated by the intervention of another person such as a family member or police (Grisham, Frost, Steketee, Kim, & Hood, 2006).

Certain personality or cognitive characteristics (e.g., perfectionism and uncertainty) are common to HD and OCD as well as other OCSDs (Abramowitz & Deacon, 2006; Phillips, Stein, et al., 2010). However, hoarding patients do not report concerns about the overimportance or overcontrol of thoughts as is seen in thought-action fusion in patients with OCD (Abramowitz & Deacon, 2006; Mataix-Cols et al., 2010; Phillips, Stein, et al., 2010). In fact, Timpano and Schmidt (2013) found that difficulty exerting self-control is associated with increased severity of symptoms in hoarding disorder.

Overall, while symptoms (difficulty discarding and excessive acquisition) of HD are correlated with symptoms of OCD in both clinical and nonclinical samples, symptoms of HD are equally as strongly correlated with non-OCD symptoms, such as depression and anxiety. This correlation suggests a nonspecific link between HD and emotional disorders in general rather than HD and OCD alone (Abramowitz, Wheaton, & Storch, 2008).

Mataix-Cols and colleagues (2010) have proposed that hoarding may have manifestations as part of OCD, which distinguish it from non-OCD HD. In the OCD case, the hoarding behavior is driven mainly by prototypical obsessions (e.g., fear of contamination) or is the result of avoidance of compulsions (e.g., not discarding in order to avoid prolonged washing rituals). Additionally, the hoarding behavior is generally unwanted and highly distressing, and there is no interest in most of the hoarded items (i.e., no sentimental or intrinsic value). Finally, in hoarding within OCD, excessive acquisition is typically not present, or related to a specific obsession (and not because of a desire to possess the items as is the case of HD).

When these guidelines appear to fit the symptoms of hoarding, the hoarding may be better conceptualized as a symptom of OCD (i.e., a compulsion). However, in most patients with OCD (60–80%), hoarding cannot be subsumed or better accounted for by other OCD symptoms. In those cases a diagnosis of HD is warranted.

Comorbidity

In a comorbidity study using *DSM-5* HD criteria, MDD was the most common comorbid condition, occurring in over half of people with HD (Frost, Steketee, & Tolin, 2011). In a community-based study of HD, 36% of participants had comorbid MDD, 24% had comorbid generalized anxiety disorder, 20% had comorbid social phobia, and 18% had comorbid OCD (Pertusa et al., 2008). In an earlier study of hoarding behaviors, Wu and Watson (2005) reported that hoarding symptoms correlated nearly as strongly with depression ($r = .38$) as with nonhoarding OCD symptoms ($r = .42$). Hoarding patients with comorbid depression display an increase in depressive symptoms (sadness and anhedonia) when discarding items as compared to hoarding patients without comorbid depression (Hall, Tolin, Frost, & Steketee, 2013). In addition, isolation or avoidance of role obligations due to fatigue and apathy may dominate the clinical picture in patients with comorbid HD and depression.

Hoarding symptoms are relatively common in OCD, with 20–40% of patients with OCD endorsing hoarding symptoms. However, these symptoms are seldom severe or interfering at the level of the other obsessions and compulsions (Foa et al., 1995). In community samples of severe HD, 17–25% also meet criteria for OCD (Pertusa et al., 2008). In patients presenting for treatment in an OCD clinic, clinical levels of hoarding as a symptom are present in approximately 5% of cases (Foa et al., 1995; Mataix-Cols, Rauch, Manzo, Jenike, & Baer, 1999). It is not clear however, whether hoarding is a consequence of other OCD fears such as contamination or harm or of a separate comorbid condition.

A great number of individuals with clinical levels of hoarding do not display other symptoms of OCD (88% in one study; Pertusa et al., 2008). However, this does not fully rule out the possibility that hoarding is a variant of OCD. In addition to clinical studies of patients with OCD, several correlational studies have shown that hoarding is not strongly associated with other OCD symptom clusters. In a study of clinical and nonclinical OCD and anxiety samples, hoarding as a symptom tended to correlate more weakly with other OCD symptoms than the other symptoms of OCD correlated with each other (Abramowitz et al., 2008). Hoarding is also comorbid with impulse control disorders such as compulsive shopping or gambling. About 25%–40% of treatment-seeking compulsive buyers show significant symptoms of hoarding, and in a nationally representative German sample, two-thirds of hoarding patients had compulsive buying symptoms (Mueller, Mitchell, Crosby, Glaesmer, & de Zwaan, 2009; Mueller et al., 2007). Hoarding is more common among individuals with compulsive gambling behaviors (Frost, Meagher, & Riskind, 2001) and occurs frequently in other OCSD clinical populations (HPD and SPD; Samuels et al., 2002; Stein, Grant, et al., 2010).

HD also frequently occurs within the context of several personality disorders (OCPD, dependent personality disorder, and schizotypal personality disorder; Frost, Steketee, Williams, & Warren, 2000). Approximately a third of hoarders meet criteria for OCPD (Phillips, Stein, et al., 2010), though after the OCPD hoarding criterion is excluded, patients with HD have no more OCPD traits than in the general population (Pertusa et al., 2008, 2010). Additionally, in individuals with OCPD, hoarding severity is not correlated with OCPD severity (Frost & Gross, 1993; Phillips, Stein, et al., 2010). Overall, hoarding, much like other emotional disorders, is comorbid with OCSDs as well as anxiety, mood, personality, and certain impulse control disorders.

Course of Illness

HD commonly onsets in adolescence and has a chronic course with very little waxing and waning, which is distinct from the variable course of OCD (Grisham et al., 2006). HD has a progressive course, and retrospective studies suggest that, like OCD, anxiety and mood disorders, hoarding symptoms usually first emerge in childhood or early adolescence. However, hoarding symptoms do not typically become clinically interfering until middle age (Frost & Gross, 1993).

Familiality

Studies show that hoarding appears to run in families, with approximately 50% of HD patients having a first-degree relative with hoarding problems (Frost & Gross, 1993; Phillips, Stein, et al., 2010). HD is more common in first-degree relatives of HD patients than in first-degree relatives of OCD patients without hoarding symptoms (Samuels et al., 2007, 2008). In a small case-control study of individuals with HD and without comorbid OCD, a quarter of the participants had a self-reported family history of OCD (Pertusa et al., 2008), suggesting a potential familial link between hoarding and OCD.

Genetic and Environmental Risk Factors

Iervolino and colleagues (2009) studied the prevalence and heritability of hoarding behaviors in a sample of over 5,000 twins (90% female). Genetic factors accounted for approximately 50% of the variance in hoarding, while nonshared environmental factors and measurement error accounted for the other 50% (Iervolino et al., 2009). The authors concluded that HD is highly heritable, at least in women, with environmental factors also contributing to the variance.

Genetic studies of hoarding have been conducted in patients with other disorders such as Tourette's disorder or OCD (Samuels et al., 2007; Zhang et al., 2002). Results have been inconsistent but suggest that hoarding may be etiologically distinct from OCD and Tourette's (Pertusa et al., 2010). Similar to the other OCSDs, an increased prevalence of stressful life events in patients with hoarding, as compared with nonhoarding, OCD patients has been found (Landau et al., 2011). In one study, approximately 50% of patients with HD without OCD linked the onset of their hoarding difficulties to stressful live events, and the number of traumatic events was correlated with HD severity (Landau et al., 2011).

Neural Substrates

Studies of the neural substrates of hoarding have been done in samples of people who present with clinical levels of hoarding both with and without concurrent OCD. HD shows a unique pattern of abnormal resting-state brain function that does not overlap with that of nonhoarding OCD (Saxena, 2008). Hoarding appears to be mediated by frontal-limbic circuits involving the cingulate cortex, ventromedial prefrontal cortex, and limbic structures, similar to PTSD or phobias (An et al., 2009; Tolin, Kiehl, Worhunsky, Book, & Maltby, 2009). In a recent study of HD, OCD, and healthy control participants, participants with HD exhibited abnormal biphasic activity in the anterior cingulate cortex and insula related to problems in identifying the emotional significance of a stimulus, generating appropriate emotional response, or regulating affective state during decision-making (Tolin et al., 2012). In a study of acquisition and decision-making, the anterior cingulate cortex was only engaged during personal acquisition decisions (Wang, Seidler, Hall, & Preston, 2012).

OCD without hoarding symptoms, by contrast, is characterized by hyperactivation of the frontostriatal system (see detailed description earlier) rather than frontal-limbic systems (Saxena, 2008). This neurocircuitry evidence indicates that hoarding appears to have a distinct neural substrate from OCD and might share neural substrates with a wide range of emotional disorders (Phillips, Stein, et al., 2010; Saxena, 2008).

Biomarkers

To date, no data are available in the biomarker validator domain.

Temperamental Antecedents

Patients with HD share characteristics such as increased sense of responsibility, increased indecisiveness, and perfectionism with OCD (Frost & Gross, 1993; Mataix-Cols et al., 2010; Steketee et al., 2003). Patients with HD also share features with compulsive buyers such as difficulties making decisions, dysfunctional beliefs about possessions, and emotional attachments to objects (Mueller et al., 2007, 2009).

Cognitive and Emotional Processing

Neuropsychological studies of HD suggest deficits in information processing, including processing speed, executive functioning, spatial and selective attention, memory, and categorization/classification

(Grisham, Brown, Savage, Steketee, & Barlow, 2007; Kyrios et al., 2004; Wincze, Steketee, & Frost, 2007). Compared to patients with OCD, patients with HD show significantly greater problems with categorization of objects, slower reaction time, problems with attention, decision-making and impulsivity, and a distinctive pattern of memory deficits (Grisham et al., 2007; Hartl et al., 2004). Individuals with hoarding problems exhibit excessive responsibility tied to the fate of possessions, whereas in OCD the sense of responsibility is tied to other concerns, such as the fear of harm to self or others (Grisham, Steketee, & Frost, 2008; Steketee et al., 2003). In addition to the neuropsychological findings, deficits in information processing is a central component of the cognitive-behavioral model of HD, which suggests that hoarding is associated with deficits in information processing, beliefs about exaggerated meaning of possessions (value, meaning, uniqueness), underlying distorted core beliefs, and emotional reinforcement (both positive and negative) of hoarding behaviors (Mataix-Cols et al., 2010; Phillips, Stein et al., 2010; Steketee, Frost & Kyrios, 2003).

Treatment Response

Preliminary evidence from uncontrolled or wait-list comparison trials suggests that community-solicited individuals with HD may respond to SRIs (Saxena, 2011; Saxena, Brody, Maidment, & Baxter, 2007). There is also evidence of effectiveness for CBT involving ERP, motivational interviewing, skills training, and hoarding-specific cognitive restructuring (Muroff et al., 2009; Tolin, Frost, & Steketee, 2007). Hoarding symptoms in patients with OCD tend to be less responsive than other OCD symptoms to evidence-based treatments for OCD, that is, ERP (Abramowitz, Franklin, Schwartz, & Furr, 2003; Mataix-Cols et al., 2002) and SRIs (Stein, Carey, et al., 2008).

Conclusion

The research to date on HD suggests that it is distinct from OCD, with the evidence across validators reviewed supporting different etiological mechanisms in both disorders. HD is prevalent and has major public health consequences, and the clinical implications of severe hoarding warrant its addition to DSM-5. HD as a new diagnostic category in DSM-5 more accurately captures the majority of cases where hoarding occurs outside of OCD. HD criteria need to be evaluated in large clinical samples, and some of the validators discussed (e.g., biomarkers and familiality) need to be more carefully studied.

Hair Pulling and Skin Picking Disorder

Hair pulling disorder (HPD) and skin picking disorder (SPD) are both recognized in DSM-5 as psychological conditions that involve repetitive grooming behaviors. HPD is characterized by DSM-5 as the recurrent pulling of one's hair and associated impairment or distress in social, occupational, or academic functioning. Recently, HPD has been estimated to occur in 3 million individuals in the United States (Duke, Keeley, Geffken, & Storch, 2010); however, the true prevalence of HPD in the general population is not known, since large epidemiological studies have not been conducted. Given its prevalence and significant comorbidity with other psychiatric conditions, HPD is considered to be a significant public health concern (Flessner, Woods, Franklin, Keuthen, & Piacentini, 2009; Keuthen et al., 2001).

SPD is characterized by recurrent skin picking that results in visible tissue damage and, at times, scarring. Patients with SPD use their fingernails (and sometimes tweezers) to pick hair from their head and face (Grant & Odlaug, 2009). In some cases, skin picking can lead to infections and even require surgical interventions (Odlaug & Grant, 2008). Individuals with SPD spend significant amounts of time picking, with some patients engaging in the behavior for many hours a day (Odlaug & Grant, 2008). As a result of the picking and tissue damage, patients with SPD experience significant distress, functional impairment, or both (Wilhelm et al., 1999). SPD is estimated to occur in approximately 2% of dermatology patients (Arnold, Auchenbach, & McElroy, 2001) and 5% of clinical samples (Grant & Odlaug, 2009).

Over the past 35 years (since the publication of DSM-III), there has been increasing interest and research on the prevalence, assessment, and treatment of HPD and SPD (Stein, Grant, et al., 2010). Given these findings, DSM-5 has revised the diagnostic criteria for HPD and included diagnostic criteria for SPD. For HPD, the most notable revision is that patients no longer need to endorse prior tension to, or subsequent gratification from, hair pulling (Stein, Grant, et al., 2010). Additionally, since many HPD patients disguise their hair loss, there is no longer a criterion stating that the degree of hair loss is "noticeable" (Stein, Grant, et al., 2010). Taking these changes into account, *DSM-5* conceptualizes HPD as the recurrent pulling out of one's hair resulting in hair loss, consequential distress, or functional impairment, and repeated attempts at reducing hair-pulling behaviors. The diagnostic criteria for SPD in *DSM-5* mirror those of HPD: recurrent skin picking resulting in skin lesions, clinically significant distress or functional impairment, and repeated attempts to decrease or stop skin picking.

The growing literature on these grooming disorders has not only influenced their diagnostic criteria but also highlighted their phenomenological similarities to OCD. As a result, researchers and clinicians alike have considered whether HPD and SPD would be more accurately categorized as OCSDs rather than impulse control disorders (Phillips, Stein, et al., 2010). Therefore, the extant research on the 11 validators will now be reviewed for both grooming disorders to demonstrate the empirical support for their inclusion on the obsessive-compulsive spectrum.

Symptom Comparison

HPD, SPD, and OCD all involve repetitive behaviors in response to urges. These behaviors tend to be anxiety relieving, often are symmetrical, and possess ritualistic characteristics (Grant & Potenza, 2006; Lochner et al., 2005; Stein, Simeon, Cohen, & Hollander, 1995; Tukel et al., 2007). Additionally, the repetitive motor symptoms of individuals with SPD parallel certain compulsions in OCD, such as tapping (Stein, Chamberlain, & Fineberg, 2006; Stein, Flessner, et al., 2008). Two critical symptom differences distinguish these disorders from OCD. First, following the repetitive behavior, individuals with the grooming disorders can experience a sense of gratification (Phillips, Stein, et al., 2010), whereas individuals with OCD experience a reduction in anxiety. Second, neither grooming disorder is associated with obsessional preoccupation prior to the repetitive behavior (Phillips, Stein, et al., 2010). In sum, HPD, SPD, and OCD all involve repetitive or ritualistic behaviors in response to urges, but the anxiolytic

function of the behaviors and presence of obsessional phenomena distinguish the grooming disorders from OCD.

Comorbidity

Lovato and colleagues (2012) examined a large OCD sample (*N* = 901) and found that approximately 19% engaged in either HPD or skin picking. Accumulating evidence also suggests that these grooming disorders are more prevalent in individuals with OCD than in healthy controls (Calikuşu, Yücel, Polat, & Baykal, 2003; Christenson & Mansueto, 1999; Jaisoorya, Janardhan-Reddy, & Srinath, 2003). Additionally, compared to patients with panic disorder or social phobia, HPD occurred significantly more frequently in patients with OCD (Richter, Summerfeldt, Antony, & Swinson, 2003). SPD also occurred more frequently in those with OCD than in patients with panic disorder (Richter et al., 2003). Further, OCD and the grooming disorders tend to have similar patterns of comorbidity with mood, anxiety, and personality disorders (Christenson & Mansueto, 1999). However, depression was found to be comorbid significantly more frequently with OCD than with HPD (Lochner et al., 2005), and SPD was found to be comorbid more frequently with nail-biting and HPD, whereas OCD was found to be comorbid more frequently with BDD (Grant & Odlaug, 2009). Taken together, the literature provides conflicting evidence on the comorbidity patterns associated with OCD and the grooming disorders.

Course of Illness

For HPD, research has consistently demonstrated a narrow age of onset that occurs near puberty (Christenson, Mackenzie, & Mitchell, 1991; Keuthen et al., 2001). SPD similarly has been shown to start in early adolescence (Grant & Odlaug, 2009). OCD has been shown to have a bimodal onset, with an early peak around age 10 and a later onset at age 19 (Geller, 2006; Geller et al., 1998). Despite the broader age distribution of onset in OCD, Grant, Mancebo, Eisen, and Rasmussen (2010) found that the age of onset of SPD (13.9 years old) was not significantly different from that of OCD (15.4 years old). Furthermore, patients with OCD and comorbid grooming disorders were found to have a younger age of onset (10 years) than that of individuals without HPD or skin picking (13 years). This indicates that these patients may possess similar risk factors that contribute to an early development and escalation of symptoms (Lovato et al., 2012). In addition to age of onset, research has found that HPD and OCD possess a similarly chronic course (Keuthen et al., 2001). Little research has examined the course of SPD.

Familiality

Bienvenu and colleagues (2000) found increased rates of HPD and skin picking in first-degree relatives of OCD probands, compared to rates found in relatives of healthy controls. Cullen and colleagues (2001) similarly demonstrated that skin picking occurs at a significantly higher rate in the first-degree relatives of patients with OCD. OCD has also been found to occur more frequently in the families of probands with HPD (Lenane et al., 1992; Schlosser, Black, Blum, & Goldstein, 1994). In a recent study with a large sample size, Bienvenu and colleagues (2012) demonstrated that HPD occurred in 4% of the OCD-affected relatives and in none of the control relatives. Similarly, skin picking occurred in 17% of the OCD-affected relatives and in only 4% of the control relatives. Taken together, the increased comorbidity and familiality of the grooming disorders with OCD supports their inclusion on the obsessive-compulsive spectrum.

Environmental Risk Factors and Genetic Links

Environmental and genetic risk factors for the grooming disorders have not been well examined. Moreover, the genetic links between OCD and grooming disorders have been very difficult to identify (Chamberlain et al., 2007; Hemmings et al., 2006). Some researchers have found that patients with the same rare gene variant, SAPAP3 (a protein that helps brain cells communicate via the glutamate chemical messenger system), may present with HPD or OCD (Abelson et al., 2005; Zuchner et al., 2006, 2009).

Neural Substrates

Some empirical evidence has found similarities in neural substrates between OCD and the grooming disorders. Most notably, altered functioning in the cortico-striatal-thalamic circuitry has been found to be associated with OCD and HPD (Saxena & Rauch, 2000). However, recent imaging studies suggest that the brain regions involved in HPD, such as the cerebellum and amygdalohippocampal formation, tend *not* to be implicated in OCD (Chamberlain et al., 2008; Keuthen et al., 2007). O'Sullivan and colleagues (1997) found that the left putamen volume was significantly smaller in those with HPD than that in healthy controls, but Stein, Coetzer, Lee, Davis, and Bouwera (1997), using a similarly designed study, did not replicate these findings. The imaging studies examining HPD have had small sample sizes and their results have been inconsistent.

Temperamental Antecedents

In one relevant study, Lochner and colleagues (2005) administered temperament questionnaires to patients with HPD and OCD. Both diagnostic groups were found to report higher harm avoidance scores than published norms, and the OCD group reported lower novelty seeking than that of the HPD group (Lochner et al., 2005).

Cognitive and Emotional Processing

In neuropsychological studies, similar cognitive impairments have been demonstrated in HPD and OCD patients. Both diagnostic groups showed significant increases in the number of between-search errors at the harder levels of difficulty on the Cambridge Neuropsychological Test Automated Battery (CANTAB) spatial working memory task (Chamberlain et al., 2007). Additionally, impairments in spatial memory for OCD and HPD patients have been documented using the stylus maze task (Rettew, Cheslow, Rapoport, Leonard, & Lenane, 1991). Additionally, in a comprehensive examination of visuospatial abilities, memory, and executive functioning, Bohne, Keuthen, Tuschen-Caffier, and Wilhelm (2005) found that HPD and OCD patients are not characterized by generalized neuropsychological dysfunction. Rather, HPD and OCD patients' visuospatial abilities, memory, and (most) executive functions were comparable to those of healthy controls. Minor differences between the diagnostic groups were found in tests of executive functioning, with HPD patients perseverating longer on the object alternation task and the OCD group showing impaired learning on the Wisconsin Card Sorting Test (Bohne et al., 2005).

Chamberlain and colleagues (2007) also documented minor differences in the neuropsychological impairments of the two groups: patients with OCD possessed significantly greater deficits in cognitive flexibility, whereas patients with HPD possessed significantly greater impairment in the inhibition of their motor response. Additional research is needed to not only examine whether impaired inhibition of motor responses occurs across all proposed OCSDs (Phillips, Stein, et al., 2010) but also compare the neurocognitive functioning/emotional processing of OCD and SPD.

Treatment Response

In terms of pharmacotherapy response for HPD and OCD, the SRI clomipramine has been found to be more effective than desipramine (Leonard et al., 1989), and the augmentation of SRIs with neuroleptics (i.e., dopamine blockers) has been shown to be useful in both disorders (Chamberlain, Odlaug, Boulougouris, Fineberg, & Grant, 2009; Stein & Hollander, 1992). Despite these similarities, significant pharmacotherapy response differences have been found between OCD and HPD. Most importantly, there is little evidence that SSRIs are an effective treatment for HPD (Bloch et al., 2007). Recent research suggests that HPD (and perhaps SPD as well) can be effectively treated by using the following as monotherapy: low-dose atypical neuroleptics, n-acetylcysteine, or naltrexone, all of which are ineffective for OCD (Chamberlain et al., 2009; Grant, Odlaug, & Kim, 2009; Walsh & McDougle, 2005). In terms of psychosocial interventions, habit reversal is the most efficacious treatment for HPD and SPD (Himle, Woods, Piacentini, & Walkup, 2006; Woods et al., 2006), whereas ERP is the gold-standard treatment for OCD (Abramowitz, 1997). Broadly speaking, both interventions encourage patients to resist performing a compulsion or repetitive grooming behavior.

As demonstrated by the reviewed literature on HPD and SPD, there is significant overlap between these grooming disorders and OCD, which merits their placement in the OCSD category. Similarities have been observed in comorbidity patterns, symptom similarities, neurocircuitry, and family history. Additionally, research has found that in relation to impulse control disorders, like pathological gambling, HPD possesses different neural underpinnings and tends not to be comorbid with other impulse control disorders (Grant & Kim, 2003; McElroy, Soutullo, Beckman, Taylor, & Keck, 1998). This evidence adds to the claim that HPD is not better classified as an impulse control disorder (Grant & Kim, 2003; McElroy et al., 1998). The literature suggests that these grooming disorders share core phenomenological features with OCD and are aptly categorized as OCSDs.

Olfactory Reference Syndrome

Olfactory reference syndrome (ORS) is a psychological condition in which one erroneously believes that one is emitting a foul or offensive bodily odor (e.g., halitosis, genital odor, or flatulence). Patients with ORS often (1) report delusions of reference (e.g., believing that their offensive odor leads other people to take special notice of them), (2) perform ritualistic and repetitive behaviors that alleviate the anxiety associated with their preoccupation (e.g., smelling their breath or armpits), and (3) excessively try to mask the purported smell (e.g., repeated showering; Pryse-Phillips, 1971). In Begum and McKenna's (2011) recent review of the literature on ORS, the disorder tends to start at approximately 21 years of age, and the average age at presentation is 29 years. When considering the symptoms of ORS, an important distinction needs to be made from the olfactory hallucinations associated with schizophrenia. For ORS to be appropriate, the false belief of emitting a bad odor must be the only delusional belief that the patient possesses. If other schizophrenia symptoms are present, then ORS should no longer be considered.

Although symptoms of ORS have been discussed for over a century (Sutton, 1919; Tilley, 1895), this psychological condition has never been recognized as a distinct syndrome in *DSM*. In *DSM-5*, the recommendation is to diagnose the symptoms of ORS as a somatic type of a delusional disorder, and indeed it is noted that the most common somatic delusions are those in which the person believes he/she "emits a foul odor" (p. 92). ORS is also discussed in the "Glossary of Cultural Concepts of Distress" section, in reference to *taijin kyofusho* ("interpersonal fear disorder" in Japanese). This cultural syndrome is characterized by anxiety and avoidance of interpersonal situations because of fears that one's appearance or actions will be offensive to others (e.g., a foul body odor).

ORS undoubtedly shares symptoms with other disorders, such as OCD, delusional disorder, social phobia, BDD, and hypochondriasis. It has been hypothesized that ORS should be included in the OCSDs (Feusner, Phillips, & Stein, 2010). However, the relationship of ORS to these suggested disorders, and its inclusion on the obsessive-compulsive spectrum, has only been minimally examined (Feusner, Phillips, et al., 2010). As a result, its diagnostic categorization remains unknown. Including diagnostic criteria for ORS in future iterations of *DSM* might motivate researchers to not only improve the assessment and treatment of this debilitating condition but also to determine the diagnostic category or spectrum (OCSD) that most accurately characterizes this psychological disorder.

Conclusion and Future Directions

One of the most significant changes in the transition from *DSM-IV* to *DSM-5* is the formation of a new superordinate category: obsessive-compulsive spectrum disorders, or OCSD. This shift entailed four major conceptual changes. First, OCD was removed from the anxiety disorders category. Second, HD was recognized as a syndrome independent of OCD or OCPD. Third, BDD was moved from the somatoform disorders category and HPD was moved from the impulse control disorder category. Finally, SPD was identified as a distinct disorder, rather than being diagnosed as an impulse control disorder not otherwise specified (NOS). A careful examination of 11 validators reveals that there are major similarities between the OCSDs, but at the same time several prominent differences. A wealth of research and expert opinions identified several core features that are shared by these disorders, predominantly related to the core symptoms of OCD. These core features across OCSDs are the patterns of obsessions and preoccupations and/or compulsions and repetitive behaviors. These may result in the manifestation of clinical symptoms such as acquisition of objects, hair pulling, skin picking, or repetitive mental rituals.

Although the creation of a spectrum of OCSDs is supported by the literature, the clinical, diagnostic, epidemiological, and public health effects of this transition to an OCSD are yet to be determined. However, the changes may be beneficial in terms of generating research attention for disorders that previously received less attention. Additionally, this change may lead to improved assessment and, subsequently, empirically validated treatments. Thus, these modifications may ultimately be beneficial for clinicians, as well as for patients and their families.

Several issues still require further attention. First, the American Psychiatric Association approved only some of the changes proposed by the OCSD task force, rejecting, for example, the recommendation that hypochondriasis and OCPD "could potentially be included with OCSDs, as they have some similarities to OCD, although evidence for their relatedness to OCD is more mixed and less persuasive" (Phillips, Stein, et al., 2010, p. 543). In addition, disorders such as ORS still require more research attention before being included in *DSM* or the OCSD category. Lastly, although BDD, HD, HPD, and SPD are included in the OCSD category, future research on the neurobiology, epidemiology, phenomenology, and therapeutic mechanisms associated with these disorders is needed in order to enhance our understanding of these conditions and ultimately improve early diagnosis and treatment.

References

Abelson, J. F., Kwan, K. Y., O'Roak, B. J., Baek, D. Y., Stillman, A. A., Morgan, T. M., et al. (2005). Sequence variants in SLITRK1 are associated with Tourette's syndrome. *Science, 310,* 317–320.

Abramovitch, A., Dar, R., Schweiger, A., & Hermesh, H. (2011). Neuropsychological impairments and their association with obsessive-compulsive symptom severity in obsessive-compulsive disorder. *Archives of Clinical Neuropsychology, 26,* 364–376.

Abramowitz, J. S. (1997). Effectiveness of psychological and pharmacological treatments for obsessive-compulsive disorder: A quantitative review. *Journal of Consulting and Clinical Psychology, 65,* 44–52.

Abramowitz, J. S., & Deacon, B. J. (2006). Psychometric properties and construct validity of the obsessive–compulsive inventory—revised: Replication and extension with a clinical sample. *Journal of Anxiety Disorders, 20,* 1016–1035.

Abramowitz, J. S., Franklin, M. E., Schwartz, S. A., & Furr, J. M. (2003). Symptom presentation and outcome of cognitive-behavioral therapy for obsessive-compulsive disorder. *Journal of Consulting and Clinical Psychology, 71,* 1049–1057.

Abramowitz, J. S., Wheaton, M. G., & Storch, E. A. (2008). The status of hoarding as a symptom of obsessive-compulsive disorder. *Behaviour Research and Therapy, 46,* 1026–1033.

Alexander, G. E., DeLong, M. R., & Strick, P. L. (1986). Parallel organization of functionally segregated circuits linking basal ganglia and cortex. *Annual Review of Neuroscience, 9,* 357–381.

An, S. K., Mataix-Cols, D., Lawrence, N. S., Wooderson, S., Giampietro, V., Speckens, A., et al. (2009). To discard or not to discard: The neural basis of hoarding symptoms in obsessive compulsive disorder. *Molecular Psychiatry, 14,* 318–331.

Andrews, G., Goldberg, D. P., Krueger, R. F., Carpenter, W. T., Hyman, S. E., Sachdev, P., et al. (2009). Exploring the feasibility of a meta-structure for DSM-V and ICD-11: Could it improve utility and validity? *Psychological Medicine, 39,* 1993–2000.

Arnold, L. M., Auchenbach, M. B., & McElroy, S. L. (2001). Psychogenic excoriation. Clinical features, proposed diagnostic criteria, epidemiology and approaches to treatment. *CNS Drugs, 15,* 351–359.

Bannon, S., Gonsalvez, C. J., Croft, R. J., & Boyce, P. M. (2002). Response inhibition deficits in obsessive-compulsive disorder. *Psychiatry Research, 110,* 165–174.

Bartz, J. A., & Hollander, E. (2006). Is obsessive-compulsive disorder an anxiety disorder? *Progress in Neuropsychopharmacology and Biological Psychiatry, 30,* 338–352.

Begum, M., & McKenna, P. (2011). Olfactory reference syndrome: A systematic review of the world literature. *Psychological Medicine, 41,* 453–461.

Bienvenu, O. J., Samuels, J. F., Riddle, M. A., Hoehn-Saric, R., Liang, K. Y., Cullen, B. A., et al. (2000). The relationship of obsessive-compulsive disorder to possible spectrum disorders: Results from a family study. *Biological Psychiatry, 48,* 287–293.

Bienvenu, O. J., Samuels, J. F., Wuyek, L. A., Liang, K. Y., Wang, Y., Grados, M. A., et al. (2012). Is obsessive-compulsive disorder an anxiety disorder, and what, if any, are spectrum conditions? A family study perspective. *Psychological Medicine, 42,* 1–13.

Bloch, M. H., Landeros-Weisenberger, A., Dombrowski, P., Kelmendi, B., Wegner, R., Nudel, J., et al. (2007). Systematic review: Pharmacological and behavioral treatment for trichotillomania. *Biological Psychiatry, 62,* 839–846.

Bloch, M. H., Landeros-Weisenberger, A., Kelmendi, B., Coric, V., Bracken, M. B., & Leckman, J. F. (2006). A systematic review: Antipsychotic augmentation with treatment refractory obsessive-compulsive disorder. *Molecular Psychiatry, 11,* 622–632.

Bloch, M. H., Landeros-Weisenberger, A., Rosario, M. C., Pittenger, C., & Leckman, J. F. (2008). Meta-analysis of the symptom structure of obsessive-compulsive disorder. *American Journal of Psychiatry, 165,* 1532–1542.

Bohne, A., Keuthen, N., Tuschen-Caffier, B., & Wilhelm, S. (2005). Cognitive inhibition in trichotillomania and obsessive-compulsive disorder. *Behaviour Research and Therapy, 43,* 923–942.

Bradshaw, J. L., & Sheppard, D. M. (2000). The neurodevelopmental frontostriatal disorders: Evolutionary adaptiveness and anomalous lateralization. *Brain and Language, 73*(2), 297–320.

Bucci, P., Mucci, A., Volpe, U., Merlotti, E., Galderisi, S., & Maj, M. (2004). Executive hypercontrol in obsessive-compulsive disorder: Electrophysiological and neuropsychological indices. *Clinical Neurophysiology, 115,* 1340–1348.

Buhlmann, U., Etcoff, N. L., & Wilhelm, S. (2008). Facial attractiveness ratings and perfectionism in body dysmorphic disorder and obsessive-compulsive disorder. *Journal of Anxiety Disorders, 22,* 540–547.

Buhlmann, U., Glaesmer, H., Mewes, R., Fama, J. M., Wilhelm, S., Brahler, E., et al. (2010). Updates on the prevalence of body dysmorphic disorder: A population-based survey. *Psychiatry Research, 178,* 171–175.

Buhlmann, U., Marques, L. M., & Wilhelm, S. (2012). Traumatic experiences in individuals with body dysmorphic disorder. *Journal of Nervous and Mental Disease, 200,* 95–98.

Buhlmann, U., McNally, R. J., Etcoff, N. L., Tuschen-Caffier, B., & Wilhelm, S. (2004). Emotion recognition deficits in body dysmorphic disorder. *Journal of Psychiatric Research, 38,* 201–206.

Buhlmann, U., Wilhelm, S., McNally, R. J., Tuschen-Caffier, B., Baer, L., & Jenike, M. A. (2002). Interpretive biases for ambiguous information in body dysmorphic disorder. *CNS Spectrums, 7,* 435–436, 441–433.

Calikuşu, C., Yücel, B., Polat, A., & Baykal, C. (2003). The relation of psychogenic excoriation with psychiatric disorders: A comparative study. *Comprehensive Psychiatry, 44,* 256–261.

Catapano, F., Perris, F., Fabrazzo, M., Cioffi, V., Giacco, D., De Santis, V., et al. (2010). Obsessive-compulsive disorder with poor insight: A three-year prospective study. *Progress in Neuropsychopharmacology and Biological Psychiatry, 34,* 323–330.

Cavedini, P., Zorzi, C., Piccinni, M., Cavallini, M. C., & Bellodi, L. (2010). Executive dysfunctions in obsessive-compulsive patients and unaffected relatives: Searching for a new intermediate phenotype. *Biological Psychiatry, 67,* 1178–1184.

Chamberlain, S. R., Blackwell, A. D., Fineberg, N. A., Robbins, T. W., & Sahakian, B. J. (2005). The neuropsychology of obsessive compulsive disorder: The importance of failures in cognitive and behavioural inhibition as candidate endophenotypic markers. *Neuroscience and Biobehavioral Reviews, 29,* 399–419.

Chamberlain, S. R., Fineberg, N. A., Blackwell, A. D., Clark, L., Robbins, T. W., & Sahakian, B. J. (2007). A neuropsychological comparison of obsessive-compulsive disorder and trichotillomania. *Neuropsychologia, 45,* 654–662.

Chamberlain, S. R., Fineberg, N. A., Blackwell, A. D., Robbins, T. W., & Sahakian, B. J. (2006). Motor inhibition and cognitive flexibility in obsessive-compulsive disorder and trichotillomania. *American Journal of Psychiatry, 163,* 1282–1284.

Chamberlain, S. R., Menzies, L. A., Fineberg, N. A., Campo, N., Suckling, J., Craig, K., et al. (2008). Grey matter abnormalities in trichotillomania: Morphometric magnetic resonance imaging study. *British Journal of Psychiatry, 193,* 216–221.

Chamberlain, S. R., Odlaug, B. L., Boulougouris, V., Fineberg, N. A., & Grant, J. E. (2009). Trichotillomania: Neurobiology and treatment. *Neuroscience and Biobehavioral Reviews, 33,* 831–842.

Christenson, G. A., Mackenzie, T. B., & Mitchell, J. E. (1991). Characteristics of 60 adult chronic hair pullers. *American Journal of Psychiatry, 148,* 365–370.

Christenson, G. A., & Mansueto, C. S. (1999). Trichotillomania: Descriptive characteristics and phenomenology. In D. J. Stein, S. R. Chamberlain & E. Hollander (Eds.), *Trichotillomania* (pp. 1–41). Washington, DC: American Psychiatric Press.

Clark, D. A. (2004). *Cognitive-behavioral therapy for OCD.* New York: Guilford Press.

Cororve, M. B., & Gleaves, D. H. (2001). Body dysmorphic disorder: A review of conceptualizations, assessment, and treatment strategies. *Clinical Psychology Review, 21,* 949–970.

Crerand, C. E., Franklin, M. E., & Sarwer, D. B. (2006). Body dysmorphic disorder and cosmetic surgery. *Plastic and Reconstructive Surgery, 118,* 167e–180e.

Crerand, C. E., Phillips, K. A., Menard, W., & Fay, C. (2005). Nonpsychiatric medical treatment of body dysmorphic disorder. *Psychosomatics, 46,* 549–555.

Cullen, B. A., Samuels, J. F., Bienvenu, O. J., Grados, M., Hoehn-Saric, R., & Hahn, J. (2001). The relationship of pathologic skin picking to obsessive-compulsive disorder. *Journal of Nervous and Mental Disease, 189,* 193–195.

Deckersbach, T., Savage, C. R., Phillips, K. A., Wilhelm, S., Buhlmann, U., Rauch, S. L., et al. (2000). Characteristics of memory dysfunction in body dysmorphic disorder. *Journal of the International Neuropsychological Society, 6,* 673–681.

Denys, D., Tenney, N., van Megen, H. J., de Geus, F., & Westenberg, H. G. (2004). Axis I and II comorbidity in a large sample of patients with obsessive-compulsive disorder. *Journal of Affective Disorders, 80,* 155–162.

Denys, D., Zohar, J., & Westenberg, H. G. (2004). The role of dopamine in obsessive-compulsive disorder: Preclinical and clinical evidence. *Journal of Clinical Psychiatry, 65*(Suppl. 14), 11–17.

Didie, E. R., Tortolani, C. C., Pope, C. G., Menard, W., Fay, C., & Phillips, K. A. (2006). Childhood abuse and neglect in body dysmorphic disorder. *Child Abuse & Neglect, 30,* 1105–1115.

Duke, D., Keeley, M., Geffken, G., & Storch, E. (2010). Trichotillomania: A current review. *Clinical Psychology Review, 30,* 181–193.

Dunai, J., Labuschagne, I., Castle, D. J., Kyrios, M., & Rossell, S. L. (2010). Executive function in body dysmorphic disorder. *Psychological Medicine, 40,* 1541–1548.

Eisen, J. L., Phillips, K. A., Coles, M. E., & Rasmussen, S. A. (2004). Insight in obsessive compulsive disorder and body dysmorphic disorder. *Comprehensive Psychiatry, 45,* 10–15.

Eisen, J. L., Pinto, A., Mancebo, M. C., Dyck, I. R., Orlando, M. E., & Rasmussen, S. A. (2010). A 2-year prospective follow-up study of the course of obsessive-compulsive disorder. *Journal of Clinical Psychiatry, 71,* 1033–1039.

El Mansari, M., & Blier, P. (2006). Mechanisms of action of current and potential pharmacotherapies of obsessive-compulsive disorder. *Progress in Neuropsychopharmacology and Biological Psychiatry, 30,* 362–373.

Fallon, B. A., Qureshi, A. I., Laje, G., & Klein, B. (2000). Hypochondriasis and its relationship to obsessive-compulsive disorder. *Psychiatric Clinics of North America, 23,* 605–616.

Ferrao, Y. A., Miguel, E., & Stein, D. J. (2009). Tourette's syndrome, trichotillomania, and obsessive-compulsive disorder: How closely are they related? *Psychiatry Research, 170,* 32–42.

Feusner, J. D., Bystritsky, A., Hellemann, G., & Bookheimer, S. (2010). Impaired identity recognition of faces with emotional expressions in body dysmorphic disorder. *Psychiatry Research, 179,* 318–323.

Feusner, J. D., Moller, H., Altstein, L., Sugar, C., Bookheimer, S., Yoon, J., et al. (2010). Inverted face processing in body dysmorphic disorder. *Journal of Psychiatric Research, 44,* 1088–1094.

Feusner, J. D., Moody, T., Hembacher, E., Townsend, J., McKinley, M., Moller, H., et al. (2010). Abnormalities of visual processing and frontostriatal systems in body dysmorphic disorder. *Archives of General Psychiatry, 67,* 197–205.

Feusner, J. D., Phillips, K. A., & Stein, D. (2010). Olfactory reference syndrome: Issues for DSM-V. *Depression and Anxiety, 27,* 592–599.

Feusner, J. D., Townsend, J., Bystritsky, A., & Bookheimer, S. (2007). Visual information processing of faces in body dysmorphic disorder. *Archives of General Psychiatry, 64,* 1417–1425.

Fineberg, N. A., Brown, A., Reghunandanan, S., & Pampaloni, I. (2012). Evidence-based pharmacotherapy of obsessive-compulsive disorder. *International Journal of Neuropsychopharmacology, 12,* 1173–1191.

Fineberg, N. A., Sharma, P., Sivakumaran, T., Sahakian, B., & Chamberlain, S. R. (2007). Does obsessive-compulsive personality disorder belong within the obsessive-compulsive spectrum? *CNS Spectrums, 12,* 467–482.

Flessner, C. A., Woods, D. W., Franklin, M. E., Keuthen, N. J., & Piacentini, J. (2009). Cross-sectional study of women with trichotillomania: A preliminary examination of pulling styles, severity, phenomenology, and functional impact. *Child Psychiatry and Human Development, 40,* 153–167.

Foa, E. B., Kozak, M. J., Goodman, W. K., Hollander, E., Jenike, M. A., & Rasmussen, S. A. (1995). DSM-IV field trial: Obsessive-compulsive disorder. *American Journal of Psychiatry, 152,* 90–96.

Frare, F., Perugi, G., Ruffolo, G., & Toni, C. (2004). Obsessive-compulsive disorder and body dysmorphic disorder: A comparison of clinical features. *European Psychiatry, 19,* 292–298.

Frost, R. O., & Gross, R. C. (1993). The hoarding of possessions. *Behaviour Research and Therapy, 31,* 367–381.

Frost, R. O., Meagher, B. M., & Riskind, J. H. (2001). Obsessive-compulsive features in pathological lottery and scratch ticket gamblers. *Journal of Gambling Studies, 17,* 5–19.

Frost, R. O., Steketee, G., & Grisham, J. (2004). Measurement of compulsive hoarding: Saving inventory–revised. *Behaviour Research and Therapy, 42,* 1163–1182.

Frost, R. O., Steketee, G., & Tolin, D. F. (2011). Comorbidity in hoarding disorder. *Depression and Anxiety, 28,* 876–884.

Frost, R. O., Steketee, G., Williams, L. F., & Warren, R. (2000). Mood, personality disorder symptoms and disability in obsessive compulsive hoarders: A comparison with clinical and nonclinical controls. *Behaviour Research and Therapy, 38,* 1071–1081.

Geller, D. A. (2006). Obsessive-compulsive and spectrum disorders in children and adolescents. *Psychiatric Clinics of North America, 29,* 353–370.

Geller, D. A., Biederman, J., Jones, J., Park, K., Schwartz, S., Shapiro, S., et al. (1998). Is juvenile obsessive-compulsive disorder a developmental subtype of the disorder? A review of the pediatric literature. *Journal of the American Academy of Child & Adolescent Psychiatry, 37,* 420–427.

Goodman, W. K., Price, L. H., Rasmussen, S. A., Mazure, C., Delgado, P., Heninger, G. R., et al. (1989). The Yale-Brown Obsessive Compulsive Scale. II. Validity. *Archives of General Psychiatry, 46,* 1012–1016.

Goodman, W. K., Price, L. H., Rasmussen, S. A., Mazure, C., Fleischmann, R. L., Hill, C. L., et al. (1989). The Yale-Brown Obsessive Compulsive Scale. I. Development, use, and reliability. *Archives of General Psychiatry, 46,* 1006–1011.

Grant, J. E., & Kim, S. W. (2003). Comorbidity of impulse control disorders in pathological gamblers. *Acta Psychiatrica Scandinavica, 108,* 203–207.

Grant, J. E., Mancebo, M., Eisen, J. L., & Rasmussen, S. A. (2010). Impulse-control disorders in children and adolescents with obsessive-compulsive disorder. *Psychiatry Research, 175,* 109–113.

Grant, J. E., & Odlaug, B. L. (2009). Update on pathological skin picking. *Current Psychiatry Reports, 11,* 283–288.

Grant, J. E., Odlaug, B. L., & Kim, S. W. (2009). N-acetylcysteine, a glutamate modulator, in the treatment of trichotillomania: A double-blind, placebo-controlled study. *Archives of General Psychiatry, 66,* 756–763.

Grant, J. E., & Potenza, M. N. (2006). Compulsive aspects of impulse-control disorders. *Psychiatric Clinics of North America, 29,* 539–551.

Grisham, J. R., Brown, T. A., Savage, C. R., Steketee, G., & Barlow, D. H. (2007). Neuropsychological impairment associated with compulsive hoarding. *Behaviour Research and Therapy, 45,* 1471–1483.

Grisham, J. R., Frost, R., Steketee, G., Kim, H., & Hood, S. (2006). Age of onset of compulsive hoarding. *Journal of Anxiety Disorders, 20,* 675–686.

Grisham, J. R., Steketee, G., & Frost, R. O. (2008). Interpersonal problems and emotional intelligence in compulsive hoarding. *Depression and Anxiety, 25,* E63-E71.

Gunstad, J., & Phillips, K. A. (2003). Axis I comorbidity in body dysmorphic disorder. *Comprehensive Psychiatry, 44*(4), 270–276.

Hall, B. J., Tolin, D. F., Frost, R. O., & Steketee, G. (2013). An exploration of comorbid symptoms and clinical correlates of clinically significant hoarding symptoms. *Depression and Anxiety, 30,* 67–76.

Hanes, K. R. (1998). Neuropsychological performance in body dysmorphic disorder. *Journal of the International Neuropsychological Society, 4,* 167–171.

Harrison, B. J., Soriano-Mas, C., Pujol, J., Ortiz, H., Lopez-Sola, M., Hernandez-Ribas, R., et al. (2009). Altered corticostriatal functional connectivity in obsessive-compulsive disorder. *Archives of General Psychiatry, 66,* 1189–1200.

Hartl, T. L., Frost, R. O., Allen, G. J., Deckersback, T., Steketee, G., Duffacy, S. R., et al. (2004). Actual and perceived memory deficits in individuals with compulsive hoarding. *Depression and Anxiety, 20,* 59–69.

Hemmings, S. M., Kinnear, C. J., Lochner, C., Seedat, S., Corfield, V. A., Moolman-Smook, J. C., et al. (2006). Genetic correlates in trichotillomania: A case-control association study in the South African Caucasian population. *Israel Journal of Psychiatry and Related Sciences, 43,* 93–101.

Himle, M. B., Woods, D. W., Piacentini, J. C., & Walkup, J. T. (2006). Brief review of habit reversal training for tourette syndrome. *Journal of Child Neurology, 21,* 719–725.

Hollander, E., Allen, A., Kwon, J., Aronowitz, B., Schmeidler, J., Wong, C., et al. (1999). Clomipramine vs desipramine crossover trial in body dysmorphic disorder: Selective efficacy of a serotonin reuptake inhibitor in imagined ugliness. *Archives of General Psychiatry, 56,* 1033–1039.

Hollander, E., Kim, S., & Zohar, J. (2007). OCSDs in the forthcoming DSM-V. *CNS Spectrums, 12,* 320–323.

Hollander, E., Zohar, J., Sirovatka, P. J., & Regier, D. A. (Eds.) (2011). *Obsessive-compulsive spectrum disorders: Refining the research agenda for DSM-V.* Washington, DC: American Psychiatric Publishing.

Hudziak, J. J., Van Beijsterveldt, C. E., Althoff, R. R., Stanger, C., Rettew, D. C., Nelson, E. C., et al. (2004). Genetic and environmental contributions to the child behavior checklist obsessive-compulsive scale: A cross-cultural twin study. *Archives of General Psychiatry, 61,* 608–616.

Iervolino, A. C., Perroud, N., Fullana, M. A., Guipponi, M., Cherkas, L., Collier, D. A., et al. (2009). Prevalence and heritability of compulsive hoarding: A twin study. *American Journal of Psychiatry, 166,* 1156–1161.

Insel, T. R. (1990). Phenomenology of obsessive compulsive disorder. *Journal of Clinical Psychiatry, 51*(Suppl.), 4–8; discussion 9.

Ipser, J. C., Sander, C., & Stein, D. J. (2009). Pharmacotherapy and psychotherapy for body dysmorphic disorder. *Cochrane Database of Systematic Reviews* (1), CD005332.

Jaisoorya, T. S., Janardhan-Reddy, Y. C., & Srinath, S. (2003). The relationship of obsessive-compulsive disorder to putative spectrum disorders: Results from an Indian study. *Comprehensive Psychiatry, 44,* 317–323.

Katerberg, H., Delucchi, K. L., Stewart, S. E., Lochner, C., Denys, D. A., Stack, D. E., et al. (2010). Symptom dimensions in OCD: Item-level factor analysis and heritability estimates. *Behavior Genetics, 40,* 505–517.

Keuthen, N. J., Fraim, C., Deckersbach, T., Dougherty, D. D., Baer, L., & Jenike, M. A. (2001). Longitudinal follow-up of naturalistic treatment outcome in patients with trichotillomania. *Journal of Clinical Psychiatry, 62,* 101–107.

Keuthen, N. J., Makris, N., Schlerf, J. E., Martis, B., Savage, C. R., McMullin, K., et al. (2007). Evidence for reduced cerebellar volumes in trichotillomania. *Biological Psychiatry, 61,* 374–381.

Koran, L. M., Abujaoude, E., Large, M. D., & Serpe, R. T. (2008). The prevalence of body dysmorphic disorder in the united states adult population. *CNS Spectrums, 13,* 316–322.

Koran, L. M., Hanna, G. L., Hollander, E., Nestadt, G., & Simpson, H. B. (2007).

Practice guideline for the treatment of patients with obsessive-compulsive disorder. *American Journal of Psychiatry, 164*(Suppl. 7), 5–53.

Krishna, R., Udupa, S., George, C. M., Kumar, K. J., Viswanath, B., Kandavel, T., et al. (2011). Neuropsychological performance in OCD: A study in medication-naive patients. *Progress in Neuropsychopharmacology and Biological Psychiatry, 35*, 1969–1976.

Kuelz, A. K., Hohagen, F., & Voderholzer, U. (2004). Neuropsychological performance in obsessive-compulsive disorder: A critical review. *Biological Psychology, 65*, 185–236.

Kyrios, M., Frost, R. O., & Steketee, G. (2004). Cognitions in compulsive buying and acquisition. *Cognitive Therapy and Research, 28*, 241–258.

Landau, D., Iervolino, A. C., Pertusa, A., Santo, S., Singh, S., & Mataix-Cols, D. (2011). Stressful life events and material deprivation in hoarding disorder. *Journal of Anxiety Disorders, 25*, 192–202.

LaSalle, V. H., Cromer, K. R., Nelson, K. N., Kazuba, D., Justement, L., & Murphy, D. L. (2004). Diagnostic interview assessed neuropsychiatric disorder comorbidity in 334 individuals with obsessive-compulsive disorder. *Depression and Anxiety, 19*, 163–173.

Lawrence, N. S., Wooderson, S., Mataix-Cols, D., David, R., Speckens, A., & Phillips, M. L. (2006). Decision making and set shifting impairments are associated with distinct symptom dimensions in obsessive-compulsive disorder. *Neuropsychology, 20*, 409–419.

Lenane, M. C., Swedo, S. E., Rapoport, J. L., Leonard, H., Sceery, W., & Guroff, J. J. (1992). Rates of obsessive-compulsive disorder in first degree relatives of patients with trichotillomania: A research note. *Journal of Child Psychology, Psychiatry, and Allied Disciplines, 33*, 925–933.

Leonard, H., Swedo, S. E., Rapoport, J. L., Koby, E. V., Lenane, M. C., Cheslow, D. L., et al. (1989). Treatment of obsessive-compulsive disorder with clomipramine and desipramine in children and adolescents: A double-blind crossover comparision. *Archives of General Psychiatry, 46*, 1088–1092.

Lochner, C., Seedat, S., du Toit, P. L., Nel, D. G., Niehaus, D., Sandler, R., et al. (2005). Obsessive-compulsive disorder and trichotillomania: A phenomenological comparison. *BMC Psychiatry, 5*, 1–10.

Lovato, L., Ferrao, Y., Stein, D. J., Shavitt, R., Fontenelle, L., Vivan, A., et al. (2012). Skin picking and trichotillomania in adults with obsessive-compulsive disorder. *Comprehensive Psychiatry, 53*, 562–568.

Mataix-Cols, D., Billottia, D., Fernández de la Cruza, L., & Nordsletten, A. E. (2012). The London field trial for hoarding disorder. *Psychological Medicine, 43*(4), 1–11.

Mataix-Cols, D., Fernández de la Cruza, L., Nakaoa, T., & Pertusa, A. (2011). Testing the validity and acceptability of the diagnostic criteria for hoarding disorder: A DSM-5 survey. *Psychological Medicine, 41*, 2475–2484.

Mataix-Cols, D., Frost, R. O., Pertusa, A., Clark, L. A., Saxena, S., Leckman, J. F., et al. (2010). Hoarding disorder: A new diagnosis for DSM-V? *Depression and Anxiety, 27*, 556–572.

Mataix-Cols, D., & Pertusa, A. (2012). Annual research review: Hoarding disorder: Potential benefits and pitfalls of a new mental disorder. *Journal of Child Psychology and Psychiatry, 53*, 608–618.

Mataix-Cols, D., Rauch, S. L., Baer, L., Eisen, J. L., Shera, D. M., Goodman, W. K., et al. (2002). Symptom stability in adult obsessive-compulsive disorder: Data from a naturalistic two-year follow-up study. *American Journal of Psychiatry, 159*, 263–268.

Mataix-Cols, D., Rauch, S. L., Manzo, P. A., Jenike, M. A., & Baer, L. (1999). Use of factor analyzed symptom dimensions to predict outcome with serotonin reuptake inhibitors and placebo in the treatment of obsessive-compulsive disorder. *American Journal of Psychiatry, 156*, 1409–1416.

Mataix-Cols, D., Wooderson, S., Lawrence, N., Brammer, M. J., Speckens, A., & Phillips, M. L. (2004). Distinct neural correlates of washing, checking, and hoarding symptom dimensions in obsessive-compulsive disorder. *Archives of General Psychiatry, 61*, 564–576.

McElroy, S. L., Soutullo, C. A., Beckman, D. A., Taylor, P., & Keck, P. E. (1998). DSM-IV intermittent explosive disorder: A report of 27 cases. *Journal of Clinical Psychiatry, 59*, 203–210.

McLaughlin, N. C. R., & Greenberg, B. D. (2011). Other biological approaches to OCD. In G. Steketee (Ed.), *The Oxford handbook of obsessive-compulsive and spectrum disorders* (pp. 307–321). New York: Oxford Univertsity Press.

Melloni, M., Urbistondo, C., Sedeno, L., Gelormini, C., Kichic, R., & Ibanez, A. (2012). The extended fronto-striatal model of obsessive compulsive disorder: Convergence from event-related potentials, neuropsychology and neuroimaging. *Frontiers in Human Neuroscience, 6*, 1–24.

Menzies, L., Chamberlain, S. R., Laird, A. R., Thelen, S. M., Sahakian, B. J., & Bullmore, E. T. (2008). Integrating evidence from neuroimaging and neuropsychological studies of obsessive-compulsive disorder: The orbitofronto-striatal model revisited. *Neuroscience and Biobehavioral Reviews, 32*, 525–549.

Monzani, B., Rijsdijk, F., Anson, M., Iervolino, A. C., Cherkas, L., Spector, T., et al. (2012). A twin study of body dysmorphic concerns. *Psychological Medicine, 42*, 1949–1955.

Monzani, B., Rijsdijk, F., Iervolino, A. C., Anson, M., Cherkas, L., & Mataix-Cols, D. (2012). Evidence for a genetic overlap between body dysmorphic concerns and obsessive-compulsive symptoms in an adult female community twin sample. *American Journal of Medical Genetics. Part B, Neuropsychiatric Genetics, 159B*, 376–382.

Morselli, E., & Jerome, L. (2001). Dysmorphophobia and taphephobia: Two hitherto undescribed forms of insanity with fixed ideas. *History of Psychiatry, 12*, 103–107.

Mueller, A., Mitchell, J. E., Crosby, R. D., Glaesmer, H., & de Zwaan, M. (2009). The prevalence of compulsive hoarding and its association with compulsive buying in a german population-based sample. *Behaviour Research and Therapy, 47*, 705–709.

Mueller, A., Mueller, U., Albert, P., Mertens, C., Silbermann, A., Mitchell, J. E., et al. (2007). Hoarding in a compulsive buying sample. *Behaviour Research and Therapy, 45*, 2754–2763.

Muroff, J., Steketee, G., Rasmussen, J., Gibson, A., Bratiotis, C., & Sorrentino, C. (2009). Group cognitive behavioral treatment for compulsive hoarding: A preliminary trial. *Depression and Anxiety, 26*, 634–640.

Murray, C. J., & Lopez, A. D. (1996). *The global burden of disease: A comprehensive assessment of mortality and disability from diseases, injuries, and risk factors in 1990 and projected to 2020.* Cambridge, MA: Harvard University Press.

National Collaborating Centre for Mental Health (NCCMH) (2006). *Obsessive-compulsive disorder: Core interventions in the treatment of obsessive-compulsive disorder and body dysmorphic disorder.* Leicester and London, UK: The British Psychological Society and the Royal College of Psychiatrists. [Full Guideline]

Nestadt, G., Samuels, J., Riddle, M., Bienvenu, O. J., 3rd, Liang, K. Y., LaBuda, M., et al. (2000). A family study of obsessive-compulsive disorder. *Archives of General Psychiatry, 57*, 358–363.

Neziroglu, F., Khemlani-Patel, S., & Yaryura-Tobias, J. A. (2006). Rates of abuse in body dysmorphic disorder and obsessive-compulsive disorder. *Body Image, 3*, 189–193.

Nielen, M. M., den Boer, J. A., & Smid, H. G. (2009). Patients with obsessive-compulsive disorder are impaired in associative learning based on external feedback. *Psychological Medicine, 39*, 1519–1526.

Obsessive Compulsive Cognitions Working Group (OCCWG). (1997). Cognitive assessment of obsessive compulsive disorder. *Behaviour Research and Therapy, 35*, 667–681.

Obsessive Compulsive Cognitions Working Group (OCCWG). (2003). Psychometric validation of the obsessive beliefs questionnaire and the interpretations of intrusions inventory: Part 1. *Behaviour Research and Therapy, 41*, 863–878.

Obsessive Compulsive Cognitions Working Group (OCCWG). (2005). Psychometric validation of the obsessive beliefs questionnaire and the interpretations of intrusions inventory: Part 2: Factor analyses and testing of a brief version. *Behaviour Research and Therapy, 43*, 1527–1542.

Odlaug, B. L., & Grant, J. E. (2008). Clinical characteristics and medical complications of pathologic skin picking. *General Hospital Psychiatry, 30*, 61–66.

Okasha, A. (2003). Diagnosis of obsessive-compulsive disorder: A review. In Mario Maj, Norman Sartorius, Ahmed Okasha, & JosephZohar (Eds.), *Obsessive-compulsive disorder* (2nd ed., Vol. 4, pp. 1–41). Chichester, UK: John Wiley & Sons.

O'Sullivan, R. L., Rauch, S. L., Breiter, H. C., Grachev, I. D., Baer, L., Kennedy, D. N., et al. (1997). Reduced basal ganglia volumes in trichotillomania measured via morphometric magnetic resonance imaging. *Biological Psychiatry, 42*, 39–45.

Pavan, C., Vindigni, V., Semenzin, M., Mazzoleni, F., Gardiolo, M., Simonato, P., et al. (2006). Personality, temperament and clinical scales in an italian plastic surgery setting: What about body dysmorphic disorder? *International Journal of Psychiatry in Clinical Practice, 10*, 91–96.

Penades, R., Catalan, R., Rubia, K., Andres, S., Salamero, M., & Gasto, C. (2007). Impaired response inhibition in obsessive compulsive disorder. *European Psychiatry, 22*, 404–410.

Pertusa, A., Frost, R. O., Fullana, M. A., Samuels, J., Steketee, G., Tolin, D., et al. (2010).

Refining the diagnostic boundaries of compulsive hoarding: A critical review. *Clinical Psychology Review 30*, 371–386.

Pertusa, A., Fullana, M. A., Singh, S., Alonso, P., Menchon, J. M., & Mataix-Cols, D. (2008). Compulsive hoarding: OCD symptom, distinct clinical syndrome, or both? *American Journal of Psychiatry Research, 165*, 1289–1298.

Phillips, K. A. (1991). Body dysmorphic disorder: The distress of imagined ugliness. *American Journal of Psychiatry, 148*, 1138–1149.

Phillips, K. A. (2005a). Olanzapine augmentation of fluoxetine in body dysmorphic disorder. *American Journal of Psychiatry, 162*, 1022–1023.

Phillips, K. A. (2005b). Placebo-controlled study of pimozide augmentation of fluoxetine in body dysmorphic disorder. *American Journal of Psychiatry, 162*, 377–379.

Phillips, K. A. (2007). Suicidality in body dysmorphic disorder. *Primary Psychiatry, 14*, 58–66.

Phillips, K. A., & Dufresne, R. G. (2000). Body dysmorphic disorder. A guide for dermatologists and cosmetic surgeons. *American Journal of Clinical Dermatology, 1*, 235–243.

Phillips, K. A., Dufresne, R. G., Jr., Wilkel, C. S., & Vittorio, C. C. (2000). Rate of body dysmorphic disorder in dermatology patients. *Journal of the American Academy of Dermatology, 42*, 436–441.

Phillips, K. A., Gunderson, C. G., Mallya, G., McElroy, S. L., & Carter, W. (1998). A comparison study of body dysmorphic disorder and obsessive-compulsive disorder. *Journal of Clinical Psychiatry, 59* 568–575.

Phillips, K. A., & Hollander, E. (2008). Treating body dysmorphic disorder with medication: Evidence, misconceptions, and a suggested approach. *Body Image, 5*, 13–27.

Phillips, K. A., & McElroy, S. L. (2000). Personality disorders and traits in patients with body dysmorphic disorder. *Comprehensive Psychiatry, 41*, 229–236.

Phillips, K. A., McElroy, S. L., Keck, P. E., Jr., Hudson, J. I., & Pope, H. G., Jr. (1994). A comparison of delusional and nondelusional body dysmorphic disorder in 100 cases. *Psychopharmacology Bulletin, 30*, 179–186.

Phillips, K. A., & Menard, W. (2006). Suicidality in body dysmorphic disorder: A prospective study. *American Journal of Psychiatry, 163*, 1280–1282.

Phillips, K. A., Menard, W., Fay, C., & Weisberg, R. (2005). Demographic characteristics, phenomenology, comorbidity, and family history in 200 individuals with body dysmorphic disorder. *Psychosomatics, 46*, 317–325.

Phillips, K. A., Menard, W., Quinn, E., Didie, E. R., & Stout, R. L. (2012). A 4-year prospective observational follow-up study of course and predictors of course in body dysmorphic disorder. *Psychological Medicine, 43*, 1–9.

Phillips, K. A., Pagano, M. E., Menard, W., & Stout, R. L. (2006). A 12-month follow-up study of the course of body dysmorphic disorder. *American Journal of Psychiatry, 163*, 907–912.

Phillips, K. A., Pinto, A., Hart, A. S., Coles, M. E., Eisen, J. L., Menard, W., et al. (2012). A comparison of insight in body dysmorphic disorder and obsessive-compulsive disorder. *Journal of Psychiatric Research, 46*, 1293–1299.

Phillips, K. A., Pinto, A., Menard, W., Eisen, J. L., Mancebo, M., & Rasmussen, S. A. (2007). Obsessive-compulsive disorder versus body dysmorphic disorder: A comparison study of two possibly related disorders. *Depression and Anxiety, 24*, 399–409.

Phillips, K. A., Stein, D. J., Rauch, S. L., Hollander, E., Fallon, B. A., Barsky, A., et al. (2010). Should an obsessive-compulsive spectrum grouping of disorders be included in DSM-V? *Depression and Anxiety, 27*, 528–555.

Phillips, K. A., Wilhelm, S., Koran, L. M., Didie, E. R., Fallon, B. A., Feusner, J., et al. (2010). Body dysmorphic disorder: Some key issues for DSM-V. *Depression and Anxiety, 27*, 573–591.

Potenza, M. N., Koran, L. M., & Pallanti, S. (2009). The relationship between impulse-control disorders and obsessive-compulsive disorder: A current understanding and future research directions. *Psychiatry Research, 170*, 22–31.

Pryse-Phillips, W. (1971). An olfactory reference syndrome. *Acta Psychiatrica Scandinavica, 47*, 484–509.

Rachman, S. (1997). A cognitive theory of obsessions. *Behaviour Research and Therapy, 35*(9), 793–802.

Rao, N. P., Reddy, Y. C. J., Kumar, K. J., Kandavel, T., & Chandrashekar, C. R. (2008). Are neuropsychological deficits trait markers in OCD? *Progress in Neuropsychopharmacology and Biological Psychiatry, 32*, 1574–1579.

Rasmussen, S. A., & Eisen, J. L. (1988). Clinical and epidemiologic findings of significance to neuropharmacologic trials in OCD. *Psychopharmacology Bulletin, 24*, 466–470.

Rauch, S. L., Savage, C. R., Alpert, N. M., Dougherty, D., Kendrick, A., Curran, T., et al. (1997). Probing striatal function in obsessive-compulsive disorder: A PET study of implicit sequence learning. *Journal of Neuropsychiatry and Clinical Neurosciences, 9*, 568–573.

Rettew, D., Cheslow, D. L., Rapoport, J. L., Leonard, H., & Lenane, M. C. (1991). Neuropsychological test performance in trichotillomania: A further link with obsessive-compulsive disorder. *Journal of Anxiety Disorder, 5*, 225–235.

Richter, M. A., Summerfeldt, L. J., Antony, M. M., & Swinson, R. P. (2003). Obsessive-compulsive spectrum conditions in obsessive-compulsive disorder and other anxiety disorders. *Depression and Anxiety, 18*, 118–127.

Rief, W., Buhlmann, U., Wilhelm, S., Borkenhagen, A., & Brahler, E. (2006). The prevalence of body dysmorphic disorder: A population-based survey. *Psychological Medicine, 36*, 877–885.

Ruscio, A., Stein, D., Chiu, W., & Kessler, R. (2010). The epidemiology of obsessive-compulsive disorder in the National Comorbidity Survey Replication. *Molecular Psychiatry, 15*, 53–63.

Salkovskis, P. M. (1999). Understanding and treating obsessive-compulsive disorder. *Behaviour Research and Therapy, 37 Suppl 1*, S29–52.

Salkovskis, P. M., Wroe, A. L., Gledhill, A., Morrison, N., Forrester, E., Richards, C., et al. (2000). Responsibility attitudes and interpretations are characteristic of obsessive compulsive disorder. *Behaviour Research and Therapy, 38*, 347–372.

Samuels, J., Bienvenu, O. J., Grados, M. A., Cullen, B., Riddle, M. A., Liang, K. Y., et al. (2008). Prevalence and correlates of hoarding behavior in a community-based sample. *Behaviour Research and Therapy, 46*, 836–844.

Samuels, J., Bienvenu, O. J., Riddle, M. A., Cullen, B. A., Grados, M. A., Liang, K. Y., et al. (2002). Hoarding in obsessive compulsive disorder: Results from a case-control study. *Behaviour Research and Therapy, 40*, 517–528.

Samuels, J., Shugart, Y. Y., Grados, M. A., Willour, V. L., Bienvenu, O. J., Greenberg, B. D., et al. (2007). Significant linkage to compulsive hoarding on chromosome 14 in families with obsessive-compulsive disorder: Results from the OCD Collaborative Genetics Study. *American Journal of Psychiatry, 164*, 493–499.

Sarwer, D. B., Wadden, T. A., Pertschuk, M. J., & Whitaker, L. A. (1998). Body image dissatisfaction and body dysmorphic disorder in 100 cosmetic surgery patients. *Plastic and Reconstructive Surgery, 101*, 1644–1649.

Sarwer, D. B., Whitaker, L. A., Pertschuk, M. J., & Wadden, T. A. (1998). Body image concerns of reconstructive surgery patients: An underrecognized problem. *Annals of Plastic Surgery, 40*, 403–407.

Savage, C. R., Baer, L., Keuthen, N. J., Brown, H. D., Rauch, S. L., & Jenike, M. A. (1999). Organizational strategies mediate nonverbal memory impairment in obsessive-compulsive disorder. *Biological Psychiatry, 45*, 905–916.

Savage, C. R., Deckersbach, T., Wilhelm, S., Rauch, S. L., Baer, L., Reid, T., et al. (2000). Strategic processing and episodic memory impairment in obsessive compulsive disorder. *Neuropsychology, 14*, 141–151.

Saxena, S. (2008). Neurobiology and treatment of compulsive hoarding. *CNS Spectrums, 13*, 29–36.

Saxena, S. (2011). Pharmacotherapy of compulsive hoarding. *Journal of Clinical Psychology, 67*, 477–484.

Saxena, S., Brody, A. L., Maidment, K. M., & Baxter, L. R. (2007). Paroxetine treatment of compulsive hoarding. *Journal of Psychiatric Research, 41*, 481–487.

Saxena, S., & Rauch, S. L. (2000). Functional neuroimaging and the neuroanatomy of obsessive-compulsive disorder. *Psychiatric Clinics of North America, 23*, 563–586.

Schlosser, S., Black, D. W., Blum, N., & Goldstein, R. B. (1994). The demography, phenomenology, and family history of 22 persons with compulsive hair pulling. *Annals of Clinical Psychiatry, 6*, 147–152.

Shafran, R., & Rachman, S. (2004). Thought-action fusion: A review. *Journal of Behavior Therapy and Experimental Psychiatry, 35*, 87–107.

Stein, D. J., Carey, P. D., Lochner, C., Seedat, S., Fineberg, N., & Andersen, E. W. (2008). Escitalopram in obsessive-compulsive disorder: Response of symptom dimensions to pharmacotherapy. *CNS Spectrums, 13*, 492–498.

Stein, D. J., Chamberlain, S. R., & Fineberg, N. (2006). An A-B-C model of habit disorders: Hair-pulling, skin-picking, and other stereotypic conditions. *CNS Spectrums, 11*, 824–827.

Stein, D. J., Coetzer, R., Lee, M., Davis, B., & Bouwera, C. (1997). Magnetic resonance brain imaging in women with obsessive-compulsive disorder and trichotillomania. *Psychiatry Research: Neuroimaging, 74*, 177–182.

Stein, D. J., Fineberg, N. A., Bienvenu, O. J., Denys, D., Lochner, C., Nestadt, G., et al. (2010). Should OCD be classified as an anxiety disorder in DSM-V? *Depression and Anxiety, 27*(6), 495–506.

Stein, D. J., Flessner, C. A., M., F., Keuthen, N. J., C., L., & Woods, D. W. (2008). Is trichotillomania a stereotypic movement disorder? An analysis of body-focused repetitive behaviors in people with hair-pulling. *Annals of Clinical Psychiatry 20,* 194–198.

Stein, D. J., Grant, J. E., Franklin, M. E., Keuthen, N., Lochner, C., Singer, H. S., et al. (2010). Trichotillomania (hair pulling disorder), skin picking disorder, and stereotypic movement disorder: toward DSM-V. *Depression and Anxiety, 27,* 611–626.

Stein, D. J., & Hollander, E. (1992). Low-dose pimozide augmentation of serotonin reuptake blockers in the treatment of trichotillomania. *Journal of Clinical Psychiatry, 53,* 123–126.

Stein, D. J., & Lochner, C. (2006). Obsessive-compulsive spectrum disorders: A multidimensional approach. *Psychiatric Clinics of North America, 29,* 343–351.

Stein, D. J., Simeon, D., Cohen, L. J., & Hollander, E. (1995). Trichotillomania and obsessive-compulsive disorder. *Journal of Clinical Psychiatry, 56,* 28–34.

Steketee, G., Eisen, J., Dyck, I., Warshaw, M., & Rasmussen, S. (1999). Predictors of course in obsessive-compulsive disorder. *Psychiatry Research, 89,* 229–238.

Steketee, G., Frost, R., & Kyrios, M. (2003). Cognitive aspects of compulsive hoarding. *Cognitive Therapy and Research, 27,* 463–479.

Storch, E. A., Abramowitz, J., & Goodman, W. K. (2008). Where does obsessive-compulsive disorder belong in DSM-V? *Depression and Anxiety, 25,* 336–347.

Sutton, R. L. (1919). Bromidrosiphobia. *Journal of the American Medical Association, 72,* 1267–1268.

Tilley, H. (1895). Three cases of parosmia: Causes and treatment. *Lancet, 2,* 907–908.

Timpano, K. R., & Schmidt, N. B. (2013). The relationship between self-control deficits and hoarding: A multimethod investigation across three samples. *Journal of Abnormal Psychology, 122,* 13–25.

Timpano, K. R., Schmidt, N. B., Wheaton, M. G., Wendland, J. R., & Murphy, D. L. (2011). Consideration of the BDNF gene in relation to two phenotypes: Hoarding and obesity. *Journal of Abnormal Psychology, 120,* 700–707.

Tolin, D. F., Frost, R. O., & Steketee, G. (2007). An open trial of cognitive behavioral therapy for compulsive hoarding. *Behaviour Research and Therapy, 45,* 1461–1470.

Tolin, D. F., Frost, R. O., & Steketee, G. (2010). A brief interview for assessing compulsive hoarding: The Hoarding Rating Scale–interview. *Psychiatry Research, 178,* 147–152.

Tolin, D. F., Kiehl, K. A., Worhunsky, P., Book, G. A., & Maltby, N. (2009). An exploratory study of the neural mechanisms of decision making in compulsive hoarding. *Psychological Medicine, 39,* 325–336.

Tolin, D. F., Meunier, S. A., Frost, R. O., & Steketee, G. (2011). Hoarding among patients seeking treatment for anxiety disorders. *Journal of Anxiety Disorders, 25,* 43–48.

Tolin, D. F., Stevens, M. C., Villavicencio, A. L., Norberg, M. M., Calhoun, V. D., Frost, R. O., et al. (2012). Neural mechanisms of decision making in hoarding disorder. *Archives of General Psychiatry, 69,* 832–841.

Torres, A. R., Ramos-Cerqueira, A. T., Ferrao, Y. A., Fontenelle, L. F., do Rosario, M. C., & Miguel, E. C. (2011). Suicidality in obsessive-compulsive disorder: Prevalence and relation to symptom dimensions and comorbid conditions. *Journal of Clinical Psychiatry, 72,* 17–26.

Tukel, R., Oflaz, S. B., Ozyildirim, I., Aslantaş, B., Ertekin, E., Sözen, A., et al. (2007). Comparison of clinical characteristics in episodic and chronic obsessive-compulsive disorder. *Depression and Anxiety, 24,* 251–255.

Tukel, R., Polat, A., Ozdemir, O., Aksut, D., & Turksoy, N. (2002). Comorbid conditions in obsessive-compulsive disorder. *Comprehensive Psychiatry, 43,* 204–209.

Ursu, S., & Carter, C. S. (2009). An initial investigation of the orbitofrontal cortex hyperactivity in obsessive-compulsive disorder: Exaggerated representations of anticipated aversive events? *Neuropsychologia, 47,* 2145–2148.

Ursu, S., Stenger, V. A., Shear, M. K., Jones, M. R., & Carter, C. S. (2003). Overactive action monitoring in obsessive-compulsive disorder: Evidence from functional magnetic resonance imaging. *Psychological Science, 14,* 347–353.

van den Heuvel, O. A., Veltman, D. J., Groenewegen, H. J., Cath, D. C., van Balkom, A. J., van, H. J., et al. (2005). Frontal-striatal dysfunction during planning in obsessive-compulsive disorder. *Archives of General Psychiatry, 62,* 301–309.

Walsh, K. H., & McDougle, C. J. (2005). Pharmacological strategies for trichotillomania. *Expert Opinion on Pharmacotherapy, 6,* 975–984.

Wang, J. M., Seidler, R. D., Hall, J. L., & Preston, S. D. (2012). The neural bases of acquisitiveness: Decisions to acquire and discard everyday goods differ across frames, items, and individuals. *Neuropsychologia, 50,* 939–948.

Whiteside, S. P., Port, J. D., & Abramowitz, J. S. (2004). A meta-analysis of functional neuroimaging in obsessive-compulsive disorder. *Psychiatry Research: Neuroimaging, 132,* 69–79.

Wilhelm, S., Keuthen, N. J., Deckersbach, T., Engelhard, I. M., Forker, A. E., Baer, L., et al. (1999). Self-injurious skin picking: Clinical characteristics and comorbidity. *Journal of Clinical Psychiatry, 60,* 454–459.

Wilhelm, S., Phillips, K. A., Fama, J. M., Greenberg, J. L., & Steketee, G. (2011). Modular cognitive-behavioral therapy for body dysmorphic disorder. *Behavior Therapy, 42,* 624–633.

Wilhelm, S., & Steketee, G. (2006). *Cognitive therapy for obsessive compulsive disorder: A guide for professionals.* Oakland, CA: New Harbinger Publications.

Wilhelm, S., Steketee, G., Fama, J. M., Buhlmann, U., Teachman, B. A., & Golan, E. (2009). Modular cognitive therapy for obsessive-compulsive disorder: A wait-list controlled trial. *Journal of Cognitive Psychotherapy, 23,* 294–305.

Wincze, J. P., Steketee, G., & Frost, R. O. (2007). Categorization in compulsive hoarding. *Behaviour Research and Therapy, 45,* 63–72.

Woods, D. W., Flessner, C. A., Franklin, M. E., Keuthen, N. J., Goodwin, R. D., Stein, D. J., et al. (2006). The Trichotillomania Impact Project (TIP): Exploring phenomenology, functional impairment, and treatment utilization. *Journal of Clinical Psychiatry, 67,* 1877–1888.

Wu, K. D., & Watson, D. (2005). Hoarding and its relation to obsessive compulsive disorder. *Behaviour Research and Therapy, 43,* 897–921.

Zhang, H., Leckman, J. F., Pauls, D. L., Tsai, C. P., Kidd, K. K., & Campos, M. R. (2002). Genomewide scan of hoarding in sib pairs in which both sibs have Gilles de la Tourette syndrome. *American Journal of Human Genetics, 70,* 896–904.

Zuchner, S., Cuccaro, M. L., Tran-Viet, K. N., Cope, H., Krishnan, R. R., Pericak-Vance, M., et al. (2006). *SLITRK1* mutations in trichotillomania. *Molecular Psychiatry, 11,* 887–889.

Zuchner, S., Wendland, J. R., Ashley-Koch, A., Collins, A. L., Tran-Viet, K., Quinn, K., et al. (2009). Multiple rare *SAPAP3* missense variants in trichotillomania and OCD. *Molecular Psychiatry, 14,* 6–9.

7

Posttraumatic Stress Disorder and Dissociative Disorders

RICHARD J. MCNALLY

Posttraumatic Stress Disorder

Clinicians have long recognized that traumatic events can produce psychiatric symptoms in previously well-adjusted individuals, but prevailing opinion held that stress-induced symptoms are transient (Jones & Wessely, 2007). Persistent symptoms implied the presence of another neurotic or characterological disturbance.

The psychiatric sequelae of the Vietnam War altered this view. Many veterans began to report chronic symptoms, often long after reentering civilian life. Instead of viewing all of these men as suffering from preexisting conditions merely exacerbated by the war, clinicians became convinced that the war itself could cause chronic psychiatric disability (Lifton, 1973; Shatan, 1973).

Antiwar psychiatrists and leaders of Vietnam veterans' organizations lobbied for the inclusion of a "post-Vietnam syndrome" diagnosis in the then-forthcoming *DSM-III*. Advocates for the diagnosis realized that for veterans to receive treatment and psychiatric disability compensation from the Veterans Administration (VA), they had to show that veterans' problems were a direct consequence of their military service, not the manifestation of previous problems or vulnerabilities. Making this case was especially challenging when symptoms surfaced only years after the war. Indeed, no single diagnosis

in the *DSM-II* captured the delayed onset of stress-related symptoms.

Leaders of the *DSM* revision process initially opposed this proposal, maintaining that combinations of several traditional diagnoses could cover the problems of these veterans. Moreover, a goal for *DSM-III* was to devise an atheoretical system comprising diagnoses explicitly defined by their signs and symptoms rather than by often-debatable etiologies. Ratification of a post-Vietnam syndrome would be clearly inconsistent with this goal.

Veterans' advocates made common cause with mental health professionals who had been working with survivors of rape (Burgess & Holmstrom, 1974), disaster (Rangell, 1976), and concentration camps (Chodoff, 1963). Similarities in survivors' symptoms produced a consensus that any terrifying, life-threatening event could cause a chronic syndrome such as that suffered by the traumatized Vietnam veteran. An influential member of the *DSM-III* task force agreed with this consensus (Andreasen, 2004). Indeed, she had observed a similar pattern of psychiatric symptoms in her patients who had been severely burned. Her support ensured that posttraumatic stress disorder (PTSD) appeared in *DSM-III*, classified as an anxiety disorder.

Since 1980, the diagnosis has undergone changes in *DSM-III-R*, *DSM-IV*, and *DSM-5*, but its core attributes remain intact. The central idea is that a traumatic event establishes a memory that gives rise to a characteristic profile of signs and symptoms (McNally, 2003a; Rubin, Berntsen, & Bohni, 2008; Young, 1995). Natural selection ensures that people remember potentially life-threatening experiences; to forget them would be to court disaster. Accordingly, as behavioral neuroscientists have shown (McGaugh, 2003), stress hormones released during the trauma render the central features of a traumatic experience highly memorable. Yet when people continue to recall their traumas involuntarily with the full emotional force of the original experience, then psychopathology is evident. The failure of stress symptoms to abate despite the absence of danger is what justifies PTSD as a mental disorder.

According to *DSM-5*, PTSD comprises four symptomatic clusters. The *intrusion* cluster (B criteria) includes reexperiencing symptoms such as traumatic nightmares, intrusive sensory images of the trauma, and physiological reactivity to reminders of the trauma. The *avoidance* cluster (C criteria) includes efforts to avoid feelings, thoughts, and reminders of the trauma. The cluster covering *negative alterations in cognitions and mood* (D criteria) includes symptoms such as emotional numbing, distorted blame of self or others, and pervasive negative emotional states (e.g., shame and anger). The cluster covering *alterations in arousal and reactivity* (Criteria E) includes symptoms such as exaggerated startle, aggression, reckless behavior, and hypervigilance.

What Counts as a Traumatic Stressor?

To qualify for PTSD, a person must meet Criterion A: exposure to a traumatic stressor. In fact, exposure to trauma is essential to the conceptual integrity of PTSD, for two reasons (McNally, 2009). First, core symptoms of PTSD possess *intentionality* in Brentano's (1889/1984) sense of the word. That is, they possess intentional content or "aboutness." Key symptoms are not merely *caused* by trauma; they are *about* the trauma. To have intrusive images, for example, is to have intrusive images about something, namely, the trauma.

Second, many symptoms of PTSD overlap with those of other disorders (e.g., loss of pleasure in activities, insomnia), and it is the memory of the trauma that unites them into a coherent syndrome

(Young, 1995, p. 5). Dispensing with Criterion A would unravel the syndrome.

The *DSM-III* concept of PTSD presupposed that only *traumatic* stressors falling outside the boundary of everyday experience could produce the symptomatic profile of the disorder. Such canonical stressors included combat, rape, torture, and natural disasters, events that would presumably produce intense distress in anyone. Conversely, ordinary stressors falling outside this boundary presumably could not cause PTSD.

Two key findings complicated this assumptive framework. First, epidemiological studies documented that most people exposed to Criterion A traumatic stressors do not develop PTSD (Breslau, Davis, Andreski, & Peterson, 1991). Accordingly, risk factors must influence whether trauma-exposed people develop the disorder, consistent with a diathesis-stress model.

Second, other studies indicated that people who failed to meet the original *DSM-III* Criterion A could nevertheless fulfill the symptomatic criteria for PTSD. This violation of the assumptive framework occurred in two ways. Some people met criteria for PTSD even though they had not directly experienced or witnessed the trauma. For example, some people met symptomatic criteria after learning of the violent death of a loved one (e.g., Saigh, 1991). Accordingly, in 1994 the *DSM-IV* broadened the concept of trauma exposure to include being "confronted with" information about a threat to the "physical integrity" of another person.

Other reports showed that direct recipients of stressors falling short of Criterion A could apparently result in PTSD (for a review, see Dohrenwend, 2010). For example, people encountering obnoxious jokes in the workplace (McDonald, 2003), giving birth to a healthy baby after an uncomplicated delivery (Olde, van der Hart, Kleber, & van Son, 2006), and having a wisdom tooth removed (de Jongh et al., 2008) reportedly developed PTSD or PTSD symptoms.

Concern that suffering people would be denied the diagnosis and reimbursable treatment honorably motivated the conceptual bracket creep in the definition of trauma (McNally, 2003b). Yet broadening the concept had other consequences, too. It meant that nearly everyone qualifies as a trauma survivor, as Breslau and Kessler (2001) discovered. Studying residents of southeastern Michigan, they found that 89.6% of adults had been exposed to a *DSM-IV* Criterion A stressor. Other researchers reported that 4% of American adults living far from the scenes of the September 11th terrorist attacks developed apparent PTSD (Schlenger et al., 2002), seemingly from watching the events on television. Not only could one now qualify as a "trauma survivor" without having been at the scene of the trauma, one did not even have to know the people whose physical integrity had been threatened (McNally & Breslau, 2008).

Yet what should we make of people who encounter relatively minor stressors but who meet symptomatic criteria for PTSD? One possibility is that they have misunderstood questions asking about PTSD symptoms. Another possibility is that they really do have PTSD, but they carry a much higher burden of preexisting risk factors relative to people who develop the disorder only after encountering very severe events. That is, the stressor may recede into the causal background as risk factors move into the causal foreground.

Consistent with this background–foreground inversion hypothesis, McNally and Robinaugh (2011) found that the effect size between cognitive ability and PTSD caseness was much larger for women whose childhood sexual abuse was mild than for those whose abuse was moderate in severity. That is, the less severe the stressor, the more important was the risk factor of lower cognitive ability in predicting PTSD.

Yet, in an epidemiological study, Breslau, Troost, Bohnert, and Luo (2013) found that the importance of risk factors (e.g., preexisting depression, parental alcohol abuse) did not differ for less severe categories of trauma (accidents) than for more severe categories of trauma (sexual assault). Moreover, in another epidemiological study, Breslau, Chen, and Luo (2013) found that lower intelligence was not more predictive of PTSD among people exposed to less severe trauma (i.e., disasters, accidents) than among those exposed to assaultive violence. Hence, the epidemiological data indicate that vulnerability factors increase risk for PTSD irrespective of the severity of the trauma.

In any event, the *DSM-5* committee has tightened up Criterion A by requiring that people who learn of physical threats to others must be a close friend or relative of the threatened person. The committee also excluded trauma exposure via media as qualifying for Criterion A (except for people for whom such exposure is part of their vocational role). In keeping with research showing

that exposure to gruesome scenes of trauma can provoke PTSD even when the witness encounters no danger (e.g., placing human remains in body bags; Sutker, Uddo, Brailey, Vasterling, & Errera, 1994), the *DSM-5* now counts it as traumatic.

In *DSM-IV*, Criterion A comprised two components, A1 and A2. The first specified exposure to a traumatic stressor, and the second specified that the person had to respond with "intense fear, helplessness or horror" during the event. Yet this second component conflates the external event and the person's emotional response to it in the definition of a traumatic stressor. In the language of behavioral psychology, it conflates the stimulus with the response; in the language of medicine, it conflates the toxin with the host (McNally, 2009). The *DSM-5* committee wisely eliminated A2 from Criterion A.

Epidemiology and Sex Ratio

According to the National Comorbidity Survey Replication (NCS-R; Kessler et al., 2005), the lifetime prevalence rate of *DSM-IV-TR* PTSD in the United States is 6.8%. According to the NCS-R, 9.7% of women and 3.6% of men develop PTSD at some point in their lives. Men are exposed to traumatic events more often than women are (Tolin & Foa, 2006), yet the rate of PTSD is twice as great in women as in men. One hypothesis for this sex difference in PTSD prevalence is that the extremely stressful events most likely to trigger PTSD occur more often in the lives of women than in men (Cortina & Kubiak, 2006). This hypothesis, however, appears incorrect. Even when one controls for type of trauma (e.g., rape), sex differences in the severity and prevalence of PTSD remain (Tolin & Foa, 2006), implying that men and women differ in ways that influence their risk of developing PTSD following exposure to trauma.

Military personnel are at heightened risk for exposure to trauma. According to the National Vietnam Veterans Readjustment Study (NVVRS), 30.9% of all men who had served in Vietnam developed *DSM-III-R* PTSD, whereas 15.2% still had the disorder in the late 1980s when the survey occurred (Kulka et al., 1990). An additional 22.5% had partial PTSD, meaning that 53.4% of all men who had served in Vietnam developed either the full-blown or the partial form of the illness.

However, for two reasons, historians of military psychiatry suspected that the NVVRS team overestimated the prevalence of PTSD (e.g., Jones & Wessely, 2005, pp. 133–134; McNally, 2007a; Shephard, 2001, p. 392). First, only about 12.5% (King & King, 1991) of Vietnam veterans had served in direct combat roles during the Vietnam War (e.g., rifleman in an infantry platoon). The historians found it odd that twice as many men developed PTSD as were in combat roles. Even when one considers the additional 15% of men who served in combat support roles (e.g., medic) and hence could encounter danger, the prevalence rate was puzzlingly high.

Second, only 3.5% of all psychiatric casualties in Vietnam itself received a diagnosis of combat exhaustion (Marlowe, 2001, p. 86). As Marlowe (2001) put it, "Vietnam produced an extremely low proportion of proximate combat stress casualties and produced or is claimed to have produced massive numbers of postcombat casualties. Therefore, Vietnam breaks with the past normative pattern of combat and war zone stress casualty production" (p. 73). Unlike the shell shock and battle fatigue cases of World War I and World War II, the stress reactions among many Vietnam veterans became evident years later.

In response to these concerns, Dohrenwend et al. (2006) reanalyzed the NVVRS data, applying rigorous criteria for PTSD caseness. Before accepting a case as PTSD-positive, they did three things prior to recalculating prevalence estimates. First, they included only those veterans whose PTSD developed from war-related trauma, not events occurring before or after the war. Second, they included only those veterans for whom archival data were consistent with their self-reported war traumas, thereby corroborating 91% of the PTSD cases. Third, they used scores on the Global Assessment of Functioning (GAF; Spitzer, Williams, & Gibbon, 1987) scale to assess functional impairment, as impairment was not a diagnostic requirement for *DSM-III-R* PTSD. Dohrenwend et al. used GAF ratings, assigned by clinical interviewers in the NVVRS, as a proxy for the then-nonexistent *DSM* impairment criterion. They considered a veteran as impaired if he had received a rating of 1 through 7 on the 9-point GAF scale. One is the lowest level of functioning, and 9 is the highest level of functioning. The modal PTSD case was rated a 7, defined as "some difficulty in social, occupational, or school functioning, but generally functioning pretty well, has

some meaningful interpersonal relationships OR some mild symptoms (e.g., depressed mood and mild insomnia, occasional truancy, or theft within the household)" (p. 2).

Dohrenwend et al.'s (2006) adjustments reduced both the lifetime and current prevalence rates of PTSD by 40%, thereby confirming the hypothesis of the historians (McNally, 2006a). The lifetime prevalence dropped from 30.9% to 18.7% and the current prevalence rate dropped from 15.2% to 9.1%. However, had Dohrenwend et al. used a slightly more stringent definition of impairment (i.e., GAF score of 1 through 6 ["moderate" impairment]), the current prevalence estimate would have dropped by 65%, that is, from 15.2% to 5.4% (McNally, 2007b).

Taken together, these data indicate that estimates of PTSD in epidemiological samples can vary wildly, depending on the criterion for clinically impairment. This affects prevalence rates in civilian samples, too. In two epidemiological studies, Breslau and Alvarado (2007) found that requiring that symptoms produce impairment lowered the prevalence of PTSD in men by 33% and 44% and in women by 25% and 30%, respectively.

In striking contrast to previous wars, those in Iraq and Afghanistan have prompted American, British, and Dutch authorities to assess their troops before, during, and after deployment (McNally, 2012a). A comprehensive review of rigorous studies indicated that between 2.1% and 13.8% of American and British service members have developed PTSD (Sundin et al., 2010).

Smith et al. (2008) conducted the methodologically strongest study on American military personnel deployed to Iraq and Afghanistan. They used data from the U.S. Millennium Cohort, a prospective, longitudinal investigation of active duty and Reserve/National Guard personnel. Administering the PTSD Checklist (PCL; Weathers, Litz, Herman, Huska, & Keane, 1993) to 47,837 members of the Armed Forces, they found that 4.3% developed PTSD. Among those exposed to combat, 7.6% developed PTSD, whereas 1.4% of those reporting no combat exposure did so. Among military personnel who had never deployed overseas, 2.3% developed PTSD from stateside traumatic events (e.g., accidents on bases).

Methodologically, Smith et al.'s (2008) study has many strengths. As a very large population-based epidemiological survey, it avoids biases associated with convenience samples. The authors excluded subjects with predeployment PTSD, thereby providing estimates of PTSD attributable to military trauma alone and not to trauma occurring prior to subjects joining the military. Using the PCL, Hoge et al. (2004) found that as many as 5% of combat troops met criteria for PTSD prior to deploying to Iraq, whereas 12.6% qualified for PTSD following combat exposure in Iraq. If one rules out preexisting PTSD among Hoge et al.'s combatants, one obtains a deployment-attributable rate of PTSD of 7.6%—the same estimate reported by Smith et al. (2008) for combat-exposed personnel.

Finally, Smith et al. (2008) ensured that PCL data on PTSD symptoms were unconnected with subjects' official military files, thereby ensuring the confidentiality of symptom disclosure. Keeping research data separate from the service person's official records likely fosters candor among soldiers justifiably worried about the stigma of admitting mental health problems (Hoge et al., 2004).

No epidemiological study is without limitations, and Smith et al.'s is no exception. As with nearly all large epidemiological studies, Smith et al. used a questionnaire (PCL) to assess PTSD, not a structured diagnostic interview, and the PCL does not gauge impairment. Overcoming these limitations in a relatively small (*n* = 382) study, Engelhard et al. (2007) found that 21% of Dutch infantry veterans of Iraq met symptomatic criteria for PTSD on a questionnaire, but this rate dropped to 4% on structured interview that confirmed that the stressor was war related and that symptoms produced impairment. Another study that added a measure of impairment to the PCL likewise lowered prevalence estimates in American troops (Thomas et al., 2010). These two studies suggest that Smith et al.'s estimate may be too high.

On the other hand, studies show that the percentage of subjects qualifying for a PTSD diagnosis rises slightly within the first 6 to 12 months following their return from Iraq or Afghanistan (Sundin et al., 2010). Some service members may initially fail to report certain symptoms that are adaptive in a war zone (e.g., hypervigilance and numbing), yet subsequently endorse them on the PCL if symptoms fail to remit months postdeployment.

Longitudinal Course of PTSD

Acute stress symptoms are common following exposure to traumatic events. For example, studying help-seeking rape victims, Rothbaum and Foa (1993) found that 95% met PTSD symptom criteria within 2 weeks of the trauma. Symptoms waned for most of them. The proportion still meeting symptom criteria at 1, 3, and 6 months postrape declined to 63.3%, 45.9%, and 41.7%, respectively. Likewise, Rothbaum and Foa found that, among victims of nonsexual assault, 64.7% met PTSD symptom criteria 1 week after the crime, whereas the proportion still fulfilling criteria at 1, 3, 6, and 9 months postassault declined to 36.7%, 14.6%, 11.5%, and 0%, respectively.

In an Australian epidemiological survey, Chapman et al. (2012) assessed a representative sample of 8,841 subjects aged 16 through 85 years old. Using *DSM-IV* criteria, they found that 75% of the subjects had experienced at least one traumatic event, and 46% of these events concerned interpersonal trauma. Among those with a trauma history, 9.6% had developed PTSD (6.1% of the men, and 13.2% of the women). The median age of onset was 26 years old; 25% had developed the disorder by age 15, and 75% by age 42. The median time to remission was 14 years, and the projected lifetime remission rate was 92%. Chapman et al. defined remission very stringently; remitted cases had to fall short of all three symptom criteria (B: reexperiencing, C: avoidance/numbing, and D: hyperarousal) clusters, not merely fail to meet criteria for the disorder overall. These data indicate that complete recovery for well over half of those who develop PTSD will not occur for nearly a decade and a half, even though the vast majority of such individuals do recover entirely.

Symptoms of PTSD usually emerge within hours or days of the trauma, making delayed-onset PTSD extremely rare (Jones & Wessely, 2005, p. 184). In a civilian epidemiological study (Breslau et al., 1991), only 1 person among the 93 diagnosed with PTSD appeared to have a delayed onset.

People who meet criteria for PTSD only after 6 months following the trauma qualify for delayed-onset PTSD. However, few, if any, of them are symptom-free during the months following the trauma (Andrews, Brewin, Philpott, & Stewart, 2007). The modal case suffers symptoms all along, finally experiencing an increase that bumps them above the diagnostic threshold. Others may develop the full syndrome immediately following the trauma, but seek help only years later (Solomon, Kotler, Shalev, & Lin, 1989). However, such delayed help-seeking is distinguishable from delayed onset of PTSD.

In a prospective, cohort investigation, Goodwin et al. (2012) administered the PCL twice to 1,397 British military personnel who had served in Iraq. Both assessments occurred after they had finished their deployment to the war zone. The first occurred between 2004 and 2006, and the second occurred between 2007 and 2009. Soldiers completed the questionnaire in reference to symptoms during the previous month. Cases of probable PTSD had a score of at least 50 on the PCL, and cases of subthreshold PTSD had a score of 40 through 49. PCL scores can range from 17 through 85. Cases of delayed-onset PTSD qualified for the syndrome at the second assessment, but not at the first one. Although 94% of the subjects were free of PTSD at both time points, 3.5% of them developed delayed-onset PTSD. That is, of those who had PTSD, 46% met criteria only at the second assessment point. Of the 44 cases of delayed-onset PTSD, 12 already had symptoms sufficiently severe as to qualify them for subthreshold PTSD.

The number of veterans from the Vietnam era seeking treatment and service-connected disability compensation has been skyrocketing in recent years (McNally, 2006a). During fiscal years 1999 to 2004, PTSD payments increased by 148.8%, and the total number of veterans receiving compensation for PTSD increased by 79.5%, whereas the total number receiving compensation for all health problems increased by only 12.2%.

It is unclear whether this upsurge reflects true delayed-onset PTSD, delayed presentation for treatment, reactivation of symptoms among veterans approaching retirement, or, as Burkett and Whitley (1998) documented in some cases, malingering. One investigation revealed that most veterans in this cohort continued to deteriorate psychiatrically despite remaining in treatment, but then terminated treatment once they achieved 100% service-connected disability status. However, their nonpsychiatric medical visits did not decline (Department of Veterans Affairs Office of the Inspector General, 2005).

In another study, Frueh et al. (2005) consulted the military personnel files in an effort to corroborate reports of trauma exposure for 100 men recently seeking treatment for combat-related PTSD stemming from Vietnam. For only 41% of the cases did the archival data corroborate the self-reported trauma, and 7% had either never served in Vietnam or never served in the military at all. Yet the clinical assessors had diagnosed PTSD in 94% of the subjects. The uncorroborated cases reported exposure to battlefield atrocities at twice the rate of corroborated cases, and many of the former reported implausible if not impossible traumatic events (e.g., a cook who said he was a prisoner in North Vietnam).

Analyzing a huge federal data set, labor economists Angrist, Chen, and Frandsen (2010) concluded that financial need, not psychiatric disorder, is the chief cause of the recent massive increase in PTSD disability claims among Vietnam veterans. They found that the increase largely occurs among veterans whose limited vocational skills make it very difficult for them to make a decent living. Moreover, Angrist et al. found that combat exposure (and therefore PTSD) could not account for the increase in claims. Accordingly, they concluded, "This leaves the attractiveness of VDC [veterans' disability compensation] for less-skilled men and the work disincentives embedded in the VDC system as a likely explanation for our findings" (p. 824). Taken together, these data have prompted some scholars to suggest that the apparent emergence of PTSD decades after exposure to trauma may often reflect financial need rather than delayed emergence of psychiatric illness (McNally & Frueh, 2012), whereas other scholars disagree with this assessment (Marx et al., 2012).

Comorbidity

Pure PTSD is unusual, and comorbidity is common. In the NVVRS, 98.8% of the veterans who qualified for a lifetime diagnosis of PTSD also qualified for at least one other mental disorder, compared with 40.6% of those without PTSD (Kulka et al., 1990). The most common comorbid disorders in both male and female veterans with PTSD were alcohol abuse and depression, and generalized anxiety disorder (GAD) in men, and panic disorder in women.

Comorbidity is common in cases of civilian PTSD, too. Kessler, Sonnega, Bromet, Hughes, and Nelson (1995) reported lifetime comorbidity rates of 88.3% in men and 79% in women with PTSD. Major depression and alcohol dependence were among the most common comorbidities. Retrospectively reported ages of onset implied that other anxiety disorders usually preceded PTSD, whereas alcohol and mood disorders usually followed the emergence of PTSD. In a representative sample of Australians (Chapman et al., 2012), among those who developed primary PTSD, 86.4% of the men and 76.6% of the women had comorbid disorders. Anxiety disorders, mood disorders, and substance use disorders were the most common diagnoses.

Risk Factors for PTSD

For many years, research on risk factors for PTSD was de facto taboo. During the struggle to have PTSD recognized in *DSM-III*, advocates for the diagnosis were keen to emphasize that the delayed emergence of chronic psychiatric problems in Vietnam veterans was attributable to their experiences in the military, not to preexisting vulnerability factors. Advocates regarded speculation about risk factors as equivalent to blaming victims for their plight (e.g., Blank, 1985). Yet research on risk factors was inevitable once the diagnosis was firmly established in the *DSM-III*, and researchers found that only a small subset of trauma survivors developed PTSD. As epidemiologists have shown, trauma is common, yet PTSD is rare (Breslau & Kessler, 2001). Exposure to trauma is necessary, but insufficient, to cause PTSD, thereby implying the relevance of risk factors for explaining etiology.

There are two aspects to risk for PTSD (Bowman & Yehuda, 2004): risk for exposure to trauma and risk for PTSD given exposure to trauma. Regarding the former, in one study, retrospectively ascertained risk factors for exposure to trauma included extroversion, neuroticism, male sex, having less than a college education, a personal history of childhood conduct problems, and a family history of psychiatric disorder (Breslau et al., 1991). This research group also did a 3-year prospective study, finding that extroversion and neuroticism predicted exposure to trauma (Breslau, Davis, & Andreski, 1995). Black subjects had a higher rate of exposure than did Whites.

Risk factors for PTSD among those exposed to trauma include female sex (e.g., Tolin & Foa, 2006); neuroticism (e.g., Breslau et al., 1991; McFarlane, 1989); lower social support (e.g., Boscarino, 1995); lower IQ (e.g., Koenen, Moffitt, Poulton, Martin, & Caspi, 2007; Macklin et al., 1998; McNally & Shin, 1995); preexisting psychiatric illness, especially anxiety and mood

disorders (e.g., Breslau et al., 1991); family history of anxiety, mood, or substance abuse disorders (e.g., Breslau et al., 1991); neurological soft signs (e.g., nonspecific abnormalities in central nervous function; Gurvits et al., 2000); and small hippocampi (Gilbertson et al., 2002). Some risk factors, such as low social support, have been assessed after individuals have developed PTSD, making it unclear whether early symptoms alienated potential sources of support or whether lack of support impeded recovery from trauma or both.

Using data from the Dunedin longitudinal study, Koenen et al. (2008) discovered that PTSD almost never developed in response to trauma during adulthood unless the subject had received a mental disorder diagnosis, often in childhood. That is, of new cases of PTSD occurring between the ages of 26 and 32, 96% had already experienced a mental disorder and 77% had received the diagnosis before the age of 15. Anxiety, mood, and conduct disorders were the three most common syndromes that preceded adult-onset PTSD. Previous disorders may signify a preexisting vulnerability to develop PTSD in response to trauma, may themselves increase risk for exposure to trauma, or both.

Some scholars have adduced evidence suggesting that previous exposure to traumatic events sensitizes people so that they experience increased risk of developing PTSD in response to subsequent stressors (e.g., King, King, Foy, & Gudanowski, 1996). In these studies, people with PTSD are asked about previous traumatic events they had experienced prior to the trauma that triggered their disorder. Unfortunately, these researchers had not assessed how individuals had responded to their earlier trauma. Indeed, Breslau, Peterson, and Schultz (2008) have shown that previous exposure to trauma does not increase risk for PTSD in response to subsequent trauma unless the person developed PTSD in response to the first trauma. Trauma-exposed individuals who do not develop PTSD in response to the earlier event are not at heightened risk for PTSD.

The findings of Solomon, Mikulincer, and Jakob (1987) foreshadowed Breslau's findings. Solomon et al. found that prior combat exposure did not increase risk for an acute combat stress reaction among Israeli soldiers who fought in the 1982 Lebanon War unless the soldier had experienced an acute combat stress reaction during a previous war. That is, prior combat per se did not predict breakdown in response to subsequent combat.

How victims respond during a trauma may predict whether they develop PTSD. The study of peritraumatic predictors involves asking victims hours, days, weeks, or sometimes years after the event how they recall responding during the trauma. Peritraumatic dissociation predicts PTSD (e.g., Shalev, Peri, Canetti, & Schreiber, 1996). That is, people who reported feeling disconnected from their body, feeling that events were happening in slow motion, and so forth were especially likely to develop the disorder.

A trauma victim's negative appraisal of acute symptoms predicts whether the person will develop PTSD (Dunmore, Clark, & Ehlers 2001; Ehring, Ehlers, & Glucksman, 2006). For example, if trauma victims construe startle responses and nightmares as signs of personal weakness or flashbacks as signs of impending psychosis, they are at heightened risk for failing to recover from the acute effects of trauma.

Most research on risk and resilience concerns individual variables. However, group cohesion, morale, and leadership function as buffers against battlefield stress (Jones & Wessely, 2007).

Cognitive Aspects of PTSD

Researchers have investigated cognitive aspects of PTSD from both phenomenological and information-processing perspectives (McNally, 2006b).

Phenomenology of Traumatic Memory

A trauma victim might suffer from ruminative intrusive thoughts *about* the trauma, such as "Why did this have to happen to me?" or suffer from repetitive, intrusive thoughts *of* the trauma, such as vivid, sensory flashbacks of the event (Hackmann, Ehlers, Speckens, & Clark, 2004). In *DSM-5*, ruminative thoughts about the trauma no longer qualify as reexperiencing symptoms; only intrusive sensory memories do.

Memories of trauma are different from memories of other events in terms of their content and emotional qualities. Do they differ in other ways? Are they represented and processed differently (Brewin, 2011)? Porter and Peace (2007) conducted a longitudinal study of individuals in the

community who had experienced a traumatic event, often crimes. In addition to having the individuals rate the emotional qualities and vividness of the traumatic memory, they had each subject select and rate a very positive memory. Relative to memories of trauma, memories of positive events tended to fade in terms of vividness and emotional intensity, and their accuracy (relative to the baseline description) tended to diminish over the course of several years.

Do people with PTSD have more fragmented and disorganized memories of trauma than do victims without PTSD? Examples of fragmentation include unnecessary repetitions of elements in the trauma narrative or disjointed thoughts expressed by the person when recounting the trauma. One study revealed that assault victims with PTSD described their trauma in a more disorganized fashion than did victims without PTSD, and the degree of disorganization predicted subsequent PTSD pathology (Halligan, Michael, Clark, & Ehlers, 2003). Importantly, disorganization was not apparent when those suffering PTSD symptoms described a nontraumatic event dating from the time of the crime. In contrast, Rubin, Feldman, and Beckham (2004) found no evidence that memories of trauma in Vietnam veterans with PTSD are especially fragmented or that indices of fragmentation predict symptom severity. A review of 16 studies indicated that peritraumatic dissociation and memory fragmentation were most apparent on patients' subjective ratings of their memory fragmentation, but not objective rater-coded or computer-assessed measures of fragmentation (Bedard-Gilligan & Zoellner, 2012).

Autobiographical Memory Issues

As with depressed people (Williams et al., 2007), those with PTSD experience difficulty recalling specific personal memories in response to cue words on the Autobiographical Memory Test (AMT; e.g., McNally, Litz, Prassas, Shin, & Weathers, 1994). For example, in response to the word *happy*, they often recall a categoric memory exemplifying a class of events (e.g., "I'm always happy whenever the New England Patriots win") or sometimes recall an extended memory spanning more than one day (e.g., "I was happy during the summer after college graduation"). In contrast to such "overgeneral memories," those that healthy subjects recall refer to specific events (e.g., "I was happy on the day that I got married"). An overgeneral retrieval style may constitute a strategy for avoiding thinking specifically about one's emotionally disturbing past (Williams et al., 2007). It may also reflect deficits in executive control and working memory, essential to searching through one's autobiographical memory database to identify specific episodes in response to cue words (Dalgleish et al., 2007).

Overgeneral memory has important clinical correlates. Patients with PTSD who exhibit overgeneral memory are especially impaired in their problem-solving performance (Sutherland & Bryant, 2008). Brown et al. (2013) found that American combat veterans of the Afghanistan and Iraq wars who developed PTSD retrieved fewer specific memories than did healthy combat veterans of these wars. Moreover, relative to healthy combat veterans, those with PTSD likewise had difficulty envisioning specific future events.

Although Iranian combat veterans of the Iran-Iraq War with PTSD retrieved fewer specific memories than did healthy combat veterans who, in turn, retrieved fewer specific memories than did control subjects without combat exposure (Moradi, Abdi, Fathi-Ashtiani, Dalgleish, & Jobson, 2012), most studies show that PTSD, not trauma exposure alone, predicts overgeneral memory (Moore & Zoellner, 2007).

Research on trauma survivors indicates that difficulties retrieving specific memories predict PTSD (e.g., Kleim & Ehlers, 2008). To test whether overgeneral memory precedes trauma exposure as well as PTSD, Bryant, Sutherland, and Guthrie (2007) tested 60 trainee firefighters who were free of PTSD and had yet to encounter the occupational stressors common in their line of work. Four years later, all had experienced trauma, and 15% had developed PTSD. Bryant et al. found that difficulty retrieving specific memories to positive words during their training predicted severity of PTSD symptoms. Hence, an overgeneral retrieval style may be a risk factor for PTSD among those exposed to trauma. Given the high comorbidity between depression and PTSD, it can be difficult to determine which is driving the overgeneral memory effect.

Vietnam veterans with PTSD who wear war regalia, such as combat fatigues and military patches, in everyday life had especially great difficulty retrieving specific memories (McNally, Lasko, Macklin, & Pitman, 1995). Compared to healthy combat veterans, these men seemed stuck in the past. Likewise, Sutherland and Bryant (2005) reported that trauma victims with PTSD more often mention traumatic memories as self-defining than do victims without PTSD. Having one's identity intertwined with one's trauma history appears predictive of poor mental health.

To investigate this issue, Berntsen and Rubin (2006) developed the Centrality of Events Scale (CES), a questionnaire that taps how strongly survivors regard their trauma as a defining event in their lives. They found that scores on the CES positively correlated with severity of PTSD symptoms among trauma-exposed college students. Others have replicated this finding in veterans of the wars in Iraq and Afghanistan who had PTSD (Brown, Antonius, Kramer, Root, & Hirst, 2010) and women who reported histories of childhood sexual abuse (Robinaugh & McNally, 2011).

As Berntsen and Rubin (2007) concluded, findings regarding the CES "contradict the widespread view that the poor integration of the traumatic memory into one's life story is a main cause of PTSD. Instead, enhanced integration appears to be a key issue" (p. 417).

The Emotional Stroop Paradigm

People with PTSD report reexperiencing their trauma in the form of intrusive thoughts, nightmares, and flashbacks. Involuntary cognitive processes may mediate these symptoms, as the emotional Stroop paradigm suggests (McNally, 2006b).

In this paradigm, subjects are asked to view words of varying emotional significance and to name the colors in which the words are printed while ignoring the meaning of the words (Williams, Mathews, & MacLeod, 1996). *Stroop interference* occurs when the meaning of the word becomes intrusively accessible, thereby slowing the subject's naming of its color. If information related to trauma is, indeed, automatically accessed in PTSD and difficult to inhibit, subjects with the disorder ought to exhibit greater Stroop interference for trauma words than that for other words and relative to trauma-exposed people without PTSD.

In one study, Vietnam veterans with PTSD, compared to veterans without PTSD, took longer to name the colors of words related to the war (e.g., *firefight*) than to name the colors of other negative words (e.g., *filthy*), positive words (e.g., *friendship*), or neutral words (e.g., *concrete*; McNally,

Kaspi, Riemann, & Zeitlin, 1990). Similar results have occurred for subjects whose PTSD resulted from rape (Cassiday, McNally, & Zeitlin, 1992), shipwrecks (Thrasher, Dalgleish, & Yule, 1994), automobile accidents (Bryant & Harvey, 1995), and childhood sexual abuse (CSA; Dubner & Motta, 1999). Unlike those with PTSD, rape victims who have recovered following treatment do not exhibit Stroop interference for trauma words (Foa, Feske, Murdock, Kozak, & McCarthy, 1991). Actors trained to mimic the effect were unable to do so (Buckley, Galovski, Blanchard, & Hickling, 2003). Instead, they named the colors of all words slowly. However, some studies, often unpublished, failed to replicate the emotional Stroop effect in PTSD (Kimble, Frueh, & Marks, 2009).

Biological Aspects of PTSD

Biological research on PTSD has been flourishing, and reviews of this field have appeared, both narrative (Pitman et al., 2012) and meta-analytic (Pole, 2007). However, the search for biological markers of PTSD is difficult (Young, 2004). Although PTSD and trauma-exposed non-PTSD groups often differ on mean values of some measure, the groups usually overlap substantially on the measure. Ideally, a biomarker would reliably appear in the PTSD group, but seldom, if ever, in the comparison group.

Cognitive Neuroscience and the Emotional Stroop Effect

Scientists have studied the neural mechanisms mediating the emotional Stroop effect in PTSD. In a positron emission tomography (PET) experiment, Bremner et al. (2004) found that women with PTSD related to childhood sexual abuse, relative to victims without PTSD, had less anterior cingulate activation during the emotional Stroop task. The groups did not differ in terms of anterior cingulate activation while performing the standard Stroop task. Hence, the activation deficit in the PTSD group was confined to the processing of trauma-related information.

Employing functional magnetic resonance imaging (fMRI), Shin et al. (2001) found that Vietnam veterans with PTSD exhibited diminished rostral anterior cingulate activation when exposed to war-related words in the emotional

counting Stroop. In this task, subjects view displays comprising from one through four copies of a word varying in emotional valence (e.g., *firefight, firefight, firefight*). They push a key corresponding to the correct number of copies of the word (e.g., 3). Subjects will be slower to count the number of copies to the extent that the meaning of the word captures their attention.

Cognitive neuroscience research on variants of the emotional Stroop in PTSD supports a pathophysiological model that highlights abnormalities in medial prefrontal cortex (PFC) and amygdala (Bremner et al., 1999; Rauch et al., 2000; Shin, Rauch, & Pitman, 2005). The medial PFC comprises medial frontal gyrus, anterior cingulate cortex (ACC), and subcallosal cortex. The downward projections of the PFC inhibit activation of amygdala, thereby explaining why an intact PFC is vital for the extinction of conditioned fear (Milad & Quirk, 2002). Disturbing, intrusive recollections of traumatic events, accompanied by increased physiological arousal, are consistent with either a hypoactive medial PFC, a hyperresponsive amygdala, or both (Shin, Rauch, & Pitman, 2006).

Prefrontal Cortical Abnormalities

Using fMRI, Shin, Wright, et al. (2005) found that PTSD subjects exhibited increased amygdala responses and reduced medial PFC responses to photographs of fearful versus happy facial expressions. In fact, signal changes in the amygdala and symptom severity negatively correlated with signal changes in the medial PFC. These findings are consistent with those of a previous study in which briefly presented and backwardly masked (*subliminal*) fearful faces provoked increased amygdalar responses in subjects with PTSD (Rauch et al., 2000). Patients with PTSD have exhibited attenuated medial prefrontal/anterior cingulate activation while listening to audiotaped scripts of their traumatic experiences (Shin et al., 2004).

As Shin et al. (2006) noted, not only have scientists found attenuated medial PFC activation in PTSD, but they have also observed smaller ACC volumes in individuals with PTSD than those in trauma-exposed individuals without the illness (Rauch et al., 2003; Woodward et al., 2006; Yamasue et al., 2003). Furthermore, the smaller the ACC volume, the worse the symptom severity was in two of these studies (Woodward et al., 2006; Yamasue et al., 2003). Most subjects had recovered from PTSD in Yamasue et al.'s study, thereby implying that diminished ACC volume may be either a vulnerability factor or a "scar" from PTSD, rather than being a correlate of the illness.

A subsequent study suggests that the scar hypothesis is correct. Using data from Gilbertson et al.'s (2002) monozygotic twins, Kasai et al. (2008) found that reduced volume (gray matter density) in the pregenual ACC in Vietnam veterans with combat-related PTSD was absent in their combat-unexposed twins. Moreover, these PTSD cases had smaller pregenual ACC volumes than did combat veterans without PTSD and their twins. Hence, reduction in the size of this region is associated with chronic PTSD, not merely exposure to trauma or a preexisting vulnerability factor.

Taken together, these data are consistent with a model of PTSD whereby the ventromedial PFC, including the pregenual (or "emotional") region of the ACC, inhibits acquired fear responses mediated by the amygdala (Rauch, Shin, & Phelps, 2006). If smaller volume of the ACC signifies diminished function, then these data provide an anatomical clue as to why fear-related reexperiencing symptoms erupt in PTSD (Pitman et al., 2012).

Hippocampal Volume

Animal research indicates that glucocorticoid stress hormones, cortisol in humans, may produce atrophy in the hippocampus, a brain structure integral to autobiographical memory (Sapolsky, 1996). Reasoning that traumatic stress may have similar consequences, Bremner et al. (1995), using magnetic resonance imaging (MRI) methods, found that Vietnam veterans with PTSD had smaller hippocampi than those of nonveteran control subjects. These findings have been replicated among adults whose PTSD was associated with sexual and physical abuse during childhood (Bremner et al., 1997; Stein, Koverala, Hanna, Torchia, & McClarty, 1997). If diminished size is associated with diminished function, then small hippocampi may make it difficult for people with PTSD to process contextual cues signifying safety (Pitman et al., 2012).

Gurvits et al. (1996) further clarified this phenomenon by comparing hippocampal volume across three groups of subjects: Vietnam combat veterans with PTSD, Vietnam combat veterans without PTSD, and nonveteran control subjects.

The healthy combat veterans and the nonveterans did not differ in hippocampal volume. The PTSD group had smaller volume than that of the other two groups. In studies failing to replicate the small hippocampus effect (e.g., Bonne et al., 2001), PTSD symptoms tend to be less severe than in studies replicating the effect (Pitman et al., 2012).

These findings are consistent with the hypothesis that traumatic stress resulting in PTSD shrinks the hippocampus. However, there are multiple reasons to question this interpretation (McNally, 2003a, pp. 136–145). First, although cortisol is the conjectured neurotoxic agent in hippocampal atrophy, levels of this stress hormone are in the low-normal to average range for most individuals with PTSD (Yehuda, 2002).

Second, the burst of cortisol release occurring during trauma itself is part of the adaptive fight–flight response, and its duration is too brief to produce lasting damage.

Third, individuals with Cushing's syndrome, an endocrine disorder characterized by chronic cortisol output five times higher than normal, do exhibit hippocampal atrophy. Treatment, however, not only normalizes their cortisol levels but also reverses their hippocampal atrophy (Starkman et al., 1999). Therefore, chronically high levels of cortisol, if corrected, did not produce lasting damage.

Fourth, small hippocampi in PTSD appear to be a vulnerability factor for PTSD, not a consequence of traumatic stress. This conclusion comes from a landmark study by Gilbertson et al. (2002). They measured hippocampal volume in monozygotic (MZ) twin pairs: 17 pairs in which one twin developed PTSD after serving in Vietnam and whose psychiatrically healthy twin had not been in combat, and 23 twin pairs in which one twin had seen combat in Vietnam, but did not have PTSD, and whose twin had neither been in combat nor had PTSD. The results confirmed that veterans with PTSD had smaller hippocampi than those of veterans without PTSD. Most striking, however, is that the nontraumatized, healthy twins of the PTSD subjects had hippocampi just as small as the hippocampi of their brothers. These findings imply that small hippocampi may signify vulnerability for developing PTSD among individuals exposed to trauma.

Yet a meta-analysis revealed that the hippocampi of trauma-exposed subjects without PTSD are smaller than the hippocampi of subjects without trauma exposure (Woon, Sood, & Hedges, 2010). These findings are subject to three interpretations (Pitman et al., 2012). Small hippocampi may be associated with subsyndromic levels of PTSD symptoms, may increase risk for trauma exposure, or may indicate that trauma exposure alone may shrink the hippocampus to some extent.

Genetics

Researchers have studied the genetic contribution to variance in PTSD symptoms. Goldberg, True, Eisen, and Henderson (1990) studied 2,092 male MZ twin pairs who had served in the military during the Vietnam War. In the case of 715 pairs, one member served in Vietnam and the other served elsewhere. Among such pairs, the prevalence of PTSD was 16.8% in twins who had served in Vietnam and 5.0% in twins who had served elsewhere. Relative to twins who served elsewhere, twins who had experienced heavy combat in Vietnam were nine times more likely to have PTSD. By controlling for genetic variance, Goldberg et al. demonstrated the pathogenic impact of combat.

In a subsequent investigation, True et al. (1993) studied 4,042 male Vietnam-era MZ and dizygotic (DZ) twin pairs to ascertain the relative contributions of heredity, shared environment, and unique environment to variance in PTSD symptoms. The results revealed that MZ twins were more concordant for combat exposure than were DZ twins, suggesting that similar personal characteristics resulted in similar assignments. Controlling for extent of combat exposure, True et al. found that between 13% and 30% of the variance in reexperiencing symptoms was associated with genetic variation. Likewise, heritability estimates for avoidance symptoms ranged from 30% to 34%, and heritability for arousal symptoms ranged from 28% to 32%. Indices of shared environment during childhood and adolescence (e.g., family upbringing, parental socioeconomic status) were unrelated to variance in PTSD symptoms. Taken together, up to one-third of the variance in PTSD symptoms is associated with genetic variance, whereas the remaining variance is chiefly associated with unique environmental experiences (e.g., heavy combat).

Some studies put the heritability estimate for PTSD even higher. Studying female twins rather than male combat veterans, Sartor et al. (2011) found a heritability of 71% for PTSD.

Individual-specific environmental factors accounted for the remaining variance in PTSD associated with civilian trauma (e.g., accidents, sexual abuse).

In addition to Gilbertson et al.'s (2002) hippocampal twin study, other studies strongly imply genetic vulnerability for PTSD. This research team administered IQ and other neurocognitive tests to MZ twin pairs (Gilbertson et al., 2006). They tested four groups: men with combat-related PTSD from Vietnam, their identical twins with no combat exposure and no PTSD, Vietnam combat veterans who had not developed PTSD, and their identical twins with no combat exposure and no PTSD. The findings were strikingly consistent: combat veterans with PTSD and their identical twins performed in the normal range, but less well than healthy combat veterans and their twins.

This study suggests several conclusions. First, trauma exposure has minimal effect on measures of IQ or on other neurocognitive tests. Second, the striking similarity in the test scores between twins strongly implicates genetic influence on performance. Third, because the PTSD group scored within the normal range on all but one test, above-average cognitive ability appears to confer protection against PTSD. Indeed, consistent with an early study (Macklin et al., 1998), the mean IQ of the healthy combat veteran group was 118, and over 40% of this group scored in the superior range (over 120). The mean IQ of the PTSD group was 105.

Another project from this research group indicated that neurological soft signs scores are more pathological in combat veterans with PTSD than among combat veterans without PTSD (Gurvits et al., 2006). Likewise, the scores of the non-trauma-exposed identical twins of the PTSD group were more pathological than those of the identical twins of the healthy combat veterans, thereby implying that subtle neurological compromise is a genetic (or at a least constitutional) vulnerability factor for PTSD rather than being a consequence of trauma or PTSD.

Other studies have further implicated cognitive ability as a buffer against PTSD. Breslau, Lucia, and Alvarado (2006) obtained the IQ scores of 6-year-old children from either the inner city of Detroit or its suburbs. In follow-up interviews with these children at age 17, Breslau et al. assessed them for exposure to trauma and for PTSD. Subjects whose IQ at age 6 was greater than 115 were at lower risk for exposure to traumatic events by age 17, and they were at lower risk for developing PTSD if they had been exposed to trauma. Children with below-average IQ and average IQ were at similar risk for PTSD. These findings imply that the higher IQ is protective rather than lower IQ being a vulnerability factor.

Studying Vietnam veteran twins, Kremen et al. (2007) found that higher predeployment cognitive ability protected against subsequent PTSD. More specifically, the highest quartile on the cognitive ability measure had a 48% lower risk for PTSD than that of the lowest quartile. Further analyses confirmed that genetic influences on pretrauma cognitive ability accounted for 5% of the variance in PTSD, but common genes explained 100% of that relationship.

Genes associated with major depression, panic disorder, and generalized anxiety disorder account for most of the genetic variation in PTSD (Pitman et al., 2012). Variants in 17 candidate genes have been associated with PTSD in at least one study, but failures to replicate and opposite findings are common (Pitman et al., 2012). Studies on the serotonin transporter gene have been the most common, yet even here, results have been contradictory. Whereas the low-expressing short allele has most often predicted PTSD, other studies have found an association between the long allele and PTSD.

In some cases, the result depends on context. For example, in one study of community residents exposed to hurricanes, researchers found that, relative to other subjects, carriers of at least one low-expressing allele had significantly higher risk for PTSD if they lived in counties with high rates of unemployment and crime. Yet these subjects had significantly lower risk of PTSD if they lived in counties with low rates of unemployment and crime (Koenen et al., 2009). Suffice it to say, genomic findings remain provisional, requiring replication.

Resting Psychophysiological Levels

In his meta-analysis, Pole (2007) examined 58 studies providing data on baseline levels of psychophysiological arousal. Subjects with PTSD had higher resting heart rate (HR), skin conductance level (SCL), systolic blood pressure (BP), and diastolic BP relative to trauma-exposed subjects without PTSD. Studies involving PTSD subjects diagnosed by *DSM-III* had larger effect sizes than studies involving PTSD subjects diagnosed with *DSM-III-R* or *DSM-IV*. Moreover, severity of PTSD symptoms positively correlated with resting levels. One might expect that anticipatory anxiety might elevate resting levels of physiological arousal in studies in which subjects know they hear startling sounds or encounter stimuli related to their trauma. However, this appears to be incorrect. Surprisingly, resting levels of physiological arousal are lower when subjects anticipate subsequent startling or stressful stimuli than in studies not involving exposure to such stimuli. Accordingly, anticipatory anxiety cannot explain elevated levels of psychophysiology in PTSD.

Physiological Reactivity to Trauma-Related Cues

Researchers have assessed reactivity to trauma cues in two ways. In the first, subjects are exposed to standardized audiovisual stimuli relevant to traumatic events. In one study, slides and sounds of combat evoked greater HR responses in Vietnam combat veterans with PTSD than in healthy combat veterans or in veterans with other psychiatric disorders (Malloy, Fairbank, & Keane, 1983). In other work, PTSD subjects exhibited enhanced HR, systolic BP, and electromyographic (EMG) responses to audiotaped battle sounds, whereas these enhanced responses did not occur in healthy nonveterans, healthy combat veterans, combat veterans with other mental disorders, or nonveterans with specific phobias (Blanchard, Kolb, Gerardi, Ryan, & Pallmeyer, 1986; Blanchard, Kolb, Pallmeyer, & Gerardi, 1982; Pallmeyer, Blanchard, & Kolb, 1986). A meta-analysis of 17 studies showed that HR response and, to a lesser extent, skin conductance response (SCR) distinguished PTSD from control groups, and EMG and BP responses trended in the same direction.

In the second approach, researchers ask subjects to imagine traumatic events recounted in audiotaped scripts (Orr, McNally, Rosen, & Shalev, 2004). These script-driven imagery studies have revealed that combat veterans with PTSD exhibit greater HR, SCR, and facial EMG (lateral frontalis) responses than those in healthy combat veterans (Orr, Pitman, Lasko, & Herz, 1993; Pitman, Orr, Forgue, de Jong, & Claiborn, 1987; Pitman et al., 1990); this effect is more pronounced for scripts that recount the subject's personal trauma than for scripts recounting a generic trauma. Moreover, combat veterans with anxiety disorders other than PTSD do not exhibit this script-driven reactivity (Pitman et al., 1990). Similar findings have emerged in civilians whose PTSD arose from childhood sexual abuse (Shin et al., 1999) or from automobile accidents or terrorist attacks (Shalev, Orr, & Pitman, 1993).

HR reactivity to trauma scripts distinguishes PTSD subjects from non-PTSD subjects with a specificity ranging from 61% to 88% and a sensitivity of 100% (Orr et al., 1993; Pitman et al., 1987). Moreover, psychophysiological reactivity can distinguish between veterans with combat-related PTSD and veterans who are asked to fake PTSD (HR: Gerardi, Blanchard, & Kolb, 1989; EMG: Orr & Pitman, 1993).

Keane et al. (1998) conducted the largest study ever done on the psychophysiology of PTSD. Recruiting Vietnam veterans from hospitals throughout the United States, they tested 778 veterans with current PTSD, 181 with past PTSD, and 369 with no history of PTSD. During both standardized audiovisual combat presentations and autobiographical combat scenes during script-driven imagery, veterans with current PTSD had greater HR, EMG, SCL, and diastolic BP than the responses in those with no history of the disorder. The group with past PTSD tended to fall midway between the other groups in terms of physiological reactivity. The magnitudes of the effects appear smaller than in earlier studies on script-driven imagery in Vietnam veterans with PTSD (Pitman et al., 1987), and about one-third of the current PTSD group was nonreactive physiologically.

In his meta-analysis of 22 of these script-driven imagery studies, Pole (2007) reported that PTSD subjects, relative to control subjects, exhibited greater EMG responses (frontalis and corrugator muscles), HR response, SCR, and diastolic BP.

Exaggerated Startle Response

Consistent with self-reports of enhanced startle, sudden, loud tones evoke larger eyeblink EMG responses in combat veterans with PTSD than in healthy combat veterans (e.g., Morgan, Grillon, Southwick, Davis, & Charney, 1996; Orr, Lasko, Shalev, & Pitman, 1995). Likewise, civilians and veterans with PTSD tend to exhibit larger EMG magnitudes than those of people with other anxiety disorders or no disorder (Shalev, Orr, Peri, Schreiber, & Pitman, 1992). PTSD and non-PTSD groups, however, do not differ in the rates at which their EMG responses habituate to these repeated tones (Morgan et al., 1996; Orr et al., 1995; Shalev et al., 1992).

Three studies have revealed greater HR responses to loud tones in PTSD groups than in non-PTSD groups (Orr et al., 1995; Paige, Reid, Allen, & Newton, 1990; Shalev et al., 1992). One study found larger SCRs as well (Shalev et al., 1992), whereas another did not (Orr et al., 1995). Finally, SCR magnitude habituates more slowly in PTSD subjects than in non-PTSD subjects (Orr et al., 1995; Shalev et al., 1992).

An MZ twin study indicated that Vietnam veterans with PTSD exhibited larger HR responses to startlingly loud tones than those of their non-combat-exposed twins and Vietnam combat veterans without PTSD and their twins (Orr et al., 2003). These data suggest that heightened startle reactions are a consequence of PTSD rather than a vulnerability factor for the disorder.

Pole (2007) examined 25 studies measuring startle responses to auditory stimuli, usually tones or bursts of white noise. Relative to controls, PTSD subjects exhibited larger HR responses, and their SCRs took longer to decline. The delayed decline in habituation of SCRs to startling sounds implies deficit regulatory processing signifying a failure to adapt (Pole, 2007).

Noradrenergic Dysregulation

Exposure to uncontrollable stressors activates the noradrenergic (NA) system, as exemplified by the enhanced release of norepinephrine (NE) by the brainstem locus coeruleus (Charney, Deutch, Krystal, Southwick, & Davis, 1993). Southwick et al. (1993) conducted a yohimbine challenge study with Vietnam combat veterans with PTSD and healthy control subjects. Yohimbine antagonizes the alpha-2 autoreceptor. Ordinarily, release of NE activates the autoreceptor, which then brakes further NE release, thereby serving as a negative feedback mechanism. By briefly blocking the autoreceptor, yohimbine enables NE to surge unimpeded. The results revealed that 70% of the PTSD subjects experienced a yohimbine-induced panic attack, and 40% experienced a concurrent flashback. Consistent with the NE dysregulation hypothesis, yohimbine produced more pronounced biochemical and cardiovascular effects in PTSD subjects than in controls.

Current Issues

The field of traumatic stress studies remains notable for its moral passions, as it has categories—perpetrator and victim—that are absent from most other areas of psychopathology. For example, identifying vulnerability factors for panic disorder has never sparked complaints that researchers are blaming the victim, as was once routine in traumatology (e.g., Blank, 1985). Although the de facto taboo against studying vulnerability has waned, the field often remains reluctant to confront what Pinker (2007) calls "dangerous ideas"—"statements of fact or policy that are defended with evidence and argument by serious scientists and thinkers but which are felt to challenge the collective decency of the age" (Pinker, 2007, p. xxiv). The uproar incited by reanalyses showing that the NVVRS apparently overestimated the prevalence of PTSD, as we understand it today, is a case in point (Dobbs, 2009; Satel, 2007). Leading traumatologists seemingly feared that lower prevalence estimates would imperil research funding and clinical services for veterans with PTSD.

Other examples abound. When scholars interpreted the temporary increase in stress reactions among New Yorkers after the 9/11 terrorist attacks as normal emotional responses, they were accused of engaging in "minimization or outright denial of human suffering" (Marshall, 2006, p. 627). They were likened to the "conspiracy theorists who believed the moon landings had actually been elaborately staged" (Marshall, 2006, p. 626). When researchers published a meta-analysis indicating that victims of childhood sexual abuse are often resilient (Rind, Tromovitch, & Bauserman, 1998), experts in trauma and dissociation protested, and Congress issued a formal condemnation of the article (Lilienfeld, 2002). For traumatology to progress scientifically, its practitioners should not regard certain assumptions as exempt from critique. Condemning critics as either ignorant of the consequences of traumatic stress or motivated by a malicious political agenda to silence the voices of survivors is not conducive to progress. Advocacy for victims is best served by ideologically unfettered inquiry.

Debates about the ontology of PTSD persist (McNally, 2011, pp. 146–158). Is PTSD a culture-bound idiom of distress or a universal psychobiological syndrome arising throughout history in response to horrific events? Do its symptoms reflect a latent category (taxon) or a latent dimension (Ruscio, Ruscio, & Keane, 2002)? Transcending both of these debates is yet another possibility (McNally, 2012b), inspired by the potentially revolutionary work of Borsboom and his colleagues (Borsboom, 2008; Borsboom & Cramer, 2013; Borsboom, Cramer, Schmittmann, Epskamp, & Waldorp, 2011; Cramer, Waldorp, van der Maas, Borsboom, 2010), who have proposed that mental disorders are causal systems (or networks) comprising functionally interconnected symptoms that unfold over time and settle into pathological equilibria. Symptoms are not fallible indicators of a latent, unobserved entity, whether taxonic or dimensional. That is, the relation between symptoms and disorder is mereological (part/whole), not one of reflective measurement whereby symptoms index an unobserved, underlying essence. Accordingly, there is nothing more to a disorder than its network of functionally interconnected constitutive symptoms.

Moreover, the causal system approach does not rest on the implausible assumption of local independence, which specifies that the latent entity is the common cause of its symptomatic indicators, each independent of the others. Indeed, few clinicians would endorse this symptom. As for PTSD, reexperiencing symptoms likely causes avoidance of traumatic reminders, and traumatic nightmares likely cause sleep problems that result in irritability. Such functional relations among symptoms are the heart of the causal system approach, yet they violate the assumption of local independence integral to latent dimensional and categorical models of psychiatric disorder.

Inspired by Boyd's (1991) concept of homeostatic property cluster kinds, other scholars have suggested broadly similar approaches to psychiatric disorder (e.g., Kendler, Zachar, & Craver, 2011; McNally, 2011, pp. 203–207), but none has developed the computational methods to render the causal systems approach testable as have Borsboom and his colleagues. For example, they have shown how it solves the comorbidity problem in psychopathology (Cramer et al., 2010). This approach appeared too late for *DSM-5*, but it promises to revolutionize our understanding of PTSD and other mental disorders in the years to come.

Dissociative Disorders

The dissociative disorders group comprises syndromes whose chief feature is dissociation, defined as "a disruption of and/or discontinuity in the normal, subjective integration of one or more aspects of psychological functioning, including—but not limited to—memory, identity, consciousness, perception, and motor control" (Spiegel et al., 2011, p. 826). This broad definition embraces diverse phenomena that do not necessarily have a common source. For example, one self-report measure of dissociation includes mundane occurrences, such as staring off into space and being unaware of time passing, as well as eerie ones, such as failing to recognize oneself in a mirror (Bernstein & Putnam, 1986).

Other phenomena dubbed *dissociative* include feelings of unreality (depersonalization and derealization), emotional numbing, a sense of time slowing down, and reported inability to recall encoded autobiographical information too excessive to count as ordinary forgetting. Some clinical scholars regard seemingly opposite phenomena as instantiations of dissociation. Hence, they speak of reports of vivid sensory recollection of traumatic events ("dissociative flashbacks") and reports of inability to recall traumatic events ("dissociative amnesia") as instances of the same process (e.g., van der Hart & Nijenhuis, 2009). However, as McHugh (2008) has emphasized, calling phenomena dissociative "is merely a description with a professional ring masquerading as an explanation. One really knows no more about a case of amnesia or fugue by saying the patient 'dissociates' than by saying the patient behaved as though he or she couldn't remember" (p. 45).

The *DSM-5* recognizes dissociative amnesia, dissociative identity disorder (DID; formerly multiple personality disorder, MPD), depersonalization/derealization disorder, other specified dissociative disorder (e.g., dissociative trance), and unspecified dissociative disorder. Because of their presumed rarity or controversial nosological status, dissociative disorders have been omitted from major epidemiological surveys, such as the NCS-R. However, clinicians specializing in dissociative disorders hold that "dissociative disorders are common in general population samples and

psychiatric samples" (van der Hart & Nijenhuis, 2009, p. 462). For example, one representative community survey reported an annual prevalence of 1.5% of DID, 0.8% of depersonalization disorder, 1.8% of dissociative amnesia, and 4.4% of dissociative disorders not otherwise specified (DDNOS; a *DSM-IV* disorder; Johnson, Cohen, Kasen, & Brook, 2006). Subjects with personality disorders were far more likely to qualify for a dissociative disorder diagnosis than were subjects without personality disorders.

Coverage of these syndromes appears in a chapter concerning PTSD because many clinical scholars specializing in the diagnosis and treatment of dissociative disorders believe "that trauma causes dissociation" (Dalenberg et al., 2012, p. 550). Other scholars, examining the same studies, argue that the hypothesis that trauma causes dissociation is far from convincingly confirmed (Lynn et al., 2014).

Dissociative Amnesia

According to *DSM-5*, dissociative amnesia is "an inability to recall important autobiographical information, usually of a traumatic or stressful nature, that is inconsistent with ordinary forgetting." Distilling the key points of this perspective in his book entitled *Repressed Memories*, Spiegel (1997) emphasized that the nature of traumatic dissociative amnesia is such

> that it is not subject to the same rules of ordinary forgetting; it is more, rather than less, common after repeated episodes; involves strong affect; and is resistant to retrieval through salient cues. (p. 6)

That is, the more often trauma occurs and the more emotionally distressing it is for the victims, the more likely it supposedly is that they will not remember having suffered any trauma. Moreover, encoded, but dissociated, memories of trauma will not be accessible by ordinary means, such as merely interviewing people about their trauma histories. These assumptions are used to justify the use of hypnosis, guided imagery, and other methods to recover presumably inaccessible memories that supposedly are the source of the patient's symptoms. As Brown, Scheflin, and Hammond (1998) expressed it:

> Because some victims of sexual abuse will repress their memories by dissociating them

from consciousness, hypnosis can be very valuable in retrieving these memories. Indeed, for some victims, hypnosis may provide the only avenue to the repressed memories. (p. 647)

It is important to note, however, that the stress hormones, such as norepinephrine and cortisol, released during traumatic events render the experience highly memorable (McGaugh, 2003), as PTSD so dramatically illustrates. Moreover, although repeated events of a certain type (e.g., flying on airplanes, sexual abuse) may diminish the distinctiveness of any specific episode, repetition does not ordinarily abolish memory for the entire class of events, especially if the events provoked intense emotion (McNally, 2003a, pp. 26–77). Accordingly, assumptions undergirding the diagnosis of dissociative amnesia run counter to established science on emotion and memory.

Discussing the work of Jean Charcot, Pierre Janet, and Sigmund Freud, the historian of psychiatry—Borch-Jacobsen—described "the birth of a true psychiatric myth, fated to a grand future: *the patient is entirely ignorant of the trauma that caused his symptoms*" (2009, p. 30). Indeed, using Internet search engines, Pope and his colleagues were unable to identify a single case of alleged traumatic dissociative amnesia in the world literature of fiction, history, or medicine prior to 1786 (Pope, Poliakoff, Parker, Boynes, & Hudson, 2007a, 2007b). They concluded that claims of dissociative amnesia are a culture-bound idiom of distress.

As Borch-Jacobsen (2009) observed, prior to Charcot developing this idea via his hypnotic work, his hysteria patients "remembered quite clearly the psychic or mechanical shock that had triggered their hysterical paralyses and attacks. After, they would tend not to know the cause of their symptoms any longer; the era of 'dissociation of consciousness' and of 'repression' had begun" (p. 25). Unwittingly transmitting his "completely new expectation, that of post-traumatic *amnesia*" (p. 25) to his suggestible patients during hypnosis, Charcot discovered precisely what he was seeking: memories of trauma seemingly dissociated from consciousness.

Janet and Freud further developed and popularized the concepts of traumatic dissociative amnesia and repression. Despite their minor theoretical differences, they agreed that the mind protects itself by dissociating or repressing emotionally disturbing material, rendering it inaccessible to awareness. Recovery of this material, processing it emotionally, and integrating it into one's autobiographical narrative was the road to healing and symptomatic recovery, notions that resurfaced in the discredited "recovered memory therapy" of the late twentieth century (Crews, 1995, pp. 216–218).

Clinicians specializing in dissociation have claimed that survivors of diverse trauma events ranging from childhood sexual abuse to the Holocaust have exhibited dissociative amnesia (e.g., Brown et al., 1998; Brown, Scheflin, & Whitfield, 1999). Yet an extensive analysis of documented cases of trauma found no instance of victims being incapable of recalling their trauma except when they had sustained a head injury or had experienced the event in the first years of life and thus during the period of childhood amnesia (Pope, Olivia, & Hudson, 1999).

Strikingly, dissociative amnesia theorists (e.g., Brown et al., 1999) and their critics (e.g., Piper, Pope, & Borowiecki, 2000) often cite the same studies in support of their diametrically opposed conclusions. How can this be? The answer is that dissociative amnesia theorists seemingly misunderstand the very data they cite in support of their position (for an extensive review, see McNally, 2003a, pp. 186–228). For example, they have confused everyday forgetfulness following trauma for an inability to remember the trauma itself. They have confused reluctance to disclose trauma with an inability to recall it. They have confused not thinking about something for a long time with an inability to remember it. They have confused failure to encode aspects of a trauma with inability to remember trauma. They have confused childhood amnesia and organic amnesia with dissociative amnesia. Ironically, the diagnosis of dissociative amnesia remains in the *DSM-5* despite the absence of convincing evidence that the phenomenon exists.

Previously a distinct syndrome in *DSM*, *dissociative fugue* now appears as a subtype of *dissociative amnesia* in *DSM-5*. This rare condition is characterized by aimless wandering, often coupled with amnesia for parts of the journey (Kopelman, Christensen, Puffett, & Stanhope, 1994). One scholar specializing in the history of psychiatry, especially dissociative disorders, conceptualized fugue as a transient mental illness that flourishes only as long as the cultural niche that produces it remains (Hacking, 1998). He described an epidemic of fugue erupting in late nineteenth-century France, often among soldiers bored in the barracks who went on unauthorized leaves. The "epidemic" ended shortly after World War I.

Although the *DSM-5* implicates overwhelmingly stressful or traumatic events as the precipitants of dissociative fugue, trauma does not appear in most of the historical case studies. For example, Stengel (1941) described 25 cases of fugue, noting that trauma seldom triggered it. Moreover, many cases did not claim amnesia for the period when they fled. Stengel suggested that head injury, suicidal ideation, interpersonal problems, epilepsy, and growing up with disturbed parents appeared to be risk factors. In all likelihood, sudden, seemingly aimless travel has diverse antecedents.

Dissociative Identity Disorder

People diagnosed with DID act as if different personalities (a.k.a., alters, identities) seize control of the person at various times. The personalities vary in their behavior, thoughts, and feelings, and each has its own name, history, and memories. The favored interpretation of DID among specialists working with these patients is that the syndrome arises from chronic, severe sexual and physical abuse during childhood. The victim's sense of self dissociates into multiple identities, and some of these harbor the memories of trauma too horrific for the host personality to entertain consciously.

Yet embedded in this theory is a problem or a paradox. The problem is that in many cases of DID, patients had no memories of childhood abuse until therapists, using hypnosis, guided imagery, and related methods, helped them recall presumably dissociated memories of trauma (for a review, see McNally, 2003a, pp. 229–259). Yet the authenticity of these memories is questionable, for several reasons. Apart from the fact that traumatic memories are seldom, if ever, inaccessible to awareness, many patients retracted their recovered memories, especially of satanic ritual abuse. The paradox pertains to DID patients who report histories of childhood trauma that they have never forgotten. The motivation for the emergence of dissociation in general, and DID in particular, is supposedly to quarantine memories of trauma, dissociating them for awareness. Yet if these patients have remembered their trauma all too well, why, then, are they dissociative?

Case reports of MPD seldom appeared in the psychiatric literature prior to 1980s. One comprehensive review cited a mere 76 cases that had appeared in the previous 128 years (Taylor & Martin, 1944). Yet following the publication of *Sybil* (Schreiber, 1973), a bestselling book about a case of MPD that soon became a made-for-TV movie, an epidemic of diagnosed cases of MPD erupted in North America. As MPD experts Putnam, Guroff, Silberman, Barban, and Post (1986) observed, "more cases of MPD have been reported within the last 5 years than in the preceding two centuries" (p. 285).

In contrast to most previous cases that had one or two additional personalities, Sybil had 16, and in contrast to previous cases, Sybil supposedly harbored horrific memories of childhood sexual and physical abuse. As Putnam (1989) observed, "It was not until the 1970s [i.e., post-Sybil], that the first reports clearly connecting MPD to childhood trauma began to appear in single case histories" (p. 47), and he noted, "Among the first and best-known was the case of Sybil" (p. 47). It is unclear if Sybil was *the* first case of MPD tied to allegedly repressed memories of horrific childhood sexual and physical abuse, but it dramatically popularized the view that MPD arises from horrific childhood abuse of which the patient's host personality is entirely unaware prior to undergoing hypnosis. Indeed, although Taylor and Martin (1944) speculated widely about the causes of MPD after reviewing 76 cases in the world literature, they never mentioned childhood trauma as a possible antecedent. As Putnam (1989) affirmed, "The book *Sybil*, with its graphic treatment of the amnesias, fugue episodes, child abuse, and conflicts among alters, served as the template against which other patients could be compared and understood" (p. 35). He added that the book "is both detailed and accurate enough to serve as mandatory clinical reading for students of MPD" (Putnam, 1989, p. 35).

Ironically, the case that launched the MPD epidemic and the trauma theory of MPD has been debunked by recent scholarship (Borch-Jacobsen, 2009; Nathan, 2011; Rieber, 2006). Sybil's mother was neither abusive nor psychotic. Rather than being a survivor of trauma, Sybil was an imaginative only child who enjoyed a comfortable, somewhat pampered, childhood. As a young woman, she moved to New York City to pursue an artistic career, and dissatisfaction with her life led her to seek psychoanalytic treatment with the psychiatrist Cornelia Wilbur. Fascinated by the recent case depicted in *The Three Faces of Eve*, Wilbur was keen to encounter another case of multiple personality. Using hypnosis and sodium pentothal ("truth serum") and other medications, Wilbur elicited Sybil's dramatic alters and her dissociated memories of horrific childhood trauma. Recently discovered audiotapes of Wilbur's sessions with Sybil document her inadvertent shaping of Sybil's multiple personalities (Rieber, 2006). On one tape, Sybil admits to manufacturing her trauma stories and multiple personalities, but Wilbur refused to accept this admission. Remarkably, the patient who inspired the trauma theory of MPD appears never to have suffered trauma, let alone repressed it from awareness.

Publications on DID and other dissociative disorders peaked in the mid-1990s before plummeting dramatically in the early twenty-first century (Pope, Barry, Bodkin, & Hudson, 2006). Although there are countless randomized controlled trials (RCTs) testing the efficacy of medications and psychotherapies for PTSD, panic disorder, and other syndromes recognized decades ago in *DSM-III*, there has never been an RCT testing a treatment for MPD/DID (Brand, Classen, McNary, & Zaveri, 2009). Malpractice lawsuits against dissociative experts accused of inadvertently fostering false memories of trauma in patients they suspected of having DID may have reduced enthusiasm for detecting hidden multiplicity among one's caseload of patients, thereby contributing to the end of the epidemic (Acocella, 1999) and diminishing scientific interest in the syndrome.

However, Huntjens and her colleagues have recruited sufficient numbers of DID patients in The Netherlands to test hypotheses about interidentity amnesia in the cognitive psychology laboratory. Their basic strategy is to test three groups: patients diagnosed with DID, control subjects trained to simulate DID, and a nonsimulating control group. The simulators view a documentary about the disorder, and receive coaching on how to role-play DID.

In one study, subjects memorized names of animals, vegetables, and flowers (Huntjens, Postma, Peters, Woertman, & van der Hart, 2003). The DID and simulating subjects then switched to a second personality who memorized names of other animals, other vegetables, and furniture. A recall test and a recognition test 1 week later for words

they had memorized indicated that both control groups and the DID group remembered words from the first list as well as words from the second list. Therefore, the second personality remembered material encoded by the first personality, documenting interidentity transfer of information, a finding inconsistent with purported amnesia. Similar findings emerged for emotionally valenced words (Huntjens, Peters, Woertman, van der Hart, & Postma, 2007).

Testing DID and control subjects, Kong, Allen, and Glisky (2008) extended these findings, showing that interidentity transfer in DID cannot plausibly be attributable to implicit memory effects. That is, they had one personality encode words auditorily and then tested the other, amnesic personality visually. Memory transfer across identities occurred despite cross-modality (i.e., auditory versus visual) between encoding and testing.

Using a concealed information task, Huntjens, Verschuere, and McNally (2012) documented interidentity transfer of *autobiographical* information in patients diagnosed with DID. They recruited three groups of women: patients diagnosed with DID, amateur actors trained to simulate DID, and control subjects who did not simulate DID. The authors administered an autobiographical questionnaire to all subjects, asking about the name of their best friend, their favorite food, favorite sport, and so forth. The DID patients completed the questionnaire twice, once as the trauma identity who reported memories of CSA, and again as an identity reportedly amnesic for memories of abuse. (The terms *trauma identity* and *amnesic identity* denote the phenomenology of the patients. That is, the probative import of the experiment does not rest on whether the patients' memories of trauma were genuine or whether the other identity was truly amnesic for them.) For example, a DID trauma identity might have written down the words *Janet, pizza,* and *swimming* in response to questions about the name of her best friend, favorite food, and favorite sport, whereas the amnesic identity might have written down the answers *Mary, steak,* and *tennis.* The authors had subjects rate the personal emotional relevance of words drawn from these questionnaires, plus many other irrelevant words, and the DID patients did so in their amnesic identity, thus enabling the authors to select words from the trauma identity's questionnaire that the amnesic identity rated as personally irrelevant.

Two weeks later, subjects performed a concealed information task whereby they viewed a series of words in uppercase letters on a computer screen. They had to decide as quickly as possible whether they recognized the word as a member of the previously memorized target set of three words (e.g., *SUSAN, CHOCOLATE, BOWLING*) or whether the word was a nontarget word. Among the nontarget items were the three words having autobiographical significance for a DID patient's trauma identity (e.g., *Janet, pizza,* and *swimming)* and the three words having autobiographical significance for the patient's amnesic identity (e.g., *Mary, steak,* and *tennis*). The computer recorded the reaction times for the recognition/classification decisions.

The results revealed that subjects were very fast to classify irrelevant words, and they were slow to classify nontarget words that possessed autobiographical significance (e.g., their best friend's name). The slowed reaction times signified recognition of the word's personal relevance. That is, they had to inhibit the impulse to respond "yes" to the question of recognition. In the DID group, the amnesic identities performed this task, and their reaction times to respond "no" to words having considerable autobiographical significance were very slow (e.g., *Mary, steak,* and *tennis*), signifying their recognition of the personal importance of these items. Crucially, these patients were just as slow to respond to the corresponding items of their trauma identity of which they were allegedly amnesic (e.g., *Janet, pizza,* and *swimming*). These data are inconsistent with the notion of interidentity amnesia. Indeed, if the amnesic identity were truly unable to access the autobiographical material of the trauma identity, then the reaction times to classify these items would not have been as slow as those for classifying the autobiographical items of the amnesic identity. Taken together, experimental research does not support claims of interidentity amnesia in DID.

Using PET, Reinders and her colleagues have investigated central and peripheral psychophysiological responses to trauma-relevant and neutral autobiographical memory scripts in a group of 11 women diagnosed with DID (Reinders et al., 2006). That is, for each patient, the researchers developed scripts recounting a neutral event and a traumatic event that the patient said had occurred to her. They tested two identities of each of the patients. The traumatic identity had access to reported traumatic memories, whereas the neutral identity had "a degree of amnesia for traumatic memories ranging from lack of personalization of the traumatic past to total amnesia" (Reinders et al., 2006, p. 730). They used a script-driven imagery paradigm whereby each identity heard two autobiographical memory scripts, one trauma-relevant and one neutral. The results showed significantly greater increases in subjective and cardiovascular responses to trauma-relevant scripts than to neutral scripts, and these increases were larger when the traumatic identity heard the scripts than when the neutral identity heard them. The two identities also exhibited different patterns of cerebral blood flow when they listened to the trauma-relevant scripts.

Although these data indicate marked distress and psychophysiological activation to the trauma-relevant scripts, these responses do not confirm the authenticity of the memories per se. Indeed, marked psychophysiological activation occurred among (non-DID) people reporting having been abducted by space aliens when they heard scripts describing their (presumably false) memories of their most traumatic encounters with extraterrestials (McNally et al., 2004). Moreover, it is a straightforward matter for neutral identities to attenuate their responses to trauma scripts evocative for trauma identities; neutral identities merely need to distract themselves from attending to the otherwise evocative script.

Reinders et al. (2012) subsequently enrolled two groups of healthy control subjects, one scoring high on a measure of fantasy proneness, and the other scoring low on this measure. They coached both groups to simulate DID. Each simulating subject heard two autobiographical memory scripts, one neutral and one trauma-related. Reinders et al. compared the results from these two simulating control groups with those of the DID patients from their previous study. The results revealed that neither control group mimicked the cerebral or peripheral responses of the DID group when all groups heard their trauma scripts. Because the high-fantasy group failed to mimic the psychophysiology of the DID group, the authors concluded "that DID does not have a sociocultural origin" (Reinders et al., 2012, p. 1).

However, the data do not compel this conclusion. To be sure, high-fantasy proneness in healthy control subjects is insufficient to incite marked psychophysiological responses to stressful scripts in healthy people who endeavor to mimic the responses of DID patients. Yet this did not mean that elevated fantasy proneness fails to contribute to the emergence of DID in distressed individuals undergoing hypnotic interventions to elicit alter personalities that the therapist presumes harbor dissociated memories of trauma.

Depersonalization/Derealization Disorder

During a depersonalization episode, people feel emotionally numb and disconnected from their body, and they experience the world as an unreal dream (i.e., derealization). Many people experience brief episodes of depersonalization or derealization when exhausted, during marijuana intoxication, or when encountering sudden danger. However, people with depersonalization/derealization disorder experience this state unremittingly, sometimes for months or years; others experience recurrent episodes interspersed with periods of normal consciousness. The onset is usually sudden, and many people fear for their sanity.

Though appearing under the dissociative disorders rubric, this syndrome may have scant etiological or pathophysiological relation to the other dissociative disorders. This eerie disturbance in consciousness may arise from corticolimbic disconnection. For example, Sierra and Berrios (1998) have suggested that activation of the right dorsolateral prefrontal cortex and reciprocal inhibition of the anterior cingulate may produce the sensation of mind emptiness. Left prefrontal inhibition of the amygdala would foster hypoemotionality and emotional detachment from the world. Although there is more theory than data on this syndrome, research is slowly accumulating (e.g., Sierra, Medford, Wyatt, & David, 2012).

Concluding Remarks

The dissociative disorders, especially DID, are as understudied as they are controversial. Although clinicians can diagnose DID reliably (Gleaves, May, & Cardeña, 2001), controversy concerns its etiology. What are we to make of people who meet criteria for the disorder, especially those who report histories of childhood trauma? There are several possibilities. There is abundant evidence

indicating that distressed, suggestible patients can develop "memories" of abuse that never occurred, especially when their "memories" surface during psychotherapies featuring hypnosis, guided imagery, and other methods designed to recover dissociated memories of trauma but likely to foster false ones instead (For a review, see McNally, 2003a, pp. 229–259). Accordingly, this pattern likely characterizes many cases of DID, especially when they have absorbed the dramatic cultural lore and media portrayals of DID, as sociocognitive theorists have argued (Lilienfeld et al., 1999).

The Sybil case notwithstanding, many DID patients may very well have suffered traumatic abuse as children, and they may cultivated alter personalities as an imaginative means of avoiding dwelling on their distressing memories. Yet attempting to avoid thinking about something is not the same thing as being *unable* to recall it, as claims of amnesia require. Indeed, there is no convincing, replicable evidence that people who have encoded memories of trauma—corroborated memories, not the satanic abuse tales emerging under hypnosis—become incapable of recalling them, thanks to dissociation or repression. Moreover, Huntjens and her colleagues have repeatedly documented how autobiographical and emotional information readily transfers between identities in DID patients. People with trauma histories may enact a DID role and simulate amnesia, but it is doubtful if they ever develop amnesia for their traumatic memories.

As Putnam et al. (1986) have shown, many MPD/DID patients suffer from diverse symptoms, and receive diagnoses of depression, borderline personality disorder, and psychosis before finally finding a clinician who diagnoses DID. Perhaps rather than debating whether the patient "really" has DID or one of these other syndromes, clinicians should steer clear of hypnosis, conversing with alter personalities, and trolling for repressed trauma histories, as McHugh (2008) has argued. Perhaps clinicians should target the presenting symptoms of mood dysregulation, and PTSD symptoms in those with always-remembered abuse, and provide practical guidance for helping them manage their problems in the here and now.

References

Acocella, J. (1999). *Creating hysteria: Women and multiple personality disorder*. San Francisco: Jossey-Bass.

Andreasen, N. C. (2004). Acute and delayed posttraumatic stress disorders: A history and some issues. *American Journal of Psychiatry, 161*, 1321–1323.

Andrews, B., Brewin, C. R., Philpott, R., & Stewart, L. (2007). Delayed-onset posttraumatic stress disorder: A systematic review of the evidence. *American Journal of Psychiatry, 164*, 1319–1326.

Angrist, J. D., Chen, S. H., & Frandsen, B. R. (2010). Did Vietnam veterans get sicker in the 1990s? The complicated effects of military service on self-reported health. *Journal of Public Economics, 94*, 824–837.

Bedard-Gilligan, M., & Zoellner, L. A. (2012). Dissociation and memory fragmentation in post-traumatic stress disorder: An evaluation of the dissociative encoding hypothesis. *Memory, 20*, 277–299.

Bernstein, E. M., & Putnam, F. W. (1986). Development, reliability, and validity of a dissociation scale. *Journal of Nervous and Mental Disease, 174*, 727–735.

Berntsen, D., & Rubin, D. C. (2006). The centrality of event scale: A measure of integrating a trauma into one's identity and its relation to post-traumatic stress disorder symptoms. *Behaviour Research and Therapy, 44*, 219–231.

Berntsen, D., & Rubin, D. C. (2007). When a trauma becomes a key to identity: Enhanced integration of trauma memories predicts posttraumatic stress disorder symptoms. *Applied Cognitive Psychology, 21*, 417–431.

Blanchard, E. B., Kolb, L. C., Gerardi, R. J., Ryan, P., & Pallmeyer, T. P. (1986). Cardiac response to relevant stimuli as an adjunctive tool for diagnosing post-traumatic stress disorder in Vietnam veterans. *Behavior Therapy, 17*, 592–606.

Blanchard, E. B., Kolb, L. C., Pallmeyer, T. P., & Gerardi, R. J. (1982). A psychophysiological study of post-traumatic stress disorder in Vietnam veterans. *Psychiatric Quarterly, 54*, 220–229.

Blank, A. S. Jr. (1985). Irrational reactions to post-traumatic stress disorder and Viet Nam veterans. In S. Sonnenberg, A. S. Blank, Jr., & A. Talbott (Eds.), *The trauma of war: Stress and recovery in Viet Nam veterans* (pp. 69–98). Washington, DC: American Psychiatric Press.

Bonne, O., Brandes, D., Gilboa, A., Gomori, J. M., Shenton, M. E., & Pitman, R. K. (2001). Longitudinal MRI study of hippocampal volume in trauma survivors with PTSD. *American Journal of Psychiatry, 158*, 1248–1251.

Borch-Jacobsen, M. (2009). *Making minds and madness: From hysteria to depression.* Cambridge, UK: Cambridge University Press.

Borsboom, D. (2008). Psychometric perspectives on diagnostic systems. *Journal of Clinical Psychology, 64*, 1089–1108.

Borsboom, D., & Cramer, A. O. J. (2013). Network analysis: An integrative approach to the structure of psychopathology. *Annual Review of Clinical Psychology, 9*, 91–121.

Borsboom, D., Cramer, A. O. J., Schmittmann, V. D., Epskamp, S., & Waldorp, L. J. (2011). The small world of psychopathology. *PLoS ONE, 6*(11), e27407, 1–11.

Boscarino, J. A. (1995). Post-traumatic stress and associated disorders among Vietnam veterans: The significance of combat exposure and social support. *Journal of Traumatic Stress, 8*, 317–336.

Bowman, M. L., & Yehuda, R. (2004). Risk factors and the adversity-stress model. In G. M. Rosen (Ed.), *Posttraumatic stress disorder: Issues and controversies* (pp. 15–38). Chichester, UK: Wiley.

Boyd, R. (1991). Realism, anti-foundationalism and the enthusiasm for natural kinds. *Philosophical Studies, 61*, 127–148.

Brand, B. L., Classen, C. C., McNary, S. W., & Zaveri, P. (2009). A review of dissociative disorders treatment studies. *Journal of Nervous and Mental Disease, 197*, 646–654.

Bremner, J. D., Randall, P., Scott, T. M., Bronen, R. A., Seibyl, J. P., Southwick, S. M., Delaney, R. C., McCarthy, G., Charney, D. S., & Innis, R. B. (1995). MRI-based measurement of hippocampal volume in combat-related posttraumatic stress disorder. *American Journal of Psychiatry, 152*, 973–981.

Bremner, J. D., Randall, P., Vermetten, E., Staib, L., Bronen, R. A., Mazure, C., Capelli, S., McCarthy, G., Innis, R. B., & Charney, D. S. (1997). Magnetic resonance imaging-based measurement of hippocampal volume in posttraumatic stress disorder related to childhood physical and sexual abuse: A preliminary report. *Biological Psychiatry, 41*, 23–32.

Bremner, J. D., Staib, L. H., Kaloupek, D., Southwick, S. M., Soufer, R., & Charney, D. S. (1999). Neural correlates of exposure to traumatic pictures and sound in Vietnam combat veterans with and without posttraumatic stress disorder: A positron emission tomography study. *Biological Psychiatry, 45*, 806–816.

Bremner, J. D., Vermetten, E., Vythilingam, M., Afzal, N., Schmahl, C., Elzinga, B., & Charney, D. S. (2004). Neural correlates of the classic color and emotional Stroop in women with abuse-related posttraumatic stress disorder. *Biological Psychiatry, 55*, 612–620.

Brentano, F. (1984). On the origin of our knowledge of right and wrong. In C. Calhoun & R. C. Solomon (Eds.), *What is an emotion?* (pp. 205–214). New York: Oxford University Press. (Original work published 1889)

Breslau, N., & Alvarado, G. F. (2007). The clinical significance criterion in *DSM-IV* posttraumatic stress disorder. *Psychological Medicine, 37,* 1437–1444.

Breslau, N., Chen, Q., & Luo, Z. (2013). The role of intelligence in posttraumatic stress disorder: Does it vary by trauma severity? *PLoS One, 8*(6): e65391.

Breslau, N., Davis, G. C., & Andreski, P. (1995). Risk factors for PTSD-related traumatic events: A prospective analysis. *American Journal of Psychiatry, 152,* 529–535.

Breslau, N., Davis, G. C., Andreski, P., & Peterson, E. (1991). Traumatic events and posttraumatic stress disorder in an urban population of young adults. *Archives of General Psychiatry, 48,* 216–222.

Breslau, N., & Kessler, R. C. (2001). The stressor criterion in DSM-IV posttraumatic stress disorder: An empirical investigation. *Biological Psychiatry, 50,* 699–704.

Breslau, N., Lucia, V. C., & Alvarado, G. F. (2006). Intelligence and other predisposing factors in exposure to trauma and posttraumatic stress disorder: A follow-up study at age 17 years. *Archives of General Psychiatry, 63,* 1238–1245.

Breslau, N., Peterson, E. L., & Schultz, L. (2008). A second look at prior trauma and the posttraumatic stress disorder-effects of subsequent trauma: A prospective epidemiological study. *Archives of General Psychiatry, 65,* 431–437.

Breslau, N., Troost, J. P., Bohnert, K., & Luo, Z. (2013). Influence of predispositions on post-traumatic stress disorder: Does it vary by trauma severity? *Psychological Medicine, 43,* 381–390.

Brewin, C. R. (2011). The nature and significance of memory disturbance in posttraumatic stress disorder. *Annual Review of Clinical Psychology, 7,* 203–227.

Brown, A. D., Antonius, D., Kramer, M., Root, J. C., & Hirst, W. (2010). Trauma centrality and PTSD in veterans returning from Iraq and Afghanistan. *Journal of Traumatic Stress, 23,* 496–499.

Brown, A. D., Root, J. C., Romano, T. A., Chang, L. J., Bryant, R. A., & Hirst, W. (2013). Overgeneralized autobiographical memory and future thinking in combat veterans with posttraumatic stress disorder. *Journal of Behavior Therapy and Experimental Psychiatry, 44,* 129–134.

Brown, D., Scheflin, A. W., & Hammond, D. C. (1998). *Memory, trauma treatment, and the law.* New York: Norton.

Brown, D., Scheflin, A. W., & Whitfield, C. L. (1999). Recovered memories: The current weight of evidence in science and in the courts. *Journal of Psychiatry and Law, 27,* 5–156.

Bryant, R. A., & Harvey, A. G. (1995). Processing threatening information in posttraumatic stress disorder. *Journal of Abnormal Psychology, 104,* 537–541.

Bryant, R. A., Sutherland, K., & Guthrie, R. M. (2007). Impaired specific autobiographical memory as a risk factor for posttraumatic stress after trauma. *Journal of Abnormal Psychology, 116,* 837–841.

Buckley, T. C., Galovski, T., Blanchard, E. B., & Hickling, E. J. (2003). Is the emotional Stroop paradigm sensitive to malingering? A between-groups study with professional actors and actual trauma survivors. *Journal of Traumatic Stress, 16,* 59–66.

Burgess, A. W., & Holmstrom, L. L. (1974). Rape trauma syndrome. *American Journal of Psychiatry, 131,* 981–986.

Burkett, B. G., & Whitley, G. (1998). *Stolen valor: How the Vietnam generation was robbed of its heroes and its history.* Dallas, TX: Verity Press.

Cassiday, K. L., McNally, R. J., & Zeitlin, S. B. (1992). Cognitive processing of trauma cues in rape victims with post-traumatic stress disorder. *Cognitive Therapy and Research, 16,* 283–295.

Chapman, C., Mills, K., Slade, T., McFarlane, A. C., Bryant, R. A., Creamer, M., Silove, D., & Teeson, M. (2012). Remission from post-traumatic stress disorder in the general population. *Psychological Medicine, 42,* 1695–1703.

Charney, D. S., Deutch, A. Y., Krystal, J. H., Southwick, S. M., & Davis, M. (1993). Psychobiologic mechanisms of posttraumatic stress disorder. *Archives of General Psychiatry, 50,* 294–305.

Chodoff, P. (1963). Late effects of the concentration camp syndrome. *Archives of General Psychiatry, 8,* 323–333.

Cortina, L. M., & Kubiak, S. P. (2006). Gender and posttraumatic stress: Sexual violence as an explanation for women's increased risk. *Journal of Abnormal Psychology, 115,* 753–759.

Cramer, A. O. J., Waldorp, L. J., van der Maas, H. L. J., & Borsboom, D. (2010). Comorbidity: A network perspective. *Behavioral and Brain Sciences, 33,* 137–193.

Crews, F. (1995). *The memory wars: Freud's legacy in dispute.* New York: New York Review of Books.

Dalenberg, C. J., Brand, B. L., Gleaves, D. H., Dorahy, M., Loewenstein, R. J., Cardeña, E., Frewen, P. A., Carlson, E. B., & Spiegel, D. (2012). Evaluation of the evidence for the trauma and fantasy models of dissociation. *Psychological Bulletin, 138*, 550–558.

Dalgleish, T., Williams, J. M. G., Golden, A.-M. J., Perkins, N., Barrett, L. F., Barnard, P. J., Au Yeung, C., Murphy, V., Elward, R., Tchanturia, K., & Watkins, E. (2007). Reduced specificity of autobiographical memory and depression: The role of executive control. *Journal of Experimental Psychology: General, 136*, 23–42.

de Jongh, A., Olff, M., van Hoolwerff, H., Aarman, I. H. A., Broekman, B., Lindaur, R., & Boer, F. (2008). Anxiety and post-traumatic stress symptoms following wisdom tooth removal. *Behaviour Research and Therapy, 46*, 1305–1310.

Department of Veterans Affairs Office of the Inspector General. (2005). *Review of state variances in VA disability compensation payments* (#05-00765-137). Retrieved from http://www.va.gov/foia/err/standard/requests/ig.html

Dobbs, D. (2009, April). The post-traumatic stress trap. *Scientific American, 300*(4), 64–69.

Dohrenwend, B. P. (2010). Toward a typology of high-risk major stressful events and situations in posttraumatic stress disorder and related psychopathology. *Psychological Injury and Law, 3*, 89–99.

Dohrenwend, B. P., Turner, J. B., Turse, N. A., Adams, B. G., Koenen, K. C., & Marshall, R. (2006). The psychological risks of Vietnam for U.S. veterans: A revisit with new data and methods. *Science, 313*, 379–982.

Dubner, A. E., & Motta, R. W. (1999). Sexually and physically abused foster care children and posttraumatic stress disorder. *Journal of Consulting and Clinical Psychology, 67*, 367–373.

Dunmore, E., Clark, D. M., & Ehlers, A. (2001). A prospective investigation of the role of cognitive factors in persistent posttraumatic stress disorder (PTSD) after physical or sexual assault. *Behaviour Research and Therapy, 39*, 1063–1084.

Ehring, T., Ehlers, A., & Glucksman, E. (2006). Contribution of cognitive factors to the prediction of post-traumatic stress disorder, phobia, and depression after motor vehicle accidents. *Behaviour Research and Therapy, 44*, 1699–1716.

Engelhard, I. M., van den Hout, M. A., Weerts, J., Arntz, A., Hox, J. J. C. M., & McNally, R. J. (2007). Deployment-related stress and trauma in Dutch soldiers returning from Iraq: A prospective study. *British Journal of Psychiatry, 191*, 140–145.

Foa, E. B., Feske, U., Murdock, T. B., Kozak, M. J., & McCarthy, P. R. (1991). Processing of threat-related information in rape victims. *Journal of Abnormal Psychology, 100*, 156–162.

Frueh, B. C., Elhai, J. D., Grubaugh, A. L., Monnier, J., Kashdan, T. B., Sauvageot, J. A.,...Arana, G. W. (2005). Documented combat exposure of US veterans seeking treatment for combat-related post-traumatic stress disorder. *British Journal of Psychiatry, 186*, 467–472.

Gerardi, R. J., Blanchard, E. B., & Kolb, L. C. (1989). Ability of Vietnam veterans to dissimulate a psychophysiological assessment for post-traumatic stress disorder. *Behavior Therapy, 20*, 229–243.

Gilbertson, M. W., Paulus, L. A., Williston, S. K., Gurvits, T. V., Lasko, N. B., Pitman, R. K., & Orr, S. P. (2006). Neurocognitive function in monozygotic twins discordant for combat exposure: Relationship to posttraumatic stress disorder. *Journal of Abnormal Psychology, 115*, 484–495.

Gilbertson, M. W., Shenton, M. E., Ciszewski, A., Kasai, K., Lasko, N. B., Orr, S. P. & Pitman, R. K. (2002). Smaller hippocampal volume predicts pathologic vulnerability to psychological trauma. *Nature Neuroscience, 5*, 1242–1247.

Gleaves, D. H., May, M. C., & Cardeña, E. (2001). An examination of the diagnostic validity of dissociative identity disorder. *Clinical Psychology Review, 21*, 577–608.

Goldberg, J., True, W. R., Eisen, S. A., & Henderson, W. G. (1990). A twin study of the effects of the Vietnam War on posttraumatic stress disorder. *Journal of the American Medical Association, 263*, 1227–1232.

Goodwin, L., Jones, M., Rona, R. J., Sundin, J., Wessely, S., & Fear, N. T. (2012). Prevalence of delayed-onset posttraumatic stress disorder in military personnel: Is there evidence for this disorder? Results of a prospective UK cohort study. *Journal of Nervous and Mental Disease, 200*, 429–437.

Gurvits, T. V., Gilbertson, M. W., Lasko, N. B., Tarhan, A. S., Simeon, D., Macklin, M. L., Orr, S. P., & Pitman, R. K. (2000). Neurologic soft signs in chronic posttraumatic stress disorder. *Archives of General Psychiatry, 57*, 181–186.

Gurvits, T. V., Metzger, L. J., Lasko, N. B., Cannistraro, P. A., Tarhan, A. S., Gilbertson, M. W.,...Pitman, R. K. (2006). Subtle neurologic compromise as a vulnerability factor for combat-related posttraumatic stress disorder: Results of a twin study. *Archives of General Psychiatry, 63*, 571–576.

Gurvits, T. V., Shenton, M. E., Hokama, H., Ohta, H., Lasko, N. B., Gilbertson, M. W.,... Pitman, R. K. (1996). Magnetic resonance imaging study of hippocampal volume in chronic, combat-related posttraumatic stress disorder. *Biological Psychiatry, 40,* 1091–1099.

Hacking, I. (1998). *Mad travelers: Reflections on the reality of transient mental illness.* Charlottesville, VA: University of Virginia Press.

Hackmann, A., Ehlers, A., Speckens, A., & Clark, D. M. (2004). Characteristics and content of intrusive memories in PTSD and their changes with treatment. *Journal of Traumatic Stress, 17,* 231–240.

Halligan, S. L., Michael, T., Clark, D. M., & Ehlers, A. (2003). Posttraumatic stress disorder following assault: The role of cognitive processing, trauma memory, and appraisals. *Journal of Consulting and Clinical Psychology, 71,* 419–431.

Hoge, C. W., Castro, C. A., Messer, S. C., McGurk, D., Cotting, D. I., & Koffman, R. L. (2004). Combat duty in Iraq and Afghanistan, mental health problems, and barriers to care. *New England Journal of Medicine, 351,* 13–22.

Huntjens, R. J. C., Peters, M. L., Woertman, L., van der Hart, O., & Postma, A. (2007). Memory transfer for emotionally valenced words between identities in dissociative identity disorder. *Behaviour Research and Therapy, 45,* 775–789.

Huntjens, R. J. C., Postma, A., Peters, M. L., Woertman, L., & van der Hart, O. (2003). Interidentity amnesia for neutral, episodic information in dissociative identity disorder. *Journal of Abnormal Psychology, 112,* 290–297.

Huntjens, R. J. C., Verschuere, B., & McNally, R. J. (2012). Inter-identity autobiographical amnesia in patients with dissociative identity disorder. *PLoS ONE, 7*(7): e40580.

Jones, E., & Wessely, S. (2005). *Shell shock to PTSD: Military psychiatry from 1900 to the Gulf War.* Hove, UK: Psychology Press.

Jones, E., & Wessely, S. (2007). A paradigm shift in the conceptualization of psychological trauma in the 20th century. *Journal of Anxiety Disorders, 21,* 164–175.

Johnson, J. G., Cohen, P., Kasen, S., & Brook, J. S. (2006). Dissociative disorders among adults in the community, impaired functioning, and axis I and II comorbidity. *Journal of Psychiatric Research, 40,* 131–140.

Kasai, K., Yamasue, H., Gilbertson, M. W., Shenton, M. E., Rauch, S. L., & Pitman,

R. K. (2008). Evidence for acquired pregenual anterior cingulate gray matter loss from a twin study of combat-related posttraumatic stress disorder. *Biological Psychiatry, 63,* 550–556.

Keane, T. M., Kolb, L. C., Kaloupek, D. G., Orr, S. P., Blanchard, E. B., Thomas, R. G., Hsieh, F. Y., & Lavori, P. W. (1998). Utility of psychophysiological measurement in the diagnosis of posttraumatic stress disorder: Results from a Department of Veterans Affairs Cooperative Study. *Journal of Consulting and Clinical Psychology, 66,* 914–923.

Kendler, K. S., Zachar, P., & Craver, C. (2011). What kinds of things are psychiatric disorders? *Psychological Medicine, 41,* 1143–1150.

Kessler, R. C., Berglund, P., Demler, O., Jin, R., Merikangas, K. R., & Walters, E. E. (2005). Lifetime prevalence and age-of-onset distributions of DSM-IV disorders in the National Comorbidity Survey Replication. *Archives of General Psychiatry, 62,* 593–602.

Kessler, R. C., Sonnega, A., Bromet, E., Hughes, M., & Nelson, C. B. (1995). Posttraumatic stress disorder in the National Comorbidity Survey. *Archives of General Psychiatry, 52,* 1048–1060.

Kimble, M. O., Frueh, B. C., & Marks, L. (2009). Does the modified Stroop effect exist in PTSD? Evidence from dissertation abstracts and the peer reviewed literature. *Journal of Anxiety Disorders, 23,* 650–655.

King, D. W., & King, L. A. (1991). Validity issues in research on Vietnam veteran adjustment. *Psychological Bulletin, 109,* 107–124.

King, D. W., King, L. A., Foy, D. W., & Gudanowski, D. M. (1996). Prewar factors in combat-related posttraumatic stress disorder: Structural equation modeling with a national sample of female and male Vietnam veterans. *Journal of Consulting and Clinical Psychology, 64,* 520–531.

Kleim, B., & Ehlers, A. (2008). Reduced autobiographical memory specificity predicts depression and posttraumatic stress disorder after recent trauma. *Journal of Consulting and Clinical Psychology, 76,* 231–242.

Koenen, K. C., Aiello, A. E., Bakshis, E., Amstadter, A. B., Ruggiero, K. J., Acierno, R., Kilpatrick, D. G., & Galea, S. (2009). Modification of the association between serotonin transporter genotype and risk of posttraumatic stress disorder in adults by county-level social environment. *American Journal of Epidemiology, 169,* 704–711.

Koenen, K. C., Moffitt, T. E., Caspi, A., Gregory, A., Harrington, H., & Poulton, R. (2008).

The developmental mental-disorder histories of adults with posttraumatic stress disorder: A prospective longitudinal birth cohort study. *Journal of Abnormal Psychology, 117,* 460–466.

Koenen, K. C., Moffitt, T. E., Poulton, R., Martin, J., & Caspi, A. (2007). Early childhood factors associated with the development of post-traumatic stress disorder: Results from a longitudinal birth cohort. *Psychological Medicine, 37,* 181–192.

Kong, L. L., Allen, J. J. B., & Glisky, E. L. (2008). Interidentity memory transfer in dissociative identity disorder. *Journal of Abnormal Psychology, 117,* 686–692.

Kopelman, M. D., Christensen, H., Puffett, A., & Stanhope, N. (1994). The great escape: A neuropsychological study of psychogenic amnesia. *Neuropsychologia, 32,* 675–691.

Kremen, W. S., Koenen, K. C., Boake, C., Purcell, S., Eisen, S. A., Franz, C. E., Tsuang, M. T., & Lyons, M. J. (2007). Pretrauma cognitive ability and risk for posttraumatic stress disorder: A twin study. *Archives of General Psychiatry, 64,* 361–368.

Kulka, R. A., Schlenger, W. E., Fairbank, J. A., Hough, R. L., Jordan, B. K., Marmar, C. R., & Weiss, D. S. (1990). *Trauma and the Vietnam War generation: Report of findings from the National Vietnam Veterans Readjustment Study.* New York: Brunner/Mazel.

Lifton, R. J. (1973). *Home from the war: Vietnam veterans: Neither victims nor executioners.* New York: Touchstone.

Lilienfeld, S. O. (2002). When worlds collide: Social science, politics, and the Rind et al. (1998) child sexual abuse meta-analysis. *American Psychologist, 57,* 176–188.

Lilienfeld, S. O., Lynn, S. J., Kirsch, I., Chaves, J. F., Sarbin, T. R., Ganaway, G. K., & Powell, R. A. (1999). Dissociative identity disorder and the sociocognitive model: Recalling the lessons of the past. *Psychological Bulletin, 125,* 507–523.

Lynn, S. J., Lilienfeld, S. O., Merckelbach, H., Giesbrecht, T., McNally, R. J., Loftus, E. F., ... Malaktaris, A. (2014). The trauma model of dissociation: Inconvenient truths and stubborn fictions. *Psychological Bulletin, 140,* 896–910.

Macklin, M. L., Metzger, L. J., Litz, B. T., McNally, R. J., Lasko, N. B., Orr, S. P., & Pitman, R. K. (1998). Lower pre-combat intelligence is a risk factor for posttraumatic stress disorder. *Journal of Consulting and Clinical Psychology, 66,* 323–326.

Malloy, P. F., Fairbank, J. A., & Keane, T. M. (1983). Validation of a multimethod assessment of posttraumatic stress disorders in Vietnam veterans. *Journal of Consulting and Clinical Psychology, 51,* 488–494.

Marlowe, D. H. (2001). *Psychological and psychosocial consequences of combat and deployment with special emphasis on the Gulf War.* Santa Monica, CA: RAND.

Marshall, R. D. (2006). Learning from 9/11: Implications for disaster research and public health. In Y. Neria, R. Gross, R. Marshall, & E. Susser (Eds.), *9/11: Mental health in the wake of terrorist attacks* (pp. 617–639). Cambridge, UK: Cambridge University Press.

Marx, B. P., Jackson, J. C., Schnurr, P. P., Murdoch, M., Sayer, N. A., Keane, T. M., ... Speroff, T. (2012). The reality of malingered PTSD among veterans: Reply to McNally and Frueh (2012). *Journal of Traumatic Stress, 25,* 457–460.

McDonald, J. J., Jr. (2003). Posttraumatic stress dishonesty. *Employee Relations Law Journal, 28,* 93–111.

McFarlane, A. C. (1989). The aetiology of post-traumatic morbidity: Predisposing, precipitating and perpetuating factors. *British Journal of Psychiatry, 154,* 221–228.

McGaugh, J. L. (2003). *Memory and emotion: The making of lasting memories.* New York: Columbia University Press.

McHugh, P. R. (2008). *Try to remember: Psychiatry's clash over meaning, memory, and mind.* New York: Dana Press.

McNally, R. J. (2003a). *Remembering trauma.* Cambridge, MA: The Belknap Press of Harvard University Press.

McNally, R. J. (2003b). Progress and controversy in the study of posttraumatic stress disorder. *Annual Review of Psychology, 54,* 229–252.

McNally, R. J. (2006a). Psychiatric casualties of war. *Science, 313,* 923–924.

McNally, R. J. (2006b). Cognitive abnormalities in post-traumatic stress disorder. *Trends in Cognitive Sciences, 10,* 271–277.

McNally, R. J. (2007a). Can we solve the mysteries of the National Vietnam Veterans Readjustment Study? *Journal of Anxiety Disorders, 21,* 192–200.

McNally, R. J. (2007b). Revisiting Dohrenwend et al.'s revisit of the National Vietnam Veterans Readjustment Study. *Journal of Traumatic Stress, 20,* 481–486.

McNally, R. J. (2009). Can we fix PTSD in DSM-V? *Depression and Anxiety, 26,* 597–600.

McNally, R. J. (2011). *What is mental illness?* Cambridge, MA: The Belknap Press of Harvard University Press.

McNally, R. J. (2012a). Are we winning the war against posttraumatic stress disorder? *Science, 336*, 874–876.

McNally, R. J. (2012b). The ontology of posttraumatic stress disorder: Natural kind, social construction, or causal system? *Clinical Psychology: Science and Practice, 19*, 220–228.

McNally, R. J., & Breslau, N. (2008). Does virtual trauma cause posttraumatic stress disorder? *American Psychologist, 63*, 282–283.

McNally, R. J., & Frueh, B. C. (2012). Why we should worry about malingering in the VA system: Comment on Jackson et al. *Journal of Traumatic Stress, 25*, 454–456.

McNally, R. J., Kaspi, S. P., Riemann, B. C., & Zeitlin, S. (1990). Selective processing of threat cues in posttraumatic stress disorder. *Journal of Abnormal Psychology, 99*, 398–402.

McNally, R. J., Lasko, N. B., Clancy, S. A., Macklin, M. L., Pitman, R. K., & Orr, S. P. (2004). Psychophysiological responding during script-driven imagery in people reporting abduction by space aliens. *Psychological Science, 15*, 493–497.

McNally, R. J., Lasko, N. B., Macklin, M. L., & Pitman, R. K. (1995). Autobiographical memory disturbance in combat-related posttraumatic stress disorder. *Behaviour Research and Therapy, 33*, 619–630.

McNally, R. J., Litz, B. T., Prassas, A., Shin, L. M., & Weathers, F. W. (1994). Emotional priming of autobiographical memory in post-traumatic stress disorder. *Cognition and Emotion, 8*, 351–367.

McNally, R. J., & Robinaugh, D. J. (2011). Risk factors and posttraumatic stress disorder: Are they especially predictive following exposure to less severe stressors? *Depression and Anxiety, 28*, 1091–1096.

McNally, R. J., & Shin, L. M. (1995). Association of intelligence with severity of posttraumatic stress disorder symptoms in Vietnam combat veterans. *American Journal of Psychiatry, 152*, 936–938.

Milad, M. R., & Quirk, G. J. (2002). Neurons in medial prefrontal cortex signal memory for fear extinction. *Nature, 420*, 70–74.

Moore, S. A., & Zoellner, L. A. (2007). Overgeneral autobiographical memory and traumatic events: An evaluative review. *Psychological Bulletin, 133*, 419–437.

Moradi, A. R., Abdi, A., Fathi-Ashtiani, A., Dalgleish, T., & Jobson, L. (2012). Overgeneral autobiographical memory recollection in Iranian combat veterans with posttraumatic stress disorder. *Behaviour Research and Therapy, 50*, 435–441.

Morgan, C. A., III, Grillon, C., Southwick, S. M., Davis, M., & Charney, D. S. (1996). Exaggerated acoustic startle reflex in Gulf War veterans with posttraumatic stress disorder. *American Journal of Psychiatry, 153*, 64–68.

Nathan, D. (2011). *Sybil exposed: The extraordinary story behind the famous multiple personality case.* New York: Free Press.

Olde, E., van der Hart, O., Kleber, R., & van Son, M. (2006). Posttraumatic stress disorder following childbirth: A review. *Clinical Psychology Review, 26*, 1–16.

Orr, S. P., Lasko, N. B., Shalev, A. Y., & Pitman, R. K. (1995). Physiologic responses to loud tones in Vietnam veterans with posttraumatic stress disorder. *Journal of Abnormal Psychology, 104*, 75–82.

Orr, S. P., McNally, R. J., Rosen, G. M., & Shalev, A. Y. (2004). Psychophysiologic reactivity: Implications for conceptualizing PTSD. In G. M. Rosen (Ed.), *Posttraumatic stress disorder: Issues and controversies* (pp. 101–126). Chichester, UK: Wiley.

Orr, S. P., Metzger, L. J., Lasko, N. B., Macklin, M. L., Hu, F. B., Shalev, A. Y., & Pitman, R. K. (2003). Physiologic responses to sudden, loud tones in monozygotic twins discordant for combat exposure: Association with posttraumatic stress disorder. *Archives of General Psychiatry, 60*, 283–288.

Orr, S. P., & Pitman, R. K. (1993). Psychophysiologic assessment of attempts to simulate posttraumatic stress disorder. *Biological Psychiatry, 33*, 127–129.

Orr, S. P., Pitman, R. K., Lasko, N. B., & Herz, L. R. (1993). Psychophysiological assessment of posttraumatic stress disorder imagery in World War II and Korean combat veterans. *Journal of Abnormal Psychology, 102*, 152–159.

Paige, S. R., Reid, G. M., Allen, M. G., & Newton, J. E. O. (1990). Psychophysiological correlates of posttraumatic stress disorder in Vietnam veterans. *Biological Psychiatry, 27*, 419–430.

Pallmeyer, T. P., Blanchard, E. B., & Kolb, L. C. (1986). The psychophysiology of combat-induced post-traumatic stress disorder in Vietnam veterans. *Behaviour Research and Therapy, 24*, 645–652.

Pinker, S. (2007). Introduction. In J. Brockman (Ed.), *What is your dangerous idea?: Today's leading thinkers on the unthinkable* (pp. xxiii–xxxiii). New York: Harper Perennial.

Piper, A. Jr., Pope, H. G., Jr., & Borowiecki, J. J., III. (2000). Custer's last stand: Brown, Scheflin, and Whitfield's latest attempt to salvage "dissociative amnesia." *Journal of Psychiatry and Law, 28,* 149–213.

Pitman, R. K., Orr, S. P., Forgue, D. F., Altman, B., de Jong, J. B., & Herz, L. R. (1990). Psychophysiologic responses to combat imagery of Vietnam veterans with posttraumatic stress disorder versus other anxiety disorders. *Journal of Abnormal Psychology, 99,* 49–54.

Pitman, R. K., Orr, S. P., Forgue, D. F., de Jong, J. B., & Claiborn, J. M. (1987). Psychophysiologic assessment of posttraumatic stress disorder imagery in Vietnam combat veterans. *Archives of General Psychiatry, 44,* 970–975.

Pitman, R. K., Rasmusson, A. M., Koenen, K. C., Shin, L. M., Orr, S. P., Gilbertson, M. W., Milad, M. R., & Liberzon, I. (2012). Biological studies of post-traumatic stress disorder. *Nature Reviews Neuroscience, 13,* 769–787.

Pole, N. (2007). The psychophysiology of posttraumatic stress disorder: A meta-analysis. *Psychological Bulletin, 133,* 725–746.

Pope, H. G., Jr., Olivia, P. S., & Hudson, J. I. (1999). Repressed memories: The scientific status. In D. L. Faigman, D. H. Kaye, M. J. Saks, & J. Sanders (Eds.), *Modern scientific evidence: The law and science of expert testimony* (Vol. 1, Pocket Part, pp. 115–155). St. Paul, MN: West Publishing.

Pope, H. G., Jr., Poliakoff, M. B., Parker, M. P., Boynes, M., & Hudson, J. I. (2007a). Is dissociative amnesia a culture-bound syndrome? Findings from a survey of historical literature. *Psychological Medicine, 37,* 225–233.

Pope, H. G., Jr., Poliakoff, M. B., Parker, M. P., Boynes, M., & Hudson, J. I. (2007b). The authors' reply. *Psychological Medicine, 37,* 1067–1068.

Pope, H. G., Jr., Barry, S., Bodkin, A., & Hudson, J. I. (2006). Tracking scientific interest in the dissociative disorders: A study of scientific publication output 1984–2003. *Psychotherapy and Psychosomatics, 75,* 19–24.

Porter, S., & Peace, K. A. (2007). The scars of memory: A prospective, longitudinal investigation of the consistency of traumatic and positive emotional memories in adulthood. *Psychological Science, 37,* 1437–1444.

Putnam, F. W. (1989). *Diagnosis and treatment of multiple personality disorder.* New York: Guilford Press.

Putnam, F. W., Guroff, J. J., Silberman, E. K., Barban, L., & Post, R. M. (1986). The clinical phenomenology of multiple personality disorder: Review of 100 recent cases. *Journal of Clinical Psychiatry, 47,* 285–293.

Rangell, L. (1976). Discussion of the Buffalo Creek disaster: The course of psychic trauma. *American Journal of Psychiatry, 133,* 313–316.

Rauch, S. L., Shin, L. M., & Phelps, E. A. (2006). Neurocircuitry models of posttraumatic stress disorder and extinction: Human neuroimaging research—past, present, and future. *Biological Psychiatry, 60,* 376–382.

Rauch, S. L., Shin, L. M., Segal, E., Pitman, R. K., Carson, M. A., McMullin, K., Whalen, P. J., & Makris, N. (2003). Selectively reduced regional cortical volumes in post-traumatic stress disorder. *Neuroreport, 14,* 913–916.

Rauch, S. L., Whalen, P. J., Shin, L. M., McInerney, S. C., Macklin, M. L., Lasko, N. B., Orr, S. P., & Pitman, R. K. (2000). Exaggerated amygdala response to masked facial stimuli in posttraumatic stress disorder: A functional MRI study. *Biological Psychiatry, 47,* 769–776.

Reinders, A. A. T. S., Nijenhuis, E. R. S., Quak, J., Korf, J., Haaksma, J., Paans, A. M. J., Willemsen, A. T. M., & den Boer, J. A. (2006). Psychobiological characteristics of dissociative identity disorder: A symptom provocation study. *Biological Psychiatry, 60,* 730–740.

Reinders, A. A. T. S., Willemsen, A. T. M., Vos, H. P. J., den Boer, J. A., & Nijenhuis, E. R. S. (2012). Fact or factitious? A psychobiological study of authentic and simulated dissociative identity states. *PLoS ONE, 7*(6): e39279.

Rieber, R. W. (2006). *Bifurcation of the self: The history and theory of dissociation and its disorders.* New York: Springer.

Rind, B., Tromovitch, P., & Bauserman, R. (1998). A meta-analytic examination of assumed properties of child sexual abuse using college samples. *Psychological Bulletin, 124,* 22–53.

Robinaugh, D. J., & McNally, R. J. (2011). Trauma centrality and PTSD symptom severity in adult survivors of childhood sexual abuse. *Journal of Traumatic Stress, 24,* 483–486.

Rothbaum, B. O., & Foa, E. B. (1993). Subtypes of posttraumatic stress disorder and duration of symptoms. In J. R. T. Davidson & E. B. Foa (Eds.), *Posttraumatic stress disorder: DSM-IV and beyond* (pp. 23–35). Washington, DC: American Psychiatric Press.

Rubin, D. C., Berntsen, D., & Bohni, M. K. (2008). A memory-based model of posttraumatic stress disorder: Evaluating basic assumptions underlying the PTSD diagnosis. *Psychological Review, 115,* 985–1011.

Rubin, D. C., Feldman, M. E., & Beckham, J. C. (2004). Reliving emotions, and fragmentation in the autobiographical memories of veterans diagnosed with PTSD. *Applied Cognitive Psychology, 18,* 17–35.

Ruscio, A. M., Ruscio, J., & Keane, T. M. (2002). The latent structure of posttraumatic stress disorder: A taxometric investigation of reactions to extreme stress. *Journal of Abnormal Psychology, 111,* 290–301.

Saigh, P. A. (1991). The development of posttraumatic stress disorder following four different types of traumatization. *Behaviour Research and Therapy, 29,* 213–216.

Sapolsky, R. M. (1996). Why stress is bad for your brain. *Science, 273,* 749–750.

Sartor, C. E., McCutcheon, V. V., Pommer, N. E., Nelson, E. C., Grant, J. D., Duncan, A. E.,…Heath, A. C. (2011). Common genetic and environmental contributions to post-traumatic stress disorder and alcohol dependence in young women. *Psychological Medicine, 41,* 1497–1505.

Satel, S. (2007). The trouble with traumatology. *Weekly Standard, 12*(22), 14–15.

Schlenger, W. E., Caddell, J. M., Ebert, L., Jordan, B. K., Rourke, K. M., Wilson, D.,…Kulka, R. A. (2002). Psychological reactions to terrorist attacks: Findings from the National Study of Americans' Reactions to September 11. *Journal of the American Medical Association, 288,* 581–588.

Schreiber, F. R. (1973). *Sybil.* New York: Warner Books.

Shalev, A. Y., Orr, S. P., Peri, T., Schreiber, S., & Pitman, R. K. (1992). Physiologic responses to loud tones in Israeli patients with posttraumatic stress disorder. *Archives of General Psychiatry, 49,* 870–875.

Shalev, A. Y., Orr, S. P., & Pitman, R. K. (1993). Psychophysiological assessment of traumatic imagery in Israeli civilian patients with posttraumatic stress disorder. *American Journal of Psychiatry, 150,* 620–624.

Shalev, A. Y., Peri, T., Canetti, L., & Schreiber, S. (1996). Predictors of PTSD in injured trauma survivors: A prospective study. *American Journal of Psychiatry, 153,* 219–225.

Shatan, C. F. (1973). The grief of soldiers: Vietnam combat veterans' self-help movement. *American Journal of Orthopsychiatry, 43,* 640–653.

Shephard, B. (2001). *A war of nerves: Soldiers and psychiatrists in the twentieth century.* Cambridge, MA: Harvard University Press.

Shin, L. M., McNally, R. J., Kosslyn, S. M., Thompson, W. L., Rauch, S. L., Alpert, N. M.,…Pitman, R. K. (1999). Regional cerebral blood flow during script-driven imagery in childhood sexual abuse-related PTSD: A PET investigation. *American Journal of Psychiatry, 156,* 575–584.

Shin, L. M., Orr, S. P., Carson, M. A., Rauch, S. L., Macklin, M. L., Lasko, N. B.,…Pitman, R. K. (2004). Regional cerebral blood flow in the amygdala and medial prefrontal cortex during traumatic imagery in male and female Vietnam veterans with PTSD. *Archives of General Psychiatry, 61,* 168–176.

Shin, L. M., Rauch, S. L., & Pitman, R. K. (2005). Structural and functional anatomy of PTSD: Findings from neuroimaging research. In J. J. Vasterling & C. R. Brewin (Eds.), *Neuropsychology of PTSD: Biological, cognitive, and clinical perspectives* (pp. 59–82). New York: Guilford Press.

Shin, L. M., Rauch, S. L., & Pitman, R. K. (2006). Amygdala, medial prefrontal cortex, and hippocampal function in PTSD. *Annals of the New York Academy of Sciences, 1071,* 67–79.

Shin, L. M., Whalen, P. J., Pitman, R. K., Bush, G., Macklin, M. L., Lasko, N. B.,…Rauch, S. L. (2001). An fMRI study of anterior cingulate function in posttraumatic stress disorder. *Biological Psychiatry, 50,* 932–942.

Shin, L. M., Wright, C. I., Cannistraro, P. A., Wedig, M. M., McMullin, K., Martis, B.,…Rauch, S. L. (2005). A functional magnetic resonance imaging study of amygdala and medial prefrontal cortex responses to overtly presented fearful faces in posttraumatic stress disorder. *Archives of General Psychiatry, 62,* 273–281.

Sierra, M., & Berrios, G. E. (1998). Depersonalization: Neurobiological perspectives. *Biological Psychiatry, 44,* 898–908.

Sierra, M., Medford, N., Wyatt, G., & David, A. S. (2012). Depersonalization disorder and anxiety: A special relationship? *Psychiatry Research, 197,* 123–127.

Smith, T. C., Ryan, M. A. K., Wingard, D. L., Slymen, D. J., Sallis, J. F., & Kritz-Silverstein, D. for the Millennium Cohort Study Team. (2008). New onset and persistent symptoms of post-traumatic stress disorder self reported after deployment and combat exposures: Prospective population based US military cohort study. *British Medical Journal, 336,* 366–371.

Solomon, Z., Kotler, M., Shalev, A., & Lin, R. (1989). Delayed onset PTSD among Israeli veterans of the 1982 Lebanon War. *Psychiatry, 52,* 428–436.

Solomon, Z., Mikulincer, M., & Jakob, B. R. (1987). Exposure to recurrent combat stress: Combat stress reactions among Israeli soldiers in the Lebanon War. *Psychological Medicine, 17*, 433–440.

Southwick, S. M., Krystal, J. H., Morgan, C. A. Johnson, D., Nagy, L. M., Nicolaou, A., Heninger, G. R., & Charney, D. S. (1993). Abnormal noradrenergic function in posttraumatic stress disorder. *Archives of General Psychiatry, 50*, 266–274.

Spiegel, D. (1997). Foreword. In D. Spiegel (Ed.), *Repressed memories* (pp. 5–11). Washington, DC: American Psychiatric Press.

Spiegel, D., Loewenstein, R. J., Lewis-Fernandez, R., Sar, V., Simeon, D., Vermetten, E., Cardeña, E., & Dell, P. F. (2011). Dissociative disorders in DSM-5. *Depression and Anxiety, 28*, 824–852.

Spitzer, R. L., Williams, J. B. W., & Gibbon, M. (1987). DSM-III-R Axis V: Global assessment of functioning. In *Structured clinical interview for DSM-III-R, version NP-R*. New York: New York State Psychiatric Institute, Biometrics Research Department.

Starkman, M. N., Giordani, B., Gebarski, S. S., Berent, S., Shork, M. A., & Schteingart, D. E. (1999). Decrease in cortisol reverses human hippocampal atrophy following treatment of Cushing's disease. *Biological Psychiatry, 46*, 1595–1602.

Stein, M. B., Koverola, C., Hanna, C., Torchia, M. G., & McClarty, B. (1997). Hippocampal volume in women victimized by childhood sexual abuse. *Psychological Medicine, 27*, 951–959.

Stengel, E. (1941). On the aetiology of the fugue states. *Journal of Mental Science, 87*, 572–599.

Sundin, J., Fear, N. T., Iverson, A., Rona, R. J., & Wessely, S. (2010). PTSD after deployment to Iraq: Conflicting rates, conflicting claims. *Psychological Medicine, 40*, 367–382.

Sutherland, K., & Bryant, R. A. (2005). Self-defining memories in post-traumatic stress disorder. *British Journal of Clinical Psychology, 44*, 591–598.

Sutherland, K., & Bryant, R. A. (2008). Social problem solving and autobiographical memory in posttraumatic stress disorder. *Behaviour Research and Therapy, 46*, 154–161.

Sutker, P. B., Uddo, M., Brailey, K., Vasterling, J. J., & Errera, P. (1994). Psychopathology in war-zone deployed and nondeployed Operation Desert Storm troops assigned graves registration duties. *Journal of Abnormal Psychology, 103*, 383–390.

Taylor, W. S., & Martin, M. F. (1944). Multiple personality. *Journal of Abnormal and Social Psychology, 39*, 281–300.

Thomas, J. L., Wilk, J. E., Riviere, L. A., McGurk, D., Castro, C. A., & Hoge, C. W. (2010). Prevalence of mental health problems and functional impairment among active component and National Guard soldiers 3 and 12 months following combat in Iraq. *Archives of General Psychiatry, 67*, 614–623.

Thrasher, S. M., Dalgleish, T., & Yule, W. (1994). Information processing in post-traumatic stress disorder. *Behaviour Research and Therapy, 32*, 247–254.

Tolin, D. F., & Foa, E. B. (2006). Sex differences in trauma and posttraumatic stress disorder: A quantitative review of 25 years of research. *Psychological Bulletin, 132*, 959–992.

True, W. R., Rice, J., Eisen, S. A., Heath, A. C., Goldberg, J., Lyons, M. J., & & Nowak, J. (1993). A twin study of genetic and environmental contributions to liability for posttraumatic stress symptoms. *Archives of General Psychiatry, 50*, 257–264.

van der Hart, O., & Nijenhuis, E. R. S. (2009). Dissociative disorders. In P. H. Blaney & T. Millon (Eds.), *Oxford textbook of psychopathology* (2nd ed., pp. 452–481). New York: Oxford University Press.

Weathers, F., Litz, B., Herman, D., Huska, J., & Keane, T. (1993, October). *The PTSD Checklist (PCL): Reliability, validity, and diagnostic utility*. Paper presented at the Annual Convention of the International Society for Traumatic Stress Studies, San Antonio, TX.

Williams, J. M. G., Barnhofer, T., Crane, C., Hermans, D., Raes, F., Watkins, E., & Dalgleish, T. (2007). Autobiographical memory specificity and emotional disorder. *Psychological Bulletin, 133*, 122–148.

Williams, J. M. G., Mathews, A., & MacLeod, C. (1996). The emotional Stroop task and psychopathology. *Psychological Bulletin, 120*, 3–24.

Woodward, S. H., Kaloupek, D. G., Streeter, C. C., Martinez, C., Schaer, M., & Eliez, S. (2006). Decreased anterior cingulate volume in combat-related PTSD. *Biological Psychiatry, 59*, 582–587.

Woon, F. L., Sood, S., & Hedges, D. W. (2010). Hippocampal volume deficits associated with exposure to psychological trauma and posttraumatic stress disorder in adults: A meta-analysis. *Progress in Neuropsychopharmacology & Biological Psychiatry, 34*, 1181–1188.

Yamasue, H., Kasai, K., Iwanami, A., Ohtani, T., Yamada, H., Abe, O.,…Kato, N. (2003). Voxel-based analysis of MRI reveals anterior cingulate gray-matter volume reduction in posttraumatic stress disorder due to terrorism. *Proceedings of the National Academy of Sciences USA, 100,* 9039–9043.

Yehuda, R. (2002). Post-traumatic stress disorder. *New England Journal of Medicine, 346,* 108–114.

Young, A. (1995). *The harmony of illusions: Inventing post-traumatic stress disorder.* Princeton, NJ: Princeton University Press.

Young, A. (2004). How narratives work in psychiatric science: An example from the biological psychiatry of PTSD. In B. Hurwitz, T. Greenhalgh, & V. Skultans (Eds.), *Narrative research in health and illness* (pp. 382–396). Oxford, UK: Blackwell.

8

Mood Disorders
Biological Bases

SHERI L. JOHNSON,

JOELLE LeMOULT,

W. MICHAEL VANDERLIND,

AND JUTTA JOORMANN

Mood disorders have been related to multiple neurobiological deficits, and these neurobiological correlates provide insight into the psychological processes and vulnerability involved in mood disorders. For example, mood disorders have been linked to deficits in dopamine (DA), serotonin, cortisol, and a set of brain pathways involved in regulating emotional responses. DA is involved in mobilization for the pursuit of rewards, whereas one of the functions of serotonin is to regulate emotion. Cortisol is integrally involved in stress responsivity and more generally plays an important role in individuals' adaptive response to environmental change. Neurobiological findings, then, provide insights into psychological facets that have been observed in both unipolar and bipolar disorder, such as heightened sensitivity to stressors, difficulties regulating initial emotional responses, and dysregulations in motivation for reward pursuit (see Chapter 9 in this volume for review of these in unipolar disorder, and Miklowitz & Johnson, 2006 for review of these in bipolar disorder).

Although many assume that neurobiological correlates of mood disorders can automatically be interpreted as vulnerability factors, it is worth challenging this assumption. The function of neurobiological systems, whether measured in neurotransmitter systems, hormonal systems, or structural or functional activity in key brain regions, represents the cumulative lifetime effect of innate vulnerability, environmental influences, and compensatory mechanisms within the brain. Trauma and severe stress, which are well documented as correlates of mood disorders (Bendall, Jackson, Hulbert, & McGorry, 2008; Brown & Harris, 1989; Wals et al., 2005), can lead to changes in the volume of the amygdala, prefrontal cortex, and hippocampus (Davidson & McEwen, 2012). That is, the functioning of these biological systems changes dramatically over the course of development and with life experiences.

Despite the dynamic nature of neurobiological function, the bulk of the neurobiological research is reliant on cross-sectional designs that aim to document deficits among currently ill persons. Such studies cannot distinguish basic vulnerability from responses to life experiences, state-dependent features of an episode, or scars left by previous episodes. Where possible, we will consider whether neurobiological deficits can be documented during remission and whether they predict the course of disorder. Studies that provide this degree of methodological sophistication help disentangle the state-like features of disorder from trait-like features. Beyond symptom status, even a 2-month trial of antidepressant medication can change neurobiological activity (Fu et al., 2004). Thus studies of unmedicated patients will be emphasized where available. Even these deficits observed among unmedicated and asymptomatic patients, though, could reflect scars of an episode, and so we will place particular emphasis on the few available studies of unaffected family members.

Within the mood disorders literature, most research has focused on the severe forms of depressive and bipolar disorders. Although the *DSM-5* defines several milder forms of disorders, such as dysthymic disorder, bipolar II disorder, and cyclothymia, very little research has been conducted on the neurobiology of these disorders. Hence, unless noted otherwise, we will focus on studies of major depressive disorder (MDD) within unipolar depression and of bipolar I disorder, defined on the basis of at least one lifetime episode of mania (which we will abbreviate as BD) within the bipolar spectrum disorders.

Many more studies focus on depression than on bipolar disorder, perhaps because depression is so much more common than bipolar disorder. Even with the explosion of BD diagnoses among children and youth (Zimmerman, Ruggero, Chelminski, & Young, 2008), current estimates suggest that MDD affects 17% of the population (Kessler et al., 2003) and BD affects about 1% of the population (Merikangas et al., 2007). Hence, each section in this chapter will begin with a summary of findings concerning MDD, followed by coverage of parallels and distinctions documented for BD.

Genes

Much of the interest in genetic models stems from the observation that family members of people with mood disorders are at increased risk for mood disorders compared to the general population. Although this phenomenon is well documented in MDD (Shih, Belmonte, & Zandi, 2004), elevations in risk are particularly striking within BD (Alda et al., 1997). For example, a meta-analysis of 17 studies suggested that children of BD parents are at a fourfold increased risk of mood disorders compared to children of parents without a psychiatric diagnosis (LaPalme, Hodgins, & LaRoche, 1997).These studies, though, do not provide clear estimates of the heritability of disorders, because environmental risk factors could contribute to the high rates of diagnoses observed among offspring.

Twin and adoption studies, then, are preferred methods for estimating the genetic contribution

to disorder. Twin studies typically compare the concordance levels of monozygotic (MZ) and dizygotic (DZ) twins in order to estimate three sources of variance contributing to the onset of disorder: genetic variance (heritability), shared environmental variance (environmental features that are experienced by both twins within a family), and nonshared (unique) environmental variance (environmental features that are dissimilar for twins within a family). Of concern in these models, the contributions of gene by environment interactions are often collapsed into genetic variance, potentially overestimating the direct role of genes (Rutter & Silberg, 2002).

Few adoption studies are available for MDD, and several of these studies have been plagued by methodological limitations such as unstructured diagnostic measures or small sample sizes. Despite these limitations, however, adoption studies generally support the idea that MDD is at least moderately heritable (Shih, Belmonte, & Zandi, 2004; Sullivan, Neale, & Kendler, 2000).

Large-scale twin studies are available in MDD. For example, Kendler and Prescott (1999), in a study of 3,000 twin pairs, estimated that 39% of the liability for MDD was genetic. In a meta-analysis of this study and four other carefully conducted twin studies of MDD, 37% of the variance in liability to depression was due to genetic factors (Sullivan, Neale, & Kendler, 2000). Across studies, only a negligible portion of the variance can be attributed to shared environmental effects; the bulk of the remaining variance appears to be due to the nonshared environment. The heritability estimates for adolescent MDD, .40, appear comparable to those identified in adult samples (Rice, 2010).

Results from twin studies suggest that BD is highly heritable. A Finnish community-based twin sample that used structured interviews to verify diagnoses obtained a heritability estimate of 93% (Kieseppa, Partonen, Haukka, Kaprio, & Lonnqvist, 2004). A similar British study yielded a heritability estimate for BD of 85% (McGuffin et al., 2003). For both of these studies, shared environmental effects were negligible. The few available adoption studies in BD also suggest high heritability (Wender et al., 1986).

A key question is the extent to which genetic vulnerability is specific to a disorder or operates more generally to increase risk for a set of disorders. Findings of twin studies suggest strong overlap in the genetic contribution to MDD and anxiety disorders, with particularly high overlap between MDD and generalized anxiety disorder (Kendler et al., 2003). First-degree relatives of BD probands are at increased risk for schizophrenia and schizoaffective disorder compared to the general population (Lichtenstein et al., 2009). Researchers have also consistently found that first-degree relatives of BD probands are at increased risk for MDD as well as BD (Smoller & Finn, 2003). In one twin study that directly modeled the overlap in heritability of MDD and BD, 71% of the genetic liability to mania was found to be distinct from that of depression (McGuffin et al., 2003). Hence, it appears that genetic contributions to BD are related to both schizophrenia and MDD, but that separable genetic contributions are also operative.

Genetic Region Studies

The human genome contains 46 chromosomes, each of which contains thousands of genes. Individual variation between people arises from the fact that many genes can take one of several different forms, or *alleles*. The term *polymorphism* refers to a variation in the DNA sequence that occurs at a particular spot, or genetic locus, on the chromosome. Researchers have used several different methodologies to study the genetic loci involved in mood disorders. In the most common approach, *association studies* examine correlations between the presence of a particular allele of a gene and the presence of mood disorders. Candidate gene studies tend to focus on a particular gene or small set of genes of interest, whereas gene-wide association (GWA) studies examine a broad set of the most common genetic loci.

Readers should be aware, however, of the large number of nonreplications within psychiatric genetic research. For example, in a meta-analysis of BD and MDD, Kato (2007) identified 166 genetic loci that had been linked with BD and MDD in initial studies and had been examined in at least three studies. Only 6 of the 166 had been replicated in more than 75% of relevant studies. Hence, positive findings should always be taken with a grain of salt, as nonreplications appear to be more common than replications.

Despite the complexities of this area, we will briefly note some of the research on the genes involved in serotonin and DA function, given the evidence described next on how these neurotransmitters are involved in mood disorders. We will also consider evidence regarding genes relevant to brain-derived neurotrophic factor (BDNF), which has been implicated in stressor-related cell death in key neural regions such as the hippocampus and prefrontal cortex, regions implicated in mood disorders.

Genes Related to Serotonin   One of the most frequently studied genetic loci is the serotonin transporter linked polymorphic region (5-HTTLPR). This gene affects the reuptake of serotonin from the synapse. The short allele results in relatively lower serotonin function and so has been considered as a risk factor. Meta-analyses suggest that this gene polymorphism is not directly related to MDD (Anguelova, Benkelfat, & Turecki, 2003). Nonetheless, the presence of the short allele may increase the risk for MDD diagnoses and symptoms in the context of life adversity. In an initial finding, those with the short allele appeared to be more reactive to life adversity (Caspi et al., 2003). Meta-analyses have confirmed that this polymorphism can increase risk of depression in the face of early childhood adversity (Karg, Burmeister, Shedden, & Sen, 2011) or major life events (Uher & McGuffin, 2010), with particularly strong findings when adversity or life events are carefully measured. One study found that the short allele increased reactivity to life stressors only among those who also had high levels of neuroticism (Jacobs et al., 2006). Overall, then, the literature suggests that the serotonin transporter gene may interact with environmental and psychological factors to increase risk of MDD. Although a range of other serotonin-relevant genetic loci have been studied in relation to MDD, findings have been somewhat mixed (Anguelova et al., 2003). Cross-study support has been obtained for a modest link between MDD and a polymorphism influencing tryptophan hydroxylase (TPH2), an enzyme that is critical to serotonin synthesis (Gao et al., 2012).

In regard to BD, the serotonin transporter region has been studied relatively extensively. Meta-analyses of the more than 20 studies of the serotonin transporter region in BD have yielded positive but small effects (e.g., Cho et al., 2005; Lasky-Su, Faraone, Glatt, & Tsuang, 2005). Unfortunately, researchers have not examined interactions of the serotonin transporter gene with environmental risk in predicting vulnerability to BD. Readers are referred to comprehensive reviews of the literature on genes and mood disorders (e.g., Kato, 2007; Lau & Eley, 2010).

Genes Related to DA   Many studies have tested for polymorphisms in the genes modulating the sensitivity of DA receptors among persons with mood disorders. For example, a large meta-analysis revealed a correlation between a polymorphism in the DRD4.2 gene and MDD (Lopez Leon et al., 2005).

Regarding BD, a large meta-analysis suggested a link with the A1 polymorphism of the e *Taq IA1* gene, which is related to dopamine synthesis (Zou et al., 2012). No consistent findings have emerged for polymorphisms in the D1, D3, and D4 receptor genes or the dopamine transporter genes (Georgieva et al., 2002; Lopez Leon et al., 2005; Manki et al., 1996).

Genes Related to Neuroplasticity and Cellular Processes   The BDNF *val66met* gene has been a major focus of research in the mood disorders, with dozens of large-scale studies now available. Meta-analyses have not confirmed an association of this gene with MDD (Verhagen et al., 2008) or BD (Kanazawa, Glatt, Kia-Keating, Yoneda, & Tsuang, 2007).

On the other hand, researchers have consistently found evidence implicating variants of the *ANK3* gene in the vulnerability to BD (Smith et al., 2009). ANK3, a protein that is concentrated in the axons of neurons, has been shown to be an important determinant of firing rate of neurons.

Summary of Research on Gene Loci   Researchers have identified polymorphisms in the serotonin transporter gene that seem to increase risk of MDD in the context of life adversities and have found links of DRD4.2 with MDD. There is evidence that BD is modestly related to polymorphisms in the serotonin transporter gene, and variants of the *ANK1* gene. Nonetheless, the effect sizes documented have been quite small, and many genetic findings have failed to replicate. Mood disorders are likely to be due to the interactive effects of many genes, each of which explains a very small proportion of the variance.

There are several other reasons why effect sizes may be so small. Genes are likely operative within the context of key environmental risk factors; that is, a gene might be "expressed" in certain contexts. This

is perhaps best illustrated by the findings that the serotonin transporter gene is related to higher risk of depression among persons exposed to life adversity. It is also clear that ethnic groups differ in the rates of polymorphisms (Chiao & Blizinsky, 2010).

Finally, genetic polymorphisms are not likely to be directly expressed as disorders. Recognition of this issue has resulted in a recent push to investigate endophenotypes—more basic traits that may themselves serve as risk factors for psychological disorders but are presumed to capture a more fundamental vulnerability. Examples of potential endophenotypes relevant to mood disorders include tendencies toward negative mood, diminished responsivity to reward, and increased sensitivity to stress, vulnerability to circadian rhythm disruption, and neurocognitive deficits (Hasler, Drevets, Gould, Gottesman, & Manji, 2006). Each of these has a substantial heritable component, and each in turn is related to mood disorders. Endophenotypes may represent a pivotal intermediate step in the causal chain between specific genes and full-blown disorder. Next, we turn to a discussion of research on neurotransmitters, neuroendocrine function, and neuroimaging.

Neurotransmitters

Mood disorders research has tended to focus on serotonin and the catecholamines, DA and norepinephrine (NE). It was originally hypothesized that catecholamine levels were low during depression and high during mania. Serotonin was hypothesized to regulate overly high or overly low levels of the catecholamines. In accord with this idea, low serotonin was postulated to play a role in increasing risk for depression or mania.

Interest in neurotransmitter models of MDD and BD was initially fueled by the responsiveness of these conditions to medication treatments. Indeed, effective antidepressants enhance the functioning of serotonin and DA (Goodwin & Jamison, 2007). Early studies also found that reserpine, which releases amines into the synaptic cleft and thereby depletes serotonin, DA, and NE, produced symptoms of depression (Freis, 1954; Muller, Pryor, Gibbons, & Orgain, 1955), with particularly strong effects among those with a history of depression (Goodwin & Bunney, 1971).

Much of the early research on neurotransmitters focused on whether neurotransmitter levels were high or low among mood disorder samples compared to nondisturbed control samples. Most commonly, researchers assessed levels of *metabolites*, chemicals formed from the breakdown of neurotransmitters after they are released into the synaptic cleft (see Table 8.1). Unfortunately, much of the neurotransmitter research has considered plasma and urine metabolites, but such levels are poorly correlated with cerebrospinal fluid (CSF) levels of a neurotransmitter. A broader issue, though, is that neurotransmitter availability is only one component of the function of the neurotransmitter system. Consider that effective neuronal signaling involves receptors that respond to the presence of neurotransmitter in the synaptic cleft, the membranes and intracellular mechanisms that carry a signal from the receptor through the neuron to the dendrites for release of neurotransmitter, and removal of the neurotransmitter from the cleft after it has been released from the neuron. People may vary in the sensitivity and density of receptors, the function of neuronal membranes, the efficiency of metabolizing neurotransmitters in the cleft, and the rapidity of reuptake of neurotransmitter from the cleft. Availability of neurotransmitters is dependent on dietary intake of amino acids, efficiency of the cell in producing more neurotransmitter, and history of the cell firing (and thereby depleting available stores). Over time, cellular processes fine-tune the sensitivity of the receptors. For example, cell nuclei that are receiving frequent signals may trigger second messengers to tune the receptor sensitivity. In sum, many points exist in the process of neuronal signaling.

Beyond the multiple aspects of neuronal function, each neurotransmitter system is complex. For example, the serotonin and DA systems both involve different types of receptors, some of which are inhibitory and some of which are excitatory

(see Table 8.1). The density of receptor subtypes differs across the multiple serotonin and DA pathways in the brain.

A growing body of work focuses on understanding specific neuronal processes, such as efficiency of reuptake of neurotransmitters from the cleft or second-messenger processes. Single-photon emission computed tomography (SPECT) or positron emission tomography (PET) imaging can be used to assay specific components of neurotransmitter systems. In both SPECT and PET, participants are administered a radioactive tracer that binds to specific tissues, forming a radioligand. The concentration of radioligands in various brain regions can be detected by a gamma-camera, and then compared across participants or groups to assay neurotransmitter synthesis, storage, transporter (reuptake), and receptor function. Although tracers are not available for all facets of neurotransmitter function or receptor subtypes, a growing number are available for many of these aspects of the dopamine and serotonin systems. These imaging modalities assay specific facets of neurotransmitter pathways and receptor subtypes that are believed to relate to depression and mania.

An alternate research approach is to consider the overall functioning of the system. Drug challenge studies provide a means to do this. In these studies, neurotransmitter levels are experimentally manipulated, and researchers examine whether people with MDD or BD are more reactive to changes in the neurotransmitter system. Although drug challenge paradigms are helpful in understanding whether the function of a neurotransmitter system is impaired, they do not provide information on specific pathways within the serotonin system or DA system.

Undoubtedly, mood disorders will be related to interactions of multiple neurotransmitters and cellular processes. Review of the interactive and synergistic mechanisms is beyond the scope of this review (see Stockmeier, 2003).

Table 8.1 Major Metabolites and Receptor Families of Key Neurotransmitters

Neurotransmitter Subtypes	Metabolite	Major Receptors Studied in Mood Disorders
Norepinephrine	3-methoxy-4-hydroxy-phenlyglycol (MHPG)	β1, β2, α1, α2
Serotonin	5-hydroxy-indoleacetic acid (5-HIAA)	5-HT1A and 5-HT2
Dopamine	homovanillic acid (HVA)	D1 and D2

Serotonin

Serotonergic neurons originate in the raphe nucleus and are widely distributed through the brain. There are multiple serotonergic pathways in the brain, some of which are involved in mood, sleep, and appetite. Beyond these functions, serotonin appears to play a key role in cognitive control over emotion-relevant stimuli (see Carver, Johnson, & Joormann, 2008, for more discussion of this theory).

Researchers have used many different paradigms to study the serotonin system, including administration of pharmacological agents that temporarily increase serotonin levels and techniques for depleting serotonin levels. Serotonin neurons that project from the raphe to the hypothalamus trigger release of prolactin. Hence, one way to measure the responsivity of the serotonin system is by administering a drug that increases serotonin levels and then measuring prolactin responses.

Beyond studies of increased serotonin availability, there have been many studies examining the consequences of diminishing serotonin availability, typically by reducing levels of tryptophan, a serotonin precursor. In acute tryptophan depletion (ATD), persons are asked to drink a milkshake that is rich in 15 amino acids other than tryptophan, aspartic acid, and glutamic acid (Moore et al., 2000). As biological processes are engaged in processing the other amino acids, tryptophan is depleted, leading to several hour acute reduction in serotonin by 10% to 50%. Milkshakes that contain tryptophan have no effect on serotonin and so provide a control comparison. Assays are typically conducted to confirm the expected changes in tryptophan levels.

Findings of several ATD studies support the idea that serotonin improves cognitive control over emotionally based responses, particularly among vulnerable individuals. For example, Munafò, Hayward, and Harmer (2006) found that ATD led to increased attention to negative words on the emotion Stroop task among remitted depressed persons. Healthy control participants did not demonstrate cognitive changes after ATD. Hence, serotonin may facilitate the ability to inhibit attention to negative stimuli (see Carver et al., 2008, for review).

Serotonin Studies in MDD   Studies that assess prolactin response to increases in serotonin

demonstrate blunted responsivity among persons with current MDD (Cowen, 2002), as well as among persons who have recovered from MDD and those who are unmedicated (Bhagwagar, Whale, & Cowen, 2002; Flory, Mann, Manuck, & Muldoon, 1998). This blunted response is believed to be secondary to poor sensitivity of serotonergic receptors (Price et al., 1997).

ATD studies also suggest that depression is associated with diminished function of the serotonin system. Although ATD has little effect on mood or depressive symptoms among persons with no personal or family history of depression, ATD leads to a temporary return of depressive symptoms among persons with a history of depression. This effect appears among persons taking antidepressants (Booij et al., 2005; Delgado et al., 1999) as well as those who are medication-free (Flory et al., 1998; Neumeister et al., 2006). These ATD effects do not appear to be a scar from previous episodes. That is, first-degree relatives of persons with depression also appear to experience more negative affect and depressive symptoms after ATD than do those with no family history of depression (Benkelfat, Ellenbogen, Dean, Palmour, & Young, 1994; Neumeister et al., 2002). It has been hypothesized that the ATD findings reflect diminished sensitivity of serotonin receptors (Sobczak, Honig, van Duinen, & Riedel, 2002).

One caveat concerning the serotonin model of MDD is that PET studies have not provided consistent evidence for this model (Nikolaus, Antke, & Muller, 2009). Some of the cross-study discrepancies may relate to changes in serotonin function that occur with administration of medication, in that few PET studies have examined medication-naive participants.

Serotonin Studies in BD   As with MDD, multiple studies have considered the role of serotonin in BD. There is some evidence from imaging studies of diminished serotonin transmission among persons diagnosed with BD, although findings appear to be localized to certain regions of the brain (Nikolaus et al., 2009).

Several studies have examined the effects of serotonin challenges on unmedicated people with BD (see Sobczak et al., 2002 for review). Four out of seven studies have suggested that people with BD depression, like those with MDD, demonstrate blunted responses to agents that increase the availability of serotonin. This pattern has also been observed among persons with BD during well periods (Nurnberger, Berrettini, Simmons-Alling, Lawrence, & Brittain, 1990).

Research has also examined ATD among family members of persons with BD. Compared to matched controls, first-degree relatives of those with BD demonstrate elevated mood reactions and more of a decline in neurocognitive tasks after ATD (Sobczak, Honig, Nicolson, & Riedel, 1999; Sobczak et al., 2002).

Summary of Serotonin Findings   Findings suggest that both MD and BD are related to deficits in serotonin function: People vulnerable to depression and mania appear to be overly sensitive to diminished serotonin levels, and they show blunted responses to increases in serotonin. It is believed that these deficits are due to poor sensitivity of serotonin receptors, although neuroimaging studies of serotonin function have not provided consistent support for this model.

Serotonin is widely believed to help regulate a broad range of other systems in the brain. Evidence exists that serotonin is involved in regulating fluctuations in DA within the reward pathway (Navailles, Moison, Cunningham, & Spampinato, 2008) and inhibiting NE (Baumgarten & Grozdanovic, 1995). Next, we review the evidence concerning dysregulation of NE and DA among persons with mood disorders.

Norepinephrine

Norepinephrine (NE) pathways originate in the locus coeruleus and project to structures throughout the brain, including subcortical regions as well as most cortical areas (Ressler & Nemeroff, 1999). NE is released in response to stress and helps to promote general arousal, focused attention, improved concentration, and memory consolidation (Ressler & Nemeroff, 1999). At high levels, NE promotes fear and anxiety.

NE function is influenced by psychomotor activity levels, as well as by all established antidepressants (Ressler & Nemeroff, 1999). Moreover, NE neurons have bidirectional links with serotonergic and DA pathways (Ressler & Nemeroff, 1999). There is strong feedback from the cortisol system (discussed later) into the NE system. Animal research has demonstrated that chronic stress can diminish the density of NE axons in the

cortex (Kitayama et al., 1994). The function of the NE system is then highly dependent on levels of acute stress as well as on cumulative lifetime exposure to stress. As NE operates as one part of a stress-response system, some have argued that NE deficits reflect a consequence of stress and depressive symptoms rather than a risk variable.

Findings regarding NE have not been consistent. Low NE levels have been more consistently observed within BD depression than MDD (Ressler & Nemeroff, 1999), but this could reflect lower rates of antidepressant administration for people with BD. Indeed, when lifetime recurrence rates and severity are carefully controlled, people with BD and MDD appear relatively matched in NE levels during depressive periods (Altshuler et al, 1995; Schatzberg & Schildkraut, 1995). Studies have been fairly consistent in documenting high NE among manic patients, but it is not clear if this reflects the heightened arousal and activity.

Whereas the foregoing research simply considered levels of NE metabolites, more sophisticated research has used two pharmacological paradigms: one in which NE production is lowered, the other in which NE receptors are stimulated. To lower NE production, researchers have used medications that diminish tyrosine hydroxylase (TH), a critical enzyme for the synthesis of NE. Early research demonstrated that medications that diminished TH produced symptoms of depression among people with a history of depression (Delgado et al., 1993) but not among people with no depression history (Heninger, Delgado, & Charney, 1996). Among people with a history of depression, findings appeared to be specific to those taking antidepressants that target NE; results have not been consistent regarding the effects of NE depletion among unmedicated people who have recovered from depression (Heninger et al., 1996). Hence, it might be that NE deficits are most important among people whose treatment has involved NE manipulation. Other research has suggested that adequate NE levels are needed for effective antidepressant action (Charney, 1998). These findings suggest that NE is more intricately involved in treatment response than in the etiology of disorder.

Other research has focused on the sensitivity of one of the NE receptor subtypes, the α_2 receptor. When α_2 receptors are stimulated, through a medication such as clonidine, growth hormone–releasing hormone is increased. Studies have suggested that depressed persons show less of a growth-hormone release in response to clonidine than do those without depression (Schatzberg & Schildkraut, 1995). This is consistent with the idea of a diminished sensitivity of one specific subtype of NE receptor.

One current theory is that NE changes occur with depressive and manic states, but that these changes are part of stress-related responses. It is thought that adequate function of NE is needed for effective antidepressant treatment and that for most people, NE may play a role in the maintenance of depressive symptoms more than in the initiation of symptoms (Ressler & Nemeroff, 1999).

Dopamine (DA)

Patients with Parkinson's disease and Huntington's chorea, both of which involve DA deficits, are at substantially increased risk of depression (Rogers, Bradshaw, Pantelis, & Phillips, 1998). Substantial research suggests that DA levels are reduced during both MDD and BD depression. Diminished CSF levels of the DA metabolite homovanillic acid (HVA) have been found among persons experiencing MDD (Dunlop & Nemeroff, 2007) and BD (Goodwin & Jamison, 2007). A major review suggested that BD depression is related to dopaminergic function as low as that observed in unipolar depression (Yatham, Srisurapanont, Zis, & Kusumakar, 1997).

SPECT imaging can provide an assay of more specific processes within the dopamine system. One key facet of the system is dopamine transporter (DAT binding) binding which influences reuptake of dopamine into the presynaptic cell after release. Lower DAT binding has been observed in conditions with decrements in dopamine function, such as Parkinson's disease (Antonini et al., 2003). DAT binding has been found to be diminished among persons experiencing current MDD in some studies (Hsiao, Lin, Liu, & Beck Schatz, 2013) and heightened among remitted patients with BD (see Nikolaus et al., 2009).

Other studies have experimentally manipulated DA levels. To increase DA, researchers have administered bromocriptine, a DA agonist. Several early studies suggested that bromocriptine provided relief from depressive symptoms (although side effects prevented this from being a feasible treatment for wide use; McGrath, Quitkin, & Klein, 1995; Nordin, Siwers, & Bertilsson, 1981).

Beyond relief from depression, multiple studies have suggested that DA agonists trigger manic symptoms (cf. McGrath et al., 1995; Willner, 1995). Manic symptoms in response to amphetamine, which releases catecholamines into the synaptic cleft, are more pronounced among people with BD than among healthy control participants (Anand et al., 2000).

The DA system involves a set of pathways. One of these is considered particularly important for mood disorders: The mesolimbic pathway, a tract from the ventral tegmental area with projections to the nucleus accumbens, amygdala, hippocampus, thalamus, and cingulate gyrus (Naranjo, Tremblay, & Buston, 2001). This pathway is believed to facilitate motivation and energy in the context of opportunities for reward (Salamone, Correa, Farrar, & Mingote 2007). Increased function of the mesolimbic dopamine pathway would be expected to correlate with energy, positive mood, and goal pursuit. Animal research has long implicated deficits in reward pathways in behaviors that mimic depressive symptoms, such as diminished motivation, apathy, and poor appetite (Nestler & Carlezon, 2006; Treadway & Zald, 2011). Similarly, theorists have reviewed the strong parallels between symptoms of acute mania and the types of behavior associated with overactivity of these systems (Depue & Iacono, 1989; Fowles, 1993).

Behavioral sensitization paradigms provide one way to study the mesolimbic DA pathway, and these paradigms have been applied in BD. With repeated intermittent doses of psychomotor stimulants (administered at specific intervals and doses), animals and humans develop increased behavioral responsiveness to stimulants (Sax & Strakowski, 2001). Animal research suggests that this increased sensitivity appears to be a result of more sustained release of DA within reward pathways (Kalivas, Duffy, DuMars, & Skinner, 1988). Hence, repeated exposure to medications that release DA may create greater sensitivity of reward pathways over time. First-episode patients with BD and schizophrenia demonstrate less behavioral sensitization (less behavioral change with repeated doses) than do those not diagnosed with these disorders. This finding has been interpreted as evidence that reward pathways might already be sensitized among people with BD (Strakowski, Sax, Setters, Stanton, & Keck, 1997). Findings such as these suggest the merit of examining second-messenger systems, which guide calibration of cellular responsivity in response to neuronal firing rates. Several studies suggest that aspects of second-messenger systems related to dopamine are disrupted in BD (Cousins, Butts, & Young, 2009).

Summary of Neurotransmitter Research

In sum, deficits in serotonin appear well documented in MDD and BD, and these might lead to poor cognitive, behavioral, and emotional control over responses to emotion stimuli. Serotonin also plays a key role in regulating DA function, and accordingly, depression and mania may both be related to dysregulation of the DA system. That is, increases in DA can trigger mania, and decreases in DA can trigger depression. NE disruptions may be secondary to stress responses, and restoration of NE function may affect treatment response.

Neuroendocrinology

Neuroendocrinology—the study of interactions between the endocrine and nervous systems—is critical to our understanding of both MDD and BD (e.g., Cervantes, Gelber, Ng Ying Kin, Nair, & Schwartz, 2001; Knorr, Vinberg, Kessing, & Wetterslev, 2010). A central component of the neuroendocrine system is the hypothalamic–pituitary–adrenal (HPA) axis. The complex interactions among the hypothalamus, pituitary gland, and adrenal gland play a central role in facilitating adaptive responses to changes in the environment. The hypothalamus releases corticotrophin-releasing hormone (CRH), which is transported by blood vessels to the pituitary gland and triggers the release of adrenocorticotropic hormone (ACTH). ACTH is transported by the blood to the adrenal gland where it rapidly stimulates biosynthesis of the glucocorticoid hormone, cortisol (see Figure 8.1).

Cortisol is often viewed as the primary marker of HPA axis activity. It is produced spontaneously throughout the day and is increased during challenges (Jones, Bright, & Chow, 2001). Cortisol, and the HPA axis more broadly, activate physical and psychological resources needed when responding to and recovering from stress and challenge (Miller & O'Callaghan, 2002). Direct administration of CRH in laboratory animals,

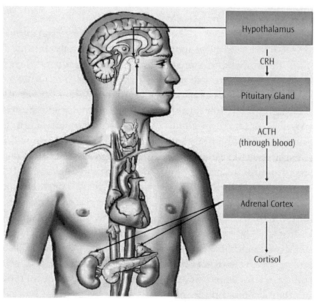

Figure 8.1 The hypothalamic–pituitary–adrenal axis (HPA axis). LifeART image copyright 2013/ca210001 Wolters Kluwer Health, Inc. Lippincott Williams & Wilkins. All rights reserved.

for example, stimulates the sympathetic nervous system (Arborelius, Owens, Plotsky, & Nemeroff, 1999). This leads to physiological changes such as increased blood pressure and heart rate that prepare people to cope with stress. Psychologically, cortisol levels have been shown to correlate with experiences of subjective stress and negative emotional states (Dickerson & Kemeny, 2004), particularly shame (Ramsay & Lewis, 2003).

The amygdala and hippocampus, two brain regions with major roles in processing emotion-relevant stimuli, have been associated with HPA axis functioning (Sullivan et al., 2004). The amygdala signals the hypothalamus to release CRH, thereby activating cortisol production. In contrast, the hippocampus down-regulates cortisol production. Together with receptors on the pituitary and hypothalamus, glucocorticoid and mineralocorticoid receptors in the hippocampus detect high cortisol levels and signal the HPA axis to decrease cortisol production. This negative feedback loop is critical to diminishing both basal cortisol and poststressor cortisol levels (Young, Haskett, Murphy-Weinberg, Watson & Akil, 1991).

The HPA axis affects many aspects of bodily function, including metabolism, immune function, and the endocrine system more broadly (e.g., Ader, Cohen, & Felten, 1995; Sapolsky, Romero, & Munck, 2000). Each of these systems interact bidirectionally. For example, cortisol affects the production of cytokines, messenger molecules that regulate immune responses (see Tsigos & Chrousos, 2002, for review). In turn, proinflammatory cytokines contribute to heightened cortisol levels by triggering activation of the HPA axis (Tsigos & Chrousos, 2002) as well as diminishing the effectiveness of the HPA negative feedback loop (Schiepers, Wichers, & Maes, 2004). Details on interactions between the endocrine, immune, and nervous systems are beyond the scope of this chapter, and readers are referred to comprehensive reviews of the topic (Slavich & Irwin, 2014; Tsigos & Chrousos, 2002).

Whereas moderate cortisol levels and responses to stress represent an adaptive and necessary response to environmental changes, excess cortisol production, stemming from chronic HPA axis activation or faulty negative feedback loops, can disrupt emotion regulation and coping (McEwen, 2008) and can damage key brain regions implicated in mood disorders (Dedovic, Duchesne, Andrews, Engert, & Pruessner, 2009). For example, the hippocampus is a brain region with a high density of glucocorticoid receptors, and increased cortisol secretion has been shown to lead to neurotoxicity in this area (Sapolsky, 2000). Excess cortisol production can also disrupt functioning in key emotion-relevant regions of the brain (e.g., the prefrontal cortex and amygdala) and can thus interfere with the ability to cope effectively with stress (Schuhmacher et al., 2012). Moreover, increasing evidence demonstrates substantial consequences of HPA axis dysregulation on cardiovascular health, immune functioning, and cognition (Hinkelmann et al., 2009; Kiecolt-Glaser, McGuire, Robles, & Glaser, 2002).

Cortisol Parameters

Researchers have studied three major facets of HPA activity in the mood disorders: basal cortisol levels, cortisol reactivity to laboratory or naturalistic stressors, and HPA responses to pharmacological challenges. We will briefly describe each, and then review evidence regarding these three types of cortisol dysfunction in mood disorders.

Cortisol is released spontaneously throughout the day (Lovallo & Thomas, 2000). Spontaneous cortisol production has a strong diurnal rhythm. In healthy individuals, cortisol levels rise rapidly after wakening and reach a peak within 30–45 minutes, called the *cortisol awakening response (CAR)*. They then gradually fall throughout the day until late afternoon, when the decline is interrupted by a brief spike. The CAR is believed to prepare the body to transition from sleep to wakefulness. Basal cortisol levels—i.e., measures of naturally occurring cortisol at a given point during the day—are thought to be influenced by baseline physiological and emotional arousal (Lovallo & Thomas, 2000).

In a second commonly used approach, researchers measure cortisol responses to naturally occurring (Peeters, Nicholson, & Berkhof, 2003) or standardized laboratory stressors. Laboratory paradigms include cognitive stress tasks (e.g., anagrams or difficult arithmetic problems) or the Trier Social Stress Test, in which participants deliver a speech and perform mental arithmetic in front of an audience (Kirschbaum, Pirke, & Hellhammer, 1993). In stress studies, cortisol reactivity and recovery levels poststress are contrasted with a baseline period.

A third facet of HPA axis dysregulation is measured using the dexamethasone suppression test (DST). Some researchers attribute the over-production of cortisol to faulty negative feedback mechanisms (Porter & Gallagher, 2006), and the DST is one way to measure functioning of this feedback system. Dexamethasone acts on the pituitary gland to suppress the release of ACTH, such that the adrenal gland releases less cortisol. After dexamethasone injection, healthy individuals show lower cortisol. Failure to suppress cortisol secretion after dexamethasone injection indicates impaired feedback regulation at the pituitary gland and hyperactivity of the HPA axis (Carroll, 1982). Dexamethasone administration can be administered alone, known as the CRH challenge test, or it can be coupled with an injection of CRH, known as the dex/CRH test. Both tests provide a window into the function of the HPA axis in response to a challenge. In considering DST, though, it is important to note that these methods have been criticized because dexamethasone does not cross the blood–brain barrier, and the levels of dexamethasone used during these tests far exceed naturalistically occurring levels (Carroll et al., 1981).

We now turn to evidence that both MDD and BD are linked to disruptions in the function of the HPA axis. Readers should be aware, however, of the substantial inconsistencies within this field. Inconsistencies have been attributed to the severity or subtype of depression, medication use, comorbid anxiety or medical conditions, personality factors such as neuroticism, and variations in methodological rigor. Whenever possible, meta-analytic results are presented; however, these too should be interpreted with caution given the inherent publication bias associated with positive findings.

Neuroendocrine Findings in MDD

Although findings of individual studies on basal HPA activity have been inconsistent, results from several meta-analyses suggest that people with MDD have higher baseline cortisol values compared to their nondepressed counterparts, particularly in the afternoon (Knorr et al. 2010; Stetler & Miller, 2011). Fewer studies have examined the more specific CAR. Many of these studies show an increased CAR in MDD (Bhagwagar, Hafizi, & Cowen, 2005; Vreeburg et al., 2009); however, some findings have suggested that MDD is associated with a blunted CAR (Huber, Issa, Schik, & Wolf, 2006; Stetler & Miller, 2005).

In regard to acute stress reactivity, a meta-analysis of seven studies indicated that depressed individuals exhibit less cortisol reactivity in response to stress and slower cortisol recovery poststress compared to nondepressed individuals (Burke, Davis, Otte, & Mohr, 2005). The profile of blunted cortisol stress reactivity appears most pronounced among older and more severely depressed participants (Burke et al., 2005) and among those with chronic MDD (Booij, Bouma, de Jonge, Ormel, & Oldehinkel, 2013).

Many patients with depression fail to exhibit the usual suppression of cortisol production in response to the DST (see Stetler & Miller, 2011, for a meta-analysis) or dex/CRH test (see Mokhtari, Arfken, & Boutro, 2013, for a meta-analysis). Despite the overall profile of findings, some heterogeneity of results has been observed. Cortisol nonsuppression is more commonly found among people with psychotic depression and, when present, predicts a more severe course (see Arana, Baldessarini, & Ornsteen, 1985, for review).

As noted earlier, proinflammatory cytokines can both trigger HPA axis activation and hinder effective HPA axis feedback loops (see Pariante, 2004, for review). In a meta-analysis, higher levels of proinflammatory cytokines, especially tumor necrosis factor (TNF)-α and interleukin (IL)-6, were observed in MDD (Dowlati et al., 2010), potentially contributing to the heightened basal cortisol levels seen among some people with MDD.

Studies have also been conducted to examine whether cortisol dysregulation is only observed during ill periods. Findings of one meta-analyses indicate that 56% of participants demonstrated similar cortisol levels from pre- to posttreatment, with no significant difference between those who did and did not respond to treatment (McKay & Zakzanis, 2010).

Beyond the potential for state-dependent and treatment effects, another concern is that HPA axis dysfunction could reflect the cumulative lifetime effect of stressors and depressive episodes. To test this, investigators have assessed HPA axis functioning in samples of depressed children. Parallel with findings among adults, findings of a meta-analysis indicated that compared to children without depression, children with depression showed higher basal cortisol levels, less suppression of cortisol production after DST, and elevated cortisol secretion in response to acute laboratory stressors (Lopez-Duran, Kovacs, & George, 2009). One caveat, though, is that cortisol reactivity to stress may depend on pubertal development. In one study of dysphoric youth, prepubertal children exhibited cortisol hyporeactivity to laboratory stressors, whereas postpubertal adolescents displayed hyperreactivity (Hankin, Badanes, Abela, & Watamura, 2010).

There is some evidence that HPA axis dysregulation can also be documented among at-risk samples of nondepressed infants, children, and adolescents with a family history of depression (see Guerry & Hastings, 2011, for a review). Evidence for elevated basil cortisol levels in at-risk offspring is most consistent; however, some studies have also found excess cortisol secretion in response to a laboratory stressor among nondepressed children whose parents had a history of depression (Ashman, Dawson, Panagiotides, Yamada, & Wilkinson, 2002; Feldman et al., 2009).

Given that not all persons with MDD or at risk for MDD demonstrate cortisol abnormalities, a key question is whether cortisol parameters can predict the course of depression. Among remitted participants, elevated cortisol responses to the dex/CRH test (Aubry et al., 2007; Zobel et al., 2001; Zobel, Yassouridis, Frieboes, & Holsboer, 1999) and larger cortisol responses to stress (Morris, Rao, & Garber, 2012) predict worsening of depressive symptoms over the next 6–12 months. Different cortisol parameters have been found to be predictive in younger samples. Rao et al. (1996) found that elevations in evening cortisol predicted a recurrent course of the disorder at a 7-year follow-up assessment within the sample of depressed adolescents. Cortisol dysregulation has also been found to predict the development of depressive symptoms among those at risk for the disorder by virtue family history (see Guerry & Hastings, 2011, for review). More specifically, elevated morning (Goodyer, Herbert, Tamplin, & Altham, 2000) and evening cortisol levels (Essex, Klein, Cho, & Kalin, 2002; Halligan, Herbert, Goodyer, & Murray, 2007) predicted future mental health difficulties in at-risk children.

Beyond prospective research, several researchers have begun to examine the interplay between genetic and neuroendocrine factors. Polymorphisms in BDNF and 5-HTTLPR genes have been shown to influence HPA axis activity and stress-related outcomes (Goodyer, Croudace, Dudbridge, Ban, & Herbert, 2010). For example, participants homozygous for the short 5-HTTLPR allele who had experienced significant stressful life events exhibited cortisol hyperreactivity to stress (Alexander et al., 2009). At-risk individuals homozygous for the short 5-HTTLPR allele with elevated morning cortisol levels were more likely to experience a future depressive episode (Goodyer, Bacon, Ban, Croudace, & Herbert, 2009).

Taken together, findings suggest the HPA axis is dysregulated in depression, that such dysregulation is related to many other key risk factors for depression. These findings dovetail well with the extensive literature linking stress and depression.

Neuroendocrine Findings in BD

Research examining HPA axis functioning in patients with BD is growing, yet results remain more mixed than for MDD, and meta-analyses are not available. Several studies have found increased basal cortisol levels during both depressed and hypomanic episodes compared to controls (e.g., Cervantes et al., 2001). Other studies, however, suggest no group effects (Watson, Gallagher, Ritchie, Ferrier, & Young, 2004) or lower plasma cortisol levels among those experiencing a first manic episode (Valiengo et al., 2012).

Despite inconsistencies in the adult literature, elevated baseline cortisol levels during the afternoon have been observed more consistently among unaffected adolescents who have a parent diagnosed with BD (Ellenbogen, Hodgins, & Walker, 2004; Ellenbogen, Hodgins, Walker, Couture, & Adam, 2006), although this pattern appears more consistent among the adolescents who are less quarrelsome (Ellenbogen et al., 2013). The elevated afternoon cortisol levels observed in this sample were found to persist into late adolescence and young adulthood (Ellenbogen, Santo, Linnen, Walker, & Hodgins, 2010) and to predict the onset of a mood disorder (Ellenbogen, Hodgins, Linnen, & Ostiguy, 2011).

Results from the dex/CRH test clearly suggest a dysregulated negative feedback system among persons with BD (e.g., Watson, Gallagher, et al., 2004; Watson, Thompson, Ritchie, Ferrier, & Young, 2006) and in rapid-cycling BD regardless of mood state (Watson, Gallagher, et al., 2004; Watson, Thompson, Malik, Ferrier, & Young, 2004). Abnormal DST results are more reliably observed in BD depression than MDD (Rush, Giles, Schlesser, & Orsulak, 1997). Higher levels of ACTH after CRH administration were found to predict future manic episodes among euthymic BD participants (Vieta et al., 1999).

Proinflammatory cytokines, which are centrally involved in HPA axis dysregulation, have also been examined in BD (see Duffy, Lewitzka, Doucette, Andreazza, & Grof, 2012, for review). Compared to controls, an excess of proinflammatory cytokines have been found among people with BD who were currently manic (Kim, Jung, Myint, Kim, & Park, 2007) and currently depressed (O'Brien, Scully, Scott, & Dinan, 2006).

Summary of Neuroendocrine Findings across MDD and BD

Multiple studies indicate that functioning of the HPA axis is abnormal in MDD and BD. There are, however, many inconsistencies in the literature, which has been attributed to divergent methodologies and samples. Across both disorders, pharmacological challenge studies provide the most consistent evidence for a deficit, indicating that negative feedback mechanisms responsible for maintaining homeostatic levels of cortisol are impaired among those with mood disorders. Although sparse, research on remitted and at-risk populations also suggests that abnormalities in the HPA axis precede and influence the course of depressive or manic symptoms. Moreover, genetic factors appear to increase vulnerability to HPA axis dysregulation.

Diurnal cortisol secretion and stress-induced HPA axis activation represent adaptive responses to environmental changes. There are significant effects, however, of chronic cortisol elevation, including degeneration of glucocorticoid receptors in the hippocampus and possible hippocampal atrophy, further perpetuating the impaired HPA feedback mechanisms (Lee, Ogle, & Sapolsky, 2002; Stokes, 1995). Continued stress exposure may also negatively influence the serotonin system, which appears to reduce stress adaptation and subsequently increase vulnerability to depression. Studies suggest that there may be critical periods early in life when glucocorticoid receptors may be more susceptible (as reviewed in Heim & Nemeroff, 2001). Exposure to adversity, trauma, or abuse in childhood may promote abnormalities in HPA axis functioning that result in altered responses to later stressors. This may explain why early stressful life events are often associated with substantial heightened vulnerability to later depression. Future research is needed, however, to better understand these developmental processes and to clearly identify how dysfunctions in the HPA system contribute to the onset, maintenance, and recurrence of affective disorders.

Brain Region Research

As noted in Chapter 4, neuroimaging technology provides a way to examine the structural and functional brain correlates of affective disorders. Whereas magnetic resonance imaging (MRI) allows researchers to study the density and volume of brain regions (the structure), functional imaging allows researchers to study how activity within brain regions changes during specific time periods or tasks. One of the first functional neuroimaging techniques was PET. Researchers can use tracers that bind to analogues of glucose to measure metabolic activity in brain regions. The main disadvantages of PET, however, are that images are acquired slowly over the course of minutes, and the spatial resolution is poor (about 1 cm). As such, researchers have focused more on functional magnetic resonance imaging (fMRI) recently, which localizes brain activity on a second-by-second basis and within millimeters. fMRI studies measure changes in blood oxygenation level in a brain region. When nerve cells are active, they consume oxygen. The blood oxygen level–dependent (BOLD) contrast compares differences in oxygenation over time as individuals complete tasks such as viewing emotion-relevant stimuli compared to neutral stimuli Higher BOLD signal intensities arise from decreases in the concentration of deoxygenated hemoglobin.

Brain Regions Involved in Emotion

MDD and BD are considered to be disorders of emotion and its regulation. Consequently, brain areas and neural circuits that have been associated with the generation and regulation of emotional states have received much attention in research on affective disorders (see Davidson, Pizzagalli, & Nitschke, 2009, for a review). Over the past decade, theorists have posited that emotional behavior is linked to the functioning of two neural systems, a ventral system and a dorsal system (see Figure 8.2). The *ventral system* involves brain regions that are important for identifying the emotional significance of a stimulus and producing affect; the *dorsal system* is important for

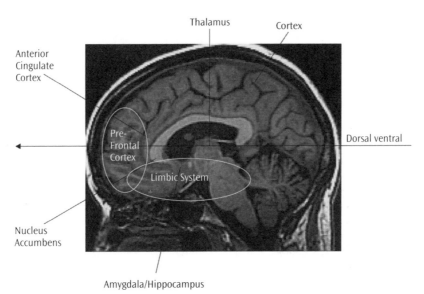

Figure 8.2 Brain regions involved in emotion and emotional disorders: thalamus, cortex, amygdala, hippocampus.

executive function, including selective attention, planning, and effortful regulation of affective states. Adaptive emotional behavior is posited to depend on the integrity and balanced interaction of these systems (Ochsner & Gross, 2005).

Most of the work on the ventral system within mood disorders focuses on the amygdala and the hippocampus. Most of the work on the dorsal system in mood disorders focuses on the prefrontal cortex (PFC) and, more specifically, the dorsolateral PFC (DLPFC) and the ventromedial PFC (VMPFC). Nonetheless, these brain regions interact with many different divisions of the PFC and other brain regions (e.g., anterior cingulate cortex) in important ways that have repercussions for understanding emotion. The following material will provide an oversimplified focus on key regions.

The amygdala has been shown to play a prominent role in emotionally mediated attention and in assigning emotional significance to stimuli. The amygdala projects to certain areas of the anterior cingulate cortex (ACC), and the ACC in turn has been shown to mediate subjective experience of emotion and emotional reaction to stimuli (Lindquist, Wager, Kober, Bliss-Moreau, & Barrett, 2012). The hippocampus has traditionally been labeled the "memory hub," but hippocampal activity also seems to subserve cognitive responding to emotional states (Femenía, Gómez-Galán, Lindskog, & Magara, 2012). The DLPFC appears to be involved in the

regulation of emotion and to modulate amygdala activity via the VMPFC (see Yamawaki, Okada, Okamoto, & Liberzon, 2012, for a review).

Given the importance of reward responsivity in MDD (Eshel & Roiser, 2010) and BD (Johnson, Edge, Holmes, & Carver, 2012), researchers have also begun to attend to areas implicated in the anticipation of and response to reward. These areas include the amygdala, ventral striatum, ACC, and orbitofrontal cortex (OFC). The PFC has also received attention in this area, as it is associated with cognitive control over reward-related functioning in limbic and paralimbic structures (Pizzagalli, Dillon, Bogdan, & Holmes, 2011).

MDD

Neuroimaging studies provide evidence of a hyperactive ventral system (more specifically, the amygdala) and a hypoactive dorsal system (DLPFC; see Disner, Beevers, Haigh, & Beck, 2011 for a review) as well as deficits in areas primarily associated with the processing of rewarding stimuli (Davidson et al., 2009; Smoski et al., 2009). Evidence for these deficits is drawn from structural studies, PET studies, and fMRI studies of responses to emotion challenges.

Studies on the Amygdala Structural studies of the amygdala have yielded inconsistent findings.

Indeed, researchers have found that depression is related to smaller (Caetano et al., 2004; Frodl et al., 2008), larger (Frodl et al., 2002, 2003) or comparably sized amygdalae (Hajek et al., 2009) as compared those in to nondepressed groups. Evidence suggests that these cross-study discrepancies might be tied to family history and medication effects.

Saleh and colleagues (2012) compared amygdala sizes among participants with a history of depression and those with no history of psychopathology. Within each diagnostic group, first-degree family history status was stratified. Among persons with no family history of depression, currently depressed individuals had larger amygdalae than those of nondepressed individuals. Conversely, among individuals with a family history of depression, currently depressed individuals had smaller amygdalae than those of nondepressed individuals.

Medication effects may also explain inconsistencies in the literature. In a meta-analysis, Hamilton, Siemer, and Gotlib (2008) reported that, among depressed individuals, those on medication showed elevations in amygdala volume whereas those who were unmedicated showed diminished amygdala volume. Taken together, these findings on amygdala size may reflect the interactive effects of family history, medication exposure, and acute phases of depression.

Studies on the functional activation of the amygdala are more consistent than structural findings. Findings from PET studies indicate that increased baseline amygdala activation in depression is positively correlated with depression severity (e.g., Drevets, Bogers, & Raaichle, 2002). Despite exceptions (Townsend et al., 2010), most fMRI findings suggest that clinical depression is characterized by hyperactivation of the amygdala in response to negative stimuli (see Hamilton et al., 2012, for a meta-analysis). Similar findings have been observed among unmedicated depressed individuals (Siegle, Thompson, Carter, Steinhauer, & Thase, 2007) and among depressed adolescents (Perlman, Simmons, et al., 2012).

To ensure that amygdala hyperactivation is not a state-dependent feature of depression, studies of high-risk persons (i.e., unaffected individuals who have a family member with a history of MDD) are particularly important. Increased amygdala activation to fearful faces has been found among high-risk samples in response to the tryptophan depletion paradigms described above (van der Veen, Evers,

Deutz, & Schmitt, 2007). Similar results were found in response to distracting negative stimuli during a cognitive task (Monk et al., 2008). Last, adolescent daughters of mothers with a history of depression also showed greater amygdala activation during a sad-mood induction task compared to their low-risk counterparts (Joormann, Cooney, Henry, & Gotlib, 2012). Taken together, these findings suggest that amygdala response to emotional stimuli may serve as an endophenotype for depression.

Although MDD and MDD risk appear to be associated with amygdala hyperactivity, there is somewhat paradoxical evidence that greater amygdala activity predicts a more positive outcome within depressed populations. That is, two studies found that greater activation to emotional stimuli predicted more recovery at follow-up assessments (Canli et al., 2005; Siegle, Carter, & Thase, 2006).

In sum, amygdala hyperactivity appears characteristic of MDD and at-risk populations. However, within disordered populations, hyperactivity in the amygdala appears to predict greater recovery from depression.

Studies on the Hippocampus   Depression has been robustly associated with a tendency to remember more negative memories Joormann, 2009; Phillips, Hine, & Thorsteinsson, 2010), and this type of bias is posited to play a crucial role in the etiology and maintenance of depression (Beck, 1976). As such, an increasing number of brain region studies have focused on structural and functional abnormalities in the hippocampus, given the central role it plays in memory. Research on structural anomalies is sparse. However, there is some evidence that depression is associated with reduced hippocampal volume (e.g., Amico et al., 2011; Caetano et al., 2004). Further, diminished hippocampal gray matter volume has also been documented in never-depressed individuals who have a family history of MDD (Amico et al., 2011; Chen, Hamilton, & Gotlib, 2010).

fMRI studies also suggest hippocampal deficits in depression. For example, diminished hippocampal activity during cognitive tasks has been observed in MDD (e.g., Milne, MacQueen, & Hall, 2012) and in unmedicated depressed samples (Young et al., 2012), particularly during a recollection memory task. Thus, abnormalities in the structure and function of the hippocampus are congruent with the large literature documenting mood-congruent memory biases in MDD.

Studies on the ACC   MDD has been associated with volume reductions in the ACC (e.g., Amico et al., 2011). In regard to functioning, a meta-analysis of PET and fMRI studies suggested that clinical depression was associated with increased metabolic activity in the ACC at baseline (Sacher et al., 2012). ACC activity is also greater among depressed persons during exposure to emotional stimuli (Gotlib et al., 2005) and during cognitive tasks (Desseilles et al., 2009; Dichter, Felder, & Smoski, 2009; Mitterschiffthaler et al., 2008). Finally, low reactivity in the ACC and high reactivity in the amygdala in response to affective words predicted recovery in depressed individuals with cognitive-behavioral therapy (Siegle et al., 2006).

Studies on the DLPFC   Depression is related to structural abnormalities in the DLPFC, such as reduced neuron and glial count and size (e.g., Chana, Landau, Beasley, Everall, & Cotter, 2003; Rajkowska, 2000). Among nondepressed individuals, reduced DLPFC volume was apparent among those with a family history of depression but not in those with no family history of depression (Amico et al., 2011).

PET studies have consistently found decreased DLPFC activation in depressed individuals as compared to healthy individuals (see Drevets, 1998; Mayberg, Keightley, Mahurin, & Brannan, 2004). Congruently, Hamilton and colleagues (2012) reported that clinical depression was characterized by hypoactivity in the DLPFC in response to negative stimuli. Similar results have been observed among unmedicated participants (Siegle et al., 2007; Zhong et al., 2011), depressed adolescents (Perlman, Simmons, et al., 2012), remitted adults (Hooley, Gruber, Scott, Hiller, & Yurgelun-Todd, 2005; Kerestes et al., 2012), and never-depressed individuals with negative cognitive styles (Zhong et al., 2011). Schaefer, Putnam, Benca, and Davidson (2006) also found that depression is associated with diminished DLPFC activity in response to both erotica and positive emotion faces. Finally, increased DLPFC activity, as well as VMPFC activity, predicted greater response to CBT treatment in a depressed sample (Ritchey, Dolcos, Eddington, Strauman, & Cabeza, 2011) and longer symptom-free periods in a remitted sample (Kerestes et al., 2012).

Studies on Reward Processing   In regard to regions involved in reward processing, depressed children and adults both show decreased activation in reward-related brain areas (e.g., ventral striatum and caudate) when making reward-related decisions, anticipating rewards, and after receiving reward (Forbes et al., 2006; Smoski et al., 2009). Keedwell, Andrew, Williams, Brammer, and Phillips (2005) found that a decreased response in the ventral striatum to happy stimuli was related to anhedonia in depression (see also Epstein et al., 2006). Finally, in a study in which depressed adolescents played a game with monetary incentives, reward gain on a preceding trial predicted caudate hypoactivity during reward anticipation on the subsequent trial (Olino et al., 2011). This finding suggests that depression is associated with less anticipation of rewards continuing in the future.

Findings on reward responsivity outside of acute stages of depression are mixed. For example, Schaefer et al. (2006) reported that the hypoactivation of the prefrontal cortex, the basal ganglia, insula, and hippocampus in response to positive stimuli normalized after successful treatment with antidepressant medication. In contrast, findings of two studies indicate that remitted individuals continue to display ventral striatum hypoactivity in response to pleasant stimuli (McCabe, Cowen, & Harmer, 2009) and after receipt of reward (Dichter, Kozink, McClernon, & Smoski, 2012). Despite some inconsistencies, it appears that ventral striatal responses to reward receipt may not be state dependent.

Few studies have investigated activation in reward-related brain areas in healthy relatives of patients diagnosed with depressive disorders. In one notable exception, daughters of mothers with a history of depression exhibited reduced putamen and left insula activity during reward anticipation and greater ACC activity in response to punishment than their low-MDD risk counterparts (Gotlib et al., 2010). Thus, there is preliminary evidence that abnormal neural activity in anticipation of or in response to rewards and punishment may serve as a biological marker for depression risk.

Studies on Connectivity   Aside from specific brain region studies, research has also begun to explore depression-related abnormalities in the functional connections between brain regions. For example, Hamilton and colleagues (Hamilton, Chen, Thomason, Schwartz, & Gotlib, 2011) used an analytic technique that allows one to estimate the degree to which activity in one brain region predicts subsequent activity in a different region. The authors found that, among depressed individuals, greater hippocampal activity predicted increased ACC activity. Further, both hippocampal and ACC activation predicted diminished dorsal cortical activity. Thus, at rest, depression is characterized by excitatory activity in limbic and paralimbic structures, which appears to inhibit activity in dorsal cortical structures.

BD

As seen throughout this chapter, research on MDD is more prevalent than research on BD. Given the more limited research on BD, in this section, we will review structural findings as a whole before turning to functional findings.

Structural Studies in BD   Most of the brain regions discussed in the section on MDD have been studied in BD. Studies investigating structural changes, for example, have reported that children with BD show diminished gray matter in the DLPFC compared to nondisordered controls (e.g., Adleman et al., 2012). Mixed results have been reported for the limbic structures, such as the amygdala and the hippocampus, among adults with BD (see Blond, Fredericks, & Blumberg, 2012, for a review). However, reduced amygdala volume in adolescents with BD has been reported fairly consistently (Usher, Leucht, Falkai, & Scherk, 2010). Finally, two recent reviews identified disruptions in the white matter connectivity between frontal regions associated with emotion regulation and limbic structures associated with emotion generation among patients with BD (Almeida & Phillips, 2013; Strakowski et al., 2012).

Parallel with the depression literature, factors such as mood state and medication use contribute to structural abnormalities seen in BD. Currently depressed BD individuals have been found to have smaller volume of the amygdala and orbitofrontal cortex than do euthymic BD individuals and healthy controls (Foland-Ross et al., 2012; Nery et al., 2009). Long-term lithium treatment has been associated with increased volume of the subgenual ACC, amygdala, and hippocampus (see Hafeman, Chang, Garrett, Sanders, & Phillips, 2012, for a review). Further, van Erp et al. (2012) reported that BD individuals treated with lithium had larger hippocampal volumes than did their nondisordered co-twins. No differences were found, however, when comparing BD individuals who were not treated with lithium and their nondisordered co-twins. Taken together, findings indicate that medication status and current mood state may moderate structural anomalies documented in BD.

Functional Studies in BD   Functional changes in BD are similar to the changes reported in MDD, especially when BD participants are in a depressed state. Currently depressed BD individuals show amygdala hyperactivity at rest and during cognitive tasks (Chang et al., 2004, Ketter et al., 2001; Krüger, Seminowicz, Goldapple, Kennedy, & Mayberg, 2003) as well as in response to emotional stimuli (Almeida, Versace, Hassel, Kupfer, & Phillips, 2010, Perlman, Almeida, et al., 2012). Studies have also reported decreased activation in the DLPFC at rest (Krüger et al., 2003), during cognitive tasks (Chang et al., 2004), and while viewing emotional faces (Yurgelun-Todd et al., 2000). This suggests that the depressed state in BD is associated with a pattern of hyperactivation in the ventral system and hypoactivation in the PFC similar to that discussed in MDD.

Euthymic BD patients have also been characterized by increased activation in ventral structures (Garrett et al., 2012; Malhi, Lagopoulos, Sachdev, Ivanovski, & Shnier, 2005; Wessa et al., 2007) and hypoactivation in frontal brain regions (Garrett et al., 2012; Hassel et al., 2008; Lagopoulos, Ivanovski, & Malhi, 2007). For example, euthymic BD individuals exhibited greater amygdala and striatum activity than did nondisordered controls during a cognitive task with distracting emotional stimuli. Yet, in the same task, DLPFC and dorsal ACC hypoactivity was observed on trials without distracting emotional stimuli (Mullin et al., 2012). Glahn et al. (2010) also reported that BD was associated with diminished DLPFC and hippocampal activity during a declarative memory task. Therefore, neural patterns associated with MDD are also observed in euthymic states of BD.

Some, but not all, research on reward processing has found that mania is associated with increased responding to positive stimuli. For example, on a task with monetary incentives, currently manic individuals exhibited increased orbitofrontal activity when expecting reward gains and decreased activity when expecting losses, whereas the opposite pattern was observed in healthy controls (Bermpohl et al., 2010). These findings have not been consistently replicated (Abler, Greenhouse, Ongur, Walter, & Heckers, 2008; Nusslock et al., 2012).

Three recent studies explored functional anomalies across all mood states (manic, depressed, euthymic) of persons with BD. Findings of one study indicated that BD is also linked to hyperactivity in the OFC across all mood states (Van der Schot, Kahn, Ramsey, Nolen, & Vink, 2010). Findings of the other two studies indicated that BD is consistently associated with hypoactivity in the PFC, particularly the DLPFC, across all mood states (Townsend & Altshuler, 2012; Townsend et al., 2010). This reduced activity in the DLPFC, a brain region associated with affect regulation, could explain sustained mood dysregulation observed in BD.

In sum, there is evidence for some trait-like functional abnormalities and some state-like abnormalities in BD. Parallel with findings in depression, BD is associated with hypoactivity in frontocortical regions and, in some states, hyperactivity in the ventral structures.

As several models emphasize that fMRI profiles may shift with episodes of the disorder (Chang, 2010), studies of children who have had fewer episodes of the disorder are particularly valuable. For example, Rich et al. (2006) reported greater activation in parts of the ventral system, including the left amygdala, ventral striatum, and ventral PFC, in children with BD when rating hostility of facial stimuli and when rating their fear of those stimuli. Groups did not differ in their brain activity patterns in response to nonemotional tasks. Children with BD also demonstrate hyperactivation in parts of the ventral striatum during cognitive tasks (Blumberg et al., 2003) and while viewing positive images (Chang et al., 2004). Finally, one study reported reduced frontopolar cortex activity during a cognitive task among a sample of never-disordered adolescents and young adults with a disordered first-degree relative (Thermenos et al., 2011). Altogether, these findings suggest that hyperactivity of the ventral system can be observed early in the course of the disease and that hypoactivation in the dorsal system may serve as an endophenotype for BD.

Studies on Neural Networks in BD In a review of eight neuroimaging studies that compared MDD and BD, deficits in connectivity of the amygdala and VMPFC appeared to be specific to the valence of the stimulus. That is, positive stimuli elicited reduced connectivity between the amygdala and VMPFC in BD, whereas negative stimuli elicited reduced connectivity of these regions in MDD (Almeida & Phillips, 2013). The authors suggested that diminished VMPFC–amygdala connectivity may contribute to sustained experiences of positive affect in BD and negative affect in MDD.

Summary

This brief overview of structural and functional findings highlights many similar abnormalities in BD and MDD. Elevated activity in the ventral system (e.g., the hippocampus and amygdala) might contribute to emotional sensitivity, whereas diminished activity of the prefrontal cortex (e.g., DLPFC) might interfere with effective goal pursuit and emotion regulation. Although these studies provide insight into the dysregulated emotion associated with affective disorders, more studies are needed that investigate whether differences in brain activation are merely correlates of the episode. More specifically, future research should continue to investigate brain structure and function in individuals who are not yet disordered but have a family history of affective disorders. So far, evidence from studies of patients with remitted MDD suggests that increased amygdala activation and decreased activation in the DLPFC in response to emotional material remain stable beyond the depressive episode. Hypoactivation in response to positive material in MDD, however, seems to normalize with recovery in some, but not all studies.

In BD, studies suggest that hyperactivation in ventral structures and hypoactivation in PFC areas remain stable after recovery and across states of depression and mania. Similarly, studies of children diagnosed with BD indicate that several functional abnormalities are present early in the course of the disorder.

Disruptions in Circadian Rhythms

Mammals have a 24-hour, or circadian, rhythm to match the cycle of the sun. The suprachiasmatic nucleus (SCN) is a key structure in guiding these circadian rhythms, receiving input from specialized ganglion cells in the retina that are activated by dawn and dusk light. The SCN sends output to other centers in the brain that help to regulate circadian rhythms. Well-synchronized and strong circadian rhythms in activity, sleep, and hormonal patterns, then, depend on exposure to light at dawn and dusk, on the strength of the signal from the SCN, as well as on strong coupling of these different brain centers. If the systems are not well synchronized, the amplitude of circadian variability diminishes (Duncan, 1996). Beyond the amplitude of the rhythm, phase shifting (in which at least one of the person's internal clocks is earlier or later than the light–dark cycle) is also one possible outcome of disturbances in these systems (Aschoff, 1983). One key way of measuring the strength of circadian rhythms is to measure core body temperature. The amplitude, or degree of daily change, in core body temperature appears attenuated for many people diagnosed with MDD (Daimon, Yamada, Tsujimoto, & Takahshi, 1992; van Londen et al., 2001). Hence, MDD appears to be related to disruptions in circadian rhythms. Although researchers have focused on a broad range of circadian rhythm disruptions within mood disorders, particularly extensive research has focused on sleep disturbance.

Sleep Disturbance

Much of the research on sleep has focused on polysomnography, or EEG indices of the distribution of sleep stages during the night. This research is key for understanding whether sleep deficits are related to an underlying disturbance in circadian rhythms, or 24-hour cycles.

Sleep Disturbance and MDD Research suggests that insomnia predicts the onset of depression over a 1-year period (Ford & Kamerow, 1989), especially for women (Dryman & Eaton, 1991). Sleep deficits may be particularly pronounced in the period just before onset (Perlis, Giles, Buysse, Tu, & Kupfer, 1997).

Polysomnography studies have identified a set of sleep disturbances among persons with MDD, such as changes in the quality and timing of rapid eye movement (REM) sleep and disturbed slow-wave sleep. The distribution of sleep phases throughout the night appears to be shifted, such that REM begins more quickly after sleep onset (shortened REM latency), there is more REM sleep (REM density) during the first few hours of sleep, and slow-wave sleep (stages 3 and 4) is more likely to occur during the second half of the night (Gillin,

Mendelson, & Kupfer, 1988). Evidence is fairly consistent that two forms of sleep disturbance persist during periods of remission: increased REM density and shortened slow-wave sleep.

Many of the sleep deficits observed during remission have been documented among unaffected family members (Giles, Kupfer, Rush, & Roffwarg, 1998). Among the half dozen studies of persons with a family history of depression, most have documented either increased REM density or shortened slow-wave sleep pared to control participants (Pillai, Kalmbach, & Ciesla, 2011).

Further evidence for a role of sleep in depressive symptoms comes from an extensive body of research on sleep deprivation. In this paradigm, persons are brought into a sleep laboratory and kept awake for an entire night (total sleep deprivation). In studies involving more than 1,000 participants, total sleep deprivation has been found to produce a temporary remission of current depressive symptoms in about 60% of patients (Wehr, 1990; Wu & Bunney, 1990). Most patients relapse with a night of sleep, although adjunct use of antidepressant medications or lithium may help to sustain the positive effects of sleep deprivation (Benedetti et al., 1997; Benedetti, Colombo, Barbini, Campori, & Smeraldi, 1999).

Sleep Disturbances and BD Sleep disturbance is common in BD, and high rates of sleep and circadian disturbance have also been reported in the unaffected offspring of those with BD (Jones, Tai, Evershed, Knowles, & Bentall, 2006; Ritter, Marx, Bauer, Lepold, & Pfennig, 2011). Parallel to findings in unipolar disorder, increased density and percentage of REM have been documented among bipolar patients in the well state compared with normal controls (Giles, Jarrett, Roffwarg, & Rush, 1987; Sitaram, Nurnberger, Gershon, & Gillin, 1982). Experimental research suggests that sleep deprivation can effectively reduce depressive symptoms among persons experiencing bipolar depression (Wu et al., 2009). Unfortunately, naturalistic and experimental studies also suggest that sleep deprivation can trigger mania among nondepressed bipolar individuals (Kivi, 1996; Knowles, Waldron, & Cairns, 1979; Wehr, Goodwin, Wirz-Justice, Breitmaier, & Craig, 1982). For example, in a naturalistic study of sleep among bipolar patients, decreases in sleep time predicted increases in mania (Leibenluft, Albert, Rosenthal, & Wehr, 1996). In experimental studies, the effects of sleep deprivation are stronger in bipolar depression than in MDD (Barbini et al., 1998). In about 10% of persons who are experiencing bipolar depression, sleep deprivation will produce manic symptoms (Colombo, Benedetti, Barbini, Campori, & Smeraldi, 1999). An increase in sleep duration also appears to predict reductions in manic symptoms (Krüger, Braunig, & Young, 1996). Two case reports have suggested that interventions to improve sleep time can diminish manic symptoms over time (Barbini et al., 2005; Wehr et al., 1998).

Summary of Circadian Research   Polysomnography indices of REM sleep disturbance have been documented among people with MDD and BD. Among those with a family history of depression, REM sleep disturbances have been found to predict onset of mood disorders. Sleep deprivation paradigms also provide strong experimental evidence for a role of sleep disturbance in mood disorders. Hence, substantial experimental and longitudinal research suggests that sleep research is critical for understanding mood disorders.

Concluding Comments

Genetic, pharmacological, neuroendocrine, neuroimaging, and sleep findings suggest that neurobiological deficits play a key role in vulnerability to mood disorders. A body of research indicates that serotonergic, neuroendocrine, and circadian deficits can be documented among unaffected family members, suggesting that these findings do not just reflect scars of the episode or medication effects. There is also clear evidence that MDD is moderately heritable and that BD is robustly heritable.

Despite the rapid gains in knowledge, several issues still pervade the field. It is not clear whether some neurobiological deficits can be detected among unaffected family members. For example, manic and depressive symptoms can be triggered by fluctuations in DA, but it is not apparent whether unaffected family members are overly sensitive to DA challenges. Neuroimaging research suggests deficits in brain regions involved in the generation and regulation of emotion, but only amygdala and hippocampal hyperactivity have been documented among unaffected family members.

Beyond the need for high-risk studies, mixed findings are particularly apparent in the quest to identify genetic loci associated with mood disorders. Effect sizes are small, and accordingly, nonreplications have been common. Nonetheless, meta-analyses provide evidence for a few loci that appear involved. Acknowledgement of the complexity of studying multiple genes with small effect sizes has inspired formation of several large collaborative networks that should provide a fruitful way to tackle this area of focus. It is hoped that progress will also be facilitated by studies examining how genes relate to specific neurobiological abnormalities.

There is also a need to identify neurobiological variables that differentiate BD and MDD. That is, remarkably parallel profiles of neurotransmitter and neuroimaging variables have been observed in BD and MDD. In some ways, this is not surprising given that many people diagnosed with BD will also experience episodes of depression during their lifetime (cf. Karkowski & Kendler, 1997), and that psychological vulnerability factors appear remarkably parallel for bipolar and unipolar depression (Cuellar, Johnson, & Winters, 2005). Nonetheless, BD is distinguished not only by the presence of manic episodes but also by substantially worse outcomes in terms of functional impairment (Goldberg & Harrow, 2011) and even all-cause mortality compared to MDD (Ösby et al., 2001). Genetic research suggests that the heritability of mania is only modestly related to the heritability of depression. This raises questions of how to identify the unique risk factors that promote expression of mania. DA levels appear to be increased during acute manic episodes, and bipolar disorder has been related to changes in the activity of the OFC as well. Neurotransmitter research provides some preliminary findings for cell membrane and second-messenger dysregulation specific to BD. Nonetheless, there is a need for studies comparing neurobiological aspects of mania and depression.

Further, some neurobiological deficits may not be specific to mood disorders. Indeed, serotonergic deficits are observed in other disorders, including alcohol dependence (Feinn, Nellissery, & Kranzler, 2005) and anxiety disorders (Lesch & Canli, 2006). Atypical patterns of both basal HPA functioning and HPA reactivity have been documented in anxiety disorders and schizophrenia (e.g., Kaneko et al., 1992; Owens, Plotsky, & Nemeroff, 1999). Amygdala hyperreactivity is also a well-documented feature of anxiety disorders (Shin et al., 2005). Hence, there is a need to consider how neurobiological deficits increase risk for a host of disorders and how to conceptualize the underlying psychological dimensions that operate across disorders (Cuthbert, 2005).

Beyond describing the limitations in neurobiological research, it is important to acknowledge some exciting work not considered here. This review has been organized in terms of research paradigms—genetic, neurotransmitter, neuroendocrine, neuroimaging, and circadian rhythm research. But some of the most exciting research findings involve links across these paradigms. For example, beyond the interactive influences of HPA axis activity noted earlier, researchers have demonstrated that polymorphisms in the serotonin transporter gene can influence cortisol (Alexander et al., 2009) and amygdala hyperreactivity (Hariri, Drabant, & Weinberger, 2006). Depleting serotonin with ATD leads to disturbed EEG sleep profiles (Haynes, McQuaid, Kelsoe, Rapaport, & Gillin, 2004). Sleep deprivation appears to improve the functioning of DA (Demontis, Fadda, Devota, Martellotta, & Fratta, 1990; Nunes, Tufik, & Nobrega, 1994). Hence, although neurobiological domains have been presented separately, a great deal of research is being conducted on how to integrate these domains.

Another recent spate of research involves the integration of biological and cognitive models of depression. Cognitive investigators have demonstrated consistently that depressed individuals attend selectively to negative stimuli over positive stimuli, a bias that presumably maintains a state of depressed mood, anhedonia, and rumination. Recent research focuses on how the biological deficits in depression can help explain these cognitive patterns. For example, polymorphisms in the serotonin transporter gene appear related to an increased bias to attend to negative material (Beevers et al., 2011). In neuroimaging research, investigators have suggested that the elevated amygdala and hippocampus activation in MDD may be related to depressed individuals' tendency to consolidate and recall negative memories (e.g., Cahill, 2000; Ramel et al., 2007; Siegle, Steinhauer, Carter, Ramel, & Thase, 2003). Drevets (2000) has posited that tonically elevated amygdala activation may be related to rumination in depression through the increased availability of negative memories. Sleep deprivation can produce improvements in cognitive correlates of depression (Benedetti et al., 2005) but can also interfere with emotion regulation (Walker & van der Helm,

2009). Hence, biological and cognitive integrative research provides helpful insights into the nature of this disorder.

Although this chapter has focused on the etiology of mood disorders, it is also clear that these biological indices are relevant for treatment outcome. This is of critical importance given the sizable proportion of patients who fail to respond to available treatments for depression and bipolar disorder (Smith, Cornelius, Warnock, Tacchi, & Taylor, 2007; Trivedi et al., 2006). As examples of how biological indices can help predict treatment outcome, polysomnography EEG indices predict worse outcome in both cognitive-behavioral therapy (Thase, Simons, & Reynolds, 1993) and interpersonal therapy (Thase et al., 1997). Activation of the rostral ACC, a critical region involved in the communications between ventral and dorsal facets of emotion regions in the brain, predicts response to antidepressant drug treatment in depression (Pizzagalli, Shackman, & Davidson, 2001). One hope is that ongoing research will help identify ways to match patients with treatments on the basis of a baseline profile of vulnerability, so as to enhance outcomes.

Most exciting, treatments that influence one system have the power to normalize activity at different levels. For example, antidepressant medications normalize EEG sleep parameters (Gillin et al., 1997; Landolt et al., 2001), amygdala hyperreactivity (Sheline et al., 2001), cortisol hypersecretion (Pariante, 2003), and activity in the DLPFC (Kennedy et al., 2001). Hence, integrative studies of how problems at each neurobiological level operate are likely to enhance clinicians' ability to build more effective treatment programs.

In sum, researchers have found a range of neurobiological deficits to be related to mood disorders, and promising research is drawing links between these different neurobiological deficits. Understanding this system as a whole is likely to have significant implications for improving treatment.

References

Abler, B., Greenhouse, I., Ongur, D., Walter, H., & Heckers, S. (2008). Abnormal reward system activation in mania. *Neuropsychopharmacology, 33*(9), 2217–2227.

Ader, R., Cohen, N., & Felten, D. (1995). Psychoneuroimmuniology: Interactions between the nervous system and the immune system. *Lancet, 345,* 99–103.

Adleman, N. E., Fromm, S. J., Razdan, V., Kayser, R., Dickstein, D. P., et al. (2012). Cross-sectional and longitudinal abnormalities in brain structure in children with severe mood dysregulation or bipolar disorder. *Journal of Child Psychology and Psychiatry, 53,* 1149–1156.

Alda, M., Grof, E., Cavazzoni, P., Duffy, A., Martin, R., Ravindran, L., et al. (1997). Autosomal recessive inheritance of affective disorders in families of responders to lithium prophylaxis? *Journal of Affective Disorders, 44,* 153–157.

Alexander, N., Kuepper, Y., Schmitz, A., Osinsky, R., Kozyra, E., & Hennig, J. (2009). Gene-environment interactions predict cortisol responses after acute stress: Implications for the etiology of depression. *Psychoneuroendocrinology, 34,* 1294–1303.

Almeida, J. R. C., & Phillips, M. L. (2013). Distinguishing between unipolar depression and bipolar depression: Current and future clinical and neuroimaging perspectives. *Biological Psychiatry, 73,* 111–118.

Almeida, J. R. C., Versace, A., Hassel, S., Kupfer, D. J., & Phillips, M. L. (2010). Elevated activity to sad facial expressions: A state marker of bipolar but not unipolar depression. *Biological Psychiatry, 67,* 414–421.

Altshuler, L. L., Post, R. M., Leverich, G. S., Mikalauskas, K., Rosoff, A., & Ackerman, L. (1995). Antidepressant-induced mania and cycle alteration: A controversy revisited. *American Journal of Psychiatry, 152,* 1130–1138.

Amico, F., Meisenzahl, E., Koutsouleris, N., Reiser, M., Möller, H., & Frodl, T. (2011). Structural MRI correlates for vulnerability and resilience to major depressive disorder. *Journal of Psychiatry & Neuroscience, 36*(1), 15–22.

Anand, A., Verhoeff, P., Seneca, N., Zoghbi, S. S., Seibyl, J. P., Charney, D. S., et al. (2000). Brain SPECT imaging of amphetamine-induced dopamine release in euthymic bipolar disorder patients. *American Journal of Psychiatry, 157,* 1108–1114.

Anguelova, M., Benkelfat, C., & Turecki, G. (2003). A systematic review of association studies investigating genes coding for serotonin receptors and the serotonin transporter: I. Affective disorders. *Molecular Psychiatry, 8,* 574–591.

Antonini, A., Benti, R., De Notaris, R., Tesei, S., Zecchinelli, A., Sacilotto, G.,…Gerundini, P. (2003). 123I-Ioflupane/SPECT binding to striatal dopamine transporter (DAT) uptake in patients with Parkinson's disease, multiple system atrophy, and progressive supranuclear palsy. *Neurological Sciences, 24,* 149–150.

Arana, G. W., Baldessarini, R. J., & Ornsteen, M. (1985). The dexamethasone suppression test for diagnosis and prognosis in psychiatry: Commentary and review. *Archives of General Psychiatry, 42,* 1193.

Arborelius L., Owens M. J., Plotsky P. M., & Nemeroff, C. B. (1999). The role of corticotropin- releasing factor in depression and anxiety disorders. *Journal of Endocrinology, 160,* 1–12.

Aschoff, J. (1983). Disorders of the circadian system as discussed in psychiatric research. In T. A. Wehr & F. K. Goodwin (Eds.), *Circadian rhythms in psychiatry* (pp. 33–51). Pacific Grove, CA: Boxwood Press.

Ashman, S. B., Dawson, G., Panagiotides, H., Yamada, E., & Wilkinson, C. W. (2002). Stress hormone levels of children of depressed mothers. *Development and Psychopathology, 14,* 333–349.

Aubry, J. M., Gervasoni, N., Osiek, C., Perret, G., Rossier, M. F., Bertschy, G., & Bondolfi, G. (2007). The DEX/CRH neuroendocrine test and the prediction of depressive relapse in remitted depressed outpatients. *Journal of Psychiatric Research, 41,* 290–294.

Barbini, B., Benedetti, F., Colombo, C., Dotoli, D., Bernasconi, A., Cigala-Fulgosi, M., et al. (2005). Dark therapy for mania: A pilot study. *Bipolar Disorders, 7,* 98–101.

Barbini, B., Colombo, C., Benedetti, F., Camori, E., Bellodi, L., & Smeraldi, E. (1998). The unipolar–bipolar dichotomy and the response to sleep deprivation. *Psychiatry Research, 79,* 43–50.

Baumgarten, H. G., & Grozdanovic, Z. (1995). Psychopharmacology of the central serotonergic system. *Pharmacopsychiatry, 28,* 73–79.

Beck, A. T. (1976). *Cognitive therapy and the emotional disorders.* Oxford, UK: International Universities Press.

Beevers, C. G., Marti, C. N., Lee, H. J., Stote, D. L., Ferrell, R. E., Hariri, A. R., & Telch, M. J. (2011). Associations between serotonin transporter gene promoter region (5-HTTLPR) polymorphism and gaze bias for emotional information. *Journal of Abnormal Psychology, 120,* 187–197.

Bendall, S., Jackson, H. J., Hulbert, C. A., & McGorry, P. D. (2008). Childhood trauma and psychotic disorders: A systematic, critical review of the evidence. *Schizophrenia Bulletin, 34,* 568–579.

Benedetti, F., Barbini, B., Florita, M., Fulgosi, M. C., Pontiggia, A., Campori, E., et al. (2005). Rapid improvement in information processing after sleep deprivation and sleep phase-advance in bipolar depression. *Clinical Neuropsychiatry: Journal of Treatment Evaluation, 2,* 180–182.

Benedetti, F., Barbini, B., Lucca, A., Campori, E., Colombo, C., & Smeraldi, E. (1997). Sleep deprivation hastens the antidepressant action of fluoxetine. *European Archives of Psychiatry and Clinical Neuroscience, 247,* 100–103.

Benedetti, F., Colombo, C., Barbini, B., Campori, E., & Smeraldi, E. (1999). Ongoing lithium treatment prevents relapse after total sleep deprivation. *Journal of Clinical Psychopharmacology, 19,* 240–245.

Benkelfat, C., Ellenbogen, M. A., Dean, P., Palmour, R. M., & Young, S. N. (1994). Mood-lowering effects of tryptophan depletion: Enhanced susceptibility in young men at genetic risk for major affective disorders. *Archives of General Psychiatry, 61,* 687–697.

Bermpohl, F., Kahnt, T., Dalanay, U., Hägele, C., Sajonz, B., et al. (2010). Altered representation of expected value in the orbitofrontal cortex in mania. *Human Brain Mapping, 31,* 958–969.

Bhagwagar, Z., Hafizi, S., & Cowen, P. J. (2005). Increased salivary cortisol after waking in depression. *Psychopharmacology, 182,* 54–57.

Bhagwagar, Z., Whale, R., & Cowen, P. (2002). State and trait abnormalities in serotonin function in major depression. *British Journal of Psychiatry, 180,* 24–28.

Blond, B. N., Fredericks, C. A., & Blumberg, H. P. (2012). Functional neuroanatomy of bipolar disorder: Structure, function, and connectivity in an amygdala–anterior paralimbic neural system. *Bipolar Disorders, 14,* 340–355.

Blumberg, H. P., Kaufman, J., Martin, A., Whiteman, R., Zhang, J. H., et al. (2003). Amygdala and hippocampal volumes in adolescents and adults with bipolar disorder. *Archives of General Psychiatry, 60,* 1201–1208.

Booij, L., Van der Does, W., Haffmans, P. M. J., Riedel, W. J., Fekkes, D., & Blom, M. J. B. (2005). The effects of high-dose and low-dose tryptophan depletion on mood and cognitive functions of remitted depressed patients. *Journal of Psychopharmacology, 19,* 267–275.

Booij, S. H., Bouma, E., de Jonge, P., Ormel, J., & Oldehinkel, A. J. (2013). Chronicity of depressive problems and the cortisol response to psychosocial stress in adolescents: The TRAILS study. *Psychoneuroendocrinology, 38*(5), 659–666.

Brown, G. W., & Harris, T. O. (1989). *Life events and illness.* New York: Guilford.

Burke, H. M., Davis, M. C., Otte, C., & Mohr, D. C. (2005). Depression and cortisol responses to psychological stress: A meta-analysis. *Psychoneuroendocrinology, 30,* 846–856.

Caetano, S. C., Hatch, J. P., Brambilla, P., Sassi, R. B., Nicolletti, M., et al. (2004). Anatomical MRI study of hippocampus and amygdala in patients with current and remitted major depression. *Psychiatry Research: Neuroimaging, 132,* 141–147.

Cahill, L. (2000). Neurobiological mechanisms of emotionally influenced, long-term memory. *Progress in Brain Research, 126,* 29–37.

Canli, T., Cooney, R. E., Goldin, P., Shah, M., Sivers, H., et al. (2005). Amygdala reactivity to emotional faces predicts improvement in major depression. *Neuroreport, 16,* 1267–1270.

Carroll, B. J. (1982). Use of the dexamethasone test in depression. *Journal of Clinical Psychiatry, 43,* 44–50.

Carroll, B. J., Feinberg, M., Greden, J. F., Tarika, J., Albala, A. A., Haskett, R. F.,…Young, E. (1981). A specific laboratory test for the diagnosis of melancholia: Standardization, validation, and clinical utility. *Archives of General Psychiatry, 38,* 15.

Carver, C. S., Johnson, S. L., & Joormann, J. (2008). Serotonergic function, two-mode models of self-regulation, and vulnerability to depression: What depression has in common with impulsive aggression. *Psychological Bulletin, 134*(6), 912–943.

Caspi, A., Sugden, K., Moffitt, T. E., Taylor, A., Craig, I. W., Harrington, H., et al. (2003). Influence of life stress on depression: Moderation by a polymorphism in the 5-HTT gene. *Science, 301,* 386–389.

Cervantes, P., Gelber, S., Ng Ying Kin, F. N. K., Nair, V. N. P., & Schwartz, G. (2001). Circadian secretion of cortisol in bipolar disorder. *Journal of Psychiatry and Neuroscience, 26,* 411–416.

Chana, G., Landau, S., Beasley, C., Everall, I. P., & Cotter, D. (2003). Two-dimensional assessment of cytoarchitecture in the anterior cingulate cortex in major depressive disorder, bipolar disorder, and schizophrenia: Evidence for decreased neuronal somal size and increased neuronal density. *Biological Psychiatry, 53,* 1086–1098.

Chang, K. (2010). Course and impact of bipolar disorder in young patients. *Journal of Clinical Psychiatry, 71,* e05.

Chang, K., Adleman, N. E., Dienes, K., Simeonova, D. J., Menon, V., & Reiss, A. (2004). Anomalous prefrontal-subcortical activation in familial pediatric bipolar disorder: A functional magnetic resonance imaging investigation. *Archives of General Psychiatry, 61,* 781–792.

Charney, D. S. (1998). Monoamine dysfunction and the pathophysiology and treatment of depression. *Journal of Clinical Psychiatry, 59,* 11–14.

Chen, M. C., Hamilton, J. P., & Gotlib, I. H. (2010). Decreased hippocampal volume in healthy girls at risk of depression. *Archives of General Psychiatry, 67,* 270–276.

Chiao, J. Y., & Blizinsky, K. D. (2010). Culture-gene coevolution of individualism-collectivism and the serotonin transporter gene. *Proceedings Biological Sciences / Royal Society, 277,* 529–537.

Cho, H. J., Meira-Lima, I., Cordeiro, Q., Michelon, L., Sham, P., Vallada, H., et al. (2005). Population-based and family-based studies on the serotonin transporter gene polymorphisms and BD: A systematic review and meta-analysis. *Molecular Psychiatry, 10,* 771–781.

Colombo, C., Benedetti, F., Barbini, B., Campori, E., & Smeraldi, E. (1999). Rate of switch from depression into mania after therapeutic sleep deprivation in bipolar depression. *Psychiatry Research, 86,* 267–270.

Cousins, D. A., Butts, K., & Young, A. H. (2009). The role of dopamine in bipolar disorder. *Bipolar Disorders, 11,* 787–806.

Cowen, P. J. (2002). Cortisol, serotonin and depression: All stressed out? *British Journal of Psychiatry, 180,* 99–100.

Cuellar, A. K., Johnson, S. L., & Winters, R. (2005). Distinctions between bipolar and unipolar depression, *Clinical Psychology Review, 25,* 307–339.

Cuthbert, B. N. (2005). Dimensional models of psychopathology: Research agenda and clinical utility. *Journal of Abnormal Psychology, 114,* 565–569.

Daimon, K., Yamada, N., Tsujimoto, T., & Takahashi, S. (1992). Circadian rhythm abnormalities of deep body temperature in depressive disorders. *Journal of Affective Disorders, 26,* 191–198.

Davidson, R. J., & McEwen, B. S. (2012). Social influences on neuroplasticity: Stress and interventions to promote well-being. *Nature Neuroscience, 15,* 689–695.

Davidson, R. J., Pizzagalli, D., & Nitschke, J. B. (2009). The representation and regulation of emotion in depression: Perspectives from affective neuroscience (pp. 218–248). In I. H. Gotlib & C. L. Hammen (Eds.), *Handbook of Depression.* New York: Guilford Press.

Dedovic, K., Duchesne, A., Andrews, J., Engert, V., & Pruessner, J. C. (2009). The brain and the stress axis: The neural correlates of cortisol regulation in response to stress. *Neuroimage, 47,* 864–871.

Delgado, P. L., Miller, H. L., Salomon, R. M., Licino, J., Heninger, G. R., & Gelenberg, A. J. (1993). Monoamines and the mechanism of antidepressant action: Effects of catecholamine depletion on mood of patients treated with antidepressants. *Psychopharmacology Bulletin, 29,* 386–396.

Delgado, P. L., Miller, H. L., Salomon, R. M., Licino, J., Krystal, J. H., Moreno, F. A., et al. (1999). Tryptophan-depletion challenge in depressed patients treated with desipramine or fluoxetine: Implications for the role of serotonin in the mechanism of antidepressant action. *Biological Psychiatry, 48,* 212–220.

Demontis, M. G., Fadda, P., Devoto, P., Martellota, M. C., & Fratta, W. (1990). Sleep deprivation increases dopamine D1 receptor agonist [3H] SCH 23390 binding and dopamine-stimulated adenylate cyclase in the rat limbic system. *Neuroscience Letters, 117,* 224–227.

Depue, R. A., & Iacono, W. G. (1989). Neurobehavioral aspects of affective disorders. *Annual Review of Psychology, 40,* 457–492.

Desseilles, M., Balteau, E., Sterpenich, V., Dang-Vu, T. T., Darsaud, A., et al. (2009). Abnormal neural filtering of irrelevant visual information in depression. *Journal of Neuroscience, 29,* 1395–1403.

Dichter, G. S., Felder, J. N., & Smoski, M. J. (2009). Affective context interferes with cognitive control in unipolar depression: An fMRI investigation. *Journal of Affective Disorders, 114,* 131–142.

Dichter, G. S., Kozink, R. V., McClernon, F. J., & Smoski, M. J. (2012). Remitted major depression is characterized by reward network hyperactivation during reward anticipation and hypoactivation during reward outcomes. *Journal of Affective Disorders, 136,* 1126–1134.

Dickerson, S. S., & Kemeny, M. E. (2004). Acute stressors and cortisol responses: A theoretical integration and synthesis of laboratory research. *Psychological Bulletin, 130,* 355–391.

Disner, S. G., Beevers, C. G., Haigh, E. A. P., & Beck, A. T. (2011). Neural mechanisms of the cognitive model of depression. *Nature Reviews Neuroscience, 12,* 467–477.

Dowlati, Y., Herrmann, N., Swardfager, W., Liu, H., Sham, L., Reim, E. K., & Lanctôt, K. L. (2010). A meta-analysis of cytokines in major depression. *Biological Psychiatry, 67,* 446–457.

Drevets, W. C. (1998). Functional neuroimaging studies of depression: The anatomy of melancholia. *Annual Review of Medicine, 49,* 341–361.

Drevets, W. C. (2000). Neuroimaging studies of mood disorders. *Biological Psychiatry, 48,* 813–829.

Drevets, W. C., Bogers, W., & Raichle, M. E. (2002). Functional anatomical correlates of antidepressant drug treatment assessed using PET measures of regional glucose metabolism. *European Neuropsychopharmacology, 12,* 527–544.

Dryman, A., & Eaton, W. W. (1991). Affective symptoms associated with the onset of major depression in the community: Findings from the US National Institute of Mental Health Epidemiologic Catchment Area Program. *Acta Psychiatria Scandinavica, 84,* 1–5.

Duffy, A., Lewitzka, U., Doucette, S., Andreazza, A., & Grof, P. (2012). Biological indicators of illness risk in offspring of bipolar parents: Targeting the hypothalamic-pituitary-adrenal axis and immune system. *Early Intervention in Psychiatry, 6,* 128–137.

Duncan, J. W. C. (1996). Circadian rhythms and the pharmacology of affective illness. *Pharmacology and Therapeutics, 71,* 253–312.

Dunlop, B. W., & Nemeroff, C. B. (2007). The role of dopamine in the pathophysiology of depression. *Archives of General Psychiatry, 64,* 327–337.

Ellenbogen, M. A., Hodgins, S., Linnen, A. M., & Ostiguy, C. S. (2011). Elevated daytime cortisol levels: A biomarker of subsequent major affective disorder. *Journal of Affective Disorders, 132,* 265–269.

Ellenbogen, M. A., Hodgins, S., & Walker, C. D. (2004). High levels of cortisol among adolescent offspring of parents with bipolar disorder: A pilot study. *Psychoneuroendocrinology, 29,* 99–106.

Ellenbogen, M. A., Hodgins, S., Walker, C. D., Couture, S., & Adam, S. (2006). Daytime cortisol and stress reactivity in the offspring of parents with bipolar disorder. *Psychoneuroendocrinology, 31,* 1164–1180.

Ellenbogen, M. A., Linnen, A. M., Santo, J. B., aan het Rot, M., Hodgins, S., & Young, S. N. (2013). Salivary cortisol and interpersonal functioning: An event-contingent recording

study in the offspring of parents with bipolar disorder. *Psychoneuroendocrinology, 38*(7), 997–1006.

Ellenbogen, M. A., Santo, J. B., Linnen, A. M., Walker, C. D., & Hodgins, S. (2010). High cortisol levels in the offspring of parents with bipolar disorder during two weeks of daily sampling. *Bipolar Disorders, 12,* 77–86.

Epstein, J., Pan, H., Kocsis, J. H., Yang, Y., Butler, T., et al. (2006) Lack of ventral striatal response to positive stimuli in depressed versus normal subjects. *American Journal of Psychiatry, 163,* 1784–1790.

Eshel, N., & Roiser, J. P. (2010). Reward and punishment processing in depression. *Biological Psychiatry, 68,* 118–124.

Essex, M. J., Klein, M. H., Cho, E., & Kalin, N. H. (2002). Maternal stress beginning in infancy may sensitize children to later stress exposure: Effects on cortisol and behavior. *Biological Psychiatry, 15,* 776–784.

Feinn, R., Nellissery, M., & Kranzler, H. R. (2005). Meta-analysis of the association of a functional serotonin transporter promoter polymorphism with alcohol dependence. *American Journal of Medical Genetics: Part B. Neuropsychiatric Genetics, 133,* 79–84.

Feldman, R., Granat, A., Pariente, C., Kanety, H., Kuint, J., & Gilboa- Schechtman, E. (2009). Maternal depression and anxiety across the postpartum year and infant social engagement, fear regulation, and stress reactivity. *Journal of the American Academy of Child & Adolescent Psychiatry, 48,* 919–927.

Femenía, T., Gómez-Galán, M., Lindskog, M., & Magara, S. (2012). Dysfunctional hippocampal activity affects emotion and cognition in mood disorders. *Brain Research, 1476,* 58–70.

Flory, J. D., Mann, J. J., Manuck, S. B., & Muldoon, M. F. (1998). Recovery from major depression is not associated with normalization of serotonergic function. *Biological Psychiatry, 43,* 320–326.

Foland-Ross, L. C., Brooks, J. O., Mintz, J., Bartzokis, G., Townsend, J., et al. (2012). Mood-state effects on amygdala volume in bipolar disorder. *Journal of Affective Disorders, 139,* 298–301.

Forbes, E. E., May, J. C., Siegle, G. J., Ladouceur, C. D., Ryan, N. D., et al. (2006). Reward-related decision-making in pediatric major depressive disorder: An fMRI study. *Journal of Child Psychology and Psychiatry, 47,* 1031–1040.

Ford, D. E., & Kamerow, D. B. (1989). Epidemiologic study of sleep disturbances and psychiatric disorders. An opportunity for prevention? *Journal of American Medical Association, 262,* 1479–1484.

Fowles, D. C. (1993). Biological variables in psychopathology: A psychobiological perspective. In P. B. Sutker & H. E. Adams (Eds.), *Comprehensive handbook of psychopathology* (2nd ed., pp. 57–82). New York: Plenum Press.

Freis, E. D. (1954). Mental depression in hypertensive patients treated for long periods with large doses of reserpine. *New England Journal of Medicine, 251,* 1006–1008.

Frodl, T., Koutsouleris, N., Bottlender, R., Born, C., Jager, M., et al. (2008). Reduced gray matter brain volumes are associated with variants of the serotonin transporter gene in major depression. *Molecular Psychiatry, 13,* 1093–1101.

Frodl, T., Meisenzahl, E., Zetzsche, T., Born, C., Jager, M., et al. (2003). Larger amygdala volumes in first depressive episode as compared to recurrent major depression and healthy control subjects. *Biological Psychiatry, 53,* 338–344.

Frodl, T., Meisenzahl, E., Zetzsche, T., Bottlender, R., Born, C., et al. (2002). Enlargement of the amygdala in patients with a first episode of major depression. *Biological Psychiatry, 51,* 708–714.

Fu, C. H., Williams, S. C., Cleare, A. J. Brammer, M. J., Walsh, N. D., Kim, J., et al. (2004). Attenuation of the neural response to sad faces in major depression by antidepressant treatment. A prospective, event-related functional magnetic resonance imaging study. *Archives of General Psychiatry, 61,* 877–889.

Gao, J., Pan, Z., Jiao, Z., Li, F., Zhao, G., Wei, Q.,...Evangelou, E. (2012). TPH2 gene polymorphisms and major depression—a meta-analysis. *PloS One, 7,* e36721.

Garrett, A. S., Reiss, A. L., Howe, M. E., Kelley, R. G., Singh, M. K., et al. (2012). Abnormal amygdala and prefrontal cortex activation to facial expressions in pediatric bipolar disorder. *Journal of the American Academy of Child & Adolescent Psychiatry, 51,* 821–831.

Georgieva, L., Dimitrova, A., Nikolov, I., Koleva, S., Tsvetkova, R., Owen, M. J., et al. (2002). Dopamine transporter gene (DAT1) VNTR polymorphism in major psychiatric disorders: Family-based association study in the Bulgarian population. *Acta Psychiatrica Scandinavica, 105,* 396–399.

Giles, D. E., Jarrett, R. B., Roffwarg, H. P., & Rush A. J. (1987). Reduced rapid eye movement latency: A predictor of recurrence in depression. *Neuropsychopharmacology, 1,* 33–39.

Giles, D. E., Kupfer, D. J., Rush, A. J., & Roffwarg, H. P. (1998). Controlled comparison of electrophysiological sleep in families of probands with unipolar depression. *American Journal of Psychiatry, 155,* 192–199.

Gillin, J. C., Mendelson, W. B., & Kupfer, D. J. (1988). The sleep disturbances of depression: Clues to the pathophysiology with special reference to the circadian rapid eye movement rhythm. In D. J. Kupfer & T. H. Monk (Eds.), *Biological rhythms and mental disorders* (pp. 27–54). New York: Guilford Press.

Gillin, J. C., Rapaport, M., Erman, M. K., Winokur, A., & Albala, B. J. (1997). A comparison of nefazodone and fluoxetine on mood and on objective, subjective and clinician-rated measures of sleep in depressed patients: A double-blind, 8-week clinical trial. *Journal of Clinical Psychiatry, 58,* 185–192.

Glahn, D. C., Robinson, J. L., Tordesillas-Gutierrez, D., Monkul, E. S., Holmes, M. K., et al. (2010). Fronto-temporal dysregulation in asymptomatic bipolar I patients: A paired associate functional MRI study. *Human Brain Mapping, 31,* 1041–1051.

Goldberg, J. F., & Harrow, M. (2011). A 15-year prospective follow-up of bipolar affective disorders: Comparisons with unipolar nonpsychotic depression. *Bipolar Disorders, 13,* 155–163

Goodwin, F. K., & Bunney, W. E. (1971). Depressions follow reserpine: A reevaluation. *Seminars in Psychiatry, 3,* 435–448.

Goodwin, F. K., & Jamison, K. R. (2007). *Manic-depressive illness.* Oxford, UK: Oxford University Press.

Goodyer, I. M., Bacon, A., Ban, M., Croudace, T., & Herbert, J. (2009). Serotonin transporter genotype, morning cortisol and subsequent depression in adolescents. *British Journal of Psychiatry, 195,* 39–45.

Goodyer, I. M., Croudace, T., Dudbridge, F., Ban, M., & Herbert, J. (2010). Polymorphisms in BDNF (Val66Met) and 5-HTTLPR, morning cortisol and subsequent depression in at-risk adolescents. *British Journal of Psychiatry, 197,* 365–371.

Goodyer, I. M., Herbert, J., Tamplin, A., & Altham, P. M. E. (2000). Recent life events, cortisol, dehydroepiandrosterone and the onset of major depression in high-risk adolescents. *British Journal of Psychiatry, 177,* 499–504.

Gotlib, I. H., Hamilton, J. P., Cooney, R. E., Singh, M. K., Henry, M L., & Joormann, J. (2010). Neural processing of reward and loss in girls at risk for major depression. *Archives of General Psychiatry, 67*, 380–387.

Gotlib, I. H., Sivers, H., Gabrieli, J. D. E., Whitfield-Gabrieli, S., Goldin, P., et al. (2005). Subgenual anterior cingulate activation to valenced emotional stimuli in major depression. *Neuroreport, 16,* 1731–1734.

Guerry, J. D., & Hastings, P. D. (2011). In search of HPA axis dysregulation in child and adolescent depression. *Clinical Child and Family Psychology Review, 14,* 135–160.

Hafeman, D. M., Chang, K. D., Garrett, A. S., Sanders, E. M., & Phillips, M. L. (2012). Effects of medication on neuroimaging findings in bipolar disorder: An updated review. *Bipolar Disorders, 14,* 375–410.

Hajek, T., Kopecek, M., Kozeny, J., Gunde, E., Alda, M., & Höschl, C. (2009). Amygdala volumes in mood disorders—Meta-analysis of magnetic resonance volumetry studies. *Journal of Affective Disorders, 115,* 395–410.

Halligan, S. L., Herbert, J., Goodyer, I., & Murray, L. (2007). Disturbances in morning cortisol secretion in association with maternal postnatal depression predict subsequent depressive symptomatology in adolescents. *Biological Psychiatry, 62,* 40–46.

Hamilton, J. P., Chen, G., Thomason, M. E., Schwartz, M. E., & Gotlib, I. H. (2011). Investigating neural primacy in major depressive disorder: Multivariate Granger causality analysis of resting-state fMRI time-series data. *Molecular Psychiatry, 16,* 763–772.

Hamilton, J. P., Etkin, A., Furman, D. J., Lemus, M. G., Johnson, R. F., & Gotlib, I. H. (2012). Functional neuroimaging of major depressive disorder: A meta-analysis and new integration of baseline activation and neural response data. *American Journal of Psychiatry, 169,* 693–703.

Hamilton, J. P., Siemer, M., & Gotlib, I. H. (2008). Amygdala volume in major depressive disorder: A meta-analysis of magnetic resonance imaging studies. *Molecular Psychiatry, 13,* 993–1000.

Hankin, B. L., Badanes, L. S., Abela, J. R., & Watamura, S. E. (2010). Hypothalamic pituitary adrenal axis dysregulation in dysphoric children and adolescents: Cortisol reactivity to psychosocial stress from preschool through middle adolescence. *Biological Psychiatry, 68,* 484–490.

Hariri, A. R., Drabant, E. M., & Weinberger, D. R. (2006). Imaging genetics: Perspectives from studies of genetically driven variation in serotonin function and corticolimbic affective processing. *Biological Psychiatry, 59,* 888–897.

Hasler, G., Drevets, W. C., Gould, T. D., Gottesman, I. I., & Manji, H. K. (2006). Toward constructing an endophenotype strategy for bipolar disorders. *Biological Psychiatry, 60,* 93–105.

Hassel, S., Almeida, J. R. C., Kerr, N., Nau, S., Ladouceur, C. D., et al. (2008). Elevated striatal and decreased dorsolateral prefrontal cortical activity in response to emotional stimuli in euthymic bipolar disorder: No associations with psychotropic medication load. *Bipolar Disorders, 10,* 916–927.

Haynes, P. L., McQuaid, J. R., Kelsoe, J., Rapaport, M., & Gillin, J. C. (2004). Affective states and EEG sleep profile in response to rapid tryptophan depletion in recently recovered nonmedicated depressed individuals. *Journal of Affective Disorders, 83,* 253–262.

Heim, C., & Nemeroff, C. B. (2001). The role of childhood trauma in the neurobiology of mood and anxiety disorders: Preclinical and clinical studies. *Biological Psychiatry, 49,* 1023–1039.

Heninger, G. R., Delgado, P. L., & Charney, D. S. (1996). The revised monoamine therapy of depression: A modulatory role of monoamines, based on new findings from monoamine depletion experiments in humans. *Pharmacopsychiatry, 29,* 2–11.

Hinkelmann, K., Moritz, S., Botzenhardt, J., Riedesel, K., Wiedemann, K., Kellner, M., & Otte, C. (2009). Cognitive impairment in major depression: Association with salivary cortisol. *Biological Psychiatry, 66,* 879–885.

Hooley, J. M., Gruber, S. A., Scott, L. A., Hiller, J. B., & Yurgelun-Todd, D. A. (2005). Activation in dorsolateral prefrontal cortex in response to maternal criticism and praise in recovered depressed and healthy control participants. *Biological Psychiatry, 57,* 809–812.

Hsiao, M. C., Lin, K. J., Liu, C. Y., & Beck Schatz, D. (2013). The interaction between dopamine transporter function, gender differences, and possible laterality in depression. *Psychiatry Research, 211,* 72–77.

Huber, T. J., Issa, K., Schik, G., & Wolf, O. T. (2006). The cortisol awakening response is blunted in psychotherapy inpatients suffering from depression. *Psychoneuroendocrinology, 31,* 900–904.

Jacobs, N., Kenis, G., Peeters, F., Derom, C., Vlietinck, R., & van Os, J. (2006). Stress-related negative affectivity and genetically altered serotonin transporter function: Evidence of synergism in shaping risk of depression. *Archives of General Psychiatry, 63,* 989–996.

Johnson, S. L., Edge, M. D., Holmes, M. K., & Carver, C. S. (2012). The behavioral activation system and mania. *Annual Review of Clinical Psychology, 8,* 243–267.

Jones, F., Bright, J., & Chow, A. (2001). *Stress: Myth, theory, and research.* New York: Pearson Education.

Jones, S. H., Tai, S., Evershed, K., Knowles, R., & Bentall, R. (2006). Early detection of bipolar disorder: A pilot familial high-risk study of parents with bipolar disorder and their adolescent children. *Bipolar Disorders, 8,* 362–372.

Joormann, J. (2009). Cognitive aspects of depression. In I. H. Gotlib & C. L. Hammen (Eds.), *Handbook of depression* (pp. 298–321). New York: Guilford Press.

Joormann, J., Cooney, R. E., Henry, M. L., & Gotlib, I. H. (2012). Neural correlates of automatic mood regulation in girls at high risk for depression. *Journal of Abnormal Psychology, 121,* 61–72.

Kalivas, P. W., Duffy, P., DuMars, L. A., & Skinner, C. (1988). Behavioral and neurochemical effects of acute and daily cocaine administration in rats. *Journal of Pharmacological Experimental Therapy, 245,* 482–492.

Kanazawa, T., Glatt, S. J., Kia-Keating, B., Yoneda, H., & Tsuang, M. T. (2007). Meta-analysis reveals no association of the Val66Met polymorphism of brain-derived neurotrophic factor with either schizophrenia or bipolar disorder. *Psychiatric Genetics, 17,* 165–170.

Kaneko, M., Yokoyama, F., Hoshino, Y., Takahagi, K., Murata, S., Watanabe, M., et al. (1992). Hypothalamic-pituitary-adrenal axis function in chronic schizophrenia: Association with clinical features. *Neuropsychobiology, 25,* 1–7.

Karg, K., Burmeister, M., Shedden, K., & Sen, S. (2011). The serotonin transporter promoter variant (5-HTTLPR), stress, and depression meta-analysis revisited: Evidence of genetic moderation. *Archives of General Psychiatry, 68,* 444–454.

Karkowski, L. M., & Kendler, K. S. (1997). An examination of the genetic relationship between bipolar and unipolar illness in an epidemiological sample. *Psychiatric Genetics, 7,* 159–163.

Kato, T. (2007). Molecular genetics of bipolar disorder and depression. *Psychiatry and Clinical Neurosciences, 61,* 3–19.

Keedwell, P. A., Andrew, C., Williams, S. C. R., Brammer, M. J., & Phillips, M. L. (2005). The neural correlates of anhedonia in major depressive disorder. *Biological Psychiatry, 58,* 843–853.

Kendler, K. S., & Prescott, C. A. (1999). A population-based twin study of lifetime major depression in men and women. *Archives of General Psychiatry, 56,* 39–44.

Kendler, K. S., Prescott, C. A., Myers, J., & Neale, M. C. (2003). The structure of genetic and environmental risk factors for common psychiatric and substance use disorders in men and women. *Archives of General Psychiatry, 60,* 929–937.

Kennedy, S. H., Evans, K. R., Krüger, S., Mayberg, H. S., Meyer, J. H., McCann, S., et al. (2001). Changes in regional brain glucose metabolism measured with positive electron tomography after paroxetine treatment of major depression. *American Journal of Psychiatry, 158,* 899–905.

Kerestes, R., Bhagwager, Z., Nathan, P. J., Meda, S. A., Ladouceur, C. D., et al. (2012). Prefrontal cortical response to emotional faces in individuals with major depressive disorder in remission. *Psychiatry Research: Neuroimaging, 202,* 30–37.

Kessler, R. C., Berglund, P., Demler, O., Jin, R., Koretz, D., Merikangas, K. R., et al. (2003). The epidemiology of major depressive disorder: Results from the National Comorbidity Survey Replication (NCS-R). *Journal of American Medical Association, 289,* 3095–3105.

Ketter, T. A., Kimbrell, T. A., George, M. S., Dunn, R. T., Speer, A. M., et al. (2001). Effects of mood and subtype on cerebral glucose metabolism in treatment-resistant bipolar disorder. *Biological Psychiatry, 49,* 97–109.

Kiecolt-Glaser, J. K., McGuire, L., Robles, T. F., & Glaser, R. (2002). Emotions, morbidity, and mortality: New perspectives from psychoneuroimmunology. *Annual Review of Psychology, 53,* 83–107.

Kieseppa, T., Partonen, T., Haukka, J., Kaprio, J., & Lonnqvist, J. (2004). High concordance of bipolar I disorder in a nationwide sample of twins. *American Journal of Psychiatry, 161,* 1814–1821.

Kim, Y. K., Jung, H. G., Myint, A. M., Kim, H., & Park, S. H. (2007). Imbalance between pro-inflammatory and anti-inflammatory cytokines in bipolar disorder. *Journal of Affective Disorders, 104,* 91–95.

Kirschbaum, C., Pirke, K. M., & Hellhammer, D. H. (1993). The "Trier Social Stress Test"—A tool for investigating psychobiological stress responses in a laboratory setting. *Neuropsychobiology, 28,* 76–81.

Kitayama, I., Nakamura, S., Yaga, T., Murase, S., Nomura, J., Kayahara, T., et al. (1994). Degeneration of locus coeruleus axons in stress-induced depression model. *Brain Research Bulletin, 35,* 573–580.

Kivi, S. A. (1996). Insomnia as a presenting symptom of mania. *Postgraduate Medicine, 99,* 143–146.

Knorr, U., Vinberg, M., Kessing, L. V., & Wetterslev, J. (2010). Salivary cortisol in depressed patients versus control persons: A systematic review and meta-analysis. *Psychoneuroendocrinology, 35,* 1275–1286.

Knowles, J. B., Waldron, J., & Cairns, J. (1979). Sleep preceding the onset of a manic episode. *Biological Psychiatry, 14,* 671–675.

Krüger, S., Braunig, P., & Young, L. T. (1996). Biological treatments of rapid-cycling bipolar disorder. *Pharmacopsychiatry, 29,* 167–175.

Krüger, S., Seminowicz, D., Goldapple, K., Kennedy, S. H., & Mayberg, H. S. (2003). State and trait influences on mood regulation in bipolar disorder: Blood flow differences with an acute mood challenge. *Biological Psychiatry, 54,* 1274–1283.

Lagopoulos, J., Ivanovski, B., & Malhi, G. S. (2007). An event-related functional MRI study of working memory in euthymic bipolar disorder. *Journal of Psychiatry & Neuroscience, 32,* 174–184.

Landolt, H. P., Raimo, E. B., Schnierow, B. J., Kelsoe, J. R., Rappaport, M. H., & Gillen, C. J. (2001). Sleep and sleep electroencephalogram in depressed patients treated with phenelzine. *Archives of General Psychiatry, 58,* 268–276.

LaPalme, M., Hodgins, S., & LaRoche, C. (1997). Children of parents with bipolar disorder: A meta-analysis of risk for mental disorders. *Canadian Journal of Psychiatry, 42,* 623–631.

Lasky-Su, J. A., Faraone, S. V., Glatt, S. J., & Tsuang, M. T. (2005). Meta-analysis of the association between two polymorphisms in the serotonin transporter gene and affective disorders. *American Journal of Medical Genetics, 133B,* 110–115.

Lau, J. Y., & Eley, T. C. (2010). The genetics of mood disorders. *Annual Review of Clinical Psychology, 6,* 313–337.

Lee, A. L., Ogle, W. O., & Sapolsky, R. M. (2002). Stress and depression: Possible links to neuron death in the hippocampus. *Bipolar Disorder, 4,* 117–128.

Leibenluft, E., Albert, P. S., Rosenthal, N. E., & Wehr, T. A. (1996). Relationship between sleep and mood in patients with rapid-cycling bipolar disorder. *Psychiatry Research, 63,* 161–168.

Lesch, K. P., & Canli, T. (2006). 5-HT$_{1A}$ receptor and anxiety-related traits. In T. Canli (Ed.), *Biology of personality and individual differences* (pp. 273–294). New York: Guilford Press.

Lichtenstein, P., Yip, B. H., Bjork, C., Pawitan, Y., Cannon, T. D., Sullivan, P. F., & Hultman, C. M. (2009). Common genetic determinants of schizophrenia and bipolar disorder in Swedish families: A population-based study. *Lancet, 373,* 234–239.

Lindquist, K. A., Wager, T. D., Kober, H., Bliss-Moreau, E., & Barrett, L. F. (2012). The brain basis of emotion: A meta-analytic review. *Behavioral and Brain Sciences, 35,* 121–143.

Lopez-Duran, N. L., Kovacs, M., & George, C. J. (2009). Hypothalamic-pituitary-adrenal axis dysregulation in depressed children and adolescents: A meta-analysis. *Psychoneuroendocrinology, 34,* 1272.

Lopez Leon, S., Croes, E. A., Sayed-Tabatabaei, F. A., Claes, S., Van Broekhoven, C., & van Duijn, C. M. (2005). The dopamine D4 receptor gene 48-base-pair repeat polymorphism and mood disorders: A meta-analysis. *Biological Psychiatry, 57,* 999–1003.

Lovallo, W. R., & Thomas, T. L. (2000). Stress hormones in psychophysiological research. In J. T. Cacioppo, L. G. Tassinary, & G. G. Bernston (Eds.), *Handbook of psychophysiology* (pp. 342–367). Cambridge, UK: Cambridge University Press.

Malhi, G. S., Lagopoulos, J., Sachdev, P. S., Ivanovski, B., & Shnier, R. (2005). An emotional Stroop functional MRI study of euthymic bipolar disorder. *Bipolar Disorders, 7,* 58–69.

Manki, H., Kanba, S., Muramatsu, T., Higuchi, S., Suzuki, E., Matsushita, S., et al. (1996). Dopamine D2, D3 and D4 receptor and transporter gene polymorphisms and mood disorders. *Journal of Affective Disorders, 9,* 7–13.

Mayberg, H. S., Keightley, M., Mahurin, R. K., & Brannan, S. K. (2004). *Neuropsychiatric aspects of mood and affective disorders.* Washington, DC: American Psychiatric Publishing.

McCabe, C., Cowen, P. J., & Harmer, C. J. (2009). Neural representation of reward in recovered depressed patients. *Psychopharmacology, 205,* 667–677.

McEwen, B. S. (2008). Central effects of stress hormones in health and disease: Understanding the protective and damaging effects of stress and stress mediators. *European Journal of Pharmacology, 583,* 174–185.

McGrath, P. J., Quitkin, F. M., & Klein, D. F. (1995). Bromocriptine treatment of relapses seen during selective serotonin reuptake inhibitor treatment of depression. *Journal of Clinical Psychopharmacology, 15*, 289–291.

McGuffin, P., Rijsdijk, F., Andrew, M., Sham, P., Katz, R., & Cardno, A. (2003). The heritability of bipolar affective disorder and the genetic relationship to MDD. *Archives of General Psychiatry, 60*, 497–502.

McKay, M. S., & Zakzanis, K. K. (2010). The impact of treatment on HPA axis activity in unipolar major depression. *Journal of Psychiatric Research, 44*, 183–192.

Merikangas, K. R., Akiskal, H. S., Angst, J., Greenberg, P. E., Hirschfeld, R. M. A., Petukhova, M., & Kessler, R. C. (2007). Lifetime and 12-month prevalence of bipolar spectrum disorder in the National Comorbidity Survey Replication. *Archives of General Psychiatry, 64*, 543–552.

Miklowitz, D. J., & Johnson, S. L. (2006). The psychopathology and treatment of bipolar disorder. *Annual Review Clinical Psychology, 2*, 199–235.

Miller, D. B., & O'Callaghan, J. P. (2002). Neuroendocrine aspects of the response to stress. *Metabolism, 51*, 5–10.

Milne, A. M. B., MacQueen, G. M., & Hall, G. B. C. (2012) Abnormal hippocampal activation in patients with extensive history of major depression: An fMRI study. *Journal of Psychiatry & Neuroscience, 37*, 28–36.

Mitterschiffthaler, M. T., Williams, S. C. R., Walsh, N. D., Cleare, A. J., Donaldson, C., et al. (2008). Neural basis of the emotional Stroop interference effect in major depression. *Psychological Medicine, 38*, 247–256.

Mokhtari, M., Arfken, C., & Boutros, N. (2013). The DEX/CRH test for major depression: A potentially useful diagnostic test. *Psychiatry Research, 208*(2), 131–139.

Monk, C. S., Klein, R. G., Telzer, E. H., Schroth, E. A., Mannuzza, S., et al. (2008). Amygdala and nucleus accumbens activation to emotional facial expressions in children and adolescents at risk for major depression. *American Journal of Psychiatry, 165*, 90–98.

Moore, P., Landolt, H.-P., Seifritz, E., Clark, C., Bhatti, T., Kelsoe, J., et al. (2000). Clinical and physiological consequences of rapid tryptophan depletion. *Neuropsychopharmacology, 23*, 601–622.

Morris, M. C., Rao, U., & Garber, J. (2012). Cortisol responses to psychosocial stress predict depression trajectories: Social-evaluative threat and prior depressive episodes as moderators. *Journal of Affective Disorders, 143*, 223–230.

Muller, J., Pryor, W., Gibbons, J., & Orgain, E. (1955). Depression and anxiety occurring during Rauwolfia therapy. *Journal of the American Medical Association, 159*, 836–839.

Mullin, B. C., Perlman, S. B., Versace, A., de Almeida, J. R. C., LaBarbara, E. J., et al. (2012). An fMRI study of attentional control in the context of emotional distracters in euthymic adults with bipolar disorder. *Psychiatry Research: Neuroimaging, 201*, 196–205.

Munafò, M. R., Hayward, G., & Harmer, C. (2006). Selective processing of social threat cues following acute tryptophan depletion. *Journal of Psychopharmacology, 20*, 33–39.

Naranjo, C. A., Tremblay, L. K., & Buston, U. E. (2001). The role of the brain reward system in depression. *Progress in Neuro-Psychopharmacology & Biological Psychiatry, 25*, 781–823.

Navailles, S., Moison, D., Cunningham, K. A., & Spampinato, U. (2008). Differential regulation of the mesoaccumbens dopamine circuit by serotonin 2C receptors in the ventral tegmental area and the nucleus accumbens: An in vivo microdialysis study with cocaine. *Neuropsychopharmacology, 33*, 237–246.

Nery, F. G., Chen, H-H., Hatch, J. P., Nicoletti, M. A., Brambilla, P., et al. (2009). Orbitofrontal cortex gray matter volumes in bipolar disorder patients: A region-of-interest MRI study. *Bipolar Disorders, 11*, 145–153.

Nestler, E. J., & Carlezon, W. A., Jr. (2006). The mesolimbic dopamine reward system in depression. *Biological Psychiatry, 59*, 1151–1159.

Neumeister, A., Hu, X. Z., Luckenbaugh, D. A., Schwarz, M., Nugent, A C., Bonne, O., et al. (2006). Differential effects of the 5-HTTLPR genotypes on the behavioral and neural responses to tryptophan depletion in patients with major depression and controls. *Archives of General Psychiatry, 63*, 978–986.

Neumeister, A., Konstantinidis, A., Stastny, J., Schwarz, M. J., Vitouch, O., Willeit, M., et al. (2002). Association between the serotonin transporter gene promoter polymorphism (5-HTTLPR) and behavioral responses to tryptophan depletion in healthy women with and without family history of depression. *Archives of General Psychiatry, 59*, 613–620.

Nikolaus, S., Antke, C., & Muller, H. W. (2009). In vivo imaging of synaptic function in the central nervous system: II. Mental and affective disorders. *Behavioural Brain Research, 204*, 32–66.

Nordin, C., Siwers, B., & Bertilsson, L. (1981). Bromocriptine treatment of depressive disorders: Clinical and biochemical effects. *Acta Psychiatrica Scandinavica, 64*, 25–33.

Nunes, G. P., Tufik, S., & Nobrega, J. N. (1994). Autoradiographic analysis of D-sub-1 and D-sub-2 dopaminergic receptors in rat brain after paradoxical sleep deprivation. *Brain Research Bulletin, 34,* 453–456.

Nurnberger, J. I., Jr., Berrettini, W., Simmons-Alling, S., Lawrence, D., & Brittain, H. (1990). Blunted ACTH and cortisol response to afternoon tryptophan infusion in euthymic bipolar patients. *Psychiatry Research, 31,* 57–67.

Nusslock, R. R., Almeida, J. R. C., Forbes, E. E., Versace, A., Frank, E., et al. (2012). Waiting to win: Elevated striatal and orbitofrontal cortical activity during reward anticipation in euthymic bipolar disorder adults. *Bipolar Disorders, 14,* 249–260.

O'Brien, S. M., Scully, P., Scott, L. V., & Dinan, T. G. (2006). Cytokine profiles in bipolar affective disorder: Focus on acutely ill patients. *Journal of Affective Disorders, 90,* 263–267.

Ochsner, K. N., & Gross, J. J. (2005). The cognitive control of emotion. *Trends in Cognitive Sciences, 9,* 242–249.

Olino, T. M., McMakin, D. L., Dahl, R. E., Ryan, N. D., Silk, J. S., et al. (2011). "I won, but I'm not getting my hopes up": Depression moderates the relationship of outcomes and reward anticipation. *Psychiatry Research: Neuroimaging, 194,* 393–395.

Ösby, U., Brandt, L., Correia, N., Ekbom, A., & Sparén, P. (2001). Excess mortality in bipolar and unipolar disorder in Sweden. *Archives of General Psychiatry, 58,* 844–850.

Owens, M. J., Plosky, P. M., & Nemeroff, C. B. (1999). The role of corticotropin-releasing factor in depression and anxiety disorders. *Journal of Endocrinology, 160,* 1–12.

Pariante, C. M. (2004). Glucocorticoid receptor function in vitro in patients with major depression. *Stress: The International Journal on the Biology of Stress, 7*(4), 209–219.

Peeters, F., Nicholson, N. A., & Berkhof, J. (2003). Cortisol responses to daily events in major depressive disorder. *Psychosomatic Medicine, 65,* 836–841.

Perlis, M. L., Giles, D. E., Buysse, D. J., Tu, X., & Kupfer, D. J. (1997). Self-reported sleep disturbance as a prodromal symptom in recurrent depression. *Journal of Affective Disorders, 42,* 209–212.

Perlman, G., Simmons, A. N., Wu, J., Hahn, K. S., Tapert, S. F., et al. (2012). Amygdala response and functional connectivity during emotion regulation: A study of 14 depressed adolescents. *Journal of Affective Disorders, 139,* 75–84.

Perlman, S. B., Almeida, J. R. C., Kronhaus, D. M., Versace, A., LaBarbara, E. J., et al. (2012). Amygdala activity and prefrontal cortex–amygdala effective connectivity to emerging emotional faces distinguished remitted and depressed mood states in bipolar disorder. *Bipolar Disorders, 14,* 162–174.

Phillips, W. J., Hine, D. W., & Thorsteinsson, E. B. (2010). Implicit cognition and depression: A meta-analysis. *Clinical Psychology Review, 30,* 691–709.

Pillai, V., Kalmbach, D. A., & Ciesla, J. A. (2011). A meta-analysis of electroencephalographic sleep in depression: Evidence for genetic biomarkers. *Biological Psychiatry, 70,* 912–919.

Pizzagalli, D. A., Dillon, D. G., Bogdan, R., & Holmes, A. J. (2011). Reward and punishment processing in the human brain: Clues from affective neuroscience and implications for depression research. In O. Vartanian & D. R. Mandel (Eds.), *Neuroscience of decision making* (pp. 199–220). New York: Psychology Press.

Pizzagalli, D., Shackman, A. J., & Davidson, R. J. (2001). The functional neuroimaging of human emotion: Asymmetric contributions of cortical and subcortical circuitry. In K. Hugdahl & R. J. Davidson (Eds.), *The assymetrical brain* (pp. 511–532). Cambridge, MA: MIT Press.

Porter, R., & Gallagher, P. (2006). Abnormalities of the HPA axis in affective disorders: Clinical subtypes and potential treatments. *Acta Neuropsychiatrica, 18,* 193–209.

Price, L. H., Malison, R. T., McDougle, C. J., McCanze-Katz, E. F., Owen, K. R., & Heninger, G. R. (1997). Neurobiology of tryptophan depletion in depression: Effects of m-chlorophenylpiperazine (mCPP). *Neuropsychopharmacology, 17,* 342–350.

Rajkowska, G. (2000). Postmortem studies in mood disorders indicate altered numbers of neurons and glial cells. *Biological Psychiatry, 48,* 766–777.

Ramel, W., Goldin, P. R., Eyler, L. T., Brown, G. G., Gotlib, I. H., & McQuaid, J. R. (2007). Amygdala reactivity and mood-congruent memory in individuals at risk for depressive relapse. *Biological Psychiatry, 61,* 231–239.

Ramsay, D., & Lewis, M. (2003). Reactivity and regulation in cortisol and behavioral responses to stress. *Child Development, 74,* 456–464.

Rao, U., Dahl, R. E., Ryan, N. D., Birmaher, B., Williamson, D. E., Giles, D. E.,…Nelson, B. (1996). The relationship between longitudinal clinical course and sleep and cortisol changes in adolescent depression. *Biological Psychiatry, 40,* 474–484.

Ressler, K. J., & Nemeroff, C. B. (1999). Role of norepinephrine in the pathophysiology and treatment of mood disorders. *Biological Psychiatry, 46,* 1219–1233.

Rice, F. (2010). Genetics of childhood and adolescent depression: Insights into etiological heterogeneity and challenges for future genomic research. *Genome Medicine, 2,* 68.

Rich, B. A., Vinton, D. T., Roberson Nay, R., Hommer, R. E., Berghorst, L. H., et al. (2006). Limbic hyperactivation during processing of neutral facial expressions in children with bipolar disorder. *Proceedings of the National Academy of Sciences of the United States of America, 103*(23), 8900–8905.

Ritchey, M., Dolcos, F., Eddington, K. M., Strauman, T. J., & Cabeza, R. (2011). Neural correlates of emotional processing in depression: Changes with cognitive behavioral therapy and predictors of treatment response. *Journal of Psychiatric Research, 45,* 577–587.

Ritter, P. S., Marx, C., Bauer, M., Lepold, K., & Pfennig, A. (2011). The role of disturbed sleep in the early recognition of bipolar disorder: A systematic review. *Bipolar Disorders, 13,* 227–237.

Rogers, M. A., Bradshaw, J. L., Pantelis, C., & Phillips, J. G. (1998). Frontostriatal deficits in unipolar major depression. *Brain Research Bulletin, 47,* 297–310.

Rush, A. J., Giles, D. E., Schlesser, M. A., & Orsulak, P. J. (1997). Dexamethasone response, thrytotropin-releasing hormone stimulation, rapid eye movement latency and subtypes of depression. *Biological Psychiatry, 41,* 915–928.

Rutter, M., & Silberg, J. (2002). Gene–environment interplay in relation to emotional and behavioral disturbance. *Annual Review of Psychology, 53,* 463–490.

Sacher, J., Neumann, J., Fünfstück, T., Soliman, A., Villringer, A., & Schroeter, M L. (2012). Mapping the depressed brain: A meta-analysis of structural and functional alterations in major depressive disorder. *Journal of Affective Disorders, 140,* 142–148.

Salamone, J. D., Correa, M., Farrar, A., & Mingote, S. M. (2007). Effort-related functions of nucleus accumbens dopamine and associated forebrain circuits. *Psychopharmacology, 191,* 461–482.

Saleh, K., Carballedo, A., Lisiecka, D., Fagan, A. J., Connolly, et al. (2012). Impact of family history and depression on amygdala volume. *Psychiatry Research, 203*(1), 24–30.

Sapolsky, R. M. (2000). Glucocorticoids and hippocampal atrophy in neuropsychiatric disorders. *Archives of General Psychiatry, 57,* 925–935.

Sapolsky, R. M., Romero, L. M., & Munck, A. U. (2000). How do glucocorticoids influence stress responses? Integrating permissive, suppressive, stimulatory, and preparative actions. *Endocrine Reviews, 21,* 55–89.

Sax, K. W., & Strakowski, S. M. (2001). Behavioral sensitization in humans. *Journal of Addictive Diseases, 20,* 55–65.

Schaefer, H. S., Putnam, K. M., Benca, R. M., & Davidson, R. J. (2006). Event-related functional magnetic resonance imaging measures of neural activity to positive social stimuli in pre- and post-treatment depression. *Biological Psychiatry, 60,* 974–986.

Schatzberg, A. F., & Schildkraut, J. J. (1995). Recent studies on norepinephrine systems in mood disorders. In F. E. Bloom & D. J. Kupfer (Eds.), *Psychopharmacology: The fourth generation of progress* (pp. 911–920). New York: Raven Press.

Schiepers, O. J. G., Wichers, M. C., & Maes M. (2004). Cytokines and major depression. *Progress in Neuro-Psychopharmacology & Biological Psychiatry, 29,* 201–217.

Schuhmacher, A., Mössner, R., Jessen, F., Scheef, L., Block, W., Belloche, A. C.,…Zobel, A. (2012). Association of amygdala volumes with cortisol secretion in unipolar depressed patients. *Psychiatry Research: Neuroimaging, 202,* 96–103.

Sheline, Y. I., Barch, D. M., Donnelly, J. M., Ollinger, J. M., Snyder, A. Z., & Mintum, M. A. (2001). Increased amygdala responses to masked emotional faces in depressed subjects resolves with antidepressant medication: An fMRI study. *Biological Psychiatry, 50,* 651–658.

Shih, R. A., Belmonte, P. L., & Zandi, P. P. (2004). A review of the evidence from family, twin, and adoption studies for a genetic contribution to adult psychiatric disorders. *International Review of Psychiatry, 16,* 260–283.

Shin, L. M., Wright, C. I., Cannistraro, P. A., Wedig, M. M., McMullin, K., Martis, B., et al. (2005). A functional magnetic resonance imaging study of amygdala and medical pre-frontal cortex responses to overtly presented fearful faces in posttraumatic stress disorder. *Archives of General Psychiatry, 62,* 273–281.

Siegle, G. J., Carter, C. S., & Thase, M. E. (2006). Use of fMRI to predict recovery from unipolar depression with cognitive behavior therapy. *American Journal of Psychiatry, 163,* 735–731.

Siegle, G. J., Steinhauer, S. R., Carter, C. S., Ramel, W., & Thase, M. E. (2003). Do the seconds turn into hours? Relationships between sustained pupil dilation in response to emotional information and self-reported rumination. *Cognitive Therapy and Research, 27*, 365–382.

Siegle, G. J., Thompson, W., Carter, C. S., Steinhauer, S. R., & Thase, M. E. (2007). Increased amygdala and decreased dorsolateral prefrontal BOLD responses in unipolar depression: Related and independent features. *Biological Psychiatry, 61*, 198–209.

Sitaram, N., Nurnberger, J. I., Jr., Gershon, E. S., & Gillin, J. C. (1982). Cholingergic reduction of mood and REM sleep: Potential model and marker of vulnerability to affective disorder. *American Journal of Psychiatry, 139*, 571–576.

Slavich, G. M., & Irwin, M. R. (2014). From stress to inflammation and major depressive disorder: A social signal transduction theory of depression. *Psychological Bulletin, 140*, 774–815.

Smith, E. N., Bloss, C. S., Badner, J. A., Barrett, T., Belmonte, P. L., Berrettini, W.,…Kelsoe, J. R. (2009). Genome-wide association study of bipolar disorder in European American and African American individuals. *Molecular Psychiatry, 14*, 755–763.

Smith, L. A., Cornelius, V., Warnock, A., Tacchi, M. J., & Taylor, D. (2007). Pharmacological interventions for acute bipolar mania: a systematic review of randomized placebo-controlled trials. *Bipolar Disorders, 9*, 551–560.

Smoller, J. W., & Finn, C. T. (2003). Family, twin and adoption studies of bipolar disorder. *American Journal of Medical Genetics Part C: Seminars in Medical Genetics, 123C*, 48–58.

Smoski, M. J., Felder, J., Bizzell, J., Green, S. R., Ernst, M., Lynch, T. R., & Dichter, G. S. (2009). fMRI of alterations in reward selection, anticipation, and feedback in major depressive disorder. *Journal of Affective Disorders, 118*, 69–78.

Sobczak, S., Honig, A., Nicolson, N. A., & Riedel, W. J. (1999). Effects of acute tryptophan depletion on mood and cortisol release in first-degree relatives of type I and type II bipolar patients and healthy matched controls. *Neuropsychopharmacology, 27*, 834–842.

Sobczak, S., Honig, A., van Duinen, M. A., & Riedel, W. J. (2002). Serotonergic dysregulation in bipolar disorders: A literature review of serotonergic challenge studies. *Bipolar Disorders, 4*, 347–356.

Stetler, C., & Miller, G. E. (2011). Depression and hypothalamic-pituitary-adrenal activation: A quantitative summary of four decades of research. *Psychosomatic Medicine, 73*, 114–126.

Stockmeier, C. A. (2003). Involvement of serotonin in depression: Evidence from postmortem and imaging studies of serotonin receptors and the serotonin transporter. *Journal of Psychiatric Research, 37*, 357–373.

Stokes, P. E. (1995). The potential role of excessive cortisol induced by HPA hyperfunction in the pathogenesis of depression. *European Neuropsychopharmacology, 5*, 77–82.

Strakowski, S. M., Adler, C. M., Almeida, J., Altshuler, L. L., Blumberg, H. P., et al. (2012). The functional neuroanatomy of bipolar disorder: a consensus model. *Bipolar Disorders, 14*, 313–325.

Strakowski, S. M., Sax, K. W., Setters, M. J., Stan-ton, S. P., & Keck, P. E. J., Jr. (1997). Lack of enhanced behavioral response to repeated d-amphetamine challenge in first-episode psychosis: Implications for sensitization model of psychosis in humans. *Biological Psychiatry, 42*, 749–755.

Sullivan, G. M., Apergis, J., Bush, D. E., Johnson, L. R., Hou, M., & LeDoux, J. E. (2004). Lesions in the bed nucleus of the stria terminalis disrupt corticosterone and freezing responses elicited by a contextual but not by a specific cue-conditioned fear stimulus. *Neuroscience, 128*, 7–14.

Sullivan, P. F., Neale, M. C., & Kendler, K. S. (2000). Genetic epidemiology of major depression: Review and meta-analysis. *American Journal of Psychiatry, 157*, 1552–1562.

Thase, M. E., Buysse, D. J., Frank, E., Chery, C. R., Cornes, C. L., Mallinger, A. G., et al. (1997). Which depressed patients will respond to interpersonal psychotherapy? The role of abnormal EEG sleep profiles. *American Journal of Psychiatry, 154*, 502–509.

Thase, M. E., Simons, A. D., & Reynolds, C. F. (1993). Psychobiological correlates of poor response to cognitive behavioral therapy: Potential indications for antidepressant pharmacotherapy. *Psychopharmacological Bulletin, 29*, 293–301.

Thermenos, H. W., Whitfield-Gabrieli, S., Giuliano, A. J., Lee, E. H., Faraone, S. V., et al. (2011). A functional MRI study of working memory in adolescents and young adults at genetic risk for bipolar disorder: Preliminary findings. *Bipolar Disorders, 13*, 272–286.

Townsend, J., & Altshuler, L. L. (2012). Emotion processing and regulation in bipolar disorder: A review. *Bipolar Disorders, 14*, 326–339.

Townsend, J., Bookheimer, S. Y., Foland-Ross, L. C., Sugar, C. A., & Altshuler, L. L. (2010). fMRI abnormalities in dorsolateral prefrontal cortex during a working memory task in manic, euthymic and depressed bipolar subjects. *Psychiatry Research: Neuroimaging, 182*, 22–29.

Townsend, J. D., Eberhart, N. K., Bookheimer, S. Y., Eisenberger, N. I., Foland-Ross, L. C., et al. (2010). fMRI activation in the amygdala and the orbitofrontal cortex in unmedicated subjects with major depressive disorder. *Psychiatry Research: Neuroimaging, 183*(3), 209–217.

Treadway, M. T., & Zald, D. H. (2011). Reconsidering anhedonia in depression: lessons from translation neuroscience. *Neuroscience and Biobehavioral Reviews, 35*, 537–555.

Trivedi, M. H., Rush, A. J., Wisniewski, S. R., Nierenberg, A. A., Warden, D., Ritz, L.,…Fava, M., & the STAR*D Study Team (2006). Evaluation of outcomes with citalopram for depression using measurement-based care in STAR*D: Implications for clinical practice. *American Journal of Psychiatry, 163*, 28–40.

Tsigos, C., & Chrousos, G. P. (2002). Hypothalamic-pituitary-adrenal axis, neuroendocrine factors and stress. *Journal of Psychosomatic Research, 53*, 865–871.

Uher, R., & McGuffin, P. (2010). The moderation by the serotonin transporter gene of environmental adversity in the etiology of depression: 2009 update. *Molecular Psychiatry, 15*, 18–22.

Usher, J., Leucht, S., Falkai, P., & Scherk, H. (2010). Correlation between amygdala volume and age in bipolar disorder—A systematic review and meta-analysis of structural MRI studies. *Psychiatry Research: Neuroimaging, 182*, 1–8.

Valiengo, L. L., Soeiro-de-Souza, M. G., Marques, A. H., Moreno, D. H., Juruena, M. F., Andreazza, A. C.,…Machado-Vieira, R. (2012). Plasma cortisol in first episode drug-naïve mania: Differential levels in euphoric versus irritable mood. *Journal of Affective Disorders. 138*, 149–152.

Van der Schot, A., Kahn, R., Ramsey, N., Nolen, W., & Vink, M. (2010). Trait and state dependent functional impairments in bipolar disorder. *Psychiatry Research: Neuroimaging, 184*, 135–142.

van der Veen, F. M., Evers, E. A., Deutz, N. E., & Schmitt, J. A. (2007). Effects of acute tryptophan depletion on mood and facial emotion perception related brain activation and performance in healthy women with and without a family history of depression. *Neuropsychopharmacology, 32*, 216–24.

van Erp, T. G. M., Thompson, P. M., Kieseppä, T., Bearden, C. E., Marino, A. C., et al. (2012). Hippocampal morphology in lithium and non-lithium-treated bipolar I disorder patients, non-bipolar co-twins, and control twins. *Human Brain Mapping, 33*, 501–510.

van Londen, L., Goekoop, J. G., Kerkhof, G. A., Zwinderman, K. H., Wiegant, V. M., & de Wied, D. (2001). Weak 24-h periodicity of body temperature and increased plasma vasopressin in melancholic depression. *European Neuropsychopharmacology, 11*, 7–14.

Verhagen, M., van der Meij, A., van Deurzen, P. A. M., Janzing, J. G. E., Arias-Vásquez, A., Buitelaar, J. K., & Franke, B. (2008). Meta-analysis of the BDNF Val66Met polymorphism in major depressive disorder: Effects of gender and ethnicity. *Molecular Psychiatry, 15*, 260–271.

Vieta, E., Martinez-De-Osaba, M. J., Colom, F., Martinez-Aran, A., Benabarre, A., & Gasto, C. (1999). Enhanced corticotropin response to corticotropin-releasing hormone as a predictor of mania in euthymic bipolar patients. *Psychological Medicine, 29*, 971–978.

Vreeburg, S. A., Hoogendijk, W. J., van Pelt, J., DeRijk, R. H., Verhagen, J., van Dyck, R.,…Penninx, B. W. (2009). Major depressive disorder and hypothalamic-pituitary-adrenal axis activity: Results from a large cohort study. *Archives of General Psychiatry, 66*, 617.

Walker, M. P., & van der Helm, E. (2009). Overnight therapy? The role of sleep in emotional brain processing. *Psychological Bulletin, 135*, 731–748.

Wals, M., Hillegers, M. H., Reichart, C. G., Verhulst, F. C., Nolen, W. A., & Ormel, J. (2005). Stressful life events and onset of mood disorders in children of bipolar parents during 14-month follow-up. *Journal of Affective Disorders, 87*, 253–263.

Watson, S., Gallagher, P., Ritchie, J. C., Ferrier, I. N., & Young, A.H. (2004). Hypothalamic-pituitary-adrenal axis function in patients with bipolar disorder. *British Journal of Psychiatry, 184*, 496–502.

Watson, S., Thompson, J. M., Malik, N., Ferrier, I. N., & Young, A. H. (2004). Temporal stability of the dex/CRH test in patients with rapid-cycling bipolar I disorder: A pilot study. *Australian and New Zealand Journal of Psychiatry, 39*, 244–248.

Watson, S., Thompson, J. M., Ritchie, J. C., Ferrier, I. N., & Young, A. H. (2006). Neuropsychological impairment in bipolar disorder: The relationship with glucocorticoid receptor function. *Bipolar Disorders, 8,* 85–90.

Wehr, R. (1990). Manipulations of sleep and phototherapy: Nonpharmacological alternatives in the treatment of depression. *Clinical Neuropharmacology, 13,* 54–65.

Wehr, R., Turner, E., Shimada, J., Lowe, C., Barker, C., & Leibenluft, E. (1998). Treatment of a rapidly cycling bipolar patient by using extended bed rest and darkness to stabilize the timing and duration of sleep. *Biological Psychiatry, 43,* 822–828.

Wehr, T. A., Goodwin, F. K., Wirz-Justice, A., Breitmaier, J., & Craig, C. (1982). 48-hour sleep-wake cycles in manic-depressive illness: Naturalistic observations and sleep deprivation experiments. *Archives of General Psychiatry, 39,* 559–565.

Wender, P. H., Kety, S. S., Rosenthal, D., Schulsinger, F., Ortmann, J., & Lunde, I. (1986). Psychiatric disorders in the biological and adoptive families of adopted individuals with affective disorders. *Archives of General Psychiatry, 43,* 923–929.

Wessa, M., Houenou, J., Paillere-Martinot, M. L., Berthoz, S., Artiges, E., et al. (2007). Fronto-striatal overactivation in euthymic bipolar patients during an emotional go/nogo task. *American Journal of Psychiatry, 164,* 638–646.

Willner, P. (1995). Sensitization of the dopamine D-sub-2- or D-sub-3-type receptors as a common pathway in antidepressant drug action. *Clinical Neuropharmacology, 18,* 49–56.

Wu, J., & Bunney, W. (1990). The biological basis of an antidepressant response to sleep deprivation and relapse: Review and hypothesis. *American Journal of Psychiatry, 147,* 14–21.

Wu, J. C., Kelsoe, J. R., Schachat, C., Bunney, B. G., Demodena, A., Golshan, S.,…Bunney, W. E. (2009). Rapid and sustained antidepressant response with sleep deprivation and chronotherapy in bipolar disorder. *Biological Psychiatry, 66,* 298–301.

Yamawaki, S., Okada, G., Okamoto, Y., & Liberzon, I. (2012). Mood dysregulation and stabilization: Perspectives from emotional cognitive neuroscience. *International Journal of Neuropsychopharmacology, 15,* 681–694.

Yatham, L. N., Srisurapanont, M., Zis, A. P., & Kusumakar, V. (1997). Comparative studies of the biological distinction between unipolar and bipolar depressions. *Life Sciences, 61,* 1445–1455.

Young, E. A., Haskett, R. F., Murphy-Weinberg, V., Watson, S. J., & Akil, H. (1991). Loss of glucocorticoid fast feedback in depression. *Archives of General Psychiatry, 48,* 693–699.

Young, K. D., Erickson, K., Nugent, A. C., Fromm, S. J., Mallinger, A. G., et al. (2012). Functional anatomy of autobiographical memory recall deficits in depression. *Psychological Medicine, 42,* 345–357.

Yurgelun-Todd, D. A., Gruber, S. A., Kanayama, G., Kilgore, W. D., Baird, A. A., & Young, A. D., (2000). fMRI during affect discrimination in bipolar affective disorder. *Bipolar Disorders, 2,* 237–248.

Zhong, M., Wang, X., Xiao, J., Yi, J., Zhu, X., et al. (2011). Amygdala hyperactivation and prefrontal hypoactivation in subjects with cognitive vulnerability to depression. *Biological Psychology, 88,* 233–242.

Zimmerman, M., Ruggero, C. J., Chelminski, I., & Young, D. (2008). Is bipolar disorder overdiagnosed? *Journal of Clinical Psychiatry, 69,* 935–40.

Zobel, A. W., Nickel, T., Sonntag, A., Uhr, M., Holsboer, F., & Ising, M. (2001). Cortisol response in the combined dexamethasone/CRH test as predictor of relapse in patients with remitted depression: A prospective study. *Journal of Psychiatric Research, 35,* 83–94.

Zobel, A. W., Yassouridis, A., Frieboes, R. M., & Holsboer, F. (1999). Prediction of medium-term outcome by cortisol response to the combined dexamethasone-CRH test in patients with remitted depression. *American Journal of Psychiatry, 156,* 949–951.

Zou, Y.-F., Wang, F., Feng, X.-L., Li, W.-F., Tian, Y.-H., Tao, J.-H.,…Huang, F. (2012). Association of DRD2 gene polymorphisms with mood disorders: A meta-analysis. *Journal of Affective Disorders, 136*(3), 229–237.

9

Depression
Social and Cognitive Aspects

RICK E. INGRAM,

CHRISTINA WILLIAMS,

KATIE L. SHARP,

AND ELISABETH J. HARFMANN

Depression is a disabling disorder that is associated with substantial emotional misery, severe interpersonal disruption, and increased risk for physical illness and death. Although depression is an "intrapsychic" disorder, it also significantly disrupts the lives of those who are close to the sufferer. Depression is frequently a chronic disorder that can last for months or years, and even after recovery it commonly reoccurs. Although there are treatments that are effective for many depressed individuals, a sizable number of cases are treatment resistant. Depression is also associated with a considerable loss of productivity in both work days lost and in diminished work quality, which combined costs the economy billions of dollars. By any indicator, depression is an extensive public health problem.

DSM-V lists several types of depression, and although these subtypes are important, the focus of this chapter is on unipolar depression—specifically the cognitive and social aspects of unipolar depression. We start with a brief overview of the history of depression and follow with an examination of the epidemiology of the disorders. Social aspects from the perspective of the life event–depression relationship are examined next, followed by a review of behavioral and interpersonal models of depression and then cognitive models. Cognitive ideas examined include schema and information-processing models, cognitive subtypes, and self-regulation models.

Early Conceptions: A Brief History of Depression

Depression is found in the earliest human records; descriptions of conditions resembling depression can be found in the Bible as well as in Egyptian writings circa 2600 B.C. The ancient Greeks provided the first casual theories of depression: melancholia was hypothesized by Hippocrates to stem from a preponderance of black bile, "darkening the spirit and making it melancholy." These ideas paved the way for the modern conceptions of depression; Araetus of Cappadocia, around 120 A.D., characterized melancholia by sadness, suicidal tendencies feelings of indifference, and psychomotor agitation. In the mid-eighteenth century, Kant suggested that emotions could not cause mental illness; rather, depression was seen as a somatic ailment. It was not until the early twentieth century that theorists such as Abraham (1911/1960) and Freud (1917/1950) associated psychological/emotional factors in a causal manner with depression.

One key question in early conceptions regarded the issue of separating mood disorders into their own diagnostic category. Into the beginning of the twentieth century, controversy raged over whether the disorders of "mood" should be separated from psychosis. Kraepelin's (1896) systematic observations of manic and schizophrenic individuals suggested that mania, which was often associated with a depressed state, should be considered a separate disorder from syndromes characterized primarily by psychosis such as schizophrenia. A similar historical debate concerned the distinction between psychopathologies with both manic and depressive states and disorders that were "just" depression. However, early depression theorists, including Freud, disregarded this distinction, between what is now seen as bipolar versus unipolar disorder.

Epidemiology of Depression

Prevalence

Several epidemiological surveys have gathered data about the prevalence rates of depression. The first was the National Institute of Mental Health Epidemiologic Catchment Area (ECA) study (Eaton & Kessler, 1985). A decade later, between 1990 and 1992, the National Comorbidity Survey (NCS; Kessler et al., 1994) was conducted using a modified version of the World Health Organization's (WHO) Composite International Diagnostic Interview (CIDI) to diagnose disorders, including depression, according to the *DSM-III* criteria. Most recently, the National Comorbidity Survey–Replication (NCS-R; Kessler et al., 2005) was conducted to survey a large number of individuals in the 48 contiguous United States. The NCS-R, however, used the criteria promulgated in the *DSM-IV* and assessed these criteria with an extended form of the CIDI (Kessler et al., 2005).

Twelve-month prevalence rates reported by the ECA are the lowest of all the surveys, with findings indicating a rate of 2.7%. The NCS, by contrast, found a 12-month prevalence rate almost twice as high, at 4.9%. The rate was higher still in the NCS-R findings, with a rate of 6.6. Lifetime prevalence rates for major depressive disorder (MDD) are again the lowest in the ECA, with a reported rate of 2.7%. The NCS rate among adults, defined as over 15 years of age, was substantially higher, with a reported rate of 15.8%. The NCS-R data are a little higher but roughly in line with the NCS, with a reported rate of 16.6%. It is important to note that differences in the various surveys reflect the use of somewhat different measures, as well as sampling differences.

Gender Differences

Compared to men, women are at a much higher risk for depression. Although female-to-male ratios differ somewhat across studies, the average ratio is close to 2:1 (Nolen-Hoeksema, 1987). For example, the NCS study found a 21.3% lifetime prevalence for women and a 12.7% rate for men. Prevalence rates for depression vary across different countries, but the gender difference remains (Nolen-Hoeksema & Hilt, 2009). The gender difference first appears in adolescence, although rates are similar for girls and boys in childhood (Garrison, Addy, Jackson, McKeown, & Waller, 1992); in fact, preadolescent boys are somewhat more prone to depression than girls (Twenge & Nolen-Hoeksema, 2002).

Age and Cohort Effects

The rate of depression also seems to vary with age. The rate of onset of the disorder increases dramatically during adolescence. Depression appears more commonly in younger than in older adults, with rates being highest for individuals from 25 to 45 years of age. Rates of first onset are considerably lower for individuals over 65 years old (Klerman, 1986; Robins, 1984; Weissman & Myers, 1978). Some data suggest that younger generations are more prone to depression than comparably aged individuals were in the past (Klerman, 1986; Klerman & Weissman, 1989); indeed, the rate of depression appears to be greater for individuals born after the mid-twentieth century (Seligman, 1990). In addition, rates of depression appear to be increasing most quickly in young men, which may decrease the discrepancy between the rate of depression in men and women (Joyce et al., 1990).

Models of Depression

Contemporary approaches to depression have become increasingly multifactorial and integrative; negative life events, genetics, biochemistry, social skills, interpersonal interactions, and cognitive processes are all involved in varying ways and to various degrees in the onset, maintenance, remission, and relapse of depressive episodes. Hence, distinctions between models have become blurred. For example, some life event models now explicitly integrate notions of vulnerability, cognitive mediation, and interpersonal behavior. Similarly, in addition to acknowledging the important role of the disruptive capacities of life events, behavioral and interpersonal models explicitly integrate cognitive constructs, and cognitive approaches assign important roles to life events as well as to interpersonal and behavioral functioning. Although integration is an important and positive trend, the examination of models here is structured according to the factors emphasized primarily by those models (e.g., cognitive processes for cognitive models).

Life Event Models

It is easy to suppose that people get depressed because bad things happen to them. This has been the basic presupposition of life event approaches to depression. *Life events* refer to sudden, or at least relatively distinctive, changes in the external environment (Paykel & Cooper, 1992). Although early research appeared to support a relatively straightforward relationship between negative life events and depression, it has become increasingly clear that the contribution of life events to depression is more complicated.

Perhaps the most extensive and influential life event research has been the work of Brown and Harris (1978, 1986). In prospective studies using the Bedford College Life Events and Difficulties Schedule (LEDS), these investigators have found that only severe events, defined as events with "marked or moderate long-term threat," are clearly related to the onset of a depressive disorder. An example would be a spouse losing his or her job. In contrast, less severe life events, such as one's spouse only being threatened with a job loss, have appeared insufficient to instigate depression. This is true even when multiple less-severe events are summed ("additivity effects"). Not surprisingly, however, these investigators have found an additivity effect for severe events (e.g., the death of a parent, and a spouse losing his or her job).

It appears that the relationship between major stressors and depression is strongest for initial depressive episodes (Mazure, 1998; Monroe & Depue, 1991). The observation that subsequent episodes can occur without major life events has

led to suggestions that recurrent episodes are only weakly linked to stress, or not at all. This idea is embodied in the idea of "kindling" (Monroe & Harkness, 2005; Post, 1992; Stroud, Davila, & Moyer, 2008)—that early occurrences of depression increase neurobiological sensitization to the point where recurrent episodes are largely initiated by these neurobiological processes. In the extreme version of this hypothesis, depression becomes autonomous and occurs independent of life stress. Monroe and Harkness (2005) have suggested a compelling alternative to this stress autonomy model. They propose a stress sensitization model in which life events continue to play an important role in the onset of depression, but the event threshold for triggering a recurrence is lowered. Hence, whereas a major event is needed to trigger a first onset, less severe (but more common) life events can initiate recurrent episodes. In this model, life stress continues to play a central role in depression, but the parameters for triggering events change as recurrences accrue. Preliminary empirical evidence examining the role of severe and less severe life events tends to support stress sensitization models (Morris, Ciesla, & Garber, 2010; Stroud, Davila, Hammen, & Vrshek-Schallhorn, 2011).

Life event researchers also distinguish between acute life events (e.g., a broken engagement) and stressors of a more chronic nature (e.g., constant arguing with a spouse, poverty, chronic problems with children or work). Recurrent depressive episodes may be linked to these chronic stressors (Monroe, 2010; Monroe, Slavich, Torres, & Gotlib, 2007). The specific *quality* of an event has also emerged as an important dimension. In particular, severe life events that signify loss appear to be most strongly associated with depression, whereas events that signify danger appear more related to anxiety disorders (e.g., Smith & Allred, 1989).

It is also important to note that stressful life events sometime instigate additional negative life events. For example, research investigating the effects of job loss and unemployment has found that economic hardship can lead to additional negative life events, such as child abuse (Justice & Duncan, 1977; Steinberg, Catalano, & Dooley, 1981) and a worsening of the spouse's mental health (Penkower, Bromet, & Dew, 1988). The occurrence of a negative life event can also worsen the quality of a marriage and, in some cases, lead to familial and marital dissolution (Liem & Liem,

1988). Vinokur, Price, and Caplan (1996) found that job loss and financial strain resulted in more negative affect and dysfunctional interactions in couples. In turn, each member's negative affect was also found to exacerbate depressive symptoms in the other partner. As a result, each partner became less socially supportive and more likely to undermine their partner's sense of self-worth. These behaviors had an additional impact on depressive symptomatology, in effect creating a vicious depression-maintaining cycle. In short, stress tends to come in bunches, and one event is not necessarily independent of other events.

Risk Factors   Although life events do precede depression, not all people exposed to even severe negative life events develop a depressive disorder. For example, in reviewing 10 studies that used the LEDS in the general population, Brown and Harris (1989) found that three-quarters of recently depressed individuals had experienced a preceding negative life event. Yet they also found that only one out of five individuals who experienced a negative life event went on to develop depression. Consequently, there have been attempts to improve the predictive value of life events by examining individual differences in the value placed on different life domains (e.g., parenting, marriage, employment). For instance, for individuals who place a high value on marriage, a negative life event related to marriage (i.e., divorce) would be predicted to have more impact for this individual. Evidence supports life event–matching hypotheses; severe negative life events that occur in domains that are particularly valued are more potent instigators of depression (e.g., Brown, Andrews, Harris, Adler, & Bridge, 1986). Likewise, some research showing that women who experienced a severe life event in a valued domain were three times more likely to develop depression than women who experienced a severe life event in a less valued domain (Brown & Harris, 1989).

Empirical work on matching hypotheses by life event researchers bears strong resemblance to work by personality and clinical psychologists investigating the interaction between negative life events and such personality variables as sociotropy/autonomy (Beck, 1987), goal orientation (Dykman, 1998; Lindsay & Scott, 2005), and perfectionism (Ahrens, 1987; Flett, Hewitt, Blankstein, & Mosher, 1995). In addition to matching strategies, life event researchers have

also sought to identify risk factors that make an individual more or less susceptible to the depressing influence of negative life events. In particular, both low social support and low self-esteem have been identified as key risk factors by life event researchers (Brown & Harris, 1989).

More recently, investigators have found that individuals possessing one or two short alleles on a gene involved in serotonin reuptake (5-HTTLPR) are more likely to become depressed, but only when they have experienced severe negative life events (Caspi et al., 2003; Karg, Burmeister, Shedden, & Sen, 2011). These findings support a gene–environment interaction model in which neither genes nor negative life events in isolation are sufficient to instigate a depressive episode, but rather the co-occurrence of both factors is required. Cognitive models of depression have also increasingly reemphasized the idea that negative cognitive patterns must be activated by life events before they eventuate in depression (Ingram, Atchley, & Segal, 2011; Ingram, Miranda, & Segal, 1998). Life events are clearly critical in many cases of depression, but mainly in the context of other factors.

Stress Generation   It has become increasingly recognized that the depressed person may generate his or her own negative life events and stress (for reviews, see Hammen, 2006; Liu & Alloy, 2010). For example, in a 1-year longitudinal study of depressed and nondepressed women, Hammen (1991) found that depressed women experienced more *dependent* negative life events, or negative events in which the depressed person was judged to have some contributory role. These dependent life events frequently involved interpersonal conflict in which depressed women were thought to be partly responsible. Moreover, these women continued to generate negative events after their depression had remitted. Since this initial study, a number of researchers have replicated the *stress generation effect* with both adult and adolescent samples, including samples restricted to men (Hammen, 2006; Liu & Alloy, 2010).

Why do depressed individuals tend to create interpersonal conflicts and other "dependent" negative life events? Given that the depressed person continues to generate such events when the depression itself has remitted, the evidence suggests that the depressed person possesses enduring characteristics or personality traits that are involved.

A number of more trait-like personality factors have been identified as being capable of generating such negative dependent life events, including neuroticism (Kendler, Gardner, & Prescott, 2003; Kercher, Rapee, & Schniering, 2009), perfectionism or high self-criticism (Cox, Clara, & Enns, 2009; Dunkley, Zuroff, & Blankstein, 2003; Shahar, Joiner, Zuroff, & Blatt, 2004), and poor interpersonal problem-solving (Davila, Hammen, Burge, Paley, & Daley, 1995).

In sum, the relationship between negative life events and depression is clear, although acute negative life events appear to have a stronger role in initial depressive episodes, while chronic events appear to be more involved with people who are experiencing recurrent depression. Increasingly, life event researchers have investigated the specific quality of negative life events, as well as matching and vulnerability characteristics of the individual. Moreover, risk factors such as short alleles on a gene involved serotonin functioning, poor social support, and low self-esteem have been identified in individuals who are most susceptible to the depressing influence of negative life events. Researchers have also begun to investigate how depressed individuals may generate their own negative life events, even when the depressed state itself remits.

Behavioral and Interpersonal Models

Behavioral Models   Behavioral and interpersonal models have been used to examine the behaviors, and especially the social behaviors, of the depressed individual. A notable early behavioral model was proposed by Lewinsohn (1974) and later reformulated (Lewinsohn, Hoberman, Teri, & Hautzinger, 1985). Lewinsohn (1974) argued that depression was due to a low rate of response-contingent positive reinforcement. When individuals fail to receive positive reinforcement that is dependent on the execution of some behavioral response (e.g., initiating a conversation), those behavioral responses become extinguished. This subsequent loss of response-based positive reinforcement deprives the individual of pleasure and leads to feelings of dysphoria. Lewinsohn also emphasized the role of social skills and maintained that, as a result of poor social skills, the depressed individual is denied access to the reinforcing properties of social relationships. Other factors were posited that might lead to a low rate of response-contingent

reinforcement. Specifically, the occurrence of negative life events—particularly events of loss, impoverishment, or excessive aversive events—diminishes the supply of potential reinforcers in the individual's environment. Indeed, as previously reviewed, severe negative life events, particularly those in which loss or interpersonal conflict is experienced, are associated with depression onset. Additionally, a decrease in the capacity to enjoy pleasant experiences or an increase in sensitivity to negative life events was seen as contributing to lower rates of response-contingent reinforcement.

To increase the predictive power of the theory, Lewinsohn et al. (1985) formulated a major revision intended to integrate existing knowledge about life events, cognitive processes, and interpersonal functioning. As such, this theory is no longer a distinctively "behavioral" model. In the revised theory, depression onset is caused by one or more stressful life events occurring in an individual who possesses inadequate coping skills or other risk factors. In these vulnerable individuals, events that disrupt major resources in life domains such as personal relationships and job tasks lead to an initial negative emotional response. Both life event disruptions and the experience of dysphoric mood lead to a decrease in response-contingent reinforcement, which has several cognitive and behavioral consequences. Cognitively, the individual becomes excessively self-focused, self-critical, pessimistic, and more aware of discrepancies between personal standards and actual accomplishments. Behaviorally, the person withdraws, has more social difficulties, and becomes less motivated. These cognitive and behavioral consequences combine to spiral the individual into an ever-deepening state of depression.

Interpersonal Models   Although the roots of the interpersonal models of behavior can be traced back to Harry Stack Sullivan (1953), the contemporary interpersonal model of depression was articulated by Coyne in 1976. Coyne argued that the occurrence of stressful life events—especially loss of significant relationships—leads to a display of depressive symptoms by the individual. These include expressions of helplessness and hopelessness, withdrawal from interactions, general slowing, and irritability and agitation. The depressed person's goal is to restore social support and gain reassurance regarding his or her self-worth and acceptance by others. Initially, the person gets what he or she wants: the social environment tends to respond with genuine concern and support, which functions to reinforce the depressed person's display of depressive symptoms.

The meaning of this social support, however, eventually becomes ambiguous. The depressed person may wonder: "Are people responding with support and reassurance because they really believe that I am worthy, or are they doing so merely because I sought it?" The depressed person, caught in this loop of uncertainty, continues to use depressive symptoms in an effort to be reassured. The persistence of such a depressive display, however, eventually becomes aversive to others, who then begin to withdraw. This leads to even further efforts by the depressed person to seek reassurance that he or she is worthwhile and is not being rejected by others. In short, a cycle based on the perceived or actual rejection by others is generated in the depressed person. This cycle is unpleasant to both the depressed person and to others who remain in the depressed person's social environment.

Coyne (1976) specifically predicted that it is excessive reassurance-seeking which culminates in feelings of hostility and aversion in others that then leads to rejection. Excessive reassurance-seeking is defined as "the relatively stable tendency to excessively and persistently seek assurances from others that one is lovable and worthy, regardless of whether such assurance has already been provided" (Joiner, Metalsky, Katz, & Beach, 1999, p. 270). Empirical evidence supports the contention that there are significant relationships between reassurance-seeking and depression. For instance, Starr and Davila (2008) conducted a meta-analysis of 38 studies and found a medium effect size for depressive symptoms and reassurance-seeking, indicating that more depressive symptoms were related to higher levels of excessively seeking reassurance. Starr and Davila (2008) also found a significant, albeit small, effect size of .14 across 16 studies examining the positive correlation between reassurance seeking and interpersonal rejection. Individuals engaging in excessive reassurance-seeking who also suffer from depression also appear to be at particular risk of being rejected (Pettit & Joiner, 2006). For example, those who report depressive symptoms but low levels of reassurance-seeking as well as anxious individuals with high levels of reassurance-seeking are not evaluated in the same

negative light by people interacting with them (Joiner & Metalsky, 1995; Pettit & Joiner, 2006). Furthermore, reassurance-seeking and depression may be more strongly linked in women. In support of this, Starr and Davila (2008) found stronger associations between reassurance-seeking and depression in samples with a higher percentage of female participants. Reassurance-seeking has also been found to interact with changes in perceived social support to predict the prospective development of depressive symptoms (Haeffel, Voelz, & Joiner, 2007).

Integrating aspects of Coyne's interpersonal theory with social-cognitive work in self-enhancement and self-consistency theory, Joiner, Alfano, and Metalsky (1992) proposed that when the mildly depressed person's reassurance-seeking is successfully rewarded by others, he or she is only temporarily satisfied. Specifically, the positive feedback elicited from others conflicts with negative self-beliefs; consequently, the depressed person doubts the validity of the feedback. This leads the depressed person to "flip-flop" and seek negative feedback that is more consistent with current self-beliefs. The combination of depression, excessive reassurance-seeking, and negative feedback-seeking then causes others to reject the person. Consistent with this view, Joiner and Metalsky (1995) found that undergraduate males who engaged in both negative feedback-seeking and reassurance-seeking were more likely to be rejected by their roommates. However, this social reaction may only occur with those closest to the depressed person; reassurance-seeking has been found to predict spouse- but not roommate-related stress (Shahar et al., 2004).

Hence, individuals with depression try both to palliate their insecurities in relationships by engaging in reassurance-seeking and to maintain a sense of consistency in self-schemas through their use of negative feedback-seeking. Such reassurance thinking is akin to Swann's research finding suggesting that people are motivated to verify even unfavorable self-perceptions (e.g., Swann, Chang-Schneider, & McClarty, 2007). The individual suffering with depression who engages in these behaviors is at particularly high risk for rejection from close others (Joiner, Alfano, & Metalsky, 1993). Thus, something inherent to the disorder of depression accounts for the social rejection experienced by these individuals. Evraire and Dozois (2011) have suggested that it is the influence of entrenched core beliefs on the information-seeking behaviors of these individuals that explains why reassurance-seeking and negative feedback-seeking lead to rejection. In support of this idea, the literature on reassurance-seeking suggests that it is not the reassurance-seeking behavior in itself that is related to depression and rejection but rather the combined influence of negative core beliefs concerning interpersonal relationships and reassurance-seeking that creates aversive social consequences. Furthermore, it is the verification of negative self-views that leads to a higher incidence of negative and emotionally distressing feedback for individuals with depression compared to those without depression (Evraire & Dozois, 2011).

Other research has extended Coyne's original theory by integrating interpersonal and stress-generation models of depression (Potthoff, Holahan, & Joiner, 1995). As described previously, the stress-generation model argues that depressed individuals play a contributory role in their own negative life events and stress (Hammen, 2006). Researchers have found that reassurance-seeking predicts subsequent levels of interpersonal stress, which in turn predicts elevated levels of depressive symptoms (Joiner, 1994; Joiner et al., 1992; Potthoff et al., 1995). Birgenheir, Pepper, and Johns (2010) found that individuals who particularly value interpersonal relationships (i.e., sociotropy) and practice reassurance-seeking demonstrate increased levels of negative interpersonal life events. Eberhart and Hammen (2010) tested a transactional model for depression on a sample of females involved in romantic relationships and found that romantic-conflict stress mediated the effects of reassurance-seeking and anxious attachment on depressive symptoms. They also found that daily-conflict stress mediated the effects of anxious and avoidant attachment styles, reassurance-seeking, and love-dependency behaviors on daily depressive symptoms. These findings support the contention that individuals' interpersonal style and their associated behaviors contribute to their depressive symptoms via their impact on stress generation.

Interpersonal models have thus focused researchers' efforts on the social consequences of depression, particularly of rejection. There remains some debate concerning the processes that lead the depressed person to be rejected. There is empirical evidence that social rejection is the result of the depressed individual's failure to meet the basic communication needs of others. Some researchers suggest that reassurance-seeking combined with social rejection, particularly in close and intimate relationships, leads to depression. Other work has integrated findings that reassurance-seeking interacts with generated life stress to predict depression.

Socioevolutionary Models   Since Coyne (1976) first proposed that depressed people act in ways that elicit rejection from others, conceptual models of depression have increasingly incorporated the role of social interactions. Evolutionary models of human psychological behavior are no exception, and they seek to identify characteristics and behaviors that demonstrate reproductive and survival advantages in human populations. As we have noted, depression confers major psychological, physical, and economic costs. From an evolutionary perspective, it is puzzling that depression remains so widespread, despite the fact that several generations have had the chance to "select" it out (Steger, 2010). Socioevolutionary models of depression attempt to explain this phenomenon by proposing that mild to moderate depressive symptoms may have conferred survival and reproductive advantages via their social functions. According to the social-risk hypothesis of depression (Allen & Badcock, 2003), depressed states evolved in order to stimulate low-risk responses when the possibility of social exclusion was perceived. Because social exclusion was a life-threatening process throughout our evolutionary history, being sensitive to rejection cues and acting to reduce social burden to the group conferred survival value. The social-risk hypothesis makes three key predictions. First, people with depressive symptoms demonstrate social impairment, which triggers depressive symptoms via negative responses from others. For example, depressed people elicit more negative affect in others through their interactions, which makes it more likely that other people will reject them (Joiner & Katz, 1999; Steger, 2010). Second, people with higher levels of depressive symptoms are more sensitive to negative social cues elicited from others. Third, social subordinate behaviors (e.g., submissiveness and reduced behavioral output) occur in the depressed individual in order to reduce their burden in the group. For example, those with greater depressive symptoms react to perceived dominance by others with exacerbated feelings of inferiority and submissiveness compared to reactions from those with fewer depressive symptoms (Zuroff, Fournier, & Moskowitz, 2007).

Cognitive Models

Cognitive models of depression emphasize that people get depressed primarily because of the way they think. Beck's (1967, 1987) well-known theory and related information-processing ideas are structured around this idea. Beck's approach is discussed here first, particularly in reference to the vulnerability aspects of this model and the diathesis-stress perspective in which this model is framed. Next reviewed are models that specify cognitively based subtypes of depression, including Abramson, Metalsky, and Alloy's (1989) hopelessness theory of depression, as well as cognitive self-regulatory approaches to depression. In this discussion it is important to note that, similar to life event and behavioral-interpersonal models, cognitive models have become increasingly integrative and have emphasized the role of life events, genetics, and behavior.

Beck's Cognitive Theory of Depression In Beck's (1967, 1987) model, depression results from the activation of a depressive *self-schema*. Self-schemas are organized mental structures which are negatively toned representations of self-referent knowledge that guide appraisal and interact with information to influence selective attention, memory search, and cognitions (Ingram et al., 1998). The content of these schemas develops from interactions that occur during childhood development (Beck, 1967, 1987; Kovacs & Beck, 1978). For example, if childhood experiences are characterized by abuse, stress, or chronic negativity, schemas may arise that guide attention to negative events, lead to the enhanced recall of negative experiences, and distort information to fit the schema (Ingram et al., 1998). Although all persons evidence schemas, those of depressed individuals are considered dysfunctional because they represent a constellation of attitudes that lead to negative perspectives about oneself, the world, and the future, or what Beck has termed the "negative cognitive triad." Schemas also underlie tacit beliefs. For instance, a depressive self-schema might contain the belief "If I am not loved and accepted by all human beings then I am worthless." Such negative beliefs are primitive, excessive, and rigid.

Depressive self-schemas also lead to negative biases or cognitive distortions, which lead to thinking errors. For instance *all-or-nothing thinking* occurs when situations are viewed in only two categories instead of on a continuum (i.e., "If I am not a complete success I'm a failure"). *Selective abstraction* occurs when negative details are focused on without taking into consideration the entire context. For instance, in conversing with a group of people, the depressed person might only notice the one person who yawned and not the others who appeared interested. *Overgeneralization* refers to sweeping judgments or predictions based on a single incident (e.g., "Because last night's date did not go well, all women find me unattractive"). In *emotional reasoning*, one thinks something must be true because one feels it to be so (e.g., "I feel ugly so I must look ugly"). *Personalization* occurs when the individual takes responsibility for the negative actions of others without considering more plausible explanations for their behaviors.

An original and fundamental aspect of Beck's model is the diathesis-stress context of negative cognition; depressive schemas lie dormant until activated by relevant stimuli: "Whether he will ever become depressed depends on whether the necessary conditions are present at a given time to activate the depressive constellation" (Beck, 1967, p. 278). Hence, stressful life events are necessary to activate negative schemas, and once activated, schemas provide access to a complex system of negative personal themes that give rise to a corresponding pattern of negative information processing that eventuates in depression (Ingram et al., 1998, 2011; Segal & Shaw, 1986). Although Beck did not view all depressions as being solely caused by depressive self-schemas, he did view the cognitive triad and negative information-processing bias to be intrinsic features of all depressions and to have causal significance.

As a diathesis factor, vulnerability is an important aspect of cognitive models because it clearly articulates ideas about causality. This idea suggests that negative cognitive factors emerge during stressful situations; this cognitive reactivity is critical for the onset, course, relapse, and recurrence of depression. Therapeutic interventions which effectively alter vulnerability should also alter the individual's chance of relapses or recurrences. In fact, Hollon, Stewart, and Strunk (2006) have summarized data to suggest that, compared to pharmacotherapy for depression, cognitive therapy is more effective in preventing relapse and recurrence. Presumably this is the case because cognitive therapy changes cognitive schemas in a way that not only brings about recovery from the disorder but also modifies the underlying cognitive vulnerability (Garratt, Ingram, Rand, & Sawalani, 2007).

Since the appearance of Beck's cognitive theory, several cognitive models of depression have emerged that explicitly incorporate constructs from experimental cognitive psychology (Ingram, 1984; Teasdale, 1988; Teasdale & Barnard, 1993) to articulate the structure and function of schemas. For example, Ingram (1984) and Teasdale and Barnard (1993) conceptualized these structures as cognitive-affective networks. Hence, in depression an appraisal of loss results in the initiation of sad emotion, which spreads activation throughout the associative linkages that make up the entire interconnected affective-cognitive network. The result of spreading activation is the heightened accessibility of the information embedded in the entire network, and the depressed individual thus becomes conscious of sad-valenced information (e.g., negative events, thoughts, and beliefs). As such, the depressed person exhibits superior attention to and encoding and recall of negatively valenced self-referential information. This type of negative information processing continues to prime the depressogenic cognitive structure, resulting in a negative "cognitive loop" that both maintains and exacerbates the depressive state. This tendency of the depressed person toward self-absorption (Ingram, 1990) leaves relatively minimal cognitive capacity available for attending to the external environment. Consequently, the individual's social interactions suffer, leading to social withdrawal. The subsequent loss of social contacts serves even further to prime the depressogenic cognitive-affective structures.

Support for many elements of Beck's model is considerable. For example, the descriptive aspects of depression noted by the model have been confirmed by numerous studies (Haaga, Dyck, & Ernst, 1991; Ingram et al., 1998). In regard to thinking about the self, depressed people report more negative (Kendall, Howard, & Hays, 1989) and less positive automatic self-referent thinking (Ingram, Slater, Atkinson, & Scott, 1990). They are highly self-critical (Cofer &

Wittenborn, 1980; Hammen & Krantz, 1976) and are likely to negatively evaluate a variety of stimuli other than the self, including imagined activities (Grosscup & Lewinsohn, 1980) and other people (Hokanson, Hummer, & Butler, 1991; Siegel & Alloy, 1990). Depressed people are also pessimistic about the future (Alloy & Ahrens, 1987). This consistent support for the cognitive triad hypothesis has led some reviewers to argue for considering it a central descriptive feature of depression, equivalent to other such well-acknowledged facts about depression as "high recurrence" and "running in families" (Haaga et al., 1991).

The evidence appears generally supportive of a systematic negative bias in information processing during depressive episodes (Haaga et al., 1991; Ingram & Holle, 1992). For example, depressed people display a tendency to direct their attention to internal, rather than external, information (Ingram, 1990), and they appear to selectively encode negative information (Ingram & Holle, 1992). Depressed individuals have also been found to recall considerably more negative than positive information (Matt, Vazquez, & Campbell, 1992). Such a process of selectively encoding negative information is presumed to be the result of a dysfunctional schema.

The diathesis-stress perspective and hence the vulnerability proposals of the model have also been borne out by an accumulating body of data. There is evidence that what are thought to be dysfunctional schemas predict depression when activated by stressful life events (Dykman & Johll, 1998; Hankin, Abramson, Miller, & Haeffel, 2004). Furthermore, proposals regarding the emergence of a negative schema under stress have begun to receive consistent and considerable support (e.g., Scher, Ingram, & Segal, 2005; Segal & Ingram, 1994). For example, Ingram and Ritter (2000) found that, when primed with a sad mood, formerly depressed individuals allocated their attentional resources toward negative stimuli, but never-depressed individuals did not. Such processes are not limited to formerly depressed adults. In a study of depressive schema activation processes in the offspring of depressed mothers, Taylor and Ingram (1999) found that these offspring evidenced significantly more negative information recall when they were primed with a sad mood than did the offspring of mothers who were not depressed. Hence, these individuals (formerly depressed people and the children of depressed mothers) are at risk for depression and appear to have dysfunctional schemas that can readily be activated by negative events.

In a similar fashion, Segal, Gemar, and Williams (1999) found that depressed patients who have recovered and who endorsed high levels of dysfunctional attitudes following a negative mood experienced more relapse than equally recovered individuals who did not respond with heightened levels of dysfunctional cognition to this mood. These results were subsequently replicated and extended by Segal et al. (2006). Other investigators have also found that negative cognitive processes elicited during negative mood inductions interact with subsequent negative life events to predict depressive symptoms (Beevers & Carver, 2003; Segal et al., 1999). These findings suggest that those who are vulnerable to depression process information as hypothesized by cognitive-diathesis-stress models and that this information processing predicts relapses. Indeed, in the data reported by Segal (Segal et al., 1999, 2006), cognitive responses predicted relapse in some cases up to 2 years after the cognitive assessment.

There is some evidence that depressive cognition has a genetic basis. For example, Beevers, Scott, McGeary, and McGeary (2009) examined whether nondepressed individuals with one or two short alleles on the 5-HTTLPR gene would show greater negative cognitive reactivity in response to a negative mood manipulation. In short, a significant positive linear relationship between number of short 5-HTTLPR alleles and a measure of the severity of negative thinking emerged, but only in the condition in which participants were exposed to a sad-mood video clip. These data suggest that genes involved in serotonergic functioning may play a role in the development of negative cognitive reactivity in response to dysphoric events. Furthermore, in a study investigating the brain regions of biased attention for both sad and happy stimuli, Beevers, Pacheco, Clasen, McGeary, and Schnyer (2010) found that volume of the lateral prefrontal cortex, an area involved in the cognitive regulation of emotion, was strongly associated with an attentional bias for emotional cues among carriers of the short 5-HTTLPR allele. Beck's model has thus received considerable support, with new information suggesting how the cognitive reactivity featured in the model is tied to neurobiological variables.

Attribution-Based Models   One of the most widely known theories of depression was originally proposed by Seligman (1975). Seligman's model was based on an observation of apparent similarity between the responses of depressed people and the conditioned behavior of laboratory dogs who did not attempt to escape after they had been unable to avoid intermittent painful electrical shocks. Seligman's extrapolated these ideas to focus on depressed persons' expectations that they are helpless to control aversive outcomes and the ensuing behavior consistent with these expectations.

Perhaps because of its simplicity, the learned-helplessness theory quickly generated a tremendous amount of data (Abramson, Seligman, & Teasdale, 1978). Although much of this research supported the fundamental tenants of the model, other research revealed the model's deficiencies. Therefore, the theory was revised to focus on people's beliefs about the causes of events (Abramson et al., 1978). In this revision, an attributional style was proposed as the critical causal variable in depression. In particular, making specific, unstable, external attributions for positive events (e.g., "I succeeded because the test was really easy"), and global, stable, and internal attributions for negative events (e.g., "I failed because I am a stupid person") was hypothesized to function as a cognitive vulnerability to depression.

Research on the various aspects of the reformulated helplessness/attributional theory of depression has provided substantial support for this theory; cross-sectional studies have shown that when individuals are depressed, they tend to make the types of attributions hypothesized by the theory (Abramson et al., 2002). Additionally, some data show that the tendency to report some of these attributions predicts negative mood reactions in response to negative events (e.g., Metalsky, Halberstadt, & Abramson, 1987; Metalsky, Joiner, Hardin, & Abramson, 1993).

A number of studies have supported the role of negative attributions in precipitating depression (Alloy, Abramson, Walshaw, & Neeren, 2006), particularly as they pertain to a subtype of depression characterized primarily by hopelessness. For instance, the Temple-Wisconsin Cognitive Vulnerability to Depression Project has provided considerable evidence (Alloy & Abramson, 1999). In this project, nondepressed university freshman were assessed on a number of cognitive measures, including measures of attributional style. These students were then followed for approximately 5 years with frequent assessments of stressful life events, cognitions, and depressive symptoms and disorders. Results showed that negative attributional styles predicted both first and subsequent depressive episodes (Alloy et al., 1999; Alloy, Abramson, Whitehouse, et al., 2006). Likewise, Sturman, Mongrain, and Kohn (2006) found that attributional styles for negative events significantly predicted symptoms of hopelessness depression when controlling for other factors. The results also indicate little correlation between attributional style and depressive symptoms that are not related to hopelessness depression, suggesting that attributional style is associated only with hopelessness depression symptoms.

Cognitive Self-Regulatory Approaches to Depression
Another useful approach derives from models for identifying how people regulate their behavior in the relative absence of external reinforcement (Bandura, 1986; 1997; Carver & Scheier, 1998). The ability to self-regulate is decidedly dependent on cognitive processes. For instance, people tend to adopt cognitive representations of desired future states that serve as guides and motives for action (e.g., Bandura, 1986). These *goal representations* serve as the benchmarks against which ongoing behavior is compared and evaluated. Variations in the representations of these goals are thought to influence motivation, performance, and affect (Caprara & Cervone, 2000). In order to understand the specific motivational and affective impact of the goal adopted, however, two additional cognitive self-regulatory variables must be considered: evaluative judgments and self-efficacy appraisals.

When people make *evaluative judgments*, they assess the relative successfulness of performance attainments. When performances fall short of standards, the effect can be motivating or disabling, depending partly on the size of the discrepancy between standard and performance. Large discrepancies generally lead to feelings of futility, dysphoria, and low motivation, and small discrepancies spur positive affect, greater persistence, and eventual goal accomplishment (Locke & Latham, 1990). However, the precise motivational effect depends on a third variable: perceived self-efficacy for the goal-relevant behavior (Bandura, 1977; 1997). *Self-efficacy appraisals* refer to people's assessments of their abilities to organize and execute specific behavioral performances (Bandura, 1997). When people judge themselves capable of an adequate performance, they may persevere even when their initial performance was substandard and dissatisfying. When people appraise themselves as inefficacious, even small goal–performance discrepancies tend to promote dysphoria and lead to a slackening, or even to an abandoning, of effort altogether (Cervone & Scott, 1995). According to Bandura (1997), a major pathway to depression occurs when individuals possess a low sense of self-efficacy for performing the actions required to realize valued goals.

There is a large literature linking individual differences in evaluative judgments (of the self and performances), goal representations, and self-efficacy judgments to depression. While in a depressive episode, depressed people are particularly self-critical in evaluating performances (e.g., Blatt, Quinlan, Chevron, McDonald, & Zuroff, 1982; Cofer & Wittenborn, 1980; Hammen & Krantz, 1976). Further, there is strong support for a relationship between efficacy judgments and depression in adults. For instance, self-efficacy for parenting (Olioff & Aboud, 1991), coping (Cozzarelli, 1993), social skills (Holahan & Holahan, 1987), and activities of personal importance (Olioff, Bryson, & Wadden, 1989) have all been related, either directly or indirectly, to depressive symptoms (see Bandura, 1997).

Similar patterns have been discovered between efficacy judgments and depression for children and adolescents. For instance, a number of investigations have linked academic self-efficacy and depression in youth (Bandura, Pastorelli, Barbaranelli, & Caprara, 1999; Scott et al., 2008). Further, other studies have demonstrated how diverse efficacy beliefs, including those for forming and maintaining social relationships, managing relationships with parents, regulating mood, and resisting negative peer pressure, can directly or indirectly influence feelings of well-being, satisfaction, and depression (e.g., Bandura, Caprara, Barbaranelli, Gerbino, & Pastorelli, 2003; Caprara, Pastorelli, Regalia, Scabini, & Bandura, 2005).

A number of goal characteristics have also been associated with depression, and some depression researchers have argued that depression can result from adopting goals that are excessively perfectionistic. Research employing attitudinal or trait-like measures of perfectionism has sometimes found that these characteristics are associated with dysphoric and depressive states (Flett,

Hewitt, & Mittelstaedt, 1991; Hewitt & Dyck, 1986; Hewitt & Flett, 1991) and that they sometimes prospectively predict depressive symptoms (Brown, Hammen, Craske, & Wickens, 1995; Flett et al., 1995). Across a number of studies, dysphoric and depressed individuals appear to hold relatively stringent performance standards in that the goals adopted exceed the performance levels judged to be possible (Ahrens, 1987). Finally, the experience of negative affect can sometimes lead to the construction of goal representations that are more perfectionistic (Cervone, Kopp, Schaumann, & Scott, 1994; Scott & Cervone, 2002). When evaluating whether a given performance level would be satisfactory or not, people appear to consult their feeling states, in effect asking themselves, "How do I feel about it?" If they are in a negative mood, they are more apt to feel dissatisfied with the considered performance and adopt higher performance standards. Interestingly, dysphoric individuals appear particularly susceptible to this affect-driven process that culminates in the construction of more perfectionistic goals (Tillema, Cervone, & Scott, 2001).

Other research has focused on the quality of the goal adopted. Dykman (1998) argued that some people are prone to adopting a validation-seeking goal orientation, which involves goals that seek "to prove or establish... basic worth, competence, and likeability" (p. 141). As a result, these individuals "continually mine the world for information relevant to their worth, competence, and likeability" (p. 153). For such individuals, then, performance situations are loaded because self-esteem is always on the line, contingent on successful performance. Not succeeding translates into appraisals of low self-worth and increased depression. In contrast, other people tend to adopt growth-seeking goals and approach performance situations with a focus on developing potential and skill. For these individuals, poor performance does not call into question self-worth; rather, subpar performance is merely viewed as a learning experience that ultimately leads to self-betterment. These growth-oriented individuals are viewed as more resilient and as less likely to develop depression in response to poor performance. Initial findings have generally supported the role of validation-seeking goal orientations in predicting changes in dysphoric symptoms, but only in the context of negative life events (Dykman, 1998; Lindsay & Scott, 2005).

Conclusions

Social and cognitive models have contributed significantly to our understanding of several key aspects of depression, although they have not been without criticism. Perhaps the key criticism is that psychological models of depression are causal models, but causality is notoriously difficult to demonstrate. Although support has begun to build for various models' proposals for causality, one of the key tasks for depression researchers is to continue to move beyond description of social and cognitive features to broaden understanding of the causal pathways of these factors. Moreover, as paradigms in behavioral science become increasingly focused on translating basic science into clinically useful ideas, it will be important to assess the linkages between the psychological variables commonly addressed in depression and biological pathways to affective disorder. Some of this work is underway, and although a comprehensive, integrated model of depression may not be obtainable in the near future, it must be an aspiration if we are to truly understand a disorder as complex as depression.

References

Abraham, K. (1911). Notes on the psychoanalytic investigation and treatment of manic-depressive insanity and allied conditions. In *Selected Papers on Psychoanalysis*. New York: Basic Books, 1960.

Abramson, L. Y., Alloy, L. B., Hankin, B. L., Haeffel, G. J., MacCoon, D. G., & Gibb, B. E. (2002). Cognitive vulnerability-stress models of depression in a self-regulatory and psychobiological context. In I. H. Gotlib, & C. L. Hammen (Eds.), *Handbook of depression* (pp. 268–294). New York: Guilford Press.

Abramson, L. Y., Metalsky, G. I., & Alloy, L. B. (1989). Hopelessness depression: A theory-based subtype of depression. *Psychological Review, 96*, 358–372.

Abramson, L. Y., Seligman, M. E. P., & Teasdale, J. (1978). Learned helplessness in humans: Critique and reformulation. *Journal of Abnormal Psychology, 87*, 49–74.

Ahrens, A. H. (1987). Theories of depression: The role of goals and the self-evaluation process. *Cognitive Therapy and Research, 11*, 665–680.

Allen, N. B., & Badcock, P. B. T. (2003). The social risk hypothesis of depressed mood: Evolutionary, psychosocial, and neurobiological perspectives. *Psychological Bulletin, 129*, 887–913.

Alloy, L. B., & Abramson, L. Y. (1999). The Temple-Wisconsin Cognitive Vulnerability to Depression (CVD) Project: Conceptual background, design, and methods. *Journal of Cognitive Psychotherapy: An International Quarterly, 13*, 227–262.

Alloy, L. B., Abramson, L. Y., Walshaw, P. D., & Neeren, A. M. (2006). Cognitive vulnerability to unipolar and bipolar mood disorders. *Journal of Social and Clinical Psychology, 25*, 726–754.

Alloy, L. B., Abramson, L. Y., Whitehouse, W. G., Hogan, M. E., Panzarella, C., & Rose, D. T. (2006). Prospective incidence of first onsets and recurrences of depression in individuals at high and low cognitive risk for depression. *Journal of Abnormal Psychology, 115*, 145–156.

Alloy, L. B., Abramson, L. Y., Whitehouse, W. G., Hogan, M. E., Tashman, N. A., Steinberg, D. L., Rose, D. T., & Donovan, P. (1999). Depressogenic cognitive styles: Predictive validity, information processing and personality characteristics, and developmental origins. *Behaviour Research and Therapy, 37*, 503–531.

Alloy, L. B., & Ahrens, A. H. (1987). Depression and pessimism for the future: Biased use of statistically relevant information in predictions for self versus others. *Journal of Personality and Social Psychology, 52*, 366–378.

Bandura, A. (1977). Self-efficacy: Toward a unifying theory of behavioral change. *Psychological Review, 84*, 191–215.

Bandura, A. (1986). *Social foundations of thought and action: A social cognitive theory.* Englewood Cliffs, NJ: Prentice-Hall.

Bandura, A. (1997). *Self-efficacy: The exercise of control.* New York: W.H. Freeman and Company.

Bandura, A., Caprara, G. V., Barbaranelli, C., Gerbino, M., & Pastorelli, C. (2003). Role of affective self-regulatory efficacy in diverse spheres of psychosocial functioning. *Child Development, 74*(3), 769–782.

Bandura, A., Pastorelli, C., Barbaranelli, C., & Caprara, G. V. (1999). Self-efficacy pathways to child depression. *Journal of Personality and Social Psychology, 76*, 258–269.

Beck, A. T. (1967). *Depression: Clinical, experimental, and theoretical aspects.* New York: Harper & Row.

Beck, A. T. (1987). Cognitive models of depression. *Journal of Cognitive Psychotherapy: An International Quarterly, 1*, 5–37.

Beevers, C. G., & Carver, C. S. (2003). Attentional bias and mood persistence as prospective predictors of dysphoria. *Cognitive Therapy and Research, 27*, 619–637.

Beevers, C. G., Pacheco, J., Clasen, P., McGeary, J. E., & Schnyer, D. (2010). Prefrontal morphology, 5-HTTLPR polymorphism and biased attention for emotional stimuli. *Genes, Brain and Behavior, 9*, 224–233.

Beevers, C. G., Scott, W. D., McGeary, C., & McGeary, J. E. (2009). Negative cognitive response to a sad mood induction: Associations with polymorphisms of the serotonin transporter (5-HTTLPR) gene. *Cognition and Emotion, 23*, 726–738.

Birgenheir, D. G., Pepper, C. M., & Johns, M. (2010). Excessive reassurance seeking as a mediator of sociotropy and negative interpersonal life events. *Cognitive Therapy Research, 34*, 185–195.

Blatt, S. J., Quinlan, D. M., Chevron, E. S., McDonald, C., & Zuroff, D. (1982). Dependency and self-criticism: Psychological dimensions of depression. *Journal of Consulting and Clinical Psychology, 50*, 113–124.

Brown, G. W., Andrews, B., Harris, T. O., Adler, Z., & Bridge, L. (1986). Social support, self-esteem and depression. *Psychological Medicine, 16*, 813–831.

Brown, G. P., Hammen, C. L., Craske, M. G., & Wickens, T. D. (1995). Dimensions of dysfunctional attitudes as vulnerabilities to depressive symptoms. *Journal of Abnormal Psychology, 104*, 431–435.

Brown, G. W., & Harris, T. (1978). *The social origins of depression: A study of psychiatric disorder in women.* New York: Free Press.

Brown, G. W., & Harris, T. (1986). Establishing causal links: The Bedford College studies of depression. In H. Katschnig (Ed.), *Life events and psychiatric disorders: Controversial issues* (pp. 201–285). Cambridge, UK: Cambridge University Press.

Brown, G. W., & Harris, T. (1989). *Life events and illness.* New York: Guilford Press.

Caprara, G. V., & Cervone, D. (2000). *Personality: Determinants, dynamics, and potentials.* Cambridge, UK: Cambridge University Press.

Caprara, G. V., Pastorelli, C., Regalia, C., Scabini, E., & Bandura, A. (2005). Impact of adolescent's filial self-efficacy on quality of family functioning and satisfaction. *Journal of Research on Adolescence, 15*, 71–97.

Carver, C. S., & Scheier, M. F. (1998). *On the self-regulation of behavior.* Cambridge, UK: Cambridge University Press.

Caspi, A., Sugden, K., Moffitt, T. E., Taylor, A., Craig, I. W., Harrington, H.,…Poulton, R. (2003). Influence of life stress on depression: Moderation by a polymorphism in the 5-HTT gene. *Science, 301,* 386–389.

Cervone, D., Kopp, D. A., Schaumann, L., & Scott, W. D. (1994). Mood, self-efficacy, and performance standards: Lower moods induce higher standards for performance. *Journal of Personality and Social Psychology, 67,* 499–512.

Cervone, D., & Scott, W. D. (1995). Self-efficacy theory of behavioral change: Foundations, conceptual issues, and therapeutic implications. In W. O'Donohue & L. Krasner (Eds.), *Theories of behavior therapy: Exploring behavior change* (pp. 349–383). Washington, DC: American Psychological Association.

Cofer, D. H., & Wittenborn, J. R. (1980). Personality characteristics of formerly depressed women. *Journal of Abnormal Psychology, 89,* 309–314.

Cox, B. J., Clara, I. P., & Enns, M. W. (2009). Self-criticism, maladaptive perfectionism, and depression symptoms in a community sample: A longitudinal test of the mediating effects of person-dependent stressful life events. *Journal of Cognitive Psychotherapy, 23*(4), 336–349.

Coyne, J. C. (1976). Toward an interactional description of depression. *Psychiatry, 39,* 28–40.

Cozzarelli, C. (1993). Personality and self-efficacy as predictors of coping with abortion. *Journal of Personality and Social Psychology, 65,* 1224–1236.

Davila, J., Hammen, C., Burge, D., Paley, B., & Daley, S. E. (1995). Poor interpersonal problem solving as a mechanism of stress generation in depression among adolescent women. *Journal of Abnormal Psychology, 104,* 592–600.

Davila, J., Stroud, C. B., & Starr, L. R. (2009). Depression in couples and families. In I. H. Gotlib & C. L. Hammen (Eds.), *Handbook of depression* (2nd ed., pp. 467–491). New York: Guilford Press.

Dunkley, D. M., Zuroff, D. C., & Blankstein, K. R. (2003). Self-critical perfectionism and daily affect: Dispositional and situational influences on stress and coping. *Journal of Personality and Social Psychology, 84,* 234–252.

Dykman, B. M. (1998). Integrating cognitive and motivational factors in depression: Initial tests of a goal-orientation approach. *Journal of Personality and Social Psychology, 74,* 139–158.

Dykman, B. M., & Johll, M. (1998). Dysfunctional attitudes and vulnerability to depressive symptoms: A 14-week longitudinal study. *Cognitive Therapy and Research* (Special Issue: *Cognitive Processes and Vulnerability to Affective Problems*), 22, 337–352.

Eaton, W. W., & Kessler, L. G. (1985) (eds.). *Epidemiologic field methods in psychiatry: The NIMH Epidemiologic Catchment Area Program.* New York: Elsevier Science.

Eberhart, N. K., & Hammen, C. L. (2010). Interpersonal style, stress, and depression: An examination of transactional and diathesis-stress models. *Journal of Social and Clinical Psychology, 29,* 23–38.

Evraire, L., & Dozois, D. J. A. (2011). An integrative model of excessive reassurance seeking and negative feedback seeking in the development and maintenance of depression. *Clinical Psychology Review, 31,* 1291–1303.

Flett, G. L., Hewitt, P. L., Blankstein, K. R., & Mosher, S. W. (1995). Perfectionism, life events, and depressive symptoms: A test of a diathesis-stress model. *Current Psychology: Developmental, Learning, Personality, Social,* 14, 112–137.

Flett, G. L., Hewitt, P. L., & Mittelstaedt, W. M. (1991). Dysphoria and components of self-punitiveness: A re-analysis. *Cognitive Therapy and Research,* 15, 201–219.

Freud, S. (1917). Mourning and melancholia. In *Collected papers* (Vol. 4). London: Hogarth Press, 1950. http://www.english.upenn. edu/~cavitch/pdf-library/Freud_ MourningAndMelancholia.pdf.

Garratt, G., Ingram, R. E., Rand, K. L., & Sawalani, G. (2007). Cognitive processes in cognitive therapy: Evaluation of the mechanisms of change in the treatment of depression. *Clinical Psychology: Science and Practice,* 14, 224–239.

Garrison, C. Z, Addy, C. L., Jackson K. L., McKeown, R. E., & Waller J. L. (1992). Major depressive disorder and dysthymia in young adolescents. *American Journal of Epidemiology,* 135, 792–802.

Grosscup, S. J., & Lewinsohn, P. M. (1980). Unpleasant and pleasant events, and mood. *Journal of Clinical Psychology,* 36, 252–259.

Haaga, D. A. F., Dyck, M. J., & Ernst, D. (1991). Empirical status of cognitive theory of depression. *Psychological Bulletin,* 110, 215–236.

Haeffel, G. J., Voelz, Z. R., & Joiner, Jr., T. E. (2007). Vulnerability to depressive symptoms: Clarifying the role of excessive reassurance seeking and perceived social support in an interpersonal model of depression. *Cognition and Emotion, 21*, 681–688.

Hammen, C. L. (1991). Generation of stress in the course of unipolar depression. *Journal of Abnormal Psychology, 100*, 555–561.

Hammen, C. L. (2006). Stress generation in depression: Reflections on origins, research, and future directions. *Journal of Clinical Psychology, 62*, 1065–1082.

Hammen, C. L., & Krantz, S. (1976). Effects of success and failure on depressive cognitions. *Journal of Abnormal Psychology, 85*, 577–586.

Hankin, B. L., Abramson, L. Y., Miller, N., & Haeffel, G. J. (2004). Cognitive vulnerability-stress theories of depression: Examining affective specificity in the prediction of depression versus anxiety in three prospective studies. *Cognitive Therapy and Research, 28*, 309–309.

Hewitt, P. L., & Dyck, D. G. (1986). Perfectionism, stress, and vulnerability to depression. *Cognitive Therapy and Research, 10*, 137–142.

Hewitt, P. L., & Flett, G. L. (1991). Dimensions of perfectionism in unipolar depression. *Journal of Abnormal Psychology, 100*, 98–101.

Hokanson, J. E., Hummer, J. T., & Butler, A. C. (1991). Interpersonal perceptions by depressed college students. *Cognitive Therapy and Research, 15*, 443–457.

Holahan, C. K., & Holahan, C. J. (1987). Self-efficacy, social support, and depression in aging: A longitudinal analysis. *Journal of Gerontology, 42*, 65–68.

Hollon, S. D., Stewart, M. O., & Strunk, D. (2006). Enduring effects for cognitive behavior therapy in the treatment of depression and anxiety. *Annual Review of Psychology, 57*, 285–315.

Ingram, R. E. (1984). Toward an information processing analysis of depression. *Cognitive Therapy and Research, 8*, 443–478.

Ingram, R. E. (1990). Self-focused attention in clinical disorders: Review and a conceptual model. *Psychological Bulletin, 107*, 156–176.

Ingram, R. E., Atchley, R., & Segal, Z. V. (2011). *Vulnerability to depression: From cognitive neuroscience to clinical strategies.* New York: Guilford Press.

Ingram, R. E., & Holle, C. (1992). Cognitive science of depression. In D. J. Stein & J. E. Young (Eds.), *Cognitive science and clinical disorders* (pp. 188–209). San Diego: Academic Press.

Ingram, R. E., Miranda, J., & Segal, Z. V. (1998). *Cognitive vulnerability to depression.* New York: Guilford Press.

Ingram, R. E., & Ritter, J. (2000). Vulnerability to depression: Cognitive reactivity and parental bonding in high-risk individuals. *Journal of Abnormal Psychology, 109*, 588–596.

Ingram, R. E., Slater, M. A., Atkinson, J. H., & Scott, W. D. (1990). Positive automatic cognition in major affective disorder. *Psychological Assessment: A Journal of Consulting and Clinical Psychology, 2*, 209–211.

Joiner, T. E. (1994). Contagious depression: Existence, specificity to depressed symptoms, and the role of reassurance-seeking. *Journal of Personality and Social Psychology, 67*, 287–296.

Joiner, T. E., Alfano, M. S., & Metalsky, G. I. (1992). When depression breeds contempt: Reassurance-seeking, self-esteem, and rejection of depressed college students by their roommates. *Journal of Abnormal Psychology, 101*, 165–173.

Joiner, T. E., Alfano, M. S., & Metalsky, G. I. (1993). Caught in crossfire: Depression, self-consistency, self-enhancement, and the response of others. *Journal of Social and Clinical Psychology, 12*, 113–134.

Joiner, T. E., & Katz, J. (1999). Contagion of depressive symptoms and mood: Meta-analytic review and explanations from cognitive, behavioral, and interpersonal viewpoints. *Clinical Psychology: Science and Practice, 6*, 149–164.

Joiner, T. E., & Metalsky, G. I. (1995). A prospective test of an integrative interpersonal theory of depression: A naturalistic study of college roommates. *Journal of Personality and Social Psychology, 69*, 778–788.

Joiner, T. E., Metalsky, G. I., Katz, J., & Beach, S. R. H. (1999). *Depression and excessive reassurance seeking. Psychological Inquiry, 10*, 269–278.

Joyce, P. R., Oakley-Browne, M. A., Wells, J. E., Bushnell, J. A. & Hornblow, A. R. (1990). Birth cohort trends in a major depression: Increasing rates and earlier onset in New Zealand. *Journal of Affective Disorders, 18*, 83–89.

Justice, B., & Duncan, D. F. (1977). Child abuse as a work-related problem. *Corrective and Social Psychiatry and Journal of Behavior Technology, Methods and Therapy, 23*, 53–55.

Karg, K., Burmeister, M., Shedden, K., & Sen, S. (2011). The serotonin transporter promoter variant (5-HTTLPR), stress, and depression meta-analysis revisited: Evidence of genetic moderation. *Archives of General Psychiatry, 68*(5), 444–454.

Kendall, P. C., Howard, B. L., & Hays, R. C. (1989). Self-referent speech and psychopathology: The balance of positive and negative thinking. *Cognitive Therapy and Research, 13*, 583–598.

Kendler, K. S., Gardner, C. O., & Prescott, C. A. (2003). Personality and the experience of environmental adversity. *Psychological Medicine, 33*, 1193–1202.

Kercher, A., Rapee, R. M., & Schniering, C. A. (2009). Neuroticism, life events and negative thoughts in the development of depression in adolescent girls. *Journal of Abnormal Child Psychology, 37*, 903–915.

Kessler, R. C., Chiu, W., Demler, O., & Walters, E. E. (2005). Prevalence, severity, and comorbidity of 12-month *DSM–IV* disorders in the National Comorbidity Survey Replication. *Archives of General Psychiatry, 62*, 617–627.

Kessler, R. C., McGonagle, K. A., Zhao, S., Nelson, C. B., Hughes, M., Eschlman, S., et al. (1994). Lifetime and 12-month prevalence of *DSM–III*–R psychiatric disorders in the United States: Results from the National Comorbidity Survey. *Archives of General Psychiatry, 51*, 8–19.

Klerman, G. (1986). The National Institute of Mental Health—Epidemiologic Catchment Area (NIMH-ECA) program: Background, preliminary findings and implications. *Social Psychiatry, 21*, 159–166.

Klerman, G., & Weissman, M. M. (1989). Increasing rates of depression. *Journal of the American Medical Association, 261*, 2229–2235.

Kovacs, M., & Beck, A. T. (1978). Maladaptive cognitive structures in depression. *American Journal of Psychiatry, 135*, 525–533.

Kraepelin, E. (1896). *Psychiatrie: Ein Lehrbuch fur Studirende und Aerzte. Funfte, vollstandig umgearbeitete Auflage*. Leipzig.

Lewinsohn, P. M. (1974). A behavioral approach to depression. In R. J. Friedman & M. M. Katz (Eds.), *The psychology of depression: Contemporary theory and research*. New York: Wiley.

Lewinsohn, P. M., & Hoberman, H., Teri, L., & Hautzinger, M. (1985). An integrative theory of depression. In S. Reiss & R. R. Bootzin (Eds.), *Theoretical issues in behavior therapy* (pp. 331–361). New York: Academic Press.

Liem, R., & Liem, J. H. (1988). The psychological effects of unemployment on workers and their families. *Journal of Social Issues, 44*, 87–105.

Lindsay, J., & Scott, W. D. (2005). Dysphoria and self-esteem following an achievement event: Predictive validity of goal orientation and personality style theories of vulnerability. *Cognitive Therapy and Research, 29*, 769–785.

Liu, R. T., & Alloy, L. B. (2010). Stress generation in depression: A systematic review of the empirical literature and recommendations for future study. *Clinical Psychology Review, 30*(5), 582–593.

Locke, E. A., & Latham, G. P. (1990). *A theory of goal setting and task performance*. Englewood Cliffs, NJ: Prentice Hall.

Matt, G. E., Vazquez, C., & Campbell, W. K. (1992). Mood-congruent recall of affectively toned stimuli: A meta-analytic review. *Clinical Psychology Review, 12*, 227–255.

Mazure, C. M. (1998). Life stressors as risk factors in depression. *Clinical Psychology: Science and Practice, 5*, 291–313.

Metalsky, G. I., Halberstadt, L. J., & Abramson, L. Y. (1987). Vulnerability to depressive mood reactions: Toward a more powerful test of the diathesis-stress and causal mediation components of the reformulated theory of depression. *Journal of Personality and Social Psychology, 52*, 386–393.

Metalsky, G. I., Joiner, T. E., Hardin, T. S., & Abramson, L. Y. (1993). Depressive reactions to failure in a naturalistic setting: A test of the hopelessness and self-esteem theories of depression. *Journal of Abnormal Psychology, 102*, 101–109.

Monroe, S. M. (2010). Recurrence in major depression: Assessing risk indicators in the context of risk estimates. In C. S. Richards & M. G. Perri (Eds.), *Relapse prevention for depression* (pp. 27–49). Washington, DC: American Psychological Association.

Monroe, S. M., & Depue, R. A. (1991). Life stress and depression. In J. Becker & A. Kleinman (Eds.), *Psychosocial aspects of depression* (pp. 101–130). Mahwah, NJ: Lawrence Erlbaum.

Monroe, S. M., & Harkness, K. L. (2005). Life stress, the "kindling" hypothesis, and the recurrence of depression: Considerations from a life stress perspective. *Psychological Review, 112*, 417–445.

Monroe, S. M., Slavich, G. M., Torres, L. D., & Gotlib, I. H. (2007). Major life events and major chronic difficulties are differentially associated with history of major depressive episodes. *Journal of Abnormal Psychology, 116*, 116–124.

Morris, M. C., Ciesla, J. A., & Garber, J. (2010). A prospective study of stress autonomy versus stress sensitization in adolescents at varied risk for depression. *Journal of Abnormal Psychology, 119*(2), 341–354.

Nolen-Hoeksema, S. (1987). Sex differences in unipolar depression: Evidence and theory. *Psychological Bulletin, 101*, 259–282.

Nolen-Hoeksema, S., & Hilt, L. M (2009). Gender differences in depression. In

I. H. Gotlib & C. Hammen (Eds.), *Handbook of depression* (2nd ed., pp. 386–404). New York: Guilford Press.

Olioff, M., & Aboud, F. E. (1991). Predicting postpartum dysphoria in primiparous mothers: Roles of perceived parenting self-efficacy and self-esteem. *Journal of Cognitive Psychotherapy, 5*, 3–14.

Olioff, T. E., Bryson, S. E., & Wadden, N. P. (1989). Predictive relation of automatic thoughts and student efficacy to depressive symptoms in undergraduates. *Canadian Journal of Behavioural Science, 21*, 353–363.

Paykel, E. S., & Cooper, Z. (1992). Life events and social stress. In E. S. Paykel (Ed.), *Handbook of affective disorders* (2nd Ed.). New York: Guilford Press.

Penkower, L., Bromet, E., & Dew, M. (1988). Husbands' layoff and wives' mental health: A prospective analysis. *Archives of General Psychiatry, 45*, 994–1000.

Pettit, J. W., & Joiner, T. E. (2006). Excessive reassurance-seeking. In J. W. Pettit & T. Joiner (Eds.), *Chronic depression: Interpersonal sources, therapeutic solutions* (pp. 55–71). Washington: American Psychological Association.

Post, R. M. (1992). Transduction of psychosocial stress into the neurobiology of recurrent affective disorder. *American Journal of Psychiatry, 149*, 999–1010.

Potthoff, J. G., Holahan, C. J., & Joiner, T. E. (1995). Reassurance seeking, stress generation, and depressive symptoms: An integrative model. *Journal of Personality and Social Psychology, 68*, 664–670.

Robins, L. (1984). Lifetime prevalence of specific psychiatric disorders in three sites. *Archives of General Psychiatry, 41*, 949–670.

Scher, C. D., Ingram, R. E., & Segal, Z. V. (2005). Cognitive reactivity and vulnerability: Empirical evaluation of construct activation and cognitive diatheses in unipolar depression. *Clinical Psychology Review, 25*, 487–510.

Scott, W. D., & Cervone, D. (2002). The influence of negative mood on self-regulatory cognition. *Cognitive Therapy and Research, 26*, 19–37.

Scott, W. D., Dearing, E., Reynolds, W. R., Lindsay, J. E., Hamill, S. K., & Baird, G. L. (2008). Cognitive self-regulation and depression: Examining self-efficacy appraisals and goal characteristics in youth of a Northern Plains tribe. *Journal of Research on Adolescence, 18*, 379–394.

Segal, Z. V., Gemar, M., & Williams, S. (1999). Differential cognitive response to a mood challenge following successful cognitive therapy or pharmacotherapy for unipolar depression. *Journal of Abnormal Psychology, 108*, 3–10.

Segal, Z. V., & Ingram, R. E. (1994). Mood priming and construct activation in tests of cognitive vulnerability to unipolar depression. *Clinical Psychology Review, 14*, 663–695.

Segal, Z. V., Kennedy, M. D., Gemar, M., Hood, K., Pedersen, R., & Buis, T. (2006). Cognitive reactivity to sad mood provocation and the prediction of depressive relapse. *Archives of General Psychiatry, 63*, 749–755.

Segal, Z. V., & Shaw, B. F. (1986). Cognition in depression: A reappraisal of Coyne & Gotlib's critique. *Cognitive Therapy and Research, 10*, 671–694.

Seligman, M. E. P. (1975). *Helplessness: On depression, development, and death.* San Francisco: Freeman.

Seligman, M. E. P. (1990). Why is there so much depression today? The waxing of the individual and the waning of the common. In R. E. Ingram (Ed.), *Contemporary psychological approaches to depression* (pp. 1–10). New York: Plenum Press.

Shahar, G., Joiner, T. E., Zuroff, D. C., & Blatt, S. J. (2004). Personality, interpersonal behavior, and depression: Co-existence of stress-specific moderating and mediating effects. *Personality and Individual Differences, 36*, 1583–1597.

Siegel, S. J., & Alloy, L. B. (1990). Interpersonal perceptions and consequences of depressive-significant other relationships: A naturalistic study of college roommates. *Journal of Abnormal Psychology, 99*, 361–363.

Smith, T. W., & Allred, K. D. (1989). Major life events in depression and anxiety. In P. C. Kendall & D. Watson (Ed.), *Anxiety and depression: Distinctive and overlapping features* (pp. 205–223). San Diego: Academic Press.

Starr, L. R., & Davila, J. (2008). Excessive reassurance seeking, depression, and interpersonal rejection: A meta-analytic review. *Journal of Abnormal Psychology, 117*, 762–775.

Steger, M. F. (2010). The social context of major depressive disorder: Sensitivity to positive and negative social interactions influences well-being. *Directions in Psychiatry, 30*, 41–52.

Steinberg, L., Catalano, R. l, & Dooley, D. (1981). Economic antecedents of child abuse and neglect. *Child Development, 52*, 975–985.

Stroud, C. B., Davila, J., Hammen, C., & Vrshek-Schallhorn, S. (2011). Severe and nonsevere events in first onsets versus recurrences of depression: Evidence for stress sensitization. *Journal of Abnormal Psychology, 120*(1), 142–154.

Stroud, C. B., Davila, J., & Moyer, A. (2008). The relationship between stress and depression in first onsets versus recurrences: A meta-analytic review. *Journal of Abnormal Psychology, 117*(1), 206–213.

Sturman, E. D., Mongrain, M., & Kohn, P. M. (2006). Attributional style as a predictor of hopelessness depression. *Journal of Cognitive Psychotherapy, 20*, 447–458.

Sullivan, H. S. (1953). *The interpersonal theory of psychiatry.* New York, NY: W.W. Norton & Co.

Swann, W. B., Jr. Chang-Schneider, C., & McClarty, K. (2007) Do people's self-views matter? Self-concept and self-esteem in everyday life. *American Psychologist, 62*, 84–94.

Taylor, L., & Ingram, R. E. (1999). Cognitive reactivity and depressotypic information processing in the children of depressed mothers. *Journal of Abnormal Psychology, 108*, 202–210.

Teasdale, J. D. (1988). Cognitive vulnerability to persistent depression. *Cognition and Emotion, 2*, 247–274.

Teasdale, J. D. & Barnard, P. J. (1993). *Affect, cognition, and change.* Hillsdale, NJ: Lawrence Erlbaum.

Tillema, J. L., Cervone, D., & Scott, W. D. (2001). Dysphoric mood, perceived self-efficacy, and personal standards for performance: The effects of attributional cues on evaluative self-judgments. *Cognitive Therapy and Research, 25*, 535–549.

Twenge, J. M., & Nolen-Hoeksema, S. (2002). Age, gender socioeconomic status, and birth cohort difference on the Children's Depression Inventory: A meta-analysis. *Journal of Abnormal Psychology, 111*, 578–588.

Vinokur, A. D., Price, R. H., & Caplan, R. D. (1996). Hard times and hurtful partners: How financial strain affects depression and relationship satisfaction of unemployed persons and their spouses. *Journal of Personality and Social Psychology, 71*, 166–179.

Weissman, M. M., & Myers, J. K. (1978). Affective disorders in a US urban community: The use of Research Diagnostic Criteria in an epidemiological survey. *Archives of General Psychiatry, 35*, 416–420.

Zuroff, D. C., Fournier, M. A., & Moskowitz, D. S. (2007). Depression, perceived inferiority, and interpersonal behavior: Evidence for the involuntary defeat strategy. *Journal of Social and Clinical Psychology, 26*, 751–778.

10

Substance Abuse
Etiological Considerations

R. O. PIHL

AND M. ABU SHAKRA

The Natural History of Drug Abuse

The medical historian Osler wrote that "the only characteristic that distinguishes man from other animals is his propensity to take drugs" (in Bean, 1951). Given current knowledge, Osler might add that there are exceptions to this statement and also that the propensity to "do drugs" is as old as human behavior. In the first instance, animal behaviorists have commonly observed various species ingesting substances for both medicinal and seemingly recreational purposes. Intoxicated behavior is seen in most animals, from elephants to the catnip-consuming pet. Some, like humans, consume hallucinogenic mushrooms—for example, Siberian deer—who then show incoordination and general intoxicated behavior. In the second instance, beginning with the earliest indications of human behavior, drugs seem to have been ingested for at least three reasons: to treat disorders both physical and mental, as purgatives, and to alter experience.

Regarding the first reason, in the area of abnormal behavior, pharmacological treatment with behavior-altering drugs is the sine qua non of modern psychiatry, and increasingly so for other professions as well. Drug treatment was known to the ancient Greeks, who viewed opium as a treatment for grief, and to early inhabitants of India, who used the snakeroot plant, a source of the current

but seldom-used antipsychotic drug reserpine, for various disorders. We are drug consumers with voracious appetites. The years between 2000 and 2010 witnessed an elevation from, respectively, 44% to 48%, 25% to 31%, and 6% to 11% in the percentage of Americans consuming at least one, two, and five prescription drugs in the past month (Gu, Dillon, & Burt, 2010). As a purgative, drugs were and are used as added inducement to reverse consumatory excesses and make one's internal environment uncomfortable for whatever organisms or wicked spirits are thought to be infesting an individual. Consistent with this approach, the ancient Egyptians regularly mixed various forms of excrement with their medicines, which likely gave rise to the frequently heard comment regarding the taste of most drugs.

In terms of altering experience, Rudgley (1994) has argued that Paleolithic drawings that festoon the dark and dank interiors of caves throughout southern Europe were inspired by fly agaric, a hallucinogenic mushroom. It seems many of the drawn geometric symbols, repeated throughout the continent, are strikingly similar to those seen in visual hallucinations produced by today's users. Rudgley also detailed how the opium poppy was cultivated and used by neolithic societies (4th millennium B.C.), as was cannabis. Indian physicians in the first millennium B.C. used cannabis as a surgical anesthetic, but perhaps the typical use was best cited by the Greek historian Herodotus, who in the fifth century B.C. described cannabis-intoxicated Scythians as "enjoying the drug so much they howl with pleasure." The Indo-Iranians of the second millennium B.C. used a plant called soma, the term later popularized by Huxley in *Brave New World* (1932), which was likely a hallucinogenic mushroom. Rudgley traced the use of fermented beverages (alcohol) to the fourth millennium B.C. Prominent mention of beer occurs in early Sumerian texts, and the Egyptians are described as being heavy users of beer and wine, as well as opium, mandrake root, hempbene, and myhrr, the latter being stimulants and occasional hallucinogens. The discovery of the New World opened new vistas of experience alteration, as some 100 species of hallucinogens were discovered, a number far exceeding what existed in the Old World. The Incas of Peru chewed daily allotments of coca leaves for intoxication and stimulation, a behavior they inherited from the Nasca culture of approximately 500 A.D. Similarly, the use of peyote derived from a cactus and of mushrooms by the Aztecs to induce hallucinations was well known. Rudgley quotes a sixteenth-century Franciscan missionary writing in the *Florentine Codex* who describes the following drug experience:

> At a banquet the first thing the Aztec Indians ate was a black mushroom, which they call Nanácatl. These mushrooms caused them to become intoxicated, to see visions and also to be provoked to lust. They ate the mushrooms before dawn when they also drank cacao. They ate the mushrooms with honey and when they began to feel excited due to the effect of the mushrooms, the Indians started dancing, while some were singing and others weeping. Thus was the intoxication produced by the mushrooms. Some Indians, who did not care to sing, sat down in their rooms, remaining there as if to think. Others, however, saw in a vision that they died and thus cried; others saw themselves being eaten by a wild beast; others imagined that they were capturing prisoners of war; others that they were rich or that they possessed many slaves; others that they committed adultery and had their heads crushed for this offence; others that they had stolen some articles for which they had to be killed, and many other visions. When this mushroom intoxication had passed, the Indians talked over amongst themselves the visions they had seen.

Notably, both positive and negative experiences are described as a result of this polydrug use, as well as overall social reinforcement, a scenario prevalent today.

These historical examples point out the very basic nature of drug-taking behavior for experience-altering reasons. This behavior is part of who we are; it is fundamental yet not necessary. For a myriad of reasons, each society can and does restrain the use of some drugs, in some way, at some point. In some societies, the use of these drugs is relegated to a privileged few: to shamen, to individuals in positions of status, to certain age groups or to men. In others, total restriction is the rule, while there are few where use is unfettered. There are those societies, like our own, that attempt to discriminate, arguably poorly and variably, allowing usage of some drugs and disapproving of others', restricting harshly in some instances and benignly in others. Finally, it is important to differentiate between drug use and abuse. Factually the use of alcohol and other drugs, particularly among adolescents, is exceedingly common, despite recent national surveys pointing to a decrease in heavy episodic alcohol consumption among young cohorts (Keyes & Miech, 2013). For example, only 10% to 20% of the approximately 85% and 50% of Americans who have respectively used licit and illicit drugs ever develop drug use problems. This finding suggests that it is not the one-timers or casual users who should glean our attention and concern but rather the fraction of those individuals who are now and will be potential abusers.

The Importance of Etiology

In working with addicted and at-risk individuals, the essential objective is to, respectively, treat and prevent addiction. Of course, preventing the problem before it has occurred is always better than dealing with the aftermath or explosion. Unfortunately, despite massive study and considerable efforts, the treatment state for substance use disorders (SUDs) remains largely pessimistic, with a general failure to blunt their prevalence and morbidity rates (Shoham & Insel, 2011). Factually the effect size of even the most well designed, theory-driven, and evidence-based available treatments is often, at best, modest. The obvious question then becomes just what is it that accounts for these impecunious effect sizes? Foremost a possible explanation pertains to substance abuse often being masked, missed, and misunderstood (Dawson, Goldstein, & Grant, 2012). Consider the example of alcohol abuse. Large-scale national surveys show that over 80% of alcoholics are never diagnosed or treated, and comorbid psychiatric disorders, if and when presented, are granted deference in terms of both diagnosis and treatment in 96% of the cases (Edlund, Booth, & Han, 2012). Clearly, this is particularly troubling considering that rarely does alcoholism occur in isolation from other forms of psychopathology. Further, among individuals who do eventually receive treatment, relapse within 3 months after treatment termination is the rule rather than the exception (Sinha, 2012). It is one thing to attempt to treat a disorder, another to successfully do so.

A tenable position postulates that when available treatments fail to induce some relief and sustainable results, the conclusion should be that something is wrong with the treatment. Many currently available treatments are based on minimal or absent etiological insight, which can render them ineffective, inefficient, and even dangerous to both patients and the field. Treatments are frequently administered under the aegis of recovered addicts proselytizing whatever general approach seemed to have worked for them. These techniques often involve elaborate social manipulations to control general behavior, with some degree of success. Nevertheless, they basically do so in the absence of knowledge of cause. The simple and clear fact is that currently available treatments are often determined by who the practitioner is and what his or her ideological beliefs are rather than by who the addicted individual is and what the context of and reason for his or her addiction might be. Perhaps this is why outcomes displaying strikingly similar trends are produced by supposedly different treatments for different drug addictions.

Preventing drug abuse has not been a slam-dunk either, and the previously discussed points are pertinent here. For example, generalized prevention programs aimed at youth, preaching abstinence, have generally been proven ineffective and, at times, to actually increase drug use. Again, despite being driven by good intent, these approaches typically lack a basis of insight into causal mechanisms as well as an understanding of adolescence.

Terms that are becoming more and more common in the lexicon of the addictions are *heterogeneous, multifactorial, interactional*, and *interdependent*. These terms are increasingly used whenever etiology of drug abuse is the topic, and they denote complexity and obviate current reductionist linear theories, be they genetic, neurobiological, social, or psychological. What is obvious at this point is that no single level of explanation is better than another or sufficient to etiologically explain SUDs. Concerning alcoholism, with many levels of etiological explanations, it is only when these levels of analyses are merged that a realistic theorization of why, how, and in whom drug abuse problems develop could be articulated (Kendler, 2012). Thus, complex multivariable interacting models are required. However, expecting any model to fit all possibilities is patently unrealistic. The field is replete with etiological models that are complex and simplistic, distal and proximal, linear and reciprocal, and all of them fail to adequately explain the individual case. In particular, linear models that postulate a direct path, with one factor presumably influencing another, that is, that rely on a particular biological state or societal disadvantage, ignore the multitude of interacting, mediating, and modulating factors that likely are involved.

A complicating factor for theories or models of drug abuse is that comorbidity, or the presence of another Axis I or II diagnosis, is the rule rather than the exception. When two or more disorders co-occur, be it concurrently or longitudinally, a distinction is often made between primary and secondary disorders, in which one disorder is thought to be responsible for the other. This distinction is deemphasized in this chapter, given that what is labeled as comorbidity may fundamentally be an artifact of shared premorbid etiological underpinnings. What follows is a discussion of critical issues to consider when investigating current factors deemed etiologically significant for substance abuse at multiple levels of analysis.

However, for any investigation of etiological underpinnings to prove meaningful, one needs to be mindful of several facts. First, how risk factors act and interact with other factors to produce which type and magnitude of effect follows a temporally dynamic gradient throughout different stages across the developmental trajectory. The developmental perspective is of paramount importance, and yet, until recently, it has been considered unnecessary and even irrelevant by most researchers and practitioners. Second, causality is a humungous conundrum and is not equivalent to correlation, neither statistically nor conceptually. Granting causative status to a risk factor is challenging, and often what one is dealing with is mere correlation rather than causation. Mistaking the former for the latter is a common fundamental logical error. Third, what we might think of as a genetic risk factor might factually be environmental, and vice versa. For example, in choosing one's peers, adolescents who are at risk to develop conduct disorder (CD) and substance misuse problems are also genetically vulnerable to select or prefer the affiliation with delinquent peers (Knafo & Jaffee, 2013). Another issue is assortative mating. Alcoholics tend to marry alcoholics. In addition, depressed women, whose offspring are typically at risk for conduct problems and/or substance misuse often have a personal history of conduct problems and antisociality, and they also tend to marry or cohabitate with antisocial men (Moffitt, 2005). Fourth, current nosology arbitrary delineates the boundaries of diagnostic categories, thereby implying that they are distinct taxa with distinct etiological mechanisms and obscuring the fact that comorbidity between mental disorders is typically normative. Fifth, whenever drug addiction is the topic, the discussion is of a disorder that is both multiphasic and heterogeneous; neither of these features is encapsulated within the *DSM-5*. In the first instance, the drug addiction trajectory begins with use, moves to established patterns of use, and ends with abuse. In each of these stages, heterogeneous effects and mechanisms are likely in play. In the second instance, multiple, and most likely distinct, risk pathways can lead different individuals to behaviorally manifest what appears to be, but is not, the same disorder.

At the Level of the Society

Culture

One's culture substantially contributes to triggering use, sculpting established patterns of drug use and possibly abuse. The breadth of these nonindividual factors is enormous, constituting at least five areas of influence. First, there is the general cultural environment that affects norms concerning drug use and that influences drug availability. Second, one's specific community affects values and norms and can support differential

drug regulations that affect access. Third, subcultures within the community that can involve the workplace, groups at school, gangs, and the like have unique influences. Fourth, family and peers provide immediate models that can be permissive or restrictive, as well as providing direct access. And finally, the drug-using context (i.e., the physical and social environment) influences drug-using practices.

Which and how much of a drug is used and misused and what the drug does, subjectively and objectively, to and for individuals can be strikingly interculturally different. This variation can determine how many individuals in each society use and/or abuse which forms of drugs and at which point in their life. Patently there are substantial intercultural differences in prevalence and persistence of substance use and abuse. The degree to which the use of certain drugs is normal or abnormal is determined by each society, often on the basis of traditions and religion, not the drugs' harmful consequences. Hence, there is great relativity as to what is considered a harmful drug. In our culture, for example, we teach, model, encourage, even idealize and favor the use of certain drugs, such as alcohol, which is deemed normative, in contrast to more relatively benign substances like hallucinogenic drugs. There are cultures, and some of our subcultures, that deem the use of hallucinogenics normative, while there are others that deem the use of both drugs highly pathological. This variability is paralleled by a large discrepancy between the prevalence rates of abuse among different cultures. These differences point to a major obvious aspect regarding causation: drug abuse begins with use, and one can neither try nor abuse what one cannot access or afford.

Concerning alcohol, it has been shown that increases in price and taxes reduce alcohol consumption, morbidity, and mortality rates (Wagenaar, Tobler, & Komro, 2010). Further, increasing the legal drinking age reduces the number of teen DWIs and traffic deaths. Alcohol prices, nonetheless, remain quite low (Albers et al., 2013). Importantly, this association is neither simple nor linear, as other cultural factors may interfere. A recent study assessing the impact of decreased alcohol taxes and a reduction in the quota on importing alcohol in Finland reported an increase in alcohol use and drinking-related consequences, particularly among those who are socioeconomically disadvantaged. However, only a small number of such consequences were demonstrated in Denmark and southern Sweden, which also had altered alcohol-related rules. The effect thus might be marginal in affluent and wealthier societies (Room et al., 2013). Also, studies show that the frequency of drinking-related consequences including physical injuries, assault (crime), and violence increased, as did so the size of alcoholic beverages permitted for sale and the times of alcohol availability for purchase (Popova, Giesbrecht, Bekmuradov, & Patra, 2009).

Societal control of drug use is more readily achieved in isolated cultures, where it becomes interwoven into the basic fabric of life. The informational and commercial borderlessness of most Western societies predestines such control efforts to limited success, as witnessed by the failure of Prohibition, the war on drugs, and the fact that cigarettes and alcohol, although prohibited to minors, are readily available to them. There are subcultures that promote and others that inhibit drug use and abuse. Drug subcultures emerge from common identities, such as age or perceived and real alienation, which in turn can promote group solidarity, or result in group dysfunction. Central to each subculture is the development of a set of shared beliefs and practices. Normative beliefs, which are perceptions of the extent to which significant others approve or disapprove of or engage in a behavior themselves, have been shown to be important predictors of drug use, particularly among adolescents and young adults (Brooks-Russell, Simons-Morton, Haynie, Farhat, & Wang, 2013). Conversely, the degree of spiritual or religious involvement has been shown in many studies to arm one against drug abuse (reviewed in Dick, 2011).

High levels of binge drinking with serious consequences by university students represent an interesting example of the role of social networks within subcultures. Psychosocial predictors of drinking by undergraduates include overestimates of others' drinking behavior and attitudes (Woodyard, Hallam, & Bentley, 2013), membership in a fraternity or sorority (Wechsler, Kuh, & Davenport, 2009), binge drinking in high school (Wechsler & Nelson, 2008), family history for alcoholism (Dager et al., 2013), and nonreligiosity (Wichers, Gillespie, & Kendler, 2013). Interestingly, although level of societal concern has varied, drinking levels and problem drinking by students have been quite consistent over time,

and college students do seem to be at greater risk for developing alcohol misuse problems than their non-college peers, although the latter seem more at risk for addiction to other drugs, including cigarettes (Blanco et al., 2008).

One social aspect in SUDs that has been viewed as a causative factor, and that theoretically could be manipulated, is poverty or neighborhood disorganization. Although poverty per se is a very weak predictor of drug abuse, when combined with neighborhood deterioration and high crime, the prediction increases substantially. One prospective study in which 4-year-olds from low-income backgrounds were followed for 5 years found that until age 6, the severity of neglect mediated the association between maternal substance dependence at baseline and a child's externalizing disorders at age 9. The latter are developmental precursors and powerful predictors of subsequent substance abuse, with the link being mediated by neighborhood crime rates (Manly, Oshri, Lynch, Herzog, & Wortel, 2013). In many industrial U.S. cities, the loss of inner-city jobs has unfortunately resulted in a situation in which the economic "success" stories (hence models for youths) are often individuals engaged in illegal activities, including the selling of drugs. Further, in this milieu, family deterioration is prevalent and prosocial training lacking. For the alienated and unemployed, the ostracism and unemployment associated with drug use are of little preventative relevance.

Culture paints the drug-taking context with expectations of response that can also dramatically determine the actual response to the drug. For example, in one study (Dobkin de Rios, 1973), when white subjects were compared to Indian subjects in their response to peyote intoxication, white participants displayed shifts in mood, whereas the Indian participants had stable mood but reverential feelings. Both groups were reflecting the expectations of their particular cultures. Another example concerns the response to cannabis: it has been shown that the intoxicating experience differs geographically, between the sexes, and with the milieu. These factors are illustrated in a series of studies conducted in Jamaica in the late 1960s and early 1970s. At this time a common belief in North America was that cannabis produced cognitive and neurological deficits, a conclusion supported by many studies. These studies, however, suffered a methodological flaw in that they used clinical, primarily "street" people, who reflected a myriad of problems as subjects. At this time, the smoking of ganga (cannabis) was almost a normative behavior in Jamaica, although the distribution of use was bimodal. In two studies with four populations, none of the expected deleterious effects of very heavy use were found (Bowman & Pihl, 1973). Rather, drug effects seemed dictated by attitude toward the drug. For example, among those who thought one should feel hunger, that occurred; among others who believed satiety was the response, that also occurred. Of course, the negative ramifications of any drug depend on the route of administration, the individual taking the drug, and the dose, as exemplified in the adage "too much of anything will eventually lead to the suppression of something."

Cultural variation that influences drug response can even occur in seemingly homogeneous groups. The first "study" of alcohol effects that one of the authors was involved in occurred in the early 1960s. Working with a small group of married college students living adjacent to the football stadium, tickets were sold to drink beer during halftime at an adjacent apartment house. This occurred at a small Midwestern college where drinking on campus was then prohibited. When the dean of students got wind of this entrepreneurial endeavor, all involved were threatened with expulsion if beer was served. However, tickets had been sold. Consequently, near-beer, an early variant of nonalcoholic beer, was hurriedly purchased from a brewery some 100 miles away and trucked to the apartment building, and bottles were opened and poured into kegs that were then pressurized. During halftime of the game, those with tickets left the stadium and came to the basement of the apartment house. Experienced drinkers quickly realized that something was wrong, demanded refunds, and returned to the game. However, many individuals, particularly freshmen, displayed drunken behavior, incoordination, falling down, loud exuberance, and some nausea and vomiting—all of this on a placebo. For these individuals, their expectations and the milieu determined their behavior and physical state. Indeed, the examples of cultural variation in response to actual drugs suggest that pharmacologically active substances are also susceptible to this placebo phenomenon.

Within many cultures, psychotropic drugs are viewed in a spiritual rather than a hedonistic way, thus greatly coloring the response. For example, many early AmerIndian societies viewed smoking tobacco as a supernatural aid, and thus the behavior was done communally and to cement agreements. Another good example of cultural determination is in the area of alcohol-related aggression. There is substantial evidence, in crime and laboratory studies, that the use of alcohol increases the likelihood of aggression. Particular pharmacological effects on brain functioning that affect this behavior have been detailed. Yet, there are societies in which, after consumption of considerable alcohol and reaching intoxication, normally aggressive individuals display a rather passive demeanor. Further, the behavioral problems frequently associated with excessive alcohol consumption are very rare in cultures where alcohol is considered a food rather than a drug, although health problems resulting from heavy consumption, such as liver disease, remain constant.

The society can model drug use in various ways. The shifting pattern of which drugs are abused is illustrative. Currently, with the exception of cannabis, prescription and some over-the-counter drugs are surpassing traditional illicit drugs in misuse (International Narcotics Control Board [INCB], 2007; Kuehn, 2007). One aspect of this trend began in the 1970s, when a common explanation for the increased use of drugs was a de facto collusion between the pharmacological industry and prescribing physicians to promote drug use (Lennard, Epstein, Bernstein, & Ransom, 1971), a view that has been revitalized (Moynihan & Cassels, 2005). The original logic was based on the fact that more than half of the individuals seeing physicians were not physically ill but suffered problems in living, which they expressed as physical complaints. Physicians were then seen as prescribing psychotropic drugs to placate the patient and to cement the role of healer. This process was viewed as encouraged by the pharmaceutical industry, where market expansion is accomplished by broadening the definition of problems requiring drug treatment. The evidence for this putative "conspiracy" included a rapid rise in the prescription of psychotropic medications, industry advertising that broadened definitions of problems requiring drug treatment, and studies showing the prescribing of these medications varied with the training and personality characteristics of doctors. The effect of these circumstances was said to be that patients no longer needed to focus on the source of their problems, thus one learned to use drugs to deal with and complement living. In effect, it was argued that an induced pharmaco-logical blindness to reality was produced—a drug culture developed that then generalized from legal to illegal use. The current mass marketing of pre-scription, over-the-counter, and social libations all promote the theme that drugs solve problems and improve quality of life. These observations are cou-pled with the theoretical proposition (Eckersley, 2005) that because Western cultures focus on the individual and materialism, where continual striv-ing for "more" is by definition unattainable, per-sonal failure can result, and thus an environment for drug use is created.

Cultural examples adroitly illustrate that defi-nitions of problems with drugs often depend on where one resides and who the user is, and that complete models of causation must be multidimen-sional. Explanations that reside purely within the individual, either physiological or psychological, do not tell the whole story. In fact, a methodologi-cal conundrum exists, as the application of more science per se cannot solve the problem of shift-ing definitions, beliefs, and attitudes. Models of etiology are therefore in themselves contextually dependent on the environment and the inherent philosophies.

The Peer Group

If one's friends use and misuse drugs, the odds of using and misusing drugs are much higher for oneself. Identification with pop subgroups instead of athletic, computer nerd, and/or religious sub-groups is much more likely to reflect a higher risk for substance use. Time spent with like friends that encourage and/or model deviancy, lack of achievement, and depressed mood are impor-tant factors in predicting problem substance use (Castellanos-Ryan, O'Leary-Barrett, & Conrod, 2013; Mason, Hitchings, & Spoth, 2007). These risk characteristics for drug abuse are the same for delinquency, teenage pregnancy, and school failure and dropout. This collection of behaviors has previously been labeled a "problem behavior syndrome." The conjoint peer behaviors and traits included in this predictive basket vary somewhat from study to study, but in approximated order of inclusion are conduct problems, slow school achievement and truancy, age at initiation, non-conformity, lack of parental support, engaging in sex, parental drug use, lack of resources at home, low Socioeconomic status neighborhoods, and

health risk behaviors. Thus, arguably, CD is the strongest predictor of both drug use initiation and progression to dependence (Sartor, Lynskey, Heath, Jacob, & True, 2007). This correlation between peer delinquency and substance use and abuse could mirror a causal chain, wherein delin-quent friends model and encourage substance use among other problem behaviors or, conversely, a youth-governed phenomenon in which individuals at risk to use and abuse substances select and/or prefer friends who model and condone use (Jaffee, Strait, & Odgers, 2012). Whatever the mecha-nisms, a temporally dynamic action and interac-tion of these processes with one another is likely to be the case. One large-scale twin study showed that along with the genetic susceptibility for dis-ruptive behavioral disorders (DBDs), peer delin-quency was the strongest vulnerability for adverse drinking trajectories (Wichers, Gardner, et al., 2013; Wichers, Gillespie, et al., 2013).

Related to this syndrome is the so-called gate-way model, which postulates that the transition from using one drug to another (more specifically from legal to illegal drugs) occurs sequentially. As such, the ascending order in use is cigarettes, alcohol, marijuana, stimulants, depressants, hal-lucinogens, cocaine, and heroin. Obviously, this progression is not inevitable and the order is vari-able, but exposure to peers who engage in drug use a step beyond one's own is seen as an important determining factor, particularly if one is strongly identified with these peers. This identification is seen as involving expectations of positive results from such drug use. Peer factors are thus central in three ways: first, in providing the drug; second, in developing attitudes about its use and effects; and third, in providing an exemplar. This peer cluster theory states not only that peers represent the most important predictor of use and progression to abuse but also that peers mediate the significance of other risk factors—for example, emotional problems and attitudes about oneself. Some research has confirmed these social-learning inter-pretations, and the consequent argument has been made that interventions should be aimed at peers. Other studies (Farrell & Danish, 1993) using lon-gitudinal designs, however, suggest that the rela-tionship is more complex, with the more frequent scenario being peer selection following drug use.

Part of the variability in studying peer and other factors in drug use arises from how "use" is defined. Studies that measure "ever used" may be selecting the wrong population for study. Drug experimentation by adolescents, even with an illegal drug such as marijuana, appears to err on the side of normality, as most adolescents have used the drug. A longitudinal study (Shedler & Block, 1990) found that adolescents who never experimented with drugs, particularly marijuana, showed indications of being more maladjusted than occasional experimenters. While experimenters do display some risk factors, heavy, escalating, and debilitating drug use should be the focus of concern.

Social modeling is a phenomenon often invoked to explain peer effects. Basically one learns by observing, and learning is more likely when the model is similar in age and other characteristics or is looked up to, and when the behavior in question is seen as rewarding. Peers alienated from school and parents and with socially conforming peers can readily adopt drug use and create a reinforcing environment where such use achieves priority. Numerous studies on modeling and drinking have shown that one's quantity consumed and drinking style vary with the behavior of one's drinking partner (Collins, Parks, & Marlatt, 1985).

The Family

Another area where modeling seems to play a role pertains to the behavior of one's parents and siblings. Drug abuse runs in families; in the case of alcohol, this has been known for millennia. The most recent evidence comes from an elegant large-scale investigation of a follow-up of nine large databases of adoptive children. Results showed that when either, versus neither, of the biological parents abused drugs, the offspring risk for drug abuse doubled, and when both did so the risk tripled (Kendler, Sundquist, et al., 2012). A slightly greater risk was found in offspring with paternal as compared to maternal drug abuse, and males seemed to be more genetically vulnerable than females. Further, a biological family history of alcoholism, criminality, or other forms of psychopathology also elevated risk in adopted offspring, and having a substance-abusing adoptive sibling was associated with greater liability than that with a substance-abusing parent (Kendler, Sundquist, et al., 2012). These findings indicate the power of familial environment in shaping the risk for drug abuse. Consistently, a subsequent analysis by the same group demonstrated that risk for SUDs

was significantly greater when the age difference was smaller. Specifically, when both siblings were born in the same year, instead of 10 years apart, the risk for drug abuse in the unaffected sibling doubled. Risk also was substantially greater when the affected proband was older and not younger than the unaffected siblings, an effect that was much more pronounced in males than in female pairs (Kendler, Ohlsson, Sundquist, & Sundquist, 2013).

Modeling of drug use occurs when parents use various drugs to relieve negative feelings, cope with stress, provide a social lubricant, and so on. As suggested earlier, this behavior also includes the giving of medications to their children for similar reasons. The most blatant example of modeling is parental abuse of illicit drugs. Often the misuse of drugs by adolescents is attributed by politicians and the popular press to the fact that the parents of these individuals are at a minimum ambivalent about drug use, are models for drug use because of their own use, or both. Indeed, many studies have consistently supported parental drug use as a risk factor for adolescent initiation of use (Pentz & Riggs, 2013). For example, adolescents with parental alcoholism, compared to those without, are more vulnerable to use and subsequently misuse drugs. Further, their age of onset of alcohol consumption is earlier and escalation to excessive drinking faster, as is the progression to the addiction. Data from community-based samples show that over half and one-fifth of the offspring of alcoholics, respectively, become alcohol and illicit drug misusers, compared to one-fourth and one-tenth of matched controls, by the time they reach young adulthood (Hussong, Huang, Serrano, Curran, & Chassin, 2012). Moreover, after adjusting for comorbid parental psychopathology, environmental stressors, and familial dysfunction, parental alcoholism stands out as a unique predictor of drug use and misuse in adolescence and early adulthood.

With the exception of cigarettes, the more family members that use drugs, the more one is likely to use them as well. In the case of cigarettes, all that seems necessary is that there be one smoker, although older brothers are more influential than younger brothers, which in general is true for all drugs of abuse (Kendler et al., 2013). Modeling aside, the simple availability of cigarettes, alcohol, marijuana, and prescription drugs within the family seems to be a contributing factor. Drug availability plus permissive parental attitudes and poor

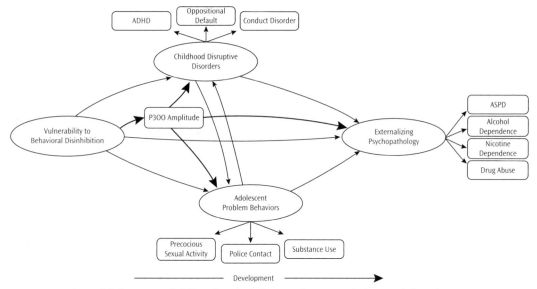

Figure 10.1 A model depicting childhood and adolescent disruptive behavioral disorders as developmental precursors for substance abuse disorders (SUDs). Reprinted from Iacono & Malone, 2011, with kind permission of John Wiley and Sons. Copyright © 2011, John Wiley and Sons.

parental support further facilitate use (Mares, Lichtwarck-Aschoff, Burk, van der Vorst, & Engels, 2012). As deviancy is a profound risk factor for substance abuse, at issue is parental behavior in the developmental internalization of rules of conduct (see Figure 10.1). One study found an indirect relationship between an alcoholic father's sensitivity in child play interactions at age 2 and the child's behavioral internalization of rules of conduct (Edwards, Eiden, & Leonard, 2006). Another study found that lack of maternal support, measured on a series of laboratory tasks, predicted drug use (Dobkin, Tremblay, & Sacchitelle, 1997).

Stress is a frequent family member in the drug-abusing family. Stressors common in families with alcoholism include high conflict, poor communication, marital discord, coercive interactions, physical abuse and neglect, economic and social deprivation, and the extremes of parenting—too authoritarian or too lax (Patock-Peckham, Cheong, Balhorn, & Nagoshi, 2001). Almost all (98%) of adolescents with drug-abusing parents are beset by at least one other environmental adversity (McLaughlin et al., 2012). The effect of abusive parenting seems more significant in abused girls than boys. In one study, even when family history of alcoholism was controlled statistically, abused girls remained at risk for drinking problems in adulthood (Widom, Ireland, & Glynn,

1995). Further, 30% of victims of abuse become abusive parents, and 80% of young adult victims escalate into manifesting a SUD (Buckingham & Daniolos, 2013). Finally, one study on a large sample of young adult female twins showed that, after controlling for familial effects of early drug use, a history of childhood sexual abuse predicted initiation of smoking and marijuana use and it very powerfully predicted early onset of alcohol use (Sartor et al., 2013).

The opposite situation to a negative family environment, of course, exists, with environments restricting the expression of problematic behaviors, such as those including religious upbringing, positive marital relationships, distance from delinquent peers, and high parental warmth and monitoring, all of which reduce the likelihood of developing SUDs (Dick & Kendler, 2012). Positive family connectedness—defined as feelings of warmth, love, and caring—significantly protected individuals from drug use as well as other harmful behaviors. But these factors also follow a temporally dynamic gradient across different stages of the developmental trajectory. For example, a longitudinal investigation following ~1,000 young adolescents for 11 years and assessing their drug consumption (specifically tobacco, alcohol, and cannabis) found that early-adolescence use was predicted by lack of parental monitoring. However, as adolescents transitioned to high school and later adolescence, it was the quality of the family relationship (indexed by shared activities, mutual regard, and positive affect between parents and adolescent offspring) that stood out and potently inversely predicted drug use. However, neither of these family factors seemed to be relevant to drug use in young adulthood (Van Ryzin, Fosco, & Dishion, 2012).

Seldom-considered but potentially significant family factors in the etiology of drug abuse are teratogenic effects. Drug use by parents can deleteriously affect intrauterine development. A mainstream and widely accepted notion has been that alcohol use during pregnancy has the consequence of fetal alcohol syndrome (FAS) and its more broad designation of FAS disorders (FASD), involving low birth weight, prematurity, infant mortality, and physical anomalies in the central nervous system development, maturation, and function (Norman et al., 2013), with similar effects reported when an infant is prenatally exposed to cocaine and cigarettes (Liu et al., 2013), methamphetamines (Twomey et al., 2013), opiates (Behnke et al., 2013), and many prescribed drugs, particularly barbiturates in addition to other common tranquilizers. However, some have argued against the causal link between drinking during pregnancy and FAS, suggesting that FAS cannot be fully explained by the effects of ethanol exposure alone, as an impoverished family environment, too, substantiates risk for FAS. Rather, FAS has been argued to be caused by certain nutritional deficiencies that ethanol exposure can exacerbate, not by a direct alcohol-induced neurotoxic effect (Ballard, Sun, & Ko, 2012). In a birth cohort study (Alati et al., 2006), children of mothers who drank during pregnancy, assessed multiple times, had an odds ratio of 2.95 for later developing adolescent problem drinking when compared with controls. Another longitudinal study showed that the effect of maternal drinking during pregnancy bore a dose–response relationship with adult offspring self-reports of problematic behaviors (Day, Helsel, Sonon, & Goldschmidt, 2013).

At the Level of the Individual

Stress and Affective Factors

When asked why they abuse substances, people frequently report that it is to reduce stress. A large epidemiological study (Dawson, Grant, & Ruan, 2005) found significant positive correlations between negative past-year events and frequency and quantity of alcohol consumption. The initiation of drinking at age 14 or younger appears to be associated with prior stressors (Dawson, Grant, & Li, 2005). Even highly "anxious" rats compared to low-"anxiety" rats show greater progression of cocaine self-administration (Dilleen et al., 2012). Women are generally more vulnerable to stress and react more negatively to adversities than men (Rosenfield & Mouzon, 2013), which is reflected in a higher lifetime prevalence of anxiety disorders and associated drug abuse (Pietrzak, Goldstein, Southwick, & Grant, 2011).

The relationship between drug abuse and stress is theorized to occur for a number of reasons. Drug abuse may be a coping strategy, an escape, or a form of self-medication. "Stress response dampening" (Sher, 1987) is a term used to describe the reduction in physiological reactivity to stressors when one is drinking. Indeed, benzodiazepines are prescribed to anxious patients to reduce reactivity, an effect shared by alcohol and other drugs. In one study (Abrams, Kushner, Medina, & Voight, 2001), patients with social anxiety given a moderate dose of alcohol decreased anxiety as well as their response to anxiety provocation. The authors concluded, as have many others, that this effect is likely reinforcing and explains the high comorbidity of the abuse of these types of drugs with panic and anxiety disorders. There is considerable evidence that severe trauma—that is, disaster, assault, combat, etc.—greatly increases the risk for drug abuse and, unsurprisingly, drug abuse is also a frequent concomitant of posttraumatic stress disorder (PTSD) (Ullman, Relyea, Peter-Hagene, & Vasquez, 2013). Substance misusers compared to nonabusers show 1.4 to 5 times the prevalence of PTSD; the Australian National Survey of Mental Health and Well-being has shown that over one-third of PTSD-diagnosed individuals show at least one or more comorbid SUDs (Mills, Teesson, Ross, & Peters, 2006). Available findings have also demonstrated that a history of physical and/or sexual abuse is reported by 55% to 99% of treatment-seeking drug abusers (Lown, Nayak, Korcha, & Greenfield, 2011). Another study on a sample of individuals who were assessed once at first grade and twice in young adulthood found that PTSD-diagnosed individuals where twice as likely to become addicted to drugs as those experiencing non-PTSD trauma and five times more than individuals who had not undergone any trauma. These findings remained substantial after controlling for childhood experiences and liability, indicating the importance of how one reacts to trauma (Reed, Anthony, & Breslau, 2007).

The transition to drug abuse is also likely modulated by other factors. For example, in one study of Vietnam veterans who had drug abuse problems associated with PTSD, there was an average of 3 1/2 years between the onset of these symptoms and the development of the drug disorder (Davidson, Swartz, Storck, Krishnan, & Hammett, 1985). Depression is likewise substantially associated with drug abuse. An epidemiological study (Grant et al., 2004) found that 20% of individuals with a mood disorder had at least one *DSM-IV* SUD. A meta-analysis of eight longitudinal studies showed that depression predicted alcohol consumption among women (Hartka et al., 1991). Consistent with the self-medication model, individuals with high levels of hopelessness reported drinking to cope with depression, which can then lead to severe alcohol problems (Grant, Beck, & Davila, 2007). In particular, women reported problems with intimacy and interpersonal stress as reasons for excessive drug consumption (Frank, Jacobson, & Tuer, 1990). However, given the importance of stress, anxiety, or depression as etiological factors, the fact that the majority of individuals who undergo these conditions do not turn to drugs for relief suggests that more than a single explanation is required.

Personality

For much of the past century, problem drug behavior was typically ascribed to an addictive personality. Indeed, a plethora of studies yielded evidence supporting a wide range of personality profiles as etiologically significant. In an earlier review (Pihl & Spiers, 1978), it was determined that 93% of this research studied exclusively patients in treatment, thus likely reflecting the characteristics of individuals who seek or are mandated to treatment, or the concomitants of the problem rather than the cause of the problem. It is highly likely that those who receive or seek treatment are more severe cases. Additionally, in these earlier studies, measures were methodologically questionable.

Fortunately, recent years have seen the development of well-constructed measures that are valid predictors tied to limited theoretical notions. These narrow approaches are starting to produce predictive information and, notably, in nonclinical populations. A consensual conclusion from many studies is that neuroticism and disinhibitory traits are precursors to SUDs (Ersche, Turton, et al., 2012; Whelan & Garavan, 2013). One prospective longitudinal report assessed a community sample of adolescents on Cloninger's four temperament dimensions at age 13, which robustly predicted drug use, disorder symptoms, age of onset for consumption of tobacco, alcohol, and illicit substances, and the number of drugs of abuse consumed at age 18. Specifically, low harm avoidance, high novelty-seeking, and persistence predicted onset of use for tobacco and illicit substances as well as the number of drugs consumed, but only novelty-seeking and persistence predicted drinking onset (Hartman, Hopfer, Corley, Hewitt, & Stallings, 2013). Another large longitudinal study of college students with the Big Five (Grekin, Sher, & Wood, 2006) has found that antisociality, novelty seeking, and negative affect predicted multiple types of substance abuse. Further, the Big Five traits of high extraversion and low openness were related to alcohol problems, low conscientiousness to illicit drug use, and high openness and low conscientiousness to tobacco symptomology. In fact, the trait of novelty seeking/sensation seeking, which is thought to reflect a lack of self-regulation, appears to be a better predictor of drug abuse than self-esteem, mental health, social bonding, or social class. Another study (Ersche, Jones, et al., 2012) assessing stimulant-dependent probands with their unaffected biological siblings and unrelated healthy individuals identified aberrations in executive functioning and behavioral control in addition to greater levels of an anxious-impulsive personality profile. These specific traits may be involved in the exploratory use preceding the abuse of the substance, while impulsivity predates the progression to compulsive use and abuse (Belin, Mar, Dalley, Robbins, & Everitt, 2008). Notably, these vulnerability traits also appear to be linked to the biological systems more directly involved in drug reinforcement.

Genetics

The evidence is massive and conclusive: SUDs are, at least, moderately heritable. The spate of adoption and twin studies, which have primarily begun arising in the early 1980s, has provided heritability estimates between 40& and 70% across the various drugs of abuse (Kendler et al., 2011). Many, but not all (Korhonen et al., 2012; Stroud et al., 2009), studies have shown these heritability estimates to vary as a function of sex. One twin study, for example, reported a stronger genetic influence on early-onset alcoholism in males, and a lesser influence on alcohol problems in women (McGue, Pickens, & Svikis, 1992). A longitudinal study following over 1,000 adolescent males and females from ages 17 to 24 found that, with age, while genetic effects became more relevant and important in men, they became less so for women, in whom environmental effects assumed more importance (Hicks et al., 2007). While these results are remarkably consistent with those of the National Epidemiologic Survey on Alcohol and Related Conditions (e.g. Hasin et al., 2007), they should not be construed as suggesting that drug use problems among women are not heritable. For example, in general, an internalizing–externalizing liability model may be operative, which postulates that males are higher on externalizing and females on internalizing factors (Eaton et al., 2013). Further, adolescent onset and adulthood onset of addictions have been associated with differential developmental etiological underpinnings, with the former showing substantial evidence for shared environmental effects and little for genetic factors, and the opposite pattern for adulthood-onset addiction (van Beek et al., 2012).

Candidate Genes Studies   The heritability estimates of addictions are analogous to those for the majority of biomedical illnesses that are widely prevalent in Western societies (Bienvenu, Davydow, & Kendler, 2011), a fact that has justified moving beyond epidemiological approaches to the delineation of specific genetic variations that predispose one to SUDs. Two paradigms have been prominent: gene association studies, which investigate the allelic variation in risk genes selected on the basis of available evidence, and genome-wide association studies (GWAS), which investigate up to a million genetic variations across the entire genome for associations with the risk for drug addiction. The power of GWAS resides in allowing an unbiased assessment of risk polymorphisms. The caveats, however, are many and extend to both the technical and, to a much greater extent, conceptual levels. Gene association studies involve many tests and therefore require very conservative significance levels.

Currently, the best available specific genetic evidence of drug abuse risk involves cigarette addiction and implicates polymorphisms in the nicotinic acetylcholine receptors (Chang et al., 2009; Chen et al., 2009). These have been robustly associated with the number of cigarettes consumed daily (Lips et al., 2010) and with serum cotinine concentrations (a long-lasting metabolite of nicotine (Munafo et al., 2012), which more objectively measures how much nicotine one inhales. Further, individuals bearing a particular minor allele show a significantly decreased puff volume in response to smoking cigarettes (Macqueen et al., 2014). Notably, these previously mentioned genetic polymorphisms have also been linked to lung cancer (Hung et al., 2008) and respiratory health phenotypes, associations that appear to be mediated by the quantity of cigarettes one consumes (Saccone et al., 2010) and the amount of smoke inhaled (Macqueen et al., 2014). This is a rather powerful example of an "outside-the-skin genetic pathway" for a cancer liability gene; the risk allele in a nicotinic receptor increases the propensity to more frequently purchase and smoke cigarettes, thereby augmenting lung cancer susceptibility (Kendler, Chen, et al., 2012).

Regarding alcohol use disorders, initial sensitivity to alcohol is an indicator of risk. To date, the only established evidence of variants affecting the sensitivity to alcohol has been variations of genes encoding alcohol dehydrogenase and aldehyde dehydrogenase 2. These variations obviate risk for and protect against the progression to alcoholism by inducing an aversive response to ethanol. As such, the presence of certain genes not only can indicate increased vulnerability but also can significantly protect against the development of the problem. Many Asians, but very few Caucasians, have this polymorphism, which affects a liver enzyme that protects sixfold against the disorder. The gene, an inactive form of mitochondrial aldehyde dehydrogenas, allows high levels of acetaldehyde to build up in the blood, resulting in negative feelings and the oft-reported response of flushing. Variants of other aldehyde genes are actually thought to enhance risk of alcoholism problems in individuals of European descent. As for other genetic variations, the best currently available evidence comes from the Collaborative Study on the Genetics of Alcoholism of affected probands along with their unaffected family members. Some attention has focused on the gamma-aminobutyric acid

(GABA) receptor subunit alpha 2, which has been correlated with adulthood SUDs (Agrawal et al., 2006), early-onset alcoholism (Enoch, 2008), and specifically an elevated frequency of drunkenness in older adolescence (Dick et al., 2013), antisocial personality disorder, CD (Dick et al., 2009), and a particular electrophysiological endophenotypic marker for disinhibition (Dick et al., 2006). Offspring of alcoholics bearing this variant have double the risk of developing CD relative to low-risk offspring and ~1.2 times the risk of becoming alcoholic. However, risk is mediated by multiple factors, such as parental monitoring, marital status, and anxiety (Dick et al., 2006). Other genes suggested to play a role in the full range of SUDs and disinhibitory disorders are the variations of endorphin, dopaminergic, and serotonergic genes (Gorwood et al., 2012; Schellekens et al., 2013).

It has been argued that these genes are not "vulnerability genes" per se but rather are "plasticity genes," meaning they render one likely to be more negatively or positively affected by, respectively, low- and high-quality environments. While the plethora of candidate genes continues to expand as genomic technology becomes more sophisticated and less expensive, explanatory value remains lacking and any transition to practice is not currently feasible (Yan et al., 2013). Further, there are abundant negative and contradictory findings. Factually, evidence against the implication of specific genetic variants has been frequent and much more robust than evidence in support of it. Even recent GWAS using very large samples, with over 90% power to identify genotypes that underlie as little as 1% of the variance in personality traits have shown no significant association of any genetic variants with personality dimensions that are 30%–60% heritable (Service et al., 2012; Verweij et al., 2010). Similarly, a recent study investigating whether specific genetic variants significantly contributed to the maximum number of alcoholic beverages consumed throughout a 24-hour period (a >50% genetic characteristic) failed to find any significant association (Kapoor et al., 2013).

The obvious question then is why is this the case when the heritability of personality traits and SUDs is indisputable? Possible explanations are many. First, it is possible that both addiction and personality risk traits are substantially polygenic, with multiple genetic variations exerting small effects that current technologies are not powerful enough to detect. Second, rendering the waters much murkier is the fact that genes interact with each other and with the environment (Dick, 2011). The study of SUDs stands to benefit greatly from appreciating that both genetic and environmental effects follow a complex and dynamic mode of action and interaction across different stages of the developmental trajectory to make up the final etiological equation. One must consider the fact that heritable and shared environmental effects tend to, respectively, increase and decrease with age. A longitudinal large-scale Swedish twin study (Baker, Maes, Larsson, Lichtenstein, & Kendler, 2011) suggested a shared vulnerability factor that mediated the association between the use of cigarettes, alcohol, and illicit substances at ages 13–14, 16–17, and 19–20. The effects of shared genetic and environmental factors were strikingly continuous, and while the genetic effects assumed more relevance and specificity with age, shared environmental factors became less important. Parental monitoring, for example, is tremendously important when children first embark into adolescence, at which stage drug use and experimentation often begin, yet genetic effects steadily and linearly occupy the driver's seat as teens progress into young adulthood, when patterns of heavy use are often developed (Palmer et al., 2013). Further, genes and shared environment can and do modulate the magnitude of each other's effects, and this malleable mode of action and interaction is determined by the nature of one's exogenous environments and genotypic architecture (Dick, 2011, Dick & Kendler, 2012).

The third reason for contradictory genetic findings is that genes are not destiny, and whenever genetic risk is the topic, the discussion is of probability and contextually shaped variations (Zhang & Meaney, 2010). In order to matter, genes need to be expressed, and whatever the mechanisms, if and when one's genetic risk is operative, it does not do so randomly or arbitrarily. Because human beings do not exist in a vacuum, environment can and does affect the expression of genes, as well as the degree of their function, much like a dimmer on a light switch. One study tells an illustrative and instructive story. Patients of prostate cancer were genotyped before and after they followed a specific diet, an exercise regimen, and meditation. The authors found that following treatment, some 300–400 genes involved in prostate cancer were down-regulated (Ornish et al., 2008). As such, searching for "the genes for SUDs" would be like fishing in turbulent water. An increasingly popular candidate mechanism has been epigenetics, where environmental events regulate the activity of transcription factors and, hence, the contextually determined genomic state (Zhang & Meaney, 2010). This mechanism involves DNA methylation, histone modifications, non-coding RNAs, and genetic imprinting (Pishva et al., 2012).

A fourth reason is that disorders, particularly addictions, are heterogeneous problems with multiple stages and pathways resulting in what deceptively appears to be, but is not, the same disorders. Heterogeneous sets of genetic variations appear to operate at macro- and micro- levels, affecting inter- and intraindividual processes across development, oblivious to the arbitrarily delineated current diagnostic boundaries. SUDs are dimensional, preceded by very early warning signs and behavioral anomalies. Many kids at risk for SUDs are described as "troublemakers"—markedly aggressive, impulsive, defiant, and frequently inattentive and overactive. Virtually half of the adult substance abusers have had a diagnosis of one or more DBDs between ages 11 and 15 (Kim-Cohen et al., 2003). Further, 75% of those afflicted with CD or oppositional defiant disorder (ODD) at age 15 or younger become substance abusers. This pattern raises serious questions around the issue of comorbidity between SUDs and other psychopathologies and the independence of disorders. Clearly, since "nosology must precede etiology," the validity of findings generated by techniques, no matter how sophisticated, will not exceed the quality of the definition of what one is actually trying to study (Pihl, 2010).

Finally, even when genes are implicated, we remain a good distance from knowing what is inherited and, most important, just what vulnerability is and how it is affected. For example, regarding alcoholism, Gordis (1996) has listed some possibilities of what is inherited: "differences in temperament, different initial sensitivity to the rewarding or aversive qualities of alcohol, different rates and routes of alcohol metabolism, different taste preferences, different signaling from peripheral sites to the brain after drinking alcohol and different abilities to relate memories of drinking experiences to their consequences" (Gordis, 1996). Overall, there is a large discrepancy between the promise of genetics in explaining and ultimately

ameliorating and preventing SUDs and current applicability. One reviewer raised the appropriate question: "Are we there yet?" (Hardy, 2013). The obvious answer is a resounding "no," and so, like young kids trapped in the back seat of the family vehicle on a summer holiday, our anticipation must be contained by the complexity of the miles yet to be traveled.

Biochemistry

Attending to the biochemical level of study is important for at least five reasons. First, genetic processes are fundamentally biochemical. Second, numerous other factors (e.g., nutrition, stress) readily affect biochemical functioning and thus, like genes, may alter individual sensitivity to various drugs. Third, drug abuse problems are increasingly being treated pharmacologically, and effective treatment often requires that knowledge of etiological biochemical underpinnings be exploited. Fourth, and most obvious, what drugs of abuse do, acutely and chronically, is produce a series of biochemical effects in the individual. Finally, drug-induced states such as tolerance and withdrawal actually alter the biochemical functioning of the individual so as to facilitate the continuance and reoccurrence of abuse. Most studies appear to focus on neurotransmitter systems including receptors and neuromodulators. Thus, our attention will focus on the dopaminergic, serotonergic, GABA, glutamate, endogenous opioid, and cannaboid and nicotine systems. Although treated separately in what follows, these systems are intractably intertwined, continually acting and interacting with each other in facilitating and inhibitory fashions.

The Dopaminergic System   The importance of the dopamine (DA) system stems primarily from its association with activation of reward, to the degree that hungry animals will prefer activating this system and will work to cause such a stimulation. An anatomical map of the dopaminergic system is illustrated in Figure 10.2.

Psychostimulants, such as cocaine, amphetamines, and alcohol, for some but not all individuals induce a positively reinforcing effect by primarily targeting the descending mesolimbic DA pathway (Volkow, Wang, Fowler, & Tomasi, 2012). A mainstream position in the literature holds that the dopaminergic projections from the ventral tegmental area (VTA) and the

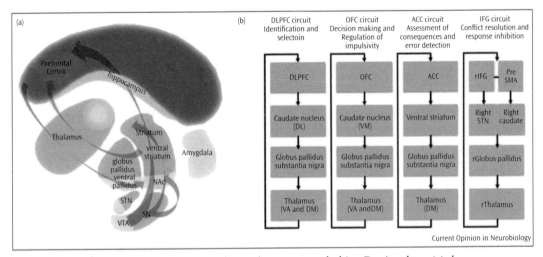

Figure 10.2 The frontostriatal circuitry of stimulus–response habits. Depicted are (a) the mesocorticolimbic dorsal anterior (DA) and (b) four frontostriatal cortical circuits postulated to play a key role in executive functioning and response regulation. DL, dorsolateral; DM, dorsomedial; VA, ventroanterior; VM, ventromedial; r, right; IFG, inferior frontal gyrus; preSMA, presomatic motor area; STN, subthalamic nucleus. Reprinted from *Current Opinion in Neurobiology*, Vol. 23, 4, Volkow, Wang, Tomasi, & Baler, Unbalanced neuronal circuits in addiction, 639–648, Copyright (2013), with permission from Elsevier.

nucleus accumbens (NAc) are required for most drugs to be reinforcing. For example, the rate of self-stimulation is dependent on the density of DA neurons (Jacobs et al., 2013), and drugs that block DA neurons, such as antipsychotics, which selectively block D2 autoreceptors, reduce drug intake (Fibiger & Phillips, 1988; McCormick, Wilson, Wilson, & Remington, 2013). But the system's function is much broader than just reward. For example, Parkinson's patients blindly injected with either active medication or placebo all showed enhanced mesolimbic DA release. Thus, the system signals not reward but rather the incentive salience of stimuli, be they rewarding, aversive, novel, or unexpected (Goodman, 2008; Pruessner et al., 2010).

Although all classes of substances appear to target the dopaminergic system, each of them appears to do so through distinct biochemical profiles (Badiani et al., 2011). For example, psychostimulants suppress dopaminergic reuptake or the inversion of DA transport process and thus prolong the effects of released dopamine, yet opiates (e.g., heroin, morphine, and alcohol in some, but not all, individuals) suppress the GABAergic interneurons, thereby indirectly recruiting the dopaminergic neurons in the VTA. Further, only one-fifth

of dopaminergic neurons, particularly in the NAc, respond to both cocaine and heroin ingestion, suggestive of different neuronal subpopulations encoding for the reinforcing influence of the two substances (Chang, Janak, & Woodward, 1998).

It has additionally been shown that not all classes of substances depend on the DA system to induce a reinforcing effect. Animal studies have found that disrupting the NAc, by whichever means, minimally affects seeking and/or consuming morphine (Sellings & Clarke, 2003) or heroin, unless the animal has a preexisting heroin addiction (Nader, Bechara, Roberts, & van der Kooy, 1994). One study even demonstrated that the chronic blockade of DA receptors potentiated the reinforced effect of low heroin doses (Goodman, 2008).

It is noteworthy that increased release of DA following acute alcohol ingestion is significantly greater in individuals who display the endophenotypic marker of increased heart rate in response to alcohol (Boileau et al., 2003). This dopamine-related increased heart rate to alcohol challenge also correlates with past histories of delinquency, aggression, pathological gambling, measures of impulsivity, increased alcohol consumption, an elevated subjective response to drinking, and better retention of memory for positive words learned before drinking (Pihl, 2010). It has further been determined that individuals who have a family history of alcoholism and display this excitatory response to alcohol respond in a similar fashion to amphetamines (Gabbay, 2005), as do alcohol-preferring rats, in whom the response has been shown to be an index of reinforcement (Bell et al., 2002). Another positron emission tomography (PET) study (Yoder et al., 2007) showed that this striatal DA release was not correlated with intoxication level per se, but rather with the subjective perception of alcohol intoxication. Further, individuals describing the effect of methylphenidate as "pleasant" (versus "unpleasant") have been found to have fewer D2 receptors, as do cocaine addicts (Buckholtz et al., 2010). Recently, mice deficient in the DA D2 autoreceptors (which inhibit DA release) were found to be hyperresponsive to cocaine and markedly motivated to seek reward (Bello et al., 2011). Further, in a process called *sensitization*, wherein the response to a stimulus is enhanced following repeated exposure to it (Kalivas & Stewart, 1991), one drug may make another similar drug more reinforcing, a phenomenon termed *cross-sensitization* (Goodman, 2008). Differential DA release mirrors positive reinforcement, which may in turn explain the increased risk for abuse in individuals displaying this stimulatory response. This also helps explain the high co-occurrence between certain forms of drug use as well as between SUDs and externalizing traits and disorders. For example, the fact that 84% of cocaine abusers also abuse alcohol (Helzer & Pryzbeck, 1988) is related to the similarity of this effect. The combination of cocaine and alcohol results in a chemical cocaethylene, which has more pronounced effects than that of each drug taken separately.

The Serotonergic System   The neurotransmitter serotonin (5-HT) is a critical regulator of human physiology and a wide spectrum of cognitive, affective, and sensory aspects of one's behavioral responses to environmental stimuli. With its at least 16 receptor subtypes, this system also modulates circadian rhythms, food and water intake, sexual behavior, and response to pain (Goodman, 2008). From an evolutionary standpoint, the serotonergic system is ancient, as it functions in neuronal development, as well as being a neurotransmitter and neuromodulator. The ascending serotonergic projections may be likened to a conductor of an orchestra, responsible for producing harmonious music from talented but individualistic soloists who would otherwise collectively produce noise (Pihl & Peterson, 1996). It is theorized that optimal 5-HT functioning leads to neurosynchrony of affect, cognition, and behavior, while 5-HT insufficiency is associated with desynchronization, psychic disharmony, behavioral dysregulation, impulsivity, and triggering of an affective state of anxiety (Hariri & Holmes, 2006). Structural and functional aberrations in this system appear to generate disinhibited behaviors in addition to exaggerated sensitivity to stress as a result of perceived or actual threat, likely via disturbing one's learning of fear associations (Hartley et al., 2012). Indeed, disinhibition is a cardinal risk factor for many SUDs, particularly early-onset alcoholism (Nigg et al., 2006), and hypersensitivity to stress and threat is at the core of vulnerability for affective disorders. Additionally, serotonin functions as a stimulator of the hypothalamic–pituitary–adrenal (HPA) axis. When this is perturbed, cortisol secretion in response to stimuli is disrupted, a feature widely observed among anxiety-disordered individuals as well as those addicted to alcohol and other drugs. For example, a striking (over 90%) decrease in central serotonergic neurotransmission has been found in male alcoholics reporting childhood abuse (Berglund, Balldin, Berggren, Gerdner, & Fahlke, 2013).

A particular polymorphism of the serotonin transporter gene has been linked to perturbed retention of fear extinction memory, anxiety, and symptoms of depression (Hartley et al., 2012). These genotypes were found to act both independently and in interaction with quality of family relations, and depressive symptoms predicted alcohol consumption patterns (Nilsson et al., 2005; Tartter & Ray, 2011) and have been linked to pathological gambling (Wilson, da Silva Lobo, Tavares, Gentil, & Vallada, 2013). Further, in a treatment study of a sample of alcoholics genotyped for a gene encoding the serotonin transporter, before receiving either ondansetron, a 5-HT transporter receptor antagonist, or placebo, it was found that those bearing the risk genotype drank the least and remained abstinent the longest (Johnson et al., 2011).

The serotonergic system also indirectly affects motivation-reward through influencing the DA system and potentiating the glutamatergic system

(Cai et al., 2013). The 5-HT receptors are found on the GABA neurons projecting from the NAc to the VTA. When stimulated, they inhibit the release of GABA, consequently disinhibiting mesolimbic DA, thereby potentiating cocaine-induced DA release. The 5-HT system has also been shown to be involved in altering both the euphorigenic and anxiogenic effects of cocaine (Aronson et al., 1995), and both increased and decreased serotonergic functioning has been related to greater alcohol use (Sari, Johnson, & Weedman, 2011).

Alcohol-induced violence has been attributed to individual variability in frontocortical serotonergic modulation. Mice showing alcohol-induced aggression have decreased availability of serotonin receptors in the prefrontal cortex (PFC). Rhesus monkeys exposed to early stress via social isolation from their mothers exhibit a decrease in the concentration of the serotonin metabolite 5-HIAA relative to mother-raised monkeys (Maestripieri, Lindell, Ayala, Gold, & Higley, 2005). However, they only did so if they bore a certain allelic variation of the gene encoding for the serotonin transporter gene. Acute and lasting reduction in serotonergic receptor availability both centrally and prefrontally hampers the ability to adapt and control one's actions and is thus a basic etiological feature of violence in response to actual or potential threat.

Animal studies have found that acute alcohol intoxication induces transient elevation of serotonergic functioning, while prolonged drinking reduces its responsivity, often resulting in greater aggression and heavier drinking (LeMarquand, Pihl, & Benkelfat, 1994a, 1994b). In and of itself, alcohol can acutely instigate aggression (Bushman & Cooper, 1990) and, in combination with decreased serotonergic functioning, likely affects aggression, be it additively or interactively (Pihl, Peterson, & Lau, 1993).

Drugs of abuse also affect 5-HT systems in various ways. Some hallucinogens, such as lysergic acid dielhylanide (LSD), dimethyltryptamine (DMT), psiolocybin, and the phenethylamines (mescaline, 3,4-methylenedioxy-N-methylamphetamine (MDMA or ecstasy]), have an affinity for 5-HT2 receptors (Titeler, Lyon, & Glennon, 1988), and blocking this abolishes the effects of these drugs. Conversely, acute use of cocaine blocks 5-HT reuptake in the short term, while chronic use likely attenuates serotonergic signaling. In one study, the level of NMDA (ecstasy) consumption

had a positive linear relationship with functional magnetic resonance imaging (fMRI) BOLD signal intensity in the occipital cortex during visual stimulation, which suggests substantial cortical responsivity, perhaps as a result of a decrease in serotonergic signaling (Benningfield & Cowan, 2013).

The GABAergic and Glutamate Systems   GABA is *the* key inhibitory neurotransmitter in the central nervous system, and the GABAergic neurons comprise a part of the mesolimbic DA system. They are, however, distributed throughout the brain (Cui, Xu, Dai, & He, 2012). Because of its high functional relevance, genes that play some role in modulating the GABAergic signaling have became exceedingly popular in the study of addictions, particularly alcoholism and DBDs (Dick et al., 2006). Benzodiazepines, barbiturates, and alcohol are known to directly affect the GABAergic system (Cui et al., 2012; Kelm, Criswell, & Breese, 2011). This effect is produced by opening chloride ion channels on GABA receptors, the major site of action for sedatives and anxiolytic agents. In fact, a drug's affinity for this action is directly linked to the sensitivity of the drug effect. The extrasynaptic $GABA_A$ receptors, which mediate GABAergic effects, in the NAc are key neural substrates for the rewarding effects of alcohol (Cui et al., 2012). Specifically, reduced $GABA_A$ receptor density appears to result from heavy alcohol consumption. This effect has been shown to contribute to tolerance, dependence, and withdrawal symptoms. The latter effect is attenuated by $GABA_A$ receptor agonists or smoking (Cosgrove et al., 2011), providing a possible explanation for the high comorbidity between heavy drinking and heavy smoking. In one fMRI study, among smokers who were more attentionally biased toward salient smoking cues, subjective negative affect during early withdrawal was stronger, and GABA levels in the dorsal anterior cingulate cortex (dACC) were lower, a deficit that has been associated with perturbed cognitive function (Janes et al., 2013). The dACC is part of the default mode network, and its task-related activation and deactivation patterns reportedly predict treatment outcome for some alcoholics (Schacht et al., 2013).

It has been known for some time that both naturally occurring anxiolytics within the brain (Sangameswaran, Fales, Friedrich, & De Blas, 1986) and naturally occurring substances that heighten anxiety (Bodnoff, Suranyi-Cadotte, Quirion, & Meaney, 1989) directly and indirectly affect GABA transmission, through their operation on anxyogenic structures like the amygdala (reviewed in Volkow, Wang, Tomasi, & Baler, 2013). Thus, individuals affected by anxiety for whatever reason should find the use of these drugs particularly reinforcing. This is seemingly the case, as individuals who suffer from phobias, panic disorders, and anxiety sensitivity show high comorbidity rates or risk for specific forms of SUDs. But the GABA system is not the whole story. Perhaps this is why pharmacological treatments for alcoholism that target GABA receptors have not received consistent support for their general effectiveness in treating withdrawal symptoms, which can last for a considerable period of time (Addolorato, Leggio, Hopf, Diana, & Bonci, 2012). An exception to this generalization might be the drug acamprosate (also referred to as Campral), which stimulates and attenuates the transmission of GABA and glutamate, respectively. Experiments with animals (Kiefer & Mann, 2010) and trials with humans (Kiefer & Mann, 2010), including a meta-analysis, support the efficacy of this drug, which proved effective in over 25 placebo-controlled, double-blind designs (Maisel, Blodgett, Wilbourne, Humphreys, & Finney, 2013). Overall, it is more effective than placebo in significantly attenuating risk relapse and increasing abstinence duration, although it does not seem to decrease the number of heavy-drinking days (Witkiewitz, Saville, & Hamreus, 2012).

To explain withdrawal symptoms and drug-induced changes in brain functioning, researchers have begun to focus on glutamate, a membrane protein that is an excitatory amino acid and a primary neurotransmitter that deals with excitatory neurotransmission. There are a number of glutamate receptors, and they are widespread throughout the central nervous system; one that may have specific relevance to the effects of alcohol and other drugs is N-methyl-D-aspartate (NMDA). The hallucinogen phencycladine, for example, binds to the recognition site normally utilized by glutamate. Glutamate receptors facilitate fast neurotransmission but can also have a negative effect, as excessive activation can produce neural degeneration. This system is implicated as the source of damage in a number of neurological disorders, including stroke, Huntington's disease, and Alzheimer's. It appears that alcohol has three effects on glutamatergic transmission: interfering with excitatory neurotransmission, promoting excitotoxicity, and impairing neurodevelopment (as in FAS). These three major effects occur through the NMDA receptor, to which alcohol seems to be an antagonist. Chronic ingestion of alcohol by experimental animals results in an increase in NMDA receptors in both limbic and cortical brain areas. This effect is transient; perhaps it is an overcompensation of the system being blocked by alcohol, as during withdrawal these receptors actually increase, and glutamate functioning in general is accelerated (Chandler et al., 2006). To a certain degree, this specific action of alcohol on the NMDA receptor explains both the symptoms of drug withdrawal and the development of brain damage, which is a common concomitant of heavy alcohol consumption. Specifically, the supersensitivity that results from alcohol blocking the receptor is displayed when alcohol is not present, and in its extreme this can result in glutamate-induced excitotoxicity (Charlet, Beck, & Heinz, 2013).

Endogenous Opioid System   The opioid system regulates the extracellular drug-induced DA release. For example, cocaine addicts show remarkable elevations in mu-opioid receptor availability, likely mirroring attenuated secretion of endogenous opioids (Goodman, 2008). The ingestion of opiate drugs results in direct stimulation of opioid receptors in the brain. The consumption of any other substance of abuse or palatable, particularly sweet food, and engaging in gambling or sexual behavior are all correlated with the secretion of endogenous opioids (Trigo, Martin-Garcia, Berrendero, Robledo, & Maldonado, 2010). This system is widespread throughout the body, with at least three types of receptors and three groups of known transmitters. Opioid receptors in the NAc appear to affect this system through the neurotransmitter DA. Stimulation appears to be reinforcing, as animals will self-administer opioids. Opiates also act both directly and indirectly on DA in the VTA.

That the endogenous opioid system is involved in the rewarding properties of heroin is exhibited by the fact that treatments aimed specifically at replacing the drug or blocking the receptors are effective. Introduced in the 1960s, methadone is a long-acting synthetic opioid that, taken orally once daily, serves as a substitute for heroin. Methadone is cross-tolerant to heroin, and the treatment is effective in attenuating some aspects of craving. However, its use is controversial, and patients receiving methadone remain at risk for relapse upon exposure to heroin-related cues (Fareed, Vayalapalli, Casarella, Amar, & Drexler, 2010). Another substitution drug, buprenorphine, was approved in 2002. It is a partial agonist that occupies all of mu-opioid receptors (Veilleux, Colvin, Anderson, York, & Heinz, 2010), thereby precluding the ability of the illicit drug's ingestion to induce an increased effect. Unfortunately, with heavy users the reduced effect can initiate withdrawal symptoms. More evidence that opiate receptors are involved in heroin addiction comes from work with drugs that block these receptors, such as naltrexone, naloxone, and nalmefene. In detoxified addicts, these drugs diminish heroin-induced positive psychoactive effects, yet regrettably, their use is generally avoided by addicts (Johansson, Berglund, & Lindgren, 2006).

Naltrexone is a nonselective opiate antagonist that at least partially acts on the midbrain by inhibiting the mu-opioid receptors, thereby decreasing alcohol-induced DA secretion in the NAc (Goodman, 2008). Approved to treat alcoholism in 1995, the use and effectiveness of this drug has been at best variable with a small effect size (Trigo, Orejarena, Maldonado, & Robledo, 2009). Clinical studies have shown that naltrexone diminishes the high from alcohol and reduces craving (Boutrel, 2008), though again, compliance is a problem.

Naltrexone also appears to be more effective in carriers of a specific allele for the opioid receptor and in women more than in men (Valenta et al., 2013). Furthermore, studies have demonstrated that individuals who displayed an excitatory response to alcohol, compared to those who did not, showed a significantly increased plasma beta-endorphin level (the most potent endogenous opioid peptide (Boileau et al., 2003). This response likely indicates positive reinforcement, successfully abolished by naltrexone (Morris, Hopwood, Whelan, Gardiner, & Drummond, 2001). To the extent that this notion is correct—that naltrexone should be selectively therapeutic, assuming compliance, with this particular at-risk population—would be a reasonable conclusion to make.

These findings and the overall state of treatment suggest that differential etiologies are involved in alcohol abuse. Thus treatments must become more directed toward individual factors, rather than homogenous approaches.

Cannaboid and Nicotine Systems

Specific marijuana receptors exist. They are distributed throughout the brain but are particularly prominent in the cerebellum, prefrontal cortex, hippocampus, and basal ganglia (Glass, Faull, & Dragunow, 1997). Endocannabinoid signaling is key in modulating affective and motivational states, which are gated by the NAc, through the excitation of cannabinoid receptors in the brain. Manipulating these receptors within the NAc, alters one's affective and motivational states, a response highly pertinent to the development of SUDs among other psychopathologies (Setiawan, Pihl, Benkelfat, & Leyton, 2012). One fMRI study has shown that chronic marijuana users and tobacco smokers both showed similar patterns of NAc activation during reward anticipation but this response, when contrasted against that seen in nonsmokers, stood out as significantly blunted. Compared to both groups, marijuana users exhibited attenuated reward anticipation signal in the caudate nucleus (Peterson et al., 1996; Pihl & Peterson, 1996). Yet, marijuana is quite low on the addiction scale; rats rarely self-administer it or place-condition to it, and it sometimes provokes a stress response. An analogy to certain food effects is also possible. For example, certain brain lipids bind to the canniboid receptors and can mimic the effects of marijuana on the brain (Peterson, Conrod, Vassileva, Gianoulakis, & Pihl, 2006). Interestingly, chocolate and cocoa powder elevate the levels of these lipids that have affinity for canniboid receptors, obscuring the distinction between drugs and foods (Pettinati et al., 2011).

Nicotine has been and still is commonly thought to be the psychoactive substance that renders cigarettes addictive (e.g., see (Changeux, 2010). However, traditional animal studies making this claim have been criticized for failing to mimic the smoking phenomena among humans: animal studies use (1) large nicotine doses and (2) ultra-high-speed infusion. Sorge and Clarke (2011) as well as others have shown that rats will self-administer much lower doses of nicotine and at a much slower rate as well. What these studies suggest, and what seems to be the case, is that nicotine in aggregation with, rather than in isolation from, other addictive ingredients found in cigarettes can and does instigate smoking addiction.

While the people who manufacture cigarettes have claimed not to know that cigarettes

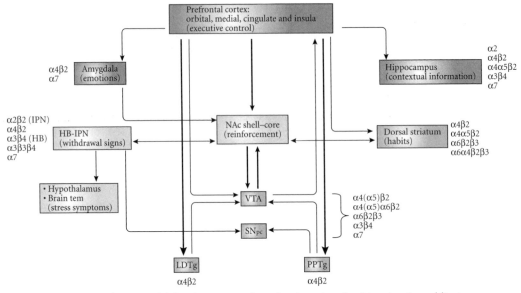

Figure 10.3 Depicted is a model for the neuronal mechanisms involved in nicotine addiction. Adapted with permission from Macmillan Publishers Ltd: *Nature Reviews Neuroscience*, Vol. 11, 6, Changeux, Nicotine addiction and nicotinic receptors: Lessons from genetically modified mice. Copyright (2010).

contain addictive substances, central nervous system effects occur within 10 seconds of inhalation. The mesolimbic reward system is activated and the DA, endogenous opioid, and glucocorticoid systems are affected, among others. Euphoric effects like those resulting from cocaine and morphine are produced. These effects are strong enough to support reward-based conditioning (Winters et al., 2012), and tolerance and withdrawal develop. It is known that the DA D2 receptors are affected, and when PET is used to measure the DA response to smoking, a strong positive correlation with a hedonic response occurs and is associated with increased DA transmission in the dorsal striatum (van Hell et al., 2010). This increase is particularly strong in those bearing a specific allele with a mu-opioid receptor A118G polymorphism (Devane et al., 1992). Figure. 10.3 depicts a model for the neuronal mechanisms involved in addiction to cigarettes.

In general, cigarette smoking activates brain areas much as cocaine does (Stein et al., 1998; Breiter et al., 1997). Further, smokers with gene variants related to low resting DA release more DA when smoking than do individuals without these variants, which suggests a genetic predisposition (di Tomaso, Beltramo, & Piomelli, 1996). The strength of cigarette smoking effects is significant;

of all forms of addictions, it is the most resistant to treatment. This observation should not be construed, however, as suggesting that cigarettes promote greater levels of physiological dependence than do other substances of abuse. A notable study by Naqvi, Rudrauf, Damasio, & Bechara (2007) found that patients who were addicted to smoking reported no interest whatsoever in smoking cigarettes after undergoing damage to the insula, which is largely involved in conscious urges (Naqvi, Rudrauf, Damasio, & Bechara, 2007).

Cognitive Aspects

Individual variation in sensitivity to drug effects can also be expressed in terms of structural and functional differences in important brain areas. Human beliefs and experiences are part of the cognitive context, and expectations of drug effect predict drug use. Luria (1980) argued that the brain reacts to stimuli in terms of context—past, current, and future. Responses are anchored in experience and learning, which in humans includes culture incorporated through language.

In drug use, cultural and social factors as well as individual experience come together to form such a context. We have referred to this elsewhere as the general expectancy set. Generally, an individual frequently using a drug is more likely to perceive less risk and to approve more of the use of that drug. Among "illicit" substances, for example, marijuana is most used and approved and is perceived as least harmful. Of course, one's attitudes toward a drug and beliefs about its use are robustly associated with changing trends of drug use behaviors. The 1980s witnessed a decline in marijuana and cocaine use in the United States that was accompanied by greater perceived risk of use. Conversely, a drastic shift of these attitudes in the other direction during much of the 1990s may have accounted for the elevated use of many illicit substances, specifically marijuana. Similarly, ecstasy use in the early 2000s dramatically decreased as a result of greater perceived danger of its use (Droungas, Ehrman, Childress, & O'Brien, 1995). Drug use is also affected by what one expects a drug to do to and for oneself, both objectively and subjectively. A large 9-year follow-up study found that among males and females, consumption of alcohol and marijuana could be predicted in adolescence and adulthood, based on early expectations of the response of positive feelings to the drugs and the alleviation of negative feelings (Stacey, Newcomb, & Bentler, 1991).

Neural reflections that correspond to differential types of expectancies are now beginning to be discovered. In one fMRI study, three groups of healthy individuals in a within-subject design were exposed to a noxious thermal stimulus, after which they ingested a potent opioid receptor agonist. Those who had positive analgesia expectations showed double the benefit from the drug, which was associated with activation of the endogenous pain regulatory system. This benefit was completely blunted among those with negative expectations, which correlated with decreased activation in brain regions involved in exacerbating pain via anxiety (Barrett, Boileau, Okker, Pihl, & Dagher, 2004). Typically, psychological factors are extremely powerful in determining what the drug does and to whom. This has been found to be the case for the anxiolytic effects of benzodiazepines, the motoric effect of deep brain stimulation on patients with Parkinson's disease, and the subjective effects of psychotrophics such as marihuana (Domino et al., 2012). In one PET study (Brody et al., 2006; Droungas et al., 1995), cocaine addicts ingested either methylphenidate (a stimulant drug) or placebo. When methylphenidate was expected, it was found to promote a significantly greater neural and subjective response than when it was not expected.

One very powerful modulator of drug expectancy is the media, which can provide young individuals with "super peers." The use of alcohol, for example, is depicted in as many as 80%–95% of Hollywood movies; in most of these movies, individuals "doing" alcohol are appealing and are attractive characters portrayed in a positive light, with their drinking typically reinforced and rarely leading to negative outcomes. One study found that watching movies in which alcohol was being used significantly and uniquely affected one's expectancies of drinking; these expectations were correlated with drinking levels and a temporal change in drinking patterns (Dal Cin et al., 2009).

Expectations regarding drug effects are far more complex than is implied by describing them as positive or negative. Some expectancies regarding a drug's effect seem completely contradictory—for example, simultaneous social facilitation and social aggression with alcohol use. Expectancies vary with the type of beverage or drug and are likely dependent on associative memory networks learned experimentally or vicariously. They play both a mediating and moderating role in the initiation or avoidance of drug use, as well as in the determination of the effect. For example, differential expectancies are a likely explanation for the greater increase in intoxication-induced aggression among drinkers of distilled beverages than among beer drinkers, with the dose controlled in both laboratory and bar (Pihl et al., 1993) studies.

Electrophysiology In alcoholics and their at-risk first-degree relatives, anomalies have been determined in electrical activity (electroencephalogram [EEG]) and wave-form responses to particular stimuli (event-related evoked potentials [ERP]), both of which are sensitive to many drugs and are often used to assess subtle cognitive risk factors. Resting EEG studies have relatively consistently pointed to the beta-band frequency in differentiating individuals at risk for disinhibitory disorders and particularly alcoholism and alcohol-related phenotypes (Dick et al., 2006; Gilmore, Malone, & Iacono, 2010). This rhythm is substantially heritable ($h = .86$), has been linked to the GABA$_A$ receptor gene, and is thought to reflect the balance between inhibitory and excitatory cell functions (Johnston, O'Malley, Bachman, & Schulenberg, 2010). Alcohol challenge studies, where repeated-measures, counterbalanced, double-blind, placebo-controlled designs are typically used, have generally found subjects who are at risk for alcoholism to have a diminished alpha response, which represents oscillation between 8 and 12 HZ and is typically associated with eyes-closed relaxation. In a 10-year follow-up study, men at high risk for alcoholism who displayed this response were more vulnerable to becoming alcoholic (Volavka et al., 1996).

The P300 wave of the visual ERP exemplifies what is arguably the best currently known endophenotypic marker for drug addiction (Bingel, Colloca, & Vase, 2011). The P300 wave is evoked when a subject responds to a distinct stimulus presented among many similar ones. In broader terms it is reflective of interindividual variability in neural inhibition or attentional regulation through the noradrenergic system (Metrik et al., 2009). The P300 amplitude has been shown to get attenuated in drug-naïve 11-year-old sons of alcoholic fathers, pointing to its heritability. This trait is also manifested in the full range of eternalizing psychopathology, which suggests that the attenuated P300 amplitude is an endophenotypic marker for low-order disinhibitory externalizing disorders (Volkow et al., 2003).

Neuropsychological Studies A wide variety of behavioral and psychological tests are thought to capture specific facets of cognitive functions, some implicating specific brain localization and systems. Both addicted and some at-risk individuals (sons of alcoholics) perform abnormally on these tests. Thus, it appears that a preexisting vulnerability can trigger drug use, which in turn is further exacerbated by drug use. At-risk individuals with insignificant or no exposure to substances of abuse also show mild to moderate neuropsychological deficits. These impairments have been found in five broad categories of cognitive performance: executive functions, which encompass abstracting, planning, and problem-solving abilities; language-based skills; attentional and memory processing; psychomotor integration; and visuoperceptual analysis and learning (Pihl, Smith, & Farrell, 1984).

These deficits have also been found in individuals with CD or ADHD. In one study of aggressive boys (Murdoch, Pihl, & Ross, 1988), particular deficits were shown on neuropsychological tests that had been previously demonstrated via

imaging studies to involve dorsolateral aspects of the frontal cortex. Similar performances in children with ADHD have led to a flurry of interest in the role of the frontal lobes in impulse-control problems. Further, certain drugs (particularly alcohol) acutely impair these cognitive functions (Porjesz et al., 2005). This may be a central factor in explaining the high correlation between intoxicated behavior and violence. A recent study found that stimulant-addicted individuals exhibited marked cognitive deficits across all domains of cognitive functioning (attention, visual memory, response control, emotional functioning, psychosocial functioning, etc.) compared to their unaffected siblings and unrelated healthy controls. Anomalies in executive functioning and inhibitory control, in addition to augmented levels of anxious-disinhibited traits, have been detected in individuals addicted to psychostimulants and their unaffected siblings, but to a significantly greater extent in the addicted individuals. This finding may point to neurotoxic or other ancillary effects of persistent drug misuse that may underlie this scale of dysfunction (Miller & Rockstroh, 2013). These commonalities have been proposed by the authors as endophentoypic markers for addiction to psychostimulants, reflected as a neurodevelopmental perturbation of prefrontal functioning (Iacono & Malone, 2011).

In another study, boys with and without an alcoholic parent demonstrated a disinhibitory response on laboratory tests assessing impulsivity, which predicted the onset of SUDs most robustly when a family history of alcohol use disorders (AUDs) was present (Gao & Raine, 2009). Consistently, nonaddicted adults with a family history of alcoholism showed greater impulsivity levels and worse executive functioning than that of individuals without this family history. The same study also showed that the more alcoholic family members one had, the worse one's executive functioning (Pihl, Peterson, & Finn, 1990; Tarter, Jacob, & Bremer, 1989).

However, whether these neuropsychological disturbances are a triggering mechanism for or a consequence of drug use and misuse remains unclear. Clearly, the heavy consumption of most drugs is neurotoxic; this is the case even for marijuana (Seguin, Pihl, Harden, Tremblay, & Boulerice, 1995). A recent longitudinal prospective study assessed a birth cohort at age 13 (prior to initiating marijuana use) and again every 3 years thereafter until subjects were in their late 30s. Persistent marijuana consumption was associated with deterioration of global facets of neuropsychological functioning. Dysfunction was particularly pronounced among those with adolescent-onset cannabis use, with longer use having a dose-dependent relationship with neurocognitive deterioration that is partially irreversible by abstinence (Pihl et al., 1990). Thus, always a concern in these observed associations is the direction they take and the degree to which they are causally mediated, and by which environmental and genetic mechanisms.

Neuroimagery   Over the past two decades, the fantastic growth of neuroimaging studies investigating addictive phenomena has been in and of itself addictive. The field's love affair with these exponentially advancing technologies is strikingly similar to that of children with candy. Unfortunately, the rapid pace at which findings have been produced far exceeds their usefulness for practice; gaining information is one thing, gaining insight another, and one would err in assuming otherwise (Braff & Braff, 2013). In spite of massive amounts of information, we remain far from delineating the causal neural mechanisms underlying SUDs. Patently, neuroimaging technologies are not beyond methodological reproach and are factually fraught with complications. This chapter does not elaborate on this issue, and interested readers are referred to other studies on tis topic (e.g., Abbott, 2009; Vul, Harris, Winkielman, & Pashler, 2009; Vul & Pashler, 2012).

What follows is a discussion of conceptual issues regarding why it is that we know so much about the brain of addicted individuals but very little about what this information really means. First, as discussed earlier, most neuroimaging studies have ascertained samples of abstinent or current addicts. This is problematic for drawing etiological conclusions given the indisputable fact that drugs of abuse are neurotoxic; they hijack the central nervous system and remodel it, both functionally and structurally (Benningfield & Cowan, 2013), and only some of the effects are reversible (Meier et al., 2012). Absent knowledge of how the brain looked like before one started to use and abuse the drug, determining via a snapshot of the addicted brain which neural fingerprints are of the triggering mechanisms and which are of the drug becomes exceedingly difficult, if not logically implausible. As such, information produced by these studies will at best teach us something about the explosion of addiction but nothing about its causality, the latter being a fundamental question that the neuroimaging field must systematically address. For example, according to a recent meta-analysis, MRI studies generally converge in showing that individuals addicted to stimulants exhibit marked gray matter (GM) shrinkage in prefrontal cortical areas that play a role in inhibitory control and consciousness (Ersche, Jones, et al., 2012). This GM reduction has also been consistently shown to bear a dose-dependent relationship with the duration of exposure to stimulants. These are certainly intriguing findings, but their explanatory power is absent. It is additionally clear that replication of findings is often an issue. The same meta-analysis (Ersche, Jones, et al., 2012) found that while some studies report volumetric increase of the basal ganglia (a key modulator of behavioral regulation) in individuals addicted to psychostimulants compared to healthy ones, others have found a decrease, and still others, no change at all.

Another main barrier to greater understanding of substance addiction has been the widely accepted notion that most drugs of abuse converge on the same reward pathway, namely the ascending mesolimbic pathway. What different drugs do to and for the same individual, and what the same drug does to different individuals are strikingly heterogeneous and depend on the class of drug ingested and the person who ingests them. Neurobiologically, two specific brain systems, among possibly others, have been proposed to mediate intra- and interindividual responses to drugs: the fear-processing system and the cue-for-reward system, which respectively reflect negative reinforcement such as self-medication, and positive reinforcement, through which the user is energized (Gierski et al., 2013). Some drugs, like psychostimulants, appear to switch the cue for the reward system "on." Others like opiates, switch the fear system "off." Yet others, like alcohol, can be positively reinforcing for some individuals—energizing and stimulating—and negatively reinforcing for others, through dampening their negative emotional state (Battista, Stewart, & Ham, 2010; Pihl, 2010; Pihl & Peterson, 1995). The extent to which individuals experience these effects in response to drugs is interindividually varied and puts individuals at different forms of risk for SUDs. A recent illustrative example is a prospective study in which, compared to light drinkers, heavy drinkers were found to display more of a stimulant effect, which predicted binge drinking and a higher likelihood, after 2 years, of being diagnosed with an AUD (King, de Wit, McNamara, & Cao, 2011).

A highly germane observation relates to the fact that SUDs rarely appear in isolation. They almost always co-occur with either externalizing (i.e., disruptive-disinhibitory) or internalizing (i.e., anxious-depressive) symptoms or disorders and occasionally they occur with both types. To a considerable extent, the externalizing and internalizing factors are behaviorally and likely neurobiologically distinct, with the former corresponding to the reward cue system and the latter to the fear system. The amygdala is central to negative reinforcement, which, among other regions (e.g., the hippocampus/parahippocampus; Servaas et al., 2013), involves the fear-processing system (Li et al., 2013). This brain structure develops much earlier and faster than those underlying higher cognitive functions, and it governs primitive fight-or-flight responses to actual or perceived threat. Inefficient functioning at any point in the fear circuit can result in over-responsivity to events and an exaggerated secretion of stress hormones, which further deteriorates the functioning of this network. Importantly, many individuals reporting coping motives for drug abuse are anxiety-sensitive, a cardinal feature of and a causal risk factor for both anxiety disorders and the abuse of alcohol and whatever other drugs that may dampen one's stress. These disorders have been repeatedly correlated by a large bulk of evidence with exaggerated amygdalae activation in response to stimuli signaling threat. In a large study of adult female twins, personality traits were related to drinking motives and symptoms of an AUD (Littlefield et al., 2011). A genetic relationship was found with coping (i.e., stress dampening) motives and AUD symptoms (Littlefield et al., 2011). Conversely, in at-risk individuals whose response to drugs is mediated by the cue-for-reward system, at the core of their liability there seems to reside a fundamental problem of impulse control. This is analogous to having a stuck gas pedal and broken brakes, the latter being the prefrontal cortex and the former, the limbic system. With the limbic system hyperactivated and the prefrontal cortex hypoactivated, the scale is tipped against a calculated rational response and in favor of a risky one (Zucker, Heitzeg, & Nigg, 2011).

Generally, most brain-imaging studies have found marked neural functional and anatomical aberration within the frontostriatal circuits in addicted individuals. This makes sense, given that these circuits subserve the core clinical feature of many cases of SUDs, that is, the impulsive and compulsive seeking of the drug. These individuals tend to use and abuse psychostimulant drugs, including alcohol. Thus, understanding what leads an individual to express these different traits and how they determine different risk profiles associated with SUDs should have great explanatory power. In general, unfortunately, the field has been somewhat myopic concerning this issue, as evidenced by the fact that the ascertaining of study samples has often been based on whether symptoms of or risk for SUDs are present, rarely on the questions of why and how.

To overcome these hurdles and address the fundamental question regarding the cause of addiction risk, some studies have resorted to parsing at-risk individuals, an approach which can and does provide substantial explanatory power of causal mechanisms that may substantiate or obviate risk. Following this logic, perhaps the most elegant studies conducted thus far have been those in which individuals with a specific form of SUD are contrasted against their full biological nonaddicted siblings and the sibling pair is then contrasted against healthy, unrelated controls. Combined with brain-imaging techniques, this approach is now aiding in the delineation of neural endophenotypic familial markers for SUDs (Ersche, Williams, Robbins, & Bullmore, 2013). One study detected dysconnectivity between the "go" and "stop" neural circuitries governing inhibitory control in both stimulant-addicted probands and their unaffected biological siblings compared to healthy controls (Ersche, Jones, et al., 2012). Using fractional anisotropy (a method by which one examines the density of axonal fibers conveying signals between neural structures), the same study also identified anomalies in the integrity of axonal fibers neighboring a brain structure associated with behavioral regulation (the inferior frontal cortex), a deficit that was much more pronounced in the affected probands and significantly associated with impulsivity scores (Ersche, Jones, et al., 2012). The authors suggested that this shared aberrance between affected probands and their nonaddicted siblings represents a familial endophenotypic marker for risk of addiction to psychostimulants. It is possible that once the at-risk individual transitions from initial drug use into established patterns of heavy use, the already fatigued "stop" networks become more and more fatigued; consequently, the "go" networks are hyperactivated and unrestrained, leading to escalation into addiction. But this risk marker does not necessarily suggest that one is doomed. The same study showed that the neurostructural integrity of multiple regions was disrupted in the addicted probands but not in their nonaddicted siblings. For example, the addicted probands showed a volumetric reduction in the orbitofrontal cortex, which is associated with behavioral compulsivity and rigidity. As such, it is not the mere presence of a risk factor that seems to pull the trigger but rather the disrupted balance between risk and protective factors, the latter being the intact structural integrity of certain regions that was seen in the nonaddicted probands but not their addicted siblings (for a review see Volkow & Baler, 2012).

In another study, three groups of cocaine abusers, recreational users, and healthy nonusers underwent fMRI scanning while performing a task assessing cognitive control (Smith, Simon Jones, Bullmore, Robbins, & Ersche, 2014). Disrupted performance, as indexed by marked selective bias to cocaine cues, was seen only in the addicted group; the other two groups performed normally and similarly to one another. Further, the cocaine abusers showed prefrontal and orbitofrontal hyperactivation, while the recreational users showed hypoactivation, which is indicative of an intact ability to control one's responses (Smith et al., 2014). These findings suggest that the potential abusers among recreational users might be distinguishable on the basis of inherited neural perturbations.

Finally, recent findings highlight the paramount importance of appreciating the complexity of addictive phenomena by showing that even the basic construct of impulsivity, which accounts for many cases of SUDs and the substantially co-occurring DBDs (e.g., CD, ODD, and ADHD), is also strikingly complex and multifaceted. In one fMRI study a motor inhibition task was administered and the performance of 14-year-olds contrasted. Results showed that the performances of those who had ADHD symptoms, compared with those who abused tobacco, alcohol, or illicit substances, were behaviorally indistinguishable but were neurally distinct. Neurofunctional

aberrations in multiple minimally overlapping cortical and subcortical networks were identified, and distinct subtypes of the impulsive phenotype were demonstrated (Whelan et al., 2012).

To summarize, despite some recent encouraging findings, the neuroimaging literature on SUDs is fragmented, laden with inconsistent and contradictory information, and replete with findings that raise more questions than answers. The causal bases of the association between SUDs and neural phenomena, assuming that such bases exist to begin with, which we do not know for a fact (Miller, 1996, 2010), remain to be elucidated and compellingly articulated. This might be attributed in part to technical issues, which technological advancement may obviate. Mostly, though, the conundrum that the neuroimaging field directly confronts today is conceptual. Careful parsing of subjects and longitudinal designs in which multiple snapshots of the brain are captured across different developmental stages are required if the great potential of brain imaging techniques to inform the etiology of SUDs is to be fully realized.

Summary

Diagnoses, when based on purely behavioral definitions, do not explain a phenomenon. But they can and will, if and when based on etiology. The latter is not captured by a system like the *DSM*'s, which was designed to produce agreement among observers and to ensure that everybody seeing a psychiatrist has a diagnostic pigeonhole. This chapter has addressed multiple levels of analysis— from the cultural to the psychological, and from the genetic to the neurobiological. What can generally be concluded with clarity and certainty is that we remain neither clear nor certain about what causes SUDs, in whom and how. The poet and writer Khalil Gibran wrote that "a little knowledge that acts is worth infinitely more than much knowledge that is idle." Gibran's words echo when the exponentially thickening volumes of available information are contrasted against the efficacy of available treatments for drug addiction. SUDs are heterogeneous, multiphasic, and multifactorial disorders, with perturbations in various multilevel mechanisms comprising whatever the final etiological equation is. Marrying the multiple levels of analysis to produce a cohesive and coherent conceptual framework, both methodologically and logically, has proven to be a very difficult nut to crack. One barrier has been the strikingly complex nature of SUDs, and another, the huge conceptual conundrum. Heavily reductionist theories and tactics should be, at least partially, held accountable. Evidence showing that genes are not destiny suggests that to hunt for "*the* genes for SUDs" would be fishing in turbulent waters. The collective fascination with advanced technologies does not justify the state of myopia, if not virtual blindness, concerning these observations. Furthermore, evidence illustrating that cultural and individual variables modulate and are modulated by neural factors demonstrates that psychological phenomena, like SUDs, do have neural foundations. However, correlation does not mean causation. Needed are longitudinal studies that span the developmental stages preceding the disorder's full-fledged manifestation. Such studies, however, are too few, and studies making causal claims, too many. As someone once said, more dangerous than ignorance is false knowledge. The history of psychiatry is replete with examples of disastrous treatments that in the longer term damaged both the patient and the field.

It should be clear that to unequivocally define and explain a psychological phenomenon such as drug addiction, one must understand the what and how of causation, the latter being a most fundamental question that the field can no longer afford to ignore. Current relabeling of the phenomenon does not and cannot obviate understanding etiology. The motivational-systems story of SUDs is illustrative and instructive. In a study of ~300 substance-abusing women who completed an extensive battery of personality and symptom inventories, four interrelated factors stood out: anxiety sensitivity, sensation seeking, impulsivity, and hopelessness (Conrod et al., 2013). These factors were shown by cluster analysis to be unique and associated with distinct psychopathological profile, comorbidity patterns, and distinctive SUDs. From the standpoint of pathology, these findings suggest that the form of drug abuse and co-occurring disorders may have the same underlying etiology. It is what the drug does for the individual that produces differential effects that explains the commonality. A randomized prevention trial based on these four motivational systems was administered by trained staff, and demonstrated enduring positive outcomes in preventing the onset of SUDs and comorbid psychopathologies in at-risk adolescents (Conrod et al., 2013).

We will be doomed to repeat history unless we recognize that SUDs, like other forms of psychopathology, are fuzzy and messy natural phenomena with no neatly delineated boundaries and no single explanation accounting for them. SUDs are neurodevelopmental disorders caused by temporally dynamic and strikingly complex macro- and micro-level modes of action and interaction of biological and environmental factors across different stages of the developmental trajectory. For the sake of affected individuals, their families, and the field, it is our hope that we come to appreciate these issues more than we do now.

References

Abbott, A. (2009). Brain imaging studies under fire. *Nature*, *457*(7227), 245.

Abrams, K., Kushner, M., Medina, K. L., & Voight, A. (2001). The pharmacologic and expectancy effects of alcohol on social anxiety in individuals with social phobia. *Drug and Alcohol Dependence*, *64*(2), 219–231.

Addolorato, G., Leggio, L., Hopf, F. W., Diana, M., & Bonci, A. (2012). Novel therapeutic strategies for alcohol and drug addiction: focus on GABA, ion channels and transcranial magnetic stimulation. *Neuropsychopharmacology*, *37*(1), 163–177.

Agrawal, A., Edenberg, H. J., Foroud, T., Bierut, L. J., Dunne, G., Hinrichs, A. L.,...Dick, D. M. (2006). Association of GABRA2 with drug dependence in the collaborative study of the genetics of alcoholism sample. *Behavior Genetics*, *36*(5), 640–650.

Alati, R., Al Mamun, A., Williams, G. M., O'Callaghan, M., Najman, J. M., & Bor, W. (2006). In utero alcohol exposure and prediction of alcohol disorders in early adulthood: A birth cohort study. *Archives of Geneeral Psychiatry*, *63*(9), 1009–1016.

Albers, A. B., DeJong, W., Naimi, T. S., Siegel, M., Shoaff, J. R., & Jernigan, D. H. (2013). Minimum financial outlays for purchasing alcohol brands in the U.S. *American Journal of Preventive Medicine*, *44*(1), 67–70.

Aronson, S. C., Black, J. E., McDougle, C. J., Scanley, B. E., Jatlow, P., Kosten, T. R.,...Price, L. H. (1995). Serotonergic mechanisms of cocaine effects in humans. *Psychopharmacology (Berlin)*, *119*(2), 179–185.

Badiani, A., Belin, D., Epstein, D., Calu, D., & Shaham, Y. (2011). Opiate versus psychostimulant addiction: the differences do matter. *Nature Reviews Neuroscience, 12*(11), 685–700.

Baker, J. H., Maes, H. H., Larsson, H., Lichtenstein, P., & Kendler, K. S. (2011). Sex differences and developmental stability in genetic and environmental influences on psychoactive substance consumption from early adolescence to young adulthood. *Psychological Medicine, 41*(9), 1907–1916.

Ballard, M. S., Sun, M., & Ko, J. (2012). Vitamin A, folate, and choline as a possible preventive intervention to fetal alcohol syndrome. *Medical Hypotheses, 78*(4), 489–493.

Barrett, S. P., Boileau, I., Okker, J., Pihl, R. O., & Dagher, A. (2004). The hedonic response to cigarette smoking is proportional to dopamine release in the human striatum as measured by positron emission tomography and [11C]raclopride. *Synapse, 54*(2), 65–71.

Battista, S. R., Stewart, S. H., & Ham, L. S. (2010). A critical review of laboratory-based studies examining the relationships of social anxiety and alcohol intake. *Current Drug Abuse Review, 3*(1), 3–22.

Bean, W. B. (1951). *Osler Aphorisms*. Springfield, IL: Thomas.

Behnke, M., Smith, V. C., Levy, S., Ammerman, S. D., Gonzalez, P. K., Ryan, S. A.,…Carlo, W. A. (2013). Prenatal substance abuse: Short- and long-term effects on the exposed fetus. *Pediatrics, 131*(3), e1009–e1024.

Belin, D., Mar, A. C., Dalley, J. W., Robbins, T. W., & Everitt, B. J. (2008). High impulsivity predicts the switch to compulsive cocaine-taking. *Science, 320*(5881), 1352–1355.

Bell, R. L., Rodd-Henricks, Z. A., Webster, A. A., Lumeng, L., Li, T. K., McBride, W. J., & Murphy, J. M. (2002). Heart rate and motor-activating effects of orally self-administered ethanol in alcohol-preferring (P) rats. *Alcoholism: Clinical and Experimental Research, 26*(8), 1162–1170.

Bello, E. P., Mateo, Y., Gelman, D. M., Noain, D., Shin, J. H., Low, M. J.,…Rubinstein, M. (2011). Cocaine supersensitivity and enhanced motivation for reward in mice lacking dopamine D2 autoreceptors. *Nature Neuroscience, 14*(8), 1033–1038.

Belsky, D. W., Moffitt, T. E., Baker, T. B., Biddle, A. K., Evans, J. P., Harrington, H.,…Williams, B. (2013). Polygenic risk and the developmental progression to heavy, persistent smoking and nicotine dependence: Evidence from a 4-decade longitudinal study—Developmental progression of smoking behavior. *Journal of the American Medical Association Psychiatry, 70*(5), 534–542.

Benningfield, M. M., & Cowan, R. L. (2013). Brain serotonin function in MDMA (ecstasy) users: Evidence for persisting neurotoxicity. *Neuropsychopharmacology, 38*(1), 253–255.

Berglund, K. J., Balldin, J., Berggren, U., Gerdner, A., & Fahlke, C. (2013). Childhood maltreatment affects the serotonergic system in male alcohol-dependent individuals. *Alcoholism, Clinical and Experimental Research, 37*(5), 757–762.

Bienvenu, O. J., Davydow, D. S., & Kendler, K. S. (2011). Psychiatric "diseases" versus behavioral disorders and degree of genetic influence. *Psychological Medicine, 41*(1), 33–40.

Bingel, U., Colloca, L., & Vase, L. (2011). Mechanisms and clinical implications of the placebo effect: Is there a potential for the elderly? A mini-review. *Gerontology, 57*(4), 354–363.

Blanco, C., Okuda, M., Wright, C., Hasin, D. S., Grant, B. F., Liu, S. M., & Olfson, M. (2008). Mental health of college students and their non-college-attending peers: Results from the National Epidemiologic Study on Alcohol and Related Conditions. *Archives of General Psychiatry, 65*(12), 1429–1437.

Bodnoff, S. R., Suranyi-Cadotte, B. E., Quirion, R., & Meaney, M. J. (1989). Role of the central benzodiazepine receptor system in behavioral habituation to novelty. *Behavioral Neuroscience, 103*(1), 209–212.

Boileau, I., Assaad, J. M., Pihl, R. O., Benkelfat, C., Leyton, M., Diksic, M.,…Dagher, A. (2003). Alcohol promotes dopamine release in the human nucleus accumbens. *Synapse, 49*(4), 226–231.

Boutrel, B. (2008). A neuropeptide-centric view of psychostimulant addiction. *British Journal of Pharmacology, 154*(2), 343–357.

Bowman, M., & Pihl, R. O. (1973). Cannabis: Psychological effects of chronic heavy use. A controlled study of intellectual functioning in chronic users of high potency cannabis. *Psychopharmacologia, 29*(2), 159–170.

Braff, L., & Braff, D. L. (2013). The neuropsychiatric translational revolution: Still very early and still very challenging. *Journal of the American Medical Association Psychiatry, 70*(8), 777–779.

Breiter, H. C., Gollub, R. L., Weisskoff, R. M., Kennedy, D. N., Makris, N., Berke, J. D.,…Hyman, S. E. (1997). Acute effects of cocaine on human brain activity and emotion. *Neuron, 19*(3), 591–611.

Brody, A. L., Mandelkern, M. A., London, E. D., Childress, A. R., Lee, G. S., Bota, R. G., … Jarvik, M. E. (2002). Brain metabolic changes during cigarette craving. *Archives of General Psychiatry, 59*(12), 1162–1172.

Brody, A. L., Mandelkern, M. A., Olmstead, R. E., Scheibal, D., Hahn, E., Shiraga, S.,…McCracken, J. T. (2006). Gene variants of brain dopamine pathways and smoking-induced dopamine release in the ventral caudate/nucleus accumbens. *Archives of General Psychiatry, 63*(7), 808–816.

Brooks-Russell, A., Simons-Morton, B., Haynie, D., Farhat, T., & Wang, J. (2013). Longitudinal relationship between drinking with peers, descriptive norms, and adolescent alcohol use. *Prevention Science*, 1–9.

Buckholtz, J. W., Treadway, M. T., Cowan, R. L., Woodward, N. D., Li, R., Ansari, M. S.,…Zald, D. H. (2010). Dopaminergic network differences in human impulsivity. *Science, 329*(5991), 532.

Buckingham, E. T., & Daniolos, P. (2013). Longitudinal outcomes for victims of child abuse. *Current Psychiatry Reports, 15*(2), 342.

Bushman, B. J., & Cooper, H. M. (1990). Effects of alcohol on human aggression: An integrative research review. *Psychological Bulletin, 107*(3), 341–354.

Cai, X., Kallarackal, A. J., Kvarta, M. D., Goluskin, S., Gaylor, K., Bailey, A. M.,…Thompson, S. M. (2013). Local potentiation of excitatory synapses by serotonin and its alteration in rodent models of depression. *Nature Neuroscience, 16*(4), 464–472.

Castellanos-Ryan, N., O'Leary-Barrett, M., & Conrod, P. J. (2013). Substance use in childhood and adolescence: A brief overview of developmental processes and their clinical implications. *Journal of the Canadian Academy of Child and Adolescent Psychiatry, 22*(1), 41–46.

Chandler, L. J., Carpenter-Hyland, E., Hendricson, A. W., Maldve, R. E., Morrisett, R. A., Zhou, F. C.,…Szumlinski, K. K. (2006). Structural and functional modifications in glutamateric synapses following prolonged ethanol exposure. *Alcoholism, Clinical and Experimental Research, 30*(2), 368–376.

Chang, J. Y., Janak, P. H., & Woodward, D. J. (1998). Comparison of mesocorticolimbic neuronal responses during cocaine and heroin self-administration in freely moving rats. *Journal of Neuroscience, 18*(8), 3098–3115.

Chang, L., Rapoport, S. I., Nguyen, H. N., Greenstein, D., Chen, M., & Basselin, M. (2009). Acute nicotine reduces brain arachidonic acid signaling in unanesthetized rats. *Journal of Cerebral Blood Flow and Metabolism, 29*(3), 648–658.

Changeux, J.-P. (2010). Nicotine addiction and nicotinic receptors: Lessons from genetically modified mice. *Nature Reviews Neuroscience, 11*(6), 389–401.

Charlet, K., Beck, A., & Heinz, A. (2013). The dopamine system in mediating alcohol effects in humans. *Current Topics in Behavioral Neuroscience, 13*, 461–488.

Chen, L. S., Johnson, E. O., Breslau, N., Hatsukami, D., Saccone, N. L., Grucza, R. A.,…Bierut, L. J. (2009). Interplay of genetic risk factors and parent monitoring in risk for nicotine dependence. *Addiction, 104*(10), 1731–1740.

Collins, R. L., Parks, G. A., & Marlatt, G. A. (1985). Social determinants of alcohol consumption: The effects of social interaction and model status on the self-administration of alcohol. *Journal of Consulting and Clinical Psychology, 53*(2), 189–200.

Conrod, P. J., O'Leary-Barrett, M., Newton, N., Topper, L., Castellanos-Ryan, N., Mackie, C., & Girard, A. (2013). Effectiveness of a selective, personality-targeted prevention program for adolescent alcohol use and misuse: a cluster randomized controlled trial. *Journal of the American Medical Association Psychiatry, 70*(3), 334–342.

Cosgrove, K. P., Esterlis, I., Mason, G. F., Bois, F., O'Malley, S. S., & Krystal, J. H. (2011). Neuroimaging insights into the role of cortical GABA systems and the influence of nicotine on the recovery from alcohol dependence. *Neuropharmacology, 60*(7–8), 1318–1325.

Cui, Y., Xu, J., Dai, R., & He, L. (2012). The interface between inhibition of descending noradrenergic pain control pathways and negative affects in post-traumatic pain patients. *Upsala Journal of Medical Sciences, 117*(3), 293–299.

Dager, A. D., Anderson, B. M., Stevens, M. C., Pulido, C., Rosen, R., Jiantonio-Kelly, R. E.,…Austad, C. S. (2013). Influence of alcohol use and family history of alcoholism on neural response to alcohol cues in college drinkers. *Alcoholism, Clinical and Experimental Research, 37*(s1), E161–E171.

Dal Cin, S., Worth, K. A., Gerrard, M., Gibbons, F. X., Stoolmiller, M., Wills, T. A., & Sargent, J. D. (2009). Watching and drinking: Expectancies, prototypes, and friends' alcohol use mediate the effect of exposure to alcohol use in movies on adolescent drinking. *Health Psychology, 28*(4), 473.

Davidson, J., Swartz, M., Storck, M., Krishnan, R. R., & Hammett, E. (1985). A diagnostic and family study of posttraumatic stress disorder. *American Journal of Psychiatry, 142*(1), 90–93.

Dawson, D. A., Goldstein, R. B., & Grant, B. F. (2012). Factors associated with first utilization of different types of care for alcohol problems. *Journal of Studies on Alcohol and Drugs*, 73(4), 647–656.

Dawson, D. A., Grant, B. F., & Li, T. K. (2005). Quantifying the risks associated with exceeding recommended drinking limits. *Alcoholism, Clinical and Experimental Research*, 29(5), 902–908.

Dawson, D. A., Grant, B. F., & Ruan, W. J. (2005). The association between stress and drinking: Modifying effects of gender and vulnerability. *Alcohol and Alcoholism*, 40(5), 453–460.

Day, N. L., Helsel, A., Sonon, K., & Goldschmidt, L. (2013). The association between prenatal alcohol exposure and behavior at 22 years of age. *Alcoholism, Clinical and Experimental Research*, 37(7), 1171–1178.

Devane, W. A., Hanus, L., Breuer, A., Pertwee, R. G., Stevenson, L. A., Griffin, G.,…Mechoulam, R. (1992). Isolation and structure of a brain constituent that binds to the cannabinoid receptor. *Science*, 258(5090), 1946–1949.

di Tomaso, E., Beltramo, M., & Piomelli, D. (1996). Brain cannabinoids in chocolate. *Nature*, 382(6593), 677–678.

Dick, D. M. (2011). Gene-environment interaction in psychological traits and disorders. *Annual Review of Clinical Psychology*, 7, 383–409.

Dick, D. M., & Kendler, K. S. (2012). The impact of gene-environment interaction on alcohol use disorders. *Alcohol Research: Current Reviews*, 34(3), 318–324.

Dick, D. M., Bierut, L., Hinrichs, A., Fox, L., Bucholz, K. K., Kramer, J.,…Foroud, T. (2006). The role of GABRA2 in risk for conduct disorder and alcohol and drug dependence across developmental stages. *Behavior Genetics*, 36(4), 577–590.

Dick, D. M., Cho, S. B., Latendresse, S. J., Aliev, F., Nurnberger, J. I., Edenberg, H. J.,…Bucholz, K. (2013). Genetic influences on alcohol use across stages of development: GABRA2 and longitudinal trajectories of drunkenness from adolescence to young adulthood. *Addiction Biology*, May 20.

Dick, D. M., Latendresse, S. J., Lansford, J. E., Budde, J. P., Goate, A., Dodge, K. A.,…Bates, J. E. (2009). Role of GABRA2 in trajectories of externalizing behavior across development and evidence of moderation by parental monitoring. *Archives of General Psychiatry*, 66(6), 649–657.

Dilleen, R., Pelloux, Y., Mar, A. C., Molander, A., Robbins, T. W., Everitt, B. J.,…Belin, D.

(2012). High anxiety is a predisposing endophenotype for loss of control over cocaine, but not heroin, self-administration in rats. *Psychopharmacology (Berlin)*, 222(1), 89–97.

Dobkin de Rios, M. (1973). Curing with ayahuasca in an urban slum. In M. Harner (Ed.), *Hallucinogens and shamanism* (pp. 147–164). London: Oxford Press.

Dobkin, P. L., Tremblay, R. E., & Sacchitelle, C. (1997). Predicting boys' early-onset substance abuse from father's alcoholism, son's disruptiveness, and mother's parenting behavior. *Journal of Consulting and Clinical Psychology*, 65(1), 86–92.

Domino, E. F., Evans, C. L., Ni, L., Guthrie, S. K., Koeppe, R. A., & Zubieta, J. K. (2012). Tobacco smoking produces greater striatal dopamine release in G-allele carriers with mu opioid receptor A118G polymorphism. *Progress in Neuropsychopharmacology & Biological Psychiatry*, 38(2), 236–240.

Droungas, A., Ehrman, R. N., Childress, A. R., & O'Brien, C. P. (1995). Effect of smoking cues and cigarette availability on craving and smoking behavior. *Addictive Behaviors*, 20(5), 657–673.

Eaton, N. R., Krueger, R.F., Markon, K.E., Keyes, K.M., Skodol, A.E., Wall, M.,…Grant, B.F. (2013). The structure and predictive validity of the internalizing disorders. *Journal of Abnormal Psychology*, 122(1), 86–92.

Eckersley, R. M. (2005). "Cultural fraud": The role of culture in drug abuse. *Drug and Alcohol Review*, 24(2), 157–163.

Edlund, M. J., Booth, B. M., & Han, X. (2012). Who seeks care where? Utilization of mental health and substance use disorder treatment in two national samples of individuals with alcohol use disorders. *Journal of Studies on Alcohol and Drugs*, 73(4), 635–646.

Edwards, E. P., Eiden, R. D., & Leonard, K. E. (2006). Behaviour problems in 18- to 36-month old children of alcoholic fathers: Secure mother-infant attachment as a protective factor. *Developmental Psychopathology*, 18(2), 395–407.

Enoch, M.A. (2008). The role of GABA(A) receptors in the development of alcoholism. *Pharmacology, Biochemistry, & Behavior*, 90(1), 95–104.

Ersche, K. D., Jones, P. S., Williams, G. B., Turton, A. J., Robbins, T. W., & Bullmore, E. T. (2012). Abnormal brain structure implicated in stimulant drug addiction. *Science*, 335(6068), 601–604.

Ersche, K. D., Turton, A. J., Chamberlain, S. R., Muller, U., Bullmore, E. T., & Robbins, T. W. (2012). Cognitive dysfunction and anxious-impulsive personality traits are endophenotypes for drug dependence. *American Journal of Psychiatry, 169*(9), 926–936.

Ersche, K. D., Williams, G. B., Robbins, T. W., & Bullmore, E. T. (2013). Meta-analysis of structural brain abnormalities associated with stimulant drug dependence and neuroimaging of addiction vulnerability and resilience. *Current Opinion in Neurobiology, 23*(4), 615–624.

Fareed, A., Vayalapalli, S., Casarella, J., Amar, R., & Drexler, K. (2010). Heroin anticraving medications: a systematic review. *American Journal of Drug & Alcohol Abuse, 36*(6), 332–341.

Farrell, A. D., & Danish, S. J. (1993). Peer drug associations and emotional restraint: Causes or consequences of adolescents' drug use? *Journal of Consulting and Clinical Psychology, 61*(2), 327–334.

Fibiger, H. C., & Phillips, A. G. (1988). Mesocorticolimbic dopamine systems and reward. *Annals of the New York Academy of Sciences, 537*, 206–215.

Frank, S. J., Jacobson, S., & Tuer, M. (1990). Psychological predictors of young adults' drinking behaviors. *Journal of Personality and Social Psychology, 59*(4), 770–780.

Gabbay, F. H. (2005). Family history of alcoholism and response to amphetamine: sex differences in the effect of risk. *Alcoholism, Clinical and Experimental Research, 29*(5), 773–780.

Gao, Y., & Raine, A. (2009). P3 event-related potential impairments in antisocial and psychopathic individuals: a meta-analysis. *Biological Psychology, 82*(3), 199–210.

Gierski, F., Hubsch, B., Stefaniak, N., Benzerouk, F., Cuervo-Lombard, C., Bera-Potelle, C.,…Limosin, F. (2013). Executive functions in adult offspring of alcohol-dependent probands: Toward a cognitive endophenotype? *Alcoholism, Clinical and Experimental Reseach, 37*(Suppl 1), E356–363.

Gilmore, C. S., Malone, S. M., & Iacono, W. G. (2010). Brain electrophysiological endophenotypes for externalizing psychopathology: a multivariate approach. *Behavior Genetics, 40*(2), 186–200.

Glass, M., Faull, R. L. M., & Dragunow, M. (1997). Cannabinoid receptors in the human brain: a detailed anatomical and quantitative autoradiographic study in the fetal, neonatal and adult human brain. *Neuroscience, 77*(2), 299–318.

Goodman, A. (2008). Neurobiology of addiction. An integrative review. *Biochemical Pharmacology, 75*(1), 266–322.

Gordis, E. (1996). Alcohol research: At the cutting edge. *Archives of General Psychiatry, 53*(3), 199–201.

Gorwood, P., Le Strat, Y., Ramoz, N., Dubertret, C., Moalic, J. M., & Simonneau, M. (2012). Genetics of dopamine receptors and drug addiction. *Human Genetics, 131*(6), 803–822.

Grant, B. F., Stinson, F. S., Dawson, D. A., Chou, S. P., Dufour, M. C., Compton, W.,…Kaplan, K. (2004). Prevalence and co-occurrence of substance use disorders and independent mood and anxiety disorders: Results from the National Epidemiologic Survey on Alcohol and Related Conditions. *Archives of General Psychiatry, 61*(8), 807–816.

Grant, D. M., Beck, J. G., & Davila, J. (2007). Does anxiety sensitivity predict symptoms of panic, depression, and social anxiety? *Behaviour Research and Therapy, 45*(9), 2247–2255.

Grekin, E. R., Sher, K. J., & Wood, P. K. (2006). Personality and substance dependence symptoms: Modeling substance-specific traits. *Psychology of Addictive Behaviors, 20*(4), 415–424.

Gu, Q., Dillon, C.F., & Burt, V. L. (2010). Prescription drug use continues to increase: U.S. prescription drug data for 2007-2008. *NCHS Data Brief, 42*, 1–8.

Hardy, J. (2013). Psychiatric genetics: Are we there yet? *Journal of the American Medical Association Psychiatry, 70*(6), 569–570.

Hariri, A. R., & Holmes, A. (2006). Genetics of emotional regulation: The role of the serotonin transporter in neural function. *Trends in Cognitve Science, 10*(4), 182–191.

Hartka, E., Johnstone, B., Leino, E.V., Motoyoshi, M., Temple, M. T., & Fillmore, K. M. (1991). A meta-analysis of depressive symptomatology and alcohol consumption over time. *British Journal of Addiction, 86*(10), 1283–1298.

Hartley, C. A., McKenna, M. C., Salman, R., Holmes, A., Casey, B. J., Phelps, E. A., & Glatt, C. E. (2012). Serotonin transporter polyadenylation polymorphism modulates the retention of fear extinction memory. *Proceedings of the National Academy of Sciences U S A, 109*(14), 5493–5498.

Hartman, C., Hopfer, C., Corley, R., Hewitt, J., & Stallings, M. (2013). Using Cloninger's Temperament Scales to predict substance-related behaviors in adolescents: A prospective longitudinal study. *American Journal on Addictions, 22*(3), 246–251.

Hasin, D. S., Stinson, F. S., Ogburn, E., & Grant, B. F. (2007). Prevalence, correlates, disability, and comorbidity of DSM-IV alcohol abuse and dependence in the United States: results from the National Epidemiologic Survey on Alcohol and Related Conditions. *Archives of General Psychiatry, 64*(7), 830–842.

Helzer, J. E., & Pryzbeck, T. R. (1988). The occurrence of alcoholism with other psychiatric disorders in the general population and its impact on treatment. *Journal of Studies in Alcohol, 49,* 219–224.

Hicks, B. M., Blonigen, D. M., Kramer, M. D., Krueger, R. F., Patrick, C. J., Iacono, W. G., & McGue, M. (2007). Gender differences and developmental change in externalizing disorders from late adolescence to early adulthood: A longitudinal twin study. *Journal of Abnormal Psychology, 116*(3), 433–447.

Hung, R. J., McKay, J. D., Gaborieau, V., Boffetta, P., Hashibe, M., Zaridze, D.,…Brennan, P. (2008). A susceptibility locus for lung cancer maps to nicotinic acetylcholine receptor subunit genes on 15q25. *Nature, 452*(7187), 633–637.

Hussong, A. M., Huang, W., Serrano, D., Curran, P. J., & Chassin, L. (2012). Testing whether and when parent alcoholism uniquely affects various forms of adolescent substance use. *Journal of Abnormal Child Psychology, 40*(8), 1265–1276.

Iacono, W. G., & Malone, S. M. (2011). Developmental endophenotypes: Indexing genetic risk for substance abuse with the P300 brain event-related potential. *Child Development Perspectives, 5*(4), 239–247.

Jacobs, M. M., Okvist, A., Horvath, M., Keller, E., Bannon, M. J., Morgello, S., & Hurd, Y. L. (2013). Dopamine receptor D1 and postsynaptic density gene variants associate with opiate abuse and striatal expression levels. *Molecular Psychiatry, 8*(11), 1205–1210.

Jaffee, S. R., Strait, L. B., & Odgers, C. L. (2012). From correlates to causes: Can quasi-experimental studies and statistical innovations bring us closer to identifying the causes of antisocial behavior? *Psychological Bulletin, 138*(2), 272–295.

Janes, A. C., Jensen, J. E., Farmer, S. L., Frederick, B. D., Pizzagalli, D. A., & Lukas, S. E. (2013). GABA levels in the dorsal anterior cingulate cortex associated with difficulty ignoring smoking-related cues in tobacco-dependent volunteers. *Neuropsychopharmacology, 38*(6), 1113–1120.

Johansson, B. A., Berglund, M., & Lindgren, A. (2006). Efficacy of maintenance treatment with naltrexone for opioid dependence: A meta-analytical review. *Addiction, 101*(4), 491–503.

Johnson, B. A., Ait-Daoud, N., Seneviratne, C., Roache, J. D., Javors, M. A., Wang, X. Q.,…Li, M. D. (2011). Pharmacogenetic approach at the serotonin transporter gene as a method of reducing the severity of alcohol drinking. *American Journal of Psychiatry, 168*(3), 265–275.

Johnston, L. D., O'Malley, P. M., Bachman, J. G., & Schulenberg, J. E. (2010). *Monitoring the future: National survey results on drug use, 1975–2009. Volume I: Secondary school students* (NIH Publication No. 10-7584). Bethesda, MD: National Institute on Drug Abuse (NIDA).

Kalivas, P. W., & Stewart, J. (1991). Dopamine transmission in the initiation and expression of drug- and stress-induced sensitization of motor activity. *Brain Research Brain Research Reviews, 16*(3), 223–244.

Kapoor, M., Wang, J.-C., Wetherill, L., Le, N., Bertelsen, S., Hinrichs, A. L.,…Dick, D. (2013). A meta-analysis of two genome-wide association studies to identify novel loci for maximum number of alcoholic drinks. *Human Genetics, 132*(10), 1141–1151.

Kelm, M. K., Criswell, H. E., & Breese, G. R. (2011). Ethanol-enhanced GABA release: A focus on G protein-coupled receptors. *Brain Research Review, 65*(2), 113–123.

Kendler, K. S. (2012). Levels of explanation in psychiatric and substance use disorders: Implications for the development of an etiologically based nosology. *Molecular Psychiatry, 17*(1), 11–21.

Kendler, K. S., Aggen, S. H., Knudsen, G. P., Roysamb, E., Neale, M. C., & Reichborn-Kjennerud, T. (2011). The structure of genetic and environmental risk factors for syndromal and subsyndromal common DSM-IV axis I and all axis II disorders. *American Journal of Psychiatry, 168*(1), 29–39.

Kendler, K. S., Chen, X., Dick, D., Maes, H., Gillespie, N., Neale, M. C., & Riley, B. (2012). Recent advances in the genetic epidemiology and molecular genetics of substance use disorders. *Nature Neuroscience, 15*(2), 181–189.

Kendler, K. S., Ohlsson, H., Sundquist, K., & Sundquist, J. (2013). Within-family environmental transmission of drug abuse: A Swedish national study. *Journal of the American Medical Association Psychiatry, 70*(2), 235–242.

Kendler, K. S., Sundquist, K., Ohlsson, H., Palmer, K., Maes, H., Winkleby, M. A., & Sundquist, J. (2012). Genetic and familial environmental influences on the risk for drug abuse: A national Swedish adoption study. *Archives of General Psychiatry, 69*(7), 690–697.

Keyes, K. M., & Miech, R. (2013). Age, period, and cohort effects in heavy episodic drinking in the US from 1985 to 2009. *Drug and Alcohol Dependence, 132*(1-2), 140–148.

Kiefer, F., & Mann, K. (2010). Acamprosate: How, where, and for whom does it work? Mechanism of action, treatment targets, and individualized therapy. *Current Pharmaceutical Design, 16*(19), 2098–2102.

Kim-Cohen, J., Caspi, A., Moffitt, T. E., Harrington, H., Milne, B. J., & Poulton, R. (2003). Prior juvenile diagnoses in adults with mental disorder: Developmental follow-back of a prospective-longitudinal cohort. *Archives of General Psychiatry, 60*(7), 709–717.

King, A. C., de Wit, H., McNamara, P. J., & Cao, D. (2011). Rewarding, stimulant, and sedative alcohol responses and relationship to future binge drinking. *Archives of General Psychiatry, 68*(4), 389–399.

Knafo, A., & Jaffee, S. R. (2013). Gene-environment correlation in developmental psychopathology. *Develomental Psychopathology, 25*(1), 1–6.

Korhonen, T., Latvala, A., Dick, D. M., Pulkkinen, L., Rose, R. J., Kaprio, J., & Huizink, A. C. (2012). Genetic and environmental influences underlying externalizing behaviors, cigarette smoking and illicit drug use across adolescence. *Behavior Genetics, 42*(4), 614–625.

Kuehn, B. M. (2007). Prescription drug abuse rises globally. *Journal of the American Medical Association, 297*(12), 1306–1306.

LeMarquand, D., Pihl, R. O., & Benkelfat, C. (1994a). Serotonin and alcohol intake, abuse, and dependence: Clinical evidence. *Biological Psychiatry, 36*(5), 326–337.

LeMarquand, D., Pihl, R. O., & Benkelfat, C. (1994b). Serotonin and alcohol intake, abuse, and dependence: Findings of animal studies. *Biological Psychiatry, 36*(6), 395–421.

Lennard, H. L., Epstein, L. J., Bernstein, A., & Ransom, D. C. (1971). *Mystification and drug misuse: Hazards in using psychoactive drugs.* San Francisco: Jossey-Bass.

Li, H., Penzo, M. A., Taniguchi, H., Kopec, C. D., Huang, Z. J., & Li, B. (2013). Experience-dependent modification of a central amygdala fear circuit. *Nature Neuroscience, 16*(3), 332–339.

Lips, E. H., Gaborieau, V., McKay, J. D., Chabrier, A., Hung, R. J., Boffetta, P.,…Brennan, P. (2010). Association between a 15q25 gene variant, smoking quantity and tobacco-related cancers among 17 000 individuals. *International Journal of Epidemiology, 39*(2), 563–577.

Littlefield, A. K., Agrawal, A., Ellingson, J. M., Kristjansson, S., Madden, P. A., Bucholz, K. K.,…Sher, K.J. (2011). Does variance in drinking motives explain the genetic overlap between personality and alcohol use disorder symptoms? A twin study of young women. *Alcoholism, Clinical and Experimental Research, 35*(12), 2242–2250.

Liu, J., Lester, B. M., Neyzi, N., Sheinkopf, S. J., Gracia, L., Kekatpure, M., & Kosofsky, B. E. (2013). Regional brain morphometry and impulsivity in adolescents following prenatal exposure to cocaine and tobacco. *Journal of the American Medical Association Pediatrics, 167*(4), 348–354.

Lown, E.A., Nayak, M.B., Korcha, R.A., & Greenfield, T.K. (2011). Child physical and sexual abuse: A comprehensive look at alcohol consumption patterns, consequences, and dependence from the National Alcohol Survey. *Alcoholism, Clinical and Experimental Research, 35*(2), 317–325.

Luria, A. R. (1980). *Higher cortical functions in man.* (Basil Haigh, trans.), (2nd ed.) New York: Basic Books.

Macqueen, D. A., Heckman, B. W., Blank, M. D., Janse Van Rensburg, K., Park, J. Y., Drobes, D. J., & Evans, D. E. (2014). Variation in the alpha 5 nicotinic acetylcholine receptor subunit gene predicts cigarette smoking intensity as a function of nicotine content. *Pharmacogenomics Journal, 14*(1), 70–76.

Maestripieri, D., Lindell, S. G., Ayala, A., Gold, P. W., & Higley, J. D. (2005). Neurobiological characteristics of rhesus macaque abusive mothers and their relation to social and maternal behavior. *Neuroscience & Biobehavioral Reviews, 29*(1), 51–57.

Maisel, N. C., Blodgett, J. C., Wilbourne, P. L., Humphreys, K., & Finney, J. W. (2013). Meta-analysis of naltrexone and acamprosate for treating alcohol use disorders: When are these medications most helpful? *Addiction, 108*(2), 275–293.

Manly, J. T., Oshri, A., Lynch, M., Herzog, M., & Wortel, S. (2013). Child neglect and the development of externalizing behavior problems: associations with maternal drug dependence and neighborhood crime. *Child Maltreatment, 18*(1), 17–29.

Mares, S. H., Lichtwarck-Aschoff, A., Burk, W. J., van der Vorst, H., & Engels, R. C. (2012). Parental alcohol-specific rules and alcohol use from early adolescence to young adulthood. *Journal of Child Psycholology & Psychiatry, 53*(7), 798–805.

Mason, W. A., Hitchings, J. E., & Spoth, R. L. (2007). Emergence of delinquency and depressed mood throughout adolescence as predictors of late adolescent problem substance use. *Psychology of Addictive Behaviors, 21*(1), 13.

McCormick, P. N., Wilson, V. S., Wilson, A. A., & Remington, G. J. (2013). Acutely administered antipsychotic drugs are highly selective for dopamine D2 over D3 receptors. *Pharmacology Research, 70*(1), 66–71.

McGue, M., Pickens, R. W., & Svikis, D. S. (1992). Sex and age effects on the inheritance of alcohol problems: A twin study. *Journal of Abnormal Psychology, 101*(1), 3–17.

McLaughlin, K. A., Green, J. G., Gruber, M. J., Sampson, N. A., Zaslavsky, A. M., & Kessler, R. C. (2012). Childhood adversities and first onset of psychiatric disorders in a national sample of US adolescents: Childhood adversities and psychiatric disorders. *Archives of General Psychiatry, 69*(11), 1151–1160.

Meier, M. H., Caspi, A., Ambler, A., Harrington, H., Houts, R., Keefe, R. S.,…Moffitt, T. E. (2012). Persistent cannabis users show neuropsychological decline from childhood to midlife. *Proceedings of the National Academy of Sciences U S A, 109*(40), E2657–2664.

Metrik, J., Rohsenow, D.J., Monti, P. M., McGeary, J., Cook, T. A., de Wit, H.,…Kahler, C. W. (2009). Effectiveness of a marijuana expectancy manipulation: Piloting the balanced-placebo design for marijuana. *Experimental and Clinical Psychopharmacology, 17*(4), 217–225.

Miller, G. A. (1996). How we think about cognition, emotion, and biology in psychopathology. *Psychophysiology, 33*(6), 615–628.

Miller, G. A. (2010). Mistreating psychology in the decades of the brain. *Perspectives in Psychological Science, 5*(6), 716–743.

Miller, G. A., & Rockstroh, B. (2013). Endophenotypes in psychopathology research: Where do we stand? *Annual Review of Clinical Psychology, 9*, 177–213.

Mills, K. L., Teesson, M., Ross, J., & Peters, L. (2006). Trauma, PTSD, and substance use disorders: Findings from the Australian National Survey of Mental Health and Well-Being. *American Journal of Psychiatry, 163*(4), 652–658.

Moffitt, T. E. (2005). The new look of behavioral genetics in developmental psychopathology: Gene-environment interplay in antisocial behaviors. *Psychology Bulletin, 131*(4), 533–554.

Morris, P. L., Hopwood, M., Whelan, G., Gardiner, J., & Drummond, E. (2001). Naltrexone for alcohol dependence: A randomized controlled trial. *Addiction, 96*(11), 1565–1573.

Moynihan, R., & Cassels, A. (2005). *Selling sickness: How the world's biggest pharmaceutical companies are turning us all into patients.* New York: Nation Books.

Munafo, M. R., Timofeeva, M. N., Morris, R. W., Prieto-Merino, D., Sattar, N., Brennan, P.,…Davey Smith, G. (2012). Association between genetic variants on chromosome 15q25 locus and objective measures of tobacco exposure. *Journal of the National Cancer Institute, 104*(10), 740–748.

Murdoch, D. D., Pihl, R., & Ross, D. (1988). The influence of dose, beverage type, and sex of interactor on female bar patrons' verbal aggression. *Substance Use & Misuse, 23*(9), 953–966.

Nader, K., Bechara, A., Roberts, D. C., & van der Kooy, D. (1994). Neuroleptics block high- but not low-dose heroin place preferences: Further evidence for a two-system model of motivation. *Behavioral Neuroscience, 108*(6), 1128–1138.

Naqvi, N. H., Rudrauf, D., Damasio, H., & Bechara, A. (2007). Damage to the insula disrupts addiction to cigarette smoking. *Science, 315*(5811), 531–534.

Nigg, J. T., Wong, M. M., Martel, M. M., Jester, J. M., Puttler, L. I., Glass, J. M.,…Zucker, R. A. (2006). Poor response inhibition as a predictor of problem drinking and illicit drug use in adolescents at risk for alcoholism and other substance use disorders. *Journal of the American Academy of Child & Adolescent Psychiatry, 45*(4), 468–475.

Nilsson, K. W., Sjoberg, R. L., Damberg, M., Alm, P. O., Ohrvik, J., Leppert, J.,…Oreland, L. (2005). Role of the serotonin transporter gene and family function in adolescent alcohol consumption. *Alcoholism, Clinical & Experimental Research, 29*(4), 564–570.

Norman, A. L., O'Brien, J. W., Spadoni, A. D., Tapert, S. F., Jones, K. L., Riley, E. P., & Mattson, S. N. (2013). A functional magnetic resonance imaging study of spatial working memory in children with prenatal alcohol exposure: Contribution of familial history of alcohol use disorders. *Alcoholism, Clinical & Experimental Research, 37*(1), 132–140.

Ornish, D., Magbanua, M. J., Weidner, G., Weinberg, V., Kemp, C., Green, C.,…Carroll, P. R. (2008). Changes in prostate gene expression in men undergoing an intensive nutrition and lifestyle intervention. *Proceedings of the National Academy of Sciences U S A, 105*(24), 8369–8374.

Palmer, R., Young, S., Corley, R., Hopfer, C., Stallings, M., & Hewitt, J. (2013). Stability and change of genetic and environmental effects on the common liability to alcohol, tobacco, and cannabis DSM-IV dependence symptoms. *Behavior Genetics, 43*(5), 374–385.

Patock-Peckham, J. A., Cheong, J., Balhorn, M. E., & Nagoshi, C. T. (2001). A social learning perspective: A model of parenting styles, self-regulation, perceived drinking control, and alcohol use and problems. *Alcoholism, Clinical & Experimental Research, 25*(9), 1284–1292.

Pentz, M. A., & Riggs, N. R. (2013). Longitudinal relationships of executive cognitive function and parent influence to child substance use and physical activity. *Prevention Science, 14*(3), 229–237.

Peterson, J. B., Conrod, P., Vassileva, J., Gianoulakis, C., & Pihl, R. O. (2006). Differential effects of naltrexone on cardiac, subjective and behavioural reactions to acute ethanol intoxication. *Journal of Psychiatry & Neuroscience, 31*(6), 386–393.

Peterson, J. B., Pihl, R. O., Gianoulakis, C., Conrod, P., Finn, P. R., Stewart, S. H.,…Bruce, K. R. (1996). Ethanol-induced change in cardiac and endogenous opiate function and risk for alcoholism. *Alcoholism, Clinical & Experimental Research, 20*(9), 1542–1552.

Pettinati, H. M., Silverman, B. L., Battisti, J. J., Forman, R., Schweizer, E., & Gastfriend, D. R. (2011). Efficacy of extended-release naltrexone in patients with relatively higher severity of alcohol dependence. *Alcoholism, Clinical & Experimental Research, 35*(10), 1804–1811.

Pietrzak, R. H., Goldstein, R. B., Southwick, S. M., & Grant, B. F. (2011). Prevalence and axis I comorbidity of full and partial posttraumatic stress disorder in the United States: Results from wave 2 of the National Epidemiologic Survey on Alcohol and Related Conditions. *Journal of Anxiety Disorders, 25*(3), 456–465.

Pihl, R. (2010). Mental disorders are brain disorders: You think? *Canadian Psychology/Psychologie Canadienne, 51*(1), 40.

Pihl, R. O., & Peterson, J. (1996). Characteristics and putative mechanisms in boys at risk for drug abuse and aggression. *Annals of the New York Academy of Science, 794*, 238–252.

Pihl, R. O., & Peterson, J. B. (1995). Alcoholism: The role of different motivational systems. *Journal of Psychiatry & Neuroscience, 20*(5), 372–396.

Pihl, R. O., & Spiers, P. (1978). Individual characteristics in the etiology of drug abuse. *Progress in Experimental Personality Research, 8*, 93–195.

Pihl, R. O., Peterson, J. B., & Lau, M. A. (1993). A biosocial model of the alcohol-aggression relationship. *Journal of Studies on Alcohol Supplement, 11*, 128–139.

Pihl, R. O., Peterson, J., & Finn, P. (1990). Inherited predisposition to alcoholism: Characteristics of sons of male alcoholics. *Journal of Abnormal Psychology, 99*(3), 291–301.

Pihl, R. O., Smith, M., & Farrell, B. (1984). Alcohol and aggression in men: A comparison of brewed and distilled beverages. *Journal of Studies on Alcohol, 45*(3), 278–282.

Pishva, E., Kenis, G., Lesch, K. P., Prickaerts, J., Steinbusch, H. M., van den Hove, D. L.,…Rutten, B. P. (2012). Epigenetic epidemiology in psychiatry: A translational neuroscience perspective. *Translational Neuroscience, 3*(2), 196–212.

Popova, S., Giesbrecht, N., Bekmuradov, D., & Patra, J. (2009). Hours and days of sale and density of alcohol outlets: Impacts on alcohol consumption and damage: A systematic review. *Alcohol and Alcoholism, 44*(5), 500–516.

Porjesz, B., Rangaswamy, M., Kamarajan, C., Jones, K. A., Padmanabhapillai, A., & Begleiter, H. (2005). The utility of neurophysiological markers in the study of alcoholism. *Clinical Neurophysiology, 116*(5), 993–1018.

Pruessner, J. C., Dedovic, K., Pruessner, M., Lord, C., Buss, C., Collins, L.,…Lupien, S. J. (2010). Stress regulation in the central nervous system: Evidence from structural and functional neuroimaging studies in human populations—2008 Curt Richter Award Winner. *Psychoneuroendocrinology, 35*(1), 179–191.

Reed, P. L., Anthony, J. C., & Breslau, N. (2007). Incidence of drug problems in young adults exposed to trauma and posttraumatic stress disorder: Do early life experiences and predispositions matter? *Archives of General Psychiatry, 64*(12), 1435–1442.

Room, R., Bloomfield, K., Gmel, G., Grittner, U., Gustafsson, N.-K., Mäkelä, P.,…Wicki, M. (2013). What happened to alcohol consumption and problems in the Nordic countries when alcohol taxes were decreased and borders opened? *International Journal of Alcohol and Drug Research, 2*(1), 77–87.

Rosenfield, S., & Mouzon, D. (2013). Gender and mental health. In C. S. Aneshensel, J. C. Phelan, & A. Bierman (Eds.), *Handbook of the sociology of mental health* (pp. 277–296). New York: Springer.

Rudgley, R. (1994). *Essential substances.* New York: Kodansha.

Saccone, N. L., Culverhouse, R. C., Schwantes-An, T. H., Cannon, D. S., Chen, X., Cichon, S.,…Bierut, L. J. (2010). Multiple independent loci at chromosome 15q25.1 affect smoking quantity: A meta-analysis and comparison with lung cancer and COPD. *PLoS Genet*, *6*(8), pii: e1001053.

Sangameswaran, L., Fales, H. M., Friedrich, P., & De Blas, A. L. (1986). Purification of a benzodiazepine from bovine brain and detection of benzodiazepine-like immunoreactivity in human brain. *Proceedings of the National Academy of Sciences*, *83*, 9236–9240.

Sari, Y., Johnson, V. R., & Weedman, J. M. (2011). Role of the serotonergic system in alcohol dependence: From animal models to clinics. *Progress in Molecular Biology and Translational Science*, *98*, 401–443.

Sartor, C. E., Lynskey, M. T., Heath, A. C., Jacob, T., & True, W. (2007). The role of childhood risk factors in initiation of alcohol use and progression to alcohol dependence. *Addiction*, *102*(2), 216–225.

Sartor, C. E., Waldron, M., Duncan, A. E., Grant, J. D., McCutcheon, V. V., Nelson, E. C.,…Heath, A. C. (2013). Childhood sexual abuse and early substance use in adolescent girls: The role of familial influences. *Addiction*, *108*(5), 993–1000.

Schacht, J. P., Anton, R. F., Randall, P. K., Li, X., Henderson, S., & Myrick, H. (2013). Effects of a GABA-ergic medication combination and initial alcohol withdrawal severity on cue-elicited brain activation among treatment-seeking alcoholics. *Psychopharmacology (Berlin)*, *227*(4), 627–637.

Schellekens, A. F., Franke, B., Ellenbroek, B., Cools, A., de Jong, C. A., Buitelaar, J. K., & Verkes, R. J. (2013). COMT Val158Met modulates the effect of childhood adverse experiences on the risk of alcohol dependence. *Addiction Biology*, *18*(2), 344–356.

Seguin, J. R., Pihl, R. O., Harden, P. W., Tremblay, R. E., & Boulerice, B. (1995). Cognitive and neuropsychological characteristics of physically aggressive boys. *Journal of Abnormal Psychology*, *104*(4), 614–624.

Sellings, L. H., & Clarke, P. B. (2003). Segregation of amphetamine reward and locomotor stimulation between nucleus accumbens medial shell and core. *Journal of Neuroscience*, *23*(15), 6295–6303.

Servaas, M. N., van der Velde, J., Costafreda, S. G., Horton, P., Ormel, J., Riese, H., & Aleman, A. (2013). Neuroticism and the brain: A quantitative meta-analysis of neuroimaging studies investigating emotion processing. *Neuroscience & Biobehavioral Reviews*, *37*(8), 1518–1529.

Service, S. K., Verweil, K. J., Lahti, J., Congdon, E., Ekelund, J., Hintsanen, M.,…Freimer, N. B. (2012). A genome-wide meta-analysis of association studies of Cloninger's Temperament Scales. *Translational Psychiatry*, *2*, e116.

Setiawan, E., Pihl, R. O., Benkelfat, C., & Leyton, M. (2012). Influence of the OPRM1 A118G polymorphism on alcohol-induced euphoria, risk for alcoholism and the clinical efficacy of naltrexone. *Pharmacogenomics*, *13*(10), 1161–1172.

Shedler, J., & Block, J. (1990). Adolescent drug use and psychological health. A longitudinal inquiry. *American Psychology*, *45*(5), 612–630.

Sher, K. J. (1987). Stress response dampening. In H. T. Blane & K. E. Leonard (Eds.), Psychological theories of drinking and alcoholism (pp. 227–271). New York: Guilford Press.

Shoham, V., & Insel, T. R. (2011). Rebooting for whom? Portfolios, technology, and personalized intervention. *Perspectives on Psychological Science*, *6*(5), 478–482.

Sinha, R. (2012). How does stress lead to risk of alcohol relapse? *Alcohol Research*, *34*(4), 432–440.

Smith, D. G., Simon Jones, P., Bullmore, E. T., Robbins, T. W., & Ersche, K. D. (2014). Enhanced orbitofrontal cortex function and lack of attentional bias to cocaine cues in recreational stimulant users. *Biological Psychiatry*, *75*(2), 124–131.

Sorge, R. E., & Clarke, P. B. (2011). Nicotine Self-Administration *Animal Models of Drug Addiction* (pp. 101–132). New York: Humana Press.

Stacy, A., Newcomb, M., & Bentler, P. (1991). Cognitive motivation and drug use: A 9 year longitudinal study. *Journal of Abnormal Psychology*, *100*, 502–515.

Stein, E. A., Pankiewicz, J., Harsch, H. H., Cho, J. K., Fuller, S. A., Hoffmann, R. G.,…Bloom, A. S. (1998). Nicotine-induced limbic cortical activation in the human brain: a functional MRI study. *American Journal of Psychiatry*, *155*(8), 1009–1015.

Stroud, L. R., Paster, R. L., Goodwin, M. S., Shenassa, E., Buka, S., Niaura, R.,…Lipsitt, L. P. (2009). Maternal smoking during pregnancy and neonatal behavior: A large-scale community study. *Pediatrics*, *123*(5), e842–848.

Tarter, R. E., Jacob, T., & Bremer, D. A. (1989). Cognitive status of sons of alcoholic men. *Alcoholism, Clinical & Experimental Research*, *13*(2), 232–235.

Tartter, M. A., & Ray, L. A. (2011). The serotonin transporter polymorphism (5-HTTLPR) and alcohol problems in heavy drinkers: Moderation by depressive symptoms. *Frontiers in Psychiatry*, 2, 49.

Titeler, M., Lyon, R. A., & Glennon, R. A. (1988). Radioligand binding evidence implicates the brain 5-HT2 receptor as a site of action for LSD and phenylisopropylamine hallucinogens. *Psychopharmacology (Berlin)*, 94(2), 213–216.

Trigo, J. M., Martin-Garcia, E., Berrendero, F., Robledo, P., & Maldonado, R. (2010). The endogenous opioid system: A common substrate in drug addiction. *Drug and Alcohol Dependence*, 108(3), 183–194.

Trigo, J. M., Orejarena, M. J., Maldonado, R., & Robledo, P. (2009). MDMA reinstates cocaine-seeking behaviour in mice. *European Neuropsychopharmacology*, 19(6), 391–397.

Twomey, J., LaGasse, L., Derauf, C., Newman, E., Shah, R., Smith, L.,…Roberts, M. (2013). Prenatal methamphetamine exposure, home environment, and primary caregiver risk factors predict child behavioral problems at 5 years. *American Journal of Orthopsychiatry*, 83(1), 64–72.

Ullman, S. E., Relyea, M., Peter-Hagene, L., & Vasquez, A. L. (2013). Trauma histories, substance use coping, PTSD, and problem substance use among sexual assault victims. *Addiction Behavior*, 38(6), 2219–2223.

Valenta, J. P., Job, M. O., Mangieri, R. A., Schier, C. J., Howard, E. C., & Gonzales, R. A. (2013). µ-Opioid receptors in the stimulation of mesolimbic dopamine activity by ethanol and morphine in Long-Evans rats: A delayed effect of ethanol. *Psychopharmacology (Berlin)*, 228(3), 389–400.

van Beek, J. H., Kendler, K. S., de Moor, M. H., Geels, L. M., Bartels, M., Vink, J. M.,…Boomsma, D. I. (2012). Stable genetic effects on symptoms of alcohol abuse and dependence from adolescence into early adulthood. *Behavior Genetics*, 42(1), 40–56.

van Hell, H. H., Vink, M., Ossewaarde, L., Jager, G., Kahn, R. S., & Ramsey, N. F. (2010). Chronic effects of cannabis use on the human reward system: An fMRI study. *European Neuropsychopharmacology*, 20(3), 153–163.

Van Ryzin, M. J., Fosco, G. M., & Dishion, T. J. (2012). Family and peer predictors of substance use from early adolescence to early adulthood: An 11-year prospective analysis. *Addiction Behavior*, 37(12), 1314–1324.

Veilleux, J. C., Colvin, P. J., Anderson, J., York, C., & Heinz, A. J. (2010). A review of opioid dependence treatment: pharmacological and psychosocial interventions to treat opioid addiction. *Clinical Psychology Review*, 30(2), 155–166.

Verweij, K. J., Zietsch, B. P., Lynskey, M. T., Medland, S. E., Neale, M. C., Martin, N. G.,…Vink, J. M. (2010). Genetic and environmental influences on cannabis use initiation and problematic use: a meta-analysis of twin studies. *Addiction*, 105(3), 417–430.

Volavka, J., Czobor, P., Goodwin, D., Gabrielli, W., Penick, E., Mednick, S., Jensen, P., Knop, J., & Schulsinger, F. (1996). The electroencephalogram after alcohol administration in high risk men and the development of alcohol use disorders ten years later. *Archives of General Psychiatry*, 53, 258–263.

Volkow, N. D., & Baler, R. D. (2012). To stop or not to stop? *Science*, 335(6068), 546–548.

Volkow, N. D., Wang, G. J., Fowler, J. S., & Tomasi, D. (2012). Addiction circuitry in the human brain. *Annual Review of Pharmacology & Toxicology*, 52, 321–336.

Volkow, N. D., Wang, G. J., Tomasi, D., & Baler, R. D. (2013). Unbalanced neuronal circuits in addiction. *Current Opinion in Neurobiology*, 23(4), 639–648.

Volkow, N.D., Wang, G.J., Ma, Y., Fowler, J.S., Zhu, W., Maynard, L.,…Swanson, J.M. (2003). Expectation enhances the regional brain metabolic and the reinforcing effects of stimulants in cocaine abusers. *Journal of Neuroscience*, 23(36), 11461–11468.

Vul, E., & Pashler, H. (2012). Voodoo and circularity errors. *Neuroimage*, 62(2), 945.

Vul, E., Harris, C., Winkielman, P., & Pashler, H. (2009). Puzzlingly high correlations in fMRI studies of emotion, personality, and social cognition. *Perspectives on Psychological Science*, 4(3), 274–290.

Wagenaar, A. C., Tobler, A. L., & Komro, K. A. (2010). Effects of alcohol tax and price policies on morbidity and mortality: A systematic review. *American Journal of Public Health*, 100(11), 2270–2278.

Wechsler, H., & Nelson, T. F. (2008). What we have learned from the Harvard School of Public Health College Alcohol Study: Focusing attention on college student alcohol consumption and the environmental conditions that promote it. *Journal of Studies on Alcohol and Drugs*, 69(4), 481–490.

Wechsler, H., Kuh, G., & Davenport, A. E. (2009). Fraternities, sororities and binge drinking: Results from a national study of American colleges. *NASPA Jounal*, 46(3), 763–784.

Whelan, R., & Garavan, H. (2013). Fractionating the impulsivity construct in adolescence. *Neuropsychopharmacology, 38*(1), 250–251.

Whelan, R., Conrod, P. J., Poline, J. B., Lourdusamy, A., Banaschewski, T., Barker, G. J.,…Garavan, H. (2012). Adolescent impulsivity phenotypes characterized by distinct brain networks. *Nature Neuroscience, 15*(6), 920–925.

Wichers, M., Gardner, C., Maes, H. H., Lichtenstein, P., Larsson, H., & Kendler, K. S. (2013). Genetic innovation and stability in externalizing problem behavior across development: A multi-informant twin study. *Behavior Genetics, 43*(3), 191–201.

Wichers, M., Gillespie, N. A., & Kendler, K. S. (2013). Genetic and environmental predictors of latent trajectories of alcohol use from adolescence to adulthood: A male twin study. *Alcoholism, Clinical & Experimental Research, 37*(3), 498–506.

Widom, C. S., Ireland, T., & Glynn, P. J. (1995). Alcohol abuse in abused and neglected children followed-up: Are they at increased risk? *Journal of Studies on Alcohol, 56*(2), 207–217.

Wilson, D., da Silva Lobo, D. S., Tavares, H., Gentil, V., & Vallada, H. (2013). Family-based association analysis of serotonin genes in pathological gambling disorder: Evidence of vulnerability risk in the 5HT-2A receptor gene. *Journal of Molecular Neuroscience, 49*(3), 550–553.

Winters, B. D., Kruger, J. M., Huang, X., Gallaher, Z. R., Ishikawa, M., Czaja, K.,…Dong, Y. (2012). Cannabinoid receptor 1-expressing neurons in the nucleus accumbens. *Proceedings of the National Academy of Scieices U S A, 109*(40), E2717–2725.

Witkiewitz, K., Saville, K., & Hamreus, K. (2012). Acamprosate for treatment of alcohol dependence: Mechanisms, efficacy, and clinical utility. *Therapeutics and Clinical Risk Management, 8,* 45–53.

Woodyard, C. D., Hallam, J. S., & Bentley, J. P. (2013). Drinking norms: Predictors of misperceptions among college students. *American Journal of Health Behavior, 37*(1), 14–24.

Yan, J., Aliev, F., Webb, B. T., Kendler, K. S., Williamson, V. S., Edenberg, H. J.,…Dick, D. M. (2013). Using genetic information from candidate gene and genome-wide association studies in risk prediction for alcohol dependence. *Addiction Biology.*

Yoder, K. K., Constantinescu, C. C., Kareken, D. A., Normandin, M. D., Cheng, T. E., O'Connor, S. J., & Morris, E. D. (2007). Heterogeneous effects of alcohol on dopamine release in the striatum: a PET study. *Alcoholism: Clinical and Experimental Research, 31*(6), 965–973.

Zhang, T. Y., & Meaney, M. J. (2010). Epigenetics and the environmental regulation of the genome and its function. *Annual Review of Psychology, 61,* 439–466, C431–433.

Zucker, R. A., Heitzeg, M. M., & Nigg, J. T. (2011). Parsing the undercontrol/disinhibition pathway to substance use disorders: A multilevel developmental problem. *Child Development Perspectives, 5*(4), 248–255.

11

Substance-Related and Addictive Disorders
Diagnosis, Comorbidity, and Psychopathology

JESSICA R. SKIDMORE,

SUSAN R. TATE,

MICHELLE L. DRAPKIN,

AND SANDRA A. BROWN

Substance use disorders (SUDs, including alcohol and other drug related disorders) are among the most common psychiatric conditions in the United States, with over 8% of individuals aged 12 or older meeting the *DSM-IV* criteria for any substance abuse or dependence in the past year (Substance Abuse and Mental Health Services Administration Office of Applied Studies, 2012). Of those, approximately 13% met criteria for both alcohol and another SUD. According to the findings of a nationally representative epidemiology study, rates of alcohol use disorders in 2011 (6.5%) were lower than in 2002 through 2010 (range = 7.1%–7.7%), and rates of SUDs in 2011 (2.5%) were also lower than most years between 2002 and 2010 (range = 2.8%–3.0%). A large, nationally representative survey of over 40,000 adults aged 18 years or older conducted in 2001–2002 found that the 12-month prevalence of any SUD was 9.35% (8.46% for alcohol and 2.00% for other drugs, with cannabis being the most prevalent; Grant et al., 2004). Compared to the 1991–1992 survey data, these rates reflected an increase in alcohol abuse (from 3.03% to 4.65%) and a decrease in alcohol dependence (from 4.38% to 3.81%). The prevalence of cannabis use disorders increased from 1.2% to 1.5% despite the fact that prevalence of marijuana use did not change.

Research suggests that behavioral addictions, specifically pathological gambling, are similar to SUDs in their neurological impact and pathways (Regard, Knoch, Gütling, & Landis, 2003; Rugle & Melamed, 1993). According to the findings of a large, nationally representative study (Petry, Stinson, & Grant, 2005), the lifetime prevalence of pathological gambling was less than 1%. Of those individuals who met diagnostic criteria for pathological gambling, 73% met lifetime criteria for an alcohol use disorder (25% alcohol abuse, 48% alcohol dependence), and 38% met lifetime criteria for an SUD (27% substance abuse, 11% substance dependence).

In addition, a variety of other psychiatric disorders are highly comorbid with SUDs. In this chapter, we review the epidemiology, diagnostic criteria, related risk factors and problems, and comorbidities of SUDs and pathological gambling; the etiology of these disorders is discussed elsewhere in this volume (see Chapter 10). It should be noted that the research presented here is unintentionally biased toward alcohol use disorders, as alcohol is the most commonly used intoxicating substance and the bulk of the extant literature has investigated alcohol use disorders and then attempted to generalize to other substances of abuse. We will mention when other substances have been studied more specifically in relation to points we are presenting.

Evolution of the Diagnosis

The diagnostic category of SUDs (including alcohol and other drug-related disorders) is broad and varied. Over the past 60 years these diagnoses have evolved rather dramatically, beginning with the *DSM-I* in 1953, when SUDs were grouped under sociopathic personality disturbances, along with the paraphilias (then known as "sexual deviations") and antisocial personality disorder (then known as "antisocial and dissocial reactions"). This early categorization of SUDs reflected the social climate, which conceptualized individuals with SUDs as social deviants. *DSM-II* made small changes to the SUD diagnosis, maintaining its consistency with personality disorders and sexual deviations although removing the sociopathic categorization. *DSM-III* included tobacco/nicotine dependence for the first time, and few significant changes were made to the diagnostic parameters until *DSM-III-R*, when the diagnoses were refined based on empirically bound criteria. In this edition, SUDs were separated from personality disorders and paraphilias, and a major revision was to include the notion of abuse versus dependence and to add the concept of physiological dependence (i.e., withdrawal and tolerance). *DSM-IV* did not add substantial changes but rather allowed for listing specifiers (i.e., with or without physiological dependence) that appeared more relevant to some substances (e.g., alcohol, opiates) than others (e.g., hallucinogens, inhalants). Additionally, social consequences were moved from the dependence criteria to the abuse criteria.

DSM-5

In May 2013, the fifth edition of the *DSM* was released with several empirically supported changes to the substance-related disorders diagnostic criteria. Given research that suggested that the abuse category was less reliable than the dependence category (Langenbucher, Labouvie, & Morgenstern, 1996) and that the abuse and dependence categories were not necessarily hierarchical (Schuckit, Smith, Danko, Bucholz, & Reich, 2001; Schuckit et al., 2005), these categories were removed. Instead, there is now a single substance use disorder category with specifiers based on an unweighted symptom count. Two to three symptoms constitute a mild specifier, four to five symptoms suggest moderate severity, and six or more symptoms indicate a severe SUD. In the *DSM-IV*, a single symptom was needed for a substance abuse diagnosis, and three symptoms were needed for a substance dependence disorder. The new criteria are in high concordance with other internationally accepted diagnostic systems (most notably *ICD-10*). Finally, two criteria were changed: the symptom related to legal problems was removed and a craving symptom was added (Jones, Gill, & Ray, 2012; see also Denis, Fatséas, & Auriacombe, 2012; Hasin, Fenton, Beseler, Park, & Wall, 2012; Saha et al., 2012, for analyses related to the development of *DSM-5*).

Gambling disorder is the single non-substance-related addiction to be included in the *DSM-5* SUDs category, and its diagnostic criteria are largely overlapping with SUDs. Gambling was previously included as an impulse control disorder (pathological gambling), but research suggests there are certain commonalities between gambling disorders and SUDs and that this reclassification could potentially improve prevention and intervention efforts (Petry, 2006). Although Internet and sex addictions were considered, the *DSM-5* work groups did not believe that there was enough empirical evidence for these diagnoses to be included.

Clinical Subtyping for Substance Use Disorders

One concern with SUD diagnoses is the amount of diagnostic heterogeneity. To resolve this problem, and to approach a greater level of specificity, a variety of clinical typologies, particularly for individuals with alcohol use disorders, has been proposed (Epstein, Labouvie, McCrady, Jensen, & Hayaki, 2002). These include unidimensional and multidimensional typologies.

Clinical subtyping began as early as 1850. Babor (1996) has indicated that during the "prescientific era" clinicians used their clinical experiences and intuition to subdivide individuals with alcohol use disorders into a variety of typologies. Babor and Lauerman (1986) reviewed the literature and found 39 different classifications proffered during that era, none of which had an empirical foundation nor was investigated empirically. Bowman and Jellinek (1941) consolidated them into a more meaningful, parsimonious typology: steady versus intermittent drinkers, with subtypes within each of exogenous (external causes) versus endogenous (internal causes). Jellinek (1960) later reformulated these subtypes into what he called *species*: alpha, beta, gamma, delta, and epsilon. Of these, Jellinek focused most on delta and gamma subtypes as he considered these to be most prevalent. The primary differences in these subtypes were etiological ("delta alcoholics" were more socially and economically focused whereas "gamma alcoholics" were more psychologically at risk) and behavioral ("delta alcoholics" could not abstain whereas "gamma alcoholics" had loss of control when drinking). Babor (1996) pointed out that although Jellinek's species-like typology gained a lot of popularity, it still lacked empirical validation and support.

Jellinek's work later spurred others to seek more empirically supported systems. A common typological distinction is based on family history. Individuals with a history of alcoholism in a first-degree relative generally have an earlier age of onset to drinking and a faster progression to alcoholism than individuals without a family history (e.g., Frances, Timm, & Bucky, 1980). Another unidimensional typology is based on concurrent psychopathology, with a common distinction between alcoholics with or without antisocial personality disorder (ASPD). The co-occurrence of ASPD is similarly associated with earlier age of onset and faster progression to alcoholism (e.g., Parella & Filstead, 1988).

A variety of multidimensional typologies have also been proffered. One prominent example is Cloninger's neurobiological model, which differentiates between two genetically driven subtypes, simply termed Type 1 and Type 2. Cloninger, Bohman, and Sigvardsson (1981) developed this model on the basis of data from an all-male Swedish adoptee sample, and it was, therefore, one of the first data-driven typologies. Type 1 alcoholics are characterized as having a later onset of alcohol-related problems (after age 25) and more psychological (as opposed to physiological) dependence, and as experiencing guilt associated with their use. Type 2 alcoholics by contrast have an earlier onset of alcohol-related problems and often have more extensive behavioral problems associated with their use, this type is also more severe and is associated with a positive family history for alcoholism. Cloninger's subtypes were limited to male alcoholics, although they have been reasonably replicated in females (Glenn & Nixon, 1991).

Babor, Hofmann, DelBoca, and Hesselbrock (1992) proposed a second multidimensional model: Type A and Type B alcoholics. The Type A/B dichotomy is based on 17 different characteristics of alcoholics, covering genetic, biological, psychological, and sociocultural aspects. These characteristics included family history of dependence, age of onset, and severity of dependence. Type A was similar to Cloninger's Type 1, with a later onset of alcohol dependence, fewer problems in childhood, and less psychopathology. Type B was similar to Cloninger's Type 2, with an earlier onset of alcohol dependence, more severe problems in childhood (particularly conduct disorder), greater levels of psychopathology, and is more severe and associated with more chronic consequences and poor treatment outcomes. The Type A/B typology has been replicated in both male and female alcoholics as well as across cultural groups (e.g., Hesselbrock, Hesselbrock, & Segal, 2000; Schuckit, Anthenelli, Bucholz, Hesselbrock, & Tipp, 1995).

Using data from a large, nationally representative sample, Moss, Chen, and Yi (2007) sought to empirically derive clinical subtypes of respondents with alcohol-dependence. Five clusters were identified. The "Young Adult Subtype" was the most prevalent cluster and was characterized by relatively young age ($M = 24.5$ years), early onset of dependence ($M = 19.5$ years), low probability of ASPD, and moderate probability of family history of alcohol dependence. The "Functional Subtype" was characterized by older age ($M = 41$ years), later initiation of drinking ($M = 18.5$ years), and later dependence onset ($M = 37$ years), as well as low probability of ASPD and moderate probability of family history. The "Intermediate Familial Subtype" was characterized by older age ($M = 37$ years), age of onset of drinking at about 17, and onset of dependence around 32; these individuals had a moderately elevated risk of ASPD and an elevated risk of family history. The "Young Antisocial Subtype" was characterized by young age ($M = 26.4$ years), onset of drinking around 15.5 years, and onset of dependence around 18.4 years; these individuals had the highest probability of ASPD and an elevated probability of family history. Finally, the "Chronic Severe Subtype" was the least prevalent of the five clusters and was characterized by older age ($M = 37.8$ years), with onset of drinking around 16 years old, and onset of dependence around 29 years old; individuals in this subtype had an elevated probability of ASPD and the highest probability of family history.

Few typology systems have been developed outside of the alcohol arena. One widely accepted distinction pertains to smokers. Shiffman, Kassel, Paty, and Gnys (1994) found differences in smokers they labeled as regular smokers versus "chippers." The subtypes are based both on quantity of cigarettes smoked and on reported motivation for smoking. Chippers are distinct from regular smokers as they typically smoke five or fewer cigarettes a day and do not meet *DSM-IV* criteria for nicotine dependence. Regular smokers report more habitual and addictive motives whereas chippers are mostly socially motivated to smoke.

All of the typologies described here are interesting from a clinical and a research standpoint, and although no system yet developed has been refined enough to allow for true clinical or research utility, some research suggests that subtype is a moderator of pharmacological treatment of alcohol dependence (Pettinati et al., 2000; Kranzler, Feinn, Armeli, & Tennen, 2012). It is the hope that eventually treatments might be oriented toward a specific subtype, designed to intervene at different points in the progression of an SUD, or geared toward more preventative measures in individuals who are not yet symptomatic but evidence various "characteristics" of a known subtype.

Risk Factors for Addictive Disorders

Family History

Researchers have examined the relationship between probands with SUDs and the incidence of these disorders in their relatives. The familial link for alcohol use disorders is widely established in the research literature (e.g., Merikangas, 1990; Prescott & Kendler, 1999), and several studies have found a potentially stronger heritability for illicit drug use than for alcohol (e.g., Jang, Livesley, & Vernon, 1995). Merikangas and colleagues (1998) found an "8-fold increased risk of drug disorders among relatives of probands with drug disorders across a wide range of specific substances, including opiates, cocaine, cannabis, and sedatives, compared with that of relatives of controls" (p. 977).

Disentangling the heritability of SUDs remains a challenge. The well-documented familial association can be attributable to both genetic and environmental factors. The genetic factors may be metabolic, physiological, and/or psychological, whereas the environmental factors may be specific (e.g., increased exposure to substances) or general (i.e., environment that creates global risk factors for psychiatric disorders). Researchers have determined via twin studies that the genetic risks for SUDs are largely nonspecific (Kendler, Jacobson, Prescott, & Neale, 2003). However, there are some unique family determinants that are critical in predicting adolescents who will develop SUDs, such as family environment, and in particular, exposure to parental SUDs (Biederman, Faraone, Monuteaux, & Feighner, 2000). Additionally, research suggests that family history of drug and alcohol dependence is associated with a more recurrent course of the respective disorders, greater impairment, and greater service utilization (Milne et al., 2009).

Family history of problem gambling is a risk factor for gambling behavior and pathological gambling, especially for males (Black, Monahan, Temkit, & Shaw, 2006; King, Abrams, & Wilkinson, 2010). As with SUDs, the relations between genetics and environmental influences is complex. A twin study found that genetic factors explained significant variance (with the remainder being explained by nonshared environment) in gambling behaviors for men, but not for women, for whom nonshared and shared environments were the greatest predictors of gambling (Beaver et al., 2010). A preliminary meta-analysis reported weak heritability findings for problem gambling, however, the impact of family history may be greater for individuals with more severe gambling problems (Walters, 2001).

Level of Response to Alcohol

One mechanism by which heredity influences an individual's propensity to develop an alcohol use disorder is by influencing his or her level of response to alcohol. Responsivity has been evaluated by giving a challenge dose of alcohol and assessing body sway and subjective perception of alcohol effects, two correlated indicators of intoxication. Lower response to alcohol, or the need for a higher number of drinks for an effect, has been associated with family history of alcoholism (Schuckit, 1985; Schuckit & Gold, 1988), development of tolerance (the need for increased amounts to achieve the desired effect or a diminished effect in response to the same amounts) to alcohol (Lipscomb, Carpenter, & Nathan, 1979; Nathan, & Lipscomb, 1979), and a fourfold greater likelihood of future alcohol dependence (Schuckit, 1994a). Level of response to alcohol appears to be a unique predictor of alcohol use disorders above and beyond a variety of other risk factors (Trim, Schuckit, & Smith, 2009) and is a robust predictor in both young and middle-aged groups (Schuckit, Smith, Anderson, & Brown, 2004; Schuckit et al., 2012). Notably, level of response to alcohol was not related to any other psychiatric diagnosis (including other SUDs) in the 10 years following the initial alcohol challenge (Schuckit, 1994a). Level of response to alcohol also appears to be genetically mediated (Heath et al., 1999; Hinckers et al., 2006). Schuckit and Smith (2000) have asserted, though, that level of response is only one mechanism in the context of a variety of other variables (e.g., personality) that help account for one's risk to develop an alcohol use disorder.

Neurophysiological Factors: Event-Related Potentials

Chronic heavy alcohol consumption leads to deleterious effects on the brain and central nervous system. Event-related potentials (ERPs) represent the relationship between behavioral performance and cerebral activity, assessed electroencephalographically. A particularly fruitful area of research has involved the P300 component of ERPs, commonly assessed utilizing a detection task for infrequent stimuli in a series of regular stimuli. A number of studies have yielded evidence for heritability of the P300 ERP (e.g., Katsanis, Iacono, McGue, & Carlson, 1997; O'Connor, Morzorati, Christian, & Li, 1994). Reduced amplitude and delayed latency for the P300 ERP have been detected in alcoholic individuals (Hansenne, 2006) as well as in cocaine-dependent and opioid-dependent individuals (Moeller et al., 2004; Singh, Basu, Kohli, & Prabhakar, 2009). Moreover, this pattern has also been demonstrated in non-alcohol-dependent children, adolescents, and adults with alcohol-dependent relatives (e.g., Polich, Pollock, & Bloom, 1994; van der Stelt, Gunning, Snel, & Kok, 1998). These findings are generally interpreted as reflecting memory, attention, and inhibition disturbances. As a consequence of this body of research, reduced P300

amplitude has come to be considered a marker of heightened risk for development of alcohol dependence. Research has also identified amplitude deficits for the N400 component, which is related to semantic processing, among individuals with alcohol dependence (Porjesz et al., 2002) and among children of individuals with alcohol dependence (Roopesh et al., 2009), suggesting that the N400 component may also serve as a risk indicator for the development of an alcohol use disorder.

Alcohol and Drug Expectancies

A highly productive area of research on risk factors for substance use has focused on *expectancies*, defined as beliefs about the anticipated effects of alcohol or other substance use. Individuals develop beliefs about the effects of substance use on social, affective, cognitive, and motor functioning and self-report questionnaires are commonly used to assess these expectancies (e.g., Brown, Christiansen, & Goldman, 1987; Leigh & Stacy, 1993). Expectations about the effects of alcohol and other substances are learned in part from family, peer, and media influences (e.g., Brown, Creamer, & Stetson, 1987; Brown, Tate, Vik, Haas, & Aarons, 1999) even prior to personal use of a given substance. Alcohol expectancies have been shown to predict initiation, progression, and problem use, as well as posttreatment relapse (e.g., Brown, Goldman, & Christiansen, 1985; Connors, Tarbox, & Faillace, 1993; Smith, Goldman, Greenbaum, & Christiansen, 1995), with elevated risk associated with expectations that alcohol use will have positive effects.

Although less extensively studied than alcohol, expectancy measures have also been developed for other substances (Alfonso & Dunn, 2007; Jaffe & Kilbey, 1994; Schafer & Brown, 1991). Marijuana expectancies are similar to alcohol expectancies, with common domains (e.g., social and sexual facilitation, tension reduction, cognitive and behavioral impairment). Consistent with the different pharmacological effects of stimulants, cocaine expectancies include unique domains (e.g., anxiety, increased energy or arousal). Unlike many risk factors, expectancies may be modifiable. Interventions can utilize information about individual's expectancies (e.g., expectations of tension reduction or social facilitation) to challenge expectancies and develop alternative skills for achieving the desired effects.

Cognitive Distortions and Gambling

Significant research has examined the role of cognitive distortions in the development and maintenance of pathological gambling (Fortune & Goodie, 2012). One such distortion is the gambler's fallacy, which is the belief that despite the random nature of a process a certain outcome can be expected (e.g., if a roulette ball has landed on black five times then it will land on red on the following turn). This cognitive bias is viewed as one of the causes of "chasing losses" (a symptom of pathological gambling). Another distortion is overconfidence about one's ability, which is not based on objective reality and this overconfidence has been found to be related to pathological gambling across multiple studies (Goodie, 2005; Lakey, Goodie, Lance, Stinchfield, & Winters, 2007). Illusory correlations, or superstitions, are another distortion; pathological gamblers often believe that their personal luck will impact the outcome of gambling (Petry, 2004). Heavy gamblers also are more likely to remember their wins rather than their losses, a phenomenon referred to as "interpretive control" (Toneatto, Blitz-Miller, Calderwood, Dragonetti, & Tsanos, 1997). Finally, the illusion of control bias is also highly related to pathological gambling, in that pathological gamblers, compared to controls, are less able to distinguish between situations in which they have control and those in which they have no control (Goodie, 2005). Although these types of cognitive distortions are not specific to gambling, they play a role in its initiation and continuation.

Peer Influences

The influence of peers on substance use during adolescence is clear from decades of research (e.g., Newcomb, & Bentler, 1986; Shoal, Gudonis, Giancola, & Tarter, 2007; Wills, Resko, Ainette, & Mendoza, 2004); however, not all peer influences are equal, as peers perceived as more similar exert a greater impact (Vik, Grizzle, & Brown, 1992). Greater peer involvement with substances, higher perceptions of peer use, and greater perceived peer acceptance of substance use are risk factors for adolescent substance involvement (Epstein & Botvin, 2002). Additionally, peers may also influence expectancies about positive reinforcement from substance use and perceptions of negative attitudes toward school by peers have been linked to

earlier onset of cigarette and marijuana use among adolescents (Bryant & Zimmerman, 2002). Social context can exert powerful effects, with increased alcohol consumption occurring in adolescents in the presence of other adolescents who are drinking (Curran, Stice, & Chassin, 1997) and greater exposure to peer use leading to adoption of values and beliefs that foster a substance use lifestyle (Tapert, Stewart, & Brown, 1999). Socializing with substance-using peers provides greater access to substances and environments supportive of risky and deviant behaviors (Brown, Vik, & Creamer, 1989). Such peer connection mediates the influence of parental alcoholism, family conflict, and socioeconomic adversity on adolescent substance abuse (e.g., Fergusson & Horwood, 1999). More broadly, peer delinquency and positive attitudes about delinquency have also been associated with substance use in adolescents (e.g., Chassin, Pillow, Curran, Moline, & Barrera, 1993) and increased exposure to stressful situations (Tate, Patterson, Nagel, Anderson, & Brown, 2007).

Gender Differences in Addictive Disorders

Although men and women share commonalities in substance use and SUDs, important differences exist. Men consume greater quantities and abuse substances at higher rates than women, but this gender gap is narrowing for both alcohol and illicit drugs (e.g., Nelson, Heath, & Kessler, 1998).

A number of studies provide evidence of accelerated development of alcohol problems and dependence in women when compared to men, referred to as *telescoping* (e.g., Randall et al., 1999; Wojnar, Wasilewski, Matsumoto, & Cedro, 1997). Specifically, at similar levels of alcohol consumption, women experience problems faster, meet criteria for an alcohol use disorder in a shorter time, and present for treatment earlier. Findings of accelerated progression for women for other substances are limited but have been documented for cannabis and opiates (Hernandez-Avila, Rounsaville, & Kranzler, 2004; Kosten, Rounsaville, & Kleber, 1985).

Research shows that women are more vulnerable to many physical consequences of alcohol use and abuse. Higher blood alcohol concentrations occur in women after consumption of equivalent amounts of alcohol because of differences in metabolism of alcohol in both the stomach and liver and differences in body water. These differences in absorption and metabolism of alcohol have led to lower standards for the definition of moderate and heavy drinking for women compared to men. Women develop liver disease more quickly than men and have higher rates of liver-related mortality (Gavaler & Arria, 1995; Hall, 1995), and they may also experience more alcohol-induced brain damage (Hommer, Momenan, Kaiser, & Rawlings, 2001; Mann et al., 2005). Increased risk of breast cancer has also been associated with moderate to heavy alcohol consumption in numerous studies (Chen, Rosner, Hankinson, Colditz, & Willett, 2011; Singletary & Gapstur, 2001).

Among the most troubling physical impacts involving women are the teratogenic effects of substances. Among children born to women consuming significant amounts of alcohol during pregnancy, fetal alcohol syndrome (FAS) involves physical (facial dysmorphology and small stature) and neuropsychological (mental retardation and attention impairment) effects that continue throughout life. Less severe fetal alcohol effects (FAE) also occur with lower levels of alcohol consumption. In addition to alcohol, other substances have documented teratogenic effects. Use of cocaine during pregnancy is associated with slow fetal growth, low birth weight, early labor, spontaneous abortion, and sudden infant death syndrome (Fox, 1994; Zuckerman et al., 1989). Infants born to mothers who are opiate dependent are also addicted, requiring treatment for withdrawal; they are also more likely to be premature, experience respiratory illness, and be underweight, and they have an increased mortality risk (Bolton, 1983; Ostrea & Chavez, 1979). Women who smoke cigarettes or abuse alcohol or drugs also experience increased rates of other types of gynecologic and obstetric problems (Collins, 1993).

In addition to physical effects, alcohol-abusing women experience more psychiatric comorbidity than men (Helzer, Burnham, & McEvoy, 1991). Women who abuse substances meet criteria for depression and anxiety disorders more frequently than their male counterparts, who are more likely to meet criteria for ASPD (Hesselbrock & Hesselbrock, 1993). Finally, relationships between victimization and substance use have been documented. Women with childhood histories or victimization (physical, sexual, or neglect) are more likely to develop alcohol and drug problems (Widom, Ireland, & Glynn, 1995; Wilsnack, Vogeltanz, Klassen, & Harris, 1997).

There are also significant gender differences in gambling behaviors and related problems. As early as adolescence, boys report more gambling and experience a greater number of gambling-related problems than girls. For both female and male adolescents, gambling is related to higher alcohol use and rates of alcohol use disorders, but only for girls is gambling related to depression, suggesting more psychiatric problems for adolescent female gamblers (Desai, Maciejewski, Pantalon, & Potenza, 2005). A national survey of gambling found that men and women were equally likely to gamble in the past year but that men gamble more frequently and have greater wins and losses (Welte, Barnes, Wieczorek, Tidwell, & Parker, 2002). However, some research suggests that, similar to the closing gender gap for alcohol use, an increasing number of women are gambling and suffering from problems related to their gambling. Additionally, female pathological gamblers appear to be at greater risk for mood and anxiety disorders such as depression, dysthymia, and panic disorder whereas male pathological gamblers are at greater risk for SUDs (Desai & Potenza, 2008; Wenzel & Dahl, 2009).

Risks Associated with Addictive Disorders

Interpersonal Aggression and Violence

Research has demonstrated a clear link between interpersonal aggression and substance use involvement; individuals who abuse a variety of intoxicating substances are more likely to perpetrate or be the victim of interpersonal aggression (e.g., Bushman, & Cooper, 1990; Chermack & Giancola, 1997). Friedman, Kramer, Kreisher, and Granick (1996) termed substance use an "interactionist risk factor" in association with violence, such that substance use does not directly lead to violence or criminal behavior but may amplify a variety of other factors to create a high-risk situation for committing crimes or engaging in violent acts (p. 379). Furthermore, it is unclear whether it is the acute or chronic effects of substance use that lead to aggressive behaviors. Giancola (2000) proffered a conceptual framework, pointing to executive functioning as both a mediator and a moderator of alcohol-related aggression. Specifically, alcohol interferes acutely with executive functioning, and drinking is more likely to lead to aggressive behaviors in individuals with low executive functioning.

Several substances have been associated with violence, those with the most evidence are alcohol, cocaine/crack, and amphetamines. A large body of research has demonstrated an association between alcohol use and a variety of levels of aggressive behavior, including verbal aggression (e.g., O'Farrell, Murphy, Neavins, & Van Hutton, 2000), familial/marital aggression including child abuse (e.g., Caetano, Schafer, & Cunradi, 2001; Keller, El-Sheikh, Keiley, & Liao, 2009), sexual aggression (Davis, Morris, George, Martell, & Heiman, J., 2006; Ramisetty-Mikler, Caetano, & McGrath, 2007), homicide (Klatsky & Armstrong, 1993), and suicide (Brent, Perper, & Allman, 1987; Kerr, Subbaraman, & Ye, 2011). Roizen (1993) demonstrated that perpetrators had consumed alcohol in 28% to 86% of homicide cases and 30% to 70% of suicide attempts. Experimental paradigms have also shown that acute alcohol administration leads to more aggressive behavior across a variety of situations (Giancola & Chermack, 1998; Hoaken, Assaad, & Pihl, 1998).

Amphetamine and cocaine use are related to interpersonal aggression, although the hypothesized mechanisms differ. Acute amphetamine intoxication frequently leads to aggressive behavior, whereas prolonged amphetamine use results in a psychotic-like disorder, which in turn leads to aggressive behavior (Baker & Dawe, 2005). Cocaine intoxication is associated with increased paranoia and irritability, often leading to interpersonal aggression (Murray et al., 2003).

Sexual Behavior

Alcohol and drug use also have been shown to result in sexual dysfunction (O'Farrell, Choquette, Cutter, & Birchler, 1997; Simons & Carey, 2001). In a community epidemiological sample of over 3,000 adults, Johnson, Phelps, and Cottler (2004) found that the most common sexual dysfunction associated with alcohol and marijuana use was anorgasmia, whereas other illicit drug use resulted in painful sex and reduced sexual pleasure. However, neither drugs nor alcohol was associated with reduced sex drive. The mechanism for the association between chronic substance use and sexual dysfunction is thought to be hormonal (Bannister & Lowosky, 1987; Van Thiel et al., 1980). These effects likely abate after prolonged periods of abstinence (Schiavi, Stimmel, Mandeli, & White, 1995).

In addition to sexual dysfunction resulting from substance use, a common problem is the spread of sexually transmitted diseases resulting from increased sexual risk-taking, including but not limited to lack of condom use (Koopman, Rosario, & Rotheram-Borus, 1994; Leichliter, Williams, & Bland, 2004). In contrast, one study, using a diary method, found that alcohol consumption prior to sex was not predictive of condom use; individuals followed their typical patterns of condom use or nonuse when intoxicated (Leigh et al., 2008). Thus, substance users may demonstrate low rates of condom use in general, but this may not be caused specifically by intoxication. Substance-related risky sexual behavior is particularly salient in adolescent populations and substance use has been associated with an earlier onset of sexual activity (Bentler & Newcomb, 1986). The relationship between substance use and sexual risk-taking is appreciably stronger in white than in black adolescents (Cooper, Peirce, & Huselid, 1994).

Neurocognitive Impairment

Chronic, sustained substance use often results in significant cognitive impairment. The etiology of such impairment is thought to involve interactions among a variety of factors, including neurotoxicity, malnutrition, and trauma, and varies depending on the substance abused (Lundqvist, 2005).

Although impairments may remediate following cessation of use (Zinn, Stein, & Swartzwelder, 2004), abstinence successfully diminishes the cognitive impairment in only a portion of the cases. Rourke and Løberg (1996) found that 45% of individuals with alcohol-dependence still evidenced cognitive impairment after 3 weeks of sustained abstinence; 15% were still impaired at a year of abstinence. Methamphetamine-dependent individuals also demonstrated impairments during the first 3 weeks of abstinence (Kalechstein, Newton, & Green, 2003). A body of research supports that this may be a result of permanent frontal lobe damage (Dao-Castellana et al., 1998; Moselhy, Georgiou, & Kahn, 2001). Adolescent substance use is hypothesized to interfere with normal brain development, causing a variety of cognitive impairments (Hanson, Medina, Padula, Tapert, & Brown, 2011; Tapert & Brown, 1999), for example, one study found that during a 3-week period of abstinence from marijuana, adolescents' attention deficits persisted (Hanson, Winward, Schweinsburg, Medina, Brown, & Tapert, 2010).

Findings related to cocaine use are similar. O'Malley, Adamse, Heaton, and Gawin (1992) found that 50% of individuals with cocaine use disorder were cognitively impaired, compared to 15% of the control subjects, and severity of the impairment was associated with recency of cocaine use. Jovanovski, Erb, and Zakzanis (2005) conducted a meta-analysis of 15 studies and found that cocaine use had its most substantial cognitive effects on attention and visual and working memory. The results for executive functioning tests across studies were mixed, but overall researchers consistently found deficits in the areas of the brain (i.e., anterior cingulated gyrus and orbitofrontal cortex) that control both attention and executive functioning. Chronic cannabis use has a similar deleterious effect on both attentional processes and executive functioning, whereas opiates may more specifically affect impulse control (Lundqvist, 2005).

Mental Health Comorbidity and Addictive Disorders

Individuals with SUDs experience high levels of psychiatric comorbidity as documented by numerous large-scale epidemiological studies (Grant et al., 2004; Kessler, Crum, Warner, & Nelson, 1997). Explanations for the co-occurrence include the following: (a) base rates of common psychiatric disorders naturally result in co-occurrence (Schuckit, 1994b); (b) comorbidity may increase the likelihood of seeking treatment or being referred to treatment (Schuckit, 1994b); (c) substance use may precipitate disorders directly (Sato, 1992) or exacerbate subthreshold symptoms to diagnostic levels (Negrete, 1989); (d) common genetic factors exist (e.g., Fu et al., 2002; Prescott, Aggen, & Kendler, 2000); and (e) shared environmental risk factors exist (e.g., trauma; childhood abuse or neglect, life stress). Finally, substance intoxication and withdrawal states can resemble psychiatric symptoms, particularly depression, anxiety, and psychotic symptoms (Bacon, Granholm, & Withers, 1998; Schuckit, 1994b).

Comorbidity complicates diagnosis, treatment, and clinical course. Difficulties arise in differentiating psychiatric symptoms that are independent of substance use from those that are substance induced. Constructing a time line for a patient's life that incorporates dates of abstinence and ages when substance use and other mental health symptoms occurred can clarify whether symptoms persist during periods of abstinence (Bacon et al., 1998; Schuckit, 1994b). In addition to diagnostic complications, substance use can diminish the effectiveness of treatment efforts. Pharmacotherapy for comorbid disorders can be compromised, as substance use may decrease medication adherence, cause serious side effects, and potentiate some psychotropic medications increasing potential for overdose (Catz, Heckman, Kochman, & DiMarco, 2001; National Institute on Alcohol Abuse and Alcoholism [NIAAA], 2005). Additionally, alcohol or substance use is associated with increases in suicidal thoughts and attempts, necessitating a focus on crisis management rather than other therapeutic goals (e.g., Claassen et al., 2007; Goldstein & Levitt, 2006; Shen et al., 2006).

Mood Disorders

Symptoms of major depressive disorder, dysthymic disorder, and bipolar disorder frequently co-occur with SUDs. The comorbidity of mood disorders and SUDs begins early, among persons with SUDs who are ages 11 to 17 years, increased risk of mood disorders has been documented across substance categories (alcohol, marijuana, other; Roberts, Roberts, & Xing, 2007). Cocaine and amphetamine withdrawal often include depression symptoms that persist beyond the acute withdrawal phase, and alcohol use disorders are commonly accompanied by depressive symptoms. Many adults with SUDs initiating addiction treatment report clinical levels of depression, although these symptoms remit for many following weeks or months of abstinence (Brown & Schuckit, 1988; Brown et al., 1998). To ascertain the prevalence of comorbid alcohol dependence and major depression independent of alcohol effects, researchers using data from a national epidemiological survey compared the prevalence of a current major depression diagnosis (past year) among adults who were formerly alcohol dependent to that of those without a history of alcohol dependence. A history of alcohol dependence (more than a year prior) increased the risk of current major depressive disorder 4.2 times (Hasin & Grant, 2002), supporting a strong association between these two disorders that is not solely a result of intoxication or withdrawal states. In the same national survey (undertaken in 2001–2002) assessing 12-month prevalence, the odds of having an independent mood disorder were increased over fourfold (OR = 4.5) for adults with any substance dependence diagnosis relative to adults without substance dependence (Grant et al., 2004). Lifetime prevalence of depressive disorders among adults with cocaine use disorders in research treatment samples range up to 50% (e.g., Carroll, Rounsaville, Gordon, & Nich, 1994). There is also an elevated comorbidity between pathological gambling and mood disorders. Specifically, a meta-analysis found that 37% of individuals with a gambling disorder also experienced a mood disorder (Lorains, Cowlishaw, & Thomas, 2011).

Anxiety Disorders

In contrast to the clear association between mood disorders and SUDs, the relationship is less clear for anxiety disorders. Adding to the complexity of evaluating research findings, studies have differed with respect to the disorders that were included under the umbrella of anxiety.

The tension reduction hypothesis (TRH) proposed that alcohol is consumed for its ability to reduce tension and anxiety, suggesting an association between anxiety and alcohol use disorders that has intuitive anecdotal appeal. However, empirical studies with alcohol-dependent samples have not consistently supported this conceptualization (e.g., Langenbucher, & Nathan, 1990). In an extensive review of prevalence, family history, and disorder onset, Schuckit and Hesselbrock (1994) concluded that anxiety disorders (panic disorder, agoraphobia, obsessive-compulsive disorder, social phobia, and generalized anxiety disorder) did not occur at higher than general-population rates when "temporary, but at times severe, substance-induced anxiety syndromes" were excluded. In a sample of youth aged 11 to 17 years, substance dependence was associated with increased likelihood of an anxiety disorder (OR = 2.2, 95% CI = 1.2–4.3), but after controlling for other comorbid disorders,

the relationship was not significant (OR = 1.0, 95% CI = 0.4–2.8; Roberts et al., 2007). In an adult sample, Schuckit and colleagues (1997) reported an increased risk of panic disorder and social phobia disorders (but not agoraphobia or obsessive-compulsive disorders) among alcohol-dependent adults compared to controls. The lifetime rate for independent anxiety disorders (agoraphobia, panic disorder, obsessive-compulsive disorder, and social phobia) was significantly higher for participants with alcohol-dependence (9.4%) than for controls (3.7%). A nationally representative epidemiological study reported a lifetime prevalence of 19.4% for any anxiety disorder (agoraphobia, social phobia, simple phobia, panic disorder, obsessive-compulsive disorder) among adults with alcohol dependence and 28.3% among adults with other drug dependence compared to 14.6% in this combined community and institutional sample (Regier et al., 1990). In a large study including data from Canada, Germany, Mexico, the Netherlands, and the United States, 32% of individuals with alcohol dependence and 35% of those with drug dependence met criteria for an anxiety disorder (generalized anxiety disorder, panic disorder, and phobic disorders were combined; Merikangas et al., 1998). Across countries, the onset of anxiety disorders preceded the onset of the alcohol use disorder for the majority of participants. A large, nationally representative study reported increased odds of 2.8 for any independent anxiety disorder (panic disorder with and without agoraphobia, social phobia, specific phobia, generalized anxiety disorder) in adults with any substance dependence diagnosis (Grant et al., 2004). Among pathological gamblers, 37% experienced a co-occurring anxiety disorder (Lorains et al., 2011).

Posttraumatic stress disorder (PTSD) has received substantial research and clinical attention in recent years but was not included in the anxiety disorders in the preceding studies. As many as 89% of patients with an SUD report they have experienced a traumatic event in their lifetime (Farley, Golding, Young, Mulligan, & Minkoff, 2004) and the rate of PTSD among individuals in addiction treatment has been reported to be 30% to 59% (Stewart, Conrod, Samoluk, Pihl, & Dongier, 2000). Studies document that among men with PTSD, alcohol use disorders are the most commonly occurring comorbid disorder, with other SUDs also being very prevalent.

Among women with PTSD, depression and other anxiety disorders are most common, followed by alcohol use disorders (e.g., Kessler, Sonnega, Bromet, Hughes, & Nelson, 1995; Kulka et al., 1990). Individuals with PTSD may use substances in self-medication efforts to relieve PTSD symptoms, and over time PTSD symptoms may come to trigger cravings for alcohol and drugs (Chilcoat & Breslau, 1998; Jacobsen, Southwick, & Kosten, 2001). Research findings have been mixed on this conceptualization of the relations between substances and PTSD (e.g., Bremner, Southwick, Darnell, & Charney, 1996; Freeman & Kimbrell, 2004).

Schizophrenia and Other Psychoses

Among individuals with schizophrenia, between 40% and 50% also meet criteria for one or more SUDs (e.g., Blanchard, Brown, Horan, & Sherwood, 2000; Regier et al., 1990). Comorbidity rates are slightly lower for women but substantially higher (80% to 90%) in male homeless and incarcerated samples. A nationally representative epidemiological study sampling both community and institutional populations found individuals with schizophrenia had 4.6 times the odds of having an SUD compared to the general population (Regier et al., 1990). SUDs among those diagnosed with schizophrenia take a heavy toll, with higher rates of homelessness, criminal offenses, medical problems, suicide, poorer treatment compliance, and rehospitalization when compared to patients with schizophrenia without SUDs (Blanchard et al., 2000; Dixon, 1999). Moreover, individuals with schizophrenia experience more difficulty using prevalent self-help substance treatment resources, such as Alcoholics Anonymous or Narcotics Anonymous (Noordsy, Schwab, Fox, & Drake, 1996).

Eating Disorders

Co-occurrence of SUDs and eating disorders has been observed in both clinical and population samples (Holderness, Brooks-Gunn, & Warren, 1994; Wolfe & Maisto, 2000). Generally, individuals who primarily restrict intake (anorexia nervosa, restricting type) have lower rates of SUDs than patients with other types of eating disorders (bulimia nervosa and anorexia nervosa, binge-eating/purging type). A review of mortality associated with psychiatric disorders observed the highest risk of premature death from both natural and unnatural causes in the SUDs and eating disorders (Harris & Barraclough, 1998), and co-occurrence of these disorders may place patients at even higher risk (Keel et al., 2003). One study sought to explain the relation between substance dependence and eating disorders and found that acting rashly when distressed (negative urgency) was more likely among a group of eating-disordered women than among control women. Additionally, individuals with comorbid SUD and eating disorders reported high levels of positive expectancies for both alcohol and eating/dieting and these findings have been replicated with young girls (Fischer, Settles, Collins, Gunn, & Smith, 2012).

Attention-Deficit/Hyperactivity Disorder (ADHD)

High rates of comorbidity for ADHD and SUDs have been documented in numerous studies (e.g., Clure et al., 1999; Ohlmeier et al., 2007); however, questions remain about the association between these disorders. Based on data from a survey of over 4,000 youths aged 11 to 17, Roberts and colleagues (2007) found no increase in odds of ADHD among youth with SUDs. Findings were the same after adjusting for other comorbid non-substance-related disorders. A recent study of childhood risk factors found that ADHD was predictive of earlier initiation of alcohol use but was not predictive of time from first drink to onset of alcohol dependence (Sartor, Lynskey, Heath, Jacob, & True, 2007). In contrast, Wilens, Biederman, Mick, Faraone, and Spencer (1997) found ADHD was associated with earlier onset of SUDs independent of other psychiatric disorders and ADHD has been shown to increase the likelihood of nicotine dependence (Ohlmeier et al., 2007; Wilens, 2004). A recent meta-analysis examined longitudinal studies that followed children with and without ADHD into adolescence and adulthood, and children with ADHD were more likely to use and develop nicotine, alcohol, marijuana, and cocaine use disorders (Lee, Humphreys, Flory, Liu, & Glass, 2011). However, questions remain about whether it is ADHD specifically or the presence of other disorders that frequently accompany the diagnosis (mood, anxiety, externalizing disorders) that increases risk for development of SUDs.

Recent research suggests that the hyperactivity and impulsivity components of ADHD pose more risk for substance use problems than does the inattention component (Elkins, McGue, & Iacono, 2007). Given that ADHD symptoms first appear during childhood, early identification and treatment for ADHD may alter progression of substance use and problems that typically occurs later.

Conduct Disorder (CD) and Antisocial Personality Disorder (ASPD)

Extensive research has verified a relationship between SUDs and CD and ASPD. A large prospective twin study assessed CD at age 11 and found an increased risk of initiating tobacco, alcohol, and illicit drug use by age 14 for adolescents with CD (Elkins et al., 2007). A diagnosis of CD by 14 years of age quadrupled the odds of nicotine dependence and more than quintupled the odds of alcohol or cannabis dependence by age 18 (Elkins et al., 2007). Other studies have found similar results, with CD predicting both early alcohol initiation and transition to alcohol dependence (e.g., Pardini, White, Stouthamer-Loeber, 2007; Sartor et al., 2007). Additionally, it appears that among these adolescents, gambling occurs as one of several behavioral problems (Barnes, Welte, Hoffman, & Tidwell, 2011; Welte, Barnes, Tidwell, & Hoffman, 2009). ASPD is characterized by continuation into adulthood of CD problems, and high rates of comorbidity with SUDs have also been observed. In a nationally representative epidemiological study, the lifetime prevalence of ASPD was 2.6% in the general sample, increasing to 14.3% among adults with alcohol dependence and 17.8% for adults with other drug dependence. Among adults with ASPD, 83.6% met criteria for an SUD (Regier et al., 1990). Among a sample of individuals presenting for treatment of pathological gambling, almost 17% met criteria for ASPD and gamblers with ASPD began gambling earlier and reported more severe gambling than those without ASPD (Pietrzak, & Petry, 2005).

Concluding Remarks

In this chapter, we have reviewed the available information on diagnosis, risk factors, associated psychopathology, and comorbidities for substance-related disorders. SUDs are a significant public health problem because of the associated health, social, and legal consequences related to these disorders. The variety of risk factors and comorbid disorders make SUDs multifaceted and complex, and they require the implementation of efficacious prevention and intervention strategies. In regard to assessment of individuals with SUDs, close attention should be paid to other potentially dangerous behaviors or risk factors, such as risky sexual behavior and interpersonal aggression and violence. Among individuals with gambling disorders, thorough assessment of other substance use is important, as a large number likely have comorbid SUDs. Given the high prevalence and frequent comorbidities, assessing for SUDs is paramount for treatment of any disorder. Developing a clear understanding of the relations between substance use and symptoms of other disorders is necessary for diagnosis and treatment planning. As SUDs are multiply determined, a careful assessment involving the aspects discussed in this chapter would enable more precise treatment recommendations.

Acknowledgment

Preparation of this chapter was supported in part by a NIAAA T32 training grant (5T32AA013525-08) to Jessica R. Skidmore, Ph.D.

References

Alfonso, J., & Dunn, M. E. (2007). Differences in the marijuana expectancies of adolescents in relation to marijuana use. *Substance Use & Misuse, 42,* 1009–1025.

Babor, T. F. (1996). The classification of alcoholics: Typology theories from the 19th century to the present. *Alcohol Health & Research World, 20,* 6–17.

Babor, T. F., Hofmann, M., DelBoca, F. K., & Hesselbrock, V. M. (1992). Types of alcoholics: I. evidence for an empirically derived typology based on indicators of vulnerability and severity. *Archives of General Psychiatry, 49,* 599–608.

Babor, T. F., & Lauerman, R. J. (1986). *Classification and forms of inebriety: Historical antecedents of alcoholic typologies.* New York: Plenum Press.

Bacon, A., Granholm, E., & Withers, N. (1998). Substance-induced psychosis. *Seminars in Clinical Neuropsychiatry, 3,* 70–79.

Baker, A., & Dawe, S. (2005). Amphetamine use and co-occurring psychological problems: Review of the literature and implications for treatment. *Australian Psychologist, 40,* 88–95.

Bannister, P., & Lowosky, M. S., (1987). Ethanol and hypogonadism. *Alcohol, 22,* 213–217.

Barnes, G. M., Welte, J. W., Hoffman, J. H., & Tidwell, M. O. (2011). The co-occurrence of gambling with substance use and conduct disorder among youth in the United States. *American Journal on Addictions, 20,* 166–173.

Beaver, K. M., Hoffman, T., Shields, R. T., Vaughn, M. G., DeLisi, M., & Wright, J. P. (2010). Gender differences in genetic and environmental influences on gambling: Results from a sample of twins from the national longitudinal study of adolescent health. *Addiction, 105,* 536–542.

Bentler, P. M., & Newcomb, M. D. (1986). Personality, sexual behavior, and drug use revealed through latent variable methods. *Clinical Psychology Review, 6,* 363–385.

Biederman, J., Faraone, S. V., Monuteaux, M. C., & Feighner, J. A. (2000). Patterns of alcohol and drug use in adolescents can be predicted by parental substance use disorders. *Pediatrics, 106,* 792–797.

Black, D. W., Monahan, P. O., Temkit, M., & Shaw, M. (2006). A family study of pathological gambling. *Psychiatry Research, 141,* 295–303.

Blanchard, J. J., Brown, S. A., Horan, W. P., & Sherwood, A. R. (2000). Substance use disorders in schizophrenia: Review, integration, and a proposed model. *Clinical Psychology Review, 20,* 207–234.

Bolton, P. J. (1983). Drugs of abuse. In D. F. Hawkins (Ed.), *Drugs and pregnancy: Human teratogenesis and related problems* (pp. 180–210). Edinburgh: Churchill Livingston.

Bowman, K. M., & Jellinek, E. M. (1941). Alcohol addiction and its treatment. *Quarterly Journal of Studies on Alcohol, 2,* 98–176.

Bremner, J. D., Southwick, S. M., Darnell, A., & Charney, D. S. (1996). Chronic PTSD in Vietnam combat veterans: Course of illness and substance abuse. *American Journal of Psychiatry, 153,* 369–375.

Brent, D., Perper, J., & Allman, C. (1987). Alcohol, firearms, and suicide among youth: Temporal trends in Allegheny County, Pennsylvania, 1960–1983. *Journal of the American Medical Association, 257,* 3369–3372.

Brown, R. A., Monti, P. M., Myers, M. G., Martin, R. A., Rivinus, T., Dubreuil, M. E., & Rohsenow, D. J. (1998). Depression among cocaine abusers in treatment: Relation to cocaine and alcohol use and treatment outcome. *American Journal of Psychiatry, 155,* 220–225.

Brown, S. A., Christiansen, B. A., & Goldman, M. S. (1987). The alcohol expectancy questionnaire: An instrument for the assessment of adolescent and adult alcohol expectancies. *Journal of Studies on Alcohol, 48,* 483–491.

Brown, S. A., Creamer, V. A., & Stetson, B. A. (1987). Adolescent alcohol expectancies in relation to personal and parental drinking patterns. *Journal of Abnormal Psychology, 96,* 117–121.

Brown, S. A., Goldman, M. S., & Christiansen, B. A. (1985). Do alcohol expectancies mediate drinking patterns of adults? *Journal of Consulting and Clinical Psychology, 53,* 512–519.

Brown, S. A., & Schuckit, M. A. (1988). Changes in depression among abstinent alcoholics. *Journal of Studies on Alcohol, 49,* 412–417.

Brown, S. A., Tate, S. R., Vik, P. W., Haas, A. L., & Aarons, G. A. (1999). Modeling of alcohol use mediates the effect of family history of alcoholism on adolescent alcohol expectancies. *Experimental and Clinical Psychopharmacology, 7,* 20–27.

Brown, S. A., Vik, P. W., & Creamer, V. A. (1989). Characteristics of relapse following adolescent substance abuse treatment. *Addictive Behaviors, 14,* 291–300.

Bryant, A. L., & Zimmerman, M. A. (2002). Examining the effects of academic beliefs and behaviors on changes in substance use among urban adolescents. *Journal of Educational Psychology, 94,* 621–637.

Bushman, B. J., & Cooper, H. M. (1990). Effects of alcohol on human aggression: An intergrative research review. *Psychological Bulletin, 107,* 341–354.

Caetano, R., Schafer, J., & Cunradi, C. B. (2001). Alcohol-related intimate partner violence among white, black, and Hispanic couples in the United States. *Alcohol Research & Health, 25,* 58–65.

Carroll, K. M., Rounsaville, B. J., Gordon, L. T., & Nich, C. (1994). Psychotherapy and pharmacotherapy for ambulatory cocaine abusers. *Archives of General Psychiatry, 51,* 177–187.

Catz, S. L., Heckman, T. G., Kochman, A., & DiMarco, M. (2001). Rates and correlates of HIV treatment adherence among late middle-aged and older adults living with HIV disease. *Psychology, Health & Medicine, 6,* 47–58.

Chassin, L., Pillow, D. R., Curran, P. J., Molina, B. S. G., & Barrera, M. (1993). Relation of parental alcoholism to early adolescent substance use: A test of three mediating mechanisms. *Journal of Abnormal Psychology, 102,* 3–19.

Chen, W. Y., Rosner, B., Hankinson, S. E., Colditz, G. A., & Willett, W. C. (2011). Moderate alcohol consumption during adult life, drinking patterns, and breast cancer risk. *Journal of the American Medical Association, 306,* 1884–1890.

Chermack, S. T., & Giancola, P. R. (1997). The relation between alcohol and aggression: An integrated biopsychosocial conceptualization. *Clinical Psychology Review, 17,* 621–649.

Chilcoat, H. D., & Breslau, N. (1998). Investigations of causal pathways between PTSD and drug use disorders. *Addictive Behaviors, 23,* 827–840.

Claassen, C. A., Trivedi, M. H., Rush, A. J., Husain, M. M., Zisook, S., Young, E.,…Alpert, J. (2007). Clinical differences among depressed patients with and without a history of suicide attempts: Findings from the STAR*D trial. *Journal of Affective Disorders, 97,* 77–84.

Cloninger, C. R., Bohman, M., & Sigvardsson, S. (1981). Inheritance of alcohol abuse: Cross-fostering analysis of adopted men. *Archives of General Psychiatry, 38,* 861–868.

Clure, C., Brady, K. T., Saladin, M. E., Johnson, D., Waid, R., & Rittenbury, M. (1999). Attention deficit/hyperactivity disorder and substance use: Symptoms pattern and drug choice. *American Journal of Drug and Alcohol Abuse, 25,* 441–448.

Collins, R. (1993). Women's issues in alcohol use and cigarette smoking. In J. Baer, G. Marlatt, & R. McMahon (Eds.), *Addictive behaviors across the life span: Prevention, treatment, and policy issues* (pp. 274–306). Thousand Oaks, CA: Sage Publications.

Connors, G. J., Tarbox, A. R., & Faillace, L. A. (1993). Changes in alcohol expectancies and drinking behavior among treated problem drinkers. *Journal of Studies on Alcohol, 54,* 676–683.

Cooper, M. L., Peirce, R. S., & Huselid, R. F. (1994). Substance use and sexual risk taking among black adolescents and white adolescents. *Health Psychology, 13,* 251–262.

Curran, P. J., Stice, E., & Chassin, L. (1997). The relation between adolescent alcohol use and peer alcohol use: A longitudinal random coefficients model. *Journal of Consulting and Clinical Psychology, 65,* 130–140.

Dao-Castellana, M., Samson, Y., Legault, F., Martinot, J. L., Aubin, H. J., Crouzel, C.,…Syrota, A. (1998). Frontal dysfunction in neurologically normal chronic alcoholic subjects: Metabolic and neuropsychological findings. *Psychological Medicine, 28,* 1039–1048.

Davis, K. C., Morris, J., George, W. H., Martell, J., & Heiman, J. R. (2006). Men's likelihood of sexual aggression: The influence of alcohol, sexual arousal, and violent pornography. *Aggressive Behavior, 32,* 581–589.

Denis, C., Fatséas, M., & Auriacombe, M. (2012). Analyses related to the development of DSM-5 criteria for substance use related disorders: 3. An assessment of pathological gambling criteria. *Drug and Alcohol Dependence, 122,* 22–27.

Desai, R. A., Maciejewski, P. K., Pantalon, M. V., & Potenza, M. N. (2005). Gender differences in adolescent gambling. *Annals of Clinical Psychiatry, 17,* 249–258.

Desai, R. A., & Potenza, M. N. (2008). Gender differences in the associations between past-year gambling problems and psychiatric disorders. *Social Psychiatry and Psychiatric Epidemiology, 43,* 173–183.

Dixon, L. (1999). Dual diagnosis of substance abuse in schizophrenia: Prevalence and impact on outcomes. *Schizophrenia Research, 35,* s93–s100.

Elkins, I. J., McGue, M., & Iacono, W. G. (2007). Prospective effects of attention-deficit/ hyperactivity disorder, conduct disorder, and sex on adolescent substance use and abuse. *Archives of General Psychiatry, 64,* 1145–1152.

Epstein, E. E., Labouvie, E., McCrady, B. S., Jensen, N. K., & Hayaki, J. (2002). A multi-site study of alcohol subtypes: Classification and overlap of unidimensional and multi-dimensional typologies. *Addiction, 97,* 1041–1053.

Epstein, J. A., & Botvin, G. J. (2002). The moderating role of risk-taking tendency and refusal assertiveness on social influences in alcohol use among inner-city adolescents. *Journal of Studies on Alcohol, 63,* 456–459.

Farley, M., Golding, J. M., Young, G., Mulligan, M., & Minkoff, J. R. (2004). Trauma history and relapse probability among patients seeking substance abuse treatment. *Journal of Substance Abuse Treatment, 27,* 161–167.

Fergusson, D. M., & Horwood, L. J. (1999). Prospective childhood predictors of deviant peer affiliations in adolescence. *Journal of Child Psychology and Psychiatry, 40,* 581–592.

Fischer, S., Settles, R., Collins, B., Gunn, R., & Smith, G. T. (2012). The role of negative urgency and expectancies in problem drinking and disordered eating: Testing a model of comorbidity in pathological and at-risk samples. *Psychology of Addictive Behaviors*, 26, 112–123.

Fortune, E. E., & Goodie, A. S. (2012). Cognitive distortions as a component and treatment focus of pathological gambling: A review. *Psychology of Addictive Behaviors*, 26(2), 298–310.

Fox, C. H. (1994). Cocaine use in pregnancy. *Journal of the American Board of Family Practices*, 7, 225–228.

Frances, R. J., Timm, S., Bucky, S. (1980). Studies of familial and non-familial alcoholism. *Archives of General Psychiatry*, 37, 564–566.

Freeman, T., & Kimbrell, T. (2004). Relationship of alcohol craving to symptoms of posttraumatic stress disorder in combat veterans. *Journal of Nervous and Mental Disease*, 192, 389–390.

Friedman, A. S., Kramer, S., Kreisher, C., & Granick, S. (1996). The relationships of substance abuse to illegal and violent behavior, in a community sample of young adult African American men and women (gender differences). *Journal of Substance Abuse*, 8, 379–402.

Fu, Q., Heath, A. C., Bucholz, K. K., Nelson, E., Goldberg, J., Lyons, M. J.,…Eisen, S. A. (2002). Shared genetic risk of major depression, alcohol dependence, and marijuana dependence: Contribution of antisocial personality disorder in men. *Archives of General Psychiatry*, 59, 1125–1132.

Gavaler, J. S., & Arria, A. M. (1995). Increased susceptibility of women to alcoholic liver disease: Artifactual or real? In P. Hall (Ed.), *Alcoholic liver disease: Pathology and pathogenesis* (2nd ed., pp 123–133). London: Edward Arnold.

Giancola, P. R. (2000). Executive functioning: A conceptual framework for alcohol-related aggression. *Experimental and Clinical Psychopharmacology*, 8, 576–597.

Giancola, P. R., & Chermack, S. T. (1998). Construct validity of laboratory aggression paradigms: A response to Tedeschi and Quigley (1996). *Aggression and Violent Behavior*, 3, 237–253.

Glenn, S. W., & Nixon, S. J. (1991). Applications of Cloninger's subtypes in a female alcoholic sample. *Alcoholism: Clinical and Experimental Research*, 15, 851–857.

Goldstein, B. I., & Levitt, A. J. (2006). Is current alcohol consumption associated with increased lifetime prevalence of major depression and suicidality? Results from a pilot community survey. *Comprehensive Psychiatry*, 47, 330–333.

Goodie, A. S. (2005). The role of perceived control and overconfidence in pathological gambling. *Journal of Gambling Studies*, 21, 481–502.

Grant, B. F., Stinson, F. S., Dawson, D. A., Chou, P., Dufour, M. C., Compton, W.,…Kaplan, K. (2004). Prevalence and co-occurrence of substance use disorders and independent mood and anxiety disorders: Results from the national epidemiologic survey on alcohol and related conditions. *Archives of General Psychiatry*, 61, 807–816.

Hall, P. M. (1995). Factors influencing individual susceptibility to alcoholic liver disease. In P. Hall (Ed.), *Alcoholic liver disease: Pathology and pathogenesis* (2nd ed., pp. 299–316). London: Edward Arnold.

Hansenne, M. (2006). Event-related brain potentials in psychopathology: Clinical and cognitive perspectives. *Psychologica Belgica*, 46, 5–36.

Hanson, K. L., Medina, K. L., Padula, C. B., Tapert, S. F., & Brown, S. A. (2011). Impact of adolescent alcohol and drug use on neuropsychological functioning in young adulthood: 10-year outcomes. *Journal of Child & Adolescent Substance Abuse*, 20, 135–154.

Hanson, K. L., Winward, J. L., Schweinsburg, A. D., Medina, K. L., Brown, S. A., & Tapert, S. F. (2010). Longitudinal study of cognition among adolescent marijuana users over three weeks of abstinence. *Addictive Behaviors*, 35, 970–976.

Harris, E. C., & Barraclough, B. (1998). "Excess mortality of mental disorder": Erratum. *British Journal of Psychiatry*, 173, 272–272.

Hasin, D. S., Fenton, M. C., Beseler, C., Park, J. Y., & Wall, M. M. (2012). Analyses related to the development of DSM-5 criteria for substance use related disorders: 2. Proposed DSM-5 criteria for alcohol, cannabis, cocaine and heroin disorders in 663 substance abuse patients. *Drug and Alcohol Dependence*, 122, 28–37.

Hasin, D. S., & Grant, B. F. (2002). Major depression in 6050 former drinkers: Association with past alcohol dependence. *Archives of General Psychiatry*, 59, 794–800.

Heath, A. C., Madden, P. A. F., Bucholz, K. K., Dinwiddie, S. H., Slutske, W. S., Bierut, L. J.,…Martin, N. G. (1999). Genetic differences in alcohol sensitivity and the inheritance of alcoholism risk. *Psychological Medicine*, 29, 1069–1081.

Helzer, J. E., Burnham, A., & McEvoy, L. T. (1991). Alcohol abuse and dependence. In L. N. Robbins & D. A. Regier (Eds.), *Psychiatric* disorders in America: The Epidemiology Catchment Area Study (pp. 81–115). New York: Free Press.

Hernandez-Avila, C., Rounsaville, B. J., & Kranzler, H. R. (2004). Opioid-, cannabis- and alcohol-dependent women show more rapid progression to substance abuse treatment. Drug and Alcohol Dependence, 74, 265–272.

Hesselbrock, M. N., & Hesselbrock, V. M. (1993). Depression and antisocial personality disorder in alcoholism: Gender comparison. In Lisansky, E. S., & Nirenberg, T. D. (Eds.), Women and substance abuse (pp. 142–161). Westport, CT: Ablex Publishing.

Hesselbrock, V., Hesselbrock, M. N., & Segal, B. (2000). Multivariate phenotypes of alcohol dependence among Alaskan natives—type A/ type B. Alcoholism: Clinical & Experimental Research, 24, 107a.

Hinckers, A. S., Laucht, M., Schmidt, M. H., Mann, K. F., Schumann, G., Schuckit, M. A., & Heinz, A. (2006). Low level of response to alcohol as associated with serotonin transporter genotype and high alcohol intake in adolescents. Biological Psychiatry, 60, 282–287.

Hoaken, P. N. S., Assaad, J., & Pihl, R. O. (1998). Cognitive functioning and the inhibition of alcohol-induced aggression. Journal of Studies on Alcohol, 59, 599–607.

Holderness, C. C., Brooks-Gunn, J., & Warren, M. P. (1994). Co-morbidity of eating disorders and substance abuse review of the literature. International Journal of Eating Disorders, 16, 1–34.

Hommer, D. W., Momenan, R., Kaiser, E., & Rawlings, R. R. (2001). Evidence for a gender-related effect of alcoholism on brain volumes. American Journal of Psychiatry, 158, 198–204.

Jacobsen, L. K., Southwick, S. M., & Kosten, T. R. (2001). Substance use disorders in patients with posttraumatic stress disorder: A review of the literature. American Journal of Psychiatry, 158, 1184–1190.

Jaffe, A. J., & Kilbey, M. M. (1994). The cocaine expectancy questionnaire (CEQ): Construction and predictive utility. Psychological Assessment, 6, 18–26.

Jang, K. L., Livesley, W. J., & Vernon, P. A. (1995). Alcohol and drug problems: A multivariate behavioural genetic analysis of co-morbidity. Addiction, 90(9), 1213–1221.

Jellinek, E. M. (1960). Alcoholism: A genus and some of its species. Canadian Medical Association Journal, 81, 1341–1345.

Johnson, S. D., Phelps, D. L., & Cottler, L. B. (2004). The association of sexual dysfunction and substance use among a community epidemiological sample. Archives of Sexual Behavior, 33, 55–63.

Jones, K. D., Gill, C., & Ray, S. (2012). Review of the proposed DSM-5 substance use disorder. Journal of Addictions & Offender Counseling, 33, 115–123.

Jovanovski, D., Erb, S., & Zakzanis, K. K. (2005). Neurocognitive deficits in cocaine users: A quantitative review of the evidence. Journal of Clinical and Experimental Neuropsychology, 27, 189–204.

Kalechstein, A. D., Newton, T. F., & Green, M. (2003). Methamphetamine dependence is associated with neurocognitve impairment in the initial phases of abstinence. Journal of Neuropsychiatry and Clinical Neurosciences, 15, 215–220.

Katsanis, J., Iacono, W. G., McGue, M. K., & Carlson, S. R. (1997). P300 event-related potential heritability in monozygotic and dizygotic twins. Psychophysiology, 34, 47–58.

Keel, P. K., Dorer, D. J., Eddy, K. T., Franko, D., Charatan, D. L., & Herzog, D. B. (2003). Predictors of mortality in eating disorders. Archives of General Psychiatry, 60, 179–183.

Keller, P. S., El-Sheikh, M., Keiley, M., & Liao, P. (2009). Longitudinal relations between marital aggression and alcohol problems. Psychology of Addictive Behaviors, 23, 2–13.

Kendler, K. S., Jacobson, K. C., Prescott, C. A., & Neale, M. C. (2003). Specificity of genetic and environmental risk factors for use and abuse/dependence of cannabis, cocaine, hallucinogens, sedatives, stimulants, and opiates in male twins. American Journal of Psychiatry, 160, 687–696.

Kerr, W. C., Subbaraman, M., & Ye, Y. (2011). Per capita alcohol consumption and suicide mortality in a panel of US states from 1950 to 2002. Drug and Alcohol Review, 30, 473–480.

Kessler, R. C., Crum, R. M., Warner, L. A., & Nelson, C. B. (1997). Lifetime co-occurrence of DSM-III-R alcohol abuse and dependence with other psychiatric disorders in the national comorbidity survey. Archives of General Psychiatry, 54, 313–321.

Kessler, R. C., Sonnega, A., Bromet, E., Hughes, M., & Nelson, C. B. (1995). Posttraumatic stress disorder in the national comorbidity survey. Archives of General Psychiatry, 52, 1048–1060.

King, S. M., Abrams, K., & Wilkinson, T. (2010). Personality, gender, and family history in the prediction of college gambling. Journal of Gambling Studies, 26, 347–359.

Klatsky, A. L., & Armstrong, M. A. (1993). Alcohol use, other traits, and risk of unnatural death: A prospective study. *Alcoholism: Clinical and Experimental Research, 17*, 1156–1162.

Koopman, C., Rosario, M., & Rotheram-Borus, M. (1994). Alcohol and drug use and sexual behaviors placing runaways at risk for HIV infection. *Addictive Behaviors, 19*, 95–103.

Kosten, T. R., Rounsaville, B. J., & Kleber, H. D. (1985). Ethnic and gender differences among opiate addicts. *International Journal of the Addictions, 20*, 1143–1162.

Kranzler, H. R., Feinn, R., Armeli, S., & Tennen, H. (2012). Comparison of alcoholism subtypes as moderators of the response to sertraline treatment. *Alcoholism: Clinical and Experimental Research, 36*, 509–516.

Kulka, R. A., Schlenger, W. E., Fairbank, J. A., Hough, R. L., Jordan, B. K., Marmar, C. R.,…Weiss, D. S. (1990). *Trauma and the Vietnam war generation: Report of findings from the national Vietnam Veterans Readjustment Study.* Philadelphia: Brunner/Mazel.

Lakey, C. E., Goodie, A. S., Lance, C. E., Stinchfield, R., & Winters, K. C. (2007). Examining DSM-IV criteria for pathological gambling: Psychometric properties and evidence from cognitive biases. *Journal of Gambling Studies, 23*, 479–498.

Langenbucher, J., Labouvie, E., & Morgenstern, J. (1996). Measuring diagnostic agreement. *Journal of Consulting and Clinical Psychology, 64*, 1285–1289.

Langenbucher, J. W., & Nathan, P. E. (1990). Alcohol, affect, and the tension-reduction hypothesis: The reanalysis of some crucial early data. In W. M. Cox (Ed.), *Why people drink: Parameters of alcohol as a reinforcer* (pp. 131–168). New York: Gardner Press.

Lee, S. S., Humphreys, K. L., Flory, K., Liu, R., & Glass, K. (2011). Prospective association of childhood attention-deficit/hyperactivity disorder (ADHD) and substance use and abuse/dependence: A meta-analytic review. *Clinical Psychology Review, 31*, 328–341.

Leichliter, J. S., Williams, S. P., & Bland, S. D. (2004). Sexually active adults in the United States: Predictors of sexually transmitted diseases and utilization of public STD clinics. *Journal of Psychology & Human Sexuality, 16*, 33–50.

Leigh, B. C., & Stacy, A. W. (1993). Alcohol outcome expectancies: Scale construction and predictive utility in higher order confirmatory models. *Psychological Assessment, 5*, 216–229.

Leigh, B. C., Vanslyke, J. G., Hoppe, M. J., Rainey, D. T., Morrison, D. M., & Gillmore, M. R. (2008). Drinking and condom use: Results from an event-based daily diary. *AIDS and Behavior, 12*, 104–112.

Lipscomb, T. R., Carpenter, J. A., & Nathan, P. E. (1979). Static ataxia: A predictor of alcoholism? *British Journal of Addiction, 74*, 289–294.

Lorains, F. K., Cowlishaw, S., & Thomas, S. A. (2011). Prevalence of comorbid disorders in problem and pathological gambling: Systematic review and meta-analysis of population surveys. *Addiction, 106*, 490–498.

Lundqvist, T. (2005). Cognitive consequences of cannabis use: Comparison with abuse of stimulants and heroin with regard to attention, memory and executive functions. *Pharmacology, Biochemistry and Behavior, 81*, 319–330.

Mann, K., Ackermann, K., Croissant, B., Mundle, G., Nakovics, H., & Diehl, A. (2005). Neuroimaging of gender differences in alcohol dependence: Are women more vulnerable? *Alcoholism: Clinical and Experimental Research, 29*, 896–901.

Merikangas, K. R. (1990). The genetic epidemiology of alcoholism. *Psychological Medicine, 20*, 11–22.

Merikangas, K. R., Mehta, R. L., Molnar, B. E., Walters, E. E., Swendsen, J. D., Auilar-Gaziola, S.,…Kessler, R. C. (1998). Comorbidity of substance use disorders with mood and anxiety disorders: Results of the international consortium in psychiatric epidemiology. *Addictive Behaviors, 23*, 893–908.

Milne, B. J., Caspi, A., Harrington, H., Poulton, R., Rutter, M., & Moffitt, T. E. (2009). Predictive value of family history on severity of illness: The case for depression, anxiety, alcohol dependence, and drug dependence. *Archives of General Psychiatry, 66*, 738–747.

Moeller, F. G., Barratt, E. S., Fischer, C. J., Dougherty, D. M., Reilly, E. L., Mathias, C. W., & Swann, A. C. (2004). P300 event-related potential amplitude and impulsivity in cocaine-dependent subjects. *Neuropsychobiology, 50*, 167–173.

Moselhy, H. F., Georgiou, G., & Kahn, A. (2001). Frontal lobe changes in alcoholism: A review of the literature. *Alcohol and Alcoholism, 36*, 357–368.

Moss, H. B., Chen, C. M., & Yi, H. (2007). Subtypes of alcohol dependence in a nationally representative sample. *Drug and Alcohol Dependence, 91*, 149–158.

Murray, H. W., Patkar, A. A., Mannelli, P., DeMaria, P., Desai, A. M., & Vergare, M. J. (2003). Relationship of aggression, sensation seeking, and impulsivity, with severity of cocaine use. *Addictive Disorders & their Treatment, 2,* 113–121.

Nathan, P. E., & Lipscomb, T. R. (1979). Studies in blood alcohol level discrimination: Etiologic cues to alcoholism. In N. A. Krasnegor (Ed.), *Behavioral analysis and treatment of substance abuse* (pp. 178–190). Washington, DC: NIDA.

National Institute on Alcohol Abuse and Alcoholism (NIAAA). (2005). *Harmful interactions: Mixing alcohol with medicines* (NIH Publication No. 03-5329). Rockville, MD: National Institute of Health.

Negrete, J. C. (1989). Cannabis and schizophrenia. *British Journal of Addiction, 84,* 349–351.

Nelson, C. B., Heath, A. C., & Kessler, R. C. (1998). Temporal progression of alcohol dependence symptoms in the U.S. household population: Results from the National Comorbidity Survey. *Journal of Consulting and Clinical Psychology, 66,* 474–483.

Newcomb, M. D., & Bentler, P. M. (1986). Substance use and ethnicity: Differential impact of peer and adult models. *Journal of Psychology: Interdisciplinary and Applied, 120,* 83–95.

Noordsy, D. L., Schwab, B., Fox, L., & Drake, R. E. (1996). The role of self-help programs in the rehabilitation of persons with severe mental illness and substance use disorders. *Community Mental Health Journal, 32,* 71–81.

O'Connor, S., Morzorati, S., Christian, J. C., & Li, T. K. (1994). Heritable features of the auditory oddball event-related potential: Peaks, latencies, morphology and topography. *Electroencephalography & Clinical Neurophysiology: Evoked Potentials, 92,* 115–125.

O'Farrell, T. J., Choquette, K. A., Cutter, H. S. G., & Birchler, G. R. (1997). Sexual satisfaction and dysfunction in marriages of male alcoholics: Comparison with nonalcoholic maritally conflicted and nonconflicted couples. *Journal of Studies on Alcohol, 58,* 91–99.

O'Farrell, T. J., Murphy, C. M., Neavins, T. M., & Van Hutton, V. (2000). Verbal aggression among male alcoholic patients and their wives in the year before and two years after alcoholism treatment. *Journal of Family Violence, 15,* 295–310.

Ohlmeier, M. D., Peters, K., Kordon, A., Seifert, J., Te Wildt, B., Wiese, B.,…Schneider, U. (2007). Nicotine and alcohol dependence in patients with comorbid attention-deficit/hyperactivity disorder (ADHD). *Alcohol and Alcoholism, 42,* 539–543.

O'Malley, S., Adamse, M., Heaton, R. K., & Gawin, F. H. (1992). Neuropsychological impairment in chronic cocaine abusers. *American Journal of Drug and Alcohol Abuse, 18,* 131–144.

Ostrea, E. M., & Chavez, C. J. (1979). Perinatal problems (excluding neonatal withdrawal) in maternal drug addiction: A study of 830 cases. *Journal of Pediactrics, 94,* 292–2295.

Pardini, D., White, H. R., & Stouthamer-Loeber, M. (2007). Early adolescent psychopathology as a predictor of alcohol use disorders by young adulthood. *Drug and Alcohol Dependence, 88,* S38–S49.

Parella, D. P, & Filstead, W. J. (1988). Definition of onset in the development of onset-based alcoholism typologies. *Journal of Studies on Alcohol, 49,* 85–92.

Petry, N. M. (2004). Depot formulations: Will pharmacological advances improve treatment options and outcomes for substance abusers? *Addiction, 99,* 1475–1476.

Petry, N. M. (2006). Should the scope of addictive behaviors be broadened to include pathological gambling? *Addiction, 101,* 152–160.

Petry, N. M., Stinson, F. S., & Grant, B. F. (2005). Comorbidity of DSM-IV pathological gambling and other psychiatric disorders: Results from the national epidemiologic survey on alcohol and related conditions. *Journal of Clinical Psychiatry, 66,* 564–574.

Pettinati, H. M., Volpicelli, J. R., Kranzler, H. R., Luck, G., Rukstalis, M. R., & Cnaan, A. (2000). Sertraline treatment for alcohol dependence: Interactive effects of medication and alcoholic subtype. *Alcoholism: Clinical and Experimental Research, 24,* 1041–1049.

Pietrzak, R. H., & Petry, N. M. (2005). Antisocial personality disorder is associated with increased severity of gambling, medical, drug and psychiatric problems among treatment-seeking pathological gamblers. *Addiction, 100*(8), 1183–1193.

Polich, J., Pollock, V. E., & Bloom, F. E. (1994). Meta-analysis of P300 amplitude from males at risk for alcoholism. *Psychological Bulletin, 115*(1), 55–73.

Porjesz, B., Begleiter, H., Wang, K., Almasy, L., Chorlian, D. B., Stimus, A. T.,…Reich, T. (2002). Linkage and linkage disequilibrium mapping of ERP and EEG phenotypes. *Biological Psychology, 61,* 229–248.

Prescott, C. A., Aggen, S. H., & Kendler, K. S. (2000). Sex-specific genetic influences on the comorbidity of alcoholism and major depression in a population-based sample of US twins. *Archives of General Psychiatry, 57,* 803–811.

Prescott, C. A., & Kendler, K. S. (1999). Genetic and environmental contributions to alcohol abuse and dependence in a population-based sample of male twins. *American Journal of Psychiatry, 156*(1), 34–40.

Ramisetty-Mikler, S., Caetano, R., & McGrath, C. (2007). Sexual aggression among white, black, and Hispanic couples in the U.S.: Alcohol use, physical assault and psychological aggression as its correlates. *American Journal of Drug and Alcohol Abuse, 33,* 31–43.

Randall, C. L., Roberts, J. S., Del Boca, F. K., Carroll, K. M., Connors, G. J., & Mattson, M. E. (1999). Telescoping of landmark events associated with drinking: A gender comparison. *Journal of Studies on Alcohol, 60,* 252–260.

Regard, M., Knoch, D., Gütling, E., & Landis, T. (2003). Brain damage and addictive behavior: A neuropsychological and electroencephalogram investigation with pathologic gamblers. *Cognitive and Behavioral Neurology, 16,* 47–53.

Regier, D. A., Farmer, M. E., Rae, D. S., Locke, B. Z., Keither, S. J., Judd, L. L., & Goodwin, F.K. (1990). Comorbidity of mental disorders with alcohol and other drug abuse: Results from the Epidemiologic Catchment Area (ECA) Study. *Journal of the American Medical Association, 264,* 2511–2518.

Roberts, R. E., Roberts, C. R., & Xing, Y. (2007). Comorbidity of substance use disorders and other psychiatric disorders among adolescents: Evidence from an epidemiologic survey. *Drug and Alcohol Dependence, 88,* S4–S13.

Roizen, J. (1993). *Issues in the epidemiology of alcohol and violence* (NIH research Monograph No. 24, No. 93-3496). Rockville, MD: US Department of Health and Human Services.

Roopesh, B. N., Rangaswamy, M., Kamarajan, C., Chorlian, D. B., Stimus, A., Bauer, L. O.,...Porjesz, B. (2009). Priming deficiency in male subjects at risk for alcoholism: The N4 during a lexical decision task. *Alcoholism: Clinical and Experimental Research, 33,* 2027–2036.

Rourke, S. B., & Løberg, T. (1996). Neurobehavioral correlates of alcoholism. In I. Grant & K. A. Adams (Eds.), *Neuropsychological assessment of neuropsychiatric disorders* (2nd ed., pp. 423–485). New York: Oxford University Press.

Rugle, L., & Melamed, L. (1993). Neuropsychological assessment of attention problems in pathological gamblers. *Journal of Nervous and Mental Disease, 181,* 107–112.

Saha, T. D., Compton, W. M., Chou, S. P., Smith, S., Ruan, W. J., Huang, B.,...Grant, B. F. (2012). Analyses related to the development of DSM-5 criteria for substance use related disorders: 1. Toward amphetamine, cocaine and prescription drug use disorder continua using item response theory. *Drug and Alcohol Dependence, 122,* 38–46.

Sartor, C. E., Lynskey, M. T., Heath, A. C., Jacob, T., & True, W. (2007). The role of childhood risk factors in initiation of alcohol use and progression to alcohol dependence. *Addiction, 102,* 216–225.

Sato, M. (1992). A lasting vulnerability to psychosis in patients with previous methamphetamine psychosis *Annals of the New York Academy of Sciences* (pp. 160–170). New York: New York Academy of Sciences.

Schafer, J., & Brown, S. A. (1991). Marijuana and cocaine effect expectancies and drug use patterns. *Journal of Consulting and Clinical Psychology, 59,* 558–565.

Schiavi, R. C., Stimmel, B. B., Mandeli, J., & White, D. (1995). Chronic alcoholism and male sexual function. *American Journal of Psychiatry, 152,* 1045–1051.

Schuckit, M. A. (1985). Ethanol-induced changes in body sway in men at high alcoholism risk. *Archives of General Psychiatry, 42,* 375–379.

Schuckit, M. A. (1994a). Low level of response to alcohol as a predictor of future alcoholism. *American Journal of Psychiatry, 151,* 184–189.

Schuckit, M. A. (1994b). The relationship between alcohol problems, substance abuse, and psychiatric syndromes. In T. A. Widiger, A. J. Frances, H. A. Pincus, M. B. First, R. Ross, & W. Davis (Eds.), *DSM-IV sourcebook* (Vol. 1, pp. 45–66). Washington, DC: American Psychiatric Association.

Schuckit, M. A., Anthenelli, R. M., Bucholz, K. K., Hesselbrock, V. M., & Tipp, J. (1995). The time course of development of alcohol-related problems in men and women. *Journal of Studies on Alcohol, 56,* 218–225.

Schuckit, M. A., & Gold, E. O. (1988). A simultaneous evaluation of multiple markers of ethanol/placebo challenges in sons of alcoholics and controls. *Archives of General Psychiatry, 45,* 211–216.

Schuckit, M. A., & Hesselbrock, V. (1994). Alcohol dependence and anxiety disorders: What is the relationship? *American Journal of Psychiatry, 151,* 1723–1734.

Schuckit, M. A., & Smith, T. L. (2000). The relationships of a family history of alcohol dependence, a low level of response to alcohol and six domains of life functioning to the development of alcohol use disorders. *Journal of Studies on Alcohol, 61*(6), 827–835.

Schuckit, M. A., Smith, T. L., Anderson, K. G., & Brown, S. A. (2004). Testing the level of response to alcohol: Social information processing model of alcoholism risk—A 20-year prospective study. *Alcoholism: Clinical and Experimental Research, 28*, 1881–1889.

Schuckit, M. A., Smith, T. L., Danko, G. P., Bucholz, K. K., & Reich, T. (2001). Five-year clinical course associated with DSM-IV alcohol abuse or dependence in a large group of men and women. *American Journal of Psychiatry, 158*, 1084–1090.

Schuckit, M. A., Smith, T. L., Danko, G. P., Kramer, J., Godinez, J., Bucholz, K. K.,…Hesselbrock, V. (2005). Prospective evaluation of the four DSM-IV criteria for alcohol abuse in a large population. *American Journal of Psychiatry, 162*, 350–360.

Schuckit, M. A., Smith, T. L., Kalmijn, J., Trim, R. S., Cesario, E., Saunders, G.,…Campbell, N. (2012). Comparison across two generations of prospective models of how the low level of responses to alcohol affects alcohol outcomes. *Journal of Studies on Alcohol and Drugs, 73*, 195–204.

Schuckit, M. A., Tipp, J. E., Bucholz, K. K., Nurnberger, J. I., Hesselbrock, V. M., Crowe, R. R., & Kramer, J. (1997). The life-time rates of three major mood disorders and four major anxiety disorders in alcoholics and controls. *Addiction, 92*, 1289–1304.

Shen, X., Hackworth, J., McCabe, H., Lovett, L., Aumage, J., O'Neil, J., & Bull, M. (2006). Characteristics of suicide from 1998-2001 in a metropolitan area. *Death Studies, 30*, 859–871.

Shiffman, S., Kassel, J. D., Paty, J. A., & Gnys, M. (1994). Smoking typology profiles of chippers and regular smokers. *Journal of Substance Abuse, 6*, 21–35.

Shoal, G. D., Gudonis, L. C., Giancola, P. R., & Tarter, R. E. (2007). Delinquency as a mediator of the relation between negative affectivity and adolescent alcohol use disorder. *Addictive Behaviors, 32*, 2747–2765.

Simons, J. S., & Carey, M. P. (2001). Prevalence of sexual dysfunction: Results from a decade of research. *Archives of Sexual Behavior, 30*, 177–219.

Singh, S. M., Basu, D., Kohli, A., & Prabhakar, S. (2009). Auditory P300 event-related

potentials and neurocognitive functions in opioid dependent men and their brothers. *American Journal on Addictions, 18*, 198–205.

Singletary, K. W., & Gapstur, S. M. (2001). Alcohol and breast cancer: Review of epidemiologic and experimental evidence and potential mechanisms. *Journal of the American Medical Association, 286*, 2143–2151.

Smith, G. T., Goldman, M. S., Greenbaum, P. E., & Christiansen, B. A. (1995). Expectancy for social facilitation from drinking: The divergent paths of high-expectancy and low-expectancy adolescents. *Journal of Abnormal Psychology, 104*, 32–40.

Stewart, S. H., Conrod, P. J., Samoluk, S. B., Pihl, R. O., & Dongier, M. (2000). Posttraumatic stress disorder symptoms and situation-specific drinking in women substance abusers. *Alcoholism Treatment Quarterly, 18*, 31–47.

Substance Abuse and Mental Health Services Administration. (2012). *Results from the 2011 National Survey on Drug Use and Health: Summary of National Findings* (NSDUH Series H-44, HHS Publication No. (SMA) 12-4713). Rockville, MD: Substance Abuse and Mental Health Services Administration.

Tapert, S. F., & Brown, S. A. (1999). Neuropsychological correlates of adolescent substance abuse: Four-year outcomes. *Journal of the International Neuropsychological Society, 5*, 481–493.

Tapert, S. F., Stewart, D. G., & Brown, S. A. (1999). Drug abuse in adolescence. In A. J. Goreczny & M. Hersen (Eds.), *Handbook of pediatric and adolescent health psychology* (pp. 161–178). Needham Heights, MA: Allyn & Bacon.

Tate, S. R., Patterson, K. A., Nagel, B. J., Anderson, K. G., & Brown, S. A. (2007). Addiction and stress in adolescents. In M. Al'Absi (Ed.), *Stress and addiction: Biological and psychological mechanisms* (pp. 249–262). San Diego: Academic Press

Toneatto, T., Blitz-Miller, T., Calderwood, K., Dragonetti, R., & Tsanos, A. (1997). Cognitive distortions in heavy gambling. *Journal of Gambling Studies, 13*, 253–266.

Trim, R. S., Schuckit, M. A., & Smith, T. L. (2009). The relationships of the level of response to alcohol and additional characteristics to alcohol use disorders across adulthood: A discrete-time survival analysis. *Alcoholism: Clinical and Experimental Research, 33*, 1562–1570.

van der Stelt, O., Gunning, W. B., Snel, J., & Kok, A. (1998). Event-related potentials during visual selective attention in children of alcoholics. *Alcoholism: Clinical and Experimental Research*, 22, 1877–1889.

Van Thiel, D. H., Gavaler, J. S., Eagan, P. K., Chiao, Y. B., Cobb, C. F., & Lester, R. (1980). Alcohol and sexual function. *Pharmacology and Biochemistry of Behavior*, 13, 125–129.

Vik, P. W., Grizzle, K. L., & Brown, S. A. (1992). Social resource characteristics and adolescent substance abuse relapse. *Journal of Adolescent Chemical Dependency*, 2, 59–74.

Walters, G. D. (2001). Behavior genetic research on gambling and problem gambling: A preliminary meta-analysis of available data. *Journal of Gambling Studies*, 17, 255–271.

Welte, J. W., Barnes, G. M., Tidwell, M. O., & Hoffman, J. H. (2009). Association between problem gambling and conduct disorder in a national survey of adolescents and young adults in the United States. *Journal of Adolescent Health*, 45, 396–401.

Welte, J. W., Barnes, G. M., Wieczorek, W. F., Tidwell, M. C., & Parker, J. (2002). Gambling participation in the US—Results from a national survey. *Journal of Gambling Studies*, 18, 313–337.

Wenzel, H. G., & Dahl, A. A. (2009). Female pathological gamblers—A critical review of the clinical findings. *International Journal of Mental Health and Addiction*, 7, 190–202.

Widom, C. S., Ireland, T., & Glynn, P. J. (1995). Alcohol abuse in abused and neglected children followed up: Are they at increased risk? *Journal of Studies on Alcohol*, 56, 207–217.

Wilens, T. E. (2004). Impact of ADHD and its treatment on substance abuse in adults. *Journal of Clinical Psychiatry*, 65, 38–45.

Wilens, T. E., Biederman, J., Mick, E., Faraone, S. V., & Spencer, T. (1997). Attention deficit hyperactivity disorder (ADHD) is associated with early onset substance abuse. *Journal of Nervous and Mental Disease*, 185, 475–482.

Wills, T. A., Resko, J. A., Ainette, M. G., & Mendoza, D. (2004). Role of parent support and peer support in adolescent substance use: A test of mediated effects. *Psychology of Addictive Behaviors*, 18, 122–134.

Wilsnack, S. C., Vogeltanz, N. D., Klassen, A. D., & Harris, T. R. (1997). Childhood sexual abuse and women's substance abuse: National survey findings. *Journal of Studies on Alcohol*, 58, 264–271.

Wojnar, M., Wasilewski, D., Matsumoto, H., & Cedro, A. (1997). Differences in the course of alcohol withdrawal in women and men: A Polish sample. *Alcoholism: Clinical and Experimental Research*, 21, 1351–1355.

Wolfe, W. L., & Maisto, S. A. (2000). The relationship between eating disorders and substance use: Moving beyond co-prevalence research. *Clinical Psychology Review*, 20, 617–631.

Zinn, S., Stein, R., & Swartzwelder, H. S. (2004). Executive functioning early in abstinence from alcohol. *Alcoholism: Clinical and Experimental Research*, 28, 1338–1346.

Zuckerman, B., Frank, D. A., Hingson, R., Amaro, H., Levenson, S. M., Kayne, H., et al. (1989). Effects of maternal marijuana and cocaine use on fetal growth. *New England Journal of Medicine*, 320, 762–768.

12

Schizophrenia
Presentation, Affect and Cognition, Pathophysiology, and Etiology

ANGUS MACDONALD, III

For a young graduate student named Susan, undergoing a psychotic break was "like turning on a faucet to a torrent of details" (Weiner, 2003). Strange new questions arose. What lay behind superficial appearances? What did the person really mean when they said "Hello"? What was the secret message behind the ad on the passing bus? What was the significance of the falling leaf? According to Susan, the world became suffused with new meanings, like light—in this case an overwhelming, sinister, and saturating light. She could no longer attend classes. She no longer met with friends. Movies contained scripts that had been hidden just for her. She changed her name, broke off contacts with her family, gave away her things, and disguised her identity. After 6 months of this torment—terrified, alone, and exhausted—she gave up her efforts to resist the Central Intelligence Agency's plot; instead, she began a sequence of ever-more harrowing suicide attempts that eventually came to the attention of the police, and from there, a psychiatric emergency room. Thus began what for Susan and her family would become a lifelong struggle with schizophrenia, one of the most disruptive and distressing illnesses of any kind.

While Susan's case is not rare, people with schizophrenia have many different symptoms. What they have in common is that their lives are interrupted, and in many cases their hopes, dreams, and plans undergo irrevocable changes. This chapter will discuss the etiology, pathophysiology, and affective and cognitive deficits associated with schizophrenia. Chapter 13 will then further address the social aspects of the disorder.

Nosology

Schizophrenia is a syndrome that involves a collection of symptoms that appear to be unrelated but that actually co-occur in many patients. In *DSM-IV* and *DSM-5*, the diagnosis of schizophrenia requires two or more of the following symptoms: delusions (believing something that most people don't and despite evidence to the contrary); hallucinations (perceiving something that is not present); disorganized speech; disorganized or catatonic behavior; or negative symptoms, such as lacking normal emotional responses to events, having reduced levels of motivation, or exhibiting a disrupted flow of speech. In an effort to reduce the heterogeneity of outcomes of people diagnosed with the disorder, the criteria also include a minimum duration and rule-outs for other conditions.

These criteria are not without controversy, as we shall see. For starters, there was some discussion as to whether cognitive dysfunction should be considered as a criterion for schizophrenia (Keefe & Fenton, 2007). Using, or at least investigating the use of, a dimensional approach to organizing what are now different psychotic disorders was also among the recommendations of the *DSM-5* research planning conference for schizophrenia (for review see Krueger & MacDonald, 2005; van Os & Tamminga, 2007). However, these changes will have to wait for a later date to be incorporated, if ever. Therefore, the diagnostic criteria that remain in place today largely derive from those put forward in the Research Diagnostic Criteria (Spitzer, Endicott, & Robins, 1975), a forerunner to *DSM-III*, published in 1979. The *DSM-III* criteria supplanted more vague descriptions of schizophrenia that existed in *DSM-II*. The *DSM-III* criteria also harmonized practice in the United States with psychiatric practices in Europe, which had maintained the more rigorous, descriptive traditions of German psychiatrist Emil Kraepelin (1856–1926), a man frequently recognized as the founder of modern psychiatry.

History of the Clinical Disorder

Allusions to psychoses can be found in many cultures the world over. For example, psychotic symptoms are mentioned in many classical Greek and Roman works (Evans, McGrath, & Milns, 2003). However, in these classical sources, there does not appear to be any conceptualization of schizophrenia as a coherent disease per se. The construct of schizophrenia that we use today derives largely from the work of Kraepelin. By all accounts, Kraepelin was an active man with training in experimental psychology and a keen appreciation of the importance of collecting data. Beginning in 1886, while practicing in Estonia, and soon afterward while leading the psychiatry departments at the University of Heidelberg and then Munich, he compiled detailed clinical histories with a particularly keen ear for his patients' experiences of their illness over time. These accounts led him to differentiate schizophrenia, which he called *dementia praecox* (literally *premature madness*), from manic-depressive insanity. This aspect of the description remains a fundamental organizing principle of the *DSM-V* to this day. Even so, the validity of this distinction—now referred to as the Kraepelinian dichotomy—has never been fully embraced, for reasons we will consider later. Kraepelin had a tremendous influence on twentieth-century psychiatry through the work of his prolific students and through his frequently revised *Textbook on Psychiatry* (*Lehrbuch der Psychiatrie*). A pattern of psychotic symptoms over time, rather than any particular cluster of symptoms, was the hallmark of dementia praecox, and

he believed it was progressive and largely untreatable (Kraepelin, 1919/1971).[1]

A contemporary of Kraepelin, Swiss psychiatrist Eugene Bleuler (1857–1939), is credited with coining the term *schizophrenia* and further characterizing it. In his treatise on the disorder, he argued vehemently against the Kraepelinian view of inevitable deterioration and felt the term dementia praecox misled trainees (particularly English ones for some reason) to focus on the wrong aspect of the disease entity. He used the term schizophrenia to delineate a " 'splitting' of the different psychic functions" of the mind (Bleuler, 1911/1950, p. 8).

One unanticipated side effect of this new word has been a fusing, now common in public discourse, between schizophrenia and multiple personalities (or dissociative identity disorder [DID]). Students of psychiatry and clinical psychology grind their teeth when they hear references to schizophrenia as a "split personality." But the confusion is illuminating because it can serve to remind us about an essential, phenomenological aspect of schizophrenia. Consider this experience:

Despite the "usual" voices, alien thoughts and paranoia, what scared me the most was a sense that I had lost myself, a constant feeling that my self no longer belonged to me. What made such an existential orientation even more intolerable is the voices incessantly telling me that the only way to reunite with my real self is to commit suicide. So I tried. Still, nothing had happened. I was simply sectioned again, detached from my real self, observing what was being done to me in a third-person perspective....Even though I am now stabilized on a new medication, I still

---

1. A tragic consequence of Kraepelin's prognosis for schizophrenia would play itself out within a few decades as the ideas of eugenics gained in popularity. In an era when gene expression was only beginning to be understood, the eugenics philosophy held that the health of a population could be improved through policies that reduced reproduction of so-called unhealthy genotypes and increased reproduction among those with presumably healthy genotypes. Within this context, Kraepelin became an active proponent of eugenics and "mental hygiene." Interested readers are referred to Shepherd's (1995) treatment of this aspect of early psychiatry. This history plays an often unspoken role in the late adoption in America of theories of schizophrenia that emphasized the importance of genetic liability, because many U.S. thinkers still recoiled from this eugenic interpretation.

cannot accept the diagnosis. The medication helps the observing self dominate over the suffering self, but the real "me" is not here any more. I am disconnected, disintegrated, diminished. (Kean, 2009, p. 1034)

This experience captures the splitting of the mind and a fracturing sense of self that Bleuler took to be a core feature of schizophrenia. Although it has elements of dissociation, it is not a description of separate personalities as in DID.

Epidemiology

Schizophrenia, as based on accepted definitions, occurs in all populations studied. This was the prominent conclusion of the World Health Organization's (WHO's) coordinated study of schizophrenia at different sites around the world, conducted in the context of the Cold War and a vocal antipsychiatry movement (Jablensky et al., 1992). These sites were in developing and developed nations, East and West, and in urban and rural districts. The rate of people who fulfilled these harmonized criteria for schizophrenia over their lifetime (called *lifetime morbid risk*) was similar across sites and approximately 1%. One change in this simple set of conclusions is a downward revision of this rate, with the median lifetime morbid risk across 132 studies calculated to be .72% (Saha, Chant, Welham, & McGrath, 2005). According to population-based epidemiological studies, the highest incidence (first occurrence) of schizophrenia is at age 20–24 years for men and 25–29 years for women (Kirkbride et al., 2006), although the first symptoms of psychosis might appear several years beforehand (Häfner et al., 1994). While men have an earlier onset and a more severe course, there is no difference in the median estimates of lifetime morbid risk for the disorder between men and women (McGrath, Saha, Chant, & Welham, 2008). Thus, women gradually "catch up" to men with more later-onset cases. Previously there was some thought that by the age of 40 or 50 people exited the risk period for schizophrenia, but more recently it has been suggested that this is an arbitrary distinction and that cases of schizophrenia in older, and even elderly, patients may occur, although these cases may have a different symptom profile (Howard, Rabins, Seeman, & Jeste, 2000). While rare cases

of schizophrenia and schizophrenia-like symptoms in early childhood have been reported, the earliest onsets of schizophrenia cases is early puberty (Remschmidt & Theisen, 2012). Thus, while the traditional view of schizophrenia as a disorder of late adolescence and young adulthood is still accurate for most cases, our understanding must incorporate this wider risk period.

The WHO epidemiological study has also been corrected with regard to several other risk factors that are now accepted, such as whether one is an immigrant or grew up in an urban or a rural environment (McGrath et al., 2008). Other risk factors, such as father's age at conception, cannabis use in adolescence, and season of birth in higher latitudes, will be addressed further when we examine the etiology of schizophrenia. However, it is one thing to locate where schizophrenia happens, and quite another to locate the construct of schizophrenia amid the broader symptoms of psychopathology.

Locating the Constructs of Schizophrenia and Psychosis

Definitions and Clinical Constructs

There is perennial discussion about how to think about schizophrenia. On the one hand, it is a *diagnosis*. As a diagnosis it is a closed construct we can use to define who has it and who does not have it. On the other hand, schizophrenia is a *syndrome*. Syndromes are different from diagnoses. Syndromes are open concepts without necessary and sufficient conditions for membership. Syndromes present a way to systematize the symptoms and other measurable signs that often, but do not necessarily, co-occur. This discussion profoundly influences our thinking about schizophrenia, from this chapter's title to whether or not this or that grant's inclusion criteria are appropriate for funding. For some, this argument over the construct is a silly semantic distraction that detracts from the work of solving the problem. For others, this is a debate about the very nature of the disorder itself without which the problem cannot be solved. To start, it will be useful to agree on several distinctions that might otherwise be confusing, based on their use.

Psychosis, originally from the Greek *psyche* ("mind" or "soul") and *-osis* (an "abnormality" or "derangement") is a broad term for describing the state of "losing touch with reality." Psychosis describes symptoms. In *DSM-5, psychotic symptoms* include delusions, hallucinations, and formal thought disorder consisting of disorganized thinking and speaking. Psychotic symptoms are present in many psychiatric illnesses other than schizophrenia, including bipolar disorder, dementia, drug-induced psychosis, and a number of physiological conditions such as delirium.

The *schizophrenia spectrum* is a term that was first used in the late 1960s by several authors and refers to the marginal conditions of schizophrenia and, therefore, something short of a clear case of the disorder (Erlenmeyer-Kimling & Nicol, 1969; Kety, Rosenthal, Wender, & Schulsinger, 1971). Its early use was in the context of studying the partial penetrance of genes associated with genetic liability, and it served as shorthand for describing someone who appeared to have a genetic vulnerability to schizophrenia, that is, someone with *schizotaxia*, but who had yet to fully *decompensate* (Meehl, 1962). The term *schizophrenia spectrum* is now often used in a manner that is almost synonymous with a dimensional approach to psychosis—that is, a continuum of symptom expression, including a range of clinical and subclinical symptoms and prodromal states that may or may not ever manifest as a clear case. It may also refer to diagnostic entities similar to schizophrenia, including schizophreniform disorder, schizotypal, schizoid, paranoid and avoidant personality disorders, and, of course, schizophrenia. Out of practice and deference to Kraepelin, authors generally do not include affective disorders, such as bipolar disorder, as part of the schizophrenia spectrum even though these can be accompanied by psychotic features. *Schizoaffective disorder*, the construct to which we now turn, is included in the spectrum.

One thing that discussions of schizophrenia—singular, plural, or in spectrum—rarely clarify is whether the fundamental Kraepelinian distinction between dementia praecox and manic-depressive insanity exists in nature. Although not the first to observe the phenomenon (Kraepelin himself was apparently aware of such cases), Kasanin (1933) receives credit, or blame, for coining the term *schizoaffective* to describe patients who have features of both schizophrenia and bipolar disorder or depression. Thus, the very construct of schizoaffective disorder presents a grave challenge to the original dichotomy of dementia praecox and

manic-depressive insanity. The construct was originally incorporated into *DSM-I* as a subtype, eventually gaining the status of a separate disease entity.[2] This disorder survives despite a lack of evidence for any differences in etiology, pathophysiology, or cognitive or affective functioning and for only occasional differences in treatment outcome between patients with schizophrenia and those with schizoaffective disorder. Thus, while the schizoaffective diagnosis appears to occupy an intermediate place between schizophrenia and the mood disorders based on symptoms (Laursen, Agerbo, & Pedersen, 2009), there does not appear to be anything particularly "special" about this place. Currently, the schizoaffective construct remains in the lexicon because it has become a convenient way to describe patients with a mixed presentation.

Statistical Analyses and Empirical Constructs

There are increasing numbers of scientific, particularly statistical, tools that have been turned toward this question of whether schizophrenia exists in nature separate from other entities. This work, using the kind of large databases of which Emil Kraepelin would have been particularly fond, purports to examine the *meta-structure* of psychopathology. Meta-structure is the efficient description of the relationships between and among various observed symptoms using factor and clustering procedures to infer the underlying, or latent, constructs that account for the observed symptoms. If schizophrenia and bipolar disorders were distinct constructs, for example, this approach could show the patterns of symptom co-occurrence that could only be accounted for by this distinction. To test this possibility, Markon (2010) examined data from the British psychiatric epidemiological survey of over 7,000 adults wherein items derived from diagnostic criteria, including psychosis screening questions, were analyzed together to find the factor and cluster structures underlying the most common combinations of symptoms that people experienced. As illustrated in Figure 12.1A, a factor defined by paranoia,

---

2. Another "intermediate" diagnosis whose origin is relevant to schizophrenia is *borderline personality disorder*. The borderline here was that between psychosis and neurosis. In current practice, borderline personality disorder is rarely conceptualized as part of the psychotic spectrum although antipsychotic medications are prescribed in some cases.

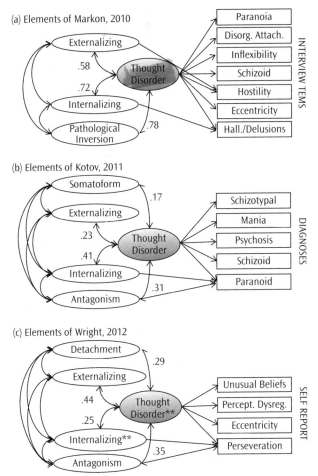

Figure 12.1 Models of the meta-structure of psychopathology. Ovals indicate the latent symptom dimensions that were inferred from factor and cluster analytic procedures. Rectangles show the observed indicator variables measured for thought disorder/psychoticism listed in order of strength of their relationship to the latent dimension; additional indicator variables were used for the other latent symptom dimensions. Correlations between Thought Disorder and the other latent symptom dimensions are illustrated. *In Kotov et al. (2011), Axis I psychotic diagnosis, including schizophrenia, could not be further distinguished because of hierarchical diagnostic rules. **For consistency with other factors in the figure, Wright et al.'s (2012) use of the terms *psychoticism, disinhibition*, and *negative affect* were relabeled *thought disorder, externalizing*, and *internalizing*, respectively. Disorg. Attach. = disorganized attachment; Hall. = hallucinations; Percept. Dysreg. = perceptual dysregulation.

eccentricity, unstable relationships, inflexibility, and social and physical anhedonia was uniquely associated with a cluster referred to as "Thought Disorder." Interestingly, hostility, a common symptom of bipolar disorder, defined *both* the Thought Disorder factor, which represented psychosis, and an Externalizing factor, which represented the tendency to act out on impulses. In contrast, hallucinations and delusions defined *both* Thought Disorder and an Internalizing factor, which represented the tendency to react aversively to stressors. The finding is consistent with Kraepelin' and Bleuler's work in so far as they acknowledged that prominent psychotic symptoms of schizophrenia, such as delusions and hallucinations, are not unique to those with this disorder. However, the high level of covariation between Thought Disorder and all the other latent psychopathology factors suggests more of a general vulnerability component rather than a distinct entity such as schizophrenia existing in a subset of people. But perhaps this was the wrong sample in which to find a distinction.

While Markon's work occurred in a large sample that doubtless included many past, present, and future psychosis patients, most respondents would not have had any of these symptoms. A more specific focus on psychiatric patients and their complaints is also needed because this is, after all, the subset of the population of greatest concern. To examine the meta-structure across 28 diagnoses from *DSM-IV*, Kotov and colleagues (2011) examined co-occurrence patterns from diagnostic interviews of 2,900 adults referred for outpatient treatment. As illustrated in Figure 12.1B, the meta-structure of psychosis that arose was similar to the pattern found in the general population by means of item-level data: a latent construct emerged defined by *both* psychosis (including schizophrenia and schizoaffective disorder) and mania, as well as three other schizophrenia-spectrum diagnoses—schizotypal, schizoid, and paranoid personality disorders—and for convenience it was again labeled Thought Disorder. In this case, the schizophrenia cluster and mania loaded on Thought Disorder with the same strength (.70, .72, respectively). The relationships between the various latent factors, which again included Externalizing and Internalizing and others, were attenuated relative to Markon's results, perhaps because the application of diagnostic thresholds weakens these relationships.

Other analyses agree with this general structure. A smaller sample of schizophrenia patients, their first-degree relatives, and controls showed a similar picture (Tackett, Silberschmidt, Krueger, & Sponheim, 2008), as did a large sample of undergraduates (Wright et al., 2012, illustrated in Figure 12.1C). Therefore, across a number of studies using a variety of modeling approaches and populations, evidence for a nosological, or symptom-based, dichotomy between schizophrenia and bipolar affective disorder has yet to emerge. Instead, there appears to be a pattern of covariation in the symptoms in both disorders that suggests elements of impaired cognitive and affective processing.

Conceptualizing Schizophrenia

A theme of this chapter is that schizophrenia is neither a disease entity nor a group of disease entities (for additional, convergent evidence, see MacDonald, 2013). For most purposes it is useful to understand schizophrenia as an open concept. As a syndrome, schizophrenia is a collection of symptoms that may appear to be superficially unrelated but whose co-occurrence in many patients suggests a shared etiology of some kind. Open concepts frustrate precise definitions. While one can impose definitions, they remain artificial because there are no necessary or sufficient conditions for membership in a class described by an open concept. Any boundary for the class should be taken with a grain of salt. Members of an open concept have a "family resemblance," one to the next, and we recognize members of the class because they are similar to this or that exemplar.

Understanding schizophrenia as an open concept is not to deny its existence, or to suggest the construct is useless or even harmful. In fact, *most concepts are open concepts*, and we build our understanding of the concept through experience rather than through definitions. In natural language, concepts with natural boundaries are the exception rather than the rule. Thus, while natural boundaries between schizophrenia and other disorders may not exist, open concepts like schizophrenia or the schizophrenia spectrum are useful for guiding the study of the causes and treatment of an illness. We can now turn to its internal structure and the challenge of understanding the differences among patients with schizophrenia.

Clinical Presentation and Structure of Symptoms

If we have located the construct of schizophrenia as a delineated space on a schizophrenia spectrum with a certain level of symptom severity and no clear boundaries that exist in nature, there still remains a high level of heterogeneity among patients diagnosed with the illness in terms of its presenting symptoms and its prognosis. This is another kind of challenge to the construct of schizophrenia, because it suggests that there may be different kinds of schizophrenia. Indeed, as early as 1911, Bleuler and others were concerned about this level of heterogeneity and sought out meaningful subgroups of patients within the larger diagnosis (see, e.g., Bleuler, 1911/1950). Bleuler wrote of different schizophrenias, as one might discuss different cancers. These different schizophrenias, or subtypes as they came to be known, included *paranoid* patients, whose presentation was dominated by preoccupation with delusions or auditory hallucinations; *catatonic* patients, who were immobile or, in improved cases, showed flat affect and little motivation; and *undifferentiated* (or, for Bleuler, *hebephrenic*) patients, who did not fall conveniently into either of those categories but also did not have a milder form of the illness (referred to as *simple schizophrenia*). While subtypes of schizophrenia are still used in the popular press, they have been used inconsistently over time, do not appear to track familial risk, and have provided little additional guidance for differential treatment. Thus, Bleuler's typology of schizophrenia survived in some form or other through *DSM-IV* but was retired from *DSM-5*.

Another way to cope with heterogeneity is to examine the important axes, or dimensions, along which patients vary. Although this is related to the previous topic examining how schizophrenia fits within the broader structure of mental disorders, this approach uses statistical tools to ask how differences among patients with schizophrenia could be characterized by a few different trait factors. The use of this approach can be dated to the mid-twentieth century (Wittenborn & Holzberg, 1951); the most influential schemes that guide thinking today date from the 1980s and delineate two factors: positive symptoms and negative symptoms. Subsequent schemes have added more dimensions, such as disorganization, excitement, and depression (for review, and three further dimensions, see Peralta & Cuesta, 2001). *Positive symptoms* are so called because they are thought to be symptoms patients have that they did not have before they became ill. Such symptoms include persecutory ideation and other sorts of delusions and hallucinations that can involve various senses, although auditory hallucinations are the most common ones. Consider the experience of one student:

> (Rats) gnawed relentlessly on my neurons, causing massive degeneration. This was particularly upsetting to me, as I depended on a sharp mind for my work in neuroscience. The rats spent significant periods of time consuming brain matter in the occipital lobe of my brain.... So I sought means of ridding my body of them. I bled them out through self-cutting and banging my head until the skin broke, bloody. Continually, I kept my brain active, electrocuting the rats that happened to be feasting on the activated neurons.

> "As a neuroscientist, how can you believe all this?" the doctors queried.
> "Because it is all of the Deep Meaning.... The Deep Meaning transcends scientific logic." (Stefanidis, 2006, p. 422)

These are the kinds of symptoms that feature most prominently in the press and film. Unabomber Ted Kaczynski published a persecutory diatribe arguing that his assassinations were a reasonable response to the threat to human freedom from technology. Nobel-prize winner John Nash's delusions that he was helping hunt down communists featured prominently in the Hollywood film *A Beautiful Mind*.

To say that positive symptoms constitute a dimension is to make at least two assertions. First, if someone has one of these symptoms, then they are at increased risk for the others, perhaps because they share a common causal factor. Second, in the great variety of experiences patients report, there is a continuum, from those with many of these symptoms to those who suffer from none of them. As in Stefanidis's (2006) example, most delusions and hallucinations have a negative valence: They are frequently disturbing, they are sometimes positive (generally grandiose), and are almost never emotionally neutral. Thus, they can be quite intrusive, although many patients with chronic symptoms somehow learn to adapt.

Negative symptoms are thought to be capacities patients lose when they became ill. Negative symptoms include blunted affect, emotional withdrawal, motor retardation, and anhedonia, or the inability to experience pleasure. It is ironic that positive symptoms are frequently scary, whereas this other aspect of the disorder is marked by abnormally reduced emotion. Consider this patient's report of her inability to experience pleasure:

> [T]his nothingness of the self is permanently there. Not a single drug or therapy has ever helped with such nothingness. By nothingness, I mean a sense of emptiness, a painful void of existence that only I can feel. My thoughts, my emotions, and my actions, none of them belong to me anymore. This omnipotent and omnipresent emptiness has taken control of everything. I am an automaton, but nothing is working inside me. (Kean, 2009, p. 1034)

The motivations of wanting and fearing are fundamental to living organisms and these seem to be strongly effected by negative symptoms. Many patients with negative symptoms also report reduced desires and aversions, but their experiences of pleasure and perhaps pain are unaffected (Gard, Kring, & Gard, 2007), which could be what this example is describing.

Disorganization symptoms are the dimension of inattention and formal thought disorder. One prominent example of this is *incoherence*, also known as *word salad*. When asked the question, "Why do people comb their hair?" one patient responded, "Because it makes a twirl in life, my box is broken help me blue elephant. Isn't lettuce brave? I like electrons, hello please!" (Videbeck, 2010). While incoherence is an extreme form of disorganization, more common forms include distractible speech; when asked, "Do you have problems keeping your attention on things?" the patient responded, "I don't know...What was that again?" Sometimes patients experience thought blocking, in which the patient stops in the middle of a thought and cannot finish the sentence. There are a number of problems patients experience in communicating, such as illogicality and a tendency to lose one's train of thought, known as derailment. This dimension also includes inappropriate affect, such as when a patient giggles while describing his or her suicide attempt (Peralta & Cuesta, 1999).

Two other symptom dimensions that frequently emerge from factor analyses are excitement (sometimes called *mania*) and depression (Peralta & Cuesta, 2001). Obviously, these two factors are not specific to schizophrenia. Our consideration of models of personality and psychopathology described here might even suggest that these two factors are manifestations of positive and negative emotionality (or extraversion and neuroticism) and are therefore prominent dimensions of *normal* personality variation (e.g., Markon, 2010; Wright et al., 2012). Also, within the context of the meta-structure of psychopathology and our conclusion that schizophrenia is an open concept, one might well wonder whether the positive, negative, and disorganization dimensions are dimensions of schizophrenia or dimensions of psychosis more broadly.

Other sources of variability between patients may require clinical attention, such as cognitive impairments and suicidality. The lifetime risk of suicide among people with schizophrenia is about 6.6%, which is much higher than in the general population and is indistinguishable from the rate (about 6.7%) among people with unipolar depression, a condition for which suicidal ideation constitutes an actual symptom (Nordentoft, Mortensen, & Pedersen, 2011). Of course, the number of suicide attempts among patients is far higher still.

Symptoms can be thought of as retrospective and global reports of various mental phenomena such as experiences and reactions to those experiences. One way to understand these phenomena may be to examine the cognitive and affective mechanisms that lead to the experiences that are later reported as symptoms.

Cognition and Affect in Schizophrenia

Two traditions, from clinical science and experimental psychology, have been used to evaluate cognition and affect in schizophrenia, in part to understand the relationships between thought and affect and in part to provide a translational link to the biological basis of the disorder. First, the clinical neuropsychological approach is discussed.

Neuropsychological Approach to Deficits in Schizophrenia

The neuropsychological approach to schizophrenia is characterized by the use of standardized behavioral tests known to be sensitive to brain injuries. The goal of this approach is to compare the pattern of performance in schizophrenia patients to patterns in patients with a variety of brain injuries to determine, by analogy, the brain abnormalities that might relate to schizophrenia.

By the turn of the twenty-first century, R. Walter Heinrichs and his students had built up a large database of neuropsychological studies published on schizophrenia. They coded the studies in a manner that allowed them to calculate each task's effect size, which is the difference between the means of the patient and control groups measured in standard deviation units (Heinrichs, 2001, 2005). While the study of schizophrenia was no longer young, few scholars had stood back to examine the broader patterns that were present. Meta-analysis of a large literature was still relatively rare, and some observers still believed that patients with schizophrenia might be spared the kind of impairments often seen in neurological disorders. In some studies, one could even find scholars suggesting that schizophrenia was a kind of creative genius. Heinrichs and his students used their systematic approach to this neuropsychological testing literature to bury these presumptions. They showed that, across a wide range of tests, in every category of thinking they examined, that patients performed worse on average than controls. Patients performed worst on global verbal memory (Cohen's effect size = −.1.41) and performed least badly on block design (Cohen's effect size = −.46, Heinrichs & Zakzanis, 1998). Between these two extremes, there was little systematic sense to patients' behavioral impairments. For example, nonverbal domains other than block design—from simple motor skills to other measures of performance IQ—were also among the most impaired (with effect sizes of −1.30 and −1.26, respectively). In addition to these domains they examined selective verbal memory, nonverbal memory, attention, general intelligence, spatial ability, executive functioning, and language functioning. None of these broader domains appeared to be selectively spared or differentially impaired. The average effect size across this assortment of neuropsychological tests was found to be about −.92; patients performed almost a full standard deviation below the level of controls (Heinrichs, 2005). In comparing this effect size, Heinrichs has reported that this deficiency is larger than in other domains with quantitative metrics, such as patients' levels of impairments in neuroimaging, electrophysiological, and even molecular biological studies. This pattern of widespread behavioral impairments in patients with schizophrenia can be thought of as a *generalized deficit* (Chapman & Chapman, 1973). Despite medication and despite improvements in measurement of more specific domains of dysfunction, this generalized deficit still remains the most prominent feature of behavior on neuropsychological tests in patients with schizophrenia. Indeed, it is so prominent that cognitive impairments were even proposed as a diagnostic criterion (Keefe & Fenton, 2007).

Does the generalized deficit relate to patients' symptom expression? Dominguez and colleagues (2009) reviewed this literature by dividing neuropsychological tasks into nine domains of performance (executive control, speed of processing, verbal working memory, etc.) and comparing their relationship with positive, negative, disorganized, and depressed symptoms across 58 studies. In this approach, positive and depressive symptoms showed few systematic relationships with performance across cognitive domains, whereas negative symptoms were correlated with the cognitive domains, $r = −.08$ to $−.25$, and disorganization symptoms were correlated, $r = −.12$ to $−.29$. Although the various domains correlated in a rather narrow range, negative symptoms were most highly correlated with verbal fluency whereas disorganization was most highly correlated with reasoning and problem-solving and attention/vigilance. Thus, these off-the-shelf tests suggest that performance across domains, perhaps corresponding to the generalized deficit, is somewhat linked to negative and disorganization symptoms. These tests, however, do not provide very much insight into the nature of delusion, hallucinations, and other positive symptoms or even the symptoms they are correlated with, for that matter. Let us then consider an alternative approach that might provide a complementary set of tools.

Cognitive-Experimental Approach to Deficits in Schizophrenia

The pattern of finding a generalized deficit across a broad swathe of neuropsychological tests presents a challenge to behavioral researchers. Logically, the domain or domains with the largest effect sizes should provide guidance for choosing processes to be examined in detail. This examination might then isolate the brain networks and predisposing cognitive processes that underlie symptoms. However, when so many facets of behavioral performance are impaired, and nearly every suspicion falls on nearly every brain region thought to support those processes according to clinical neuropsychological lore, there is no clear path to follow.

A different approach that also emphasizes behavioral performance is called the *cognitive-experimental approach.* Instead of using a broad battery of well-standardized tests to find a relative impairment, this approach uses a confirmatory hypothesis-driven approach to test theories about the mechanisms underlying the various symptoms of schizophrenia. While experimental studies of schizophrenia patients have been conducted since the outset—indeed, Kraepelin trained in the laboratory of the founder of experimental psychology, Wilhelm Wundt—the modern tradition of cognitive-experimental psychopathology grows from the work of pioneers like David Shakow and Saul Mednick (1958), who applied new theories of information processing and learning, respectively, to the study of schizophrenia.

To follow one such pioneer, Shakow's work focused on a phenomenon wherein patients responded faster to a probe following an irregular delay than to one after a consistent delay, whereas controls showed the opposite pattern (Rodnick & Shakow, 1940); this phenomenon came to be called *reaction time crossover*. Notice here that patients' performance is *relatively spared* on the irregular delay, the condition that is in fact more difficult for controls. Shakow conceptualized this reaction time crossover as a failure to maintain alertness or maintain set over time, and found it was related to patients' level of disorganization symptoms (Rosenthal, Lawlor, Zahn, & Shakow, 1960).

As cognitive theory continued to develop, the construct of maintaining set fell out of favor and became subsumed within other psychological constructs; one such generalization was context processing. Context processing was introduced by Jonathan Cohen and colleagues to bring into a single framework the extant literatures on executive control, attention, and working memory (Cohen & Servan-Schreiber, 1992; Servan-Schreiber, Cohen, & Steingard, 1996). This theory, expressed as a formal computer model, posited that context processing was the goal-dependent modulation of activity in task-dedicated circuits to support "nondominant" or underlearned responses. The representation and maintenance of the context, generally goals or task-relevant information no longer present in the environment, required constant updating. A reverberating circuit in dorsolateral prefrontal cortex (DLPFC) accomplished this, and the strength of the update depended on a signal-to-noise ratio that was believed to depend on the neurotransmitter dopamine. This theory suggested, and the data supported, a mechanism by which patients' might fail across a number of different kinds of tests, for example, by losing the context of a sentence and getting derailed by the dominant meaning of a word, leading to a word salad (Cohen, Barch, Carter, & Servan-Schreiber, 1999). Indeed, by modifying a continuous performance task, the authors demonstrated that patients' performance was relatively spared on a condition that did not require context processing relative to a second condition that required extra context processing. Reminiscent of Shakow's findings, the extent to which patients were impaired correlated with their disorganization symptoms (see MacDonald, 2008, for further discussion). This approach to understanding disorganization symptoms continues to morph and generalize to incorporate additional phenomena, including some perceptual tasks that would appear to be quite distinct from failures to maintain set or context processing (Phillips & Silverstein, 2003). Another fly in the ointment here is that while these constructs may provide some insight into the disorganization symptom dimension, their correlations with symptoms are not consistently higher than those with neuropsychological measures. In addition, this series of theories provides little insight into the other symptoms of schizophrenia; the theory is not yet general enough to explain the reason why these symptoms appear together.

Therefore, it is important to note that other cognitive-experimental approaches are continuing to develop, and these theories are naturally broadening to incorporate the methods and theories of cognitive neuroscience, which we will address subsequently. Several theories are aimed at understanding positive symptoms, such as persecutory ideation. One such theory that has been somewhat generative suggests that persecutory ideation is the result of an interaction between abnormal affective experiences, which are associated with anxiety, and poor reasoning skills that lead persecuted individuals to jump to conclusions (Freeman, 2007). In the absence of anxiety, someone prone to jump to conclusions would not become persecuted, although they might carry around a number of other odd beliefs. In the absence of a jumping-to-conclusions bias, evidence would be scrutinized more thoroughly and explanations for an emotional experience would be more realistic.

A central test of the jumping-to-conclusions bias is called the *beads test*, in which participants have the opportunity to draw color beads from a virtual jar until they decide to guess the predominant color of beads in the jar. One way to perform the task would be to draw half or even more of the beads from the jar to ensure that one's early draws were not flukes. While few people actually draw that many beads, one study found that patients draw fewer beads before being willing to guess, that patients who are currently delusional are those most likely to draw few beads, and that this trait is largely stable over time (So et al., 2012). Thus, a combination of affective experiences and a failure to censor or reign in unlikely explanations of those experiences may capture a complementary aspect of schizophrenia that is mechanistically distinct from what underlies negative and disorganization symptoms.

In many respects, the cognitive-experimental approach to the behavioral level of analysis is the natural domain within which to demonstrate the relationship between the psychological mechanisms underlying moment-to-moment experiences and the global, frequently retrospective reports of symptoms. The approach incorporates and modifies tools to examine specific hypotheses as opposed to using well-standardized testing batteries. This flexibility is also a grave challenge, as many paradigms will not behave in the manner expected; even here it can be difficult to distinguish between specific deficits in a hypothesized mechanism and the generalized deficit (see Chapman & Chapman, 1973). Despite these challenges, one measure of the success of the cognitive-experimental approach is that it has become an integral component of cognitive neuroscientific studies that use these tasks to challenge specific brain regions and networks during imaging. We now turn our attention to the important findings from this level of analysis.

Systems and Cognitive Neuroscience of Schizophrenia

A widely accepted view is that schizophrenia is a disease of the brain. However, since all mental disorders involve neuronal functions, this is not a particularly helpful revelation. Further, it is not yet clear what kind of brain disease it might be. There is no single insult to the brain or any single structure or neurotransmitter that is uniquely responsible. Therefore, one of the challenges is to link the symptoms of schizophrenia and the problems in cognition and affect to particular facets of brain functioning.

It would be helpful to know that a handful of regions show slowed responses, relative decreases or increases in activation, or weaker connectivity in schizophrenia. Unfortunately, and despite a great deal of effort, this kind of pithy conclusion is not yet possible from the fragmented literature arising from the various methods used to study the neural processes in people with schizophrenia.

Electroencephalography

Scalp electrodes can reveal a number of different aspects of the *timing* of brain functions. One method, called electroencephalography (EEG), focuses on the frequencies and strengths of different brain waves. Findings based on this technique have indicated that schizophrenia involves a reduction of the power of brain waves across a broad spectrum; impairments in the gamma spectrum (which has a frequency of electrical brainwaves in the 30–80 Hz range) may be particularly telling (Gandal, Edgar, Klook, & Siegel, 2012). This frequency is responsible for cognitive coordination (Phillips & Silverstein, 2003) and for binding thoughts from different parts of the brain together into a coherent percept (Gonzalez-Burgos & Lewis, 2008). Another way of using scalp electrodes is to examine event-related potentials, which speak to the timing of brain responses to environmental perturbations. Unsurprisingly, this technique has shown that many waveforms have a reduced magnitude in patients. The stand-outs in this crowd, due to either popularity of study or ease of reliable measurement, are reductions in the P1, MMN, and P300 waveforms (for review, see Ford et al., 2012). The P1 is a very early component associated with the perception of a stimulus; the MMN, which stand for mismatch negativity, is an early waveform interpreted as showing an impairment in the early, nonvolitional capacity to redirect attention; and the P300 is a component interpreted as indicating a capacity for attentional orientation. Thus, there is ample evidence that schizophrenia affects of the timing of a number of important processes in the brain, some of which dovetails with evidence of early perceptual impairments, and some of which suggests top-down failures of cognitive control processes.

Structure and Connectivity

If there are timing dysfunctions in the brain, what brain *regions* are most affected? Magnetic resonance imaging (MRI) has been the tool of choice for addressing this kind of question in recent years because MRI instruments can be tuned to examine several aspects of brain anatomy: structure and structural connectivity, and function and functional connectivity. Beginning with structure, a highly replicated and completely unspecific finding is that patients have reductions in intracranial, whole brain, and total gray and white matter volumes and increases in ventricular volumes (De Peri et al., 2012). Early efforts to show more specific abnormalities indicated a consistent loss of gray matter in the superior temporal lobes, a region implicated in auditory sensory processing

(Shenton, Dickey, Frumin, & McCarley, 2001). Inevitably, methods have evolved, and there are now several quantitative reviews examining the literature using whole-brain, voxel-by-voxel analyses called *voxel-based morphometry* (Chan, Di, McAlonan, & Gong, 2011; Ellison-Wright, Glahn, Laird, Thelen, & Bullmore, 2008). These reviews, reporting on two to three dozen studies, have found consistent reductions in gray matter in thalamus and limbic regions such as the insula, anterior cingulate, uncus, and amygdala. While the thalamus is an essential cortico-cortico relay network, these limbic regions are thought to work together in a salience network, responsible for evaluating stimuli for rewards and threats in the environment. Of course, the picture is not entirely consistent and there are other regions where even these reviews differ, such as whether reductions in left inferior frontal gyrus or the cerebellum are reliably reduced in first-episode patients. The impact of chronicity has also been examined, with chronic patients continuing to show gray matter loss in some of these same limbic regions, such as the insula, but also starting to show gray matter compromised in executive control regions such as the inferior and dorsolateral prefrontal cortex, and in a region that becomes more active when the brain is not engaged in a task known as the the medial prefrontal gyrus. Although far fewer studies have directly compared schizophrenia and bipolar patients, they do appear to be similar in showing reductions in whole brain volume and a number of other features compared to controls (De Peri et al., 2012). However, schizophrenia patients may show more gray matter volume reduction, whereas bipolar patients may have more white matter reduction.

White matter is composed of myelinated axons carrying information across the brain. An imaging technique known as diffusion tensor imaging can be used to quantify the extent to which these axon fiber tracts are organized coherently, like rope, or incoherently, like lint. Unsurprisingly, the vast majority of this literature has found evidence for less coherence in the axon fiber tracts of patients with schizophrenia, with some evidence suggesting that the connections between frontal lobe regions are particularly compromised (Pettersson-Yeo, Allen, Benetti, McGuire, & Mechelli, 2011). A shortcoming of both this structural connectivity literature and the structural abnormalities described above is that very few studies have

reported how differences among schizophrenia patients relate to their symptom presentations, therefore making it difficult to tell a more refined story about the relationship between structure and symptoms. Nevertheless, we will try to rectify this when we turn to functional neuroimaging.

Function and Functional Networks

Functional imaging of the brain began in the 1970s (Ingvar & Franzen, 1974), with a marked increase in interest in imaging following the advent of functional magnetic resonance imaging (fMRI) in the early 1990s. However, a concern soon arose as to whether differences in brain activity between patients and controls caused differences in performance, or whether differences in performance, strategy, or motivation reduced the demands on regions that healthy participants used to perform the task (e.g., Ebmeier, Lawrie, Blackwood, Johnstone, & Goodwin, 1995). This causality confound still bedevils the field, increasing the challenge of extracting a coherent meaning from the literally thousands of fMRI studies of schizophrenia patients that have been published to date.

Despite this confound there are a number of conclusions from studies that have begun to link the heterogeneity in patients' symptoms to differences in functioning across the brain (for review of symptom–activation relationships, see Goghari, Sponheim, & MacDonald, 2010). For example, the occurrence of auditory hallucinations corresponds to activity in the superior temporal gyrus, an area we found also to have structural abnormalities. Thus, one of the most common symptoms in schizophrenia may reflect processing at the earliest sensory inputs into the brain. Positive symptoms more generally also appear to be related to abnormalities in the medial prefrontal cortex, a region associated with self-awareness and ideas about others' state of mind. Reduced activation in ventral striatum, a region associated with reward-processing, appears to correlate with the extent to which negative symptoms are expressed. Negative symptoms have also been associated with blunted amygdala responses. Both of these regions are involved in the salience network described earlier. Consistent with behavioral work, disorganization has been related to impairments of activation of the prefrontal cortex, a region of the brain implicated in executive functioning.

While these findings begin to fit within our picture of schizophrenia, they also highlight a major flaw in this literature which, in part because of small sample sizes, has largely neglected the need to examine the relationships between brain activity and patient heterogeneity in symptoms and functioning. This situation is beginning to improve, and several large data sets are currently being collected to enable more definitive testing of these relationships. In the meantime, our next step is to go below the level of systems and look more closely at molecular neurobiology.

Cellular Pathophysiology and Neuropharmacology of Schizophrenia

A growing literature has examined the brain's structure at a still more molecular level, scrutinizing which neurons and glia are present and how patients' neuronal cells may be subtly different from those of healthy controls. This work has relied on brain tissues from people who have donated this organ upon their death, and it reminds us of the importance of this kind of generosity for solving important mental health challenges. Since people live with schizophrenia for many years before passing away, patients' brains reflect not only the causes of the disorder but also the sequelae of chronic illness and the use of medication. These caveats notwithstanding, a number of telling findings have emerged. Complementing this work, neuropharmacology addresses the chemical compounds that affect neurotransmission, including but not limited to neurotransmitters. There are a number of candidates for study, with no reason to think that any one neurotransmitter can account for patients' heterogeneity or is more fundamental to the disorder. This has not always been the case; for many years, schizophrenia was thought to be a problem uniquely associated with problems in the transmission of dopamine (DA).

The origin of the *dopamine hypothesis* of schizophrenia is useful to relay because it provides a nutmeg of consolation for students of psychopathology frustrated by what little we now know of schizophrenia after more than a century of scientific scrutiny. In the mid-twentieth century, psychiatry had to be contented with many vagaries and empirical observations, which is a polite way of saying experiments guided by chance and providence. There was plenty of incentive and opportunity for experimentation: thousands and thousands of patients with schizophrenia were permanently housed on the sprawling, overcrowded campuses of state hospitals. In this atmosphere, a class of compounds that had originally been developed for the textile industry in the nineteenth century and tested for possible antimalarial and anesthetic properties during World War I eventually came to the attention of a team of French psychiatrists (cf. López-Muñoz et al., 2005). After some tinkering, the compound that would eventually be known as chlorpromazine proved to be surprisingly good at reducing patients' concerns about, and the occurrence of, delusions and hallucinations. Though it was hailed as a wonder drug, soon its side effects began to overshadow its successes. This, in turn, led to attempts to find compounds similar to chlorpromazine that did not have such severe side effects; these would become known as typical antipsychotics. Interestingly, these drugs were used in the treatment of schizophrenia starting in the mid-1950s, long before it was understood how they worked. The definitive result underpinning the first dopamine hypotheses of schizophrenia was not published until the mid-1970s, when it was demonstrated that clinical effects of the various antipsychotic drugs available at that time strongly correlated with the extent to which they blocked DA receptors (Seeman & Lee, 1975). This illustrates that treatments can be viable even if the cause of the condition is unknown or even misunderstood. While the dopamine hypothesis accounted for a number of observations about psychosis at the time, the façade of this simple explanation would not stand indefinitely, despite several revisions (for a review of various dopamine hypotheses as well as a modern rendering of the hypotheses, see Howes & Kapur, 2009).

A challenge to the reigning hypothesis built around the *therapeutic* effects of dopamine antagonists came from the *psychomimetic* (psychosis inducing) effects of another drug known as phencyclidine (PCP, or "angel dust"). Phencyclidine was originally developed as a tranquilizer; however, people who used the drug showed transient schizophrenia-like symptoms, and patients who were given the drug showed long-lasting symptom exacerbations even at very low doses (Luby, Gottlieb, Cohen, Rosenbaum, & Domino, 1962). When evidence emerged that phencyclidine and similar compounds such as ketamine ("special K") increased the activity of the N-methyl-D-aspartate, or NMDA, receptors on glutamatergic neurons (Vincent, Kartalovski, Geneste, Kamenka, & Lazdunski, 1979), it brought into focus an alternative *glutamate hypothesis* (Javitt & Zukin, 1991). Pyramidal neurons are pervasive and can be thought of as the primary working neurons and connections of the cortex. This glutamate hypothesis was parsimonious insofar as it explained how a single dysfunction might result in numerous, correlated impairments in different brain systems and relate to the degradation of white matter tracks described earlier. Reinforcing this theory, postmortem studies began to show that pyramidal neurons in patients' brains had shorter axons, tighter cell-packing, and fewer NMDA receptors on their dendrites (see Lin, Lane, & Tsai, 2012, for review). It then became necessary to explain away the primary basis of the dopamine hypothesis, which could be done if the effectiveness of typical dopaminergic antipsychotic drugs was simply the result of dopaminergic modulation of glutamate, or even secondary to their sedative effects. Despite this promise, only a few new pharmaceuticals have been developed on the basis of these findings. This low yield is in part due to the difficulty of safely modulating the activity of one of the most fundamental cell types of the brain.

A third pathophysiological and neuropharmacological hypothesis is largely built on postmortem brain tissue observations but also incorporates gene expression and brain network connectivity data. In this case, the abnormalities of interest are in the γ-aminobutyric acid (GABA) interneurons that inhibit activity in other neurons, primarily pyramidal neurons. This hypothesis is therefore known as the *GABA hypothesis*. These neurons, and in particular a subset of them known as basket and chandelier cells, contain parvalbumin. Parvalbumin maintains the tone of pyramidal neurons that is needed to resonate appropriately in the gamma frequency. This frequency, it will be recalled from above, underlies cognitive coordination and stimulus binding. Originally based on postmortem studies of patients, the GABA hypothesis incorporates the roles of dopamine and glutamate, proposing that perturbations of these neurotransmitter systems are downstream from the dysconnectivity that results from a failure to maintain the tone of pyramidal neurons (see Gonzalez-Burgos & Lewis, 2008, for review). While this hypothesis suggests a new neurotransmitter system to target with pharmaceuticals, this promise has yet to be realized. In the meantime, it provides an elegant example of how multiple methods and data from many levels of analysis can be synthesized into a comprehensive account of a mental illness.

This section provides only a taste of an extensive literature on the neuroscience, pathophysiology, and pharmacology of schizophrenia. Before moving on to explore the causes of these neural abnormalities, it is useful to make two general observations. The first is that while the hypotheses are competing in the scientific community, they need not actually compete in the brain. That is, the hypotheses may all contain a nonmutually exclusive portion of the truth, and other mechanisms may be in play besides. While it is parsimonious to think that the neural basis of schizophrenia is simple, nature frustrates this hope. Research can be hypothesis-driven without making the naïve assumption that there is, at the core, a single abnormality. The second observation is that, given evidence of the kind described here, schizophrenia is often considered more organic than many other disorders described in this text. This classification brings with it many implicit assumptions about the condition and those who suffer from it. For example, it suggests that the true pathology of schizophrenia is to be found in neurons and that treatments for schizophrenia will require medicine to change those neurons. The distinction between psychological and organic causes for a disorder may be appealing, but it is increasingly untenable given our understanding of the tight relationships between the software and hardware of the brain. The brain limits the cognitive mechanisms that can be implemented, but those same neurons also reflect the traces of the cognitive mechanisms that have been required of them. In fact, all disorders addressed in this textbook have or will have neural correlates; all symptoms will respond to medicine, either real or hypothetical. Sometimes the symptoms of schizophrenia appear to be more biologically based, but this may be simply because new biological methods are often brought to bear here first before expanding to other diagnoses. In the final analysis, schizophrenia is unlikely to prove a special case of mental illness in this regard.

Etiology of Schizophrenia

In reviewing findings on the causes of schizophrenia, we will follow the simplified scheme of classifying causes as either genetic or environmental.

Genetic Risks for Schizophrenia

Some of the first examinations of the etiology of schizophrenia were family studies conducted by the protégées of Emil Kraepelin in the 1910s (see Kendler & Zerbin-Rüdin, 1996). Family studies allow inferences to be made through the use quantitative genetics, based on the association between degree of genetic relatedness and level of risk. These earliest studies showed that patients' siblings were at a markedly increased risk of illness relative to the general population, but the studies were largely neglected until the 1960s when a new generation of scholars began to examine whether genes might play a role in the etiology of schizophrenia. Gottesman (1991) combined these data across studies to show a compelling relationship: third-degree relatives, such as patients' first cousins, who share about 12.5% of their genes, show a 2% risk of developing the disorder compared to .7% in the general population. Second-degree relatives, such as uncles and nieces, share about 25% of their genes and have a 2–6% *risk*, whereas first-degree relatives, such as siblings, including fraternal twins, have a 6–17% *risk*, but patients' monozygotic twins, who share 100% of their genes, have nearly a 50% risk. These data are interpreted in the parlance of quantitative genetics as indicating the heritability of the *liability to schizophrenia*. Liability can be thought of as the diathesis to schizophrenia, that is, it is necessary but not sufficient for developing the illness. These data, along with information about the prevalence of schizophrenia in the general population, show that the liability is 80% heritable in most populations, which is to say 80% of the variance in liability in that population is associated with variance in genes across the whole genome.

The data do not tell us how heritable *schizophrenia* is. For example, the likelihood that you will develop schizophrenia if a monozygotic co-twin has the illness is only about 50%. These findings suggest a phenomenon called *reduced penetrance*. Simply inheriting the genetic liability for the illness is generally insufficient to cause the illness. Something additional is needed. Thus, the diathesis-stress model suggests some kind of environmental stressor might be required in addition to the diathesis to make the disorder become manifested. We will review a number of such proposed stressors later, but it is worth noting that luck—the chance factors that govern whether or not this or that gene is expressed in the body's cells—also counts as an "environmental" contribution within this model.

Quantitative genetic studies provide the impetus for *molecular genetic research*, and this has now become one of the fastest developing domains of the schizophrenia literature. Rather than asking *whether* genes contribute to the illness, this research asks *which* genes contribute. The hope is not simply that identifying these genes will be interesting, but that the functions of those genes will suggest treatments, or even a cure. The thrust of the story of the molecular genetics of schizophrenia is threefold: identifying genes involved in the illness requires very large samples of patients and controls, and more markers across the genome, because there are likely to be many, many genes that convey a little bit of risk.

In the 1990s, the molecular genetics of schizophrenia consisted largely of linkage studies that used measures of recombination frequency, rather than a specific physical distance along each chromosome, to detect regions of various chromosomes that might be associated with risk for schizophrenia. By the end of this era, there were a number of promising findings, such as a portion of chromosome 2p12-q22.1 that was consistently linked to the illness (Lewis et al., 2003). However, the method precluded identifying specific genes and thus precluded understanding the specific pathways to illness.

In the 2000s, attention turned to specific genetic markers known as single-nucleotide polymorphisms, or SNPs, which formed the basis of the candidate gene approach. In this method, SNPs on a number of candidate genes were selected for closer scrutiny because they were thought to be involved in a putative neural mechanism. SNP markers on a number of genes came to light, including genes relevant to DA (e.g., catechol-O-methyltransferase [COMT]), glutamate (e.g., neuregulin [NRG1]), GABA (e.g., glutamic acid decarboxylase 1 [GAD1]), and neurodevelopment (e.g., disrupted in schizophrenia 1 [DISC1]), among others. While a number of early studies using this method provided excited results, researchers worried about the low replicability of many findings, particularly those derived from small sample sizes ($Ns < 1000$).

A series of new findings shook up this a priori approach to gene discovery when genotyping technology advanced and genome-wide association studies (GWAS) became practical. Genome-wide association studies do not examine a few markers in selected genes. Instead, they look at markers across all chromosomes to identify any gene with a sufficiently strong association to an illness. However examining so many markers presents the statistical problem of multiple comparisons, the clearest solution to which is an increase in sample sizes. Large consortia formed to obtain the sample sizes required for replicable results, and these have begun to make progress on the problem, with some surprising results. For example, schizophrenia risk was associated with genes in 6p22 that code for histones (Shi et al., 2009). Histones are spools around which strands of DNA are curled, and as such they play a fundamental role in ordering and regulating gene expression. If histones do indeed turn out to play a role in the schizophrenia diathesis, and the region is indeed associated with the illness in other samples, this would be a largely nonspecific risk factor.

Another nonspecific risk factor that has come to light is DNA copy number variations (CNVs). CNVs are places where a sequence of nucleotides varies within a population, such that some individuals may have few repeats and others may have very many copies of the sequence, or where a fragment of DNA is missing. CNVs are associated with many other mental and physical illnesses. Some CNVs convey a high degree of risk for schizophrenia, but these are rare even among populations of patients (Walsh et al., 2008). Therefore, alone they account for only a small amount of the genetic liability to the illness over a population.

Molecular genetic studies of schizophrenia originally set out to establish which genes contribute to risk for the illness. Instead they discovered that many genes—likely numbering in the thousands—are statistically associated with the illness, and that many of these genes are quite common in the general population as well. In addition, all the genes that have so far been associated with schizophrenia together account for a very small proportion of the variance in schizophrenia in the population, suggesting that more complicated interactions and pathways will have to be taken into account. Instead of implicating a specific genetic or molecular mechanism of risk, these studies suggest that a number of mechanisms may be relevant to the diathesis for schizophrenia and psychosis more broadly. The job of untangling these findings enough to turn them into treatment options remains a daunting task.

Environmental and Other Risks for Schizophrenia

In the decades following World War II, clinical practice in the United States was dominated by psychodynamic, and therefore primarily environmental, explanations of psychosis. One tragic consequence of this bias was the growth of a myth of a *schizophrenogenic mother*. The schizophrenogenic mother was said to have defective interactions with her children and a number of other vague and at times conflicting shortcomings as a parent that led the future patient to learn something that eventually manifested as the illness. The unintended result of these strongly environmental theories of schizophrenia was that the parents of patients, already struggling with the day-to-day difficulties of supporting their ill son or daughter, were further saddled by the guilt of perhaps having caused the illness to begin with. This is the cautionary environmentalists' tale, much as the history of eugenics is a caution of overinterpreting genetic causal factors.

The fundamental observation that still requires an environmental, or nongenetic, account of the etiology of schizophrenia is that the concordance between monozygotic twins is about 50%. Since this is less than 100%, it is thought that there must be some nongenetic cause that leads to the ultimate manifestation. Table 12.1 lists eight additional risk factors that have been established

Table 12.1 Nongenetic Risk Factors Associated with Schizophrenia

Risk Factor	Odds Ratio
Migrant status	4.6
Older fathers	3.8
Toxoplasmosis gondii exposure	2.7
Prenatal famine	2.3
Lifetime cannabis use	2.1
Obstetrical complications	1.8
Urban rearing	1.7
Winter or spring birth	1.1

Note: For full citations, see MacDonald and Schulz (2009). Odds ratios are calculated as the increased odds of someone with the risk factor developing the condition, where 1.0 is the general population risk.

through large meta-analyses. None of these risk factors implicates defective parenting, and most of them implicate either pre- or perinatal events (older fathers, prenatal famine, obstetrical complications, winter or spring birth) or other biological risk factors (*Toxoplasmosis gondii* exposure, lifetime cannabis use). That is, they are unlikely to affect one's learning regimen. Of the two others, migrant status and urban rearing, is it unclear what aspect of these very general risk factors convey risk at this time, although an argument can be made for stress or anxiety. Importantly, even the most reliably potent risk factors—such as migrant status or older fathers—only moderately increases risk; most patients are not migrants or the offspring of older fathers.

Another question that arises with a great deal of regularity is whether brain injuries cause schizophrenia. Many researchers who use neuroimaging and therefore screen patients for head injuries have observed that patients with schizophrenia are far more likely than controls to report an errant baseball bat or harrowing bicycle accident that left them with a concussion. According to published case studies, head injuries can only in rare instances lead to psychosis, and these psychoses generally have fewer negative symptoms (Fujii & Fujii, 2012). These findings would seem to suggest that a schizophrenia patient with few negative symptoms could be indistinguishable from a patient with head injury–induced psychosis. However, this kind of question is tricky to study rigorously in sufficiently large samples to come to a definitive conclusion.

Finally, careful readers will note that our classification of genetic and environmental causation is, like other convenient distinctions raised in this chapter, to be taken with a grain of salt. For example, evidence for these risk factors does not rule out the possibility that a great deal of the reduced concordance between monozygotic twins is simply due to chance; such twins may have inherited differences in the strength of expressing certain genes, a phenomenon known as methylation. Thus, even nongenetic causes may involve the genome in some ways. Another way in which the genetic–environmental distinction may be misleading is in the context of gene–environment correlations and gene–environment interactions. For example, cannabis use may only be a risk factor for people with a particular diathesis. Thus, the reader should be prepared to critique such simplistic classifications.

Conclusion

The symptoms of schizophrenia constitute a devastating, serious, and persistent syndrome that affects a remarkably high proportion of the human race. It can affect all aspects of life, indeed shortening life itself through increased suicidality and other health consequences. Numerous theories of the nature of the illness have arisen and have fallen in the 100 years since its description and coinage by Kraepelin and Bleuler. Were these progenitors alive today, they would survey the legacy of their work with a mixture of pride and disappointment.

There is much to be proud of in the century of work that has expanded our knowledge of how different symptoms dimensions relate to each other and to other disorders, how these relate to cognitive functions and brain networks, and how these brain networks are in turn influenced by biochemical processes. The fact that these processes may not be specific to schizophrenia per se but may be relevant to disorders beyond that strict definition does not detract from those accomplishments. It is ironic, however, that much of the progress in treating the illness has proceeded entirely independent of the psychopathological science regarding it. Pharmacological treatment discoveries, although never coincidences, have only in recent years been built on our understanding of the causes of the disorder. It is also ironic that psychosocial treatments, used rarely in the past, have become increasingly acceptable within this new zeitgeist of nonspecificity of symptoms and broad sources of causation. Thus, while the construct introduced to psychiatry 100 years ago is certainly showing signs of aging, it is sure to provide a reference point for thinking about psychosis far into the future.

References

Bleuler, E. (1950). *Dementia praecox or the group of schizophrenias* (Trans. J. Zinkin). New York: International Universities Press (original work published 1911).

Chan, R. C. K., Di, X., McAlonan, G. M., & Gong, Q. (2011). Brain anatomical abnormalities in high-risk individuals, first-episode, and chronic schizophrenia: An activation likelihood estimation meta-analysis of illness progression. *Schizophrenia Bulletin*, 37(1), 177–188.

Chapman, L. J., & Chapman, J. P. (1973). Problems in the measurement of cognitive deficit. *Psychological Bulletin*, 79, 380–385.

Cohen, J. D., Barch, D. M., Carter, C., & Servan-Schreiber, D. (1999). Context-processing deficits in schizophrenia: Converging evidence from three theoretically motivated cognitive tasks. *Journal of Abnormal Psychology, 108*(1), 120–133.

Cohen, J. D., & Servan-Schreiber, D. (1992). Context, cortex and dopamine: A connectionist approach to behavior and biology in schizophrenia. *Psychological Review, 99*(1), 45–77.

De Peri, L., Crescini, A., Deste, G., Fusar-Poli, P., Sacchetti, E., & Vita, A. (2012). Brain structural abnormalities at the onset of schizophrenia and bipolar disorder: A meta-analysis of controlled magnetic resonance imaging studies. *Current Pharmaceutical Design, 18*(4), 486–494.

Dominguez, M. D. G., Viechtbauer, W., Simons, C. J. P., van Os, J., & Krabbendam, L. (2009). Are psychotic psychopathology and neurocognition orthogonal? A systematic review of their associations. *Psychological Bulletin, 135*(1), 157–171.

Ebmeier, K. P., Lawrie, S. M., Blackwood, D. H. R., Johnstone, E. C., & Goodwin, G. M. (1995). Hypofrontality revisited: A high resolution single photon emission computer tomography study in schizophrenia. *Journal of Neurology, Neurosurgery and Psychiatry, 58*, 452–456.

Ellison-Wright, I., Glahn, D. C., Laird, A. R., Thelen, S. M., & Bullmore, E. (2008). The anatomy of first-episode and chronic schizophrenia: An anatomical likelihood estimation meta-analysis. *American Journal of Psychiatry, 165*(8), 1015–1023.

Erlenmeyer-Kimling, L., & Nicol, S. (1969). Comparison of hospitalization measures in schizophrenic patients with and without a family history of schizophrenia. *British Journal of Psychiatry, 115*(520), 321–334.

Evans, K., McGrath, J., & Milns, R. (2003). Searching for schizophrenia in ancient Greek and Roman literature: A systematic review. *Acta Psychiatrica Scandinavica, 107*(5), 323–330.

Ford, J. M., Dierks, T., Fisher, D. J., Herrmann, C. S., Hubl, D., Kindler, J.,...van Lutterveld, R. (2012). Neurophysiological studies of auditory verbal hallucinations. *Schizophrenia Bulletin, 38*(4), 715–723.

Freeman, D. (2007). Suspicious minds: The psychology of persecutory delusions. *Clinical Psychology Review, 27*(4), 425–457.

Fujii, D., & Fujii, D. C. (2012). Psychotic disorder due to traumatic brain injury: Analysis of case studies in the literature. *Journal of Neuropsychiatry and Clinical Neurosciences, 24*(3), 278–289.

Gandal, M. J., Edgar, J. C., Klook, K., & Siegel, S. J. (2012). Gamma synchrony: Towards a translational biomarker for the treatment-resistant symptoms of schizophrenia. *Neuropharmacology, 62*(3), 1504–1518.

Gard, D., Kring, A., & Gard, M. (2007). Anhedonia in schizophrenia: Distinctions between anticipatory and consummatory pleasure. *Schizophrenia Research, 93*(415), 253–260.

Goghari, V. M., Sponheim, S. R., & MacDonald, A. W. (2010). The functional neuroanatomy of symptom dimensions in schizophrenia: A qualitative and quantitative review of a persistent question. *Neuroscience and Biobehavioral Reviews, 34*(3), 468–486.

Gonzalez-Burgos, G., & Lewis, D. A. (2008). GABA neurons and the mechanisms of network oscillations: Implications for understanding cortical dysfunction in schizophrenia. *Schizophrenia Bulletin, 34*(5), 944–961.

Gottesman, I. I. (1991). *Schizophrenia genesis: The origins of madness.* New York: W.H. Freeman.

Häfner, H., Maurer, K., Löffler, W., Fätkenheuer, B., an der Heiden, W., Riecher-Rössler, A.,...Gattaz, W. F. (1994). The epidemiology of early schizophrenia. Influence of age and gender on onset and early course. *British Journal of Psychiatry Supplement, 23*, 29–38.

Heinrichs, R. W. (2001). *In search of madness: Schizophrenia and neuroscience.* New York: Oxford University Press.

Heinrichs, R. W. (2005). The primacy of cognition in schizophrenia. *American Psychologist, 60*(3), 229–242.

Heinrichs, R. W., & Zakzanis, K. K. (1998). Neurocognitive deficit in schizophrenia: A quantitative review of the evidence. *Neuropsychology, 12*(3), 426–445.

Howard, R., Rabins, P. V, Seeman, M. V., & Jeste, D. V. (2000). Late-onset schizophrenia and very-late-onset schizophrenia-like psychosis: An international consensus. The International Late-Onset Schizophrenia Group. *American Journal of Psychiatry, 157*(2), 172–178.

Howes, O. D., & Kapur, S. (2009). The dopamine hypothesis of schizophrenia: Version III—The final common pathway. *2009, 35*(3), 549–562.

Ingvar, D. H., & Franzen, G. (1974). Distribution of cerebral activity in chronic schizophrenia. *Lancet*, 1484–1486.

Jablensky, A., Sartorius, N., Ernberg, G., Anker, M., Korten, A., Cooper, J. E.,…Bertelsen, A. (1992). Schizophrenia: manifestations, incidence and course in different cultures. A World Health Organization ten-country study. *Psychological Medicine Monograph Supplement*, *20*, 1–97.

Javitt, D. C., & Zukin, S. R. (1991). Recent advances in the phencyclidine model of schizophrenia. *American Journal of Psychiatry*, *148*, 1301–1308.

Kasanin, J. (1933). The acute schizoaffective psychoses. *American Journal of Psychiatry*, *90*(1), 97–126.

Kean, C. (2009). Silencing the self: Schizophrenia as a self-disturbance. *Schizophrenia Bulletin*, *35*(6), 1034–1036.

Keefe, R. S. E., & Fenton, W. S. (2007). How should DSM-V criteria for schizophrenia include cognitive impairment? *Schizophrenia Bulletin*, *33*(4), 912–920.

Kendler, K. S., & Zerbin-Rüdin, E. (1996). Abstract and review of "Zur Erbpathologie der Schizophrenie" (Contribution to the genetics of schizophrenia). 1916. *American Journal of Medical Genetics*, *67*(4), 343–346.

Kety, S. S., Rosenthal, W., Wender, P. H., & Schulsinger, F. (1971). Mental Illness in the biological and adoptive families of adopted schizophrenics. *American Journal of Psychiatry*, *128*(3), 302–306.

Kirkbride, J. B., Fearon, P., Morgan, C., Dazzan, P., Morgan, K., Tarrant, J.,…Jones, P. B. (2006). Heterogeneity in incidence rates of schizophrenia and other psychotic syndromes: Findings from the 3-center AeSOP study. *Archives of General Psychiatry*, *63*(3), 250–258.

Kotov, R., Ruggero, C. J., Krueger, R. F., Watson, D., Yuan, Q., & Zimmerman, M. (2011). New dimensions in the quantitative classification of mental illness. *Archives of General Psychiatry*, *68*(10), 1003–1011.

Kraepelin, E. (1971). *Dementia praecox and paraphrenia* (Trans. R M. Barclay). Edinburgh: Livingston (original work published 1919).

Krueger, R. F., & MacDonald, A. W. I. (2005). Dimensional approaches to understanding and treating psychosis. *Psychiatric Annals*, *35*, 31–34.

Laursen, T. M., Agerbo, E., & Pedersen, C. B. (2009). Bipolar disorder, schizoaffective disorder, and schizophrenia overlap: A new comorbidity index. *Journal of Clinical Psychiatry*, *70*(10), 1432–1438.

Lewis, C. M., Levinson, D. F., Wise, L. H., DeLisi, L. E., Straub, R. E., Hovatta, I.,…Faraone, S. V. (2003). Genome scan meta-analysis of schizophrenia and bipolar disorder, part II: Schizophrenia. *American Journal of Human Genetics*, *73*(1), 34–48.

Lin, C.-H., Lane, H.-Y., & Tsai, G. E. (2012). Glutamate signaling in the pathophysiology and therapy of schizophrenia. *Pharmacology, Biochemistry, and Behavior*, *100*(4), 665–677.

López-Muñoz, F., Alamo, C., Cuenca, E., Shen, W., Clervoy, P., & Rubio, G. (2005). History of the discovery and clinical introduction of chlorpromazine. *Annals of Clinical Psychiatry*, *17*(3), 113–135.

Luby, E. D., Gottlieb, J. S., Cohen, B. D., Rosenbaum, G., & Domino, E. F. (1962). Model psychoses and schizophrenia. *American Journal of Psychiatry*, *119*, 61–67.

MacDonald, A. W. (2008). Building a clinically relevant cognitive task: Case study of the AX paradigm. *Schizophrenia Bulletin*, *34*(4), 619–628.

MacDonald, A. W. (2013). What kind of a thing is schizophrenia? Specific causation and general failure modes. In S. M. Silverstein, B. Moghaddam, & T. Wykes (Eds.), *Schizophrenia: Evolution and synthesis* (pp. 24–48). Cambridge, MA: MIT Press.

MacDonald, A. W., & Schulz, S. C. (2009). What we know: Findings that every theory of schizophrenia should explain. *Schizophrenia Bulletin*, *35*(3), 493–508.

Markon, K. E. (2010). Modeling psychopathology structure: A symptom-level analysis of axis I and II disorders. *Psychological Medicine*, *40*(2), 273–288.

McGrath, J., Saha, S., Chant, D., & Welham, J. (2008). Schizophrenia: A concise overview of incidence, prevalence, and mortality. *Epidemiologic Reviews*, *30*, 67–76.

Mednick, S. A. (1958). A learning theory approach to research in schizophrenia. *Psychological Bulletin*, *55*(5), 316–327.

Meehl, P. E. (1962). Schizotaxia, schizotypy, schizophrenia. *American Psychologist*, *17*, 827–838.

Nordentoft, M., Mortensen, P. B., & Pedersen, C. B. (2011). Absolute risk of suicide after first hospital contact in mental disorder. *Archives of General Psychiatry*, *68*(10), 1058–1064.

Peralta, V., & Cuesta, M. J. (1999). Dimensional structure of psychotic symptoms: An item-level analysis of SAPS and SANS symptoms in psychotic disorders. *Schizophrenia Research*, *38*(1), 13–26.

Peralta, V., & Cuesta, M. J. (2001). How many and which are the psychopathological dimensions of schizophrenia? Issues influencing their ascertainment. *Schizophrenia Research*, *49*(3), 269–285.

Pettersson-Yeo, W., Allen, P., Benetti, S., McGuire, P., & Mechelli, A. (2011). Dysconnectivity in schizophrenia: Where are we now? *Neuroscience and Biobehavioral Reviews*, *35*(5), 1110–1124.

Phillips, W. A. & Silverstein, S. M. (2003). Convergence of biological and psychological perspectives on cognitive coordination in schizophrenia. *Behavioral and Brain Sciences*, *26*(1), 65–82; discussion 82–137.

Remschmidt, H., & Theisen, F. (2012). Early-onset schizophrenia. *Neuropsychobiology*, *66*(1), 63–69.

Rodnick, E. H., & Shakow, D. (1940). Set in schizophrenia as measured by a composite reaction time index. *American Journal of Psychiatry*, *97*, 214–255.

Rosenthal, D., Lawlor, W. G., Zahn, T. P., & Shakow, D. (1960). The relationship of some aspects of mental set to degree of schizophrenic disorganization. *Journal of Personality*, *28*, 26–38.

Saha, S., Chant, D., Welham, J., & McGrath, J. (2005). A systematic review of the prevalence of schizophrenia. *PLoS Medicine*, *2*(5), 413–433.

Seeman, P., & Lee, T. (1975). Antipsychotic drugs: Direct correlation between clinical potency and presynaptic action on dopamine neurons. *Science*, *188*(4194), 1217–1219.

Servan-Schreiber, D., Cohen, J. D., & Steingard, S. (1996). Schizophrenic deficits in the processing of context: A test of a theoretical model. *Archives of General Psychiatry*, *53*, 1105–1112.

Shenton, M. E., Dickey, C. C., Frumin, M., & McCarley, R. W. (2001). A review of MRI findings in schizophrenia. *Schizophrenia Research*, *49*(1–2), 1–52.

Shepherd, M. (1995). Two faces of Emil Kraepelin. *British Journal of Psychiatry*, *167*(2), 174–183.

Shi, J., Levinson, D. F., Duan, J., Sanders, A. R., Zheng, Y., Pe'er, I.,…Gejman, P. V. (2009). Common variants on chromosome 6p22.1 are associated with schizophrenia. *Nature*, *460*(7256), 753–757.

So, S. H., Freeman, D., Dunn, G., Kapur, S., Kuipers, E., Bebbington, P.,…Garety, P. A. (2012). Jumping to conclusions, a lack of belief flexibility and delusional conviction in psychosis: A longitudinal investigation of the structure, frequency, and relatedness of reasoning biases. *Journal of Abnormal Psychology*, *121*(1), 129–139.

Spitzer, R. L., Endicott, J., & Robins, E. (1975). Research diagnostic criteria. *Psychopharmacology Bulletin*, *11*(3), 22–25.

Stefanidis, E. (2006). Being rational. *Schizophrenia Bulletin*, *32*(3), 422–423.

Tackett, J. L., Silberschmidt, A. L., Krueger, R. F., & Sponheim, S. R. (2008). A dimensional model of personality disorder: Incorporating DSM Cluster A characteristics. *Journal of Abnormal Psychology*, *117*(2), 454–459.

Van Os, J., & Tamminga, C. (2007). Deconstructing psychosis. *Schizophrenia Bulletin*, *33*(4), 861–862.

Videbeck, S. R. (2010). *Psychiatric-mental health nursing* (4th ed.). Philadelphia: Lippincott Williams & Wilkins.

Vincent, J. P., Kartalovski, B., Geneste, P., Kamenka, J. M., & Lazdunski, M. (1979). Interaction of phencyclidine (" angel dust ") with a specific receptor in rat brain membranes Neurobiology : *Proceedings of the National Academy of Sciences*, *76*(9), 4678–4682.

Walsh, T., McClellan, J. M., McCarthy, S. E., Addington, A. M., Pierce, S. B., Cooper, G. M.,…Sebat, J. (2008). Rare structural variants disrupt multiple genes in neurodevelopmental pathways in schizophrenia. *Science (New York)*, *320*(5875), 539–543.

Weiner, S. K. (2003). First person account: Living with the delusions and effects of schizophrenia. *Schizophrenia Bulletin*, *29*(4), 877–879.

Wittenborn, J. R., & Holzberg, J. D. (1951). The generality of psychiatric syndromes. *Journal of Consulting Psychology*, *15*(5), 372–380.

Wright, A. G. C., Thomas, K. M., Hopwood, C. J., Markon, K. E., Pincus, A. L., & Krueger, R. F. (2012). The hierarchical structure of DSM-5 pathological personality traits. *Journal of Abnormal Psychology*, *121*(4), 951–957.

13

Social Functioning and Schizophrenia

JILL M. HOOLEY

Impaired social functioning is a fundamental feature of schizophrenia. Recognized in the early clinical descriptions of the disorder, deterioration of social relations remains one of the defining characteristics of the syndrome. A century ago, Emil Kraepelin noted the lack of concern for social convention that characterized the schizophrenia patient, remarking that:

> The patients no longer have any regard for their surroundings; they do not suit their behavior to the situation in which they are, they conduct themselves in a free and easy way, laugh on serious occasions, are rude and impertinent towards their superiors, challenge them to duels, lose their deportment and personal dignity; they go about in untidy and dirty clothes, unwashed, unkempt, go with a lighted cigar into church, speak familiarly with strangers, decorate themselves with gay ribbons. (Kraepelin, 1919, p. 34)

Though contemporary writers might describe these difficulties less vividly, it is acknowledged that everyday social encounters often present considerable challenges to individuals with this disorder. Withdrawal and social isolation form part of the clinical profile of schizophrenia. Impairment in social or occupational functioning is also necessary for the diagnosis to be made in *DSM-5*.

This chapter provides a survey of the literature concerning social functioning in schizophrenia, tracing progress in the field over time. We begin by considering the nature of social exchanges and by describing the social problems experienced by patients with schizophrenia. We then discuss factors that are associated with better or worse social functioning, focusing particularly on the role of gender, and also positive and negative symptoms. Consideration of the possible link between symptoms and social dysfunction naturally raises the question of whether interpersonal difficulties characterize patients before symptoms even develop. Accordingly, we review the literature concerning social impairments in the premorbid phases of the illness. We also consider the interpersonal functioning of those who are simply at a statistically higher risk for the development of the disorder but who are otherwise psychiatrically well.

Following a review of the early literature we turn our attention toward newer areas of research. These involve the role of neurocognition in social functioning, as well as such topics as emotion perception and other aspects of social cognition. Finally, we consider the role of the patient's social environment in the course of schizophrenia, ending with a discussion of the treatment options that are available to help patients and their families function more effectively in the face of this illness.

This is a broad topic that covers a range of different research areas. Thus our literature review must be more selective than exhaustive. We are often unable to consider many interesting and important aspects of the topics that are discussed. Wherever possible, however, we draw readers' attention to articles that do provide more detailed consideration of specific issues.

Interpersonal Adjustment and Schizophrenia

The subjective reports of schizophrenia patients are full of references to the difficulties they experience during ordinary social interactions. These difficulties are also mirrored in the comments of their family members: The ex-wife of "Jon," a patient with schizophrenia, puts it this way:

> Some aspects of Jon's illness were particularly puzzling. I knew he was highly intelligent and perfectly at ease when it came to discussing complicated philosophical issues or analyzing the works of sophisticated artists. Why then was he at a loss when it came to dealing with everyday human relationships? He didn't seem to be able to get the feel of people, to interpret their gestures correctly. Instead of relying on that intuitive understanding we usually have of what other people are trying to convey, he built up intricate theories that often led him to erroneous interpretations. It took me a long time to understand that this continuous theorizing might be his way of grappling with his own uncertainty and bewilderment. It was as though some strange deficiency prevented him from understanding some things that seem perfectly obvious to most people. When I finally grasped this, I started spelling out those "obvious" things, even though I started to sound very stilted to myself. It was like explaining the most obvious and familiar aspects of our life on Earth to an extraterrestrial. (Anonymous, 1994, p. 228)

Relationships have been classified as a function of the interpersonal needs that they serve (Bennis, Schein, Berlew, & Steele, 1964). Instrumental relationships are task-oriented and goal-driven. Work and service relationships such as purchasing an item in a store, asking for directions, giving appropriate information in a job interview, or

dealing with those responsible for processing disability benefits primarily subserve instrumental role needs (see Liberman, 1982).

People with schizophrenia show significant impairment in their instrumental relationships (see Wallace, 1984, for a review of the early literature). For example, those with the illness are frequently unable to finish school or to achieve the level of education they desire. Jeffrey's illness began while he was attending college:

> To say that my freshman year was arduous is an understatement. I didn't finish my first year, my first semester marks were relatively low, and I was placed on academic probation. Although present, the first signs of schizophrenia (loss of motivation, withdrawal from others, and confused thought processes) went undiagnosed. Because of this, I failed or withdrew from all college classes. (DeMann, 1994, pp. 579–580)

Another patient describes a problem with an instrumental relationship more specifically:

> After graduation I enrolled at a college near home. I stayed only 2 years. It was difficult for me to deal with ordinary situations, such as a problem with a teacher. (Herrig, 1995, p. 339)

Many individuals with schizophrenia are also unable to hold a job for sustained periods of time. Only about 10%–20% of patients are employed (Marwaha & Johnson, 2004), and when they do work it is often at an employment level that is lower than that of their parents. This phenomenon is referred to as downward social drift (see Hass & Garratt, 1998). Jon, the patient described earlier, had his first breakdown when he was in the army. He left the army and later found part-time work. Finding that to be too much, he subsequently gave up work entirely and stayed at home reading, writing, and doing household chores while his wife went out to work (Anonymous, 1994).

Deficits are also very much apparent in the social-emotional domain. In contrast to the task-oriented or goal-directed nature of instrumental interpersonal relationships, social-emotional aspects of relationships are driven more by the needs of the relationship itself. Social-emotional exchanges might therefore include such things as asking how a spouse or partner feels, greeting a relative, going to an event with a friend, or chatting at a party (Liberman, 1982). Although these sorts of transactions are everyday occurrences for most of us, they are not routine for the person with schizophrenia. The patient quoted earlier dealt with this difficulty as follows:

> I wanted to blend in in the classroom as though I were a desk. I never spoke. I didn't participate in any extracurricular activities or have any close friends. (Herrig, 1995, p. 339)

Perhaps the most striking evidence that schizophrenia patients are impaired in the social-emotional domain is the fact that the great majority of them never marry. This is conventional wisdom among clinicians. It also is well supported by empirical data. For example, Nanko and Moridaira (1993) found that only 35% of a large sample of outpatients with schizophrenia had ever been married. Rates of marriage are also much lower in patients with schizophrenia than in those with other severe forms of mental illness such as bipolar disorder (Mueser et al., 2010). Notably, males with the disorder are particularly unlikely to marry. Although precise rates vary across studies, it is clear that schizophrenia severely reduces the probability of marriage for men; it compromises this probability less for women (Häfner, 2003; Hass & Garratt, 1998).

General descriptions of the problems experienced by patients with schizophrenia are important and informative. However, they tell us little about what these patients actually do in social situations. Fortunately, researchers have explored the interpersonal deficits associated with schizophrenia in an effort to understand their nature and possible origins. It is this literature that we turn to next.

Measuring Social Behavior

Social Competence

Social competence is "a context-related and more or less subjective judgment or evaluation of observed behavior or social role performance" (Appelo et al., 1992, p. 419). In general, it reflects how well we consider people to be doing in everyday social situations. Often used interchangeably with terms such as *social role functioning* or *social role adjustment*, it is the most global level of analysis. As we have already seen, subjective accounts and clinical observations highlight the problems

in social competence that are so fundamental to schizophrenia. Studies that have examined social competence more formally have also reached similar conclusions.

One instrument for assessing social competence is the Social Competence Scale (Zigler & Phillips, 1961). This rather heterogeneous measure considers age of onset, education, marital status, occupation, and employment history to yield a composite social functioning score. As might be expected, patients with schizophrenia typically score lower on the Social Competence Scale than do psychiatric patients with other disorders (e.g., Schwartz, 1967). Adolescents at risk for schizophrenia also appear to score more poorly on this instrument, relative both to nonpsychiatric controls and to adolescents at risk for mood disorders (Dworkin et al., 1990).

On other measures of global social functioning (see Yager & Ehmann, 2006, for a review), such as the Social Adjustment Scale[1] (SAS-II; Schooler, Hogarty, & Weissman, 1986) and the Quality of Life Scale[2] (QLS; Heinrichs, Hanlon, & Carpenter, 1984), patients with schizophrenia again score worse than either nonpatient controls or patients diagnosed with mood disorders (see Bellack, Morrison, Wixted, & Mueser, 1990). Moreover, impaired social functioning relative to controls on the SAS-II is found even in patients who are experiencing their first episodes of illness (Ballon, Kaur, Marks, & Cadenhead, 2007). Global difficulties in social competence thus seem to be characteristic of those diagnosed with schizophrenia at all stages of the illness.

---

1. Originally developed for use with affectively disturbed patients (Weissman, Paykel, Siegal, & Klerman, 1971), the SAS was later revised for use with more chronically ill samples (SAS-II; Schooler, Hogarty, & Weissman, 1986). Using a semi-structured interview, 52 items are used to measure interpersonal performance in five domains. These include work, relationships with household members, relationships with other relatives, leisure and recreational activities, and personal well-being.

2. The 21 items on this scale are rated by an interviewer after talking with the patient. Ratings cover four dimensions: interpersonal relations, instrumental role functioning (primarily occupational, student, or homemaker roles), intrapsychic functioning (i.e., cognitive, affective, and motivational functioning), and common objects and activities (which assesses whether the patient reads newspapers, possesses a wallet, or is otherwise involved with the objects and activities of everyday life).

Social Skills   Social skills represent a level of social functioning that is more molecular than the broad concept of social competence. They have been described as the "specific verbal, nonverbal and paralinguistic (e.g., voice tone) behavioral components that together form the basis for effective communication" (Mueser, Bellack, Morrison, & Wade, 1990, p. 138). Social skills include the ability to give and obtain information, and to express and exchange attitudes, opinions, and feelings. These skills, which are apparent in the everyday conversations, encounters, and relationships that people have with each other, are thought to be critical to social competence.

In the research lab, social skills are often investigated using role-play techniques. In role-playing, the patient interacts with a confederate in a prescribed situation (such as an exchange with a shopping clerk or a staged argument with a loved one). Thus, a researcher interested in exploring social competence may rate role-playing activities on various dimensions of social skills scales. These more "microsocial" (see Milev, Ho, Arndt, & Andreasen, 2005, p. 503) ratings may focus raters' attention on specific nonverbal skills such as the appropriateness of gaze, duration of speech, meshing (e.g., the smoothness of turn-taking and pauses in the conversation) or the expressiveness and congruence of facial expression (see Mueser, Bellack, Douglas, & Morrison, 1991). Verbal skills, which are evaluated in the context of the social situation being enacted, are also considered.

Typically viewed as a measure of response capabilities rather than as a reflection of behavior occurring in the natural environment, role-play nevertheless appears to be a valid method for the study of interpersonal behavior (see Mueser & Bellack, 1998). Behavior during role-play is strongly correlated with more global measures of social competence such as the SAS-II and the QLS. Judges' ratings of verbal and nonverbal behavior also differentiate patients with schizophrenia from mood-disordered patients and healthy control groups (Bellack, Morrison, Mueser, Wade, & Sayers, 1990).

Social skills research, relying heavily on role-playing tasks, has also provided useful information about more specific social deficiencies of patients with schizophrenia. For example, in conversation, schizophrenia patients show weaker verbal (e.g., clarity, negotiation, and persistence) and nonverbal skills (e.g., interest, fluency, and affect) than do nonpatient controls (Bellack, Sayers, Mueser, & Bennett, 1994). Compared with patients diagnosed with mood disorders or with nonpatient controls, they also tend to be less assertive when challenged. Moreover, although in the face of criticism normal and psychiatric controls tend to apologize or explain, patients with schizophrenia tend to deny making errors or to simply lie (Bellack, Mueser, Wade, Sayers, & Morrison, 1992). In many cases, however, overall social performance of patients with schizophrenia is compromised more by mild impairments across a range of component skill areas rather than by marked problems in any one domain (see Mueser, Bellack, Douglas, & Morrison, 1991).

Social Problem-Solving   The ability to successfully recognize an interpersonal problem, formulate a solution, and take action is fundamental to social success. Social problem-solving, another element of social competence, can be examined in a number of different ways. The Means-Ends Problem Solving (MEPS) procedure presents research participants with hypothetical interpersonal problem situations and measures how well they are able to conceptualize and generate effective solutions for the resolution of each problem. In an early series of studies, Platt and Spivack (1972, 1974) reported that, compared with a control sample of hospital employees, patients with schizophrenia were less able to provide appropriate and potentially effective solutions to the problems under consideration.

These findings are difficult to interpret, however, for two reasons. First, prior to the development of *DSM-III*, the diagnostic criteria for schizophrenia in the United States were very broad (Professional Staff, 1974). Second, the performance of the schizophrenia patients was compared only with that of normal controls. The interpersonal functioning of patients with schizophrenia could be compromised by such factors as pathology in general, institutionalization, or stigma. Comparing schizophrenia patients with patients suffering from other psychiatric disorders provides valuable information about the extent to which any differences found are specific to schizophrenia or are characteristic of psychiatric patients in general.

With respect to the first problem, we now know that patients diagnosed by means of newer (post-*DSM-III*) diagnostic criteria for schizophrenia demonstrate problems in the area of interpersonal problem-solving. Donahoe et al. (1990) developed the Assessment of Interpersonal Problem-Solving Skills (AIPSS) to examine this issue in depth. The AIPSS consists of a number of brief videotaped vignettes, most of which depict some form of interpersonal problem (e.g., someone arrives for a scheduled job interview only to learn that the interviewer has left for the day). After viewing each vignette, one is asked whether there is a problem in the scene and, if so, to describe what the problem is. (This aspect of the test is thought to tap *receiving skills*). The participant is then asked what he or she would do about the problem. (This is considered to be a measure of *processing skills*). Finally, *sending skills* are assessed when the participant is asked to role-play for the examiner what he or she would do in that specific situation to minimize any negative consequences. In this last respect, the AIPSS shows overlap with other indicators of social functioning, because the ability to implement and enact a solution to a specific problem necessarily relies on social skills.

As might be expected, patients with schizophrenia performed more poorly on the AIPSS relative to controls (Bowen et al., 1994; Donahoe et al., 1990). Bellack and his colleagues (1994) have also reported that inpatients with schizophrenia show deficits on social problem-solving tasks. More specifically, relative to controls, the schizophrenia patients generated solutions that were rated by judges as being less appropriate and less likely to be able to be implemented. The patients were also generally less assertive and less able to recognize poor problem solutions that were unlikely to work. Nonetheless, it warrants mention that these difficulties also characterized patients with bipolar disorder. Both patient groups performed less well than controls, and no significant differences between the patient groups were found.

Overall, then, there appears to be ample evidence demonstrating that patients with schizophrenia exhibit a wide range of problems across a diverse array of social domains when compared with control subjects. There is also evidence that, even when compared to patients with other forms of psychiatric disorders (such as mood disorders), patients with schizophrenia still show more impairments (Bellack, Morrison, Wixted, et al., 1990; Bellack et al.,1992; Mueser et al., 2010), although this is not always the case (e.g., Bellack et al., 1994). It is quite likely that the factors that underlie poor social problem-solving in patients with schizophrenia (e.g., cognitive impairments) are not the same as the factors associated with poor social functioning in patients with bipolar disorder (e.g., acute symptoms). More data on the extent to which problems remain when patients show clinical improvement would be informative. Although social impairments appear to be stable over time in people with schizophrenia (Cornblatt et al., 2007; Mueser, Bellack, Douglas, & Morrison, 1991), less is known about the long-term stability of skill deficits in other diagnostic groups. However, even in older patient samples (age 50 years or more), social functioning deficits are still more marked in patients with schizophrenia than they are in those with major mood disorders (Mueser et al., 2010).

Gender and Interpersonal Functioning

Gender is a variable often neglected in studies of schizophrenia. However, a sizeable literature suggests that the course of the illness is more benign in women than in men. For example, female patients have a characteristically later age of onset of the illness (Abel, Drake, & Goldstein, 2010; Häfner, Maurer, Löffler, & Rieche-Rössler, 1993). Men show a peak in the incidence of schizophrenia between 20 and 24 years of age. For women, the peak in the number of new cases during these ages is less marked, and the onset of schizophrenia is instead more broadly distributed throughout the 20s and early 30s. Females also have shorter and less frequent psychotic episodes, and show a better response to treatment than do their male counterparts (see Leung & Chue, 2000).

The "advantages" conferred upon females with schizophrenia also extend into the interpersonal realm. Evidence suggests that, compared with males, female patients have a milder range of interpersonal problems and are characterized by better social functioning. Both Dworkin (1990) and Perry, Moore, and Braff (1995) have reported that females with schizophrenia, as a group, scored significantly better than males with schizophrenia on the Social Competency Index (Zigler & Phillips, 1961), and Andia and her colleagues (1995) found that women with schizophrenia were more likely than men with the disorder to have been married, to live independently, and to be employed, despite having similar symptom profiles. Moreover, females in this last study had higher levels of social functioning even though they were being maintained on lower doses of antipsychotic medication than the male patients.

Similar gender differences have also been reported by other research groups. In a study using a role-play test, Mueser and his colleagues (1990) reported a clear advantage for female patients across a range of different measures. Although they did not differ from male patients with respect to their symptoms, females with schizophrenia were more skilled than males in the appropriateness of the duration of their speech (very short or very long responses were rated less favorably), their meshing or turn-taking abilities during conversations, aspects of their verbal content in specific role play scenarios, and their overall social skills. There is also evidence that the relationship between gender and social skill may be specific to schizophrenia. In the study just described, gender was unrelated to social skill in either the affective control or the normal control groups.

Gender differences are not universally documented. Indeed, in the study just described, no differences were found between the male and female schizophrenia patients on measures of social adjustment such as the SAS-II and the QLS. More global measures of social adjustment may simply be less sensitive to gender differences than laboratory-based assessments are. Overall, however, when gender differences are found, the results typically point toward better interpersonal functioning in females with schizophrenia (see Hass & Garratt, 1998).

Why do women score better on measures of social adaptation? With respect to marriage, differences in the age of onset of the illness may provide a partial explanation. As we have noted, more men than women develop schizophrenia in their early 20s (Abel et al., 2010). Women may therefore be more likely to marry (which warrants a higher rating on some social competence scales) and have children before the development of the disorder. Gold (1984) has also suggested that a given degree of psychosocial handicap will have a more detrimental influence on the marriage prospects of men than it will on women. Even today, men are still expected to take the lead in the courtship process. For this reason, the passive man with schizophrenia is likely to be less successful in dating than the passive woman with schizophrenia. Relevant here is Planansky and Johnston's (1967) finding that women who married men with schizophrenia rated themselves as being much more active in the pursuit of their husbands during courtship than did the wives of men who did not have a psychiatric illness.

Societal explanations also exist for the female advantage in social functioning. Gender differences in social roles or in society's tolerance for deviant behaviors may result in greater or earlier social morbidity in males. For example, withdrawn behavior or idiosyncratic thought processes may be either detected earlier or tolerated less in males than in women. This could result in earlier and more severe disruption of social roles. And, as already noted, meeting social role expectations might be easier for the woman with schizophrenia than the man with the disorder. However, as Mueser et al. (1990) have observed, these advantages may be consequences, rather than causes, of women's greater social skillfulness. In the Mueser et al. study, female patients were evaluated using the same behavioral criteria that were applied to the male patients. No social bias was therefore operating. Nonetheless, the female patients did show social skills advantages. At the more general level, these advantages may allow them to navigate the social world in a manner that engenders more tolerance and less hostility from others than that experienced by their male counterparts. To the extent that we create our social environments, the social environments of females with schizophrenia may be more benign than those of males with schizophrenia.

Finally, the social advantages apparent in female patients may simply reflect the fact that, for reasons that are not fully clear, women tend to have a somewhat milder form of illness. Related to this, some authors have speculated about the neuroprotective properties of estrogen (Rao & Kőlsch, 2003). Because of its ability to reduce the sensitivity of D2 dopamine receptors, estrogen may exert a weak neuroleptic-like effect on symptoms (Kulkani et al., 2008). Females may also be less susceptible than males to structural brain abnormalities that could lead to developmental problems and greater impairment in functioning (Abel et al., 2010). Interestingly, the social functioning advantages that are apparent in women with schizophrenia are not seen in older patients (Mueser et al., 2010). This may be because of reduced estrogen production in older women.

The Relation Between Social Functioning and Clinical Symptoms

Schizophrenia is characterized by a number of symptoms such as hallucinations, delusions, affective flattening, and anhedonia. Each or all of these might be expected to be associated with interpersonal difficulties. In the following section we examine the evidence as a function of two major symptom groupings: positive and negative.

Developed in an attempt to explain the heterogeneity in schizophrenia, the division between positive and negative symptoms (Andreasen & Olsen, 1982) is based on whether the symptoms of the disorder are florid, or rather represent a "defect" or failure to display a "normal" behavior. Symptoms such as delusions, hallucinations, formal thought disorder, or bizarre behavior are thus regarded as positive symptoms, while alogia (greatly reduced speech or speech conveying very little information), affective flattening, avolition (apathy), and anhedonia are characteristic negative symptoms (Kirkpatrick et al., 2006). Negative symptoms that are enduring and that do not reflect efforts to cope with positive symptoms are also termed *deficit symptoms* (Carpenter, Heinrichs, & Wagman, 1988).

Positive Symptoms

Positive symptoms in general do not appear to be particularly related to social adjustment (Bellack, Morrison, Wixted, et al., 1990; Bora et al., 2006; Perry et al., 1995; see also Dworkin, 1990). However, reports of associations between more positive symptoms and impaired social competency can be found (Appelo et al., 1992; Corrigan & Toomey, 1995). This suggests that intact thought processes may be necessary for effective social functioning. Precisely which symptoms might compromise which domains of interpersonal functioning and under what circumstances, however, are questions in need of further investigation.

Negative Symptoms

Examining the association between negative symptoms and social functioning is not as straightforward as it might first appear. As Dworkin (1992) has noted, many ratings on the Scale for the Assessment of Negative Symptoms (SANS; Andreasen, 1982) are based on the patient's behavior during an interview. Yet an interview is an interpersonal situation. Moreover, the ratings that are made are based on behavioral indicators such as unchanging facial expression, decreased spontaneous movements, and poor eye contact. These behavioral indicators of negative symptoms could thus actually be the result of social skills deficits.

Recognizing this problem, what does an examination of the current literature tell us about the association between negative symptoms and social adjustment or social skills? Perhaps not surprisingly, negative symptoms have been linked to poorer social functioning, particularly when more global measures of social adjustment are used (e.g., Appelo et al., 1992; Blanchard, Mueser & Bellack, 1998; Bora et al., 2006; Pinkham & Penn, 2006). Moreover, even in first-episode patients, the presence of more severe negative symptoms is associated with having a smaller social network with fewer friends (Thorup et al., 2006).

In a focused examination of the role of negative symptoms, Bellack and his colleagues (Bellack, Morrison, Mueser & Wade, 1989; see also Bellack, Morrison, Wixted, & Mueser, 1990) administered the SANS to a sample of inpatients with schizophrenia. These patients were then further divided into a group that had more severe negative symptoms and a group that had less severe negative symptoms (i.e., positive symptom and mixed symptom patients, see Andreasen & Olsen, 1982). Consistent with prediction, the patients with negative symptoms were found to be significantly more impaired on the SAS-II and the QLS than were the other schizophrenia patients or the control patients with schizoaffective disorder or bipolar disorder.

Less compelling, however, are the data linking negative symptoms with more specific social deficits. Jackson et al. (1989) reported impressive associations between negative symptoms and social skills during a role-play task. Corrigan and his colleagues (Corrigan, Green, & Toomey, 1994) also found that patients' scores on a scale assessing blunted affect, emotional withdrawal, and motor retardation were negatively correlated with their performance on a social cue recognition task. However, Appelo et al. (1992) concluded that negative symptoms did not explain specific skill deficits in their sample of schizophrenia patients, and no compelling links between negative symptoms and problem solving ability were reported by Bellack et al. (1994). Finally, using the Physical

Anhedonia Scale and the Social Anhedonia Scale (see Chapman, Chapman, & Raulin, 1976), Blanchard, Bellack, and Mueser (1994) found no relationship between either of these two anhedonia scales and measures of social skill in their patient samples.

Overall, the findings suggest that, although negative symptoms may not be particularly associated with any specific social skill deficit, they do predict unemployment (Marwaha & Johnson, 2004), reduced social network size (Thorup et al., 2006), and diminished social competence more broadly. This raises the question of whether the social deficits of patients with schizophrenia can be explained solely by negative symptoms.

The answer is "probably not," for the following reasons. First, although schizophrenia patients with negative symptoms generally perform less well than schizophrenia patients with non-negative symptoms on measures of interpersonal skill, the latter still perform less well than affectively ill or community control groups (Bellack et al., 1989; Bellack, Morrison, Wixted, & Mueser, 1990; Dworkin, 1990; Dworkin et al., 1991). This suggests that social impairments are associated with schizophrenia in general and are not linked only to the negative symptoms of the disorder.

Second, in Dworkin's (1990) study of twins with schizophrenia, male patients showed greater asociality and withdrawn behavior, as well as poorer premorbid social competence than female patients did. This, as we have seen, is in keeping with the generally better social functioning of female than of male patients. However, Dworkin found no significant differences between the sexes with respect to the symptoms that they exhibited. The differences in social functioning found in this sample are therefore not easily explained simply by differences in symptoms (see also Andia et al., 1995).

In summary, these results suggest that negative symptoms and social functioning may reflect different processes in the development and manifestation of schizophrenia. Negative symptoms may exacerbate the poor interpersonal abilities of those with schizophrenia. However, negative symptoms alone do not provide a full explanation for the interpersonal deficits that characterize the disorder. Rather, the data point to the likely existence of some more focal deficit that is related to social functioning.

Are Social Deficits Apparent Before the Onset of Schizophrenia?

If the social deficits that characterize people with schizophrenia are simply a consequence of the symptoms of disorder (or are secondary to the effects of medications and hospitalization), we would not expect them to be observable prior to the onset of the illness. However, information about patients' interpersonal functioning prior to the development of the disorder suggests that interpersonal difficulties often appear long before any psychiatric illness is diagnosed. A large number of studies with a wide range of research designs have demonstrated that people with schizophrenia show social deficits in the premorbid stages of their illness. Moreover, these social deficits resemble the deficits that characterize them in the morbid phase of the illness (see Amminger & Mutschlechner, 1994; Childers & Harding, 1990; Gureje, Aderibigbe, Olley, & Bamidele, 1994). Importantly, interpersonal deficits have also been found to characterize individuals who are simply at a heightened risk for developing the disorder. In other words, interpersonal difficulties may predate any signs of illness, often by many years.

One way to examine this issue is to explore the premorbid adjustment of currently diagnosed patients using retrospective reports. One scale used for this purpose is the Premorbid Adjustment Scale (PAS; Cannon-Spoor, Potkin, & Wyatt, 1982). The PAS is concerned with such issues as how many friends the person had in childhood and the nature of his or her interactions with the opposite sex during adolescence. These assessments are made on the basis of a review of school records or from an interview with the patient or a close relative.

Using this approach, Cannon and colleagues (1997) interviewed the mothers of 70 patients with schizophrenia, 28 patients with bipolar disorder, and 100 healthy controls. Mothers were asked to report on their children's adjustment in several areas, including social functioning. Compared with the mothers of both the healthy controls and the patients with bipolar disorder, mothers of patients with schizophrenia reported that their children were significantly less sociable and more withdrawn in their childhood and adolescent social relationships. Differences in the premorbid social adjustment of the patients with bipolar disorder were also apparent when compared to the healthy controls. However, overall, they were less impaired than the schizophrenia group and they continued to do quite well in school despite their social problems.

Similar findings have been noted by researchers who have compared the early social functioning of people with schizophrenia to that of people with other psychiatric conditions or that of healthy controls. In general, retrospective studies of this type have shown that patients with schizophrenia do have poorer premorbid social histories—marked by greater social isolation and inability—than those of psychiatric controls (e.g., Gureje et al., 1994) or healthy controls (e.g., Cannon-Spoor et al., 1982).

Of course, retrospective investigations are not without methodological problems. One concern is the accuracy of the historical reports. Memory does not improve with time. Moreover, potential biases such as the tendency to reinterpret and remember the past in a manner that is more consistent with present events may compromise data obtained from retrospective studies (but see Brewin, Andrews, & Gotlib, 1993; see also Maughan & Rutter, 1997). Because of this, those interested in the premorbid functioning of patients with schizophrenia have sought alternative avenues of exploration.

In a creative series of studies, Walker and her colleagues (e.g., Walker & Lewine, 1990) examined home movies of people diagnosed with schizophrenia. These home movies featured the patients and their healthy siblings interacting during childhood, *years before* any psychiatric difficulties became apparent in one of the children. Despite this, independent raters, who did not know which child later developed schizophrenia, were able to successfully identify the vulnerable child. This is all the more striking when we consider that the Walker and Lewine sample was selected to include patients whose parents reported that their children showed no unusual behavior or signs of illness when they were growing up! Although raters were given no specific instructions about how to evaluate the children in the home movies, they indicated that their decisions were frequently guided by interpersonal aspects of the children's behavior. In particular, such behaviors as decreased social responsiveness, reduced eye contact, and lack of positive affect were mentioned, although other factors, such as motor behavior, also influenced the decisions.

Other evidence of premorbid social deficits in schizophrenia comes from examinations of high-risk populations. In the classic form of high-risk investigation, the offspring of parents with diagnosed schizophrenia are recruited in childhood and then studied prospectively. These children, who are presumed to be at heightened risk for psychiatric disorder themselves, can be followed closely as they mature. In this way, high-risk studies hold the potential to provide valuable information about the manner in which schizophrenia-like social deficits may develop in the absence of overt psychiatric symptoms.

Consistent with results obtained using retrospective reports, data from high-risk studies provide further evidence that those at risk for schizophrenia experience problems in their early social functioning. Using data from the New York High-Risk Project, Dworkin and his colleagues reported that adolescents at risk for schizophrenia are rated as being less socially competent than adolescents who are at risk for affective illness (Dworkin et al., 1990, 1991; Dworkin, Lewis, Cornblatt, & Erlenmeyer-Kimling, 1994). These evaluations, made by trained raters, were based on information from interviews conducted with the adolescents themselves and also from interviews with their parents. More specifically, the adolescents at risk for schizophrenia also reported significantly poorer peer relationships and fewer hobbies and interests relative to the adolescents at risk for mood disorders. In other words, among high-risk adolescents, those who later succumbed to schizophrenia had poorer peer relationships even before they became ill.

Impairments in social adjustment have also been reported in adolescents at high risk for the development of schizophrenia (e.g., Hans, Auerbach, Asarnow, Styr, & Marcus, 2000; Hans, Marcus, Henson, Auerbach, & Mirsky, 1992). Although the data tell us little about why these adolescents have fewer friends, they do suggest that social difficulties predate the onset of the disorder. They also again highlight the importance of gender differences. Watt and his colleagues used archival school records to rate comments made by teachers of children who later developed schizophrenia. Overall, the boys who went on to develop schizophrenia were rated as being more antisocial and abrasive; the "pre-schizophrenia" girls by contrast, tended to be more introverted and socially insecure (Watt, 1978; Watt & Lubensky, 1976).

The methodology of most of the early high-risk investigations involved selecting participants on the basis of their genetic relatedness to an identified patient. However, other research designs can also be used. One option is to select subjects who score high on measures known to be predictive of later schizophrenia. Another involves studying people who are considered to be at high risk for developing schizophrenia because they are already showing some of the prodromal (early clinical) signs of the disorder.

In an example of the former approach, Zborowski and Garske (1993) selected male subjects who scored high on a self-report measure of schizotypic traits involving perceptual aberrations and magical ideation (the Per-Mag Scale; see Chapman, Chapman, & Miller, 1982; Chapman, Chapman, Kwapil, Eckblad, & Zinser, 1994). These males were then compared to control male undergraduates who had low scores on the same self-report scale. Although the two groups were comparable with respect to their age and class rank, the groups differed in important ways when they interacted with a female research assistant in a videotaped interview. Males high on the Per-Mag scale showed more odd behavior during the interview. They were also rated as being more avoidant. Interestingly, the female interviewers reported that, when interacting with the hypothetically schizophrenia-prone males, they felt more anxious, angrier, and less curious than when interacting with the control males. These data suggest that undergraduate males who are not psychiatrically ill but who are at statistically higher risk for the development of schizophrenia show interpersonal anomalies during social interactions. Importantly, their odd and avoidant behavior also appears to create social discomfort for those with whom they interact.

Given that social impairments are associated with both genetic and behavioral high risk for the development of schizophrenia, it should come as little surprise that social difficulties also characterize those who have prodromal positive symptoms but who are not psychotic (Ballon et al., 2007; Cornblatt et al., 2007). Moreover, these social deficits may be an omen for what is to come. Cornblatt and colleagues (2007) have reported that social impairments measured in the prodrome predicted the presence of psychosis 1 year later. This raises the possibility that impaired social functioning could be an early marker for schizophrenia. Of course, whether social functioning deficits reflect a vulnerability to the disorder or simply create the kinds of stressful circumstances that might trigger the onset of schizophrenia is not resolved. Social difficulties may be a manifestation of an underlying diathesis, a behavioral marker that engenders increased social stress (perhaps from irritated peers or family), or both.

Regardless, research has identified poor premorbid social functioning as a negative prognostic sign. Retrospective studies have linked poorer premorbid social functioning to a more chronic clinical course and more frequent hospitalizations (Cannon-Spoor et al., 1982). In contrast, good premorbid functioning has been shown to be predictive of more complete remissions after an episode of illness (Amminger & Mutschlechner, 1994). Premorbid functioning is also predictive of the level of community functioning and adjustment that can be attained once the illness has developed (Childers & Harding, 1990). Simply put, social difficulties, whether indexed via measures of premorbid adjustment or through other global assessments, appear to signal serious clinical problems in the future.

Exploring the Role of Cognition in Social Dysfunction

An extensive literature documents the difficulties that patients with schizophrenia experience in aspects of their neurocognitive functioning relative to healthy controls (see Heinrichs, 2005). For example, in reaction-time studies that require subjects to respond to a stimulus as quickly and appropriately as possible, patients with schizophrenia do poorly compared with controls (see Nuechterlein, 1977). They also show deficits on the Continuous Performance Task (CPT; e.g., Cornblatt, Lenzenweger, & Erlenmeyer-Kimling, 1989). This requires the subject to attend to a series of letters or numbers and then to detect an intermittently presented target stimulus that appears on the screen along with other letters or numbers. On the span of apprehension task (SOA), which measures the number of stimuli that can be attended to, apprehended, and reported in a single brief exposure, patients with schizophrenia also perform less well than psychiatric and nonpsychiatric controls (e.g., Neale, 1971; Neale, McIntyre, Fox, & Cromwell, 1969). However, manic patients do sometimes exhibit SOA deficits that are indistinguishable from those of schizophrenia patients (Strauss, Prescott, Gutterman, & Tune, 1987).

Problems in neurocognitive functioning are further revealed in studies that involve working memory (Park, Holzman & Goldman-Rakic, 1995), backward masking (Green, Nuechterlein, & Mintz, 1994), or other cognitive demands such as sensory gating (e.g., Grillon, Courchesne, Ameli, Geyer, & Braff, 1990). There is also evidence that attentional dysfunctions may be indicators of a biological susceptibility to at least some forms of schizophrenia (Cornblatt, Lenzenweger, Dworkin, & Erlenmeyer-Kimling, 1992).

Given the neurocognitive deficits that are often associated with schizophrenia, it is reasonable to ask if they might serve as "rate limiters" (see Bellack, 1992) for how well patients can function in a social domain. Intuitively, this is a very plausible idea. The interpersonal skills that most of us take for granted depend on a wide range of cognitive operations. They are also much more complex than we typically appreciate. For example, entering into a conversation requires us to selectively focus our attention on the appropriate stimulus (our conversational partner) while at the same time filtering out the rest of the background noise that is around us. In addition, in order to respond appropriately we need to remember what our partner has said, and to generate a comment of our own that is related and on-topic. This places obvious demands on our memory systems and on higher-level information-processing and executive skills. Moreover, all of this must be done while simultaneously processing the multiple verbal and nonverbal cues that our partner generates.

The conversational abilities of even healthy subjects can be easily disrupted. Barch and Berenbaum (1994) asked college students to complete a complex processing task while at the same time talking to an interviewer. The students' performance under this condition was then compared to their performance during a control interview that did not have a concurrent task. Under the condition of reduced processing capacity, the students' conversational skills showed marked impairment. More specifically, they spoke less, showed less syntactic complexity in their language, and said "um" and "ah" significantly more than they did during the control interview. This experimental manipulation reveals just how important certain facets of information processing are likely to be to

smooth social performance. They also suggest that those who more ordinarily lack sufficient cognitive resources to meet competing demands might well be expected to experience difficulties making sense of and navigating the interpersonal world. A personal comment from a patient with schizophrenia highlights this struggle:

> I have trouble concentrating and keeping my mind on one thing at a time, especially when I'm with people. I can hear what they're saying, but I can't keep up with them and make sense of the conversation. I lose my grip on being part of the conversation and drift off. It's not so bad when I'm talking with just one other person, but if I'm trying to tune in to a conversation with several people, things come in too fast and I get lost. It's hard for me to contribute to a conversation when the ideas get blurred. (Liberman, 1982, p. 78)

Neurocognition and Social Functioning

Does the performance of schizophrenia patients on neurocognitive tasks correlate with their abilities in the social domain? Drawing conclusions from the literature is complicated by the range of cognitive measures that are used and the different measures of social functioning that have been employed. Nonetheless, it is clear that neurocognition and social functioning are indeed linked.

A patient's ability to function in the community, for example, is linked to the kind of executive-functioning skills that are assessed by tasks such as the Wisconsin Card Sort Test (WCST; Heaton, 1981). In this task the subject is presented with four key cards that show different shapes, colors, and quantities (e.g., a red triangle, three blue squares, two yellow circles). The subject is presented with a card from a deck and asked to match it to a key card according to a matching principle that is not revealed by the tester (e.g., color, number, shape). The only feedback the subject receives is whether the match they have made is correct or incorrect. After the subject has been successful over several trials, the matching principle is suddenly changed and a formerly correct response is now incorrect. The subject is required to discover the new matching principle and sort the cards according to that until it changes again.

The WCST involves abstract conceptual learning and problem-solving. Although healthy controls are able to complete the WCST without much problem, patients with schizophrenia often experience difficulties with it. Further, patients' performance on the WCST is predictive of their functioning in the community. In a meta-analytic review, Green and colleagues (Green, Kern, Braff, & Mintz, 2000) reported a modest relation (r = .23) between card-sorting performance and global social functioning. This association suggests that the kinds of skills tapped by the WCST (executive functioning, concept formation, and cognitive flexibility) are also necessary for good social competence (see also Jaeger & Douglas, 1992; Lysaker, Bell, & Beam-Goulet, 1995).

Memory skills are important not only for social competence in general (e.g., Goldman et al., 1993) but also for social problem-solving. Poor memory has been related to greater social skill impairments in patients with schizophrenia and schizoaffective disorder but not in patients with mood disorders (Mueser, Bellack, Douglas, & Wade, 1991). Memory has also been found to be linked to the ability to implement solutions in a role-play task (Bellack et al., 1994).

Consistent with these observations, Green et al.'s (2000) review has highlighted the role of memory in the functional outcome of patients with schizophrenia. The ability to learn new psychosocial skills (such as might be taught in a rehabilitation program) is predicted by immediate verbal memory, which is the ability to hold a limited amount of information (e.g., a phone number) in memory for a short time. Secondary verbal memory, which involves the ability to acquire and recall information after a delay (e.g., lists of words, stories), is also important. Secondary verbal memory predicts community functioning at the global level; it also predicts both performance on social problem solving tasks and psychosocial skill acquisition. Overall, however, immediate verbal memory appears to be a little more strongly associated with functional outcome in schizophrenia (r = .40) than secondary verbal memory (r = .29).

Another neurocognitive domain that emerges with some frequency in the functional outcome literature concerns vigilance. Vigilance, or sustained attention, is a process that is often measured using the CPT. Green and colleagues (2000) have reported an effect size of r = .20 between vigilance and functional outcome, and have provided solid support for the association between vigilance and social problem-solving as measured by the AIPSS.

The link between attentional dysfunction and interpersonal deficits is also suggested by results of one of the high-risk projects described earlier. As part of a comprehensive assessment battery, subjects from the New York High-Risk Project were tested on a wide array of attentional measures, allowing a single "attentional index" score to be assigned. Consistent with findings discussed earlier for diagnosed patients, children's attention scores were found to be highly correlated with two factors derived from the Personality Disorders Examination (PDE; Loranger, Susman, Oldham, & Russakoff, 1987) and measured in adulthood. These factors reflected a relative insensitivity to other individuals, coupled with an indifference to their feelings, and an avoidance of interpersonal interactions whenever possible (see Cornblatt et al., 1992). Thus, children who exhibited deficits in their attentional skills were, as adults, less socially sensitive and more socially indifferent, and also more socially avoidant. Using data from a second sample in this same project, Dworkin et al. (1993) were further able to demonstrate that childhood attentional dysfunction was predictive of significantly poorer social competence when the children reached adolescence. Thus, even in those simply at high risk for schizophrenia, the link between attention and interpersonal performance is apparent. Among children at risk as well as in adults with schizophrenia, deficits in attention are associated with deficits in social competence and social skills.

To summarize, research findings implicate card-sorting performance, immediate memory, secondary verbal memory, and sustained attention/vigilance in the functional outcomes of patients with schizophrenia. These functional outcomes include global functioning in the community, social problem-solving, and psychosocial skill acquisition. The effect sizes associated with the neurocognitive variables, while quite modest, are far from trivial. However, knowledge in this area is limited by the range of predictor measures used (Green et al., 2000). The mechanisms through which neurocognition is linked to functional outcome in schizophrenia also remain unknown. However, one promising potential mediator is social cognition (Kee, Kern, & Green, 1998; Schmidt, Mueller, & Roder, 2011). It is to this topic that we now turn.

Social Cognition in Schizophrenia

Traditional measures of neurocognition leave much of the variability in social functioning unaccounted for (Penn, Corrigan, Bentall, Racenstein, & Newman, 1997). This has prompted the search for other factors that might lead to greater understanding of the cognitive underpinnings of impaired social functioning in schizophrenia. Of central importance here has been the study of social cognition.

Social cognition is concerned with the mental operations that underlie the capacity to process and apply social information (Kohler, Walker, Martin, Healy, & Moberg, 2010). It is a broad construct that includes many different abilities. Unlike nonsocial cognition, which involves the kind of tasks described earlier (e.g., card sorting, CPT), it concerns stimuli that are personally relevant. Moreover, although social cognition obviously requires nonsocial cognitive skills, it also involves other skills (see Couture, Penn, & Roberts, 2006). These include the ability to perceive and make correct inferences about the emotions of others (emotion perception), the ability to pick up social cues (social knowledge), the ability to understand that others have mental states that differ from one's own and make correct inferences about another person's intentions or beliefs (theory of mind), and the ability to use causal attributions to draw conclusions about social events that occur (attributional style). Because skills in these domains are considered more proximal to social behavior than the skills traditionally assessed in neurocognitive paradigms, they have become an active focus of interest with respect to competent social functioning in schizophrenia.

Emotion Perception

People who have schizophrenia struggle with the kinds of social processing tasks that most of us perform with relative ease. A case in point is emotion perception (see Edwards, Jackson, & Pattison, 2002; Kohler et al., 2010). Those with the disorder have problems identifying specific emotions in faces. They also have difficulties making judgments about differences in emotional expressiveness—again, typically in faces. A recent meta-analysis suggests that compared to controls, the effect sizes associated with these performance deficits in patients with schizophrenia are large in magnitude ($d = 0.89$ for facial emotion identification; $d = 1.09$ for differentiation; see Kohler et al., 2010). Whether emotion perception problems represent a specific deficit or reflect the fact that patients with schizophrenia perform poorly across a wide range of tasks is not yet resolved (Chapman & Chapman, 1978; see also Penn et al., 1997).

Patients with schizophrenia are also impaired relative to healthy controls in their ability to recognize emotion being conveyed in speech (e.g., Hooker & Park, 2002). In some instances, they may fail to comment on emotional expression at all (e.g., Cramer, Bowen, & O'Neill, 1992; Hellewell, Connell, & Deakin, 1994). Deficits in face perception and face affect recognition have also been demonstrated in psychosis-prone, schizotypic individuals (e.g., Germine & Hooker, 2011; Poreh, Whitman, Weber, & Ross, 1994).

Problems with emotion recognition are related to the presence of both negative symptoms (e.g., Mueser et al., 1996) and positive symptoms (Poole, Tobia, & Vinogradov, 2000). In each case, higher levels of symptoms are associated with more difficulties in emotion perception. However, deficits in emotion perception are unrelated to medication status or to education (Kohler et al., 2010). To the extent that education can be regarded as a proxy measure for cognitive ability, this lack of association suggests that neurocognitive impairments may not explain the emotion perception deficits that are characteristic of schizophrenia.

Finally, as might be expected, there is a link between emotion recognition deficits and interpersonal functioning. Mueser et al. (1996) noted strong associations between schizophrenia patients' abilities to identify facial emotions from photographs and nurses' ratings of those patients' social skills in a hospital setting. A similar correlation between better performance on tasks of emotion recognition and better social functioning has also been reported by other researchers (e.g., Hooker & Park, 2002; Ihnen, Penn, Corrigan, & Martin, 1998; Poole et al., 2000). Such findings highlight how integral the ability to identify and distinguish different emotions is for successful social adjustment.

Social Perception and Knowledge

Being successful in interpersonal situations requires social knowledge. It is hard to imagine how a person who lacked a basic understanding of the structure and rules of social interactions could participate fluidly and competently in social exchange. Given the interpersonal difficulties associated with schizophrenia, it is not surprising that people with the disorder often perform poorly on tests that measure social perception or social knowledge.

In an interesting early study, Cutting and Murphy (1990) gave patients multiple-choice questions that were designed to tap two knowledge domains. The first concerned practical knowledge (e.g., "Why is it not safe to drink tap water in some countries?"). The second assessed knowledge in a more social domain (e.g, "How would you tell a friend politely that they had stayed too long?"). For this latter question, the answer choices included "There's no more coffee left," or "You'd better go. I'm fed up with you staying too long," or (correct answer) "Excuse me. I've got an appointment with a friend. " Compared with bipolar and unipolar depressed controls, the patients with schizophrenia showed significant impairment on the social knowledge test. Interestingly, the nonsocial knowledge test did not discriminate between the patients with schizophrenia and those with bipolar disorder, although both of these patient groups scored significantly worse than the depressed patients.

Social knowledge can also be assessed in other ways. The Schema Component Sequencing Task (SCST; Corrigan & Addis, 1995) contains 12 sets of cards. Each set contains five to eight cards that describe the component actions involved in different social situations (e.g., going shopping, getting a job). The person completing the test is presented with the cards in a mixed-up order. He or she is then required to arrange the cards in the order that makes sense for the successful completion of the social task. Compared to nonclinical controls, patients with schizophrenia take longer to sort the cards and are less likely to put them in the correct order (Pinkham & Penn, 2006). Moreover, in the study just described, sorting time and accuracy on the SCST were highly correlated with interpersonal skill measured during a conversational role play. As Pinkham and Penn (2006) noted, "to interact effectively, one needs to know the rules that govern social settings." (p. 176).

Theory of Mind

Frith (1992) was the first to suggest that people with schizophrenia might have difficulties

understanding the mental states of others, a skill that he referred to as "theory of mind." Research since then has confirmed that patients with schizophrenia do indeed have theory of mind (ToM) deficits.

In an early study, Corcoran, Mercer, and Frith (1995) explored how well patients with schizophrenia and patients with other psychiatric conditions were able to pick up hints made by others. Schizophrenia patients, depressed or anxious psychiatric controls, and healthy normal controls were given brief scenarios that featured interactions between two characters. At the end of each scenario, one of the characters dropped a very obvious hint (e.g., "I want to wear that blue shirt but it's creased."). Subjects were then asked to say what the character meant and what he or she was hinting at. If the subject failed to get the hint, an even more obvious cue was given (e.g., "It's in the ironing basket."). Consistent with a ToM deficit, the patients with schizophrenia did poorly on this task, scoring significantly lower than subjects in the two control groups. Findings such as this again bring to mind the comment, made earlier, of the ex-wife of "Jon": "It was as though some strange deficiency prevented him from understanding some things that seem perfectly obvious to most people" (Anonymous, 1994).

A more advanced ToM test is the Faux-Pas Recognition test (Baron-Cohen, O'Riordan, Stone, Jones, & Plaisted, 1999). Developed for use in autism research, this test requires the experimenter to read stories to the research subject and then ask the subject whether someone in the story said something that they should not have said. The subject is also asked additional questions so that the experimenter can confirm that the subject understands why the faux pas comment should not have been made and why the person who made the faux pas comment might have said it. Compared to healthy controls, patients with schizophrenia perform poorly on the Faux Pas test (Hooker, Bruce, Lincoln, Fisher, & Vinogradov, 2011; Zhu et al., 2007). Moreover, although impaired performance on this test is correlated with worse social functioning, faux-pas recognition appears to be unrelated to the presence of clinical symptoms.

In addition to being characteristic of patients with chronic schizophrenia, ToM deficits can also be seen in first-episode patients (see Bora & Pantelis, 2013; Bora, Yücel, & Pantelis, 2009a, for meta-analyses). In each case the effect sizes are large relative to healthy controls. The effects sizes associated with ToM impairments are also remarkably similar across the first episode *(d = 1.0)* and chronic *(d = 1.1)* patient groups. These findings suggest that ToM difficulties are unlikely to result from factors such as illness progression or long-term medication use. It is also unlikely that ToM problems result from the presence of severe symptoms, because they have been noted in remitted patients (Herold, Tényi, Lénárd, & Trixler, 2002). Although the effect sizes are much smaller, ToM impairments can even be detected in first-degree relatives of patients with schizophrenia as well as in people at clinical high risk for the disorder (Bora & Pantelis, 2013; Janssen, Krabbendam, Jolles, & van Os, 2003). Taken together, these findings provide further support for the independence of ToM impairments and clinical state.

It again warrants mention that ToM difficulties are not specific to schizophrenia. They are found in patients with disorders such as autism and are present in patients with bipolar disorder (Bora, Yücel & Pantelis, 2009b). For example, Donahoe and colleagues (2012) reported that, relative to healthy controls, patients with bipolar disorder and patients with schizophrenia performed equally badly on the Reading the Mind in the Eyes Test (Baron-Cohen, Wheelwright. Hill, Raste, & Plumb, 2001). This requires participants to identify the emotion being depicted when only the eye region of a given face is shown. However, on another ToM task (hinting task), the performance of the bipolar patients was intermediate between the performance of the controls and the performance of the schizophrenia patients. In other words, the bipolar patients were much less impaired. The differences just reported also remained when IQ and symptom severity were statistically controlled. Findings such as these suggest that the decoding of mental state (eyes task) is impaired in both bipolar disorder and schizophrenia, although the former group of patients may have more mild impairments in the area of mental-state reasoning (hinting task). They are also consistent with the idea that, rather than being entirely distinct disorders, schizophrenia and bipolar disorder may lie on a spectrum of neurodevelopmental/affective pathology, with bipolar disorder involving less cognitive impairment and schizophrenia (along with autism) reflecting more neurodevelopmental compromise and more

cognitive difficulties (Craddock & Owen, 2010; Smoller, 2013).

Attributional Style

Yet another domain of social cognition concerns how people tend to explain the causes of events that happen in their lives. This is referred to as attributional style (AS). Within schizophrenia, it has been demonstrated that patients who have persecutory delusions or paranoid ideation tend to blame other people, rather than the situation itself, when there is a negative circumstance that demands an explanation (see Bentall, Corcoran, Howard, Blackwood, & Kinderman, 2001). For example, if we encounter a person who acts in an unfriendly way toward us, we might make an attribution that they are rude. On the other hand, if we subsequently learn that they received bad news just before we met them, we would likely correct our initial impression. People with persecutory delusions, however, typically fail to update or modify their initial impressions, retaining the blaming attribution. A strong need for early closure, impairments in cognitive flexibility, and deficits in ToM are possible factors that could prevent people with schizophrenia from countering natural biases in attribution style (see Couture et al., 2006).

To date, relatively little research has explored the link between AS and social functioning in schizophrenia, Lysaker, Lancaster, Nees, and Davis (2004) have noted an association between social dysfunction and a tendency toward seeing life events as being caused unstable factors. However, the direction of this effect is unclear. Although particular biases in affective style might create social problems, it is equally possible that social rejection creates biases in attributional style. Until more work is done in this area, the importance of AS for our understanding of social adjustment in schizophrenia remains in question.

Taken together, across a wide range of social-cognitive tasks, patients with schizophrenia appear to perform poorly. Not only do they have difficulties with respect to reading emotional cues, but they also appear to be less socially facile. They fail to spot the kinds of subtle (or not so subtle) social hints that most of us detect without difficulty. Compounding these problems, they also have impairments in gaze perception, perceiving a face with an averted gaze as making eye contact with them (Hooker & Park, 2005; Tso, Mui, Taylor, & Deldin, 2012). Since the days of Kraepelin we have known that navigating the social world presents serious challenges for those with schizophrenia. As a result of research efforts spanning several decades, we now know much more about the elements of social functioning that are most severely compromised.

Is Social Cognition a Better Predictor of Social Behavior Than Neurocognition?

It is important to keep in mind that a considerable proportion of the variance in social cognition is explained by nonsocial cognition (Vauth, Rüsch, Wirtz, & Corrogan, 2004); intact cognitive functions are clearly required for a person to perform well on tests of social cognition. Although social cognition and neurocognition are related, evidence suggests that they are largely distinct constructs (Allen, Strauss, Donohue, & van Kammen, 2007; Sergi et al., 2007). There is reason to believe that, because of their greater ecological validity, measures of social cognition will prove more predictive of overall social functioning than measures of nonsocial cognition (neurocognition).

In an early consideration of this issue Corrigan and Toomey (1995) administered a battery of nonsocial cognition measures to a sample of patients with schizophrenia and schizoaffective disorder. The measures of nonsocial cognition included a measure of vigilance (the degraded stimulus form of the CPT), a measure of immediate memory (Digit Span Distractibility Task), a measure of secondary memory (the Rey Auditory Learning Test), and a measure of conceptual flexibility (the WCST). In addition, a measure of social cognition, the Social Cue Recognition Test (SCRT), was also administered. The SCRT consisted of eight video-taped vignettes that featured two or three people interacting in a social situation. After viewing the vignettes, subjects were asked to answer a series of true–false questions about the interpersonal cues they saw in the interactions. The measures of nonsocial and social cognition were then correlated with performance on a measure of interpersonal problem-solving, the AIPSS. Social cue sensitivity was found to be related to receiving (detecting a problem), processing (coming up with a solution), and sending (role-playing the solution) skills. In contrast, none of the nonsocial cognitive variables

predicted performance on the AIPSS. These findings suggested that measures of social cognition were more strongly associated with interpersonal problem-solving skills than were measures of nonsocial cognition.

Subsequent research has provided further support for this conclusion. Pinkham and Penn (2006) administered several tests of neurocognition (assessing overall intellectual functioning, immediate memory, and executive functioning) and several tests of social cognition (assessing emotion recognition, social knowledge, and theory of mind) to outpatients with schizophrenia as well as to nonclinical controls. These variables were then used to predict interpersonal skill as measured in a role-play test that involved talking to a confederate. For the patients with schizophrenia, the measures of social cognition accounted for almost twice as much variance in interpersonal skill as the measures of neurocognition did.

As these and other studies illustrate, measures of social cognition contribute additional variance to functional outcome in schizophrenia over that contributed by measures of neurocognition (see also Brekke, Kay, Kee, & Green, 2005; Sergi, Rassovsky, Nuechterlein, Green, 2006). A recent meta-analysis has provided further support for the validity of social cognition over neurocognition as a predictor of community functioning (Fett et al., 2011). Interestingly, it was ToM measures that showed the strongest associations with functional outcome. Consistent with this, Maat, Fett, and Derks (2012) have observed that performance on the hinting task (also a ToM measure) was the best predictor of quality of life in large sample of patients with schizophrenia. In short, there is good support for the idea that social cognition is a critical mediator in the link between neurocognition and social functioning in schizophrenia (see Schmidt et al., 2011). Neurocognitive impairments may lead to problems with social cognition, which in turn exert a negative influence on social functioning.

The Social Consequences of Schizophrenia Patients' Social Difficulties

The focus so far has been on the interpersonal functioning of patients diagnosed with schizophrenia. Schizophrenia is a disorder characterized by a considerable range of social problems. Although the nature of the social difficulties that are observed tends to vary from study to study, one conclusion can be safely drawn. Patients with schizophrenia are less skilled and less fluid in complex interpersonal situations than people in the general population. In many cases, they are also more impaired than patients with other severe psychiatric conditions.

This may be one reason why interacting with a person with schizophrenia does not seem to be easy for the average person. Earlier, we described the results of a study in which female interviewers interacted with male college students who scored high on two scales associated with increased risk for schizophrenia (Zborowski & Garske, 1993). Even though the male students only showed schizotypic traits, interacting with them resulted in more anger, increased anxiety, and less interest on the part of the female interviewers than did interactions with males who did not exhibit these schizotypic traits.

In another study, Nisenson, Berenbaum, and Good (2001) had student research assistants form brief friendships with schizophrenia patients at a local inpatient psychiatric facility. Although the students were specifically selected because of their congenial dispositions, over the course of the 2 weeks of the study, the amount of negativity that the students expressed toward the patients increased significantly. Findings such as these lend credence to the idea that interacting with patients with schizophrenia may present a considerable social challenge.

Blanchard and Panzarella (1998) have speculated on how affective flattening, one characteristic symptom of schizophrenia, may disrupt interpersonal functioning. They hypothesized that diminished emotional expressiveness in the person with schizophrenia may be interpreted by others as reflecting a lack of feeling. In other words, family, friends, and coworkers may interpret blunted affect as apathy or insensitivity. To the extent that this interpretation is made, it might be expected to damage interpersonal relations. Indeed, Blanchard and Panzarella (1998) reported preliminary findings that highlight how readily observers misinterpret the feelings of someone with schizophrenia on the basis of facial cues.

Misinterpretation does, in fact, appear to be the most accurate description of what happens. There is no evidence that the affective flattening that we see in schizophrenia patients represents a lack of true emotional experiences. Patients with schizophrenia are less expressive facially than controls are when they view emotional film clips or engage in social role-play. However, they report experiencing emotion at equal or greater levels (Aghevli, Blanchard, & Horan, 2003; Berenbaum & Oltmans, 1992; Kring, Kerr, Smith, & Neale. 1993). Indeed, in some studies, patients with schizophrenia actually appear to be more aroused (as measured by skin conductance) by emotional stimuli than healthy controls (Kring & Neale, 1996). Thus, there appears to be a lack of congruence between the expressive and the subjective experience response systems of emotion in schizophrenia. The lack of affective expression among schizophrenic patients may not be due to an underlying experiential deficiency, but rather may represent a failure to express the emotions that are being experienced in a manner that is detectable by others.

Interpersonal Stress and the Onset of Schizophrenia

Social interaction is a two-way street. People who suffer from schizophrenia have social problems that tend to make those with whom they interact feel uncomfortable. However, in the other direction, patients with schizophrenia are also sensitive to the social environments in which they live. Indeed, after World War II, schizophrenia was widely considered to be caused by problems in parenting. By the 1950s many of the theories of the development of schizophrenia were concerned with pathological family dynamics that were viewed as causally related to the onset of the illness (e.g., Bateson, Jackson, Haley, & Weakland, 1956; Fromm-Reichmann, 1948; Lidz, Fleck, & Cornelison, 1965). However, the lack of subsequent empirical support for these theories led them to lose popularity long ago.

Today, it is widely accepted that problems in the family environment do not cause schizophrenia in the absence of any genetic diathesis for the disorder. However, in an important study, Tienari and his colleagues (2004) have demonstrated that people at high genetic risk for schizophrenia may be especially sensitive to high levels of family disorganization compared to those at low genetic risk.

Over the course of a longitudinal study, Tienari and his colleagues collected data on the psychiatric outcomes of children born to mothers with schizophrenia but adopted at an early age. A comparison sample consisted of children who were adopted early in life but who had no particular genetic risk for schizophrenia. After observing, testing, and interviewing the adoptive parents of the children, the researchers made ratings of the family environment. They then looked at the number of children who went on to develop schizophrenia or schizophrenia spectrum disorders (less severe psychotic disorders that are thought to be related to schizophrenia) in adulthood.

The results were quite striking. For the children at low genetic risk, being raised in a healthy or disorganized family environment made little difference to their eventual psychiatric outcomes. In both cases, about 4% of the children went on to develop schizophrenia or schizophrenia spectrum disorders. For the children who were at high genetic risk for schizophrenia, however, this was not the case. When they were raised in a healthy family environment, the rates of schizophrenia in the high genetic risk group were comparable to those of the low-risk group (4.4%). However, when they were raised in an aversive family environment, 18.6% of the high-risk children went on the develop schizophrenia or schizophrenia-related illnesses as adults.

Tienari et al.'s findings are exciting because they highlight the importance of gene–environment interaction in the development of schizophrenia. More specifically, they suggest that genetic factors may play a role in determining how susceptible to the possible adverse effects of dysfunctional family environments each of us may be. Perhaps most importantly, however, these findings illustrate the protective effects that can result from living in a healthy family environment, even for those at high genetic risk.

Interpersonal Stress and Relapse

Decades ago, Brown and his colleagues noticed that the social environment into which patients with schizophrenia were discharged after they left the hospital was significantly associated with how well patients fared psychiatrically over the next several months (Brown, Monck, Carstairs & Wing, 1962). In later work, Brown and his coworkers attempted to quantify the aspects of the family environment that were associated with patients relapsing or remaining well after a hospital stay. The result of these efforts was the construct of expressed emotion (EE).

EE reflects the extent to which the relatives of a psychiatric patient talk about that patient in a critical, hostile, or emotionally overinvolved way during an interview conducted in the patient's absence. This interview, which is termed the Camberwell Family Interview (CFI), asks the relative a series of semi-structured, open-ended questions about the patient's previous and current psychiatric difficulties. Most important, it provides the family member with an opportunity to talk about the index patient's functioning in the months prior to the hospitalization.

The central aspect of EE is criticism. Criticism is rated if there is a statement of frank dislike of something the patients does. This is illustrated in the following comment, which was made to the author by a mother whose son suffered from schizophrenia.

> It gets on my nerves when I tell him to do something and he says "Yes, I will" and he won't. We'd like to have rules and with him we never have it. It's so aggravating.

Criticism can also be rated when, by virtue of changes in voice tone, speed of speech, or other vocal cues, criticism is implicit in what is being said (e.g., "He gets completely out of it and *nasty*."). If the family member makes six or more critical remarks during the CFI or expresses any evidence of hostility (a more extreme form of criticism) or shows marked emotional overinvolvement toward the patient (a dramatic, overprotective or excessively self-sacrificing response to the patient's illness) he or she is characterized as being high in EE (see Leff & Vaughn, 1985, for more details about EE assessment).

A series of studies conducted all over the world have established that high EE (especially high criticism) is a robust and reliable predictor of early relapse in schizophrenia (see Butzlaff & Hooley, 1998). Patients who return home to live with relatives who are rated as being high in EE have relapse rates that are more that double those of patients who return home to live with low-EE relatives (e.g., 50–60% versus 20–30%). Interestingly, this association is not unique to schizophrenia. EE has also been shown to predict poor outcome in patients with mood disorders, anxiety disorders, eating disorders, and substance abuse disorders (see Hooley, 2007, for a review).

Although the prevalence of high EE in families varies across cultures (Jenkins & Karno, 1992), high EE tends to be normative in Europe and the United States. It has been measured not only in the relatives of psychiatric patients but also in psychiatric staff involved in supervising and treating patients (Berry, Barrowclough, & Haddock, 2011). In many cases, high levels of EE may be a natural response to the stress of prolonged caretaking and continued exposure to psychopathology. EE levels do seem to increase in families where patients have been ill for longer periods of time (Hooley & Richters, 1995). Nisenson et al.'s (2001) findings of increased negativity in the students who visited schizophrenia inpatients also lends credence to this notion that criticism and hostility might develop as a consequence of continued interaction with a disturbed patient.

High EE may also be a reaction to the symptoms (or to the social or behavioral disturbances) of the patients themselves. Hooley and colleagues have demonstrated that the spouses of psychiatric patients who have more negative symptoms are less happy with their relationships than are spouses who are married to patients with more positive symptoms (Hooley, Richters, Weintraub, & Neale, 1987). This may be because negative symptoms, as discussed earlier, are associated with more interpersonal deficits on the part of patients, and these interpersonal difficulties may generate tension within a marital relationship. Another possibility is that spouses who live with patients who have more pronounced positive symptoms are, because of the unusual nature of the symptoms, more likely to view such patients as being psychiatrically ill and thus remain more sympathetic and understanding (Hooley & Gotlib, 2000). In contrast, one unfortunate consequence of many negative symptoms (e.g., apathy or poor self-care) is that they may not readily be attributed to severe mental illness. Families may thus be more likely to blame patients for negative symptoms in a way that they would not blame them for positive symptoms. Several empirical studies have now provided data consistent with this attributional model (see Barrowclough & Hooley, 2003, for a review). Moreover, experience suggests that family members are much more likely to complain about patients' generally low levels of activity and lack of cleanliness than they are to complain about delusions or hallucinations. That relatives may be inclined to blame patients for negative symptoms is further suggested by their spontaneous comments:

Always lacking in energy. She's what I call lazy....Sitting around for her is her life.

The problem is he is lazy. He doesn't want to work, that's all.

Finally, characteristics of the relatives themselves may also be important. Hooley (1998) has shown that relatives who have a more internally based locus of control make more critical remarks about patients than do relatives with a more external locus of control. Personality characteristics such as flexibility and tolerance also appear to be negatively related to high-EE attitudes (Hooley & Hiller, 2000). Certain personality characteristics may thus render relatives more or less likely to become high EE in the face of the stress of coping with psychiatric impairment.

How might all of these observations be integrated? Taken together, these findings are consistent with the notion that high-EE relatives are people who (not unreasonably) find disturbed behavior difficult to accept. Perhaps because they believe that patients are capable of controlling certain aspects of their symptoms or problem behaviors, these relatives then make efforts to encourage patients to behave differently. These efforts may be well intentioned and designed to help patients function at a higher level. In some cases, these interventions may be helpful and be well received by patients. In other cases, patients may be unable (or possibly unwilling) to change in the way that the relative wants. The relative's level of frustration may rise, tolerance may decrease, and, over time, critical attitudes (and later, hostility) may be the inevitable result. According to this formulation, relatives' characteristics and patient factors interact over time to produce high levels of tension in the household and to create stress for the relative and the patient alike.

Precisely why patients are more likely to relapse in the face of high EE is still an unanswered question. However, within a diathesis-stress framework (Nuechterlein & Dawson, 1984; Zubin & Spring, 1977), EE is generally assumed to be a form of psychosocial stress. In a series of studies Hooley and colleagues have used functional magnetic resonance imaging (fMRI) to explore what happens in the brains of people who are emotionally healthy and people who are vulnerable to psychopathology when they are directly exposed to personal criticisms (Hooley, Gruber, Scott, Hiller & Yurgelun-Todd, 2005; Hooley et al., 2009; Hooley, Siegle & Gruber, 2012). Overall, the findings suggest that, compared to healthy controls, those with a vulnerability to psychopathology show less engagement of prefrontal areas (e.g., dorsolateral prefrontal cortex) and more activation in limbic regions (e.g., amygdala) during exposure to criticism. Both of these are key brain regions with regard to emotion processing. They are also brain areas that are implicated in many forms of psychopathology.

It may also be that people with schizophrenia have difficulties coping with negative affect because they lack the social skills to reduce or deflect it. However, research suggests that patients with schizophrenia are not invariably impaired in the face of high EE-type behavior (Bellack et al., 1992; Mueser et al., 1993). For example, in a role-play in which the confederate takes on different emotional attitudes, patients with schizophrenia were just as likely to lie and not apologize to a benign partner as to a partner mimicking high EE attitudes. Nonetheless, within a transactional framework, behaviors such as lying or failing to apologize could provide targets for criticism from family members who might be predisposed to high EE attitudes. To the extent that patients with critical relatives may lack the skills needed to effectively manage affectively charged situations, this may lead to an escalation of negative attitudes, ultimately culminating in relapse.

Psychosocial Approaches to Treatment

Schizophrenia is a disorder with strong biological underpinnings. Yet even when medications result in symptomatic improvement, social deficits still remain (Bellack et al., 2004). This speaks to the importance of psychosocial treatments (Mueser, Deavers, Penn, & Cassisi, 2013). Although no strategy alone is sufficient to treat schizophrenia, as Bellack and Mueser (1993) have noted, "psychosocial interventions can play a critical role in a comprehensive intervention program and are probably necessary components if treatment is to improve the patient's overall level of functioning, quality of life, and compliance with prescribed treatments" (p. 318).

Developed in the 1970s, one of the most frequently used treatments aimed at the correction of interpersonal deficits in schizophrenia involves *social skills training* (SST). SST programs are designed to teach patients a wide variety of interpersonal skills. These may range from very basic behavioral skills (e.g., eye contact or turn taking) to more elaborate sequences of behaviors such as those involved in being assertive. In SST, complex social sequences of social behaviors like making friends or interviewing for a job are broken down into their component parts. These parts are then further reduced to more basic elements. After being first taught by instruction and modeling to perform the component elements, patients then learn to combine them in a more smooth and fluid manner through further instruction coupled with reinforcement and feedback.

The value of SST for patients with schizophrenia was initially the subject of debate (Mueser & Penn, 2004; Pilling et al., 2002). However, two meta-analytic reviews now support the efficacy of SST for improving social competence, although there is clearly room for improvement. Pfammatter, Junghan, and Brenner (2006) reported that SST resulted in post-treatment improvements in social skill acquisition (effect size $d = .77$) and assertiveness ($d = .43$) as well as in social functioning ($d = .39$). Improvements in skill acquisition ($d = .52$) and social functioning ($d = .32$) were also apparent in follow-up studies. Importantly, rates of rehospitalization were also reduced ($d = .48$). A later review of 23 randomized controlled trials by Kurtz and Mueser (2008) also showed that skills training had beneficial effects on social and daily living skills ($d = .52$) as well as community functioning ($d = 0.52$). Benefits to negative symptoms ($d = .40$) and to relapse rates ($d = .23$) were also apparent.

In light of the neurocognitive deficits associated with schizophrenia, it should come as little surprise that cognitive remediation therapy is also now a focus of attention. Studies in this area often involve repeated practice on cognitive tasks, or the learning of compensatory strategies (e.g., Wykes et al., 2007). The results overall appear to be positive. Cognitive remediation is associated with post-treatment improvements in attention ($d = .32$), memory ($d = .36$), and executive functioning ($d = .28$); social cognition ($d = .20$) and social functioning ($d = .49$) also improve (see Pfammatter et al., 2006). An even more recent meta-analysis of 40 randomized controlled trials involving 2,104 participants reported significant effect sizes for cognitive remediation for improving global cognitive functioning (d = .45), social cognition (d = .65), and psychosocial functioning (d = .42), as well as smaller and less durable effects on reducing symptoms (d = .18; see Wykes, Huddy, Cellard, McGurk, & Czobor, 2011).

These findings highlight the link between neurocognition and social cognition and the importance of neurocognition for functional outcome. It is also encouraging that cognitive remediation therapy is associated with durable improvements even when it is given to people who have been suffering from schizophrenia for some time (Wykes et al., 2007). Nonetheless, having more symptoms is associated with smaller benefits overall (Wykes et al., 2011). The benefits of cognitive remediation for older patients (40 years or more) also appear to be much more limited (Kontis, Huddy, Reeder, Landau, & Wykes, 2013).

Although cognitive remediation therapy leads to improvements in social cognition, new treatment approaches are now targeting social cognition more specifically. This makes sense because measures of social cognition are better predictors of functional outcome than measures of neurocognition.

In general, efforts to ameliorate social cognition deficits in schizophrenia take one of two forms. Some interventions are highly specific and target a single domain such as facial affect recognition (see Wolwer et al., 2005). Other treatment programs are much more broad-based and target multiple domains. An example here is Social Cognition and Interaction Training (SCIT; Penn, Roberts, Combs, & Sterne, 2007). This is an 18- to 24-week group-based intervention designed to improve emotion perception, attributional bias, and theory of mind abilities (see Combs et al., 2007, 2009). Horan and colleagues (2009) have also developed a social cognitive skills training program that aims to improve skills in four domains (facial affect perception, social perception, attributional style, and theory of mind). This treatment approach incorporates aspects of the SCIT program but also includes new training exercises.

Most of the research in this area is in its early stages, and randomized controlled trials with adequate follow-up assessments are still very much needed. Nonetheless, some preliminary findings appear promising. The only meta-analysis published to date suggests that social cognitive training produces moderately large improvements in facial affect recognition (d = 0.71) and discrimination (d = 1.01) and enhances theory of mind skills (d = 0.46). However, at least as currently delivered, social cognitive training does not seem to produce significant changes in positive or negative symptoms or improve social perception skills or attributional style (Kurtz & Richardson, 2012).

Finally, it warrants mention that psychosocial interventions targeted at helping families cope with schizophrenia also provide clinical benefits. As already discussed, family attitudes are predictive of relapse in schizophrenia. When families are given the skills to help them cope with the stress of living with a loved one with schizophrenia, they can become a vital resource in efforts to help patients stay well.

Typically, family-based interventions begin by educating relatives about the symptoms, etiology, treatment, and prognosis of schizophrenia. Families are then provided with family-based therapy, in either an individual family context (e.g., Leff, Kuipers, Berkowitz, Eberlein-Vries, & Sturgeon, 1982, Tarrier et al., 1988) or in a group containing patients and relatives from several families (e.g., McFarlane et al., 1995).

Psychosocial interventions that have involved families of patients with schizophrenia have been remarkably successful. Meta-analyses (e.g., Pfammatter et al., 2006) indicate that such approaches improve relatives' knowledge about the disorder (r = .39), reduce levels of EE (r = .59), improve patients' social functioning (r = .38) and result in decreased rates of relapse (r = .42) at 6- to 12-month follow-up. Although much still remains to be understood about how such interventions work, findings such as these highlight the key role that relatives can play in the clinical course of schizophrenia.

Summary and Concluding Remarks

Difficulties in the interpersonal domain characterize schizophrenia patients in all stages of the illness. Although the extent and nature of social difficulties vary considerably from one individual to another, males appear to be particularly likely to experience difficulties in their social relationships. Social difficulties also frequently predate the illness, are found in those who are risk for schizophrenia, and remain present even during periods of symptom remission.

Although the symptoms of schizophrenia compromise social functioning to some degree, there is reason to believe that the social difficulties experienced by many patients with schizophrenia are important in their own right. Precisely why they are such a central feature of the illness is not clear. Interpersonal impairments seem, at least to some degree, to be related to neurocognitive deficits, particularly those involving attention/vigilance and aspects of memory. Difficulties in these areas may also underlie some problems in more social areas of cognition. However, social cognition is distinct from neurocognition. Importantly, it appears to serve as a mediator between neurocogniton and functional outcome.

It is also likely that schizophrenia patients' difficulties in relating to and understanding the social world seriously limit the extent to which they can develop supportive interpersonal relationships. Patients with schizophrenia do not pick up obvious social hints. They are also often emotionally unexpressive and hard for others to "read." Together, these and other characteristics may conspire to make interactions with schizophrenia patients less rewarding for those who live or work with them. This is unfortunate, because patients with schizophrenia, like many other patients, appear to be at higher risk of relapse when they live in emotionally stressful home environments. Helping patients improve their social skills and helping families cope with the stress of a schizophrenic relative is clearly important for many reasons.

Understanding the nature and origins of social-functioning impairments in schizophrenia is hindered by the variability in social-functioning measures used in different studies. Social adjustment is a broad concept that encompasses performance on lab-based tasks of social skill as well as global functioning in the community. As noted by others (Cohen, Forbes, Mann, & Blanchard, 2006; Green et al., 2000), different types of cognitive deficits are associated with different domains of social functioning. Unfortunately, the majority of research investigations do not involve both lab-based and community-based assessments (but see Addington & Addington, 1999; Addington, McClearly, & Monroe-Blum, 1998, for exceptions).

The extent to which particular social difficulties are specific to schizophrenia is also not always clear. This speaks to the need for appropriate psychiatric control samples. More information about the stability of interpersonal functioning in general and skill deficits in particular is also needed. Longitudinal investigations are the exception rather than the rule in this research area. Perhaps most important, however, is the question of *why* social deficits are so characteristic of patients with schizophrenia.

Going forward, some of the most exciting directions will be those designed to increase our understanding of the "social brain." Neuroimaging methods are being used to explore the neural circuitry associated with emotion perception, theory of mind, and other social cognition skills (see Germine, Garrido, Bruce, & Hooker, 2011; Hooker et al., 2012; Lee, Farrow, Spence, & Woodruff, 2004; Li et al., 2012). As research advances we will be able to integrate findings from different areas of study into a more cohesive framework. For example, one brain region that is activated during theory of mind tasks is the ventromedial prefrontal cortex (VMPFC). This is a brain area that is also known to be structurally and functionally abnormal in schizophrenia. Linking these two observations, Hooker and colleagues (2011) have shown that reduced gray matter volume in the VMPFC is associated with greater theory of mind impairment. As we learn more about the neural circuitry that supports effective social functioning, we will gain a greater understanding of why the social world can be so mysterious to people with schizophrenia. We may also develop new insights about how to enhance current remediation efforts—perhaps in ways that could ultimately be used to restore functioning in compromised brain regions.

References

Abel, K. M., Drake, R., & Goldstein, J. M. (2010). Sex differences in schizophrenia. *International Review of Psychiatry, 22,* 417–428.

Addington, J., & Addington, D. (1999). Neurocognitive and social functioning in schizophrenia. *Schizophrenia Bulletin, 25,* 173–182.

Addington, J., McClearly, L., & Monroe-Blum, H. (1998). Relationship between cognitive and social dysfunction in schizophrenia. *Schizophrenia Research, 34,* 59–66.

Aghevli, M. A., Blanchard, J. J., & Horan, W. P. (2003). The expression and experience of emotion in schizophrenia: A study of social interaction. *Psychiatry Research*, *119*, 261–270.

Allen, D. N., Strauss, G. P., Donohue, B., & van Kammen, D. P. (2007). Factor analytic support for social cognition as a separable cognitive domain in schizophrenia. *Schizophrenia Research*, *93*, 325–333.

Amminger, G. P., & Mutschlechner, R. (1994). Social competence and adolescent psychosis. *British Journal of Psychiatry*, *165*, 273.

Andia, A. N. Zisook, S., Heaton, R. K., Hesselink, J., Jernigan, T., Kuck, J., Morganville, J., & Braff, D. L. (1995). Gender differences in schizophrenia. *Journal of Nervous and Mental Disease*, *183*, 522–528.

Andreasen, N. C. (1982). Negative symptoms in schizophrenia: Definition and reliability. *Archives of General Psychiatry*, *39*, 784–788.

Andreasen, N. C., & Olsen, S. (1982). Negative v. positive schizophrenia. *Archives of General Psychiatry*, *39*, 789–794.

Anonymous (1994). First person account: Life with a mentally ill spouse. *Schizophrenia Bulletin*, *20*, 227–229.

Appelo, M. T., Woonings, F. M. J., van Nieuwenhuizen, C. J., Emmelkamp, P. M. G., Slooff, C. J., & Louwens, J. W. (1992). Specific skills and social competence in schizophrenia. *Acta Psychiatrica Scandinavica*, *85*, 419–422.

Ballon, J.S., Kaur, T., Marks., I. I., & Cadenhead, K. S. (2007). Social functioning in young people at risk for schizophrenia. *Psychiatry Research*, *151*, 29–35.

Baron-Cohen, S., O'Riordan, M., Stone, V., Jones, R., & Plaisted, K. (1999). Recognition of faux pas by normally developing children and children with Asperger syndrome or high functioning autism. *Journal of Autism and Developmental Disorders*, *29*, 407–418.

Baron-Cohen, S., Wheelwright, S., Hill, J., Raste, Y., & Plumb, I. (2001). The "Reading the Mind in the Eyes" Test revised version: a study with normal adults, and adults with Asperger syndrome or high-functioning autism. *Journal of Child Psychology and Psychiatry*, *42*, 241–251.

Barrowclough, C. M., & Hooley, J. M. (2003). Attributions and expressed emotion: A review. *Clinical Psychology Review*, *23*, 849–880.

Bateson, G., Jackson, D., Haley, J., & Weakland, J. (1956). Toward a theory of schizophrenia. *Behavioral Science*, *1*, 251–264.

Barch, D., & Berenbaum, H. (1994). The relationship between information processing and language production. *Journal of Abnormal Psychology*, *103*, 241–250.

Bellack, A. S. (1992). Cognitive rehabilitation for schizophrenia: Is it possible? Is it necessary? *Schizophrenia Bulletin*, *18*, 43–50.

Bellack, A. S., Morrison, R. L., Mueser, K. T., & Wade, J. (1989). Social competence in schizoaffective disorder, bipolar disorder, and negative and non-negative schizophrenia. *Schizophrenia Research*, *2*, 391–401.

Bellack, A. S., Morrison, R. L., Mueser, K. T., Wade, J. H., & Sayers, S. L. (1990). Role play for assessing the social competence of psychiatric patients. *Psychological Assessment*, *2*, 248–255.

Bellack, A. S., Morrison, R. L., Wixted, J. T., & Mueser, K. T. (1990). An analysis of social competence in schizophrenia. *British Journal of Psychiatry*, *156*, 809–818.

Bellack, A. S., & Mueser, K. T. (1993). Psychosocial treatment for schizophrenia. *Schizophrenia Bulletin*, *19*, 317–336.

Bellack, A. S., Mueser, K. T., Wade, J., Sayers, S., & Morrison, R. L. (1992). The ability of schizophrenics to perceive and cope with negative affect. *British Journal of Psychiatry*, *160*, 473–480.

Bellack, A. S., Sayers, M., Mueser, K. T., & Bennett, M. (1994). Evaluation of social problem solving in schizophrenia. *Journal of Abnormal Psychology*, *103*, 371–378.

Bellack, A. S., Schooler, N. R., Marder, S. R., Kane, J. M., Brown, C. H., & Yang, Y. (2004). Do clozapine and risperidone affect social competence and problem solving? *American Journal of Psychiatry*, *161*, 364–367.

Bennis, W. G., Schein, E. H., Berlew, D. E., & Steele, F. I. (1964). *Interpersonal dynamics: Essays and readings on human interaction*. Homewood, IL: Dorsey Press.

Bentall, R. P., Corcoran, R., Howard, R., Blackwood, N., & Kinderman, P. (2001). Persecutory delusions: A review and theoretical interpretation. *Clinical Psychology Review*, *21*, 1143–1192.

Berenbaum, H., & Oltmans, T. F. (1992). Emotional experience and expression in schizophrenia and depression. *Journal of Abnormal Psychology*, *101*, 37–44.

Berry, K. B., Barrowclough, C., & Haddock, G. (2011). The role of expressed emotion in relationships between psychiatric staff and people with a diagnosis of psychosis: A review of the literature. *Schizophrenia Bulletin*, *37*, 958–972.

Blanchard, J. J., Bellack, A. S., & Mueser, K. T. (1994). Affective and social-behavioral correlates of physical and social anhedonia in schizophrenia. *Journal of Abnormal Psychology*, *103*, 719–728.

Blanchard, J. J., Mueser, K.T., & Bellack, A. S. (1998). Anhedonia, positive and negative affect, and social functioning in schizophrenia. *Schizophrenia Bulletin, 24,* 413–424.

Blanchard, J. J., & Panzarella, C. (1998). Affect and social functioning in schizophrenia. In K. T. Mueser & N. Tarrier (Eds.). *Handbook of social functioning in schizophrenia* (pp. 181–196). Boston: Allyn & Bacon.

Bora, E., Eryavuz, A., Kayahan, B., Sungu, G., & Veznedaroglu, B. (2006). Social functioning, theory of mind and neurocognition in outpatients with schizophrenia; mental state decoding may be a better predictor of social functioning than mental state reasoning. *Psychiatry Research, 145,* 95–103.

Bora E., & Pantelis, C. (2013). Theory of mind impairments in first-episode psychosis, individuals and ultra-high risk for psychosis, and in first-degree relatives of schizophrenia: Systematic review and meta-analysis. *Schizophrenia Research, 144,* 31–36.

Bora, E., Yücel, M., & Pantelis, C. (2009a). Theory of mind impairment in schizophrenia: Meta-analysis. *Schizophrenia Research, 109,* 1–9.

Bora, E., Yücel, M., & Pantelis, C. (2009b). Theory of mind impairment: A distinct trait marker for schizophrenia spectrum disorders and bipolar disorder? *Acta Psychiatrica Scandinavica, 120,* 253–264.

Bowen, L., Wallace, C. J., Glynn, S. M., Nuechterlein, K. H., Lutzker, J. R., & Kuehenl, T. G. (1994). Schizophrenic individuals cognitive functioning and performance in interpersonal interactions and skills training procedures. *Journal of Psychiatric Research, 28,* 289–301.

Brekke, J. S., Kay, D. D., Kee, K. S., & Green, M. F. (2005). Biosocial pathways to functional outcome in schizophrenia. *Schizophrenia Research, 80,* 213–225.

Brewin, C. R., Andrews, B., & Gotlib, I. H. (1993). Psychopathology and early experience: A reappraisal of retrospective reports. *Psychological Bulletin, 113,* 82–98.

Brown, G. W., Monck, E. M., Carstairs, G. M., & Wing, J. K. (1962). Influence of family life on the course of schizophrenic illness. *British Journal of Preventive and Social Medicine, 16,* 55–68.

Butzlaff, R. L., & Hooley, J. M. (1998). Expressed emotion and psychiatric relapse. *Archives of General Psychiatry, 55,* 547–552.

Cannon, M., Jones, P., Gilvarry, C., Rifkin, McKenzie, K., Foester, A., & Murray, R. M. (1997). Premorbid social functioning in schizophrenia: Similarities and differences. *American Journal of Psychiatry, 154,* 1544–1550.

Cannon-Spoor, H. E., Potkin, S. G., & Wyatt, R. J. (1982). Measurement of premorbid adjustment in chronic schizophrenia. *Schizophrenia Bulletin, 8,* 470–484.

Carpenter, W. T., Heinrichs, D. W., & Wagman, A. M. I. (1988). Deficit and nondeficit forms of schizophrenia: The concept. *American Journal of Psychiatry, 145,* 578–583.

Chapman, L. J., & Chapman, J. P. (1978). The measurement of differential deficit. *Journal of Psychiatric Research, 14,* 303–311.

Chapman, L. J., Chapman, J. P., Kwapil, T. R., Eckblad, M., & Zinser, M. (1994). Putatively psychosis-prone subjects ten years later. *Journal of Abnormal Psychology, 103,* 171–183.

Chapman, L. J., Chapman, J. P., & Miller, E. N. (1982). Reliabilities and intercorrelations of eight measures of proneness to psychosis. *Journal of Consulting and Clinical Psychology, 50,* 187–195.

Chapman, L. J., Chapman, J.P., & Raulin, M. L. (1976). Scale for physical and social anhedonia. *Journal of Abnormal Psychology, 85,* 374–382.

Childers, S. E., & Harding, C. M. (1990). Gender, premorbid social functioning, and long-term outcome in DSM-III schizophrenia. *Schizophrenia Bulletin, 16,* 309–318.

Cohen, A. S., Forbes, C. B., Mann, M. C., & Blanchard, J. J. (2006). Specific cognitive deficits and differential domains of social functioning impairments in schizophrenia. *Schizophrenia Research, 81,* 227–238.

Combs, D. R., Adams, S. D., Penn, D. L., Roberts, D., Tiegreen, J., & Stem, P. (2007). Social Cognition and Interaction Training (SCIT) for inpatients with schizophrenia spectrum disorders: Preliminary findings. *Schizophrenia Research, 91,* 112–116.

Combs, D. R., Elerson, K., Penn, D. L., Tiegreen, J. A., Nelson, A., Ledet, S. N., & Basso, M. R. (2009). Stability and generalization of Social Cognition and Interaction Training (SCIT) for schizophrenia: Six-month follow-up results. *Schizophrenia Research, 112,* 196–197.

Corcoran, R., Mercer, G., & Frith, C.D. (1995). Schizophrenia, symp tomatology and social inference: Investigating "theory of mind" in people with schizophrenia. *Schizophrenia Research, 17,* 5–13.

Cornblatt, B. A., Auther, A. M., Niendam, T., Smith, C. W., Zinberg, J., Bearden, C. E., & Cannon, T. D. (2007). Preliminary findings for two new measures of social and role functioning in the prodromal phase of schizophrenia. *Schizophrenia Bulletin, 33*(3), 688–702.

Cornblatt, B. A., Lenzenweger, M. F., Dworkin, R. H., & Erlenmeyer-Kimling, L. (1992). Childhood attentional dysfunctions predict social deficits in unaffected adults at risk for schizophrenia. *British Journal of Psychiatry, 161*(Suppl. 18), 59–64.

Cornblatt, B. A., Lenzenweger, M. F., & Erlenmeyer-Kimling, L. (1989). The continuous performance test, identical pairs version: II. Contrasting attentional profiles in schizophrenic and depressed patients. *Psychiatry Research, 29*, 65–85.

Corrigan, P. W., & Addis, I. B. (1995). The effect of cognitive complexity on a social sequencing task in schizophrenia. *Schizophrenia Research, 16*, 137–144.

Corrigan, P. W., Green, M. F., & Toomey, R. (1994). Cognitive correlates to social cue perception in schizophrenia. *Psychiatry Research, 53*, 141–151.

Corrigan, P. W., & Toomey, R. (1995). Interpersonal problem solving and information processing in schizophrenia. *Schizophrenia Bulletin, 21*, 395–403.

Couture, S. M., Penn, D. L., & Roberts, D. L. (2006). The functional significance of social cognition in schizophrenia: A review. *Schizophrenia Bulletin, 32*, 44–63.

Craddock, N., & Owen, M. J. (2010). The Kraepelinian dichotomy—going, going…but still not gone. *British Journal of Psychiatry, 196*, 92–95.

Cramer, P., Bowen, J., & O'Neill, M. (1992). Schizophrenics and social judgment: Why do schizophrenics get it wrong? *British Journal of Psychiatry, 160*, 481–487.

Cutting, J., & Murphy D. (1990). Impaired ability of schizophrenics, relative to manics or depressives, to appreciate social knowledge about their culture. *British Journal of Psychiatry, 157*, 355–358.

DeMann, J. A. (1994). First person account: The evolution of a person with schizophrenia. *Schizophrenia Bulletin, 20*, 579–582,

Donahoe, C. P., Carter, M. J., Bloem, W. D., Hirsch, G. L, Laasi, N., & Wallace, C. J. (1990). Assessment of interpersonal problem-solving skills. *Psychiatry, 53*, 329–339.

Donahoe, G., Duignan, A., Hargreaves, A., Morris, D. W., Rose, E., Robertson, D., Cummings, E. Moore, S., Gill, M., & Corvin, A. (2012). Social cognition in bipolar disorder versus schizophrenia: Comparability in mental state decoding deficits. *Bipolar Disorders, 14*, 743–748.

Dworkin, R. H. (1990). Patterns of sex difference in negative symptoms and social functioning consistent with separate dimensions of schizophrenic psychopathology. *American Journal of Psychiatry, 147*, 347–349.

Dworkin, R. H. (1992). Affective deficits and social deficits in schizophrenia: What's what? *Schizophrenia Bulletin, 18*, 59–64.

Dworkin, R. H., Bernstein, G., Kaplansky, L. M., Lipsitz, J. D., Rinaldi, A., Slater, S. L., Cornblatt, B. A., Erlenmeyer-Kimling, L. (1991). Social competence and positive and negative symptoms: A longitudinal study of children and adolescents at risk for schizophrenia and affective disorder. *American Journal of Psychiatry, 148*, 1182–1188.

Dworkin, R. H., Cornblatt, B. A., Friedmann, R., Kaplansky, L. M., Lewis, J. A., Rinaldi, A., Shilliday, C., & Erlenmeyer-Kimling, L. (1993). Childhood precursors of affective vs. social deficits in adolescents at risk for schizophrenia. *Schizophrenia Bulletin, 19*, 563–576.

Dworkin, R. H., Green, S. R., Small, N. E. M. Warner, M. L., Cornblatt, B. A., & Erlenmeyer-Kimling, L. (1990). Positive and negative symptoms and social competence in adolescents at risk for schizophrenia and affective disorder. *American Journal of Psychiatry, 147*, 1234–1236.

Dworkin, R. H., Lewis, J. A., Cornblatt, B. A., & Erlenmeyer-Kimling, L. (1994). Social competence deficits in adolescents at risk for schizophrenia. *Journal of Nervous and Mental Disease, 182*, F103–108.

Edwards, J., Jackson, H. J., & Pattison, P. E. (2002). Emotion recognition via facial expression and affective prosody in schizophrenia: A methodological review. *Clinical Psychology Review, 22*, 789–832.

Fett, A-K., Viechtbauer, W., Dominguez, M., Penn, D. L., van Os, J., & Krabbendam, L. (2011). The relationship between social cognition and neurocognition with functional outcomes in schizophrenia: A meta-analysis. *Neuroscience and Biobehavioral Reviews, 35*, 573–588.

Frith, C. (1992). *The cognitive neuropsychology of schizophrenia*. Hove, UK: Psychology Press.

Fromm-Reichmann, F. (1948). Notes on the development of treatment of schizophrenics by psychoanalytic psychotherapy. *Psychiatry, 11*, 263–273.

Germine, L. T., Garrido, L., Bruce, L., & Hooker, C. (2011). Social anhedonia is associated with neural abnormalities during face emotion processing. *Neuroimage, 58*, 935–945.

Germine, L. T., & Hooker, C. I. (2011). Face emotion recognition is related to individual differences in psychosis proneness. *Psychological Medicine, 41*, 937–847.

Gold, D. D. (1984). Late age of onset schizophrenia: Present but unaccounted for. *Comprehensive Psychiatry, 25*, 225–237.

Goldman, R. S., Axelrod, B. N., Tandon, R., Ribeiro, S. C. M., Craig, K., & Berent, S. (1993). Neuropsychological prediction of treatment efficacy and one-year outcome in schizophrenia. *Psychopathology, 126*, 122–126.

Green, M. F., Kern, R. S., Braff, D. L., & Mintz, J. (2000). Neurocognitive deficits and functional outcome in schizophrenia: Are we measuring the "right stuff"? *Schizophrenia Bulletin, 26*, 119–136.

Green, M. F., Nuechterlein, K. H., & Mintz, J. (1994). Backward masking in schizophrenia and mania: I. Specifying a mechanism. *Archives of General Psychiatry, 51*, 939–944.

Grillon, C., Courchesne, E., Ameli, R., Geyer, M. A., & Braff, D. L. (1990). Increased distractibility in schizophrenic patients: Electrophysiologic and behavioral evidence. *Archives of General Psychiatry, 47*, 171–179.

Gureje, O., Aderibigbe, Y. A., Olley, O., & Bamidele (1994). Premorbid functioning in schizophrenia: A controlled study of Nigerian patients. *Comprehensive Psychiatry, 35*, 437–440.

Häfner, H. (2003). Gender differences in schizophrenia. *Psychoneuroendocrinology, 28*, 17–54.

Häfner, H., Maurer, K., Löffler, W., & Rieche-Rössler, A. (1993). The influence of age and sex on the onset and early course of schizophrenia. *British Journal of Psychiatry, 162*, 80–86.

Hans, S. L., Auerbach, J. G., Asarnow, J. R., Styr, B., & Marcus, J. (2000). Social adjustment of adolescents at risk for schizophrenia: The Jerusalem Infant Development Study. *Journal of the Academy of Child and Adolescent Psychiatry, 39*, 1406–1414.

Hans, S. L., Marcus, J., Henson, L., Auerbach, J. G., & Mirsky, A. F. (1992). Interpersonal behavior of children at risk for schizophrenia. *Psychiatry, 55*, 314–335.

Hass, G. L., & Garratt, L. S. (1998). Gender differences in social functioning. In K. T. Mueser & N. Tarrier (Eds.). *Handbook of social functioning in schizophrenia* (pp. 149–180). Boston: Allyn & Bacon.

Heaton, R. K. (1981). *Wisconsin Card Sort manual*. Odessa, FL: Psychological Assessment Resources.

Heinrichs, D. W., Hanlon, T. E., & Carpenter, W. T. (1984). The Quality of Life Scale: An instrument for rating the schizophrenic deficit syndrome. *Schizophrenia Bulletin, 12*, 388–398.

Heinrichs, R. W. (2005). The primacy of cognition in schizophrenia. *American Psychologist, 60*, 229–242.

Hellewell, J. S. E., Connell, J., & Deakin, J. F. W. (1994). Affect judgment and facial recognition memory in schizophrenia. *Psychopathology, 27*, 255–261.

Herold, R., Tényi, T., Lénárd, K., & Trixler, M. (2002). Theory of mind deficits in people with schizophrenia in remission. *Psychological Medicine, 32*, 1125–1129.

Herrig, E. (1995). First person account: A personal experience. *Schizophrenia Bulletin, 21*, 339–342.

Hooker, C. I., Bruce, L., Fisher, M., Verosky, S. C., Miyakawa, A., & Vinogradov, S. (2012). Neural activity during emotion recognition after combined cognitive plus social cognitive training in schizophrenia. *Schizophrenia Research, 139*, 53–59.

Hooker, C. I., Bruce, L., Lincoln, S. H., Fisher, M., & Vinogradov, S. (2011). Theory of mind skills are related to gray matter volume in the ventromedial prefrontal cortex in schizophrenia. *Biological Psychiatry, 70*, 1169–1178.

Hooker, C., & Park, S. (2002). Emotion processing and its relationship to social functioning in schizophrenia patients. *Psychiatry Research, 112*, 41–50.

Hooker, C., & Park, S. (2005). You must be looking at me: The nature of gaze perception in schizophrenia. *Cognitive Neuropsychology, 10*, 327–345.

Hooley, J. M. (1998). Expressed emotion and locus of control. *Journal of Nervous and Mental Disease, 186*, 374–378.

Hooley, J. M. (2007). Expressed emotion and relapse of psychopathology. *Annual Review of Clinical Psychology, 3*, 349–372.

Hooley, J. M., & Gotlib, I. H. (2000). A diathesis-stress conceptualization of expressed emotion and clinical outcome. *Applied and Preventive Psychology, 9*, 135–151.

Hooley, J. M., Gruber, S. A., Parker, H., Guillaumot, J., & Rogowska, J., & Yurgelun-Todd, D. A. (2009). Cortico-limbic response to personally-challenging emotional stimuli after complete recovery from major depression. *Psychiatry Research: Neuroimaging, 172*, 83–91.

Hooley, J. M., Gruber, S. A., Scott, L. A., Hiller, J. B., & Yurgelun-Todd, D. A. (2005). Activation in dorsolateral prefrontal cortex in response to maternal criticism and praise in recovered depressed and healthy control participants. *Biological Psychiatry*, *57*, 809–812.

Hooley, J. M., & Hiller, J. B. (2000). Expressed emotion and personality. *Journal of Abnormal Psychology*, *109*, 40–44.

Hooley, J. M., & Richters, J. E. (1995). Expressed emotion: A developmental perspective. In D. Cicchetti & S. L. Toth (Eds.). *Rochester symposium on developmental psychopathology, volume 6: Emotion, cognition, and representation* (pp. 133–166). Rochester, NY: University of Rochester Press.

Hooley, J. M., Richters, J. E., Weintraub, S., & Neale, J. M. (1987). Psychopathology and marital distress: The positive side of positive symptoms. *Journal of Abnormal Psychology*, *96*, 27–33.

Hooley J. M., Siegle, G. J., & Gruber, S. A. (2012). Affective and neural reactivity to criticism in individuals high and low on perceived criticism. *PLoS ONE, 7*(9), e44412.

Horan, W. P., Kern, R. S., Shokat-Fadai, K., Sergi, M. J., Wynn, J. K., & Green, M. F. (2009). Social cognitive skills training in schizophrenia: An initial efficacy study of stabilized outpatients. *Schizophrenia Research*, *107*, 47–54.

Ihnen, G. H., Penn, D. L., Corrigan, P. W., & Martin, J. (1998). Social perception and social skill in schizophrenia. *Psychiatry Research*, *80*, 275–286.

Jackson, H. J., Minas, I.H., Burgess, P.M., Joshua, S.D., Charisiou, J., & Campbell, I.M. (1989). Negative symptoms and social skills performance in schizophrenia. *Schizophrenia Bulletin*, *2*, 457–463.

Jaeger, J., & Douglas, E. (1992). Neuropsychiatric rehabilitation for persistent mental illness. *Psychiatric Quarterly*, *63*, 71–94.

Janssen, I., Krabbendam, L., Jolles, J., & van Os, J. (2003). Alterations in theory of mind in patients with schizophrenia and non-psychotic relatives. *Acta Psychiatrica Scandinavica*, *108*, 110–117.

Jenkins, J. H., & Karno, M. (1992). The meaning of expressed emotion: Theoretical issues raised by cross-cultural research. *American Journal of Psychiatry*, *149*, 9–21.

Kee, K. S., Kern, R. S., & Green, M.F. (1998). Perception of emotion and neurocognitive functioning in schizophrenia. *Psychiatry Research*, *81*, 57–65.

Kirkpatrick, B., Fenton, W., Carpenter, W. T., & Marder, S. R. (2006). The NIMH-MATRICS consensus statement on negative symptoms. *Schizophrenia Bulletin*, *32*, 296–303.

Kohler, C. G., Walker, J. B., Martin, E. A. Healy, K. M., & Moberg, P. J. (2010). Facial emotion perception in schizophrenia: A meta-analytic review. *Schizophrenia Bulletin*, *36*, 1009–1019.

Kontis, D., Huddy, V., Reeder, C., Landau, S., & Wykes, T. (2013). Effects of age and cognitive reserve on cognitive remediation therapy outcome in patients with schizophrenia. *American Journal of Geriatric Psychiatry*, *21*, 218–230.

Kraepelin, E. (1919) *Dementia praecox and paraphrenia*. E and S Livingstone; Edinburgh, UK. Reprinted by the Classics of Medicine Library, Birmingham, AL, 1989.

Kring, A. M., Kerr, S. L., Smith, D. A., & Neale, J. M. (1993). Flat affect in schizophrenia does not reflect diminished subjective experience of emotion. *Journal of Abnormal Psychology*, *102*, 507–517.

Kring, A. M., & Neale, J. M. (1996). Do schizophrenic patients show a disjunctive relationship among expressive, experiential, and psychophysiological components of emotion? *Journal of Abnormal Psychology*, *105*, 249–257.

Kulkani, J., de Castella, A., Fitzgerald, P. B., Gurvich, C. T., Bailey, M., Bartholomeusz, C., & Burger, H. (2008). Estrogen in severe mental illness: A potential new treatment approach. *Archives of General Psychiatry*, *65*, 955–960.

Kurtz, M. M., & Mueser, K. T. (2008). A meta-analysis of controlled research on social skills training for schizophrenia. *Journal of Consulting and Clinical Psychology*, *76*, 491–504.

Kurtz, M. M., & Richardson, C. L. (2012). Social cognitive training for schizophrenia: A meta-analytic investigation of controlled research. *Schizophrenia Bulletin*, *38*, 1092–1104.

Lee, K-H., Farrow, T. F. D., Spence, S. A., & Woodruff, P. W. R. (2004). Social cognition, brain networks and schizophrenia. *Psychological Medicine*, *34*, 391–400.

Leff, J. P., Kuipers, L., Berkowitz, R., Eberlein-Vries, R., & Sturgeon, D. (1982). A controlled trial of social intervention in schizophrenia families. *British Journal of Psychiatry*, *141*, 121–134.

Leff, J., & Vaughn, C. (1985). *Expressed emotion in families*. New York: Guilford Press.

Leung, A., & Chue, P. (2000). Sex differences in schizophrenia, a review of the literature. *Acta Psychiatrica Scandinavica*, *101*, 3–38.

Li, H, Chan, R. C. K., Gong, Q., Liu, Y., Liu, S., Shum, D., & Ma, Z. (2012). Facial emotion processing in patients with schizophrenia and their non-psychotic siblings: A functional magnetic resonance imaging study. *Schizophrenia Research, 134*, 143–150.

Liberman, R. P. (1982). Assessment of social skills. *Schizophrenia Bulletin, 8*, 62–83.

Lidz, T., Fleck, S., & Cornelison, A. R., (1965). *Schizophrenia and the family.* New York: International Universities Press.

Loranger, A. W., Susman, V. L., Oldham, J. M., & Russakoff, L. M. (1987). The personality disorder examination: A preliminary report. *Journal of Personality Disorders, 1*, 1–13.

Lysaker, P., Bell, M., & Beam-Goulet, J. (1995). Wisconsin Card Sort Test and work performance in schizophrenia. *Schizophrenia Research, 56*, 45–51.

Lysaker, P. H., Lancaster, R. S., Nees, M. A., & Davis, L. W. (2004). Attributional style and symptoms as predictors of social function in schizophrenia. *Journal of Rehabilitation Research and Development, 41*, 225–232.

Maat, A., Fett, A-K., Derks, E., and GROUP Investigators (2012). Social cognition and quality of life in schizophrenia. *Schizophrenia Research, 137*, 212–218.

Marwaha, S., & Johnson, S. (2004). Schizophrenia and employment. *Social Psychiatry and Psychiatric Epidemiology, 39*, 337–349.

Maughan, B., & Rutter, M. (1997) Retrospective reporting of childhood adversity: Issues in assessing long-term recall. *Journal of Personality Disorders, 11*, 19–33.

McFarlane, W. R., Lukens, E., Link, B, Dushay, R., Deakins, S. A., Newmark, M., Dunne, E. J., Horen, B., & Toran, J. (1995). Multiple-family groups and psychoeducation in the treatment of schizophrenia. *Archives of General Psychiatry, 52*, 679–687.

Milev, P., Ho, B-C., Arndt, S., & Andreasen, N. C. (2005). Predictive values of neurocognition and negative symptoms on functional outcome in schizophrenia: A longitudinal first-episode study with a 7-year follow-up. *American Journal of Psychiatry, 162*, 495–5006.

Mueser, K. T., & Bellack, A. S. (1998). Social skills and social functioning. In K. T. Mueser & N. Tarrier (Eds.), *Handbook of social functioning in schizophrenia* (pp. 79–96). Boston: Allyn & Bacon.

Mueser, K.T, Bellack, A. S., Douglas, M. S., & Morrison, R. L. (1991). Prevalence and stability of social skill deficits in schizophrenia. *Schizophrenia Research, 5*, 167–176.

Mueser, K. T., Bellack, A. S., Douglas, M. S., & Wade, J. H. (1991). Prediction of social skill acquisition in schizophrenia and major affective disorder patients from memory and symptomatology. *Psychiatry Research, 37*, 281–296.

Mueser, K. T., Bellack, A. S., Morrison, R. L., & Wade, J. H. (1990). Gender, social competence, and symptomatology in schizophrenia: A longitudinal analysis. *Journal of Abnormal Psychology, 99*, 138–147.

Mueser, K. T., Bellack, A. S., Wade, J. H., Sayers, S. L., Tierney, A., & Haas, G. (1993). Expressed emotion, social skill, and response to negative affect in schizophrenia. *Journal of Abnormal Psychology, 102*, 339–351.

Mueser, K. T., Deavers, F., Penn, D. L., & Cassisi, J. (2013). Psychosocial treatments for schizophrenia. *Annual Review of Clinical Psychology, 9*, 465–497.

Mueser, K. T., Doonan, R., Penn, D. L., Blanchard, J. J., Bellack, A. S., Nishith, P., & DeLeon, J. (1996). Emotion recognition and social competence in chronic schizophrenia. *Journal of Abnormal Psychology, 105*, 271–275.

Mueser, K. T., & Penn, D. L. (2004). Letter to the editor. *Psychological Medicine, 34*, 1365–1367.

Mueser, K. T., Pratt, S. I., Bartels, S. J., Forester, B., Wolfe, R., & Cather, C. (2010). Neurocognition and social skill in older persons with schizophrenia and major mood disorders: An analysis of gender and diagnosis effects. *Journal of Neurolinguistics, 23*, 297–317.

Nanko, S., & Moridaira, J. (1993). Reproductive rates in schizophrenic outpatients. *Acta Psychiatrica Scandanavica, 87*, 400–404.

Neale, J. M. (1971). Perceptual span in schizophrenia. *Journal of Abnormal Psychology, 77*, 196–204.

Neale, J. M., McIntyre, C. W., Fox, R., & Cromwell, R. L. (1969). Span of apprehension in acute schizophrenics. *Journal of Abnormal Psychology, 74*, 593–596.

Nisenson, L., Berenbaum, H., & Good, T. (2001). The development of interpersonal relationships in individuals with schizophrenia. *Psychiatry, 64*, 111–125.

Nuechterlein, K. H. (1977). Reaction time and attention in schizophrenia: A critical evaluation of the data and theories. *Schizophrenia Bulletin, 3*, 373–428.

Nuechterlein, K. H., & Dawson, M. E. (1984). A heuristic vulnerability/stress model of schizophrenic episodes. *Schizophrenia Bulletin, 10*, 300–312.

Park, S., Holzman, P.S., & Goldman-Rakic, P.S. (1995). Spatial working memory deficits in the relatives of schizophrenic patients. *Archives of General Psychiatry, 52*, 821–828.

Penn, D. L., Corrigan, P. W., Bentall, R. P., Racenstein, J. M., & Newman, L. (1997). Social cognition in schizophrenia. *Psychological Bulletin, 121,* 114–132.

Penn, D. L., Roberts, D. L., Combs, D., & Sterne, A. (2007). Best practices: The development of the social cognition and interaction training program for schizophrenia spectrum disorders. *Psychiatric Services, 58,* 449–451.

Perry, W., Moore, D., & Braff, D. (1995). Gender differences on thought disturbance measures among schizophrenic patients. *American Journal of Psychiatry, 152,* 1298–1301.

Pfammatter, M., Junghan, U. M., & Brenner, H. D. (2006). Efficacy of psychological therapy in schizophrenia: Conclusions from meta-analyses. *Schizophrenia Bulletin, 32, S1,* S64–S80.

Pilling, S., Bebbington, P., Kuipers, E., Garety, P., Geddes, J. R., Martindale, B., Orbach, G., & Morgan, C. (2002). Psychological treatments in schizophrenia: II Meta-analyses of randomized controlled trials of social skills training and cognitive remediation. *Psychological Medicine, 32,* 783–791.

Pinkham, A. E., & Penn, D. L. (2006). Neurocognitive and social cognitive predictors of interpersonal skill in schizophrenia. *Psychiatry Research, 143,* 167–178.

Planansky, K., & Johnston, R. (1967). Mate selection in schizophrenia. *Acta Psychiatrica Scandinavica, 43,* 397–409.

Platt, J. J., & Spivack, G. (1972). Problem-solving thinking of psychiatric patients. *Journal of Consulting and Clinical Psychology, 39,* 148–151.

Platt, J. J., & Spivack, G. (1974). Means of solving real-life problems: I. Psychiatric patients vs. controls and cross-cultural comparisons of normal females. *Journal of Community Psychology, 2,* 45–48.

Poole, J. H., Tobia, F. C., & Vinogradov, S. (2000). The functional relevance of affect recognition errors in schizophrenia. *Journal of the International Neuropsychological Society, 6,* 649–658.

Poreh, A., Whitman, D., Weber, M., & Ross, T. (1994). Facial recognition in hypothetically schizotypic college students. *Journal of Nervous and Mental Disease, 182,* 503–507.

Professional Staff of the United States–United Kingdom Cross-National Project. (1974). The diagnosis and psychopathology of schizophrenia in New York and London. *Schizophrenia Bulletin, 1* (Experimental Issue No. 11), 80–102.

Rao, M. L., & Kőlsch, H. (2003). Effects of estrogen on brain development and neuroprotection—implications for negative symptoms in schizophrenia. *Psychoneuroendocrinology, 28,* 83–96.

Schmidt, S. J., Mueller, D. R., & Roder, V. (2011). Social cognition as a mediator variable between neurocognition and functional outcome in schizophrenia: Empirical review and new results by structural equation modeling. *Schizophrenia Bulletin, 37*(Suppl. 2), S41–S54.

Schooler, N., Hogarty, G. E., & Weissman, M. M. (1986). Social Adjustment Scale II (SAS-II). In W. A Hargreaves, C. C. Atkinson, & J. E. Sorenson, (Eds.). *Resource materials for community mental health program evaluators* (DHEW No. 79-328; pp. 290–303). Washington, DC: U.S. Government Printing Office.

Schwartz, S. (1967). Diagnosis, level of social adjustment and cognitive deficits. *Journal of Abnormal Psychology, 72,* 446–450.

Sergi, M. J., Rassovsky, Y., Nuechterlein, K., H., & Green, M. F. (2006). Social perception as a mediator of the influence of early visual processing on functional status in schizophrenia. *American Journal of Psychiatry, 163,* 448–454.

Sergi, M. J., Rassovsky, Y., Widmark, C., Reist, C., Erhart, S., Braff, D. L., Marder, S. R., & Green, M. F. (2007). Social cognition in schizophrenia: Relationships with neurocognition and negative symptoms. *Schizophrenia Research, 90,* 316–324.

Smoller, J. W. (2013). Disorders and borders: psychiatric genetics and nosology. *American Journal of Medical Genetics Part B Neuropsychiatric Genetics, 162B,* 559–579.

Strauss, M. E., Prescott, C. A., Gutterman, D. F., & Tune, L. E. (1987). Span of apprehension deficits in schizophrenia and mania. *Schizophrenia Bulletin, 13,* 699–704.

Tarrier, N., Barrowclough, C., Vaughn, C., Bamrah, J., Porceddu, K., Watts, S., & Freeman, H. (1988). The community management of schizophrenia: a controlled trial of a behavioral intervention with families to reduce relapse. *British Journal of Psychiatry, 153,* 532–542.

Thorup, A., Petersen, L., Jeppesen, Øhlenschlæger, J., Christensen, T., Krarup, G., Jørgensen, P., & Nordentoft, M. (2006). Social network among young adults with first episode schizophrenia spectrum disorders. *Social Psychiatry and Psychiatric Epidemiology, 41,* 761–770.

Tienari, P. A., Wynne, L. C., Sorri, A., Lahti, I., Lasky, K., Moring, J., Naarala, M., Nieminen, P., & Wahlberg, K.-E. (2004). Genotype-environment interaction in schizophrenia-spectrum disorder. *British Journal of Psychiatry, 184,* 216–222.

Tso, I. F., Mui, M. L., Taylor, S. F., & Deldin, P. J. (2012). Eye contact perception in schizophrenia: Relationship with symptoms and socioemotional functioning. *Journal of Abnormal Psychology, 121,* 616–627.

Vauth, R., Rűsch, N., Wirtz, M., & Corrogan, P. W. (2004). Does social cognition influence the relation between neurocognitive deficits and vocational functioning in schizophrenia? *Psychiatry Research, 128,* 155–165.

Walker, E., & Lewine, R. J. (1990). Prediction of adult-onset schizophrenia from childhood home movies of the patients. *American Journal of Psychiatry, 147,* 1052–1056.

Wallace, C. J. (1984). Community and interpersonal functioning in the course of schizophrenic disorders. *Schizophrenia Bulletin, 10,* 233–257.

Watt, N. F. (1978). Patterns of childhood social development in adult schizophrenics. *Archives of General Psychiatry, 35,* 160–165.

Watt, N. F., & Lubensky, A. W. (1976). Childhood roots of schizophrenia. *Journal of Consulting and Clinical Psychology, 44,* 363–375.

Weissman, M. M., Paykel, E. S., Siegal, R., & Klerman, G. L. (1971). The social role performance of depressed women: Comparisons with a normal group. *American Journal of Orthopsychiatry, 41,* 390–405.

Wolwer, W., Frommann, Haufmann, S., Piaszek., A., Streit, M., & Gaebel, W. (2005). Remediation of impairments in facial affect recognition in schizophrenia: Efficacy and specificity of a new training program. *Schizophrenia Research, 80,* 295–303.

Wykes, T., Huddy, V., Cellard, C., McGurk, S. R., & Czobor, P. (2011). A meta-analysis of cognitive remediation for schizophrenia: Methodology and effect sizes. *American Journal of Psychiatry, 168,* 472–485.

Wykes, T., Reeder, C., Landau, S., Everitt, B., Knapp, M., Patel, A., & Romeo, R. (2007). Cognitive remediation therapy in schizophrenia: Randomised controlled trial. *British Journal of Psychiatry, 190,* 421–427.

Yager J. A., & Ehmann, T. S. (2006). Untangling social function and social cognition: A review of concepts and measurement. *Psychiatry, 69,* 47–68.

Zborowski, M. J., & Garske, J. P. (1993). Interpersonal deviance and consequent social impact in hypothetically schizophrenia-prone men. *Journal of Abnormal Psychology, 102,* 482–489.

Zhu, C-Y., Lee, T. M. C., Li, X-S., Jing, S-C., Wang, Y-G., & Wang, K. (2007). Impairments of social cues recognition and social functioning in Chinese people with schizophrenia. *Psychiatry and Clinical Neurosciences, 61,* 149–158.

Zigler, E., & Phillips, L. (1961). Social competence and outcome in psychiatric disorder. *Journal of Abnormal and Social Psychology, 63,* 264–271.

Zubin, J., & Spring, B. J. (1977). Vulnerability: A new view of schizophrenia. *Journal of Abnormal Psychology, 86,* 103–126.

14

Paranoid and Delusional Disorders

PAUL H. BLANEY

The words *paranoid* and *delusions* are often paired, and each is on occasion used to presume the other. Still, they may be distinguished: there are delusions other than paranoid ones, and some paranoid ideation does not qualify as delusional. Each word is mentioned in one *DSM-5* diagnostic category name—paranoid personality disorder (PPD), and delusional disorder (DD), respectively—but they both denote clinical phenomena seen in schizophrenia and other mental disorders as well.

Delusions, including paranoid ones, are also seen in many medical conditions—at least 70 in one count (Cummings, 1985), most notably senile dementia as in Alzheimer's. Delusions may be precipitated by use of (or withdrawal from) certain psychoactive drugs (e.g., amphetamines) and drugs not usually classed as psychoactive. Given treatment implications, correct diagnosis is crucial (cf. Soreff, 1987). This chapter focuses mainly on conditions that seem unrelated to specific medical problems or drug effects.

Paranoia

To be paranoid generally means to suspect or believe that one (or one's group) is being intentionally targeted for harm—especially betrayal—by some other person(s). In this context, even to merely suspect is also to expect, so there is an openness to any information that seems consistent with the imputed threat. A paranoid individual may see a nonexistent threat—or notice a real threat that others miss. In the language of developmental psychopathology, the individual has a hostile attributional bias, that is, an inclination to view others' behavior as arising from hostility toward oneself (see the discussion of stressor antecedents below).

This definition is narrower than some. Some definitions involve a focus on, for instance, interpersonal hypersensitivity, unforgivingness, resistance to correction, rigidity, humorlessness, referentiality, need for autonomy, and arrogance (cf. Bernstein & Useda, 2007; Blaney, 1999). In lay usage, the meanings stray even farther afield.

The intensity of clinical paranoia may be linked to various biases: (a) exaggerated assessment of the risk of impending betrayal, (b) skewed judgment regarding what constitutes betrayal, (c) the view that it is especially terrible to be betrayed (cf. Koehler & Gershoff, 2003), and (d) overreaction to betrayal that one perceives has occurred. One might view them as facets of a single paranoid dynamic, but such a view is not clearly warranted. For example, overreaction to mistreatment may not always be linked to an exaggerated perception of risk, and one can as easily overreact to real as to imagined mistreatment.

Within Section II of *DSM-5,* paranoia is evident in most PPD criteria, as well as in some schizotypal PD criteria. Within Section III, PPD itself is absent from the alternative model for personality disorders (PDs), though paranoia is discernible within the factor-based *PD-Trait Specified* option in the form of a *suspiciousness* facet (listed under Negative Affectivity and Detachment domains). That facet is also one of six traits that contribute to the Section III diagnosis of schizotypal PD.

Paranoia is also prominent in the persecutory and jealous subtypes of DD (i.e., DD-persecutory and DD-jealous), as well as in persecutory delusions common in schizophrenia. To simplify, the threshold for delusion is crossed when an unwarranted suspicion becomes a belief. The discussion in the next subsections spans the range from mere suspiciousness to full delusionality.

Perceived Threat

Paranoia involves sensitivity to danger. When strong emotions arise from exaggerated threat perception, other persons may judge the emotions to be excessive and be dismissive of them. Empathy is best achieved when the observer takes the individual's perspective—by imagining how *I* would feel if actually confronted with whatever the delusional person suspects (or believes) he or she confronts.

While various clinical writers have identified a particular *response to* perceived threat as *the* paranoid one, the particular response varies from writer to writer: for some, it a fearful, furtive, and avoidant response, but for others it is hostile and angry—perhaps involving preemptive antagonism. Each presumption thus narrows the definition of paranoia in a way that is not universally shared.

That paranoia can entail fear and/or hostility is evident in the descriptions of both PPD and DD in *DSM.* Of the seven *DSM-5* PPD criteria, one mentions that the person may be "reluctant to confide in others because of unwarranted *fear*" and another that he or she may be "quick to react *angrily*" (p. 649, italics added). Unsurprisingly, there is evidence of comorbidity between PPD and both anxiety and antisocial diagnoses (Ekselius, Lindström, von Knorring, Bodlund, & Kullgren, 1994; Reich & Braginsky, 1994; Røysamb et al., 2011). Regarding DD, the fearful thread is evident in the statement that the patient may avoid leaving "his house except late at night…dressed in clothes quite different from his normal attire"

(*DSM-IV-TR*, p. 324). On the other hand, the person with DD-persecutory may be "resentful and angry and may resort to violence" (*DSM-5*, p. 92). This fearful–hostile distinction obviously tracks generic responses to danger: flight and fight.

The form that paranoia takes in a given individual may depend on dispositional factors, and indeed, Shapiro (1965) and Benjamin (1996) have proposed two variants of paranoid personality: fearful and hostile. It may also depend on the nature of the threat; for example, a fearful response may be most likely if one perceives the nemesis to be extremely powerful. We turn now to close examination of these two threads.

Fear and Anxiety   Persecutory delusions may entail a sense of serious—even mortal—danger. Still, in many cases the delusions apparently develop gradually, and in their earlier stages the fear is simply of marginalization (cf. Masillo et al., 2012; Rhodes & Jakes, 2010). Studies of PPD and suspiciousness in the context of attachment theory have generally shown associations with anxious, insecure, and avoidant attachment (cf. Crawford et al., 2007; Westen, Nakash, Thomas, & Bradley, 2006).

Tone, Goulding, and Compton (2011) have discussed the overlap between paranoia and social anxiety. Both involve expectations of negativity from others, and both involve referential thinking (see later discussion). However, while socially anxious persons anticipate negative evaluations from others, paranoid individuals often expect more serious harm. And while socially anxious individuals blame others' negativity on themselves, paranoid individuals often attribute it to others' ill will.

While perceived vulnerability may fuel anxiety, Freeman, Garety, Kuipers, Fowler, and Bebbington (2002) have suggested that this is a two-way street. That is, anxiety may also fuel, or at least shape, persecutory ideation. The key is that "a person having unusual experiences…interprets them in line with their emotional state. If they are anxious it is more likely that the interpretation will be of threat" (Freeman & Garety, 2006, p. 409). Thus Freeman and colleagues have proposed a delusion-as-explanation model in which preexisting anxiety may guide the explanation. Freeman et al. (2002) have relied on anxiety theory also in accounting for the persistence of persecutory beliefs in persons who are never actually harmed: As with anxiety, persecutory delusions may endure because the individual takes "actions designed to reduce the threat, but which actually prevent disconfirmatory evidence being received or fully processed" (p. 339).

Freeman et al. (2012) reported longitudinal findings indicating that, among persons lacking evidence of paranoia initially, those who showed high initial worry were far more likely to show evidence of paranoia later than were those with low initial worry; other indicants of distress were also predictive of subsequent paranoia. See Freeman (2007) for further evidence of a close tie between paranoia and anxiety.

Fearful paranoia can have dire implications for family members (cf. Ulzen & Carpentier, 1997). For example, a parent may view her or his children as co-targets and keep them in seclusion to protect them from imagined threats.

Hostility   As noted, the expectation of harm may lead to preemptive attacks. Paranoia may involve self-fulfilling prophesies. Even when judgments of another person's ill-will are unwarranted, the paranoid individual may engage in preemptive behaviors that eventually engender real ill-will. This puts into perspective the aphorism that even paranoids have enemies. Evidence for this kind of dynamic emerges from a study of the peer relations of adolescents, indicating that those with PPD characteristics initiated more bullying and other uncooperative behaviors (Natsuaki, Cicchetti, & Rogosh, 2009).

Lay stereotypes link psychosis with violence. These are influenced by lurid cases in the media, but a number of systematic studies have confirmed a relation between delusions—especially persecutory—and aggressive behavior (e.g., Björkly, 2002; Fresán et al., 2005; Mojtabai, 2006; Van Dongen, Buck, & van Marle, 2012). Studying individuals who had committed homicide and had received a diagnosis of schizophrenia, Laajasalo and Häkkänen (2006) found that nearly 90% had delusions, and in most of those cases the delusions were persecutory. Family members may be those most at risk of harm. In one series of delusional individuals who had committed homicide, about two-thirds had killed a family member (Benezech, Yesavage, Addad, Bourgeois, & Mills, 1984; see also Kennedy, Kemp, & Dyer, 1992).

As noted, paranoia may have fearful and hostile variants. A case can be made that the angry overtones are more prominent or common—drawing upon research using interpersonal and factor-based

models of personality. Within the interpersonal circumplex model, PPD has most commonly been positioned empirically in the region between the hostile-cold-quarrelsome and ambitious-dominant poles (e.g., Clifton, Turkheimer, & Oltmanns, 2005; Monsen, Hagtvet, Havik, & Eilertsen, 2006; see also Podubinski, Daffern, & Lee, 2012). Among five-factor model (FFM) studies (e.g., De Fruyt, De Clercq, van de Wiele, & Van Heeringen, 2006; Trull, Widiger, & Burr, 2001), PPD usually shows particularly high correlations with the facet of hostility. However, one impressive factor-analytic study allocated paranoia to internalizing as well as to antagonistic tendencies (Kotov et al., 2011).

As also noted, Freeman and Garety (2006) have proposed that paranoia may grow out of unexplained anxiety. Boden and Berenbaum (2012) have proposed a similar account that involves anger as well. Specifically, they suggested that the root of suspiciousness is a lack of emotional clarity, in which both the source and the nature of emotional arousal tend to be unclear to persons susceptible to suspiciousness. Both the specific emotion that is experienced (anxiety or anger) and the perception of the cause of that emotion (e.g., a mean boss) grow out of an attempt to account for the emotional experience.

Perceived Harm

Here we discuss responses to harm that (one perceives) has already occurred. In the coverage of PPD, *DSM-5* offers just one response-to-harm criterion: "Persistently bears grudges (i.e., is unforgiving of insults, injuries, or slights)" (p. 649). *DSM-5* also notes that the patient with DD "may engage in litigious or antagonistic behavior" (p. 92). Such actions are characteristic of *querulous paranoia*, in which the person is preoccupied with gaining redress. The clinical picture in such cases may entail a toxic mix of obsessive grievance, angry confrontation, and self-righteous disdain for the views of all other persons. *Litigious* applies when the person files cases within the legal system, rather than just pestering the nemesis or complaining to media and public officials. Such persons— sometimes referred to as vexatious litigants or querulants—may be so persistent and infuriating that they garner contempt-of-court citations. Some behave assaultively when pleas are denied (d'Orbán, 1985; Mullen & Lester, 2006). Apart from discussions of querulous paranoia, relevant research on intense responses to perceived harm is found within literatures on such far-flung topics as posttraumatic embitterment disorder (e.g., Dobricki & Maercker, 2010; Linden, Baumann, Rotter, & Shippan, 2008) and forgivingness (e.g., Mullet, Neto, & Revière, 2005).

When the perceived harm involves behavior that is clearly lawful (e.g., a business partner terminates a relationship as permitted under the partnership agreement), it may be unclear how realistically wronged the individual is entitled to feel. Paranoid individuals can accuse others of "breaking" commitments that were not clearly made in the first place. If such matters were simple, breach-of-contract trials would always be brief (they are not), and civil juries would always reach consensus quickly (they do not).

One of the PPD criteria within *ICD-10* focuses on the individual's excessive sense of personal rights, and Veale (2002) has suggested that the litigious individual is one who elevates fairness above all other values. Related to this, Haslam, Reichert, and Fiske (2002) have reported empirical findings indicating that PPD may reflect a relationship pattern called "market pricing" which is "based on a model of proportionality and organized with reference to ratios and rates, such as wages and cost/benefit calculations" (p. 21). Vohs, Baumeister, and Chin (2007) have coined the term *sugrophobia* to describe intense fear of exploitation in the marketplace.

Some querulous individuals view themselves as advocates of the oppressed—that is, their persecutory preoccupations are partly vicarious and altruistic. The distinction between the querulous paranoid and the passionate activist may be clearer in the abstract than in reality, and there may be a fine line between, say, having a circumscribed persecutory/grandiose delusion and being a valiant whistle-blower (cf. Mullen & Lester, 2006).

Trust

The word *mistrustful* is a quasi-synonym for paranoid, though not all mistrust pertains to suspecting that one is intentionally targeted for harm. One may be generally mistrustful because one believes it's a dog-eat-dog world and we're all vulnerable (no targeting). Or one may mistrust a particular person because one believes him or her to be inexperienced and incompetent (no perception

of harmful intent). One might assume that these kinds of mistrust are merely less severe forms of paranoia, although there is evidence that interpersonal cynicism and persecutory ideation are somewhat distinct (Waller, 1999, Table 9.4). See Chan (2009) for a fuller discussion of the diverse phenomena encompassed by mistrust. In any case, paranoia involves an active mistrust that goes beyond merely not trusting.

The widely shared presumption that it is good to be a trusting person underlies the notion that paranoia is dysfunctional (Harper, 1996), but it is difficult to specify the boundaries of healthy trust. To say that reasonable concern about exposure to risk comprises the adaptive counterpart to paranoia begs a key question: What, in this context, is reasonable? Even among the well-functioning, my excessive suspiciousness my be your due caution, and my trustingness may be your gullibility. Anyone may overestimate or underestimate another's good will on occasion. There is, for all of us, a trade-off between vigilance and vulnerability.

When a person who lives in an inhospitable and chaotic neighborhood shows signs of cynicism, it may have more to do with the living situation than with personal dispositions (cf. Ellett, Freeman, & Garety, 2008; King, 2012). Even a context that is merely competitive may warrant considerable vigilance (Kramer & Messick, 1999). Our society provides us with institutional mechanisms for managing concerns about victimization. For example, a physician or psychologist may purchase malpractice insurance. And an entrepreneur may hire an attorney to review a contract before signing it—in which case the attorney is the "designated paranoid." Our ability to behave in a trusting way in the marketplace rests in part on our belief that the legal system will provide recourse if someone attempts to betray us.

The situation is somewhat different when it comes to companionship and love. There is no way to ensure that relationships will never be the source of pain, and no judge can make someone love another person. One might preserve a relationship by jealous, possessive means, but coercion may corrode the mutuality that makes a relationship worth having.

Considerable media attention has been given to the notion that the neuropeptide oxytocin may be the "trust hormone," or the "moral molecule." Much of the research has been essentially behavioral—relying on versions of a paradigm referred to as the trust game. Recent reviews (Campbell, 2010; MacDonald & MacDonald, 2010; Van IJzendoorn & Bakermans-Kranenburg, 2012) confirm that the "trust hormone" claim, while not exactly frivolous, oversimplifies what occurs within a complex, far-reaching system. There are contexts in which oxytocin's effects are not exclusively prosocial (e.g., Radke & de Bruijn, 2012), though preliminary research has suggested that intranasal oxytocin may be useful in lessening paranoia-relevant symptoms among patients with schizophrenia (Pedersen et al., 2011). Other hormones have also been shown to have trust-relevant effects (cf. Riedl & Javor, 2012).

Delusions

Insofar as psychosis is defined by a loss of contact with reality, to have a delusion is to have a psychotic condition. However, delusional states may wax and wane. Even a stable delusional belief may be circumscribed, coherent, and nonbizarre, such that the individual does not present as generally psychotic; in such cases a diagnosis of DD is likely appropriate. Persons with DD often do not the fit the usual profile for schizophrenia; they are often married and self-supporting, and the mean age of onset in various studies is usually much later than with schizophrenia—in the late 30s or early 40s (Grover, Biswas, & Avasthi, 2007), perhaps even later among women (Wustmann, Pillman, & Marneros, 2011). Still, what would now be considered DD has sometimes been viewed as a mild form of schizophrenia, and Pillman, Wustmann and Marneros (2012) reported that nearly 20% of individuals who initially warranted a DD diagnosis eventually received a schizophrenia diagnosis.

A delusion is, by common definition, a false belief that has emotional significance to the person, held in defiance of the evidence at hand. Thus there are two key aspects: *significance* and *falsity*.

Regarding emotional significance, Kinderman and Bentall have observed that the delusions most commonly seen "reflect an intense preoccupation with the individual's position in the social universe" (2007, p. 280), and Rhodes and Jakes (2000) have noted that most delusions are related to specific personal goals or motives. Conversely, "[n]o one develops the delusion that popcorn comes from barley or that pavement just happens

to be made of worn-out carpet" (MacDonald, 2008, p. 719).

The falsity criterion is both crucial and problematic. When a clinician is making judgments regarding the falsity of a patient's beliefs, subjectivity and uncertainty may be minimized, but they generally cannot be eliminated. Consider the following two examples: A man's wife often comes home late from work, and he believes she is unfaithful. An Arab immigrant is sure he is being trailed by the FBI. In each instance, especially if the patient seems eccentric or overwrought, the clinician might be skeptical about his claim and favor a hypothesis of delusional pathology. Still, it would be risky to deem these patients' beliefs categorically false. Consider two others: A musically untrained woman asserts that her compositions will someday be on everyone's playlist—if not in this century then in the next. An amateur cosmologist asserts that the earth will explode on February 17, 2946. In each case, even if a clinician—perhaps having obtained expert opinion regarding these assertions—is comfortable with a diagnosis involving delusionality, it strictly speaking cannot be based on a determination of falsity—not, at least, within the lifetime of anyone now living. And consider two final cases: The depressed person believes himself to be uniquely evil and loathsome. The person with body dysmorphic disorder (BDD) is certain that he is ugly and repulsive. In both cases, the beliefs relate to the application of inappropriate standards; rather than defying truth, the patient is embracing unreasonable norms of virtue or beauty (cf. Coltheart, Langdon, & McKay, 2011).

Illogicality is arguably a good alternative or supplement to the falsity criterion, but it has its own limitations (cf. Kinderman & Bentall, 2007). *Implausibility* is another, and a good one, though of course implausibly dire or boastful claims sometimes prove accurate (cf. Menuck, 1992; Mullen & Lester, 2006).

Attributes of Delusions

Delusional pathology is not categorical; there is instead a continuum of delusionality. Terms such as *overvalued ideation, delusion-like beliefs,* and *strongly held ideas* denote partial delusionality. *Cognitive distortions* and *biases*, while often viewed as specific to depression, may also describe ideation that lies midway on this continuum.

Though falsity is, as noted, an important attribute in defining delusionality, there are others that may loom larger in any given clinical case. Researchers have offered various lists, ranging as long as 16 (Hurn, Gray, & Hughes, 2002). Shorter attribute lists are ensconced in standardized instruments useful in assessing individuals across a broad range of content and severity (e.g., Eisen et al., 1998; Peters, Joseph, & Garety, 1999). If only on the basis of their frequency in the literature, the following attributes may be deemed canonical: *bizarreness, distress, conviction, insight, involvement,* and *preoccupation.* (Some of these collapse two or more attributes found on longer lists.) These six will briefly be discussed in order, followed by one that is not so regularly listed: *narrative complexity.*

Bizarreness   Bizarre delusions have long been viewed as indicative of schizophrenia, but under *DSM-5* bizarreness is a specifier that can be applied to DD delusions (such that DD is now distinguished by the absence of other schizophrenic symptoms more than by any quality of the delusion).

Sometimes bizarreness is blatant and undeniable. For example: A woman, born in 1974, claims that she was impregnated by Elvis prior to his death in 1977 and that she has been carrying his baby ever since but has postponed the birth out of concern that the happy event will upset the earth's gravitational field. In other instances bizarreness is less blatant, and concerns have arisen about whether it can be assed reliably. In fact, interrater reliability estimates for bizarreness have ranged from .28 to .85 (Cermolacce, Sass, & Parnas, 2010). That the range extends so low gives evidence that there are serious problems with this delusion attribute; that the range reaches so high suggests that those problems may have solutions. Note that agency delusions (discussed later) are usually deemed bizarre.

Distress   This is commonly listed as a variable associated with delusions, though this may reflect our reluctance to deem any condition pathological unless there is distress involved. There is evidence that one may hold beliefs that are at least quasi-delusional without incurring distress (e.g., Cella, Vellante, & Preti, 2012; Larøi, Van der Linden, DeFruyt, van Os, & Aleman, 2006; McCreery & Claridge, 2002; Preti, Bonventre,

Ledda, Petretto, & Masala, 2007). It might seem that only grandiose delusions would not be distressing, but some people embrace personal identities involving victimization or terrible illness with apparent gusto; even a grievance or an affliction can give one's life meaning. Persons who embrace aberrant beliefs may be proud of their open-mindedness, and suspicious persons may be proud that they are not naïve.

Conviction   This too is on most lists—though sometimes the terms employed are *imperviousness to feedback, certainty, commitment, inflexibility, fixity, doxasitic strength, incorrigibility,* or *firmly sustained.* Conviction may be self-perpetuating; as Rhodes and Jakes (2004, p. 216) noted regarding a group of patients whom they studied intensively, from their viewpoint "they encountered, often on a daily basis, objects, events and people that confirmed their beliefs." There is evidence suggesting that delusions having a religious component tend to entail strong conviction (cf. Appelbaum, Robbins, & Roth, 1999).

Brett-Jones, Garety, and Hemsley (1987) have developed an interactive procedure for assessing delusional conviction. In it, the individual is probed with hypothetical contradictions of the delusional belief and asked, "How do you think you would react if this [contradictory event] really happened?" The reliance on an interactive format seems apt, given that delusions usually do not exist in a social vacuum. Most persons who entertain a distressing false belief will have been challenged in that belief by other persons who might usually be trusted. For example, friends will have dismissed the worries of someone with a persecutory delusion, and physicians will have tried to reassure someone with a somatic delusion. In this light, a high level of conviction may reflect the individual having drifted away from the back-and-forth interaction with significant others that most of us rely on to keep perspective in our daily lives. The notion that paranoid individuals are particularly rigid and brittle may relate to interpersonal dynamics of this sort. To be committed to any delusion—persecutory or otherwise—is to mistrust those who question it. Wholesale rejection of others' views may bespeak a kind of arrogance even if the delusion itself is not grandiose.

Of course, just because a person favors his or her own beliefs over those of family, friends, and experts does not itself mean that they are false.

Sometimes (though not usually) it is the minority of one who sees the world most clearly.

In some cases it's a minority of two who jointly fail so see the world clearly, as when a married couple are enmeshed but are isolated from other persons. The disorder has been called *shared psychotic disorder*, and earlier still *folie à deux*. Often, one of the persons is dominant, and he or she works to limit the other's exposure to outside influence. The nondominant person may share the delusional views when the two are together, but the tenuousness of his or her conviction becomes evident when they are separated. *DSM-5* offers "delusional symptoms in partner of individual with delusional disorder" (p. 122) as a diagnostic option which acknowledges the asymmetry of conviction. Instances involving more than two persons have been reported, as in *folie à trois* (e.g., Maizel, Knobler, & Herbstein, 1990).

Insight   Regarding delusions, the lack of insight denotes unawareness that one's belief is in error (cf. Phillips, Price, Greenberg, & Rasmussen, 2003). Some writers equate low insight with high conviction. The fact that delusions may vary on insight, even within an individual across time, has been apparent at least since Sacks, Carpenter, and Strauss's (1974) description of the "double awareness phase"—a term provided by a patient regarding her own experience of wavering between embracing a delusional belief and recognizing its delusionality. Such experiences are apparently not uncommon (Campbell & Morrison, 2007). In this vein, patients with BDD may show insight regarding their appearance, then lose it upon looking at themselves in the mirror (Phillips, 2005). Similarly, persons with obsessive-compulsive disorder (OCD) may lose perspective when threatened (Kozak & Foa, 1994), and persons with panic disorder may be unable during an attack to consider noncatastrophic explanations (Beck & Rector, 2002).

Still, lack of insight is often cited as differentiating persons with persistent delusions from persons having a nonpsychotic condition. While noting that persons with either DD or social anxiety disorder may "focus on being rejected by or offending others," *DSM-5* indicates that what differentiates the two conditions is the fact that "many individuals with social anxiety disorder have good insight that their beliefs are out of proportion" (p. 207). However, as noted below, in the case

of some obsessive-compulsive and related disorders (OCRDs) even a true lack of insight does not always qualify the individual for a DD diagnosis under *DSM-5*.

Involvement   This may encompass *emotional* involvement, which is indistinguishable from distress (discussed earlier). More importantly, it also encompasses *behavioral* involvement, that is, the presence of delusion-related actions, or "pressure to act upon beliefs" (*DSM-5*, p. 743).

Behavioral involvement is most noteworthy when discrepant with insight, as when the individual can acknowledge that his or her "belief" is not true, yet acts as if it were. Especially when the behavior is self-destructive, it may be unwise to view a condition as categorically nondelusional on the basis that the individual regularly verbalizes insight.

Preoccupation   This feature addresses the extent to which the ideation consumes the individual's mental life—such that thought processes are in a rut. Adjectives that reflect this include *obsessive*, *pervasive*, *recurring*, *persistent*, *perseverative*, *ruminative*, and *intrusive*. Preoccupation can, of course, be a problem even in the absence of suspiciousness or false beliefs.

To be unduly preoccupied with something is obviously to obsesses about it, but *DSM-5* draws a barrier between DD diagnoses and OCRD diagnoses—specifying, for example, that a person who qualifies for OCD may not qualify for DD, even if insight is absent. There is one point at which *DSM-5* does implicitly acknowledge the continuity between delusional preoccupation and obsessionality: in indicating that the subdelusional version of DD-jealous is to be viewed as an "other" form of OCRD (p. 264). In addition, *DSM-5* notes that a diagnosis of a psychotic condition may take priority over the OCRD diagnoses of trichotillomania (hair-pulling) and excoriation (skin-picking) disorder.

Narrative Complexity   Full-blown delusions can be full of detail and texture. To give a persecutory example, the person does not merely believe that someone wishes to do him harm: he believes that a particular person (real or fictional) wishes to harm him in a particular way and by particular means. Thus, some delusional patients may be described as having "a tendency to develop elaborate constructions around their fears" (Stopa, Denton, Wingfield, & Taylor, 2013).

The term *conspiracy theorist* is often used casually to describe persons whose suspicions evince narrative complexity, especially when such suspicions span diverse topics. Though perhaps apt, the degree of delusionality may depend on whether the individual is isolated in his or her belief or is part of a trusted group of mistrusters. Persons who embrace conspiracy theories often manifest a strange mix of paranoid cynicism and gullible trust.

Delusionality in *DSM-5* Section III of *DSM-5* (pp. 743–744) provides "Clinician-Rated Dimensions of Psychosis Symptom Severity" in which severity of delusions is coded (concurrently) in terms of two of the previously discussed attributes: distress and behavioral involvement. In contrast, in the context of OCDR specifiers (pp. 237, 243, and 247), delusionality is linked with absence of insight. It is unclear why delusionality is handled so differently in these two contexts.

Delusional Themes

The foregoing features are those on which delusion and delusion-like symptomatology vary, regardless of thematic content. We turn now to such content. Various *DSM-5* passages mention the following: erotomanic, jealous, persecutory, somatic, grandiose, invulnerability, guilt, worthlessness, religious, and referential. On this list, the first five comprise the major DD subtypes, grandiose is also associated with manic states (as is invulnerability), and guilt and worthlessness are associated with depressive states. Any of these may be seen in schizophrenia.

In the real clinical world, a given delusion often qualifies under two or more content headings (e.g., Cannon & Kramer, 2011), perhaps occasioning a "mixed" label in the DD context. Someone who falsely believes that his or her body is malfunctioning because a nemesis has poisoned the person does not have two delusions, one somatic and one persecutory, but rather a single delusion in which the two themes are organized (cf. Rhodes, Jakes, & Robinson, 2005). Grandiose and persecutory themes are easily interwoven: One must be quite special to attract the attention that persecution entails, and having a strong sense of entitlement may incline one to define an unremarkable slight as a profound insult.

We turn to a discussion of those thematic categories of delusion listed here, plus others (agentic and misidentification). In the course of doing so, we also address the question: How does *DSM-5* handle the less-than-delusional variants of each?

Erotomanic In lay usage, erotomanic often denotes rampant sexual desire and/or behavior. Here it instead denotes the belief that a specific other person—usually someone implausibly grand and distant—is in love with oneself. The traditional name is *de Clérambault syndrome*.

DD-erotomanic may account for a tiny fraction of DD cases (de Portugal, González, Haro, Autonell, & Cervilla, 2008; Grover et al., 2007). As a result, research may depend on archival sources (e.g., Brüne, 2001). Many of the cases are, nonetheless, extraordinarily fascinating—for example, one in which the erotomanic belief was so firmly held as to lead to death by starvation (Aviv, 2011). *DSM-5* offers no clear home for a nonpsychotic variant. The closest approximation is narcissistic PD, where the individual may be "preoccupied with fantasies of...ideal love" (p. 669). There is also at least one striking commonality between DD-erotomanic and borderline personality disorder (BPD): In some cases of each, individuals may engage in stalking behavior.

Jealous In this context, jealous is not a synonym of envious. Rather, it refers to the belief is that one's partner is unfaithful (as in "jealous lover"). The clinical problem may lie in an excessive preoccupation with the *possibility* of betrayal, or it may lie in an excessive response to *real* betrayal (cf. McKenna, 1984)—a distinction which jealousy researchers (e.g., Parrott, 1991) refer to as suspicious versus reactive jealousy—though the two are by no means mutually exclusive. The classic label for DD-jealous is often said to be *Othello syndrome*, though Shakespeare's Othello manifested reactive jealousy while DD-jealous leans toward the suspicious variant.

As noted, in *DSM-5* (p. 264) nondelusional jealousy may warrant an OCRD/other diagnosis. Suspicion of infidelity also comprises one of the seven PPD criterion (A7, p. 649)—one that may be somewhat distinct from the other six (cf. Fogelson et al., 1999; Thomas, Turkheimer, & Oltmanns, 2003). Some jealous individuals may qualify for BPD, though not if jealousy is the sole symptom.

Persecutory   Coverage here is brief, as this discussion is a minor elaboration of the earlier section on paranoia.

Persecution is arguably a poor summary term, as here the phenomena encompass humiliation, exploitation, victimization, rejection, exclusion, betrayal, etc.—none of which are necessarily implied by *persecution*. Anything to which one aspires, one can believe another person is aiming to interfere with. Anything one dreads, one can believe someone else is working to bring about. *Betrayal* is noteworthy, as the belief that someone has wantonly breached an obligation (to oneself) is a common aspect of such delusions.

DD-persecutory (along with DD-jealous) and PPD may be viewed, respectively, as the delusional and nondelusional loci within the nonschizophrenia region of the persecutory/paranoid dimension. As noted, persecutory symptoms are also criteria for schizotypal PD, reflecting their putative relevance to the schizophrenia spectrum. Of all major schizophrenia symptoms, the persecutory delusion is likely the most common (e.g., McGrath et al., 2004).

Somatic   Delusions involving one's body are noted under four *DSM-5* diagnostic headings: schizophrenia, depression, DD-somatic, and BDD. Though DD itself is uncommon, somatic cases make up a substantial subset within that group (Grover et al., 2007). The nondelusional counterpart of DD-somatic consists of conditions found in the *DSM-5* somatic symptom and related disorders grouping, especially *somatic symptom disorder*, and perhaps *illness anxiety disorder* as well.

BDD poses some interesting issues. In the years prior to *DSM-5*, BDD was grouped with somatic (i.e., somatoform) disorders, and was the most extensively researched among them. Persons whose BDD reached delusional severity—perhaps a majority of BDD cases (Mancuso, Knoesen, & Castle, 2009)—were said to have two disorders: BDD and DD-somatic. *DSM-5* changed this by moving BDD to the OCRD grouping, and by giving priority to the BDD (over the DD) diagnosis. Thus a person who might previously have received comorbid DD and BDD diagnoses is now diagnosed with BDD plus a specifier that insight is absent. This contrasts with what has occurred with the new counterparts of somatoform conditions with which BDD was previously grouped in *DSM-IV-TR*—somatic symptom disorder and

illness anxiety disorder; in these instances, when ideation is deemed delusional, it is a psychosis diagnosis that now takes precedence.

Anorexic persons, too, may have perseverative, reality-defying somatic beliefs. In one study 28% of those with restrictive anorexia nervosa were deemed delusional (Konstantakopoulos et al., 2012). *DSM-5* ignores such a possibility: It does not offer the insight-absent specifier that is available for some OCRDs, and it certainly does not mention any possibility of delusionality, even though it acknowledges that "individuals with anorexia nervosa frequently either lack insight into or *deny* the problem" (p. 340, italics added). The word *deny* is perhaps telling, given its association with pre-*DSM-III* neurotic (rather than psychotic) conditions—this in spite of the fact that some emaciated patients' belief that they weigh too much may border on the bizarre. (Some traditions die slowly.) Especially if behavioral involvement is considered (as the Delusions rating scale provided by *DSM-5* on p. 743 suggests it should be), the high death rates associated with BDD and anorexia indicate that at their worst they are among the most severe—and certainly the most perilous—of delusional conditions.

Grandiose and Invulnerable   Beliefs that one is truly special and invincible define the content of DD-grandiose and are also characteristic of manic states. Such delusions may be especially common among highly religious persons (Suhail & Ghauri, 2010). DD-erotomanic may be viewed as a variant of DD-grandiose, as in DD-erotomanic the fantasied suitor is typically grand. No *DSM-5* diagnosis captures subdelusional grandiosity very well. The best options are hypomanic state and narcissistic PD.

Guilt and Worthlessness   These are sometimes referred to as *self-denigrating* or *negative-self* delusions (Rhodes et al., 2005). They may be viewed as extreme versions of cognitive distortions characteristic of depressive states. Self-denigrating delusions do not play a role in diagnostic criteria for DD, but a large fraction of patients warranting a DD diagnosis show comorbid depressive disorders (Grover et al., 2007). BDD is, in effect, appearance-oriented self-denigration.

Religious Preoccupations   having to do with religion are not uncommon, evident in perhaps 20%–25% of psychotic inpatients (Raja, Azzoni, & Lubich, 2000; Siddle, Haddock, Tarrier, & Faragher, 2002), though the percentage may fluctuate with societal attitudes (Stompe, Ortwein-Swoboda, Ritter, & Schanda, 2003). Preoccupations in OCD often have religious overtones as well (cf. Abramowitz, 2008). It is not clear that a delusion may be solely religious; most such delusions are likely also persecutory, grandiose, or guilty.

Determining that religious beliefs are delusional is complicated by their inherently irrefutable nature. While it is always important to view beliefs against the backdrop the patient's cultural context, this is especially the case for religious beliefs. Consider the devout Christian who asserts: "Each week I drink the blood of a man who was murdered 2000 years ago, and whose mother and father were, respectively, a virgin and the creator of the universe." This person would likely be viewed as bizarrely delusional by an observer who is totally unfamiliar with the traditional Christian narrative.

Referential   Overestimation of the extent to which others notice oneself is a common bias (Gilovich, Medvec, & Savitsky, 2000). Delusions (and ideas) of reference may be viewed as an exaggerated form of this bias. Two variants have been noted (Startup & Startup, 2005): communication (e.g., messages in the public media are directed at the self), and observation (e.g., others are secretly observing or gossiping about oneself).

Rosse, Kendrick, Wyatt, Isaac, and Deutsch (1994) employed a task in which research participants viewed pictures of faces that varied with respect to the direction of gaze, and the participant's task was to decide whether the pictured person's gaze was directed at oneself. Schizophrenic individuals, especially those with paranoid schizophrenia, showed a distinctive tendency to misperceive the gaze as directed at self. Recent studies (e.g., Bucci, Startup, Wynn, Baker, & Lewin., 2008; Freeman, Pugh, Vorontsova, Antley, & Slater, 2010; Walss-Bass, Fernandes, Roberts, Service, & Velligan, 2013) have employed more elaborate stimulus settings for the assessment of referential inferences.

Some writers view excessive self-focus as *the* defining element of paranoia (Fenigstein, 1996), Supporting a paranoid-referential linkage, there is factor analytic research suggesting that referential ideation may be subsumed under mistrust (e.g., Chmielewski & Watson, 2008), and there is experimental evidence suggesting that increasing someone's self-focus may increase his or her sense of being taken advantage of (cf. Ellett & Chadwick, 2007; Kramer, 1994). Some assessment devices focus on referential experiences that have inherently paranoid overtones (e.g., Wong et al., 2012).

Still, diverse beliefs can be referential (cf. Lenzenweger, Bennett, & Lilenfeld, 1997; Wuthrich & Bates, 2006). For example, a grandiose individual may believe that others are eyeing oneself with awe or envy. However, there is evidence that even the tendency to have pleasant referential thoughts is associated with paranoia as well as with narcissism (Cicero & Kerns, 2011).

Referentiality is ensconced in the name of an unofficial diagnostic entity, *olfactory reference syndrome*, in which one is preoccupied with the belief that others are noticing one's body odor and are judging it to be foul (Feusner, Phillips, & Stein, 2010). This condition is sometimes viewed as a variant of BDD, which is in turn associated with a tendency to misperceive others' facial expressions as conveying contempt toward oneself (Buhlmann, Etcoff, & Wilhelm, 2006).

Agentic   This delusional domain lacks standardized terminology, and it should be noted that *agency delusions* is simply the term that is favored here. The closest synonym for agency is *loss of boundary* (i.e., self versus non-self). Both *bizarre* and *Schneiderian* (or *first-rank*) delusions overlap with this domain, as do *delusions of disintegration* (Foulds & Bedford, 1975). However labeled, the domain of agency delusions consists of (a) beliefs about *being influenced* (reduced agency), and (b) beliefs about *influencing* (excessive agency). At first glance, these two may seem to be opposites, but there is evidence that they are functionally linked (cf. Hauser et al., 2010).

It is the first that is often called *delusions of influence* (alternatively, *passivity experiences*), referenced in the *DSM-5* mention of "[d]elusions that express a loss of control over mind or body" (p. 87). Included (with alternative labels) are *delusions of control* (or *external control* or *alien control experiences*, i.e., of body movements), *delusions of thought control* (insertion or withdrawal), *delusions of emotional control* (or *made emotions*), and *somatic passivity experiences* (i.e., somatosensory experiences, arguably hallucinations). The influence acts on experience itself, so the delusion that powerful others are, say, manipulating one's bank accounts would not qualify as a delusion of influence.

The second subgroup has no standard name, and discussions of agency delusions often give it scant attention. The prime instance of it is *thought broadcasting*. *Magical thinking*, a term commonly used in describing subpsychotic manifestations (as in schizotypal PD), overlaps with this subgroup. Thus in *DSM-5* magical thinking is said to involve the belief that "one's thoughts, words, or actions will cause or prevent a specific outcome in some way that defies…laws of cause and effect" (p. 824). A common near-synonym is *aberrant beliefs*.

An individual can have both an agency delusion and a persecutory one, and a belief can be both agentic and paranoid (e.g., that a nemesis controls one's subjective experience). Still, the empirical relationship between these two belief-types is unclear. They often are grouped with one another (and with hallucinations) in a single positive-symptom factor (e.g., Serretti et al., 2001), but it has been suggested that when artificial factor-analytic constraints are absent, agency delusions emerge as distinct (Stuart, Malone, Currie, Klimidis, & Minas, 1995), and indeed such distinctness has emerged repeatedly (e.g., Allardyce, McCreadie, Morrison, & van Os, 2007; Kimhy, Goetz, Yale, Corcoran, & Malaspina, 2005; Peralta & Cuesta, 1999). Agency delusions are arguably in a class by themselves, perhaps with distinctive causes (see later discussion of the comparator model). There is evidence that that, within schizophrenia, they may be associated with reduced cortical thickness in the inferior parietal lobe (Venkatasubramanian, Jayakumar, Keshavan, & Gangadhar, 2011).

As agency delusions are rarely mentioned in discussions of DD, one might surmise that they are specific to the schizophrenia spectrum. Such ideation is, however, also seen in OCD, as when an individual believes he or she must perform a ritual to prevent some distal outcome (cf. Berle, Blaszczynski, Einstein, & Menzies, 2006; Bocci & Gordon, 2007). In this vein, there are reports of elevations on measures of magical thinking in some OCRDs (cf. Einstein & Menzies, 2004; Fear, Sharp, & Healy, 2000; Lavender, Shubert, de Silva, & Treasure, 2006).

As noted, *DSM-5* acknowledges that some OCD patients lack insight, but it indicates that they

should be given a "with absent insight/delusional beliefs" specifier rather than any psychotic diagnosis. *DSM-5* (p. 238) asserts that such persons comprise a small fraction of OCD patients, but some research (Matsunaga et al., 2002) suggests the low-insight fraction may be as high as one third. OCD is a diverse category, and delusional-like mentation is likely more common in some forms than in others (cf. Lee & Telch, 2005).

Misidentification   These are usually classed as *monothematic* delusions, denoting their circumscribed, focal nature. They include *Cotard* (the belief that one is dead), *Fregoli* (a person in one's world is someone one knows but cannot recognize, as that person is in disguise), *mirrored-self-misidentification* (the person one sees in the mirror is an imposter), *somatoparaphrenia* (part of one's body is not one's own), and *Capgras*. Capgras patients believe that at least one other person—usually a loved one—is not who that person claims to be, but is instead an imposter who looks, sounds, and acts just like that person. The patient may also have a pervasive feeling that things are not as they should be. More progress has been made in understanding Capgras than is the case with most delusions, as noted below.

Research on Delusions

The literature on delusions is focused more on symptom than on diagnosis; much of it resides in a *DSM*-free zone. Much of it is paranoia-relevant, if only because cases of schizophrenia with persecutory delusions dominate study samples. However, results from such studies may be viewed as shedding light on paranoia, on delusionality, or on schizophrenia—and it is often not obvious which is the most apt way to interpret a given set of findings. There are various ways of dealing with this quandary.

One option is to compare delusional versus nondelusional cases of schizophrenia, though persons with nondelusional schizophrenia may have a history of, or a future course involving, delusions. Another approach focuses on cases of DD, but DD is uncommon. Another option is to focus on persons whose delusions are distinctly nonpersecutory (e.g., grandiose), but studies of such samples are uncommon. A related approach focuses on delusionality in conditions not traditionally viewed as psychotic, such as BDD (e.g.,

Mancuso et al., 2009; Phillips, McElroy, Keck, Hudson, & Pope, 1994). There are assessment tools which facilitate this, most notably the Brown Assessment of Beliefs Scale (BABS; Eisen et al., 1998), an interview-based instrument that can be administered whenever there is a "dominant belief (obsession, concern, idea, worry, or delusion) that has preoccupied the patient" (p. 103).

Another alternative examines the correlates of *proneness* to delusions. Such research typically involves nonclinical samples, identified by responses on inventories. The developers of any such inventory is caught between two considerations. On the one hand, items that allude to blatantly deviant beliefs may set off alarms in persons who are already somewhat guarded. On the other hand, the less deviant-seeming an item is, the greater the likelihood that some persons who endorse it are doing so for reasons unrelated to pathology (cf. Freeman et al., 2010). For example, persons endorsing mildly worded items about being targeted for harm may sometimes be expressing accurate threat appraisals. In this vein, the fact that African Americans may score well above non-Hispanic Whites on measures of paranoid tendencies (Combs, Penn, & Fenigstein, 2002) cannot be assumed to reflect undue suspiciousness.

Three overlapping research traditions pertain to delusion-proneness: suspiciousness, aberrant beliefs, and delusion-like beliefs. The first provides a possible analogue for the persecutory/paranoid side of the equation, the second is most relevant to agency delusions, and the third addresses delusions broadly. Overviews of these three are now provided, with a focus on assessment.

Suspiciousness   Any measure of PPD tendencies is relevant here. Among non-PPD scales, one that is widely used is Fenigstein and Vanable's (1992) Paranoia Scale, which correlates highly with continuous measures of PPD (Useda, 2002). Others are Rawlings and Freeman's (1996) Paranoia/Suspiciousness Questionnaire, and McKay, Langdon, and Coltheart's (2006) Persecutory Ideation Questionnaire. In addition, mistrust and suspiciousness subscales are found in multiscale instruments that have emerged from a close examination of the entire PD domain (cf. Clark, Livesley, Schroeder, & Irish, 1996). Also relevant are certain subscales of schizotypal PD instruments, for example, the Schizotypal Personality Questionnaire (SPQ; Raine, 1991).

Items in such scales are diverse. For example, in some the focus is external (e.g., "I am sure I get a raw deal from life"). In some the relevance is oblique (e.g., "No one really cares much what happens to you"). Some address fearful wariness (e.g., "I tend not to be on guard. . ."—reverse scored). Some tap referentiality (e.g., "I have often felt that strangers were looking at me critically"). (These examples are from Fenigstein and Vanable's [1992] scale, which was in turn based on the Minnesota Multiphasic Personality Inventory.)

As noted, people may be wary about endorsing such self-report items. There is evidence that the interview format may *increase* guardedness (cf. Mohr & Leonards, 2005). A more promising alternative is reliance on informants' reports; those who know individuals well may be more aware of—or more willing to acknowledge—some PPD-related features (high hostility, low altruism) than are the individuals themselves (Miller, Pilkonis, & Clifton, 2005).

Aberrant Beliefs   Research in this area (cf. Chapman & Chapman, 1988) arose specifically to tap beliefs that may lie on a continuum with delusions—primarily those involving agency and referentiality. The seminal measure is Eckblad and Chapman's (1983) Magical Ideation Scale, an example item from which is "Some people can make me aware of them just by thinking about me." Similarly, the SPQ (Raine, 1991) includes a Magical Thinking subscale, an example item from which is "Do you believe in telepathy (mind-reading)?"

DD patients may not have distinctive levels of aberrant beliefs (Fear, Sharp, & Healy, 1996), and correlations between self-reports of suspiciousness and of aberrant beliefs have usually been modest (e.g., Chan et al., 2011; Horan, Brown, & Blanchard, 2007). This parallels findings, noted earlier, regarding the distinctness of persecutory versus agency delusions.

Delusion-like Beliefs   The key instruments are the 40-item Peters et al. Delusions Inventory (PDI; Peters et al., 1999) and its short form (PDI-21; Peters, Joseph, Day, & Garety, 2004), both of which have been widely used. The PDI softens delusional belief queries by prefacing them with wording such as "Do you ever feel as if...?" Follow-up questions allow for the assessment of distress, preoccupation, and conviction. The PDI covers most traditional delusion themes, including self-denigration. Thus high scores reflect in part how diverse one's quasi-delusional ideation is, and a person who has one circumscribed delusion could receive a low PDI score. Although persecution is central to delusion research generally, just 2 of the 21 short-form items relate directly to it: "Do you ever feel as if you are being persecuted?" and "Do you ever feel as if there is a conspiracy against you?" A third may also be relevant: "Are you often worried that your partner may be unfaithful?"

Comment   Research on nonpatients who obtain elevated scores on instruments such as the PDI has been strongly advocated (e.g., Freeman, 2007), on the basis that it allows the researcher to observe quasi-delusional processes uncomplicated by frank psychosis. However, healthy persons who hold such beliefs may possess protective attributes that account for their good mental health (cf. Warman & Martin, 2006), in which case the study of such persons may tell more about protective factors than about delusion-proneness.

Roots of Paranoia and Delusions

As noted, the literatures on paranoia and delusions are intertwined. This is especially the case for etiological and risk factors. Accordingly, various studies addressing both issues are summarized together here. These all address aspects of persons' lives that appear to put them at risk for the development of these kinds of pathology.

Personal and Social Characteristics

Migration   There is evidence that migrants are vulnerable to paranoid disorders (cf. Bentall, Corcoran, Howard, Blackwood, & Kinderman, 2001; Selten, Cantor-Graae, & Kahn, 2007). Harassment or marginalization may have preceded immigration, and relocation may not have provided the anticipated relief. The development of the paranoia is often gradual, concomitant with growing frustration in the new locale (cf. Maizel et al., 1990). Janssen et al. (2003) have reported that, among persons showing no delusional ideation at baseline, subsequent development of such ideation was predicted by perceived discrimination.

Sensory Impairments   Though findings are not entirely consistent (cf. van der Werf et al., 2007), it has long been asserted that persons with sensory, especially hearing, impairments may incur an increased risk for delusions (e.g., Cooper & Curry, 1976; Fuchs, 1999). The usual explanation is tied to referential thinking: When you cannot hear what nearby people are saying, it is easy to surmise that they are saying things about you that they do not want you to hear. Of course, as persons with such impairments may be especially susceptible to exclusion and victimization (Rounds, 1996), hypersensitivity may be warranted.

Developmental Processes

Stressor Antecedents   Varese et al. (2012) have concluded from a meta-analysis that exposure to various kinds of childhood adversities substantially increases the risk of psychosis. The studies summarized next focus on paranoia- and delusion-related outcome variables.

In a large, longitudinal study, Johnson, Cohen, Chen, Kasen, and Brook (2006) addressed parental maltreatment as a predictor of PDs. Among 12 PDs assessed, rates of PPD showed the most dramatic rise as a function of problematic parental child-rearing behaviors. Rates of PPD were exceptionally high (relative even to other PDs) when many types of aversive parental behavior had been observed during the child-rearing period.

Yang, Ullrich, Roberts, and Coid (2007) reported that the experience of institutionalized care (hence disrupted parenting) during childhood is predictive of PPD symptoms among adults. In a study of children documented by age 12 as having experienced maltreatment and evaluated for PD symptoms during adolescence, Natsuaki et al. (2009) reported that maltreated children were underrepresented among those showing low PPD. Relying on archival data regarding a sample of patients with severe mental illness, Choi, Reddy, and Spaulding (2012) reported that histories of childhood sexual abuse and emotional maltreatment were predictive of clinical ratings of suspiciousness/hostility. Nonlongitudinal findings confirming such relationships are myriad; recent examples include those from Ashcroft, Kingdon, and Chadwick (2012), Fisher, Appiah-Kusi, and Grant (2012), Murphy, Shevlin, Adamson, Cruddas, and Houston (2012), and Saha et al. (2011). Such effects are not confined to paranoid ideation. Perkins and Allen (2006) reported a relation between paranormal beliefs and self-reported childhood physical abuse in undergraduates, and Lataster et al. (2006) reported associations in a sample of adolescents between aberrant beliefs and both sexual trauma and bullying.

Given that children should be able to trust caregivers to provide care and protection, any form of child abuse or neglect counts as betrayal, and repeated betrayals during the formative years would seem likely to foster expectations of future betrayal. While this would suggest a direct stressor-to-paranoia path, there may also be pathways involving the effects of stressors on anxiety or self-esteem (cf. Fisher et al., 2012; Kesting, Bredenpohl, Klenke, Westermann, & Lincoln, 2013), perhaps with lasting neurochemical disregulation.

A study by Holmes and Steel (2004) is a rare instance of experimental research in this area. Students who had been previously assessed on various measures, including aberrant beliefs, were shown a disturbing video (focusing on traffic accidents) and were asked to report spontaneously occurring intrusions related to that film during the week following. The correlation between preassessed aberrant beliefs and frequency of intrusions was noteworthy for its strength ($r = .5$). This suggests that delusion-prone individuals may be especially susceptible to the effects of trauma.

The summary presented here draws from diverse and unconnected literatures. There is an extensive, focused research tradition that is also relevant: on *hostile attributional style*. Persons with this tendency, when in a situation in which another person's intent is ambiguous, tend to impute hostility. This style is arguably a childhood counterpart of adult paranoia, and it is often evident in children who have been abused. It also predicts the later development of aggressive behavior patterns; see Dodge (2006) and Tone and Davis (2012) for reviews.

Genetic Contributions There are a number of relevant twin studies involving comparisons of the within-pair correlations for monozygotic pairs with those for dizygotic pairs (r_{MZ} vs. r_{DZ}). Among studies in which a measure of PPD characteristics, trust, or suspiciousness has been considered, several have suggested modest but reliable genetic effects (Coolidge, Thede, & Jang, 2004; Jang, Livesley, Angleitner, Riemann, &Vernon,

2002; Kendler et al., 2006; Oskarsson, Dawes, Johannesson, & Magnusson, 2012; Shikishima, Hiraishi, & Ando, 2006), though Jang, Livesley, and Vernon (1996) reported mixed results, and two studies have suggested no genetic effect (Gustavsson, Pedersen, Åsberg, & Schalling, 1996; Torgersen et al., 2000). Regarding aberrant beliefs, MacDonald, Pogue-Geile, Debski, and Manuck (2001) reported results unsupportive of a genetic effect. Studies of delusion-like beliefs have yielded results that are more consistently indicative of a genetic effect (Jacobs, Myin-Germeys, Derom, Vlietinck, & van Os, 2005; Linney et al., 2003; Varghese et al., 2013).

A number of studies have inquired whether suspiciousness or aberrant beliefs tend to be relatively common among nonschizophrenic members of families in which there is a member with schizophrenia, and findings are generally positive in both cases (e.g., Chang & Lenzenweger, 2005; Nicolson et al., 2003; Tarbox, Almasy, Gur, Nimgaonkar, & Pogue-Geile, 2012; Yaralian et al., 2000). Tarbox et al. (2012) suggested that, when self-reporting, relatives of schizophrenic individuals may minimize their own deviant thinking, yielding underestimates of concordance in such studies.

To summarize twin and family studies, the majority point to genetic contributions, but as there are negative results, and as effects are never large, the most reasonable inference is that the genetic contribution is modest (see also Bentall et al., 2001). Little relevant molecular genetic research has been reported, and the few positive findings that have reported (cf. Debnath, Das, Bera, Nayak, & Chaudhuri, 2006; Schulze et al., 2005; Sun, Jayathilake, Zhao, & Meltzer, 2012) appear not to have been replicated.

Evolutionary Influences

Evolutionary models typically view biological malfunctions as adaptive processes that are defective or that have been repurposed maladaptively. In the case of paranoia, the adaptive function presumably involves alertness to danger, especially from other persons (Schlager, 1995). Otherwise stated, a "detect hostile others" system may be overactive in paranoia (Gilbert, 2001, p. 23). Perhaps ancestrally set thresholds for threat detection mechanisms cause excessive false alarms in the context of some modern environments (Schlager, 1995).

Human societies have long been hierarchically organized; low-status individuals have reason to fear exploitation from above, and those with high status may fear being displaced (Gilbert, Boxall, Cheung, & Irons, 2005; Kramer & Messick, 1999). Mistrustful biases may confer an adaptive advantage in the face of uncertainty, since survival may be better served by seeing threat where there is none than by failing to see threat where it exists (cf. Haselton & Nettle, 2006; Vohs et al., 2007). The range of possible dangers to consider within such a framework is wide, and the evolutionary processes relevant to, say, romantic disloyalty may not be the same as those relevant to financial fraud.

The foregoing, once articulated, may seem obvious as a framework for how paranoid biases may be the product of evolution. However, the value of an evolutionary approach lies in its ability to generate testable hypotheses that go beyond the obvious. An experimental study reported by Schaller, Park, and Mueller (2003) was based on the premise that a darkness-threat link may have its basis in evolution. Hypothesizing that darkness may increase a sense of vulnerability to members of out-groups, these researchers asked students to rate in-group and out-group members with respect to danger-relevant and anger-irrelevant traits in two conditions: lights on and lights off. As predicted, out-group derogation was evident in the lights-off condition for ratings of danger-relevant characteristics only, an effect that was specific to individuals who possessed a generalized view of the world as a dangerous place. Thus this research suggests that an evolutionarily valenced cue (darkness) and a personal variable (dangerousness beliefs) interact to elicit a hostile response (out-group derogation).

Sequelae of Paranoia and Delusionality

Here we discuss prospective and quasi-prospective research in which aspects of delusionality or paranoia are treated as predictors of later outcome.

Chapman, Chapman, Kwapil, Eckblad, and Zinser (1994) and Kwapil, Miller, Zinser, Chapman, and Chapman (1997) reported that college students who eventually show signs of

psychosis were, prior to that outcome, characterized by high levels of aberrant beliefs, especially when social anhedonia was also present. Poulton et al. (2000) reported that the presence at age 11 of a group of features encompassing aberrant beliefs, unusual perceptual experiences, and suspiciousness was predictive of schizophreniform disorder at age 26. Cannon et al. (2001) examined childhood psychiatric records and found that the variable most predictive of later schizophrenia was abnormal suspiciousness or sensitivity. Welham et al. (2009) reported that item endorsements relevant to paranoia ("I am suspicious" in females, and "I feel that others are out to get me" in males) at age 14 were predictive of a diagnosis of nonaffective psychosis at age 21.

Fiedler, Oltmanns, and Turkheimer (2004) have reported that, among military personnel, high levels of self- and peer-reported PPD features were predictive of discharge for unsatisfactory behavior or performance. Regarding physical health, there are findings which suggest that persons with various paranoid diagnoses have a higher incidence of a wide variety of medical conditions than do nonclinical controls (Dalmau, Bergman, & Brismar, 1998). There is also considerable research on the relation between suspiciousness or cynicism and physical health (cf. Bunde & Suls, 2006; Miller, Smith, Turner, Guijarro, & Hallet, 1996.) For example, Jackson, Kubzansky, Cohen, Jacobs, and Wright (2007) reported that cynical hostility was related to indicators of chronic obstructive pulmonary disease. Examination of the scales in question strongly suggests their relevance to suspiciousness—with hostile overtones.

Although much research has suggested that patients with paranoid schizophrenia have better prognoses than those with other forms of schizophrenia, Salinas, Paul, and Newbill (2002) have suggested that much of that research lacked appropriate controls, and that when such controls are provided this effect does not emerge. In a schizophrenia study reported by Harrow et al. (2004), delusional beliefs were predictive of poor occupational outcomes, especially when there was a strong emotional commitment to the delusional belief.

Findings described in this section are drawn from diverse research traditions. As most are longitudinal studies, in many cases very large, they deserve to be taken seriously, and together they indicate that aspects of paranoia and delusionality foster, or are markers of variables that foster, diverse negative outcomes over time.

Theoretical Perspectives and Related Research

Models of delusional and paranoid conditions may be assigned to three groupings: motivational, explanationist, and deficit/bias. Motivational models assume that faulty beliefs arise from self-protective needs. An explanationist model assumes that delusions arise from normal processing of abnormal experiences; if there is a motive involved, it is merely to make sense of strange perceptions. Deficit/bias models posit a diminished wherewithal to see reality clearly; some bias models also incorporate motivational factors, and specific deficit models have arisen to account for misidentification delusions (two-process model) and delusions of influence (comparator model). Note that a similar array of models has arisen in the study of confabulation (cf. Fotopoulou, 2010).

These three approaches are now discussed, with a special subsection devoted to one motivation-related issue: projective defenses.

Motivational Approaches

Based on broader research within psychology, one can assert with confidence that motives sometimes influence beliefs. Paranoid and delusional ideation is surely not exempt. However, this says little about the specific role of motivations in the pathological nature of some beliefs. Crucial questions remain: Does the aberrancy of delusional beliefs have motivational sources? If so, what are they?

In the classic Freudian view of paranoia (cf. Bone & Oldham, 1994), the individual deals with unacceptable impulses by projecting them; see the discussion of projection that follows. Freud argued that homosexual impulses lay at the root of paranoia, and that the individual denies the presence of those impulses and imputes his or her own self-condemnation to others.

In Shapiro's (1965) view, the individual is seen as dealing with a deep sense of vulnerability by viewing the world as eyeing him or her menacingly: "the paranoid person is continuously occupied and concerned with the threat of being subjected to some external control or some external infringement of his will" (p. 82). Shapiro described paranoia as a state of emergency mobilization, requiring that spontaneous responses be replaced with intentional ones and that tender and playful emotions in particular be cast aside. The individual in this kind of humorless, hyperpurposive state assumes that others are as he or she is— and that others' laughter is purposive rather than spontaneous.

In Millon and Davis's (1996) account of PPD, the focus is on the avoidance of dependency and the drive toward autonomy. A key aspect of the internal economy in PPD lies in the "dependence on self for both stimulation *and* reinforcement" (p. 700). Persons with PPD "find reinforcements within themselves. Accustomed to self-determination, they use their active fantasy world to create a self-enhanced image and rewarding existence apart from others" (p. 700). However, this self-reliance and isolation leave such individuals "bereft of the reality checks that might restrain their suspicions and fantasies" (p. 700) and ultimately leave them vulnerable to delusional thinking.

Projection

This term is used in diverse ways. The lowest common denominator is the element of *ascription* of one's own traits, goals, etc. to others; this is sometimes referred to as *social* or *attributive projection*, and it is akin to what social psychologists refer to as the *false consensus effect*. Projection is sometimes assumed also to entail *disowning* of one's attributes that are ascribed to others, that is, via denial, repression, or suppression from awareness. Further, projection is sometimes defined in a way that focuses on the ascription (and perhaps disowning) only of one's own *negative* characteristics—perhaps all of them, or only interpersonal ones (e.g., disloyalty), or only those in a particular domain (e.g., particular sexual desires).

Simple ascription is widespread and it occurs outside awareness (Krueger, 2007). It may be viewed it as an information-processing heuristic, perhaps not involving defensive motivations. In potentially adversarial situations, those who behave antagonistically are likely to assume others are also behaving likewise (Krueger, 2007). Hostile intents may thus nourish a tendency to attribute hostile intents to others—perhaps accounting for a special tie between paranoia and hostility.

To go beyond ascription toward disowning is to move toward models that imply defensive processes. Such a model arose in a research report by Newman, Duff, and Baumeister (1997), who addressed "the act of perceiving in other people those characteristics that one wishes to deny in oneself" (p. 980). Their research showed that defensive people tend to (a) avoid dwelling on their own unacceptable traits and (b) employ those unacceptable traits in characterizing other persons' behaviors. This need not represent a general tendency to see the worst in others, only a tendency to see one's own suppressed, undesirable attributes in others. In their model, the ascription is not motivated, but the disowning is.

Miceli and Castelfranchi (2003) have suggested that ascription may also be motivated and have suggested three ways that ascription might aid disowning. First, someone must be at fault, and blaming the other person is an alternative to blaming oneself. Second, criticizing an aspect of oneself in another is an irrational but still-potent way of asserting one's innocence regarding that aspect. Third, whatever negative feelings arise from one's awareness of the attribute in oneself can be "explained" by the presence of the attribute in another person.

Schimel, Greenberg, and Martens (2003) have similarly suggested two possibilities: that in ascribing a trait to another one can attribute the accessibility of the trait to the other and stop thinking about it, and that by increasing one's negative perception of another one may view oneself more favorably by comparison. In support of these possibilities, Schimel et al. reported research in which student participants were given feedback that they harbored a specific negative trait (or not) and were given the opportunity to ascribe that trait to an ambiguous target (or not). As predicted, persons led to believe they had the trait rated the other as having more of that trait than did those not given that feedback, a finding that did not generalize to other negative attributes. Among persons led to believe they had the negative trait, the opportunity to ascribe that trait to another reduced the negativity of self-ratings on that trait (see also Govorun, Fuegen & Payne, 2006).

Such research suggests that ascription is sometimes motivated, if only in the service of disowning. It offers hope for an intellectually rigorous account in which defensive projection plays a key role in clinical paranoia, a hope that currently remains unfulfilled.

Explanationist Approaches

The major entry here is Maher's (e.g., 1988, 2005) anomalous experience model. *Explanationism* (cf. Pacherie, Green, & Bayne, 2006) is a newer idiom that captures the approach particularly well. In Maher's words: "Where the patient may differ from a normal observer is not in the manner of drawing inference from evidence but in the kinds of perceptual experience that provide the evidence from which the inference is to be drawn" (2005, p. 137). Thus delusions are reasonable attributions and conjectures, and no bias, thought disorder, or defensive process need be posited. In all persons, unexpected or puzzling information calls for an explanation, and this is surely the case for anomalous experiences (e.g., hallucinations). Explanations, once established, are not easily abandoned, for reasons that are again not particularly pathological: "nobody changes beliefs easily" (Maher, 1988, p. 31).

Consider the individual who has memory loss coupled with anosognosia (unawareness of the deficit). Unable to keep track of things, the person may explain their "disappearance" by inferring that they have been stolen. When items are lost frequently, explanations may develop into elaborated beliefs regarding the robbers. This appears to be what commonly occurs among patients with Alzheimer's disease (cf. Mizrahi, Starkstein, Jorge, & Robinson, 2006). Similar accounts can be offered for how delusions would arise from sensory impairments or, especially, from hallucinations.

However, such explanationism appears to have limitations. First, some delusions are profoundly implausible (Pacherie et al., 2006), even given a particular anomalous experience (McKay, 2012). In the words of Fine, Craigie, and Gold (2005, p. 160), in many cases "the explanations produced by patients with delusions to account for their anomalous thoughts are not just incorrect; they are nonstarters." The assertion that people are reluctant to change beliefs hardly accounts for delusional persons' inattentiveness to gross contradictions between their delusion and their remaining beliefs (Bayne & Pacherie, 2005).

Second, delusional understandings often appear not to arise from reflection on what was experienced, but rather to come with the experience itself (e.g., Gipps & Fulford, 2004). Rhodes and Jakes (2004) conducted detailed interviews with delusional persons and concluded that some delusion-related "experiences are intrinsically imbued with ideas from their first appearance" (p. 216).

Further, Chapman and Chapman (1988) noted that some persons' delusional beliefs have no apparent relationship to any unusual experience, and some persons who have unusual experiences develop nondeviant explanations for them, for example, attributing critical inner voices to one's own conscience. Frith (1999) has pointed to experimental procedures that create anomalous experience, to which acute schizophrenics, but not controls, respond with delusional attributions.

Finally, pure explanationism may not provide the simplest account for the fact that delusions—including those in Alzheimer's (Migliorelli et al., 1995)—are so often persecutory. It is difficult to dismiss the basic motivational premise: that persecutory attributions help maintain self-respect by externalizing blame (see later discussion).

Still, the modest claim that an explanation process often plays a role in delusion formation is widely accepted, and Maher's (e.g., 1988) model has had exceptional heuristic value. In addition, it helps humanize delusional persons who might otherwise be viewed as quite alien. It does so by acknowledging the irrationality of much everyday thinking and by underscoring the challenge that any of us would face were we to be bombarded with incomprehensible experiences.

Deficits and Biases

These approaches depart from pure explanationism in positing some kind of processing anomaly. Such models usually assume that the anomaly is broad, providing the seedbed for the delusion but extending beyond the delusional domain. The following subsections address selected models that are receiving current research attention.

Theory of Mind (ToM)   The touchstone of Frith's (e.g., 1992) model is that the human mind is characterized by a system—theory of mind (ToM)—that facilitates inferences about the mental processes of other persons, that is, mentalism. He proposed that individuals in whom that system is defective are susceptible to delusions. Standardized ToM assessment approaches are diverse. Some ask one to discern others' intentions, some address the ability to perceive that another person holds an inaccurate belief, some assess the ability to infer

another's character from a behavior sample, and some assess comprehension of irony and metaphor.

Various reviews (e.g., Bentall & Taylor, 2006; Freeman, 2007; Sprong, Schothorst, Vos, Hox, & van Engeland, 2007) have concluded that ToM deficits may be found in schizophrenia, including paranoid schizophrenia, but they are not clearly related to the presence of delusions per se. Recent research has raised two possibilities: that, among individuals with auditory hallucinations, delusion formation is most likely when ToM deficits are present (Bartels-Velthuis, Blijd-Hoogewys, & van Os, 2011) and that, among schizophrenic individuals, delusional tendencies are associated with overmentalizing—that is, an excessive engagement in ascribing mental states to other individuals (Montag et al., 2011).

Jumping to Conclusions and Need for Closure   Garety (1991) and colleagues (e.g., Garety, Kuipers, Fowler, Freeman, & Bebbington, 2001) have offered multifactorial explanations for delusion formation. A key element involves reasoning/judgment biases in situations in which information is incomplete and ambiguous. Much of this tradition revolves around a specific laboratory procedure in which, in the original version, individuals are asked to draw beads from a jar and to guess (on the basis of the color of the beads drawn) whether it comes from a jar containing mainly red or mainly green beads. Studies using this task or variants of it (reviewed by Bentall & Taylor, 2006; Fine, Gardner, Craigie, & Gold, 2007; Freeman, 2007) have shown that the number of draws of beads required for the individual to reach a conclusion is distinctively low among delusional persons. This is referred to as the jumping to conclusions effect (JTC), and it has been widely (if not universally) replicated.

Given the implication that delusional persons arrive at conclusions in a distinctive way, JTC may be said to challenge a pure explanationist view of delusion. JTC does not represent the kind of caution that might be expected of a wary individual, and indeed there are suggestions that the JTC effect may be hardest to demonstrate in the case of specifically persecutory delusions (McKay, Langdon & Coltheart, 2007). Delusion-prone individuals may show JTC, suggesting that it functions as a vulnerability factor (e.g., Colbert & Peters, 2002). Findings regarding the persistence of JTC when delusional states have remitted are mixed (Colbert, Peters, & Garety, 2006; Lincoln, Ziegler, Mehl, & Rief, 2010;

Woodward, Munz, LeClerc, & Lecomte, 2009). In addition, JTC may be unrelated to delusional conviction and to belief inflexibility (So et al., 2012; see also Moritz et al., 2010).

The underlying process is unclear. One possibility is that JTC reflects an intolerance for uncertainty or a need for closure. There is research indicating that self-reported need for closure characterizes delusional patients (e.g., Colbert et al., 2006; McKay et al., 2007; but see White & Mansell, 2009). However, need for closure is apparently unrelated to JTC (e.g., McKay et al., 2007; Moritz et al., 2010). The two may thus be independently related to delusionality. Similarly, intolerance for uncertainty may also be related to delusion-proneness, though not to JTC (White & Mansell, 2009). A self-report scale has been developed specifically to address JTC tendencies, but its relation to the standard behavioral measure is modest (van der Gaag et al., 2013).

Various studies have aimed at pinpointing the nature of the JTC effect. Speechley, Whitman, and Woodward (2010) have offered findings indicating that it may be accounted for by the tendency of persons with delusions to "show a greater preference for whichever option is supported by the current incoming data" (p. 15). JTC and ToM measures are correlated with one another, as one would expect if they both reflect a single bias or deficit (Langdon, Ward, & Coltheart, 2010).

Intentionality Bias This involves a readiness to attribute purposiveness even to meaningless events. Blakemore et al. (2003) demonstrated such a bias among patients with persecutory delusions. They did so using a computer-generated series of on-screen interactions between two nondescript icons, varying the extent to which the interaction between the icons was normatively perceived to be contingent. In the key condition, those with persecutory delusions tended to see purposiveness in the icons (e.g., that one "followed" or "watched" the other). Russell, Reynaud, Herba, Morris, and Corcoran (2006) and Tschacher and Kupper (2006) have reported related findings. This is perhaps a kind of over-mentalizing, one in which even inanimate objects have minds of their own, one which could amplify the sense that intent lies behind other persons' behaviors.

Attributional Bias The roots of this model (e.g., Bentall, Kinderman, & Kaney, 1994;

Kinderman & Bentall, 1996, 1997) lie in the study of the aspect of social cognition that pertains to our explanations for what befalls us. This model pertains to persecutory delusions—to their content rather than their delusionality (cf. Blackwood, Howard, Bentall, & Murray, 2001). It appears to have developed independent of the tradition of research on hostile attributional style in developmental psychopathology, mentioned earlier.

In its simplest form, the claim is that patients with persecutory delusions have an exaggerated self-serving bias, in which they tend to attribute negative outcomes externally, especially to other persons (as opposed to situations), and to attribute `positive outcomes internally. Garety and Freeman (1999; see also Freeman, 2007) have reviewed considerable evidence indicating that, compared with controls, those with persecutory delusions more often attribute the causes of negative events externally and that the external causes tend to be persons. There is less evidence for a tendency to take credit for positive events.

This model has a motivational aspect involving self-esteem maintenance, as is evident in the assertion that when "negative self-representations are primed by threatening events, leading to discrepancies between the self-representations and self-ideals, external…attributions for the threatening events are elicited. These attributions are self-protective in the sense that they reduce the patient's awareness of discrepancies between the self and self-ideals, but carry the penalty of activating schemata that represent threats from others" (Bentall & Kaney, 1996, p. 1231).

Summarizing then-existing research, Garety and Freeman (1999) concluded that persons with persecutory delusions are heterogeneous with respect to self-esteem, and that it is much clearer that persons with persecutory delusions tend to externalize blame for negative events than that externalizing serves a defensive function. Based on reviews of some of the same research, Bentall and colleagues have acknowledged that empirical support for their model has been mixed but argued that it remains reasonable to assume that "the paranoid patient's tendency to make external-personal attributions for negative events…partly reflects a defensive avoidance of making internal attributions…which might otherwise lead to the kind of catastrophic escalation of discrepancies between self-representations and ideals found in depressed patients" (Bentall et al., 2001, p. 1170). They have suggested the possibility "that these patients might be locked into an intense struggle to maintain positive self-representations that often fails" (p. 1166). This may ring true clinically but is notably "hard to test" (Freeman, 2007, p. 434).

Bentall and Taylor (2006) have concluded that "the available findings suggest that self-esteem plays an important role in paranoia, but that the relationships between paranoia, self-esteem, attributions, and beliefs about deservedness of persecution are highly complex and non-linear" (p. 286). Perhaps relevant is Raes and Van Gucht's (2009) report of an association between paranoia and self-reported self-esteem instability, in a nonpatient adolescent sample. In addition, it has been reported that among patients persecutory ideation is associated modestly with implicit, but not explicit, self-esteem (Valiente et al., 2011), though some findings call this claim into question (Cicero & Kerns, 2011). Recent findings have indicated that attributing negative events to another person is seen mainly when individuals are currently paranoid, and that such individuals may also attribute positive events to another person (Aakre, Seghers, St-Hilaire, & Docherty, 2009).

Person Perception Bias   There is a diverse research tradition pertaining to the active perceptual processes involved in viewing another person, usually the face. It often addresses interpersonal hypervigilance or the tendency to make inferences about other persons on the basis of little information. Relevant research sometimes tracks eye movements and gaze fixations in response to standard stimuli, processes that are presumably automatic and unintentional. Sometimes note is taken of differential ocular response (or accuracy in identification) as a function of the facial expression (e.g., angry versus neutral).

Green, Williams, and Hemsley (2000) reviewed earlier studies and concluded that deluded schizophrenics show restricted scanpaths, longer fixations, and less emotion identification accuracy. Green, Williams, and Davidson (2001), using facial pictures with happy, sad, neutral, angry, and fearful expression, found that delusion-prone individuals showed delayed identification of angry facial expressions. Green, Williams, and Davidson (2003) employed a similar procedure and, in addition, monitored visual scanpath. Delusion-prone persons showed fewer fixations to facial expressions of anger and fear and showed poorer

affect accuracy, particularly in response to fear. Arguedas, Green, Langdon, and Coltheart (2006) employed a task in which pairs of face pictures were presented side by side (half happy-neutral, half angry-neutral), and the task was to respond to a dot appearing on the screen where a picture had just been, with reaction time as the dependent variable. Delusion-prone persons showed selective attention to, and difficulty disengaging attention from, angry faces.

Research by Peer, Rothmann, Penrod, Penn, and Spaulding (2004) addressed the perceptions of negative emotions in faces that, by normative judgment, lack those emotions. Among participants with severe mental illness, assessed paranoia was associated with the tendency to misperceive disgust. Although an effect for anger was not found in the Peer et al. study, results reported by Combs, Michael, and Penn (2006) have suggested an association between paranoia and the misperception of anger. Larøi, D'Argembeau, and Van der Linden (2006) added a memory component, employing a task in which individuals were first shown faces with happy, neutral, or angry expressions. Delusion-prone nonpatients were distinctively successful in recalling angry faces.

A study by Bucci et al. (2008) considered interpretations of hand and body gestures. Patients with referential delusions of communication were distinguished from other patients and controls by their tendency to interpret incidental movements as gestures (see Intentionality Bias, earlier)—and gestures as signs of rejection. In their research, Hooker et al. (2011) focused on trustworthiness judgments of neutral faces. Among patients with schizophrenia, degree of paranoia was associated with the extent to which such judgments shifted toward untrustworthiness when exposure was preceded by an unrelated threat prime.

These diverse studies may be viewed as suggesting active, perhaps automatic, processes that could be expected to perpetuate whatever expectations an individual might bring to an interpersonal context. Thus, some individuals may have biases that contribute to the anomalous experiences for which their delusional beliefs are explanations. There is also fMRI evidence that, while schizophrenics without paranoid symptoms process facial information in a way that is similar to normal controls, paranoid symptoms are associated with distinctive cortical processes, especially in assessing threat (e.g., Pinkham, Hopfinger, Pelphrey, Piven, &

Penn, 2008). For a related overview, see Huang, Xu, and Chan (2011).

Bias Against Disconfirmatory Evidence Focusing on the clinical characteristics often called rigidity or inflexibility, Woodward, Moritz, Cuttler, and Whitman (2006) have reported research on the rejection of contrary evidence. They proposed that delusional individuals are characterized by a bias against disconfirmatory evidence (BADE). Their task involved a series of comic-strip-like stimuli. For each one, the participant was first shown one picture and was asked to rate for plausibility each of several descriptions of what it portrayed, then more cards were shown, followed by more ratings. The tasks were constructed such that the initial card would elicit endorsement of a description that would later become implausible. Currently delusional schizophrenic patients tended not to down-rate the plausibility of descriptions that they had reasonably chosen after the initial card, even after it had ceased to be plausible. Note that this BADE manifestation is not specific to the individual's delusion. See also the study by Woodward, Moritz, and Chen (2006).

Woodward, Buchy, Moritz, and Liotti (2007) have reported associations between BADE (assessed with sentence stimuli) and variables relevant to delusion-proneness in nonclinical samples. Colbert, Peters, and Garety (2010) have reported similar results with respect to personal (but nondelusion-relevant) beliefs, and Moritz et al. (2010) have shown BADE to be related to self-reported need for closure.

The Two-Factor Approach

Maher's explanationism has been the centerpiece of most accounts of delusions in recent decades, but the two-factor model is perhaps becoming its successor. It grew out of research on Capgras syndrome (which, as noted, involves the belief that a loved one is an imposter).

Most people, when confronted with familiar versus unfamiliar faces, show greater skin conductance responses to the former; however, that familiar–unfamiliar difference is absent in Capgras patients (Brighetti, Bonifacci, Borlimi, & Ottaviani, 2007; Ellis, Lewis, Moselhy, & Young, 2000: Ellis, Young, Quayle, & de Pauw, 1997; Hirstein & Ramachandran, 1997). In the prevailing account of this effect, face recognition involves two cortical pathways, involving figural and affective recognition, respectively, with the latter disrupted in Capgras syndrome. The patient is said to "explain" the lack of an affective response to the loved one by experiencing the loved one as an imposter.

The importance of this account notwithstanding, it does not fully solve the Capgras puzzle, for reasons related to those discussed earlier regarding explanationism generally. In particular, "this person looks like my loved one but is an imposter" is not the only conclusion one could draw from lack of an affective response to the beloved. Why does the Capgras patient choose one that is so implausible? Some patients have a relevant neuropsychological anomaly (ventromedial frontal lesions) but do not show symptoms of Capgras (Coltheart, Menzies & Sutton, 2010). Why is this so?

In suggesting an answer to these questions Coltheart, Langdon, and McKay (2007) have posited two deficits: one from loss of the limbic pathway involved in affective recognition (noted earlier), the other from disruption of a right frontal function involved in the rejection of implausible hypotheses. That is, the first deficit determines the delusional content, and the second accounts for the fact that the delusion is adopted and maintained. McKay (2012) has offered a modification of this model, in which the second factor involves not a belief evaluation system but rather a bias in which one discounts preexisting beliefs in deference to accommodating the evidence of the senses.

Coltheart et al. (2010) have suggested that their two-factor model offers a template that may be useful in accounting for other monothematic delusions, and perhaps for delusions more generally—albeit with varying pairs of factors. For example, delusions of alien abduction (cf. Clancy, McNally, Schachter, Lenzenweger, & Pitman, 2002) may emerge from having sleep paralysis experiences plus a predisposition to favor New Age beliefs. Coltheart et al. have also noted the possible relevance of the two-factor approach to delusions of external control (see next section). Of course, one could take their proposal beyond two factors, as three or more risk factors could be called upon within a similar framework. Various theorists (e.g., Freeman et al., 2010) have, in fact, proposed models involving multiple contributing factors.

The Comparator Model

The relevance of this model, which is sometimes referred to as the *forward model of action awareness*, is primarily to agency delusions, especially those involving passivity (i.e., reduced agency). It does not address experiences involving excessive agency except insofar as diminished action awareness opens the door to diverse agency misattributions (cf. Maeda et al., 2012). Although the comparator model is based on understandings of normal perception that date to the nineteenth century and which Feinberg (1978) had suggested were relevant to psychotic symptoms, the key impetus came from Frith's (1992) focus on "an impairment [in schizophrenia] in the ability to distinguish changes due to our own actions and changes due to external events" (p. 81).

To understand the underlying nonpathological process, consider the following three phenomena. When one turns one's head, the room is not perceived as moving in the opposite direction but as stable. When one strokes one's arm, the sensation is attenuated in comparison with what would occur were the same movement externally caused. When one speaks, one's voice does not sound as loud (nor does it generate as much cortical activity) as when a similar noise comes from another source (cf. Ford, Gray, Faustman, Roach, & Mathalon, 2007). In all cases, the sensory dampening is automatic and compelling. In the comparator (or efference copy) model, these effects are accounted for by the initiation, concurrent with the action, of an efference copy (or corollary discharge) comprising the predicted sensory effect of that action—a copy with which the actual sensory effect is then routinely compared. Normally, the related attenuation of self-generated stimulation increases the relative salience of externally caused sensations (Shergill, Samson, Bays, Frith, & Wolpert, 2005)—an adaptive effect given that it is more important that one note environmentally generated than self-generated stimuli (cf. Heinks-Maldonado et al., 2007). A normal sense of agency is said to emerge from the match between the predicted sensation (the efference model) and the actual sensory feedback resulting from the action.

Frith and Dolan (2000) have suggested that delusions of external control may arise from repeated failures to generate accurate sensory expectations and from the absence of agency-confirming matches. Several studies have shown that schizophrenics are unusually inclined to confuse the results of their own actions with external events (see Farrer et al., 2004; Frith, Blakemore, & Wolpert, 2000; Haggard, Martin, Taylor-Clarke, Jeannerod, & Franck, 2003). In some cases, such effects are specific to patients with delusions of influence (Jeannerod et al., 2003; Schnell et al., 2008). There also is evidence that related effects are present in nonpsychotic persons who show schizotypal features (Asai & Tanno, 2007), delusion-proneness (Teufel, Kingdon, Ingram, Wolpert, & Fletcher, 2010), and prodromal psychotic features (Hauser et al., 2010).

This comparator model accounts for the anomalous experience, but not necessarily for the delusion. There is a neurological condition, referred to as *anarchic limb* (or alien limb) *syndrome*, in which, say, a hand apparently behaves against the person's wishes. Typically, the affected individual does not embrace a delusional explanation, even though the movements are distressing and even frightening (Frith et al., 2000; Spence, 2002). Noting that patients with haptic deafferentiation might be predicted (in a one-factor model) to have delusions of external control but do not, Coltheart et al. (2010, 2011) have suggested the relevance of their two-factor model in this situation. That is, to have delusions of control, one must have both a deficit related to the efference copy system and a second deficit—perhaps in a belief evaluation system.

Considerable attention has been given to the cerebral localization of problems noted in such models; for relevant discussions, see Heinks-Maldonado et al. (2007), Pacherie et al. (2006), Schnell et al. (2008), and Taber and Hurley (2007). For further discussion of the comparator model itself, see Carruthers (2012), Frith (2012), and Pynn and DeSouza (2013).

Final Comment

This chapter reflects an attempt to do justice to two topics—paranoid disorders and delusional disorders—viewed as distinct phenomena, while drawing on rich research and clinical literatures in which they often are not treated as distinct. The two have an inherent linkage: to embrace even a nonpersecutory delusion is usually to be uncommonly untrusting of the views that most other persons claim to hold.

It is disconcerting that neither *paranoid* nor *delusional* is used with complete consistency in the literature. In this chapter, paranoia has been understood in terms of the individual's experience of being threatened or wronged by virtue of another's ill intent or malice. The discourse on delusions has focused on the several delusionality-relevant aspects of beliefs (e.g., falsity, conviction, and narrative complexity). As such, it raises the possibility that two persons might be viewed as highly delusional for rather different reasons; for instance, one may hold a belief with wavering conviction but be totally preoccupied with it, while another holds the identical belief with total conviction but be able to put it aside for extended periods.

While such a polythetic approach may not be a satisfactory endpoint, it does suggest greater research attention to the origins of these aspects of delusionality, rather than of delusions per se. Paranoia, too, may need to be deconstructed. For instance, it may be that attention should be given separately to hyperalertness to possible harm or betrayal, and to excessive reactivity once harm or betrayal is perceived to have occurred.

References

Aakre, J. M., Seghers, J. P., St-Hilaire, A., & Docherty, N. (2009). Attributional style in delusional patients: A comparison of remitted paranoid, remitted, nonparanoid, and current paranoid patients with nonpsychiatric controls. *Schizophrenia Bulletin, 35*, 994–1002.

Abramowitz, J. S. (2008). Scrupulosity. In J. S. Abramowitz, D. McKay, & S. Taylor (Eds.), *Clinical handbook of obsessive-compulsive disorder and related problems* (pp. 156–172). Baltimore: Johns Hopkins.

Allardyce, J., McCreadie, R. G., Morrison, G., & van Os, J. (2007). Do symptom dimensions or categorical diagnoses best discriminate between known risk factors for psychosis. *Social Psychiatry and Psychiatric Epidemioliology, 42*, 429–437.

Appelbaum, P. S., Robbins, P. C., & Roth, L. H. (1999). Dimensional approach to delusions: Comparison across types and diagnoses. *American Journal of Psychiatry, 156*, 1938–1943.

Arguedas, D., Green, M. J., Langdon, R., & Coltheart, M. (2006). Selective attention to threatening faces in delusion-prone individuals. *Cognitive Neuropsychiatry, 11*, 557–575.

Asai, T., & Tanno, Y. (2007). The relationship between the sense of self-agency and schizotypal personality traits. *Journal of Motor Behavior, 39*, 162–168.

Ashcroft, K., Kingdon, D. G., & Chadwick, P. (2012). Persecutory delusions and childhood emotional abuse in people with a diagnosis of schizophrenia. *Psychosis: Psychological, Social and Integrative Approaches, 4*, 168–171.

Aviv, R. (2011). God knows where I am. *The New Yorker, 87* (15), 56–65.

Bartels-Velthuis, A. A., Blijd-Hoogewys, E. M. A, & van Os, J. (2011). Better theory-of-mind skills in children hearing voices mitigate the risk of secondary delusion formation. *Acta Psychiatrica Scandinavica, 124*, 193–197.

Bayne, T., & Pacherie, E. (2005). In defence of the doxastic conception of delusions. *Mind & Language, 20*, 163–188.

Beck, A. T., & Rector, N. A. (2002). Delusions: A cognitive perspective. *Journal of Cognitive Psychotherapy, 16*, 455–468.

Benezech, M., Yesavage, J. A., Addad, M., Bourgeois, M., & Mills, M. (1984). Homicide by psychotics in France: A five-year study. *Journal of Clinical Psychiatry, 45*, 85–86.

Benjamin, L. S. (1996). *Interpersonal diagnosis and treatment of personality disorders* (2nd ed.). New York: Guilford Press.

Bentall, R. P., Corcoran, R., Howard, R., Blackwood, N., & Kinderman, P. (2001). Persecutory delusions: A review and theoretical integration. *Clinical Psychology Review, 21*, 1143–1192.

Bentall, R. P., & Kaney, S. (1996). Abnormalities of self-representation and persecutory delusions: A test of a cognitive model of paranoia. *Psychological Medicine, 26*, 1231–1237.

Bentall, R. P., Kinderman, P., & Kaney, S. (1994). The self, attributional processes and abnormal beliefs: Towards a model of persecutory delusions. *Behaviour Research and Therapy, 32*, 331–341.

Bentall, R. P., & Taylor, J. L. (2006). Psychological processes and paranoia: Implications for forensic behavioural science. *Behavioural Sciences and the Law, 24*, 277–294.

Berle, D., Blaszczynski, A., Einstein, D. A., & Menzies, R. G. (2006). Thought-action fusion in schizophrenia: A preliminary investigation. *Behavior Change, 23*, 260–269.

Bernstein, D. P., & Useda, J. D. (2007). Paranoid personality disorder. In W. O'Donohue, K.A. Fowler, & S. O. Lilienfeld (Eds.), *Personality disorders: Toward the DSM-V* (pp. 41–62). Thousand Oaks, CA: Sage.

Björkly, S. (2002). Psychotic symptoms and violence toward others—a literature review of some preliminary findings: Part 1. Delusions. *Aggression and Violent Behavior, 7*, 617–631.

Blackwood, N. J., Howard, R. J., Bentall, R. P., & Murray, R. M. (2001). Cognitive neuropsychiatric models of persecutory delusions. *American Journal of Psychiatry, 158*, 527–539.

Blakemore, S. J. (2003). Deluding the motor system. *Consciousness and Cognition, 12*, 647–655.

Blakemore, S-.J., Sarfati, Y., Basin, N., & Decety, J. (2003). The detection of intentional contingencies in simple animations in patients with delusions of persecution. *Psychological Medicine, 33*, 1433–1441.

Blaney, P. (1999). Paranoid and delusional disorders. In T. Millon, P. H. Blaney, & R. Davis (Eds.), *Oxford textbook of psychopathology* (pp. 339–361). New York: Oxford University Press.

Bocci, L., & Gordon, P. K. (2007). Does magical thinking produce neutralizing behaviour? An experimental investigation. *Behaviour Research and Therapy, 45*, 1823–1833.

Boden, M. T., & Berenbaum, H. (2012). Facets of emotional clarity and suspiciousness. *Personality and Individual Differences, 53*, 426–430.

Bone, S., & Oldham, J. M. (1994). Paranoia: Historical considerations. In J. M. Oldham & S. Bone (Eds.), *Paranoia: New psychoanalytic perspectives* (pp. 3–15). Madison, CT: International Universities Press.

Brett-Jones, J. R., Garety, P. A., & Hemsley, D. R. (1987). Measuring delusional experiences: A method and its application. *British Journal of Clinical Psychology, 26*, 257–265.

Brighetti, G., Bonifacci, P., Borlimi, R., & Ottaviani, C. (2007). "Far from the heart far from the eye": Evidence from the Capgras delusion. *Cognitive Neuropsychiatry, 12*, 189–197.

Brüne, M. (2001). De Clérambault's syndrome (erotomania) in an evolutionary perspective. *Evolution and Human Behavior, 22*, 409–415.

Bucci, S., Startup, M., Wynn, P., Baker, A., & Lewin, T. (2008). Referential delusions of communication and interruptions of gestures. *Psychiatry Research, 15*, 27–34.

Buhlmann, U., Etcoff, N. L., & Wilhelm, S. (2006). Emotion recognition bias for contempt and anger in body dysmorphic disorder. *Journal of Psychiatric Research, 40*, 105–111.

Bunde, J., & Suls, J. (2006). A quantitative analysis of the relationship between the Cook-Medley Hostility Scale and traditional coronary artery disease risk factors. *Health Psychology, 25*, 493–500.

Campbell, A. (2010). Oxytocin and human social behavior. *Personality and Social Psychology Review, 14*, 281–295.

Campbell, M. L. C., & Morrison, A. P. (2007). The subjective experience of experiencing paranoia: Comparing the experiences with psychosis and individuals with no psychiatric history. *Clinical Psychology and Psychotherapy, 14*, 63–77.

Cannon, B. J., & Kramer, L. M. (2011). Delusion content across the 20th century in an American psychiatric hospital. *International Journal of Social Psychiatry, 58*, 323–327.

Cannon, M., Walsh, E., Hollis, C., Kargin, M., Taylor, E., Murray, R. M., & Jones, P. B. (2001). Predictors of later schizophrenia and affective psychosis among attendees at a child psychiatry department. *British Journal of Psychiatry, 178*, 420–426.

Carruthers, G. (2012). The case for the comparator model as an explanation of the sense of agency and its breakdowns. *Consciousness and Cognition, 21*, 30–45.

Cella, M., Vellante, M., & Preti, A. (2012). How psychotic-like are paranormal beliefs? *Journal of Behavior Therapy and Experimental Psychiatry, 43*, 897–900.

Cermolacce, M., Sass, L., & Parnas, J. (2010). What is bizarre in bizarre delusions? A critical review. *Schizophrenia Bulletin, 36*, 667–679.

Chan, M. E. (2009). "Why did you hurt me?" Victim's interpersonal betrayal attribution and trust implications. *Review of General Psychology, 13*, 262–274.

Chan, R. C. K., Li, X., Lai, M., Li, H., Wang, Y., Cui, J.,…Raine, A. (2011). Exploratory study on the base-rate of paranoid ideation in a non-clinical Chinese sample. *Psychiatry Research, 85*, 254–260.

Chang, B. P., & Lenzenweger, M. F. (2005). Somatosensory processing and schizophrenia liability: Proprioception, exteroceptive sensitivity, and graphesthesia performance in the biological relatives of schizophrenia patients. *Journal of Abnormal Psychology, 114*, 85–95.

Chapman, L. J., & Chapman, J. P. (1988). The genesis of delusions. In T. F. Oltmanns & B. A. Maher (Eds.), *Delusional beliefs* (pp. 167–183). New York: John Wiley & Sons.

Chapman, L. J., Chapman, J. P., Kwapil, T. R., Eckblad, M., & Zinser, M. C. (1994). Putatively psychosis-prone subjects 10 years later. *Journal of Abnormal Psychology, 103*, 171–183.

Chmielewski, M., & Watson, D. (2008). The heterogeneous structure of schizotypal personality disorder: Item-level factors of the Schizotypal Personality Questionnaire and their associations with obsessive-compulsive disorder symptoms, dissociative tendencies, and normal personality. *Journal of Abnormal Psychology, 117,* 364–376.

Choi, K.-H., Reddy, L. F., & Spaulding, W. (2012) Child abuse rating system for archival information in severe mental illness. *Social Psychiatry and Psychiatric Epidemiology, 47,* 1271–1279.

Cicero, D. C., & Kerns, J. G. (2011). Unpleasant and pleasant referential thinking: Relations with self-processing, paranoia, and other schizotypal traits. *Journal of Research in Personality, 45,* 208–218.

Clancy, S., McNally, R. J., Schachter, D. L., Lenzenweger, M. F., & Pitman, R. K. (2002). Memory distortion in people reporting abduction by aliens. *Journal of Abnormal Psychology, 111,* 455–461.

Clark, L. A., Livesley, W. J., Schroeder, M. L., & Irish, S. L. (1996). Convergence of two systems for assessing specific traits of personality disorder. *Psychological Assessment, 8,* 294–303.

Clifton, A., Turkheimer, E., & Oltmanns, T. F. (2005). Self- and peer perspectives on pathological personality traits and interpersonal problems. *Psychological Assessment, 17,* 123–131.

Colbert S. M., & Peters, E. R. (2002). Need for closure and jumping-to-conclusions in delusion-prone individuals. *Journal of Nervous & Mental Disease, 190,* 27–31.

Colbert, S. M., Peters, E. R., & Garety, P. A. (2006). Need for closure and anxiety in delusions: A longitudinal investigation in early psychosis. *Behaviour Research and Therapy, 44,* 1385–1396.

Colbert, S. M., Peters, E. R., & Garety, P. A. (2010). Delusions and belief flexibility in psychosis. *Psychology and Psychotherapy, 83,* 45–57.

Coltheart, M., Langdon, R., & McKay, R. (2007). Schizophrenia and monothematic delusions. *Schizophrenia Bulletin, 33,* 642–647.

Coltheart, M., Langdon, R., & McKay, R. (2011). Delusional belief. *Annual Review of Psychology, 62,* 271–298.

Coltheart, M., Menzies, P., & Sutton, J. (2010). Abductive inference and delusional belief. *Cognitive Neuropsychiatry, 13,* 261–287.

Combs, D. R., Michael, C. O., & Penn, D. L. (2006). Paranoia and emotion perception across the continuum. *British Journal of Clinical Psychology, 45,* 10–31.

Combs, D. R., Penn, D. L., & Fenigstein, A. (2002). Ethnic differences in subclinical paranoia: An expansion of norms of the Paranoia Scale. *Cultural Diversity and Ethnic Minority Psychology, 8,* 248–256.

Coolidge, F. L., Thede, L. L., & Jang, K. L. (2004). Are personality disorders psychological manifestations of executive function deficits? Bivariate heritability evidence from a twin study. *Behavior Genetics, 34,* 75–84.

Cooper, A. F., & Curry, A. R. (1976). The pathology of deafness in the paranoid and affective psychoses of later life. *Journal of Psychosomatic Research, 20,* 97–105.

Crawford, T. N., Livesley, W. J., Jang, K. L., Shaver, P. R., Cohen, P., & Ganiban, J. (2007). Insecure attachment and personality disorder: A twin study of adults. *European Journal of Personality, 21,* 191–208.

Cummings, J. L. (1985). Organic delusions: Phenomenology, anatomical correlations, and review. *British Journal of Psychiatry, 146,* 184–197.

Dalmau, A. B., Bergman, B. K., & Brismar, B. G. (1998). Somatic morbidity among patients diagnosed with affective psychoses and paranoid disorders: A case-control study. *Psychosomatics, 39,* 253–262.

Debnath, M., Das, S. K., Bera, N. K., Nayak, C. R., & Chaudhuri, T. K. (2006). Genetic associations between delusional disorder and paranoid schizophrenia: A novel etiologic approach. *Canadian Journal of Psychiatry, 51,* 342–349.

De Fruyt, F., De Clercq, B. J., van de Wiele, L., & Van Heerington, K. (2006). The validity of Cloninger's psychobiological model versus the five-factor model to predict DSM-IV personality disorders in a heterogeneous psychiatric sample: Domain facet and residualized descriptions. *Journal of Personality, 74,* 479–510.

de Portugal, E., González, N., Haro, J. M., Autonell, J., & Cervilla, J. A. (2008). A descriptive case-register study of delusional disorder. *European Psychiatry, 23,* 125–133.

Dobricki, M., & Maercker, A. (2010). (Post-traumatic) embitterment disorder: Critical evaluation of its stressor criterion and a proposed revised classification. *Nordic Journal of Psychiatry, 64,* 147–152.

Dodge, K. A. (2006). Translational science in action: Hostile attributional style and the development of aggressive behavior problems. *Development and Psychopathology, 18,* 791–814.

d'Orbán, P. T. (1985). Psychiatric aspects of contempt of court among women. *Psychological Medicine, 15,* 597–607.

Einstein, D. A., & Menzies, R. G. (2004). Role of magical thinking in obsessive-compulsive symptoms in an undergraduate sample. *Depression and Anxiety, 19,* 174–179.

Eisen, J. L., Phillips, K. A., Baer, L., Beer, D. A., Atala, D. K., & Rasmussen, S. A. (1998). The Brown Assessment of Beliefs Scale: Reliability and validity. *American Journal of Psychiatry, 155,* 102–108.

Ekselius, L., Lindström, von Knorring, L., Bodlund, O., & Kullgren, G. (1994). Comorbidity among the personality disorders in DSM-III-R. *Personality and Individual Differences, 17,* 155–160.

Ellett, L., & Chadwick, P. (2007). Paranoid cognitions, failure, and focus of attention in college students. *Cognition and Emotion, 21,* 558–576.

Ellett, L., Freeman, D., & Garety, P. A. (2008). The psychological effect of an urban environment on individuals with persecutory delusions: The Camberwell walk study. *Schizophrenia Research, 99,* 77–84.

Ellis, H. D., Lewis, M. B., Moselhy, H. F., & Young, A. W. (2000). Automatic without autonomic responses to familiar faces: Differential components of covert face recognition in a case of Capgras delusion. *Cognitive Neuropsychiatry, 5,* 255–269.

Ellis, H. D., Young, A. W., Quayle, A. H., & de Pauw, K. W. (1997). Reduced autonomic responses to faces in Capgras delusion. *Proceedings of the Royal Society: Biological Sciences, B264,* 1085–1092.

Farrer, C., Franck, N., Frith, C. D., Decety, J., Georgieff, N., d'Amato, T., & Jeannerod, M. (2004). Neural correlates of action attribution in schizophrenia. *Psychiatry Research, 131,* 31–44.

Fear, C., Sharp, H., & Healy, D. (1996). Cognitive processes in delusional disorders. *British Journal of Psychiatry, 168,* 61–67.

Fear, C., Sharp, H., & Healy, D. (2000). Obsessive-compulsive disorder with delusions. *Psychopathology, 33,* 55–61.

Feinberg, I. (1978). Efference copy and corollary discharge: Implications for thinking and its disorders. *Schizophrenia Bulletin, 4,* 636–640.

Fenigstein, A. (1996). Paranoia. In C. G. Costello (Ed.), *Personality characteristics of the personality disordered* (pp. 242–275). New York: John Wiley & Sons.

Fenigstein, A., & Vanable, P. A. (1992). Paranoia and self-consciousness. *Journal of Personality and Social Psychology, 62,* 129–138.

Feusner, J. D., Phillips, K. A., & Stein, D. J. (2010). Olfactory reference syndrome: Issues for DSM-V. *Depression and Anxiety, 27,* 592–599.

Fiedler, E. R., Oltmanns, T. F., & Turkheimer, E., (2004). Traits associated with personality disorders and adjustment to military life: Predictive validity of self and peer reports. *Military Medicine, 169,* 207–211.

Fine, C., Craigie, J., & Gold, I. (2005). The explanation approach to delusion. *Philosophy, Psychiatry, & Psychology, 12,* 159–163.

Fine, C., Gardner, M., Craigie, J., & Gold, I. (2007). Hopping, skipping, or jumping to conclusions? Clarifying the role of the JTC bias in delusions. *Cognitive Neuropsychiatry, 12,* 46–77.

Fisher, H. L., Appiah-Kusi, E., & Grant, C. (2012). Anxiety and negative self-schemas mediate the association between childhood maltreatment and paranoia. *Psychiatry Research, 196,* 323–324.

Fogelson, D. L., Nuechterlein, K. H., Asarnow, R. F., Payne, D. L., Subotnik, K. L., & Giannini, C. A. (1999). The factor structure of schizophrenia spectrum personality disorders: Signs and symptoms in relatives of psychotic patients from the UCLA family members study. *Psychiatry Research, 87,* 137–146.

Ford, J. M., Gray, M., Faustman, W. O., Roach, B. J., & Mathalon, D. H. (2007). Dissecting corollary discharge dysfunction in schizophrenia. *Psychophysiology, 44,* 522–529.

Fotopoulou, A. (2010). The affective neuropsychology of confabulation and delusion. *Cognitive Neuropsychiatry, 15,* 38–63.

Foulds, G. A., & Bedford, A. (1975). Hierarchy of classes of personal illness. *Psychological Medicine, 5,* 181–192.

Freeman, D. (2007). Suspicious minds: The psychology of persecutory delusions. *Clinical Psychology Review, 27,* 425–457.

Freeman, D., & Garety, P. (2006). Helping patients with paranoid and suspicious thoughts: A cognitive-behavioural approach. *Advances in Psychiatric Treatment, 12,* 404–415.

Freeman, D., Garety, P. A., Kuipers, E., Fowler, D., & Bebbington, P. E. (2002). A cognitive model of persecutory delusions. *British Journal of Cognitive Psychology, 41,* 331–347.

Freeman, D., Pugh, K., Vorontsova, F., Antley, A., & Slater, M. (2010). Testing the continuum of delusional beliefs: An experimental study using virtual reality. *Journal of Abnormal Psychology, 119,* 83–92.

Freeman, D., Stahl, D., McManus, S., Meltzer, H., Brugha, T., Wiles, N., & Bebbington, P.

(2012). Insomnia, worry, anxiety and depression as predictors of the occurrence and persistence of paranoid thinking. *Social Psychiatry and Psychiatric Epidemiology*, 47, 1195–1203.

Fresán, A., Apiquian, R., de la Fuente-Sandoval, C., Löyzaga C., García-Anaya, M., Meyenberg, N., & Niccolini, H. (2005). Violent behavior in schizophrenic patients: Relationship witch clinical symptoms. *Aggressive Behavior*, 31, 511–520.

Frith, C. D. (1992). *The cognitive neuropsychology of schizophrenia*. Hove, UK: Lawrence Erlbaum.

Frith, C. (1999). Commentary on Garety & Freeman II: "Cognitive approaches to delusions: A critical review of theories and evidence." *British Journal of Clinical Psychology*, 38, 19–321.

Frith, C. (2012). Explaining delusions of control: The comparator model 20 years on. *Consciousness and Cognition*, 21, 52–54.

Frith, C., Blakemore, S.-J., & Wolpert, D. M. (2000). Explaining the symptoms of schizophrenia: Abnormalities in the awareness of action. *Brain Research Reviews*, 31, 357–363.

Frith, C., & Dolan, R. J. (2000). The role of memory in the delusions associated with schizophrenia. In D. L. Schacter & E. Scarry (Eds.), *Memory, brain, & belief* (pp. 115–135). Cambridge, MA: Harvard University Press.

Fuchs, T. (1999). Life events in late paraphrenia and depression. *Psychopathology*, 32, 60–69.

Garety, P. (1991). Reasoning and delusions. *British Journal of Psychiatry*, 159(Suppl. 14), 14–18.

Garety, P. A., & Freeman, D. (1999). Cognitive approaches to delusions: A critical review of theories and evidence. *British Journal of Cognitive Psychology*, 38, 113–154.

Garety, P. A., Kuipers, E., Fowler, D., Freeman, D., & Bebbington, P. E. (2001). A cognitive model of the positive symptoms of psychosis. *Psychological Medicine*, 31, 189–195.

Gilbert, P. (2001). Evolutionary approaches to psychopathology: The role of natural defences. *Australian and New Zealand Journal of Psychiatry*, 35, 17–27.

Gilbert, P., Boxall, M., Cheung, M., & Irons, C. (2005). The relation of paranoid ideation and social anxiety in a mixed clinical population. *Clinical Psychology and Psychotherapy*, 12, 124–133.

Gilovich, T., Medvec, V. H., & Savitsky, K., (2000). The spotlight effect in social judgment: An egocentric bias in estimates of the salience of one's own actions and appearance. *Journal of Personality and Social Psychology*, 78, 211–222.

Gipps, R. G. T., & Fulford, K. W. M. (2004). Understanding the clinical concept of delusion: From an estranged to an engaged epistemology. *International Review of Psychiatry*, 16, 225–235.

Govorun, O., Fuegen, K., & Payne, B. K. (2006). Stereotypes focus defensive projection. *Personality and Social Psychology Bulletin*, 32, 781–793.

Green, M. J., Williams, L. M., & Davidson, D. J. (2001). Processing of threat-related affect is delayed in delusion-prone individuals. *British Journal of Clinical Psychology* 40, 157–165.

Green, M. J., Williams, L. M., & Davidson, D. (2003). Visual scanpaths and facial affect recognition in delusion-prone individuals: Increased sensitivity to threat? *Cognitive Neuropsychiatry*, 8, 19–41.

Green, M. J., Williams, L. M., & Hemsley, D. R. (2000). Cognitive theories of delusion formation: The contribution of visual scanpath research. *Cognitive Neuropsychiatry*, 5, 63–74.

Grover, S., Biswas, P, & Avasthi, A. (2007). Delusional disorder: Study from North India. *Psychiatry and Clinical Neurosciences*, 61, 462–470.

Gustavsson, J. P., Pedersen, N. L., Åsberg, M., & Schalling, D. (1996). Exploration in to the sources of individual differences in aggression-, hostility- and anger-related (AHA) personality traits. *Personality and Individual Differences*, 21, 1067–1071.

Haggard, P., Martin, F., Taylor-Clarke, M., Jeannerod, M., & Franck, N. (2003). Awareness of action in schizophrenia. *Cognitive Neuroscience and Neuropsychology*, 14, 1081–1085.

Harper, D. J. (1996). Deconstructing "paranoia": Towards a discursive understanding of apparently unwarranted suspicion. *Theory & Psychology*, 6, 423–448.

Harrow, M., Herbener, E. S., Shanklin, A., Jobe, T. H., Rattenbury, F., & Kaplan, K. J. (2004). Follow-up of psychotic outpatients: Dimensions of delusions and work functioning in schizophrenia. *Schizophrenia Bulletin*, 30, 147–161.

Haselton, M. G., & Nettle, D. (2006). The paranoid optimist: An integrative evolutionary model of cognitive biases. *Personality and Social Psychology Review*, 10, 47–66.

Haslam, N., Reichert, T., & Fiske, A. P. (2002). Aberrant social relations in the personality disorders. *Psychology and*

Psychotherapy: Theory Research and Practice, 75, 19–31.

Hauser, M., Knoblich, G., Repp, B. H., Lautenschlager, M., Gallinat, J., Heinz, A., & Voss, M. (2010). Altered sense of agency in schizophrenia and the putative psychotic prodrome. *Psychiatry Research, 186,* 170–176.

Heinks-Maldonado, T. H., Mathalon, D. H., Houde, J. F., Gray, N., Faustman, W. O., & Ford, J. M. (2007). Relationship of imprecise corollary discharge in schizophrenia to auditory hallucinations. *Archives of General Psychiatry, 64,* 286–296.

Hirstein, W., & Ramachandran, V. S. (1997). Capgras syndrome: A novel probe for understanding the neural representation of the identity and familiarity of persons. *Proceedings of the Royal Society of London, Series B, 264,* 437–444.

Holmes, E. A., & Steel, C. (2004). Schizotypy: A vulnerability factor for traumatic intrusions. *Journal of Nervous and Mental Diseases, 192,* 28–34.

Hooker, C. I., Tully, L. M., Verosky, S. C., Fisher, M., Holland, C., & Vinogradov, S. (2011). Can I trust you? Negative affective priming influences social judgments in schizophrenia. *Journal of Abnormal Psychology, 120,* 98–107.

Horan, W. P., Brown, S. W., & Blanchard, J. J. (2007). Social anhedonia and schizotypy: The contribution of individual differences in affective traits, stress, and coping. *Psychiatry Research, 149,* 147–156.

Huang, J., Xu, T., & Chan, R. C. K. (2011). Do patients with schizophrenia have a general or specific deficit in the perception of social threat? A meta-analytic study. *Psychiatry Research, 185,* 1–8.

Hurn, C., Gray, N. S., & Hughes, I. (2002). Independence of "reaction to hypothetical contradiction" from other measures of delusional ideation. *British Journal of Clinical Psychology, 41,* 349–360.

Jackson, B., Kubzansky, L. D., Cohen, S., Jacobs, D. R., Jr., & Wright, R. J. (2007). Does harboring hostility hurt? Associations between hostility and pulmonary function in the coronary artery risk development in (young) adults (CARDIA) study. *Health Psychology, 26,* 333–340.

Jacobs, N., Myin-Germeys, I., Derom, C., Vlietinck, R., & van Os, J. (2005). Deconstructing the familiality of the emotive component of psychotic experiences in the general population. *Acta Psychiatrica Scandinavica, 112,* 394–401.

Jang, K. L., Livesley, W. J., Angleitner, A., Riemann, R., & Vernon, P. A. (2002). Genetic and environmental influences on the covariance of facets defining the domains of the five-factor model of personality. *Personality and Individual Differences, 33,* 83–101.

Jang, K. L., Livesley, W. J., & Vernon, P. A. (1996). The genetic basis of personality at different ages: A cross-sectional twin study. *Personality and Individual Differences, 21,* 299–301.

Janssen, I., Hanssen, M., Bak, M., Bijl, R. V., De Graff, R., Vollebergh, W., . . . van Os, J. (2003). Discrimination and delusional ideation. *British Journal of Psychiatry, 182,* 71–76.

Jeannerod, M., Farrer, C., Franck, N., Fourneret, P., Posada, A., Daprati, E., & Georgieff, N. (2003). Action recognition in normal and schizophrenic subjects. In T. Kircher & D. Anthony (Eds.), *The self in neuroscience and psychiatry* (pp. 380–406). New York: Cambridge University Press.

Johnson, J. G., Cohen, P., Chen, H., Kasen, S., & Brook, J. S. (2006). Parenting behaviors associated with risk for offspring personality disorder during adulthood. *Archives of General Psychiatry, 63,* 579–587.

Kendler, K. S., Czajkowski, N., Tambs, K., Torgersen, S., Aggen, S. H., Neale, M. C., & Reichborn-Kjennerud, T. (2006). Dimensional representations of DSM-IV Cluster A personality disorders in a population-based sample of Norwegian twins: A multivariate study. *Psychological Medicine, 36,* 1583–1591.

Kennedy, H. G., Kemp, L. I., & Dyer, D. C. (1992). Fear and anger in delusional (paranoid) disorder: The association with violence. *British Journal of Psychiatry, 160,* 488–492.

Kesting, M. L., Bredenpohl, M., Klenke, J., Westermann, S., & Lincoln, T. M. (2013). The impact of social stress on self-esteem and paranoid ideation. *Journal of Behavior Therapy and Experimental Psychiatry, 44,* 122–128.

Kimhy, D., Goetz, R., Yale, S., Corcoran, C., & Malaspina, D. (2005). Delusions in individuals with schizophrenia: Factor structure, clinical correlates, and putative neurobiology. *Psychopathology, 38,* 338–344.

Kinderman, P., & Bentall, R. P. (1996). Self-discrepancies and persecutory delusions: Evidence for a defensive model of paranoid ideation. *Journal of Abnormal Psychology, 105,* 106–114.

Kinderman, P., & Bentall, R. P. (1997). Causal attributions in paranoia and depression: Internal, personal, and situational attributions for negative events. *Journal of Abnormal Psychology, 106,* 341–345.

Kinderman, P., & Bentall, R. P. (2007). The functions of delusional beliefs. In M. C. Chung, K. W. M. Fulford, & G. Graham (Eds.), *Reconceiving schizophrenia* (pp. 274–294). New York: Oxford University Press.

King, K. (2012). Aggravating conditions: Cynical hostility and neighborhood ambient stressors. *Social Science & Medicine, 75,* 2258–2266.

Koehler, J. J., & Gershoff, A. D. (2003). Betrayal aversion: When agents of protection become agents of harm. *Organizational Behavior and Human Decision Processes, 90,* 244–261.

Konstantakopoulos, G., Varsou, E., Dikeos, D., Ioannidi, N., Gonidakis, F., Papadimitriou, G., & Oulis, P. (2012). Delusionality of body image beliefs in eating disorders. *Psychiatry Research, 200,* 482–488.

Kotov, R., Ruggero, C. J., Krueger, R. F., Watson, D., Yuan, Q., & Zimmerman, M. (2011). New dimensions in the quantitative classification of mental illness. *Archives of General Psychiatry, 68,* 1003–1011.

Kozak, M. J., & Foa, E. B. (1994). Obsessions, overvalued ideas, and delusions in obsessive-compulsive disorder. *Behavior Research and Therapy, 32,* 343–353.

Kramer, R. M. (1994). The sinister attribution error: Paranoid cognition and collective distrust in organizations. *Motivation and Emotion, 18,* 199–230.

Kramer, R. M., & Messick, D. M. (1999). Getting by with a little help from our enemies: Collective paranoia and its role in intergroup relations. In C. Sedikides, J. Schopler, & C. Insko (Eds.), *Intergroup cognition and intergroup behavior* (pp. 233–255). Mahwah, NJ: Lawrence Erlbaum Associates.

Krueger, J. I. (2007). From social projection to social behavior. *European Review of Social Psychology, 18,* 1–35.

Kwapil, T. R., Miller, M. B., Zinser, M. C., Chapman, J., & Chapman, L. J. (1997). Magical ideation and social anhedonia as predictors of psychosis proneness: A partial replication. *Journal of Abnormal Psychology, 106,* 491–495.

Laajasalo, T., & Häkkänen, H. (2006). Excessive violence and psychotic symptomatology among homicide offenders with schizophrenia. *Criminal Behaviour and Mental Health, 26,* 242–253.

Langdon, R., Ward, P. B., & Coltheart, M. (2010). Reasoning anomalies associated with delusions in schizophrenia. *Schizophrenia Bulletin, 36,* 321–330.

Larøi, F., D'Argembeau, A., & Van der Linden, M. (2006). The effects of angry and happy expressions on recognition memory for unfamiliar faces in delusion-prone individuals. *Journal of Behavior Therapy and Experimental Psychiatry, 37,* 271–282.

Larøi, F., Van der Linden, M., DeFruyt, F., van Os, J., & Aleman, A. (2006). Associations between delusion proneness and personality structure in non-clinical participants: Comparison between young and elderly samples. *Psychopathology, 39,* 218–226.

Lataster, T., van Os, J., Drukker, M., Henquet, C., Feron, F., Gunther, N., & Myin-Germeys, I. (2006). Childhood victimisation and developmental expression of non-clinical delusional ideation and hallucinatory experiences. *Social Psychiatry and Psychiatric Epidemiology, 41,* 423–428.

Lavender, A., Shubert, I., de Silva, P., & Treasure, J. (2006). Obsessive-compulsive beliefs and magical ideation in eating disorders. *British Journal of Clinical Psychology, 45,* 331–342.

Lee, H.-J. & Telch, M. J. (2005). Autogenous/ reactive obsessions and their relationship with OCD symptoms and schizotypal personality features. *Anxiety Disorders, 19,* 793–805

Lenzenweger, M. F., Bennett, M. E., & Lilenfeld, L. R. (1997). The Referential Thinking Scale as a measure of schizotypy: Scale development and initial construct validation. *Psychological Assessment, 9,* 452–463.

Lincoln, T. M., Ziegler, M., Mehl, S., & Rief, W. (2010). The jumping to conclusions bias in delusions: Specificity and changeability. *Journal of Abnormal Psychology, 119,* 40–49.

Linden, M., Baumann, K., Rotter, M., & Shippan, B. (2008). Diagnostic criteria and the standardized diagnostic interview for posttraumatic embitterment disorder (PTED). *International Journal of Psychiatry in Clinical Practice, 12,* 93–96.

Linney, Y. M., Murray, R. M., Peters, E. R., MacDonald, A. M., Rijsdijk, F., & Sham, P. C. (2003). A quantitative genetic analysis of schizotypal personality traits. *Psychological Medicine, 33,* 803–816.

MacDonald, A. W., III. (2008). A sneaking suspicion: The semantics of emotional beliefs and delusions. *Behavioral and Brain Sciences, 31,* 719–720.

MacDonald, A. W., III., Pogue-Geile, M. F., Debski, T. T., Manuck, S. (2001). Genetic and environmental influences on schizotypy: A community-based twin study. *Schizophrenia Bulletin, 27,* 47–58.

MacDonald, K., & Mac Donald, T. M. (2010). The peptide that binds: A systematic review of oxytocin and its prosocial effects in humans. *Harvard Review of Psychiatry, 18,* 1–21.

Maeda, T., Kato, M., Muramatsu, T., Iwashita, S., Mimura, M., & Kashima, H. (2012). Aberrant sense of agency in patients with schizophrenia: Forward and backward over-attribution of temporal causality during intentional action. *Psychiatry Research, 198,* 1–6.

Maher, B. (1988). Anomalous experience and delusional thinking: The logic of explanations. In T. F. Oltmanns & B. A. Maher (Eds.), *Delusional beliefs* (pp. 15–33). New York: John Wiley & Sons.

Maher, B. (2005). Delusional thinking and cognitive disorder. *Integrative Physiological & Behavioral Science, 40,* 136–146.

Maizel, S., Knobler, H. Y., & Herbstein, R. (1990). Folie à trois among two Soviet-Jewish immigrant families to Israel. *British Journal of Psychiatry, 157,* 290–292.

Mancuso, S. G., Knoesen, N. P., & Castle, D. J. (2009). Delusional versus nondelusional body dysmorphic disorder. *Comprehensive Psychiatry, 51,* 177–182.

Masillo, A., Day, F., Laing, J., Howes, O., Fusar-Poli, P., Byrne, M.,…Valmaggia, L. R. (2012). Interpersonal sensitivity in the at-risk mental state for psychosis. *Psychological Medicine, 42,* 1835–1845.

Matsunaga, H., Kiriike, N., Matsui, T., Oya, K., Iwasaki, Y., Koshimune. K.,…Stein, D. J. (2002). Obsessive-compulsive disorder with poor insight. *Comprehensive Psychiatry, 43,* 150–157.

McCreery, C., & Claridge, G. (2002). Healthy schizotypy: The case of out-of-the-body experiences. *Personality and Individual Differences, 32,* 141–154.

McGrath, J. A., Nestadt, G., Liang, K.-L., Lasseter, V. K., Wolyniec, P. S., Fallin, M. D.,…Pulver, A. E. (2004). Five latent factors underlying schizophrenia: Analysis and relationship to illnesses in relatives. *Schizophrenia Bulletin, 30,* 855–873.

McKay, R. (2012). Delusional inference. *Mind & Language, 27,* 330–355.

McKay, R., Langdon, R., & Coltheart, M. (2006). The Persecutory Ideation Questionnaire. *The Journal of Nervous and Mental Disease, 194,* 628–631.

McKay, R., Langdon, R., & Coltheart, M. (2007). Jumping to delusions? Paranoia, probabilistic reasoning, and need for closure. *Cognitive Neuropsychiatry, 12,* 362–376.

McKenna, P. J. (1984). Disorders with overvalued ideas. *British Journal of Psychiatry, 145,* 579–585.

Menuck, M. N. (1992). Differentiating paranoia and legitimate fears. *American Journal of Psychiatry, 149,* 140–141.

Miceli, M., & Castelfranchi, C. (2003). The plausibility of defensive projection: A cognitive analysis. *Journal for the Theory of Social Behaviour, 33,* 279–301.

Migliorelli, R., Petracca, G., Tesón, A., Sabe, L., Leiguarda, R., & Sarkstein, S. E. (1995). Neuropsychiatric and neuropsychological correlates of delusions in Alzheimer's disease. *Psychological Medicine, 25,* 505–513.

Miller, J. D., Pilkonis, P. A., & Clifton, A. (2005). Self- and other-reports of traits from the five-factor model: Relations to personality disorder. *Journal of Personality Disorders, 19,* 400–419.

Miller, T. Q., Smith, T. W., Turner, C. W., Guijarro, M. L., & Hallet, A. J. (1996). A meta-analytic review of research on hostility and physical health. *Psychological Bulletin, 119,* 322–248.

Millon, T., & Davis, R. D. (1996). *Disorders of personality: DSM-IV and beyond.* New York: John Wiley & Sons.

Mizrahi, R., Starkstein, S. E., Jorge, R., & Robinson, R. G. (2006). Phenomenology and clinical correlates of delusions in Alzheimer disease. *American Journal of Geriatric Psychiatry, 14,* 573–581.

Mohr, C., & Leonards, U. (2005). Does contextual information influence positive and negative schizotypy scores in healthy individuals? The answer is maybe. *Psychiatry Research, 136,* 135–141.

Mojtabai, R. (2006). Psychotic-like experience and interpersonal violence in the general population. *Social Psychiatry and Psychiatric Epidemiology, 41,* 183–190.

Monsen, J. T., Hagtvet, K. A., Havik, O. E., & Eilertsen, D. E. (2006). Circumplex structure and personality disorder correlates of the interpersonal problems model (IIP-C): Construct validity and clinical implications. *Psychological Assessment, 18,* 165–173.

Montag, C., Dziobek, I., Richter, I. S., Neuhaus, K., Lehmann, A., Sylla, R.,…Gallinat, J. (2011). Different aspects of theory of mind in paranoid schizophrenia: Evidence from a video-based assessment. *Psychiatry Research, 186,* 203–209.

Moritz, S., Veckenstedt, R., Hottenrott, B, Woodward, T. S., Randjbar, S., & Lincoln, T. M. (2010). Different sides of the same coin? Intercorrelations of cognitive biases in schizophrenia. *Cognitive Neuropsychiatry, 15,* 406–421.

Mullen, P. E., & Lester, G. (2006). Vexatious litigants and unusually persistent complainants and petitioners: From querulous paranoia to querulous behaviour. *Behavioral Sciences and the Law, 24,* 333–349.

Mullet, E., Neto, F., & Revière, S. (2005). Personality and its effects on resentment, revenge, forgiveness, and self-forgiveness. In E. L. Worthington (Ed.), *Handbook of forgiveness,* (pp. 159–181). New York: Taylor & Francis.

Murphy, J., Shevlin, M., Adamson, G., Cruddas, S., & Houston, J. (2012) Memories of childhood threat, fear of disclosure and paranoid ideation: A mediation analysis using a nonclinical sample. *Journal of Aggression, Maltreatment & Trauma, 21,* 459–476.

Natsuaki, M. N., Cicchetti, D., & Rogosh, F. A. (2009). Examining the developmental history of child maltreatment, peer relations, and externalizing problems among adolescents with symptoms of paranoid personality disorder. *Development and Psychopathology, 21,* 1181–1193.

Newman, L. S., Duff, K. J., & Baumeister, R. F. (1997). A new look at defensive projection: Thought suppression, accessibility, and biased person perception. *Journal of Personality and Social Psychology, 72,* 980–1001.

Nicolson, R., Brookner, F. B., Lenane, M., Gochman, P. G., Ingraham, L. J., Egan, M. F.,…Rapoport, J. L. (2003). Parental schizophrenia spectrum disorders in childhood-onset and adult-onset schizophrenia. *American Journal of Psychiatry, 160,* 490–495.

Oskarsson, W., Dawes, C., Johannesson, M., & Magnusson, P. K. E. (2012). The genetic origins of the relationship between psychological traits and social trust. *Twin Research and Human Genetics, 15,* 21–33.

Pacherie, E., Green, M., & Bayne, T. (2006). Phenomenology and delusions: Who put the "alien" in alien control? *Consciousness and Cognition, 15,* 566–577.

Parrott, W. G. (1991). The motive for the arousal of romantic jealousy: Its cultural origin. In. P. Salovey (Ed.), *The psychology of jealousy and envy* (pp. 3–30). New York: Guilford Press.

Pedersen, C. A., Gibson, C. M., Rau, S. W., Salimi, K., Smedley, K. L. Casey, R. L.,…Penn, D. L. (2011). Intranasal oxytocin reduces psychotic symptoms and improves theory of mind and social perception in schizophrenia. *Schizophrenia Research, 132,* 50–53.

Peer, J. E., Rothmann, T. L., Penrod, R. D., Penn, D. L., & Spaulding, W. D. (2004). Social cognitive bias and neurocognitive deficit in paranoid symptoms: Evidence for an interaction effect and changes during treatment. *Schizophrenia Research, 71,* 463–471.

Peralta, V., & Cuesta, M. J. (1999) Factor structure and clinical validity of competing models of positive symptoms in schizophrenia. *Biological Psychiatry, 44,* 107–114.

Perkins, S. L., & Allen, R. (2006). Childhood physical abuse and differential development of paranormal belief systems. *Journal of Nervous and Mental Disease, 194,* 349–355.

Peters, E., Joseph, S., Day, S., & Garety, P. (2004). Measuring delusional ideation: The 21-item PDI (Peters et al. Delusions Inventory). *Schizophrenia Bulletin, 30,* 1005–1022.

Peters, E., Joseph, S., & Garety, P. A. (1999). Measurement of delusional ideation in the normal population: Introducing the PDI (Peters et al. Delusions Inventory). *Schizophrenia Bulletin, 25,* 553–576.

Phillips, K. A. (2005). *The broken mirror.* Oxford, UK: Oxford University Press.

Phillips, K. A., McElroy, S. L., Keck, P. E., Jr., Hudson, J. I., & Pope, H. G., Jr. (1994). A comparison of delusional and nondelusional body dysmorphic disorder in 100 cases. *Psychopharmacology Bulletin, 30,* 179–186.

Phillips, K. A., Price, L. H., Greenberg, B. D., & Rasmussen, S. A. (2003). Should the DSM diagnostic groupings be changed? In K. A. Phillips, M. B. First, & H. A. Pincus (Eds.), *Advancing DSM: Dilemmas in psychiatric diagnosis* (pp. 57–84). Washington, DC: American Psychiatric Association.

Pillmann, F., Wustmann, T., & Marneros, A. (2012). Acute and transient psychotic disorders versus persistent delusional disorders: A comparative longitudinal study. *Psychiatry and Clinical Neurosciences, 66,* 44–52.

Pinkham, A. E., Hopfinger, J. B., Pelphrey, K. A, Piven, J., & Penn, D. L. (2008). Neural bases for impaired social cognition in schizophrenia and autism spectrum disorders. *Schizophrenia Research, 99,* 164–175.

Podubinski, T., Daffern, M., & Lee, S. (2012). A prospective examination of the stability of hostile-dominance and its relationship to paranoia over a one-year follow-up. *Personality and Individual Differences, 52,* 586–590.

Poulton, R., Caspi, A., Moffitt, T. E., Cannon, M., Murray, R., & Harrington, H. (2000). Children's self-reported psychotic symptoms and adult schizophrenic disorder. *Archives of General Psychiatry, 57,* 1053–1058.

Preti, A., Bonventre, E., Ledda, V., Petretto, D. R., & Masala, C. (2007). Hallucinatory experiences, delusional thought proneness, and psychological distress in a nonclinical population. *Journal of Nervous and Mental Disease, 195,* 484–491.

Pynn, L. K., & DeSouza, J. F. X. (2013). The function of efference copy signals: Implications for symptoms of schizophrenia. *Vision Research, 76,* 124–133.

Radke, S., & de Bruijn, E. R. A. (2012). The other side of the coin: Oxytocin decreases the adherence to fairness norms. *Frontiers in Human Neuroscience, 6,* Article 193.

Raes, F., & Van Gucht, D. (2009). Paranoia and instability of self-esteem in adolescents. *Personality and Individual Differences, 47,* 928–932.

Raine, A. (1991). The SPQ: A scale for the assessment of schizotypal personality based on DSM-III-R criteria. *Schizophrenia Bulletin, 17,* 555–564.

Raja, M., Azzoni, A., & Lubich, L. (2000). Religious delusion. *Schweizer Archiv für Neurologie und Psychiatrie, 151,* 22–29.

Reich, J., & Braginsky, Y. (1994). Paranoid personality traits in a panic disorder population: A pilot study. *Comprehensive Psychiatry, 35,* 260–264.

Rhodes, J. E., & Jakes, S. (2000). Correspondence between delusions and personal goals: A qualitative analysis. *British Journal of Medical Psychology, 73,* 211–225.

Rhodes, J. E., & Jakes, S. (2004). Evidence given for delusions during cognitive behavior therapy. *Clinical Psychology and Psychotherapy, 11,* 207–218.

Rhodes, J. E., & Jakes, S. (2010). Perspectives on the onset of delusions. *Clinical Psychology and Psychotherapy, 17,* 136–146.

Rhodes, J. E., Jakes, S., & Robinson, J. (2005). A qualitative analysis of delusional content. *Journal of Mental Health, 14,* 383–398.

Riedl, R., & Javor, A. (2012). The biology of trust: Integrating evidence from genetics, endocrinology, and functional brain imaging. *Journal of Neuroscience, Psychology, and Economics, 5,* 63–91.

Rosse, R. B., Kendrick, K., Wyatt, R. J., Isaac, A., & Deutsch, S. I. (1994). Gaze discrimination in patients with schizophrenia: Preliminary report. *American Journal of Psychiatry, 151,* 919–921.

Rounds, D. L. (1996). Victimization of Individuals with legal blindness: Nature and forms of victimization. *Behavioral Sciences and the Law, 14,* 29–40.

Røysamb, E., Kendler, K. S., Tambs, K., Ørstavik, R. E., Neale, M. C., Aggen, S. H.,…Reichborn-Kjennerud, T. (2011). The joint structure of *DSM-IV* Axis I and Axis II

disorders. *Journal of Abnormal Psychology, 120,* 198–209.

Russell, T. A., Reynaud, E., Herba, C., Morris, R., & Corcoran, R. (2006). Do you see what I see? Interpretations of intentional movement in schizophrenia. *Schizophrenia Research, 81,* 101–111.

Sacks, M. H., Carpenter, W. T., & Strauss, J. S. (1974). Recovery from delusions: Three phases documented by patient's interpretation of research procedures. *Archives of General Psychiatry, 30,* 117–120.

Saha, S., Varghese, D., Slade, T., Degenhardt, L., Mills, K., McGrath, J., & Scott, J. (2011). The association between trauma and delusional-like experiences. *Psychiatry Research, 189,* 259–264.

Salinas, J. A., Paul, G. L., & Newbill, W. A. (2002). Is paranoid status prognostic of good outcomes? It depends. *Journal of Consulting and Clinical Psychology, 70,* 1029–1039.

Schaller, M., Park, J. H., & Mueller, A. (2003). Fear of the dark: Interactive effects of beliefs about danger in ambient darkness on ethnic stereotypes. *Personality and Social Psychology Bulletin, 29,* 637–649.

Schimel, J., Greenberg, J., & Martens, A. (2003). Evidence that projection of a feared trait can serve a defensive function. *Personality and Social Psychology Bulletin, 29,* 969–979.

Schlager, D. (1995). Evolutionary perspectives on paranoid disorder. *Psychiatric Clinics of North America, 18,* 263–279.

Schnell, K., Heekeren, K., Daumann, J., Schnell, T., Schnitker, R., Möller-Hartman, W., & Gouzoulis-Mayfrank, E. (2008). Correlation of passivity symptoms and dysfunctional visuomotor action monitoring in psychosis. *Brain, 131,* 2873–2797.

Schulze, T. G., Ohlraun, S., Czerski, P. M., Schumacher, J., Kassem, L., Deschner, M.,…Rietschel, M. (2005). Genotype-phenotype studies in bipolar disorder showing association between the DAOA/G30 locus and persecutory delusions: A first step toward a molecular genetic classification of psychiatric phenotypes. *American Journal of Psychiatry, 162,* 2101–2108.

Selten, J., Cantor-Graae, E., & Kahn, R. S. (2007). Migration and schizophrenia. *Current Opinion in Psychiatry, 20,* 111–115.

Serretti, A., Rietschel, M., Lattuada, E., Krauss, H., Schulze, T. G., MQQQller, D.J.,…Smeraldi, E. (2001). Major psychoses symptomatology: Factor analysis of 2241 psychotic subjects. *European Archives of*

Psychiatry and Clinical Neuroscience, 251, 193–198.

Shapiro, D. (1965). *Neurotic styles.* New York: Basic Books.

Shergill, S. S., Samson, G., Bays, P. M., Frith, C. D., & Wolpert, D. M. (2005). Evidence for sensory prediction deficits in schizophrenia. *American Journal of Psychiatry, 162,* 2384–2386.

Shikishima, C., Hiraishi, K., & Ando, J. (2006). Genetic and environmental influences on general trust: A test of a theory of trust with behavioral genetic and evolutionary psychological approaches. *Japanese Journal of Social Psychology, 22,* 48–57 [abstract].

Siddle, R., Haddock, G., Tarrier, N., & Faragher, E. B. (2002). Religious delusions in patients admitted to hospital with schizophrenia. *Social Psychiatry and Psychiatric Epidemiology, 37,* 130–138.

So, S. H., Freeman, D., Dunn, G., Kapur, S., Kuipers, E., Bebbington, P.,…Garety, P. A. (2012). Jumping to conclusions, a lack of belief flexibility and delusional conviction in psychosis: A longitudinal investigation of the structure, frequency, and relatedness of reasoning biases. *Journal of Abnormal Psychology, 121,* 129–139.

Soreff, S. M. (1987). Paranoia. In S. M. Soreff & G. N. McNeil (Eds.), *Handbook of psychiatric differential diagnosis* (pp. 318–363). Littleton, MA: PSG Publishing.

Speechley, W. J., Whitman J. C., & Woodward, T. S. (2010). The contribution of hypersalience to the "jumping to conclusions" bias associated with delusions. *Journal of Psychiatry and Neuroscience, 35,* 7–17.

Spence, S. A. (2002). Alien motor phenomena: A window on to agency. *Cognitive Neuropsychiatry, 7,* 211–220.

Sprong, M., Schothorst, P., Vos, E., Hox J., & van Engeland, H. (2007). Theory of mind in schizophrenia: Meta-analysis. *British Journal of Psychiatry, 191,* 5–13.

Startup, M., & Startup, S. (2005). On two kinds of delusion of reference. *Psychiatry Research, 137,* 87–92.

Stompe, T., Ortwein-Swoboda, G., Ritter, K., & Schanda, H. (2003). Old wine in new bottles? Stability and plasticity of the contents of schizophrenic delusions. *Psychopathology, 36,* 6–12.

Stopa, L., Denton, R., Wingfield, M., & Taylor, K. N. (2013). The fear of others: A qualitative analysis of interpersonal threat in social phobia and paranoia. *Behavioural and Cognitive Psychotherapy, 41,* 188–209.

Stuart, G. W., Malone, V., Currie, J., Klimidis, S., & Minas, I. H. (1995). Positive and negative symptoms in neuroleptic-free psychotic inpatients. *Schizophrenia Research, 16,* 175–188.

Suhail, K., & Ghauri, S. (2010). Phenomenology of delusions and hallucinations in schizophrenia by religious convictions. *Mental Health, Religion & Culture, 13,* 245–259.

Sun, J., Jayathilake, K., Zhao, Z, & Meltzer, H. Y. (2012). Investigating association of four gene regions (GABRB3, MAOB, PAH, and SLC6A4) with five symptoms in schizophrenia. *Psychiatry Research, 198,* 202–206.

Taber, K. H., & Hurley, R. A. (2007). Neuroimaging in schizophrenia: Misattributions and religious delusions. *Journal of Neuropsychiatry & Clinical Neurosciences, 19,* 1–4.

Tarbox, S. I., Almasy, L., Gur, R. E., Nimgaonkar, V. L., & Pogue-Geile, M. F. (2012). The nature of schizotypy among multigenerational multiplex schizophrenia families. *Journal of Abnormal Psychology, 121,* 396–406.

Teufel, C., Kingdon, A., Ingram, J. N., Wolpert D. M., & Fletcher, P. C. (2010). Deficits in sensory prediction are related to delusional ideation in healthy individuals. *Neuropsychologia, 14,* 4169–4172.

Thomas, C., Turkheimer, E., & Oltmanns, T. F. (2003). Factorial structure of pathological personality as evaluated by peers. *Journal of Abnormal Psychology, 112,* 81–91.

Tone, E. B., & Davis, J. S. (2012). Paranoid thinking, suspicion, and risk for aggression: A neurodevelopmental perspective. *Development and Psychopathology, 24,* 1031–1046.

Tone, E. B., Goulding, S. M., & Compton, M. T. (2011). Associations among perceptual anomalies, social anxiety, and paranoia in a college student sample. *Psychiatry Research, 188,* 258–263.

Torgersen, S., Lygren, S., Øien, P. A., Skre, I., Onstad, S., Edvardsen, J.,…Kringlen, E. (2000). A twin study of personality disorders. *Comprehensive Psychiatry, 41,* 416–425.

Trull, T. J., Widiger, T. A., & Burr, R. (2001). A structured interview for the assessment of the five-factor model of personality: Facet-level relations to the Axis II personality disorders. *Journal of Personality, 69,* 175–198.

Tschacher, W., & Kupper, Z. (2006). Perception of causality in schizophrenia spectrum disorder. *Schizophrenia Bulletin, 32,* S106–S112.

Ulzen, T. P. M., & Carpentier, R. (1997). The delusional parent: Family and multisystemic issues. *Canadian Journal of Psychiatry, 42,* 617–622.

Useda, J. D. (2002). The construct validity of the Paranoid Personality Disorder Features Questionnaire (PPDFQ): A dimensional assessment of paranoid personality disorder. (Doctoral dissertation, University of Missouri-Columbia, 2001). *Dissertation Abstracts International, 62*(9-B), 4240.

Valiente, C., Cantero, D., Vázquez, C., Sanchez, Á., Provencio, M., & Espiosa, R. (2011). Implicit and explicit self-esteem discrepancies in paranoia and depression. *Journal of Abnormal Psychology, 120,* 691–699.

van der Gaag, M., Schütz, C., ten Napel, A., Landa, Y., Delespaul, P., Bak, M.,…de Hert, M. (2013). Development of the Davos Assessment of Cognitive Biases Scale (DACOBS). *Schizophrenia Research, 144,* 63–71.

van der Werf, M., van Boxtel, M., Verhey, F., Jolles, J., Thewissen, V., & van Os, J. (2007). Mild hearing impairment and psychotic experiences in a normal aging population. *Schizophrenia Research, 92,* 180–186.

Van Dongen, J. D. M., Buck, N. M. L., & van Marle, H. J. C. (2012). Delusional distress partly explains the relation between persecutory ideations and inpatient aggression on the ward. *Psychiatry Research, 200,* 779–783.

Van IJzendoorn, M. H., & Bakermans-Kranenburg (2012). A sniff of trust: Meta-analysis of the effects of intranasal oxytocin administration on face recognition, trust to in-group, and trust to out-group. *Psychoneuroendocrinology, 37,* 438–443.

Varese, F., Smeets, F., Drukker, M., Lieverse, R., Lataster, T., Viechtbauer, W., . . .Bentall, R. P. (2012). Childhood adversities increase the risk of psychosis: A meta-analysis of patient-control, prospective- and cross-sectional cohort studies. *Schizophrenia Bulletin, 38,* 661–671.

Varghese, D., Wray, N. R., Scott, J. G., Williams, G. M, Najman, J. M., & McGrath, J. J. (2013). The heritability of delusional-like experiences. *Acta Psychiatrica Scandinavica, 127,* 48–52.

Veale, D. (2002). Over-valued ideas: A conceptual analysis. *Behavior Research and Therapy, 40,* 383–400.

Veale, D. (2004). Advances in a cognitive behavioural model of body dysmorphic disorder. *Body Image, 1,* 113–125.

Venkatasubramanian, G., Jayakumar, P. N., Keshavan, M. S., & Gangadhar, B. N. (2011). Schneiderian first rank symptoms and inferior parietal lobule cortical thickness in antipsychotic-naïve schizophrenia. *Progress in Neuro-Psychopharmacology & Biological Psychiatry, 35,* 40–46.

Vohs, K. D., Baumeister, R. F., & Chin, J. (2007). Feeling duped: Emotional, motivational, and cognitive aspects of being exploited by others. *Review of General Psychology, 11,* 127–141.

Waller, N. G. (1999). Search for structure in the MMPI. In S. E. Embretson & S. L. Hershberger (Eds.), *The new rules of measurement: What every psychologist and educator should know* (pp. 186–216). Mahwah, NJ: Lawrence Erlbaum.

Walss-Bass, C., Fernandes, J. M., Roberts, D. L., Service, H., & Velligan, D. (2013). Differential correlations between plasma oxytocin and social cognitive capacity and bias in schizophrenia. *Schizophrenia Research, 147,* 387–392.

Warman, D. M., & Martin, J. M. (2006). Cognitive insight and delusion proneness: An investigation using the Beck Cognitive Insight Scale. *Schizophrenia Research, 84,* 297–304.

Welham, J., Scott, J., Williams, G., Naiman, J., Bor, W., O'Callaghan, M., & McGrath, J. (2009). Emotional and behavioural antecedents of young adults who screen positive for non-affective psychosis: A 21-year birth cohort study. *Psychological Medicine, 39,* 625–634.

Westen, D., Nakash, O., Thomas, C., & Bradley, R. (2006). Clinical assessment of attachment patterns and personality disorder in adolescents and adults. *Journal of Consulting and Clinical Psychology, 74,* 1065–1085.

White, L. O., & Mansell, W. (2009). Failing to ponder? Delusion-prone individuals rush to conclusions. *Clinical Psychology and Psychotherapy, 16,* 111–124.

Wong, G. H. Y., Hui, C. L. M., Tang, J. Y. M., Chiu, C. P. Y., Lam, M. M. L., Chan, S. K. W.,…Chen, E. Y. H. (2012). Screening and assessing ideas and delusions of reference using a semi-structured interview scale: A validation study of the Ideas of Reference Interview Scale (IRIS) in early psychosis patients. *Schizophrenia Research, 135,* 158–163.

Woodward, T. S., Buchy, L., Moritz, S., & Liotti, M. (2007). A bias against disconfirmatory evidence is associated with delusion proneness in a nonclinical sample. *Schizophrenia Bulletin, 33,* 1023–1028.

Woodward, T. S., Moritz, S., & Chen, E. (2006). The contribution of a cognitive bias against disconfirmatory evidence (BADE) to delusions: A study in an Asian sample with first episode schizophrenia spectrum disorders. *Schizophrenia Research, 83,* 297–298.

Woodward, T. S., Moritz, W., Cuttler, C., & Whitman, J. C. (2006). The contribution of a cognitive bias against disconfirmatory evidence (BADE) to delusions in schizophrenia. *Journal of Clinical and Experimental Neuropsychology, 28*, 605–617.

Woodward, T. S., Munz, M., LeClerc, C., & Lecomte, T. (2009). Change in delusions is associated with change in "jumping to conclusions." *Psychiatry Research, 170*, 124–127.

Wustmann, T., Pillman, F., & Marneros, A. (2011). Gender-related features of persistent delusional disorders. *European Archives of Psychiatry and Clinical Neuroscience, 261*, 29–36.

Wuthrich, V. M., & Bates, T. C. (2006). Confirmatory factor analysis of the three-factor structure of the schizotypal personality questionnaire. *Journal of Personality Assessment, 87*, 292–304.

Yang, M., Ullrich, S., Roberts, A., & Coid, J. (2007). Childhood institutional care and personality disorder traits in adulthood: Findings from the British national surveys of psychiatric morbidity. *American Journal of Orthopsychiatry, 77*, 67–75.

Yaralian, P. S., Raine, A., Lencz, T., Hooley, J. M., Bihrle, S. E., Mills, S., & Ventura, J. (2000). Elevated levels of cognitive-perceptual deficits in individuals with a family history of schizophrenia spectrum disorders. *Schizophrenia Research, 46*, 57–63.

Part III

OTHER CLINICAL SYNDROMES

15

Sexual Dysfunctions

DONALD S. STRASSBERG,

JULIA E. MACKARONIS,

AND MICHAEL A. PERELMAN

Sexual dysfunctions, conditions that impair the desire or ability to achieve sexual satisfaction, are among the most prevalent of the distressing emotional and behavioral problems facing those seeking treatment from mental health professionals and health clinicians. The National Health and Social Life Survey (NHSLS; Laumann, Gagnon, Michael, & Michaels, 1994; Laumann, Paik, & Rosen, 1999) reported a prevalence rate for all sexual disorders of 31% for men and 43% for women. Because of its research methodology, including a sample size of 3,000 U.S. men and women, aged 18 to 59, the use of a national probability sample with a 79% response rate, and the use of 90-minute in-person interviews, the NHSLS has been heralded by many as the best source of prevalence data on sexual disorders in the United States in decades.

Still, the NHSLS is not without its critics (e.g., Bancroft, Loftus, & Long, 2003), and the meaningfulness of at least some of its data has been called into question (Graham, 2007). For example, Laumann et al. (1999) specified that a sexual difficulty had to have been experienced for "several months or longer" during the previous year. As reasonable as this seems, it is possible that a significant subgroup of their participants labeled "dysfunctional" actually had been experiencing a relatively transient sexual difficulty rather than a chronic dysfunction (Graham, 2007). Data from

other large-scale surveys suggest that this may well be the case, particularly for women's sexual complaints (Mercer et al., 2003).

What we are left with is the reality that *any* particular label or operational definition (including its duration criterion) is imperfect and subject to alternative interpretations. Still, rates of sexual dysfunctions even substantially less than those reported by the NHSLS would indicate that many men, women, and their partners deal with sexual difficulties. Throughout this chapter, we will attempt to identify the source of the prevalence data provided. It should be understood, however, that for every dysfunction discussed, there are often several (sometimes quite discrepant) published and frequently cited prevalence figures (e.g., Lewis et al., 2010). The reader is advised to consider the various sources of these figures in evaluating their meaningfulness and to treat them, at best, as estimates. *DSM-5* organizes sexual dysfunctions roughly according to the sexual response cycle, as originally proposed by Masters and Johnson (1966) and Helen Singer Kaplan (1979)—that is, desire, arousal, and orgasm. The utility of this organizational structure, particularly its applicability to women, has been the subject of much debate (Basson, 2005; Sand & Fisher, 2007; Working Group for a New View of Women's Sexual Problems, 2001). Additionally, the new-to-*DSM-5* diagnosis of female sexual interest/arousal disorder (SIAD; described later in the chapter) combines difficulties occurring at both the interest and arousal phases of the cycle. Still, as it is the most commonly used way of categorizing sexual dysfunctions, this structure will be used throughout this chapter, especially in providing definitions of the disorders. While they can be treated as separate for descriptive and didactic purposes, as we do in this chapter, in reality these "stages" frequently co-occur or are etiologically linked, both within individuals and even between members of a couple.

Although the identified and hypothesized psychosocial (including both individual and dyadic features) and biological (including disease, disorder, and medication effects) causes and treatments of these various dysfunctions can differ, there is also a great deal of etiological and treatment overlap. Therefore, before discussing each of the male and female dysfunctions individually, we will consider these disorders as a group in terms of (a) the most commonly identified psychosocial and biological factors that have been demonstrated or hypothesized to play a significant role as proximal and/or distal causes in their development and/or maintenance and (b) generic issues in their assessment and treatment.

The difference between the prevalence rates for the various sexual disorders and the numbers of people seeking treatment for these conditions makes very clear that most men and women with a sexual dysfunction never seek treatment for these problems (Laumann et al., 1999). This occurs despite the intrapsychic (e.g., Tomlinson & Wright, 2004) and interpersonal costs the disorders often exact and the availability of effective treatments for many of them. There are many reasons for individuals not seeking treatment. First, unlike the men and women portrayed in some contemporary television shows, many people have never learned to be comfortable talking about things sexual—not in the abstract, and especially not when it concerns them personally. Even couples who have been together for many years, and have experienced physical intimacy hundreds of times, are often reluctant to reveal their sexual desires, fears, and concerns to each other. In fact, this lack of honest communication about sex between partners often contributes to sexual problems (Kelly, Strassberg, & Kircher, 1990; Shabsigh, Perelman, Laumann, & Lockhart, 2004) and is frequently a target in treatment. It is no surprise then that

the first prescription medications to be heavily marketed through the Internet were those for the treatment of a sexual disorder, erectile dysfunction (ED). The anonymity of the Internet allowed millions of men to receive treatment for their sexual disorder without ever having to talk to a receptionist, nurse, doctor, or pharmacist.

Despite the ongoing controversy regarding the possible overuse of medical approaches to conceptualizing and treating sexual problems (discussed later in the chapter), there is no doubt that the multimedia advertisements for ED drugs have increased our thinking about, and discussion of, sexual functioning in general and sexual dysfunctions in particular. With more and more people recognizing and seeking help for their sexual problems, it is more important than ever that clinicians in the health and mental health fields understand the nature of sexual disorders and be prepared to engage their clients in an informed discussion of these problems. Of course, such a dialogue requires that the treatment provider, as well as his or her patient, be able and willing to speak comfortably about sexual matters.

Etiology

Decades ago, it was common to assume that sexual dysfunctions were almost always the result of an underlying psychological or relationship problem. Later, such dysfunctions were routinely viewed as having a medical etiology. Today, clinicians recognize the important independent and interactive roles in sexual dysfunctions played by cognitive, behavioral, affective, relational, medical, and situational or contextual factors (Binik, Bergeron, & Khalife, 2006; Janssen, 2011). They understand that, in any given individual, the existence of almost any sexual dysfunction can be the result of any one or combination of these factors (e.g., Perelman, 2009; Waldinger, 2008). We will next provide an overview of some of the most common etiologies for sexual dysfunctions, as a group.

Organic Causes of Sexual Dysfunctions

Rewarding sexual activity requires the adequate functioning of at least three organ systems: cardiovascular, hormonal, and neurological (Janssen, 2011). Virtually any structural defect, disease process, medication, or even treatment that significantly compromises any of these systems can, potentially, interfere with a man or woman's ability to successfully function sexually. It is important to note that the impact on sexual desire or function resulting from any of the many drugs, conditions, and treatments described here can vary substantially from one person to another. For example, as few as 10% of men on an antihypertensive medication might experience significant ED, leaving 90% of men with little or no sexual effect. This is true, to varying degrees, with virtually all of these biological/organic elements. Even something as dramatic as radical prostate surgery will not leave every patient with an erection insufficient for intercourse. Because any of these drugs, conditions, or treatments *can* impact sexual functioning, in the assessment of a sexual problem it is important that their possible role be thoroughly explored in each case. However, the mere existence of one or more of these organic risk factors is not in and of itself proof of its etiological significance. Of course, the appearance of a sexual problem soon after the introduction of a new drug or about the same time as the likely beginning of a new medical problem substantially increases (though still does not prove) its likely importance.

Drugs

A wide variety of medications, listed below, have been linked to one or more sexual problems. Given how many people regularly use these drugs, it is obvious that, as stated, they do not always significantly interfere with sexual function and pleasure. Also, this list is not exhaustive. Rather, it represents the drugs most often implicated in sexual problems. For a review indicating how sexual side effects are best assessed and treated, see Segraves and Balon (2010).

- Antidepressants (MAOIs, tricyclics, SSRIs)
- Antiepileptics
- Beta-blockers
- Antihypertensives
- Anxiolytics
- Antipsychotics (especially conventional antipsychotics)
- Anticholinergics
- Anticonvulsants
- Substances of abuse (alcohol, opioids, stimulants, sedative-hypnotics, cannabis)

- Cholesterol lowering medications
- Antihistamines and decongestants
- Anorectic agents
- Diuretics
- Hormone blockers (Lupron, Zoladex)
- Hormonal contraceptives
- Tranquilizers
- Analgesics, including codeine

Medical Illnesses, Treatments, Procedures, Conditions, and Changes

Virtually any medical illness, condition, treatment, or change that impacts neurological, hormonal, or cardiovascular functioning can, potentially, negatively affect some aspect of a man or woman's sexual functioning (e.g., Celik et al., 2013). Many of the most common of these or those having the most impact are listed below. Of course, not everyone affected by these conditions will be sexually impacted by them, nor will all those sexually affected necessarily show the same type or degree of dysfunction (for many of these illnesses, clinicians can seek out literature specifically addressing what sexual side effects may result from the disease and/or its treatment; e.g., for a review of the sexual consequences of cancer survivorship, see Brotto and Kingsberg, 2010). Further, the co-occurrence of any medical condition and a sexual dysfunction need not prove a cause–effect relationship. Given how many medical conditions can affect sexual functioning and how commonly they occur, however, it is important that the clinician explore for their presence (both currently and in the past) in history taking.

- Alcoholism or substance abuse (acute and chronic)
- Diabetes
- Hypothalamopituitary dysfunction
- Neurological or vascular pathology (e.g., multiple sclerosis; Parkinson's disease)
- Diseases affecting the sexual organs (congenital anomalies or malformations, cysts, trauma, tumor, infection)
- Spinal cord injury
- Pituitary, adrenal, or thyroid malfunction
- Cardiovascular disease (e.g., atherosclerosis, myocardial infraction [MI], stroke)
- Hormonal imbalance
- Kidney or liver infection, dysfunction, or failure

- Almost any chronic or debilitating disease (e.g., arthritis)
- Insomnia
- Prostate disease, prostatitis, or benign prostatic hyperplasia (BPH)
- Menopause
- Dialysis
- Hysterectomy or oophorectomy
- Mastectomy
- Prostatectomy
- Pelvic surgery, trauma, or radiation
- Rectal surgery
- General surgery
- Radiation therapy
- Chemotherapy
- Episiotomy scarring
- Rigid hymen
- Metabolic syndrome

Psychosocial and Cultural Causes of Sexual Disorders and Dysfunctions

For both men and women, a variety of proximal and distal psychosocial and cultural variables have been identified as risk factors for sexual problems (e.g., Althof et al., 2005).

Historical and cultural
- Sexual, physical, or emotional abuse as a child or adolescent
- Religious orthodoxy, sex-negative messages growing up
- Sexual assault as an adult
- Antisexual cultural rites and rituals

Intrapsychic
- Depression
- Anxiety disorders (e.g., obsessive-compulsive disorder [OCD], performance anxiety)
- Psychosis
- Low self-esteem
- Poor body image
- Anger
- Sex guilt
- Sexual orientation conflict
- Stress (e.g., from work or family responsibilities)
- Other sexual dysfunction(s)

Relationship
- Infidelity
- Trust issues
- Anger at partner

- Lack of affection for or by partner
- Lack of sexual interest in, or attraction to, partner
- Partner sexual dysfunction
- Partner psychopathology
- Fear (e.g., of pregnancy, commitment, sexually transmitted infections [STIs], rejection)
- Intimacy deficits
- Jealousy
- Partner sexual skill deficit
- Boring sexual routine
- Communication problems (sexual or nonsexual)
- Desire discrepancy or other sexual compatibility issues
- Power struggles
- Too busy (i.e., physical intimacy not prioritized)
- Infertility
- Value and priority or related couple differences (e.g., in-laws, religion, children, money)

Biopsychosocial Dual-Control Models

Increasingly, clinicians from many disciplines support "dual-control" biopsychosocial-cultural models in understanding the development and maintenance of sexual dysfunctions (Bancroft, Graham, Janssen, & Sanders, 2009; Kaplan, 1995; Metz & McCarthy, 2007; Perelman, 2009; 2011; Pfaus, 2009). This viewpoint is consistent with a combination or integrated treatment approach to the management of sexual disorders (Althof, 2006; Banner & Anderson, 2007; Brock et al., 2007; Metz & McCarthy, 2007; Perelman, 2009; Rosen et al., 2004; Walkup et al., 2008).

Although integrating mind and body predates Descartes, Bancroft and Janssen (2000) along with colleagues at the Kinsey Institute (Graham, Heiman, Janssen, Sanders) have articulated a "dual-control" biopsychosocial theory (Bancroft et al., 2009; Graham, Sanders, & Milhausen, 2006). The central feature of that model is understanding that "sexual response and associated arousal occurs in a particular individual, in a particular situation, is ultimately determined by the balance between two systems in that individual's brain, the sexual activation or excitation system and the sexual inhibition system, each of which has a neurobiological substrate (Bancroft, 2009, p. 15)."

Perelman described an alternative dual-control model, the sexual tipping point (STP), that focused on clinical applications that he developed in association with Kaplan, who had first described the role of "sexual incitors and suppressors" (Kaplan, 1995; Perelman, 2012a). The STP model illustrates both intra- and interindividual variability, which is key to appreciating concepts of psychosocial-cultural and biological predispositions and thresholds. The sexual tipping point is the characteristic threshold for an expression of a sexual response for any man or woman, which may vary dynamically within and between any given sexual experience. The specific threshold for the sexual response is determined by multiple factors for any given moment or circumstance, with one factor or another dominating, while others recede in importance.

Essentially, all the biopsychosocial-cultural models of sexual dysfunction provide a compelling argument for optimizing patient care through a combination treatment that integrates sex counseling and sexual pharmaceuticals (Perelman, 2009). Patients whose dysfunction is based on deep-seated psychosocial and emotional issues may not be amenable to simple single-agent pharmacological therapeutics, while those who have physical issues related to age, illness, etc. are unlikely to be fully helped by sex counseling or therapy exclusively. Sex therapists working together with medical providers who prescribe pharmacological agents may be able to help patients previously untreatable by counseling methods alone. Reciprocally, counseling helps a physician optimize the efficacy of pharmaceuticals within the context and limitations of an individual's own sexual tipping point (Perelman, 2011).

Assessment of Sexual Dysfunctions

A careful assessment of any sexual dysfunction can be challenging, always requiring, at a minimum, a careful history of the presenting complaint and generally much more. In both the assessment and treatment of sexual dysfunctions, it is very important that the therapist be seen as nonjudgmental. Remember that clients are attempting to discuss very sensitive matters, information that they have likely never shared with anyone else (even their partners) and almost certainly not in detail with a stranger.

Interviews should, whenever possible, include the symptomatic individual and his or her partner, with at least some of the interview time being spent with each partner individually. For unpartnered individuals who present with sexual complaints, it is important to keep in mind that such persons may in fact have avoided relationships specifically because of their sexual difficulties. Among the questions clinicians would like to be able to answer after the interviews and other information gathering (e.g., lab tests and other medical findings) are complete are as follows:

1. Is the problem truly a sexual disorder?
2. To what extent is the etiology organic, psychosocial-cultural, or mixed?
3. Is the locus of problem in one partner or both?
4. Is the problem generalized or situational (i.e., partner specific)?
5. Is the presenting sexual problem primary (i.e., the individual has always had the problem) or secondary (i.e., there was a time when the person did not have the problem)? If secondary, is it in response to another dysfunction in the symptomatic client or his or her partner?

In general, the following information should be gathered during the interview(s) from each partner's perspective:

1. What is the sexual problem?
2. How long has the problem been a problem?
3. How distressed (if at all) is the person by the problem, and how distressed does the person think his or her partner is?
4. How does the person explain the problem (i.e., what does he or she think has caused or is maintaining the problem)?
5. What, exactly, actually takes place when the couple is sexual (i.e., a detailed description of their typical sexual interaction)? What has the couple tried, and with what success, to solve the sexual problem?
6. What is at stake for each or for the relationship if the problem does not get solved? What, if anything, is at stake if it does?
7. Are there any sexual secrets (e.g., extramarital relationships [romantic or sexual], homosexual feelings)?
8. What about nonsexual secrets (e.g., one wanting out of the relationship)?

9. What, if anything, makes the problem better and what makes it worse?

10. How does each person see the quality of the nonsexual relationship (e.g., emotional intimacy, communication)?

11. What are each partner's health problems and nonsexual sources of stress?

12. What competes with sex (e.g., work, kids, hobbies, friends) for each partner's time and energy?

13. Why are they seeking treatment now?

14. When was sex best in this relationship? Why? What was different?

15. What were each partner's previous (or concurrent) sexual relationships like?

16. What are each partner's sexual fantasies?

17. What would each partner like sexually that he or he is not currently receiving and what in their current sexual life would they like to stop?

18. How was the topic of sex treated in their family of origin?

19. Does either partner have any history of sexual, physical, or other abuse?

20. How willing is each partner to engage in treatment?

21. Does the nonsymptomatic partner blame him- or herself for the problem (e.g., "If only I were attractive or sexy enough…")?

22. What psychological strengths do each partner and the relationship bring to treatment?

23. What treatment outcome does each person hope to see? How optimistic is each of the partners about achieving this outcome? How realistic are these hopes and expectations?

A thorough evaluation of a sexual disorder will often require the involvement and cooperation of one or more health care professionals, including urologists, gynecologists, physical therapists, and endocrinologists, in addition to the sex therapist. Also, client treatment expectations need to be assessed (see question 23, above) and, where appropriate, adjusted so that they can be optimistic yet realistic.

General Issues in the Treatment of Sexual Dysfunctions

As mentioned, many men and women experiencing a sexual dysfunction will never seek treatment for this problem. The NHSLS found that while in general men and women who reported a sexual disorder also described a lower quality of life than their sexually functional counterparts, only 20% of the women and 10% of the men reporting a dysfunction had ever sought medical consultation for the problem (Laumann et al., 1999). Many of those who ultimately do seek treatment will consult a sex therapist or psychotherapist only as a last resort. Prior to this, they will have likely sought treatment from a physician, usually a general practitioner, or (increasingly) tried to "fix" the problem themselves using information and/or products obtained from the Internet or other media. Some individuals may feel that seeing a mental health professional for a sexual problem is an admission that the problem is psychological in nature, something many of those with a sexual dysfunction would prefer to avoid (i.e., they would much prefer a medical etiology and treatment). Also, by the time they find their way to a therapist, the failure of previous attempts to resolve the problem may have left them discouraged and pessimistic about the chances of any practitioner being of much help. While there is much anecdotal and some empirical research evidence (Almas & Landmark, 2010; Heiman & Meston, 1997) demonstrating the efficacy of the psychological treatment of many (although not all) sexual dysfunctions, a recent meta-analysis concluded that treatment efficacy is only clearly supported for two of these disorders: female desire (termed SIAD) and female orgasmic difficulties (Frühauf, Gerger, Schmidt, Munder, & Barth, 2013).

The most significant development in sexology since the mid-1990s has been the *medicalization* of sexual problems: the movement toward viewing these disorders from a disease, or at least a physiological, perspective, and the dramatically increased use of pharmaceuticals in their treatment (Bancroft, 2000; Graham, 2007; Perelman, 2001, 2007a; Rowland, 2007; Uckert, Mayer, Jonas, & Stief, 2006). The pros and cons of this development have fueled a very heated debate within academic and clinical sexology (e.g., Althof, 2006; Rowland, 2007; Tiefer, 2007). Despite the many limitations associated with the view that prescribing a pill is a necessary and sufficient intervention for something as complex as a sexual dysfunction, it is undoubtedly the case that pharmacological interventions for some of these sexual problems can be effective and are here to stay. This has led many researchers and clinicians to look for means by which to *integrate* medical and psychosocial perspectives into a more comprehensive approach to understanding and treating sexual dysfunctions (e.g., Althof, 2006; McCarthy & Fucito, 2005; Perelman, 2005a; Rosen, 2000; Rowland, 2007; Strassberg, 1994).

William Masters, the famous sex researcher and therapist, was fond of saying, "There are no unaffected partners in sexual dysfunctions." We know that a sexual dysfunction in one person can precipitate or exacerbate a dysfunction in his or her partner (e.g., Goldstein et al., 2005; Shabsigh, Anastasiades, Cooper, & Rutman, 2006) and that sexual dysfunctions almost always impact and/or are often impacted by the quality of a relationship (Fisher et al., 2005). Consequently, failure to consider relationship issues in the assessment and treatment of sexual dysfunctions can result in a woefully incomplete understanding of the problem(s) and in treatment that is ultimately less effective (e.g., Kelly et al., 1990; Kelly, Strassberg, & Turner, 2004; Perelman, 2007b). Consequently, the involvement of the partner of the symptomatic client in treatment is widely believed to play an important, even critical, facilitative role in sex therapy (Masters & Johnson, 1970). Some therapists go as far as to require a partner's involvement in both the assessment and treatment phases of sex therapy. Of course, clinicians will encounter clients without a partner or with partners who are unwilling to participate in treatment, preferring, perhaps, to believe they play no role in the sexual problem and simply wanting the *sick one* to be *fixed*. In fact, most sexually dysfunctional men and women first present alone. Although having to assess and/or treat sexually dysfunctional clients by themselves can make a difficult clinical task more challenging, most therapists will work with what they have, making the necessary adjustments along the way. Fortunately, it is *sensitivity to partner issues* on the part of the therapist and *partner cooperation and participation* that are likely the key variables—not necessarily partner attendance during the office visits (Perelman, 2003). Stephenson, Rellini, and Meston (2013), for example, found that for women with sexual dysfunctions, those with lower pretreatment relationship satisfaction benefitted less from individual cognitive-behavioral therapy (CBT). Even when their sexual functioning did improve, their sexual distress did not diminish. Functional sex within

the context of a bad relationship, it seems, can still be quite distressing.

One important strategy in treating a sexual dysfunction is to help the symptomatic individual and his or her partner to recognize that symptom removal need not be a requisite for an improved sex life. In many cases, an unnecessarily limited sexual script (i.e., their blueprint for what constitutes "good sex") prevents couples from learning to accommodate to whatever their current sexual situation might be. By insisting on how sex *should* be, one or both members of the couple often fail to enjoy what is currently available to them sexually and put added pressure on themselves and/or each other to get things "right," often making it less likely that things will get better. Relatedly, clinicians may find the distinction between *objective* and *functional* definitions of sexual dysfunction to be useful. Given the paucity of population-level data on sexual functioning, *objective* definitions of sexual dysfunction are practically nonexistent (i.e., how much time is clearly "too long" to take to reach orgasm?), whereas *functional* definitions focus on whether an individual's sexuality is working for them and their partner (Nathan, 2010).

It is well known among therapists that *sometimes a problem is also a solution*. Although no one knows how often a sexual problem *solves* some other individual or dyadic issue or results in a secondary gain, it undoubtedly occurs some of the time. For example, a wife's loss of interest in sex (i.e., Sexual Interest/Arousal Disorder) could, even without her awareness, serve to protect the fragile self-esteem of her partner who suffers from ED. Or, a man's ED may help reassure his partner of his fidelity. Therefore, therapists must understand what is at stake for both partners and for the relationship should the dysfunction no longer exist, and be alert for the possibility of contradictory objectives (Hartmann & Waldinger, 2006; Potts, Gavey, Grace, & Vares, 2003).

Therapists must also understand what is at stake if therapy fails. There are instances in which it seems clear, often because one partner has said so, that a failure to fix the sexual problem will end the relationship. In other cases, it seems equally clear that, for any of a variety of reasons (some healthier than others), the viability of the relationship is not at risk no matter what the outcome of treatment is. Having more at stake in treatment (i.e., the continuation of the relationship) can sometimes serve as an important motivator for one or both partners. More often, however, the relationship being at stake is negatively prognostic because (a) it is usually evidence of serious dissatisfaction with the relationship, and (b) it increases the demands and anxiety of treatment, thereby working precisely in the wrong direction.

Most current approaches to sex therapy are cognitive-behavioral in nature (Strassberg & Mackaronis, 2014), which often include therapist-assigned exercises (e.g., sensate focus) adapted from Masters and Johnson (1970) and Kaplan (1974) that have both diagnostic and therapeutic value. These are guided couples' exercises, with both proscriptions and prescriptions, done in the privacy of the clients' own home. They help each person to identify what is sensually pleasing to them and their partner and to communicate that to each other. As essentially in vivo systematic desensitization assignments, early sensate focus exercises are designed to be more sensual than sexual and usually prohibit genital touching. After the first few basic exercises, the assignments become more genitally focused and are individualized to the couple as a function of the specific sexual problem with which they present and their responses to the previous assignments. Therapy sessions are used to thoroughly process behaviors, thoughts, and feelings associated with the previous period's homework assignments and to give instructions on the next exercises. In terms of efficacy, in a meta-analysis of 20 randomized controlled studies on the effect of psychological interventions mentioned earlier, Frühauf and colleagues (2013) found effect sizes across all included studies to be moderate for both reductions in symptom severity ($d = .58$) and increases in sexual satisfaction ($d = .47$), Again, though, given the notable variability between studies, the strongest effect sizes were for female arousal and female orgasmic disorders in particular.

When medication or other medical interventions are indicated in the treatment of a sexual dysfunction, these should be undertaken by medical practitioners trained and experienced in these procedures, ideally as part of an overall approach to treatment that includes consultation with, or the direct involvement of, a mental health practitioner skilled in the treatment of sexual disorders. This multidisciplinary approach is increasingly recognized as the most likely to be effective in the long term (Simopoulos & Trinidad, 2013). One of the reasons why those with a sexual disorder often discontinue even effective medical interventions is the failure to integrate their use within meaningful individual or couples' counseling or sex therapy (Perelman, 2005a).

Ultimately, the goal of treatment for a sexual dysfunction, whether medical, psychosocial, or some combination of both, will be to restore or create a situation in which the symptomatic individual and his or her partner can engage in and enjoy a mutually rewarding and satisfying sexual relationship. Sometimes medication and/or brief sex therapy or counseling are insufficient for this goal. Such cases may require an intense exploration of the relationship and/or the psychosocial histories of one or both partners through extended individual and/or couples' therapy to achieve lasting and meaningful change. When sex therapy is at least part of the intervention, it is often, as mentioned earlier, cognitive-behavioral in nature with goals, in addition to symptom removal, typically including the removal of spectatoring (i.e., when an individual focuses on themselves from a third-party perspective; Masters & Johnson, 1970), self-defeating pessimism, unrealistic fears, inhibitions, and expectations, while facilitating intimacy, support, permission giving, sex education, improved communication (sexual and other), and attitude change and helping to make sex fun (McCarthy & McCarthy, 2003).

In the preceding overview, we have described some of the general etiological and treatment perspectives that have been developed in the last several decades, through both research and clinical experience, regarding the sexual disorders. We will now describe in some detail, each of the primary types of sexual dysfunction, relying primarily on the organizational scheme used in the *DSM-5*.

Disorders of Sexual Desire

Definition

Our interest in sex, often termed *libido*, can vary substantially, not only from one of us to another but also within the same person, from one day to the next, from one partner to the next, and as we age. We can reveal our level of interest in several ways, including how often we think about sex and, assuming we have an appealing partner available to us, how often we initiate sex with that partner or choose to respond to his or her sexual overtures.

Among both men and women, there are some who appear to have very little, if any, such interest. They rarely or never think or fantasize about sex and they rarely or never initiate sex or want to respond to the sexual initiations of their partners. A small proportion of men and women who meet this description self-identify as asexual, and they typically report no distress at their level of sexual interest; for characterization of asexually identified individuals, see Prause and Graham (2007), and Brotto, Knudson, Inskip, Rhodes, and Erskine (2010). But for those wishing a significant interest in sex, low or absent desire for sex can be a serious problem for them and their partner. It is one of the more difficult sexual disorders to define, in part because it is hard to say just what level of interest in sex is normal and how far from that one's interest must be to be labeled disordered.

Importantly, standards used to define abnormally low desire in men are increasingly suspected of being inappropriate for defining the problem in women (Brotto, 2010; Carvalheira, Brotto, & Leal, 2010). The *DSM-5* reflects this changing understanding by synthesizing two distinct diagnoses for women from *DSM-IV-TR*—hypoactive sexual desire disorder (HSDD) and female sexual arousal disorder (FSAD)—into one new diagnostic category, female Sexual Interest/Arousal Disorder (SIAD). This approach, however, has not been without its critics (DeRogatis, Clayton, Rosen, Sand, & Pyke, 2011). SIAD captures both distressingly low interest *and* arousal in women, but we discuss it most thoroughly in this first section on disorders of sexual desire.

Examining the now outdated *DSM-IV-TR* criteria for both male and female Hypoactive Sexual Desire Disorder (HSDD) can give readers a sense of the definitional difficulties inherent in this area of psychopathology: "Persistently or recurrently deficient (or absent) sexual fantasies and desire for sexual activity. The judgment of deficiency is made by the clinician, taking into account factors that affect sexual functioning, such as age and the context of the person's life" (p. 541). Of course, as with virtually all *DSM* diagnoses, female SIAD and male HSDD (shortened below as SIAD/HSDD) currently require that the low desire must "cause marked distress or interpersonal difficulty." Among the problems with this definition of desire disorders, especially as it applies to women, were how to define *deficient* (especially when it is left to the clinician to decide) and whether sexual

fantasies and other signs of *intrinsic* desire for sex are the best ways to assess sexual interest (Basson, Althof, David, Fugl-Meyer, & Goldstein, 2004). Further discussion of issues associated with the definition of SIAD/HSDD will come later in this section.

Nature and Prevalence

It is hard to go through the checkout stand at the supermarket and not see several magazines (mostly aimed at women) whose covers scream about new ways to "spice up your love life." The frequency of encountering such articles implies that many people's love lives need some spicing up. Still, given the definitional limits of the *DSM's* criteria for SIAD/HSDD, it is not surprising that arriving at an accurate estimate of the number of men and women who experience distressingly low interest in sex has proven particularly challenging.

Among the questions asked of the interviewees in the NHSLS was the following: "During the last 12 months, has there ever been a period of several months or more when you lacked interest in having sex?" Thirty-three percent of women and 16% of men answered this question affirmatively. Others have reported comparable figures (e.g., Hayes, Bennett, Fairley, & Dennerstein, 2006; Mercer et al., 2003). Because the NHSLS respondents were not asked about individual or relationship *distress* associated with their lack of desire, it is not clear how many cases would have met *DSM-5* criteria for SIAD/HSDD. The most recent data on low sexual desire in women, from a nationally representative sample, indicated that while large percentages of premenopausal and menopausal women report low sexual desire (26.7% and 56.4%, respectively), much smaller percentages of women meet DSM criteria for a desire disorder; West et al., 2008). Still, it seems clear that many men, and even more women, experience substantial periods of time in which they feel little, if any, interest in sex.

While both men's and women's sexual function is often impacted by the context in which sex occurs (e.g., Perelman 2005c, 2007b), few would disagree with the belief that, in general, sexuality is more often contextual for women than it is for men. This is particularly the case with respect to female sexual desire (Bancroft et al., 2003; Basson, 2006). Researchers and clinicians generally accept absent, low, or diminished interest in sex to be the most common sexual concern expressed by women, irrespective of age. It is also the most controversial sexual complaint, with a heated debate currently centering on the issue of perceived inadequacies in the way in which this disorder has traditionally been conceptualized and defined (Basson, 2006). What was most controversial about the *DSM-IV-TR* diagnosis of HSDD for women was whether the relative or even absolute absence of sexual fantasies or other examples of *spontaneous yearning* for sex in a woman is evidence of low, or even nonexistent, sexual desire (Basson, 2006). In order to take into account the fact that many women may report experiencing desire only *after* sexual arousal, Basson (2010) has suggested that the most useful criteria for defining low sexual desire in women might be *both* "a marked absence of sexual thinking, fantasizing, self-stimulation, or conscious yearning for the physical experience. . .beyond a normative lessening with relationship duration and with age *and* the inability to trigger desire by becoming sexually aroused" (p. 164).

There is little argument that the *DSM-5* criteria for HSDD fits well for men with the disorder. Sexual fantasies and intrinsic interest in sex seem part of the makeup of most men from puberty through most of their lives, although there is usually a decrease in the frequency and urgency as men age. With women, however, many have argued that the situation is likely to be more complex. This issue is, perhaps, best understood as two overlapping distribution curves, with the median of the men's curve shifted toward a more easily engendered spontaneous sexual interest/desire than the median of the women's curve.

Basson (2006) and others have argued that overt interest in sex can be minimal or even absent in many women who otherwise report normal sexual functioning including average or above levels of sexual satisfaction. To make sense of this, Basson has focused on a distinction between *spontaneous* and *responsive* sexual desire. While women often report low levels (compared to that of men) of *spontaneous* desire, many of these women, nevertheless, describe themselves as being able to be sexually *responsive* to (i.e., aroused by) sexual or even nonsexual (e.g., romantic) overtures by their partner. That is, many women may sense desire only once the sexual experience is underway. Accordingly, it may have been inappropriate to label some women as suffering from

HSDD, although they might well have fit many of the *DSM-IV-TR* criteria for the disorder. The *DSM-5* criteria for SIAD attempt to take the lessons from this controversy into account in several ways: first, by using polythetic criteria (to reflect the fact that women present with different constellations of symptoms); second, by using duration criteria (such that normative fluctuations in sexual interest/arousal are not inadvertently pathologized); and third, by adding descriptive contextual factors (nodding to the reality that factors such as relationship quality may have a real and clinically significant impact on sexual interest/arousal). The basic *DSM-5* criteria for SIAD include (a) a lack of sexual interest/arousal, of at least 6 months' duration, manifested by at least three of five indicators that (b) cause clinically significant distress or impairment. Importantly, while "absent/reduced sexual/erotic thoughts or fantasies" are one of the five indicators, this need not be part of the woman's clinical presentation in order for her to be diagnosed with SIAD.

Again, this diagnostic approach is not without its critics, and concerns include how this new definition will impact diagnostic precision (DeRogatis, Clayton, Rosen, Sand, & Pyke, 2011).

A number of studies have demonstrated that women's motivations for having sex are more varied and sometimes quite different from those of men. In particular, compared to men's sexual motivations, women's motivations are more likely to be more frequently relationship focused (e.g., increasing emotional intimacy) and less related to physical urges. For example, Meston and Buss (2007) found that men were significantly more likely than women to endorse having sex for physical reasons, such as "I wanted to achieve an orgasm," and "It feels good." Women, in contrast, exceeded men on only 3 of over 200 reasons people gave for having sex, including "I wanted to express my love for the person" and "I realized that I was in love."

It seems clear that many of the reasons and incentives some women have for sexual activity have little to do with intrinsic physical demands for sexual release, and that their desire may be experienced only once sexual stimulation has begun and arousal is experienced. While arousal and desire can co-occur and reinforce each other for all people, this may be particularly true for women. Further, compared to men, women's subjective arousal appears to be far less associated with, and influenced by, genital vasocongestion

(Laan, Everared, van der Velde, & Geer, 1995), and their distress about sex less associated with specific desire, arousal, or orgasm difficulties (Bancroft et al., 2003).

The implications of these sex differences for the absolute and relative prevalence figures for desire disorders in men and women reported by studies such as the NHSLS are unclear. It is quite apparent, however, that by any current standard of defining hypoactive sexual desire, far more women than men present clinically with this complaint (Basson, 2006).

Sexual Desire Discrepancies

Because human beings differ substantially from each other in their levels of various appetites (e.g., food), it should come as no surprise that we also differ substantially in our levels of interest in and desire for sex. Given this, it is hardly unlikely that two people who happen to fall in love and choose to spend their lives together might differ in the frequency of partnered sex they desire, even though neither might meet diagnostic criteria for a sexual desire disorder. For example, imagine a couple that had found each other at around age 35 for both. The man reports that he has long desired, and engaged in, partnered sex about three to five times a week. His partner has, across several previous partners, never wanted sex more than about once a week. The absolute levels of these individuals' libido could not, in any meaningful sense, be labeled as abnormal, yet the *discrepancy* or disparity in their desire for sex could certainly be experienced as dysfunctional to the relationship.

No one knows how many couples experience a sexual desire discrepancy sufficient to cause significant relationship distress, but there must be many. Certainly some (perhaps most) such couples eventually work out a compromise they can both live with regarding the frequency of sex, just as they do with the many other issues with which their preferences may not coincide. In other couples, one partner ultimately determines sexual frequency, with the other having to "learn to live with it" as best he or she can. Still other men and women may turn to extra-relationship "affairs" or masturbation as means of coping with the discrepancy.

Although there is no *DSM* category for couples experiencing such desire discrepancies, the potential distress they can cause is no less important or less clinically meaningful. Empirical research has shown, for example, that partner incompatibility, measured in a variety of ways, is typically significantly correlated with women's sexual distress (Witting et al., 2008). However, given how little clinicians understand about the nature or causes of sexual drive, particularly when it occurs within the *normal* range, helping couples to accommodate to substantially different levels of this drive can be very challenging. Certainly a good place to start is to help such couples understand that there is nothing abnormal about their respective libidos, and that the only *problem* they have, albeit not an unimportant one, is how to manage their different levels of sexual appetite.

Etiology

The independent and interactive etiological contributions of organic (e.g., debilitating disease), psychological (particularly depression), and relationship (e.g., anger) factors in sexual dysfunctions described earlier in this chapter are applicable to both male and female sexual desire disorders. Desire disorders can also be the cause or the effect of other sexual dysfunctions in the individual, his or her partner, or both. Sex-negative messages while growing up or a history of sexual abuse is believed to be particularly likely to lead to a general disinterest in sex.

SIAD in Women

Given the relatively strong contextual nature of women's sexual desire (Bancroft et al., 2003; Basson, 2006), it is especially likely that (compared to men) their sexual disinterest is related to their particular life and relationship circumstances, particularly when desire was previously much higher. Stress associated with work, home, or child care responsibilities and negative feelings toward their partner often underlie many cases of a lack or loss of women's sexual desire. All too frequently, partners whose approach to sex is, purposely or not, self-centered, unskilled, uncommunicative, unromantic, or too genitally focused can leave women with little reason to appreciate or look forward to sexual encounters. Although several studies have examined the effects of age on sexual desire in women, no simple relationship has been identified (Hayes et al., 2007; Tessler-Lindau et al., 2007). The role of hormonal contraceptives is similarly complicated; in a recent review, Burrows and colleagues (2012) noted that small percentages of women report *increases or decreases* in sexual desire as an apparent result of contraceptive use. When decreases in sexual desire occur, it may be the result of the decrease in androgens associated with the increase in sex hormone-binding globulin (SHBG) that occur with oral contraceptives (Panzer et al., 2006). Additionally, a team conducting fMRI research has found that, when compared with women without sexual complaints, women with distress about low sexual desire spend significantly more time attending to their physiological responses to sexual stimuli (perhaps while spectatoring; Arnow et al., 2009), which raises intriguing questions for future research about whether such monitoring is a cause, product, or symptom of desire complaints.

HSDD in Men

Although less common and far less studied than in women, men too can experience "persistently or recurrently deficient (or absent) sexual/erotic thoughts or fantasies and desire for sexual activity" (*DSM-5*'s criteria for male HSDD; see p. 440), and for similar reasons (DeRogatis et al., 2012). Prevalence rates of HSDD for men under 45 years of age are estimated to be around 2% or less (*DSM-5*). However, this rate increases significantly with age, especially after age 60.

Men with HSDD (or their partners) often suspect testosterone insufficiency as the reason for their lack of sexual interest, although clear insufficiencies are rarely found. When a man reports low or absent desire and screening levels of testosterone *are* found to be low or absent, it is important to ensure the thorough assessment of endocrine function, particularly when desire was once much higher.

Because, in many cultures, men are *expected* to have a strong (perhaps even insatiable) sexual appetite, those with little or no demonstrable interest in partner-oriented sex frequently have partners (men or women) who are quite distressed. These partners often wonder whether their male partner (a) no longer finds them sexually appealing, (b) no longer loves them, (c) is having an affair, (d) is angry with them, or (e) is planning on leaving them. While any of these reasons could be playing a role in a man's change in desire, often none are involved.

Treatment

In general, treatment of sexual desire problems in men or women can be challenging, largely as a function of how little is understood about (a) the nature and development of normal sexual desire, (b) what constitutes abnormally low sexual desire or its etiology, and (c) how to change someone's level of sexual desire, particularly when that level has remained fairly constant across time, situations, and partners. Still, a recent meta-analysis of the treatment literature found psychological interventions for women with desire complaints were among the most reliably effective in the treatment of any of the sexual dysfunctions (Frühauf et al., 2013).

As with other male and female sexual dysfunctions, desire disorders come in different subtypes; it will be important to differentiate among them to maximize treatment effectiveness and efficiency. Desire disorders can be primary/lifelong or acquired, situational (e.g., partner specific), or generalized (occurring under all circumstances and conditions, including self-stimulation). In general, the prognosis is better for the acquired and/or situational variants than for those that are lifelong, generalized, or both (Maurice, 2006). As described earlier, the etiology of SIAD/HSDD is often as complex as, or more so, than that of other sexual dysfunctions, particularly so by the time the mental health clinician sees the person or couple. For these reasons, assessment will usually require a detailed psychological, relationship, and medical history, and may necessitate a medical workup. On a hopeful note, Frühauf and colleagues (2013) noted in their meta-analysis that psychotherapy for women with SIAD had some of the largest effect sizes for decreases in symptom severity ($d = .91$) and increases in sexual satisfaction ($d = .51$). Additionally, Brotto and Woo (2010) have described how CBT for low desire in both men and women can be augmented by mindfulness-based components. The practice of mindfulness is nonjudgmental awareness oriented to the present "here-and-now" moment (for a succinct description of mindfulness, see Brotto, 2011), and has been studied in the treatment of several other sexual dysfunctions, details of which will be provided in the relevant sections below.

For men, if testosterone insufficiency is evident, its supplementation can be helpful. However, adding testosterone for men with average levels of the hormone rarely increases sexual interest significantly. In addition, while useful clinically, there is a continuing debate within urological circles regarding the safety and efficacy of long-term testosterone augmentation (Morgentaler, 2007). Although also controversial, exogenous testosterone (via patches) has been demonstrated to be of some value for women who experience a decrease in sexual desire following surgically-induced menopause (e.g., after bilateral oophorectomy and hysterectomy; Braunstein et al., 2005; Shifren et al., 2000; Simon, 2005), for postmenopausal women with complaints regarding low desire (Davis & Braunstein, 2012), and for other groups of androgen-deficient women (Bolour & Braunstein, 2005; Burger & Papalia, 2006; Dennerstein, Coochak, Barton, & Graziottin, 2006). For premenopausal women with SIAD, the role of testosterone is still incompletely understood (Stuckey, 2008), but treatment with bupropion (Segraves, Clayton, Croft, Wolf, & Warnock, 2004) and apomorphine (Caruso et al., 2004) has shown some promise. There are other nonhormonal drugs in different stages of development for sexual indications, including bremelanotide, flibanserin, Librido, and Lybridos for HSDD; Femprox for FSAD, desvenlafaxine and vilazadone for FOD; and ospemifene for dyspareunia. The efficacy and safety of these drugs for a sexual indication, of course, require further documentation before any U.S. Food and Drug Administration (FDA) approval would be granted. However, given the contextual nature of the disorder(s) it is likely that the most effective treatment would be one that combines the use of such pharmaceuticals with appropriate and effective counseling. Finally, clinicians interested in treating individuals suffering from these conditions exclusively with pharmaceuticals would be well-served by familiarizing themselves with views that articulate the potential risks to the patient and society that medicalization of these biopsychosocial disorders may represent.

Male Sexual Arousal Disorder: Erectile Disorder

Nature and Etiology

For as long as clinicians and researchers have been tracking such information, erectile dysfunction (ED), formerly known as impotence, has been the most common sexual complaint of men seeking medical or psychotherapeutic help for a sexual problem. ED refers to a condition in which the man is unable to obtain or maintain a penile erection sufficient to engage fully in intercourse. The condition can range from the man only occasionally losing some of his erection during intercourse to his inability to achieve even a partial erection.

It is interesting to note that although ED may be less prevalent than premature ejaculation (PE), it is more likely to lead a man to seek professional treatment. There are likely several reasons for this. First, the inability to obtain or maintain an erection sufficient for intercourse is obviously a serious detriment to a man's ability to engage fully in couple-oriented sexual interactions. But nearly as important is the role that erections seem to play in many men's overall self-concept. In many cultures, including ours, a man's view of himself as generally capable, empowered, useful, or manly is often tied closely with his erectile capacity. Also, the widespread discussions of Viagra and the other ED medications by late-night TV personalities, as well as the ubiquitous presence of commercials for these products, have undoubtedly increased the number of men and couples seeking treatment for ED.

When a man becomes aroused, through either physical stimulation (e.g., he or someone else stroking his penis) or psychological stimulation (e.g., via fantasy or viewing sexually provocative material), smooth muscles within the chambers of the penis (i.e., the corpora cavernosa) relax, thereby permitting additional blood into these chambers, resulting in an erection. Erection requires that a man's hormonal, vascular, and neurological systems are functioning properly. Failure in any of these systems, whether due to disease (e.g., diabetes, multiple sclerosis [MS], hypertension, kidney disease, cardiovascular or prostate problems), injury (e.g., pelvic trauma), medical treatment (e.g., prostate surgery, dialysis), or medication (e.g., antidepressants, antihypertensives), can result in difficulty obtaining or maintaining a functional erection (Rosen, Wing, Schneider, & Gendrano, 2005). For this reason, and because of the many cardiovascular comorbidities associated with ED, it is essential that men experiencing ED, *particularly when it is chronic and not situation-specific*, receive a careful and thorough medical evaluation.

In addition to the many possible medical causes for ED, psychological factors are often of etiological significance. For example, when a man is depressed, anxious, angry, or distracted, the body's ability to direct blood flow to the penis can be compromised (Hale & Strassberg, 1990). Therefore, almost any significant intrapsychic or interpersonal source of subjective distress or relationship discord can impact erectile capacity. Men with a diagnosable anxiety disorder, particularly obsessive-compulsive disorder, or mood disorder, particularly major depression, are at higher risk for ED, independent of the effects of medication associated with the treatment of these emotional disorders. Other psychological risk factors include fear (e.g., of pregnancy, STIs, commitment); a history of physical, sexual, or emotional abuse; low self-esteem; and conflict over sexual orientation. Many relationship issues such as anger at, or loss of sexual interest in, one's partner can also underlie ED. It is important to note that psychological problems in the individual or the relationship can *result from* as well as *cause* ED (or any other sexual dysfunction).

Frequently, both medical *and* psychological factors combine to create or maintain erection difficulties. For example, even if a man's initial episodes of ED result from purely physiological factors (e.g., being too tired, having consumed too much alcohol, starting a new medication), once he has experienced erectile difficulty (as virtually every man has, on occasion), he now has a new reason to be concerned during sex: the possibility that he may again experience an episode of ED. This concern about one's ability to function sexually, termed *performance anxiety*, by Masters and Johnson (1970), can, by itself, be enough of a distraction and source of distress to maintain ED or any other sexual dysfunction indefinitely. This performance anxiety, which is very often a feature of ED by the time the man presents for treatment, is frequently a central target of treatment of the dysfunction. Also, it is increasingly recognized that various lifestyle choices can impact a man's sexual functioning (Millett et al., 2006). In particular, alcohol abuse, obesity, smoking, and lack of exercise have been implicated in the etiology and maintenance of ED (Rosen et al., 2005).

Finally, other sexual dysfunctions, in either the man or his partner, can be etiologically related to ED. For example, it is not uncommon for a man who has PE, or whose partner has little interest in sex, to eventually develop ED as a direct result of these other conditions (Hall, Shackelton, Rosen, & Araujo, 2010). Such comorbidities with ED can make accurate diagnosis and effective treatment more challenging.

Prevalence and Demographics

Published estimates of the prevalence of ED, like those for all other sexual dysfunctions, vary widely. In large part, this variability is a function of the ages of the men surveyed, the specific definition of the disorder used, as well as the sampling and data collection methods used (i.e., interview versus anonymous questionnaire). The National Health and Social Life Survey (Laumann et al., 1999) reported ED prevalence rates ranging from 5.6% for men ages 18 to 24, to just over 20% for men ages 50 to 59, with a rate across all ages surveyed (18 to 59) of 10.4%. In contrast, other large-scale surveys of American adult males have found overall prevalence rates ranging from 18.4% (Selvin, Burnett, & Platz, 2007) to 33.7% (Shaeer & Shaeer, 2012), whereas the Massachusetts Male Aging Study (Feldman, Goldstein, Hatzichristou, Krane, & McKinlay, 1994) found that about half of its sample of 1,290 men ages 40 to 70 reported some degree of ED, with about 35% reporting complete ED. All large-scale surveys in this area report a substantial positive relationship between age and rates of ED. This increase in ED with age is largely the result of the greater frequency of age-associated medical conditions that can impact sexual functioning, the larger number of medications taken by older men that can interfere with erections (Albersen, Orabi, & Lue, 2012), and androgen deficiency (Wylie & Kenney, 2010). Yet getting older does not necessarily result in ED. Many men are sexually potent well into their 70s or even beyond. Furthermore, men of any age will overwhelmingly support the statement, "I am not too old for sex" (Perelman, Shabsigh, & Lockhart, 2002). Rosen et al. (2005) offer the following summary of the evidence from epidemiological studies of ED. ED is highly prevalent in aging men, affecting approximately 50% of all men older than 60. For many men, ED first manifests itself in their 40s and 50s but increases markedly in frequency and severity after age 60. Yet the degree of bother associated with ED is inversely related to aging, so distress and treatment-seeking are usually higher in younger men and middle-aged men. Further, Rosen et al. concluded that the prevalence and incidence of ED are highly correlated with the presence of known risk factors and comorbidities, in particular cardiovascular comorbidities (e.g., hypertension, hypercholesterolemia), diabetes mellitus, the metabolic syndrome, depression, and lower urinary tract symptoms (LUTS).

Medical Treatments

Fortunately, the number and variety of ED treatments currently available make it very likely that, for almost any man with the disorder, irrespective of the problem's severity or etiology, significant help is possible. Of course, although many men with ED may be well on their way to recovery with a pill, a brief course of sex therapy, or both, others may require longer term individual or couples' therapy or more invasive medical and surgical procedures to effectively treat their ED (Hatzimouratidis & Hatzichristou, 2005).

Oral Medications By far the most popular and most preferred ED treatments are the oral PDE-5 inhibitors (sildenafil [Viagra], vardenafil [Levitra], tadalafil [Cialis]) that cause the smooth muscles of the penis to relax, facilitating maintenance of increased blood flow within the penis (Braun et al., 2000). These drugs, while highly effective, do not work for everyone. On average, about two-thirds of men with ED will be sufficiently responsive to at least one of these oral medications to engage in intercourse. The dopamine agonist, apomorphine, has also been found to be effective in treating ED (Eardley et al., 2010). Response to each of these medications often improves with practice, and some men respond to one when they have failed with another (e.g., Brisson, Broderick, Thiel, Heckman, & Pinkstaff, 2006; Dean et al., 2006). The more physiologically compromised the man (e.g., following radical prostatectomy or after many years of uncontrolled diabetes), the less likely that oral medications alone will be successful.

Primary care providers write most prescriptions for ED medications. Unfortunately, these providers usually lack the time for a thorough evaluation of all relationship issues, even if the partner (atypically) joins the patient for the office visit. Some clinicians effectively resolve this conundrum by spending an extra few minutes with the patient during the evaluation visit as well as recognizing the importance of follow-up and liaison consultation. They will ask the man questions not only about himself but also about his partner and their relationship (Perelman, 2003).

For men for whom the oral medications are unsuccessful or contraindicated (e.g., those taking nitrates for angina), several other medical treatments are available, including testosterone supplementation, vacuum devices, urethral suppositories, penile injections of vasodilators, penile implants, and vascular reconstructive surgery. Although often effective, all these medical and surgical treatments have side effects, sometimes quite serious ones, and should be undertaken only after a serious weighing of the pros and cons of each intervention.

Testosterone Replacement Therapy (TRT) Supplementation of exogenous testosterone via oral, injectable, and transdermal (patches or gel) administration can be effective in treating men whose ED is related to abnormally low testosterone production (Hajjar, Kaiser, & Morley, 1997). In addition to its effects on erectile capacity, testosterone replacement therapy (TRT) for hypogonadal men has also been demonstrated to have positive effects on mood, energy levels, and libido (Meikle, Arver, Dobs, Sanders, & Mazer, 1996; Shabsigh, 1997). Given the variety of causes of testosterone deficiency, a complete medical history, physical exam, and laboratory studies are critical. It is also important that men receiving exogenous testosterone be monitored regularly to ensure that its levels remain within normal limits.

Although TRT is probably safe for most hypogonadal men, there are several traditionally important contraindications for its use, including known or suspected carcinoma of the breast or prostate, and bladder outlet obstruction resulting from an enlarged prostate. However, as indicated earlier, these contraindications have become controversial in and of themselves over the past decade, as some advocates of testosterone augmentation even provide replacement therapy for men previously diagnosed with prostate cancer (Morgentaler, Lipshultz, Bennett, Sweeney, Avila, & Khera, 2011). Men who are attempting to father a child may also wish to avoid TRT because of its association with reduced sperm count.

Vacuum Devices Mechanical vacuum devices work by creating a partial vacuum around the penis, causing blood to be drawn into the penis, resulting in erection. The device consist of three parts: a plastic cylinder, which goes around the penis and against the stomach wall; a pump (both manual and electrical models are available, depending on how much one is willing to spend) to draw air from the cylinder; and a heavy elastic band, which, once the penis is erect, is placed around the base of the penis to maintain the erection (i.e., prevent blood from flowing out of the penis). The band is kept in place until intercourse is completed.

Although the use of vacuum devices is generally safe and there are no specific conditions that would necessarily interfere with their use, caution should be exercised by men if they are using blood thinners, have diminished penile sensation, or have a history of bleeding disorders, Peyronie's disease (abnormal and potentially painful curvature of the penis), or priapism (potentially dangerous erections lasting several hours or longer). However, vacuum devices are also being experimented on with men with Peyronie's disease to attempt to reduce the degree of curvature (Levine, 2007) and in penile rehabilitation following prostate cancer therapy (Pahlajani, Raina, Jones, Ali, & Zippe, 2012). The clinician is again reminded to review the relevant literature and consult with appropriate medical colleagues when the sexual disorder involves significant organic disease processes.

Typically, after a man has had some practice with a vacuum device, it will take him about 10 to 20 minutes to obtain an erection adequate for penetration. This time delay, the mechanical nature of the procedure, and the cosmetic changes in the penis (i.e., superficial vein swelling and a decrease in temperature) make vacuum devices unacceptable to substantial numbers of men who have tried this approach. Other reasons for discontinuation of the device include the failure to achieve adequate rigidity, penile pain, bruising, and failure to ejaculate (although orgasm is not usually impaired). Finally, the erection achieved with vacuum devices tends to hinge at the point of the constriction ring, resulting in an erection that is somewhat different from "normal." Despite the drawbacks associated with the use of vacuum devices, many men are sufficiently satisfied with this inexpensive and completely reversible procedure to continue its use (Baltaci, Avdos, Kosar, & Anafarta, 1995; Bosshardt, Farwerk, Sikora, Sohn, & Jakse, 1995; Levine & Dimitriou, 2001).

Although these devices are available in some stores and through the Internet, it is advisable for the man to have its use described and supervised by a sexual medicine physician before trying it at home. Also, it often requires some practice with the vacuum device before adequate erections can be achieved reliably.

Urethral Suppositories   Men who fail to achieve an adequate erection with one of the oral ED drugs may be helped by the medication prostaglandin (alprostadil) when administered via small pellets inserted into the urethra (marketed under the name MUSE). No needles are involved, and the process is preferred by some as less invasive than penile injections. The prescription medication is absorbed through the urethral mucosa and into the surrounding erectile tissue. Men for whom the procedure is effective report obtaining an erection within 10 to 30 minutes of application. It is recommended that the first dose of MUSE be administered in the physician's office. The most common side effect is burning in the urethra, but others (e.g., dizziness, minor bleeding, testicular aching) have also been noted. Some female partners of men using urethral suppositories have reported vaginal itching or burning. Because prostaglandin can cause uterine contractions, men having intercourse with pregnant women should not use these urethral suppositories unless condoms or other barrier devices are also used.

Penile Injections   This technique involves injection at-home of one or more drugs (e.g., papaverine, prostaglandin, phentolamine) directly into the corpus cavernosa of the penis of the ED patient, producing vascular dilation and a relaxation of smooth muscle. The result is an erection beginning in 5 to 20 minutes and lasting from 30 minutes to several hours, which may subside only as the drug wears off, as opposed to following orgasm. These injections have been shown to produce satisfactory erections in men with varied ED etiologies, with an overall success rate of over 75% (e.g., Alexandre, Lemaire, Desvaux, & Amar, 2007).

There are a number of side effects associated with penile injections, including pain (usually mild) at the site of the injection, bruising at the injection site (after repeated injections), infection, bleeding, dizziness, and rapid heart rate. Among the most serious possible side effects is corporal fibrosis (tissue scarring), which can develop into Peyronie's disease (Bella, Perelman, Brant, & Lue, 2007). Additionally, the patient should be warned about the possibility of priapism, which, while infrequent, occurs at a significantly greater rate than with PDE-5s (e.g., Viagra). Careful titration of the drugs used and the combining of small amounts of several drugs (rather than larger amounts of a single drug) can help reduce the number and seriousness of some of the side effects. The most serious possible side effects are more common among men who use injections more frequently and over a longer period of time. Because of its efficacy, and despite its many possible side effects, many men with ED report being quite satisfied with their use of penile injections (Alexandre et al., 2007).

Penile Prosthesis   A surgical implant (penile prosthesis), because of its invasiveness and cost, is usually used when a man's ED has failed to respond to alternative interventions. In such cases, the erectile problem usually has an organic etiology, such as a non-nerve-sparing radical prostatectomy for treating prostate cancer. A penile prosthesis is a surgically implanted device designed to provide an artificial erection. The most basic prosthesis consists of a pair of malleable rods surgically implanted within the penis' spongy tissue (i.e., the corpus cavernosa). This type of implant results in a penis that is always semi-rigid (i.e., essentially, a permanent erection). Alternative devices, commonly favored by men, are various hydraulic, inflatable prostheses (Dhar, Angemeier, & Montague, 2006). These systems include self-contained, simultaneously implanted reservoir systems from which the man can pump fluid into (and out of) inflatable chambers surgically implanted in his penis' corpus cavernosa. The result is an *on-demand* erection that is more natural and can be more easily hidden than a permanent erection. In general, patient satisfaction with implants is high (Lux, Reyes-Vallejo, Morgentaler, & Levine, 2007), although postoperative infections, mechanical failures, and other problems can occur, in addition to the fact that implants preclude spontaneously occurring erection.

Vascular Reconstructive Surgery   In cases in which a man's ED is the result of a blockage of blood vessels serving the penis, vascular reconstructive surgery (a bypass procedure) may be performed. Because of the technical difficulties, costs, and inconsistent outcomes, this procedure has been infrequently performed (Sohn, Hatzinger, Goldstein, & Krishnamurti, 2013). The surgery is most commonly performed, and is most likely to be effective, with young men whose ED results from trauma to the pelvic area.

Psychological Treatment

When ED is primarily the result of psychological factors (e.g., stress, performance anxiety, depression, relationship issues), sex therapy, psychotherapy, or couples' counseling may be necessary, and sometimes sufficient, to remedy the problem. If, after careful assessment, a man's ED appears psychological but independent of any significant psychopathology (e.g., major depression) or serious relationship problems, then a course of time-limited sex therapy may be an appropriate place to start (e.g., Althof, 2000; Kaplan, 1974). As described earlier, sex therapy for ED usually begins with sensate focus and other "non-demand" exercises that become more genitally focused and individualized as the treatment progresses.

For men whose ED appears to be secondary to serious psychopathology, individual psychotherapy is often the best course to follow. In most cases, this would mean that interventions aimed specifically at the sexual dysfunction would not take place until there has been substantial progress in treating the underlying psychopathology. Although medication may be necessary in the treatment of some forms of psychopathology (e.g., SSRI antidepressants for major depression), it will be important to use drugs that, while effectively impacting the psychological disorder, are the least likely to exacerbate the ED or to create additional sexual problems (Clayton et al., 2002; Rosen, Lane, & Menza, 1999). There are empirical data both supportive of (Heiman & Meston, 1997; Melnik, Soares, & Nasello, 2008) and nonsupportive of (Frühauf et al., 2013) the efficacy of psychological approaches to the treatment of ED.

For some men, relationship dynamics appear to be the primary cause of their ED. For these men, a course of couples' counseling may be a necessary first step in the treatment program. For example, there is probably very little to be gained (and perhaps much to lose) in attempting sex therapy in a relationship characterized by much anger, resentment, suspicion, or jealousy. Assuming that the dysfunctional relationship dynamics can be successfully addressed, sex therapy can then begin.

Finally, regardless of any medical approach that might be used as a primary intervention for a man's ED, some form of sexual counseling is likely to optimize response to treatment for both the man and his partner (Grellet & Faix, 2011; Leiblum, 2002; Perelman, 2005c). At the very least, the expectations these men and their partners have for any medical intervention should be thoroughly explored and, where appropriate, adjusted so as to be realistic. Further, medical interventions often require fairly strict adherence to protocols that are more likely to be followed when men or couples are monitored and supported. Couples may also benefit from sex counseling if an initial medical approach fails and other treatment approaches need to be considered.

Perhaps most importantly, a satisfying sexual relationship requires more than genitals that function well (Grellet & Faix, 2011). Simply put, there is more to good sex than a firm penis. Many couples wherein the man has suffered from ED for months or years have, either before or after the ED appeared, developed a sexual relationship that was dysfunctional in more ways than is evident from the presenting complaint. Sex counseling or therapy can help men or couples dealing with ED to integrate the medical treatment they may receive into a more meaningful, mutually satisfying, intimate relationship (Perelman, 2005a, 2007b).

Female Sexual Arousal Disorder: Female Sexual Interest and Arousal Disorder (SIAD)

Definition and Nature

In principle, when a woman experiences sexual arousal, there is an increase in blood flow to her genital area (vasocongestion) that helps to prepare her body for intercourse. Central to the changes taking place are the secretion of vaginal lubricants and the swelling of labial tissue. But the situation can be more complicated than this. Unlike men, women can demonstrate the physiological signs of arousal (i.e., vaginal swelling, lubrication) yet may experience little or no subjective arousal. Alternatively, they may feel sexually "turned on" without necessarily evidencing the physiological signs of sexual excitement.

DSM-5 explicitly incorporates female sexual arousal difficulties into the broader category of Female Sexual Interest/Arousal Disorder (SIAD) in several of the six possible symptoms of the disorder: "absent/reduced sexual excitement/pleasure during sexual activity (on at least 75% or more of sexual encounters)" and "absent/reduced genital and/or non-genital physical changes during sexual activity (on at least 75% or more of sexual

encounters)." The definition also includes duration and severity criteria, contextual factors, and associated features. We have explored earlier why HSDD was incorporated into SIAD; for a review of why FSAD was also incorporated into SIAD, see Graham (2010b).

Further, as discussed, many women may not experience sexual desire until they have first started experiencing sexual arousal (Basson, 2006). Women who are unable to experience sexual arousal are, therefore, at a particular disadvantage, because they may never experience much desire either, and the entire sexual response cycle never has a chance to get started or for its various components to become mutually reinforcing. It is not surprising then that, for women, sexual arousal difficulty is often comorbid with a desire problem or difficulty achieving orgasm. Basson (2010) has further described several themes that have emerged from her work with women with and without desire and arousal concerns, including (a) most women situate desire in the context of wanting to be emotionally close to a partner, (b) the environmental and relationship context in which sexual acts play out is of vital importance, (c) many women with low sexual desire or arousal describe difficulty being able to focus on in-the-moment physical and sexual sensations, and (d) some women become increasingly avoidant of sexual activity as desire or arousal complaints persist.

Until recently, the arousal component of SIAD has received much less attention in the empirical and clinical literatures than have desire or orgasm difficulties, despite the fact that many women of all ages complain of lubrication difficulties and lack of subjective arousal (West, Vinikoor, & Zolnoun, 2004). It is likely that the recent success of oral medications in the treatment of male sexual arousal disorder has inspired more clinicians, and especially researchers, to pay closer attention to the female sexual arousal complaints (Graham, Sanders, Milhausen, & McBride, 2004).

Prevalence

Because of the overlap of arousal and desire sexual difficulties for women, many symptomatic women and their treating clinicians have difficulty distinguishing these problems. As a result, it has been difficult to establish an accurate prevalence figure specifically and uniquely when HSDD and FSAD were treated as separate diagnostic categories in *DSM-IV-TR*. Prevalence estimates for arousal difficulties range from a low of the NHSLS's 21% to about 40% (West et al., 2004), and the shift to SIAD in *DSM-5* was in part to aid in the validity and reliability of diagnosing women with interest and/or arousal difficulties (see Brotto, 2010, for a thorough review of these issues). It remains to be seen, however, whether this change in *DSM-5* to merge desire and arousal complaints will be clinically useful; a recent study found that 75% of women reporting sexual difficulties failed to meet criteria for a *DSM-IV-TR*-defined sexual dysfunction, and even higher percentages of such individuals failed to meet criteria for a *DSM-5*-defined sexual dysfunction (Sarin, Amsel, & Binik, 2013).

Etiology

There are many identified and suspected possible causes for a woman's inability to reliably respond to sexual stimulation with the physiological or psychological signs of arousal. Because effective treatment can often be closely tied to accurate identification of the causes for the dysfunction, a woman experiencing difficulty achieving sexual arousal should receive a thorough psychosocial and medical evaluation by clinicians familiar with female sexual health issues. Because almost all of the physiological and medical, psychological, and relationship etiologies for SIAD overlap those described in the opening section of this chapter or in the following section on female orgasmic dysfunction, they will be only very briefly mentioned here.

Among the possible organic causes for SIAD are hormone deficiencies, substance or alcohol abuse, medications (e.g., SSRIs), diseases (e.g., diabetes, MS), and aging (Perelman, 2007a). Many women notice a change in their sexual functioning during and following menopause (brought about surgically or naturally), including vaginal dryness that can result from decreasing estrogen, progesterone, and testosterone levels (e.g., Goldstein, 2007; Nappi, Verde, Polatti, Genazzani, & Zara, 2002; Schwenkhagen, 2007).

The psychological causes of SIAD include sex-negative attitudes and beliefs (Nobre & Pinto-Gouveia, 2006), particularly those learned early; stress and fatigue (e.g., from home and child care, work); distraction (Dove & Wiederman, 2000); negative emotions (depression, anxiety, shame, guilt); history of abuse or assault; conflicts about and sexual orientation.

Relevant relationship issues include a lack of communication, romance, or intimacy; a self-centered or technically inept partner; boring and short sexual routines; and the loss of love, respect, or trust in a partner.

Treatments

Like most sexual dysfunctions, as there is no single cause for SIAD, there currently is no single solution that works for all women.

Medical   A wide variety of medical treatments have been found to have benefit for subgroups of women with SIAD (Perelman, 2007a). For some, nothing more sophisticated than an external lubricant may be all that is necessary. Change of medication (to one known to have fewer sexual side effects) can help, as can hormone replacement. Consistent with the estrogen-based treatments mentioned earlier, rigorous research has also indicated that for postmenopausal women, intravaginal application of dehydroepiandrosterone (a molecular precursor of both androgens and estrogens) can have a globally positive impact on sexual functioning, from physiological issues like vaginal dryness (Labrie et al., 2009b), to arousal (both sensation and lubrication) and orgasm (Labrie et al., 2009a). Topical alprostadil or Eros therapy (a vacuum-pump device designed to enhance clitoral engorgement; Billups et al., 2001) may increase blood flow to the clitoris and vagina. Finally, despite their efficacy in treating ED, oral medications have not, in general, been found to be particularly helpful in most cases of SIAD (Basson, McInnes, Smith, Hodgson, & Koppiker, 2002; Berman, Berman, Toler, Gill, & Haughie, 2003; Caruso, Intelisano, Lupo, & Agnello, 2001), including a drug (Flibanserin) specifically formulated to treat low desire or arousal (for a review of the FDS's conclusions regarding this drug, see Perelman, 2014). One exception to this is the suggestion in some studies that sildenafil may be helpful to some women with SSRI-induced sexual arousal disorder (e.g., Hensley & Nurnberg, 2002).

Psychological   Psychological treatment, via individual psychotherapy, relationship therapy, or sex therapy, usually involves identifying and addressing, if possible, the individual inhibitions (e.g., those associated with childhood abuse) and/or interpersonal factors (e.g., lack of sexual or emotional attraction to the partner, sexual boredom) that inhibit arousal and increase the conditions that facilitate it. Older women may need to learn to ask for more direct and intense stimulation (e.g., more foreplay, use of a vibrator) to reach a level of arousal that was more easily reached at a younger age. Two studies on the impact of mindfulness-based interventions on arousal complaints have also been promising. A group-based brief mindfulness intervention was tested in a sample of women presenting with arousal difficulties secondary to gynecological cancer; women reported significant improvements in a wide variety of indices of sexual functioning (Brotto et al., 2008). Another study compared CBT versus mindfulness-based therapy in a sample of women with histories of childhood sexual abuse and quite high levels of sexual distress, including arousal difficulties. While both groups benefitted from treatment, women receiving mindfulness training also reported significantly greater concordance between subjective and genital arousal post-treatment (Brotto, Seal, & Rellini, 2012).

Persistent Genital Arousal Disorder

A recently identified and uncommon female problem, one that does not yet appear in the *DSM*, has been termed *persistent sexual arousal* (PSA; Goldmeier & Leiblum, 2006; Leiblum, 2007) and, more recently, *persistent genital arousal disorder* (PGAD; Goldmeier, Mears, Hiller, & Crowley, 2009) or *restless genital syndrome* (ReGS; Waldinger et al., 2009). It is characterized by physical feelings of spontaneous and persistent genital arousal that occur without any physical stimulation or even conscious awareness of sexual desire, that can persist for hours, days, or (rarely) even longer, and do not subside with the woman's orgasm. These genital sensations are typically experienced as unwanted and distressing. Early theorizing postulated that PGAD had some overlap with hypersexuality (a condition characterized by high levels of psychological sexual desire and often accompanied by frequent sexuality activity; perhaps because some women with PGAD do engage in frequent sexual behavior in attempts at symptom relief; Anzellotti et al., 2010). Research indicates, however, that these are unrelated

conditions. In fact, many women with PGAD may begin to avoid sexual activity, in attempts to avoid triggering an episode of their uncomfortable and uncontrollable physiological symptoms.

Women with PGAD present with a level of dysfunction roughly between the levels found in healthy women and women presenting with complaints regarding low arousal (Leiblum & Seehuus, 2009). There is evidence that both withdrawal from SSRIs (Leiblum & Goldmeier, 2008) and physiological abnormalities such as pelvic varices and small fiber sensory neuropathy are associated with PGAD (for a helpful diagram of possible etiological pathways to PGAD, see Waldinger et al., 2009). One team of researchers recently found that 12 out of 18 women presenting with PGAD had sacral spinal cysts with the potential to have produced their PGAD symptoms (Komisaruk & Lee, 2012). One theoretical model posits that women with PGAD may be at the high end of a continuum of genital arousal in women, who then experience "cognitive narrowing" (i.e., an intensification of focus on their symptoms) that is maintained and perpetuated by anxiety (Leiblum & Chivers, 2007). At present, assessment for static mechanical hyperesthesia (Waldinger et al., 2009) and pelvic ultrasounds (Goldmeier et al., 2009) are recommended for diagnoses, and in cases where SSRI withdrawal is possibly causal, anecdotal evidence suggests that restarting a course of SSRIs may be useful (Goldmeier et al., 2009). Research in neuroscience may provide additional insight in the coming years. One fascinating case study has been reported in which a woman's PGAD appeared to be related to hyperconnectivity between several brain regions, and her symptoms remitted following antiepileptic therapy (Anzellotti et al., 2010). For interested readers, Facelle, Sadeghi-Nejad, and Goldmeier (2013) have written the most comprehensive review to date regarding characterization, etiology, and physiological, pharmacological, and psychological treatment options for PGAD.

Orgasm Disorders

Definition and Overview

Both men and women can experience adequate sexual desire, arousal and excitement yet still be unable to reach orgasm, be able to do so only in very restricted circumstances (e.g., masturbation) or with great difficulty, or (uncommonly) reach orgasm well before they would have preferred. These orgasmic disorders can be lifelong or acquired and generalized or situational. They are very common in both men and women; however, women experience a greater prevalence of delayed and inhibited orgasm, whereas for men, the prevalence of a rapidly occurring orgasm is greater (Bancroft et al., 2003; Perelman, McMahon, & Barada, 2004).

Orgasmic Disorders in Men

The various male orgasmic disorders are the most common sexual dysfunctions for men. The spectrum of these dysfunctions extends from premature ejaculation (PE) (termed early ejaculation in the *DSM-5*) through various degrees of delayed ejaculation (termed male orgasmic disorder in *DSM-IV* and delayed ejaculation in *DSM-5*; Perelman et al., 2004). This chapter uses a variety of conventional names describing male orgasmic or ejaculatory disorders. All investigators agree on what is being named, but they do not necessarily agree on the names themselves (Perelman et al., 2004).

Premature Ejaculation (aka Early Ejaculation)

Definition and Prevalence   According to the liberal criteria used in the NHSLS, PE is the most common male sexual disorder, estimated to affect as many as 30% of U.S. men (Laumann et al., 1994, 1999). However, more restrictive diagnostic criteria, such as that used by the *DSM-5*, limit the prevalence of PE to less than 5%. Although to date no serious studies have investigated "premature orgasm," or orgasm experienced as occurring too early, in women, very quick orgasms in women, with little buildup and negligible sensation and satisfaction, have been described. In men, PE is most often a lifelong condition, experienced from the very beginning of sexual activity; less often, it can develop after a period (of even years) of satisfactory sexual activity (Segraves, 2006; Waldinger, 2008).

PE has proven to be more difficult to define and assess than one might expect (Serefoglu & Saitz, 2012). *DSM-5* defines premature (early) ejaculation as the "persistent or recurrent pattern of ejaculation occurring during partnered sexual activity within approximately one minute of vaginal penetration and before the individual wishes it" (p. 443). The condition also has to have been present for at least 6 months and has to be experienced on all, or almost all, occasions. These definitional elements (particularly the 1-minute time frame) represent a significant change from the vagueness of previous *DSM* editions and may result in far fewer men meeting diagnostic criteria for the disorder.

The *DSM-5* criteria are quite close to those which emerged from the International Society for Sexual Medicine's meeting of leading experts on PE (Sharlip, Hellstrom, & Broderick, 2008, p. 340). Further, the *DSM-5* criteria are, in general, consistent with most operational definitions of PE described in the research literature, which, based on self-reports, include (a) self-reports of *time* from penetration to orgasm of less than 60–120 seconds, depending on the study; (b) degree of *satisfaction* with time to orgasm; and (c) sense of *control* over the occurrence of orgasm during sexual stimulation. These measures involve a great deal of subjectivity, or even guesswork, yet they form the basis of most of our empirical evidence regarding the nature of PE and the efficacy of various treatment approaches. Some researchers have gone beyond such self-reports and have included partner evaluations (e.g., Strassberg, deGouveia Brazao, Rowland, Tan, & Slob, 1999) and objective timing of orgasmic latency (e.g., Strassberg, Mahoney, Schaugaard, & Hale, 1990). Of note, *DSM-5* criteria for PE are exclusive to men engaging in heterosexual intercourse; a more inclusive definition might broaden penetration to include anal and oral penetration for men engaging in same-sex sexual acts.

Etiology   There is little doubt that there is a subgroup of men who are less able to tolerate significant levels of physical genital stimulation than most other men, and that these men also tend to report less control over the onset of their orgasm and less sexual satisfaction (Strassberg, Kelly, Carroll, & Kircher, 1987). What remains unclear and debated is (a) whether rapid ejaculators actually experience less control over their orgasm than other men, and (b) the etiology of rapid ejaculation (Buvat, 2011; Patrick et al., 2005; Patrick, Rowland, & Rothman, 2007; Waldinger, 2002).

Masters and Johnson (1970) argued that PE was the result of early (e.g., adolescent) ejaculatory experiences in which reaching a quick orgasm was of value (e.g., to avoid being interrupted by an adult while masturbating or during early attempts at intercourse). The primary flaw in this argument is that concerns about interruption during early sexual experiences are so ubiquitous that it is unlikely that such experiences would be far more characteristic of any one group of men than others. In contrast, Kaplan (1974) argued that premature ejaculators were, for psychological reasons (i.e., anxiety), less able than others to recognize the physical sensations that indicated one was precipitously close to reaching orgasm (i.e., the "point of ejaculatory inevitability"). As a result, these men could not learn to modulate and delay their level of arousal (e.g., through slowing down thrusting) until it was too late. However, there is compelling evidence that rapid ejaculators are no less able than others to assess their level of sexual arousal (Strassberg et al., 1987).

A number of other theories have been put forth over the years explaining PE as the consequence of a variety of intra- and interpersonal psychological problems, including unresolved Oedipal conflicts, anger, passive-aggressiveness, and performance anxiety. However, there is little if any empirical support for any of these hypotheses (Strassberg et al., 1987).

One of the more parsimonious etiological theories of PE presumes that the amount of physical genital stimulation most men can tolerate before their orgasmic reflex is triggered is primarily a *physiologically determined, normally distributed* threshold (Waldinger, 2011), tending to characterize each man from puberty on, across virtually all types of genital stimulation, including masturbation (Strassberg, 1994; Strassberg et al., 1990). Men on the low side of this distribution would represent those we refer to as premature ejaculators, whereas men at the other end of the distribution would represent those currently diagnosed as having an *orgasm phase disorder* (discussed later). Consistent with this hypothesis is the fact that in most clinically significant cases of rapid ejaculation, men report that they have always had the problem, across both time and partners. Further, these men reach orgasm more quickly than normal controls even in masturbation (Strassberg et al., 1990). Consistent with this physiologically determined explanation of most primary PE, there is some evidence for genetic influences in the development of the disorder (Buvat, 2011).

There is little doubt that men who reach orgasm relatively quickly report lower levels of *control* over the onset of their orgasms than do other men (e.g., Rowland, Cooper, & Slob, 1997; Rowland, Strassberg, deGouveia Brazao, & Slob, 2000; Strassberg et al., 1999). What remains unclear is whether this is simply a perceptual side effect of reaching orgasm so quickly. That is, many—perhaps most—men whose orgasmic latency during intercourse is at least average still report that they wish they could last longer during intercourse (e.g., Grenier & Byers, 1997). If these men possessed substantially more genuine control over their level of arousal than rapid ejaculators, why are they not able to prolong intercourse as long as they would like, or at least longer than they currently can? The higher (relative to PEs) levels of control these men report may not represent greater actual control, but just the *perception* of greater control, owing to their higher arousal threshold and therefore their ability to last longer during intercourse.

There are many reasons why any man would prefer to have substantial control over the timing of his orgasm. Such control could allow him to extend his arousal as long as he desired, including the ability to engage in intercourse long enough so that his female partner has the best opportunity to experience orgasm during the act. Yet, because intercourse appears to be a generally more efficient technique for men to reach orgasm than for women, many men (including many non-rapid ejaculators) will have difficulty persisting long enough for their partner to climax at or before the time that they do. For rapid ejaculators (per multiple definitions), this is particularly challenging, as their average time to orgasm during intercourse, typically 2 minutes or less, is substantially less time than most women typically require (Patrick et al., 2005; Waldinger & Schweitzer, 2006a, 2006b).

Many men, including those whose ejaculatory latencies fall well within the normal range (approximately 4 to 7 minutes), have learned a variety of cognitive and behavioral techniques by which to prolong their sexual arousal without reaching orgasm. The cognitive techniques usually involve some sort of distraction, attempting to focus their attention on something other than the psychological state or physical sensations associated with their current sexual interaction. Although there is little direct empirical evidence of the effectiveness of distraction during intercourse, the virtual universality of the use of the technique and extensive anecdotal data suggest that it probably is of some value to at least a significant number of men, both premature ejaculators and otherwise. But even when effective, its use comes at a price, as it may interfere with attention to the ideation and sensations that make the sex act so pleasurable. Imagining one's partner as unattractive or STI infected, doing math problems or thinking about one's hated boss or financial woes might well help to prolong the sex, but just what is it then that one has now managed to prolong? For those men with a stronger biological predisposition to PE, distraction can be antithetical to success, as they are even less likely to note and respond to premonitory sensations and thus be even less likely to be able to delay the onset of orgasm.

Cognitive distraction is not the only way men have learned to control their sexual arousal prior to orgasm. Simply slowing or stopping thrusting, penile withdrawal, changing intercourse positions, thrusting in a "circular motion," or ejaculating prior to intercourse are all self-reported to prolong intercourse (e.g., Grenier & Byers, 1997). It is not surprising that some men with a history of PE eventually go on to develop ED as a direct result of the anxiety, disappointment, and discouragement they experience from their low orgasmic threshold.

Treatment   It is clear that only a small percentage of men with PE, both in absolute terms and compared to those with ED, ever seek treatment for it, despite the increasing availability of effective treatments (Waldinger, 2008). There are likely several reasons for this. Most men with PE are able to engage in penetrative sexual acts (albeit briefly) and achieve orgasm during such acts. Consequently, many of these men may not see their short orgasmic latency as a dysfunction since they are unaware of how long other men are able to last or because their own sexual satisfaction is not necessarily impacted. Even men concerned about their partner's lack of orgasm during the brief period of intercourse may view this as the woman's problem, not theirs. Still other men with PE are unaware of the existence of effective treatment and others are uncomfortable at the prospect of disclosing their sexual problem to anyone, even a health or mental health practitioner.

Masters and Johnson (1970), Kaplan (1974), and others have popularized the squeeze (Semens, 1956) and stop-start techniques as behavioral treatments for clinical levels of PE. Whether these procedures may lengthen intercourse simply because of the delays or reduction in stimulation they produce (i.e., by slowing down or stopping intercourse) or whether they actually change the orgasmic threshold (i.e., the absolute amount of physical stimulation a man can sustain without reaching orgasm) remains unclear. It should be noted that while there is substantial clinical and some research evidence (Berner & Gunzler, 2012; Metz, Pryor, Nesvacil, Abuzzahab, & Koznar, 1997) demonstrating the efficacy of these techniques, at least in the short term, a recent empirical review failed to support such efficacy (Frühauf et al., 2013). While some cognitive approaches to treating PE have also been described, their effectiveness remains to be demonstrated empirically (Rowland & Cooper, 2011).

Other procedures suggested by therapists for treating serious PE also rely on reducing the level of physical stimulation experienced by the man during intercourse and are identical to techniques many men seem to learn on their own. These include (1) experimenting with different intercourse positions to find one that may produce less stimulation (e.g., female superior or side-by-side positions), (2) using one (or more) condoms, or (3) using a desensitizing cream. As mentioned, when considering these interventions, one must weigh the relative costs and benefits associated with the lengthening of intercourse while reducing arousal during the process. This is especially true for the last two of these three techniques.

The newest of the approaches used clinically in the treatment of serious PE is medication. For many years, those prescribing psychoactive medications for psychiatric problems noted that, in many instances, these drugs interfered with some aspect of the patient's sexual functioning, usually reducing their ability to obtain or maintain an erection or to achieve orgasm. In particular, the SSRI class of antidepressants (e.g., Prozac) was well-known for lengthening the time it took a man to reach orgasm, in many cases preventing him from doing so (e.g., Rowland et al., 1997; Strassberg et al., 1999). At the same time, a number of clinical reports began to appear in which clinicians described success in the off-label use of antidepressant medication to treat PE, using an often-unwanted drug side effect as a desirable therapeutic effect. These case reports were eventually followed by sophisticated, double-blind, placebo-controlled studies in which the efficacy of antidepressants (e.g., SSRIs, clomipramine) in treating PE was clearly demonstrated (e.g., Strassberg et al., 1999). There can be differential effects on ejaculatory latency of these various medications, as well as different side-effect profiles (Montejo, Llorca, Izquierdo, & Rico-Villademoros, 2001; Waldinger & Olivier, 2004; Waldinger, Zwinderman, & Olivier, 2004). Recently, considerable commercial effort has been expended in the development of the SSRI dapoxetine, which, though currently lacking regulatory approval for use, reportedly delays ejaculation with less adverse events than those with other serotinergic agents (Hatzimouratidis et al., 2010; Pryor et al., 2006; Waldinger et al., 2004). This may be due to its rapid metabolism within the body. There is also very preliminary evidence that injections of hyaluronic acid can be effective in increasing ejaculatory latency (Littara, et al., 2013); however, less intrusive methods are much more likely to be practiced by most physicians and sex therapists.

Delayed Ejaculation

Delayed ejaculation (DE; termed male orgasmic disorder [MOD] in *DSM-IV-TR*) is probably the least common and least understood of all the male sexual dysfunctions (Perelman et al., 2004). DE refers to an alteration of ejaculation and/or orgasm that ranges from varying delays in ejaculatory latency to a complete inability to ejaculate. This difficulty or inability must occur despite adequate sexual stimulation and a conscious desire to achieve orgasm. Confusion regarding DE is partially related to the fact that, though usually occurring simultaneously, ejaculation and orgasm are separate physiological phenomena. Orgasm is usually coincident with ejaculation, but is a central sensory event that has significant subjective variation. For purposes of simplicity, in this chapter, orgasm and ejaculation are used synonymously when discussing DE. In the *DSM-5*, the diagnosis of DE requires that distress be associated with the undesired marked infrequency of absence of ejaculation.

Prevalence   Although DE is the least common male sexual dysfunction in most clinical settings, the NHSLS still found that nearly 8% of men reported the "inability to achieve an orgasm" over at least a 2-month period in the previous year. Other surveys have generally reported prevalence figures near or somewhat lower than this (e.g., Rosen & Leiblum, 1995). Kaplan (1974) classified male orgasmic disorder into four severity categories: (1) *mild*—men who can achieve orgasm during vaginal intercourse, but only under certain conditions (e.g., only in certain positions or only after an unusually long time); (2) *moderate*—men who cannot ejaculate during intercourse but can via other forms of partner stimulation (e.g., fellatio or manual stimulation); (3) *severe*—men who can achieve orgasm only when alone; and (4) *most severe*—men who are unable to ejaculate under any circumstances. As with most disorders, the milder forms of MOD are more common than the more severe forms. MOD can be secondary to ED or a partner's sexual problem (e.g., SIAD).

Although men with DE typically have no difficulty attaining or maintaining erections and can engage in intercourse longer than their nondysfunctional counterparts, thereby providing their partners with extended stimulation and a greater chance to reach their own orgasm, the men and their partners rarely see this as an advantage (Apfelbaum, 2000). In fact, most such couples find sex hard work, a "chore" that, at best, is anticipated with very mixed feelings (Hartmann & Waldinger, 2006). Further, partners of men with MOD are inclined to blame themselves for the problem. Given men's reputation for reaching orgasm quickly and reliably, it is easy for a woman to assume that her partner's inability to do so must be the result of his finding her inadequately attractive, sexy, or appealing or proof of her poor technique. Perhaps as a result of these potential difficulties, men with DE typically report less coital activity, higher levels of relationship distress, greater sexual dissatisfaction, more anxiety about their sexual performance, lower subjective arousal, and more general health issues when compared to sexually functional men (Abdel-Hamid & Saleh, 2011; Rowland, Van Diest, Incrocci, & Slob, 2005).

Etiology   There are a number of possible organic causes of delayed orgasm (usually leading to generalized MOD), including hypogonadism, thyroid disorders, pituitary conditions (e.g., Cushing's syndrome), diseases affecting the nervous system (e.g., strokes, MS, diabetic neuropathy), prostate surgery, and substance or alcohol abuse. Several classes of medication can also impact orgasmic capacity, including tricyclic antidepressants (e.g., clomipramine), phenothiazines (e.g., chlorproma-zine), thiazides, and beta-blockers (Montejo et al., 2001). So common are the effects on orgasm of some of these drugs (e.g., clomipramine) that, as described previously, they are used therapeutically to extend the ejaculatory latency of men with PE (Strassberg et al., 1999).

The length of time a male can engage in vaginal intercourse before triggering his orgas-mic reflex (intravaginal ejaculatory latency time [IELT]) varies across a largely biologically deter-mined continuum for both humans (Waldinger & Schweitzer, 2006a, 2006b) and other animals (Waldinger & Olivier, 2005). Earlier, we argued that for many men with lifelong, generalized PE, the condition probably represents a physiological fact of life: These men simply have a lower orgas-mic threshold than the average man. Similarly, it seems likely that for many men with lifelong generalized (i.e., occurring with both self- and partner stimulation) MOD, their relatively long ejaculatory latencies result from a physiologically determined high orgasmic threshold (Hartmann & Waldinger, 2006; Perelman, 2006b; Perelman & Rowland, 2006; Strassberg et al., 1990). Many of these men may simply fall at the other end of the spectrum from those with PE, and may present with significant distress when their time to orgasm is significantly longer than that for not only most men but also their female partners. It is important to also note that IELT informa-tion alone may not capture the psychological component of MOD (Jern, Gunst, Sandqvist, Sandnabba, & Santtila, 2010); the same IELT may feel more or less under an individual's con-trol depending on other factors (e.g., what their preferred time to orgasm would be for a particu-lar sexual encounter).

Many men with secondary MOD can mas-turbate to orgasm, whereas others, for multiple reasons, will not or cannot. Interestingly, corre-lational evidence suggests that masturbatory fre-quency and style may be predisposing factors for MOD, because a substantial portion of men who present with coital delayed orgasm typically report high levels of activity using an idiosyncratic mas-turbatory style (e.g., an especially firm hand grip; Perelman, 2005b, 2006b), possibly with related penile irritation (e.g., skin abrasion as a result of an especially firm hand grip) as well (Abdel-Hamid & Saleh, 2011). For the many men who only have difficulty achieving orgasm during intercourse,

the orgasmic threshold or other physiological ele-ments are less likely to be etiologically significant. Among the psychological features suggested in such cases are a variety of fears (of loss of control, pregnancy, STDs, castration, incest), paraphilic interests, abuse history, and conflicts over sexual orientation (Hartmann & Waldinger, 2006). Relationship issues can include anger at or loss of sexual interest in one's partner. There also appears to be increased likelihood of MOD as men age (Blanker et al., 2001). In some cases, age related physical changes in a man's partner (e.g., a vagina loosing much of its ability to contract around a penis) can make it more it more difficult for him to reach orgasm during intercourse, particularly when associated with his requiring more intense penile stimulation as a function of his aging.

Female Orgasmic Disorder

Definition

The *DSM-5* definition of female orgasmic disorder (FOD) requires delay in, absence of, or markedly reduced orgasmic sensations for at least 6 months and occurring in at least 75% of occasions of sex-ual activity.

The diagnosis also now contains a variety of specifiers (e.g., lifelong versus acquired). Interested readers may consult Graham (2010a) for a detailed review of the research leading to the decision to update the definition from *DSM-IV-TR* to include more specifiers regarding the subjective experience of orgasm.

Prevalence

In clinical settings, many women report having difficulty experiencing orgasm reliably. For some, this difficulty is experienced only during inter-course, whereas for others it extends to all forms of partner stimulation and even to masturbation when alone. In the NHSLS (Laumann et al., 1994, 1999), *problems reaching orgasm* in the past year were reported by 24% of the women surveyed. By this definition, however, many women whose sexual functioning is quite normal could be inap-propriately described as dysfunctional. The reason for this is that, in several important ways, women are at an orgasmic disadvantage (compared to men) during heterosexual intercourse. For many, perhaps most, women, intercourse alone fails to provide a level of sexual stimulation sufficient to reach orgasm. This is likely the result of a penis in a vagina failing to provide the clitoris, the source of most women's most intense sexual stimulation, with sufficient direct contact. Further, even for those women for whom intercourse alone could, if engaged in long enough, provides adequate stimulation for orgasm, their male partners are often unable to maintain active thrusting sufficiently long, before they reach orgasm, for the female to reach orgasm.

This largely physiologically determined male–female difference in the relative effectiveness of coitus in evoking an orgasm is the source of many couples' distress, leaving many men and women feeling disappointed and defining themselves or each other as sexually dysfunctional, despite the fact that this difference is quite statistically commonplace and can be viewed as *normal*. Unfortunately, many couples fail to recognize the normality of this male–female difference.

There are, of course, women who truly experience an orgasmic dysfunction—having difficulty reaching orgasm reliably with *any* type of partner sexual stimulation or, in some cases, even with self-stimulation. It is unclear how many of the 24% of women in the NHSLS who reported orgasm problems would meet this stricter criterion.

Etiology

One particularly important consideration regarding female orgasmic difficulties is emerging research on population-based female orgasmic rates. One recent study of a large sample of adult female twins, for example, found that orgasm rates are highly heritable, but are at best only weakly correlated with a variety of other sexual traits (e.g., libido and frequency of sexual fantasy), and the authors noted that these findings cast doubt on the idea that low rates of orgasm, especially during partnered sexual activity, are biologically unusual (Zietsch, Miller, Bailey, & Martin, 2011). Population rates aside, however, any of the psychological (e.g., depression, abuse history) or relationship (e.g., anger) factors described earlier in this chapter can be, and often are, at issue in a woman's orgasm disorder, as can any of the possible organic causes responsible for male orgasmic disorder described earlier. Unique to women are the orgasmic and other sexual problems associated

with the medical and psychological consequences of mastectomy and medically induced menopause (e.g., Kedde, van de Wiel, Weijmar Schultz, & Wijsen, 2013).

Some have said that women are more complicated sexually than are men. There is certainly some truth to this generalization, particularly regarding the ease of orgasmic response. For most men, on most occasions, applying friction to the penis (via his partner's hand, mouth, vagina, etc.) will be sexually arousing and likely to result in an orgasm. For women, it can be more complicated, in several respects. Women can differ dramatically from one another in the particular type of stimulation that might be most effective. Further, any given woman might find that the most effective form of stimulation can change from one day to the next or even from one moment to the next within a sexual episode. For a woman to maximize her sexual arousal, therefore, she must (a) know what will arouse her, (b) be willing and able to share this information with her partner, and (c) have a partner who cares about her sexual pleasure and is (d) willing and able to "hear" her and behave accordingly (Kelly et al., 1990). Difficulty at any of these steps can easily interfere with a woman's chances of experiencing sexual arousal sufficient for orgasm.

Unfortunately, some women have never learned what works best for them sexually (i.e., produces the most sexual arousal). Such learning usually takes place via self-stimulation or experimentation with types (i.e., places in and around their vulva, pressures, and timing) of partner stimulation—opportunities available to most women but not always explored as they are by most men. Among women who have learned what constitutes effective sexual stimulation for them, not all become comfortable sharing such information with their partners. For heterosexual couples in particular, some women will not ask for what they want sexually because they perceive that their male partners are uncaring about the woman's sexual needs, whereas others see their male partners as hypersensitive about such feedback, believing that the man will see himself as a poor lover for not instinctively knowing what she wants or needs. And, for women of all sexual orientations, there are those who fear the lack of control they may experience during orgasm and (consciously or not) inhibit the *letting go* that is often necessary to achieve orgasm. Relatedly, emotional intelligence (i.e., skills relating to identifying and regulating the emotions of oneself and others) is positively correlated with both frequency of orgasm during intercourse and masturbation (Burri, Cherkas, & Spector, 2009), thus, relative deficits in emotional intelligence may be worthy therapy targets for women with orgasmic complaints.

Some partners of women who are anorgasmic in partnered sex are, in fact, ill-equipped as lovers. Many of these men are simply uninformed about what their female partner or women in general need sexually and may be unaware of their ignorance. Others are uninformed, know it, but are unwilling to "ask directions" because they think they are *supposed* to know what to do. Some male sexual partners may be selfish, caring little about anything but their own sexual pleasure. As a final note, female orgasm rates during partnered non-intercourse sexual activity (e.g., cunnilingus) and individual masturbation are strongly correlated ($r = .50$), but both those orgasm rates correlate only weakly with orgasm rates during intercourse ($r = .22$ and $r = .16$, respectively; Zietsch, et al., 2011). Thus, if a heterosexual couple's goal is female orgasm during intercourse, even women who are orgasmic in other domains may have difficulty translating that orgasmic potential to intercourse.

As noted previously, relationship dynamics can play an important role in many cases of sexual dysfunction. For many women, it can be difficult to give herself sufficiently to her partner and the sexual experience if she is conflicted in her feelings toward her partner. Experiencing anger, jealousy, distrust, or fear toward a partner, or perceiving the partner to be insensitive, unsupportive, or uncommitted can easily interfere with a woman's sexual pleasure sufficiently to inhibit orgasm.

Treatment

The treatment of male or female orgasmic disorder is usually dependent on the specific nature of the dysfunction (e.g., under what circumstances the person can and cannot reach orgasm) and the identified or suspected etiological elements (e.g., intrapsychic versus interpersonal dynamics; Meston, 2006). First, of course, organic factors that might be responsible for the disorder should be ruled out or addressed; as an example, Corona and colleagues (2010) noted that evaluations of hormonal milieu can be useful for men presenting with either PE or DE. Individual therapy or couples' counseling may

first need to occur before the sexual disorder can be the therapeutic focus. Communications training, sex education, especially helping the couple to appreciate what is normal, and sensate focus exercise are frequently used.

A recent clinical trial explored the utility of bupropion in treating men with lifelong DE, but results revealed only limited benefits (Abdel-Hamid & Saleh, 2011). For men who experience DE as a result of prostate cancer or its treatment, vibrators may be of use in amplifying stimulation (Nelson, Ahmed, Valenzuela, Parker, & Mulhall, 2007; Perelman, 2008; Tajkarimi & Burnett, 2011).

Nathan (2010) wisely observed that many women presenting with orgasmic dysfunction did not meet *DSM-IV-TR* criteria for female orgasmic disorder, which specified that orgasmic dysfunction could only be diagnosed in the presence of adequate sexual stimulation, precisely because their sexual activities were marked by inadequate sexual stimulation. The removal of stipulations about sexual stimulation from the diagnosis in *DSM-5* may make classification easier, but clinicians will still encounter many cases of female orgasmic disorder in the context of inadequate sexual stimulation. For women who present with primary, generalized orgasmic dysfunction, treatment often begins with a program of physical and psychological self-exploration, designed to help her identify, first on her own, then with her partner, what types of stimulation produce the most arousal (Barbach, 1975; Heiman & LoPiccolo, 1988). Frühauf and colleagues (2013) also reported in their meta-analysis that, like women with SIAD, women with FOD typically respond well to treatment, with moderate effect sizes (both $ds = .46$) for both reductions in symptom severity and increases in sexual satisfaction across over a dozen studies. When the woman or man is able to reach orgasm under at least some conditions, therapy is often directed at helping the patient to transfer, through successive approximations, this responsiveness from one condition to others.

Sexual Pain Disorders

Nature and Definition

In the *DSM*, sexual pain disorders are listed under sexual dysfunctions. While the experience of pain during intercourse, a condition much more common among women than men, can obviously interfere with satisfying sex, considering these disorders as *sexual dysfunctions* has recently come under some criticism. In particular, Binik (2005) has argued that disorders such as dyspareunia and vaginismus have more in common with pain disorders affecting other parts of the body than they do with other sexual problems and should, therefore, be conceptualized and treated as are other pain disorders. This interesting idea has generated substantial discussion in the literature (e.g., Strassberg, 2005).

Female Genitopelvic Pain/Penetration Disorder

DSM-IV-TR distinguished between two sources of female pain during intercourse, vaginismus and dyspareunia. *Vaginismus* was defined as the persistent or recurrent involuntary contraction of the musculature of the outer third of the vaginal barrel when penetration (e.g., by a penis, tampon, speculum) is anticipated, making intercourse painful or impossible. *Dyspareunia* was defined as pain on intercourse from some cause other than vaginismus. However, in practice, this diagnostic distinction was often difficult or impossible to make reliably (Binik, 2010a, 2010b).

In contrast, *DSM-5* has combined these conditions under female genitopelvic pain/penetration disorder (GPPPD), involving, on at least half of occasions, the inability to have vaginal intercourse, pain during intercourse, marked fear of intercourse, and/or marked tensing of pelvic muscles during attempted vaginal penetration.

Of note, *DSM-IV-TR* (but not *DSM-5*) required that the source of the pain be identified as organic, psychological, or mixed, but in reality such distinctions are often very difficult if not impossible to make (Payne, Bergeron, Khalife, & Binik, 2005). As a final observation on nomenclature, GPPPD represents a conscious shift away from the term *sexual pain*, which, as others have noted, "implies that sex is the originating problem rather than the context in which the pain is usually, although not always, provoked" (Bergeron, Meana, Binik, & Khalifé, 2010, p. 197).

The most common forms of GPPPD fall under the category of vulvodynia (Harlow & Stewart, 2003), characterized by chronic vulvar discomfort or pain (e.g., burning, stinging, irritation) that is not the result of infection or skin disease.

Although burning sensations are the most common symptom, the type and severity of symptoms are highly individualized. Pain may be constant or intermittent, localized or diffuse. Careful diagnosis is particularly important and requires more than psychological evaluation. Bergeron et al. (2010) recommend three physical tests as well: "(1) a careful gynecological history, (2) a cotton-swab palpation of the vestibular area with the woman rating her pain at various sites, and (3) vaginal and cervical cultures to exclude the possibility of infection-related pain" (p. 203).

There are two main subtypes of vulvodynia. Generalized vulvodynia is pain in different areas of the vulva (e.g., the labia, vestibule, clitoris, mons pubis, perineum, inner thighs) at different times. Vulvar pain may be constant or occur intermittently. Touch or pressure may or may not prompt it, but can make the pain worse. Vulvar vestibulitis syndrome (VVS) is pain only in the vestibule (i.e., the entrance to the vagina). Often a burning sensation, this type of vulvar pain comes on only after touch or pressure, such as during intercourse, and, as such, is also referred to as provoked vestibulodynia (PVD). For some women with particularly severe VVS, even exercising (e.g., bike riding or jogging) can be quite painful. In acute forms of VVS, it is sometimes possible to identify a precipitating cause, whereas in chronic cases, etiology is very difficult to determine.

There are many possible medical conditions that can result in painful intercourse, including vaginal birth delivery (Paterson, Davis, Khalifé, Amsel, & Binik, 2009), vaginal dryness (common in postmenopausal women), vulvovaginal atrophy (VVA; thinning of the vaginal lining in postmenopausal women), side effects of drugs such as antihistamines and tamoxifen, an allergic reaction to spermicides or douches, endometriosis, a history of recurrent yeast infections, certain vaginal skin diseases (e.g., lichen planus), urinary tract infections, STDs (e.g., genital herpes), and genetic susceptibility to inflammatory disorders. Several good reviews of this research have been published (Latthe, Mignini, Gray, Hills, & Kahn, 2006; Payne, Binik, Amsel, & Khalife, 2005; Pukall, Payne, & Kao, 2005; Weijmar Schultz et al., 2005). For many of these medical corollaries of sexual pain (e.g., endometriosis and menopause), pain may be a result of estrogen levels that are insufficient for generating the genital vasocongestion necessary for sexual activity to be comfortable (Basson, 2010). It is also worth noting that sexual pain often understandably co-occurs with other sexual problems; for example, post-menopausal women with VVA are several times more likely to also suffer from sexual dysfunction than women without VVA (Levine, Williams, & Hartmann, 2008). Several studies have also indicated that, as is the case with other chronic pain problems, once pain is experienced, it can be perpetuated and amplified by pain-related psychological phenomenon such as anxiety about pain and pain catastrophizing (Desrochers, Bergeron, Khalifé, Dupuis, & Jodoin, 2009; Meana & Lykins, 2009) and anxiety reduction associated with avoidance of sexual activity.

For coital pain not associated with a medical condition, a number of risk factors have been suggested, including childhood physical or sexual abuse or adult sexual trauma (Binik, Meana, Berkely, & Khalife, 1999; Latthe et al., 2006), inadequate foreplay, female sexual interest or arousal disorder, and an extended time period without intercourse. A number of these risk factors are supported by empirical research, including having a history of sexual abuse, relationship distress, and psychological characteristics like catastrophic thinking and trait anxiety (Kao et al., 2012; Landry & Bergeron, 2011; Leclerc, Bergeron, Binik, & Khalifé, 2010). Recent research has also emphasized the potential importance of both automatic and deliberate disgust-based reactions to sexual acts among women with sexual pain (Borg, de Jong, & Schultz, 2010).

For vaginismus, etiology is believed to be similar to that of other causes of GPPPD and include negative sexual attitudes, religious orthodoxy, and lack of sex education. Childhood sexual abuse has clearly been empirically demonstrated to be a risk factor for vaginismus (Reissing, Binik, Khalife, Cohen, & Amse, 2004) and, as with sexual pain more broadly, disgust-based reactions may contribute an important psychological component (Reissing, 2011; van Overveld et al., 2013). Additionally, both harm avoidance and pain catastrophizing may play significant roles in the etiology and maintenance of vaginismus (Borg, Peters, Schultz, & de Jong, 2012).

Treatment of Sexual Pain Disorders

Given their nature, it is critically important that the assessment of all female sexual pain disorders include a careful and comprehensive gynecological exam. Because they will often be quite fearful of such exams, women with these disorders may need to be prepared for a gynecological assessment. Further, a practitioner skilled in these assessments and sensitive to the patients' concerns should perform the evaluation.

There is much similarity in the variety of approaches that have been described in the treatment of all the female sexual pain disorders. Both medical and psychosocial (couples' therapy, behavior therapy, sex therapy) treatments have been described in the clinical and research literatures (Binik et al., 2006). In cases in which the coital pain is associated with a known medical condition, the appropriate treatment for that condition may be sufficient to relieve the pain—for example, external lubricants (for vaginal dryness), antifungals (for vaginal yeast infections), antibiotics (for urinary tract infections or sexually transmitted infections), steroid creams (for skin disease), and medication or surgery (for endometriosis).

When, as is often the case, no obvious medical cause exists for the sexual pain, the most effective treatment approach is far less clear (Binik et al., 2006). Treatments are directed toward alleviation of symptoms and may provide little, partial, or complete relief. Among the many medical treatments that have been used, with at least some success, are the following: topical creams, oral medications (e.g., acyclovir, tricyclic antidepressants, anxiolytics, anticonvulsants), biofeedback (McKay et al., 2001), physical therapy, cognitive-behavioral sex therapy, pain management (injections, nerve blocks, acupuncture, hypnosis), local anesthetic agents (e.g., lidocaine), topical estrogen, electrical stimulation of the vaginal vestibular area (Nappi et al., 2003), biofeedback, and surgery. Even local Botox injections have met with some success (Ghazizadeh & Nikzad, 2004). Tan and colleagues (2012) have provided a comprehensive review of the treatment options for vulvovaginal atrophy in particular, with estrogen preparations emerging as the options with the most empirical support to date.

Some of the best-controlled treatment research on sexual pain has been done on VVS (e.g., Goldstein & Goldstein, 2006). A number of therapies have resulted in significant clinical improvement (ter Kuile & Weijenborg, 2006). In one important study, vestibulectomy produced better short-term results in pain reduction at both post-treatment and 6-month follow-up than either biofeedback or group CBT (Bergeron et al., 2001), and at 2.5 year follow-up, vestibulectomy maintained its pain reduction benefit, although all three forms of treatment were equally effective in their impact on sexual functioning (Bergeron, Khalife, Glazer, & Binik, 2008). With respect to vestibulectomy, however, Bergeron and colleagues (2010) have described that clinicians would be wise to consider whether patients see such surgery as a "quick fix," with attendant strong pro-surgery motivation and unrealistic expectations. Another recent randomized control trial also provided support for CBT (as compared with supportive psychotherapy), including the finding that treatment gains were maintained at 1-year follow-up (Masheb, Kerns, Lozano, Minkin, & Richman, 2009). Contemporary recommendations for vulvodynia are that a multidisciplinary approach is warranted, including education, therapy, and pelvic floor physiotherapy (Sadownik, Seal, & Brotto, 2012). With vaginismus, Masters and Johnson (1970) and others have reported success rates as high as 90% (or more), with full penetration during intercourse as the criterion, using behavioral exercises (e.g., sensate focus) and vaginal dilators (Jeng, Wang, Chou, Shen, & Tzeng, 2006; Schnyder, Schnyder-Luthi, Ballinari, & Blaser, 1998), therapist-aided exposure (ter Kuile et al., 2009), and CBT (ter Kuile et al., 2007). Other reviews, however, suggest this high success rate is atypical (e.g., Heiman & Meston, 1997).

It is important to understand that women with a sexual pain disorder can respond quite differently to these different treatments. It can take time and patience, for both the patient and the practitioner, to find a treatment or combination of treatments that will significantly decrease the pain.

Male Sexual Pain Disorders

Although not described in *DSM-IV-TR*, nor receiving as much attention as women's sexual pain in the medical literature, men, too, can experience genital pain associated with erection or orgasm that can interfere with or prevent intercourse. The etiology of male sexual pain disorders is often medical in nature. For example, sexual pain, especially postejaculatory pain, is a common feature of chronic prostatitis or chronic pelvic pain syndrome (CPPS), affecting as many as 75% of men with the disorder. Peyronie's disease, priapism,

STIs (e.g., genital herpes), penile skin infections, and benign prostatic hyperplasia (BPH; benign enlargement of the prostate) are also often associated with painful erections or ejaculation. These are almost always treated with medication or, in some cases, surgery. Even here, however, urology is increasingly recognizing the importance of psychosocial and cultural issues in terms of both the impact and the treatment of these painful conditions (Bella et al., 2007). Additionally, a number of postorgasmic pain problems for men are initially organic in nature, yet fail to resolve even when the underlying disease state has been repaired. For these men, like many of the women suffering pain disorders, the muscle clenching in anticipation of potential sexual pain can actually create the pain in the absence of continuing organic pathology. These situations can often be resolved with a psychoeducational approach that combines relaxation training with counseling. Adjunctive physical therapy can also help ameliorate the problem. Finally, men who are sexual with other men may report pain associated with receptive anal intercourse, that is, anodyspareunia. Treatment for this can be similar to the treatment for vaginismus.

Sex and Aging

There is little doubt that aging can negatively affect sexual functioning (e.g., Wylie & Kenney, 2010). This should come as no surprise given that many of the medications and illnesses we've discussed as potentially negatively impacting sexual function are far more typical in lives of older men and women that they are of those younger. Throughout this chapter, we have touched on the impact of aging in the context of several of the specific sexual dysfunctions. Here, we would like to provide an overview of this issue through the results of a recent, ambitious, and important study. Using a national probability sample of over 3,000, the University of Chicago's National Social Life, Health, and Aging Project (NSHAP) examined, more comprehensively than ever before, the sexual lives of men and women ages 57 to 85. This team of researchers (Tessler-Lindau et al., 2007) interviewed 1,550 women and 1,455 men for about 2 hours in their own homes, about such issues as the frequency with which they were sexual, the types of sex in which they engaged, the sexual problems (if any) they experienced, the availability of sex partners, and the state of their general health.

The findings of this survey provide reason to be both optimistic (i.e., about how many older Americans are still reporting regular and satisfying sexual lives) and yet concerned (i.e., about the frequency of untreated sexual complaints in this population). Some of the NSHAP's most interesting findings include the following: While the likelihood of remaining sexual decreases with age, many older Americans are sexually active. Specifically, among those ages 57 to 64, 73% (84% of men, 62% of women) reported still being sexual. This figure dropped to 53% (67% of men, 39% of women) among respondents age 65 to 74. But even among those between 75 and 85 years of age, 26% (38% of men, 17% of women) were still sexually active. Note that women were significantly less likely than men to report being sexually active at every age surveyed. In large part, these male–female differences were likely a function of the sex differences in the availability of intimate partners. For example, more than three-quarters (78%) of men aged 75 to 85 had a spouse or other intimate relationship, while only 40% of women in that age group had a partner. In addition, women surveyed were more likely than men to rate sex as "not at all important" (35% versus 13% of men).

Nearly half of those who were sexually active reported at least one sexual problem, with 43% of women reporting diminished desire, 39% vaginal dryness, and 24% the inability to climax, while 37% of men reported erectile difficulties. Despite the frequency of sexual problems, only about a third of the men and just a fifth of the women in the study had discussed sex with a doctor since age 50. Still, 14% percent of all men reported using medication or supplements to help improve sexual function.

In summary, results from NSHAP and other surveys (Cain et al., 2003; Feldman et al., 1994; Howard, O'Neill, & Travers, 2006) provide reason for at least guarded optimism regarding the potential for satisfying sex throughout our lives. Clinicians should be careful not to assume that because men or women have reached the sixth or even seventh decade of life that sex is something in which they are uninterested or of which they are incapable. They should also be prepared to ask about and address the many treatable impediments to satisfying sex facing their older patients.

Concluding Comments

Researchers know more about the nature and etiology of male and female sexual dysfunctions than ever before. New diagnostic procedures and treatments are being developed constantly. Literally thousands of research and clinical articles on sexual dysfunctions appear every year in dozens of quality scientific journals, and there are more medical and mental health professionals devoting their professional careers to understanding and treating sexual disorders than ever before. As a consequence, the millions of couples in this country and around the world who experience a sexual dysfunction are more likely than ever to have their problems accurately diagnosed and effectively treated.

And yet, there is so much that clinicians and researchers have yet to learn about both normal and dysfunctional sexual behaviors, as they have only just started to scratch the surface of understanding the neurocognitive mechanisms underlying normal, dysfunctional, and atypical expressions of sexuality. In addition, new treatment approaches that include genetic reengineering, nanotechnology, and stem cell research are currently being developed. Like earlier medical approaches, all of these are likely to be enhanced when integrated with good sexual counseling.

Like all other animals, we humans are designed to be sexual. Unlike most other species, however, we can appreciate the many ways in which our sexuality can increase the quality of our lives as individuals and as couples well beyond its procreative value. The more we learn about ourselves as sexual beings, the more we recognize that our sexuality is far more complex than for most other organisms. We truly are biopsychosocial creatures, and this is no more obvious than when we try to understand ourselves as sexual beings. As a result, the number and variety of possible etiological facors in a sexual dysfunction can make its accurate diagnosis and ultimate treatment challenging.

It is clear that a *complete* understanding of even the *functional* varieties of sexual thoughts, feelings, and behaviors is still beyond our reach. This is even more the case for the dysfunctional varieties. Still, the knowledge base keeps growing and with it come increased opportunities to understand sexual problems. Perhaps, most importantly, there are substantial data showing that many, though not all, of these dysfunctions can respond to thoughtful and professionally administered treatment.

References

Abdel-Hamid, I. A., & Saleh, E.-S. (2011). Primary lifelong delayed ejaculation: Characteristics and response to bupropion. *Journal of Sexual Medicine, 8,* 1772–1779.

Albersen, M., Orabi, H., & Lue, T. F. (2012). Evaluation and treatment of erectile dysfunction in the aging male: A mini-review. *Gerontology, 58,* 3–14.

Alexandre, B., Lemaire, A., Desvaux, P., & Amar, E. (2007). Intracavernous injections of prostaglandin E1 for erectile dysfunction: Patient satisfaction and quality of sex life on long-term treatment. *Journal of Sexual Medicine, 4,* 426–431.

Almas, E., & Landmark, B. (2010). Non-pharmacological treatment of sexual problems: A review of research literature 1970–2008. *Sexologies, 19,* 202–211.

Althof, S. E. (2000, June). The patient with erectile dysfunction: Psychological issues. *Nurse Practitioner* (Suppl.), 11–13.

Althof, S. E. (2006). Sexual therapy in the age of pharmacotherapy. *Annual Review of Sex Research, 17,* 1–17.

Althof, S. E., Leiblum, S. R., Chevret-Measson, M., Hartman, U., Levine, S. E., McCabe, M., et al. (2005). Psychological and interpersonal dimensions of sexual function and dysfunction. *Journal of Sexual Medicine, 2,* 793–818.

Anzellotti, F., Franciotti, R., Bonanni, L., Tamburro, G., Perrucci, M. G., Thomas, A.,…Onofrj, M. (2010). Persistent genital arousal disorder associated with functional hyperconnectivity of an epileptic focus. *Neuroscience, 167,* 88–96.

Apfelbaum, B. (2000). Retarded ejaculation: A much misunderstood syndrome. In R. C. Rosen & S. R. Leiblum (Eds.), *Principles and practice of sex therapy* (3rd ed., pp. 205–241). New York: Guilford Press.

Arnow, B. A., Millheiser, L., Garrett, A., Lake Polan, M., Glover, G. H., Hill, K. R.,…Desmond, J. E. (2009). Women with hypoactive sexual desire disorder compared to normal females: A functional magnetic resonance imaging study. *Neuroscience, 158,* 484–502.

Baltaci, S., Avdos, K., Kosar, A., & Anafarta, K. (1995). Treating erectile dysfunction with a vacuum tumescence device: A retrospective analysis of acceptance and satisfaction. *British Journal of Urology, 76,* 757–760.

Bancroft, J. (2000). The medicalization of female sexual dysfunction: The need for caution. *Archives of Sexual Behavior, 31,* 451–453.

Bancroft, J. (2009). *Human sexuality and its problems* (3rd ed.). London: Churchill Livingstone.

Bancroft, J., Graham, C. A., Janssen, E., & Sanders, S. A. (2009). The dual control model: Current status and future directions. *Journal of Sex Research, 42,* 121–142.

Bancroft, J., & Janssen, E. (2000). The dual control model of male sexual response: A theoretical approach to centrally mediated erectile dysfunction. *Neuroscience and Biobehavioral Reviews, 24,* 571–579.

Bancroft, J., Loftus, J., & Long, J. S. (2003). Distress about sex: A national survey of women in heterosexual relationships. *Archives of Sexual Behavior, 32,* 193–208.

Banner, L. L., & Anderson, R. U. (2007). Integrated sildenafil and cognitive-behavior sex therapy for psychogenic erectile dysfunction: A pilot study. *Journal of Sexual Medicine, 4,* 1117–1125.

Barbach, L. G. (1975). *For yourself: The fulfillment of female sexuality*. Garden City, NY: Doubleday.

Basson, R. (2005). Women's sexual dysfunction: Revised and expanded definitions. *Canadian Medical Association Journal, 172,* 1327–1333.

Basson, R. (2006). Sexual and arousal disorders in women. *New England Journal of Medicine, 354,* 497–506.

Basson, R. (2010). Women's difficulties with low sexual desire, sexual avoidance, and sexual aversion. In S. B. Levine (Ed.), *Handbook of clinical sexuality for mental health professionals* (2nd ed., pp. 159–179). New York: Routledge/Taylor & Francis Group.

Basson, R., Althof, S., David, S., Fugl-Meyer, K., & Goldstein, I. (2004). Summary of the recommendations on sexual dysfunctions in women. *Journal of Sexual Medicine, 1,* 24–34.

Basson, R., McInnes, R., Smith, M. D., Hodgson, G., & Koppiker, N. (2002). Efficacy and safety of sildenafil citrate in women with sexual dysfunction associated with female sexual arousal disorder. *Journal of Women's Health & Gender-Based Medicine, 11,* 367–377.

Bella, A. J., Perelman, M. A., Brant, W. O., & Lue, T. F. (2007). Peyronie's disease. *Journal of Sexual Medicine, 4,* 1527–1538.

Bergeron, S., Binik, Y. M., Khalife, S., Pagidas, K., Glazer, H. I., Meana, M., et al. (2001). A randomized comparison of group cognitive-behavioral therapy, surface electromyographic feedback, and vestibulectomy in the treatment of dyspareunia resulting from vulvar vestibulitis. *Pain, 91,* 297–306.

Bergeron, S., Khalife, S., Glazer, H. I., & Binik, Y. M. (2008). Surgical and behavioral treatments for vestibulodynia: Two-and-one-half year follow-up and predictors of outcome. *Obstetrics & Gynecology, 111,* 159–166.

Bergeron, S., Meana, M., Binik, Y. M., & Khalifé, S. (2010). Painful sex. In S. B. Levine (Ed.), *Handbook of clinical sexuality for mental health professionals* (2nd ed., pp. 193–214). New York: Routledge/Taylor & Francis Group.

Berman, J. R., Berman, L. A., Toler, S. M., Gill, J., & Haughie, S. (2003). Safety and efficacy of sildenafil citrate for the treatment of female sexual arousal disorder: A double-blind, placebo controlled study. *Journal of Urology, 170,* 2333–2338.

Berner, M., & Gunzler, C. (2012). Efficacy of psychosocial interventions in men and women with sexual dysfunctions: A systematic review of controlled trials. Part 1: The efficacy of psychosocial interventions for male sexual dysfunction. *Journal of Sexual Medicine, 9,* 3089–3107.

Billups, K. L., Berman, L., Berman, J., Metz, M. E., Glennon, M. E., & Goldstein, I. (2001). A new pharmacological vacuum therapy for female sexual dysfunction. *Journal of Sex & Marital Therapy, 27,* 435–441.

Binik. Y. M. (2005). Should dyspareunia be retained as a sexual dysfunction in DSM-V? A painful classification decision. *Archives of Sexual Behavior, 34,* 11–21.

Binik, Y. M. (2010a). The DSM diagnostic criteria for vaginismus. *Archives of Sexual Behavior, 39,* 278–291.

Binik, Y. M. (2010b). The DSM diagnostic criteria for dyspareunia. *Archives of Sexual Behavior, 39,* 292–303.

Binik, Y. M., Bergeron, S., & Khalife, S. (2006). Dyspareunia and vaginismus: So-called sexual pain. In S. R. Leiblum (Ed.), *Principles and practice of sex therapy* (4th ed., pp. 124–156). New York: Guilford Press.

Binik, Y. M., Meana, M., Berkely, K., & Khalife, S. (1999). The sexual pain disorders: Is the pain sexual or is the sex painful? *Annual Review of Sex Research, 10,* 210–235.

Blanker, M. H., Bohnen, A. M., Groeneveld, F. P., Frans, P. M. J., et al. (2001). Correlates of erectile and ejaculatory dysfunction in older Dutch men: A community-based study. *Journal of the American Geriatrics Society, 49,* 436–442.

Bolour, S., & Braunstein, G. (2005). Testosterone therapy in women: A review. *International Journal of Impotence Research, 17,* 399–408.

Borg, C., de Jong, P. J., & Schultz, W. W. (2010). Vaginismus and dyspareunia: Automatic vs. deliberate disgust responsivity. *Journal of Sexual Medicine, 7,* 2149–2157.

Borg, C., Peters, M. L., Schultz, W. W., & de Jong, P. J. (2012). Vaginismus: Heightened harm avoidance and pain catastrophizing cognitions. *Journal of Sexual Medicine, 9,* 558–567.

Bosshardt, R. J., Farwerk, R., Sikora, R., Sohn, M., & Jakse, G. (1995). Objective measurement of the effectiveness, therapeutic success and dynamic mechanisms of the vacuum device. *British Journal of Urology, 75,* 786–791.

Braun, W., Wassmer, G., Klotz, T., Reifenrath, B., Mathers, M., & Englemann, U. (2000). Epidemiology of erectile dysfunction: Results of the "Cologne male survey." *International Journal of Impotence Research, 12,* 305–311.

Braunstein, G. D., Sundwall, D. A., Katz, M., Shifren, J. L., Buster, J. E., Simon, J. A., et al. (2005). Safety and efficacy of a testosterone patch for the treatment of hypoactive sexual desire disorder in surgically menopausal women: A randomized, placebo-controlled trial. *Archives of Internal Medicine, 165,* 1582–1589.

Brisson, T. E., Broderick, G. A., Thiel, D. D., Heckman, M. G., & Pinkstaff, D. M. (2006). Vardenafil rescue rates of sildenafil l nonresponders: Objective assessment of 327 patients with erectile dysfunction. *Urology, 68,* 397–401.

Brock, G., Carrier, S., Casey, R., Tarride, J. E., Elliott, S., Dugre, H., et al. (2007). Can an educational program optimize PDE5i therapy? A study of Canadian primary care practices. *Journal of Sexual Medicine, 4,* 1404–1413.

Brotto, L. A. (2010). The DSM diagnostic criteria for hypoactive sexual desire disorder in women. *Archives of Sexual Behavior, 39,* 221–239.

Brotto, L. A. (2011). Non-judgmental, present-moment, sex…as if your life depended on it. *Sexual and Relationship Therapy, 26,* 215–216.

Brotto, L. A., Heiman, J. R., Goff, B., Greer, B., Lentz, G. M., Swisher, E.,...Blaricom, A. (2008). A psychoeducational intervention for sexual dysfunction in women with gynecologic cancer. *Archives of Sexual Behavior, 37,* 317–329.

Brotto, L. A., & Kingsberg, S. A. (2010). Sexual consequences of cancer survivorship. In S. B. Levine (Ed.), *Handbook of clinical sexuality for mental health professionals* (2nd ed., pp. 329–347). New York: Routledge/Taylor & Francis Group.

Brotto, L. A., Knudson, G., Inskip, J., Rhodes, K., & Erskine, Y. (2010). Asexuality: A mixed-methods approach. *Archives of Sexual Behavior, 39,* 599–618.

Brotto, L. A., Seal, B. N., & Rellini, A. (2012). Pilot study of a brief cognitive behavioral versus mindfulness-based intervention for women with sexual distress and a history of childhood sexual abuse. *Journal of Sex & Marital Therapy, 38,* 1–27.

Brotto, L. A., & Woo, J. S. T. (2010). Cognitive-behavioral and mindfulness-based therapy for low sexual desire. In S. R. Leiblum (Ed.), *Treating sexual desire disorders: A clinical casebook* (pp. 149–164). New York: Guilford Press.

Burger, H. G., & Papalia, M. A. (2006). A clinical update on female androgen insufficiency: Testosterone testing and treatment in women presenting with low sexual desire. *Sexual Health, 3,* 73–78.

Burri, A. V., Cherkas, L. M., & Spector, T. D. (2009). Emotional intelligence and its association with orgasmic frequency in women. *Journal of Sexual Medicine, 6*(7), 1930–1937.

Burrows, L. J., Basha, M., & Goldstein, A. T. (2012). The effects of hormonal contraceptives on female sexuality: A review. *Journal of Sexual Medicine, 9,* 2213–2223.

Buvat, J. (2011). Pathophysiology of premature ejaculation. *Journal of Sexual Medicine, 4,* 316–327.

Cain, V. S., Johannes, C. B., Avia, N. E., Mohr, B., Schocken, M., Skurnick, J., et al. (2003). Sexual functioning and practices in a multi-ethnic study of midlife women: Baseline results from SWAN (Study of Women's Health across the Nation). *Journal of Sex Research, 40,* 266–276.

Caruso, S., Agnello, C., Intelisano, G., Farina, M., De Mari, L., & Cianci, A. (2004). Placebo-controlled study on efficacy and safety of daily apomorphine SL intake in premenopausal women affected by hypoactive sexual desire disorder and sexual arousal disorder. *Urology, 63,* 955–959.

Caruso, S., Intelisano, G., Lupo, L., & Agnello, C. (2001). Premenopausal women affected by sexual arousal disorder treated with sildenafil l: A double-blind, cross-over, placebo-controlled study. *BJOG: An International Journal of Obstetrics and Gynaecology, 108,* 623–628.

Carvalheira, A. A., Brotto, L. A., & Leal, I. (2010). Women's motivations for sex: Exploring the diagnostic and statistical manual, fourth edition, text revision criteria for hypoactive sexual desire and female sexual arousal disorders. *Journal of Sexual Medicine, 7*(4 Pt. 1), 1454–1463.

Celik, D. B., Poyraz, E. C., Bingol, A., Indiman, E., Ozakbas, S., & Kaya, D. (2013). Sexual dysfunction in multiple sclerosis: Gender differences. *Journal of the Neurological Sciences, 324,* 17–20.

Clayton, A. H., Pradko, J. F., Croft, H. A., Montano, C. B., Leadbetter R. A., Bolden-Watson, C., et al. (2002). Prevalence of sexual dysfunction among new antidepressants. *Journal of Clinical Psychiatry, 63,* 357–366.

Corona, G., Jannini, E. A., Lotti, F., Boddi, V., De Vita, G., Forti, G.,...Maggi, M. (2010). Premature and delayed ejaculation: Two ends of a single continuum influenced by hormonal milieu. *International Journal of Andrology, 34,* 41–48.

Davis, S. R., & Braunstein, G. D. (2012). Efficacy and safety of testosterone in the management of hypoactive sexual desire disorder in postmenopausal women. *Journal of Sexual Medicine, 9,* 1134–1148.

Dean, J., Hackett, G. I., Gentile, V., Pirozzi-Farina, F., Rosen, R. C., Zhao, Y., et al. (2006). Psychosocial outcomes and drug attributes affecting treatment choice in men receiving sildenafil citrate and tadalafil for the treatment of erectile dysfunction: Results of a multicenter, randomized open-label, crossover study. *Journal of Sexual Medicine, 3,* 651–661.

Dennerstein, L., Coochak, P., Barton, J., & Graziottin, A. (2006). Hypoactive sexual desire disorder in menopausal women: A survey of western European women. *Journal of Sexual Medicine, 3,* 212–222.

DeRogatis, L. R., Clayton, A. H., Rosen, R. C., Sand, M., & Pyke, R. E. (2011). Should sexual desire and arousal disorders in women be merged? *Archives of Sexual Behavior, 40,* 217–219.

DeRogatis, L., Rosen, R. C., Goldstein. I., Werneburg, B., Kempthorne-Rawson, J., & Sand, M. (2012). Characterization of hypoactive sexual desire disorder (HSDD) in men. *Journal of Sexual Medicine, 9*, 812–820.

Desrochers, G., Bergeron, S., Khalifé, S., Dupuis, M.-J., & Jodoin, M. (2009). Fear avoidance and self-efficacy in relation to pain and sexual impairment in women with provoked vestibulodynia. *Clinical Journal of Pain, 25*, 520–527.

Dhar, N. B., Angemeier, K. W., & Montague, D. K. (2006). Long-term mechanical reliability of AMS 700CX/CXM inflatable penile prosthesis. *Journal of Urology, 176*, 2599–2601.

Dove, N. L., & Wiederman, M. W. (2000). Cognitive distraction and women's sexual functioning. *Journal of Sex & Marital Therapy, 26*, 67–78.

Eardley, I., Donatucci, C., Corbin, J., El-Megiegy, A., Hatzimouratidis, K. et al. (2010). Pharmacotherapy for erectile dysfunction. *Journal of Sexual Medicine, 7*, 524–540.

Facelle, T. M., Sadeghi-Nejad, H., & Goldmeier, D. (2013). Persistent genital arousal disorder: Characterization, etiology, and management. *Journal of Sexual Medicine, 10*, 439–450.

Feldman, H. A., Goldstein, I., Hatzichristou, D. G., Krane, R. J., & McKinlay, J. B. (1994). Impotence and its medical and psychosocial correlates: Results of the Massachusetts Male Aging Study. *Journal of Urology, 151*, 54–61.

Fisher, W., Rosen, R. C., Mollen, M., Brock, G., Karlin, G., Pomerville, P., et al. (2005). Improving the sexual quality of life of couples affected by erectile dysfunction: A double blind, randomized, placebo-controlled trial of vardenafil l. *Journal of Sexual Medicine, 2*, 699–708.

Frühauf, S., Gerger, H., Schmidt, H., Munder, T., & Barth, J. (2013). Efficacy of psychological interventions for sexual dysfunction: A systematic review and meta-analysis. *Archives of Sexual Behavior*, 1–19.

Ghazizadeh, S., & Nikzad, M. (2004). Botulinum toxin in the treatment of refractory vaginismus. *Obstetrics and Gynecology, 104*, 922–925.

Goldmeier, D., & Leiblum, S. R. (2006). Persistent genital arousal in women—a new syndrome entity. *International Journal of STDs and AIDS, 17*, 215–216.

Goldmeier, D., Mears, A., Hiller, J., & Crowley, T. (2009). Persistent genital arousal disorder: A review of the literature and recommendations for management. *International Journal of STD & AIDS, 20*, 373–377.

Goldstein, A. T., & Goldstein, I., (2006). Sexual pain disorders within the vulvar vestibule: Current techniques. In I. Goldstein, C. M. Meston, S. R. Davis, & A. M. Traish (Eds.), *Women's sexual function and dysfunction: Study, diagnosis, and treatment* (pp. 587–596). New York: Taylor & Francis.

Goldstein, I. (2007). Current management strategies of the postmenopausal patient with sexual health problems. *Journal of Sexual Medicine, 4*(Suppl. 3), 235–253.

Goldstein, I., Fisher, W. A., Sand, M., Rosen, R. C., Mollen, M., Brock, G., et al. (2005). Women's sexual function improves when partners are administered vardenafil for erectile dysfunction: A prospective, randomized, double-blind, placebo-controlled trial. *Journal of Sexual Medicine, 2*, 819–832.

Graham, C. A. (2007). Medicalizations of women's sexual problems: A different story? *Journal of Sex & Marital Therapy, 33*, 443–447.

Graham, C. A. (2010a). The DSM diagnostic criteria for female orgasmic disorder. *Archives of Sexual Behavior, 39*, 256–270.

Graham, C. A. (2010b). The DSM diagnostic criteria for female sexual arousal disorder. *Archives of Sexual Behavior, 39*, 240–255.

Graham, C. A., Sanders, S. A., & Milhausen, R. R. (2006). The sexual excitation/sexual inhibition inventory for women: Psychometric properties. *Archives of Sexual Behavior, 35*, 397–409.

Graham, C. A., Sanders, S. A., Milhausen, R. R., & McBride, K. R. (2004). Turning on and turning off: A focus group study of the factors that affect women's sexual arousal. *Archives of Sexual Behavior, 33*, 527–538.

Grellet, L., & Faix, A. (2011). What exactly are we trying to cure when we treat someone for an erectile dysfunction. *Sexologies, 20*(1), 8–11.

Grenier, G., & Byers, E. S. (1997). The relationship among ejaculatory control, ejaculatory latency, and attempts to prolong heterosexual intercourse. *Archives of Sexual Behavior, 26*, 27–47.

Hajjar, R. R., Kaiser, F. E., & Morley, J. E. (1997). Outcomes of long-term testosterone replacement in older hypogonadal males: A retrospective analysis. *Journal of Clinical Endocrinology and Metabolism, 82*, 3793.

Hale, V. E., & Strassberg, D. S. (1990). The role of anxiety on sexual arousal. *Archives of Sexual Behavior, 19*, 569–581.

Hall, S. A., Shackelton, R., Rosen, R. C., & Araujo, A. B. (2010). Risk factors for incident erectile dysfunction among community-dwelling men. *Journal of Sexual Medicine, 7*, 712–722.

Harlow, B. L., & Stewart, E. G., (2003). A population-based assessment of chronic unexplained vulvar pain. Have we underestimated the prevalence of vulvodynia? *Journal of the American Medical Women's Association, 58,* 82–88.

Hartmann, U., & Waldinger, M. D. (2006). Treatment of delayed ejaculation. In S. R. Leiblum (Ed.), *Principles and practice of sex therapy* (4th ed., pp. 241–276). New York: Guilford Press.

Hatzimouratidis, K., Amar, E., Eardley, I., Giuliano, F., Hatzichristou, D., Montorsi, F., &…Wespes, E. (2010). Guidelines on male sexual dysfunction: Erectile dysfunction and premature ejaculation. *European Urology, 57,* 804–814.

Hatzimouratidis, K., & Hatzichristou, D. G. (2005). A comparative review of the options for treatment of erectile dysfunction: Which treatment for which patient. *Drugs, 65,* 1621–1650.

Hayes, R. D., Bennett, C. M., Fairley, C. K., & Dennerstein, L. (2006). What can prevalence studies tell us about female sexual difficulty and dysfunction? *Journal of Sexual Medicine, 3,* 589–595.

Hayes, R. D., Dennerstein, L., Bennett, C. M., Koochaki, P. E., Leiblum, S. R., & Graziottin, A. (2007). Relationship between hypoactive sexual desire disorder and aging. *Fertility and Sterility, 87,* 107–112.

Heiman, J. R., & Meston, C. M. (1997). Empirically validated treatment for sexual dysfunction. In R. Rosen, C. Davis, & H. Ruppel (Eds.), *Annual Review of Sex Research* (pp. 148–194). Mount Vernon, IA: Society for the Scientific Study of Sexuality.

Heiman, J. R., & LoPiccolo, J. (1988). *Becoming orgasmic: A sexual and personal growth program for women.* New York: Simon & Schuster (Fireside).

Hensley, P. L., & Nurnberg, H. G. (2002). SSRI female dysfunction: A female perspective. *Journal of Sex & Marital Therapy, 28,* 143–153.

Howard, J. R., O'Neill, S., & Travers, C. (2006). Factors affecting sexuality in older Australian women: Sexual interest, sexual arousal, relationships and sexual distress in older Australian women. *Climateric, 9,* 355–367.

Janssen, E. (2011). Sexual arousal in men: A review and conceptual analysis. *Hormones and Behavior, 59,* 708–716.

Jeng, C. J., Wang, L. R., Chou, C. H., Shen, J., & Tzeng, C. R. (2006). Management and outcome of primary vaginismus. *Journal of Sex & Marital Therapy, 32,* 379–387.

Jern, P., Gunst, A., Sandqvist, F., Sandnabba, N. K., & Santtila, P. (2010). Using ecological momentary assessment to investigate associations between ejaculatory latency and control in partnered and non-partnered sexual activities. *Journal of Sex Research, 48*(4), 316–324.

Kao, A., Binik, Y. M., Amsel, R., Funaro, D., Leroux, N., & Khalifé, S. (2012). Biopsychosocial predictors of postmenopausal dyspareunia: The role of steroid hormones, vulvovaginal atrophy, cognitive-emotional factors, and dyadic adjustment. *Journal of Sexual Medicine, 9,* 2066–2076.

Kaplan, H. S. (1974). *The new sex therapy.* New York: Brunner/Mazel.

Kaplan, H. S. (1979). *Disorders of sexual desire.* New York: Brunner/Mazel.

Kaplan, H. S. (1995). *The sexual desire disorders: Dysfunctional regulation of sexual motivation.* New York: Brunner/Mazel.

Kedde, H., van de Wiel, H. B. M., Weijmar Schultz, W. C. M., & Wijsen, C. (2013). Sexual dysfunction in young women with breast cancer. *Support Care Cancer, 21,* 271–280.

Kelly, M. P., Strassberg, D. S., & Kircher, J. R. (1990). Attitudinal and experiential correlates of anorgasmia. *Archives of Sexual Behavior, 19,* 165–177.

Kelly, M. P., Strassberg, D. S., & Turner, C. M. (2004). Communication and associated relationship issues in female anorgasmia. *Journal of Sex & Marital Therapy, 30,* 1–14.

Komisaruk, B. R., & Lee, H.-J. (2012). Prevalence of sacral spinal (tarlov) cysts in persistent genital arousal disorder. *Journal of Sexual Medicine, 9,* 2047–2056.

Laan, E., Everaerd, W., van der Velde, J., & Geer, J. H. (1995). Determinants of subjective experience of sexual arousal in women: Feedback from genital arousal and erotic stimulus content. *Psychophysiology, 32,* 444–451.

Labrie, F., Archer, D., Bouchard, C., Fortier, M., Cusan, L., Gomez, J.-L.,…Balser, J. (2009a). Effect of intravaginal dehydroepiandrosterone (Prasterone) on libido and sexual dysfunction in postmenopausal women. *Menopause, 16*(5), 923–931.

Labrie, F., Archer, D., Bouchard, C., Fortier, M., Cusan, L., Gomez, J.-L.,…Balser, J. (2009b). Intravaginal dehydroepiandrosterone (Prasterone), a physiological and highly efficient treatment of vaginal atrophy. *Menopause, 16*(5), 907–922.

Landry, T., & Bergeron, S. (2011). Biopsychosocial factors associated with dyspareunia in a community sample of adolescent girls. *Archives of Sexual Behavior, 40*, 877–889.

Latthe P., Mignini, L., Gray, R., Hills, R., & Kahn, K. (2006). Factors predisposing women to chronic pelvic pain: Systematic review. *British Medical Journal, 332*, 749–755.

Laumann, E. O., Gagnon, J. H., Michael, R. T., & Michaels, S. (1994). *The social organization of sexuality: Sexual practices in the United States.* Chicago: University of Chicago Press.

Laumann, E. O., Paik, A., & Rosen, R. C. (1999). Sexual dysfunction in the United States: Prevalence and predictors. *Journal of the American Medical Association, 28*, 537–544.

Leclerc, B., Bergeron, S., Binik, Y. M., & Khalifé, S. (2010). History of sexual and physical abuse in women with dyspareunia: Association with pain, psychosocial adjustment, and sexual functioning. *Journal of Sexual Medicine, 7*, 971–980.

Leiblum, S. R. (2002). After sildenafil l: Bridging the gap between pharmacologic treatment and satisfying sexual relationships. *Journal of Clinical Psychiatry, 63*, 17–22.

Leiblum, S. R. (2007). Persistent genital arousal disorder: Perplexing, distressing, and under-recognized. In S. R. Leiblum (Ed.), *Principles and practice of sex therapy* (4th ed., pp. 54–84). New York: Guilford Press.

Leiblum, S. R., & Chivers, M. L. (2007). Normal and persistent genital arousal in women: New perspectives. *Journal of Sex & Marital Therapy, 33*, 357–373.

Leiblum, S. R., & Goldmeier, D. (2008). Persistent genital arousal disorder in women: Case reports of association with anti-depressant usage and withdrawal. *Journal of Sex & Marital Therapy, 34*, 150–159.

Leiblum, S. R., & Seehuus, M. (2009). FSFI scores of women with persistent genital arousal disorder compared with published scores of women with female sexual arousal disorder and healthy controls. *Journal of Sexual Medicine, 6*, 469–473.

Levine, L. A. (2007). *State of the art lecture: Peyronie's disease, surgical review.* Paper presented at the Sexual Medicine Society of North America, Inc., 14th Annual Scientific Program Committee, Anaheim, CA.

Levine, L. A., & Dimitriou, R. J. (2001). Vacuum constriction and external erection devices in erectile dysfunction. *Urologic Clinics of North America, 28*, 335–341.

Levine, K. B., Williams, R. E., & Hartmann, K. E. (2008). Vulvovaginal atrophy is strongly associated with female sexual dysfunction among sexually active postmenopausal women. *Menopause, 15*(4 Pt. 1), 661–666.

Lewis, R. W., Fugl-Meyer, K. S., Corona, G., Hayes, R. D., A. R., Laumann, Moreira, E. D., et al. (2010). Definitions/epidemiology/risk factors for sexual dysfunction. *International Journal of Sexual Medicine, 7*, 1598–1607.

Littara, A., Palmieri, B., Rottigni, V., & Iannitti, T. (2013). A clinical study to assess the effectiveness of a hyaluronic acid-based procedure for treatment of premature ejaculation. *International Journal of Impotence Research, 25*, 117–120.

Lux, M., Reyes-Vallejo, L., Morgentaler, A., & Levine, L. A. (2007). Outcomes and satisfaction rates for the redesigned 2-piece penile prosthesis. *Journal of Urology, 177*, 262–266.

Masheb, R. M., Kerns, R. D., Lozano, C., Minkin, M. J., & Richman, S. (2009). A randomized clinical trial for women with vulvodynia: Cognitive-behavioral therapy vs. supportive psychotherapy. *Pain, 141*, 31–40.

Masters, W. H., & Johnson, V. E. (1966). *Human sexual responses.* Boston: Little, Brown.

Masters, W. H., & Johnson, V. E. (1970). *Human sexual inadequacy.* Boston: Little, Brown.

Maurice, W. L. (2006). Sexual desire disorders in men. In S. R. Leiblum (Ed.), *Principles and practice of sex therapy* (4th ed., pp. 181–211). New York: Guilford Press.

McCarthy, B., & Fucito, L. (2005). Integrating medication, realistic expectations, and therapeutic interventions in the treatment of male sexual dysfunction. *Journal of Sex & Marital Therapy, 31*, 319–328.

McCarthy, B. W., & McCarthy, E. (2003). *Rekindling desire: A step by step program to help low-sex and no-sex marriages.* New York: Brunner-Routledge.

McKay, E., Kaufman, R. H., Doctor, U., Berkova, Z., Glazer, H., & Redko, V. (2001). Treating vulvar vestibulitis with electromyographic biofeedback of pelvic floor musculature. *Journal of Reproductive Medicine, 46*, 337–342.

Meana, M., & Lykins, A. (2009). Negative affect and somatically focused anxiety in young women reporting pain with intercourse. *Journal of Sex Research, 46*, 80–88.

Meikle, A. W., Arver, S., Dobs, A. S., Sanders, S. W., & Mazer, N. A. (1996). Androderm: A permeation-enhanced, non-scrotal testosterone transdermal system for the treatment of male hypogonadism. In S. Bhasin (Ed.), *Pharmacology, biology, and clinical applications of androgens* (pp. 449–457). New York: Wiley-Liss.

Melnik, T., Soares, B. O., & Nasello, A. (2008). The effectiveness of psychological interventions for the treatment of erectile dysfunction: Systematic review and meta-analysis, including comparisons to sildenafil treatment, intracavernosal injection, and vacuum devices. *Journal of Sexual Medicine, 5,* 2562–2574.

Mercer, C. H., Fenton, K. A., Johnson, A. M., Wellings, K., MacDowell, W., Mcmamus, S., et al. (2003). Sexual function problems and help seeking behaviour in Britain: National probability sample survey. *British Medical Journal, 327,* 426–427.

Meston, C. M. (2006). Female orgasmic disorder: Treatment strategies and outcome results. In I. Goldstein, C. M. Meston, S. R. Davis, & A. M. Traish (Eds.), *Women's sexual function and dysfunction: Study, diagnosis, and treatment* (pp. 449–461). New York: Taylor & Francis.

Meston, C. M., & Buss, D. M. (2007). Why humans have sex. *Archives of Sexual Behavior, 36,* 477–507.

Metz, M. E., & McCarthy, B. W. (2007). The "good-enough sex" model for couple sexual satisfaction. *Sexual & Relationship Therapy, 22,* 351–362.

Metz, M. E., Pryor, J. L., Nesvacil, L. J., Abuzzahab, S. F., & Koznar, J. (1997). Premature ejaculation: A psychophysiological review. *Journal of Sex and Marital Therapy, 23,* 3–23.

Millett, C., Wen, L. M., Rissel, C., Smith, A., Richters, J., Grulich, A., et al. (2006). Smoking and erectile dysfunction: Findings from a representative sample of Australian men. *Tobacco Control, 15,* 73–74.

Montejo, A. L., Llorca, G., Izquierdo, J. A., & Rico-Villademoros, F. (2001). Incidence of sexual dysfunctions associated with antidepressant agents: A prospective multi-center study of 1022 outpatients. Spanish Working Group for the Study of Psychotropic-Related Sexual Dysfunction. *Journal of Clinical Psychiatry, 62,* 10–21.

Morgentaler, A. (2007). Testosterone replacement therapy and prostate cancer. *Urologic Clinics of North America, 34,* 555–563.

Morgentaler, A., Lipshultz, L. I., Bennett, R., Sweeney, M., Avila, D., & Khera, M. (2011). Testosterone therapy in men with untreated prostate cancer. *Journal of Urology, 185,* 1256–1261.

Nappi, R. E., Ferdeghini, P., Abbiati, I., Vercesi, C., Farina, C., & Polatti, F. (2003). Electrical stimulation (ES) in the management of sexual pain disorders. *Journal of Sex & Marital Therapy, 29,* 103–110.

Nappi, R. E., Verde, J. B., Polatti, F., Genazzani, A. R., & Zara, C. (2002). Self-reported symptoms in women attending menopause clinics. *Gynecology and Obstetrics Investigations, 53,* 181–187.

Nathan, S. G. (2010). When do we say a woman's sexuality is dysfunctional? In S. B. Levine (Ed.), *Handbook of clinical sexuality for mental health professionals* (2nd ed., pp. 143–158). New York: Routledge/Taylor & Francis Group.

Nelson, C. J., Ahmed, A., Valenzuela, R., Parker, M., & Mulhall, J. P. (2007). Assessment of penile vibratory stimulation as a management strategy in men with secondary retarded orgasm. *Urology, 69,* 552–555.

Nobre, P. J., & Pinto-Gouveia, J. (2006). Dysfunctional sexual beliefs as vulnerability factors for sexual dysfunction. *Journal of Sex Research, 43,* 68–75.

Pahlajani, G., Raina, R., Jones, S., Ali, M., & Zippe, C. (2012). Vacuum erection devices revisited: Its emerging role in the treatment of erectile dysfunction and early penile rehabilitation following prostate cancer therapy. *Journal of Sexual Medicine, 9,* 1182–1189.

Panzer, C., Wise, S., Fantini, G., Kang, G., Munarriz, R., Guay, A., & Goldstein, I. (2006). Impact of female contraceptives on sex hormone-binding globulin and androgen levels: A retrospective study of women with sexual dysfunction. *Journal of Sexual Medicine, 3,* 104–113.

Paterson, L. Q. P., Davis, S. N. P., Khalifé, S., Amsel, R., & Binik, Y. M. (2009). Persistent genital and pelvic pain after childbirth. *Journal of Sexual Medicine, 6,* 215–221.

Patrick, D. L., Althof, S. E., Pryor, J. L., Rosen, R., Rowland, D. L., Ho, K. F., et al. (2005). Premature ejaculation: An observational study of men and their partners. *Journal of Sexual Medicine, 2,* 358–367.

Patrick, D. L., Rowland, D. L., & Rothman, M. (2007). Interrelationships among measures of premature ejaculation: The central role of perceived control. *Journal of Sexual Medicine, 4,* 780–788.

Payne, K. A., Bergeron, S., Khalife, S., & Binik, Y. M. (2005). Sexual pain disorders: Assessment, treatment strategies, and outcome results. In I. Goldstein, C. M. Meston, S. R. Davis, & A. M. Traish (Eds.), *Women's sexual function and dysfunction: Study, diagnosis, and treatment* (pp. 471–479). New York: Taylor & Francis.

Payne, K. A., Binik, Y. M., Amsel, R., & Khalife, S. (2005). When sex hurts, anxiety and fear orient attention towards pain. *European Journal of Pain*, 9, 427–436.

Perelman, M. A. (2001). The impact of the new sexual pharmaceuticals on sex therapy. *Current Psychiatry Reports*, 3, 195–201.

Perelman, M. A. (2003). Sex coaching for physicians: Combination treatment for patient and partner. *International Journal of Impotence Research*, 15, S67–S74.

Perelman, M. A. (2005a). Combination therapy for sexual dysfunction: Integrating sex therapy and pharmacotherapy. In R. Balon & R. T. Seagraves (Eds.), *Handbook of sexual dysfunction* (pp. 67–109). Boca Raton, FL: Taylor & Francis.

Perelman M. A. (2005b). Idiosyncratic masturbation patterns: A key unexplored variable in the treatment of retarded ejaculation by the practicing urologist. *Journal of Urology*, 173, 340.

Perelman, M. A. (2005c). Psychosocial evaluation and combination treatment of men with erectile dysfunction. *Urologic Clinics of North America*, 32, 441–445.

Perelman, M. A. (2006b). A new combination treatment for premature ejaculation: A sex therapist's perspective. *Journal of Sexual Medicine*, 3, 1004–1012.

Perelman, M. A. (2007a). Clinical application of CNS-acting agents in FSD. *Journal of Sexual Medicine*, 4, 280–290.

Perelman, M. A. (2007b). The impact of relationship variables on the etiology, diagnosis and treatment of erectile dysfunction. *Advances in Primary Care Medicine: Clinical Update*, 3, 3–6.

Perelman, M. A. (2009). The sexual tipping point: A mind/body model for sexual medicine. *Journal of Sexual Medicine*, 6, 629–632.

Perelman, M. A. (2011). The sexual tipping point: A mind/body model for the past, present and future. *Journal of Sexual Medicine*, 8, 87.

Perelman, M. A. (2012a). Helen Singer Kaplan's legacy and the future of sexual medicine. *Journal of Sexual Medicine*, 9, 227.

Perelman, M. A. (2008). Integrated sex therapy: Interplay of behavioral, cognitive, and medical approaches. In C. C. Carson, I. Goldstein, & R. S. Kirby (Eds.), *Textbook of erectile dysfunction* (2nd ed., pp. 298–305). London: Informa Healthcare.

Perelman, M. A. (2014). The history of sexual medicine. In D. L. Tolman & L. M. Diamond (Eds.), *American Psychological Association handbook of sexuality and psychology* (Vol. 2) (pp. 137–179). Washington, DC: American Psychological Association.

Perelman, M. A., McMahon, C., & Barada, J. (2004). Evaluation and treatment of the ejaculatory disorders. In T. Lue (Ed.), *Atlas of male sexual dysfunction* (pp. 127–157). Philadelphia: Current Medicine.

Perelman, M. A., & Rowland, D. L. (2006). Retarded ejaculation. *World Journal of Urology*, 24, 645–652.

Perelman, M., Shabsigh, R., & Lockhart, D. (2002). An investigation of attitudes in men with erectile dysfunction, using a common methodology, in six countries. *International Journal of Impotence Research*, 14, S60.

Pfaus, J. G. (2009). Pathways of sexual desire. *Journal of Sexual Medicine*, 6, 1506–1533.

Potts, A., Gavey, N., Grace, V. M., & Vares, T. (2003). The downside of Viagra: Women's experiences and concerns. *Sociology of Health & Illness*, 25, 697–719.

Prause, N., & Graham, C. A. (2007). Asexuality: Classification and characterization. *Archives of Sexual Behavior*, 36, 341–356.

Pryor, J. L., Althof, S. E., Steidle, C., Rosen, R. C., Hellstrom, W. J., Shabsigh, R., et al. (2006). Efficacy and tolerability of dapoxetine in treatment of premature ejaculation: An integrated analysis of two double-blind, randomized controlled trials. *Lancet*, 368, 929–937.

Pukall, C., Payne, K. A., & Kao, K. (2005). Dyspareunia. In R. Balon & R. T. Seagraves (Eds.), *Handbook of sexual dysfunction* (pp. 249–272). Boca Raton, FL: Taylor & Francis.

Reissing, E. D. (2011). Consultation and treatment history and causal attributions in an online sample of women with lifelong and acquired vaginismus. *Journal of Sexual Medicine*, 9, 251–258.

Reissing, E. D., Binik, Y. M., Khalife, S., Cohen, D., & Amse, R. (2004). Vaginal spasm, pain, and behavior: An empirical investigation of the diagnosis of vaginismus. *Archives of Sexual Behavior*, 33, 5–17.

Rosen, R. C. (2000). Medical and psychological interventions for erectile dysfunction: Toward a combined treatment approach. In S. R. Leiblum & R. C. Rosen (Eds.), *Principles and practice of sex therapy* (3rd ed., pp. 276–304). New York: Guilford Press.

Rosen, R. C., Fisher, W. A., Eardley, I., Niederberger, C., Nadel, A., & Sand, M. (2004). The multinational Men's Attitudes to Life Events and Sexuality (MALES) study: I. Prevalence of erectile dysfunction and related health concerns in the general population. *Current Medical Research Opinion*, 20, 607–617.

Rosen, R. C., Lane, R. M., & Menza, M. (1999). Effects of SSRIs on sexual function: A critical review. *Journal of Clinical Psychopharmacology, 19,* 67–85.

Rosen, R. C., & Leiblum, S. R. (1995). Treatment of sexual dysfunction: An integrated approach. *Journal of Consulting and Clinical Psychology, 63,* 877–890.

Rosen, R. C., Wing, R., Schneider, S., & Gendrano, N., III. (2005). Epidemiology of erectile dysfunctions: The role of medical comorbidities and lifestyle factors. *Urologic Clinics of North America, 32,* 403–417.

Rowland, D. J. (2007). Will medical solutions to sexual problems make sexological care and science obsolete? *Journal of Sex & Marital Therapy, 33,* 385–397.

Rowland, D., & Cooper, S. (2011). Practical tips for sexual counseling and psychotherapy in premature ejaculation. *Journal of Sexual Medicine, 4,* 342–352.

Rowland, D. J., Cooper, S. E., & Slob, A. K. (1997). Penile sensitivity in men with primary premature ejaculation. *Journal of Urology, 158,* 187–188.

Rowland, D. J., Strassberg, D. S., deGouveia Brazao, C. A., & Slob, A. K. (2000). Ejaculatory latency and control in men with premature ejaculation: An analysis across sexual activities using multiple sources of information. *Journal of Psychosomatic Research, 48,* 68–77.

Rowland, D., Van Diest, S., Incrocci, L., & Slob, A. K. (2005). Psychosexual factors that differentiate men with inhibited ejaculation from men with no dysfunction or another sexual dysfunction. *Journal of Sexual Medicine, 2,* 383–389.

Sadownik, L. A., Seal, B. N., & Brotto, L. A. (2012). Provoked vestibulodynia: Women's experience of participating in a multidisciplinary vulvodynia program. *Journal of Sexual Medicine, 9,* 1086–1093.

Sand, M., & Fisher, W. A. (2007). Women's endorsement of models of female sexual response: The Nurses' Sexuality Study. *Journal of Sexual Medicine, 4,* 708–719.

Sarin, S., Amsel, R., & Binik, Y. (2013). Disentangling desire and arousal: A classificatory conundrum. *Archives of Sexual Behavior, 1,* 1–22.

Schnyder, U., Schnyder-Luthi, C., Ballinari, P., & Blaser, A. (1998). Therapy for vaginismus: In vivo versus in vitro desensitization. *Canadian Journal of Psychiatry, 43,* 941–944.

Schwenkhagen, A. (2007). Hormonal changes in menopause and implications on sexual health. *Journal of Sexual Medicine, 4,* 220–226.

Segraves, R. T. (2006). Rapid ejaculation: A review of nosology, prevalence and treatment. *International Journal of Impotence Research, 18,* 24–32.

Segraves, R. T., & Balon, R. (2010). Recognizing and reversing sexual side effects of medications. In S. B. Levine (Ed.), *Handbook of clinical sexuality for mental health professionals* (2nd ed., pp. 311–327). New York: Routledge/Taylor & Francis Group.

Segraves, R. T., Clayton, A., Croft, H., Wolf, A., & Warnock, J. (2004). Bupropion sustained release for the treatment of hypoactive sexual desire disorder in premenopausal women. *Journal of Clinical Psychopharmacology, 24,* 339–342.

Selvin, E., Burnett, A. L., & Platz, E. A. (2007). Prevalence and risk factors for erectile dysfunction in the US. *American Journal of Medicine, 120,* 151–157.

Semens, J. H. (1956). Premature ejaculation: A new approach. *Southern Medical Journal, 49,* 353–358.

Serefoglu, E. C., & Saitz, T. R. (2012). New insights on premature ejaculation: A review of definition, classification, prevalence, and treatment. *Asian Journal of Andrology, 14,* 822–829.

Shabsigh, R. (1997). The effects of testosterone on the cavernous tissue and erectile function. *World Journal of Urology, 15,* 21.

Shabsigh, R., Anastasiades, A., Cooper, K. L., & Rutman, M. P. (2006). Female sexual dysfunction, voiding symptoms and depression: Common findings in partners of men with erectile dysfunction. *World Journal of Urology, 24,* 653–656.

Shabsigh, R., Perelman, M. A., Laumann, E. O., & Lockhart, D. C. (2004). Drivers and barriers to seeking treatment for erectile dysfunction: A comparison of six countries. *British Journal of Urology International, 94,* 1055–1065.

Shaeer, O., & Shaeer, K. (2012). The Global Online Sexuality Survey (GOSS): The United States of America in 2011. Chapter I: Erectile dysfunction among English-speakers. *Journal of Sexual Medicine, 9*(12), 3018–3027.

Sharlip, I. D., Hellstrom, W. J., & Broderick, G. A. (2008) The ISSM definition of premature ejaculation: A contemporary, evidence-based definition. *Journal of Urology,* (Suppl.), 179, 340, abstract 988.

Shifren, J. L., Braunstein, G. D., Simon, J. A., Casson, P. R., Buster, J. E., Redmond, G. P., et al. (2000). Transdermal testosterone treatment in women with impaired sexual dysfunction after oophorectomy. *New England Journal of Medicine, 343,* 682–688.

Simon, J. (2005). Testosterone patch increases sexual activity and desire in surgically menopausal women with hypoactive sexual desire disorder. *Journal of Clinical Endocrinology and Metabolism, 90,* 5226–5233.

Simopoulos, E. F., & Trinidad, A. C. (2013). Male erectile dysfunction: Integrating psychopharmacology and psychotherapy. *General Hospital Psychiatry, 35,* 33–38.

Sohn, M., Hatzinger, M., Goldstein, I., & Krishnamurti, S. (2013). Standard operating procedures for vascular surgery in erectile dysfunction: Revascularization and venous procedures. *Journal of Sexual Medicine, 10,* 172–179.

Stephenson, K. R., Rellini, A. H., & Meston, C. M. (2013). Relationship satisfaction as a predictor of treatment response during cognitive behavioral sex therapy. *Archives of Sexual Behavior, 42,* 143–152.

Strassberg, D. S. (1994). A physiologically based model of early ejaculation: A solution or a problem? *Journal of Sex Education and Therapy, 20,* 215–217.

Strassberg, D. S. (2005). A rose by any other name: Should dyspareunia be reclassified? *Archives of Sexual Behavior, 34,* 48–49.

Strassberg, D. S., & Mackaronis, J. M. (2014). Sexuality and Psychotherapy. In D. L. Tolman & L. M. Diamond (Eds.), *American Psychological Association handbook of sexuality and psychology* (Vol. 2, pp. 105–135). Washington, DC: American Psychological Association.

Strassberg, D. S., deGouveia Brazao, C. A., Rowland, D. L., Tan, P., & Slob A. K. (1999). Clomipramine in the treatment of rapid (premature) ejaculation. *Journal of Sex and Marital Therapy, 25,* 89–102.

Strassberg, D. S., Kelly, M. P., Carroll, C., & Kircher, J. C. (1987). The psychophysiological nature of premature ejaculation. *Archives of Sexual Behavior, 16,* 327–336.

Strassberg, D. S., Mahoney, J. M., Schaugaard, M., & Hale, V. E. (1990). The role of anxiety in premature ejaculation: A psychophysiological model. *Archives of Sexual Behavior, 19,* 251–257.

Stuckey, B. G. A. (2008). Female sexual function and dysfunction in the reproductive years: The influence of endogenous and exogenous sex hormones. *Journal of Sexual Medicine, 5,* 2282–2290.

Tajkarimi, K., & Burnett, A. L. (2011). The role of genital nerve afferents in the physiology of the sexual response and pelvic floor function. *Journal of Sexual Medicine, 8,* 1299–1312.

Tan, O. M. D., Bradshaw, K. M. D., & Carr, B. R. M. D. (2012). Management of vulvovaginal atrophy-related sexual dysfunction in postmenopausal women: An up-to-date review. *Menopause, 19,* 109–117.

ter Kuile, M. M., Bulté, I., Weijenborg, P. T. M., Beekman, A., Melles, R., & Onghena, P. (2009). Therapist-aided exposure for women with lifelong vaginismus: A replicated single-case design. *Journal of Consulting and Clinical Psychology, 77,* 149–159.

ter Kuile, M. M., van Lankveld, J. J., de Groot, E., Melles, R., Neffs, J., & Zandbergen, M. (2007). Cognitive-behavioral therapy for women with lifelong vaginismus: Process and prognostic factors. *Behavior, Research and Therapy, 45,* 359–373.

ter Kuile, M. M., & Weijenborg, P. T. M. (2006). A cognitive-behavioral group program for women with vulvar vestibulitis syndrome (VVS); factors associated with treatment success. *Journal of Sex & Marital Therapy, 32,* 199–213.

Tessler-Lindau, S., Schumm, P., Laumann, E. O., Levinson, W., O'Muircheartaigh, C., & Waite, L. J. (2007). A study of sexuality and health among older adults in the United States. *New England Journal of Medicine, 357,* 762–774.

Tiefer, L. (2007). Sexuopharmacology: A fateful new element in sexual scripts. In M. Kimmel (Ed.), *The sexual self: The construction of sexual scripts* (pp. 239–248). Nashville, TN: Vanderbilt University Press.

Tomlinson, J., & Wright, D. (2004). Impact of erectile dysfunction and its subsequent treatment. *British Medical Journal, 328,* 1037–1039.

Uckert, S., Mayer, M. E., Jonas, U., & Stief, C. G. (2006). Potential future options in the pharmacotherapy of female sexual dysfunction. *World Journal of Urology, 24,* 630–638.

van Overveld, M., de Jong, P. J., Peters, M. L., van Lankveld, J., Melles, R., & ter Kuile, M. M. (2013). The Sexual Disgust Questionnaire; a psychometric study and a first exploration in patients with sexual dysfunctions. *Journal of Sexual Medicine, 10,* 396–407.

Waldinger, M. D. (2002). The neurobiological approach to premature ejaculation. *Journal of Urology, 168,* 2359–2367.

Waldinger, M. D. (2008). Premature ejaculation: Different pathophysiologies and etiologies determine its treatment. *Journal of Sex & Marital Therapy, 34,* 1–13.

Waldinger, M. D. (2011). Toward evidence-based genetic research on lifelong premature ejaculation: A critical evaluation of methodology. *Korean Journal of Urology, 52,* 1–8.

Waldinger, M. D., & Olivier, B. (2004). Utility of selective serotonin reuptake inhibitors in premature ejaculation. *Current Opinion in Investigational Drugs, 5,* 743–747.

Waldinger, M. D., & Olivier, B. (2005). Animal models of premature and retarded ejaculation. *World Journal of Urology, 23,* 115–118.

Waldinger, M. D., & Schweitzer, D. H. (2006a). Changing paradigms from a historical DSM-III and DSM-IV view toward an evidence-based definition of premature ejaculation. Part I: Validity of DSM-IV-TR. *Journal of Sexual Medicine, 3,* 682–692.

Waldinger, M. D., & Schweitzer, D. H. (2006b). Changing paradigms from a historical DSM-III and DSM-IV view toward an evidence-based definition of premature ejaculation. Part II: Proposals for DSM-V and ICD-11. *Journal of Sexual Medicine, 3,* 693–705.

Waldinger, M. D., Venema, P. L., van Gils, A. P. G., & Schweitzer, D. H. (2009). New insights into restless genital syndrome: Static mechanical hyperesthesia and neuropathy of the nervus dorsalis clitoridis. *Journal of Sexual Medicine, 6,* 2778–2787.

Waldinger, M. D., Zwinderman, A. H., & Olivier, B. (2004). On-demand treatment of premature ejaculation with clomipramine and paroxetine: A randomized, double-blind fixed-dose study with stopwatch assessment. *European Urology, 46,* 510–515.

Walkup, J. T., Albano, A. M., Piacentini, J., Birmaher, B., Compton, S., Sherrill, J., et al. (2008). Cognitive behavioral therapy, sertraline, or a combination in childhood anxiety. *New England Journal of Medicine, 359,* 2753–2766.

Weijmar Schultz, W., Basson, R., Binik, Y., Eschenback, D., Wesselmann, U., & Van Lankveld, J. (2005). Women's sexual pain and its management. *Journal of Sexual Medicine, 2,* 301–316.

West, S. L., D'Aloisio, A. A., Agans, R. P., Kalsbeek, W. D., Borisov, N. N., & Thorp, J. M. (2008). Prevalence of low sexual desire and hypoactive sexual desire disorder in a nationally representative sample of us women. *Archives of Internal Medicine, 168,* 1441–1449.

West, S. L., Vinikoor, L. C., & Zolnoun, D. (2004). A systematic review of the literature on female sexual dysfunction prevalence and predictors. *Annual Review of Sex Research, 15,* 40–172.

Witting, K., Santtila, P., Varjonen, M., Jern, P., Johansson, A., von der Pahlen, B., & Sandnabba, K. (2008). Female sexual dysfunction, sexual distress, and compatibility with partner. *Journal of Sexual Medicine, 5,* 2587–2599.

Working Group for a New View of Women's Sexual Problems. (2001). A new view of women's sexual problems. In E. Kaschak & L. Tiefer (Eds.), *A new view of women's sexual problems* (pp. 1–8). New York: Haworth Press.

Wylie, K., & Kenney, G. (2010). Sexual dysfunction and the aging male. *Maturitas, 65,* 23–27.

Zietsch, B. P., Miller, G. F., Bailey, J. M., & Martin, N. G. (2011). Female orgasm rates are largely independent of other traits: Implications for "female orgasmic disorder" and evolutionary theories of orgasm. *Journal of Sexual Medicine, 8,* 2305–2316.

16

Eating Disorders

HOWARD STEIGER,

JENNIFER S. COELHO,

LEA THALER,

AND FREDERIQUE VAN DEN EYNDE

Eating disorders (EDs) are polysymptomatic syndromes, defined by maladaptive attitudes and behaviors around eating, weight, and body image, but typically accompanied by disturbances of self-image, mood, impulse regulation, and interpersonal functioning. The current system of psychiatric diagnosis, *DSM-5*, includes four official ED syndromes—anorexia nervosa (AN), bulimia nervosa (BN), the formerly provisional diagnosis, binge eating disorder (BED), and a new classification—avoidant/restrictive food intake disorder (ARFID). There are two additional categories addressing atypical ED variants that do not fulfill criteria for one of the four syndromes noted but that nonetheless constitute a significant detriment to individuals' adjustment—other specified feeding and eating disorder (OSFED) and unspecified feeding and eating disorder (USFED). Revisions embodied in *DSM-5* ED criteria have been motivated by various concerns about aspects of the performance of the *DSM-IV-TR* criteria for the EDs—a main one being that a majority of eating-disordered individuals were classified as having the rather vaguely defined, eating disorder not otherwise specified (EDNOS). A main goal in the recent revision of diagnostic criteria for the EDs has been to reduce the proportion of eating-disordered individuals who would formerly have been classified as having an EDNOS, by redistributing them (as much as possible) among the four other, more specific diagnoses. In this chapter, we review pathognomonic features of the different *DSM-5* ED syndromes, as well as findings on concurrent traits and comorbid psychopathology. We also discuss the factors—biological, psychological and social—that are believed to explain ED development.

Defining Characteristics

Anorexia Nervosa (AN)

AN is defined by a relentless pursuit of thinness. Formerly attributed to a morbid fear of the consequences of eating, usually expressed as a dread of weight gain or obesity, *DSM-5* restates the concern of affected individuals without it being mandatory that there be intense fear of weight gain, although such fears are noted as a commonly present feature. What is required is that individuals restrict energy intake relative to requirements (leading to a markedly low body weight), experience a fear of weight gain or loss of control over weight gain or display persistent behavior to avoid weight gain (even though at a markedly low weight), and experience either a disturbance in the way in which their body weight or shape is experienced, undue influence of body weight or shape on self-evaluation, or persistent lack of recognition of the seriousness of a currently low body weight. The modifications described respond to the reality that people with AN, especially those who are very young or who are from Asian or African cultures, do not always espouse fears of fatness or weight gain as a rationale for their food-refusal and self-induced emaciation. *DSM-5* also drops the criterion sign of amenorrhea, it having been regarded as nondefinitive, providing only an imprecise reflection of nutritional status, and inappropriate in the case of males.

To provide an illustrative example, we describe "Joannie." Joannie, a 17-year-old high school student, eats a restricted range of "safe" foods, mainly vegetables, or an occasional spoonful of yoghurt and a few nuts. She avoids eating with her family or friends, so that she will be able to fully control what, how much, and when she eats. She exercises at least 2 hours a day (on the treadmill) and never eats before 6 PM, so as to be sure not to have time to overeat during any given day. Joannie is 5'4" tall and weighs 88 pounds, giving her a body mass index (BMI: Kg/m^2 or lbs/in^2 703) of 15.1—meaning that she is so thin as to border on emaciation. Her weight has dropped in recent months from an average of 128 pounds. Joannie compulsively insists that her fingertips have to touch when she circles her thighs with her hands, and when she feels that she has eaten something too rich in calories, even when it may have been what most people would call a small snack, Joannie purges by vomiting or by taking laxatives.

Although Joannie shows no binge eating (thus far), over half of people with AN eventually develop binge-eating episodes—that is, periodic dyscontrol over eating, or incapacity to satiate. In consideration of this reality, *DSM-5* (like *DSM-IV-TR*) draws a distinction between AN, restricting subtype (AN-R), in which there is restriction of food intake but no binge-eating or purging, and AN, binge-eating/purging (AN-B/P) subtype, in which (as the label implies) regular binge or purge episodes occur. Joannie would be diagnosable as having AN-B/P subtype, because she regularly purges.

Bulimia Nervosa (BN)

A defining feature of BN is binge eating (i.e., appetitive dyscontrol) followed by an effort to compensate for calories consumed through self-induced vomiting, laxative misuse, intensive exercise, fasting, or other means. BN occurs in people with normal or above-normal body weight and who therefore by definition do not have AN. Binge-purge episodes occur at least once weekly in the *DSM-5* definition (rather than twice weekly as was required in *DSM-IV-TR*). Regardless, such episodes typically occur far more frequently and can, when the disorder is severe, occur many times daily. AN and BN share in common a core preoccupation with body shape and weight, and the compulsion to restrict food intake. Excessive dietary restraint in people with BN eventually gives way to appetitive dysregulation and binge eating. In BN, binges are characterized by consumption, with a terrifying sense of dyscontrol, of excessive, sometimes massive, quantities of calories. Binge eating can provoke profound feelings of shame, anxiety, or depression, and dramatic shifts in the sufferer's sense of self-worth and well-being. This lends to BN a characteristic unpredictability or lability, as people with this syndrome tend to shift rapidly (depending upon felt control over eating) from a sense of well-being, expansiveness, or excitability, to profound despair, irritability, and depression.

Kiera serves as a "prototype." Kiera, aged 29, a recent graduate from law school, is serving as an apprentice in a law firm. People know her to be very hard working but a bit of a "thrill seeker." She has had a number of short-lived relationships, drinks alcohol fairly regularly, and dabbles with cocaine use when it is offered to her. Although she has a slim-normal frame, she is conscious of her weight and tries to keep her food intake down, often skipping breakfast and eating green salads for lunch. After supper, especially if she has been drinking (but often when not), Kiera often finds she cannot stop eating, and she goes from two portions of her supper to eating cookies, cakes, food leftovers, and just about everything else she has to eat in her pantry and fridge. She then forces herself to vomit several times, sometimes using a toothbrush to provoke gagging. After a binge-purge episode, she feels very badly about herself. At such times, she can bruise her thighs with her fists; once she burned her upper arm with a lit cigarette.

The validity of BN as a unique diagnostic entity is well supported (Wonderlich, Joiner, Keel, Williamson, & Crosby, 2007). However, *DSM-5* has dropped a dubious distinction, made in *DSM-IV-TR*, between purging and nonpurging bulimic subtypes.

Binge Eating Disorder (BED)

Like BN, BED is characterized by recurrent eating binges. However, in BED compensatory behaviors (such as vomiting, exercise, or fasting) are absent, so that BED is commonly associated with or leads to obesity. Defining characteristics include eating more rapidly than normal, eating until uncomfortably full, eating when not hungry, eating alone because of embarrassment around the quantity one eats, or feeling intense distress (guilt, disgust, or depression) after eating. Despite initial concerns that BED might not be a "mental" disorder, findings support the conclusion that BED and non-BED obese individuals differ in the sense that the former group displays higher overall caloric intake, additional pathological eating behaviors (such as chaotic or emotional eating), additional indices of comorbid psychopathology, and poorer response to treatment (Wonderlich, Gordon, Mitchell, Crosby, & Engel, 2009). Notably, BED also emerges as a distinct disorder in familial-aggregation and genetic studies (Javaras et al., 2008).

Avoidant/Restrictive Food Intake Disorder (ARFID)

ARFID, a new diagnosis in *DSM-5*, evolved from what was originally conceived to be a characteristic eating problem of children, feeding disorder of infancy or early childhood—effectively the "picky eater" syndrome. The diagnostic concept has been retooled to make it applicable across the lifespan. ARFID comprises a range of conditions in which people become severely blocked in the ability to nourish themselves adequately, not because of concerns about weight gain or body image, but because of such things as intense aversion to certain food tastes or textures, preoccupation with nutritional value of certain foods, or inordinate fears that eating will cause indigestion or vomiting. ARFID syndromes differ from variants of AN in which people show "persistent behavior to avoid weight gain" that is anchored to body-image concerns. Someone who eats a rigidly restricted range of foods because of a compulsive effort to consume only healthy, natural foods (colloquially described as "orthorexia"), if they fail to nourish themselves adequately, would often meet ARFID criteria.

Feeding and Eating Disorders Not Elsewhere Classified (FEDNEC)

As we noted earlier, a problem with the *DSM-IV-TR* classification system was that it classified a disproportionate number of individuals within the EDNOS category—largely representing "partial" or "subthreshold" anorexic or bulimic syndromes, or BED. According to most available evidence, EDNOS syndromes account for comparable levels of distress, psychiatric comorbidity, and health-service usage to those in fully syndromic ED variants (Fairburn et al., 2007). In modifying existing criteria for AN and BN (as described earlier) and introducing BED as a formal diagnosis, the proposed *DSM-5* classification aims to reduce the number of individuals who will meet OSFED or USFED criteria.

Are *DSM* diagnostic distinctions valid? Available efforts to develop valid ED classifications using taxometric methods, latent class analyses, or other statistical classification techniques have provided fairly good support for AN, BN, and BED as phenomenologically distinct entities (Wonderlich et al., 2007). Not only is each broad category at least partly discriminable using empirical methods, but there is also evidence to suggest that the categories may "breed true" within families. In addition, there is quite convincing support for the boundary between "restricter" and "binger/purger" variants of AN, and between BED and BN. However, there is mixed support for the distinction between anorexic- and normal-weight variants of binge-purge syndromes (i.e., AN-binge/purge type versus BN), and literally no validation of the distinction between syndromic versus subsyndromic forms of BN (i.e., BN versus bulimia-spectrum EDNOS).

Historical Perspectives

The English physician Richard Morton is often credited with having introduced AN to the medical literature. In 1689, he documented two adolescent cases, one a boy, the other a girl, both suffering "nervous consumption," "want of appetite," and weight loss, in the absence of any apparent medical cause (Gordon, 1990, p. 12). Well-elaborated reports on AN emerged again in an 1860 account by the French physician Marcé and in independent reports (published in 1870) by Sir William Gull and Charles Lasègue. Gull is credited with coining the term "anorexia nervosa," but all three described a syndrome characterized by food refusal, onset in adolescence, amenorrhea, and lack of concern for consequences of not eating (Gordon, 1990). Intriguingly, reports on AN became relatively common through the nineteenth and twentieth centuries, but a pivotal diagnostic element—fear of weight gain—was first acknowledged only in accounts emerging well into the twentieth century. Late "entry" of this characteristic has been taken to suggest that fears of weight gain may not be essential to AN but, rather, may constitute only a contemporary rationale for instances of self-starvation, shaped by contemporary cultural values.

The first formal reports on BN emerged much more recently, in roughly concurrent, 1979 publications by Igoin in France, Boyadjieva and Achkova in Bulgaria, and Robert Palmer and Gerald Russell in England (Vandereycken, 1994). Having been formally recognized in the late 1970s, BN is widely thought to be a recently developing ED variant. Indeed, after an exhaustive review of available historical and cross-cultural data, Keel and Klump (2003) concluded that AN and BN have distinct temporal and geographical distributions, with AN showing a relatively modest increase in incidence over the years, and occurring frequently in geographical areas that are quite untouched by the "culture of slimness." In contrast, BN appears to have increased dramatically in prevalence during the latter part of the twentieth century and mainly in industrialized cultures. Updating this impression, recent reviews suggest that the incidence of AN has been surprisingly stable over the past four decades, whereas BN incidence seems to have increased markedly over the second half of the twentieth century, and then to have declined slightly since that time (Currin, Schmidt, Treasure, & Jick, 2005; Keel, Heatherton, Dorer, Joiner, & Zalta, 2006; Smink, van Hoeken, & Hoek, 2012).

The phenomenon of binge eating among the obese was described by Stunkard (1959) over 50 years ago. However, BED has a rather short history in diagnostic nosology, having been introduced in 1994 in *DSM-IV* as a provisional ED diagnosis, and as an official ED for the first time in *DSM-5*.

Epidemiology

Studies emanating from various industrialized countries suggest that strictly defined AN affects from .5% to just under 1% of young (school-aged) females, with an incidence of approximately 8 cases per 100,000 of the population per year (Hoek & van Hoeken, 2003). Point prevalences obtained for BN in young-adult females range from 1% to 2%, with an incidence of at least 12 cases per 100,000 of the population per year (Hoek & van Hoeken, 2003; Keski-Rahkonen et al., 2007). BED, a substantially more prevalent disorder, reportedly affects 3.5% of females and 2.0% of males in the United States (Hudson, Hiripi, Pope, & Kessler, 2007). In corroboration, a recent study by our group, implicating a carefully stratified sample of 1,501 women aged 20 to 40 in the area of Montreal, Canada, documented a 3.7% rate of BED (Gauvin, Steiger, & Brodeur, 2009). Full-threshold ED syndromes aside, it appears that subthreshold EDs (i.e., disorders formerly classified as EDNOS) may affect at least 10% of young females (e.g., Stice, Marti, Shaw, & Jaconis, 2009).

The median age of onset of an ED is between 18 and 21 years of age; onset of AN typically occurs by the mid-teens, BN and BED by early adulthood (Hudson et al., 2007). Although AN and BN occur about 10 times more frequently in women than in men, BED displays a more even gender distribution, with a male/female ratio of roughly 2:3. Although it is widely believed that EDs are disorders of affluent, urban society, data show no significant linkage with either socioeconomic status or urbanicity (Swanson, Crow, Le Grange, Swendsen, & Merikangas, 2011).

Comorbid Psychopathology

Paradoxically, it seems that if one assertion can be made about EDs, it is that they are often not just about eating. Rather, EDs frequently co-occur with mood, anxiety, substance abuse, personality, and other psychiatric disorders.

Mood Disorders

Among comorbid tendencies noted in individuals with EDs, mood disorders figure prominently.

Hudson et al. (2007) found lifetime rates of mood disorder to be 42% in adults with AN (2.4 times the risk in matched normal eaters), 70% in adults with BN (a 7.8-fold increased risk), and 46% in adults with BED (a 3.1-fold greater risk). A similar pattern emerged for adolescents with bulimic ED variants: 49.9% of those with BN (a 5.7-fold greater risk) and 45.3% of those with BED (a 4.6-fold risk) were observed to report presence of a mood disorder (Swanson et al., 2011). Notably, mood disorders were not as pronounced in adolescents with AN (10.9%, a 0.7-fold risk). In a similar vein, findings suggest that mood disorder rates may be substantially lower in community-based samples than they are in treatment-seeking ones (Blinder, Cumella, & Sanathara, 2006). In other words, factors related to age, social standing, and recruitment all seem to influence the extent to which comorbid psychopathology becomes apparent in people with EDs. Coaggregation of EDs with other mood disorder variants is also noted: A community study by Zaider, Johnson, and Cockell (2000) points to an important affinity between EDs and dysthymia. Other evidence has shown a strong association between BN and seasonal affective disorder (SAD), implying cyclical season-dependent recurrences in depressed mood, which parallel seasonal variations in binge-purge behaviors (Ghadirian, Marini, Jabalpurwala, & Steiger, 1999).

Various areas of etiological overlap can be postulated to explain the convergence between mood disorders and EDs. Pertinent to questions of shared causality, a twin study by Wade, Bulik, Neale, and Kendler (2000) has attributed shared risk for AN and mood disorders about equally to genetic and environmental factors, such as shared family and developmental determinants.

Anxiety Disorders

Anxiety disorders are also common in individuals with EDs (e.g., Hudson et al., 2007; Kaye, Bulik, Thornton, Barbarich, & Masters, 2004), the most commonly occurring ones appearing to be obsessive–compulsive disorder (reported to occur in 41% of people with an ED) and social phobia (reported in 20%) (Kaye et al., 2004). Hudson et al. (2007) found that 47% of people with AN displayed a lifetime anxiety disorder (a 1.9-fold greater risk than that in matched controls), and 80% of those with

BN (an 8.6-fold greater risk) and 65% of people with BED (a 4.3-fold greater risk) had a lifetime anxiety disorder. AN was observed to co-occur especially often with specific phobia, whereas BN and BED were associated with increased risks for most anxiety disorders. Reportedly, some anxiety disorders precede the onset of ED symptoms (such as social phobia), whereas others (such as panic disorder and generalized anxiety disorder) tend to emerge in concurrence with or after ED development (Godart et al., 2003; Pallister & Waller, 2008).

To account for high rates of comorbidity between eating and anxiety disorders, Pallister and Waller (2008) presented a shared transmission model, proposing that cognitions and environmental experiences increase the likelihood of cognitive avoidance strategies, which can take the form of disordered eating behaviors, anxiety-related behaviors, or both. A pattern suggesting shared heredity is that anxiety appears to be prominent in the familial pedigrees of individuals prone to AN, with increased rates of anxiety disorders being noted in the non-eating-disordered, first-degree relatives of AN participants (Strober, Freeman, Lampert, & Diamond, 2007).

Posttraumatic Stress Disorder

Evidence associates bulimic ED variants with exposure to traumatic stress. Modal figures suggest that about 30% of adults with BN report unwanted sexual experiences during childhood, and more than half report childhood physical maltreatment (Wonderlich, Brewerton, Jocic, Dansky, & Abbott, 1997). Various investigators have concluded that victimization experiences have a significant role in the development of BN. Consistent with a link between EDs and adverse (or traumatic) life experiences, findings have suggested a striking co-occurrence between EDs and posttraumatic stress disorder (PTSD). One study found PTSD symptoms in about half of women with AN, BN, or EDNOS (Gleaves, Eberenz, & May, 1998). The National Comorbidity Survey reported lifetime PTSD to occur in 45% of individuals with BN, compared to only 12% of those with AN (Hudson et al., 2007).

Various pathways, direct or indirect, might account for an etiological link between the EDs and traumatic events. Traumata directly affecting the body may have direct consequences for body image and, in turn, for eating and weight-control behaviors. Alternatively, abusive experiences might affect self-, mood-, and impulse regulation and in these ways, indirectly heighten risk of maladaptive eating behavior. For instance, our group has documented a tendency for people with BN who report past abuse to show greater abnormalities on indices reflecting serotonin and cortisol functions (Steiger, Bruce, & Groleau, 2011; Steiger et al., 2001). Such results could imply neurobiological sequelae of childhood abuse that could heighten risk of overreactivity to stress, and of self- and appetitive dysregulation.

Substance Use Disorders

Studies associate binge-eating symptomatology more strongly with substance use disorders than they do restrictive or purging symptoms in the absence of binge-eating (see Bulik et al., 2004). Relevant findings show that 10% to 55% of women with BN abuse substances, whereas 25% to 40% of females with alcohol dependence show some form of ED (often in the bulimia spectrum). Not surprisingly, studies examining psychopathological implications of substance abuse in the EDs report that concurrent substance abuse predicts greater psychiatric comorbidity of various forms. Substance abusers in eating-disordered samples have been found to have significantly more comorbid psychiatric diagnoses (Lilenfeld et al., 1998), exhibit more impulsivity and perfectionism (Bulik et al., 2004), and have a greater likelihood of exposure to genetic and developmental risks (Richardson et al., 2008).

Personality Disorders

Among various comorbid propensities seen in the EDs, that with personality disorders (PDs) is arguably the strongest (see Cassin & von Ranson, 2005; Lilenfeld, Wonderlich, Riso, Crosby, & Mitchell, 2006). A meta-analysis found 58% of women with EDs to have a PD, compared to 28% of a comparison group (Rosenvinge, Martinussen, & Ostensen, 2000). Furthermore, although individuals with AN and BN exhibited comparable rates of DSM Cluster C (anxious-fearful) PDs (45% and 44%, respectively), individuals with BN showed higher proportions of Cluster B (dramatic-erratic) PDs (44% overall) and borderline PD (31%).

The literature on this topic concurs on the following points: (1) PDs are frequently present in individuals with anorexic and bulimic symptomatology; (2) restrictive symptomatology seems to be associated with a high concentration of anxious-fearful PD diagnoses (characterized by anxiousness, orderliness, introversion, and preference for sameness); (3) ED variants characterized by binge–purge symptoms coincide with more heterogeneous PD subtypes than do restrictive forms, and with higher rates of dramatic-erratic PDs (characterized by prominent attention- and sensation-seeking, extroversion, mood lability, and impulsivity); and (4) PD comorbidity in BED is comparable to that seen in BN, although the loading of dramatic-erratic PDs, like borderline personality disorder, may be less pronounced. Taken together, it appears that the dietary over-control that characterizes restrictive AN is paralleled by generalized overcontrol, as a personality or adaptive style. Binge/purge symptomatology, in contrast, affects people who evince quite heterogeneous personality traits, although dysregulatory traits (e.g., affective instability, impulsivity) are overrepresented.

Malnutrition can have adverse effects on personality functioning (Keys, Brozek, Henschel, Mickelson, & Taylor, 1950), and this raises the concern that apparent personality problems seen in individuals with EDs may reflect "state" disturbances associated with an active ED, and not "trait" tendencies. In other words, caution is warranted concerning the use of PD diagnoses in individuals with an active ED. Nonetheless, various findings suggest that personality problems seen in individuals with an ED often exist independently of the ED. For example, one investigation reported that 26% of women who recovered from AN or BN showed some form of ongoing PD (Matsunaga et al., 2000).

Etiology

It is widely held that EDs have a multidimensional etiology, including genetic liabilities (affecting mood, behavioral controls, sensitivity to reward, energy metabolism and appetite), developmental processes (conducive to self-image or adjustment problems, or excessive concerns with achievement and social approval), environmental stresses (such as perinatal insults or childhood traumata), state-related effects (owing to the nutritional and mental status), and ultimately, social inducements toward intensive dieting (e.g., Jacobi, Hayward, de Zwaan, Kraemer, & Agras, 2004; Steiger & Bruce, 2007; Striegel-Moore & Bulik, 2007; Treasure, Claudino, & Zucker, 2010). The following sections review the various social, psychological, and biological factors that have been thought to contribute to risk for ED development.

Sociocultural Context

Western social values associate slimness with cultural ideals of success, beauty, power, and self-control, and this association likely underlies the tendency for people in the West—especially young females—to be dissatisfied with their bodies. There is little doubt that internalization of the "thin ideal" plays a direct role in the development of body-image preoccupations and clinical EDs (see Jacobi et al., 2004). A multisite, cross-cultural survey indicates that increased exposure to Western media is associated with a smaller ideal body weight and increased body dissatisfaction (Swami et al., 2010). Likewise, a meta-analytic review has concluded that exposure to media images of thinness is associated with increased body dissatisfaction and eating-disorder symptoms (Grabe, Ward, & Hyde, 2008).

Even with these findings, the role of culture in ED development can be overstated. First, effect sizes reflecting the impact of exposure to media images on body satisfaction are modest (Swami et al., 2010). Second, cross-cultural research indicates that AN-like disorders, characterized by food refusal, are prevalent in diverse (non-Western) contexts (Keel & Klump, 2003). If we assume that sociocultural factors are a central part of ED pathogenesis, the question still remains: Why do relatively few individuals develop a clinically significant ED, despite such widespread body dissatisfaction and valuation of the "thin ideal"? To answer this question, we need to consider additional sources of vulnerability, conveyed by psychological, developmental, and biological processes.

Psychological Factors

The first psychometric studies on the EDs, published in the mid-1970s, led to an association of AN with such traits as obsessionality, social

anxiety, introversion, neuroticism, and depression. These same reports introduced a distinction between EDs characterized solely by restriction of food intake (i.e., AN-R) and variants implicating binge eating and purging (AN-B/P subtype). Individuals with the AN-R subtype were described as conforming, obsessional, and emotionally and socially reserved, whereas those with AN-B/P were thought to be prone to impulsivity, antisociality, and externalization (Sohlberg & Strober, 1994). Later studies on BN broadened the boundaries of an association between binge eating and impulsive or erratic characteristics (Vitousek & Manke, 1994), and the stage was set for belief in a systematic distinction, on associated personality characteristics, between ED variants characterized by restriction (i.e., AN-R) and variants characterized by binge eating and/or purging (i.e., BN or AN-BP).

Although the fit proves to be imperfect, contemporary studies continue to find restricter and binger/purger groups to differ along the lines stated (see Cassin & von Ranson, 2005; Lilenfeld et al., 2006). Findings show individuals with BN to be more novelty seeking than people with restricting or binge/purge variants of AN, individuals with restricting forms of AN to be more reward dependent (or concerned with social approval) than those with BN or AN-B/P subtype, and individuals with AN to have stronger loadings on measures of persistence (largely compulsive personality) than individuals with BN (Bulik, Sullivan, Weltzin, & Kaye, 1995; Díaz-Marsá, Carrasco, & Sáiz, 2000). These findings support belief in a systematic coaggregation (at a group level) between AN-R and anxious, approval-seeking, compulsive traits, and between ED variants characterized by binge eating and/or purging (AN-BP and BN) and emotionality, risk taking, or oppositionality.

However, a caveat is needed here: Use of average traits in diagnostic subgroups risks obscuring meaningful within-subtype heterogeneities. For example, studies have shown that AN, BN, and EDNOS variants all evince substantial within-diagnosis heterogeneity as to comorbid personality traits (see Claes et al., 2012; Westen & Harnden-Fischer, 2001; Wonderlich et al., 2005). Studies point remarkably consistently to three broad, psychopathology-defined ED subphenotypes (Steiger et al., 2009; Wonderlich et al., 2005): (1) psychologically intact (although perhaps perfectionistic), (2) overregulated (compulsive and inhibited), and (3) dysregulated (impulsive and reactive). As a generality, AN-R subtype coincides with the overregulated personality profile, whereas binge eating/purging ED variants seem to occur with about the same probability with any of the three profiles. Highlighting the clinical importance of the trait-based distinctions noted, investigators have associated the "dysregulated" characteristic with increased comorbidity (e.g., depression, self-mutilation, drug abuse), more developmental disturbances (e.g., child abuse, attachment problems), and poorer treatment outcome (see Duncan et al., 2005; Steiger & Bruce, 2007).

Specific Traits

1. Perfectionism In assessment of perfectionistic traits, individuals with AN, BN, and BED have all been found to have higher self-rated perfectionism scores than those of healthy controls—and this is especially true for aspects of perfectionism that are associated with the setting of high personal standards and goals, being overly self-critical, or overly concerned with others' judgements (Bardone-Cone et al., 2007; Steele, O'Shea, Murdock, & Wade, 2011). Perfectionistic tendencies appear to predate ED onset (Fairburn, Cooper, Doll, & Welch, 1999), persist after recovery (Lilenfeld et al., 2006), be common in the non-eating-disordered relatives of those who develop an ED (Lilenfeld et al., 2000; Woodside et al., 2002), and correspond to severity of such symptoms as dietary restraint and overevaluation of shape and weight.

2. Impulsivity People with binge/purge ED variants display higher levels of self-reported trait impulsivity and engage in more impulsive behaviors than those with restrictive ED variants or normal eaters (Claes, Vandereycken, & Vertommen, 2006; Favaro et al., 2005; Rosval et al., 2006). For example, multi-impulsivity (i.e., engaging in more than one behavior, such as self-mutilation, substance abuse, suicide attempts, shoplifting) has been linked to purging behaviors in women with EDs (Favaro et al., 2005) and with BN (Newton, Freeman, & Munro, 1993). Furthermore, pronounced impulsivity in BN and in "binge-purge" ED variants has been linked, in some reports, to more severe eating disturbances (binge eating, vomiting, laxative abuse, and drive for thinness), body-image problems, and generalized psychopathology, including substance abuse, self-injurious

behaviors, and "borderline traits" (e.g., Wiederman & Pryor, 1996). There has also been some evidence favoring the notion that impulsivity may be a temporal antecedent to BN onset (e.g., Wonderlich, Connolly, & Stice, 2004).

3. Body-Image Disturbances Disturbance in the way one experiences one's body weight or shape constitutes a defining characteristic of AN and BN, and it is hypothesized to have a fundamental role in the etiology and maintenance of these disorders. Thus it is striking that there has been controversy over the importance and, indeed, occurrence of body-image disturbance in AN and BN. Empirical findings have supported conflicting conclusions: Some highlight clear-cut tendencies of eating-disordered individuals to overestimate bodily proportions or to have unusually harsh attitudes toward their bodies (e.g., Favaro et al., 2012). Others show no differences in perception of body image between eating-disordered individuals and controls, or they suggest that emotional and attentional factors (and not perceptual ones) explain the evident preoccupations with body and body image seen in people with EDs (Espeset et al., 2011).

4. Dietary Restraint Cognitive components of dietary restraint—or restrictive eating attitudes (e.g., the expectation that it is important or desirable to eat low-calorie foods or to compensate when one eats)—are thought to make a fundamental contribution to the development and maintenance of EDs (e.g., Fairburn, Cooper, & Shafran, 2003). Overvaluing slim appearance and dietary control have a clear role in supporting the excessive dieting often seen in patients with an ED. Paradoxically, chronic attempts to restrain eating often increase individuals' susceptibility to overeating. Polivy and Herman, pioneers in the study of the effects of attempted dietary restraint, have demonstrated that diverse triggers lead to overeating in individuals who are attitudinally restrained. These triggers, identified mainly through laboratory studies in nonclinical populations, include (1) beliefs that one has exceeded an allowable calorie limit, (2) negative affect, (3) feelings of self-inadequacy, or (4) global disinhibition, as is induced by alcohol consumption (Polivy & Herman, 1993). Recent findings from a longitudinal study suggest further that depression interacts with dieting status, such that individuals who both diet and report high

levels of depression are more likely to display later onset of binge-eating (Goldschmidt, Wall, Loth, Le Grange & Neumark-Sztainer, 2012).

5. **Emotion Dysregulation** Negative emotions play an important role in the maintenance of binge-eating symptoms. Affect-regulation models of BN posit that negative emotions trigger binge episodes and that binge eating serves to alleviate negative affect, if only temporarily. Support for such models comes mainly from functional analyses of binge-eating antecedents and consequences (usually performed using online experience-sampling procedures) (Berg et al., 2013; Engelberg, Steiger, Gauvin, & Wonderlich, 2007; Haedt-Matt & Keel, 2011; Steiger, Lehoux, & Gauvin, 1999). Affect-regulating properties of binge-purge episodes may be ingredients in the tendency of binge eating to become entrenched and self-perpetuating.

6. **Neurocognition** Neurocognitive performance in people with an ED appears to differ from that in healthy subjects, with some patterns of neurocognitive functioning proposed to serve as "endophenotypes" or "biomarkers." Numerous neurocognitive domains have been studied in ED populations, and a wide range of tasks has been used. The presence of an ED has generally been associated with impairment in higher-level cognitive functions, such as active memory, attention, and problem-solving (e.g., Zakzanis, Campbell, & Polsinelli, 2010). However, currently there is insufficient evidence to suggest that people with a bulimic disorder have altered neurocognitive performance (Van den Eynde et al., 2011).

In research on AN, evidence suggests specific impairments in the ability to shift perceptual or problem-solving sets flexibly ("set-shifting" abilities) or to apprehend global organizing principles in favor of attention to details, called "central coherence" (Holliday, Tchanturia, Landau, Collier, & Treasure, 2005; Roberts, Tchanturia, & Treasure, 2013). Various groups have demonstrated that people with a lifetime history of AN, and their unaffected siblings have poorer set-shifting and central-coherence abilities than those of healthy comparison groups (Galimberti et al., 2013; Roberts, Tchanturia, Stahl, Southgate, & Treasure, 2007; Tenconi et al., 2010). Although weak set-shifting and central coherence have been proposed as endophenotypes for the EDs, recent research has questioned the disorder specificity

of these observations, suggesting that presence of coexisting depression may be a confounding factor (Giel et al., 2012).

Decision-making is another function that has received attention in ED research (Galimberti et al., 2013). However, here the potential impact of co-occurring problems, such as substance dependence in people with bulimic symptoms, needs to be ruled out. As for "state" or "trait" questions, longitudinal studies report improved neuropsychological performance coincident with ED-symptom remission (Lauer, Gorzewski, Gerlinghoff, Backmund, & Zihl, 1999). Whether a "trait" or a "state," preliminary data indicate that cognitive remediation therapy (Tchanturia et al., 2008), which uses cognitive exercises to improve eating-disordered patients' thinking processes, may lead to an improvement in neurocognitive functioning (Tchanturia et al., 2008).

Developmental Factors

Theories on Family Dynamics

Early theories often construed AN as a phobic-obsessional adaptation to familial intrusions and overprotectiveness, conceptualizing food refusal as a child's means of self-assertion in the face of excessive familial controls or emotional investment. In contrast, early models of BN conveyed a view of children's frantic struggles to satisfy needs in disengaged or neglectful families (e.g., Humphrey, 1991). In such views, bulimic eating patterns were thought to play a self- and mood-regulatory function and to be a response to chaotic family interactions tinged, alternately, with desperate attempts to affiliate, and hostile rejections and blaming. Aside from having dubious empirical support, such portrayals of the family's role in ED development are overly saturated with blame and guilt induction.

The thinking on the role of family functioning in the EDs has shifted quite dramatically in recent years. Based on the strength of evidence suggesting that family functioning, although perhaps implicated, does not have a central etiological role, the Academy for Eating Disorders (AED) has taken the following stance: "It is the position of the AED that whereas family factors can play a role in the genesis and maintenance of eating disorders, current knowledge refutes the idea that they are either the exclusive or even the primary mechanisms that underlie risk. Thus, the AED stands firmly against any etiologic model of eating disorders in which family influences are seen as the primary cause of anorexia nervosa or bulimia nervosa, and condemns generalizing statements that imply families are to blame for their child's illness" (le Grange, Lock, Loeb, & Nicholls, 2010, p. 1).

Empirical Findings on Family Functioning

This well-warranted proviso should not be taken to mean, however, that there is no empirical evidence suggesting that EDs coincide systematically with variations in family functioning. On the contrary, cross-sectional studies have tended to associate AN with families evincing high levels of enmeshment or lack of separation, and bulimic ED variants with familial tensions, disengagement, lack of nurturance, and hostility (Humphrey, 1991). Similarly, families of individuals with a BED have been characterized as being incohesive, unexpressive, conflictual, and controlling (see Hodges, Cochrane, & Brewerton, 1998; Jacobi et al., 2004). However, the interpretation of such findings and their application in causal modeling need to be nuanced by judicious consideration of the limitations of available family research. First, most of the pertinent findings have been generated through cross-sectional or retrospective designs, meaning that observations risk being contaminated by the effects on family functioning of living with an eating-disordered member. Indeed, the few prospective family studies that exist, designed to identify temporal sequences with causal implications, provide weak evidence at best of a priori involvement of family-functioning variables in risk for ED development (see Beato-Fernández, Rodríguez-Cano, Belmonte-Llario, & Martínez-Delgado, 2004; Nicholls & Viner, 2009; Shoebridge & Gowers, 2000). Second, effects observed, even if repeatable, need not represent family dynamics that act etiologically but may instead constitute markers of heritable "traits" (such as anxiousness or impulsivity) that are present in various family members. Such traits might tend to shape family interaction patterns and co-occur with risk of ED development, without themselves having any specific causal implication. Third, interpretation of significant results is obfuscated by the lack of psychiatric control groups in most studies, rendering it impossible to specify the extent to which

observed problems in family functioning constitute an ED-specific factor or a nonspecific risk for generalized problems of adjustment.

Family dynamics may not *cause* EDs, but they might represent important factors in maintaining an ED. In keeping with this view, many current treatment paradigms mobilize the family as a potential resource in therapy. Treatment-outcome studies have highlighted that involvement of families in treatment improves outcomes, especially in the case of younger ED patients (Eisler, Simic, Russell, & Dare, 2007; Lock, Couturier, & Agras, 2006).

Biological Factors

Data from recent neurobiological, genetic-epidemiological, and molecular-genetic studies have led to increasing consideration of the importance of biological determinants and maintaining factors in the EDs. This section reviews the pertinent findings.

Neurobiological Alterations

Various neurobiological systems have been postulated to contribute to susceptibility to ED development.

Serotonin Serotonin(5-hydroxytryptamine[5-HT]) is a regulator of mood, social behavior, impulsivity, and eating behavior—with increased 5-HT activity promoting appetite suppression and underactivity promoting excessive, binge-like eating. 5-HT thus becomes an obvious candidate for a causal role in the EDs. Various 5-HT anomalies have been reported in patients with AN, including alterations on central and peripheral 5-HT indices (see Kaye, 2008; Steiger, Bruce, & Groleau, 2011, for a review). Moreover, several findings indicate persistent 5HT-system anomalies in individuals who have recovered from AN, long after weight restoration. In BN, studies have shown anomalies on measures indicating reduced platelet binding of serotonin uptake inhibitors, altered brain receptor sensitivity and transporter activity, and diminished neuroendocrine responses to serotonin precursors and agonists. In BED, studies have documented similar, disorder-relevant 5-HT alterations. Moreover, as in AN, persistent 5-HT anomalies have been documented in samples of individuals who are fully recovered from bulimia, with relevant studies revealing persistently altered 5-HT_{2A} receptor binding and reduced platelet paroxetine-binding. Providing a striking indication that such results implicate heredity, one study by our group showed that unaffected first-degree relatives of patients with BN had anomalous peripheral uptake of 5-HT compared to that in relatives of control women (Steiger et al., 2006).

Other Neurotransmitters and Neuropeptides   There are putative pathophysiological roles for several other biological systems; dopamine (DA) influences reward-driven behaviors, novelty seeking, executive control, affect, and food ingestion (see Bello & Hajnal, 2010; Broft, Berner, Martinez, & Walsh, 2011). Similarly, DA-system assays have suggested functional alterations in individuals with active AN, active BN, and partially recovered (i.e., weight-restored) AN. For instance, Frank and colleagues (2005) found that individuals who had recovered from AN displayed increased binding of D2/D3 receptors in the anteroventral striatum, a region that organizes responses to reward stimuli. In parallel, studies of BN have documented decreased DA metabolites, DA transporter (DAT) availability (Kaye, Fudge, & Paulus, 2009), and striatal activity during tasks involving reward (Wagner et al., 2010) and self-regulatory control (Marsh et al., 2009, 2011).

Neurotrophins act in cellular proliferation and survival, synaptic activity, and neural plasticity. One widely studied neurotrophin, brain-derived neurotrophic factor (BDNF), is also an important regulator of food intake and energy homeostasis and thus constitutes a plausible candidate affecting ED (Mercader et al., 2007; Monteleone Zanardini, et al., 2006). Supporting evidence shows serum BDNF to be reduced in people with AN or BN (Monteleone, 2011). Furthermore, molecular-genetic findings indicate a recurrent association of the BDNF Val66Met polymorphism with BN.

The hypothalamic–pituitary–adrenal (HPA) axis is the body's main stress-response system. Findings in AN and BN indicate various HPA-axis alterations (Brambilla, 2003)—some perhaps due to effects of malnutrition, some to comorbid mood and anxiety problems, some to posttraumatic effects, and some due directly to having an ED. Several studies link pronounced psychopathology in ED sufferers to pronounced anomalies in HPA-axis functioning (Bruce, Steiger, & Israël, 2012; Díaz-Marsá, Carrasco, Basurte, Sáiz, López-Ibor, & Hollander, 2008).

Cholecystokinin (CCK), a peptide secreted by the gut, acts on the hypothalamus to produce satiety. Suggestive of a possible facilitating effect on bulimic behavior, plasma CCK levels have been observed to be low in BN (Pirke, Kellner, Friess, Krieg, & Fichter, 1994). Like CCK, peptide YY (PYY) is a gut peptide involved in appetite regulation. And like CCK, PYY has been found to be low, after eating, in BN (Monteleone, Martiadis, et al., 2005). Likewise, abnormally low levels of leptin, a hormone secreted by fat cells that regulates appetite and energy expenditure, have been documented in women with active AN (Grinspoon et al., 1996) and in those with normal-weight BN (Brewerton, Lesem, Kennedy, & Garvey, 2000). Finally, there is some evidence for a role of ghrelin, which affects short-term regulation of appetite and long-term regulation of energy balance, in BED (Monteleone, Fabrazzo, et al., 2005).

Sex Hormones   Given the sex distribution of EDs, one enticing hypothesis has been that sex hormones, androgens and estrogens, may impact risk for ED development. In support of this are findings derived from opposite-sex twin pairs (in which the female co-twin is exposed to more testosterone, in utero, than are females from a same-sex twin pair) that point to a significant role of androgen in buffering against risk of ED development (Culbert, Breedlove, Burt, & Klump, 2008). A related study associated second-digit/fourth-digit finger length ratios (an indirect measure of intrauterine androgen exposure) with levels of ED symptomatology in women. Other studies support a role of sex hormones in structuring risk of ED development, by showing apparent activating effects of puberty on genetic risk for ED development (Klump et al., 2012).

Neuroimaging Studies

AN   A catalogue of brain-imaging studies in individuals with AN has now accumulated, with results pointing to altered resting brain activity and brain-activation responses provoked by disorder-relevant stimuli. Here, diverse brain regions are implicated, often those known to be involved in the processing of emotions and of food- and body-related stimuli—the amygdala, parahippocampal and cingulate gyrus, and insular, medial prefrontal, orbitofrontal, parietal, medial, and inferior temporal cortices (Kaye et al., 2009; Pietrini et al., 2011; Zhu et al., 2012). There has been particular interest in the idea that altered activity in the insular cortex has a role in AN. For example, provocation studies have reported greater insula (and sometimes anterior cingulate) activation in AN than in control participants after provocation with food images or body-size comparisons. One exception to such indications of increased insular activity in response to disorder-relevant stimulation in AN is a study by Wagner and colleagues (2008) on gustatory processing in AN, which showed that individuals who had recovered from AN displayed lower neural activation in the insula after sucrose and water administration than that in healthy female controls. A possible explanation for this deviation from an expected result of overactivation may be that this study, unlike others cited, addressed recovered (instead of actively anorexic) individuals and consequently may have reflected "scarring" effects or other adaptations resulting from long-term exposure to effects of severe malnutrition.

In addition to body and food images, a number of other exposure paradigms have been used to investigate specific brain activation patterns in people with AN with regard to such constructs as self-identity (McAdams & Krawczyk, 2014) and social cognition (McAdams & Krawczyk, 2011). For both constructs, the (medial) frontal cortex appears to play a central role. Lower brain activation in this area in response to a theory of mind task may be associated with poorer treatment outcome (Schulte-Rüther, Mainz, Fink, Herpertz-Dahlmann, & Konrad, 2012). Finally, fMRI research on the neural correlates of neurocognitive patterns such as set-shifting confirms impairments in corticoid-subcortical circuits (Zastrow et al., 2010).

Several studies investigating brain activity patterns in people with AN whose weight is restored provide an interesting potential to control for confounding effects of concurrent malnutrition. The studies show lasting anomalies in frontal cortex resting state (Cowdrey, Filippini, Park, Smith, & McCabe, 2014), insula response to pain anticipation (Strigo et al., 2013), and ventral striatum response to reward processing (Cowdrey, Park, Harmer, & McCabe, 2011; Wagner et al., 2008). Although few longitudinal studies have been completed, Vocks and colleagues showed that therapy for body-image concerns can lead to changes in body-relevant areas, such as the medial prefrontal cortex and the extrastriatal body area (Vocks et al., 2011).

BN   There are a few activation studies targeting voluntary control processes and response inhibition problems in individuals with BN. Uher and colleagues (2004) reported decreased dorsolateral prefrontal activation in BN during cognitive performance. Likewise, Marsh et al. (2009) reported that, compared to controls, bulimic women failed to activate frontostriatal circuits on the Simon Spatial Incompatibility Task, which requires the inhibition of "primed" responses. Finally, Wagner et al. (2010) assessed brain-imaging response to a monetary reward task and found evidence for altered functioning of the anterior ventral striatum in recovered BN participants during the task. Taken together, these findings show evidence of frontal hypoactivation in BN linked to cognitive disinhibition or impulsivity.

Genetics

Family and Twin Studies   For culture-bound syndromes or social epidemics, EDs appear to be surprisingly heritable. Genetic-epidemiological studies have shown that the EDs are subject to familial transmission, with findings consistently indicating increased liability for an ED among the female relatives of individuals with an ED compared to those of comparison groups (e.g., Strober, Freeman, Lampert, Diamond, & Kaye, 2000). Furthermore, available twin studies provide unequivocal support for the idea that there is a genetic diathesis for EDs. Heritability estimates generated in such studies have ranged from 33% to 84% for AN, 28% to 83% for BN, and 41% to 57% for BED (Thornton, Mazzeo, & Bulik, 2011). The same studies have shown contribution from the shared environment (e.g., shared family environment) to often be surprisingly small. In other words, findings indicate an undeniable etiological contribution to ED development from genetic determinants.

Molecular Genetics   Despite evidence of a genetic role in EDs, definitive causal DNA variations have not yet been isolated, and nonreplication seems to be more the exception than the rule in molecular-genetic studies. However, results from such studies in eating-disordered individuals are suggestive, with enough consistencies to allow guarded generalizations.

Candidate-Gene Studies Evidence of anomalous functioning of main monamine neurotransmitter systems in the EDs has prompted examination into associations between EDs and polymorphisms acting on 5-HT, DA, norepinephrine, and other neuroregulatory systems (see Clarke, Weiss, & Berrettini, 2012; Pinheiro, Root, & Bulik, 2009; Scherag, Hebebrand, & Hinney, 2010, for full reviews). For AN, there appears to be some association with genes relevant to the 5-HT transporter and to certain 5-HT receptors (e.g., 5-HT$_{2A}$ and 5-HT$_{2C}$). Likewise, some findings reveal possible associations with certain dopamine-system genes. For instance, DAT, DRD2, DRD4, catechol-O-methyl transferase, and a short-allele variant of the 3'-UTR VNTR polymorphism have all been linked to binge-eating or BN. Furthermore, molecular-genetic findings show a recurrent though inconsistent association of the BDNF Val66Met polymorphism with BN. A meta-analysis concluded that eating-disorder risk is 36% higher in Met-allele carriers of the BDNF Val66Met polymorphism than it is in Val/Val carriers (González, Mercader, de Cid, Urretavizcaya, & Estivill, 2007).

Other candidate-gene studies have examined polymorphisms in appetite-related genes, such as the Agouti-related protein gene (AgRP). Two available studies associated the same AgRP variant with AN (Clarke et al., 2012). Not surprisingly, given the sex-based distribution of the EDs, there have been additional indications that genes acting on certain aspects of estrogen activity could contribute to risk of AN (see Pinheiro et al., 2009). This possibility would be consistent with known effects of estrogens in the etiology of AN.

Genome-wide Association (GWA) Studies GWA studies attempt to identify genomic regions that harbor genes that influence risk of ED development. A first study of this type, evaluating 192 families with at least two relatives affected by AN, showed no statistically significant findings for overall association, but it did yield evidence of a susceptibility locus on chromosome 1 when the sample was restricted to relative pairs exhibiting restricting AN (Grice et al., 2002). More recent results of GWA studies in the EDs have provided mixed results. An association study examining over 5,000 single-nucleotide polymorphisms (SNPs) judged to be likely candidate genes for AN in 1,085 individuals with AN and 677 control individuals found no statistically significant associations with AN for any SNP or haplotype block (Pinheiro et al., 2010). In contrast, a Wellcome Trust Consortium study, involving 1,033 AN cases and 3,733 pediatric control cases, genotyped 610,000 SNP markers across the entire genome and found associations of HTRD1 (coding for serotonin receptor 1D) and OPRD1 (coding for delta-opioid receptor) (Brown et al., 2007). In another GWA study of AN, Nakabayashi et al. (2009) identified 10 novel loci showing association with AN. There is much less work of this type for BN. However, available studies have suggested some promising findings in linkage analyses, with some evidence suggesting a region of interest on chromosome 10 (see Bulik & Tozzi, 2004).

Genes and Correlated Traits A third molecular-genetic approach explores the extent to which genetic information accounts for variations in comorbid traits (e.g., compulsivity, affective instability, or impulsivity) that may indirectly contribute to risk. Here the assumption is made that genetic information may help explain trait-linked vulnerabilities and, hence, subphenotypic (e.g., trait-based) variations better than they do phenotypic variations (like the ultimate presence or absence of an ED). Studies of this type have reported that bulimic individuals who carry low-function 5HTTLPR alleles display more harm avoidance (Monteleone, Santonastaso, et al., 2006), anxiety (Ribasés et al., 2008), affective instability, impulsivity, sensation seeking (Steiger et al., 2007), and dissocial-impulsive tendencies (Steiger et al., 2008, 2009). Likewise, a couple of studies involving bulimic samples have supported an association between the G allele of the -1428G/A promoter polymorphism of the 5HT2A receptor gene and heightened impulsivity in eating-disordered patients (Bruce et al., 2005; Nishiguchi et al., 2001). A study from our group associated variations of a polymorphism acting on monoamine oxidase activity with different levels of suicidality and self-injuriousness in a mixed anorexic/bulimic sample (Steiger, Fichter, et al., 2011). Also implicating the 5-HT system in trait variations found in people with BN is a study reporting an association between the -995A/-759T/-697C/ Cys23 haplotype of the 5HT2C gene and traits of hostility, obsessive-compulsiveness, somatization, depression, anxiety, phobic anxiety, and paranoid ideation (Ribasés et al., 2008). Relevant to the dopamine system, Thaler and colleagues (2012) found interaction effects (DRD2 DAT and DRD4 COMT) that predict greater novelty seeking and binge eating in women with BN.

Gene–Environment   Interactions   Interactions between genotypes and developmental stressors, as would suggest the environmental activation of genetic susceptibilities, have been documented in various disorders. Providing the first available study of this type, Caspi, Sugden, and Moffitt (2003) reported that a functional polymorphism in the promoter region of the serotonin transporter (5-HTT) gene moderated the influence of stressful life events on depression. In the same vein, our group has shown that bulimic women carrying low-function alleles of 5HTTLPR, when they report childhood abuse, display more novelty seeking, affective instability (Steiger et al., 2007), and dissocial (impulsive-aggressive) behavior (Steiger et al., 2008). A similar interaction implicating low-function 5HTTLPR alleles and familial/developmental stress has been linked to AN (Karwautz et al., 2011) and to binge-eating behavior in a large-scale community study (Akkermann et al., 2012). Similar interaction effects implicating other neural systems have also been documented. One of our findings indicated that, in BN, the DRD2 Taq1A polymorphism interacts with childhood abuse to moderate manifestations of novelty seeking (Groleau et al., 2012). Likewise, in two controlled comparisons, our group observed that BN was disproportionately associated with the combination of a low-function variant of the glucorticoid receptor polymorphism, *Bcl*I—implying reduced stress accommodation—and exposure to childhood abuse (Steiger et al., 2011, Steiger, et al., 2012). We inferred from these observations that traumatic stress may have especially detrimental effects in individuals disposed to lower modulation of stress responses.

With respect to AN, one could envisage several possible gene–environment interactions (Klump & Gobrogge, 2005). Given its association with dieting and pubertal development, it is plausible that AN may often depend on amplification of etiological genetic effects due to malnutrition, dieting,

and/or hormonal effects occurring at puberty. Or, associated genotypes might influence individuals' tendency to place themselves in high-risk (e.g., high-achievement or body-focused) environments. In addition, there remains the possibility that genotypic variations cause individuals to indirectly activate environmental risks, as might occur when mothers with AN, because of their own nutritional status, expose their fetuses to increased perinatal and obstetrical risks (Bulik, 2005).

EDs and Epigenetics   Newly discovered epigenetic mechanisms are believed to register environmental exposures on the genome and, in doing so, to constitute a physical substrate for genetic by environmental (G E) interactions. Epigenetic effects have been postulated to link such environmental stressors as perinatal "insults" or childhood abuse to various mental illness phenotypes, among them, eating disorders (Campbell, Mill, Uher, & Schmidt, 2011; Pietri, Schmidt, Kas, & Campbell, 2012; Toyokawa, Uddin, Koenen, & Galea, 2012). A main mechanism involved in epigenetic regulation of gene expression is DNA methylation—that is, the addition of methyl to specific genomic regions, called CpG islands. Methylated CpGs in genes reduce access of the transcriptional machinery to the DNA and, in turn, block gene expression. Various factors (e.g., childhood stress, nutritional status, maternal diet during gestation, perinatal complications, and current stressors) have been thought to influence DNA methylation. The likelihood that some or all of these factors act etiologically in the EDs has mobilized much recent interest in the possible contribution of epigenetic processes to ED development and maintenance (see Campbell et al., 2011; Pietri et al., 2012). In one of the first epigenetic studies in the EDs, Frieling, Römer, and Scholz (2010) reported excess methylation of main dopamine-system genes (*DRD2* and *DAT*) in people with AN and BN. We have also generated new data on methylation in regulatory regions of various targeted gene promoters: In one study, we observed bulimic women with a history of suicidality to show hypermethylation in the exon 1C region of the glucocorticoid receptor (GR) gene (Steiger et al., 2013). In another, we observed hypermethylation of the DRD2 promoter in bulimic women with Borderline Personality Disorder, and a trend towards hypermethylation in bulimic women with a history of childhood sexual abuse (Groleau et al., 2013). Even more recently, we evaluated BDNF promoter (exon 4) methylation in data from 64 women with BN and 32 normal eaters to reveal hypermethylation of specific CpG sites in BN—especially when there had been prior childhood abuse (Thaler et al., 2014).

In other words, psychopathological expressions in our sample of bulimic women seemed to be associated with predictable increases in DNA methylation, in regions that would (predictably) correspond to increased risk of eating symptoms and common comorbid symptoms.

Toward an Integrated Etiological Concept

If the material reviewed above supports one assertion, it is that the EDs are likely to have diverse causal and maintaining factors. Contemporary clinician-scientists, inspired by an accumulating body of data attesting to this point, have attempted to achieve an integrated biopsychosocial perspective on eating and related disorders (see Jacobi et al., 2004; Steiger & Bruce, 2007; Striegel-Moore & Bulik, 2007; Treasure et al., 2010). In general form, these models assume that EDs are multiply determined by complex interactions among (1) constitutional factors (e.g., hereditary processes affecting mood, temperament, and appetite); (2) psychological and developmental processes (influencing general personality development and specific attitudes toward eating and body image); (3) social factors (including cultural emphasis on thinness and broad social influences on self-image); and, finally, (4) the secondary effects, in biological, psychological, and social spheres, of maladaptive eating practices themselves.

The advent of genetic-epidemiological, molecular-genetic, brain imaging, neurobiological, and neuropsychological studies has resulted in an increased appreciation of the extent to which biology, and especially hereditary traits, act in risk of ED development. However, this does not mean that there has been a simple pendulum swing away from an emphasis on sociocultural or developmental processes and toward modeling that is more psychobiologically oriented. Rather, contemporary multidimensional models use new psychobiological data to attempt to elaborate a properly neurodevelopmental perspective on the EDs. Biologically informed, multidimensional models are, arguably, responsible for a very positive development

in etiological thinking: Eating disorders cease to be viewed as expressions of "superficial body consciousness," "capriciousness," or "stubborn oppositionality" in affected people and as responses to "dysfunctional," "overinvolved," or "toxic" families. Instead, they are understood to represent the activation, by environmental stresses (and, almost invariably, pressures promoting too much dieting), of real physical vulnerabilities to ED development, borne by susceptible people. Such people do not "ask" to get an ED or "bring the ED on themselves." Rather, such people develop eating disorders because they bear real vulnerabilities that get "switched on" by specifiable environmental factors.

To help clarify the roles in ED development of various putative risk factors that have been discussed in this chapter, we introduce a concept that we believe provides a useful heuristic. The concept, supported by various available studies on the structure of ED pathology, is that, in the EDs, variables that bear directly on eating symptoms (restricting, bingeing, vomiting, body dissatisfaction, etc.) tend to map onto one factor or cluster, those that load onto generalized psychopathology (e.g., depression, anxiety, impulsivity, perfectionism) tend to cohere onto another. Furthermore, and more importantly, severity of eating symptoms in the EDs is often surprisingly independent of severity of comorbid components. In other words, individuals displaying severe comorbid disturbances need not display correspondingly severe eating symptoms, and vice versa.

To assist in elaborating the preceding concept and in discussing hypothetical causal interactions among eating-specific and generalized components of pathology in the EDs, we have listed in Table 16.1 the various factors thought to be relevant to each component. Hypothetical eating-specific risk factors are listed in the left-hand column of Table 16.1. These are presumed to impinge directly on bodily components of self-representation and on eating-specific cognitions and behaviors. They include (1) biological factors related to bodily appearance and appetite regulation, (2) psychological and developmental processes linked to concern with body image or weight (e.g., identifications with weight-conscious parents and peers), and (3) social values that heighten concerns with weight and bodily appearance. Together, these factors are presumed to constitute the ingredients—biological, psychological, and social—of marked

Table 16.1 Putative Biological, Psychological, Developmental, and Social Risk Factors for Development of Eating Disorders*

	Eating-Specific Factors (Direct Risk Factors)	Generalized Factors (Indirect Risk Factors)
Biological factors	ED-specific genetic risk Physiognomy and body weight Appetite regulation Energy metabolism Gender	Genetic risk for associated disturbance Temperament Impulsivity Neurobiology (e.g., 5-HT mechanisms) Gender
Psychological factors	Poor body image Maladaptive eating attitudes Maladaptive weight beliefs Specific values or meanings assigned to food, body Overvaluation of appearance	Poor self-image Inadequate coping mechanisms Self-regulation problems Unresolved conflicts, deficits, posttraumatic reactions Identity problems Autonomy problems
Developmental factors	Identifications with body-concerned relatives, or peers Aversive mealtime experiences Trauma affecting bodily experience	Overprotection Neglect Felt rejection, criticism Traumata Object relationships (interpersonal experience)
Social factors	Maladaptive family attitudes to eating, weight Peer-group weight concerns Pressures to be thin Body-relevant insults, teasing Specific pressures to control weight (e.g., through ballet, athletic pursuits) Maladaptive cultural values assigned to body	Family dysfunction Aversive peer experiences Social values detrimental to stable, positive self-image Destabilizing social change Values assigned to gender Social isolation Poor support network Impediments to means of self-definition

* Factors are separated into those thought to contribute to eating-specific pathology and to generalized psychopathology. Factors shown are meant to be illustrative, not exhaustive.

concerns with eating, weight, and body image. We assume that various forms of interaction and modulation occur "vertically" among factors shown in Table 16.1, and that together, such effects control overall strength of eating-related concerns. However, we also assume that alone these factors may not create sufficiently strong predisposition to explain development of a clinical ED.

A second group of factors, assumed to be nonspecific to eating (i.e., to underlie generalized susceptibilities or maladjustments) but to be important components of vulnerability to ED development, are depicted in the right-hand column of Table 16.1. These include (1) biological processes (e.g., neurotransmitter abnormalities, genetic susceptibilities) influencing temperament, mood, and impulse regulation, (2) psychological

and developmental processes that shape general "self" development and self-concept (e.g., familial overprotection, developmental neglect, childhood traumata), and (3) sociocultural influences pertinent to overall self-image. (Again, we assume various forms of interaction, on the vertical dimension, among factors listed in Table 16.1—controlling presence and strength of generalized vulnerability and/or maladaptation.) Although nonspecific, such factors might interact (horizontally and diagonally) with eating-specific agents to contribute to risk of developing a clinical ED, as follows:

1. Generalized constitutional vulnerabilities (e.g., inherited susceptibilities of one's serotonin system) may, along with predictable effects on mood and impulse regulation (acting on the right side of Table 16.1), confer vulnerability to disorders of

satiation, and hence bulimic eating patterns, in individuals disposed by social pressures emphasizing thinness (shown on the left side of Table 16.1) to restrict their food intake. Such tendencies might, in part, explain an affinity of bulimic eating syndromes for manifestations suggesting mood or impulse dyscontrol and, in part, account for the demonstrated importance, as a causal antecedent, of dieting in bulimic syndromes. We have found that stress seems to adversely affect serotonin function, and developmental stressors (e.g., childhood abuse) may have lasting effects into adulthood on later 5-HT function (see Steiger, Bruce & Groleau, 2011). The stage becomes set for a cascade of maladaptive potentials: Genetic susceptibilities associated with variants of serotonin polymorphisms that confer less resiliency of the 5-HT system may become amplified by adverse developmental experiences, increasing potentials for pathogenic serotonin-system dysregulation. The further challenge to the system created by intensive dieting, influenced by social pressures to stay slim, may be sufficient to activate neurobiological potentials and corresponding psychopathological expressions—in the form of symptoms like depression, anxiety, impulsivity, and dietary disinhibition (binge eating).

2. Given a social context that overvalues thinness and that links body-esteem to overall self-esteem, especially in women, generalized self-image problems in females, and especially the propensity to be perfectionistic or overly sensitive to social approval (all shown on the left side of Table 16.1), might indirectly heighten susceptibility to intensive dieting and eventually to pathological eating practices. In this eventuality, one would expect, as tends to be the case, that perfectionism, self-criticism, reward dependence, and related characteristics tend to load heavily in individuals who are prone to AN. Consider effects that might occur in a hypothetical example: An insecure adolescent girl, with a genetic predisposition toward anxious, perfectionistic traits, might begin to diet to bolster her self-esteem. Weight loss produces various social rewards, as peers and parents pay her more positive attention. However, because dieting also leads to alteration of neurotransmitter function, a normal consequence of dieting, one effect might be an exacerbation of latent propensities toward anxiety and obsessionality and, gradually, increasing preoccupation with thinness. The adolescent's "natural" tendency to demand too much of herself

might become amplified, under new biological influences, into full-blown obsession—and intensive dieting gradually evolves into a full-blown ED. Based on currently available data, such effects are most likely to occur in people who, because of unique hereditary susceptibilities, are particularly vulnerable to ED development.

A main implication of the view we present here is that generalized susceptibilities, though not representing a specific ingredient, are almost certain to enhance vulnerability to ED development. Furthermore, once an ED has developed, biopsychosocial consequences may promote development of increasingly more severe and more entrenched eating habits and generalized disturbances. For instance, if the affected individual was not highly obsessional or affectively unstable to start with, he or she soon becomes so, under the influence of increasing dietary dysregulation.

Conclusions

Our thinking in this chapter has been structured around the concept that eating disorders, and the generalized psychopathological tendencies that coincide with them, have multiple and often shared biological, psychological, and social determinants. This means that comorbid traits need to be understood as an integral part of the ED syndrome, tightly woven into its complex of causes and symptoms, and relevant as an expression of, and influence on, the ED's biopsychosocial mix.

Indeed, it may be that we can never fully segregate "having an eating disorder" (in either phenomenological or etiological respects) from "concurrent psychopathological trait tendencies." Rather, psychopathological phenomena (like impulsivity, compulsivity, or perfectionism) may be at least as relevant to defining ED syndromes as any one of a number of superficially more relevant aspects of ED phenomenology (like presence of body dissatisfaction, binge eating or laxative abuse). Indeed, available data argue that the psychopathological variations may be the stronger predictors of clinical phenomenology, neurobiological substrates, sexual abuse history, treatment outcome, prognosis, and other aspects.

If EDs are indeed as multiply determined as available data suggest, pathways to them will likely be immensely heterogeneous. Following from this line of thinking, we propose that what may be of greatest interest about the EDs is, in fact, their tendency to have diverse and interleaved causes. The study of the EDs may inform theory on the way in which many forms of maladjustment represent a collision between sociocultural pressures and psychobiological vulnerabilities. In other words, in understanding the pathogenesis of the EDs, we may be learning generally about psychobiological processes that render vulnerable individuals permeable to maladaptive social influences and values. In social contexts, such vulnerabilities may often become manifest in the form of extreme susceptibility, especially in young females, to social ideals of thinness, self-control, and achievement. However, the same generalized vulnerabilities may, in other contexts and life stages, account for diverse maladaptive investments that may equally reflect the adverse impacts of social ideals on self-concept.

References

Akkermann, K., Kaasik, K., Kiive, E., Nordquist, N., Oreland, L., & Harro, J. (2012). The impact of adverse life events and the serotonin transporter gene promoter polymorphism on the development of eating disorder symptoms. *Journal of Psychiatric Research*, 46, 38–43.

Bardone-Cone, A. M., Wonderlich, S. A., Frost, R. O., Bulik, C. M., Mitchell, J. E., Uppala, S., & Simonich, H. (2007). Perfectionism and eating disorders: Current status and future directions. *Clinical Psychology Review*, 27, 384–405.

Beato-Fernández, L., Rodríguez-Cano, T., Belmonte-Llario, A., & Martínez-Delgado, C. (2004). Risk factors for eating disorders in adolescents. A Spanish community-based longitudinal study. *European Child & Adolescent Psychiatry*, 13, 287–294.

Bello, N. T., & Hajnal, A. (2010). Dopamine and binge eating behaviors. *Pharmacology, Biochemistry, and Behaviour*, 97, 25–33.

Berg, K. C., Crosby, R. D., Cao, L., Peterson, C. B., Engel, S. G., Mitchell, J. E., & Wonderlich, S. A. (2013). Facets of negative affect prior to and following binge-only, purge-only, and binge/purge events in women with bulimia nervosa. *Journal of Abnormal Psychology*, 122, 111–118.

Blinder, B. J., Cumella, E. J., & Sanathara, V. A. (2006). Psychiatric comorbidities of female inpatients with eating disorders. *Psychosomatic Medicine*, 68, 454–462.

Brambilla, F. P. M. (2003). Physical complications and physiological aberrations in eating disorders: A review. In M. Maj, L. Lopez-Ibor, & N. Sartorius (Eds.), *Eating disorders* (pp. 139–192). Chichester, UK: John Wiley & Sons.

Brewerton, T. D., Lesem, M. D., Kennedy, A., & Garvey, W. T. (2000). Reduced plasma leptin concentrations in bulimia nervosa. *Psychoneuroendocrinology*, 25, 649–658.

Broft, A. I., Berner, L. A., Martinez, D., & Walsh, B. T. (2011). Bulimia nervosa and evidence for striatal dopamine dysregulation: A conceptual review. *Physiology & Behavior*, 104, 122–127.

Brown, K. M., Bujac, S. R., Mann, E. T., Campbell, D. A., Stubbins, M. J., & Blundell, J. E. (2007). Further evidence of association of OPRD1 & HTR1D polymorphisms with susceptibility to anorexia nervosa. *Biological Psychiatry*, 61, 367–373.

Bruce, K. R., Steiger, H., Joober, R., Ng Ying Kin, N. M., Israel, M., & Young, S. N. (2005). Association of the promoter polymorphism -1438G/A of the 5-HT2A receptor gene with behavioral impulsiveness and serotonin function in women with bulimia nervosa. *American Journal of Medical Genetics Part B: Neuropsychiatric Genetics*, 137, 40–44.

Bruce, K. R., Steiger, H., & Israël, M. (2012). Cortisol responses on the dexamethasone suppression test among women with bulimia-spectrum eating disorders: Associations with clinical symptoms. *Progress in Neuro-Psychopharmacology and Biological Psychiatry*, 38, 241–246.

Bulik, C. M. (2005). Exploring the gene–environment nexus in eating disorders. *Journal of Psychiatry & Neuroscience*, 30, 335–339.

Bulik, C. M., Klump, K. L., Thornton, L., Kaplan, A. S., Devlin, B., & Fichter, M. M. (2004). Alcohol use disorder comorbidity in eating disorders: A multicenter study. *Journal of Clinical Psychiatry*, 65, 1000–1006.

Bulik, C. M., Sullivan, P. F., Weltzin, T. F., & Kaye, W. H. (1995). Temperament in eating disorders. *International Journal of Eating Disorders*, 17, 251–261.

Bulik, C. M., & Tozzi, F. (2004). The genetics of bulimia nervosa. *Drugs Today (Barc).* 40, 741–749.

Campbell, I. C., Mill, J., Uher, R., & Schmidt, U. (2011). Eating disorders, gene–environment interactions and epigenetics. *Neuroscience & Biobehavioral Reviews*, 35, 784–793.

Caspi, A. Sugden, K., & Moffitt, T. E., (2003). Influence of life stress on depression: Moderation by a polymorphism in the 5-HTT. *Genetic Science*, 301, 386–389.

Cassin, S. E., & von Ranson, K. M. (2005). Personality and eating disorders: A decade in review. *Clinical Psychology Review, 25,* 895–916.

Claes, L., Fernandez-Aranda, F., Jiménez-Murcia, S., Agüera, Z., Granero, R., Sánchez, I., & Menchón, J. M. (2012). Personality subtypes in male patients with eating disorder: Validation of a classification approach. *Comprehensive Psychiatry, 53,* 981–987.

Claes, L., Vandereycken, W., & Vertommen, H. (2006). Pain experience related to self-injury in eating disorder patients. *Eating Behaviors, 7,* 204–213.

Clarke, T. K., Weiss, A. R. D., & Berrettini, W. H. (2012). The genetics of anorexia nervosa. *Clinical Pharmacology & Therapeutics, 91,* 181–188.

Cowdrey, F. A., Filippini, N., Park, R. J., Smith, S. M., & McCabe, C. (2014). Increased resting state functional connectivity in the default mode network in recovered anorexia nervosa. *Human Brain Mapping, 35*(2), 483–491.

Cowdrey, F. A, Park, R. J., Harmer, C. J., & McCabe, C. (2011). Increased neural processing of rewarding and aversive food stimuli in recovered anorexia nervosa. *Biological Psychiatry, 70,* 736–743.

Culbert, K. M., Breedlove, S. M., Burt, S. A., & Klump, K. L. (2008). Prenatal hormone exposure and risk for eating disorders: A comparison of opposite-sex and same-sex twins. *Archives of General Psychiatry. 65,* 329–336.

Currin, L., Schmidt, U., Treasure, J., & Jick, H. (2005). Time trends in eating disorder incidence. *British Journal of Psychiatry, 186,* 132–135.

Díaz-Marsá, M., Carrasco, J. L., Basurte, E., Sáiz, J., López-Ibor, J. J., & Hollander, E. (2008). Enhanced cortisol suppression in eating disorders with impulsive personality features. *Psychiatry Research, 158,* 93–97.

Díaz-Marsá, M., Carrasco, J. L., & Sáiz, J. (2000). A study of temperament and personality in anorexia and bulimia nervosa. *Journal of Personality Disorders, 14,* 352–359.

Duncan, A. E., Neuman, R. J., Kramer, J., Kuperman, S., Hesselbrock, V., Reich, T., & Bucholz, K. K. (2005). Are there subgroups of bulimia nervosa based on comorbid psychiatric disorders? *International Journal of Eating Disorders, 37,* 19–25.

Eisler, I., Simic, M., Russell, G., & Dare, C. (2007). A randomized controlled treatment trial of two forms of family therapy in adolescent anorexia nervosa: A five-year follow-up. *Journal of Child Psychology and Psychiatry 48,* 552–560.

Engelberg, M. J., Steiger, H., Gauvin, L., & Wonderlich, S. A. (2007). Binge antecedents in bulimic syndromes: An examination of dissociation and negative affect. *International Journal of Eating Disorders, 40,* 531–536.

Espeset, E. M. S., Nordbø, R. H. S., Gulliksen, K. S., Skårderud, F., Geller, J., & Holte, A. (2011). The concept of body image disturbance in anorexia nervosa: An empirical inquiry utilizing patients' subjective experiences. *Eating Disorders, 19,* 175–193.

Fairburn, C. G., Cooper, Z., Bohn, K., O'Connor, M. E., Doll, H. A., & Palmer, R. L. (2007). The severity and status of eating disorder NOS: Implications for DSM-V. *Behavior Research & Therapy, 45,* 1705–1715.

Fairburn, C. G., Cooper, Z., Doll, H. A., & Welch, S. L. (1999). Risk factors for anorexia nervosa: Three integrated case-control comparisons. *Archives of General Psychiatry, 56,* 468–476.

Fairburn, C. G., Cooper, Z., & Shafran, R. (2003). Cognitive behaviour therapy for eating disorders: A "transdiagnostic" theory and treatment. *Behaviour Research & Therapy, 41,* 509–528.

Favaro, A., Santonastaso, P., Manara, R., Bosello, R., Bommarito, G., Tenconi, E., & Di Salle, F. (2012). Disruption of visuospatial and somatosensory functional connectivity in anorexia nervosa. *Biological Psychiatry, 72,* 864–870.

Favaro, A., Zanetti, T., Tenconi, E., Degortes, D., Ronzan, A., Veronese, A., & Santonastaso, P. (2005). The relationship between temperament and impulsive behaviors in eating disordered subjects. *Eating Disorders, 13,* 61–70.

Frank, G. K., Bailer, U. F., Henry, S. E., Drevets, W., Meltzer, C. C., & Price, J. C. (2005). Increased dopamine D2/D3 receptor binding after recovery from anorexia nervosa measured by positron emission tomography and [(11)C]Raclopride. *Biological Psychiatry, 58,* 908–912.

Frieling, H., Römer, K. D., & Scholz, S. (2010). Epigenetic dysregulation of dopaminergic genes in eating disorders. *International Journal of Eating Disorders, 43,* 577–583.

Galimberti, E., Fadda, E., Cavallini, M. C., Martoni, R. M., Erzegovesi, S., & Bellodi, L. (2013). Executive functioning in anorexia nervosa patients and their unaffected relatives. *Psychiatry Research, 208*(3), 238–244.

Gauvin, L., Steiger, H., & Brodeur, J.-M. (2009). Eating-disorder symptoms and syndromes in a sample of urban-dwelling Canadian women: Contributions toward a population health perspective. *International Journal of Eating Disorders, 42*, 158–165.

Ghadirian, A. M., Marini, N., Jabalpurwala, S., & Steiger, H. (1999). Seasonal mood patterns in eating disorders. *General Hospital Psychiatry, 21*, 354–359.

Giel, K. E., Wittorf, A., Wolkenstein, L., Klingberg, S., Drimmer, E., & Schönenberg, M. (2012). Is impaired set-shifting a feature of "pure" anorexia nervosa? Investigating the role of depression in set-shifting ability in anorexia nervosa and unipolar depression. *Psychiatry Research, 200*, 538–543.

Gleaves, D. H., Eberenz, K. P., & May, M. C. (1998). Scope and significance of posttraumatic symptomatology among women hospitalized for an eating disorder. *International Journal of Eating Disorders, 24*, 147–156.

Godart, N. T., Flament, M. F., Curt, F., Perdereau, F., Lang, F., & Venisse, J-L. (2003). Anxiety disorders in subjects seeking treatment for eating disorders: A DSM-IV controlled study. *Psychiatry Research, 117*, 245–258.

Goldschmidt, A. B., Wall, M., Loth, K. A., Le Grange, D., & Neumark-Sztainer, D. (2012). Which dieters are at risk for the onset of binge eating? A prospective study of adolescents and young adults. *Journal of Adolescent Health, 51*, 86–92.

Gordon, R. A. (1990). *Anorexia and bulimia: Anatomy of a social epidemic.* Cambridge, MA: Blackwell.

Grabe, S., Ward, L. M., & Hyde, J. S. (2008). The role of the media in body image concerns among women: A meta-analysis of experimental and correlational studies. *Psychological Bulletin, 134*, 460–476.

Gratacòs, M., González, J. R., Mercader, J. M., de Cid, R., Urretavizcaya, M., & Estivill, X. (2007). Brain-derived neurotrophic factor Val66Met and psychiatric disorders: meta-analysis of case-control studies confirm association to substance-related disorders, eating disorders, and schizophrenia. *Biological Psychiatry, 61*, 911–922.

Grice, D. E., Halmi, K. A., Fichter, M. M., Strober, M., Woodside, D. B., Treasure, J. T.,…Berrettini, W. H. (2002). Evidence for a susceptibility gene for anorexia nervosa on chromosome 1. *American Journal of Human Genetics, 70*, 787–792.

Grinspoon, S., Gulick, T., Askari, H., Landt, M., Vignati, L., & Bowsher, R. (1996). Serum leptin levels in women with anorexia nervosa. *Journal of Clinical Endocrinology and Metabolism, 81*, 3861–3863.

Groleau, P., Steiger, H., Joober, R., Bruce, K. R., Israel, M., Badawi, G., Zeramdini, N., & Sycz, L. (2012). Dopamine-system genes, childhood abuse, and clinical manifestations in women with bulimia-spectrum disorders. *Journal of Psychiatric Research, 46*, 1139–1145.

Groleau, P., Joober, R., Israel, M., Zeramdini, N., DeGuzman, R., & Steiger, H. (2014). Methylation of the dopamine D2 receptor (DRD2) gene promoter in women with a bulimia-spectrum disorder: Associations with borderline personality disorder and exposure to childhood abuse. *Journal of Psychiatric Research, 48*, 121–127.

Haedt-Matt, A. A., & Keel, P. K. (2011). Revisiting the affect regulation model of binge eating: A meta-analysis of studies using ecological momentary assessment. *Psychological Bulletin, 137*, 660–681.

Hodges, E. L., Cochrane, C. E., & Brewerton, T. D. (1998). Family characteristics of binge-eating disorder patients. *International Journal of Eating Disorders, 23*, 145–151.

Hoek, H. W., & van Hoeken, D. (2003). Review of the prevalence and incidence of eating disorders. *International Journal of Eating Disorders, 34*, 383–396.

Holliday, J., Tchanturia, K., Landau, S., Collier, D., & Treasure, J. (2005). Is impaired set-shifting an endophenotype of anorexia nervosa? *American Journal of Psychiatry, 162*, 2269–2275.

Hudson, J. I., Hiripi, E., Pope, H. G., Jr, & Kessler, R. C. (2007). The prevalence and correlates of eating disorders in the National Comorbidity Survey Replication. *Biological Psychiatry, 61*, 348–358.

Humphrey, L. L. (1991). Object relations and the family system: An integrative approach to understanding and treating eating disorders. In C. Johnson (Ed.), *Psychodynamic treatment of anorexia nervosa and bulimia* (pp. 322–353). New York: Guilford Press.

Jacobi, C., Hayward, C., de Zwaan, M., Kraemer, H. C., & Agras, W. S. (2004). Coming to terms with risk factors for eating disorders: Application of risk terminology and suggestions for a general taxonomy. *Psychological Bulletin, 130*, 19–65.

Javaras, K. N., Laird, N. M., Reichborn-Kjennerud, T., Bulik, C. M., Pope, H. G., Jr, & Hudson, J. I. (2008). Familiality and heritability of binge eating disorder: Results of a case-control family study and a twin study. *International Journal of Eating Disorders, 41*, 174–179.

Karwautz, A. F., Wagner, G., Waldherr, K., Nader, I. W., Fernandez-Aranda, F., Estivill, X., Holliday, J., Collier, D. A. & Treasure, J. L. (2011). Gene–environment interaction in anorexia nervosa: Relevance of non-shared environment and the serotonin transporter gene. *Molecular Psychiatry, 16,* 590–592.

Kaye, W. H. (2008). Neurobiology of anorexia and bulimia nervosa. *Physiological Behaviour. 94,* 121–135.

Kaye, W. H., Bulik, C. M., Thornton, L., Barbarich, N., & Masters, K. (2004). Comorbidity of anxiety disorders with anorexia and bulimia nervosa. *American Journal of Psychiatry, 161,* 2215–2221.

Kaye, W. H., Fudge, J. L., & Paulus, M. (2009). New insights into symptoms and neurocircuit function of anorexia nervosa. *Nature Review of Neuroscience, 10,* 573–584.

Keel, P. K., Heatherton, T. F., Dorer, D. J., Joiner, T. E., & Zalta, A. K. (2006). Point prevalence of bulimia nervosa in 1982, 1992, and 2002. *Psychological Medicine, 36,* 119–127.

Keel, P. K., & Klump, K. L. (2003). Are eating disorders culture bound syndromes? Implications for conceptualizing their etiology. *Psychological Bulletin, 129,* 747–769.

Keski-Rahkonen A., Hoek, H. W., Susser, E. S., Linna, M. S., Sihvola, E., & Raevuori, A. (2007). Epidemiology and course of anorexia nervosa in the community. *American Journal of Psychiatry, 164,* 1259–1265.

Keys, A., Brozek, J., Henschel, A., Mickelson, O., & Taylor, H. (1950). *The biology of human starvation.* Minneapolis: University of Minnesota Press.

Klump, K. L., Culbert, K. M., Slane, J. D., Burt, S. A., Sisk, C. L., & Nigg, J. T. (2012). The effects of puberty on genetic risk for disordered eating: Evidence for a sex difference. *Psychological Medicine, 42,* 627–637.

Klump, K. L., & Gobrogge, K.L. (2005). A review and primer of molecular genetic studies of anorexia nervosa. *International Journal of Eating Disorders, 37,* 543–548.

Lauer, C. J., Gorzewski, B., Gerlinghoff, M., Backmund, H., & Zihl, J. (1999). Neuropsychological assessments before and after treatment in patients with anorexia nervosa and bulimia nervosa. *Journal of Psychiatric Research, 33,* 129–138.

le Grange, D., Lock, J., Loeb, K., & Nicholls, D. (2010). Academy for eating disorders position paper: The role of the family in eating disorders. *International Journal of Eating Disorders, 43,* 1–5.

Lilenfeld, L. R., Kaye, W. H., Greeno, C. G., Merikangas, K. R., Plotnicov, K., & Pollice, C. (1998). A controlled family study of anorexia and bulimia nervosa: Psychiatric disorders in first-degree relatives and effects of proband comorbidity. *Archives of General Psychiatry, 55,* 603–610.

Lilenfeld, L. R., Stein, D., Bulik, C. M., Strober, M., Plotnicov, K., & Pollice, C. (2000). Personality traits among currently eating disordered, recovered and never ill first-degree female relatives of bulimic and control women. *Psychological Medicine, 30,* 1399–1410.

Lilenfeld, L. R., Wonderlich, S., Riso, L. P., Crosby, R., & Mitchell, J. (2006). Eating disorders and personality: A methodological and empirical review. *Clinical Psychology Review, 26,* 299–320.

Lock, J., Couturier, J., & Agras, W. S. (2006). Comparison of long term outcomes in adolescents with anorexia nervosa treated with family therapy. *American Journal of Child and Adolescent Psychiatry, 45,* 666–672.

Marsh, R., Horga, G., Wang, Z., Wang, P., Klahr, K. W., Berner, L. A., Walsh, B. T., & Peterson, B. S. (2011). An fMRI study of self-regulatory control and conflict resolution in adolescents with bulimia nervosa. *American Journal of Psychiatry, 168,* 1210–1220.

Marsh, R., Steinglass, J. E., Gerber, A. J., Graziano O'Leary, K., Wang, Z., Murphy, D., Walsh, B. T., & Peterson, B. S. (2009). Deficient activity in the neural systems that mediate self-regulatory control in bulimia nervosa. *Archives of General Psychiatry, 66,* 51–63.

Matsunaga, H., Kaye, W. H., McConaha, C., Plotnicov, K., Pollice, C., & Rao, R. (2000). Personality disorders among subjects recovered from eating disorders. *International Journal of Eating Disorders, 27,* 353–357.

McAdams, C. J., & Krawczyk, D. C. (2011). Impaired neural processing of social attribution in anorexia nervosa. *Psychiatry Research, 19,* 454–463.

McAdams, C. J., & Krawczyk, D. C. (2014). Who am I? How do I look? Neural differences in self-identity in anorexia nervosa. *Social, Cognitive and Affective Neuroscience, 9*(1), 12–21.

Mercader, J. M., Ribasés, M., Gratacòs, M., González, J. R., Bayés, M., de Cid, R., Badía, A., Fernández-Aranda, F., & Estivill, X. (2007). Altered brain-derived neurotrophic factor blood levels and gene variability are associated with anorexia and bulimia. *Genes, Brain and Behavior, 6,* 706–716.

Monteleone, P. (2011). New frontiers in endocrinology of eating disorders. In R. A. H. Adan & W. H. Kaye (Eds.), *Behavioral Neurobiology of Eating Disorders* (pp. 189–208). Berlin, Heidelberg: Springer.

Monteleone, P., Fabrazzo, M., Tortorella, A., Martiadis, V., Serritella, C., & Maj, M. (2005). Circulating ghrelin is decreased in non-obese and obese women with binge eating disorder as well as in obese non-binge eating women, but not in patients with bulimia nervosa. *Psychoneuroendocrinology*, *30*, 243–250.

Monteleone, P., Martiadis, V., Rigamonti, A. E., Fabrazzo, M., Giordani, C., & Muller, E. E. (2005). Investigation of peptide YY and ghrelin responses to a test meal in bulimia nervosa. *Biological Psychiatry*, *57*, 926–931.

Monteleone, P., Santonastaso, P., Mauri, M., Bellodi, L., Erzegovesi, S., & Fuschino, A. (2006). Investigation of the serotonin transporter regulatory region polymorphism in bulimia nervosa: Relationships to harm avoidance, nutritional parameters, and psychiatric comorbidity. *Psychosomatic Medicine*, *68*, 99–103.

Monteleone, P., Zanardini, R., Tortorella, A., Gennarelli, M., Castaldo, E., & Maj, M. (2006). The 196G/A (val66-met) polymorphism of the BDNF gene is significantly associated with binge eating behavior in women with bulimia nervosa or binge eating disorder. *Neuroscience Letters*, *406*, 133–137.

Nakabayashi, K., Komaki, G., Tajima, A., Ando, T., Ishikawa, M., Nomoto, J.,…Shirasawa, S. (2009). Identification of novel candidate loci for anorexia nervosa at 1q41 and 11q22 in Japanese by a genome-wide association analysis with microsatellite markers. *Journal of Human Genetics*, *54*, 531–537.

Newton, J. R., Freeman, C. P., & Munro, J. (1993). Impulsivity and dyscontrol in bulimia nervosa: Is impulsivity an independent phenomenon or a marker of severity? *Acta Psychiatrica Scandinavia*, *87*, 389–394.

Nicholls, D. E., & Viner, R. M. (2009). Childhood risk factors for lifetime anorexia nervosa by age 30 years in a national birth cohort. *Journal of the American Academy of Child & Adolescent Psychiatry*, *48*, 791–799.

Nishiguchi, N., Matsushita, S., Suzuki, K., Murayama, M., Shirakawa, O., & Higuchi, S. (2001). Association between 5HT2A receptor gene promoter region polymorphism and eating disorders in Japanese patients. *Biological Psychiatry*, *50*, 123–128.

Pallister, E., & Waller, G. (2008). Anxiety in the eating disorders: Understanding the overlap. *Clinical Psychology Review*, *28*, 366–386.

Pinheiro, A. P., Bulik, C. M., Thornton, L. M., Sullivan, P. F., Root, T. L., Bloss, C. S.,…Woodside, D. B. (2010). Association study of 182 candidate genes in anorexia nervosa. *American Journal of Medical Genetics B Neuropsychiatric Genetics*, *153*, 1070–1080.

Pinheiro, A. P., Root, T., & Bulik, C. M. (2009). The genetics of anorexia nervosa: Current findings and future perspectives. *International Journal of Child & Adolescent Health*, *2*, 153–164.

Pietri, E., Schmidt, U., Kas, M. & Campbell, I. (2012). Epigenetics and eating disorders. *Current Opinion in Clinical Nutritional and Metabolic Care*, *15*, 330–335.

Pietrini, F., Castellini, G., Ricca, V., Polito, C., Pupi, A., & Faravelli, C. (2011). Functional neuroimaging in anorexia nervosa: a clinical approach. *European Psychiatry*, *26*, 176–182.

Pirke, K. M., Kellner, M. B., Friess, E., Krieg, J. C., & Fichter, M. M. (1994). Satiety and cholecystokinin. *International Journal of Eating Disorders*, *15*, 63–69.

Polivy, J., & Herman, C. (1993). Etiology of binge eating: Psychological mechanisms. In C. G. Fairburn & G. T. Wilson (Eds.), *Binge eating: Nature, assessment, and treatment* (pp. 173–205). New York: Guilford Press.

Ribasés, M., Fernández-Aranda, F., Gratacòs, M., Mercader, J. M., Casasnovas, C., Núñez, A., Vallejo, J., & Estivill, X. (2008). Contribution of the serotoninergic system to anxious and depressive traits that may be partially responsible for the phenotypical variability of bulimia nervosa. *Journal of Psychiatric Research*, *42*, 50–57.

Richardson, J., Steiger, H., Schmitz, N., Joober, N., Bruce, K. R., Israel, M.,…deGuzman, R. (2008). Relevance of the 5HTTLPR polymorphism and childhood abuse to increased psychiatric comorbidity in women with bulimia-spectrum disorders. *Journal of Clinical Psychiatry*, *69*, 981–990.

Roberts, M. E., Tchanturia, K., Stahl, D., Southgate, L., & Treasure, J. (2007). A systematic review and meta-analysis of set-shifting ability in eating disorders. *Psychological Medicine*, *37*, 1075–1084.

Roberts, M. E., Tchanturia, K., & Treasure, J. L. (2013). Is attention to detail a similarly strong candidate endophenotype for anorexia nervosa and bulimia nervosa? *World Journal of Biological Psychiatry*, *14*(6), 452–463.

Rosenvinge, J. H., Martinussen, M., & Ostensen, E. (2000). The comorbidity of eating disorders and personality disorders: A meta-analytic review of studies published between 1983 and 1998. *Eating & Weight Disorders*, *5*, 52–61.

Rosval, L., Steiger, H., Bruce, K., Israël, M., Richardson, J., & Aubut, M. (2006). Impulsivity in women with eating disorders: Problem of response inhibition, planning or attention? *International Journal of Eating Disorders, 39*, 590–593.

Scherag, S., Hebebrand, J., & Hinney, A. (2010). Eating disorders: The current status of molecular genetic research. *European Child & Adolescent Psychiatry, 19*, 211–226.

Schulte-Rüther, M., Mainz, V., Fink, G. R., Herpertz-Dahlmann, B., & Konrad, K. (2012) Theory of mind and the brain in anorexia nervosa: Relation to treatment outcome. *Journal of the American Academy of Child & Adolescent Psychiatry, 51*, 832–841.

Shoebridge, P., & Gowers, S. G. (2000). Parental high concern and adolescent-onset anorexia nervosa. A case-control study to investigate direction of causality. *British Journal of Psychiatry, 176*, 132–137.

Smink, F. R., van Hoeken, D., & Hoek, H. W. (2012). Epidemiology of eating disorders: Incidence, prevalence and mortality rates. *Current Psychiatry Reports, 14*, 406–414.

Sohlberg, S., & Strober, M. (1994). Personality in anorexia nervosa: An update and a theoretical integration. *Acta Psychiatrica Scandinavica, 89*, 1–15.

Steele, A. L., O'Shea, A., Murdock, A., & Wade, T. D. (2011). Perfectionism and its relation to overevaluation of weight and shape and depression in an eating disorder sample. *International Journal of Eating Disorders, 44*, 459–464.

Steiger, H., & Bruce, K. R. (2007). Phenotypes, endophenotypes, and genotypes in bulimia spectrum eating disorders. *Canadian Journal of Psychiatry, 52*, 220–227.

Steiger, H., Bruce, K. R., & Groleau, P. (2011). Neural circuits, neurotransmitters, and behavior: Serotonin and temperament in bulimic syndromes. In W. H. Kaye & R. Adan (Eds.), *Current topics in behavioral neuroscience: Behavioral neurobiology of eating disorders* (pp. 125–138). Heidelberg: Springer.

Steiger, H., Bruce, K., Gauvin, L., Groleau, P., Joober, R., Israel, M., Richardson, J., & Ng Yin Kin, N. M. K. (2011). Contributions of the glucocorticoid receptor polymorphism (Bcl1) and childhood abuse to risk of bulimia nervosa. *Psychiatry Research, 187*, 193–197.

Steiger, H., Fichter, M., Bruce, K., Joober, R., Badawi, G., Richardson, J.,…Bachetzky, N. (2011). Molecular-genetic correlates of self-harming behaviors in eating-disordered women: Findings from a combined Canadian–German sample. *Progress in Neuropsychopharmacology & Biological Psychiatry, 35*, 102–106.

Steiger, H., Gauvin, L., Israël, M., Koerner, N., Ng Ying Kin, N. M. K., Paris, J., & Young, S. N. (2001). Association of serotonin and cortisol indices with childhood abuse in bulimia nervosa. *Archives of General Psychiatry, 58*, 837–843.

Steiger, H., Gauvin, L., Joober, R., Israel, M., Ng Ying Kin, N. M. K., & Bruce, K. (2006). Intrafamilial correspondences on platelet [3H-] paroxetine-binding indices in bulimic probands and their unaffected first-degree relatives. *Neuropsychopharmacology, 31*, 1785–1792.

Steiger, H., Gauvin, L., Joober, R., Israel, M., Badawi, G., Groleau, P., Bruce, K. R., Ng Yin Kin, N. M. K., Sycz, L., & Ouelette, A-S. (2012). Interaction of the BclI glucocorticoid receptor polymorphism and childhood abuse in Bulimia Nervosa (BN): Relationship to BN and to associated trait manifestations. *Journal of Psychiatric Research, 46*, 152–158.

Steiger, H., Joober, R., Israël, M., Young, S. N., Ng Ying Kin, N. M. K., & Gauvin, L. (2005). The 5HTTLPR polymorphism, psychopathological symptoms, and platelet [3H-] paroxetine binding in bulimic syndromes. *International Journal Eating Disorders, 37*, 57–60.

Steiger, H., Labonté, B., Groleau, P., Turecki, G., & Israel, M. (2013). Methylation of the glucocorticoid receptor gene promoter in bulimic women: Associations with borderline personality disorder, suicidality and exposure to childhood abuse. *International Journal of Eating Disorders, 46*, 246–255.

Steiger, H., Lehoux, P., & Gauvin, L. (1999). Impulsivity, dietary restraint, and the urge to binge in bulimic eating syndromes. *International Journal of Eating Disorders, 26*, 261–274.

Steiger, H., Richardson, J., Joober, R., Gauvin, L., Israel, M., Bruce, K. R., Ng Ying Kin, N. M. K., Howard, H., & Young, S. N. (2007). The 5HTTLPR polymorphism, prior maltreatment, and dramatic-erratic personality manifestations in women with bulimic syndromes. *Journal of Psychiatry & Neuroscience, 32*, 354–362.

Steiger, H., Richardson, J., Joober, R., Israel, M., Bruce, K. R., Ng Ying Kin, N. M. K.,…Gauvin, L. (2008). Dissocial behavior, the 5HTTLPR polymorphism and maltreatment in women with bulimic syndromes. *American Journal of Medical Genetics, 147*, 128–130.

Steiger, H., Richardson, J., Schmitz, N., Joober, R., Israel, M., Bruce, K. R.,…Anestin, A. (2009). Association of trait-defined, eating-disorder sub-phenotypes with (biallelic and triallelic)

5HTTLPR variations. *Journal of Psychiatric Research*, 43, 1086–1094.

Stice, E., Marti, C. N., Shaw, H., & Jaconis, M. (2009). An 8-year longitudinal study of the natural history of threshold, subthreshold, and partial eating disorders from a community sample of adolescents. *Journal of Abnormal Psychology*, 118, 587–597.

Striegel-Moore, R. H., & Bulik, C. M. (2007). Risk factors for eating disorders. *American Psychology*, 62,181–198.

Strigo, I. A., Matthews, S. C., Simmons, A. N., Oberndorfer, T., Klabunde, M., Reinhardt, L. E., & Kaye, W. H. (2013). Altered insula activation during pain anticipation in individuals recovered from anorexia nervosa: Evidence of interoceptive dysregulation. *International Journal of Eating Disorders*, 46, 23–33.

Strober, M., Freeman, R., Lampert, C., & Diamond, J. (2007). The association of anxiety disorders and obsessive compulsive personality disorder with anorexia nervosa: Evidence from a family study with discussion of nosological and neurodevelopmental implications. *International Journal of Eating Disorders*, 40, 46–51.

Strober, M., Freeman, R., Lampert, C., Diamond, J., & Kaye, W. (2000). Controlled family study of anorexia nervosa and bulimia nervosa: Evidence of shared liability and transmission of partial syndromes. *American Journal of Psychiatry*, 157, 393–401.

Stunkard, A. J. (1959). Eating patterns and obesity. *Psychiatry Quarterly*, 33, 284–295.

Swami, V., Frederick, D. A., Aavik, T., Alcalay, L., Allik, J., & Anderson, D. (2010). The attractive female body weight and female body dissatisfaction in 26 countries across 10 world regions: Results of the International Body Project I. *Personality and Social Psychology Bulletin*, 36, 309–325.

Swanson, S. A., Crow, S. J., Le Grange, D., Swendsen, J. & Merikangas, K. R. (2011). Prevalence and correlates of eating disorders in adolescents: Results from the National Comorbidity Survey Replication Adolescent Supplement. *Archives of General Psychiatry*, 68, 714–723.

Tchanturia, K., Davies, H., Lopez, C., Schmidt, U., Treasure, J., & Wykes, T. (2008). Neuropsychological task performance before and after cognitive remediation in anorexia nervosa: A pilot case-series. *Psychological Medicine*, 38, 1371–1373.

Tenconi, E., Santonastaso, P., Degortes, D., Bosello, R., Titton, F., Mapelli, D., & Favaro, A. (2010). Set-shifting abilities, central coherence, and handedness in anorexia nervosa patients, their unaffected siblings and healthy controls: Exploring putative endophenotypes. *World Journal of Biological Psychiatry*, 11, 813–823.

Thaler, L., Groleau, P., Badawi, G., Sycz, L., Zeramdini, N., Too, A.,…Steiger, H. (2012). Epistatic interactions amongst dopaminergic genes in bulimia nervosa (BN): Relationship to eating- and personality-related psychopathology. *Progress in Neuro-Psychopharmacology & Biological Psychiatry*, 39, 120–128.

Thaler, L., Gauvin, L., Joober, R., Groleau, P., de Guzman, R., Ambalavanan, A., Israel, M., Samantha, W., Steiger, H. (2014). Methylation of BDNF in women with bulimic eating syndromes: Associations with childhood abuse and borderline personality disorder, *Progress in Neuropsychopharmacology & Biological Psychiatry*, doi:10.1016/j.pnpbp.2014.04.010

Thornton, L. M., Mazzeo, S. E., & Bulik, C. M. (2011). The heritability of eating disorders: Methods and current findings. *Current Topics in Behavioral Neuroscience*, 6, 141–156.

Toyokawa, S., Uddin, M., Koenen, K. C., & Galea, S. (2012). How does the social environment "get into the mind"? Epigenetics at the intersection of social and psychiatric epidemiology. *Social Science & Medicine*, 74, 67–74.

Treasure, J., Claudino, A. M., & Zucker, N. (2010). Eating disorders. *Lancet*, 375, 583–593.

Uher, R., Murphy, T., Brammer, M. J., Dalgleish, T., Phillips, M. L., Ng, V. W.,…Treasure, J. (2004). Medial prefrontal cortex activity associated with symptom provocation in eating disorders. *American Journal of Psychiatry*, 161, 1238–1246.

Van den Eynde, F., Guillaume, S., Broadbent, H., Stahl, D., Campbell, I. C., Schmidt, U., & Tchanturia, K. (2011). Neurocognition in bulimic eating disorders: A systematic review. *Acta Psychiatrica Scandinavia*, 124, 120–40.

Vandereycken, W. (1994). Emergence of bulimia nervosa as a separate diagnostic entity: Review of the literature from 1960 to 1979. *International Journal of Eating Disorders*, 16, 105–116.

Vitousek, K., & Manke, F. (1994). Personality variables and disorders in anorexia nervosa and bulimia nervosa. *Journal of Abnormal Psychology*, 103, 137–147.

Vocks, S., Schulte, D., Busch, M., Grönemeyer, D., Herpertz, S., & Suchan, B. (2011). Changes in neuronal correlates of body image processing by means of cognitive-behavioural body image therapy for eating disorders: A randomized controlled fMRI study. *Psychological Medicine, 41,* 1651–1663.

Wade, T. D., Bulik, C. M., Neale, M., & Kendler, K. (2000). Anorexia nervosa and major depression: Shared genetic and environmental risk factors. *American Journal of Psychiatry, 157,* 469–471.

Wagner, A., Aizenstein, H., Mazurkewicz, L., Fudge, J., Frank, G. K., Putnam, K.,…Kaye, W. H. (2008) Altered insula response to taste stimuli in individuals recovered from restricting-type anorexia nervosa. *Neuropsychopharmacology, 33,* 513–523.

Wagner, A., Aizenstein, H., Venkatraman, V. K., Bischoff-Grethe, A., Fudge, J., May, J. C.,…Kaye, W. H. (2010). Altered striatal response to reward in bulimia nervosa after recovery. *International Journal of Eating Disorders,43,* 289–294.

Westen, D., & Harnden-Fischer, J. (2001). Personality profiles in eating disorders: Rethinking the distinction between axis I and axis II. *American Journal of Psychiatry, 58,* 547–562.

Wiederman, M. W., & Pryor, T. (1996). Multi-impulsivity among women with bulimia nervosa. *International Journal of Eating Disorders, 20,* 359–365.

Wonderlich, S. A., Brewerton, T. D., Jocic, Z., Dansky, B. S., & Abbott, D. W. (1997). Relationship of childhood sexual abuse and eating disorders. *Journal of the American Academy of Child & Adolescent Psychiatry, 36,* 1107–1115.

Wonderlich, S., Connolly, K., & Stice, E. (2004). Impulsivity as a risk factor for eating disorder behavior: Assessment implications with adolescents. *International Journal of Eating Disorders, 36,* 172–182.

Wonderlich, S. A., Crosby, R. D., Joiner, T., Peterson, C. B., Bardone-Cone, A., & Klein, M. (2005). Personality subtyping and bulimia nervosa: Psychopathological and genetic correlates. *Psychological Medicine, 35,* 649–657.

Wonderlich, S. A., Gordon, K. H., Mitchell, J. E., Crosby, R. D., & Engel, S. G. (2009). The validity and clinical utility of binge eating disorder. *International Journal of Eating Disorders, 42,* 687–705.

Wonderlich, S. A., Joiner, T. E., Jr., Keel, P. K., Williamson, D. A., & Crosby, R. D. (2007). Eating disorder diagnoses: Empirical approaches to classification. *American Psychologist, 62,* 167–180.

Woodside, D. B., Bulik, C. M., Halmi, K. A., Fichter, M. M., Kaplan, A., & Berrettini, W. H. (2002). Personality, perfectionism, and attitudes toward eating in parents of individuals with eating disorders. *International Journal of Eating Disorders, 31,* 290–299.

Zaider, T. I., Johnson, J. G., & Cockell, S. J. (2000). Psychiatric comorbidity associated with eating disorder symptomatology among adolescents in the community. *International Journal of Eating Disorders, 28,* 58–67.

Zakzanis, K. K., Campbell, Z., & Polsinelli, A. (2010). Quantitative evidence for distinct cognitive impairment in anorexia nervosa and bulimia nervosa. *Neuropsycholology, 4,* 89–106.

Zastrow, A., Kaiser, S., Stippich, C., Walther, S., Herzog, W., Tchanturia, K.,…Friederich, H. C. (2010). Neural correlates of impaired cognitive-behavioral flexibility in anorexia nervosa. *American Journal of Psychiatry, 166,* 608–616.

Zhu, Y., Hu, X., Wang, J., Chen, J., Guo, Q., Li, C., & Enck, P. (2012). Processing of food, body and emotional stimuli in anorexia nervosa: A systematic review and meta-analysis of functional magnetic resonance imaging studies. *European Eating Disorder Reviews, 20,* 439–450.

17

Developmental Psychopathology

THOMAS M. ACHENBACH

The discipline of *developmental psychopathology* originated primarily with efforts to understand maladaptive functioning between birth and maturity. (For brevity, I use "children" in reference to this entire period.) A key goal of the first book on developmental psychopathology (Achenbach, 1974, 1982) was to advance understanding, prevention, and treatment of psychopathology by conceptualizing maladaptive functioning in relation to developmental sequences, developmental processes, and the tasks, problems, and achievements characterizing particular developmental periods.

Because there had been relatively little empirical research on child psychopathology and because developmental changes are so salient between birth and maturity, developmental psychopathology initially focused primarily on children. The developmental approach was especially important for counteracting tendencies to view disorders as encapsulated entities that were the same at all ages. As an example, the *DSM* diagnostic criteria for what has become known as attention deficit hyperactivity disorder (ADHD) were the same regardless of age. This meant that the same behaviors were defined as symptoms of ADHD and that the same number of symptoms were required to meet the diagnostic threshold at all ages. Even though the population base rates, meanings, and consequences of the criterial symptoms might differ

greatly for different ages, ADHD was viewed as a disorder whose nature, manifestations, and diagnostic criteria remained essentially the same across all developmental periods.

Although it is now recognized that adults might also have ADHD problems, the concept of ADHD as a fixed disease entity nevertheless implies that the same symptoms can be used to diagnose ADHD at such ages as 20 and 50, as at such ages as 2, 6, 10, and 14. The definition of disorders according to the same symptoms for different ages thus implies that the underlying essences remain the same across developmental periods. This view also implies that the same diagnostic criteria identify the essence of ADHD in males and females and in settings as different as home, school, and work. Moreover, the same criteria for ADHD are applied to information from different sources such as parent, teacher, and self-reports, plus observations in clinical and everyday settings. Although the ADHD criteria require that "several inattentive or hyperactive–impulsive symptoms are present in two or more settings" (*DSM-5*, p. 60), no assessment operations are specified for determining whether the symptoms occur in two or more settings.

The example of ADHD is particularly emblematic of child psychopathology, because ADHD has long been publicized as a common condition that significantly impairs children's functioning and achievement. ADHD was also assumed to be limited to childhood and to be "outgrown" by about the age of 18. Although *DSM-5* includes a slightly lower diagnostic threshold for ages ≥17, the lack of more developmentally differentiated evidence-based diagnostic criteria for ADHD and other disorders argues for a developmental framework for understanding psychopathology in adulthood as well as in childhood. Physical and cognitive changes may be slower and less salient during adulthood than during childhood, but the study of adult psychopathology needs to take account of aspects of adaptive and maladaptive functioning that characterize adults of different ages.

Models for Psychopathology

During much of the twentieth century, psychopathology was viewed from the perspectives of theories that purported to explain the causes of many aspects of functioning, normal as well as abnormal. Psychoanalytic and learning theories were the most ambitious and influential explanatory theories. More recently, the term *model* has become widely used for systematic representations of phenomena, including psychopathology. Although some models may purport to represent the causes of phenomena, the goal of many models is to represent phenomena in ways that are useful without necessarily explaining the causes of the phenomena. Because phenomena can be modeled in multiple ways, different models for the same phenomena can be evaluated in terms of their utility for particular purposes and for particular users, without implying that only one model is correct while all other models for the phenomena must be wrong.

The increasing replacement of broad explanatory theories with multiple models may be at least partly attributable to methodological advances that take account of a multiplicity of variables. Quantitative genetic research, for example, has moved from seeking to explain disorders on the basis of one or a few genetic abnormalities to modeling a multiplicity of genetic factors, each of which may have very modest effects and may interact in numerous ways with other genetic as well as environmental factors. Molecular genetic research also models numerous genetic abnormalities, each of which may contribute in small and

heterogeneous ways even to diagnostic phenotypes that have traditionally been viewed as categorical and likely to have quite specific genetic causes, such as autism and schizophrenia (Morrow et al., 2008; Stefansson et al., 2008). Although progress in neuroimaging has raised expectations for discoveries of specific neuroanatomical causes for particular disorders, neuroimaging studies are also pointing toward ever more complex interactions among numerous variables that require multiple models.

At this stage of our knowledge, it appears that phenotypic as well as genotypic representations of psychopathology are more fruitfully viewed in terms of models than in terms of broad explanatory theories. The following sections address two prominent approaches to phenotypic modeling of psychopathology.

Diagnostic Models

The American Psychiatric Association's *DSM* and the World Health Organization's *ICD* provide the most widely used diagnostic models for psychopathology. The *DSM* and *ICD* comprise diagnostic categories, plus criteria for determining whether the problems reported for individuals fit particular diagnostic categories. The *DSM* and *ICD* are constructed by panels of experts who—with input from others—decide on the diagnostic categories and the criteria for each category. Most diagnostic criteria require diagnosticians to make yes-or-no judgments about whether a case meets each criterion and then a yes-or-no judgment about whether the case qualifies for the diagnosis. A task force appointed by the American Psychiatric Association recommended use of dimensional criteria for *DSM-5* (Helzer et al., 2008), but *DSM-5* retains the yes-or-no format.

Although the *DSM-5* is said to provide "operationalized diagnostic criteria" (Narrow et al., 2013, p. 71), it does not actually provide assessment operations for determining whether individuals meet criteria for diagnoses, other than specifying that intelligence tests are needed to determine whether individuals have low enough IQs to qualify for diagnoses of intellectual impairment. Nor does the *ICD* specify assessment operations. For most diagnoses, people making the diagnoses must decide what assessment data to obtain, from whom, by what means, and how to combine the data. They must also decide what diagnostic conclusions to draw from contradictory data, such as a teacher's report that a child cannot concentrate versus a parent's report that the child concentrates intensely on video games. To ensure that criteria are validly and reliably assessed and aggregated, assessment operations must be standardized, as addressed in the following sections.

Operationalizing Diagnostic Models   In order to operationalize diagnostic models in uniform and testable ways, standardized diagnostic interviews (SDIs) have been developed. The basic goal of SDIs is to translate each criterion for each diagnosis into one or more questions that can lead to a yes-or-no answer about whether an individual meets that criterion. One type of SDI is designated as "structured," because it comprises highly structured, very specific questions that require simple yes-or-no answers, with no need for clinical probing or interpretation. Structured SDIs are designed to be administered by computers and by interviewers who—although trained to administer the SDI—need no clinical training. Because respondents' answers are taken pretty much at face value to determine whether diagnostic criteria are met, structured SDIs are also known as "respondent based."

The Diagnostic Interview Schedule (DIS; Robins, Helzer, Croughan, & Ratcliff, 1981) is one of the most widely used SDIs for research on adult diagnoses. The DIS has spawned other structured SDIs, such as the World Health Organization's (1992) Composite International Diagnostic Interview (CIDI), which is widely used in international studies. A version of the DIS for assessing children, the Diagnostic Interview Schedule for Children (DISC; Shaffer et al., 2000), is also widely used.

A second type of SDI is designated as "semi-structured," because these SDIs require more flexible questioning, probing, and interpretation by the interviewer. To administer a semi-structured SDI, interviewers need to be clinically trained—as well as being trained to give the SDI—and need to translate respondents' answers into the yes-or-no judgments that ultimately determine which diagnostic criteria are met. An example is the Schedule for Affective Disorders and Schizophrenia (SADS; Endicott & Spitzer, 1978), which also has a children's version, the Kiddie-SADS (K-SADS; Kaufman et al., 1997). Because interviewers' clinical judgments determine whether diagnostic criteria are met, semi-structured SDIs are also known as "interviewer based."

SDIs were developed to operationalize the explicit diagnostic criteria that were introduced in *DSM-III*. Although SDIs can be fairly readily administered to most adults, efforts to extend SDIs to children have encountered issues that are highlighted by a developmental approach to psychopathology. One issue is the age or developmental level at which children can be expected to tolerate and give valid answers to lengthy SDIs. Although versions of SDIs have been developed for administration to children as young as 6 years (Reich, 2000), research has shown that many children as old as 11 do not understand and respond accurately to many SDI questions (Breton et al., 1999).

Considering that children may not have the concepts of psychopathology on which SDIs focus and that children may not be able or willing to give accurate answers to questions about hundreds of diagnostic criteria, it was recognized that SDIs were also needed to obtain parents' reports regarding their children's problems. Numerous disagreements were then found between parent and child reports on the SDIs (Jensen et al., 1999). The disagreements between children and their parents have raised questions about whether a diagnostic criterion is met if the child answers "yes" but the parent answers "no," and vice versa. To further challenge the operationalization of diagnostic criteria, separate interviews with a child's mother and father often yield different conclusions about whether the yes-or-no criteria are met for particular diagnoses. Although it is not realistic to expect most teachers to submit to lengthy SDIs, data obtained from teachers by other means may also disagree with data from children and parents.

In order to test the reliability of children's responses to SDIs, SDIs have been administered to children on two occasions separated by intervals brief enough (e.g., 1 to 2 weeks) to make it unlikely that their true diagnoses would change. (Note that "reliability" refers both to test–retest consistencies in the level of problems reported, e.g., the number of symptoms reported, and to consistencies in the rank ordering of individuals' scores, e.g., as measured by correlation coefficients.) It has been found that children often report fewer symptoms on the second occasion than on the first, causing the second interview to yield fewer diagnoses than the first (Jensen et al., 1995). Although it may not be surprising that children's yes-or-no responses to diagnostic questions are not very reliable, the same tendency among children to report fewer symptoms at the second interview than at the first has also been found for the children's parents. Moreover, adults interviewed about themselves also report fewer symptoms at the second interview.

Found in many studies of children and adults, the decline in reported symptoms from a first to a second interview has come to be called the *test-retest attenuation effect*. Note that—according to the categorical *DSM* model—a symptom count does not represent a score on a continuous psychometric dimension. Instead, a diagnostic threshold is defined by a prespecified number of symptoms from the list of criterial symptoms for a diagnosis. Consequently, a decline of even one reported symptom can change a diagnostic conclusion from "yes" to "no." The test–retest attenuation effect thus often causes the number of diagnoses to decline from first to second administrations of SDIs. Furthermore, meta-analyses of studies that reported diagnoses made from SDIs and from clinical evaluations of the same people have yielded only low to moderate agreement between SDI and clinical diagnoses for both child and adult cases (Rettew, Doyle, Achenbach, Dumenci, & Ivanova, 2009). Equally important, the few studies that have reported diagnoses of the same individuals made independently from two different SDIs—such as the DISC and K-SADS—have found that the different SDIs often yielded different diagnoses (e.g., Cohen, O'Connor, Lewis, Velez, & Malachowski, 1987). Even though SDIs are widely considered to provide gold-standard diagnoses, diagnoses made from them are likely to be significantly affected by the type of interviewee (e.g., mother, father, self), by whether it is the first or second interview, and by the particular SDI that is used.

What some may view as mere methodological quirks of SDIs actually raise more fundamental questions about diagnostic models. The findings that informants often disagree about whether diagnostic criteria are met, that second administrations of SDIs tend to yield fewer diagnoses than first administrations, and that different diagnoses may be produced by different SDIs mean that SDI diagnoses cannot be taken at face value as error-free revelations of actual disorders. Consequently, diagnostic models and SDIs need to be understood as subject to errors of measurement, just as other models and assessment procedures are. Disagreements between informants, test–retest attenuation, and differences between results obtained from different assessment instruments are also relevant to other models for psychopathology. The following sections present models that do not depend on assumptions of error-free revelations of categorical disorders via yes-or-no diagnostic criteria. These models stem from a bottom-up, empirically based approach that has grown out of the developmental study of psychopathology.

Empirically Based Models

A significant impetus to the emergence of developmental psychopathology as a discipline was concern about the big gaps between the prevailing diagnostic models and the behavioral, emotional, and social problems for which children needed help. *DSM-I*—which was the official U.S. diagnostic system until 1968—provided only the following two diagnostic categories for child psychopathology: Adjustment Reaction of Childhood and Schizophrenic Reaction, Childhood Type. Children seen in outpatient mental health services tended to be diagnosed as having Adjustment Reaction of Childhood, whereas extremely disturbed children tended to be diagnosed as having Schizophrenic Reaction, Childhood Type.

To determine whether more differentiated patterns of psychopathology could be identified than were implied by the two *DSM-I* diagnostic categories, several researchers took advantage of the electronic computers that became available in the 1960s to factor analyze ratings of problems reported for actual samples of children (Achenbach, 1966; Conners, 1969; Miller, 1967; Quay, 1964). Despite differences between rating instruments, sources of data, samples of children, and analytic methods, subsequent reviews of these efforts revealed considerable convergence on two broad-band groupings of problems that came to be designated as "Internalizing" or "Overcontrolled" and "Externalizing" or "Undercontrolled," plus more numerous narrow-band syndromes than were reflected in the two *DSM-I* diagnostic categories (Achenbach & Edelbrock, 1978; Quay, 1979). The Internalizing grouping comprised problems such as sadness, fears, withdrawal, and somatic complaints without known medical cause. The Externalizing grouping, by contrast, comprised problems such as fighting, lying, and stealing. The factor-analytically derived broad-band groupings and narrow-band syndromes provided models comprising the co-occurring problem items themselves. The word *syndrome* is used throughout this chapter to mean a set of co-occurring characteristics, based on the Greek meaning of syndrome as "the act of running together" (Gove, 1971, p. 2320). Consequently, syndromes may include categorical diagnoses, but are not limited to such diagnoses.

Operationalizing Empirically Based Models The factor-analytic studies worked "from the bottom up" by analyzing ratings of problems for actual samples of children. Within a particular study, the factor-analytically derived models could thus be operationalized by aggregating ratings of the items comprising each model. For example, individual children could be given scores for an Internalizing model by summing each child's ratings on the problems comprising the version of the Internalizing model derived from particular factor analyses. However, to operationalize empirically based models for research and clinical applications beyond each initial research study, assessment instruments needed to be developed that could be completed by informants in new settings. Analogous to the development of SDIs, the development of more broadly applicable assessment instruments for empirically based models required that the problems comprising the models be formatted for ratings by informants such as parents, teachers, and children. However, the development of instruments for assessing empirically based models differed from the development of SDIs in the following ways:

1. The models assessed by SDIs consisted of diagnostic constructs formulated by panels of experts, whereas the empirically based models consisted of problem items found to co-occur in factor analyses of ratings of children.
2. The diagnostic criteria assessed by SDIs were selected by the experts to represent the diagnostic models formulated by the experts, whereas the problem items for assessing the empirically based models were the items that had been factor analyzed to derive the empirically based models.
3. The wording of SDI criteria required translations into terms understandable by informants such as parents, teachers, and children, whereas the wording of items for assessing the empirically based models could be retained from the wording that was used to obtain informants' ratings for the factor analyses.

The empirically based approach markedly reduced the gap between models for psychopathology and procedures for assessing children in terms of those models. The straightforward adaptation of the items to instruments that could be self-administered or administered by interviewers with no special training fostered the development of many rating instruments that were briefer, more economical, and more practical for use in more diverse clinical and research contexts than the SDIs, which often included thousands of questions (Shaffer et al., 2000). Although the advance of empirically based models was initially fueled by the lack of developmentally credible diagnostic models for child psychopathology, empirically based models are now applied to adult psychopathology as well. The following sections address facets of assessment and understanding of psychopathology that are being advanced by the empirically based approach stemming from developmental psychopathology.

Quantification of Psychopathology

DSM-I and *DSM-II* comprised diagnostic categories that were specified in terms of narrative descriptions without explicit criteria or decision rules. Beginning with *DSM-III*, the official diagnostic categories have been defined by sets of yes-or-no criteria. For each diagnostic category, an explicit decision rule specifies the number and combination of criteria that individuals must be judged to meet in order to qualify for a diagnosis.

The empirically based models, by contrast, are derived mainly by quantitative methodology that uses measures of associations among item ratings as input. Factor-analytic methods have been widely used, but methods such as cluster analysis, item response theory, and latent class analysis are also used. Whether the problem items are rated yes-or-no or are rated on Likert scales such as *0 = not true, 1 = somewhat or sometimes true, 2 = very true or often true*, etc., correlations between items can be used to quantify the degree to which ratings of each item tend to increase or decrease in relation to ratings of each other item. When factor-analytic methodology is applied to correlations among items rated for large samples of individuals, the end products are "factors" (dimensions, vectors) on which each item has a "loading." An item's loading on a factor is analogous to a correlation coefficient that indicates how strongly ratings of that item are associated with that factor. Factor analyses of problem item ratings tend to yield factors on which items that assess particular kinds of problems load highly, while items that assess other kinds of problems have low loadings. For example, in factor analyses of ratings of both child and adult problems, a factor is often found on which aggressive behaviors such as "gets in many fights," "physically attacks people," and "threatens to hurt people" have high loadings.

The items that load highly on a factor can be used to form a dimensional scale for scoring individuals in terms of the sum or some other aggregation of the ratings on these items. The set of co-occurring items can be given a descriptive label such as "Aggressive Behavior," which can be viewed a "syndrome" (Gove, 1971). Problem items that load highly on other factors can be similarly used to construct scales that provide scores for syndromes that can be given descriptive labels such as "Attention Problems," "Anxiety," and "Depression."

Note that the empirically based approach quantifies the basic information about the presence of problems in terms of quantitative ratings, the associations among problems in terms of quantitative correlations, the aggregation of problems into syndromes via multivariate statistical methods, and the assessment of individuals in terms of quantitative scales. As discussed later, quantitative norms are used to evaluate the degree of deviance indicated by an individual's scale score in relation to norms for the individual's age and gender, the type of informant, and the relevant society.

Advantages of Quantification

Quantification has multiple advantages over modeling and assessment of psychopathology in terms of yes-or-no diagnostic models and yes-or-no criteria for each model. One advantage is that models derived from quantitative procedures such as factor analysis make use of data on associations among problems reported for actual samples of individuals rather than depending on particular experts' memories, judgments, and inferences concerning the co-occurrence of particular problems.

A second advantage is that informants' reports are not forced into yes-or-no choices that are hard for most people to make and may be especially vulnerable to individual differences in "yea-saying"

and "nay-saying" response sets. For example, suppose that an SDI question is designed to obtain a yes-or-no answer from a mother and a father about whether their child meets the ADHD criterion "is often distracted by extraneous stimuli." A mother and father might agree that their child is often distracted when doing homework but not when playing video games. However, when forced to make a yes-or-no choice, a parent who thinks about the child's distractibility while doing homework might answer "yes" to the question about distraction. By contrast, a parent who thinks about the child's concentration on video games might answer "no." The result is 100% disagreement about whether the child meets the diagnostic criterion, despite the parents' complete agreement that the child is easily distracted when doing homework but not when playing video games.

If the diagnostic criterion is quantified on even a simple Likert scale such as "0 = not true, 1 = somewhat or sometimes true, 2 = very true or often true," both parents would be apt to rate the child 1, yielding 100% agreement. However, even if one parent rated the child 1 and the other parent rated the child 0 or 2, disagreement would be much less than 100%. When diagnoses are defined by multiple yes-or-no criterial items, differences in yea-saying versus nay-saying response sets can lead to many disagreements, even if the informants actually agree that problems occur occasionally or in mild to moderate degree. Meta-analyses show that quantitative criteria yield significantly better reliability and validity than categorical criteria for assessment of psychopathology (Markon, Chmielewski, & Miller, 2011).

A third advantage is that quantification reduces the adverse consequences of the test–retest attenuation effect. Recall that informants tend to report fewer problems on a second SDI than on an initial SDI. Because a report of even one fewer criterial problems can change a categorical diagnostic conclusion from yes to no, second SDIs tend to yield fewer diagnoses than initial SDIs. Test–retest attenuation effects have also been found on quantitative assessment instruments. However, quantitative scales measure the *degree to which* problems are reported rather than requiring yes-or-no diagnoses. Consequently, a small reduction in scale scores from the initial rating of problems to a second rating need not dictate a change from "sick" to "well." Instead, test–retest attenuation of scale scores—which has been found to account for very small percentages of variance in the scale scores (e.g., Achenbach & Rescorla, 2001)—typically leaves individuals' second scale scores in the same range (e.g., high, medium, or low) as that of their initial scores. SDIs that operationalize categorical diagnostic models, by contrast, must treat a difference between an initial symptom count that reaches a diagnostic threshold and a subsequent count that falls one symptom below the threshold as a change from "sick" to "well."

A fourth advantage of quantitative criteria for psychopathology is that scale scores can be normed for each gender in different age ranges. By assessing representative population samples of males and females of different ages, we can identify gender and age differences in scale scores that are large enough to warrant different standard scores and clinical cut points.

Quantification has a fifth advantage with respect to differences between reports by different informants. As mentioned previously, when SDIs were initially developed for assessing children, it was discovered that diagnoses made from SDIs administered to the children did not agree with diagnoses made from SDIs that were used to obtain parents' yes-or-no reports of the children's problems. Because differences were also found between quantitative ratings of children's problems by parents, teachers, and the children themselves, meta-analyses of correlations between different informants' ratings of children were done to determine the typical levels of agreement (Achenbach, McConaughy, & Howell, 1987). For pairs of informants who played similar roles vis-à-vis the children (pairs of parents, teachers, mental health workers, observers), the mean correlation was found to be 0.60. For pairs of informants who played different roles vis-à-vis the children (e.g., parent versus teacher, teacher versus mental health worker), the mean correlation was found to be 0.27. And for children's reports of their own problems versus reports by parents, teachers, and mental health workers, the mean correlation was 0.22.

The meta-analytic findings have been subsequently borne out by so many additional studies that they are considered to be among "the most robust findings in clinical child research" (De los Reyes & Kazdin, 2005, p. 483). Cited in over 3,700 publications (Google Scholar, 2013), the meta-analytic findings have led to widespread recognition by researchers and clinicians that assessment of children's problems requires data from multiple sources, such as mothers, fathers, teachers, and children themselves. Instruments for assessing child psychopathology, the design of interventions, evaluations of outcomes, epidemiology, and models for child psychopathology increasingly take account of data from multiple sources.

Meta-analyses have also shown only modest agreement between self-ratings of adult psychopathology and ratings by collaterals who knew the adults who were being assessed, such as spouses, partners, family members, friends, and therapists (Achenbach, Krukowski, Dumenci, & Ivanova, 2005). The need to obtain and integrate data from multiple sources—first identified in developmental psychopathology research on children—is now increasingly recognized for adult psychopathology as well. Consequently, quantitative methodology is used to rigorously document relations between data from different sources and is also used in clinical and research applications of multi-informant assessment, as discussed later.

Hierarchical (Multitier) Models

The number of diagnostic categories has greatly increased from *DSM-I* through *DSM-5*. Since the introduction of explicit diagnostic criteria and decision rules in *DSM-III*, research has shown that many individuals meet criteria for multiple diagnostic categories (Costello, Edelbrock, Kalas, Kessler, & Klaric, 1982). Called "comorbidity," the apparent co-occurrence of multiple disorders in the same individuals could potentially shed light on etiological factors common to the comorbid disorders. However, for psychopathology for which no gold-standard biomarkers are known, apparent comorbidity might also reflect a lack of valid boundaries between diagnostic categories. As an example, in three studies, a mean of 92% of children who met *DSM-III* criteria for conduct disorder (CD) also met criteria for oppositional defiant disorder (ODD; Faraone, Biederman, Keenan, & Tsuang, 1991; Spitzer, Davies, & Barkley, 1990; Walker et al., 1991). These findings indicated that the diagnostic criteria probably did not validly mark boundaries between different disorders. Although subsequent editions of the *DSM* were intended to reduce the apparent comorbidity between CD and ODD, the lack of gold-standard markers leaves open the question of where and how boundaries between diagnostic categories should be drawn.

Confusion created by assumptions of categorical differences between disorders and homogeneity within each category is further illustrated by the 15 *DSM-5* criterial symptoms for CD. Among the 15 criterial symptoms, there are subsets of symptoms that are labeled "Aggression to People and Animals," "Destruction of Property," "Deceitfulness or Theft," and "Serious Violations of Rules." Only 3 of the 15 criteria need to be met for an individual to be diagnosed as having CD. Consequently, some individuals may qualify for CD because they are judged to engage in aggressive behavior. Others may qualify because they are judged to engage in deceitfulness or theft. And still others may qualify because they violate rules or display various combinations of the criterial behaviors for CD. Many factor-analytic studies have yielded separate, though correlated, syndromes for aggressive behaviors versus nonaggressive rule-breaking behaviors (e.g., Ivanova, et al., 2013; Loeber & Schmaling, 1985). This evidence thus suggests that a basic distinction should be made between aggressive and nonaggressive conduct problems instead of lumping them together as equivalent criteria for the single category of CD. Factor-analytic studies have also yielded other syndromes that differ from *DSM* diagnostic categories, although some factor-analytically derived syndromes do approximate sets of problems corresponding to the symptom criteria for *DSM* categories.

The progressive increase in the number of *DSM* diagnostic categories from *DSM-I* through *DSM-5* may reflect taxonomic splitting, additions of newly discovered disorders, or both. However, the lack of evidence that *DSM* diagnostic criteria validly mark gold-standard boundaries between categorical disorders and the findings that many people meet criteria for multiple disorders argue for quantitative approaches that do not require assumptions of rigid boundaries between particular sets of problems. For example, positive correlations are often found between scores that people obtain on different syndromes. Such correlations do not necessarily mean that the people have multiple comorbid disorders, each of which is defined by a different syndrome. Instead, the correlations indicate that individuals who score relatively high on certain syndromes also tend to score relatively high on certain other syndromes. When individuals' syndrome scores are displayed on profiles, various patterns of high and low scores can be seen (e.g., Achenbach & Rescorla, 2001).

Furthermore, when correlations between multiple factor-analytically derived syndromes are themselves factor analyzed, the resulting factors (called "second-order" factors because they reflect correlations among the initial "first-order" syndromes) comprise broad-band groupings of problems. The broad-band Internalizing and Externalizing groupings mentioned earlier were identified in one of the first factor-analytic studies of child psychopathology (Achenbach, 1966) and have since been repeatedly found in studies of adult as well as child psychopathology (Krueger & Markon, 2006).

Because first-order factor analyses are applied to large numbers of specific problem items and second-order factor analyses are applied to correlations between smaller numbers of first-order factors, the results can be used to construct hierarchical (or multitier) models. The models can include large numbers of very specific problem items at the most molecular level. The large numbers of problem items can then be aggregated into smaller numbers of moderately specific syndromes of co-occurring problems. The syndromes can be subsequently aggregated into a few broad-band groupings such as those designated as Internalizing and Externalizing. A total problem score can also be computed by summing ratings on all the problem items to yield a very broad measure of psychopathology. Figure 17.1 illustrates such a hierarchy derived from ratings of 6- to 18-year-olds. The syndromes were derived from exploratory factor analyses (EFAs) and were supported by confirmatory factor analyses (CFAs; Achenbach, 2009).

Quantitatively derived hierarchical models like that illustrated in Figure 17.1 avoid the need for forced choices between diagnostic categories, because individuals are rated on each problem item and the ratings of items comprising each syndrome are summed to yield scores on the syndromes. All individuals thus obtain scores on all syndromes. Because many patterns of low, medium, and high syndrome and broad-band scores are possible, the patterns document the kinds of problems reported for each individual rather than requiring interpretations in terms of separate but potentially comorbid disorders.

The broad-band Internalizing and Externalizing groupings reflect correlations among subsets of syndromes that may share certain genetic and/or other etiological influences (Kendler, Prescott, Myers, & Neale, 2003; Krueger & Markon, 2006). Hierarchical models that embody multiple levels

Total Problems							
Broad-Band Groupings of Syndromes							
Internalizing						Externalizing	
Factor-Analytically Derived Cross-Informant Syndromes							
Anxious/ Depressed	Withdrawn/ Depressed	Somatic Complaints	Social Problems	Thought Problems	Attention Problems	Rule-Breaking Behavior	Aggressive Behavior
Examples of Problem Items[a]							
Cries	Enjoys little	Aches, pains	Clumsy	Can't get	Acts young	Bad	Argues
Fears	Lacks energy	Eye problems	Gets teased	mind off	Can't	companions	Attacks
Feels	Rather be	Feels dizzy	Jealous	thoughts	concentrate	Breaks rules	people
unloved	alone	Headaches	Lonely	Hears things	Can't sit still	Lacks guilt	Disobedient
Feels too	Refuses to	Nausea	Not liked	Repeats acts	Confused	Lies, cheats	Fights
guilty	talk	Overtired	Prefers	Sees things	Daydreams	Sets fires	Loud
Talks or	Sad	Stomach-	younger	Strange	Fails to finish	Steals	Mean
thinks of	Secretive	aches	kids	behavior	Impulsive	Swearing	Screams
suicide	Shy, timid	Tired	Too	Strange	Inattentive	Truant	Temper
Worries	Withdrawn	Vomiting	dependent	ideas	Stares	Vandalism	Threatens

[a]Abbreviated versions of items for obtaining parent, teacher, and self-ratings of 6–18–year olds.

Figure 17.1 Hierarchical model of empirically based assessment levels. Adapted from Achenbach, 2009. Copyright © 2009 by Thomas M. Achenbach. Used with permission of the author.

of specificity, ranging from individual problems to narrow-band syndromes, broad-band groupings of syndromes, and total problem scores, avoid issues of boundaries and comorbidity between disorders. This is because the lowest level in the hierarchy can accommodate a lot of differentiation among specific problems, while higher levels reflect associations among particular subsets of problems and syndromes of problems.

Multi-Informant Assessment of Psychopathology

As mentioned previously, early SDIs for childhood disorders revealed poor agreement between children's reports of their problems and reports by their parents. Meta-analyses of cross-informant correlations subsequently showed that agreement between various combinations of informants is typically too low to warrant accepting any one informant's report as an accurate substitute for reports by the person being assessed or by other informants. Consequently, comprehensive assessment and understanding of psychopathology require that data be systematically obtained from

informants who know the person being assessed, as well as from the person being assessed.

To compare reports by different informants, it is important for the different informants to respond to parallel questions in a standard format, with appropriate variations for the type of informant. As an example of variations, self-report instruments are worded in the first person and may include a few items not likely to be ratable by other informants, such as "My heart pounds or races." Instruments for completion by other informants are worded in the third person and may include a few items not likely to be ratable by the person being assessed, such as "Stares blankly." Additional variations may be needed to assess problems ratable by informants who play different roles with respect to the person being assessed. For example, parents but not teachers may be asked to rate problems such as "Cruel to animals," whereas teachers but not parents may be asked to rate problems such as "Sleeps in class."

Diagnostic conclusions based on multi-informant data often differ markedly from conclusions based only on self-reports. For example, Meyer et al. (2001) found that 70% of diagnoses based only on self-reports were wrong when compared with diagnoses based on multi-informant data. Furthermore, the chance-corrected agreement (kappa coefficient) was only 18% between diagnoses based on self-reports versus diagnoses based on multi-informant data. Although it might seem cumbersome to obtain data from multiple informants, U.S. national survey findings showed that over 80% of randomly selected adults were willing to nominate collateral informants who, in turn, were willing to complete rating instruments parallel to those completed by the person being assessed (Achenbach, Newhouse, & Rescorla, 2004; Achenbach & Rescorla, 2003). The optimal kind and number of informants, as well as the methods for comparing and using their reports, will, of course, depend on the clinical or research purposes for obtaining the data.

Cross-Informant Syndromes

Both the similarities and differences between informants' reports are important for assessing individuals for clinical purposes. They are also important for constructing models of psychopathology that take account of multiple perspectives. One approach to constructing such models has been to derive syndromes separately from ratings of large samples of people by informants who play different roles with respect to the people being assessed. Because the relevant informants, the problems appropriate for rating by the informants, and the syndromes formed by the problems may vary with development, syndromes have been derived separately for different age groups. As an example, parallel parent, teacher, and self-ratings of 6- to 18-year-olds have been factor analyzed separately to derive syndromes on the basis of ratings by each type of informant (Achenbach & Rescorla, 2001).

The syndromes derived from parent, teacher, and self-ratings were compared to identify items that loaded significantly on analogous syndromes derived from ratings by at least two kinds of informants. The items that loaded significantly on versions of a syndrome derived from ratings by at least two kinds of informants were then used to define a *cross-informant syndrome construct* (latent variable) of the syndrome. Each syndrome construct is operationalized in terms of items that are worded appropriately for each type of informant, such as first-person wording for self-ratings and third-person wording for parent and teacher

ratings. Moreover, items that are ratable by only one kind of informant and that loaded significantly on a syndrome derived from ratings by that kind of informant are also included in the operational definition of the syndrome construct rated by that kind of informant. For example, the item "Disrupts class discipline," which is rated only by teachers, loaded significantly on the version of the "Attention Problems" syndrome derived from teacher ratings. The lack of the item "Disrupts class discipline" on the parent and self-rating instruments means that it is included in the Attention Problems syndrome scale scored only from teacher ratings.

For ages 6–18, eight cross-informant syndrome constructs were derived from parent, teacher, and self-ratings. As illustrated in Figure 17.1, in addition to Attention Problems, the cross-informant syndromes are designated as Anxious/Depressed, Withdrawn/Depressed, Somatic Complaints, Social Problems, Thought Problems, Rule-Breaking Behavior, and Aggressive Behavior. Second-order factor analyses of the syndromes yielded a broad-band Internalizing grouping comprising the Anxious/Depressed, Withdrawn/Depressed, and Somatic Complaints syndromes, plus an Externalizing grouping comprising the Rule-Breaking Behavior and Aggressive Behavior syndromes.

The syndromes and the items comprising each syndrome are displayed on profiles that show the syndrome scale scores standardized in relation to norms for a child's age, gender, the type of informant (parent, teacher, or self), and the user-selected society, as explained later. Figure 17.2 illustrates a profile that displays item ratings and syndrome scores for a 15-year-old boy rated by his father (all personal identifying data are fictitious).

Syndromes Found for Different Age Periods To take account of developmental differences, multiple studies have used procedures like those just described to derive syndromes from rating instruments designed for ages 1½–5, 18–59, and ≥60 years (Achenbach et al., 2004; Achenbach & Rescorla, 2000, 2003). Like the rating instruments for ages 6–18, the rating instruments for each of the other age periods comprise developmentally appropriate items designed to be rated by informants who are knowledgeable about the functioning of the people being assessed. For ages 1½–5, parallel rating instruments are designed

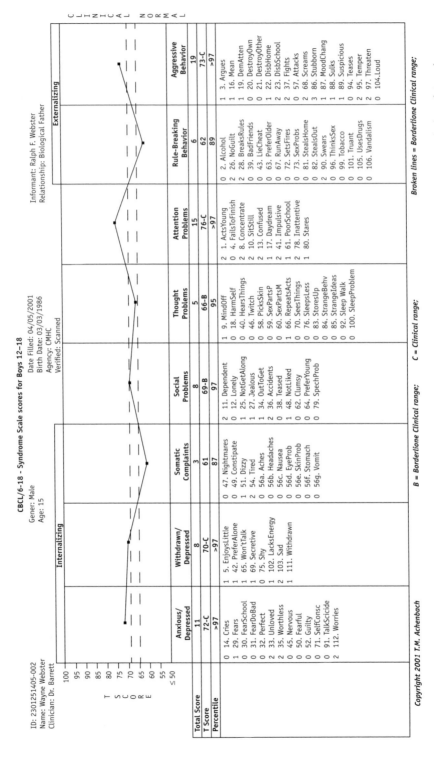

Figure 17.2 Computer-scored syndrome profile from CBCL completed for a 15-year-old boy by his father. Personal identifying data are fictitious. Reprinted from Achenbach & Rescorla, 2001. Copyright © 2001 by Thomas M. Achenbach and Leslie A. Rescorla. Used with permission of the author.

Table 17.1 Cross-Informant Syndromes Found for Different Age Periods

Syndrome	Age Periods in Years			
	1½–5	6–18	18–59	≥60
Emotionally Reactive	Y			
Anxious/Depressed	Y	Y	Y	Y
Somatic Complaints	Y	Y	Y	Y
Withdrawn[a]	Y	Y	Y	
Social Problems		Y		
Thought Problems		Y	Y	Y
Attention Problems	Y	Y	Y	
Rule-Breaking Behavior		Y	Y	
Aggressive Behavior	Y	Y	Y	
Intrusive			Y	
Worries				Y
Functional Impairment				Y
Memory/Cognition Problems				Y
Irritable/Disinhibited				Y

Note. A Sleep Problems syndrome was found in parents' ratings of 1½- to 5-year-olds.

[a]Designated as "Withdrawn/Depressed" for ages 6–18.

for completion by parent figures and by preschool teachers and caregivers who see children in group settings. For ages 18–59 and ≥60, parallel rating instruments are designed for self-ratings and ratings by collaterals such as spouses, partners, family members, friends, therapists, and staff in residential settings occupied by the people being assessed, such as treatment facilities, retirement communities, and nursing homes.

Table 17.1 lists cross-informant syndromes derived from ratings by different kinds of informants for each age period. Although the items comprising the syndromes differ somewhat, developmentally appropriate versions of the Anxious/Depressed and Somatic Complaints syndromes were found for all age periods. Versions of the Withdrawn, Attention Problems, and Aggressive Behavior syndromes were found for ages 1½–59. Versions of the Thought Problems syndrome were found for ages 6 to >90 years, while certain other syndromes were found for only a single age period, including Emotionally Reactive for ages 1½–5, Social Problems for ages 6–18, Instrusive for ages 18–59, and Worries, Functional Impairment, Memory/Cognition Problems, and Irritable/Disinhibited for ages 60 to over 90. A Sleep Problems syndrome comprising items rated only by parent figures was also found for ages 1½–5. A few other syndromes have been found in ratings by clinical interviewers, classroom observers, and administrators of individual ability and

achievement tests (McConaughy & Achenbach, 2001, 2004, 2009).

Practical Applications of Multi-Informant Assessment

To facilitate use of data from multiple informants, the software for scoring the cross-informant syndromes displays side-by-side comparisons of ratings of each problem item by the different informants. The software also displays Q correlations between the 0-1-2 ratings of problem items by each pair of informants, such as mother versus father, each parent versus each teacher, and self-ratings versus ratings by other informants. (Q correlations are computed by applying the formula for the Pearson product-moment correlation to sets of items rated by two individuals. Note that Q correlations are statistical measures of similarity between two sets of scores, whereas "Q sorts" are methods for sorting descriptors of individuals into normal distributions.) To help users evaluate the magnitude of the Q correlation between each pair of informants, the software also displays the 25th percentile, mean, and 75th percentile Q correlations obtained for large reference samples of pairs of particular kinds of informants, such as mothers versus fathers. The software describes the Q correlation between a particular pair of informants as "below average" if it is less than the 25th percentile of the correlations in the reference group, "average" if it is between the 25th and 75th percentiles, and "above average" if it is greater than the 75th percentile.

To make it easy for users to compare syndrome scores obtained from ratings by different informants, the software also displays bar graphs of scale scores from all informants. Figure 17.3 illustrates the bar graph comparisons of syndrome scores obtained from mother, father, teacher, and self-ratings of the 15-year-old boy whose profile of syndromes scored from his father's ratings was displayed in Figure 17.2. Each bar is standardized for the age and gender of the person who was rated, plus the kind of informant (e.g., parent, teacher, self), and the user-selected society. (A society is a population of people who live in a particular political jurisdiction where a particular language is dominant. Many societies are countries but some are not, such as Puerto Rico and Flanders, the Flemish-speaking area of Belgium.)

In addition to bar graphs for the syndrome scales, the software scores and provides multi-informant bar graph comparisons for Internalizing, Externalizing, and Total Problems scales. The software also scores and provides multi-informant bar graph comparisons for DSM-oriented scales. The DSM-oriented scales were constructed by having experts from many societies identify items that they judged to be very consistent with particular DSM diagnostic categories. The items identified by most experts as being very consistent with a DSM category were aggregated into a scale for that category. Like the empirically based "bottom-up" scales, the expert judgment "top-down" DSM-oriented scales are displayed in relation to norms for age, gender, the type of informant, and the user-selected society.

Research Applications of Multi-Informant Assessment

Because informant reports of psychopathology so often differ and because there is no litmus test for most kinds of psychopathology, research as well as clinical services must take account of informant variance. One focus of such research has been on identifying reasons for discrepancies between reports by different informants. Although some have blamed informant discrepancies on measurement error, there is plenty of evidence that measurement error does not explain most informant discrepancies (De Los Reyes, 2011).

An especially illuminating line of research has used correlations between informants' ratings of monozygotic (MZ) versus dizygotic (DZ) twins to test the degree to which differences between informants' ratings reflect "informant biases" versus differences in the genetically and environmentally influenced aspects of the twins' functioning that may be captured by different informants' ratings. As an example, Dutch researchers compared Internalizing and Externalizing scores obtained from mothers' and fathers' ratings of 3,501 pairs of 3-year-old twins (Van der Valk, Van den Oord, Verhulst, & Boomsma, 2001). Based on correlations between ratings of MZ and DZ twins, genetic modeling showed that discrepancies between mothers' and fathers' ratings validly reflected different genetically influenced aspects of the children's functioning rather than informant biases. Longitudinal analyses of parents' ratings of Dutch twins have also shown that discrepancies between mothers' and fathers' ratings validly reflect genetically influenced aspects of their children's functioning over multiple developmental periods (Bartels, Boomsma, Hudziak, van Beijsterveldt, & van den Oord, 2007; Bartels, van den Oord, Hudziak, Rietveld, van Beijsterveldt, & Boomsma, 2004).

Genetic analyses of cross-informant correlations have been extended to ratings of Dutch twins by their mothers and teachers, who saw the children in the very different settings of home versus school and were also apt to have very different mindsets stemming from their different roles, training, experience, and objectives vis-à-vis the children (Derks, Hudziak, van Beijsterveldt, Dolan, & Boomsma, 2006). Based on ratings of the empirically based Attention Problems syndrome for over 2,000 pairs of twins, Derks et al. analyzed MZ and DZ correlations into genetically versus environmentally influenced aspects of the variance that was common to both kinds of raters versus specific to each kind of rater. Derks et al. found that 32% of the variance in mothers' Child Behavior Checklist (CBCL) ratings and teachers' Teacher's Report Form (TRF) ratings reflected genetically influenced aspects of Attention Problems scores that were common to mother and teacher ratings. The additional 9% of variance that was common to ratings by mothers and teachers reflected environmentally influenced aspects of Attention Problems scores.

Of the rater-specific variance, 45% was accounted for by genetic factors and 14% by

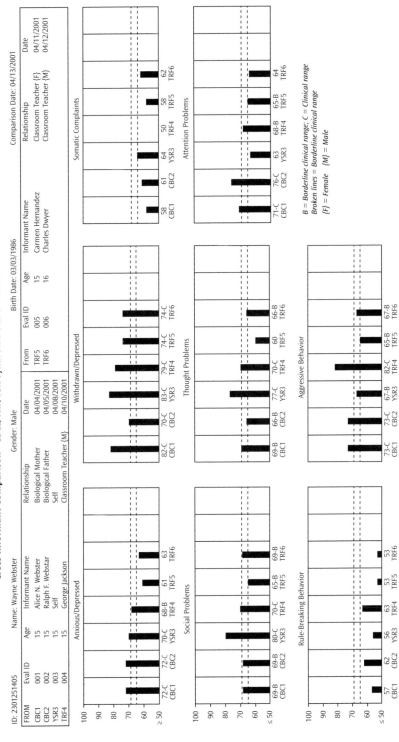

Figure 17.3 Cross-informant comparisons of syndrome scores for a 15-year-old boy. Personal identifying data are fictitious. Reprinted from Achenbach & Rescorla, 2001. Copyright © 2001 by Thomas M. Achenbach and Leslie A. Rescorla. Used with permission of the author.

environmental factors in mothers' ratings, while 23% was accounted for by genetic factors and 36% by environmental factors in teachers' ratings. These findings thus showed that differences between ratings by informants as different as mothers versus teachers validly reflected differences in genetic and environmental effects. These and other genetic findings not only support the validity and utility of multi-informant data, but they also contribute to our understanding of genetic and environmental influences on functioning with different interaction partners in different settings across multiple developmental periods (Bartels et al., 2007).

The Importance of Norms for Evaluating Psychopathology

Since the first successful tests for clinical assessment of intelligence were constructed by Binet and Simon (1905), it has been recognized that norms are needed to provide metrics for identifying children whose cognitive development is sufficiently retarded to warrant special education. Yes-or-no criteria for psychopathology imply that disorders can be identified as present-versus-absent without the benefit of norms. However, findings that population base rates for particular behaviors differ by age argue for using age-based norms to evaluate reports of behaviors that are used as criteria for psychopathology. As an example, *DSM-5* criteria for diagnosing ADHD include "often has difficulty sustaining attention in tasks or play activities" and "often has difficulty waiting his or her turn." These behaviors are only to be judged as meeting diagnostic criteria if they "have persisted for at least 6 months to a degree that is maladaptive and inconsistent with developmental level" (p. 59). However, no norms or other metrics are provided for determining whether the behaviors are "maladaptive or inconsistent with developmental level." Nor are norms or other metrics provided for determining how the total number of criteria that the diagnostician deems to be met compares with the number that would be within the normal range versus clinical range for particular ages, nor for males versus females, nor for reports by different informants such as parents versus teachers. Although norms have been used to evaluate intelligence test scores for over a century, they have not yet been incorporated into official criteria for diagnosing psychopathology.

The derivation of empirically based syndromes separately for preschool children, school-age children, adults, and the elderly takes account of major developmental differences with respect to the relevant informants, the problems to be rated, and the syndromal patterning of problems. However, even within each age period, scale scores may differ for males versus females. Moreover, scale scores may differ between informants who see the people being assessed in different settings, have different mindsets, and rate somewhat different items. To take account of possible age, gender, and informant differences in scale scores, it is necessary to assess large population samples from which distributions of scale scores can be generated for individuals of each gender at different ages who are rated on the age-appropriate instruments by each relevant kind of informant. Because it cannot be assumed that syndrome findings and norms for any single society would be the same as for other societies, it is also important to test the syndromes and distributions of scale scores in the populations of other societies.

U.S. Age, Gender, and Informant-Specific Norms for Psychopathology

To obtain data from which to construct norms for the syndrome, *DSM*-oriented, Internalizing, Externalizing, and Total Problems scales, interviewers visited homes that were selected to be representative of the 48 contiguous states. For households that agreed to participate, one household member was randomly selected for assessment with standardized rating instruments appropriate for that individual's age. For ages 1½–5 and 6–18, a parent figure was first asked to rate the child. For ages 18–59 and ≥60, the person to be assessed was first asked to complete a self-rating instrument. Interviewers then asked for consent to request completion of parallel rating forms by other informants (preschool teachers and daycare providers for ages 1½–5; teachers for ages 6–18; youths to complete self-report instruments for ages 11–18; adult collaterals nominated by the assessed adults for ages 18–59 and 60–98). After consent was granted, interviewers asked the 11- to 18-year-old youths and the adult collaterals to complete the appropriate instruments.

To create what epidemiologists call "healthy" samples for constructing norms, the researchers used data for all the assessed individuals for whom no mental health, substance abuse, or major special education services were reported for the preceding 12 months. The data were used to compute cumulative frequency distributions of scores for each scale as a basis for assigning percentiles and normalized *T* scores to each raw score on the scales. As was illustrated in Figure 17.2, raw scale scores are displayed on profiles in relation to the *T* score metrics. Beneath the profile, the software also displays the percentile and *T* score equivalent of each raw scale score obtained by an individual from ratings by each kind of informant, plus the 0-1-2 ratings of each problem item belonging to the syndrome or *DSM*-oriented scale (Achenbach et al., 2004; Achenbach & Rescorla, 2000, 2001, 2003).

Multicultural Norms for Psychopathology

The empirically based syndromes were derived from ratings of Anglophone people who resided mainly in the United States. To apply the syndromes and scales to people from other societies, it is necessary to test whether the syndrome models fit ratings of people in those societies. It is also necessary to compare scale scores for population samples from different societies and to construct different sets of norms to take account of important societal differences between mean scores. Translations of the rating forms are available in over 90 languages and multicultural norms have been constructed for over 55 societies (Achenbach & Rescorla, 2014).

Models embodying the syndromes listed in Table 17.1 have been supported by CFAs for population samples in 56 societies (Ivanova et al., 2010, 2011, 2013; Rescorla et al., 2012).The CFA findings thus provide evidence that the empirically based syndrome models are applicable to ratings of problems in at least those 56 societies. Although additional problems and syndrome models might also be applicable in particular societies, the standard sets of Likert-rating items and the CFA-supported syndrome models provide a common data language for assessing, researching, and communicating about psychopathology across societies that differ greatly in cultures, religions, languages, ethnicities, economic structures, political systems, and geographical regions.

Q correlations averaging in the 0.70s have been found between the mean ratings of problem items from different societies for each kind of informant (Rescorla et al., 2012, 2014). These large correlations indicate that the same problems tend to receive relatively low, medium, or high ratings across societies. Analyses of variance (ANOVAs) have revealed that age and gender differences in scale scores are similar in most societies. However, the ANOVAs have yielded large enough differences between scale scores from different societies to argue against using a single set of norms for all societies.

The mean Total Problems scores from all societies that have provided data for a particular instrument have been found to be approximately normally distributed, with most societies having mean Total Problems scores within ±1 *SD* of the "omnicultural mean" (Ellis & Kimmel, 1992), that is, the mean of the mean Total Problems scores from all available societies. Mean scores on the scales at lower levels in hierarchies like the one illustrated in Figure 17.1 are also normally distributed across societies.

To take account of the differences between societies having relatively low, intermediate, or high problem scores, three sets of norms have been incorporated into the software for scoring the syndrome, *DSM*-oriented, Internalizing, Externalizing, and Total Problems scales (Rescorla et al., 2012). To provide norms for societies having low problem scores, data were aggregated from all the societies whose mean Total Problems scores were more than one *SD* below the omnicultural mean. For each scale, cumulative frequency distributions for the aggregated data were then computed, and percentiles and normalized *T* scores were assigned to scale scores based on the cumulative frequency distributions. The same procedure was followed to obtain percentiles and *T* scores for norms based on data aggregated from societies having Total Problems scores more than one *SD* above the omnicultural mean.

The inclusion of three sets of multicultural norms in the scoring software enables users to select norms appropriate for raters from the societies for which normative data are available. Individuals' scale scores can therefore be displayed on profiles like the one in Figure 17.2 and in cross-informant comparisons like those in Figure 17.3 in relation to user-selected norms for low-scoring, medium-scoring, and high-scoring societies. Scale scores for a particular individual can be displayed in relation to different sets of norms (Rescorla et al., 2012). For example, an immigrant girl living in the United States can be rated by her parents on instruments that have been translated into her parents' native language. The scale scores derived from her parents' ratings can then be displayed in relation to norms for the parents' home societies. If the girl attends a U.S. school, her teachers' ratings can be displayed in relation to U.S. norms for teachers' ratings. And if the girl is old enough to complete a self-report instrument, her scale scores can be displayed in relation to both U.S. norms and norms for her home society. The user can thus determine whether the girl's scores are clinically elevated according to any or all of the informants' ratings in relation to the different sets of norms.

Competencies and Adaptive Strengths

Although the study of psychopathology focuses mainly on maladaptive behaviors, emotions, and thoughts, understanding of people's functioning also requires assessment of their competencies and adaptive strengths. Like psychopathology, competencies and adaptive strengths are best viewed from multiple perspectives in relation to developmental processes, periods, and norms. Several instruments for obtaining ratings of problems also assess competencies and adaptive strengths in terms of ratings and other information provided by the people being assessed and by people who know them.

As an example, the CBCL/6-18 and Youth Self-Report (Achenbach & Rescorla, 2001) (YSR) include items for reporting the sports and nonsports activities that a child most likes to participate in, organizations the child belongs to, the child's jobs and chores, number of close friends, contacts with friends, how well the child gets along with significant others, how well the child plays and works alone, and various aspects of school functioning. Scores for activities, social, school, and total competence scales are based on combinations of what is reported and ratings of the child's functioning. The TRF obtains teachers' ratings of performance in academic subjects, plus ratings of adaptive strengths in school, including how hard the child is working, how appropriately the child is behaving, how much the child is learning, and how happy the child is.

For ages 18–59, adaptive strengths items are scored on scales for relations with friends, family members, and spouse or partner, as well as functioning in work and educational programs. Self-ratings and collateral ratings are also obtained for personal strengths, such as "Makes good use of his/her opportunities," "Works up to abilities," and "Is a happy person." The competence, adaptive functioning, and personal strengths scales have been found to discriminate significantly between people referred for mental health or substance use services and demographically matched people who have not been referred for services (Achenbach & Rescorla, 2001, 2003). Like the scales for psychopathology, the scales for competencies and adaptive strengths have age-, gender-, and informant-specific norms. The normed scales thus enable users to evaluate individuals in terms of their favorable characteristics as well as their problems. In some cases, competencies and adaptive strengths may mitigate the effects of problems. In other cases, interventions may be needed to strengthen adaptive functioning as well as to reduce problems. As addressed in the following sections, longitudinal research has shown that early adaptive strengths, as well as problems and risk factors, affect the developmental course of psychopathology.

Research Findings on the Development of Psychopathology

Longitudinal research is essential for tracing the developmental course of psychopathology, for identifying risk and protective factors, and for designing preventive and therapeutic interventions. Because there are so many potentially relevant variables and because their manifestations may change across the course of development, models for psychopathology are needed that reflect actual patterns of problems at different developmental periods but that can also be empirically linked across developmental periods. Because longitudinal research requires long-term commitments by investigators and by participants to complete multiple assessments, it is essential that the models for psychopathology be operationalized via procedures that can be economically applied on multiple occasions at different developmental periods and in various contexts.

Because each longitudinal study has idiosyncrasies that may limit the generalizability of its findings, developmental understanding of psychopathology can be best advanced by including a core set of standardized models and assessment procedures in studies that may differ in various other ways. The following sections provide an overview of several longitudinal studies that have applied a common core set of models and assessment procedures to large population samples in the United States and the Netherlands.

U.S. National Longitudinal Study

The U.S. National Longitudinal Study initially assessed a nationally representative sample of 2,734 4- to 16-year-olds on the basis of home interviews in which parents rated their children's problems and competencies and reported on many child and family variables. Subsequent assessments 3, 6, and 9 years later included parent, teacher, and self-ratings on instruments that assessed empirically based models for psychopathology, plus reports of signs of disturbance, such as suicidal behavior, mental health services, trouble with the law, substance abuse, and being fired from a job.

Scores on scales for empirically based syndromes significantly predicted scores on the corresponding syndrome scales and various signs of disturbance at 3-, 6-, and 9-year intervals, after controlling for numerous demographic and other variables (Achenbach, Howell, McConaughy, & Stanger, 1995a, 1995b, 1995c, 1998; Wadsworth & Achenbach, 2005). The empirically based syndrome models for psychopathology and the assessment procedures for operationalizing them thus revealed considerable continuity in patterns of problems from early childhood to adolescence and from adolescence to young adulthood. The findings also showed that the empirically based syndrome scores could predict signs of disturbance that were not included in the syndrome models. Parent, teacher, and self-ratings on competence and adaptive strengths scales added significantly to the prediction of signs of disturbance, especially to the prediction of total disturbance scores, which aggregated the different signs of disturbance.

Developmental Course of Relations Between Psychopathology and Socioeconomic Status In addition to testing the developmental continuity and predictive power of the empirically based models, the U.S. National Longitudinal Study tested hypotheses that required data spanning multiple developmental periods in a representative population sample. As an example, Wadsworth and Achenbach (2005) tested the hypothesis that factors associated with socioeconomic status (SES) contribute to differences in levels of psychopathology. It was found long ago that major disorders are more prevalent among lower-SES than upper-SES adults (e.g., Hollingshead & Redlich, 1958). However, cross-sectional studies of adults cannot explain the extent to which the higher prevalence results from "downward drift" in SES among adults whose psychopathology impairs their ability to maintain higher SES or instead results from a higher incidence of psychopathology among lower-SES people.

To prevent the possible contribution of downward drift from confounding research on relations between SES and psychopathology, it is necessary to compare the developmental courses of psychopathology for children whose families differ in SES. This excludes downward drift as an explanation, because children's psychopathology is not apt to cause their families' SES to drift downward.

Over the 9 years of the U.S. National Longitudinal Study, it was found that the scores of significantly more children from low-SES than from high-SES families increased from the normal to the clinical range on the Anxious/Depressed, Somatic Complaints, Thought Problems, Rule-Breaking Behavior, and Aggressive Behavior syndromes. These findings indicated that low SES predicts developmental increases in the problems modeled by these syndromes. However, it was also found that, among children who obtained clinically elevated scores on the Withdrawn and Somatic Complaints syndromes at a particular assessment point, fewer from low-SES than from higher-SES families subsequently obtained scores in the normal range. For these particular kinds of problems, the evidence thus indicated a greater "cumulative prevalence" of elevated problem scores among lower- than higher-SES children. In other words, there was a greater developmental accumulation of elevated scores among children from lower- than from higher-SES families. Both the greater incidence and greater cumulative prevalence of particular kinds of problems thus contributed to the higher prevalence of psychopathology among those born into lower SES families than among higher SES families.

Zuid Holland Longitudinal Study

A Dutch longitudinal study started with parents' ratings of their 4- to 16-year-old children on Dutch translations of the instruments that were used for assessing the empirically based syndrome models and competencies in the U.S. study (Verhulst, Akkerhuis, & Althaus, 1985). The Dutch parents also reported on child and family variables like those assessed in the U.S. study. The Dutch children's teachers completed the TRF, and 11- to 16-year-olds completed the YSR. The sample was selected to be representative of 4- to 16-year-olds living in the Province of Zuid (South) Holland. The participants were then reassessed at four 2-year intervals, followed by 6- and 10-year intervals, over a total of 24 years, when the oldest participants were 40 years old. At every assessment, Dutch translations of developmentally appropriate versions of the U.S. instruments were completed by participants and by informants who knew the participants. SDIs were also administered to adult participants, and the participants and other informants provided data on signs of disturbance and other aspects of functioning. The participants' own children were eventually assessed with the instruments that had been used to assess the participants when they were children. The participants' childhood scores were found to significantly predict their children's scores (van Meurs, Reef, Verhulst, & van der Ende, 2009).

For 1,365 participants rated by their parents at the initial assessment and rated by themselves 24 years later, high scores on all the empirically based syndromes rated by their parents significantly predicted high scores 24 years later on the self-rated counterparts of the syndromes, with the exception of the Thought Problems and Attention Problems syndromes (Reef, Diamantopoulou, van Meurs, Verhulst, & van der Ende, 2009). These findings thus indicated homotypic continuity (i.e., consistency of low, medium, or high scores on the same syndromes) over 24 years for the Anxious/Depressed, Withdrawn, Somatic Complaints, Rule-Breaking Behavior, and Aggressive Behavior syndromes, despite the difference in raters (parents initially, self 24 years later). Although not significantly predicted by parents' initial ratings on the Thought Problems syndrome, adults' self-ratings on this syndrome were significantly predicted by parents' initial ratings on the Anxious/Depressed, Attention Problems, Rule-Breaking Behavior, and Aggressive Behavior syndromes. Adults' self-ratings on the Attention Problems syndrome were significantly predicted by parents' initial ratings on the Anxious/Depressed and Thought

Problems syndromes. The significant prediction of adult Thought Problems and Attention Problems ratings from scores on other syndromes thus indicated heterotypic continuity for these kinds of problems. The parents' initial ratings also significantly predicted DSM diagnoses made from SDIs administered to the participants 24 years later (Reef, Diamantopoulou, van Meurs, Verhulst, & van der Ende, 2010).

Multi-informant Ratings from Age 4 to 40 Years Ratings of the participants by multiple informants at all seven assessment points enabled the research team to compute agreement between ratings by 12,059 informant pairs when the participants were assessed at various ages from 4 to 40 years (van der Ende, Verhulst, & Tiemeier, 2012). Cross-informant correlations between ratings of Internalizing and Externalizing problems were computed from parent, teacher, adult partner, and self-ratings. The magnitudes of the cross-informant correlations were similar to those found previously in meta-analyses of cross-informant correlations (Achenbach et al., 1987, 2005) and depended more on the kinds of informant pairs than on the age of the participants or on whether the ratings were for Internalizing or Externalizing problems. Participants were found to rate themselves higher on the problem scales than their parents, teachers, or partners rated them. Multicultural comparisons of parents' CBCL ratings versus youths' YSR ratings have also shown that youths rated themselves higher than parents rated them on counterpart problem scales in 25 very diverse societies (Rescorla et al., 2013). The differences found between self-versus-informant ratings of people of different ages and in diverse societies further underscore the need for multi-informant assessment of psychopathology.

Dutch versus U.S. Developmental Trajectories   The use of parallel assessment instruments in the Zuid Holland and U.S. longitudinal studies has enabled researchers to rigorously compare developmental trajectories for psychopathology in the Netherlands and the United States. As an example, the data used in the previously described Wadsworth and Achenbach (2005) test of associations between SES and the development of psychopathology were compared with data from the Zuid Holland study to determine whether conclusions would differ for the U.S. versus Dutch populations (Van Oort, van der Ende, Wadsworth, Verhulst, & Achenbach, 2011). Comparisons of this sort are especially important, because smaller economic differences and more equal access to health care for lower- versus upper-SES families in countries such as the Netherlands than in the United States could affect associations between SES and the development of psychopathology.

Parents' ratings of 833 U.S. children and 708 Dutch children were compared for assessments spanning 9 years in both societies. After correcting for chance differences, only minor Dutch-U.S. differences were found between tendencies for the incidence and cumulative prevalence of clinically elevated scores on certain syndromes to be higher for children from lower-SES families than from higher-SES families. Although more detailed data on SES, plus data from more societies, might support other conclusions, the similarity of findings in Dutch and U.S. population samples are consistent with findings from a review of studies in 15 societies where empirically based problem scale scores were consistently found to be higher for children of lower- than for higher-SES families (Achenbach & Rescorla, 2007).

Generation R Longitudinal Study

Another Dutch longitudinal study started with 8,880 women living in Rotterdam who were assessed during pregnancy. ("R" in "Generation R" stands for Rotterdam.) The pregnant women were assessed via ultrasound, blood and urine samples, and questionnaires, while fathers of the children were assessed via blood samples and questionnaires. Over the first 5 postnatal years, the children were assessed via biological, observational, questionnaire, and other measures, and they are continuing to be assessed at later ages. Numerous Generation R findings of associations between prenatal and postnatal variables have been published (reviewed by Tiemeier et al., 2012). The Generation R study's use of standardized rating instruments from the family of instruments used in the U.S. and Zuid Holland longitudinal studies enables researchers to analyze the developmental course of psychopathology in terms of the empirically based models used in those studies as well as in many other studies.

As an example, mothers and fathers rated Generation R children on the CBCL/1½–5 at ages 3 and 5. Children who were identified as having small subcortical volumes via brain imaging at postnatal age 6 weeks were found to have significantly higher Internalizing problem scores than those of other children on the CBCL at age 3 (Herba et al., 2010). Furthermore, at age 5, elevated Internalizing scores were found for children who carried the short allele of the 5-HTTLPR polymorphism in the promoter region of the serotonin transporter gene (5-HTT, SLC6A4) *and* whose mothers reported high levels of anxiety at prenatal assessments and/or postnatal assessments (Tiemeier et al., 2012). This finding is important because previous studies have yielded inconsistent results regarding interactions between the short allele of the 5-HTTLPR polymorphism and individuals' own stressful experiences during childhood. Caspi et al. (2003) initially reported that carriers of the short allele were at elevated risk for developing depression after maltreatment and other stressful childhood experiences. However, several subsequent studies failed to support this gene by environment (G E) interaction (e.g., Risch et al., 2009), while other studies concluded that inclusion of chronic illnesses as stressors and use of observational data on stress provided support for the G E interaction (e.g., Caspi, Hariri, Holmes, Uher, & Moffitt, 2010).

Because serotonin appears at about 5 weeks after conception, differences in serotonin transporter availability related to the 5-HTTLPR polymorphism could affect vulnerability to effects of prenatal stressors such as maternal anxiety. The Generation R findings that mothers' anxiety during either the prenatal or postnatal period (with prenatal anxiety controlled) predicted subsequent elevations in age 5 CBCL Internalizing scores for children with the short allele suggest that maternal anxiety can affect children with the short allele by both prenatal intrauterine processes and postnatal environmental processes. Furthermore, when mothers had high anxiety either prenatally or postnatally, children with two short alleles obtained higher CBCL Internalizing scores than those of children with a single short allele who, in turn, obtained higher Internalizing scores than those of children with no short alleles. However, children whose mothers did not report much anxiety either prenatally or postnatally obtained low Internalizing scores, regardless of whether they had 0, 1, or 2 short alleles. In other words, high prenatal and postnatal maternal anxiety levels were associated with high age 5 Internalizing scores, but short alleles appeared to exacerbate Internalizing problems only among children whose mothers reported high anxiety either pre- or postnatally.

Although the Generation R findings indicate that the short and long 5-HTTLPR alleles differentially affect children's reactions to pre- and postnatal stress, the effects were very small. Technological advances in many facets of research, such as genetic and neuroimaging methods, are greatly increasing the power of research to detect very small effects of this sort. Each small effect may be important, but the many small effects are further complicated by myriad interactions among them. Consequently, developmentally appropriate multivariate phenotypic models and standardized procedures for assessing them are needed to provide common foci across studies of the many potentially relevant variables and the interactions among them.

Summary and Conclusions

The discipline of developmental psychopathology originated primarily with efforts to understand maladaptive functioning between birth and maturity. However, its concepts, strategies, and findings are relevant across the life span. The developmental approach counteracts tendencies to view disorders as encapsulated entities that are the same at all ages. It also fosters empirically based models derived from multivariate statistical analyses of problems rated for large samples of individuals on developmentally appropriate assessment instruments. The "bottom-up," empirically based models for psychopathology differ from "top-down," diagnostic models that are constructed on the basis of expert judgments.

The empirically based models consist of syndromes of co-occurring problems that are operationalized by summing ratings of the constituent problem items. Each individual obtains standardized scores on syndromes appropriate for the individual's age. The syndrome scores are displayed on profiles in relation to norms for the individual's age and gender, the type of informant who provided the ratings, and the user's choice of society.

By contrast, diagnostic models are operationalized via standardized diagnostic interviews (SDIs), which are designed to obtain yes-or-no answers regarding whether each criterion for each diagnostic category is met. Fixed decision rules are then applied to the SDI responses to determine whether the person being assessed meets enough criteria for particular disorders.

Quantification of psychopathology has the following advantages: (a) quantitative derivation of models from measures of problems reported or rated for large samples of people can capture actual patterns of co-occurring problems, as seen by various informants; (b) informants are not required to fit their knowledge of the person being assessed into yes/no responses, which may be especially vulnerable to yea-saying and nay-saying response sets and which magnify disagreements between informants; (c) quantitative criteria for psychopathology yield significantly better reliability and validity than categorical criteria; (d) quantification reduces the adverse consequences of test–retest attenuation effects; (e) quantification facilitates construction of hierarchical models that can prevent artifactual comorbidity, which may result from rigid borders between diagnostic categories as well as from arbitrary splitting and lumping of categories; and (f) quantification provides rigorous methods for coping with the ubiquitous differences between reports of psychopathology by different informants.

Comprehensive assessment for both research and clinical purposes requires data from multiple informants. Different kinds of informants—such as parents versus teachers—are apt to have different knowledge of the person being assessed. To take account of both the differences and similarities in what is assessed by different informants, cross-informant syndromes have been derived from ratings by different kinds of informants. Each syndrome comprises a core set of items ratable by different kinds of informants and may also include items that are specific to particular kinds of informants.

Practical applications of multi-informant assessment include bar graphs that provide side-by-side displays of scores obtained from multiple informants on syndrome scales normed for the age and gender of the person being assessed, the type of informant, and the user-selected society.

Understanding people's functioning requires assessment of competencies and adaptive strengths. Several of the instruments described in this chapter assess age-appropriate competencies and adaptive strengths, as well as problems. The competencies and strengths are scored on scales that are normed for the age and gender of the person being assessed and the type of informant. Longitudinal research has shown that scores for competencies and adaptive strengths contribute to the long-term prediction of signs of disturbance.

Longitudinal studies from the United States and the Netherlands were used to illustrate research on the development of psychopathology. These studies have included assessments ranging from the prenatal period to age 40. The studies have documented the power of numerous variables assessed by standardized instruments to predict long-term outcomes related to psychopathology. The studies have also revealed very similar developmental sequences in different societies.

References

Achenbach, T. M. (1966). The classification of children's psychiatric symptoms: A factor-analytic study. *Psychological Monographs, 80*(7, Serial No. 615).

Achenbach, T. M. (1974). *Developmental psychopathology.* New York: Ronald Press.

Achenbach, T. M. (1982). *Developmental psychopathology* (2nd ed.) New York: Wiley.

Achenbach, T. M. (2009). *The Achenbach System of Empirically Based Assessment (ASEBA): Development, findings, theory, and applications.* Burlington, VT: University of Vermont, Research Center for Children, Youth, and Families.

Achenbach, T. M., & Edelbrock, C. (1978). The classification of child psychopathology: A review and analysis of empirical efforts. *Psychological Bulletin, 85,* 1275–1301.

Achenbach, T. M., Howell, C. T., McConaughy, S. H., & Stanger, C. (1995a). Six-year predictors of problems in a national sample of children and youth: I. Cross-informant syndromes. *Journal of the American Academy of Child & Adolescent Psychiatry, 34,* 336–347.

Achenbach, T. M., Howell, C. T., McConaughy, S. H., & Stanger, C. (1995b). Six-year predictors of problems in a national sample of children and youth: II. Signs of disturbance. *Journal of the American Academy of Child & Adolescent Psychiatry, 34,* 488–498.

Achenbach, T. M., Howell, C. T., McConaughy, S. H., & Stanger, C. (1995c). Six-year predictors of problems in a national sample: III. Transitions to young adult syndromes. *Journal of the American Academy of Child & Adolescent Psychiatry, 34,* 658–669.

Achenbach, T. M., Howell, C. T., McConaughy, S. H., & Stanger, C. (1998). Six-year predictors of problems in a national sample: IV. Young adult signs of disturbance. *Journal of the American Academy of Child & Adolescent Psychiatry, 37,* 718–727.

Achenbach, T. M., Krukowski, R. A., Dumenci, L., & Ivanova, M. Y. (2005). Assessment of adult psychopathology: Meta-analyses and implications of cross-informant correlations. *Psychological Bulletin, 131,* 361–382.

Achenbach, T. M., McConaughy, S. H., & Howell, C. T. (1987). Child/adolescent behavioral and emotional problems: Implications of cross-informant correlations for situational specificity. *Psychological Bulletin, 101,* 213–232.

Achenbach, T. M., Newhouse, P. A., & Rescorla, L. A. (2004). *Manual for the ASEBA older adult forms & profiles.* Burlington, VT: University of Vermont, Research Center for Children, Youth, and Families.

Achenbach, T. M., & Rescorla, L. A. (2000). *Manual for the ASEBA preschool forms & profiles.* Burlington, VT: University of Vermont, Research Center for Children, Youth, and Families.

Achenbach, T. M., & Rescorla, L. A. (2001). *Manual for the ASEBA school-age forms & profiles.* Burlington, VT: University of Vermont, Research Center for Children, Youth, and Families.

Achenbach, T. M., & Rescorla, L. A. (2003). *Manual for the ASEBA adult forms & profiles.* Burlington, VT: University of Vermont, Research Center for Children, Youth, and Families.

Achenbach, T. M., & Rescorla, L. A. (2007). *Multicultural understanding of child and adolescent psychopathology: Implications for mental health assessment.* New York: Guilford Press.

Achenbach, T. M., & Rescorla, L. A. (2014). *Multicultural guide for the ASEBA forms & profiles for ages 1½–59.* Burlington, VT: University of Vermont, Research Center for Children, Youth, and Families.

Bartels, M., Boomsma, D. I., Hudziak, J. J., van Beijsterveldt, T. C. E. M., & van den Oord, E. J. C. G. (2007). Twins and the study of rater (dis)agreement. *Psychological Methods, 12,* 451–466.

Bartels, M., van den Oord, E. J. C. G., Hudziak, J. J., Rietveld, M. J. H., van Beijsterveldt, T. C. E. M., & Boomsma, D. I. (2004). Genetic and environmental mechanisms underlying stability and change in problem behaviors at the ages 3, 7, 10, and 12. *Developmental Psychology, 40,* 852–867.

Binet, A., & Simon, T. (1905). New methods for the diagnosis of the intellectual level of subnormals. *L'Année Psychologique, 12,* 191–244. 1916. In A. Binet & T. Simon (Trans.). (1916). *The development of intelligence in children.* Baltimore: Williams & Wilkins.

Breton, J-J., Bergeron, L., Valla, J-P., Berthiaume, C., Gaudet, N., Lambert, J., et al. (1999). Quebec child mental health survey: Prevalence of DSM-III-R mental health disorders. *Journal of Child Psychology & Psychiatry, 40,* 375–384.

Caspi, A., Hariri, A. R., Holmes, A. Uher, R., & Moffitt, T. E. (2010). Genetic sensitivity to the environment: The case of the serotonin transporter gene and its implications for studying complex diseases and traits. *American Journal of Psychiatry, 167,* 509–527.

Caspi, A., Sugden, K., Moffitt, T. E., Taylor, A., Craig, I. W., Harrington, H., et al. (2003). Influence of life stress on depression: Moderation by a polymorphism in the 5-HTT gene. *Science, 301,* 386–389.

Cohen, P., O'Connor, P., Lewis, S., Velez, C.N., & Malachowski, B. (1987). Comparison of DISC and K-SADS-P interviews of an epidemiological sample of children. *Journal of the American Academy of Child & Adolescent Psychiatry, 26,* 662–667.

Conners, C. K. (1969). A teacher rating scale for use in drug studies with children. *American Journal of Psychiatry, 126,* 884–888.

Costello, A., Edelbrock, C., Kalas, R., Kessler, M., & Klaric, S. A. (1982). *Diagnostic Interview Schedule for Children (DISC)* (Contract No. RFP-DB-81-0027). Bethesda, MD: National Institute of Mental Health.

De Los Reyes, A. (2011). Introduction to the special section: More than measurement error: Discovering meaning behind informant discrepancies in clinical assessments of children and adolescents. *Journal of Clinical Child and Adolescent Psychology, 40,* 1–9.

De Los Reyes, A., & Kazdin, A. E. (2005). Informant discrepancies in the assessment of childhood psychopathology: A critical review, theoretical framework, and recommendations for further study. *Psychological Bulletin, 131,* 483–509.

Derks, E. M., Hudziak, J. J., van Beijsterveldt, T. C. E. M., Dolan, C. V., & Boomsma, D. I. (2006). Genetic analyses of maternal and teacher ratings on attention problems in 7-year-old Dutch twins. *Behavior Genetics, 36,* 833–844.

Ellis, B. B., & Kimmel, H. D. (1992). Identification of unique cultural response patterns by means of item response theory. *Journal of Applied Psychology, 77,* 177–184.

Endicott, J., & Spitzer, R. L. (1978). A diagnostic interview. *Archives of General Psychiatry, 35,* 837–844.

Faraone, S. V., Biederman, J., Keenan, K., & Tsuang, M. T. (1991). A family genetic study of girls with DSM-III attention deficit disorder. *American Journal of Psychiatry, 148,* 112–117.

Gove, P. (Ed.). (1971). *Webster's third new international dictionary of the English language.* Springfield, MA: Merriam.

Helzer, J. E., Kraemer, H. C., Krueger, R. F., Wittchen, H. -U., Sirovatka, P. J., & Regier, D. A. (Eds.). (2008). *Dimensional approaches in diagnostic classification: Refining the research agenda for DSM-V.* Washington, DC: American Psychiatric Association.

Herba, C. M., Roza, S. J., Govaert, P., van Rossum, J., Hofman, A., Jaddoe, V., et al. (2010). Infant brain development and vulnerability to later internalizing difficulties: The Generation R Study. *Journal of the American Association of Child and Adolescent Psychiatry, 49,* 1053–1063.

Hollingshead, A. B., & Redlich, F. C. (1958). *Social class and mental illness.* New York: Wiley.

Ivanova, M. Y., Achenbach, T. M., Rescorla, L. A., Bilenberg, N., Bjarnadottir, G., Denner, S., et al. (2011). Syndromes of preschool psychopathology reported by teachers and caregivers in 14 societies using the Caregiver Teacher Report Form (C-TRF). *Journal of Early Childhood and Infant Psychology, 7,* 87–103.

Ivanova, M. Y., Achenbach, T. M., Rescorla, L. A., Harder, V. S., Ang, R. P., Bilenberg, N., et al. (2010). Preschool psychopathology reported by parents in 23 societies. Testing the seven-syndrome model of the Child Behavior Checklist for Ages 1.5-5. *Journal of the American Academy of Child & Adolescent Psychiatry, 49,* 1215–1224.

Ivanova, M. Y., Achenbach, T. M., Rescorla, L. A., Turner, L. V., Au, A., Caldas, J. C., et al. (2013). Syndromes of self-reported psychopathology for ages 18-59 in 28 societies. Submitted.

Jensen, P., Roper, M., Fisher, P., Piacentini, J., Canino, G., Richters, J., et al. (1995). Test-retest reliability of the Diagnostic Interview Schedule for Children (DISC 2.1): Parent, child, and combined algorithms. *Archives of General Psychiatry, 52,* 61–71.

Jensen, P. S., Rubio-Stipec, M., Canino, G., Bird, H. R., Dulcan, M., Schwab-Stone, M., et al. (1999). Parent and child contributions to diagnosis of mental disorder: Are both informants always necessary? *Journal of the American Academy of Child & Adolescent Psychiatry, 38*, 1569–1579.

Kaufman, J., Birmaher, B., Brent, D., Rao, U., Flynn, C., Moreci, P., et al. (1997). Schedule for Affective Disorders and Schizophrenia for School-Age Children-Present and Lifetime Version (K-SADS-PL): Initial reliability and validity data. *Journal of the American Academy of Child & Adolescent Psychiatry, 36*, 980–988.

Kendler, K. S., Prescott, C. A., Myers, J., & Neale, M. C. (2003). The structure of genetic and environmental risk factors for common psychiatric and substance use disorders in men and women. *Archives of General Psychiatry, 60*, 929–937.

Krueger, R. F., & Markon, D. E. (2006). Reinterpreting comorbidity: A model-based approach to understanding and classifying psychopathology. *Annual Review of Clinical Psychology, 2*, 111–133.

Loeber, R., & Schmaling, K. B. (1985). Empirical evidence for overt and covert patterns of antisocial conduct problems: A meta-analysis. *Journal of Abnormal Child Psychology, 13*, 337–352.

Markon, K. E., Chmielewski, M., & Miller, C. J. (2011). The reliability and validity of discrete and continuous measures of psychopathology: A quantitative review. *Psychological Bulletin, 137*, 856–879.

McConaughy, S. H., & Achenbach, T. M. (2001). *Manual for the semi-structured clinical interview for children and adolescents* (2nd ed.). Burlington, VT: University of Vermont, Research Center for Children, Youth, and Families.

McConaughy, S. H., & Achenbach, T. M. (2004). *Manual for the test observation form for ages 2-18.* Burlington, VT: University of Vermont, Research Center for Children, Youth, and Families.

McConaughy, S. H., & Achenbach, T. M. (2009). *Manual for the ASEBA direct observation form.* Burlington, VT: University of Vermont, Research Center for Children, Youth, and Families.

Meyer, G. J., Finn, S. E., Eyde, L. D., Kay, G. G., Moreland, K. L., Dies, R. R., et al. (2001). Psychological testing and psychological assessment: A review of evidence and issues. *American Psychologist, 56*, 128–165.

Miller, L. C. (1967). Louisville Behavior Checklist for males, 6-12 years of age. *Psychological Reports, 21*, 885–896.

Morrow, E. M., Yoo, S-Y., Flavell, S. W., Kim, T-K., Lin, Y., Hill, R. S., et al. (2008). Identifying autism loci and genes by tracing recent shared ancestry. *Science, 321*, 218–223.

Narrow, W. E., Clarke, D. E., Kuramoto, S. J., Kraemer, H. C., Kupfer, D. J., Greiner, L., et al. (2013). DSM-5 field trials in the United States and Canada, part III: Development and reliability testing of a cross-cutting symptom assessment for DSM-5. *American Journal of Psychiatry, 170*, 71–82.

Quay, H. C. (1964). Personality dimensions in delinquent males as inferred from the factor analysis of behavior ratings. *Journal of Research in Crime and Delinquency, 1*, 33–37.

Quay, H. C. (1979). Classification. In H. C. Quay & J. S. Werry (Eds.), *Psychopathological disorders of childhood* (2nd ed., pp. 1–42). New York: Wiley.

Reef, J., Diamantopoulou S., van Meurs, I., Verhulst, F., & van der Ende, J. (2009). Child to adult continuities of psychopathology: A 24-year follow-up. *Acta Psychiatrica Scandinavica, 120*, 230–238.

Reef, J., Diamantopoulou, S., van Meurs, I., Verhulst, F., & van der Ende, J. (2010). Predicting adult emotional and behavioral problems from externalizing problem trajectories in a 24-year longitudinal study. *Journal of European Child and Adolescent Psychiatry, 19*, 577–585.

Reich, W. (2000). Diagnostic interview for children and adolescents (DICA). *Journal of the American Association of Child and Adolescent Psychiatry, 39*, 59–66.

Rescorla, L. A., Achenbach, T. M., Ivanova, M. Y., Turner, L. V., Au, A., Bellina, M., et al. (2014). Problems and adaptive functioning reported by adults in 17 societies. Submitted.

Rescorla, L. A., Ginzburg, S., Achenbach, T. M., Ivanova, M. Y., Almqvist, F., Bilenberg, N., et al. (2013). Cross-informant agreement between parent-reported and adolescent self-reported problems in 25 societies. *Journal of Clinical Child and Adolescent Psychology, 42*, 262–273.

Rescorla, L. A., Ivanova, M. Y., Achenbach, T. M., Begovac, I., Chahed, M., Drugli, M. B., et al. (2012). International epidemiology of child and adolescent psychopathology: 2. Integration and applications of dimensional findings from 44 societies. *Journal of the American Academy of Child & Adolescent Psychiatry, 51*, 1273–1283.

Rettew, D. C., Doyle, A., Achenbach, T. M., Dumenci, L., & Ivanova, M. (2009). Meta-analyses of agreement between diagnoses made from clinical evaluations and standardized diagnostic interviews.

International Journal of Methods in Psychiatric Research, 18, 169–184.

Risch, N., Herrell, R., Lehner, T., Liang, K. Y., Eaves, L., Hoh, J., et al. (2009). Interaction between the serotonin transporter gene (5-HTTLPR), stressful life events, and risk of depression: A meta-analysis. *Journal of the American Medical Association, 301*, 2462–2471.

Robins, L. N., Helzer, J. E., Croughan, J., & Ratcliff, K. S. (1981). National Institute of Mental Health Diagnostic Interview Schedule: Its history, characteristics, and validity. *Archives of General Psychiatry, 38*, 381–389.

Shaffer, D., Fisher, P., Lucas, C. P., Dulcan, M. K., & Schwab-Stone, M. E. (2000). NIMH Diagnostic Interview Schedule for Children version IV (NIMH DISC-IV): Description, differences from previous versions, and reliability of some common diagnoses. *Journal of the American Academy of Child & Adolescent Psychiatry, 39*, 28–38.

Spitzer, R. L., Davies, M., & Barkley, R. A. (1990). The DSM-III-R field trial of disruptive behavior disorders. *Journal of the American Academy of Child & Adolescent Psychiatry, 29*, 690–697.

Stefansson, H., Rujescu, D., Cichon, S., Pietiläinen, O. P. H., Ingason, A., Steinberg, S., et al. (2008). Large recurrent microdeletions associated with schizophrenia. *Nature, 455*, 232–236.

Tiemeier, H., Velders, F. P., Szekely, E., Roza, S. J., Dieleman, G., Jaddoe, V. W. V., et al. (2012). The Generation R Study: A review of design, findings to date, and a study of the 5-HTTLPR by environmental interaction from fetal life onward. *Journal of the American Association of Child and Adolescent Psychiatry, 51*, 1119–1135.

van der Ende, J., Verhulst, F., & Tiemeier, H. (2012). Agreement of informants on emotional and behavioral problems from childhood to adulthood. *Psychological Assessment, 24*, 293–300.

Van der Valk, J. C., van den Oord, E. J. C. G., Verhulst, F. C., & Boomsma, D. I. (2001). Using parental ratings to study the etiology of 3-year-old twins' problem behaviors: Different views or rater bias? *Journal of Child Psychology and Psychiatry, 42*, 921–931.

van Meurs, I., Reef, J., Verhulst, F. C., & van der Ende, J. (2009). Intergenerational transmission of child problem behaviors: A longitudinal, population-based study. *Journal of the American Association of Child and Adolescent Psychiatry, 48*, 138–145.

Van Oort, F. V. A., van der Ende, J., Wadsworth, M. E., Verhulst, F. C., & Achenbach, T. M. (2011). Cross-national comparison of the link between socioeconomic status and emotional and behavioral problems in youths. *Social Psychiatry and Psychiatric Epidemiology, 46*, 167–172.

Verhulst, F. C., Akkerhuis, G. W., & Althaus, M. (1985). Mental health in Dutch children: (I) A cross-cultural comparison. *Acta Psychiatrica Scandinavica Supplementum, 72*, 323, 1–108.

Wadsworth, M. E., & Achenbach, T. M. (2005). Explaining the link between low socioeconomic status and psychopathology: Testing two mechanisms of the social causation hypothesis. *Journal of Consulting and Clinical Psychology, 73*, 1146–1153.

Walker, J. L., Lahey, B. B., Russo, M. F., Frick, P. J., Christ, M. A. G., McBurnett, K., et al. (1991). Anxiety, inhibition, and conduct disorder in children: I. Relations to social impairment. *Journal of the American Academy of Child & Adolescent Psychiatry, 30*, 187–191.

World Health Organization. (1992). *Mental disorders: Glossary and guide to their classification in accordance with the tenth revision of the international classification of diseases* (10th ed.). Geneva: World Health Organization.

18

Attention Deficit Hyperactivity Disorder (ADHD)

HANNEKE VAN EWIJK

AND JAAP OOSTERLAAN

Individuals with attention deficit hyperactivity disorder (ADHD) suffer from persistent and age-inappropriate levels of inattention, hyperactivity, and/or impulsivity, occurring in multiple situations, to such a degree that symptoms have a severely detrimental impact on their daily life functioning. Throughout the past three decades, scientific interests in ADHD and knowledge about the disorder have grown exponentially. While a large body of research is available on ADHD, the number of unanswered questions is possibly even more substantial. ADHD has proven to be a heterogeneous disorder, causing a difficult challenge for researchers to create a consistent image of the disorder. The past two decades have been characterized by an increase in concerns about the validity of ADHD and stigmatization of patients diagnosed with the disorder (Mueller, Fuermaier, Koerts, & Tucha, 2012). This chapter covers the etiology, prevalence, and treatment of ADHD, as well as the neurobiological underpinnings and neuropsychological dysfunction often observed in patients. We hope to convey the heterogeneity of ADHD, and provide an extensive and critical overview of our current understanding of the disorder.

A Short History

It is frequently thought that ADHD is a "twenty-first century disorder," caused by the abundant stimuli that are part of the current information technology society (e.g., TV, smartphones, social media), resulting in an information overload too intense for many children to cope with. Although a range of societal factors might potentially contribute to the number of children diagnosed with ADHD, ADHD-like symptoms were reported as early as 1902 (Spencer, Biederman, & Mick, 2007). Early reports of ADHD-like behavior were primarily focused on children's malfunctioning and mainly targeted symptoms of hyperactivity and impulsivity. For decades, these children were described as having minimal brain damage (MBD), which was later nuanced to minimal brain dysfunctioning. In 1968, *DSM-II* introduced a childhood mental disorder characterized by hyperactivity, labeled "hyperkinetic reaction of childhood." With the release of *DSM-III* in 1980, symptoms of inattention were also recognized as part of the disorder, and even became the major focus. The condition was renamed as "attention deficit disorder," and it could either be diagnosed with or without hyperactivity. *DSM-IV* again redefined the diagnosis in 1994, distinguishing the predominantly inattentive (ADHD-I) and predominantly hyperactive-impulsive (ADHD-H) subtypes, as well as the combined subtype (ADHD-C), which describes children showing both inattentive and hyperactive-impulsive symptoms. Although debate is ongoing regarding the validity of this distinction (Coghill & Seth, 2011), the *DSM-5* retains these subtypes, which are now called *presentations*. The current version of an alternative classification system, *ICD-10*, recognizes a set of symptoms very similar to *DSM* combined presentation, which has been labeled "hyperkinetic disorder."

Prevalence, Course, Comorbidities, and Functional Impact

Prevalence

The most recent estimate, based on a large number of studies, is that about 6%–7% of children worldwide suffer from (any presentation of) ADHD (Willcutt, 2012). However, prevalence rates of ADHD vary dramatically between studies. Reported rates in different countries have ranged from as low as 1% to as high as 20% among school-aged children. Some of this variability is most likely attributable to a rise in clinical referrals and diagnoses over recent years, as shown by a U.S. national survey from the past two decades (Robison, Sclar, Skaer, & Galin, 1999; Visser, Bitsko, Danielson, Perou, & Blumberg, 2010). However, other factors may also play a role. One is the method or classification system used to determine ADHD diagnoses (Spencer et al., 2007). The two most commonly used diagnostic classification systems, *ICD* and *DSM*, focus on slightly different aspects of the disorder, and even within these systems, different versions have employed different diagnostic criteria. Furthermore, many studies—and possibly also clinical practitioners—tend to apply diagnostic criteria far too loosely (discussed later in this chapter), resulting in inflated prevalence rates (Willcutt, 2012).

In general, males are two to three times more likely to be diagnosed with ADHD than females (Ramtekkar, Reiersen, Todorov, & Todd, 2010; Willcutt, 2012). Among all individuals with ADHD (children and adults alike), females are more likely to meet criteria for the inattentive presentation, while males are more likely to be diagnosed with the combined presentation (Willcutt, 2012). Because inattentive behavior is less disturbing and burdensome for the family and school than hyperactive-impulsive behavior, and the fact that girls with ADHD are less likely to suffer from accompanying disruptive disorders (Spencer, Biederman, & Mick, 2007), girls may be underdiagnosed with ADHD. Hence, it is possible that the prevalence of ADHD may not differ between boys and girls as much as previously thought, but rather reflects lower rates of clinical referrals for girls.

Developmental Course

ADHD was initially recognized as only a childhood disorder and was thought to largely remit in adolescence. However, recent literature shows that in a large number of cases, at least some symptoms persist into adulthood. Rates are highly dependent on the definition of persistence used (i.e., full *DSM* diagnosis needed, or more lenient criteria used). Pooled estimates from follow-up studies show that at age 25, ~15% of ADHD patients still meet full criteria for ADHD, while a much larger percentage, ~65%, meets criteria for "ADHD in partial remission" (Faraone, Biederman, & Mick, 2006). A recent follow-up study even reported persistent ADHD (meeting full criteria) in 70% of adolescents (Langley et al., 2010). Interestingly, ADHD prevalence is estimated at 5% in young adulthood (Willcutt, 2012), and at 3-4% in old age (Michielsen et al., 2012), percentages very similar to prevalence rates in childhood and adolescence. Altogether, these numbers show a fairly consistent image of the persistence of symptoms, and indicate that ADHD is best described as a disorder that originates in childhood, and often—at least partly—persists into adulthood.

Comorbidities and Functional Impact

More often than not, ADHD patients experience comorbid disorders and problems (Gillberg et al., 2004; Spencer, Biederman, & Mick, 2007). Externalizing disorders most frequently reported in children with ADHD include oppositional defiant disorder (ODD) and conduct disorder (CD), with estimates around 60% for ODD and ~40% for CD (Connor, Steeber, & McBurnett, 2010). Although often less expected, children with ADHD frequently also experience serious internalizing problems, such as mood or anxiety disorders (estimates varying between 15% and 45%; Elia, Ambrosini, & Berrettini, 2008; Spencer, Biederman, & Mick, 2007). Other comorbidities frequently associated with pediatric or adolescent ADHD include autism spectrum disorders (65–80% show several symptoms of autistic disorder; Gillberg et al., 2004), learning disabilities including reading disorder (15–45%; Sexton, Gelhorn,

Bell, & Classi, 2012; Spencer, Biederman, & Mick, 2007), sleep disorders (25–50%; Corkum, Tannock, & Moldofsky, 1998), tic disorders (8–33%; Kadesjö & Gillberg, 2003; MTA Cooperative Group, 1999; Palumbo, Spencer, Lynch, Co-Chien, & Faraone, 2004; Steinhausen et al., 2006), substance use disorders (1.35–2.36 times increased chance of developing nicotine dependence or alcohol or drug abuse; Charach, Yeung, Climans, & Lillie, 2011) and developmental coordination disorder (~50%; Gillberg et al., 2004). Adults with ADHD are reported to have a 1.5–7 times increased likelihood of developing mood, anxiety, and substance use disorders (Kessler et al., 2006).

Even in the absence of comorbid disorders, ADHD has a major impact on the patient's life, as well as on society as a whole. Children with ADHD often suffer from poor social skills leading to conflicted peer relationships, low self-esteem, adverse academic outcome, and injuries and accidents, and these children are frequently seen as a burden on their families (Coghill et al., 2008; Pardini & Fite, 2010). In adolescence, ADHD patients have been shown to start smoking at an earlier age and smoke more on a daily basis (S. S. Lee, Humphreys, Flory, Liu, & Glass, 2011; McClernon & Kollins, 2008), and to engage in risky sexual behavior more often (Flory, Molina, Pelham, Gnagy, & Smith, 2006). When looking at adult or lifetime ADHD, it is clear that the disorder has a strong negative impact on an individual's overall functioning, including a lower socioeconomic status, marital difficulties, and general health problems (Biederman et al., 1993, 2006; Sawyer et al., 2002). Occurrence of antisocial behaviors, including theft, assault, vandalism or disorderly conduct, is highly increased in adults with lifetime ADHD, and a higher number of individuals is arrested, convicted, and incarcerated (Barkley, Fischer, Smallish, & Fletcher, 2004; Biederman et al., 2006; Küpper et al., 2012). Mental health problems are reported in the majority of adults with ADHD, including depression, anxiety disorder, antisocial personality disorder and substance use disorder (Biederman et al., 2006; Küpper et al., 2012). In the workplace, individuals with ADHD suffer from poor productivity, absenteeism, and general occupational underachievement or unemployment, partly as a result of other comorbid mental health problems as mentioned before (Küpper et al., 2012). In the United States, it has been shown that ADHD has a

substantial economic impact with overall national costs estimated at \$143–676 billion (Doshi et al., 2012). Most of these costs were due to loss of productivity and income loss in adults, and extra costs in health care and education in children with ADHD.

It has to be noted, however, that most literature discussed in this paragraph is based on clinical samples. It is likely that a selection bias, in combination with loosely applied diagnostic criteria, has inflated prevalence rates and risks for comorbid difficulties in ADHD, limiting generalization of these findings to the general population.

Current Diagnostic Issues

The validity of ADHD and its three presentations is a prominent topic of discussion. Several limitations can be pointed out in the current diagnostic criteria and procedures that appear to play a large role in the controversy regarding the existence and validity of the disorder.

First, both symptom dimensions of ADHD—inattention and hyperactive/impulsive behavior—should be seen as continua ranging from normal to severely abnormal behavior. While ADHD patients typically have more severe symptoms of inattention and hyperactivity/impulsivity than is typical in the "normal" population, the cut-off between "normal variation" and "abnormal behavior" is rather arbitrary. Furthermore, several consensus guidelines emphasize the importance of strictly adhering to standard diagnostic criteria for the diagnosis of ADHD, such as those defined by *DSM* or *ICD* (Kendall, Taylor, Perez, & Taylor, 2008; Pliszka, 2007; Seixas, 2013; Wolraich et al., 2011). However, important criteria, including impairment, pervasiveness, and differential diagnostics, are easily and often overlooked in the diagnostic process, which can lead to overdiagnosis of the disorder. For example, if symptoms only exist in the classroom situation but not at home, this might indicate that there are specific problems at school that are causing hyperactive behavior, not ADHD. Likewise, children may have trouble concentrating because of conflicts at home between their parents, or impulsive symptoms in an adult may better be accounted for by borderline personality disorder or mania. Somatic conditions can also be a direct cause of ADHD-like symptoms. In such cases, it is important to acknowledge the actual cause of the behavioral symptoms and target the intervention accordingly. A recent meta-analysis showed that the estimated prevalence based on symptoms alone (without accounting for additional criteria such as impairment) was much higher than prevalence estimates based on full *DSM* criteria (Willcutt, 2012). These data underline the importance of strictly adhering to diagnostic criteria in order to guarantee the validity of the diagnosis. Since many ADHD rating scales omit diagnostic criteria like functional impairment, all guidelines agree that assessment should always include a full clinical interview, preferably a family interview (Seixas, 2013).

Evaluating *adult* ADHD creates some extra challenges because diagnostic criteria were originally defined to evaluate children's behavior. Until recently, most symptom definitions were unmistakably targeted at children, such as "runs about or climbs excessively in situations in which it is inappropriate." It is clear that such symptoms should be adapted to match similar adult behaviors, for example, focusing on subjective feelings of restlessness instead of inappropriate hyperactive behavior. While the current *DSM-5* includes a few examples targeted at adolescents or adults, *ICD-10* and *DSM-IV-TR* do not provide an adapted formulation for adults. Therefore, until recently, it was up to the researcher or clinician to translate the diagnostic criteria into adult behaviors, making assessment highly subjective and weakening the validity of the diagnosis in adulthood. Another issue in the diagnostic process of adult ADHD assessment arises from the criterion that symptoms must be present before the age of 12. With increasing age it becomes more difficult to correctly remember the exact age of onset of symptoms, and opportunities to use informants from different settings (e.g. teachers, parents) are reduced. It is important for practitioners to keep these issues in mind while diagnosing adults with ADHD. Unfortunately, given the lack of research on the validity of diagnostic criteria for adults, assessment of adult ADHD will remain highly subjective until more research is conducted.

Another issue that is receiving prominent attention is the validity of the two symptom dimensions of ADHD as they are currently defined (Milich, Balentine, & Lynam, 2001; Willcutt et al., 2012). While this two-dimensional approach can be useful in creating behavioral profiles of the disorder, it is unclear to what extent these dimensions cover other types of variance in the disorder (Milich et al., 2001). For example, differences in behavioral symptoms, demographic information, and comorbidities can clearly be distinguished between both symptom dimensions. However, neuropsychological deficits exist equally within both dimensions, and no clear distinction can be made. These findings suggest that other factors in the classification of the disorder are still being overlooked and that the current division into two dimensions might not be optimal in guiding future research on the disorder. Alternatively, defining ADHD presentations on the basis of neurocognitive deficits rather than behavioral symptoms might be a viable option (e.g. Sonuga-Barke, Bitsakou, & Thompson, 2010), but this needs to be further explored.

Treatment

Standard Treatment of ADHD

It is widely accepted that either *behavioral therapy, medication*, or a *combination of both* is most beneficial for most patients. Behavioral therapy and medication have both been established as evidence-based treatments and show large effects on improvement of behavioral symptoms. Most treatment guidelines recommend starting with either behavioral therapy (in preschool children or children with moderate symptom severity) or medication (in cases with severe symptoms or comorbidities, or if high levels of family stress are present) or a combination of both. If only one type of treatment is given, it is recommended that a second type of intervention be added if the first does not provide sufficient improvement (Graham et al., 2011; Kendall et al., 2008; Pliszka, 2007; Wolraich et al., 2011). In all cases, psychoeducation about ADHD and the various treatment options is indicated for the parent as well as the child, at the start and throughout the course of treatment.

Behavioral therapy has been recognized as a well-established stand-alone treatment option for pediatric ADHD, mostly using positive and negative reinforcement to increase desired behavior and decrease undesired behavior (Fabiano et al., 2009; P. C. Lee, Niew, Yang, Chen, & Lin, 2012; Pelham & Fabiano, 2008). Different types of evidence-based behavioral treatments have been identified, each targeting the child with ADHD in a different setting: behavioral parent training, classroom management, and peer interventions. A meta-analysis has shown that behavioral therapy in ADHD not only ameliorates behavioral symptoms of the disorder but also has moderate effects on comorbid oppositional and conduct behavior as well as social behavior outcomes (Van der Oord, Prins, Oosterlaan, & Emmelkamp, 2008). Behavioral treatment in *adults* with ADHD lacks proper investigation, but preliminary reports are positive (Knouse, Cooper-Vince, Sprich, & Safren, 2008).

Medication treatment for pediatric as well as adult ADHD typically involves either stimulants (such as methylphenidate or Ritalin®) or nonstimulants (such as atomoxetine or Strattera®) and is believed to enhance neurotransmission of dopamine (stimulants only) and norepinephrine (stimulants and atomoxetine) in the brain. A few other pharmacological options are available, including mixed amphetamine salts and lisdexamfetamine dimesylate (LDX), but these are all clearly framed as second-line options (Seixas, 2013). Immediate-release stimulants exert their effects within 1 hour after ingestion and are effective for approximately 3–5 hours, whereas extended-release stimulants and atomoxetine are effective for 8–10 hours and require only once-daily dosing.

The beneficial effect of both stimulants and atomoxetine on ADHD symptoms has been well documented (Castells et al., 2011; Faraone & Buitelaar, 2010). Pharmacological treatment often not only ameliorates core symptoms but can also have a beneficial effect on comorbid oppositional defiant behavior, social behavior, quality of life, classroom behavior, cognitive functions, and productivity at school or work (but there is no effect on overall academic achievement; Chamberlain et al., 2011; Coghill, 2010; Langberg & Becker, 2012; Molina et al., 2009; Pietrzak, Mollica, Maruff, & Snyder, 2006; Prasad et al., 2013; Van der Oord et al., 2008). However, there is little and inconsistent evidence for the *long-term* beneficial effects of medication beyond 2 years of use (Langberg & Becker, 2012; van de Loo-Neus, Rommelse, & Buitelaar, 2011).

In general, stimulants and atomoxetine are well-tolerated drugs. Most frequently reported side effects include headache, decreased appetite, insomnia, and abdominal pain, but these are uncommon and generally mild (Findling, 2008). Atomoxetine is more often associated with nausea

and sedation than stimulants and is slightly less effective, but it holds the advantage of being less likely to lead to medication misuse or diversion (Findling, 2008; Pliszka, 2007) and it may decrease comorbid tics (Cortese et al., 2013). Stimulants and atomoxetine may sometimes lead to reductions in weight and height gain in children, possibly due to a loss of appetite (Cortese et al., 2013), although some authors have suggested that the growth reduction is related to ADHD itself (Faraone, Biederman, Morley, & Spencer, 2008). So-called drug holidays (taking children off medication during weekends or holidays) are often advised, as they may be helpful in normalizing side effects, including reductions in height and weight gain (Pliszka, 2007).

While serious concerns have been raised regarding health risks for children using medication for ADHD, most of these concerns lack scientific support. Small cardiovascular effects of ADHD drugs have been reported, including slightly elevated blood pressure and heart rate, but there is currently no evidence that ADHD drugs increase the risk for serious cardiovascular events (Pliszka, 2007). The validity of other concerns, including an elevated risk for suicidal thoughts, psychosis, and substance use disorders, is still largely unclear. It is important to be clear that there is *currently* no evidence of this kind, but of course, future research may prove different (Graham et al., 2011; Pliszka, 2007; van de Loo-Neus et al., 2011). In all cases, risk management of possible adverse effects is of highest concern, at the start of as well as throughout treatment (Cortese et al., 2013; Graham et al., 2011; Pliszka, 2007; Warren et al., 2009).

When directly comparing the efficacy of medication treatment with behavioral therapy, a large hallmark study (the Multimodal Treatment Study of Children with ADHD [MTA]) reported that behavioral treatment is effective in reducing core symptoms of ADHD, but it is not as effective as a strict medication management program (MTA Cooperative Group, 1999); this finding is supported by more recent studies (Van der Oord et al., 2008). Combining pharmacological treatment and behavioral therapy does not seem to have an additional effect on reducing ADHD symptoms (Pliszka, 2007; Van der Oord et al., 2008), but it may have an additional short-term effect on internalizing symptoms, social skills, parent–child relations, and reading achievement (Molina et al., 2009).

Alternative Treatment Methods

Currently, behavior therapy and pharmacological treatment are the only two evidence-based treatments for ADHD. However, these treatment options offer incomplete symptom relief in over 30% of patients (Swanson et al., 2001). Behavioral therapy is relatively cost-intensive (Jensen et al., 2005), and nonpharmacological treatments are often favored by parents, thus there is an increasing interest in alternative treatment options. Although none of these alternative treatment methods are sufficiently investigated to draw robust conclusions, we will discuss the most promising ones.

The role of *nutrition* in ADHD has provoked controversy in both research and the media. One meta-analysis of 10 studies noted that some children with ADHD (~30%) may respond to a *restriction diet*, leaving out synthetic food colors or other additives (Nigg, Nikolas, & Burt, 2010). Two specific dietary elements are seen as promising targets. First, increasing evidence shows that ADHD symptoms could be reduced by leaving out *artificial food colors* from the diets of children with ADHD (Nigg et al., 2010). Second, lower plasma and blood concentrations of *polyunsaturated fatty acids* have been found in children with ADHD (Gillies, Sinn, Lad, Leach, & Ross, 2012). Preliminary results suggest that supplementation of these acids, in particular omega-3, can improve ADHD symptoms in some children (Bloch & Qawasmi, 2011; Sonuga-Barke et al., 2013). Unfortunately, only a small number of good-quality studies are available and conclusions are inconsistent (Gillies et al., 2012; Sonuga-Barke et al., 2013). It is important to note that results of these studies are difficult to interpret. First, participants are often preselected to maximize compliance to the strict diet, which reduces generalizability of findings to *all* families with ADHD. Second, children on a restriction diet are not only limited in their food intake but also receive much more attention and structure at home, which can also have a beneficial effect on their behavior. Also, placebo effects cannot be ruled out in studies using a restriction diet.

Another popular alternative treatment option for ADHD is *neurofeedback (NF) training*. During NF training, children learn to control specific brainwave patterns as measured by electroencephalography (EEG), using real-time audio or video feedback. Several studies showed improvement in ADHD-related behavior after extensive NF training (Lofthouse, Arnold, Hersch, Hurt, & DeBeus, 2012; Moriyama et al., 2012), leading many (commercial) health care suppliers to offer NF as stand-alone ADHD treatment. Unfortunately, the limited quality of current NF research prevents the drawing of valid conclusions, and NF can currently only be described as a "promising" treatment for ADHD (Lofthouse, Arnold, Hersch, et al., 2012; Lofthouse, Arnold, & Hurt, 2012; Loo & Makeig, 2012). The same holds for *cognitive training* (e.g., working memory training) in children with ADHD. The limited evidence available shows promising results regarding symptom improvement as rated by parents, however, without generalization to classroom behavior (Rutledge, van den Bos, McClure, & Schweitzer, 2012).

Taken together, effective treatment of ADHD involves many considerations, and treatment protocols should always be tailored and evaluated on an individual basis. Personal characteristics of the patient (such as symptom severity, comorbid problems and the patient's social environment) should be weighed together with advantages and disadvantages of the available treatment options in order to set up an individual treatment plan.

Etiology and Risk Factors

During the past two decades, a large number of investigators have attempted to find a single cause or theory for the etiology of ADHD (e.g., Barkley, 1997; Sergeant, 2005; Sergeant, Geurts, Huijbregts, Scheres, & Oosterlaan, 2003). While several factors, for example, heritability, have been found to play a substantial role, the "single-cause" approach has proven unsuccessful in explaining even a minority of the occurrences of the disorder. Currently, ADHD is best described as a multifactorial disorder, in which a variety of factors, and combinations of these factors, contribute to the overall risk of developing the disorder. A large number of risk factors have been identified, and an increasing number of studies are investigating complex interactions between these risk factors. The current notion is that in most cases, ADHD is caused by an interaction between risk genes and environmental factors. However, even with this multifactorial approach only a small proportion of the variance in ADHD symptoms can be explained.

Genetic Influences

Twin and adoption studies have consistently reported high heritability rates, with, on average, 76% of the variance in ADHD symptoms being explained by genetic factors (Biederman & Faraone, 2005). While this suggests that the disorder is for the most part caused by risk genes, an unsatisfactory low percentage of them have been identified so far. Over the past two decades, a considerable number of studies have tried to identify specific genes associated with ADHD, resulting in abundant but often conflicting literature. A meta-analysis showed that only six of the many proposed candidate genes could consistently be linked to the risk for ADHD, with disappointingly low effect sizes (odds ratios 1.11–1.33; Gizer, Ficks, & Waldman, 2009). These include dopamine transporter and receptor genes (*DAT1/SLC6A3, DRD4, DRD5*), serotonin transporter and receptor genes (*5-HTT/SLC6A4, HTR1B*), and the *SNAP25* gene involved in neurotransmission.

Using genome-wide association studies (GWAS), in which the whole genome is investigated instead of a small number of specifically selected genes, several attempts have been made to obtain a complete picture of the genes involved in ADHD. Unfortunately, GWAS require extraordinary large data sets and are generally underpowered. While GWAS in ADHD research have identified 85 candidate genes in total, GWAS have unfortunately not significantly increased our understanding of ADHD risk genes, given the limited consistency between results. A review of these studies adopted a different methodology and managed to integrate current findings into a network involved in neurite outgrowth, which included 53% of these candidate genes. These data suggest that, in ADHD patients, small alterations in the outgrowth of axons and dendrites in the brain caused by these risk genes may play a large role in the development of the disorder (Poelmans, Pauls, Buitelaar, & Franke, 2011).

Environmental Risk Factors

Several environmental risk factors have been implicated in ADHD. In this context, the term *environment* may be interpreted in a broad way, encompassing everything, other than the genotype, that can influence a child's development. Environmental risk factors for ADHD are generally divided into two domains: neurobiological and psychosocial factors.

Neurobiological factors often associated with ADHD can for a large part be characterized as complications during pregnancy or delivery. They include maternal smoking or alcohol use during pregnancy, eclampsia, fetal distress, premature birth, poor maternal health, and higher maternal age (Bhutta, Cleves, Casey, Cradock, & Anand, 2002; Biederman & Faraone, 2005; Linnet et al., 2003). Many of these factors can lead to hypoxia in the fetal brain. Notably, the basal ganglia, a brain structure often implicated in ADHD, is particularly sensitive to the effects of hypoxia (Froehlich et al., 2011).

Psychosocial factors often associated with ADHD include poor socioeconomic status, family dysfunction (including maternal mental disorders, paternal criminality, marital problems, and in-home conflict), and large family size (Banerjee, Middleton, & Faraone, 2007; Biederman & Faraone, 2005). Concerns have arisen that media use might lead to ADHD-like behavioral problems (Christakis, Zimmerman, DiGiuseppe, & McCarty, 2004). While there is some evidence for a relationship between media use and ADHD, no conclusions can be drawn regarding the direction of this relationship (Banerjee et al., 2007; Huizinga, Nikkelen, & Valkenburg, 2013).

It is important to note that while a large number of neurobiological and psychosocial factors have been associated with ADHD, the effect sizes and odds ratios are generally small, indicating that none of these factors act as strong, independent predictors of the disorder. Furthermore, while many of these factors are strongly associated with the *presence* of ADHD in a family, they should not automatically be considered direct *causes* of ADHD. For example, while maternal smoking may directly cause ADHD through neurobiological alterations in the fetal brain, it is also possible that the mother's predisposition to smoke during pregnancy is a result of her having ADHD or a vulnerability to it, which is transferred to the child genetically. Moreover, it is important to state that while these factors are consistently linked to an increased risk for the development of ADHD, many children who have experienced one or more of these risk factors do not develop ADHD and, conversely, not all children with ADHD show one or more of these risk factors.

Gene by Environment Interactions

While a variety of risk genes and environmental factors have been linked to ADHD, none of them fully explains the risk for developing the disorder. For example, it is possible that in a monozygotic twin pair, sharing 100% of their genotype at birth, one child develops ADHD while the other does not. Such a situation would result from a gene by environment (G x E) interaction, meaning that the effect of specific genes may vary because of differences in the environment. For example, one twin might have experienced hypoxia during birth while the other did not, resulting in one twin with and one without ADHD. Another example of G x E interaction is that a specific environment (such as maternal smoking or alcohol use during pregnancy) may be damaging to many infants, but more specifically so to those infants who carry specific risk genes, making them more vulnerable to the adverse effects of this environment.

Given the large variation in implicated risk genes and environmental factors, most hypotheses on G x E interactions have only received attention in a single study, resulting in literature with limited overlap. A literature review showed that, overall, psychosocial factors seem to interact with ADHD risk genes, primarily with *DAT1* and *5-HTT*, in the development of the disorder (Nigg et al., 2010). Unfortunately, because of the limited overlap between studies, it is unclear whether this interaction exists for all psychosocial factors or only specific ones. For neurobiological factors, even less overlap was found. Findings for maternal smoking or alcohol use during pregnancy are highly inconsistent and suggest that if an interaction with risk genes does occur, this may cause hyperactive behavior, but not necessarily the full range of ADHD symptoms.

Heterogeneity in Etiology

While some risk factors for ADHD have been identified and replicated, possibly a far higher number remain unknown, and we have only just begun to unravel the complex interactions between these different risk factors. One of the causes for the large inconsistency between findings thus far may be the heterogeneity of behavioral symptoms of the disorder. In linking specific risk genes to a behavioral outcome (i.e., phenotype), heterogeneity in phenotype considerably reduces power to

find risk genes. In this context, during the past decade, researchers have suggested that the field move toward identification of "endophenotypes" or intermediate phenotypes (Castellanos & Tannock, 2002). *Endophenotypes* refer to heritable traits that are more strongly associated with the genotype than the phenotypical manifestation and less influenced by environmental factors than the phenotype. Examples of endophenotypes are neurocognitive deficits or specific neurobiological abnormalities that are characteristic for ADHD. Identification of endophenotypes may provide useful direction in the search for candidate risk genes for the disorder and be useful in itself for understanding underlying mechanisms of dysfunction. Although identifying risk genes may not uncover the full complex multifactorial etiology of the disorder, it may be a first step toward clarifying the neurobiological underpinnings of ADHD.

Neurocognitive and Neurobiological Abnormalities

Given the high heritability rates of ADHD, the disorder is suspected to have an important neurobiological basis. With advancing research techniques, considerable progress has been made in unraveling the neurobiological underpinnings of the disorder, although a lot of uncertainty remains. This field of research can roughly be divided into two domains: abnormalities in neurocognitive functioning and neurobiological abnormalities as measured by neuroimaging techniques.

Neurocognitive Abnormalities

The search for neurocognitive deficits in ADHD has been on the fast track in recent years, resulting in a large number of studies, and a variety of neurocognitive functions suggested to be deficient in ADHD. Early neurocognitive studies into ADHD have primarily attempted to objectify the symptoms of inattention, motor restlessness, and impulsivity (e.g. Corkum & Siegel, 1993; Kuehne, Kehle, & McMahon, 1987; Porrino et al., 1983). In general, this seems a fruitful approach, as patients with ADHD are often found to be impaired on neurocognitive measures of sustained attention, motor restlessness, and impulsivity (Alderson, Rapport, & Kofler, 2007; Huang-Pollock, Karalunas, Tam, & Moore, 2012; Huizenga, van Bers, Plat, van den

Wildenberg, & van der Molen, 2009; Losier, McGrath, & Klein, 1996; Rapport et al., 2009). However, effect sizes are generally small, findings remain inconsistent, and neurocognitive measures have not proven useful aids in the diagnosis of ADHD. Moreover, it is questionable whether these neurocognitive measures adequately represent the behavioral symptoms of the disorder (e.g., Nigg, 2000). More recent neurocognitive studies have adopted a broader perspective and investigated a large variety of neurocognitive functions in children and adults with ADHD. The most consistently found deficits involve executive functions and include behavioral inhibition, planning, working memory, and set-shifting (Willcutt, Doyle, Nigg, Faraone, & Pennington, 2005). Furthermore, problems with delay aversion and social cognition (i.e., emotion perception), as well as a large variability in reaction times, are often seen in ADHD patients (Huang-Pollock, et al., 2012; Luman, Oosterlaan, & Sergeant, 2005; Sonuga-Barke, Sergeant, Nigg, & Willcutt, 2008; Tamm et al., 2012; Uekermann et al., 2010). Effect sizes for most neurocognitive functions lie in the medium range (Willcutt et al., 2005). Given the large variety of neurocognitive deficits implicated in ADHD, it is possible that a more general deficit may underlie poor performance across tasks. Some evidence exists that a general processing deficit (Alderson et al., 2007), attentional lapses during task performance (Tamm et al., 2012), or motivational deficits (Konrad, Gauggel, Manz, & Scholl, 2000) may underlie poor performance on many neurocognitive tasks. However, more research is needed to clarify this issue.

It is interesting to note that while a number of ADHD patients are impaired on one or multiple neurocognitive functions, another substantial group of patients does not show any neurocognitive deficit at all (Nigg et al., 2010; Willcutt et al., 2005). Moreover, neurocognitive problems seem to be independent of the developmental course of ADHD (i.e., persistence versus remission of symptoms later in life; van Lieshout, Luman, Buitelaar, Rommelse, & Oosterlaan, 2013), suggesting that these deficits may not share the same etiology as the behavioral symptoms of the disorder. Altogether, this issue warrants more attention in future research.

Neurobiological Abnormalities

Neuroimaging techniques can be useful tools to elucidate the neurobiological mechanisms that underlie the behavioral and neurocognitive deficits observed in ADHD. One of the most used imaging techniques is magnetic resonance imaging (MRI), allowing in vivo three-dimensional imaging of brain structure and function.

Brain volumes, as measured by structural MRI, have been studied for decades, and many brain regions have been suggested to be reduced in ADHD. In general, ADHD patients often show a reduced overall brain volume (Nakao, Radua, Rubia, & Mataix-Cols, 2011) and reduced thickness of the cortex (Almeida et al., 2010; Narr et al., 2009; Shaw et al., 2006) compared to healthy controls. Reductions in more specific regions are also observed, most consistently in structures within the basal ganglia, including the striatum (Frodl & Skokauskas, 2012; Nakao et al., 2011). Others include the prefrontal cortex, corpus callosum, anterior cingulate cortex, amygdala, and cerebellum (Frodl & Skokauskas, 2012; Valera, Faraone, Murray, & Seidman, 2007). Volume reductions mostly show medium effect sizes and are often more pronounced in the right hemisphere (Frodl & Skokauskas, 2012; Valera et al., 2007).

In general, structural brain abnormalities in ADHD are viewed as reflecting a developmental delay, rather than a static deficit. Converging evidence shows that volume reductions may normalize around mid- to late adolescence, most particularly in structures within the basal ganglia (Frodl & Skokauskas, 2012; Nakao et al., 2011; Silk, Vance, Rinehart, Bradshaw, & Cunnington, 2009). A large longitudinal study also showed a developmental delay in cortical thickness in children with ADHD (Shaw et al., 2007). The authors showed that in typically developing children, the development of cortical thickness follows a growth curve described by an increase in thickness during childhood, reaching peak thickness at around 7–8 years of age, and a subsequent decrease in thickness during adolescence. Patients with ADHD showed a similarly shaped growth curve that was delayed by approximately 3 years, reaching peak thickness at around 10–11 years of age. Consistent with previously described literature on volume reductions in ADHD, these results suggest that ADHD might, at least partly, be due to a delay in brain maturation (Rubia, 2007), and that some of the brain abnormalities in ADHD might resolve in adolescence. Independent of this catch-up in brain maturation, long-term pharmacological treatment seems to have positive effects on brain structure.

Brain volume reductions are less pronounced in treated patients than in treatment-naïve patients, and volumes of several brain regions seem to even normalize to similar volumes to those in healthy controls (Frodl & Skokauskas, 2012; Schweren, de Zeeuw, & Durston, 2013).

Using functional MRI, brain activation can be investigated during performance of cognitive tasks. Converging evidence suggests that patients with ADHD show reduced brain activity during tasks that tap into cognitive processes such as attention, response inhibition, and reward anticipation. These reductions in activity are most frequently found in frontal, parietal, and temporal brain regions as well as the basal ganglia (Cortese et al., 2012; Dickstein, Bannon, Castellanos, & Milham, 2006; Hart, Radua, Nakao, Mataix-Cols, & Rubia, 2013). Interestingly, many of these regions overlap with brain regions found to be reduced in volume.

In line with findings of altered brain activity in ADHD patients, electroencephalography (EEG) studies show abnormal electrical brain activity in children, adolescents, and adults with ADHD. The P300, an event-related potential (ERP) component thought to represent attentional and executive functioning, has a decreased amplitude in patients with ADHD (Szuromi, Czobor, Komlosi, & Bitter, 2011). Increased theta activity (associated with drowsiness or cortical underactivation) and reduced beta activity (associated with a less attentive state) are often found, indicative of brain immaturity. While this pattern may reflect a developmental delay in childhood ADHD, similar EEG abnormalities in adults with ADHD suggest that at least some of these abnormalities may persist throughout life (Tye, McLoughlin, Kuntsi, & Asherson, 2011).

Positron emission tomography (PET) and single photon emission computed tomography (SPECT) have been used to study the neurochemistry of the ADHD brain. Components of catecholamine signaling systems are encoded by risk genes implicated in ADHD and play a large role in the neurochemistry of the disorder (Caylak, 2012; Durston & Konrad, 2007; Madras, Miller, & Fischman, 2005). One of these components, dopamine (DA), is highly active in the striatum, and striatal DA levels play a pivotal role in the regulation of psychomotor activity and reward-seeking behavior (Spencer et al., 2005). Another component implicated in ADHD is norepinephrine (NE),

which plays an important role in the regulation of attention and behavior and is mainly effective in the (pre)frontal cortex (Arnsten & Li, 2005; Madras et al., 2005). PET studies have shown dysregulation of both DA and NE in ADHD and suggest underactivity of these neurotransmitters in cortical regions but overactivity in subcortical regions (Ernst, Zametkin, Matochik, Jons, & Cohen, 1998; Fusar-Poli, Rubia, Rossi, Sartori, & Balottin, 2012; Madras et al., 2005; Spencer et al., 2005; Swanson, Castellanos, Murias, LaHoste, & Kennedy, 1998). Most effective pharmacological treatments for ADHD are thought to ameliorate behavioral symptoms of the disorder by optimizing neurotransmission in catecholamine signaling systems, consequently normalizing DA and NE levels in the striatum and frontal cortex (Arnsten & Li, 2005; Madras et al., 2005).

Disturbed Connectivity

Abnormalities in brain structure and function are predominantly found in (pre)frontal cortical regions and the basal ganglia. These findings have led to a prominent theory that neurobiological deficits in ADHD are mainly located in the so-called frontostriatal circuit (Bush, Valera, & Seidman, 2005; Durston & Konrad, 2007), which includes brain regions in and between the frontal cortex and the striatum, a component within the basal ganglia. Concurrent with this theory, the perspective on neuropathology in ADHD has shifted from identifying local deficiencies to studying connectivity between brain regions. Brain regions are interconnected through a large number of white matter tracts and can constitute a functional network of activation during a cognitive task. Consequently, one local deficiency (either cortical or subcortical) could disturb the whole functional network, indirectly causing a reduction in brain activation in another, more distant brain region and its functioning.

Structural as well as functional brain connectivity can be measured using various MRI techniques. Diffusion tensor imaging (DTI) is a relatively new MRI technique, allowing in vivo measurement of the microstructural integrity of brain white matter. DTI studies are just beginning to emerge in ADHD research and are still limited by some methodological issues. However, converging evidence points to reduced microstructural organization and integrity of white matter tracts in children and adults with ADHD (van Ewijk, Heslenfeld, Zwiers, Buitelaar, & Oosterlaan, 2012). Alterations have most consistently been found in several white matter tracts in frontostriatal regions and the cerebellum (de Zeeuw et al., 2011; van Ewijk et al., 2012), but results from different studies are still inconsistent. Findings from functional connectivity studies suggest that during rest as well as during cognitive tasks, patients with ADHD display altered (usually less coherent) connectivity between brain regions and might fail to suppress task-irrelevant activation in these networks during performance of cognitive tasks (Konrad & Eickhoff, 2010). While connectivity research in ADHD is still fairly new and needs to be interpreted with caution, it is currently a prominent topic in research and shows great potential in unraveling the neurobiological underpinnings of the disorder.

Conclusions

ADHD is one of the most frequently diagnosed childhood psychiatric disorders. It is known to often persist into adulthood, causing severe impairment in the patient, the patient's family, and social environment, as well as in school or work functioning. This chapter has summarized the current knowledge and literature on different aspects of ADHD. Advancement has been made in the clinical conceptualization of ADHD throughout the past century, and a standard treatment protocol is now well established, encompassing behavioral treatment and/or medication. Alternative treatment options are being sought, but well set-up and replicated studies proving its efficacy are still lacking. Many factors have been identified that may play a role in the etiology and development of the disorder, including several risk genes, environmental factors, neurocognitive deficits, and brain abnormalities. However, these factors only explain a small proportion of the variance, and a coherent model integrating all of these factors is still missing.

In this chapter, we have emphasized the important role of etiological and phenotypical heterogeneity, which has created a challenge in the diagnosis of ADHD as well as in research into the different mechanisms underlying the disorder. This heterogeneity in research findings might indicate that the current classification of ADHD and its

three presentations may, despite the clinical value, not provide optimal guidance for identifying the underlying mechanisms. However, in research as well as in clinical practice, diagnostic criteria for ADHD are often misinterpreted or applied very loosely, possibly resulting in overdiagnosis of the disorder. Only after implementation of consistent use of diagnostic criteria can new advances be made toward resolving current heterogeneity and producing more clarity in the etiology and clinical manifestation of the disorder.

References

Alderson, R. M., Rapport, M. D., & Kofler, M. J. (2007). Attention-deficit/hyperactivity disorder and behavioral inhibition: A meta-analytic review of the stop-signal paradigm. *Journal of Abnormal Child Psychology, 35,* 745–758.

Almeida, L. G., Ricardo-Garcell, J., Prado, H., Barajas, L., Fernandez-Bouzas, A., Avila, D., et al. (2010). Reduced right frontal cortical thickness in children, adolescents and adults with adhd and its correlation to clinical variables: A cross-sectional study. *Journal of Psychiatric Research, 44,* 1214–1223.

Arnsten, A. F., & Li, B. M. (2005). Neurobiology of executive functions: Catecholamine influences on prefrontal cortical functions. *Biological Psychiatry, 57,* 1377–1384.

Banerjee, T. D., Middleton, F., & Faraone, S. V. (2007). Environmental risk factors for attention-deficit hyperactivity disorder. *Acta Paediatrica, 96,* 1269–1274.

Barkley, R. A. (1997). Behavioral inhibition, sustained attention, and executive functions: Constructing a unifying theory of adhd. *Psychological Bulletin, 121,* 65–94.

Barkley, R. A., Fischer, M., Smallish, L., & Fletcher, K. (2004). Young adult follow-up of hyperactive children: Antisocial activities and drug use. *Journal of Child Psychology and Psychiatry and Allied Disciplines, 45,* 195–211.

Bhutta, A. T., Cleves, M. A., Casey, P. H., Cradock, M. M., & Anand, K. J. (2002). Cognitive and behavioral outcomes of school-aged children who were born preterm: A meta-analysis. *Journal of the American Medical Association, 288,* 728–737.

Biederman, J., & Faraone, S. V. (2005). Attention-deficit hyperactivity disorder. *Lancet, 366,* 237–248.

Biederman, J., Faraone, S. V., Spencer, T., Wilens, T., Norman, D., Lapey, K. A., et al. (1993). Patterns of psychiatric comorbidity, cognition, and psychosocial functioning in adults with attention deficit hyperactivity disorder. *American Journal of Psychiatry, 150,* 1792–1798.

Biederman, J., Monteaux, M. C., Mick, E., Spencer, T., Wilens, T. E., Silva, J. M., et al. (2006). Young adult outcome of attention deficit hyperactivity disorder: A controlled 10-year follow-up study. *Psychological Medicine, 36,* 167–179.

Bloch, M. H., & Qawasmi, A. (2011). Omega-3 fatty acid supplementation for the treatment of children with attention-deficit/hyperactivity disorder symptomatology: Systematic review and meta-analysis. *Journal of the American Academy of Child & Adolescent Psychiatry, 50,* 991–1000.

Bush, G., Valera, E. M., & Seidman, L. J. (2005). Functional neuroimaging of attention-deficit/hyperactivity disorder: A review and suggested future directions. *Biological Psychiatry, 57,* 1273–1284.

Castellanos, F. X., & Tannock, R. (2002). Neuroscience of attention-deficit/hyperactivity disorder: The search for endophenotypes. *Nature Reviews Neuroscience, 3,* 617–628.

Castells, X., Ramos-Quiroga, J. A., Rigau, D., Bosch, R., Nogueira, M., Vidal, X., et al. (2011). Efficacy of methylphenidate for adults with attention-deficit hyperactivity disorder: A meta-regression analysis. *CNS Drugs, 25,* 157–169.

Caylak, E. (2012). Biochemical and genetic analyses of childhood attention deficit/hyperactivity disorder. *American Journal of Medical Genetics Part B, Neuropsychiatric Genetics, 159B,* 613–627.

Chamberlain, S. R., Robbins, T. W., Winder-Rhodes, S., Muller, U., Sahakian, B. J., Blackwell, A. D., et al. (2011). Translational approaches to frontostriatal dysfunction in attention-deficit/hyperactivity disorder using a computerized neuropsychological battery. *Biological Psychiatry, 69,* 1192–1203.

Charach, A., Yeung, E., Climans, T., & Lillie, E. (2011). Childhood attention-deficit/hyperactivity disorder and future substance use disorders: Comparative meta-analyses. *Journal of the American Academy of Child & Adolescent Psychiatry, 50,* 9–21.

Christakis, D. A., Zimmerman, F. J., DiGiuseppe, D. L., & McCarty, C. A. (2004). Early television exposure and subsequent attentional problems in children. *Pediatrics, 113,* 708–713.

Coghill, D. (2010). The impact of medications on quality of life in attention-deficit hyperactivity disorder: A systematic review. *CNS Drugs, 24,* 843–866.

Coghill, D., & Seth, S. (2011). Do the diagnostic criteria for adhd need to change? Comments on the preliminary proposals of the DSM-5 ADHD and disruptive behavior disorders committee. *European Child and Adolescent Psychiatry, 20,* 75–81.

Coghill, D., Soutullo, C., d'Aubuisson, C., Preuss, U., Lindback, T., Silverberg, M., et al. (2008). Impact of attention-deficit/hyperactivity disorder on the patient and family: Results from a european survey. *Child and Adolescent Psychiatry and Mental Health, 2,* 31.

Connor, D. F., Steeber, J., & McBurnett, K. (2010). A review of attention-deficit/hyperactivity disorder complicated by symptoms of oppositional defiant disorder or conduct disorder. *Journal of Developmental and Behavioral Pediatrics, 31,* 427–440.

Corkum, P., & Siegel, L. S. (1993). Is the continuous performance task a valuable research tool for use with children with attention-deficit/hyperactivity disorder? *Journal of Child Psychology and Psychiatry, 34,* 1217–1239.

Corkum, P., Tannock, R., & Moldofsky, H. (1998). Sleep disturbances in children with attention-deficit/hyperactivity disorder. *Journal of the American Academy of Child & Adolescent Psychiatry, 37,* 637–646.

Cortese, S., Holtmann, M., Banaschewski, T., Buitelaar, J., Coghill, D., Danckaerts, M., et al. (2013). Practitioner review: Current best practice in the management of adverse events during treatment with ADHD medications in children and adolescents. *Journal of Child Psychology and Psychiatry and Allied Disciplines, 54*(3), 227–246.

Cortese, S., Kelly, C., Chabernaud, C., Proal, E., Di Martino, A., Milham, M. P., et al. (2012). Toward systems neuroscience of ADHD: A meta-analysis of 55 fMRI studies. *American Journal of Psychiatry, 169*(10), 1038–1055.

de Zeeuw, P., Mandl, R. C. W., Pol, H., Hilleke, E., van Engeland, H., & Durston, S. (2011). Decreased frontostriatal microstructural organization in attention deficit/hyperactivity disorder. *Human Brain Mapping, 33,* 1941–1951.

Dickstein, S. G., Bannon, K., Castellanos, F. X., & Milham, M. P. (2006). The neural correlates of attention deficit hyperactivity disorder: An ALE meta-analysis. *Journal of Child Psychology and Psychiatry and Allied Disciplines, 47,* 1051–1062.

Doshi, J. A., Hodgkins, P., Kahle, J., Sikirica, V., Cangelosi, M. J., Setyawan, J., et al. (2012). Economic impact of childhood and adult attention-deficit/hyperactivity disorder in the United States. *Journal of the American Academy of Child & Adolescent Psychiatry, 51,* 990–1002.

Durston, S., & Konrad, K. (2007). Integrating genetic, psychopharmacological and neuroimaging studies: A converging methods approach to understanding the neurobiology of ADHD. *Developmental Review, 27,* 374–395.

Elia, J., Ambrosini, P., & Berrettini, W. (2008). ADHD characteristics: I. Concurrent co-morbidity patterns in children and adolescents. *Child and Adolescent Psychiatry and Mental Health, 2,* 15.

Ernst, M., Zametkin, A. J., Matochik, J. A., Jons, P. H., & Cohen, R. M. (1998). Dopa decarboxylase activity in attention deficit hyperactivity disorder adults. A [fluorine-18] fluorodopa positron emission tomographic study. *Journal of Neuroscience, 18,* 5901–5907.

Fabiano, G. A., Pelham, W. E., Jr., Coles, E. K., Gnagy, E. M., Chronis-Tuscano, A., & O'Connor, B. C. (2009). A meta-analysis of behavioral treatments for attention-deficit/hyperactivity disorder. *Clinical Psychology Review, 29,* 129–140.

Faraone, S. V., Biederman, J., & Mick, E. (2006). The age-dependent decline of attention deficit hyperactivity disorder: A meta-analysis of follow-up studies. *Psychological Medicine, 36,* 159–165.

Faraone, S. V., Biederman, J., Morley, C. P., & Spencer, T. J. (2008). Effect of stimulants on height and weight: A review of the literature. *Journal of the American Academy of Child & Adolescent Psychiatry, 47,* 994–1009.

Faraone, S. V., & Buitelaar, J. (2010). Comparing the efficacy of stimulants for ADHD in children and adolescents using meta-analysis. *European Child and Adolescent Psychiatry, 19,* 353–364.

Findling, R. L. (2008). Evolution of the treatment of attention-deficit/hyperactivity disorder in children: A review. *Clinical Therapeutics, 30,* 942–957.

Flory, K., Molina, B. S. G., Pelham Jr, W. E., Gnagy, E., & Smith, B. (2006). Childhood ADHD predicts risky sexual behavior in young adulthood. *Journal of Clinical Child and Adolescent Psychology, 35,* 571–577.

Frodl, T., & Skokauskas, N. (2012). Meta-analysis of structural MRI studies in children and adults with attention deficit hyperactivity disorder indicates treatment effects. *Acta Psychiatrica Scandinavica, 125,* 114–126.

Froehlich, T. E., Anixt, J. S., Loe, I. M., Chirdkiatgumchai, V., Kuan, L., & Gilman, R. C. (2011). Update on environmental risk factors for attention-deficit/hyperactivity disorder. *Current Psychiatry Reports, 13,* 333–344.

Fusar-Poli, P., Rubia, K., Rossi, G., Sartori, G., & Balottin, U. (2012). Striatal dopamine transporter alterations in ADHD: Pathophysiology or adaptation to psychostimulants? A meta-analysis. *American Journal of Psychiatry, 169,* 264–272.

Gillberg, C., Gillberg, I. C., Rasmussen, P., Kadesjo, B., Soderstrom, H., Rastam, M., et al. (2004). Co-existing disorders in ADHD—implications for diagnosis and intervention. *European Child and Adolescent Psychiatry, 13*(Suppl. 1), I80–I92.

Gillies, D., Sinn, J., Lad, S. S., Leach, M. J., & Ross, M. J. (2012). Polyunsaturated fatty acids (PUFA) for attention deficit hyperactivity disorder (ADHD) in children and adolescents. *Cochrane Database of Systematic Reviews, 7,* CD007986.

Gizer, I. R., Ficks, C., & Waldman, I. D. (2009). Candidate gene studies of ADHD: A meta-analytic review. *Human Genetics, 126,* 51–90.

Graham, J., Banaschewski, T., Buitelaar, J., Coghill, D., Danckaerts, M., Dittmann, R. W., et al. (2011). European guidelines on managing adverse effects of medication for ADHD. *European Child and Adolescent Psychiatry, 20,* 17–37.

Hart, H., Radua, J., Nakao, T., Mataix-Cols, D., & Rubia, K. (2013). Meta-analysis of functional magnetic resonance imaging studies of inhibition and attention in attention-deficit/hyperactivity disorder: Exploring task-specific, stimulant medication, and age effects. *Journal of the American Medical Association Psychiatry, 70,* 185–198.

Huang-Pollock, C. L., Karalunas, S. L., Tam, H., & Moore, A. N. (2012). Evaluating vigilance deficits in ADHD: A meta-analysis of CPT performance. *Journal of Abnormal Psychology, 121,* 360–371.

Huizenga, H. M., van Bers, B. M., Plat, J., van den Wildenberg, W. P., & van der Molen, M. W. (2009). Task complexity enhances response inhibition deficits in childhood and adolescent attention-deficit/hyperactivity disorder: A meta-regression analysis. *Biological Psychiatry, 65,* 39–45.

Huizinga, M., Nikkelen, S. W. C., & Valkenburg, P. M. (2013). Children's media use and its relation to attention, hyperactivity, and impulsivity. In D. Lemish (Ed.), *The Routledge international handbook of children, adolescents and media* (pp. 179–185). New York: Routledge.

Jensen, P. S., Garcia, J. A., Glied, S., Crowe, M., Foster, M., Schlander, M., et al. (2005). Cost-effectiveness of ADHD treatments: Findings from the multimodal treatment study of children with ADHD. *American Journal of Psychiatry, 162,* 1628–1636.

Kadesjö, B., & Gillberg, C. (2003). The comorbidity of ADHD in the general population of Swedish school-age children. *Journal of Child Psychology and Psychiatry, 42,* 487–492.

Kendall, T., Taylor, E., Perez, A., & Taylor, C. (2008). Guidelines: Diagnosis and management of attention-deficit/hyperactivity disorder in children, young people, and adults: Summary of NICE guidance. *British Medical Journal, 337,* 751–753.

Kessler, R. C., Adler, L., Barkley, R., Biederman, J., Conners, C. K., Demler, O., et al. (2006). The prevalence and correlates of adult ADHD in the United States: Results from the National Comorbidity Survey Replication. *American Journal of Psychiatry, 163,* 716–723.

Knouse, L. E., Cooper-Vince, C., Sprich, S., & Safren, S. A. (2008). Recent developments in the psychosocial treatment of adult ADHD. *Expert Review of Neurotherapeutics, 8,* 1537–1548.

Konrad, K., & Eickhoff, S. B. (2010). Is the ADHD brain wired differently? A review on structural and functional connectivity in attention deficit hyperactivity disorder. *Human Brain Mapping, 31,* 904–916.

Konrad, K., Gauggel, S., Manz, A., & Scholl, M. (2000). Lack of inhibition: A motivational deficit in children with attention deficit/hyperactivity disorder and children with traumatic brain injury. *Child Neuropsychology, 6,* 286–296.

Kuehne, C., Kehle, T. J., & McMahon, W. (1987). Differences between children with attention deficit disorder, children with specific learning disabilities, and normal children. *Journal of School Psychology, 25,* 161–166.

Küpper, T., Haavik, J., Drexler, H., Ramos-Quiroga, J. A., Wermelskirchen, D., Prutz, C., et al. (2012). The negative impact of attention-deficit/hyperactivity disorder on occupational health in adults and adolescents. *International Archives of Occupational and Environmental Health, 85,* 837–847.

Langberg, J. M., & Becker, S. P. (2012). Does long-term medication use improve the academic outcomes of youth with

attention-deficit/hyperactivity disorder? *Clinical Child and Family Psychology Review, 15,* 215–233.

Langley, K., Fowler, T., Ford, T., Thapar, A. K., van den Bree, M., Harold, G., et al. (2010). Adolescent clinical outcomes for young people with attention-deficit hyperactivity disorder. *British Journal of Psychiatry, 196,* 235–240.

Lee, P. C., Niew, W. I., Yang, H. J., Chen, V. C., & Lin, K. C. (2012). A meta-analysis of behavioral parent training for children with attention deficit hyperactivity disorder. *Research in Developmental Disabilities, 33,* 2040–2049.

Lee, S. S., Humphreys, K. L., Flory, K., Liu, R., & Glass, K. (2011). Prospective association of childhood attention-deficit/hyperactivity disorder (ADHD) and substance use and abuse/dependence: A meta-analytic review. *Clinical Psychology Review, 31,* 328–341.

Linnet, K. M., Dalsgaard, S., Obel, C., Wisborg, K., Henriksen, T. B., Rodriguez, A., et al. (2003). Maternal lifestyle factors in pregnancy risk of attention deficit hyperactivity disorder and associated behaviors: Review of the current evidence. *American Journal of Psychiatry, 160,* 1028–1040.

Lofthouse, N., Arnold, L. E., Hersch, S., Hurt, E., & DeBeus, R. (2012). A review of neurofeedback treatment for pediatric ADHD. *Journal of Attention Disorders, 16,* 351–372.

Lofthouse, N., Arnold, L. E., & Hurt, E. (2012). Current status of neurofeedback for attention-deficit/hyperactivity disorder. *Current Psychiatry Reports, 14,* 536–542.

Loo, S. K., & Makeig, S. (2012). Clinical utility of EEG in attention-deficit/hyperactivity disorder: A research update. *Neurotherapeutics, 9,* 569–587.

Losier, B. J., McGrath, P. J., & Klein, R. M. (1996). Error patterns on the continuous performance test in non-medicated and medicated samples of children with and without ADHD: A meta-analytic review. *Journal of Child Psychology and Psychiatry and Allied Disciplines, 37,* 971–987.

Luman, M., Oosterlaan, J., & Sergeant, J. A. (2005). The impact of reinforcement contingencies on ADHD: A review and theoretical appraisal. *Clinical Psychology Review, 25,* 183–213.

Madras, B. K., Miller, G. M., & Fischman, A. J. (2005). The dopamine transporter and attention-deficit/hyperactivity disorder. *Biological Psychiatry, 57,* 1397–1409.

McClernon, F. J., & Kollins, S. H. (2008). ADHD and smoking: From genes to brain to behavior. *Annals of the New York Academy of Sciences, 1141*, 131–147.

Michielsen, M., Semeijn, E., Comijs, H. C., van de Ven, P., Beekman, A. T., Deeg, D. J., et al. (2012). Prevalence of attention-deficit hyperactivity disorder in older adults in the Netherlands. *British Journal of Psychiatry, 201*, 298–305.

Milich, R., Balentine, A. C., & Lynam, D. R. (2001). ADHD combined type and ADHD predominantly inattentive type are distinct and unrelated disorders. *Clinical Psychology Science and Practice, 8*, 463–488.

Molina, B. S., Hinshaw, S. P., Swanson, J. M., Arnold, L. E., Vitiello, B., Jensen, P. S., et al. (2009). The MTA at 8 years: Prospective follow-up of children treated for combined-type ADHD in a multisite study. *Journal of the American Academy of Child & Adolescent Psychiatry, 48*, 484–500.

Moriyama, T. S., Polanczyk, G., Caye, A., Banaschewski, T., Brandeis, D., & Rohde, L. A. (2012). Evidence-based information on the clinical use of neurofeedback for ADHD. *Neurotherapeutics, 9*, 588–598.

MTA Cooperative Group. (1999). A 14-month randomized clinical trial of treatment strategies for attention-deficit/hyperactivity disorder. *Archives of General Psychiatry, 56*, 1073–1086.

Mueller, A. K., Fuermaier, A. B. M., Koerts, J., & Tucha, L. (2012). Stigma in attention deficit hyperactivity disorder. *Attention Deficit and Hyperactivity Disorder, 4*, 101–114.

Nakao, T., Radua, J., Rubia, K., & Mataix-Cols, D. (2011). Gray matter volume abnormalities in ADHD: Voxel-based meta-analysis exploring the effects of age and stimulant medication. *American Journal of Psychiatry, 168*, 1154–1163.

Narr, K. L., Woods, R. P., Lin, J., Kim, J., Phillips, O. R., Del'Homme, M., et al. (2009). Widespread cortical thinning is a robust anatomical marker for attention deficit/hyperactivity disorder (ADHD). *Journal of the American Academy of Child & Adolescent Psychiatry, 48*, 1014.

Nigg, J. T. (2000). On inhibition/disinhibition in developmental psychopathology: Views from cognitive and personality psychology and a working inhibition taxonomy. *Psychological Bulletin, 126*, 220–246.

Nigg, J. T., Nikolas, M., & Burt, S. A. (2010). Measured gene-by-environment interaction in relation to attention-deficit/hyperactivity disorder. *Journal of the American Academy of Child & Adolescent Psychiatry, 49*, 863–873.

Palumbo, D., Spencer, T., Lynch, J., Co-Chien, H., & Faraone, S. V. (2004). Emergence of tics in children with ADHD: Impact of once-daily Oros® methylphenidate therapy. *Journal of Child and Adolescent Psychopharmacology, 14*, 185–194.

Pardini, D. A., & Fite, P. J. (2010). Symptoms of conduct disorder, oppositional defiant disorder, attention-deficit/hyperactivity disorder, and callous-unemotional traits as unique predictors of psychosocial maladjustment in boys: Advancing an evidence base for DSM-V. *Journal of the American Academy of Child & Adolescent Psychiatry, 49*, 1134–1144.

Pelham, W. E., Jr., & Fabiano, G. A. (2008). Evidence-based psychosocial treatments for attention-deficit/hyperactivity disorder. *Journal of Clinical Child and Adolescent Psychology, 37*, 184–214.

Pietrzak, R. H., Mollica, C. M., Maruff, P., & Snyder, P. J. (2006). Cognitive effects of immediate-release methylphenidate in children with attention-deficit/hyperactivity disorder. *Neuroscience and Biobehavioral Reviews, 30*, 1225–1245.

Pliszka, S. (2007). Practice parameter for the assessment and treatment of children and adolescents with attention-deficit/hyperactivity disorder. *Journal of the American Academy of Child & Adolescent Psychiatry, 46*, 894–921.

Poelmans, G., Pauls, D. L., Buitelaar, J. K., & Franke, B. (2011). Integrated genome-wide association study findings: Identification of a neurodevelopmental network for attention deficit hyperactivity disorder. *American Journal of Psychiatry, 168*, 365–377.

Porrino, L. J., Rapoport, J. L., Behar, D., Sceery, W., Ismond, D. R., & Bunney, W. E., Jr. (1983). A naturalistic assessment of the motor activity of hyperactive boys. I. Comparison with normal controls. *Archives of General Psychiatry, 40*, 681–687.

Prasad, V., Brogan, E., Mulvaney, C., Grainge, M., Stanton, W., & Sayal, K. (2013). How effective are drug treatments for children with ADHD at improving on-task behaviour and academic achievement in the school classroom? A systematic review and meta-analysis. *European Child and Adolescent Psychiatry, 22*, 203–216.

Ramtekkar, U. P., Reiersen, A. M., Todorov, A. A., & Todd, R. D. (2010). Sex and age differences in attention-deficit/hyperactivity disorder symptoms and diagnoses: Implications for DSM-V and ICD-11. *Journal of the American Academy of Child & Adolescent Psychiatry, 49*, 217–228 e211–213.

Rapport, M. D., Bolden, J., Kofler, M. J., Sarver, D. E., Raiker, J. S., & Alderson, R. M. (2009). Hyperactivity in boys with attention-deficit/ hyperactivity disorder (ADHD): A ubiquitous core symptom or manifestation of working memory deficits? *Journal of Abnormal Child Psychology, 37*, 521–534.

Robison, L. M., Sclar, D. A., Skaer, T. L., & Galin, R. S. (1999). National trends in the prevalence of attention-deficit/hyperactivity disorder and the prescribing of methylphenidate among school-age children: 1990-1995. *Clinical Pediatrics, 38*, 209–217.

Rubia, K. (2007). Neuro-anatomic evidence for the maturational delay hypothesis of ADHD. *Proceedings of the National Academy of Sciences U S A, 104*, 19663–19664.

Rutledge, K. J., van den Bos, W., McClure, S. M., & Schweitzer, J. B. (2012). Training cognition in ADHD: Current findings, borrowed concepts, and future directions. *Neurotherapeutics, 9*, 542–558.

Sawyer, M. G., Whaites, L., Rey, J. M., Hazell, P. L., Graetz, B. W., & Baghurst, P. (2002). Health-related quality of life of children and adolescents with mental disorders. *Journal of the American Academy of Child & Adolescent Psychiatry, 41*, 530–537.

Schweren, L. J., de Zeeuw, P., & Durston, S. (2013). MR imaging of the effects of methylphenidate on brain structure and function in attention-deficit/hyperactivity disorder. *European Neuropsychopharmacology, 23*(10), 1151–1164.

Seixas, N. (2013). Change, challenges, and core values. *Annals of Occupational Hygiene, 57*, 3–5.

Sergeant, J. A. (2005). Modeling attention-deficit/ hyperactivity disorder: A critical appraisal of the cognitive-energetic model. *Biological Psychiatry, 57*, 1248–1255.

Sergeant, J. A., Geurts, H., Huijbregts, S., Scheres, A., & Oosterlaan, J. (2003). The top and the bottom of ADHD: A neuropsychological perspective. *Neuroscience and Biobehavioral Reviews, 27*, 583–592.

Sexton, C. C., Gelhorn, H. L., Bell, J. A., & Classi, P. M. (2012). The co-occurrence of reading disorder and ADHD: Epidemiology, treatment, psychosocial impact, and economic burden. *Journal of Learning Disabilities, 45*, 538–564.

Shaw, P., Eckstrand, K., Sharp, W., Blumenthal, J., Lerch, J., Greenstein, D., et al. (2007). Attention-deficit/hyperactivity disorder is characterized by a delay in cortical maturation. *Proceedings of the National Academy of Sciences U S A, 104*, 19649–19654.

Shaw, P., Lerch, J., Greenstein, D., Sharp, W., Clasen, L., Evans, A., et al. (2006). Longitudinal mapping of cortical thickness and clinical outcome in children and adolescents with attention-deficit/ hyperactivity disorder. *Archives of General Psychiatry, 63*, 540.

Silk, T. J., Vance, A., Rinehart, N., Bradshaw, J. L., & Cunnington, R. (2009). Structural development of the basal ganglia in attention deficit hyperactivity disorder: A diffusion tensor imaging study. *Psychiatry Research, 172*, 220–225.

Sonuga-Barke, E. J., Bitsakou, P., & Thompson, M. (2010). Beyond the dual pathway model: Evidence for the dissociation of timing, inhibitory, and delay-related impairments in attention-deficit/hyperactivity disorder. *Journal of the American Academy of Child & Adolescent Psychiatry, 49*, 345–355.

Sonuga-Barke, E. J., Brandeis, D., Cortese, S., Daley, D., Ferrin, M., Holtmann, M., et al. (2013). Nonpharmacological interventions for ADHD: Systematic review and meta-analyses of randomized controlled trials of dietary and psychological treatments. *American Journal of Psychiatry, 170*, 275–289.

Sonuga-Barke, E. J., Sergeant, J. A., Nigg, J., & Willcutt, E. (2008). Executive dysfunction and delay aversion in attention deficit hyperactivity disorder: Nosologic and diagnostic implications. *Child and Adolescent Psychiatric Clinics of North America, 17*, 367–384, ix.

Spencer, T. J., Biederman, J., Madras, B. K., Dougherty, D. D., Bonab, A. A., Livni, E., et al. (2007). Further evidence of dopamine transporter dysregulation in ADHD: A controlled PET imaging study using altropane. *Biological Psychiatry, 62*, 1059–1061.

Spencer, T. J., Biederman, J., Madras, B. K., Faraone, S. V., Dougherty, D. D., Bonab, A. A., et al. (2005). In vivo neuroreceptor imaging in attention-deficit/hyperactivity disorder: A focus on the dopamine transporter. *Biological Psychiatry, 57*, 1293–1300.

Spencer, T. J., Biederman, J., & Mick, E. (2007). Attention-deficit/hyperactivity disorder: Diagnosis, lifespan, comorbidities, and neurobiology. *Journal of Pediatric Psychology, 32*, 631–642.

Steinhausen, H. C., Nøvik, T. S., Baldursson, G., Curatolo, P., Lorenzo, M. J., Rodrigues Pereira, R., et al. (2006). Co-existing psychiatric problems in ADHD in the adore cohort. *European Child and Adolescent Psychiatry, 15*, 25–29.

Swanson, J., Castellanos, F. X., Murias, M., LaHoste, G., & Kennedy, J. (1998). Cognitive neuroscience of attention deficit hyperactivity disorder and hyperkinetic disorder. *Current Opinion in Neurobiology, 8*, 263.

Swanson, J., Kraemer, H. C., Hinshaw, S. P., Arnold, L. E., Conners, C. K., Abikoff, H. B., et al. (2001). Clinical relevance of the primary findings of the MTA: Success rates based on severity of ADHD and ODD symptoms at the end of treatment. *Journal of the American Academy of Child & Adolescent Psychiatry, 40*, 168–179.

Szuromi, B., Czobor, P., Komlosi, S., & Bitter, I. (2011). P300 deficits in adults with attention deficit hyperactivity disorder: A meta-analysis. *Psychological Medicine, 41*, 1529–1538.

Tamm, L., Narad, M. E., Antonini, T. N., O'Brien, K. M., Hawk, L. W., Jr., & Epstein, J. N. (2012). Reaction time variability in ADHD: A review. *Neurotherapeutics, 9*, 500–508.

Tye, C., McLoughlin, G., Kuntsi, J., & Asherson, P. (2011). Electrophysiological markers of genetic risk for attention deficit hyperactivity disorder. *Expert Reviews in Molecular Medicine, 13*, e9.

Uekermann, J., Kraemer, M., Abdel-Hamid, M., Schimmelmann, B. G., Hebebrand, J., Daum, I., et al. (2010). Social cognition in attention-deficit hyperactivity disorder (ADHD). *Neuroscience and Biobehavioral Reviews, 34*, 734–743.

Valera, E. M., Faraone, S. V., Murray, K. E., & Seidman, L. J. (2007). Meta-analysis of structural imaging findings in attention-deficit/hyperactivity disorder. *Biological Psychiatry, 61*, 1361–1369.

van de Loo-Neus, G. H., Rommelse, N., & Buitelaar, J. K. (2011). To stop or not to stop? How long should medication treatment of attention-deficit hyperactivity disorder be extended? *European Neuropsychopharmacology, 21*, 584–599.

Van der Oord, S., Prins, P. J., Oosterlaan, J., & Emmelkamp, P. M. (2008). Efficacy of methylphenidate, psychosocial treatments and their combination in school-aged children with ADHD: A meta-analysis. *Clinical Psychology Review, 28*, 783–800.

van Ewijk, H., Heslenfeld, D. J., Zwiers, M. P., Buitelaar, J. K., & Oosterlaan, J. (2012). Diffusion tensor imaging in attention deficit/hyperactivity disorder: A systematic review and meta-analysis. *Neuroscience and Biobehavioral Reviews, 36*, 1093–1106.

van Lieshout, M., Luman, M., Buitelaar, J., Rommelse, N., & Oosterlaan, J. (2013). Does neurocognitive functioning predict future or persistence of ADHD? A systematic review. *Clinical Psychology Review, 33*(4), 539–560.

Visser, S., Bitsko, R., Danielson, M., Perou, R., & Blumberg, S. (2010). Increasing prevalence of parent-reported attention-deficit/hyperactivity disorder among children—United States, 2003 and 2007. *Morbidity and Mortality Weekly Report, 59*, 1439–1443.

Warren, A. E., Hamilton, R. M., Belanger, S. A., Gray, C., Gow, R. M., Sanatani, S., et al. (2009). Cardiac risk assessment before the use of stimulant medications in children and youth: A joint position statement by the Canadian Paediatric Society, the Canadian Cardiovascular Society, and the Canadian Academy of Child and Adolescent Psychiatry. *Canadian Journal of Cardiology, 25*, 625–630.

Willcutt, E. G. (2012). The prevalence of DSM-IV attention-deficit/hyperactivity disorder: A meta-analytic review. *Neurotherapeutics, 9*, 490–499.

Willcutt, E. G., Doyle, A. E., Nigg, J. T., Faraone, S. V., & Pennington, B. F. (2005). Validity of the executive function theory of attention-deficit/hyperactivity disorder: A meta-analytic review. *Biological Psychiatry, 57*, 1336–1346.

Willcutt, E. G., Nigg, J. T., Pennington, B. F., Solanto, M. V., Rohde, L. A., Tannock, R., et al. (2012). Validity of DSM-IV attention deficit/hyperactivity disorder symptom dimensions and subtypes. *Journal of Abnormal Psychology, 121*, 991–1010.

Wolraich, M., Brown, L., Brown, R. T., DuPaul, G., Earls, M., Feldman, H. M., et al. (2011). ADHD: Clinical practice guideline for the diagnosis, evaluation, and treatment of attention-deficit/hyperactivity disorder in children and adolescents. *Pediatrics, 128*, 1007–1022.

19

Autism and Autism Spectrum Disorders

FRED R. VOLKMAR

AND KEVIN PELPHREY

Autism and related conditions–previously termed the pervasive developmental disorders (PDDs) and more recently the autism spectrum disorders (ASDs)—share significant difficulties in social development and interaction associated with problems in communication and behavior. These conditions have been the source of great interest for decades, but only with the official recognition of autism in 1980 in DSM-III did research begin to increase. Over time this increase has been quite dramatic, with several thousand scientific papers appearing each year. Despite this increase, research in some areas is quite limited, but overall, very significant progress has been made in understanding and treating these conditions.

Diagnostic Concepts

Autistic disorder (also referred to as childhood autism or infantile autism) is the prototypic disorder of the group and the one that has been the focus of most of the available research. Research is much less extensive on the broader "spectrum" of disorders (ASDs), and caution should be used in generalizing results from more "classic" autism to this larger population.

The syndrome was initially described by Leo Kanner (1943), and all subsequent definitions have kept some degree of continuity with his emphasis on two key features: autism (lack of social interest and engagement from the time of birth), and what he termed resistance to change or insistence on sameness (difficulties with change, stereotyped movements). Kanner's work prefigures much current research, which aims to understand genetic and brain mechanisms of social vulnerability coupled with an overengagement in the nonsocial world. Other diagnostic concepts were proposed before and after 1943. Both ICD-10 and DSM-IV explicitly recognized a number of these, although DSM-5 is returning to a more unitary model, potentially at some price in term of restricted coverage. Conditions included in ICD-10 and DSM-IV were Asperger's disorder, characterized by serious social vulnerability associated with perseverative interests, good vocabulary, and motor clumsiness, and two "disintegrative conditions" in which skills were dramatically lost. One of these conditions, Rett's disorder, is now known to be a single-gene disorder. In the other, childhood disintegrative disorder, autism has its apparent onset after years of clearly normal development. Finally, there was a "subthreshold" category: PDD not otherwise specified, for cases not meeting specific criteria for one of these conditions but with problems that seem best viewed as related to autism (see Volkmar & Lord, 2007, for a review).

The DSM-IV and ICD-10 definitions are very similar; criteria focus on problems in social interaction, communication, and play, and, in addition, on unusual environmental responses and restricted-repetitive interests. The onset of the condition must be before age 3 years. Social problems are weighted more heavily than other factors. The polythetic *ICD-10/DSM-IV* approach allows for over 2,000 combinations of the 12 diagnostic criteria provided.

DSM-5 differs from its predecessor in a number of ways. For autism, two overarching decisions for *DSM-5* have had significant impact: the decision to derive the definitions from reanalyses of research diagnostic instruments, and the decision to remove all subthreshold categories throughout the manual. For autism, the decision was to move to a more unitary construct—autism spectrum disorder. This reflected concern about reliability and validity of more fine-grained distinctions and an awareness of the growing body of research on the complex genetic bases of autism (Lord et al., 2012). The move toward a more rational name for the overall category is praiseworthy, as is the attempt to provide ratings for dimensions of dysfunction. Other aspects of the new system may prove problematic (Volkmar & Reichow, 2013). Social-communication features are now grouped in one category, while the restricted interest category has changed to include unusual sensitivities. In addition, there are many fewer ways for a diagnosis to be achieved, and *DSM-5* may differentially exclude more cognitively able and less "classic" cases. Consistent with *DSM-5* generally, no subthreshold categories are provided, but there is a new condition called "social-communication disorder." The rational for this category and its actual use in practice remain to be determined. A large data reanalysis of items collected as part of research diagnostic assessments was performed, but a true field trial was not actually conducted apart from some work on reliability; using the data available, diagnostic accuracy was good if both historical information and direct research assessment instruments were available (but decreased when they were not). A major unanswered question is how well items derived from research-based instruments—and which require considerable training in administration/interpretation—can readily be extrapolated to more typical clinical settings (Volkmar & Reichow, 2013).

Prevalence, Gender, and Cultural Perspectives

Several complications arise in the interpretation of epidemiological studies. Prevalence estimates can vary dramatically if different diagnostic approaches are used. DSM-IV and ICD-10 criteria were designed to be relatively "neutral" to IQ—that is, a goal was for criteria to work reasonably well in both lower and higher cognitive-functioning individuals. The tendency to equate autism spectrum disorders (i.e., autism and related conditions) with more classical autism is yet another problem given the tendency to rely on school diagnoses rather than on results of actual independent assessment. Thus school settings may use the autism label to justify services (the problem of diagnostic substitution). Other factors influencing prevalence estimates include greater public awareness and recognition. In general, in epidemiological studies higher rates have been obtained when smaller samples are studied (presumably reflecting better case finding). On balance, the median rate of strictly defined autistic disorder is about 1 per 800, but if a broader autism spectrum definition is used this rises to the order of 1 in 150 (Fombonne, 2005). The apparent increase in prevalence of the condition likely reflects the many factors noted earlier, although there may also be some slight increase relative to specific genetic mechanisms, for example, higher risk for older fathers of having a child with autism (Puleo et al., 2012).

There is a strong gender predominance in autism, with males being three to five times more likely to have the condition. When females have autism they tend, on balance, to be more cognitively impaired, suggesting a complex interaction of severity with genetic risk and gender. Kanner's (1943) original paper noted a preponderance of well-educated and successful parents; this has not been confirmed in subsequent studies that controlled for referral bias. Autism appears, particularly in younger children, to be remarkably the same in individuals from various countries, but cultural practices regarding special education and treatment may have a significant impact on outcome (Brown & Rogers, 2003). There is little research on cultural or ethnic differences. Some early suggestion of increased risk in immigrant families has not generally been supported in the literature (Fombonne, 2005).

Historical Perspectives

It is likely that some of the first reports of autism may have been those of so-called feral children (Wolff, 2004). It is a tribute to the genius of Leo

Kanner that he was able to identify a central distinguishing feature (autism or lack of social engagement) that differentiated the condition from other developmental problems. Unfortunately, there were two aspects of his early report that have turned out to be somewhat misleading: his mention of high levels of professional attainment in parents, and his mistaken impression of normal intellectual levels (based on better nonverbal than verbal abilities) and sometimes unusual ability. His impression of parents as successful and emotionally distant contributed to notions of disturbed parent–child relationships as a cause of autism in the 1950s. Finally, his use of the word *autism* suggested to many a point of continuity with schizophrenia, and indeed, in *DSM-II* (i.e., until 1980) autism was considered to be a feature of childhood schizophrenia. Diagnostic ambiguity complicated much available research until work in the 1970s clarified the strong genetic and brain basis of autism. Its first inclusion in *DSM-III* marked a critical moment in research, which has steadily increased since that time.

Diagnostic practice has varied over the years. Early attempts were made to operationalize Kanner's definition, and Rutter's (1978) approach, which specified social and cognitive features as well as unusual behavioral responses, proved highly influential for *DSM-III*.

In addition to changes in diagnostic practice, significant shifts in clinical work and research have occurred. It has become apparent that structured, intensive intervention programs (of various types) are associated, on balance, with improved outcomes, for example, regarding the number of adults who are self-sufficient and independent (Howlin, 2014). However, some children remain in need of considerable support in adulthood. Basic research advances have occurred in a number of areas, but those in genetics and neurobiology have been the most important and are discussed subsequently.

Onset and Course

Kanner (1943) initially described autism as congenital. With one important qualification, the observation of regression in some cases, subsequent research has been largely consistent with this view. Many parents are worried about the child's development in the first year of life and the vast majority (90%) are worried about it by age 2. Common concerns include possible deafness, social deviance or lack of engagement, odd interests in the nonsocial world, and language delay (Chawarska, Klin, & Volkmar, 2008). Despite the apparent early onset, issues of diagnosis in infants remain complex. The complexities arise from the relative dearth of robust screening instruments and approaches until the infant reaches about 18 months, and even when concerns arise, diagnostic stability is clearly the case by age 3. The most common situation is one in which a child seemingly moves from more to less strictly defined autism, or vice versa. It is not uncommon for a child to have the social-communicative features of autism at 18–24 months but not to express the unusual restricted interests and repetitive behaviors until age 36 months. Often such children have some unusual interests, such as in fans or lights, that may presage the development of the more typical repetitive interests and behaviors.

Although autism is probably congenital, rarely, a child who seems classically autistic makes considerable progress and loses the diagnosis. A further complexity is introduced by the phenomenon of regression, typically reported in about 20% of cases. However, parental experiences of regression sometimes are clouded by failure to note early delays; sometimes development slows and the pattern of apparent regression is actually more one of relative stagnation (e.g., a child seems to say a few words and then doesn't progress at expected rates). Less commonly, a significant and major regression occurs. This phenomenon remains poorly understood but appears to be a relatively bad prognostic sign. In some rare cases the child develops normally until 4 or 5 years of age and then has, over a relatively short period of time, a catastrophic loss of skills often associated with anxiety and development of autistic presentation; the specific term for this phenomenon (childhood disintegrative disorder [CDD]) was included in *DSM-IV* but has been excluded in *DSM-5*. Development of newer approaches to diagnosis, such as those based on measures like neural correlates of the visual processing of face images (McPartland et al., 2011), may be important in this regard.

The ability to diagnose autism early in life has important implications for treatment as it seems likely that for many individuals earlier intervention leads to better outcome (Howlin, 2014). The issue assumes added urgency with the awareness that recurrence risk in younger siblings may approach 20%. Although delays in diagnoses remain frequent, the increased awareness of professionals and the lay public along with important changes in social policy (e.g., in the United States the mandate for schools to provide intervention starting at age 3) appear to have fostered better early identification. Both social interest and reports of behavior problems may increase as the child approaches the primary school years. In adolescence some individuals become highly motivated and make gains while others seem to lose skills. Epilepsy is relatively common in individuals with more "classic" autism, with peaks of onset in early childhood and again in adolescence; treatment of the seizures may complicate service provision. It is sadly the case that, despite the vast increase in research on autism, there is vanishingly little on adults in general and on their treatment needs in particular.

Psychological Perspectives

The social disturbance in autism is highly distinctive and consistently emerges as a, if not the, defining feature of the condition (Carter, Davis, Klin, & Volkmar, 2005). The social problems seen in autism are in marked contrast to normative social development where, from the moment of birth, the typically developing infant is interested in the human face and voice. From the perspectives of both psychology and neurobiology, the challenge is in understanding how these deficits arise and what their implications are for learning and development. There have been significant shifts in theoretical views over the decades since its first description.

The earliest theoretical approaches conceptualized autism as a disorder that arose within the context of deviant caretaking experience. A few early investigators did note the unusual pattern of variability in intellectual skills—often with some peak skills in nonverbal areas and occasional unusual or "savant" abilities (e.g., in memory, drawing, calendar calculation (Hermelin, 2001). Over time, a body of research began to suggest that autism was a brain-based disorder with a strong genetic component. In addition, work within developmental psychology made it clear that from the moment of birth the typically developing infant was remarkably social (raising questions about theoretical notions like a normative "autistic phase"

of development). By the 1970s and into 1980s theoretical approaches shifted to specific processes like perception, language, and attention. Although helpful in stimulating research, these approaches did not yield strong conceptual models for understanding the social dysfunction which appears to be the hallmark of the disorder. Indeed, in some ways it is only in recent years that the emphasis of psychological models began to shift to approaches emphasizing social information processing (paralleling, in some respects, the growing appreciation for the role of the social brain in the pathogenesis of these conditions (Brothers, 1990). The potential for examining possible genetic and brain mechanisms has given added urgency to these endeavors. Several theoretical approaches have been used in the past two decades.

The most productive theoretical model for research has been the theory of mind (ToM) hypothesis (Baron-Cohen, 1995). Social difficulties are viewed as a function of a basic difficulty in intersubjectivity, that is, of understanding the mental life of self and others. This view emphasizes that individuals with autism have major problems in understanding the intention, desires, and beliefs of others and in predicting others' behavior. Individuals with ASD, who are capable of understanding false beliefs when explicitly prompted to do so, are less capable of spontaneously anticipating an actor's behavior on the basis of the actor's false belief (Senju, Southgate, White, & Frith, 2009) or of taking the protagonist's innocent intentions into account to exculpate for accidental harms (Moran et al., 2011). Children with ASD are significantly impaired when interpreting pretense (Bigham, 2008), less able to make inferences based on event scripts in comprehending narratives (Nuske & Bavin, 2011), and worse at taking on another person's visual perspective, especially when it involves understanding that different people may experience seeing the same object differently at the same time (Hamilton, Brindley, & Frith, 2009). This model has focused on many of the significant communication problems in autism, for example, with pragmatic language, figurative language, and implied meaning. Some treatment approaches have been developed using it.

However, some problems arise given the very strong relationship of ToM skills to overall language ability. Another problem arises in that more cognitively able ASD individuals can do usual ToM problems but remain significantly socially impaired (Dahlgren & Trillingsgaard, 1996). A final, major, problem arises in that many of the earliest social manifestations of autism arise, in development well before ToM skills are typically manifest. Despite these limitations, this theoretical approach has generated a truly impressive body of research.

A different approach has centered on the group of "forward planning" and organizational skills subsumed under the term *executive functioning* (EF). These skills help the individual integrate the range of subtasks and the multitask processing allowing for efficient cognitive functioning in dealing with complex stimuli—like those involved in social interaction. The EF hypothesis in autism focuses on the many difficulties with perseveration, set-shifting, and organization (Corbett et al., 2009). EF skills appear to involve brain regions such as the dorsolateral prefrontal cortex that might also be involved in autism. A considerable body of work has indeed shown the persistent EF difficulties in individuals with autism. At a more global level, however, problems for the EF hypothesis arise given that these difficulties are not unique to autism, and levels of severity do not relate to degree of social impairment in a straightforward manner (Dawson et al.,1998). Put another way, executive functions are common in autism but seem more likely to be a consequence, rather than a fundamental cause, of the basic social difficulty (McGonigle-Chalmers & Alderson-Day, 2010; Zandt, Prior, & Kyrios, 2009).

Other approaches focus somewhat more directly on social skills. For example, the weak central coherence hypothesis (Frith, 1989) suggests that difficulty in understanding and integrating information into meaningful wholes results in problems with selective attention and appreciation of social meaning. Although of great interest, this approach has not had the same degree of empirical research as other models. Support for this approach comes from the identification of cognitive tasks in which individuals with autism may perform faster than typically developing individuals, for example, finding hidden shapes in drawings—a result not expected if weak central coherence is the case. This hypothesis is also consistent with the clinical observation that individuals with autism have difficulties using context, for example, in understanding narratives. Empirical support has been rather limited, and some investigators (Mottron, Burack, Iarocci, Belleville, & Enns, 2003) suggest that overarching language-decoding difficulties better account for fragmented perceptions. It could be argued that apparent problems with central coherence arise from autism, that is, individuals with autism may not, from the first days of life, be drawn to those socially based "framing" activities like face perception or eye contact that set the stage for subsequent learning. A slightly different model also centers on social deficits as the central aspect of autism. In the enactive mind the early development of cognition is viewed within the context of social experience as the early "frame" that helps shape how the infant perceives and acts on the world. In this model, an early deficit in social orientation leads to an overengagement and interest in the nonsocial world—that is, rather than using social contact as a beginning point for learning and using early social engagement as a way of exploring the world, the infant with autism looks for meaning in other ways, for example, in the search for simple contingencies (see Klin, Lin, Gorrindo, Ramsay, & Jones, 2009).

Biological Perspectives

Our understanding of the biological basis of autism has increased dramatically in the last decade. Progress has occurred in several areas, including genetics (State & Levitt, 2011) and neuroanatomy. Attempts have been made to link specific brain regions and processes to observed psychological phenomena. Genetic studies have revealed a large number of leads for genes potentially involved in the condition, many of which are related to cell-to-cell connections in the brain. At present, the significance of these findings remains unclear, but there is long-term potential for clarifying specific mechanisms that impact the brain generally and in specific regions.

The nature of the social brain in autism has been a major focus of research interest over the past decade. The term *social neuroscience* has been used in studying brain mechanisms that underlie social skills. Social perception refers to "the initial stages in the processing of information that culminates in the accurate analysis of the dispositions and intentions of other individuals" (Allison, Puce, & McCarthy, 2000, p. 1). Social perceptions are an ontogenetic and phylogenetic prequel to more sophisticated aspects of social cognition, including ToM skills. Successful social perception involves three distinct but interrelated social cognition abilities: (1) individuating and recognizing other people, (2) perceiving their emotional states, and (3) analyzing their intentions and motivations. Successful social perception, in turn, facilitates a fourth and more sophisticated aspect of social cognition: (4) representing another person's perceptions and beliefs, or "theory of mind."

Social perception has been of interest to psychologists for decades. For example, a major focus of Fritz Heider's (1958) work was the description of cognitive mechanisms for the perception of social objects. In collaboration with Mary-Ann Simmel, he provided elegant experimental demonstrations of the ways in which the perception of people differs from the perception of objects, particularly with regard to the attributions we make for each category of visual stimulus (Heider & Simmel, 1944). Psychological scientists commonly divvy up human cognitive abilities into memory, attention, reasoning, perception, etc. Our textbooks help to consecrate these categories, but nature does not respect the boundaries. Humans are, at their core, social and affective beings, but these essential characteristics have often been treated as sources of noise to be excluded from controlled experiments in the laboratories of cognitive psychologists. New discoveries have provided strong evidence for the need for new approaches regarding the unique ways in which the brain processes social information.

Neuroscientists became deeply interested in social perception when it was discovered that neurons within the temporal cortex and amygdaloidal complex of monkeys were sensitive to and selective for social objects (e.g., faces and hands) and complex social stimuli (actions in a social context and direction of gaze). On the basis of these seminal findings, researchers began to consider the possibility of a network of brain regions dedicated to processing social information. The label "social brain" was coined by Leslie Brothers (1990) and served to capture elegantly the core, emerging idea. The social brain is defined as the complex network of areas that enables us to recognize other individuals and to evaluate their mental states (e.g., intentions, dispositions, desires, and beliefs). The key idea is that human beings, in response to the unique computational demands of their highly social environments, have evolved cognitive mechanisms and associated, dedicated neural systems supporting such abilities as recognizing other agents and their

actions, individuating others, perceiving the emotional states of others, analyzing the intentions and dispositions of others, sharing attention with one another, and representing another person's perceptions and beliefs. Brothers (1990) emphasized the contributions of the superior temporal sulcus (STS), amygdala, orbital frontal cortex (OFC), and fusiform gyrus (FFG) to social perception. In humans, the STS region, particularly the right posterior STS, analyzes biological motion cues, including eye, hand, and other body movements, to interpret and predict the actions and intentions of others (e.g., Pelphrey, Morris, & McCarthy, 2005). The FFG, located in the ventral occipitotemporal cortex, contains a region termed the fusiform face area (FFA), which has been implicated in face detection (identifying a face as a face) and face recognition (identifying one's friend versus a stranger) (e.g., Kanwisher, McDermott, & Chun, 1997). The OFC has been strongly implicated in social reinforcement and reward processes more broadly (e.g., Rolls, 2000, 2009). Finally, the amygdala, a complex structure that is highly interconnected with cortical (including the STS and FFG) and other subcortical brain structures, has been implicated in helping to recognize the emotional states of others through analysis of facial expressions, as well as in multiple aspects of the experience and regulation of emotion.

To understand social brain function, we must be as attentive to the interconnections of neuroanatomical structures as we are to their individual contributions. Currently, in humans, much is known about the roles played by the individual brain regions, but very little is known about the ways in which they are interconnected, and thus even less is known about how they interact functionally. However, we can take some initial guidance from the monkey brain. Here, it is known that the STS region has reciprocal connections to the amygdala, which is connected to the OFC (Amaral, Price, Pitkanen, & Carmichael, 1992). The STS is also connected with the OFC, which is connected to the prefrontal cortex, itself connected to the motor cortex and the basal ganglia, thus completing what Allison and colleagues (2000) described as a pathway from social perception to social action.

More recent neuroimaging work in adult humans has revealed a small but remarkably consistent set of cortical regions in and around the posterior parietal cortex associated with thinking about other people's thoughts, or "theory of mind"; bilateral temporoparietal junction (TPJ), medial PFC, and posterior cingulate cortex (PC). The medial PFC is recruited during the processing of many kinds of information about people (Amodio & Frith, 2006), whereas the right TPJ is recruited selectively for thinking about thoughts (Saxe & Kanwisher, 2003).

Sabbagh (2004) reviewed evidence for an orbitofrontal/medial temporal circuit and argued that the ability to decode others' mental states from observable cues is different from the ability to reason about others' mental states. Using animations of rigid geometric shapes that depict social interactions versus false-belief stories, Gobbini, Koralek, Bryan, Montgomery, and Haxby (2007) showed that the two tasks activated distinctly different neural systems: The social animations activated a "social perception" system comprised of the STS, the frontal operculum, and inferior parietal lobule, whereas the false-belief stories activated a "mental state reasoning system" consisting of the TPJ, the anterior paracingulate cortex, and the posterior cingulate cortex or precuneus.

There is now clear behavioral and neuroimaging evidence for deficits in both the social perception and mental state reasoning systems in ASD. We review selected behavioral and neuroimaging evidence from the empirical record next.

The Social Perception System

Eye-tracking studies demonstrate that toddlers with ASD fail to orient to the social significance of biological motion; instead, they focus on nonsocial, physical contingencies, contingencies that are disregarded by neurotypical peers (Klin et al., 2009). In the auditory domain, Rutherford, Baron-Cohen, and Wheelwright (2002) showed that adults with ASD have difficulty decoding and extracting mental state information from vocalizations. With respect to visual signals, Kaiser et al. (2010), in an fMRI study, found that when young children were shown point-light displays of coherent versus scrambled biological motion, children with ASD, compared to unaffected siblings and typically developing peers, exhibited hypoactivation in the FFG, amygdala, ventromedial PFC, ventrolateral PFC, and posterior STS *in response to coherent motion.*

Other methods (e.g., evoked potential response to faces) have been used and suggest differences in face processing that converge with findings from the fMRI study mentioned earlier (McPartland & Pelphrey, 2012). These findings indicate widespread disruption of the social perception system in young children with ASD. Eye-gaze shifts that are difficult (versus easy) to decode (e.g., when a target shows up, the actor looks toward empty space, rather than the target) were found to differentially activate the STS region in typical adults but not in adults with ASD (Pelphrey et al., 2005). In addition, in fMRI research, activation of the FFG, but not the amygdala, can be altered to a normal level in individuals with ASD by compelling people with ASD to perform visual scanpaths that involve fixating on the eyes of a fearful face (Perlman, Hudac, Pegors, Minshew, & Pelphrey, 2011). With respect to auditory signals, individuals with ASD (versus controls) fail to activate the voice-selective regions of the STS in response to vocal sounds (Gervais et al., 2004).

The behavioral deficit in mental state reasoning in ASD has been linked to less activation in the TPJ region (Lombardo, Chakrabarti, Bullmore, & Baron-Cohen, 2011). Participants were asked to judge, "How likely is the British Queen to think that keeping a diary is important?" (mental state reasoning) or "How likely is the British Queen to have bony elbows?" (physical reasoning). In typical individuals, the TPJ region activated more strongly to mental state reasoning than physical reasoning; however, in individuals with ASD, there was no such selective activation in this region. Interestingly, there was no interaction between group and judgment condition in the dorsomedial PFC to the specific stimuli employed.

Genetics

The strong genetic basis of autism was suggested by the results of the first study contrasting rates of autism in identical and fraternal twins (Folstein & Rutter, 1978). Over the next several decades, evidence on the strong genetic basis of the condition continued to accumulate, and it gradually became clear that autism was likely a polygenic disorder. This task has been complicated by changes in diagnostic conceptualizations of the condition and the awareness that the broader autism phenotype moves past traditional boundaries of the condition. Unfortunately, research on the broader phenotype has lagged in important respects and there is not, as yet, agreement on the best approaches to characterize it. That being said, a large body of work, using rather different methodologies, has suggested that a number of potential genes (many involving synaptic connections) may be involved (Abrahams & Geschwind, 2008). It is of interest that genetic variants associated with autism have been linked to a number of different disorders. As Rutter and Thapar (2014) point out, these issues are complicated. Hopefully, over time, the expression of specific genes and genetic mechanisms can be studied in animal models.

In summary, it is clear that there is a very strong genetic contribution to autism, and potential leads have been identified in terms of specific genetic mechanisms. There has also been recognition that a broad spectrum of difficulties may be inherited, although the lack of good metrics relevant to functioning in this populations remains an obstacle for research.

References

Abrahams, B. S., & Geschwind, D. H. (2008). Advances in autism genetics: On the threshold of a new neurobiology [erratum appears in *Nature Reviews Genetics* 2008;9(6):493]. *Nature Reviews Genetics, 9*(5), 341–355.

Allison, T., Puce, A., & McCarthy, G. (2000). Social perception from visual cues: Role of the STS region. *Trends in Cognitive Sciences, 4,* 267–278.

Amaral, D. G., Price, J. L., Pitkanen, A., & Carmichael, S. T. (1992). Anatomical organization of the primate amygdaloid complex. In J. P. Aggleton (Ed.), *The amygdala: Neurobiological aspects of emotion, memory, and mental dysfunction* (pp. 1–66). New York: Wiley-Liss.

Amodio, D. M., & Frith, C. D. (2006). Meeting of minds: The medial frontal cortex and social cognition. *Nature Reviews Neuroscience, 7,* 268–277.

Baron-Cohen, S. (1995). What is theory of mind, and is it impaired in ASC? In S. Bölt & J. Hallmayer (Eds.), *Autism spectrum conditions: FAQs on autism, Asperger syndrome, and atypical autism answered by international experts* (pp. 136–138). Cambridge, MA: Hogrefe Publishing.

Bigham, S. (2008). Comprehension of pretense in children with autism. *British Journal of Developmental Psychology, 26,* 265–280.

Brothers, L. (1990). The social brain: A project for integrating primate behavior and neurophysiology in a new domain. *Concepts in Neuroscience, 1,* 27–51.

Brown, J. R., & Rogers, S. J. (2003). Cultural issues in autism. In R. L. Hendren, S. Ozonoff, & S. Rogers (Eds.), *Autism spectrum disorders* (pp. 209–226). Washington, DC: American Psychiatric Press.

Carter, A. S., Davis, N. O., Klin A., & Volkmar, F. R. (2005). Social development in autism. In F. R. Volkmar, A. Klin, R. Paul, & D. J. Cohen (Eds.), *Handbook of autism and pervasive developmental disorders* (Vol. 1, pp. 312–334). Hoboken, NJ: Wiley.

Chawarska, K., Klin, A., & Volkmar, F. (2008). *Autism spectrum disorders in infants and toddlers: Diagnosis, assessment, and treatment.* New York: Guilford Press.

Corbett, B. A., Constantine, L. J., Hendren, R., Rocke, D., & Ozonoff, S. (2009). Examining executive functioning in children with autism spectrum disorder, attention deficit hyperactivity disorder and typical development. *Psychiatry Research, 166,* 210–222.

Dahlgren, S. O., & Trillingsgaard, A. (1996). Theory of mind in non-retarded children with autism and Asperger's syndrome: A research note. *Child Psychology & Psychiatry & Allied Disciplines, 37,* 759–763.

Dawson, G., Meltzoff, A. N. Osterling, J., Rinaldi, J., & Brown, E. (1998). Children with autism fail to orient to naturally occurring social stimuli. *Journal of Autism and Developmental Disorders, 28,* 479–485.

Folstein, S., & Rutter, M. (1978). Genetic influences and infantile autism. *Annual Progress in Child Psychiatry & Child Development, 1978,* 437–441.

Fombonne, E. (2005). Epidemiological studies of pervasive developmental disorders. In F. R. Volkmar, A. Klin, R. Paul, & D. J. Cohen (Eds.), *Handbook of autism and pervasive developmental disorders* (Vol. 1, pp. 42–69). Hoboken, NJ: Wiley.

Frith, U. (1989). *Autism: Explaining the enigma.* London: Basil Blackwell.

Gervais, H., Belin, P., Boddaert, N., Leboyer, M., Coez, A., Sfaello, I., et al. (2004). Abnormal cortical voice processing in autism. *Nature Neuroscience, 7,* 801–802.

Gobbini, M. I., Koralek, A. C., Bryan, R. E., Montgomery, K. J., & Haxby, J. V. (2007). Two takes on the social brain: A comparison of theory of mind tasks. *Journal of Cognitive Neuroscience, 19,* 1803–1814.

Hamilton, A. F. D. C., Brindley, R., & Frith, U. (2009). Visual perspective taking impairment in children with autistic spectrum disorder. *Cognition, 113,* 37–44.

Heider, F. (1958). *The psychology of interpersonal relations.* New York: John Wiley & Sons.

Heider, F., & Simmel, M. (1944). An experimental study of apparent behavior. *American Journal of Psychology, 57,* 243–259.

Hermelin, B. (2001). *Bright splinters of the mind: A personal story of research with autistic savants.* London: Jessica Kingsley.

Howlin, P. (2014). Outcomes in adults with autism spectrum disorders. In F. R. Volkmar, R. Paul, S. R. Rogers, & K. A. Pelphrey (Eds.), *Handbook of autism and pervasive developmental disorders, 4th ed.* Hoboken, NJ: Wiley.

Kaiser, M. D., Hudac, C. M., Shultz, S., Lee, S. M., Cheung, C., Berken, A. M., et al. (2010). Neural signatures of autism. *Proceedings of the National Academy of Sciences of the United States of America, 107,* 21223–21228.

Kanner, L. (1943). Autistic disturbances of affective contact. *Nervous Child, 2,* 217–250.

Kanwisher, N., McDermott, J., & Chun, M. M. (1997). The fusiform face area: A module in human extrastriate cortex specialized for face perception. *Journal of Neuroscience, 17,* 4302–4311.

Klin, A., Lin, D. J., Gorrindo, P., Ramsay, G., & Jones, W. (2009). Two-year-olds with autism fail to orient towards human biological motion but attend instead to non-social, physical contingencies. *Nature, 459,* 257–261.

Lombardo, M. V., Chakrabarti, B., Bullmore, E. T., & Baron-Cohen, S. (2011). Specialization of right temporo-parietal junction for mentalizing and its relation to social impairments in autism. *NeuroImage, 56,* 1832–1838.

Lord, C., Petkova, E., Hus, V., Gan, W., Lu, F., et al. (2012). A multisite study of the clinical diagnosis of different autism spectrum disorders. *Archives of General Psychiatry, 69,* 306–313.

McGonigle-Chalmers, M., & Alderson-Day, B. (2010). Free classification as a window on executive functioning in autism spectrum disorders. *Journal of Autism and Developmental Disorders, 40*(7), 844–857.

McPartland, J. C., & Pelphrey, K. A. (2012). The implications of social neuroscience for social disability. *Journal of Autism and Developmental Disorders, 42,* 1256–1262.

McPartland, J. C., Reichow, B., & Volkmar, F. R. (2012). Sensitivity and specificity of proposed DSM-5 diagnostic criteria for autism spectrum disorder. *Journal of the American Academy of Child & Adolescent Psychiatry, 51,* 368–383.

McPartland, J. C., Wu, J., Bailey, C. A., Mayes, L. C., Shultz, R. T., & Klin, A. (2011)

Atypical neural specialization for social percepts in autism spectrum disorders. *Social Neuroscience, 6,* 436–451.

Moran, J. M., Young, L. L., Saxe, R., Lee, S. M., O'Young, D., Mavros, P. L., & Gabrieli, J. D. (2011). Impaired theory of mind for moral judgment in high-functioning autism. *Proceedings of the National Academy of Sciences of the United States of America, 108,* 2688–2692.

Mottron, L., Burack, J. A., Iarocci, G., Belleville, S., & Enns, J. T. (2003). Locally oriented perception with intact global processing among adolescents with high-functioning autism: Evidence from multiple paradigms. *Journal of Child Psychology & Psychiatry & Allied Disciplines, 44*(6), 904–913.

Nuske, H. J., & Bavin, E. L. (2011). Narrative comprehension in 4- to 7-year-old children with autism: Testing the Weak Central Coherence account. *International Journal of Language & Communication Disorders, 46,* 108–119.

Pelphrey, K. A., Morris, J. P., & McCarthy, G. (2005). Neural basis of eye gaze processing deficits in autism. *Brain, 128,* 1038–1048.

Puleo, C. M., Schmeidler, J., Reichenberg, A., Kolevzon, A., Soorya, L. V., Buxbaum, J. D., & Silverman, J. M. (2012). Advancing paternal age and simplex autism. *Autism, 16,* 367–380.

Perlman, S. B., Hudac, C. M., Pegors, T., Minshew, N. J., & Pelphrey, K. A. (2011). Look me in the eye: An experimental manipulation of activity in the face processing system of individuals with autism. *Social Neuroscience, 6,* 22–30.

Rolls, E. T. (2000). The orbitofrontal cortex and reward. *Cerebral Cortex, 10,* 284–294.

Rolls, E. T. (2009). Prefrontal contributions to reward encoding. In L. R. Squire (Ed.), *Encyclopedia of neuroscience* (pp. 895–903). Oxford, UK: Academic Press.

Rutherford, M. D., Baron-Cohen, S., & Wheelwright, S. (2002). Reading the mind in the voice: A study with normal adults and adults with Asperger syndrome and high functioning autism. *Journal of Autism and Developmental Disorders, 32,* 189–194.

Rutter, M. (1978). Diagnosis and definitions of childhood autism. *Journal of Autism & Developmental Disorders, 8,* 139–161.

Rutter, M., & Thapar, A. (2014). Genetics of autism spectrum disorder. In F. R. Volkmar, R. Paul, S. J. Rogers, & K. A. Pelphrey (Eds.), *Handbook of autism and pervasive developmental disorders, 4th ed.* Hoboken, NJ: John Wiley.

Sabbagh, M. A. (2004). Understanding orbitofrontal contributions to theory-of-mind reasoning: Implications for autism. *Brain and Cognition, 55,* 209–219.

Saxe, R., & Kanwisher, N. (2003). People thinking about thinking people: The role of the temporo-parietal junction in "theory of mind." *Neuroimage, 19,* 1835–1842.

Senju, A., Southgate, V., White, S., & Frith, U. (2009). Mindblind eyes: An absence of spontaneous theory of mind in Asperger syndrome. *Science, 325,* 883–885.

State, M. W., & Levitt, P. (2011). The conundrums of understanding genetic risks for autism spectrum disorders. *Nature Neuroscience, 14,* 1499–1506.

Volkmar, F. R., & Lord, C. (2007). Diagnosis and classification. In F. Volkmar (Ed.), *Autism and pervasive developmental disorders* (2nd ed., pp. 1–13). Cambrdige, UK: Cambridge University Press.

Volkmar, F. R., & Reichow, B. (2013). Autism in DSM-5: Progress and challenges. *Molecular Autism, 4,* 13.

Wolff, S. (2004). The history of autism. *European Child & Adolescent Psychiatry, 13,* 201–208.

Zandt, F., Prior, M., & Kyrios, M. (2009). Similarities and differences between children and adolescents with autism spectrum disorder and those with obsessive compulsive disorder: Executive functioning and repetitive behaviour. *Autism, 13,* 43–57.

20

Somatic Symptom and Related Disorders

THEO K. BOUMAN

Somatic sensations and bodily symptoms are part and parcel of everyday life, with about 75% of the general population experiencing some form of mild to severe physical complaint in any given month, and about one third reporting at least one general physical symptom over the previous year (Escobar et al., 2010). In most cases these symptoms subside spontaneously, but in about 25% of the sufferers they persist for a longer period, prompting them to contact their doctors for medical care. Studies in various countries around the world have found between 20% and 50% of the physical symptoms in primary and secondary care to be medically unexplained (see, e.g., Kroenke, 2003). Although many of these patients will be satisfied with negative medical examination results, a significant subgroup will continue to be concerned about the possibility of a yet-undiagnosed physical disease. These individuals are likely to continue to seek help for their physical symptoms, demand more physical examinations and specialist referrals, undergo laboratory tests, and, in rare cases, end up on an operating table. At the extreme, such illness behavior can seriously interfere with life activities and goals, resulting in clinically significant impairment. In these cases, in which somatic symptoms play a major part in an individual's life, a diagnosis in the *DSM-5* category of *somatic symptom and related disorders* becomes likely. Patients satisfying criteria for this diagnostics category will be found in medical rather than mental health care settings. When exhibiting persistent somatic symptoms and high levels of psychosocial distress, they are considered to be difficult patients by health care providers (Hinchey & Jackson, 2011; Van Wilgen, Koning, & Bouman, 2013). These conditions are generally distressing for the patient and those close to the person, are difficult to handle by health care providers, and lead to high costs in health care and high economic costs (e.g., sick leave) (Barsky, Orav, & Bates, 2005).

In the following sections a brief introduction will be given into the nature and classification of somatic symptom and related disorders, along with a discussion of auxiliary constructs. Next, each of these disorders listed in *DSM-5* will be discussed according to their clinical picture, historical roots, contemporary theoretical models, etiology, and course. This is followed by sections on diagnostic issues and general theoretical perspectives.

General Features

The feature that these *DSM-5* disorders share in common is the presence of at least one somatic symptom with either an established or an unclear medical etiology. This somatic condition is associated with psychological distress and psychosocial dysfunction on cognitive, behavioral, and emotional levels. The disorders are therefore defined by the presence of somatic, psychological, and behavioral characteristics (Dimsdale & Creed, 2010), rather than by the absence of an explanation for somatic symptoms. The *DSM-5* chapter on the somatic symptom and related disorders (SSRD) group consists of (a) somatic symptom disorder (SSD), (b) illness anxiety disorders (IAD), (c) functional neurological symptom disorder, (d) psychological factors affecting medical conditions, and (e) factitious disorder. A diagnosis of one of these SSRD can be made in addition to a general medical condition regardless of whether the latter is a well-recognized disease or a functional somatic syndrome, such as fibromyalgia or chronic fatigue syndrome.

Generally speaking, reliable information on the prevalence of these and similar conditions is usually limited. This is largely because epidemiological studies have used various and ever-changing diagnostic criteria, as well as a large variety of samples drawn from the general population or from specific medical settings. The assumed low base rates of these conditions in the general population are another obstacle to obtaining reliable prevalence rates. De Waal, Arnold, Eekhof, and Van Hemert (2004) estimated a prevalence of about 16% for the diagnostic group of *DSM-IV* somatoform disorders in general practice.

Development of the *DSM* Classification

The *DSM* classification of disorders in which somatic symptoms predominate has a long and complex history with lot of controversy and debate. *DSM-I* identified the group of *psychophysiologic autonomous and visceral disorders*, consisting of reactions that "represent the visceral expression of affect which may be thereby largely prevented from being conscious. The symptoms are due to a chronic and exaggerated state of normal physiological expression of emotion, with the feeling, or subjective part being repressed" (p. 41). In later *DSM* versions, disorders previously classified in one single category as neuroses (anxiety neurosis, neurotic depression, hypochondriasis, and hysteria) were reclassified in four separate categories: anxiety disorders, mood disorders, somatoform disorders, and dissociative disorders.

The broad descriptive classification of *somatoform disorders* put forward in *DSM-IV* originated from the *DSM-III* effort to rid psychiatric taxonomy of the concept of neurosis with its etiological psychodynamic connotations. *DSM-IV* stated that the common feature of the somatoform disorders is the presence of physical symptoms that suggest a general medical condition (hence, the term *somatoform*) and are not fully explained

by a general medical condition, nor by the direct effects of substance or by another mental disorder (e.g., anxiety disorder or depression). Therefore, by definition, somatoform disorders could only be diagnosed by exclusion. As an additional diagnostic requirement, these physical symptoms and the related illness behaviors should result in substantial personal, social, and occupational impairment. It is important to note that the physical symptoms should not be feigned or voluntarily produced, as is the case in malingering or factitious disorder.

The closest counterpart to the somatic symptom and related disorders section in *DSM-5* is, therefore, the *DSM-IV-TR* section entitled "somatoform disorders." The hallmark disorders within that somatoform grouping were

- somatization disorder,
- undifferentiated somatoform disorder,
- conversion disorder,
- pain disorder,
- hypochondriasis, and
- body dysmorphic disorder.

The dissatisfaction with the emphasis on medically unexplained symptoms as a common denominator, the unreliability of the diagnoses, and the overlap between symptoms of diagnostic categories (Kroenke, Sharpe, & Sykes, 2007) prompted the *DSM-5* task force to take a new stance. The emphasis shifted from functional (even unexplained) somatic symptoms to maladaptive cognitions, emotions, and behaviors related to somatic symptoms of whatever nature. In contrast to *DSM-IV-TR*, the hallmark disorders within the corresponding *DSM-5* section are

- somatic symptom disorder,
- illness anxiety disorder,
- conversion disorder,
- psychological factors affecting medical condition, and
- factitious disorder.

While this chapter is structured around the *DSM-5* list, the clinical and research literatures relate more clearly to the *DSM-IV-TR* categories, so it is important to briefly spell out the correspondences between them:

- *DSM-5* somatic symptom disorder is the coalescence of somatization disorder, undifferentiated somatoform disorder, pain disorder, and hypochondriasis. Of these three, pain disorder is the only one to be somewhat differentiated within somatic symptom disorder—by means of a specifier rather than a distinct disorder.

- *DSM-5* illness anxiety disorder is derived from two *DSM-IV-TR* sources: the illness subtype within simple phobia (which was and is an anxiety disorder) and hypochondriasis.
- Conversion disorder largely remains, but with a new name: functional neurological symptom disorder.
- Factitious disorder is new to this *DSM-5* grouping, having had its own chapter in *DSM-IV-TR*.
- Psychological factors affecting medical condition were part of the *DSM-IV-TR* Appendix, entitled "Other conditions that may be the focus of clinical attention."
- Finally, in *DSM-5*, body dysmorphic disorder has been located in a new chapter, obsessive-compulsive and related disorders.

In conclusion, the history of *DSM* classification shows a shift from mere somatic symptom count and the assumption of etiological factors to a more descriptive approach and the acknowledgment of psychological factors that are associated with any type of somatic symptoms.

Auxiliary and Historical Concepts

The interplay between body and mind is probably one of the most enigmatic of all clinical, empirical, and philosophical topics. In the Western world, scholars traditionally sought to understand this relationship by deciphering how body and mind influence each other. Despite the evidence for considerable comorbidity and phenomenological overlap between psychological and somatic disorders, the Cartesian mind–body dualism is still implicitly or explicitly influential. This may be partly due to the traditional division of labor (at least in the twenty-first century in the Western world) between medical and psychological disciplines, each claiming (or hoping) to answer some of the questions in the realm of body and mind. Such dualistic models, however, are a serious obstacle to our understanding of the complex area described in this chapter, since their basic premise is untenable. There is broad agreement among

most contemporary researchers that genetic, environmental, behavioral, cognitive, and physiological variables interact at any time (commonly referred to as the *biopsychosocial model*; Engel, 1960). Hence, current theories of somatic symptom (and indeed of most other) disorders seek to account for this interplay, although they may differ in their emphasis on the contributions of its components. We will now briefly mention some frequently used concepts meant to highlight the relationship between somatic symptoms and the ways the individual deals with these.

The distinction between *disease* and *illness* reflects the traditional debate on the assumed objective and subjective nature of somatic symptoms and complaints. In a conceptual analysis of these and related terms, Boyd (2000, p. 10) states: "Disease then, is the pathological process, deviation from a biological norm. Illness is the patient's experience of ill health, sometimes when no disease can be found. Sickness is the role negotiated with society." However simple these distinctions seem to be, when the author analyzes their dictionary, practical, and philosophical status, the concepts appear to be rather elusive, often being used interchangeably.

When addressing the mind–body interaction, the concept of *somatization*, originally coined by Stekel (1943), plays an important role. Lipowsky (1988) defines somatization as a tendency to experience and express psychological distress in the form of somatic symptoms that individuals misinterpret as serious physical illness and for which they seek medical help. This definition reflects the current view of somatization as a complex interactive psychopathological process, rather than a discrete group of disorders. Kellner (1986) states that somatization is neither a discrete clinical entity nor the result of a single pathological process; instead, it cuts across diagnostic categories, such as depression, anxiety, and SSRD. Somatization, therefore, is not a diagnosis but an explanatory process.

A related concept is that of *psychosomatic disorders*, which have been defined as medical conditions in which psychological factors are assumed to play an etiological role. Alexander (1950) described seven classic psychosomatic illnesses: bronchial asthma, ulcerative colitis, thyrotoxicosis, essential hypertension, rheumatoid arthritis, neurodermatitis, and peptic ulcer. The psychosomatic concept has been criticized as being unhelpful (Lipowsky, 1988) because it presupposes that these disorders are caused by a single and identifiable psychogenic etiology and, as such, are incompatible with contemporary multicausal models and the ensuing empirical evidence.

In medical contexts clinicians often refer to *medically unexplained symptoms (MUS)* or *functional somatic symptoms* or *syndromes (FSS)*. MUS refers to physical symptoms for which no clear or consistent organic pathology can be demonstrated. Implicitly or explicitly psychological causes for these symptoms are assumed. FSS implies a disturbance or alteration in bodily functions, rather than in anatomical structure. However, this begs the question if it implies that the symptoms cannot be explained by routine medical examinations or, more specifically, by specialist diagnostic procedures. Then again, it remains unclear what kind of explanation has to be excluded for these terms to be applicable. Interestingly, every medical specialty has its own set of unexplained symptoms and syndromes, such as atypical chest pain in cardiology and irritable bowel syndrome in gastroenterology (Kanaan, Lepine, & Wessely, 2007; Stone, 2009). Wessely, Nimnuan, and Sharpe (1999) postulated that the existence of specific somatic syndromes is largely an artifact of medical specialization, in view of the considerable overlap in phenomenology, similar diagnostics criteria for different syndromes, and many patients having multiple somatic symptoms. It appears that the application of either of these concepts depends on the medical or psychiatric context in which the patient is encountered. Many functional syndromes described in general medicine are similar to syndromes described in various psychiatric categories, adding to their diagnostic confusion and unclear communication with patients.

Thus the domain of body–mind interaction contains many competing and often overlapping concepts and hence presents many challenges for conceptual clarification. Authors tend to choose their terminology according to their theoretical frame of reference, the clinical or research context, and philosophical versus empirical arguments. Many have criticized these and related concepts on the basis of their lack of patient acceptability, their lack of conceptual clarity, and the implicit mind–body dualism (e.g., Creed et al., 2010). Mentioning and analyzing these concepts, Eriksen, Kirkengen, and Vetlesen (2013) went even further, gloomily stating that "despite the fact that these efforts remain medically, scientifically and politically legitimate, it remains equally obvious that this activity does not steer the sciences towards a deeper insight or better knowledge concerning these phenomena" (p. 591).

Overview of Somatic Symptom and Related Disorders

Somatic Symptom Disorder

Clinical Picture   The *DSM-5* diagnosis of *somatic symptom disorder* (SSD) encompasses four previous *DSM-IV* disorders: pain disorder, somatization disorder, hypochondriasis, and undifferentiated somatoform disorder. This new diagnosis is a typical example of lumping, based on the claim by a group of experts, in which the similarities of the four disorders outweigh their differences (Dimsdale & Creed, 2010). The central issue in this disorder is the presence of somatic symptoms that are distressing and result in a significant disruption of daily life. These symptoms can be either normal bodily sensations or medically unexplained symptom. They may be localized (as in pain) or nonspecific (as in fatigue). In order to qualify for the diagnosis of SSD the patient should in addition exhibit misattributions, excessive concern, anxiety, or preoccupation related to the symptoms. When this condition lasts for at least 6 months it is specified as *persistent*, whereas a duration of less than 6 months allows for the diagnosis of *brief SSD*. *DSM-5* mentions one specifier, namely SSD with predominant pain (previously pain disorder).

SSD has already been criticized because its criteria might be met too easily: if one is suffering from a medical illness and (quite understandably) is worrying about it a lot, one would already qualify for the diagnosis (Frances, 2013). It remains to be seen if these criteria will appear to be overinclusive, since in clinical practice patients with established diseases who are overly concerned might also be assigned the SSD diagnosis. Another complicating factor is that SSD may show high comorbidity with another medical condition. Other authors specifically criticize Criterion B ("excessive thoughts, feelings, and behaviors related to somatic symptoms or associated health concerns") because its three components blur into each other, are difficult to differentiate, and depend on the clinician's subjective assessment (First, 2011), thus precluding a reliable assessment. From a communicative point of view, it might be difficult for SSD to be accepted as a diagnosis by both health care professionals and patients since it has a very abstract connotation and is not embedded in everyday language (cf. Starcevic, 2006). In addition, SSD as a category is part of the chapter on *somatic symptom and related disorders*. It is fair to assume that this unfortunate nomenclature will lead to substantial semantic confusion both in research and in clinical practice.

Because this diagnostic category has only come into existence with the advent of *DSM-5*, is has not yet been part of a research tradition. However, in order to be provide an overview of theoretical perspectives, prevalence, onset and course, we will dwell on the knowledge available on the earlier *DSM-IV* diagnoses of pain disorder, somatization disorder, and hypochondriasis, all three of which contribute to the full picture of SSD. Having said this, it would have been helpful if *DSM-5*, to retain historical scientific continuity, would have also included specifiers for polysymptomatic and hypochondriacal variants, in addition to the pain specifier.

Somatic Symptom Disorder: The Somatization Disorder Legacy

The *DSM-IV* diagnosis of somatization disorder required a relatively large number of somatic symptoms, in various categories, that were medically unexplained and were not being feigned. In order to qualify for this diagnosis, the patient needed to have been suffering from this condition for many years. In contrast to this, in *DSM-5*, SSD emphasizes the individuals' ways of responding to at least one distressing somatic symptom, which can be either medically explained or unexplained. *DSM-5* thereby puts the weight on psychological rather than medical aspects of the disorder.

For many years, somatization disorder has been a rather unsatisfying diagnosis for which numerous alternatives and variants have been proposed. Surveying the literature may, therefore, be rather confusing because of the many (seemingly) synonymous concepts that have been proposed. Examples are *somatization, abridged somatization disorder* (Escobar, Waitzkin, Silver, Gara, & Holman, 1998), *multisomatoform disorder* (Jackson & Kroenke, 2008), *functional somatic symptoms, body distress disorder,* or *medically unexplained symptoms*.

The disorder has a low prevalence and leads to frequent and multiple medical consultations, a complex medical history, and alterations of the person's lifestyle, such as frequent absences from work or school, and excessive use of drugs and alcohol.

Historical Perspectives Somatization disorder builds upon the classical concepts of hysteria and dissociation and has a historical link with conversion disorder. These features will be discussed in this chapter under the heading Conversion Disorder, together with theoretical insights into the underlying mechanisms.

In the middle of the nineteenth century, the French physician Pierre Briquet described a polysymptomatic somatic condition, for many decades known as Briquet's syndrome. Guze and Perley (1963) redefined this syndrome as *somatization disorder* in the 1960s, as a precursor of the *DSM-III* diagnostic criteria. In subsequent revisions of the *DSM*, the number of somatic symptoms required in order to assign the diagnosis has gradually been reduced—for instance, from at least 13 out of 35 symptoms in *DSM-III-R* to only 8 symptoms divided over four symptom clusters in *DSM-IV-TR*. As mentioned earlier, in *DSM-5* this reduction has been furthered, to the requirement of at least one somatic symptom.

Predominant Pain (Previously Pain Disorder)

Pain is ipso facto a subjective phenomenon and constitutes the most common complaint of individuals presenting to a physician (Ford, 1995). Psychological factors such as cognitions, emotions, and attention are involved in the onset, maintenance, or exacerbation of pain, and they therefore complicate differential diagnosis (Kroenke et al., 2007). Although there is a considerable overlap between the *DSM-IV* diagnosis of pain disorder and the *DSM-5* diagnosis of SSD with predominant pain as a specifier, the latter has dropped the criterion that the pain should not be intentionally feigned. Also, the *DSM-IV* specifiers of pain being associated with psychological factors and/or a general medical condition have been omitted.

For a better understanding of the central phenomenon of this diagnostic category we will briefly go into pain itself. Chronic pain, in particular, is often associated with major changes in behavior, such as decreased activity and somatic preoccupation (Pilowsky, Chapman, & Bonica, 1977). What ultimately brings people into treatment is not so much the intensity of perceived pain, but rather the psychological costs of their pain management (Dahl, Wilson, & Nilsson, 2004). In their attempt to struggle against chronic pain, people put their lives on hold and become increasingly disconnected from their family, friends, work, and recreation (Dahl & Lundgren, 2007).

Common pain locations are back, head, abdomen, and chest, and most research has been conducted in low-back pain. The estimated prevalence of chronic pain (irrespective of its location) in the general population is substantial, and it is a relatively common phenomenon affecting adults of all ages. Benedek (2007) has estimated that 25%–30% of the U.S. population suffers from some form of a chronic pain condition. Australian researchers (Blyth et al., 2001), interviewing over 17,000 randomly selected adult members of the general population, found that 17.1% of males and 20% of females reported having chronic pain. This condition was related to receiving disability or unemployment benefits and experiencing psychological distress and interference with daily activities. Among European adults, 19% (from a sample of over 46,000 recruited in 15 countries) reported having chronic pain of moderate to severe intensity; few individuals were seen by a pain specialist, and almost 50% experienced inadequate pain management (Breivik et al., 2006). Chronic pain prevalence in primary care varies considerably across the world, with a mean of about 22% (range 6%–40%) and chances of recovery after 12 months of about 50% (Gureje, Simon, & Von Korff, 2001).

Historical Perspectives   Throughout history, there has been considerable speculation concerning the nature and cause of pain. For instance, Aristotle thought pain was an emotion, not a sensation; Descartes viewed it as a result of physical stimuli impinging on the body; Epictetus saw it as the result of cognitive activity; and religious leaders looked at it as a test of faith imposed by God or as punishment for sins (Turk, Meichenbaum, & Genest, 1983). A commonality of these early theories is a unidimensional view of pain. Theories were based on either organic or psychological causes, and few attempted to integrate the two. It was not until the twentieth century that Cartesian dualism was seriously questioned and multidimensional theories of pain began to develop.

Contemporary Theoretical Perspectives   Pain itself serves protective and survival purposes for the organism, in which the peripheral and central nervous systems are involved. Brain areas related to emotions have a modulating effect on the processing of pain stimuli (nociception). In chronic pain, the immediate physical cause has subsided, and psychological and behavioral aspects are thought to influence the experience of pain. Melzack and Wall (1965) formulated the gate-control theory, stating that the spinal cord functions as a gate in which some factors increase pain sensations, and other factors lead to a decrease.

Fordyce's (1976) behavioral theory states that maladaptive pain behavior is acquired through respondent conditioning (*sensory pain*) and maintained through operant conditioning (*psychological pain*). Verbal reports and nonverbal expressions of pain are maintained because of associated positive (e.g., financial benefits, attention, concern, or sympathy) and negative reinforcers (e.g., avoidance of or escape from undesirable stimuli such as work or unwanted social interaction). Additionally, in the absence of direct exposure to environmental contingencies, pain behavior may be acquired or taught through modeling (Craig, 1986). Although respondent and operant conditioning are different processes, the two may interact from the onset to further worsening of pain behavior. For instance, the avoidance of physical activity can lead to muscle fibers shortening and losing elasticity. This can be very painful and, as a consequence, individuals tend to avoid or escape from physical activity. Such avoidance and escape are negatively reinforced when they lead to a short-term decrease of pain. On the other hand, a long-term cost is also frequently incurred because avoidance and escape may exacerbate the physical condition of the individual, resulting in a vicious circle ultimately enabling chronic pain (Flor, Knost, & Birbaumer, 2002).

Social contextual variables are also thought to influence the development of chronic pain. If pain behavior is reinforced more than alternative behavior (e.g., pain coping without complaining), it is likely that it will increase and healthy behavior will decrease. It has been repeatedly found that pain behavior is particularly susceptible to social reinforcement (Flor, Kerns, & Turk, 1987). In an experimental analogue study, Sullivan, Adams, and Sullivan (2004) found that in the presence of an observer, high-pain catastrophizers showed a propensity to engage in strategies (e.g., facial displays and vocalizations) that more effectively communicate their pain. In their communal coping model it is postulated that this behavioral coping strategy is employed to elicit emotional and/ or tangible support from others, thereby positively reinforcing pain and illness behaviors and undermining successful adaptation to pain.

Contemporary information-processing models, as well as cognitive-behavioral conceptualizations, emphasize that pain behavior is due to negative or unrealistic expectations about experiencing pain, as well as to low levels of perceived competence to deal with pain. In particular, pain-catastrophizing cognitions have been found to be associated with increased pain awareness and persistence, disability, lower pain tolerance, and the failure to disengage from pain stimuli (Quartana, Campbell, & Edwards, 2009). These cognitions often lead to avoidance of particular situations, which may result in further negative expectations regarding the ability to control and cope with pain. The fear-avoidance model (Vlaeyen, Kole-Snijders, Boeren, & Van Eek, 1995) stipulates that interpreting pain as a signal of threat leads to fear and, subsequently, to the avoidance of physical activity. In the long run, this avoidance leads to inactivity and a worsened physical condition, increasing the experience of pain. Additionally, it is has been found that the expectation of intense pain will amplify the actual nociceptive input.

Differences in coping styles are particularly important for the resultant perception of pain and associated mood states (Turk, Okifuji, & Scharff, 1995) and may also affect the impact of the pain stimulus (Asmundson & Norton, 1995). Perceived competence influences how intense pain is experienced, how much disturbance it elicits, and whether the individual engages in adaptive or maladaptive coping behavior (Schermelleh-Engel, Eifert, Moosbrugger, & Frank, 1997). Coping behavior seems to be directly influenced by a person's perceived level of competence and only indirectly influenced by pain intensity and pain-related anxiety and depression.

Onset and Course   Most pain is usually of relative short duration and can be the result of tissue damage, injury, or disease. The development of chronic pain can be understood from the theoretical models discussed previously, as a complex interplay between nociceptive, cognitive, behavioral, and social factors. Chronic pain subsides after 1 year in about 50% of patients (Gureje, Simon, & Von Korff, 2001), but in some individuals it may last for many decades. In this case impaired daily functioning, sick leave, unemployment, and disability benefits may be the consequence. The course may vary substantially between individuals.

Somatic Symptom Disorder: The Hypochondriasis Legacy

The *DSM* distinguishes between health-anxious patients who suffer from at least one distressing somatic symptom (and who should be diagnosed as having SDD) and those who are free of somatic symptoms (who should be diagnosed as having illness anxiety disorder; see discussion later in this chapter). The health-anxious variant of SSD resembles the previous diagnosis of hypochondriasis (which has been abandoned in *DSM-5*), which we will discuss here to provide some insight into its clinical picture and mechanisms.

Hypochondriasis is characterized by unjustified fears or convictions that one has a serious and often fatal illness, such as heart disease, cancer, or AIDS. Patients frequently seek reassurance, check their bodies, and avoid illness-related triggers (such as bodily sensations and medical information). Merely informing the patient of the absence of a disease process or explaining the benign nature of the somatic symptoms only results in temporary relief that is followed by renewed worry over symptoms and continuing overuse of medical services (Abramowitz & Braddock, 2008). As Starcevic (2006) has stated, "Overall, hypochondriasis may be characterized less by medically unexplained symptoms than by a dysfunctional style of appraising and experiencing health, illness, and physical symptoms, and by the corresponding abnormal illness behavior" (p. 280).

Prevalence studies related to full-blown hypochondriasis yield widely varying results because of the use of diverse samples, settings, definitions, and assessment techniques. Studies using self-report questionnaires estimate the prevalence of health anxiety in the general population to be around 7% (e.g., Rief, Hessel, & Braehler, 2001). A systematic review (Creed & Barsky, 2004) found a median prevalence of 4.2% in seven primary care studies. In other studies, the full diagnosis of hypochondriasis has a prevalence of about 1% in primary care (De Waal et al., 2004;

Gureje, Ustun, & Simon, 1997). In a very large sample (n = 28.991) in UK medical specialist clinics, Tyrer et al. (2011) found a prevalence of 19.8% of health anxiety (i.e., not hypochondriasis) based on a cut-off score on a self-report measure. An Australian study (Sunderland, Newby, & Andrews, 2013) established a lifetime prevalence of 5.7% and a point prevalence of 3.4% in 8,841 members of the general population. However diverse these estimates are, given the variations in operationalization and methodology, they suggest a considerable prevalence of this condition. In most studies no consistent and significant gender differences for hypochondriasis have been found.

Historical Perspectives The concept of hypochondriasis (a Greek word meaning "below the cartilage") was derived from the humoral theories of disease and illness; it was considered a special form of melancholia resulting from an excess of black bile. In the seventeenth century, Thomas Sydenham, an English physician, argued that hypochondriasis occurred only in men and was equivalent to hysteria occurring in females. Freud (1956) suggested that hypochondriacal patients direct their libido inward, whereas healthy persons typically direct their libido at external objects. He theorized that internally directed libido would build up and result in physical symptoms. Other psychodynamic theories of hypochondriasis suggested that physical symptoms defended against low self-esteem, because a sick body is attached to fewer stigmas than a sick mind. Although psychodynamic theories provided a more comprehensive account of hypochondriasis than earlier pseudomedical theories, there is virtually no empirical evidence to support any of their underlying notions (Abramowitz & Braddock, 2008). In recent clinical and research literature, hypochondriasis as a concept has been increasingly abandoned because of its assumed stigmatizing connotation, and it has gradually been replaced by the more neutral concept of health anxiety.

Contemporary Theoretical Perspectives Cognitive-behavioral models emphasize the misinterpretation of innocuous bodily sensations, particularly if the nature and consequences of such sensations are difficult to understand by the patient. Research data are in support of the main features of the cognitive-behavioral model proposed by Warwick and Salkovskis (1990; Salkovskis & Warwick,

2001), in which they hypothesized that the onset and maintenance of hypochondriasis involves the complex interaction of cognitive, attentional, and behavioral factors. Williams (2004) provided an overview of the information-processing literature on health anxiety and found that selective attention to illness information, risk perception, misinterpretation of benign somatic symptoms, and cognitive responses to medical reassurance are well-documented maintaining factors for this condition. In a meta-analysis, Marcus, Gurley, Marchi, and Bauer (2007) found that health-anxious individuals hold dysfunctional beliefs and assumptions about illness-related constructs. Examples of these are the catastrophic interpretation of innocuous physical sensations and the belief that good health is associated with the absence of bodily symptoms. Weck, Neng, Richtberg, and Stangier (2012) observed that patients diagnosed with hypochondriasis indeed have more restrictive concepts about good health than do anxious and normal controls. However, it has not been convincingly demonstrated that triggering these assumptions leads to increased hypochondriacal concerns. In addition, patients diagnosed with hypochondriasis experience high levels of somatosensory amplification (i.e., a tendency to experience a broad range of bodily sensations as noxious, intense, and disturbing) and body vigilance (i.e., a persons' conscious attendance to internal cues) (Olatunji, Daecon, Abramowitz, & Valentiner, 2007), although these elevations were also found in patients suffering from panic disorder and generalized anxiety disorder. In their meta-analysis, Marcus and colleagues (2007) also noted the possibility that health-anxious individuals may be more sensitive to some aversive stimuli, but that there is little evidence of a positive relationship between health anxiety and the ability to perceive autonomic processes accurately.

Whereas most contemporary models focus on the individual patient, Noyes et al. (2003) tested an interpersonal model of hypochondriasis and found this condition to be associated with an insecure (especially fearful) attachment style. The researchers assume that a person may communicate his or her need for care through illness behavior.

Onset and Course It is generally believed that the onset lies in early adulthood, although in individual patients the disorder may start at any age. The course is often chronic, but remission (also known as transient hypochondriasis) can occur. For example, Barsky, Wool, Barnett, and Cleary (1994) found in a 5-year prospective study that 36.5% of patients no longer met criteria for hypochondriasis. The reasons for this transient state are not well understood (Williams, 2004).

Illness Anxiety Disorder

Clinical Picture The term *illness anxiety disorder* (IAD) was first coined in *DSM-5* to diagnose patients with no or only minimal somatic symptoms but exhibiting high illness anxiety for at least 6 months. They engage in various kinds of checking, avoiding, and reassurance-seeking behaviors and excessive health care utilization, features that are also considered typical for patients suffering from hypochondriasis. When the disorder lasts for less than 6 months the diagnosis should be *brief IAD*; another variant is *IAD without excessive health-related behaviors*. In comparison with the *DSM-IV*, this condition may be considered hypochondriasis without prominent somatic symptoms.

Historical Perspectives The *DSM-IV* diagnosis of specific phobia ("other type") mentioned the fear of contracting an illness that the individual does not have. This specifier has been deleted from *DSM-5*. Hypochondriasis, by contrast, is characterized by a preoccupation with a disease that a person believes to be present (i.e., disease conviction). Noyes, Carney, and Langbehn (2004) summarized the empirical findings on illness phobia and concluded that is a common condition in the general population, with prevalence rates as high as 4%. They also pointed to cognitive and behavioral differences between illness phobia and hypochondriasis that are related to the absence or presence of somatic illness.

Contemporary Theoretical Perspectives At present there are no specific models available for IAD, other than those for hypochondriasis. Misinterpretation of bodily symptoms leads to heightened anxiety, which in turn gives rise to anxiety-reducing behaviors such as checking, avoiding, and reassurance seeking. A research agenda for the near future would include the general question of whether the etiological and maintaining mechanisms of this condition differ from those of the traditional diagnosis of hypochondriasis and from the *DSM-5* diagnosis of SSD with excessive health anxiety.

Conversion Disorder (Functional Neurological Symptom Disorder)

Clinical Picture Patients with conversion disorder present with altered voluntary motor or sensory function that is incompatible with a known medical or neurological condition. The disorder may involve motor symptoms or deficits (e.g., paralysis), seizures or convulsions, sensory symptom or deficit (e.g., blindness, anesthesia, and aphonia), or a mixed presentation. *DSM-5* allows for eight symptom specifiers, such as *weakness or paralysis, swallowing symptoms,* and *attacks or seizures.* A classic example is "glove anesthesia," in which the patient complains of numbness of the hand; however, such a sensation does not conform to the body's innervation pattern (i.e., dermatomes). *DSM-5* requires positive evidence for the disorder and presents a list of examples of tests to establish these. A practical guideline has also been presented by Stone (2009), who has mentioned numerous tests and diagnostic considerations for so-called functional neurological symptoms.

Although most patients with conversion disorder experience extreme distress over their bodily symptoms, some patients manifest an indifference to, or lack of worry about, their symptoms (so called *belle indifference*). However, this indifference has been found to be present in patients with known medical diseases as well, so it is not exclusively a characteristic of conversion disorder (Roelofs & Spinhoven, 2007).

Though common in the nineteenth century, conversion disorder has become an exceedingly rare condition in the Western world. For example, De Waal et al. (2004) found a prevalence of 0.2% in general medical practice in The Netherlands. Conversion disorder is usually found in young people and is five times more common in women than in men. The condition is more common in persons living in rural areas and of lower socioeconomic status with limited medical or psychological knowledge. In non-Western countries, prevalence rates are significantly higher. For example, Sar, Akyüz, Dogan, and Öztü (2009) screened a considerable sample ($n = 628$) of women of the general population in a semirural area in Turkey, using *DSM*-based semi-structured interviews and questionnaires. They established a lifetime prevalence of a staggering 48.7%. Scrutinizing this article's tables, it is quite remarkable to find dizziness, fainting, and vomiting to be the most prevalent conversion symptoms, which raises the question about the precise definition and reliability of the diagnosis of conversion disorder.

In a systematic review including 27 studies over a 40-year period, Stone et al. (2005) estimated how often patients with an initial diagnosis of conversion symptoms are subsequently given a neurological diagnosis that, in hindsight, explained their original symptoms. They found a steep decline from 29% in the 1950s to only 4% in current practice. They attributed this decline to poor diagnostic quality of the initial studies, which used rather vague definitions of "hysteria."

Historical Perspectives The origin of the contemporary concept of conversion disorder can be traced back to Hippocrates in ancient Greece, when the more generic concept of *hysteria* referred to diseases caused by a "wandering womb" in women. The clinical picture consisted of a wide variety of chronic somatic symptoms and diseases. For many centuries this concept contained what came to be known as conversion disorder and somatization disorder. In the second half of the twentieth century, the polysymptomatic constellation led to the diagnosis of somatization disorder (see earlier discussion), whereas symptoms that suggested a deficit in neurological functioning, but without a neurological explanation, gave rise to the current concept of conversion disorder (see Allin, Streeruwitz, & Curtis, 2005 for a historical overview).

The nineteenth-century French neurologist Charcot demonstrated that "hysterical conversions" involving symptoms such as convulsions and paralysis could be induced by using hypnotic techniques. Based on such observations, he assumed that these symptoms originated from mental rather than physical processes. Physical symptoms were regarded as a defense mechanism against unacceptable unconscious conflicts such that massive repression had forced psychic energy to be transformed (or converted; hence the term *conversion*) into bodily symptoms (Freud, 1956). Pierre Janet first suggested a relation between conversion disorder and childhood trauma, at the end of the nineteenth century. Thus the name *conversion disorder* is a lingering vestige of the psychodynamic influence. It has been conceptualized as a dissociation of cognitive, sensory, and motor processes that occurs as an adaptation to an overwhelming traumatic experience.

In *DSM-II* it was grouped with dissociation disorder under the new diagnostic category of "hysterical neurosis." In these earlier versions of *DSM* specific psychodynamic etiological factors, in particular conflict and psychological trauma, were important diagnostic criteria. Although in some patients the symptom or deficit is believed to be related to a specific stressor, it has not been convincingly demonstrated that such a relation is typical. Accordingly, in *DSM-5* psychological etiology is not a defining criterion, though it is offered as a specifier. The definition of conversion disorder has evolved to a more etiologically neutral description of specific functional disorders in neurology, thus paralleling other medical specialist fields (Stone et al., 2010).

Contemporary Theoretical Perspectives Most research into conversion disorder and somatization disorder is still strongly influenced by Janet's concepts of dissociation and repression (Maldonado & Spiegel, 2001). Dissociation is an elusive concept that has many descriptive and explanatory definitions and is an issue of considerable controversy (Roelofs & Spinhoven, 2007). Is it generally assumed that the process of dissociation involves attentional narrowing that is triggered by traumatic events with which the individual is unable to cope.

In a small-scale study, patients diagnosed with somatization disorder, when compared to other medical patients, showed higher scores on dissociative amnesia for traumatic events, in particular for childhood emotional and physical abuse and for family conflict (Brown, Schrag, & Trimble, 2005). Patients with conversion disorder reported more physical and sexual abuse than did patients with affective disorders (Roelofs, Keijsers, Hoogduin, Näring, & Moene, 2002).

Currently, neurobiological models conceptualize this dissociative disconnection as a disturbance in the integration between neurophysiological stimuli, data processing, and explicit motor activity. In a neuroimaging (fMRI) study comparing 16 patients with motor conversion symptoms with 16 matched healthy controls, functional connectivity was found between emotional areas and motor areas of the brain (Voon et al., 2010). A similar pattern has been found in a study in which 11 patients with psychogenic nonepileptic seizures were compared with 11 healthy controls (Van der Kruijs et al., 2012). For the patients, stronger connectivity values between areas involved in emotion, executive control, and movement were observed, which were significantly associated with dissociation scores.

Conversion disorder has also been conceptualized by some as a primitive communicative learned behavior that is utilized when direct verbal communication is blocked (Maldonado & Spiegel, 2001). Despite these recent findings, however, we do not have an adequate, empirically supported theory of conversion disorder.

Onset and Course Isolated conversion symptoms are believed to be fairly common, and symptoms often disappear after a relatively brief period. Although conversion may occur at any age, the onset is typically in late childhood or early adulthood. Mace and Trimble (1996) reported on a 10-year follow-up of general hospital patients with an original diagnosis of conversion disorder and found that 59% had improved. In 15% of these patients, the psychiatric diagnosis had been changed to a known medical diagnosis.

Factitious Disorder

Clinical Picture The central element in factitious disorder is the deliberate simulation of illness for the purpose of acquiring the sick role, in the absence of obvious external rewards. Physical symptoms may be fabrications of subjective complaints (e.g., pain), self-inflicted illnesses (e.g., as a result of drug use), injections of infectious materials, deliberate self-harm, or an exaggeration of existing physical symptoms. Symptoms are under voluntary control and could apply to any part of the body (cf. Feldman & Ford, 1993). Some factitious-disordered patients are eager to undergo extensive medical procedures and even surgery, which in turn may lead to further complications. At some point the patient's deception may be identified by the medical care system. This could occur when somatic complaints cannot be explained by medical knowledge, when medical tests yield bizarre outcomes, when unexpected complications emerge, or because an illness lasts exceptionally long. In addition, the clinical picture consists of a dramatic and sometimes acute, but notably vague, presentation of symptoms. Patients also frequently lie about the nature of their symptoms and life circumstances in general (*pseudologia fantastica*). *Factitious disorder imposed on another* is diagnosed in the perpetrator when he or she presents another individual as being ill while having this inflicted upon him or her.

Factitious disorder should be distinguished from malingering, in which the patient intentionally produces symptoms with a recognizable goal, such as financial compensation or other privileges (e.g., being exempt from duties). Factitious disorder is often inaccurately considered synonymous with Münchhausen syndrome (Asher, 1951), defined by the triad of a more severe and chronic course, hospital shopping, and *pseudologia fantastica*. This more severe variant comprises about 10% of patients with factitious disorder (Feldman, Hamilton, & Deemer, 2001; Fink & Jensen, 1989). Apart from inflicting illnesses on themselves, some patients, particularly mothers, have been found to fabricate symptoms in their children to get attention from doctors. This condition is known as the Münchausen-by-proxy-syndrome (Schreier & Libow, 1993), considered by some authors as a subtype of the battered-child syndrome.

Because factitious disorder is rarely assigned as a diagnosis, its prevalence is largely unknown, although Fliege, Scholler, Rose, Willenberg, and Klapp (2002) summarized studies, suggesting a prevalence of around 0.5% in general hospital settings. Bauer and Boegner (1996) found the diagnosis to apply to 0.3% of all patients admitted to a neurological clinic over a 1-year period, and Sutherland and Rodin (1990) reported that 0.8% of consecutively referred patients in a general hospital's psychiatric service met criteria for a diagnosis of factitious disorder. The disorder is believed to be more common in men than in women, although a significant proportion of cases seem to involve young adult women who possess extensive medical knowledge, such as nurses and medical assistants (Feldman & Ford, 1993; Plassmann, 1994a).

Historical Perspectives In 1838, Gavin coined the term "factitious disorder" (Kanaan & Wessely, 2010) to indicate a subtype of malingering in which the clinical evidence had been faked. He had observed this in soldiers who wanted to be away from the battlefield and enter the ease and comfort of the hospital, where they were met with compassion. Over a century later, Asher (1951) described a few patients whom he diagnosed as having *Münchausen syndrome*, leading to an increase in reported cases. Factitious disorder was first mentioned in *DSM-III* as a diagnostic category emphasizing the aspect of illness deception, positioning it between hysteria (in which symptoms are produced unconsciously and without external motives) and malingering (consciously produced symptoms with external motives). This is assumed to allow the clinician to pathologize deception, rather than putting it in a legal context (Kanaan & Wessely, 2010).

Contemporary Theoretical Perspectives   At present, there is no specific, empirically validated model of factitious disorders. Although over the years the number of reports and published case studies of this condition has increased (cf. Plassmann, 1994a), the elusive nature of psychological symptoms has prevented systematic research in this area. Several papers have focused on the psychodynamic aspects of factitious disorders. One has proposed that affected parts of the body represent the patient's negative affect and that a highly negative self-concept paves the way to self-destruction (Plassmann, 1994a). A behavioral notion of factitious disorder suggests it to be the result of social learning and the current reinforcement of the sick role—for example, by gaining sympathy, attention, and care, and by evading responsibilities and obligations (Feldman et al., 2001). Krahn, Bostwick, and Stonnington (2008) have speculated that these patients display a deficit in emotional awareness and emotional processing, leading to a desperate search for the patient role. This seems similar to patients suffering from other SSRD, in which various degrees of deception or somatic-symptom exaggeration can also be found.

Onset and Course   Onset of the disorder is believed to be in early adulthood, and its course is often chronic. A particularly poor prognosis applies to individuals who wander from hospital to hospital, lack steady relationships and employment, are socially isolated, abuse drugs and alcohol, and display antisocial behaviors that may even result in criminal convictions. Not surprisingly, severe personality disorders, such as borderline personality disorder, are frequently diagnosed in individuals with factitious disorder (Freyberger, Nordmeyer, Freyberger, & Nordmeyer, 1994).

Psychological Factors Affecting Medical Condition

Clinical Picture   Being a very broad category, this diagnosis is considered when a patient is suffering from a medical condition and when psychological or behavioral factors adversely affect its onset, maintenance, or course.

The onset of a medical condition may be related to specific personality characteristics or coping styles (e.g., stress-related headache, Type A personality traits). Another example is evident when an individual engages in illness denial and fails to seek appropriate treatment for a serious medical condition (e.g., males at risk for testicular cancer). Refusal of medical care for cultural or religious reasons may also seriously impact an individual's health—for example, females not wanting to be examined by a male doctor, or a person's refusal to be inoculated against a serious disease because of religious convictions. In addition, some behaviors constitute a well-established health risk for the individual (e.g., sedentary life, smoking, overeating, or unsafe sex). Emotional states may affect the onset and maintenance of chronic conditions such as asthma or hypertension, and depression after a myocardial infarct predicts mortality.

On a behavioral level, the course of a disease can be influenced by the degree of compliance, which is defined as the degree to which a patient correctly follows medical advice, such as diabetes medication, physical therapy, or lifestyle changes. A study by the World Health Organization (2003) showed that in the Western world only about 50% of patients suffering from a chronic disease follow treatment recommendations. This implies that a substantial number of patients do not profit from the available health care facilities, leading to high personal and economic costs. Noncompliance can take many forms, ranging from not filling a prescription at the pharmacy to not using or underusing prescribed medication.

Historical Perspectives   Previously, *psychological factors affecting medical condition* was mentioned in the appendix of *DSM-IV-TR*, in the section of *other conditions that may be a focus of clinical attention*. The *DSM-5* criteria are very similar to those listed there. Some authors argue that this diagnostic category lacks specificity and will have virtually no impact on clinical practice (Sirri & Fava, 2013). An alternative classification has been proposed under the name of *diagnostic criteria for psychosomatic research* (Porcelli & Rafanelli, 2010). Researchers endorsing this classification claim it to be more specific and sensitive than the *DSM* classification (Fava, Fabbri, Sirri, & Wise,

2007; Guidi, Rafanelli, Roncuzzi, Sirri, & Fava, 2013).

Differential Diagnosis and Comorbidity

General Diagnostic Validity

DSM-5 (p. 309) states that "all the disorders in this chapter share a common feature: the prominence of somatic symptoms associated with significant distress and impairment." This implies that positive somatic and psychobehavioral symptom criteria are required to make the diagnosis, rather than the traditional convention of mere symptom counting, or the requirement that the somatic symptoms be medically unexplained. Although abandoning the latter feature may seem to be a step forward, it also removes a unifying principle in this diagnostic category (Sykes, 2012). The main issue is that this *DSM-5* chapter covers a broad area of somatic symptoms of various nature and origin, as well as cognitive, affective, behavioral, and social factors that play a role in the onset or maintenance of the somatic symptoms or are consequences of the somatic symptoms. Therefore, it lacks a coherent underpinning that unites its various subcategories. The somatic symptoms included may be the result of a known disease, may be medically unexplained, may be symptoms caused by psychological factors (such as stressors), or may be afflicted by the individual him- or herself. On the other hand, supporting the relevance of including any kind of somatic symptoms as criteria, Escobar et al. (2010) found in a large community study that individuals with three or more current general physical symptoms (mostly pain other functional symptoms) showed more anxiety, depression, substance abuse, and health care utilization than that of individuals with less somatic symptoms. Interestingly, the nature of these symptoms, that is, explained or unexplained, had no predictive value for the reported psychopathology.

Similar to the earlier somatoform disorders, the diagnostic validity of the somatic symptom and related disorders in relation to each other as well as to other clinical syndromes is problematic and will continue to be the focus of intense debate (Fava et al., 2007; Mayou, Kirmayer, Simon, Kroenke, & Sharpe, 2005; Rief & Sharpe, 2004; Starcevic, 2006). Despite the shift toward positive diagnostic criteria, the conceptual boundaries between somatic symptom and related disorders are still unclear, giving way to the risk of assigning mental health diagnoses to many medical patients (Frances, 2013; Sykes, 2012). In addition, some comments made by Mayou et al. (2005) on the diagnostic purposes of the somatoform disorders still hold for the SSRD: (a) their terminology remains unacceptable to patients, (b) they do not form a coherent category, (c) they lack clearly defined symptom thresholds, and (d) they will continue to cause confusion in disputes over medical-legal and insurance entitlements.

Nonetheless, there is some emerging empirical support for the revised diagnostic criteria of SSRD. For instance, Wolburg, Voigt, Braukhaus, Herzog, and Löwe (2013) showed that self-reported health status is better predicted by psychosocial features (notably health worries, health habits, and symptom attribution) than by the sole presence of somatic symptoms (i.e., somatic symptom count). The latter was a main requirement for the *DSM-IV* diagnosis of somatization disorder. The same research group reached a similar conclusion in a study involving 259 patients with somatoform disorders, stating that the inclusion of psychological symptoms (i.e., Criterion B) in the *DSM-5* SSD resulted in greater predictive value and clinical utility than that for *DSM-IV*-defined somatoform disorders (Voigt et al., 2012).

In a conceptual literature review, Voigt et al. (2010) compared various somatoform disorder diagnoses (such as these from the *DSM-IV* and *DSM-5* as well as multisomatoform disorder and body distress disorder) with regard to construct validity, descriptive validity, predictive validity, and clinical utility. Their analysis showed that *complex* SSD (encompassing multiple somatic symptoms) performs best on construct validity (reflecting current biopsychosocial models), descriptive validity (including specific psychological and behavioral maintenance factors), and clinical utility (e.g., being time limited since no evaluation of medical records is required). These findings underscore the clinical and conceptual value of *DSM-5* including psychological and behavioral factors as criteria. It should be noted, however, that the authors departed from an earlier diagnostic proposal for SDD (which has been abandoned in the *DSM*), called *complex somatic symptom disorder*, in which two or more (rather than one) somatic symptoms were required.

Differential Diagnoses Between Somatic Symptom and Related Disorders

According to *DSM-5*, the subcategories of SSRD are partly based on research evidence, but mainly on consensus within the task force. It is still an open question whether these subcategories will reach acceptable standards of reliability, which will in turn affect clinical practice and patients' rights to medical-legal entitlements. Differentiating among the various somatic symptom and related disorders using *DSM-5* criteria may be difficult because of the considerable overlap of criteria as well as the functional overlap of associated behaviors. It can thus be argued that the SSRD are not qualitatively distinct but rather merge into each other, just as was the case with their predecessors, the somatoform disorders (Kanaan et al., 2007; Wessely et al., 1999). This has been partly acknowledged in *DSM-5* by the broad SSD category. Other diagnostic categories may be considered to be traditionally narrow, such as conversion disorder and IAD. Some issues concerning potential differential diagnostic difficulties are the following.

For example, let us compare the diagnostic criteria for SSD (and in particular health-anxious patients who suffer from at least one distressing somatic symptom) and IAD (health-anxious patients who are free of somatic symptoms). It is quite remarkable that Criterion B for IAD ("Somatic symptoms are not present...") and particularly the second part of this criterion ("...or, if present, are only mild in intensity. If another medical condition is present or there is a high risk for developing a medical condition (...), the preoccupation is clearly excessive or disproportionate") resembles Criterion A for SSD ("one or more somatic symptoms that are distressing"). Criteria A, C, and D for IAD (referring to somatic preoccupations, anxiety, and health-related behaviors, respectively) on the other hand are nearly identical to the tripartite Criterion B for SSD. Since suffering from somatic symptoms and being without such symptoms is not a simple dichotomy, the lack of clear symptom thresholds will undoubtedly be reflected in the difficulty to distinguish SSD with health anxiety from IAD. This begs the question as to the required nature and severity of a somatic symptom to yield either of these two diagnoses.

Another example concerns the distinction between the criteria for conversion disorder and those for SSD. In SSD any somatic symptom that is distressing is part of Criterion A. In conversion disorder, this criterion is restricted to altered voluntary motor or sensory function. It could easily be argued that such a conversion symptom can be qualified under Criterion A for SSD as well. Probably its historical background and its puzzling nature secured conversion disorder's own place in successive *DSM*s. Formally speaking, altered function can be considered as one of the many medically unexplained symptoms that occur in each and every medical specialist area (e.g., Stone, 2009). In the case of conversion disorder, this frequently happens to be within the realm of neurology. From this it may be concluded that SSD as a category is (too) inclusive in relation to other disorders.

This list of examples could easily be continued, pointing to the fact that there are many inconsistencies in the *DSM* criteria, that the divergent validity of the SSRD diagnoses among each other will be problematic, and that this might run the risk of reducing clinical utility.

Somatic Symptom and Related Disorders and General Medical Conditions

The distinction between SSRD and "normal disease" and illness is hard to make. One problem with the criteria for all of these disorders is their reference to normative patterns of behavior and cognition that are never clearly outlined. Criteria such as "excessive time and energy devoted to these symptoms or health concerns" and "one or more somatic symptoms that are distressing" are difficult to objectify because there is no clear definition of *excessive* or of *distressing*. Even in general practice it may occasionally be difficult for a doctor to distinguish between a deviation from normality and pathology (e.g., pain associated with injury). Therefore, not only the somatic criteria but certainly also the psychobehavioral criteria depend heavily on the clinician's subjective assessment. Apart from their role in the assessment, doctors may also exert influence on the nature and magnitude of the psychobehavioral criteria. *DSM-5* is remarkably silent about the patient–doctor interaction, despite its well-documented influence on both patients' and doctors' perception and behavior (e.g., Hinchey & Jackson, 2011).

As an example, Criterion B for SSD refers to the patient being too preoccupied with, having too much anxiety about, and devoting too much time to his or her physical symptoms. It could be argued that these characteristics can only partly be attributed to the individual patient. Doctors' behaviors (and the health care system as a whole) are also determinant of the way in which individuals react to somatic symptoms (Schröder & Fink, 2010). Consider the situation in which a cardiologist fails to explain the nature and consequences to a patient who has had a heart attack. If this patient becomes overly careful with physical efforts and keeps on wondering what he might and might not do, should he be diagnosed with SSD or IAD? A similar issue has been raised with regard to the adequate medical reassurance criterion included in the *DSM-IV* diagnosis of hypochondriasis. Basically, a doctor's less-than-adequate behavior could contribute to the patient being assigned a psychiatric diagnosis.

Somatic Symptom and Related Disorders, Depression, and Anxiety

There are many similarities in the presentation of persons with SSRD, anxiety disorders, and depression (Bass & Murphy, 1995; Fava et al., 2007; Kanaan et al., 2007). All of these disorders share psychological symptoms such as negative affectivity and marked somatic symptoms. In addition, the disorders share cognitive, behavioral, affective, and pathophysiological mechanisms (Rief & Sharpe, 2004). In a meta-analytic review, Henningsen, Zimmerman, and Sattel (2003) found that a number of functional somatic syndromes were strongly related to anxiety and depression, but that they were not entirely explained by them. Similar findings were reported by Simms, Prisciandaro, Krueger, and Goldberg (2011), who used latent-structure models in a multinational sample of 5,433 primary care patients. Their results showed somatic symptoms, depression, and anxiety to each have specific predictive value regarding psychosocial dysfunction and psychiatric diagnosis. Interestingly, the three disorders were related to a general internalizing or distress factor.

In addition to (and possibly as a consequence of) this considerable psychological and somatic symptom overlap, the diagnoses themselves also show high comorbidity. In particular, comorbidity between SSRD and depressive disorder and, to a lesser extent, with dysthymic disorder has been well documented (Katon & Sullivan, 1995). For example, Rief, Hiller, Geissner, and Fichter (1995)

found high lifetime comorbidity between various somatoform disorders and depression (86%) and anxiety (43%). The absence of comorbidity was associated with higher remission rates than in cases with comorbidity. This high comorbidity has also been observed outside the Western world, for instance, in women attending community and primary health care centers in low- and middle-income countries (Shidhaye, Mendenhall, Sumathipala, Sumathipala, & Patel, 2013). More specifically, several studies have found a striking relation between pain and major depression or dysthymic disorder (Chaturvedi & Michael, 1986; France, Krishnan, Houpt, & Maltbie, 1984), and hypochondriasis shows symptom overlap and comorbidity with obsessive-compulsive disorder (Bouman, 2008).

Somatization and Personality

A number of studies have been devoted to the relationship between somatization and somatic presentations on the one hand and personality characteristics on the other hand. In particular, neuroticism, that is, the lifelong tendency to experience negative affect, has been found to be associated with anxiety and depression, as well as with high stress reactivity and the increased incidence of physical illnesses or, more generally, "distress proneness" (Deary, Chalder, & Sharpe, 2007). In a sample of 185 primary care patients, Hollifield, Tuttle, Pain, and Kellner (1999) studied the Big Five personality traits in relation to hypochondriasis and somatization. Patients high on hypochondriasis and somatization scored higher on neuroticism and lower on extraversion than those with low scores on the two disorders. In addition, somatization patients exhibited lower scores on agreeableness and conscientiousness.

SSRD and their predecessors (the somatoform disorders) share many features with personality disorders (Bass & Murphy, 1995; Tyrer, 1995) in terms of their developmental origin, persistent nature, disruptive impact on social functioning, and chronic course. A meta-analysis (Bornstein & Gold, 2008) supports this notion, showing that somatization disorder is comorbid with the majority of personality disorders. A study by Garcia-Campayo, Aldaa, Sobradiela, Olivana, and Pascuala (2007), for example, found 28.2% comorbidity between mood and anxiety disorder and personality disorders, and as high as 62.9% comorbidity between somatization disorder and (in particular, histrionic and obsessive-compulsive) personality disorders. Noyes et al. (2001) reported that a higher percentage of patients with a *DSM-IV* somatoform disorder met criteria for one or more personality disorders, especially obsessive-compulsive personality disorder, than did control patients. Somatoform patients also differed from control patients with respect to self-defeating, depressive, and negativistic personality traits and scored higher on the dimension of neuroticism and lower on the dimension of agreeableness.

Explanatory Models and Perspectives

Given that the prevalence of transitory somatic symptoms is high in the general population, an important question relates to how and why some people develop long-lasting and often debilitating conditions, whereas others do not. In this section we will discuss the etiological and maintaining factors that may be assumed to be related to the various SSRD. Again, because of the lack of a body of research, we will focus on theories and empirical evidence gathered from somatoform disorders, somatization, and medically unexplained symptoms, as well as that from specific disorders.

Etiological Factors

Genetics   In a twin study, Torgerson (1986) concluded that although somatoform disorders may have a genetic factor, transmission seems to be environmental. A few studies have concentrated on a genetic and familial component in hypochondriasis, suggesting that there is, at best, only a moderate genetic contribution. For instance, a study by Taylor, Thordarson, Jang, and Asmundson (2006) found that, after controlling for medical morbidity, environmental influences accounted for most of individual differences in health anxiety.

Life Events   The etiological role of life events has only been studied in the predecessors of specific SSRD. In particular, sexual and physical abuse, traumatization, and parental rearing style have been pinpointed as etiological factors, although these are also found in nearly all other forms of psychopathology.

Several retrospective studies have found sexual and physical abuse as well as traumatization

to be likely precursors of somatization disorder (Morrison, 1989; Roelofs & Spinhoven, 2007; Salmon & Calderbank, 1996), pain disorder (Ford & Parker, 1990), excessive health anxiety (Barsky et al., (1994), and conversion disorder (Roelofs et al., 2002; Sharma & Chaturvedi, 1995).

Craig, Boardman, Mills, Daly-Jones, and Drake (1993) found a lack of parental care during childhood illness to be the best predictor of adult somatization. Insecure attachment style may also be associated with health anxiety (Parker & Libscombe, 1980). Noyes et al. (2001) tested this hypothesis in a large sample of hypochondriacal patients and found insecure (fearful) attachment to be positively related to hypochondriasis and somatic symptoms and negatively related to satisfaction with medical care. Although there is a great lack of empirical data regarding the etiology of factitious disorder, many authors emphasize the patient's need for being taken care of. Significant physical and emotional deprivation and abuse in early life as well as extreme family tension are assumed to contribute to the development of factitious disorder (Plassmann, 1994b). Furthermore, early experiences with medical procedures and carrying a grudge against the medical profession have been mentioned as etiological factors.

Learning   The phenomenon of observational learning may be a factor involved in the acquisition of abnormal illness behavior. It is also likely that persons who develop SSRD have been exposed to negative health-related events to a greater degree than persons who do not develop these disorders. For example, some studies indicate that a significant number of persons with cardiophobia, defined as an irrational fear of heart disease, have observed heart disease and its potentially lethal effects in relatives and close friends (Eifert & Forsyth, 1996). As a result, they may also have had more exposure to heart-focused perceptions and interpretations of physical symptoms and physiological processes. Observational learning is strongly involved in acquiring pain tolerance, pain ratings, and nonverbal expressions of pain (Flor et al., 2002 Quartana, Campbell, & Edwards, 2009). Such observational learning may increase the likelihood of expressing and interpreting arousal and pain in later life. For instance, if one or both parents have heart disease, children might observe their parent's response to a heart problem. If the behavior that is modeled is maladaptive (e.g., excessive illness behavior), these children will not only be more likely to respond to stress with increased cardiovascular activity, but they will have also learned maladaptive labeling and interpretation of such somatic symptoms and have fewer adaptive coping skills.

Maintaining Factors

Cognition and Information Processing Cognitive factors are assumed to play an important role in the formation and perpetuation of SSRD. A review by Rief and Broadbent (2007) summarizes the main factors involved, which of course may vary between manifestations of SSRD. Patients suffering from SSRD generally exhibit abnormalities in symptom interpretation and illness beliefs. They engage in a catastrophic interpretation of physical symptoms and bodily sensations, and they have a general tendency to be preoccupied with and worry about health and illness. A complication is that patients tend to report multiple illness attributions, rather than a simplistic explanation. Attitudes toward health and disease are influenced by the idea that health is the absence of any physical abnormality, so the individual often sets unrealistic standards for their personal well-being. It has been suggested that selective perception of and attention to bodily sensations and changes may contribute to the acquisition of somatization behavior. Over time, these processes are likely to increase a person's ability to detect sensations that have previously remained below the threshold of perceptibility. Accordingly, the construct of somatosensory amplification (Barsky & Wyshak, 1990) has been used to describe the enhanced perceptions of innocuous bodily sensations and variations. Memory tends to be biased toward the encoding and retrieval of illness-related material. Medical explanations and illness-related experiences are more easily remembered than other information, for example, in patients with medically unexplained symptoms (Rief & Broadbent, 2007), chronic pain (Winterowd, Beck, & Gruener, 2003), and health anxiety (Marcus et al., 2007).

The current cognitive-behavioral conceptualization of hypochondriasis postulates that exposure to threatening situations helps establish maladaptive health-related assumptions and beliefs (Marcus et al., 2007; Salkovskis & Warwick, 2001). These beliefs are subsequently triggered when individuals encounter critical incidents (such as being confronted with somebody else's symptoms or even death) or in circumstances in which ambiguous bodily sensations are experienced. Thus, for otherwise healthy people, the sensations of a beating heart or chest pain may lead to a sequence of verbal and autonomic events that result in the belief that they are having a heart attack. In this instance, a fast or irregular heartbeat is not just a felt beating heart. Instead, it is an acquired and verbally mediated formulation of what it means to have a fast or irregular heartbeat or chest pain (e.g., "I have heart disease" or "I am having a heart attack"). Further health-related experiences may consolidate assumptions and beliefs through selective attention to illness-related information and through confirmatory reasoning bias. Several researchers have suggested that exposure to disease and display of somatic symptoms in the family—in combination with parental attitudes toward illness—influence the development of hypochondriacal concerns in children. These concerns are likely to continue into adulthood, particularly when persons experience and selectively attend to symptoms that they cannot easily explain or understand.

Abnormal Illness Behavior Given the current prominence of information-processing paradigms, behavioral factors involved in SSRD have received little research attention. A recent overview by Prior and Bond (2013) highlights the importance of these factors.

On a behavioral level, an important general maintaining factor of SSRD is the acquisition of the *sick role* (Parsons, 1951). This is a sociological construct referring to a role granted to an individual by society with accompanying privileges (e.g., staying home from work) and obligations (e.g., complying with medical instructions). Partly overlapping with this construct is that of illness behavior (Mechanic & Volkart, 1960), referring to the way individuals deal with somatic symptoms, check their bodies, cope with these symptoms, and engage in any kind of intervention.

Pilowsky (1993, p. 62) has defined abnormal illness behavior as "the persistence of a maladaptive mode of experiencing, perceiving, evaluating, and responding to one's own health status, despite the fact that a doctor has provided a lucid and accurate appraisal of the situation and management to be followed (if any), with opportunities for discussion, negotiation and clarification, based on adequate assessment of all relevant biological, psychological, social and cultural factors." Somatically focused (in contrast to psychologically focused) abnormal illness behavior is divided into illness-affirming and illness-denying behavior. Pilowsky (1993) states that abnormal illness behavior is not a diagnosis as such because it refers to the disagreement between the doctor and patient about the sick role to which the patient feels entitled. This positions SSRD in a societal rather than an intraindividual context. Sharpe, Mayou, and Bass (1995) maintain that the concept of abnormal illness behavior has been valuable in drawing attention to the behavioral aspects of all illnesses, but it is not specific to patients with somatic symptoms per se. Reassurance seeking, need for medical examination, avoidance of physical effort, an inactive lifestyle, and interaction with others constitute only a small part of the behavioral components of SSRD (Prior & Bond, 2013). These behaviors are associated with the individual's illness attributions (about the nature, cause, and consequences of illness), as has been established, for example, by Rief, Nanke, Emmerich, Bender, and Zech (2004) in a large sample of patients suffering from medically unexplained symptoms. In sum, abnormal illness behavior may be regarded as one of the constituting dimensions in a multidimensional conceptualization of SSRD.

Emotional Factors   In addition to cognitive and behavioral factors, emotion regulation has long been assumed to occupy a pivotal position in the onset and maintenance of persistent somatic presentations. An important role has been assigned to the concept of alexithymia (Sifneos, 1973), which refers to the difficulty in describing, recognizing, and expressing emotions. Individuals high on this trait are not very well able to perceive somatic manifestations as emotional expressions. The failure to regulate and modulate stress-related emotions may result in excessive physiological and behavioral responses, as well as increased vulnerability to disease because of prolonged physical activation. Somatoform disorders have been linked to a diminished capacity to consciously experience and differentiate emotions and express them in an adequate way, as documented in a review paper by Waller and Scheidt (2006). The ability to consciously experience emotion requires the creation of a mental representation of that state in a verbal or symbolic form. If this representation is lacking, the emotion will only be implicitly manifested by its physiological and behavioral components. This notion was supported by an experimental study in which patients suffering from somatoform disorders exhibited less emotional content and reduced theory of mind functioning in comparison to healthy controls (Subic-Wrana, Beutel, Knebel, & Lane, 2010). This deficit in emotion regulation has also been discussed in terms of attachment theory, in that inadequate (i.e., insecure) attachment styles are associated with defensive forms of processing and expressing of emotions (Noyes et al., 2003; Waller & Scheidt, 2006).

Doctor–Patient Relationship   Factors relating to doctors' behaviors and activities (so-called iatrogenic factors) frequently play a role in the onset, maintenance, or exacerbation of SSRD. For instance, a physician's failure to recognize psychological factors, and the prescription of unnecessary medical drugs and treatments are likely to reinforce the patient's illness beliefs (Mai, 2004). Unfortunately, the doctor–patient relationship is a relatively neglected area in *DSM-5*, despite the fact that around 15% of medical patients are considered to be difficult by their doctors (Hahn et al., 1996; Hinchey & Jackson, 2011). These so-called difficult patients exhibit more functional impairment, psychosocial problems, health care utilization, and dissatisfaction with care. For the physician the difficult relationship between doctor and patient is often characterized by disbelief (as in conversion symptoms), suspicion (as in factitious disorder), despair and fear (as in hypochondriasis), powerlessness (as in somatization disorder), and demoralization. In an experimental study, Van Wilgen et al. (2013) found that the more patients manifested somatic symptoms and psychosocial distress, the more negative beliefs and emotions were elicited in health care providers. In addition, doctors who consider patients to be difficult to deal with appear to be less experienced and show less psychosocial orientation (Hinchey & Jackson, 2011).

This relationship can be a negative iatrogenic component in the perpetuation of SSRD, resulting in a battle between patient and health care professional, leading away from an understanding of and solution to the complex problems. This, in turn, may foster the patient's reluctance to be referred to mental health care professionals. Such patients feel they are not being taken seriously and see themselves as being discarded as a psychiatric case. This leads to additional distress, adding to somatic symptoms in patients who already possess these as their idiom of distress. Their tendency to try to convince the doctor of their symptoms, to stick to somatic explanations of their symptoms, to request more examination (confirmatory bias), and to show poor compliance with medical regimens is seriously reinforced. This all ties in with the patient's abnormal illness behavior, discussed earlier.

Social and Cultural Aspects of Somatic Expressions   In general, culture and society comprise understudied but nevertheless important variables in the presentation of somatic symptoms. Eriksen and colleagues (2013) point to the increasing medicalization of societal and cultural problems, in which the focus is on what is *within* the patient, who is made responsible for having fallen ill and for the process of recovery. *Medicalization* here refers to the process whereby aspects of everyday life come under the influence of the medical profession. This process comes at the expense of the interplay between the individual and his or her (social and cultural) environment. Doctors play an important role, in the sense that they are socialized into and represent the biomedical system and often act "symptom interpreters."

Cultural influences on somatization processes are well documented. Based on a review of data from cross-cultural studies, Escobar, Allen, Nervi, & Gara, (2001) concluded that there is "considerable cultural variation in the expression of somatizing syndromes. The available evidence elaborates the well-accepted tenet that the presentation of personal/social distress in the form of somatic complaints appears to be the norm for most cultures" (p. 226). As an example, Farooq, Gahir, Okyere, Sheikh, and Oyebode (1995) found that Asian patients living in Great Britain reported significantly more somatic and depressive symptoms than did Caucasians. In this respect, the expression of somatic symptoms can be construed as an idiom of distress. "Idioms of distress are socially and culturally resonant means of experiencing and expressing distress in local worlds" (Nichter, 2010, p. 405), and "somatization is considered to be an important idiom through which distress is communicated" (Chaturvedi, 2013, p. 3). Nichter (2010) has presented examples of ways in which cultural idioms become apparent, such as the medical and psychiatric terminology, the use of diagnostic tests, health care seeking, and medicine-taking

behavior. In addition, the clinical presentation and experiencing of symptoms are culturally shaped and influenced by, for example, explanatory models, health care facilities, illness prototypes, and the doctor–patient relationship. Thus, the presentation of somatic symptoms often appears to be more a function of the individual's culture than of some underlying (distinct) biologically based disease process. Somatic symptoms have both an individual and a social meaning. Consequently, "there is a need for a social and cultural approach to the phenomenon of somatization that goes beyond the model of diseases and disorders" (Kirmayer & Sartorius, 2007, p. 839).

DSM-5 agrees with the assertion that the types and frequency of somatic symptoms differ across cultures and that symptom lists should be adjusted to the patient's culture. In its "glossary of cultural concepts of distress" (pp. 833–837) a few examples of such disorders are given. Culturally specific SSRD are, for example, the South Asian *dhat* syndrome (the fear of semen loss in young males), the Cambodian *khyal cap* (panic-like symptoms associated with a wind-related substance in the body), and the Chinese *shenjing shuairuo* (weakness of the nervous system), all referring to complexes of somatic and psychological symptoms. This is only the tip of the proverbial iceberg. For example, people in Africa and Southern Asia report burning hands and feet or the nondelusional experience of worms in the hands or ants in the head; such reports are virtually unheard of among individuals in Europe and North America. By comparison, Europeans and North Americans tend to be preoccupied with heart disease and cancer. Despite these differences, and the heterogeneous nature of patient populations, there is little cultural perspective included in the *DSM-5* (Fritzsche, Xudong, & Schaefert, 2011).

Conclusions

One of the most compelling conclusions arising from this chapter is that SSRD cannot be adequately understood, assessed, and treated from a single perspective. Although somatic symptoms are very common in the general population, it is still unclear why in some people such symptoms develop into an often lifelong distressing condition. Although data are emerging, we are still short of reliable information on the prevalence of SSRD, its distribution across specific groups within the population, and related cultural and gender differences.

Barlow (2002) has stated that classification of any disorder, whether dimensional or categorical, should reliably describe subgroups of any type of symptoms or behaviors that are readily identifiable by independent observers on the basis of operational definitions. There should also be clinical utility in identifying these subgroups or dimensions, such as predicting a specific response to treatment and course of the disorder, or tailoring treatment. However, these criteria are not met by the SSRD, since they appear to be a somewhat arbitrary amalgam of various conditions relating to bodily functioning and they ways in which the individual perceives and acts upon them

Both the classification of and research on SSRD could be improved by adopting a multidisciplinary approach and an integrated biopsychosocial perspective. For example, Mayou, Bass, and Sharpe (1995) proposed a classification of patients with functional somatic symptoms along five dimensions: (1) number and type of somatic symptoms; (2) mental state (mood and psychiatric disorder); (3) cognitions (e.g., symptom misinterpretations, disease conviction); (4) behavioral and functional impairment (illness behavior, avoidance, use of health services); and (5) pathophysiological disturbance (organic diseases, physiological mechanisms such as hyperventilation). Individuals may be assigned different positions on all of these dimensions across the various types of SSRD. Rather than attempting to find the "correct diagnosis," it is recommended that assessment be applied along the crucial dimensions involved in the regulation of maladaptive illness behavior and devising treatment programs based on such assessments.

Deary and colleagues (2007, p. 788) have provided an essentially cognitive-behavioral model that attempts to integrate the empirical evidence to date:

An innate tendency to somato-psychic distress and ease of distress sensitisation, combined with childhood adversity, increases both the amount of symptoms experienced and lowers the threshold for their detection. Life events and stress lead to physiological changes which produce more symptoms and set up processes of sensitisation and selective attention. This further

reduces the threshold of symptom detection. Lack of explanation or advice increases anxiety, symptoms, and symptom focus. Stress cues become associated with symptoms through classical conditioning. Avoidance of symptom provocation, and symptom-led activity patterns, lead to further sensitisation through operant conditioning. The prolonged stress of the illness experience itself further activates physiological mechanisms, producing more symptoms, sensitisation, selective attention and avoidance. The individual can thereby become locked into a vicious cycle of symptom maintenance.

Despite increasing evidence for the nature and role of the various components of this model, we are now in dire need of a test of their interrelatedness.

There are several potential avenues for future research that could help us improve our understanding and, consequently, treatment of these problems. In recent years, we have learned more about the impact of cognitive processes (attribution, attention, and memory), environmental contingencies (social and cultural correlates of illness behavior, medical practice guidelines), as well as emotion regulation. Furthermore, psychoneuroimmunological and neuroimaging models have increased our understanding of the complex nature of what has been referred to as the "mind–body interface" (Rief & Broadbent, 2007). Studying the specific interactions among psychological, somatic, and social factors, rather than viewing these factors in isolation, should help increase our understanding of this group of disorders. In that respect, the research agenda for SSRD could benefit from the emerging practice in psychological research of studying the commonalities, rather than (supposed) differences, between disorders. A transdiagnostic approach to research and treatment that focuses on the study of common processes (such as attention, reasoning, experiential avoidance) is likely to lead to an improved understanding of the relative contribution and interaction of key processes (Harvey, Watkins, Mansell, & Shafran, 2004). Such an approach, in conjunction with efforts at multidimensional classification and integrative biopsychosocial model building, is likely to increase explanatory power and treatment utility.

References

Abramowitz, J. S., & Braddock, A. E. (2008). *Psychological treatment of health anxiety and hypochondriasis: A biopsychosocial approach.* Cambridge MA: Hogrefe.

Alexander, F. (1950). *Psychosomatic medicine.* New York: Norton.

Allin, M., Streeruwitz, A., & Curtis, V. (2005). Progress in understanding conversion disorder. *Neuropsychiatric Disease and Treatment, 1,* 205–209.

Asher, R. (1951). Münchhausen's syndrome. *Lancet, i,* 339–341.

Asmundson, G. J., & Norton, G. R. (1995). Anxiety sensitivity in patients with physically unexplained chronic back pain. *Behaviour Research and Therapy, 33,* 771–777.

Barlow, D. H. (2002). *Anxiety and its disorders: The nature and treatment of anxiety and panic* (2nd ed.). New York: Guilford Press.

Barsky, A. J., Orav, E. J., & Bates, D. W. (2005). Somatization increases medical utilization and costs independent of psychiatric and medical comorbidity. *Archives of General Psychiatry, 62,* 903–910.

Barsky, A. J., Wool, C., Barnett, M. C., & Cleary, P. D. (1994). Histories of childhood trauma in adult hypochondriacal patients. *American Journal of Psychiatry, 151,* 397–401.

Barsky, A. J., & Wyshak, G. (1990). Hypochondriasis and somatosensory amplification. *British Journal of Psychiatry, 157,* 404–409.

Bass, C. M., & Murphy, M. R. (1995). Somatoform and personality disorders: Syndromal comorbidity and overlapping developmental pathways. *Journal of Psychosomatic Research, 39,* 403–427.

Bauer, M., & Boegner, F. (1996). Neurological syndromes in factitious disorder. *Journal of Nervous and Mental Diseases, 184,* 281–288.

Benedek, E. P. (2007). Cognitive therapy for chronic pain: A step-by-step guide. *Bulletin of the Menninger Clinic, 71,* 248–251.

Blyth, F. M., March, L. M., Brnabic, A. J. M., Jorn, L. R., Williamson, M., & Cousins, M. J. (2001). Chronic pain in Australia: A prevalence study. *Pain, 89,* 127–134.

Bornstein, R. F., & Gold, S. H. (2008). Comorbidity of personality disorders and somatization disorder: A meta-analytic review. *Journal of Psychopathology and Behavior Assessment, 30,* 154–161.

Breivik, H., Collett, B., Ventafridda, V., Cohen, R., & Gallacher, D. (2006). Survey of chronic pain in Europe: Prevalence, impact on daily life, and treatment. *European Journal of Pain, 10,* 287–333.

Brown, R. J., Schrag, A., & Trimble, M. R. (2005). Dissociation, childhood interpersonal trauma, and family functioning in patients with somatization disorder. *American Journal of Psychiatry, 162,* 899–905.

Bouman, T. K. (2008). Hypochondriasis. In J. S. Abramowitz, D. McKay, & S. Taylor (Eds.), *Obsessive-compulsive disorders: Subtypes and spectrum conditions.* New York: Elsevier.

Boyd, K. M. (2000). Disease, illness, sickness, health, healing and wholeness: Exploring some elusive concepts. *Journal of Medical Ethics: Medical Humanities, 26,* 9–17.

Chaturvedi, S. K. (2013). Many faces of somatic symptom disorders. *International Review of Psychiatry, 25,* 1–4

Chaturvedi, S. K., & Michael, A. (1986). Chronic pain in a psychiatric clinic. *Journal of Psychosomatic Research, 30,* 347–354.

Craig, K. D. (1986). Social modeling influences: Pain in context. In R. A. Sternbach (Ed.), *The psychology of pain* (2nd ed., pp. 67–95). New York: Raven Press.

Craig, T. K. J., Boardman, A. P., Mills, K., Daly-Jones, O., & Drake, H. (1993). The south London somatisation study. I: Longitudinal course and the influence of early life experiences. *British Journal of Psychiatry, 163,* 579–588.

Creed, F., & Barsky, A. (2004). A systematic review of the epidemiology of somatisation disorder and hypochondriasis. *Journal of Psychosomatic Research, 56,* 391–408.

Creed, F., Guthrie, E., Fink, P., Henningsen, P., Rief, W., Sharpe, M., & White, P. (2010). Is there a better term than "medically unexplained symptoms"? *Journal of Psychosomatic Research, 68,* 5–8.

Dahl, J., & Lundgren, T. (2007). *Living beyond your pain.* Oakland, CA: New Harbinger.

Dahl, J., Wilson, K. G., & Nilsson, A. (2004). Acceptance and commitment therapy and the treatment of persons at risk for long-term disability resulting from stress and pain symptoms: A preliminary randomized trial. *Behavior Therapy, 35,* 785–802.

Deary, V., Chalder, T., & Sharpe, M. (2007). The cognitive behavioural model of medically unexplained symptoms: A theoretical and empirical review. *Clinical Psychology Review, 27,* 781–797.

De Waal, M. W., Arnold, I. A., Eekhof, J. A. H., & Van Hemert, A. M. (2004). Somatoform disorders in general practice. *British Journal of Psychiatry, 184,* 470–476.

Dimsdale, J., & Creed, F. (2010). The proposed diagnosis of somatic symptom disorders in DSM-V to replace somatoform disorders in DSM-IV—a preliminary report. *Journal of Psychosomatic Research, 66,* 473–476.

Eifert, G. H., & Forsyth, J. F. (1996). Heart-focused and general illness fears in relation to parental medical history and separation experiences. *Behaviour Research and Therapy, 34*, 735–739.

Engel, G. L. (1960). A unified concept of health and disease. *Perspectives on Biological Medicine, 3*, 459–484.

Eriksen, T. E., Kirkengen, A. L., & Vetlesen A. J. (2013). The medically unexplained revisited. *Medical Health Care and Philosophy, 16*, 587–600.

Escobar, J. I., Allen, L. A., Nervi, C. H., & Gara, M. A. (2001). General and cross-cultural considerations in a medical setting for patients presenting with medically unexplained symptoms. In G. J. G. Asmundson, S. Taylor, & B. Cox (Eds.), *Health anxiety: Clinical research perspectives on hypochondriasis and related disorders* (pp. 220–245). New York: Wiley.

Escobar, J. I., Cook, B., Chen, C-N., Gara, M. A., Alegria, M., Interian, A., & Diaz, E. (2010). Whether medically unexplained or not, three or more concurrent somatic symptoms predict psychopathology and service use in community populations. *Journal of Psychosomatic Research, 69*, 1–8.

Escobar, J. I., Waitzkin, H., Silver, R., Gara, M., & Holman, A. (1998). Abridged somatization: A study in primary care. *Psychosomatic Medicine, 60*, 466–72.

Farooq, S., Gahir, M. S., Okyere, E., Sheikh, A. J., & Oyebode, F. (1995). Somatization: A transcultural study. *Journal of Psychosomatic Research, 39*, 883–888.

Fava, G. A., Fabbri, S., Sirri, L., & Wise, T. N. (2007). Psychological factors affecting medical conditions: A new proposal for DSM-V. *Psychosomatics, 48*, 103–111.

Feldman, M. D., & Ford, C. V. (1993). *Patient or pretender: Inside the strange world of factitious disorders.* New York: Wiley.

Feldman, M. D., Hamilton, J. C., & Deemer, H. N. (2001). Factitious disorder. In K. A. Phillips (Ed.), *Somatoform and factitious disorders.* Washington, DC: American Psychiatric Publishing.

Fink, P., & Jensen, J. (1989). Clinical characteristics of the Münchhausen syndrome. A review and three new cases. *Psychotherapy and Psychosomatics, 52*, 164–170.

First, M. B. (2011). Moving beyond unexplained medical symptoms in DSM-5: Great idea, problematic execution. *Psychosomatics, 52*, 594–595.

Fliege, H., Scholler, G., Rose, M., Willenberg, H., & Klapp, B. F. (2002). Factitious disorders and pathological self-harm in a hospital population: An interdisciplinary challenge. *General Hospital Psychiatry, 24*, 164–171.

Flor, H., Knost, B., & Birbaumer, N. (2002). The role of operant conditioning in chronic pain: An experimental investigation. *Pain, 95*, 111–118.

Flor, F., Kerns, R. D., & Turk, D. C. (1987). The role of spouse reinforcement, perceived pain, and activity levels of chronic pain patients. *Journal of Psychosomatic Research, 31*, 251–259.

Ford, C. V. (1995). Dimensions of somatization and hypochondriasis. *Neurologic Clinics, 13*, 241–253.

Ford, C. V., & Parker, P. E. (1990). Somatoform disorders. In M. E. Thase, B. A. Edelstein, & M. Hersen (Eds.), *Handbook of outpatient treatment of adults* (pp. 291–307). New York: Plenum Press.

Fordyce, W. E. (1976). *Behavioral methods for chronic pain and illness.* St. Louis: C. V. Mosby.

France, R. D., Krishnan, K. R. R., Houpt, J. L., & Maltbie, A. A. (1984). Differentiation of depression from chronic pain with the dexamethasone suppression test and DSM-III. *American Journal of Psychiatry, 141*, 1577–1579.

Frances, A. (2013). DSM-5 somatic symptom disorder. *Journal of Nervous and Mental Disease, 201*, 530–531.

Freud, S. (1956). *Collected papers.* London: Hogarth.

Freyberger, H., Nordmeyer, J. P., Freyberger, H. P., & Nordmeyer, J. (1994). Patients suffering from factitious disorder in the clinico-psychosomatic consultation liaison service: Psychodynamic procedures, psychotherapeutic initial care and clinico-interdisciplinary cooperation. *Psychotherapy and Psychosomatics, 62*, 108–122.

Fritzsche, K., Xudong, Z., & Schaefert, R. (2011). Crazy like us?—The proposed diagnosis of complex somatic symptom disorders in DSM-V from a cross-cultural perspective. *Journal of Psychosomatic Research, 71*, 282–283.

Garcia-Campayo, J., Aldaa, M., Sobradiela, N., Olivana, B., & Pascuala, A. (2007). Personality disorders in somatization disorder patients: A controlled study in Spain. *Journal of Psychosomatic Research, 62*, 675–680.

Guidi, G., Rafanelli, C., Roncuzzi, R., Sirri, L., & Fava, G. A. (2013). Assessing psychological factors affecting medical conditions: Comparison between different proposals. *General Hospital Psychiatry, 35*, 141–145.

Gureje, O., Simon, G. E., & Von Korff, M. (2001). A cross-national study of the course of persistent pain in primary care. *Pain, 92,* 195–200.

Gureje, O., Ustun, T. B., & Simon, G. E. (1997). The syndrome of hypochondriasis: A cross-national study in primary care. *Psychological Medicine, 27,* 1001–1010.

Guze, S. B., & Perley, M. J. (1963). Observations on the natural history of hysteria. *American Journal of Psychiatry, 119,* 960–965.

Hahn, S. R., Kroenke, K., Spitzer, R. L., Brody, D., Williams, J. B. W., Linzer, M., & Verloin de Gruy, F. (1996). The difficult patient: Prevalence, psychopathology, and functional impairment. *Journal of General Internal Medicine, 11,* 1–8.

Harvey, A., Watkins, E., Mansell, W., & Shafran, R. (2004). *Cognitive behavioural processes across psychological disorders: A transdiagnostic approach to research and treatment.* Oxford, UK: Oxford University Press.

Henningsen, P., Zimmerman, T., & Sattel, H. (2003). Medically unexplained physical symptoms, anxiety and depression: A meta-analytic review. *Psychosomatic Medicine, 65,* 528–533.

Hinchey, S. A., & Jackson, J. L. (2011). A cohort study assessing difficult patient encounters in a walk-in primary care clinic, predictions and outcomes. *Journal of General Internal Medicine, 26,* 588–594.

Hollifield, M., Tuttle, L., Pain, S., & Kellner, R. (1999). Hypochondriasis and somatization related to personality and attitudes toward self. *Psychosomatics, 40,* 387–395.

Jackson, J. L., & Kroenke, K. (2008). Prevalence, impact, and prognosis of multisomatoform disorder in primary care: A 5-year follow-up study. *Psychosomatic Medicine, 70,* 430–434.

Kanaan, R. A. A., Lepine, J. P., & Wessely, S. (2007). The association or otherwise of the functional somatic syndromes. *Psychosomatic Medicine, 69,* 855–859.

Kanaan, R. A. A., & Wessely, S. C. (2010). The origins of factitious disorder. *History of the Human Sciences, 23,* 68–85.

Katon, W., & Sullivan, M. (1995). Antidepressant treatment of functional somatic symptoms. In R. Mayou, C. M. Bass, & M. Sharpe (Eds.), *Treatment of functional somatic symptoms* (pp. 313–327). Oxford, UK: Oxford University Press.

Kellner, R. (1986). *Somatization and hypochondriasis.* New York: Praeger.

Kirmayer, L. J., & Sartorius, N. (2007). Cultural models and somatic symptoms. *Psychosomatic Medicine, 69,* 832–840.

Krahn, L. E., Bostwick, J. M., & Stonnington, C. M. (2008). Looking towards DSM-V: Should factitious disorder become of subtype of somatoform disorder? *Psychosomatics, 49,* 277–282.

Kroenke, K. (2003). Patients presenting with somatic complaints: Epidemiology, psychiatric co-morbidity and management. *International Journal of Methods in Psychiatric Research, 12,* 34–43.

Kroenke, K., Sharpe, M., & Sykes, R. (2007). Revising the classification of somatoform disorders: Key questions and preliminary recommendation. *Psychosomatics, 48,* 277–285.

Lipowsky, Z. J. (1988). Somatization: The concept and its clinical applicability. *American Journal of Psychiatry, 145,* 1358–1368.

Mace, C. J., & Trimble, M. R. (1996). Ten-year prognosis of conversion disorder. *British Journal of Psychiatry, 169,* 282–288.

Mai, F. (2004). Somatization disorder: A practical review. *Canadian Journal of Psychiatry, 49,* 652–661.

Maldonado, J. R., & Spiegel, D. (2001). Conversion disorder. In K. A. Phillips (Ed.), *Somatoform and factitious disorders.* Washington, DC: American Psychiatric Publishing.

Marcus, D. K., Gurley, J. R., Marchi, M. M., & Bauer, C. (2007). Cognitive and perceptual variables in hypochondriasis and health anxiety: A systematic review. *Clinical Psychology Review, 27,* 127–139.

Mayou, R., Bass, C. M., & Sharpe, M. (1995). Overview of epidemiology, classification and aetiology. In R. Mayou, C. M. Bass, & M. Sharpe (Eds.), *Treatment of functional somatic symptoms* (pp. 42–65). Oxford, UK: Oxford University Press.

Mayou, R., Kirmayer, L., Simon, G., Kroenke, K., & Sharpe, M. (2005). Somatoform disorders: Time for a new approach in DSM-V. *American Journal of Psychiatry, 162,* 847–855.

Mechanic, D., & Volkart, E. H. (1960). Illness behavior and medical diagnoses. *Journal of Health and Human Behavior, 1,* 86–94.

Melzack, R., & Wall, P. D. (1965). Pain mechanisms: A new theory. *Science, 50,* 971–979.

Morrison, J. (1989). Childhood sexual abuse of women with somatization disorder. *American Journal of Psychiatry, 146,* 239–241.

Nichter, M. (2010). Idioms of distress revisited. *Culture, Medicine and Psychiatry, 34,* 401–416.

Noyes, R., Carney, C. P., & Langbehn, D. R. (2004). Specific phobia of illness: Search for a new subtype. *Anxiety Disorders, 18,* 531–545.

Noyes, R., Langbehn, D. R., Happel, R. L, Stout, L. R., Muller, B. A., & Longley, S. L. (2001). Personality dysfunction among somatizing patients. *Psychosomatics, 42,* 320–329.

Noyes, R., Stuart, S. P., Langbehn, D. R., Happel, R. L., Longley, S. L., Muller, B. A., & Yagla, S. J. (2003). Test of an interpersonal model of hypochondriasis. *Psychosomatic Medicine, 65,* 292–300.

Olatunji, B., Daecon, B., Abramowitz, J. S., & Valentiner, D. (2007). Body vigilance in nonclinical and anxiety disorder samples: Structure, correlates, and prediction of health concerns. *Behavior Therapy, 38,* 392–401.

Parker, G., & Lipscombe, P. (1980). The relevance of early parental experiences to adult dependency, hypochondriasis, and utilization of primary physicians. *British Journal of Medical Psychology, 53,* 355–363.

Parsons, T. (1951). Illness and the role of the physician: A sociological perspective. *American Journal of Orthopsychiatry, 21,* 452–460.

Pilowsky, I. (1993). Aspects of abnormal illness behaviour. *Psychotherapy and Psychosomatics, 60,* 62–74.

Pilowsky, I., Chapman, C. R., & Bonica, J. J. (1977). Pain, depression, and illness behavior in a pain clinic population. *Pain, 4,* 183–192.

Plassmann, R. (1994a). Münchhausen syndromes and factitious diseases. *Psychotherapy and Psychosomatics, 62,* 7–26.

Plassmann, R. (1994b). The biography of the factitious-disorder patient. *Psychotherapy and Psychosomatics, 62,* 123–128.

Porcelli, P., & Rafanelli, C. (2010). Criteria for psychosomatic research (DCPR) in the medical setting. *Current Psychiatry Reports, 12,* 246–254.

Prior, K. N., & Bond, M. J. (2013). Somatic symptom disorders and illness behavior: Current perspectives. *International Review of Psychiatry, 25,* 5–18.

Quartana, P. J., Campbell, C. M., & Edwards, R. R. (2009). Pain catastrophizing: A critical review. *Expert Review of Neurotherapeutics, 9,* 745–758.

Rief, W., & Broadbent, E. (2007). Explaining medically unexplained symptoms—models and mechanisms, *Clinical Psychology Review, 27,* 769–780.

Rief, W., Hessel, A., & Braehler, E., 2001. Somatization symptoms and hypochondriacal features in the general population. *Psychosomatic Medicine, 63,* 595–602.

Rief, W., Hiller, W., Geissner, E., & Fichter, M. M. (1995). A two-year follow-up study of patients with somatoform disorders. *Psychosomatics, 36,* 376–386.

Rief, W., Nanke, A., Emmerich, J., Bender, A., & Zech, T. (2004). Causal illness attributions in somatoform disorders: Associations with comorbidity and illness behavior. *Journal of Psychosomatic Research, 57,* 367–371.

Rief, W., & Sharpe, M. (2004). Somatoform disorders—new approaches to classification, conceptualization and treatment. *Journal of Psychosomatic Research, 56,* 387–390.

Roelofs, K., Keijsers, G. P. J., Hoogduin, C. A. L., Näring, G. W. B., & Moene, F. C. (2002). Childhood abuse in patients with conversion disorder. *American Journal Psychiatry, 159,* 1908–1913.

Roelofs, K., & Spinhoven, P. (2007). Trauma and medically unexplained symptoms. Towards an integration of cognitive and neurobiological accounts. *Clinical Psychology Review, 27,* 798–820.

Salkovskis, P. M., & Warwick, H. M. C. (2001). Making sense of hypochondriasis: A cognitive model of health anxiety. In G. J. G. Asmundson, S. Taylor, & B. Cox (Eds.), *Health anxiety: Clinical research perspectives on hypochondriasis and related disorders* (pp. 46–64). New York: Wiley.

Salmon, P., & Calderbank, S. (1996). The relationship of childhood physical and sexual abuse to adult illness behavior. *Journal of Psychosomatic Research, 40,* 329–336.

Sar, V., Akyüz, G., Dogan, O., & Öztü, E. (2009). The prevalence of conversion symptoms in women from a general Turkish population. *Psychosomatics, 50,* 50–58.

Schermelleh-Engel, K., Eifert, G. H, Moosbrugger, H., & Frank, D. (1997). Perceived competence and anxiety as determinants of maladaptive and adaptive coping strategies of chronic pain patients. *Personality and Individual Differences, 22,* 1–10.

Schreier, H. A., & Libow, J. A. (1993). *Hurting for love: Münchhausen by proxy syndrome.* New York: Guilford Press.

Schröder, A., & Fink, P. (2010). The proposed diagnosis of somatic symptom disorder in DSM-V: Two steps forward and one step backward? *Journal of Psychosomatic Research, 68,* 95–96.

Sharma, P., & Chaturvedi, S. K. (1995). Conversion disorder revisited. *Acta Psychiatrica Scandinavica, 92,* 301–304.

Sharpe, M., Mayou, R., & Bass, C. M. (1995). Concepts, theories, and terminology. In R. Mayou, C. M. Bass, & M. Sharpe (Eds.), *Treatment of functional somatic symptoms* (pp. 3–16). Oxford, UK: Oxford University Press.

Shidhaye, R., Mendenhall, E., Sumathipala, K., Sumathipala, A., & Patel, V. (2013).

Association of somatoform disorders with anxiety and depression in women of low and middle income countries: A systematic review. *International Review of Psychiatry, 25*, 65–76.

Sifneos, P. E. (1973). The prevalence of "alexithymic" characteristics in psychosomatic patients. *Psychotherapy and Psychosomatics, 22*, 255–262.

Simms, L. J., Prisciandaro, J. J., Krueger, R. F., & Goldberg, D. P. (2011). The structure of depression, anxiety and somatic symptoms in primary care. *Psychological Medicine, 42*, 15–28.

Sirri, L., & Fava, G. A. (2013). Diagnostic criteria for psychosomatic research and somatic symptom disorders. *International Journal of Psychiatry, 25*, 19–30.

Starcevic, V. (2006). Somatoform disorders and the DSM-V: Conceptual and political issues in the debate. *Psychosomatics, 47*, 277–281.

Stekel W. (1943). *The interpretation of dreams: New developments and technique.* New York: Liveright.

Stone, J. (2009). Functional symptoms in neurology. *Neurology in Practice, 9*, 19–189.

Stone, J., LaFrance, W. C., Brown, R., Spiegel, D., Levenson, J. L., & Sharpe, M. (2010). Conversion disorder: Current problems and potential solutions for DSM-5. *Journal of Psychosomatic Research, 71*, 369–376.

Stone, J., Smyth, R., Carson, A., Lewis, S., Prescott, R., Warlow, C., & Sharpe, M. (2005). Systematic review of misdiagnosis of conversion symptoms and "hysteria." *British Medical Journal, 331*, 989–991.

Subic-Wrana, C., Beutel, M. E., Knebel, A., & Lane, R. D. (2010). Theory of mind and emotional awareness deficits in patients with somatoform disorders. *Psychosomatic Medicine, 72*, 404–411.

Sullivan, M. J. L., Adams, H., & Sullivan, M. E. (2004). Communicative dimensions of pain catastrophizing: Social cueing effects on pain behaviour and coping. *Pain, 107*, 220–226.

Sutherland, A. J., & Rodin, G. M. (1990). Factitious disorder in a general hospital setting: Clinical features and a review of the literature. *Psychosomatics, 31*, 392–399.

Sunderland, M., Newby, J. M., & Andrews, G. (2013). Health anxiety in Australia: Prevalence, comorbidity, disability and service use. *British Journal of Psychiatry, 202*, 56–61.

Sykes, R. (2012). Somatoform disorder and the DSM-V workgroup's interim proposals: Two central issues. *Psychosomatics, 53*, 334–338.

Taylor, G. J., Thordarson, D. S., Jang, K. L., & Asmundson, G. J. (2006). Genetic and environmental origins of health anxiety: A twin study. *World Psychiatry, 5*, 47–50

Torgerson, S. (1986). Genetics of somatoform disorders. *Archives of General Psychiatry, 43*, 502–505.

Turk, D. C., Meichenbaum, D., & Genest, M. (1983). *Pain and behavioral medicine: A cognitive-behavioral perspective.* New York: Guilford Press.

Turk, D. C., Okifuji, A., & Scharff, L. (1995). Chronic pain and depression: Role of perceived impact and perceived control in different age cohorts. *Pain, 61*, 93–101.

Tyrer, P. (1995). Somatoform and personality disorders: Personality and the soma. *Journal of Psychosomatic Research, 39*, 395–397.

Tyrer, P., Cooper, S., Crawford, M., Dupont, S., Green, J., Murphy, D., Salkovskis, P., et al. (2011). Prevalence of health anxiety problems in medical clinics. *Journal of Psychosomatic Research, 71*, 392–394.

Van der Kruijs, S. J. M., Bodde, N. M. G., Vaessen, M. J., Lazeron, R. H. C., Vonck, K., Boon, P., Hofman, P. A. M., Backes, W. H., Aldenkamp, A. P., & Jansen, J. F. A. (2012). Functional connectivity of dissociation in patients with psychogenic non-epileptic seizures. *Journal of Neurology and Neurosurgical Psychiatry, 83*, 239–247.

Van Wilgen, C. P., Koning, M., & Bouman, T. K. (2013). Initial responses of different health care professionals to various patients with headache: Which are perceived as difficult? *International Journal of Behavioral Medicine, 20*(3), 468–475.

Vlaeyen, J. W., Kole-Snijders, A. M., Boeren, R. G., & Van Eek, H. (1995). Fear of movement/(re)injury in chronic low back pain and its relation to behavioral performance. *Pain, 62*, 363–372.

Voigt, K., Nagel., A., Meyer, B., Langs, G., Braukhaus, C., & Löwe, B. (2010). Towards positive diagnostic criteria: A systematic review of somatoform disorder diagnoses and suggestions for future classification. *Journal of Psychosomatic Research, 68*, 403–414.

Voigt, K., Wollburg, E., Wienmann, N., Herzog, A., Meyer, B., Langs, G., & Löwe, B. (2012). Predictive validity and clinical utility of DSM-5 somatic symptom disorder—comparison with DSM-IV somatoform disorders and additional criteria for consideration. *Journal of Psychosomatic Research, 73*, 345–350.

Voon, V., Brezing, C., Gallea, C., Ameli, R., Roelofs, K., LaFrance Jr., W. C., & Hallett, M. (2010). Emotional stimuli and motor conversion disorder. *Brain, 133*, 1526–1536.

Waller, E., & Scheidt, C. E. (2006). Somatoform disorders as disorders of affect regulation: A developmental perspective. *International Review of Psychiatry*, *18*, 13–24.

Warwick, H. M. C., & Salkovskis, P. M. (1990). Hypochondriasis. *Behaviour Research and Therapy*, *24*, 597–602.

Weck, F., Neng, J. M. B., Richtberg, S., & Stangier, U. (2012). The restrictive concept of good health in patients with hypochondriasis. *Journal of Anxiety Disorders*, *26*, 792–798.

Wessely, S., Nimnuan, C., & Sharpe, M (1999). Functional somatic syndromes: One or many? *Lancet*, *354*, 936–939.

Williams, P. G. (2004). The psychopathology of self-assessed health: A cognitive approach to health anxiety and hypochondriasis. *Cognitive Therapy and Research*, *28*, 629–644.

Winterowd, C., Beck, A. T., & Gruener, D. (2003). *Cognitive therapy for chronic pain patients*. New York: Springer.

Wolburg, E., Voigt, K., Braukhaus, C., Herzog, A., & Löwe, B. (2013). Construct validity and descriptive validity of somatoform disorders in light of proposed changes for DSM-5. *Journal of Psychosomatic Research*, *74*, 18–24.

World Health Organization (2003). *Adherence to long-term therapies: Evidence for action*. Geneva: World Health Organization.

21

Sleep–Wake Disorders

CHARLES M. MORIN
AND JACK D. EDINGER

Sleep–wake disorders are common and debilitating conditions that contribute to emotional distress, social or occupational dysfunction, increased risks for injury, and serious medical illnesses (Partinen & Hublin, 2011; Roth et al., 2011). Although it has long been recognized that sleep disturbances are common symptoms of various psychopathological conditions, their significance as distinct clinical entities has been minimized or ignored by psychologists and other health care providers. However, over the past three decades, research has increasingly pointed to their importance as central factors in the etiology of many psychiatric and medical disorders and as primary disorders that occur in isolation or comorbidly with other mental and medical disorders. When sleep disorders occur as comorbid conditions, they typically warrant separate clinical attention.

This chapter highlights those sleep–wake disturbances that present either as independent syndromes occurring in isolation or comorbidly, or as etiologically important symptoms in the development of other forms of psychopathology. The initial section describes the brief history of classification systems for sleep–wake disorders. The subsequent sections describe the various sleep disorders listed in *DSM-5*, along with a summary of their epidemiology, clinical features, and etiology. Following their descriptions is a discussion of the relationships of sleep disorders to selected mental and medical disorders. The concluding section considers limitations of previous research and provides suggestions for future research.

Sleep–Wake Disorders Classification

Nosologies for the diagnosis of sleep–wake disorders have become available only within the past four decades. During this period, several divergent approaches for these disorders classification have been proposed, but research supporting the reliability and validity of these nosologies has been limited. Nonetheless, each has heuristic appeal and provides a basis for further research. The ensuing discussion describes the evolution of these nosologies and recounts the merits and limitations of the systems currently in use.

In 1979, the Association of Sleep Disorders Centers (ASDC) spawned interest in formal sleep–wake disorders classification, with the publication of their monograph *Diagnostic Classification of Sleep and Arousal Disorders* (DCSAD; Association of Sleep Disorders Centers, 1979). This system categorized disorders primarily on the basis of patients' presenting complaints. There were four global categories: disorders of initiating and maintaining sleep (DIMS), disorders of excessive daytime somnolence (DOES), sleep–wake schedule disorders, and parasomnias. Included within the DIMS were seven insomnia subtypes arising from underlying psychiatric, behavioral, or medical/neurological causes. The DOES included diagnoses reserved for sleep–wake disturbances associated with primary complaints of excessive daytime sleepiness (EDS). Sleep–wake schedule disorders included conditions resulting from a mismatch of individuals' endogenous circadian rhythms and their desired sleep–wake schedules (e.g., jet lag). Finally, the parasomnias included unusual events (e.g., seizures) or aberrant behaviors (e.g., sleepwalking) that occur during sleep.

During this same time period other professional organizations began to recognize sleep disorders and include them in their nosologies. The *ICD-9* provided a fairly global nosology that listed a number of sleep disorders of nonorganic origin and disorders of organic origin (i.e., "true" primary sleep disorders). Likewise, *DSM-III-R* included 15 diagnoses for sleep–wake disorders. Insomnias were subdivided into four categories (i.e., insomnia due to another mental disorder, insomnia due to a known organic factor, primary insomnia, and insomnia not otherwise specified—NOS), whereas the diagnoses of breathing-related sleep disorder, narcolepsy, primary hypersomnia, hypersomnia related to another mental disorder, hypersomnia related to a known organic factor, and hypersomnia NOS were reserved for those conditions characterized primarily by EDS. Also included in *DSM-III-R* were four diagnoses (sleepwalking, night terror, nightmare, and parasomnia NOS) for the parasomnias and one diagnosis, sleep–wake schedule disorder, which subsumed all types of circadian rhythm disorders (e.g., jet lag, shift work). Whereas *DSM-III-R* and DCSAD classification schemes categorized sleep–wake disorders primarily on the basis of patients' presenting complaints, the *DSM-III-R* system used broader groupings.

In contrast, subsequent systems such as the *International Classification of Sleep Disorders (ICSD/ICSD-R;* American Academy of Sleep Medicine, 1990, 1997) and *DSM-IV/DSM-IV-TR* grouped sleep disorders primarily on the basis of their pathophysiologies. For example, *DSM-IV-TR* nosology included a total of 22 disorders presumed to represent either primary sleep–wake disorders or predominant secondary symptoms arising from other psychiatric, medical, or substance abuse disorders. The initial ICSD versions included a total of 84 disorders, for much greater diagnostic specificity. However, because much has yet to be learned about the pathophysiology of many sleep disorders, the organizational structure of the original *ICSD* was replaced with a simpler, more descriptive and global classification system in the subsequent revised version of this nosology, called the *ICSD-2 (American Academy of Sleep Medicine)* 2005). Furthermore, the *ICSD-2* classification

scheme was accepted for inclusion in the *ICD-10* system as well. Although the *ICSD-2* nosology provided a more global classification system than did the original *ICSD*, it continued to delineate a fairly large number of sleep disorders. As such, it seemed to serve the needs of sleep disorder specialists more than those of general practitioners.

Since the publication of *DSM-IV-TR* and *ICSD-2*, there have been growing pressures for revising these two classification systems, both to incorporate new research findings and to make the two systems as concordant as possible. For some disorders such as insomnia, recent research has argued for a "lumping approach" wherein many of the insomnia subtypes previously listed in both *DSM-IV-TR* and *ICSD-2* are grouped into a relatively few more global insomnia disorders. For other disorders such as narcolepsy, research has suggested the need for a "splitting approach" in which the more global narcolepsy disorder is divided into distinctive subtypes. In addition, reports (Buysse et al., 1994; Ohayon & Roberts, 2001) highlighting the discordance between these systems has also led to the recognition that a more unified diagnostic approach is needed to optimize research and clinical care in the field of sleep medicine. As such, there has been considerable collaboration between the American Psychiatric Association (APA) and American Academy of Sleep Medicine (AASM) to develop revised versions of the *DSM* and *ICSD* systems that are both evidence-based and concordant. These collaborative efforts, in turn, have led to the current *DSM-5* and *ICSD-3* versions of the APA and AASM systems. Whereas the *ICSD-3* remains a somewhat more complex scheme than is the Sleep Disorders section of the *DSM-5*, these two have overlap and consistency not seen in the previous *DSM* and *ICSD* systems.

One notable area of convergence between the two systems is their abandonment of the distinction between "primary" and "secondary" forms of sleep disorders. Common to all previous sleep disorders nosologies was their underlying premise that disorders such as insomnia or hypersomnia could exist both as an independent disorder and as a symptom of various medical and psychiatric conditions (i.e., primary versus secondary). However, clinical experience and research have suggested that sleep problems occurring coincident with medical and psychiatric conditions may often develop some independence over time and thus warrant independent clinical attention. This change in opinion is reflected in the following comment provided in the 2005 NIH State of the Science Conference Statement concerning the manifestations and management of chronic insomnia in adults (National Institutes of Health [NIH], 2005):

> Most cases of insomnia are comorbid with other conditions. Historically, this has been termed "secondary insomnia." However, the limited understanding of mechanistic pathways in chronic insomnia precludes drawing firm conclusions about the nature of these associations or direction of causality. Furthermore, there is concern that the term secondary insomnia may promote under-treatment. Therefore, we propose that the term "comorbid insomnia" may be more appropriate. (p. 1050)

In view of such considerations, both the *DSM-5* and *ICSD-3* have generally moved away from distinguishing primary and secondary forms of sleep disorders and resorted to more global insomnia disorder categories that can be assigned in the presence or absence of another medical, psychiatric, or sleep disorder that could also cause sleep disturbance.

Since *DSM-5* is likely to be used much more widely by psychologists and other mental health professionals, the system listed there will be the focus of this chapter. This nosology lists eight general categories (see Table 21.1). Patients with these conditions generally report dissatisfaction with some aspect of their sleep or waking functions or both. For some patients, the sleep-focused problems may concern the quality, timing, amounts, or discontinuity in their sleep. For others, primary complaints focus more on daytime sleepiness or impairment, and for yet others, they focus on unusual behaviors occurring in sleep. The following text provides a description of each of these sleep disorder categories.

Insomnia Disorder

Insomnia disorder is characterized by a dissatisfaction with sleep quantity or quality, associated with symptoms of difficulty initiating or maintaining sleep. This condition may occur independently from or comorbidly with a psychiatric, medical, substance or medication use, or other sleep disorder (Morin & Benca, 2012). Individuals suffering from insomnia that occurs as an independent disorder often complain of mild anxiety, mood disturbances, concentration or memory dysfunction, somatic concerns, and general malaise, but such clinical symptoms do not meet the diagnostic

Table 21.1 Overview of *DSM-5* Sleep–Wake Disorders

Insomnia disorder. The predominant complaint is dissatisfaction with sleep quality or quantity, associated with difficulty falling asleep, difficulty maintaining sleep, or early morning awakening with an inability to return to sleep.

Hypersomnolence disorder. The main feature is excessive sleepiness during the day despite adequate sleep duration at night. Sleep is not refreshing, morning awakening is difficult, and there are recurrent episodes of sleep or lapses into sleep during the day.

Narcolepsy. Recurrent and uncontrollable sleep attacks during the day, with or without episodes of cataplexy (i.e., sudden loss of muscle tone triggered by strong emotions).

Breathing-related sleep disorders (BRSDs). Repeated episodes of complete (apneas) or partial cessation of breathing (hypopneas) during sleep accompanied by snoring, sleep fragmentation, decreased oxygen saturation, and excessive daytime sleepiness.

Circadian rhythm sleep-wake disorders (CRSWDs). A group of disorders characterized by a misalignment between the endogenous circadian clock and the sleep–wake schedule, resulting in undesired sleepiness when wakefulness is necessary and insomnia when sleep is needed.

Parasomnias. Abnormal behavioral events occurring during different sleep stages, such as sleepwalking, sleep terrors, nightmares, and REM behavior disorder.

Restless legs syndrome (RLS). A condition characterized by an irresistible urge to move the legs resulting from an unpleasant creeping or crawling sensation in the legs. This condition occurs mainly while siting or resting, is worst in the evening, and may cause significant problems falling asleep. It is temporarily relieved by moving or stretching the legs.

Substance/medication-induced sleep disorder. Sleep–wake disturbances associated with the use, abuse, or withdrawal of substances (e.g., alcohol, caffeine), prescribed and over-the-counter medications, and illicit drugs.

criteria for another mental disorder (Edinger & Carney, 2008; Morin & Espie, 2003). In cases of comorbid insomnia disorder, insomnia symptoms may first emerge as a consequence of the comorbid condition, but over time the insomnia develops partial or total independence from the comorbid disorder. In contrast, patients who develop insomnia disorder in isolation appear at greater risk for the subsequent development of comorbid mental disorders such as depression and anxiety disorders. In practice it is usually not possible to differentiate the causal pathways between insomnia and comorbid conditions. As such, insomnia disorder would apply for patients with comorbid conditions whenever the insomnia symptoms warrant separate treatment attention.

The sleep symptoms of insomnia may include difficulty initiating sleep; difficulty maintaining sleep, characterized by frequent awakenings or difficulty returning to sleep after an awakening; or waking up too early, well before the desired rising time, with an inability to return to sleep. Difficulties maintaining sleep occur more commonly than difficulties falling asleep, although the two sorts of sleep complaint often occur together. A complaint of nonrestorative or unrefreshing sleep may occur along with these other sleep complaints; rarely it may also occur in isolation. In the latter case the diagnosis of insomnia disorder would not apply; such cases are assigned a diagnosis of other specified insomnia disorder or unspecified insomnia disorder. The nature of the specific problems may vary over time such that individuals may present with sleep-onset complaints at one time point and subsequently with sleep maintenance difficulties or a mixture of sleep onset and maintenance problems at a later time (Morin et al., 2009). Although there are no agreed-upon quantitative cutoffs to define sleep onset and maintenance insomnia, sleep latencies and wake times during the course of the night in the 20- to 30-minute range are more characteristic of insomnia sufferers than they are of normal sleepers (Lichstein, Durrence, Taylor, Bush, & Riedel, 2003; Lineberger, Carney, Edinger, & Means, 2006).

The presence of these various sleep symptoms alone does not warrant an insomnia disorder diagnosis. Such symptoms must lead to distress or impairment in occupational, academic, social, or other important areas of waking function. Moreover, the sleep disturbance must occur during time periods when the affected individual has adequate opportunity (is allotting enough time for sleep) and circumstances (a safe and comfortable sleeping environment) for sleep. In addition, the sleep–wake disturbance must occur at least three nights per week for a period of minimally 3 months to warrant an insomnia disorder diagnosis.

Transient insomnia, due to episodic stress or sudden disruption in the usual sleep–wake schedule, is experienced by most individuals at one time or another. Between 9% and 22% of adults report chronic insomnia, and between 6% and 10% meet full *DSM* diagnostic criteria for an insomnia disorder (Morin, LeBlanc, Daley, Grégoire, & Mérette, 2006; Ohayon, 2002; Roth et al., 2011). Epidemiological surveys have shown that complaints of insomnia are age related, with an increased prevalence among middle-aged and older adults (Ohayon, 2002). In addition, sleep-onset difficulties are more common among young adults, whereas difficulties maintaining sleep, and poor-quality sleep occur more commonly among middle-aged and older individuals. Several studies have shown that insomnia complaints are more prevalent among women than among men (Ohayon, 2002), but it is not known whether such findings reflect reporting biases or actual gender differences. Unfortunately, many previous epidemiological surveys queried respondents about general sleep symptoms (e.g., difficulty falling asleep, difficulty staying asleep) but did not include questions covering full diagnostic criteria to provide accurate estimates of the prevalence of insomnia disorder. Population prevalence based on *DSM-5* criteria has not yet been established. However, with a more stringent and operational definition of insomnia in *DSM-5*, it is expected that the prevalence of insomnia disorder may be slightly lower than previously reported. Of course, insomnia is fairly prevalent in clinical venues such as primary and specialty care settings (Buysse et al., 1994).

A widely accepted etiological theory attributes this condition to a special confluence of endogenous predisposing characteristics, sleep-disruptive precipitating events, and perpetuating behaviors or circumstances (Spielman, 1986). According to this theory, vulnerabilities such as a proneness to worry, repression of disturbing emotion, physiological hyperarousal, an innate propensity toward light, fragmented sleep, or a combination of these factors may predispose certain individuals to a primary sleep disturbance. Subsequently, insomnia may develop among such individuals given sufficient stress or disruption from a precipitating event (e.g., loss of a loved one, undergoing a painful medical procedure). Insomnia may then persist when conditioned environmental cues, repetitive sleep-disruptive habits, and dysfunctional cognitions serve to perpetuate sleep disturbance long after the initial precipitating circumstances are resolved.

Clinical observations have provided much support for this model. Many individuals with insomnia disorder report an intense preoccupation with sleep and a heightened arousal as bedtime approaches (Edinger & Carney, 2008; Morin & Espie, 2003; Spielman, Conroy, & Glovinsky, 2003). Indeed, such patients report that they view bedtime as the worst time of day. A vicious cycle emerges in which repetitive unsuccessful sleep attempts reinforce the insomnia sufferer's anticipatory anxiety that, in turn, contributes to more insomnia. Through repetitive association with unsuccessful sleep efforts, the bedroom environment and presleep rituals often become cues or stimuli for poor sleep. Moreover, in some cases, formerly benign habits such as watching television, eating, or reading in bed may also reduce the stimulus value of the bed and bedroom for sleep and may further exacerbate the sleep problem. Consequently, it is common for those with insomnia disorder to report improved sleep in novel settings where conditioned environmental cues are absent and usual presleep rituals are obviated.

In addition, many with insomnia disorder admit to poor sleep habits that initially emerged as a means of dealing with their sleep disturbances. For example, poor sleep at night may lead to daytime napping or sleeping late on weekends in efforts to catch up on lost sleep. Alternatively, such individuals may lie in bed for protracted periods trying to force sleep, only to find themselves becoming more and more awake. Such findings are particularly common among middle-aged and older adults because of an age-related decline in homeostatic sleep drive and an accompanying increase in sleep fragmentation (Bliwise, 2011; Dijk, Duffy, & Czeisler, 2001). In addition, other practices, such as routinely engaging in physically or mentally stimulating activities shortly before bed or failing to adhere to a regular sleep–wake schedule, often emerge from lifestyle choices or perceived social obligations and contribute to the sleep difficulty.

Several studies have corroborated these observations and suggested that dispositional characteristics, stressful life events, and perpetuating behaviors or circumstances may all play a role in the etiology of primary insomnia. Psychometric studies have shown that persons with primary insomnia are characterized by mild anxiety, depression, and a predisposition toward worrying and the internalization of disturbing affect (Edinger et al., 2000). In addition, laboratory studies have shown that those with insomnia disorder show less daytime sleepiness and higher heart rates, higher core body temperature and cortical activation during sleep, and higher metabolic activity during the night than do age- and gender-matched controls (Bonnet & Arand, 1998, 2010; Nofzinger et al., 2006). Collectively, such studies give credibility to the assumption that predisposing characteristics (i.e., hyperarousal, worrying) may enhance the vulnerability of certain individuals to insomnia.

Similarly, several precipitating circumstances appear etiologically important, as most individuals with insomnia report that a stressful life (i.e., family, health, work) is associated with the onset of their insomnia (Bastien, Vallières, & Morin, 2004). Finally, numerous studies (for reviews, see Morin et al., 2006; Smith et al., 2002) have demonstrated the efficacy of behavioral treatments in eliminating poor sleep hygiene practices and conditioned arousal at bedtime, thus lending support to the presumed significance of those mechanisms in sustaining insomnia that occur in isolation or are comorbid with other disorders.

Although these studies provide indirect support for the etiological model for insomnia disorder, they fall short of confirming it. Studies of predisposing and precipitating factors have either failed to include appropriate control groups or have employed cross-sectional or retrospective methodologies. Moreover, whereas behavioral treatment studies provide seemingly more compelling support for the importance of conditioned arousal and poor sleep hygiene as perpetuating mechanisms, such studies have generally failed to demonstrate that sleep improvements occurred in conjunction with elimination of these sustaining factors. Hence, it is possible that such treatments are effective because they address some yet-to-be-identified dispositional characteristic and/or perpetuating agents germane to insomnia. In addition, factors other than those noted earlier may play a significant role in sustaining the sleep difficulties of at least some insomnia sufferers. Results reported by Buysse et al. (1994), for example, showed that psychiatric disorders often coexist with insomnia. As a consequence, some writers (e.g., Vgontzas, Kales, Bixler, & Vela-Bueno, 1993) have argued that such psychiatric conditions play central etiological roles in the development of most people who meet criteria for this disorder.

Hypersomnolence Disorder

Hypersomnolence disorder (also called idiopathic hypersomnia) involves excessive daytime sleepiness (EDS) despite adequate sleep duration at night. Its main manifestations include a prolonged (>9 hours) sleep episode at night that is not refreshing, difficulty awakening in the morning along with sleep inertia, and recurrent episodes of sleep or lapses into sleep during the day. Individuals with this disorder can fall asleep very rapidly and sleep very well and for a prolonged period. Nonetheless, they have great difficulty coming out of sleep, often experiencing an awakening that is characterized by confusion, followed by impaired performance and vigilance even after being awake for some time. Other features may include automatic behaviors (e.g., eating, reading, driving) that the individuals carry out with little recollection (Anderson, Pilsworth, Sharples, Smith, & Shneerson, 2007). Because of excessive sleepiness persisting even after a prolonged nocturnal sleep episode, daytime naps are frequent and often repeated throughout the day. These naps are relatively long (may last more than 1 hour), but they are not more refreshing than the nocturnal sleep episode and do not lead to improved vigilance.

Individuals with this disorder often experience major difficulties showing up at work or at school on time given their difficulties getting up in the morning. They may also fall asleep at inappropriate places or times, causing social stigma, irritations, or even risk for injuries to self or others. It is estimated that 28% of adults experience excessive sleepiness and between 2% and 5% meet criteria for hypersomnolence disorder (Ohayon, Dauvilliers, & Reynolds, 2012). The onset of this condition is most common in late adolescence and young adulthood, and it is often chronic and treatment resistant.

The etiology of this disorder is poorly understood. Reflecting this lack of knowledge, this condition is also called idiopathic hypersomnia (American Academy of Sleep Medicine, 2005).

The main differential diagnosis is with insufficient sleep syndrome, which often produces EDS. In this later case, sleep is usually refreshing but simply too short for the individual to feel rested in the morning and remain awake and alert throughout the next day. There are also normal variations in sleep requirements, and some people may need 9 or 10 hours of sleep per night; these "natural long sleepers" usually feel rested when they obtain their required sleep, whereas an individual with hypersomnolence disorder does not feel rested even after, say, 12 hours of sleep. Other sleep (e.g., sleep apnea, narcolepsy) or psychiatric disorders (e.g., the depressive phase of a bipolar disorder) may be associated with EDS, but these conditions would have their own distinctive features. For example, sudden and recurrent sleep attacks are primary features of narcolepsy, whereas daytime sleepiness usually builds up gradually in hypersomnolence. In sleep apnea, the breathing problem impairs sleep at night and is directly responsible for the EDS.

Narcolepsy

The term *narcolepsy* was first used in 1880 by the French neurologist Gélineau to describe a syndrome characterized by recurrent, irresistible daytime sleep episodes that, in some patients, were accompanied by sudden falls. Four symptoms that commonly co-occur were later identified and became regarded as the classic tetrad indicative of narcolepsy: (1) EDS and unintended sleep episodes occurring during situations (e.g., driving, at work, during conversations) when most persons typically are able to remain awake; (2) cataplexy, which consists of an abrupt and reversible decrease or loss of muscle tone (without loss of consciousness), precipitated most often by such emotions as laughter, anger, surprise, or exhilaration; (3) sleep paralysis, which involves an awakening from nocturnal or diurnal sleep with an inability to move; and (4) hypnagogic hallucinations, consisting of strong, vivid images occurring as a person is falling asleep or coming out of sleep. However, not all narcoleptics display this tetrad of symptoms.

DSM-5 describes five variants of narcoleptic phenotypes distinguished by their presenting symptom array, age of onset, associated biomarkers, and/or etiologies. These include *narcolepsy without cataplexy but with hypocretin deficiency* (a protein found in the cerebrospinal fluid; CSF);

narcolepsy with cataplexy but without hypocretin deficiency (<5% of all narcolepsy cases); *autosomal dominant cerebellar ataxia, deafness, and narcolepsy,* a late-onset (ages 30 to 40 years) variant leading to dementia; and *autosomal dominant narcolepsy, obesity, and type II diabetes,* a rare subtype having these three co-occurring disorders. Finally, *narcolepsy secondary to another medical condition* is characterized by the common wake and sleep symptoms of narcolepsy and develops as a result of an infectious process or brain trauma or tumor that destroys the hypocretin neurons in the central nervous system.

Regardless of the specific subtype, individuals with narcolepsy typically report frequent overwhelming sleepiness leading to napping throughout the day despite having obtained a seemingly adequate amount of sleep during the previous night. EDS is usually the first symptom to present, followed by cataplexy typically occurring 1 to 3 years later. The onset of narcolepsy usually occurs during adolescence or young adulthood and rarely during later adulthood. Epidemiological data suggest that onset of narcolepsy occurs most frequently between the ages of 15 and 25 years and between ages 30 and 35 years. Other symptoms of the disorder may develop several years after the onset of EDS or not at all. Between 20% and 60% of narcolepsy sufferers report very vivid and disturbing hypnagogic hallucinations at sleep onset or similar hypnopompic (upon awakening) hallucinations. A similar proportion also report sleep paralysis characterized by an inability to move or speak upon falling asleep or after awakening. Nighttime sleep often shows alterations in sleep architecture and fragmentation that reduce overall sleep efficiency and quality. Although daytime naps are often momentarily restorative, excessive sleepiness may return shortly thereafter. As the syndrome progresses, naps may lose their restorative value and even nocturnal sleep may become more and more disturbed.

Narcolepsy is a relatively rare condition, with about 5 cases in 10,000, and a slightly higher prevalence among men. Cross-cultural comparisons indicate that its prevalence varies substantially across ethnic groups, and such findings, along with studies of narcoleptic canines, suggest genetic characteristics are involved as predisposing factors (Mignot, 2011). However, nongenetic mechanisms such as infectious processes or central nervous system trauma have been implicated

as causative factors in some cases. Recent findings show that, in most cases with cataplexy and in fewer cases without cataplexy, a deficiency in the neuropeptide hypocretin system is also involved. The mechanism by which hypocretin deficiency leads to narcolepsy is only recently beginning to emerge, and data suggest a central role of hypocretin in the promotion of wakefulness. Life events may, at times, precipitate the onset of this disorder (Orellana et al., 1994), and although not viewed as causative factors, psychosocial disturbances may present as noteworthy associated features of narcolepsy. Depressed mood, impaired occupational and social functioning, and marital discord may all be caused by the EDS arising from this syndrome. In addition, individuals with narcolepsy may engage in volitional emotional constriction or avoid situations that might arouse even pleasant emotions in an effort to control cataplectic attacks. Hence, narcolepsy may contribute to significant psychosocial dysfunction.

Since the diagnosis of narcolepsy is reliant on specialized diagnostic procedures, individuals suspected of having this disorder should be referred to a sleep specialist for evaluation. Overnight sleep testing or polysomnography (PSG) along with a daytime test known as the Multiple Sleep Latency Test (MSLT) are used to diagnose narcolepsy, particularly when the condition is first recognized. PSG testing typically shows a fairly rapid onset of rapid eye movement (REM) sleep usually within 15 minutes of sleep onset (REM latency varies between 70 and 90 minutes among normal controls). The subsequent daytime MSLT, which consists of a series of four to five nap trials scheduled throughout the day, typically shows an average sleep onset of 8 minutes or less, with the occurrence of REM sleep on at least two of the naps. Data suggest that 99% of narcoleptics are positive for the human leukocyte antigen (HLA)DQB1*06:02, whereas 12%–38% of non-narcoleptics have positive findings for this antigen. Hence, a positive assay for this antigen is consistent with but does not confirm a diagnosis of narcolepsy. In some cases measuring CSF hypocretin-1 immunoreactivity is useful for the diagnosis of this condition, particularly to rule out a conversion disorder or to evaluate cases that lack cataplexy or fail treatment efforts. However, this test is only available at a limited number of centers and is generally not considered a part of the routine diagnostic process.

Breathing-Related Sleep Disorders

DSM-5 describes a variety of breathing-related sleep disorders (BRSDs) that produce significant nocturnal sleep disruption and result in sleep–wake complaints. Among these are *obstructive sleep apnea, central sleep apnea*, and *sleep-related hypoventilation*. These three vary in their presentations and underlying etiologies. They can be distinguished by specific respiratory patterns found on the diagnostic PSG. For that reason, PSG is essential in their diagnosis.

Patients with *obstructive sleep apnea* (OSA) experience repetitive partial (hypopneas) or complete (apneas) obstruction of their upper airways during sleep despite a continued diaphragmatic effort to breathe. Each such respiratory event lasts 10 seconds or longer and typically has sleep-disruptive effects. *DSM-5* criteria for the diagnosis of OSA require a minimum of 15 apneas or hypopneas per hour of sleep, regardless of accompanying sleep–wake complaints, or a minimum of five such breathing events per hour of sleep in association with snoring, snorting or gasping, or breathing pauses during sleep or daytime fatigue, sleepiness, or unrefreshing sleep despite a relatively normal sleep duration. Etiological contributors to OSA can vary across individuals and include a small oropharynx, presence of excessive or obstructive tissues in the upper airway, and intrusion of the mandible into the upper airway space. In young children OSA usually arises as a result of enlarged tonsils and adenoids. There are several variations of OSA, but all such BRSDs typically lead to repeated arousals from sleep (to restart normal breathing) and consequent reduction of sleep quality (Cao, Guilleminault, & Kushida, 2011). In children, symptoms can include hyperactivity, irritability, and behavioral problems.

The common symptoms of OSA are loud snoring, pauses in breathing, and EDS. Although some patients have insomnia, most report EDS and unintentional sleep daytime episodes. Additional symptoms may include gasping for breath during sleep, headaches upon awakening, and automatic behaviors (i.e., carrying out activities without being aware of one's actions) during wakefulness. OSA may result in such secondary psychological symptoms as dysphoria, memory disturbance, concentration problems, and irritability. In addition, it may produce serious medical consequences, including hypertension, cardiac arrhythmias,

sexual dysfunction, nocturnal enuresis, and hearing loss (Sanders & Givelber, 2006).

Patients with *central sleep apnea* (CSA) evidence repeated sleep-related events characterized by the cessation of breathing or markedly reduced airflow in the absence of respiratory effort. Patients with heart failure may have CSA in association with a Cheyne-Stokes breathing pattern, characterized by repeated crescendo–decrescendo patterns of airflow during sleep that result in the central apneas/hyponeas. In contrast, some patients may have CSA attributed to comorbid use of opioids, which reduce respiratory drive. Finally, in rare cases, CSA is idiopathic and occurs in the absence of any comorbid condition thought to interfere with breathing during sleep. Regardless of subtype, patients with CSA can present with complaints of insomnia or daytime sleepiness along with sleep fragmentation or awakenings associated with a shortness of breath. Central and obstructive sleep apneic events can occur in the same individual.

In cases of *sleep-related hypoventilation* (SRH), the diagnostic PSG shows episodes of decreased respiration associated with increased CO_2 and reduced O_2 concentration in the hemoglobin. SRH is commonly associated with such comorbid conditions as obesity, pulmonary disorders, neuromuscular or chest wall disorders, and certain medications (benzodiazepines, opioids). Individuals with SRH can present with complaints of daytime sleepiness or insomnia. Some also have headaches upon awakening; decreased mental acuity and depression are seen as well. Consequences of SRH can include pulmonary hypertension, right-sided heart failure, disproportionate increases in red blood cells, and cognitive dysfunction.

BRSDs are far more prevalent than narcolepsy. OSA, the most common BRSD, is found in 1%–2% of children and between 2% and 15% of adults depending on the particular ethnic group considered (Cao et al., 2011). OSA is relatively rare among younger women but may be found with greater frequency among postmenopausal women. Among older adults, OSA may be particularly common, although the clinical significance of mild sleep apnea in this population is unclear. CSA occurs in at least 20% of those with heart failure and in about 30% of those with chronic opioid use. Among those with SRH, comorbid forms are relatively common, whereas the congenital and idiopathic variants are relatively rare.

Circadian Rhythm Sleep–Wake Disorders

Circadian rhythm sleep–wake disorders (CRSWDs) are characterized by persistent or recurrent difficulties resulting from a mismatch between the individual's endogenous circadian (i.e., 24-hour) rhythms and the sleep–wake schedule required by occupational, school, or social demands. Because of this misalignment, a person may experience excessive sleepiness when wakefulness is necessary or insomnia when sleep is desired. Individuals with CRSWDs typically note that their sleep is disrupted or does not occur at a time that is consistent with their desired schedule. For example, alterations of the usual sleep–wake schedule due to rotating shift work or social or recreational pursuits may lead to CRSWDs. Such conditions may be intermittent or recurrent as a function of frequently changing work schedules (Zhu & Zee, 2012). For some individuals, very early or late bedtimes may, over a period of time, lead to a persistent shift (either an advance or delay) in the underlying circadian mechanisms that control the timing of the sleep period. To meet criteria for this group of disorders, an individual must demonstrate significant distress or impairment in social, occupational, or other important areas of functioning.

DSM-5 lists five subtypes of CRSWDs. The main distinguishing feature among them is the temporal pattern of disruptions of the sleep–wake schedules. The *delayed sleep phase type* is based on a pattern of repeated problems falling asleep and an inability to awaken at the desired or required time. Sleep onset can be delayed by several hours but, once sleep is initiated, it usually unfolds normally for the desired duration. In the absence of obligations in the morning, a person with this problem may go to bed at 11:00 pm, fall asleep around 3:00 am, and once asleep, stay asleep for a normal period of time. The sleep period is shifted or delayed to a later time, but its duration is essentially normal. Because of school, work, or social obligations, this delayed sleep often leads to problems arising in the morning. Thus, an individual may present with both insomnia at night and EDS. This type of condition is more common among adolescents and young adults and often runs in the family. While there may be a biological predisposition, behavioral factors (e.g., irregular sleep schedules) may also contribute to this condition (Lack & Wright, 2012).

The *advanced sleep phase type* is the opposite pattern. It is characterized by excessive sleepiness occurring long before the desired bedtime, usually followed by an early awakening and an inability to return to sleep. Because of excessive sleepiness in the evening, which can be very difficult to overcome, a person may fall asleep at 8:00 pm and sleep until 3:00 or 4:00 am. The sleep period is essentially normal but its timing is too early for conventional sleep schedules. This condition is more common among older adults, whose entire circadian rhythms tend to be advanced with aging. For an older person living alone, this may not have the same significance as for someone who is working and living with a partner.

In the *irregular sleep–wake type* of CRSWD, there is a lack of clearly recognizable sleep–wake circadian rhythm, with sleep being distributed in at least three separate episodes throughout the 24-hour period. It is based on a history of insomnia at night and excessive sleepiness during the day. The *non-24-hour sleep–wake type* is a slight variant of this pattern, which is also characterized by a lack of synchronization between the 24-hour light–dark cycle and the endogenous circadian rhythm. Unlike the previous pattern, this disorder is characterized by a gradual shift from an asymptomatic period, when the sleep phase is aligned with the nighttime period, to a period when sleep gradually drifts into the daytime and the individual has trouble staying awake during this period. This latter condition is quite common among visually handicapped individuals because of the absence of normal daylight perception.

The main features of the *shift work type* of CRSWD involve difficulties sleeping during the main sleep period (usually during off work hours during the day) and difficulties staying awake during the main awake period (usually while at work at night). Presence of both of these symptoms is required to make this diagnosis. These difficulties are usually caused by work schedules occurring outside the conventional 8:00 am–5:00 pm window. Such difficulties usually disappear when the individual reverts to a daytime schedule. The problem is that individuals engaged in rotating shift work often have repeated alterations of their sleep–wake schedules between work days and days off, which perpetuate the sleep–wake problems (Reid & Zee, 2005). Several factors can increase the risk of developing sleep–wake disorders of the shift-work type, including the so-called morning chronotype (i.e., individuals with a natural preference to get up early and who are at their best early in the day), older age (>50 years old), as well as family and environmental variables (i.e., the type of work).

There is limited information regarding the prevalence and etiology of CRSWDs. Surveys suggest that the delayed sleep phase subtype may occur in as many as 7% of all adolescents and young adults, whereas sleep–wake disorders due to work schedule demands may occur in up to 60% of all shift workers (Reid & Zee, 2005). Investigations concerning etiological factors contributing to CRSWDs have implicated (1) the neural and endocrine systems that serve as 24-hour pacemakers; (2) the coupling mechanisms that link those endogenous pacemakers to each other; and (3) the systems that synchronize endogenous circadian rhythms with externally prescribed sleep–wake schedules. The extent to which these dysfunctions are primary or secondary to behavioral and environmental factors is often uncertain. There is some debate as to whether sleep difficulties arising from conditions such as jet lag and shift work should be considered sleep disorders because behavioral and environmental factors play such a prominent etiological role in those disorders (Regestein & Monk, 1994). For this reason, CRSWD due to jet lag produced by traveling across several time zones is no longer listed in *DSM*.

Parasomnias

The term *parasomnias* refers to unusual or abnormal behaviors occurring during sleep. While these may range from fairly discrete behaviors (e.g., body rocking) to more noticeable ones (e.g., sleep talking, bruxism), *DSM-5* only recognizes a group of five such abnormal phenomena related to non-REM (NREM) or REM sleep stages.

NREM Sleep Arousal Disorders (Sleepwalking and Night Terrors)

NREM sleep arousal disorders are among the most common aberrant nocturnal behaviors (Mahowald & Bornemann, 2011; Ohayon, Guilleminault, & Priest, 1999). These phenomena can occur during any stage of NREM sleep but most typically occur during the deepest stages of sleep and represent incomplete arousals. Because of their close association with slow-wave sleep (SWS), they most typically occur in the first third of the night, when most of the night's SWS also occurs. More rarely, such events may emerge during the later sleep period. The events are usually short-lived, lasting 1 to 10 minutes, but some last up to 1 hour. Typically individuals have their eyes open and display a range of complex behaviors with varying degrees of conscious awareness and of motoric, behavioral, and autonomic arousal.

Sleepwalking and night terrors are the two most common subtypes of NREM sleep arousal disorders, and these phenomena can occur together or in isolation. Individuals with sleepwalking episodes arise from bed in a stuporous state and amble about their homes or even out of doors. Typically such sleepwalking episodes involve behaviors that are relatively routine or of low complexity, such as using the bathroom, eating, talking, or walking aimlessly. In some rare individuals sexual behaviors may also occur. In contrast, individuals with night terrors display episodes during which they suddenly emit a shrill scream, usually after sitting up in bed. Both of these conditions usually occur from SWS or deep sleep and there is usually no dream content in association with the event. Moreover, the individual is usually confused and difficult to arouse from the episode and typically has no recall of the event the next morning. At a minimum, such events cause embarrassment and may contribute to avoidance of certain situations (e.g., going on trips, overnight visits to friends' homes). In more severe cases, these parasomnias may result in injury to the affected individual or bed partner.

NREM parasomnias are more common in children than in adults, possibly because children spend a greater proportion of the night spent in SWS. From 10% to 30% of children have at least one sleepwalking episode, but only about 2% to 3% have frequent sleepwalking episodes. Between 4% and 5% of the adult population report sleepwalking episodes and approximately the same proportion experience night terrors (Mahowald & Bornemann, 2011; Ohayon et al., 1999). However, fewer than 1% of all adults have regularly occurring NREM parasomnias. In many cases, those that emerge during childhood disappear during adolescence or early adulthood. Night terrors are more common in males than in females.

Many factors have been implicated in the etiology of parasomnias. Genetic factors likely increase vulnerability to these parasomnias (Mahowald & Bornemann, 2011). Psychological trauma such as combat exposure or childhood abuse are commonly reported by individuals with these parasomnias. The occurrence of comorbid sleep disorders that cause excessive sleep fragmentation, such as the BSRDs, can trigger NREM arousal disorders. In one study, indices of anxiety were elevated among those with night terrors, whereas measures of externally directed hostility were elevated among sleepwalkers (Crisp, Matthews, Oakley, & Crutchfield, 1990). Among adults, medications often are viewed as significant contributors to parasomnias, particularly when such individuals show a recent, de novo onset (Mahowald & Bornemann, 2011). Collectively, these findings suggest that, like nightmare, these parasomnias most probably develop through multiple etiological pathways.

Nightmare Disorder

Nightmare disorder is characterized by repeated disturbing, prolonged story-like dreams that provoke anxiety, fear, or other unpleasant emotions. Typically such dreams involve threats to the individual's physical, psychological, and/or emotional well-being. Upon awakening, the individual appears fully alert, oriented, and cognizant of the arousing dream's content. Subsyndromal anxiety and depressed mood often develop as secondary features of the nightmares, leading the individual to seek clinical attention. Moreover, although nightmares are highly common and have a lifetime prevalence approaching 100% (Nielsen & Zadra, 2011), nightmare disorder is a diagnosis reserved for those whose disturbing dreams are recurrent and lead to significant impairment of functioning.

Individuals with nightmare disorder report repeated disturbing dreams that arouse them from their sleep. Nightmares arise during REM sleep, and individuals with nightmare disorder typically experience nightmare-induced awakenings during the latter half of the night, when REM sleep becomes longer and dreams are more vivid. The clinical interview may reveal dream content that reflects a recurrent theme of underlying conflicts, characteristic fears, or more general personality characteristics (Nielsen & Zadra, 2011). For example, individuals with obsessive-compulsive traits often report recurrent nightmares in which they find themselves repeatedly unable to finish an important assignment despite their persistent efforts to do so. Individuals with nightmare disorder usually experience anxiety and sleep

disturbance caused by the nightmares, as well as disruption of their daytime functioning.

Between 1% and 4% of parents report that their children have nightmares on a frequent basis (Simard, Nielsen, Tremblay, Boivin, & Montplaisir, 2008). About 2.5% of boys and 2.7% of girls in the 10- to 13-year age range report nightmares; thereafter nightmare frequency declines among males and increases among females: by age 16, 0.4% of males and 4.9% of females report nightmares (Nielsen & Zadra, 2011). These gender differences are then maintained into adulthood. Such findings may represent actual gender-specific differences in nightmare propensity or differences between women and men in their willingness to report nightmares. The frequency of nightmares decreases slightly with aging (Nielsen, Stenstrom, & Levin, 2006), although it is unclear whether this is due to poorer dream recall. Some cultures attribute nightmares to spiritual or supernatural phenomena, whereas other cultures regard nightmares as indicative of psychopathology. Consequently, nightmare disorder may be diagnosed more freely in some cultures than in others.

Early psychoanalytic theory attributed nightmares and other dreams to subconscious drives related to conflict resolution and wish fulfillment. However, because the role dreaming plays in human psychological and biological functioning remains poorly understood, our knowledge regarding the etiology of nightmare disorder remains rudimentary. Some early research suggested that individuals with frequent nightmares tend to be open, trusting, creative, and vulnerable to other mental disorders (Hartmann, 1984). More recent studies have shown reduced REM propensity in those with chronic nightmares as well as a proneness toward dissociative coping strategies (Nielsen & Zadra, 2011). Finally, observations of nightmares following exposure to traumatic events has led to the speculation that they represent efforts to connect new memories to old ones so as to integrate and synthesize such events (Hartmann, 1994). Given our limited understanding of nightmares, it is safe to assume that nightmare disorder represents a cluster of symptoms that may have a variety of etiological origins.

Rapid Eye Movement (REM) Sleep Behavior Disorder

REM behavior disorder (RBD), a new diagnosis in *DSM-5*, is characterized by abrupt and repetitive arousals associated with violent movements of the limbs occurring during REM sleep. These movements are typically associated with loud vocalizations or screaming and by vivid dreams recalled upon awakening. These movements often involve complex motor responses occurring in reaction to the perception of being attacked or in an attempt to escape from a threatening situation (dream-enactment behavior). Upon awakening, the individual is fully alert and oriented and able to recall details of a distressing dream. An interesting feature of this disorder is its occurrence during REM sleep, a period usually characterized by muscle atonia. In RBD, there is absence of muscle atonia and the individual is actually trying to act out his or her dream (Mahowald & Schenck, 2009), with potential for injuries to self or to the bed partner.

Older males (>55 years old) are at increased risk for this disorder, although it may also occur more rarely in younger individuals and in females. The main differential diagnosis is with other parasomnias, such as sleep terror and sleepwalking, nocturnal seizures, and sleep apnea. RBD is not necessarily associated with a psychiatric disorder but it has been observed more frequently among individuals treated for a psychiatric disorder. Several longitudinal studies of case series have documented a strong association between RBD (as a prodrome) and the development of subsequent neurodegenerative disorders such as Parkinson's disease (Schenck, Boeve, & Mahowald, 2013). The main interventions for this condition involve medication (e.g., benzodiazepines with anticonvulsant properties) as well preventive measures, such as securing the immediate environment by removing objects or furniture that could cause injuries.

may occur during the day but they are definitely more bothersome in the evening and worsen around bedtime; they often cause significant difficulties initiating sleep and may also interfere with sleep maintenance throughout the night. EDS may also be present, but it is not the predominant feature of this condition.

By definition, RLS occurs during wakefulness, but there is a related condition that occurs in sleep, periodic limb movements during sleep (PLMS). It is characterized by repetitive, stereotyped movements of the legs which occur in series of several movements within a regular interval of approximately 20–40 seconds. They can be associated with microarousals and cause sleep fragmentation and/or EDS; these movements do not always produce any consequence on sleep or wakefulness. Most individuals with RLS also have PLMS, but the reverse is not necessarily true.

The prevalence of RLS varies between 2% and 9% depending on the specific definitions used. Both RLS and PLMS are more frequent in females and in older adults. RLS has a strong familial aggregation with a clear genetic predisposition (Ohayon, O'Hara, & Vitiello, 2012). These conditions are associated with pregnancy, anemia, iron deficiency, some antidepressant medications (e.g., fluoxetine), and several medical conditions (e.g., renal diseases, chronic pain).

RLS is predominantly a neurological disorder and must be differentiated from leg cramps, positional discomfort, and neuropathy (Allen et al., 2003). On the psychiatric differential, it must be distinguished from a more general restlessness observed in anxiety disorders. Treatment of RLS is mostly pharmacological and involves dopaminergic agonists.

Restless Legs Syndrome

Restless legs syndrome (RLS) is characterized by frequent, repetitive, and irresistible urges to move the legs (and sometimes the arms). It is usually triggered by unpleasant and uncomfortable sensations (parasthesias) in the legs. The sensation is typically described as creeping, crawling, or itching, but it does not necessarily involve pain. Moving or stretching the legs provides some relief for as long as the activity continues (Allen, 2012). This condition occurs during wakefulness, most frequently at rest, while sitting or lying down. The symptoms

Substance/Medication-Induced Sleep–Wake Disorders

Alcohol, prescribed and over-the-counter medications, illicit drugs, and a variety of other substances (e.g., caffeine) may contribute to sleep–wake disturbances. These substances may produce insomnia, daytime sleepiness, parasomnias, or a mixture of these symptoms, either while in use or during periods of withdrawal and abstinence. When such disturbances become a predominant clinical complaint and when they are sufficiently severe to warrant clinical attention, the diagnosis of *substance/medication-induced sleep–wake disorder* is made. Most commonly, such a diagnosis would be associated with excessive use of alcohol, sedative-hypnotic medications, and stimulants (e.g., amphetamines, cocaine). It may also involve drugs prescribed for psychiatric (e.g., some SSRIs used for depression) or medical conditions (e.g., opioids for pain in patients with cancer).

Although the exact prevalence of substance/medication-induced sleep disorders is unknown, such conditions are likely to be relatively common, particularly with alcohol, because 13% of adults aged 18 to 45 years in the general population report using alcohol as a sleep aid during the course of a year and, for 15% of these individuals (or 2% of the population), alcohol is used regularly for more than 1 month (Johnson, Roehrs, Roth, & Breslau, 1998). Approximately 4% of patients presenting to sleep disorders centers are diagnosed with a substance-induced sleep disorder (Buysse et al., 1994).

Alcohol is a depressant of the central nervous system and produces a sedative effect. When used around bedtime it may hasten sleep onset and deepen sleep in the first half of the night; however, difficulties maintaining sleep are quite common in the second half of the night after the alcohol is metabolized. Alcohol intoxication may initially produce deeper sleep but, with falling blood levels, it is soon followed by periods of restlessness, fitful sleep, and awakenings. Behavioral and dietary factors often interact with alcohol abuse in altering the sleep–wake cycles. Alcohol used at bedtime may worsen sleep apnea by suppressing the respiratory drive during sleep. Heavy alcohol intake may also result in a variety of parasomnias, such as bedwetting, sleep terrors, and sleepwalking. Alcohol has a suppressant effect on REM sleep and, during acute withdrawal, vivid, disturbing dreams may emerge due to a REM rebound effect (Gillin, Drummond, Clark, & Moore, 2005). During acute withdrawal, sleep is frequently interrupted and shortened, and there is a significant loss of deep-sleep stages. Among chronic alcohol abusers, sleep disturbances may persist even during prolonged periods of abstinence and serve as the primary catalyst for relapse.

Like alcohol, sedative hypnotic medications (e.g., benzodiazepines) may contribute to a substance-induced sleep disorder. Although most sedating medications used as sleep aids are effective for transient sleep disturbances, tolerance develops with repeated and prolonged use. With short-term use, benzodiazepines improve sleep efficiency and sleep continuity but significantly reduce the amount of Stages 3–4 and REM sleep. These effects are less pronounced with the newer hypnotic agents (e.g., zolpidem, eszopiclone). Increasing the dosage of these medications may produce EDS, particularly with long-acting sleep medications. In addition, abrupt withdrawal of sedating medications may lead to rebound insomnia during which sleep disturbances worsen (Gillin et al., 2005). Clinical observations suggest that such withdrawal effects often contribute to a perceived loss of self-control in regard to sleep and encourage many individuals to continue use of hypnotics long after these drugs lose their effectiveness. Also, most benzodiazepines produce anterograde amnesia involving poor recall of the past nights' awakenings upon arising in the morning. This may explain why some insomniacs continue using these drugs for prolonged periods of time despite loss of efficacy.

The effects of cannabis on sleep have not been studied extensively. However, there is some evidence that with acute usage, cannabis decreases the time to fall asleep, increases the amount of SWS, and reduces the amount of REM sleep. The impact of cannabis on sleep decreases with repeated usage and, upon withdrawal, difficulty sleeping and strange dreams are often reported, along with a rebound effect of REM sleep (Gillin et al., 2005; Schierenbeck, Riemann, Berger, & Hornyak, 2008).

Stimulants such as amphetamines, cocaine, caffeine, and nicotine increase daytime alertness and may disrupt nighttime sleep (Arndt, Conroy, & Brower, 2012). Although they are both stimulants, caffeine and nicotine may produce paradoxical symptoms involving insomnia during nicotine withdrawal and hypersomnia during periods of heavy caffeine use (Regestein, 1989). Illicit stimulants such as cocaine and Ecstasy produce severe insomnia during acute usage, and withdrawal is associated with further sleep disturbances and unpleasant dreams (Schierenbeck et al., 2008). Most amphetamines and related stimulants also alter the sleep architecture. In addition to insomnia, these substances significantly reduce REM sleep and, upon withdrawal, there is a marked rebound of REM sleep that may be associated with depressed mood or even hallucinations. Sleep disturbances related to drug use, including stimulants, may persist for prolonged periods after withdrawal.

A variety of drugs prescribed for medical or psychiatric conditions produce insomnia or sleepiness as a prominent side effect. For example, some antidepressant drugs interfere with sleep when used at bedtime (e.g., fluoxethine) while others (e.g., mirtazapine) may produce excessive residual sleepiness during the day. Opioids used for controlling pain in cancer patients, for example, also produce significant sleepiness, which may facilitate sleep at night but interfere with wakefulness during the day. Long-acting drugs used to reduce nighttime agitation among patients with dementia may leave residual sleepiness the next day.

Relationship of Sleep–Wake Disorders to Mental and Medical Disorders

Sleep disturbances are common clinical features of several psychiatric and medical disorders (Fleming & Davidson, 2012; Manber, Haynes, & Siebern, 2012; Pearson, Johnson, & Nahin, 2006; Roth et al., 2006). The most common psychiatric conditions comorbid with insomnia are mood disorders, anxiety disorders, and substance/medication-induced sleep disorder (alcohol abuse). Comorbid diagnoses such as borderline and obsessive-compulsive personality disorders have been reported, although few data are available on these comorbidities.

Historically, the *DSM* diagnosis of sleep–wake disorder related to another mental or medical disorder has implied that the sleep–wake problem was temporally and causally related to the underlying disorder (e.g., depression, pain) and that it was of sufficient concern to the patient to warrant independent clinical attention. This attempt to distinguish between primary and secondary sleep–wake disorders has often led clinicians to treat the underlying disorder (e.g., major depression) and ignore the sleep complaint. Recognition that a causal attribution between sleep and a coexisting disorder is not always possible, and that the direction of the association may actually change over time, has led to an important paradigm shift in *DSM-5*, as stated earlier. However, it remains important to understand the interplay between sleep and various medical and psychiatric disorders. This final section provides a brief overview of the current state of knowledge about the nature of the relationship between sleep and psychiatric disorders and then summarizes typical sleep–wake complaints and EEG sleep disturbances associated with selected psychiatric and medical disorders.

Comorbidity of Sleep–Wake Disturbance and Psychopathology

The co-occurrence of sleep disturbances with psychological symptoms and psychiatric disorders can take many different forms. Sleep disturbance can be a clinical manifestation of an underlying psychiatric condition, a concurrent but functionally autonomous disorder, or even a marker of vulnerability to develop psychopathology. The nature of these relationships is complex, multifactorial, and certainly bidirectional. These associations have important implications for differential diagnosis, as well as for treatment and prevention.

As previously noted, psychological symptoms (e.g., anxiety, dysphoria, irritability) are extremely common among patients with sleep disorders, especially those with chronic insomnia. Sleep disturbance can also be a clinical feature and even a diagnostic criterion for some psychiatric disorders, for example, major depression, generalized anxiety disorder (GAD), and posttraumatic stress disorder (PTSD). The severity of sleep disturbance is sometimes, although not always, associated with the intensity of psychiatric symptomatology (Bélanger, Morin, Langlois, & Ladouceur, 2004), but it is not associated with specific diagnoses. In their milder forms, psychological symptoms are seen as correlates or consequences of chronically disturbed sleep.

The prevalence of psychological symptoms and probable psychiatric cases has been documented in several randomly selected community samples. In the National Survey of Psychotherapeutic Drug Use (Mellinger, Balter, & Uhlenhuth, 1985), about half (47%) of those who reported trouble falling or staying asleep were also judged to experience significant psychological distress, in comparison to only 11% of those who had never experienced insomnia. When clusters of symptoms were used to approximate *DSM-III* diagnoses, 21% of serious insomniacs (compared to less than 1% of those who had never had insomnia) reported symptoms resembling major depression and 13% (versus 3% for never had insomnia) presented features of generalized anxiety. Severity of reported sleep disturbances and degree of psychological distress were strongly correlated.

In the Epidemiological Catchment Area (ECA) study (Ford & Kamerow, 1989), the rate of psychiatric disorders was higher among those with sleep complaints. Forty percent of those with insomnia and 47% of those with hypersomnia were diagnosed with a psychiatric disorder, compared to a base rate of 16% among those without sleep complaints. The most common disorders in subjects with insomnia complaints were anxiety disorders (24%), major depression (14%), dysthymia (9%), alcohol abuse (7%), and drug abuse (4%). However, 60% of individuals with insomnia and 53% with hypersomnia did not have any psychiatric disorder. In a large epidemiological study ($N = 14,915$) conducted in Europe, 28% of respondents with insomnia had a current diagnosis of a mental disorder and 26% had a past psychiatric history. Chronic insomnia (more than 1 year's duration) was a predictor of a psychiatric history (Ohayon & Roth, 2003). It was also found that among cases of comorbid insomnia and mood disorders, insomnia appeared before (40%) or around the same time as (22%) mood disorder symptoms. In cases of comorbid insomnia and anxiety disorders, insomnia appeared mostly at the same time (38%) or after (34%) the anxiety disorder developed.

Several longitudinal studies have shown that persistent sleep disturbance increases the risk for new psychiatric disorders and for suicide. For example, participants in the ECA study (Ford & Kamerow, 1989) who reported persistent insomnia from baseline to the 1-year follow-up interview showed an increased risk for developing a new major depression (and, to a smaller extent, anxiety disorders) relative to those without insomnia at baseline or those with insomnia that had remitted between the two interviews. Another longitudinal study of 1,200 young adults (Breslau, Roth, Rosenthal, & Andreski, 1996) found a similar association between insomnia and the risk for new psychiatric disorders over the next 3.5 years. The gender-adjusted relative risk for new onset of major depression was four times higher among individuals with a history of insomnia at baseline relative to those without insomnia, more than twice (2.17) as high for new-onset anxiety disorders, and seven times higher for new onset of substance abuse or dependency disorders. Similar associations have been reported in more than a dozen longitudinal studies (Baglioni et al., 2011). Insomnia and sleep disturbances in general have also been linked with increased risk for suicide. In a longitudinal study conducted over a 20-year

period with 75,000 adults living in Norway, the age- and gender-adjusted hazard ratios for suicide were 1.9, 2.7, and 4.3 for persons reporting sleep problems sometimes, often, or almost every night, respectively, relative to those with no sleep problem (Bjørngaard, Bjerkeset, Romundstad, & Gunnell, 2011).

In summary, there is a high rate of comorbidity between sleep and psychiatric disorders, particularly between insomnia, and depression and anxiety. Between 50% and 80% of patients with mood or anxiety disorders also report sleep disturbances. Among randomly selected community-resident individuals, 40% to 50% of those who report sleep disturbances also report psychological symptoms or psychiatric disorders, whereas about 50% to 60% report sleep difficulties without significant psychological symptomatology. Among individuals without depression at baseline, insomnia represents a significant risk for future depression in subsequent years, with odds ratio ranging from 3.2 to 4.0. The nature of this relationship (i.e., causal, covariation, bidirectional) is more complex than is generally assumed. The specific mechanisms explaining this relationship remain unknown. Whether early detection and treatment of insomnia would prevent the onset of depression remains an important but unanswered question.

Sleep and Mood Disorders   Subjective sleep–wake complaints in mood disorders involve primarily insomnia and, less frequently, hypersomnia. Major depression and dysthymia are often characterized by difficulty falling asleep, frequent and/or prolonged nocturnal awakenings, and premature awakening in the morning with an inability to return to sleep. The early morning awakening is often seen as a classic symptom of major depression, but it is not specific or diagnostic of this condition. Most patients with major depression have mixed difficulties initiating and maintaining sleep, with reduced sleep time. They may also complain of nonrestorative sleep and of disturbing dreams.

In patients with bipolar disorder, insomnia is more typical of the manic phase, whereas extended nocturnal sleep, difficulty awakening in the morning, and daytime sleepiness are more characteristic of the depressive cycles (Kaplan & Harvey, 2009; St-Amand, Provencher, Bélanger, & Morin, 2013). In mania, there is a perception of reduced need for sleep, which is not seen as problematic by the patient. Acute sleeplessness may precede the onset of a manic episode. However, this reduced need for sleep at night may be compensated for by sleeping during the day. When EDS is involved in bipolar disorder, it is not as severe as the hypersomnia observed with other sleep disorders, such as narcolepsy. Individuals with atypical mood disorders (e.g., seasonal affective disorder) may report hypersomnolence that is manifested by extended nocturnal sleep periods, frequent but unrefreshing napping, and feelings of fatigue and lethargy. However, not all patients with seasonal depression have these clinical features (Shapiro, Devins, Feldman, & Levitt, 1994). In fact, not all patients complaining of EDS associated with mood disorders show objective evidence of hypersomnia (Billard, Partinen, Roth, & Shapiro, 1994); for some, this subjective complaint may simply reflect the underlying state of anergia.

For many patients, insomnia is prodromal to the onset of depression (Perlis, Giles, Buysse, Tsu, & Kupfer, 1997). Sleep disturbances may worsen during acute episodes of the illness and, although sleep generally improves during remission, insomnia and fatigue are the two most common residual symptoms in otherwise successfully treated patients with major depression (Nierenberg et al., 1999). For this reason, there is general agreement that treatment should specifically target both the insomnia and its comorbid psychiatric disorder (e.g., depression, anxiety) to provide optimal disease management. Indeed, clinical trials have shown that, in the context of comorbid insomnia and depressive disorders, the addition of psychological (i.e., cognitive-behavioral therapy) or pharmacological therapies for insomnia produces better outcomes (i.e., response and remission rates for both insomnia and depression) than when treating depression alone (Fava et al., 2006; Manber et al., 2008).

Most individuals with mood disorders show some form of objective EEG sleep disturbances (Manber et al., 2012). The most consistent findings across studies include sleep continuity disturbances (increased sleep latency and time awake after sleep onset, more frequent awakenings, and diminished total sleep time) and an alteration of the sleep architecture, such as reduced SWS and alterations of REM sleep features (Peterson & Benca, 2006). Of all forms of psychopathology, depression has the most pronounced effect on sleep architecture in general and on REM sleep in particular. Compared to normal controls, patients

who are depressed typically show a decrease in the amount of SWS, a type of EEG pattern that usually predominates in the first part of the night and that is associated with deep sleep. There is also evidence of several REM sleep abnormalities, including a shorter latency between sleep onset and the first REM episode, an increased proportion of time in REM sleep, and an altered temporal distribution of REM sleep and slow-wave (Stages 3–4) activity across the night. The first REM sleep period is longer and more intense (increased frequency of REMs) among patients who are depressed, whereas much of their deep sleep (Stages 3–4) is delayed and occurs after the first REM episode (Peterson & Benca, 2006).

Although earlier studies suggested that a short REM latency might be a biological marker for major depression (Kupfer & Foster, 1972), subsequent investigations have observed such REM sleep characteristics in other psychopathologies as well. Thus, the diagnostic specificity, sensitivity, and clinical utility of REM latency as a marker of depression have been challenged. REM sleep is affected by several factors, such as age, medication, and type of depression. In addition, it is unclear whether REM abnormalities are temporally linked to the acute phase of depression or represent a trait marker of a greater vulnerability to recurring depressive episodes (Cartwright, 1983; Rush et al., 1986). Several abnormal features of REM sleep and SWS may persist for prolonged periods of time after remission (Rush et al., 1986). The persistence of such sleep disturbance abnormalities in the absence of clinical depression may indicate a biological vulnerability for depression and predate the illness, or it could indicate that sleep impairments persist much longer than other depressive symptoms (Reynolds & Kupfer, 1987). In either case, persisting sleep disturbances could be a risk factor for subsequent relapse of the depression.

Sleep and Anxiety-Related Disorders Sleep complaints are quite common in several anxiety-related disorders. Such complaints are most prominent among patients with GAD, PTSD, and panic disorder. They may involve difficulties initiating and maintaining sleep, sudden and prolonged awakenings, restless sleep, intrusive thoughts during sleep, and nightmares. Complaints about daytime fatigue may also be present, but EDS is much less frequent. More than 60% of patients with GAD report at least one insomnia complaint, and for most of them insomnia is perceived as temporally linked to excessive worrying (Bélanger et al., 2004). Neither the presence nor the severity of sleep disturbances, however, is associated with GAD severity. There is significant overlap in some of the core symptoms in GAD and insomnia disorder, including sleep difficulties, daytime fatigability, poor concentration, and irritability. In insomnia disorder, the patient's focus of attention is essentially on his or her inability to sleep and on the resulting daytime consequences, whereas in GAD sleeplessness is only one among several sources of worries. Nevertheless, a separate insomnia disorder diagnosis is warranted whenever insomnia or sleep represents a significant concern for the patient and is judged to warrant treatment.

As for those with depression, anxiety may increase the perception of disrupted sleep more than the standard EEG variables reflect. Nonetheless, objective sleep abnormalities are typically present among patients who are anxious. As a group, patients with GAD take longer to fall asleep, wake up more frequently and spend more time awake at night, achieve lower sleep efficiencies, and spend less time in deep (Stages 3–4) sleep and more time in light (Stage 1) sleep (Monti & Monti, 2000). Sleep continuity disturbances are similar to those observed in major depression, whereas REM sleep may or may not be altered (Papadimitriou, Linkowski, Kerkhofs, Kempenaers, & Mendlewicz, 1988). Comparison of patients who are anxious and patients who are depressed is often difficult because of overlapping symptoms in those two subgroups, and it may be difficult to study patients who are anxious without any comorbid depressive features.

Nocturnal panic is fairly common in patients with panic disorder, with 44% to 71% reporting at least one such attack (Craske & Tsao, 2005). Such panic attacks can arise during sleep and lead to insomnia symptoms, especially sudden and prolonged awakenings (Craske & Tsao, 2005). Difficulties initiating sleep may also develop as a result of the anticipatory anxiety of having a panic attack at night. Other abnormalities may include reduced sleep time and sleep efficiency. Sleep architecture outside the panic attacks is not remarkably affected (Hauri, Friedman, & Ravaris, 1989), and there is no alteration of REM sleep. Nocturnal panic attacks typically occur during non-REM sleep, usually in the transition period from Stage

2 to SWS (Stages 3–4) (Mellman & Uhde, 1989). These attacks appear to be different from sleep terrors, which originate from SWS, in that they are less stereotyped and less intense. Because psychological factors presumably play a more limited role in triggering nocturnal panic attacks, the distinction between these attacks and those occurring during wakefulness may help delineate the biological bases of panic attacks. There is currently no clear distinction between these two forms of panic attacks. However, when panic attacks occur exclusively in sleep, it is important to consider other sleep terrors, nightmares, and sleep apnea when making the differential diagnosis.

In PTSD, which is classified separately from other anxiety disorders in *DSM-5*, patients often experience various forms of sleep disturbances, including insomnia, nightmares, and sleep terrors (Germain, 2013; Ross, Ball, Sullivan, & Caroff, 1989). Recurring traumatic dreams, the most characteristic sleep features of PTSD, can be quite intense and disabling. Patients with PTSD exhibit excessive body movements during sleep, as well as awakenings with somatic symptoms that are accompanied by startle or panic-like features often related to threatening dreams (Mellman, Kulick-Bell, Ashlock, & Nolan, 1995). These arousals do not always arise from REM sleep. Anxiety, depression, and chronic use of psychotropic medications often contribute to the findings of disturbed sleep and are difficult to tease out from the PTSD. Sleep disturbance following a traumatic event (motor vehicle accident) is a significant predictor of subsequent development of PTSD (Koren, Arnon, Lavie, & Klein, 2002). As is often the case in depression, it is also a frequent residual symptom in otherwise successfully treated patients with PTSD (DeViva, Zayfert, Pigeon, & Mellman, 2005).

Patients with other anxiety-related disorders, such as social anxiety disorder or obsessive-compulsive disorder (OCD), may also experience sleep disturbances, but such disturbances are not among the core features of the disorders. In social anxiety disorder, sleep difficulties may be associated with preoccupations about performing (e.g., musicians, athletes). In patients with OCD, sleep difficulties are usually associated with a comorbid depression or with the checking rituals (e.g., need to check the stove or alarms repeatedly at night).

Sleep and Schizophrenia Sleep disturbances are very prevalent in schizophrenia and other psychoses, although individuals with such disorders rarely report sleep as their primary difficulty. Such difficulties may involve insomnia, hypersomnia, and circadian rhythm sleep–wake disturbances. Most frequently, the sleep–wake cycle is disorganized or delayed; patients with chronic schizophrenia may go to bed very late or at irregular times in the evening and, consequently, sleep late in the morning. For some patients, there is a reversal of sleep–wake cycles, with a preference for sleeping during the day. These difficulties are partly the result of poor sleep habits, neuroleptic drugs, and chronic use of alcohol and substance abuse. Some of these features are also common among otherwise healthy persons whose circadian cycles are not paced by work and social obligations (e.g., unemployed persons living alone).

Sleep disturbances are more pronounced during acute psychotic decompensation (Neylan, van Kammen, Kelley, & Peters, 1992), and acute insomnia can be prodromal to relapse (Chemerinski et al., 2002). There is, however, significant variability of sleep disruptions across patients and within patients over the course of a psychotic exacerbation. Persistent sleep disruptions in chronic and even remitted psychotic patients are also quite frequent. The hallucinatory experiences of patients with schizophrenia once were hypothesized to be the result of intrusions of dreaming into wakefulness. Research has not supported this interpretation. In some very specific cases, however, there may be confusion between the schizophrenic hallucinations and the REM sleep–induced hallucinations of some patients with narcolepsy.

There are few reliable EEG sleep abnormalities in patients with schizophrenia that distinguish this disorder from other psychiatric disorders. Nonetheless, a meta-analysis of studies evaluating sleep in unmedicated patients with schizophrenia revealed increased sleep latency and reduced sleep time and sleep efficiency relative to healthy controls (Chouinard, Poulin, Stip, & Godbout, 2004). Sleep disturbances were worse in the neuroleptic-withdrawal group than in the never-treated group. These findings would suggest that sleep disturbances are not necessarily caused by neuroleptic drugs and may be linked to the underlying neurobiological mechanisms of schizophrenia. A shortened REM latency does occur in some patients with schizophrenia, as in major depression. One feature distinguishing patients with schizophrenia from normal controls

is that following sleep deprivation, patients with schizophrenia do not show the typical rebound of REM sleep; the clinical significance of this finding is unclear.

In summary, several psychiatric disorders are associated with significant sleep complaints that are often corroborated by objective EEG sleep disturbances. These involve sleep continuity disturbances such as trouble falling asleep and staying asleep, with corresponding reductions of sleep efficiency and total sleep time. These abnormalities are quite robust across several psychiatric disorders, especially mood and anxiety disorders, but they are essentially nonspecific. Despite the extensive literature on sleep impairments in various mental disorders, no reliable biological sleep marker has been identified for any mental disorder. Nonetheless, sleep represents a major problem for patients with psychiatric disorders. Problems with sleep may alter the course of the psychiatric disorder and often warrant an independent diagnosis and separate treatment.

Sleep–Wake Disorders and Medical Disorders Sleep–wake disturbances may arise in the context of numerous medical conditions. The subjective sleep complaint may be peripheral to or occupy an important focus in the overall clinical presentation. As for comorbid psychiatric disorders, *DSM-5* no longer makes a distinction between a primary sleep–wake disorder and one that is associated with a medical condition. Whenever sleep is a primary concern for the patient and warrants independent clinical attention, a sleep–wake disorder diagnosis is also warranted. For example, even if acute pain following an accident or surgery may be directly responsible for triggering sleep disturbances initially, poor sleep often exacerbates pain and may contribute to perpetuating it over time. With chronic pain, it often becomes difficult to determine which is the cause and which is the consequence. Thus, rather than seeing the relationship of medical and sleep disorders as being unidirectional, it is preferable to conceptualize it as bidirectional (Fleming & Davidson, 2012).

Sleep problems are much more prevalent among individuals with active medical illness (e.g., pain, obesity, coronary heart failures) than among healthy controls (Pearson et al., 2006; Taylor et al., 2007). Almost all forms of sleep–wake disorders may be found in various medical conditions. For instance, insomnia is associated with a variety of pain-related conditions (e.g., cancer, arthritis, osteoporosis, fibromyalgia), chronic obstructive pulmonary diseases, hyperthyroidism, and neurodegenerative disorders (Pearson et al., 2006; Fleming & Davidson, 2012). Obesity and coronary artery diseases are often associated with BRSDs, while diabetes and kidney diseases are almost always associated with RLS, insomnia, and EDS. Patients with neurodegenerative diseases such as Parkinson's disease often have a history of RBD. Some disorders can also be a side effect of drug treatments for medical (e.g., beta-blockers for hypertension) or psychiatric disorders (e.g., some SSRIs for depression); such conditions would then be diagnosed as a substance/medication-induced sleep–wake disorder. In addition to treating the associated medical condition, the sleep disturbance often warrants independent treatment. Increasing evidence shows that cognitive-behavioral therapy of sleep disturbances comorbid with various medical conditions (e.g., pain, cancer) produces clinical benefit even without altering the underlying medical condition (Smith, Huang, & Manber, 2005).

Conclusions

Sleep disorders are relatively common and often serious conditions that may arise as independent disorders or in the context of another psychological or medical disorder. In either case, they are often associated with significant psychological distress and impairment of social, family, or occupational functioning. Previous research has provided much information about the prevalence, nature, and etiology of sleep disorders. However, the scientific study of the syndromes discussed here is yet in its infancy. In fact, so much remains unknown about sleep–wake disorders that it is difficult to prioritize the many research questions that need to be addressed. Nevertheless, some research endeavors pertaining to sleep disturbances and their relationship to other forms of psychopathology seem paramount at this juncture.

More research about classification is needed. Although the *DSM-5* represents conceptual and practical advancements over previous classifications, validation of this system has yet to be conducted. The reliability and validity of many entities described in sleep–wake disorder nosologies remain to be tested. Moreover, it has yet to be shown that any current classification accurately characterizes the entire spectrum of sleep–wake disturbances seen in the clinical setting. There is also a need for identifying phenotypes of sleep–wake disorders. For instance, insomnia disorder is likely to include a variety of subtypes, some of which have been recognized in the *ICSD* nosology, yet these subtypes remain to be further delineated and validated.

Epidemiological studies of the various sleep–wake disorders are critical. Estimates of population prevalence, incidence, and persistence of several disorders remain unknown or are quite variable across studies. As a result, it is currently impossible to determine the numbers of adults who may require clinical attention for such conditions. Despite the increasing interest in the comorbidity of sleep and psychiatric disorders, the nature of the relationship between many sleep–wake disturbances and psychopathology remains controversial (National Institutes of Health, 2005). Fortunately, we have moved away from the simplistic view that sleep disturbances are only symptomatic of another (more important) psychiatric disorder. While increasing evidence suggests that insomnia is a risk factor for new onset of psychiatric disorders, particularly depression, additional prospective studies are needed to clarify the implications of these new findings with regard to the prognostic value of sleep disturbances for predicting the development of and recovery from different forms of psychopathology, as well as their implications for treatment and prevention.

Finally, little is known about the etiology of many disorders described in this chapter. Whereas many of these conditions appear to be associated with underlying biological and psychological vulnerabilities, the interplay of such factors in the development of these conditions is currently poorly understood. In the case of insomnia disorder, for example, little is known about hypothesized biological factors that contribute to this condition and, as noted earlier, the role of psychological traits in its etiology has been hotly debated. In contrast, it is generally accepted that sleep–wake disorders are commonly associated with many psychopathological disorders, but whether specific forms of sleep–wake disruption underlie and contribute to the development of each of these psychiatric conditions is yet to be determined. Thus, additional research with, perhaps, newer technologies and research methods will likely lead to insights into the etiologies of many currently recognized sleep–wake disorders.

References

Allen, R. P. (2012). Restless legs syndrome (Willis-Ekbom disease) and periodic limb movements. In C. M. Morin & C. A. Espie (Eds.), *The Oxford handbook of sleep and sleep disorders* (pp. 707–725). New York: Oxford University Press.

Allen, R. P., Picchietti, D., Hening, W. A., Trenkwalder, C., Walters, A., & Montplaisir, J. (2003). Restless legs syndrome: diagnostic criteria, special considerations, and epidemiology: A report from the restless legs syndrome diagnosis and epidemiology workshop at the National Institutes of Health. *Sleep Medicine, 4,* 101–119.

American Academy of Sleep Medicine. (2005). *International classification of sleep disorders–2nd edition: Diagnostic and coding manual.* Chicago: Author.

American Sleep Disorders Association. (1990). *International classification of sleep disorders (ICSD): Diagnostic and coding manual.* Rochester, MN: Author.

American Sleep Disorders Association. (1997). *International classification of sleep disorders-revised edition (ICSD-R): Diagnostic and coding manual.* Rochester, MN: Author.

Anderson, K. N., Pilsworth, S., Sharples, L. D., Smith, I. E., & Shneerson, J. M. (2007). Idiopathic hypersomnia: A study of 77 cases. *Sleep, 30,* 1274–81.

Arnedt, J. T., Conroy, D. A., & Brower, K. J. (2012). Sleep and substance use disorders. In C. M. Morin & C. A. Espie (Eds.), *The Oxford handbook of sleep and sleep disorders* (pp. 526–554). New York: Oxford University Press.

Association of Sleep Disorders Centers. (1979). Diagnostic classification of sleep and arousal disorders. *Sleep, 2,* 1–137.

Baglioni, C., Battagliese, G., Feige, B., Spiegelhalder, K., Nissen, C., Voderholzer, U.,…Riemann, D. (2011). Insomnia as a predictor of depression: a meta-analytic evaluation of longitudinal epidemiological studies. *Journal of Affective Disorders, 135,* 10–19.

Bastien, C., Vallières, A., & Morin, C. M. (2004). Precipitating factors of insomnia. *Behavioral Sleep Medicine, 1,* 50–62.

Bélanger, L., Morin, C. M., Langlois, F., & Ladouceur, R. (2004). Insomnia and generalized anxiety disorder: Effects of cognitive behavior therapy for GAD on insomnia symptoms. *Journal of Anxiety Disorders, 18,* 561–571.

Billard, M., Partinen, M., Roth, T., & Shapiro, C. (1994). Sleep and psychiatric disorders. *Journal of Psychosomatic Research, 38*(Suppl. 1), 1–2.

Bjørngaard, J. H., Bjerkeset, O., Romundstad, P., & Gunnell, D. (2011). Sleeping problems and suicide in 75,000 Norwegian adults: A 20-year follow-up of the HUNT I Study. *Sleep, 34,* 1155–1159.

Bliwise, D. L. (2011). Normal aging. In M. H. Kryger, T. Roth, & W. C. Dement (Eds.), *Principles and practice of sleep medicine* (5th ed., pp. 27–41). St. Louis: Elsevier Saunders.

Bonnet, M. H., & Arand, D. L. (1998). Heart rate variability in insomniacs and normal sleepers. *Psychosomatic Medicine, 60,* 610–615.

Bonnet, M. H., & Arand, D. L. (2010). Hyperarousal and insomnia: State of the science. *Sleep Medicine Reviews, 14,* 9–15.

Breslau, N., Roth, T., Rosenthal, L., & Andreski, P. (1996). Sleep disturbance and psychiatric disorders: A longitudinal epidemiological study of young adults. *Biological Psychiatry, 39,* 411–418.

Buysse, D. J., Reynolds, C. F., Kupfer, D. J., Thorpy, M. J., Bixler, E., Manfredi, R.,…Deborah, M. (1994). Clinical diagnoses in 216 insomnia patients using the International Classification of Sleep Disorders (ICSD), DSM-IV and ICD-10 categories: A report from the APA/NIMH DSM-IV field trial. *Sleep, 17,* 630–637.

Cao, M. T., Guilleminault, C., & Kushida, C. A. (2011). Clinical features and evaluation of obstructive sleep apnea and upper airway resistance syndrome. In M. H. Kryger, T. Roth, & W. C. Dement (Eds.), *Principles and practice of sleep medicine* (5th ed., pp. 1206–1218). St. Louis: Elsevier Saunders.

Cartwright, R. D. (1983). REM sleep characteristics during and after mood-disturbing events. *Archives of General Psychiatry, 40,* 197–201.

Chemerinski, E., Ho, B., Flaum, M., Arndt, S., Fleming, F., & Andreasen, N. C. (2002). Insomnia as a predictor for symptom worsening following antipsychotic withdrawal in schizophrenia. *Comprehensive Psychiatry, 43,* 393–396.

Chouinard, S., Poulin, J., Stip, E., & Godbout, R. (2004). Sleep in untreated patients with schizophrenia: A meta-analysis. *Schizophrenia Bulletin, 30,* 957–967.

Craske, M. G., & Tsao, J. C. (2005). Assessment and treatment of nocturnal panic attacks. *Sleep Medicine Reviews, 9,* 173–184.

Crisp, A. H., Matthews, B. M., Oakley, M., & Crutchfield, M. (1990). Sleepwalking, night terrors and consciousness. *British Medical Journal, 300,* 360–362.

DeViva, J. C., Zayfert, C., Pigeon, W. R., & Mellman, T. A. (2005). Treatment of residual insomnia after CBT for PTSD: Case studies. *Journal of Trauma Stress, 18,* 155–159.

Dijk, D. J., Duffy, J. F., & Czeisler, C. A. (2001). Age-related increase in awakenings: Impaired consolidation of NREM sleep in all circadian phases. *Sleep, 24,* 565–577.

Edinger, J. D., & Carney, C. E. (2008). *Overcoming insomnia: A cognitive-behavioral approach.* New York: Oxford University Press.

Edinger, J. D., Fins, A. I., Glenn, D. M., Sullivan, R. J., Jr., Bastian, L. A., Marsh, G. R.,…Vasilas, D. (2000). Insomnia and the eye of the beholder: Are there clinical markers of objective sleep disturbances among adults with and without insomnia complaints? *Journal of Consulting and Clinical Psychology, 9,* 398–411.

Fava, M., McCall, W. V., Krystal, A., Wessel, T., Rubens, R., Caron, J., Amato D., Roth, T. (2006). Eszopiclone co-administered with fluoxetine in patients with insomnia coexisting with major depressive disorder. *Biological Psychiatry, 59,* 1052–1160.

Fleming, L., & Davidson, J. R. (2012). Sleep and medical disorders. In C. M. Morin & C. A. Espie (Eds.), *Oxford handbook of sleep and sleep disorders* (pp. 502–525). New York: Oxford University Press.

Ford, D. E., & Kamerow, D. B. (1989). Epidemiologic study of sleep disturbances and psychiatric disorders: An opportunity for prevention? *Journal of the American Medical Association, 262,* 1479–1484.

Germain, A. (2013). Sleep disturbances as the hallmark of PTSD: Where are we now? *American Journal of Psychiatry, 170,* 372–382.

Gillin, J. C., Drummond, S., Clark, C. P., & Moore, P. (2005). Medication and substance abuse. In M. H. Kryger, T. Roth, & W. C. Dement (Eds.), *Principles and practice of sleep medicine* (4th ed., pp. 1345–1358). Philadelphia: W. B. Saunders.

Hartmann, E. (1984). *The nightmare: The psychology and biology of terrifying dreams.* New York: Basic Books.

Hartmann, E. (1994). Nightmares and other dreams. In M. H. Kryger, T. Roth, & W. C. Dement (Eds.), *Principles and practice of sleep medicine* (2nd ed., pp. 407–410). Philadelphia: W. B. Saunders.

Hauri, P. J., Friedman, M., & Ravaris, C. L. (1989). Sleep in patients with spontaneous panic attacks. *Sleep, 12,* 323–337.

Johnson, E. A., Roehrs, T., Roth, T., & Breslau, N. (1998). Epidemiology of alcohol and medication as aids to sleep in early adulthood. *Sleep, 21,* 178–186.

Kaplan, K. A., & Harvey, A. G. (2009). Hypersomnia across mood disorders: A review and synthesis. *Sleep Medicine Review 13,* 275–285.

Koren, D., Arnon, I., Lavie, P., & Klein, E. (2002). Sleep complaints as early predictors of posttraumatic stress disorder: a 1-year prospective study of injured survivors of motor vehicle accidents. *American Journal of Psychiatry, 159,* 855–857.

Kupfer, D. J., & Foster, F. G. (1972). Interval between onset of sleep and rapid-eye movement sleep as an indicator of depression. *The Lancet, 2,* 684–686.

Lack, L. C., & Wright, H. R. (2012). Circadian rhythm disorders I: Phase-advanced and phase-delayed syndromes. In C. M. Morin and C. A. Espie (Eds.), *The Oxford handbook of sleep and sleep disorders* (pp. 597–625). New York: Oxford University Press.

Lichstein, K. L., Durrence H. H., Taylor, D. J., Bush, A. J., & Riedel, B. W. (2003). Quantitative criteria for insomnia. *Behaviour Researsh and Therapy, 41,* 427–45.

Lineberger, M. D., Carney C. E., Edinger J. D., & Means M. K. (2006). Defining insomnia: Quantitative criteria for insomnia severity and frequency. *Sleep, 29,* 479–485.

Mahowald, M. W., & Bornemann, M. A. C. (2011). NREM sleep-arousal parasomnias. In M. H. Kryger, T. Roth, & W. C. Dement (Eds.), *Principles and practice of sleep medicine* (5th ed., pp. 1075–1082). St. Louis: Elsevier Saunders.

Mahowald, M. W., & Schenck, C. H. (2009). The REM sleep behavior disorder odyssey. *Sleep Medicine Reviews, 13,* 381–384.

Manber, R., Edinger, J. D., Gress, J. L., San Pedro-Salcedo, M. G., Kuo, T. F., Kalista, T. (2008). Cognitive behavioral therapy for insomnia enhances depression outcome in patients with comorbid major depressive disorder and insomnia. *Sleep, 31,* 489–495.

Manber, R., Haynes, T., & Siebern, A. T. (2012). Sleep and psychiatric disorders. In C. M. Morin and C. A. Espie (Eds.), *Oxford handbook of sleep and sleep disorders* (pp. 471–501). New York: Oxford University Press.

Mellinger, G. D., Balter, M. B., & Uhlenhuth, E. H. (1985). Insomnia and its treatment: Prevalence and correlates. *Archives of General Psychiatry, 42,* 225–232.

Mellman, T. A., & Uhde, T. W. (1989). Electroencephalographic sleep in panic disorder. *Archives of General Psychiatry, 46,* 178–184.

Mellman, T. A., Kulick-Bell, R., Ashlock, L. E., & Nolan, B. (1995). Sleep events among veterans with combat-related posttraumatic stress disorder. *American Journal of Psychiatry, 152,* 110–115.

Mignot, E. (2011). Narcolepsy: pathophysiology, and genetic predipostion. In M. H. Kryger, T. Roth, & W. C. Dement (Eds.), *Principles and practice of sleep medicine* (5th ed., pp. 938–956). St. Louis: Elsevier Saunders.

Monti, J. M., & Monti, D. (2000). Sleep disturbance in generalized anxiety disorder and its treatment. *Sleep Medicine Reviews, 4,* 263–276.

Morin, C. M., Belanger, L., Leblanc, M., Ivers, H., Savard, J., Espie, C. A.,…Grégoire, J-P. (2009). The natural history of insomnia: A population-based 3-year longitudinal study. *Archives of Internal Medicine, 169,* 447–453.

Morin, C. M., & Benca, R. (2012). Chronic insomnia. *Lancet, 379,* 1129–1141.

Morin, C. M., Bootzin, R., Buysse, D. J., Edinger, J. D., Espie, C. A., & Lichstein, K. L. (2006). Psychological and behavioral treatment for insomnia: An update of recent evidence (1998–2004). *Sleep, 29,* 1398–1414.

Morin, C. M., & Espie, C. A. (2003). *Insomnia: A clinical guide to assessment and treatment.* New York: Kluwer Academic/ Plenum Publishers.

Morin, C. M., LeBlanc, M., Daley, M., Grégoire, J-P., & Mérette, C. (2006). Epidemiology of insomnia: Prevalence, self-help treatments, consultations, and determinants of help-seeking behaviors. *Sleep Medicine, 7,* 123–130.

National Institutes of Health. (2005). National Institutes of Health State of the Science Conference Statement: Manifestations and management of chronic insomnia in adults. *Sleep, 28,* 1049–1057.

Neylan, T. C., van Kammen, D. P., Kelley, M. E., & Peters, J. L. (1992). Sleep in schizophrenic patients on and off Haloperidol therapy. *Archives of General Psychiatry, 49,* 643–649.

Nielsen, T. A., Stenstrom, P., & Levin, R. (2006). Nightmare frequency as a function of age, gender and September 11, 2001: Findings from an internet questionnaire. *Dreaming, 16,* 145–158.

Nierenberg, A. A., Keefe, B. R., Leslie, V. C., Alpert, J. E., Pava, J. A., Worthington, J. J.,…Fava, M. (1999). Residual symptoms in depressed patients who respond acutely to fluoxetine. *Journal of Clinical Psychiatry, 60,* 221–225.

Nielsen, T. A., & Zadra, A. (2011). Idiopathic nightmares and dream disturbances associated with sleep-wake transitions. In M. H. Kryger, T. Roth, & W. C. Dement (Eds.), *Principles and practice of sleep medicine* (5th ed., pp. 1106–1115). St. Louis: Elsevier Saunders.

Nofzinger E. A., Nissen, C., Germain, A., Moul, D., Hall, M., Price, J. C.,…Buysse, D. J. (2006). Regional cerebral metabolic correlates of WASO during NREM sleep in insomnia. *Journal of Clinical Sleep Medicine, 2,* 316–22.

Ohayon, M. M. (2002). Epidemiology of insomnia: What we know and what we still need to learn, *Sleep Medicine Reviews, 6,* 97–111.

Ohayon, M. M., Dauvilliers, Y., & Reynolds, C. F. (2012). Operational definitions and algorithms for excessive sleepiness in the general population: Implications for DSM-5 nosology. *Archives of General Psychiatry, 69,* 71–79.

Ohayon, M. M., Guilleminault, C., & Priest, R. G. (1999). Night terrors, sleepwalking, and confusional arousal in the general population: Their frequency and relationship to other sleep and mental disorders. *Journal of Clinical Psychiatry, 60,* 268–276.

Ohayon, M. M., O'Hara, R., & Vitiello, M. V. (2012). Epidemiology of restless legs syndrome: A synthesis of the literature. *Sleep Medicine Reviews, 16,* 283–295.

Ohayon, M. M., & Roberts, R. E. (2001). Comparability of sleep disorders diagnoses using DSM-IV and ICSD classifications with adolescents. *Sleep, 2,* 920–5.

Ohayon, M. M., & Roth, T. (2003). Place of chronic insomnia in the course of depressive and anxiety disorders. *Journal of Psychiatric Research, 37,* 9–15.

Orellana, C., Villemin, E., Tafti, M., Carlander, B., Besset, A., & Billard, M. (1994). Life events in the year preceding the onset of narcolepsy. *Sleep, 17,* S50–S53.

Papadimitriou, G. N., Linkowski, P., Kerkhofs, M., Kempenaers, C., & Mendlewicz, J. (1988). Sleep EEG recordings in generalized anxiety disorder with significant depression. *Journal of Affective Disorders, 15,* 113–118.

Partinen, M., & Hublin, C. (2011). Epidemiology of sleep disorders. In M. H. Kryger, T. Roth, & W. C. Dement (Eds.), *Principles and practice of sleep medicine* (5th ed., pp. 694–715). St. Louis: Elsevier Saunders.

Pearson, N. J., Johnson, L., & Nahin, R. L. (2006). Insomnia, trouble sleeping, and complementary and alternative medicine: Analysis of the 2002 National Health Interview Survey Data. *Archives of Internal Medicine, 166,* 1775–1782.

Perlis, M. L., Giles, D. E., Buysse, D. J., Tsu, X., & Kupfer, D. J. (1997). Self-reported sleep disturbance as prodromal symptom in recurrent depression. *Journal of Affective Disorders, 42,* 209–212.

Peterson, M. J., & Benca, R. M. (2006). Sleep in mood disorders. *Psychiatric Clinics of North America, 29,* 1009–1032.

Regestein, Q. R. (1989). Pathologic sleepiness induced by caffeine. *American Journal of Medicine, 87,* 586–588.

Regestein, Q. R., & Monk, T. (1994). Is the poor sleep of shift workers a disorder? *American Journal of Psychiatry, 148,* 1487–1493.

Reid, K. J., & Zee, P. C. (2005). Circadian disorders of the sleep-wake cycle. In M. H. Kryger, T. Roth, & W. C. Dement (Eds.), *Principles and practice of sleep medicine* (4th ed., pp. 691–701). Philadelphia: Elsevier Saunders.

Reynolds, C. F., & Kupfer, D. J. (1987). Sleep research in affective illness: State of the art circa 1987. *Sleep, 10,* 199–215.

Ross, R. J., Ball, W. A., Sullivan, K. A., & Caroff, S. N. (1989). Sleep disturbance as the hallmark of posttraumatic stress disorder. *American Journal of Psychiatry, 146,* 697–706.

Roth, T., Coulouvrat, C., Hajak, G., Lakoma, M. D., Sampson, N. A., Shahly, V.,…Kessler, R. C. (2011). Prevalence and perceived health associated with insomnia based on DSM-IV-TR; International Statistical Classification of Diseases and Related Health Problems, Tenth Revision; and Research Diagnostic Criteria/ International Classification of Sleep Disorders, second edition criteria: Results from the America Insomnia Survey. *Biological Psychiatry, 69,* 592–600.

Roth, T., Jaeger, S., Jin, R., Kalsekar, A., Stang, P. E., & Kessler, R. C. (2006). Sleep problems, comorbid mental disorders, and role functioning in the national comorbidity survey replication. *Biological Psychiatry, 60,* 1364–1371.

Rush, A. J., Erman, M. K., Giles, D. E., Schlesser, M. A., Carpenter, G., Vasavada, N., & Roffwarg, H. P. (1986). Polysomnographic findings in recently drug-free and clinically remitted depressed patients. *Archives of General Psychiatry, 43,* 878–884.

Sanders, M. H., & Givelber, R. J. (2006). Overview of obstructive sleep apnea in adults. In T. L. Lee-Chiong (Ed.), *Sleep: A comprehensive handbook* (pp. 231–247). Hoboken, NJ: John Wiley & Sons.

Schenck, C. H., Boeve, B. F., & Mahowald M. W. (2013). Delayed emergence of a Parkinsonian disorder or dementia in 81% of older males initially diagnosed with idiopathic REM sleep behavior disorder (RBD): 16-year update on a previously reported series. *Sleep Medicine, 14*(8), 744–748.

Schierenbeck, T., Riemann, D., Berger, M., & Hornyak, M. (2008). Effect of illicit recreational drugs upon sleep: Cocaine, ecstasy and marijuana. *Sleep Medicine Reviews, 12,* 381–390.

Shapiro, C. M., Devins, G. M., Feldman, B., & Levitt, A. J. (1994). Is hypersomnolence a feature of seasonal affective disorder? *Journal of Psychosomatic Research, 38*(Suppl. 1), 49–54.

Simard, V., Nielsen, T. A., Tremblay, R. E., Boivin, M., & Montplaisir, J. Y. (2008). Longitudinal study of bad dreams in preschool children: Prevalence, demographic correlates, risk, and protective factors. *Sleep, 31,* 62–70.

Smith, M. T., Huang, M. I., & Manber, R. (2005). Cognitive behavior therapy for chronic insomnia occurring within the context of medical and psychiatric disorders. *Clinical Psychology Review, 25,* 559–592.

Smith, M. T., Perlis, M. L., Park, A., Smith, M. S., Pennington, J., Giles, D. E., & Buysse D. J. (2002). Comparative meta-analysis of pharmacotherapy and behavior therapy for persistent insomnia. *American Journal of Psychiatry, 159,* 5–11.

Spielman, A. J. (1986). Assessment of insomnia. *Clinical Psychology Review, 6,* 11–25.

Spielman, A., Conroy, D., & Glovinsky, P. B. (2003). Evaluation of insomnia. In M. L. Perlis & K. L. Lichstein (Eds.), *Treating sleep disorders: Principles and practice of behavioral sleep medicine* (pp. 190–213). Hoboken, NJ: John Wiley & Sons.

St-Amand, J., Provencher, M. D., Bélanger, L., & Morin, C. M. (2013). Sleep disturbances in bipolar disorder during remission. *Journal of Affective Disorders, 146,* 112–119.

Taylor, D. J., Mallory, L. J., Lichstein, K. L., Durrence, H. H., Riedel, B. W., & Bush, A. J. (2007). Comorbidity of chronic insomnia with medical problems. *Sleep, 30,* 213–218.

Vgontzas, A. N., Kales, A., Bixler, E. O., & Vela-Bueno, A. (1993). Sleep disorders related to another mental disorder (nonsubstance/ primary): A DSM-IV literature review. *Journal of Clinical Psychiatry, 54,* 256–259.

Zhu, L., & Zee, P. C. (2012). Circadian rhythm sleep disorders. *Neurology Clinics, 30,* 1167–1191.

22

Paraphilia, Gender Dysphoria, and Hypersexuality

JAMES M. CANTOR

AND KATHERINE S. SUTTON

Few mental health or behavioral phenomena arouse greater public emotion or fascination than does this family of conditions. Consensual paraphilias, such as the erotic interest in pain, have given rise to entire subcultures, analogous to the gay communities of previous decades. Nonconsensual paraphilias, such as the erotic interest in children or in rape, motivate persons to engage in sexual offenses, leading legislatures to enact increasingly putative and lengthy sentences and to establish publicly accessible registries of offenders. Cases of transsexualism, of "sex addiction" (often termed *hypersexuality* in the research literature), and of highly unusual paraphilias (such as erotic interest in nonhuman animals or in being an amputee) have been featured in contemporary entertainment media and documentaries (e.g., Lawrence, 2006; Reay, Attwood, & Gooder, 2013; Williams & Weinberg, 2003).

Neuroanatomical and genetic research on these conditions has lagged behind that of other behavioral phenomena. Thus, this chapter necessarily emphasizes description over etiology. Great care must be taken when generalizing findings regarding individuals with paraphilic interests; much of what we know about the nonconsensual paraphilias derives from research on sex offenders. More recently, mutual support groups for self-identified pedophiles working to remain offense-free as well as professionally led groups for pedophiles

unknown to law enforcement have emerged (e.g., Beier et al., 2009). Such groups may provide a new window on nonoffending pedophiles, but research on their participants is just beginning to emerge. Similarly, reports of hypersexuality (also termed *sex addiction* and *sexual compulsivity*) frequently rely on self-referral and self-diagnosis from individuals who already presume the validity of analogies between sexual behavior and drug or alcohol use. Although the *ICD-10* includes the category *Excessive Sexual Drive* and *Excessive Masturbation*, the *DSM-5* contains no equivalent, nor an applicable catch-all category.

Paraphilias

Paraphilias refer broadly to any powerful and persistent sexual interest other than sexual interest in copulatory or precopulatory behavior with morphologically typical, consenting, adult human partners. Although some paraphilic interests have been reported in women, the paraphilias occur nearly exclusively in men.

A fundamental change introduced in *DSM-5* is its distinction between a paraphilia and a paraphilic disorder. With the introduction of the *DSM-5*, paraphilias are not diagnosable disorders unto themselves. The more restrictive term, *Paraphilic Disorder*, is reserved by *DSM-5* for the subset of individuals who experience distress or impairment or who harm or risk harm to others, because of their paraphilic interest. Thus, the existing literature includes samples that would now be said to have a paraphilia but not a paraphilic disorder (such as surveys of cross-dressing social groups) and includes samples that would now be said to have both a paraphilia and be diagnosable with a paraphilic disorder (such as phallometric studies of convicted, pedophilic child molesters). Thus, among the paraphilic individuals in the studies reviewed here, some would and some would not have received a *DSM-5* diagnosis.

Paraphilias may be classified under two broad headings: (a) those in which the sexually interesting *object* is something other than phenotypically normal humans between the ages of physical maturity and physical decline, and (b) those in which the sexually interesting *activity* is something other than copulatory or precopulatory behavior with a consenting partner.

Object Paraphilias

Erotic Age-Preferences

The erotic age-preferences are termed according to the level of physical development of an individual's most preferred sexual object (Blanchard et al., 2009). *Pedophilia* refers to the strong or preferential sexual interest in specifically prepubescent children (i.e., children showing Tanner stage 1 features, typically age 10 and younger). *Hebephilia* refers to the equivalent interest in pubescent children (Tanner stages 2–3, typically ages 11–14). Because pedophilia and hebephilia can co-occur or be difficult to distinguish, authors have used *pedohebephilia* as a superordinate category to refer to both. *Ephebophilia* refers to strong sexual interest in persons in adolescence or late puberty (Tanner stage 4, typically ages 15 to physical maturity), and *teleiophilia* refers to the erotic age preference toward adults between reaching physical maturity but before physical decline (Tanner stage 5, typically ages, 17–45). Finally, there also exist individuals whose primary sexual interests are for elderly persons, termed *gerontophilia*. Pedophilia, hebephilia, and gerontophilia are typically referred to as paraphilias, but ephebophilia and teleiophilia are not.

The typical behaviors of pedophilic and hebephilic men consist of touching the breasts, buttocks, or genitals of the child or inducing the child (such as with bribes or threats) to touch or fellate the offender. Abduction and violent sexual abuse of children are comparatively rare. Some pedophilic men report experiencing an interest in children that is romantic as well as erotic (Wilson & Cox, 1983). Pedophilia and hebephilia supply the motivation behind a substantial proportion of cases of child molestation, but these erotic age-preferences are not synonymous with sexual offenses against children (Seto, 2004, 2008). Some cases of child molestation, especially those involving incest, are committed in the absence of any identifiable deviant erotic age-preference (e.g., Freund, Watson, & Dickey, 1991); in such cases, the child is a sexual target of convenience to the offender. Conversely, there are men with no known records of sexual contact with a child who present to clinicians seeking assistance in dealing with their erotic interest in children.

Although pedophilia is more widely discussed, hebephilia may be the more widespread social and clinical problem. The modal age of victims of sexual offenses in the United States is 13–14 years (Snyder, 2000; Vuocolo, 1969). In anonymous surveys of social organizations of persons who acknowledge having an erotic interest in children, attraction to children of pubescent ages is more frequently reported than is attraction to those of prepubescent ages (e.g., Bernard, 1975; Wilson & Cox, 1983). In samples of sexual offenders recruited from clinics and correctional facilities, the hebephilic men typically outnumber the pedophilic men (e.g., Cantor et al., 2004; Gebhard, Gagnon, Pomeroy, & Christenson, 1965; Studer, Aylwin, Clelland, Reddon, & Frenzel, 2002).

The Internet includes sites dedicated to sexual depictions of elderly women, catering to gerontophilic consumers. An unknown proportion of sexual offenders are gerontophilic; reviews suggests that 2%–7% of rape victims are elderly women (Ball, 2005), and homosexual gerontophilic sexual offending also exists (Kaul & Duffy, 1991). Sexual homicides of the elderly show evidence of greater brutality, even though the victims are less likely or able to resist or protect themselves (Safarik, Jarvis, & Nussbaum, 2002).

Fetishism

Fetishism denotes a heterogeneous group of paraphilias in which the individuals' strongest sexual interest is focused on classes of objects or features of objects other than the external reproductive organs of phenotypically normal human beings. The term does not apply to erotic interests that include the mere use of objects, such as dildos, costumes, or ropes; it applies to instances where those objects represent the central feature rather than a supportive role in sexual activity. Although fetishism is sometimes discussed as an erotic interest in an arbitrary object, many fetishes involve objects that are highly gender-specific (e.g., shoes, underwear) or are closely related to people (e.g., urine, feces, body parts). Chalkley and Powell (1983) reviewed the files of all cases over a 20-year period who met criteria for a nontransvestic fetishes in a teaching hospital. Forty-eight cases were identified, and the objects included clothing (58.3%), rubber and rubber items (22.9%), footwear (14.6%), body parts (14.6%), leather and leather items (10.4%), and soft materials and fabrics (6.3%).

Stuff-Fetishism   *Stuff-fetishism* refers to the erotic interest in specific materials, such as rubber, leather, or fur. Individuals with this fetish will seek out items composed of those materials for use during masturbation, such as in a case described by Gosselin and Wilson (1980, pp. 50–51):

> After fifteen years of marriage, Mr. W.'s wife died. He made no serious attempt to acquire another partner, because he was "pretty much able to look after himself" and the appearance of his house bore this out.... [H]e kept in his house a complete "rubber room" lined throughout with curtain of the same material and containing two large cupboards full of rubber garments, gas masks, photographic and other equipment. He has in the past visited prostitutes to play out some aspect of his fantasies, but now does not do so, feeling that he has all he needs for sexual satisfaction without leaving his house.

Stuff-fetishists who choose clothing rather than other items made of their preferred material can be difficult to distinguish from *clothing-fetishists* (described later). For stuff-fetishism, it is the material (its texture and scent, etc.) rather than the form of the object that is of primary interest; in clothing-fetishism, it is the form of the object (such as the shape of a women's shoe) that is of primary importance.

Clothing-Fetishism   The garments chosen by clothing-fetishists are often emblematic of gender: high-heeled shoes, bras, or panties. The behaviors of clothing-fetishists include kissing and licking the garment, rubbing it against their genitals, and wearing it. A heterosexual male's wearing of a female-typical article of clothing, such as a shoe or pantyhose, resembles fetishistic transvestism; however, a clothing-fetishist dons the garment in order to interact with it physically, whereas a fetishistic transvestite employs garments in order to assist his mental imagery of taking on feminine characteristics. Clothing-fetishism also occurs among homosexual men; their erotic interests pertain to, for example, men's underwear or masculine footwear such as boots or wingtip shoes (Weinberg, Williams, & Calhan, 1994). Unlike many activity paraphilias (described later), the expression of clothing-fetishism does not itself involve any nonconsenting persons; however, some individuals commit theft to obtain garments from people (e.g., Anonymous, Chambers, & Janzen, 1976; Revitch, 1978). Because this behavior occurs despite the relative ease with which such garments could be purchased, such thefts may indicate that the process of the theft is part of these individuals' paraphilic interest or may represent an erotic interest specifically in clothing that has already been worn by someone (Weinberg et al., 1994). As noted in a case described by Grant (1953, p. 144):

> If I buy the kind of shoes I prefer and ask a woman I know to wear them for me, it doesn't have the same appeal as if they were her own shoes. I guess this is because they don't seem to be as much a part of her.

Transvestism   *Transvestism*, also called *fetishistic transvestism*, refers to a male's erotic interest in wearing feminine attire, makeup, and wigs. There is sometimes an interest in being perceived as female in public; however, some men with fetishistic transvestism wear a single item, such as panties, underneath their regular attire when appearing in public. On phallometric testing, both fetishistic transvestites and clothing-fetishists show similar penile reactions to pictures of women's underwear (Freund, Seto, & Kuban, 1996). The great majority of men with fetishistic transvestism are heterosexual (e.g., Långström & Zucker, 2005). Although there exist homosexual male crossdressers, their behavior is rarely, if ever, associated with sexual arousal and is instead employed for humor or entertainment.

Partialism   In *partialism,* there is an erotic interest in a specific portion of human anatomy, such as feet or legs. The interest in the body part is described as providing the same as or greater sexual arousal than interest in the genitals (e.g., Kunjukrishnan, Pawlak, & Varan, 1988). Interestingly, partialism involving the foot frequently co-occurs with clothing-fetishism focused on shoes, as illustrated by a case described by Kunjukrishnan et al. (1988, p. 821):

> Mr. A had been masturbating regularly with fetish fantasies of smelling women's feet or sucking their toes.…He visited massage parlours and acted out his fetish fantasies with the masseuse. He usually got an erection while smelling or sucking women's feet and this was often followed by masturbation. He also asked several women that he met on the street if he could smell their feet.…When he and his wife had guests, he would often go downstairs to smell the shoes of female guests who would be upstairs talking to his wife or otherwise occupied.

There also exist homosexual male partialists, attracted to the feet or other nongenital body parts of men (Weinberg et al., 1994; Weinberg, Williams, & Calhan, 1995).

Urophilia and Coprophilia   *Urophilia* (also called *uro-langia*) refers to the erotic interest in urine. Urophilic individuals express interests in being urinated on, in clothing with urine stains or scents, and sometimes in consuming the urine of their sexual partners. *Coprophilia* (also called *coprolagnia*) refers to the analogous interest in feces. No studies have sampled urophilic or coprophilic individuals specifically; existing reports describe samples of persons who have several paraphilias, one of which is urophilia or coprophilia. Nonetheless, offers and requests for persons interested in engaging in these behaviors appear in personal ads and advertisements for prostitution or escort services. In a survey of several thousand gay men, 1% responded that they engaged in urophilic behaviors "always" or "very frequently," and 0.5% reported engaging in coprophilic behaviors that frequently (Jay & Young, 1977).

Altered Partners

Acrotomophilia   *Acrotomophilia* is the erotic interest in persons missing one or more limbs. Some acrotomophiles ask their (anatomically intact) sexual partners to mimic being an amputee during sexual intercourse (Dixon, 1983; Massie & Szajnberg, 1997; Money & Simcoe, 1986), and pornography depicting amputees in sexual or alluring poses exists both on the Internet and in print media (Elman, 1997; Waxman-Fiduccia, 1999). Dixon (1983) provided the results of a survey of individuals who subscribed to a service that distributed erotica depicting amputees: Leg amputations were preferred over arm amputations; amputations of a single limb, over double amputations; and amputations that left a stump, over amputations that left no stump. Congenital malformations of limbs received the lowest ratings. Many people sexually attracted to amputees report that they recognized their interest for the first time as a child when they saw a person or a photograph of a person missing a limb (First, 2005).

Gynandromorphophilia/Gynemimetophilia   *Gynandromorphophilia* and *gynemimetophilia* refer to the erotic interest in cross-dressed or anatomically feminized men. Individuals with such interests seek to have sexual encounters with men who are dressed as women, with postoperative male-to-female transsexuals, or with biological males whose bodies have undergone sufficient hormonal or surgical treatment to appear female but have retained the penis (Blanchard & Collins, 1993; Money & Lamacz, 1984). Pornography depicting "she-males" exists both in print media and on the Internet, and personal ads sometimes include persons seeking or offering encounters with feminized men (Blanchard & Collins, 1993; Escoffier, 2011). In convenience samples of men with this interest, approximately half refer to themselves as bisexual and half as heterosexual, but many indicate that neither term exactly captures them (Operario, Burton, Underhill, & Sevelius, 2008; Weinberg & Williams, 2010). Nonetheless, gynandromorphophilia remains largely unstudied; it is unknown precisely which aspects of feminized males correspond to the focus of gynandromorphophiles' erotic interests.

Necrophilia   The erotic interest in corpses is *necrophilia*. The paraphilia has also been called *vampirism* (e.g., Bourguignon, 1983), although others restrict "vampirism" to refer only to the erotic interest in drinking blood (e.g., Vanden Bergh & Kelly, 1964). The most extreme forms of the expression of necrophilia entail obtaining actual corpses or rendering an unwilling victim unconscious for copulation. Rosman and Resnick (1989) reviewed and tabulated the information available from 122 cases of necrophilia that were reported in the literature or made available to them by colleagues. The behaviors and behavioral fantasies of the cases included vaginal intercourse with the corpse (51%), its mutilation (29%), anal penetration of it (11%), kissing it (15%), performing fellatio or cunnilingus upon it (8%), and sucking or fondling the breasts of the corpse (8%). In some cases, mutilation of the body included cannibalism or the drinking of its blood. Thirty-four cases from the whole sample provided self-reports of their motivations: These included the desire to possess an unresisting and unrejecting partner (68%), reunions with a (presumably deceased) romantic partner (21%), sexual attraction to corpses (15%), comfort or overcoming feelings of isolation (15%), or seeking self-esteem by expressing power over a homicide victim (12%). Stein, Schlesinger, and Pinizzotto (2010) similarly tabulated information from FBI case files, wherein the paraphilic nature of the offense was ascertained by the victim's attire (or the lack of it), exposure of victims' sexual anatomy, sexual positioning of the victim, or other features. This sample largely resembled that described by Rosman and Resnick; however, many of these cases showed evidence of the victim having been raped before being killed, contesting the claim that having an unresisting partner was a central motivation.

Erotic Identity Disorders

The sexual fantasies of individuals with erotic identity disorders focus on imagery of themselves in a different form, such as men fantasizing about having the body of a woman, about having the body of a child or infant, or about being an amputee. Such individuals sometimes describe their physical bodies as incorrect and the fantasized image as their ideal self (Lawrence, 2006). The expressions of these conditions range from covert visualization during masturbation or during sexual interactions with other people; to mimicking or approximating the erotic identity through clothing, costumes, and props; to seeking medical intervention for permanent body modification to resemble the image of the erotic identity more closely.

Autogynephilia   *Autogynephilia* refers to a male's erotic interest in the image or thought of himself as

a woman (Blanchard, 1989a, 1991). During sexual intercourse with women, an autogynephilic male might imagine himself as a woman sexually interacting as a lesbian (Newman & Stoller, 1974) or imagine himself as a woman being penetrated by his partner, who is imagined as a man (Benjamin, 1966; Lukianowicz, 1959). Homosexual (and non-autogynephilic) men may also fantasize about being penetrated by a man, but the focus of their erotic imagery is on the masculine characteristics of their sexual partner, whereas the erotic imagery of autogynephilic men focuses on the feminine characteristics of themselves. Autogynephilia most frequently co-occurs with fetishistic transvestism; however, a male's erotic interest in being a woman can occur on its own, as illustrated in a case described by Blanchard (1993a, p. 70):

> The earliest sexual fantasy [the patient] could recall was that of having a woman's body. When he masturbated, he would imagine that he was a nude woman lying alone in her bed. His mental imagery would focus on his breasts, his vagina, the softness of his skin, and so on—all the characteristic features of the female physique....When questioned why he did not cross-dress at present—he lived alone and there was nothing to prevent him—he indicated that he simply did not feel strongly impelled to do so.

Some autogynephilic fantasies pertain to other aspects of being female, such as menstruating, being pregnant, lactating, or douching (Blanchard, 1991; Denko, 1976). Autogynephilia sometimes co-occurs with *gender dysphoria* (see Gender Dysphoria and Transsexualism, later in this chapter). Cases of *partial autogynephilia* have also been described: Instead of envisioning themselves entirely as female, such individuals envision themselves with a mixture of male and female anatomy (Blanchard, 1993a, 1993b).

Infantilism   *Infantilists* are sexually aroused by behaving or imaging themselves as children or infants. (In earlier decades, the term "infantilism" was used to refer more generally to any arrest of psychosexual development in childhood, which was believed to be the cause of the paraphilias in general; e.g., Stekel, 1930.) Such individuals will crawl on all fours and employ (adult-size) baby clothes, bibs, feeding bottles, pacifiers, or other props as part of acting out the fantasy of being a young child, which is often accompanied by penile erection, masturbation, and ejaculation (e.g., Bethell, 1974; Pate & Gabbard, 2003). As part of expressing their fantasies, infantilists will often wear adult-sized diapers and urinate or defecate in them. Some individuals request that sexual partners mother them, such as by rocking them, bottle-feeding them, or changing their diapers. Commercial websites have emerged that cater to individuals who refer to themselves as "adult babies" and supply adult-size baby clothes and nursery items (Pate & Gabbard, 2003). There have also been reports of individuals who wear diapers while masturbating but express no desire to seem like an infant (Malitz, 1966; Tuchman & Lachman, 1964); it is not known if these individuals were hiding such imagery from their clinicians or if these individuals had an incomplete form of infantilism (analogous to clothing-fetishism as an incomplete form of transvestism).

Apotemnophilia *Apotemnophilia* is the erotic interest in being or seeming to be an amputee (Money, Jobaris, & Furth, 1977). Some apotemnophilic individuals mimic amputeeism, in public or in private, using wheelchairs or crutches and by binding or concealing a healthy limb. There exist individuals who report that having four intact limbs makes them feel incomplete and that amputation is necessary in order for them to feel whole (Berger, Lehrmann, Larson, Alverno, & Tsao, 2005). The term *body integrity identity disorder* (BIID) has been suggested to describe individuals who seek an amputation in order to actualize a subjective sense of self (First, 2005). Lawrence (2006) has argued that BIID derives from and is secondary to apotemnophilia, citing evidence that the majority of individuals who seek limb amputation do so with an explicitly sexual motivation.

A convenience sample of 52 individuals who wanted a healthy limb removed was recruited from Internet groups; the great majority desired specifically to have a single leg removed, cut above the knee (First, 2005). Notably, the preference for this particular amputation is the same one that is reported by acrotomophiles (Dixon, 1983). Some individuals have attempted or performed self-amputation of a limb, and others have purposefully injured a limb in hopes of forcing emergency medical teams to amputate it (Bensler & Paauw, 2003; Berger et al., 2005; Money et al., 1977).

Erotic Target Location and Location Errors   The erotic fantasies of persons with erotic identity disorders pertain less to any sexual partners and more to their transformed images of themselves; some authors refer to these paraphilias as *autoerotic*. It has been hypothesized that autogynephilia represents a misdirected form of male heterosexuality (Blanchard, 1991; Ellis, 1928; Hirschfeld, 1918); that is, instead of an attraction to women in the environment, autogynephilic men experience an attraction to women internal to themselves. Freund and Blanchard (1993) referred to this characteristic as an *erotic target location error*. They hypothesized that erotic target location was a basic dimension of sexual attraction, independent of the nature of the erotic target (object) itself. They interpreted infantilism as an erotic target location error for persons whose erotic target is children, that is, infantilism as an autoerotic form of pedophilia. The hypothesis furthermore relates apotemnophilia as the autoerotic form of acrotomophilia (Lawrence, 2006, 2013).

Zoophilia/Bestiality

Zoophilia and *bestiality* are both used to refer to the erotic interest in nonhuman animals. Among 114 self-acknowledged zoophilic men in an Internet-based survey, sexual behaviors included orally stimulating the genitals of the animal (81%), vaginal penetration of the animal (75%), masturbation of the animal (68%), and being anally penetrated by the animal (52%) (Williams & Weinberg, 2003). Inducing the animal to lick the human's genitals and anal penetration of the animal have also been reported (Peretti & Rowan, 1983). On a similar survey of 82 male and 11 female zoophiles, the most commonly preferred animals were (in descending order): male dogs, female dogs, and male horses, followed by female horses (for men) or male cats (for women) (Miletski, 2001). Some zoophilics report being attracted only to certain species, to certain breeds of a species, or only to male or female members of a species (Williams & Weinberg, 2003).

Some persons who acknowledge repeatedly engaging in sex with animals describe the behavior as a form of masturbation during which they fantasize about sexual contact with humans (Peretti & Rowan, 1983). Other persons report that the behavior is part of an emotional and romantic bond with the animal, one that they believe the animal shares with them (Miletski, 2005; Williams & Weinberg, 2003). Moreover, some zoophiles report they would feel jealous if other humans or animals expressed an interest in "their" animal(s) (e.g., Earls & Lalumière, 2002; McNally & Lukach, 1991; Miletski, 2005). In describing their interviews with self-acknowledged zoophiles, Williams and Weinberg (2003) noted that some individuals professed an extreme affinity for nonhuman animals, "believing they had animal characteristics or that they felt like they were an animal" (p. 528). This suggests that there may also exist an autoerotic form of zoophilia.

Activity Paraphilias

Agonistic Sexual Behavior

Biastophilia (Paraphilic Rape)   The erotic interest in committing rape has been variously called *biastophilia, paraphilic rape,* and *paraphilic coercive disorder.* Rapists react to depictions of rape significantly more, on average, than do nonrapists on tests of penile tumescence responses, but respond significantly less than nonrapists to depictions of consensual sex (Lalumière, Harris, Quinsey, & Rice, 2005). It is not known what proportion of rapists are biastophilic, however. Although some nonparaphilic men report experiencing occasional sexual fantasies that include elements of rape (Arndt, Foehl, & Good, 1985; Crepault & Couture, 1980), biastophilic individuals prefer rape to sexual interaction with willing partners. Emphasizing this distinction, the paraphilic interest in rape has also been called *preferential rape* (Freund, Scher, & Hucker, 1983), *pathological rape,* or the *deviant rape pattern.* Rape as a primary erotic interest is illustrated by a case described by Freund (1990, p. 198):

A well-educated, well-built, and good-looking businessman used to go out at night and rape female strangers, whom he dragged into the lanes between houses. When one of his victims said she would gladly have intercourse with him if he would accompany her to her apartment, he said no, it must be here and now, and then he raped her.

The manner by which the individual obtains sexual intercourse is a central component to the erotic interest. In clinical practice, it can be difficult to distinguish an individual who committed a rape to enact a biastophilic fantasy from one who committed a rape as a kind of theft.

Sexual Sadism   *Sexual sadism* refers to the erotic interest in inflicting fear, humiliation, or suffering. Although both sadistic sexual offenders and biastophilic sexual offenders employ force, they do so with different motivations (Hirschfeld, 1938; Freund & Blanchard, 1986): Biastophiles prefer sexual activities with unwilling strangers (who must therefore be coerced into compliance). For sadistic sexual offenders, however, it is the infliction of pain and suffering per se that carries erotic value. Thus, sadistic sexual offenders will continue to apply force, sometimes in increasing magnitude, regardless of the compliance of the victims. In extreme cases, this proceeds to the death of the victim (Dietz, Hazelwood, & Warren, 1990; Gratzer & Bradford, 1995) and, further still, to the mutilation of the victim's body. Sadistic rapes do not always include penile penetration of the victim (Brittain, 1970). A review of case files in the U.S. National Center for the Analysis of Violent Crime revealed that offenses included sexual bondage (77%), anal rape (73%), forced fellatio of the offender by the victim (70%), vaginal rape (57%), penetration of victim with a foreign object (40%), blunt force trauma (60%), and the offenders' retention of a personal item belonging to the victim (40%) (Dietz et al., 1990).

There also exist individuals who seek to inflict pain or humiliation, but only on willing partners (e.g., Gosselin, 1987); this has been called the *hyperdominance pattern* of sexual behavior (Freund, Scher, Racansky, Campbell, & Heasman, 1986). It is not known whether or to what extent hyperdominance is related to sadism. Hyperdominants often express the desire to provide sexual pleasure to their submissive sexual partner(s), who are sometimes acting out their own paraphilic interests, such as fetishism, klismaphilia, or masochism. Ernulf and Innala (1995) observed discussions among individuals with such interests, one of whom described the goal of hyperdominants (p. 644):

A good top is an empath who knows how to tell with the least possible feedback exactly what will blow the bottom's mind. The top enjoys his pleasure vicariously. He has a great time. The idea is to turn the body into a sexual response machine.

Among sadistic sexual offenders, however, there is no obvious indication of a desire to provide pleasure. Although it is possible that hyperdominance and sadistic sexual offenses represent qualitatively different phenomena that resemble each other only superficially, it is also possible that such individuals (or a proportion of them) have the same erotic interests and differ in nonsexual psychological characteristics, such as antisociality, psychopathy, or the propensity to project or misinterpret the mental status of their sexual partners or victims.

Masochistic Paraphilias

Sexual Masochism   Persons with *sexual masochism* experience erotic excitement from enduring humiliation or physical pain, often enacting such fantasies (or approximations of them) alone or with sexual partners. Sufficient numbers of individuals seek opportunities to engage in these behaviors to form stable subcultures, which have been repeatedly surveyed (e.g., Ernulf & Innala, 1995; Nordling, Sandnabba, Santtila, & Alison, 2006). The majority of respondents to such surveys report the desire to undergo verbal abuse, slapping (either manually or with implements), being ordered to perform sexual acts, or being tied up or restrained. A smaller proportion of individuals seek to undergo very severe stimulation: These include torture through beatings that draw blood, branding or burning, and mummification (immobilizing the entire body with rope or other wrapping) and confinement for extended periods of time. Clinical and nonclinical samples of masochists (i.e., individuals with masochism and individuals diagnosable with *DSM-5* masochistic disorder) report interests in the same activities (cf., Freund, Seto, & Kuban, 1995). Accidental deaths have been reported from engaging in some masochistic behaviors, such as through the self-application of electricity to the genitals or other parts of the body (Cairns & Rainer, 1981).

One of the most dramatic cases of sexual masochism was that of Mr. Bernd Brandes, which was widely reported in the media. Brandes answered a personal ad placed by Mr. Armin Meiwes, asking for young, well-built men who wanted to be slaughtered and consumed (Harding, 2003). After Brandes consumed a combination of alcohol and sleeping pills, Meiwes cut off Brandes' penis and fried it for both of them to eat. Meiwes then fatally stabbed Brandes, all of which Brandes consented to, on videotape. Notably, before he was arrested, Meiwes had met with five other men who responded to his personal ad.

Autoerotic Asphyxia   *Autoerotic asphyxia* refers to the erotic interest in being suffocated, such as by being hanged or strangled. Some asphyxiophilics engage in such behaviors alone (sometimes called *asphyxiophilia*), using ropes suspended from beams or ligatures tied to doorknobs while they masturbate, whereas others engage sexual partners to purposefully restrict airflow to the lungs or blood flow to the brain as part of their sexual activities (suggesting masochism focused on suffocation). When enacted in solitude, asphyxiophilia has led to accidental deaths (Hucker & Blanchard, 1992). Some cases of asphyxiophilic fatalities have come to the attention of clinicians through lawyers or insurance companies (e.g., Cooper, 1995, 1996), as life insurance claims are payable in the event of an accidental death but not of suicide. In some fatality cases, the body of the asphyxiophilic individual is discovered naked or with his penis exposed, with pornographic magazines nearby, with dildos or other sex toys nearby, or with evidence of his having ejaculated (Hucker & Blanchard, 1992; Janssen, Koops, Anders, Kuhn, & Püschel, 2005). The condition of such corpses also suggests that asphyxiophilia is frequently comorbid with other paraphilias: The corpse is sometimes cross-dressed or wearing makeup, the content of pornographic material is of a sadomasochistic nature, or the corpse is found with self-applied gags or bindings on his hands, feet, or genitals (Blanchard & Hucker, 1991). Asphyxiophilia has also been called *hypoxyphilia,* under the presumption that hypoxia enhances sexual sensations (e.g., Uva, 1995). Such an association has not been established, however; the sexual interest might instead be focused on psychological associations with the actual behaviors, rather than with any physiological effects of hypoxia (Blanchard & Hucker, 1991).

Courtship Disorder

A specific set of the activity paraphilias—voyeurism, exhibitionism, telephone scatologia, toucheurism, frotteurism, and biastophilia—has been hypothesized to be individual symptoms of a single underlying pathology, called *courtship disorder* (Freund, 1988). As detailed below, the courtship disorder hypothesis maintains that each of the paraphilias in this set is a disordered expression of a phase of human courtship (Freund, 1976; Freund, Seeley, Marshall, & Glinfort, 1972). Biastophilia has already been described in the previous section together with sadism; the following describes the other paraphilias comprising courtship disorder.

Voyeurism   *Voyeurism* is the erotic interest in viewing an unsuspecting person or persons in typically private situations. Viewed acts include dressing or undressing, sexual intercourse, urinating, and defecating. (In some cases, it is unclear whether these latter behaviors indicate voyeurism, with the urine and feces being incidental, or indicate urophilia or coprophilia with the urine or feces being central; e.g., Collacott & Cooper, 1995.) The increased availability of affordable and easily concealed electronic devices has broadened the range of opportunities available to voyeurs for viewing unsuspecting strangers (e.g., Simon, 1997). Some cases of voyeurism have included holding cellular telephone cameras over or under the partitions of public washroom stalls, and hiding small cameras in the bedrooms of victims. Paraphilic voyeurism would not describe persons for whom the mere sight or image of a person were sufficient for eliciting sexual arousal; in paraphilic voyeurism, the means by which the individual achieves his view is an integral part of the paraphilic interest. That is, in some cases, the glance must be "stolen" to be of erotic interest.

Exhibitionism   The erotic interest in exposing one's genitals to unsuspecting strangers is *exhibitionism*. The paraphilia pertains to persons for whom there is sexual pleasure in doing so, not when the behavior is motivated by money (such as strippers) or other nonsexual reasons (such as pranks). The majority of exhibitionists masturbate to ejaculation as part of exposing their penis (Freund, Watson, & Rienzo, 1988; Langevin et al., 1979). On a questionnaire given to a sample of 185 exhibitionists, Freund et al. (1988) asked, "How would you have preferred a person to react if you were to expose your privates to him or her?" (p. 256). Of the seven possible choices, the most common response was "Would want to have sexual intercourse" (35.1%), followed by "No reaction necessary at all" (19.5%), "To show their privates also" (15.1%), "Admiration" (14.1%), and "Any reaction" (11.9%). Few exhibitionists chose "Anger and disgust" (3.8%) or "Fear" (0.5%).

Telephone Scatologia   *Telephone scatologia* refers to the erotic interest in using a telephone to expose unsuspecting persons to vulgar or sexual language or to elicit it from them. Many scatologists masturbate during the call or masturbate subsequently while recollecting the call; some telephone scatologists cross-dress or pose as female when calling (e.g., Dalby, 1988; Pakhomou, 2006). Although it was not based on any systematic observation, Mead (1975) provided an intuitive taxonomy of obscene telephone call content: (a) the "shock caller," who immediately makes obscene remarks or propositions in order provoke an emotional response from the victims; (b) the "ingratiating seducer," who fabricates a plausible story to lure the victim into conversation; and (c) the "trickster," who poses, for example, as someone conducting a survey in order to elicit sexual history or other information about the victim. A survey of 1,262 Canadian women who were employed outside the home asked respondents about their experiences of receiving obscene phone calls (Smith & Morra, 1994); 83.2% of the sample had received such calls. Of those, 84.5% of the calls came from males, 86.8% came from adults, and 73.8% were reportedly from strangers (in 7.5% of the cases, the victim knew the scatologist, and in 18.6%, the victim was unsure whether she knew the caller).

Approximately 37% of rapists have been reported to engage in obscene telephone calls (Abel, Becker, Cunningham-Rathner, Mittelman, & Rouleau, 1988), but only 5%–6% of apprehended telephone scatologists have been found to commit rape (Abel et al., 1988; Price, Kafka, Commons, Gutheil, & Simpson, 2002). Because not all obscene telephone calls are reported to authorities, it is unknown how well these individuals represent all telephone scatologists. It is also unknown whether the content or other parameters of the calls predict an individual's likelihood of committing other sexual offenses.

Telephone scatologia is sometimes described as a variant of exhibitionism (e.g., Hirschfeld, 1938; Nadler, 1968), differing by being auditory rather visual. Indeed, telephone scatologia is highly comorbid with exhibitionism (e.g., Price et al., 2002). Although telephone scatologia necessarily involves obscene telephone calls, not all obscene telephone calls are motivated by telephone scatologia; the behavior may represent a prank with no erotic value to the caller (Pakhomou, 2006).

Toucheurism and Frotteurism   *Toucheurism* and *frotteurism* refer to the erotic interest in approaching unsuspecting strangers to touch their (usually clothed) breasts, buttocks, or genital area.

Toucheurism pertains to when contact is made using the hands, and frotteurism pertains to men who press their penis against the victim, especially against the buttocks, through clothing. Frotteurs typically target women in crowded public places (e.g., streetcars), whereas toucheurs will often grab at a woman while quickly moving across her path.

The Courtship Disorder Hypothesis The courtship disorder hypothesis asserts that the usual male sexual activity cycle consists of four phases: (a) looking for and appraising potential sexual partners; (b) pretactile interaction with those partners, such as by smiling at and talking to them; (c) tactile interaction with them, such as by embracing or petting; and then (d) sexual intercourse (Freund, 1976; Freund & Blanchard, 1986). In normal courtship, each phase of the cycle leads to the next. In courtship disorder, however, one or more of these phases is exaggerated or distorted, and the cycle fails to progress from one phase to the next. According to the hypothesis, voyeurism is a rigid, isolated form of the searching phase; exhibitionism and telephone scatologia represent distortions of the pretactile phase; toucheurism and frotteurism represent pathologies of the tactile phase; and, in the preferential rape pattern, the first three courtship phases are altogether skipped.

The assertion that these six paraphilias all emerge from the same underlying disorder simplifies the interpretation of several observations: (a) The paraphilias in this set are highly comorbid with each other (Freund & Blanchard, 1986; Freund et al., 1983). (b) During laboratory testing of penile reactions to audiotaped stimuli, individuals who have shown one courtship paraphilia, but not another, nonetheless show an elevated response to stimuli representing other courtship paraphilias (Freund et al., 1983, 1986). (c) The paraphilias of courtship disorder share the propensity to target strangers (e.g., Freund et al., 1988; Gebhard et al., 1965; Mohr, Turner, & Jerry, 1964; Smith & Morra, 1994), whereas other paraphilias more often involve people known to the paraphilic individual (or involve no other person at all).

Miscellaneous Paraphilias

Klismaphilia

Klismaphilia refers to the erotic interest in enemas. Klismaphilics will entertain sexual fantasies about enemas during masturbation, self-administer enemas for masturbatory stimulation, or engage their sexual partners to administer them. Some have reported experiencing sexual arousal upon administration of clinical enemas by nursing staff, and feigning physical symptoms to justify the procedure (Denko, 1973). By contrast, the term would not apply when the enema provides a secondary rather than mandatory role—such as being forced to receive an enema as part of a masochistic fantasy—nor when only indirectly associated with sex, such as regular use in anticipation of anal intercourse. Twenty-two klismaphilics responded to an ad placed in sex-oriented periodicals as part of a survey of individuals with erotic interests in enemas (Arndt, 1991); the median frequency of enema use was twice per week, and approximately half the respondents engaged in the behavior together with their sexual partners. In describing a series of 15 cases, Denko (1976) reported that three male klismaphilics fantasized themselves as female during the enemas and that three such individuals experienced erotic enjoyment while eliciting enema-related conversation with female sales clerks (such as by asking for instructions).

Triolism

Triolism refers to the erotic interest in watching one's romantic partner engage in sexual behavior with a third party. Triolism differs from voyeurism in that the romantic partner (but not necessarily the third party) is typically aware of being observed. Some triolists want to observe the sexual activity visually (sometimes while hidden; e.g., Hirschfeld, 1938), some record the activity with cameras or audio recorders, and some want only to listen to their partners describe encounters had while the triolist was absent (Wernik, 1990).

Multiple Paraphilias and Blended Paraphilias

Individuals with one paraphilic interest often have other paraphilic interests (e.g., Abel et al., 1988; Abel & Osborn, 1992; Bradford, Boulet, & Pawlak, 1992; Freund et al., 1983). In some cases, these paraphilias function independently in the individual, such as in a man who will expose his genitals on certain occasions and who will grab the buttocks of females on other occasions. We refer to these simply as cases of comorbid or *multiple paraphilias.* Other individuals, however, possess erotic interests that deviate from typical in more than one aspect at the same time, such as men whose erotic fantasies entail being forced to cross-dress (e.g., Hucker, 1985) or a man who exposes his genitals to large dogs (McNally & Lukach, 1991), suggesting a blending of paraphilic interests.

Prevalence and Sex Ratio

Owing to their usually secretive nature, no meaningful prevalence or incidence data are available for any of the paraphilias. Numbers of persons who are charged with or convicted of certain sexual offenses have been used as estimates for some paraphilias. It is unknown what proportion of such offenders is genuinely paraphilic, however. A more sophisticated estimation has been conducted for the prevalences of transvestic fetishism, exhibitionism, and voyeurism (Långström & Seto, 2006; Långström & Zucker, 2005). These investigations analyzed responses to a representative survey of 2,450 men and women in Sweden. A total of 3.1% of the respondents reported having been sexually aroused at least one time by exposing their genitals to a stranger; of that subset, 23.7% also experienced sexual fantasies about the behavior. Of the whole sample, 7.8% reported engaging in voyeurism at least one time; of that subset, 53.4% also experienced sexual fantasies about doing so. Of the males, 2.8% reported cross-dressing that was associated with sexual arousal; an insufficient number of women reported ever having done so to support any analysis. National forensic databases have suggested rates of autoerotic deaths by asphyxia at 0.1 per million population (Sweden) to 2–4 per million (U.S.) (Byard & Winskog, 2012), but the prevalence of nonfatal practitioners remains unknown.

As previously noted, most paraphilias appear to be phenomena restricted nearly entirely to males. Notwithstanding case reports that have appeared in the literature, neither clinics, forensic institutions, nor social clubs for proponents of engaging in paraphilic behaviors report any substantial number of females with paraphilic age-preferences, courtship disorders, or fetishes. Sexual masochism is unusual among the paraphilias in that it shows a relatively high frequency of female practitioners. Breslow, Evans, and Langley (1985) surveyed

subscribers to and advertisers in a periodical catering to individuals interested in masochism or hyperdominance. Of the 81 non-prostitutes who preferred or usually preferred masochistic behaviors (termed "submissive" in the survey), 49.4% were women. Similarly, Ernulf and Innala (1995) analyzed messages on an online discussion group catering to people with the same interests: Of the 56 posts seeking to engage in masochistic acts (again termed "submissive"), 58.9% were purportedly from women.

Despite its close association with masochism, asphyxiophilia is usually viewed as a male phenomenon, owing to the lack of women among individuals who suffered accidental asphyxiophilic death. For example, the Hucker and Blanchard (1992) sample consisted of all 118 known such deaths in Ontario and Alberta, Canada, from 1974 to 1987, and only one was female. It is plausible, however, that there are women who engage in the behavior, but that they are less likely to suffer accidental death. This might occur if more male asphyxiophilics engaged in the solitary form of the behavior and more female asphyxiophilics did so in the company of a sexual partner (thereby protecting against accident).

Associated Features

We refer to the hypothetical factors that increase the probability of developing paraphilic interests as *paraphilogenic* factors. The existence of a biological predisposition to developing one or more paraphilias has been hypothesized for well over a century (e.g., Binet, 1887; Krafft-Ebing, 1886/1965), but few rigorous studies have been conducted. Some tentative conclusions can be proffered, however, primarily on the basis of investigations of individuals who have committed sexual offenses motivated by paraphilias, especially pedophilia.

IQ and Other Neuropsychological Testing

Pedophilic men and sexual offenders against children have lower IQs than nonpedophilic controls (Cantor et al., 2004; Cantor, Blanchard, Robichaud, & Christensen, 2005). The association between IQ and pedophilia appears to be independent of referral method; the same result emerges whether the pedophiles were referred by parole and probation officers, by lawyers, or by physicians and by self-referral (Blanchard et al., 2007). Consistent with these studies, pedophilic men are more likely to have repeated grades in school or to have required placement in special education classes (Cantor et al., 2006). Although several studies have administered batteries of neuropsychological tests to heterogeneous samples of sexual offenders, they have not reported results from homogeneous samples of paraphilic men. It remains unknown whether pedophiles have a general cognitive deficit (i.e., they would perform poorly on any neuropsychological test that correlates with IQ) or if they have a distinct pattern of cognitive strengths and weaknesses that might be detected by future investigations employing larger and more homogeneous samples.

It is also unknown whether and to what extent poor cognitive functioning is a characteristic specific to paraphilic age-preference or a characteristic of several (or all) paraphilias. Community-based samples of self-acknowledged paraphilics have repeatedly described highly educated and high-functioning individuals (e.g., Alison, Santtila, Sandnabba, & Nordling, 2001; Croughan, Saghir, Cohen, & Robins, 1981; Docter & Prince, 1997; Williams & Weinberg, 2003). Although it is possible that low IQ is specific to pedo- and hebephilia, it is also possible paraphilics with higher IQs are more likely to participate in interest groups and research studies.

Handedness

Handedness is of interest because of its association with very early brain development. Fetuses demonstrate a hand preference when thumb-sucking in utero (Hepper, Shahidullah, & White, 1991), and that preference predicts handedness later in life (Hepper, Wells, & Lynch, 2005). Approximately 8%–15% of the general population is non-right-handed (Hardyck & Petrinovich, 1977). Pedophilic men have been shown to be up to three times more likely to be non-right-handed (Cantor, Klassen, et al., 2005). Nonhomosexual male-to-female transsexuals (who have been shown empirically to experience autogynephilia; Blanchard, 1985, 1988, 1989b) similarly show elevated rates of non-right-handedness (Green & Young, 2001). Very little is known regarding handedness in any of the other paraphilias.

Meta-analytic review has shown homosexual men, although they are not paraphilic, to have

34% greater odds and homosexual females to have 91% greater odds of non-right-handedness than their heterosexual counterparts (Lalumière, Blanchard, & Zucker, 2000). Recent research indicates that the association between non-right-handedness and homosexuality in men is limited to individuals with no or few older brothers (Blanchard, 2008). Considered together, the findings on hand-preference and sexuality suggest that non-right-handedness might pertain to the development of all variant erotic-object interests (see Blanchard, 2008).

Non-right-handedness has commonly been interpreted as a marker for lesser than usual degrees of asymmetry between the left and right hemispheres of the brain. Therefore, Blanchard (2008) conjectured that Klar's (2004) explanation for the association of non-right-handedness and homosexuality might apply to variant erotic-object preferences in general. Klar hypothesized that "less asymmetric hemispheres may allow additional neuronal connections between different parts of the brain, thereby predisposing individuals to develop homosexuality, in contrast to the restricted possibilities allowed in the more common asymmetric hemispheric arrangement" (Klar, 2004, p. 254). Blanchard (2008) argued that the collective data on homosexual men and women, pedophiles, and transsexuals suggest that the hypothesized "additional neuronal connections" made possible by less asymmetric hemispheres might lead to an array of different psychosexual outcomes. The notion that erotic variations (paraphilic or benign) may result from atypical connections among brain regions, and not from anomalies in the brain regions themselves, is revisited in a different context in the next section.

Brain Imaging

Neuroimaging studies of paraphilias have been limited to sexual offenders. Computed tomography has been used to study sadists and pedophiles, but for the most part provided only null or inconsistent findings (Blanchard, Cantor, & Robichaud, 2006). Higher resolution images are provided by MRI, which has been applied in three investigations. All three found pedophilic men to have lower brain volumes, but in different neuroanatomical structures: Cantor et al. (2008) reported lower white matter volumes (fronto-occipital fasciculus and right arcuate fasciculus), whereas lower gray matter volumes were reported by Schiltz et al. (2007)

(amygdala, hypothalamus, substantia innominata, septal region, and bed nucleus of the stria terminalis) and by Schiffer et al. (2007) (ventral striatum and nucleus accumbens, orbitofrontal cortex, and cerebellum). Schiltz et al. (2007) and Schiffer et al. (2007) both compared pedophiles with healthy controls, whereas Cantor et al. (2008) compared pedophiles with men who had committed nonsexual crimes. It is therefore possible that the white matter differences pertain to pedophilia whereas the gray matter differences reflect differences related to having been apprehended, convicted, or incarcerated. If white matter rather than gray matter deficiencies are the neuroanatomical contributor to pedophilia, then pedophilia may be an insufficiency of connectivity among a set of topographically disparate brain regions rather than a dysfunction of those regions themselves. This would suggest for pedophilia what has previously been suggested for schizophrenia and mood disorders: "It is becoming increasingly evident that a lesion model is inappropriate and that a more relevant characterisation will be found in terms of disorders of functional interconnections between brain regions" (Frith & Dolan, 1998, p. 259).

Hormonal Assays

Studies of sexual offenders have measured the baseline levels of several hormones, including 5α-dihydrotestosterone, androstenedione, cortisol, dehydroepiandrosterone, dihydrotestosterone, estradiol, follicle-stimulating hormone, the free-androgen index, luteinizing hormone, prolactin, sex hormone-binding globulin, and testosterone (Blanchard et al., 2006). Those investigations have failed to reveal any consistent association between paraphilic sexual offenses (primarily involving pedophilia, exhibitionism, or sexual sadism) and any hormone except, potentially, testosterone: Greater levels of testosterone have been found among rapists relative to nonparaphilic controls (Giotakos, Markianos, Vaidakis, & Christodoulou, 2003; Rada, Laws, & Kellner, 1976). Other investigations have failed to detect such a difference, however (Haake et al., 2003; Rada, Laws, Kellner, Stivastava, & Peake, 1983). Lower levels of testosterone have been reported among pedophilic men by some studies (Gurnani & Dwyer, 1986; Seim & Dwyer, 1988), but no differences have been found in others (Gaffney & Berlin, 1984; Lang, Flor-Henry, &

Frenzel, 1990). It is possible that testosterone reflects the propensity to violence or aggression rather than any paraphilia.

Intimacy/Social Skills Deficits

Sex offenders may seek out sex with children because they do not have the social skills to successfully interact with adult partners and they cannot fulfill their sexual and emotional needs in relationships with peers (Seto, 2008). Sex offenders lack the capacity for intimate relationships and report themselves to be lonely (Garlick, Marshall, & Thornton, 1996; Seidman, Marshall, Hudson, & Robertson, 1994). Ward, Hudson, and Marshall (1996) found that sex offenders exhibited a wide range of insecure attachment styles, each associated with different psychological problems. Child molesters with a preoccupied attachment style were characterized by emotional neediness and profound doubts about their ability to elicit love and support from partners. Fearful dismissively attached offenders tended to distance themselves emotionally in relationships because of their fear of rejection. Both groups experienced problems with intimacy and apparently turned to sex with children because their adult relationships were compromised or unsatisfactory. The primary causal mechanism underlying their deviant sexual behavior was seen to be their insecure attachments and subsequent problems establishing satisfactory relationships with adults (Ward & Seigert, 2002).

As reviewed by Smallbone (2006), in several studies, child sex offenders have reported less secure childhood attachments than have nonsexual offenders (Marsa et al., 2004; Smallbone & Dadds, 1998) and nonoffenders (Marsa et al., 2004; Smallbone & Dadds, 1998). Similarly, according to Smallbone (2006), child sex offenders more frequently report an insecure rather than a secure adult attachment style (Jamieson & Marshall, 2000; Ward et al., 1996) and to report less secure adult attachment than that of both nonsexual offenders and nonoffenders (Marsa et al., 2004; Sawle & Kear-Colwell, 2001; Smallbone & Dadds, 1998).

Onset and Course

It is unknown whether the paraphilias share a common age at which they first manifest, or if they vary in age of onset. One should note that the age of onset of paraphilic interests does not necessary coincide with the age at which the paraphilogenic factors first operate. By way of analogy, typical (nonparaphilic) heterosexuality and typical homosexuality do not overtly manifest until puberty, but there is no reason to believe that the etiology of sexual orientation occurs at that time rather than earlier in development. The *DSM–5* describes the age of onset for the paraphilias to be during adolescence, although some of the paraphilic disorders may not be diagnosed until age 16 (in the case of pedophilic disorder) or 18 (in the case of voyeuristic disorder). These cut-offs are not meant to follow any etiological mechanism, however, and instead reflect an attempt to avoid false positives relative to typical sexual curiosity and experimentation in puberty and early adolescence.

It is unknown to what extent information about age of onset is affected by legal status of expressing paraphilic interests. It is plausible that individuals who experience paraphilic interests unassociated with sexual offending would be more willing to acknowledge awareness of their interests during childhood. The research literature supports the childhood onset of rubber fetishism (Gosselin & Wilson, 1980), cross-dressing (Brown et al., 1996), apotemnophilia (First, 2005), acrotomophilia (Dixon, 1983), homosexual or bisexual foot and shoe fetishism (Weinberg et al., 1995), and masochism and hyperdominance (Breslow et al., 1985). Moreover, paraphilics sometimes recall events from early childhood during which they became—and then remained—fascinated with the object(s) or behaviors of their future sexual interest (e.g., Dixon, 1983; Freund et al., 1995; Massie & Szajnberg, 1997; Weinberg et al., 1994, 1995).

Gender Dysphoria and Transsexualism

The term *gender dysphoria* refers to a broad class of phenomena characterized by discontent with one's biological sex, social gender, or both. In adults, it manifests as the persistent idea that one is, or should have been, a member of the opposite sex, and, in children, by pervasive patterns of behavior consistent with such a belief. The affective component of gender dysphoria is discontent with one's biological sex and the desire to possess the body of the opposite sex and to be regarded by others as a member of the opposite sex. *DSM-5* introduced *Gender Dysphoria* as the formal diagnostic term

(replacing the *DSM-IV-TR* term, *Gender Identity Disorder,* which, in turn replaced the *DSM-III-R* term, *Transsexualism*). Thus, gender dysphoria may now refer either to the broad term or the more narrowly defined diagnosis (capitalized here).

Gender dysphoria varies in severity and, at its most extreme is accompanied by a desire for surgery to simulate, as much as possible, the reproductive organs of the opposite sex. Individuals with milder forms sometimes perceive themselves to be both male and female or fluctuate between seeing themselves as one or the other.

There appear to be two, unrelated phenomena, each capable of motivating discontent with one's biological sex. The two groups experiencing these phenomena differ in sex ratio and in the age of onset, course, associated features, and, probably, the etiology of such discontent (Blanchard, 1989a, 1989b). One is associated with autogynephilia, the aforementioned paraphilic interest (of biological males) in being female. These individuals sometimes engage in erotic cross-dressing for many years before deciding to pursue permanent feminization. The other group lacks any obvious paraphilic interests but shows multiple, extremely strong or exaggerated features atypical for their biological sex.

In medical and research contexts, authors often use terms relative to a person's original biological sex, whereas community groups often use terms relative to a person's goal or ideal sex.

Autogynephilic Male-to-Females

The autogynephilic type accounts for a substantial proportion of persons seeking sex reassignment in Europe and North America (e.g., Nieder et al., 2011; Smith, van Goozen, Kuiper, & Cohen-Kettenis, 2005). The exact nature of the relation between autogynephilia and gender dysphoria is unclear. Many autogynephilic transsexuals report that their desires to be women remained the same or grew even stronger after their initial strong sexual response to that ideation had diminished or disappeared.

Insofar as autogynephilic transsexuals are erotically oriented toward other persons, they may be attracted to women, to both sexes, or to neither sex. It is likely that those individuals attracted to women constitute the prototype, and that bisexual and asexual individuals represent secondary variations. The asexual individuals represent those cases in which the autogynephilia nullifies or over-shadows the person's erotic attraction to women, and the bisexual individuals represent those cases in which the autogynephilic disorder instead gives rise to some secondary erotic interest in men that coexists with the person's basic attraction to women (Blanchard, 1985). Blanchard (1989b) has suggested that the latter phenomenon need not reflect an equal attraction to the male and female phenotypes and would perhaps be better character-ized as *pseudobisexuality*. Because autogynephilic male-to-females express the belief that "inside" they really are women, those who are attracted to women may—paradoxically—describe their erotic interests in women as "homosexual," and refer to themselves as "lesbians trapped in a man's body" (Lawrence, 2013).

Autogynephilic male-to-females are not con-spicuously cross-gendered in childhood, although the private wish to be a woman may begin to occur before puberty. They are rarely labelled as sissies by their peers; and their cross-gender behavior is typically restricted to secret, solitary cross-dressing, in garments surreptitiously bor-rowed from their mothers, sisters, or other females in their households. This type of gender dyspho-ria tends to develop more slowly and often has the character of a progressive disorder, with tempo-rary or milder methods of expressing female traits preceding more permanent and dramatic ones. Autogynephilic male-to-females usually present to clinicians in their mid-30s, and it is common for such individuals to seek professional help for the first time at age 50 or 60 years. Many auto-gynephilic male-to-females marry women and father children before their wish to live as women becomes overwhelming, thus delaying their pur-suit of sex reassignment (Blanchard, 1994).

Androphilic Male-to-Females and Gynephilic Female-to-Males

Male-to-female gender dysphorics who are sexu-ally attracted to men (i.e., who are *androphilic*) exhibit multiple overtly feminine behaviors, which were readily apparent in childhood. Such boys pre-fer girls' games and toys and female playmates, and would rather be around adult women than adult men. They often or always take female roles in fan-tasy play (e.g., princess, ballerina), and they iden-tify with glamorous female characters in television stories or other media. Some of these boys also

dress up as women; however, their cross-dressing is not experienced as sexually arousing, either in childhood or later. Even when they are not engag-ing in any obvious cross-gender behavior, boys with gender dysphoria are noticeably effeminate, which may manifest as feminine speech patterns, gestures, or gait.

Female-to-male gender dysphoric who are sexually attracted to women (i.e., are *gynephilic*) show the corresponding picture. In childhood, they express very strong preferences for boys' toys and games and a rejection of long hair and dresses in favor of short hair and trousers. They may imi-tate other male-typical behaviors, such as stand-ing to urinate. Unlike ordinary "tomboys," they do not merely enjoy some activities stereotyped as male; rather, they systematically and vehemently reject all activities, clothes, etc., that would iden-tify them to the world as female.

Gender-dysphoric boys and girls may verbally express the wish to belong to the opposite sex or state the belief that they will become members of the opposite sex when they grow up. Claims of actually being members of the opposite sex are more common in younger than in older children, probably because older children have a better understanding of gender constancy. Older children are also less likely to communicate the desire to belong to the opposite sex, an inhibition attribut-able to their greater awareness of social sanctions (Wallien et al., 2009; Zucker et al., 1993, 1999).

The course of childhood gender dysphoria is unpredictable, and the outcome is highly vari-able. In many cases, the dysphoria resolves with-out clinical intervention, usually by puberty. That is, the individuals grow up to be ordinary, non-transsexual, androphilic men (i.e., gay men) or ordinary, nontranssexual, gynephilic women (i.e., lesbians), each content with their original, biologi-cal sex. In other cases, substantial cross-gender behavior remains, but the wish for a full transi-tion to the opposite sex is weak or absent. These include gay male "drag queens," who cross-dress intermittently but extensively and who may take estrogenic medications to develop breasts, as well as biologically female "genderqueers," who may seek testosterone medication for its masculinizing effects (e.g., beard growth) but express no interest in mastectomy or pelvic surgery.

The remaining cases, who reach adulthood with their dysphoria unabated or intensified, may seek transsexual surgery and other interventions.

Both and rophilic male-to-females and gynephilic female-to-males (sometimes called in the literature *homosexual transsexuals,* relative to their biological sex) typically begin to seek sex reassignment surgery when they are in their mid-20s, by which time many of them have already begun living full-time as the opposite sex. For male-to-females, the definitive operation is the construction of a vagina and vulva. For female-to-males, the most urgent procedure is usually breast tissue reduction and construction of a male chest contour, followed by removal of the uterus and ovaries. They do not universally pursue construction of an artificial penis, which is expensive, technically difficult, and often disfiguring to the part of the body from which the donor tissue is taken.

Androphilic Female-to-Males

There is a rare but distinct group of female-to-males who are sexually orientated toward males and who say that they want to undergo sex reassignment so that they can become "gay men" (Blanchard, 1990; Dickey & Stephens, 1995). This makes the syndrome seem analogous to autogynephilic transsexualism in biological males. No one, however, has identified a distinct paraphilia (like autogynephilia) that accompanies or precedes heterosexual transsexualism in biological females; therefore, the analogy seems incomplete.

Prevalence and Sex Ratio

The prevalence of full-blown transsexualism is easier to estimate than the prevalence of lesser degrees of gender dysphoria, because transsexuals, almost by definition, must disclose their condition for medical or legal purposes. Contemporary estimates are about 1 in 12,000 for male-to-female transsexuals and 1 in 30,000–50,000 for female-to-male transsexuals (Bakker, van Kesteren, Gooren, & Bezemer, 1993; De Cuypere et al., 2007; Wilson, Sharp, & Carr, 1999). The ratio of biological males to females is around 2:1 or 3:1 (Garrels et al., 2000; Landén, Wålinder, & Lundström, 1996).

Neurological Correlates

Zhou, Hofman, Gooren, and Swaab (1995) and Kruijver et al. (2000) reported that a sex-dimorphic structure of the brain, the central subdivision of the bed nucleus of the stria terminalis (BSTc), was shifted in size toward that of the opposite sex in a small series of transsexuals examined postmortem. There are at least three reasons to be skeptical that this unconfirmed finding has conclusively identified a neurological substrate of cross-gender identity. First, significant sexual dimorphism in BSTc volume and neuron number does not develop in humans until adulthood (Chung, De Vries, & Swaab, 2002), whereas many or most transsexuals report that their feelings of gender dysphoria began in childhood. Second, all of the subjects had undergone feminizing or masculinizing hormone treatment, and such treatment has profound effects on brain volume (Hulshoff Pol et al., 2006). Third, BSTc volume has been reported to be smaller among pedophilic men than among controls (Schiltz et al., 2007), which suggests that the structure may be related to sexual anomalies in general rather than to cross-gender identity specifically.

Subsequent findings have suggested not a neuroanatomical cause of gender dysphoria itself but that two neuroanatomical phenomena are in play: one related to autogynephilia and another, independent one related to homosexuality (Cantor, 2011). Contrasting a sample consisting entirely of androphilic male-to-female transsexuals with nontranssexual males and with nontranssexual females revealed this subtype of transsexuals to be "female shifted," analogous to how homosexual men exhibit several neurological and behavioral shifts toward female-typical values (Rametti et al., 2011). Other researchers studying autogynephilic male-to-female transsexuals, however, have found no differences in sexually dimorphic brain structures (Savic & Arver, 2011).

Hypersexuality

Multiple theory-laden terms have been used to describe sexual urges or behaviors whose frequencies are sufficiently high so as to produce distress or harm, the most common of which has been "sex addiction" (Carnes, 1983). The major competing theoretical perspectives of hypersexuality include addiction (Carnes, 1983; Goodman, 1997), compulsivity (Quadland, 1983; Coleman, 2003), the dual-control model (Bancroft, 1999; Bancroft, Graham, Janssen, & Sanders, 2009), and desire dysregulation (Kafka, 2010). Although the theories make use of different terminology and treatment modalities, they contain many more similarities than differences. The word *hypersexuality* will be used to describe this condition in the following discussion.

Elevation in sexual behavior is a symptom of several conditions, including hypomania, borderline personality disorder, and disinhibiting neurological trauma or disease. Hypersexuality as a syndrome unto itself has been receiving increasing attention, but there is not yet any consensus on definition or theoretical models.

Prevalence and Sex Ratio

Estimating the prevalence of hypersexuality is hampered by the diversity of operational definitions and the lack of any meaningful distinction between typical and excessive rates of sexual urges or behaviors. Coleman (1992) offered an estimate of 5%–6% of the population being affected by "impulsive-compulsive" sexual behavior; however, it is unclear how such an estimate might be produced in the absence of reliable criteria, and it is likely that the problem may have increased following the readier access to pornography via the Internet. For comparison, a large cross-sectional study in the United States found 1.9% of males to masturbate daily, and 1.2%, more than daily (Laumann, Gagnon, Michael, & Michaels, 1994). (The survey did not ask whether these individuals experienced problems due to the frequency of their sexual activity, however). Similarly, 2%–8% of men, including adolescents, experience more than seven orgasms per week (Mick & Hollander, 2006). Although such data might be imagined to be useful in identifying a clear cut-off, sexual frequency can interact with sexual context. For example, higher sexual frequency within a stable relationship correlates with higher psychological functioning, but frequency of solo or impersonal sexual behaviors does not (Långström & Hanson, 2006). A further impediment to accurate prevalence estimates is that hypersexuality may also be confused with high-risk sexual behavior, which overlaps with but is not the same as out-of-control sexual behavior (Bancroft & Vukadinovic, 2004).

As with paraphilias, the reported samples consistently indicate a majority of males among individuals seeking assistance for potential hypersexuality—approximately three to five males per female (Black, Kehrberg, Flumerfelt, & Schlosser,

1997; Carnes, 1998). Among studies that included both male and female referrals, 60%–92% of each sample was male (Kaplan & Krueger, 2010).

Comorbidities

In studies of hypersexuality, from 83% to 100% of affected individuals also had one or more *DSM-IV* Axis I diagnoses (Black et al., 1997; Raymond, Coleman, & Miner, 2003). These include mood and anxiety disorders, substance abuse, impulse control disorders, and obsessive-compulsive disorder (Black et al., 1997; Kafka & Hennen, 2003; Kafka & Prentky, 1994, 1998; Raviv, 1993; Raymond et al., 2003; Shapira, Goldsmith, Keck, Khosla, & McElroy, 2000). Personality disorders are also common, with approximately half meeting *DSM-IV-TR* criteria (Black et al., 1997; Raymond et al., 2003). Moreover, conditions for which hypersexuality is a symptom include dementia (Fedoroff, Peyser, Franz, & Folstein, 1994), temporal lobe epilepsy (Remillard, Andermann, & Testa, 1983), and Tourette's syndrome (Kerbeshan & Burd, 1991), as well as bipolar disorder and borderline personality disorder (*DSM-IV-TR*, 2000).

Notwithstanding those associations, many individuals seeking help for hypersexuality show normal MMPI-2 profiles (Reid & Carpenter, 2009). Such discrepancies might reflect heterogeneous subtypes, the proportions of which differ between clinics or recruitment methods. The possibility that hypersexual phenomena consist of distinct subtypes has indeed been proposed (e.g., Cantor et al., 2013; Kafka, 2010; Raymond et al., 2003). In the most explicit attempt to identify clinically meaningful subtypes, referrals have been characterized as showing paraphilic hypersexuality, avoidant masturbation, and chronic adultery, with other phenomena being associated with genuine distress but not any behavioral excesses not already accounted for by other issues (Cantor et al., 2013).

Neuroimaging studies have compared patients with and without hypersexual symptomatology (Black, Muralee, & Tempi, 2005; Mendez & Shapira, 2013). For example, a study on patients with behavioral variant frontotemporal dementia found evidence of temporal lobe–limbic involvement, as well as frontal lobe involvement in those patients who also had hypersexuality. The authors of that study concluded that individuals with hypersexuality may have developmental or genetic differences in the ability of the right anterior temporal lobe to inhibit limbic and subcortical areas for sexual arousal (Mendez & Shapira, 2013).

Associated Features

Investigations of the role of testosterone have demonstrated that low levels of the hormone are consistently associated with low levels of sexual interest and behavior, suggesting that high levels would be associated with elevated sexual interest and behavior. This conclusion has not yet been examined, however (Berlin, 2008). Opioids may also play a role, as one study demonstrated a statistically significant release of internal opioids in the cingulate, the temporal, and the frontal cortex during sexual arousal in men (Frost et al., 1986). Relatedly, individuals with Parkinson's disease and who are prescribed dopamine agonists frequently display sexual acting out (Klos, Bower, Josephs, Matsumoto, & Ahlskog, 2005).

Reid, Karim, McCrory, and Carpenter (2010) found that a sample of treatment-seeking hypersexual males scored lower than controls on a self-report measure of executive functioning. However, this team subsequently found that such males scored no worse than an age-, education-, and Full Scale Intelligence Quotient (FSIQ)-matched community sample when directly tested with executive functioning measures (Reid, Garos, Carpenter, & Coleman, 2011). These investigators concluded that executive functioning may be limited to situations in which there is an opportunity for sex, but it is also possible that such individuals simply perceive and rate themselves as having less self-control as a reaction to instead of a cause of their symptom. Both studies controlled for substance abuse and ADHD, because these conditions are known to affect executive functioning and are often comorbid with hypersexuality.

Hypersexual behavior is frequently described as an addiction to sex. As a test of that comparison, Steele, Staley, Fong, and Prause (2013) used EEG to record the P300 amplitude of hypersexuals in response to sexual stimuli. Instead of finding a diminished (down-regulated) response as predicted by the addiction model, the hypersexuals showed an elevated response. Neuroimaging studies of sexual arousal in controls have demonstrated activation in areas including the prefrontal, orbitofrontal, insular, occipitotemporal, and anterior cingulate cortices, as well as in subcortical regions, including the amygdala and substantia nigra (Stoléru, Fonteille, Cornélis, Joyal, & Moulier, 2012), making these important areas to examine as potentially mediating sexually problematic behavior (Mendez & Shapira, 2013).

References

Abel, G. G., Becker, J. V., Cunningham-Rathner, J., Mittelman, M., & Rouleau, J.-L. (1988). Multiple paraphilic diagnoses among sex offenders. *Bulletin of the American Academy of Psychiatry and the Law, 16*, 153–168.

Abel, G. G., & Osborn, C. (1992). The paraphilias: The extent and nature of sexually deviant and criminal behavior. *Psychiatric Clinics of North America, 15*, 675–687.

Alison, L., Santtila, P., Sandnabba, N. K., & Nordling, N. (2001). Sadomasochistically oriented behavior: Diversity in practice and meaning. *Archives of Sexual Behavior, 30*, 1–12.

Anonymous, Chambers, W. M., & Janzen, W. B. (1976). The eclectic and multiple therapy of a shoe fetishist. *American Journal of Psychotherapy, 30*, 317–326.

Arndt, W. B. (1991). *Gender disorders and the paraphilias*. Madison, CT: International Universities Press.

Arndt, W., Foehl, J., & Good, F. (1985). Specific sexual fantasy themes: A multidimensional study. *Journal of Personality and Social Psychology, 48*, 472–480.

Bakker, A., van Kesteren, P. J., Gooren, L. J. G., & Bezemer, P. D. (1993). The prevalence of transsexualism in The Netherlands. *Acta Psychiatrica Scandinavica, 87*, 237–238.

Ball, H. N. (2005). Sexual offending on elderly women: A review. *The Journal of Forensic Psychiatry and Psychology, 16*, 127–138.

Bancroft, J. (1999). Central inhibition of sexual response in the male: A theoretical perspective. *Neuroscience and Biobehavioral Reviews, 23*, 763–784.

Bancroft, J., Graham, C. A., Janssen, E., & Sanders, S. A. (2009). The dual control model: Current status and future directions. *Journal of Sex Research, 46*, 121–142.

Bancroft, J., & Vukadinovic, Z. (2004). Sexual addiction, sexual compulsivity, sexual impulsivity, or what? Toward a theoretical model. *Journal of Sex Research, 41*, 225–234.

Beier, K. M., Neutze, J., Mundt, I. A., Ahlers, C. J., Goecker, D., Konrad, A., & Schaefer, G. A. (2009). Encouraging self-identified pedophiles and hebephiles to seek professional help: First results of the Prevention Project Dunkelfeld (PPD). *Child Abuse & Neglect, 33*, 545–549.

Benjamin, H. (1966). *The transsexual phenomenon.* New York: Julian.

Bensler, J. M., & Paauw, D. S. (2003). Apotemnophilia masquerading as medical morbidity. *Southern Medical Journal, 96,* 674–676.

Berger, B. D., Lehrmann, J. A., Larson, G., Alverno, L., & Tsao, C. I. (2005). Nonpsychotic, nonparaphilic self-amputation and the internet. *Comprehensive Psychiatry, 46,* 380–383.

Berlin, F. S. (2008). Basic science and neurobiological research: Potential relevance to sexual compulsivity. *Psychiatric Clinics of North America, 31,* 623–642.

Bernard, F. (1975). An enquiry among a group of pedophiles. *Journal of Sex Research, 11,* 242–255.

Bethell, M. F. (1974). A rare manifestation of fetishism. *Archives of Sexual Behavior, 3,* 301–302.

Binet, A. (1887). Le fétichisme dans l'amour. *Revue Philosophique, 24,* 143–167, 252–274.

Black, B., Muralee, S., & Tampi, R. R. (2005). Inappropriate sexual behaviors in dementia. *Journal of Geriatric Psychiatry and Neurology, 18,* 155–162.

Black, D. W., Kehrberg, L. L. D., Flumerfelt, D. L., & Schlosser, S. S. (1997). Characteristics of 36 subjects reporting compulsive sexual behavior. *American Journal of Psychiatry, 154,* 243–249.

Blanchard, R. (1985). Typology of male-to-female transsexualism. *Archives of Sexual Behavior, 14,* 247–261.

Blanchard, R. (1988). Nonhomosexual gender dysphoria. *Journal of Sex Research, 24,* 188–193.

Blanchard, R. (1989a). The classification and labeling of nonhomosexual gender dysphorias. *Archives of Sexual Behavior, 18,* 315–334.

Blanchard, R. (1989b). The concept of autogynephilia and the typology of male gender dysphoria. *Journal of Nervous and Mental Disease, 177,* 616–623.

Blanchard, R. (1990). Gender identity disorders in adult women. In R. Blanchard & B. W. Steiner (Eds.), *Clinical management of gender identity disorders in children and adults* (pp. 77–91). Washington, DC: American Psychiatric Press.

Blanchard, R. (1991). Clinical observations and systematic studies of autogynephilia. *Journal of Sex and Marital Therapy, 17,* 235–251.

Blanchard, R. (1993a). The she-male phenomenon and the concept of partial autogynephilia. *Journal of Sex and Marital Therapy, 19,* 69–76.

Blanchard, R. (1993b). Partial versus complete autogynephilic and gender dysphoria. *Journal of Sex and Marital Therapy, 19,* 301–307.

Blanchard, R. (1994). A structural equation model for age at clinical presentation in nonhomosexual male gender dysphorics. *Archives of Sexual Behavior, 23,* 311–320.

Blanchard, R. (2008). Review and theory of handedness, birth order, and homosexuality in men. *Laterality: Asymmetries of Body, Brain and Cognition, 13,* 51–70.

Blanchard, R., Cantor, J. M., & Robichaud, L. K. (2006). Biological factors in the development of sexual deviance and aggression in males. In H. E. Barbaree & W. L. Marshall (Eds.), *The juvenile sex offender* (pp. 77–104). New York: Guilford Press.

Blanchard, R., & Collins, P. I. (1993). Men with sexual interest in transvestites, transsexuals, and she-males. *Journal of Nervous and Mental Disease, 181,* 570–575.

Blanchard, R., & Hucker, S. J. (1991). Age, transvestism, bondage, and concurrent paraphilic activities in 117 fatal cases of autoerotic asphyxia. *British Journal of Psychiatry, 159,* 371–377.

Blanchard, R., Kolla, N. J., Cantor, J. M., Klassen, P. E., Dickey, R., Kuban, M. E., et al. (2007). IQ, handedness, and pedophilia in adult male patients stratified by referral source. *Sexual Abuse: A Journal of Research and Treatment, 19,* 285–309.

Blanchard, R., Lykins, A. D., Wherrett, D., Kuban, M. E., Cantor, J. M., Blak, T., Dickey, R., & Klassen, P. E. (2009). Pedophilia, hebephilia, and the DSM–V. *Archives of Sexual Behavior, 38,* 335–350.

Bourguignon, A. (1983). Vampirism and autovampirism. In L. B. Schlesinger & E. Revitch (Eds.), *Sexual dynamics of anti-social behavior* (pp. 278–301). Springfield, IL: Charles C. Thomas.

Bradford, J. M. W., Boulet, J., & Pawlak, A. (1992). The paraphilias: A multiplicity of deviant behaviours. *Canadian Journal of Psychiatry, 37,* 104–108.

Breslow, N., Evans, L., & Langley, J. (1985). On the prevalence and roles of females in the sadomasochistic subculture: Report of an empirical study. *Archives of Sexual Behavior, 14,* 303–317.

Brittain, R. (1970). The sadistic murderer. *Medicine, Science and the Law, 10,* 198–207.

Brown, G. R., Wise, T. N., Costa, P. T., Herbst, J. H., Fagan, P. J., & Schmidt, C. W. (1996). Personality characteristics and sexual functioning of 188 cross-dressing men. *Journal of Nervous and Mental Disease, 184,* 265–273.

Byard, R. W., & Winskog, C. (2012). Autoerotic death: Incidence and age of victims—a population-based study. *Journal of Forensic Sciences, 57*, 129–131.

Cairns, F. J., & Rainer, S. P. (1981). Death from electrocution during auto-erotic procedures. *New Zealand Medical Journal, 94*, 259–260.

Cantor, J. M. (2011). New MRI studies support the Blanchard typology of male-to-female transsexualism [Letter to the Editor]. *Archives of Sexual Behavior, 40*, 863–862.

Cantor, J. M., Blanchard, R., Christensen, B. K., Dickey, R., Klassen, P. E., Beckstead, A. L., et al. (2004). Intelligence, memory, and handedness in pedophilia. *Neuropsychology, 18*, 3–14.

Cantor, J. M., Blanchard, R., Robichaud, L. K., & Christensen, B. K. (2005). Quantitative reanalysis of aggregate data on IQ in sexual offenders. *Psychological Bulletin, 131*, 555–568.

Cantor, J. M., Kabani, N., Christensen, B. K., Zipursky, R. B., Barbaree, H. E., Dickey, R., Klassen, P. E., et al. (2008). Cerebral white matter deficiencies in pedophilic men. *Journal of Psychiatric Research, 42*, 167–183.

Cantor, J. M., Klassen, P. E., Dickey, R., Christensen, B. K., Kuban, M. E., Blak, T., et al. (2005). Handedness in pedophilia and hebephilia. *Archives of Sexual Behavior, 34*, 447–459.

Cantor, J. M., Klein, C., Lykins, A., Rullo, J. E., Thaler, L., & Walling, B. R. (2013). A treatment-oriented typology of self-identified hypersexuality referrals. *Archives of Sexual Behavior, 42*, 883–893.

Cantor, J. M., Kuban, M. E., Blak, T., Klassen, P. E., Dickey, R., & Blanchard, R. (2006). Grade failure and special education placement in sexual offenders' educational histories. *Archives of Sexual Behavior, 35*, 743–751.

Carnes, P. J. (1983). *Out of the Shadows: Understanding sexual addiction.* Minneapolis, MN: CompCare.

Carnes, P. (1998). The obsessive shadow: Profiles in sexual addiction. *Professional Counsellor, 13*, 15–17, 40–41.

Chalkley, A. J., & Powell, G. E. (1983). The clinical description of forty-eight cases of sexual fetishism. *British Journal of Psychiatry, 142*, 292–295.

Chung, W. C., De Vries, G. J., & Swaab, D. F. (2002). Sexual differentiation of the bed nucleus of the stria terminalis in humans may extend into adulthood. *Journal of Neuroscience, 22*, 1027–1033.

Coleman, E. (1992). Is your patient suffering from compulsive sexual behavior? *Psychiatric Annals, 22*, 320–325.

Coleman, E. (2003). Compulsive sexual behavior: What to call it, how to treat it? *SIECUS Report, 31*(5), 12–16.

Collacott, R. A., & Cooper, S.-A. (1995). Urine fetish in a man with learning disabilities. *Journal of Intellectual Disability Research, 39*, 145–147.

Cooper, A. J. (1995). "Auto-erotic asphyxial death: Analysis of nineteen fatalities in Alberta": Comment. *Canadian Journal of Psychiatry, 40*, 363–364.

Cooper, A. J. (1996). Auto-erotic asphyxiation: Three case reports. *Journal of Sex and Marital Therapy, 22*, 47–53.

Crepault, C., & Couture, M. (1980). Men's erotic fantasies. *Archives of Sexual Behavior, 9*, 565–581.

Croughan, J. L., Saghir, M., Cohen, R., & Robins, E. (1981). A comparison of treated and untreated male cross-dressers. *Archives of Sexual Behavior, 10*, 515–528.

Dalby, J. T. (1988). Is telephone scatologia a variant of exhibitionism? *International Journal of Offender Therapy and Comparative Criminology, 32*, 45–49.

De Cuypere, G., Van Hemelrijck, M., Michel, A., Carael, B., Heylens, G., Rubens, R., et al. (2007). Prevalence and demography of transsexualism in Belgium. *European Psychiatry, 22*, 137–141.

Denko, J. D. (1973). Klismaphilia: Enema as a sexual preference: Report of two cases. *American Journal of Psychotherapy, 27*, 232–250.

Denko, J. D. (1976). Klismaphilia: Amplification of the erotic enema deviance. *American Journal of Psychotherapy, 30*, 236–255.

Dickey, R., & Stephens, J. (1995). Female-to-male transsexualism, heterosexual type: Two cases. *Archives of Sexual Behavior, 24*, 439–445.

Dietz, P. E., Hazelwood, R. R., & Warren, J. (1990). The sexually sadistic criminal and his offenses. *Bulletin of the American Academy of Psychiatry and the Law, 18*, 163–178.

Dixon, D. (1983). An erotic attraction to amputees. *Sexuality and Disability, 6*, 3–19.

Docter, R. F., & Prince, V. (1997). Transvestism: A survey of 1032 cross-dressers. *Archives of Sexual Behavior, 26*, 589–605.

Earls, C. M., & Lalumière, M. L. (2002). A case study of preferential bestiality (zoophilia). *Sexual Abuse: A Journal of Research and Treatment, 14*, 83–88.

Ellis, H. (1928). *Studies in the psychology of sex* (Vol. 7). Philadelphia: F. A. Davis.

Elman, R. A. (1997). Disability pornography: The fetishization of women's vulnerabilities. *Violence Against Women, 3*, 257–270.

Ernulf, K. E., & Innala, S. M. (1995). Sexual bondage: A review and unobtrusive investigation. *Archives of Sexual Behavior*, 24, 631–654.

Escoffier, J. (2011). Imagining the she/male: Pornography and the transsexualization of the heterosexual male. *Studies in Gender and Sexuality*, 12, 268–281.

Fedoroff, J. P., Peyser, C., Franz, M. L., & Folstein, S. E. (1994). Sexual disorders in Huntington's disease. *Journal of Neuropsychiatry*, 6, 147–153.

First, M. B. (2005). Desire for amputation of a limb: Paraphilia, psychosis, or a new type of identity disorder. *Psychological Medicine*, 35, 919–928.

Freund, K. (1976). Diagnosis and treatment of forensically significant anomalous erotic preferences. *Canadian Journal of Criminology and Corrections*, 18, 181–189.

Freund, K. (1988). Courtship disorder: Is the hypothesis valid? *Annals of the New York Academy of Sciences*, 528, 172–182.

Freund, K. (1990). Courtship disorder. In W. L. Marshall, D. R. Laws, & H. E. Barbaree (Eds.), *Handbook of sexual assault: Issues, theories, and treatment of the offender* (pp. 195–207). New York: Plenum.

Freund, K., & Blanchard, R. (1986). The concept of courtship disorder. *Journal of Sex & Marital Therapy*, 12, 79–92.

Freund, K., & Blanchard, R. (1993). Erotic target location errors in male gender dysphorics, paedophiles, and fetishists. *British Journal of Psychiatry*, 162, 558–563.

Freund, K., Scher, H., & Hucker, S. (1983). The courtship disorders. *Archives of Sexual Behavior*, 12, 369–379.

Freund, K., Scher, H., Racansky, I. G., Campbell, K., & Heasman, G. (1986). Males disposed to commit rape. *Archives of Sexual Behavior*, 15, 23–35.

Freund, K., Seeley, H. R., Marshall, W. E., & Glinfort, E. K. (1972). Sexual offenders needing special assessment and/or therapy. *Canadian Journal of Criminology and Corrections*, 14, 3–23.

Freund, K., Seto, M. C., & Kuban, M. (1995). Masochism: A multiple case study. *Sexuologie*, 4, 313–324.

Freund, K., Seto, M. C., & Kuban, M. (1996). Two types of fetishism. *Behaviour Research and Therapy*, 34, 687–694.

Freund, K., Watson, R., & Dickey, R. (1991). Sex offenses against female children perpetrated by men who are not pedophiles. *Journal of Sex Research*, 28, 409–423.

Freund, K., Watson, R., & Rienzo, D. (1988). The value of self-reports in the study of voyeurism and exhibitionism. *Annals of Sex Research*, 2, 243–262.

Frith, C., & Dolan, R. J. (1998). Images of psychopathology. *Current Opinion in Neurobiology*, 8, 259–262.

Frost J. J., Mayberg H. S., Berlin F. S., Behal, R., Dannals, R. F., Links, J. M., et al. (1986). Alteration in brain opiate receptor binding in man following arousal using C-11 carfentinil and positron emission tomography. Proceedings of the 33rd Annual Meeting of the Society of Nuclear Medicine. *Journal of Nuclear Medicine*, 27, 1027.

Gaffney, G. R., & Berlin, F. S. (1984). Is there hypothalamic-pituitary-gonadal dysfunction in paedophilia? A pilot study. *British Journal of Psychiatry*, 145, 657–660.

Garlick, Y., Marshall, W. L., & Thornton, D. (1996). Intimacy deficits and attribution of blame among sex offenders. *Legal and Criminological Psychology*, 1, 251–288.

Garrels, L., Kockott, G., Michael, N., Preuss, W., Renter, K., Schmidt, G., et al. (2000). Sex ratio of transsexuals in Germany: The development over three decades. *Acta Psychiatrica Scandinavica*, 102, 445–448.

Gebhard, P. H., Gagnon, J. H., Pomeroy, W. B., & Christenson, C. V. (1965). *Sex offenders: An analysis of types*. New York: Harper & Row.

Giotakos, O., Markianos, M., Vaidakis, N., & Christodoulou, G. N. (2003). Aggression, impulsivity, plasma sex hormones, and biogenic amine turnover in a forensic population of rapists. *Journal of Sex and Marital Therapy*, 29, 215–225.

Goodman, A. (1997). Sexual addiction: Diagnosis, etiology, and treatment. In J. H. Lowenstein, R. B. Millman, P. Ruiz, & J. G. Langrod (Eds.), *Substance Abuse: A comprehensive textbook* (3rd ed., pp. 340–354). Baltimore: Williams & Wilkins.

Gosselin, C. C. (1987). The sadomasochistic contract. In G. W. Wilson (Ed.), *Variant sexuality: Research and theory* (pp. 229–257). London: Croom-Helm.

Gosselin, C., & Wilson, G. (1980). *Sexual variations: Fetishism, sadomasochism, and transvestism*. New York: Simon and Schuster.

Grant, V. W. (1953). A case study of fetishism. *Journal of Abnormal and Social Psychology*, 48, 142–149.

Gratzer, T., & Bradford, J. (1995). Offender and offense characteristics of sexual sadists: A comparative study. *Journal of Forensic Sciences*, 40, 450–455.

Green, R., & Young, R. (2001). Hand preference, sexual preference, and transsexualism. *Archives of Sexual Behavior*, 30, 565–574.

Gurnani, P. D., & Dwyer, M. (1986). Serum testosterone levels in sex offenders. *Journal of Offender Counseling, Services, and Rehabilitation, 11*, 39–45.

Haake, P., Schedlowski, M., Exton, M. S., Giepen, C., Hartmann, U., Osterheider, M., et al. (2003). Acute neuroendocrine response to sexual stimulation in sexual offenders. *Canadian Journal of Psychiatry, 48*, 265–271.

Harding, L. (2003, December 4). Victim of cannibal agreed to be eaten. *The Guardian.*

Hardyck, C., & Petrinovich, L. F. (1977). Left-handedness. *Psychological Bulletin, 84*, 385–404.

Hepper, P. G., Shahidullah, S., & White, R. (1991). Handedness in the human fetus. *Neuropsychologia, 29*, 1107–1111.

Hepper, P. G., Wells, D. L., & Lynch, C. (2005). Prenatal thumb sucking is related to postnatal handedness. *Neuropsychologia, 43*, 313–315.

Hirschfeld, M. (1918). *Sexualpathologie* [Sexual pathology] (Vol. 2). Bonn: Marcus & Weber.

Hirschfeld, M. (1938). *Sexual anomalies and perversions: Physical and psychological development, diagnosis and treatment* (New and rev. ed.). London: Encyclopaedic Press.

Hucker, S. J. (1985). Self-harmful sexual behavior. *Psychiatric Clinics of North America, 8*, 323–337.

Hucker, S. J., & Blanchard, R. (1992). Death scene characteristics in 118 fatal cases of autoerotic asphyxia compared with suicidal asphyxia. *Behavioral Sciences and the Law, 10*, 509–523.

Hulshoff Pol, H. E., Cohen-Kettenis, P. T., Van Haren, N. E., Peper, J. S., Brans, R. G., Cahn, W., et al. (2006). Changing your sex changes your brain: Influences of testosterone and estrogen on adult human brain structure. *European Journal of Endocrinology, 155*(Suppl. 1), S107–S114.

Jamieson, S., & Marshall, W. L. (2000). Attachment styles and violence in child molesters. *Journal of Sexual Aggression, 5*, 88–98.

Janssen, W., Koops, E., Anders, S., Kuhn, S., & Püschel, K. (2005). Forensic aspects of 40 accidental autoerotic death in Northern Germany. *Forensic Science International, 147* (Suppl.), S61–S64.

Jay, K., & Young, A. (1977). *The gay report: Lesbians and gay men speak out about sexual experiences and lifestyles.* New York: Summit Books.

Kafka, M. P. (2010). Hypersexual disorder: A proposed diagnosis for DSM-V. *Archives of Sexual Behavior, 39*, 377–400.

Kafka, M. P., & Hennen, J. (2003). Hypersexual desire in males: Are males with paraphilias different from males with paraphilia-related disorders? *Sexual Abuse: A Journal of Research and Treatment, 15*, 307–321.

Kafka, M. P., & Prentky, R. A. (1994). Preliminary observations of DSM-III-R axis I comorbidity in men with paraphilias and paraphilia-related disorders. *Journal of Clinical Psychiatry, 55*, 481–487.

Kafka, M. P., & Prentky, R. A. (1998). Attention-deficit/hyperactivity disorder in males with paraphilias and paraphilia-related disorders: A comorbidity study. *Journal of Clinical Psychiatry, 59*, 388–396.

Kaplan, M. S., & Krueger, R. B. (2010). Diagnosis, assessment, and treatment of hypersexuality. *Journal of Sex Research, 47*, 181–198.

Kaul, A., & Duffy, S. (1991). Gerontophilia: A case report. *Medicine, Science and the Law, 31*, 110–114.

Kerbeshan, J., & Burd, L. (1991). Tourette syndrome and current paraphilic masturbatory fantasy. *Canadian Journal of Psychiatry, 36*, 155–157.

Klar, A. J. S. (2004). Excess of counterclockwise scalp hair-whorl rotation in homosexual men. *Journal of Genetics, 83*, 251–255.

Klos, K. J., Bower, J. H., Josephs, K. A., Matsumoto, J. Y., & Ahlskog, J. E. (2005). Pathological hypersexuality predominantly linked to adjuvant dopamine agonist therapy in Parkinson's disease and multiple system atrophy. *Parkinsonism & Related Disorders, 11*, 381–386.

Krafft-Ebing, R. von. (1965). *Psychopathia sexualis: A medico-forensic study* (H. E. Wedeck, Trans.). New York: G. P. Putnam's Sons (Original work published 1886).

Kruijver, F. P., Zhou, J. N., Pool, C. W., Hofman, M. A., Gooren, L. J., & Swaab, D. F. (2000). Male-to-female transsexuals have female neuron numbers in a limbic nucleus. *Journal of Clinical Endocrinology and Metabolism, 85*, 2034–2041.

Kunjukrishnan, R., Pawlak, A., & Varan, L R. (1988). The clinical and forensic psychiatric issues of retifism. *Canadian Journal of Psychiatry, 33*, 819–825.

Lalumière, M. L., Blanchard, R., & Zucker, K. J. (2000). Sexual orientation and handedness in men and women: A meta-analysis. *Psychological Bulletin, 126*, 575–592.

Lalumière, M. L., Harris, G. T., Quinsey, V. L., & Rice, M. E. (2005). *The causes of rape: Understanding individual differences in male propensity for sexual aggression.* Washington, DC: American Psychological Association.

Landén, M., Wålinder, J., & Lundström, B. (1996). Prevalence, incidence, and sex ratio of transsexualism. *Acta Psychiatrica Scandinavica, 93*, 221–223.

Lang, R. A., Flor-Henry, P., & Frenzel, R. R. (1990). Sex hormone profiles in pedophilic and incestuous men. *Annals of Sex Research, 3*, 59–74.

Langevin, R., Paitch, D., Ramsay, G., Anderson, C., Kamrad, J., Pope, S., et al. (1979). Experimental studies of the etiology of genital exhibitionism. *Archives of Sexual Behavior, 8*, 307–331.

Långström, N., & Hanson, R. K. (2006). High rates of sexual behavior in the general population: Correlates and predictors. *Archives of Sexual Behavior, 35*, 37–52.

Långström, N., & Seto, M. C. (2006). Exhibitionistic and voyeuristic behavior in a Swedish national population survey. *Archives of Sexual Behavior, 35*, 427–435.

Långström, N., & Zucker, K. J. (2005). Transvestic fetishism in the general population: Prevalence and correlates. *Journal of Sex and Marital Therapy, 31*, 87–95.

Laumann, E. O., Gagnon, J. H., Michael, R. T., & Michaels, S. (1994). *The social organization of sexuality: Sexual practices in the United States*. Chicago: University of Chicago Press.

Lawrence, A. A. (2006). Clinical and theoretical parallels between desire for limb amputation and gender identity disorder. *Archives of Sexual Behavior, 25*, 263–278.

Lawrence, A. A. (2013). *Men trapped in men's bodies: Narratives of autogynephilic transsexualism*. New York: Springer.

Lukianowicz, N. (1959). Survey of various aspects of transvestism in the light of our present knowledge. *Journal of Nervous and Mental Diseases, 128*, 36–64.

Malitz, S. (1966). Another report on the wearing of diapers and rubber pants by an adult male. *American Journal of Psychiatry, 122*, 1435.

Marsa, F., O'Reilly, G., Carr, A., Murphy, P., O'Sullivan, M., Cotter, A., et al. (2004). Attachment styles and psychological profiles of child sex offenders in Ireland. *Journal of Interpersonal Violence, 19*, 228–251.

Massie, H., & Szajnberg, N. (1997). The ontogeny of a sexual fetish from birth to age 30 and memory processes: A research case report from a prospective longitudinal study. *International Journal of Psycho-Analysis, 78*, 755–771.

McNally, R. J., & Lukach, B. M. (1991). Behavioral treatment of zoophilic exhibitionism. *Journal of Behavioral Therapy and Experimental Psychiatry, 22*, 281–284.

Mead, B. T. (1975). Coping with obscene phone calls. *Medical Aspects of Human Sexuality, 9*(6), 127–128.

Mendez, M. F., & Shapira, J. S. (2013). Hypersexual behavior in frontotemporal dementia: A comparison with early-onset Alzheimer's disease. *Archives of Sexual Behavior, 42*, 501–509.

Mick, T. M., & Hollander, E. (2006). Impulsive-compulsive sexual behavior. *CNS Spectrums, 11*, 994–995.

Miletski, H. (2001). Zoophilia—Implications for therapy. *Journal of Sex Education and Therapy, 26*, 85–89.

Miletski, H. (2005). Is zoophilia a sexual orientation? A study. In A. M. Beetz & A. L. Podberscek (Eds.), *Bestiality and zoophilia: Sexual relations with animals* (pp. 82–97). West Lafayette, IN: Purdue University Press.

Mohr, J. W., Turner, R. E., & Jerry, M. B. (1964). *Pedophilia and exhibitionism*. Toronto: University of Toronto Press.

Money, J., Jobaris, R., & Furth, G. (1977). Apotemnophilia: Two cases of self demand amputation as a sexual preference. *Journal of Sex Research, 13*, 115–124.

Money, J., & Lamacz, M. (1984). Gynemimesis and gynemimetophilia: Individual and cross-cultural manifestations of a gender-coping strategy hitherto unnamed. *Comprehensive Psychiatry, 25*, 392–403.

Money, J., & Simcoe, K. W. (1986). Acrotomophilia, sex, and disability: New concepts and case report. *Sexuality and Disability, 7*, 43–50.

Nadler, R. P. (1968). Approach to psychodynamics of obscene telephone calls. *New York State Journal of Medicine, 68*, 521–526.

Newman, L. E., & Stoller, R. J. (1974). Nontranssexual men who seek sex reassignment. *American Journal of Psychiatry, 131*, 437–441.

Nieder, T. O., Herff, M., Cerwenka, S., Preuss, W. F., Cohen-Kettenis, P. T., De Cuypere, G., et al. (2011). Age of onset and sexual orientation in transsexual males and females. *Journal of Sexual Medicine, 8*, 783–791.

Nordling, N., Sandnabba, N. K., Santtila, P., & Alison, L. (2006). Differences and similarities between gay and straight individuals involved in the sadomasochistic subculture. *Journal of Homosexuality, 50*, 41–57.

Operario, D., Burton, J., Underhill, K., & Sevelius, J. (2008). Men who have sex with transgender women: Challenges to category-based HIV prevention. *AIDS & Behavior, 12*, 18–26.

Pakhomou, S. M. (2006). Methodological aspects of telephone scatologia: A case study. *International Journal of Law and Psychiatry, 29*, 178–185.

Pate, J. E., & Gabbard, G. O. (2003). Adult baby syndrome. *American Journal of Psychiatry, 160*, 1932–1936.

Peretti, P. O., & Rowan, M. (1983). Zoophilia: Factors related to its sustained practice. *Panminerva Medica, 25*, 127–131.

Price, M., Kafka, M., Commons, M. L., Gutheil, T. G., & Simpson, W. (2002). Telephone scatologia: Comorbidity with other paraphilias and paraphilia-related disorders. *International Journal of Law and Psychiatry, 25*, 37–49.

Quadland, M. C. (1983). Compulsive sexual behavior: Definition of a problem and an approach to treatment. *Journal of Sex and Marital Therapy, 11*, 121–132.

Rada, R. T., Laws, D. R., & Kellner, R. (1976). Plasma testosterone levels in the rapist. *Psychosomatic Medicine, 38*, 257–268.

Rada, R. T., Laws, D. R., Kellner, R., Stivastava, L., & Peake, G. (1983). Plasma androgens in violent and non-violent sex offenders. *Bulletin of the American Academy of Psychiatry and the Law, 11*, 149–158.

Rametti, G., Carrillo, B., Gomez-Gil, E., Junque, C., Segovia, S., Gomez, A, & Guillamon, A. (2011). White matter microstructure in female-to-male transsexuals before cross-sex hormone treatment. A diffusion tensor imaging study. *Journal of Psychiatric Research, 45*, 199–204.

Raviv, M. (1993). Personality characteristics of sexual addicts and gamblers. *Journal of Gambling Studies, 9*, 17–30.

Raymond, N. C., Coleman, E., & Miner, M. H. (2003). Psychiatric comorbidity and compulsive/impulsive traits in compulsive sexual behavior. *Comprehensive Psychiatry, 44*, 370–380.

Reay, B., Attwood, N., & Gooder, C. (2013). Inventing sex: The short history of sex addiction. *Sexuality & Culture, 17*, 1–19.

Reid, R. C., & Carpenter, B. N. (2009). Exploring relationships of psychopathology in hypersexual patients using the MMPI-2. *Journal of Sex and Marital Therapy, 35*, 294–310.

Reid, R. C., Garos, S., Carpenter, B. N., & Coleman, E. (2011). A surprising finding related to executive control in a patient sample of hypersexual men. *Journal of Sexual Medicine, 8*, 2227–2236.

Reid, R. C., Karim, R., McCrory, E., & Carpenter, B. N. (2010). Self-reported differences on measures of executive function and hypersexual behavior in a patient and community sample of men. *International Journal of Neuroscience, 120*, 120–127.

Remillard, G. M., Andermann, F., & Testa, G. F. (1983). Sexual ictal manifestations predominate in women with temporal lobe epilepsy: A finding suggesting sexual dimorphism in the human brain. *Neurology, 33*, 323–330.

Revitch, E. (1978). Sexual motivated burglaries. *Bulletin of the American Association of Psychiatry and the Law, 6*, 277–283.

Rosman, J. P., & Resnick, P. J. (1989). Sexual attraction to corpses: A psychiatric review of necrophilia. *Bulletin of the American Academy of Psychiatry and the Law, 17*, 153–163.

Safarik, M. E., Jarvis, J. P., & Nussbaum, K. E. (2002). Sexual homicide of elderly females: Linking offender characteristics to victim and crime scene attributes. *Journal of Interpersonal Violence, 17*, 500–525.

Savic, I., & Arver, S. (2011). Sex dimorphism of the brain in male-to female transsexuals. *Cerebral Cortex, 21*, 2525–2533.

Sawle, G. A., & Kear-Colwell, J. (2001). Adult attachment style and pedophilia: A developmental perspective. *International Journal of Offender Therapy and Comparative Criminology, 45*, 32–50.

Schiffer, B., Peschel, T., Paul, T., Gizewski, E., Forsting, M., Leygraf, N., et al. (2007). Structural brain abnormalities in the frontostriatal system and cerebellum in pedophilia. *Journal of Psychiatric Research, 41*, 753–762.

Schiltz, K., Witzel, J., Northoff, G., Zierhut, K., Gubka, U., Fellman, H., et al. (2007). Brain pathology in pedophilic offenders: Evidence of volume reduction in the right amygdala and related diencephalic structures. *Archives of General Psychiatry, 64*, 737–746.

Seidman, B. T., Marshall, W. L., Hudson, S. M., & Robertson, P. J. (1994). An examination of intimacy and loneliness in sex offenders. *Journal of Interpersonal Violence, 9*, 518–534.

Seim, H. C., & Dwyer, M. A. (1988). Evaluation of serum testosterone and luteinizing hormone levels in sex offenders. *Family Practice Research Journal, 7*, 175–180.

Seto, M. C. (2004). Pedophilia and sexual offenses against children. *Annual Review of Sex Research, 15*, 321–360.

Seto, M. C. (2008). *Pedophilia and sexual offending against children: Theory, assessment, and intervention.* Washington, DC: American Psychological Association.

Shapira, N. A., Goldsmith, T. D., Keck Jr., P. E., Khosla, U. M., & McElroy, S. L. (2000). Psychiatric features of individuals with problematic internet use. *Journal of Affective Disorders, 57*, 267–272.

Simon, R. I. (1997). Video voyeurs and the covert videotaping of unsuspecting victims: Psychological and legal consequences. *Journal of Forensic Sciences, 42,* 884–889.

Smallbone, S. W. (2006). An attachment-theoretical revision of Marshall and Barbaree's integrated theory of the etiology of sexual offending. In W. L. Marshall, Y. M. Fernandez, L. E. Marshall, & G. A. Serran (Eds.), *Sex offender treatment: Controversial issues* (pp. 93–107). West Sussex, UK: John Wiley & Son.

Smallbone, S. W., & Dadds, M. R. (1998). Childhood attachment and adult attachment in incarcerated adult male sex offenders. *Journal of Interpersonal Violence, 13,* 555–573.

Smith, M. D., & Morra, N. N. (1994). Obscene and threatening phone calls to women: Data from a Canadian national survey. *Gender and Society, 8,* 584–596.

Smith, Y. L. S., van Goozen, S. H. M., Kuiper, A. J., & Cohen-Kettenis, P. T. (2005). Transsexual subtypes: Clinical and theoretical significance. *Psychiatry Research, 137,* 151–160.

Snyder, H. N. (2000). *Sexual assault of young children as reported to law enforcement: Victim, incident, and offender characteristics* (Report No. NCJ 18399). Washington, DC: U.S. Department of Justice.

Steele, V. R., Staley, C., Fong, T., & Prause, N. (2013). Sexual desire, not hypersexuality is related to neurophysiological responses elicited by sexual images. *Socioaffective Neuroscience & Psychology, 3,* 20770.

Stein, M. L., Schlesinger, L. B., & Pinizzotto, A. J. (2010). Necrophilia and sexual homicide. *Journal of Forensic Sciences, 55,* 443–446.

Stekel, W. (1930). *Sexual Aberrations: The phenomenon of fetishism in relation to sex* (Vol. 1) (S. Parker, Trans.). New York: Liveright Publishing.

Stoléru, S., Fonteille, V., Cornélis, C., Joyal, C., & Moulier, V. (2012). Functional neuroimaging studies of sexual arousal and orgasm in healthy men and women: A review and meta-analysis. *Neuroscience & Biobehavioral Reviews, 36,* 1481–1509.

Studer, L. H., Aylwin, A. S., Clelland, S. R., Reddon, J. R., & Frenzel, R. R. (2002). Primary erotic preference in a group of child molesters. *International Journal of Law and Psychiatry, 25,* 173–180.

Tuchman, W. W., & Lachman, J. H. (1964). An unusual perversion: The wearing of diapers and rubber pants in a 29-year-old male. *American Journal of Psychiatry, 120,* 1198–1199.

Uva, J. L. (1995). Review: Autoerotic asphyxiation in the United States. *Journal of Forensic Sciences, 40,* 574–581.

Vanden Bergh, R. L., & Kelly, J. F. (1964). Vampirism: A review with new observations. *Archives of General Psychiatry, 11,* 543–547.

Vuocolo, A. B. (1969). *The repetitive sex offender: An analysis of the administration of the New Jersey sex offender program from 1949 to 1965.* Roselle, NJ: Quality Printing.

Wallien, M. S. C., Quilty, L. C., Steensma, T. D., Singh, D., Lambert, S. L., Leroux, A., Owen-Anderson, A., et al. (2009). Cross-national replication of the Gender Identity Interview for Children. *Journal of Personality Assessment, 91,* 545–552.

Ward, T., Hudson, S. M., & Marshall, W. L. (1996). Attachment style in sex offenders: A preliminary study. *Journal of Sex Research, 33,* 17–26.

Ward, T., & Seigert, R. J. (2002). Toward a comprehensive theory of child sexual abuse: A theory knitting perspective. *Psychology, Crime & Law, 8,* 319–351.

Waxman-Fiduccia, B. F. (1999). Sexual imagery of physically disabled women: Erotic? Perverse? Sexist? *Sexuality and Disability, 17,* 277–282.

Weinberg, M. S., & Williams, C. J. (2010). Men sexually interesting in transwomen (MSTW): Gendered embodiment and the construction of sexual desire. *Journal of Sex Research, 47,* 374–383.

Weinberg, M. S., Williams, C. J., & Calhan, C. (1994). Homosexual foot fetishism. *Archives of Sexual Behavior, 23,* 611–626.

Weinberg, M. S., Williams, C. J., & Calhan, C. (1995). "If the shoe fits…": Exploring male homosexual foot fetishism. *The Journal of Sex Research, 32,* 17–27.

Wernik, U. (1990). The nature of explanation in sexology and the riddle of triolism. *Annals of Sex Research, 3,* 5–20.

Williams, C. J., & Weinberg, M. S. (2003). Zoophilia in men: A study of sexual interest in animals. *Archives of Sexual Behavior, 32,* 523–535.

Wilson, G. D., & Cox, D. N. (1983). Personality of paedophile club members. *Personality and Individual Differences, 4,* 323–329.

Wilson, P., Sharp, C., & Carr, S. (1999). The prevalence of gender dysphoria in Scotland: A primary care study. *British Journal of General Practice, 49,* 991–992.

Zhou, J. N., Hofman, M. A., Gooren, L. J., & Swaab, D. F. (1995). A sex difference in the human brain and its relation to transsexuality. *Nature, 378,* 68–70.

Zucker, K. J., Bradley, S. J., Kuksis, M., Pecore, K., Birkenfeld-Adams, A., Doering, R. W., et al. (1999). Gender constancy judgments in children with gender identity disorder: Evidence for a developmental lag. *Archives of Sexual Behavior*, 28, 475–502.

Zucker, K. J., Bradley, S. J., Lowry Sullivan, C. B., Kuksis, M., Birkenfeld-Adams, A., & Mitchell, J. N. (1993). A gender identity interview for children. *Journal of Personality Assessment*, 61, 443–456.

Part IV

PERSONALITY DISORDERS

23

Dimensional and Model-Based Alternatives to Categorical Personality Disorders

SHANI OFRAT,

ROBERT F. KRUEGER,

AND LEE ANNA CLARK

Dimensionalizing *DSM*: The Call to Action

In 1999, the American Psychiatric Association (APA) and National Institute of Mental Health (NIMH) co-sponsored a *DSM-5* Research Planning Conference to review the extant literature and to recommend priorities for research to be undertaken in preparation for *DSM-5*. The focus was on issues that concerned *DSM-IV*[1] users and that should be researched and clarified before the publication of *DSM-5*. One of the areas in which change was clearly warranted was in developing dimensional alternatives to strictly categorical classifications. Across diagnoses, there was a cognizance that it is "important that consideration be given to advantages and disadvantages of basing part or all of *DSM-V* on dimensions rather than categories" (Rounsaville et al., 2002, p. 12). Indeed, this was such a fundamental issue that it was identified as one of seven basic nomenclature issues needing clarification before the publication of *DSM-5* (Kupfer, First, & Regier, 2002), with particular dissatisfaction noted in the personality disorders (PD) domain. The study group tasked

with identifying issues with previous *DSM*s noted that "despite the compelling impact of maladaptive personality traits, there is notable dissatisfaction with the current conceptualization and definition of the *DSM-IV* personality disorders" (First et al., 2002, p. 124). It seemed that PD was a logical first candidate for the shift in diagnostic ideology: "There is a clear need for dimensional models to be developed and their utility compared to that of existing typologies in one or more limited fields, such as personality. If a dimensional system performs well and is acceptable to clinicians, it might be appropriate to explore dimensional approaches in other domains" (Rounsaville et al., 2002, p. 13). To set these statements in historical context, it is important to review how twentieth-century psychiatry came to emphasize a strictly categorical approach to classification.

The Neo-Kraepelinian Legacy in Psychiatry

Twentieth-century psychiatry has been dominated by categorical diagnoses. This emphasis on strict diagnostic criteria and delineation between disorders culminated in the neo-Kraepelinian revolution in psychiatry in the latter part of the twentieth century (see Blashfield, 1984, for further explication of this history). Briefly, this movement was a reaction

---

1. We reference only *DSM-IV*, not *DSM-IV-TR*, because we are focused on the PD criteria, which are the same in both volumes.

to the psychoanalytic tradition that predominated in psychiatry through approximately the 1970s. Neo-Kraepelinians argued that psychiatry had deviated from the standard medical paradigm, which emphasized diagnoses as discrete clinical entities and focused on concrete presence versus absence of disorder categories. To respond to a lack of scientific rigor that characterized the psychoanalytic tradition and to move psychiatry toward the medical model, neo-Krapelinians advocated operationalizing psychiatric disorders according to a strict set of criteria that would define diagnostic entities. Regier, Narrow, Kuhl, and Kupfer (2009) traced the origins of the re-emphasis on categorical diagnosis in psychiatry to Robins and Guze's (1970) seminal work, which established specific guidelines in the quest for greater validity of psychiatric disorders, and to the Feighner Diagnostic Criteria (FDC; Feighner et al., 1972), which operationalized the extant diagnostic categories using specific criteria. The FDC then became the basis for the Research Diagnostic Criteria (RDC; Spitzer, Endicott, & Robins, 1978), which were the models for the diagnoses adopted in *DSM-III* in 1980. Robert Spitzer, the primary framer of *DSM-III*, denied that his thinking was well characterized by the label "neo-Krapelinian" per se, but, as evidenced by *DSM-III*'s shift to strict diagnostic criteria for all disorders, this line of thought had a pervasive impact on *DSM-III*. This system indeed improved upon the vignette-based diagnostic system that predated *DSM-III*, resulting in diagnoses with somewhat greater reliability than earlier versions (Blashfield, 1984).

The then-current conceptualization of diagnosis was that mental illnesses were aberrant states, separated from mental health by "zones of rarity" (Kendell & Jablensky, 2003). These constituted the metaphorical space between disease status and non-disease status, where there would be no, or at least few, cases in the intermediate space between being sick and being well. This concept was imported from the standard medical model, in which some diseases do display a zone of rarity. For example, sickle cell anemia is either present in the patient or it is not. The astute reader will note, however, that not all medical conditions follow the standard model, and many exist on a spectrum, for example, hypertension and morbid obesity.

There are many benefits to a categorical system. For example, assuming the system is reliable,

health professionals can talk about disorders with confidence that they are discussing the same constellation of symptoms. As such, they can compare successful treatments, presumably leading to better care for those suffering from the illness. Additionally, treatments that work for one person with a certain disorder can be presumed to work for another person with that same disorder, because a common diagnosis implies a common etiology. A categorical system also holds the promise of reliable diagnosis (i.e., agreement across clinicians), and reliable assessment, in turn, is a precursor to establishment of the validity of the diagnoses themselves.

The Categorical Approach to Personality Disorders in *DSM*: History and Criticisms

Versions of *DSM* before *DSM-III* suffered from a lack of clear diagnostic criteria. As a result, these early *DSMs* had poor reliability (Blashfield, 1998; Kirk & Kutchins, 1994). Subsequent *DSMs* defined diagnostic entities more clearly, by specifying the criteria that must be met to receive a diagnosis. As mentioned earlier, however, implicit in this approach is the concept of disease status, in which those who have a disorder are discrete and separate from those without the disorder. Thus, categorical approaches are appropriate only where clear distinctions between the presence and absence of disorders actually exist (Grove & Andreasen, 1989). In the case of PD, however, no study has ever (1) shown a distinction (i.e., found a "zone of rarity") between the presence and absence of PD (instead, subclinical manifestations of PD occupy the liminal zone, see e.g., Zimmerman & Coryell, 1990) or (2) documented a clear distinction between the 10 *DSM-IV* PDs (e.g., Oldham et al., 1992). This is problematic because in order to have validity, categorical classification must reflect the reality of the phenomenon in nature. That is, a valid diagnostic system must map onto the distinctions, or lack thereof, that exist in nature, that "cut nature at its joints."

Failures of the DSM-III and DSM-IV Diagnostic System in the Case of Personality Disorder

An investigation of the research data on PD diagnosis shows that the *DSM-IV* PDs suffer from all the problems predicted to arise when categorical diagnoses are implemented where true categories do not exist. The problems with PD as defined in *DSM-III, DSM-III-R,* and *DSM-IV* are well documented and generally agreed upon by clinicians and researchers. These problems include comorbidity, heterogeneity within PD categories, temporal instability, arbitrary diagnostic thresholds, widespread use of "not otherwise specified" (NOS) designation that signifies poor coverage of personality pathology, and limited clinical utility. In the following sections we discuss each of these issues in turn.

Extensive Co-occurrence and Comorbidity The average number of PD diagnoses per patient has been reported consistently as greater than one; specific point estimates range from 2.8 (Zanarini, Frankenburg, Chauncey, & Gunderson, 1987) to 4.6 (Skodol, Rosnick, Kellman, Oldham, & Hyler, 1988). *DSM-IV* PDs co-occur far more frequently than by chance alone, strongly suggesting that the boundaries between specific PD diagnoses are blurred, and *DSM*-defined PDs are not really distinct entities. Categories are meant to separate patients into meaningfully distinct groups, with different implications for treatment and research, but when most patients fit into several categories, those categories are not clinically useful distinctions.

Heterogeneity To understand the heterogeneity problem, it is necessary to understand how PD has been assessed in *DSM-III* through *DSM-5* (Section II, which reprints the criteria from *DSM-IV*). Specifically, these PD categories are polythetic, meaning that the diagnostic threshold is reached when a patient meets a certain number of criteria in a larger list. If the diagnosis dictates that the patient must meet five of nine possible criteria, the situation arises in which two patients can be diagnosed with the same PD diagnosis while sharing only one criterion. For example, Patient A can meet Criteria 1 through 5, whereas patient B meets Criteria 5 through 9. Thus, the polythetic nature of the criteria—paired with the relatively low homogeneity of some of the PD criterion sets—has led to the present situation in which patients with the same PD diagnosis may present with very different clinical pictures. If a purported advantage of categorical diagnosis is that it provides clinicians with a common language that implies a common

set of symptoms for their patients, the polythetic nature of the criteria negates this benefit by removing the descriptive value of the diagnostic category. Additionally, that two patients in the same diagnostic category can share only one criterion calls into question the validity of the diagnosis as a syndrome—a collection of criteria that recur across patients.

Lack of Temporal Stability Inherent in the definition of PD is the notion of temporal stability, or a relative lack of change over time. However, several studies have found that fewer than half of PD patients remain at or above full criteria, even over intervals as short as 1–2 years (e.g., Grilo et al., 2004). Additionally, within 2 years of initial assessment, more than half the PD patients Grilo et al. studied were in remission, defined as the presence of no more than two criteria of their initial PD for 12 consecutive months. This and other studies led Grilo et al. to conclude that PD should be conceptualized as having two distinct elements: (1) stable personality traits that in PD are pathologically skewed or exaggerated, and (2) dysfunctional behaviors that are attempts at adapting to, defending against, coping with, or compensating for these pathological traits (e.g., self-cutting to reduce affective tension, avoiding work situations involving many people because of extreme shyness; Morey et al., 2002).

However, Samuel et al. (2011) found that when assessed as dimensions, the *DSM-IV* PDs showed relative stability: There was fluctuation in the number of criteria, with the mean decreasing over time, but there was a high correlation between initial assessment and a 2-year follow-up. Thus, the lack of stability of categorical diagnoses is likely due to fluctuations in clinical state, which can cause patients to drop "below threshold" for a specific PD category and no longer meet criteria. Indeed, the reason for the mean decrease in PD in Grilo et al.'s data is likely that participants were recruited into the study because they were seeking treatment because of a particular uptick in their PD manifestations. A clear advantage of a dimensional approach to PD assessment is that it provides a more nuanced view of changes in patients' clinical pictures over time.

Arbitrary Diagnostic Thresholds There is little evidence to suggest that the number of symptoms required to make a specific PD diagnosis in the

DSM is empirically valid (e.g., see Kamphuis & Noordhof, 2009, for the lack of evidence for the borderline PD criterion cut point). That is, there is no empirical rationale for the number of criteria required to reach diagnostic threshold, as seen in borderline PD, where manifesting at least five of nine symptoms purportedly indicates the presence of this PD. To our knowledge (and two of us served recently on a *DSM* workgroup), the reason for the selection of five symptoms is that it is greater than half of the criteria. There is also no meaningful weighting of the symptoms, as they all carry equal weight toward diagnosis. For example, a patient with four criteria of nine would not receive a diagnosis, even if those symptoms were extremely debilitating and greatly affected functioning. In terms of the impact on their lives, what would be the difference between patients who endorsed four versus five symptoms? Should a treatment plan ignore maladaptive personality features because there are fewer than what is required for diagnosis? These are important empirical questions that have not been well addressed in the literature. In *DSM-IV*, there is an option to describe maladaptive personality features that do not meet full clinical criteria, but in reality this option is rarely used.

Poor Coverage   The most frequent clinical PD diagnosis is personality disorder, not otherwise specified (PDNOS; Verheul & Widiger, 2007). This is obviously unfortunate because the designation "NOS" conveys little clinical information other than that something is awry with regard to the patient's personality functioning. More specifically, it likely means that clinicians use this diagnosis frequently because—of their patients who meet the general criteria for PD—most have features of several PD diagnoses, although they may fall one or a few criteria short of the diagnostic thresholds. Patients with a diagnosis of PDNOS do not differ significantly from patients with a single specific PD diagnosis in terms of severity or Global Assessment of Functioning (GAF) scores, but they do differ significantly in the number of PD symptoms they endorse (Coccaro, 2012). Thus, in order to capture the presence of PD that produces a clinical level of impairment, but that does not reach the arbitrary diagnostic threshold set by the *DSM*, or to capture a diagnosis that is an amalgam of several *DSM* PD categories, the diagnosis of PD, NOS is the only option. This is obviously unfortunate because the designation "NOS" conveys

little clinical information other than "something is awry with regard to the patient's personality functioning."

Limited Clinical Utility   Bernstein, Iscan, and Maser (2007) asked 400 members of two professional associations, the Association for Research on Personality Disorders, and the International Society for the Study of Personality Disorders, to complete a 78-item Web survey about the clinical utility of the *DSM-IV* PDs. Of the 96 who completed the survey, 80% felt that personality dimensions or illness spectra better characterized PD than diagnostic categories. Seventy-four percent felt that the *DSM-IV*'s categorical system of PD diagnosis should be replaced. The respondents most frequently advocated an alternative system for PD that combined categories and dimensions. Interestingly, only 31.3% voted to retain the term "borderline PD" in the *DSM-5*. It is clear that clinicians and researchers alike find the current categorical conception of PD to have limited clinical utility and would welcome meaningful changes aimed at improving PD classification. We turn now to describe how dimensional approaches can solve or circumvent many of the problems with the categorical *DSM* system.

What is a Dimensional Approach to Personality/PD?

Dimensional approaches to personality and PD are based on continuous spectra of personality traits or illness spectra, in contrast to the categorical approach, which defines specific PD categories like histrionic or borderline PD. A trait dimension is defined as a continuum or spectrum along which individuals' personalities vary. One well-known dimension is extraversion–introversion, with individuals' ranging along this spectrum from extremely outgoing and friendly to quiet and reserved. Broad, higher order dimensions such as extraversion–introversion are typically referred to as trait domains, domain traits, or just domains, whereas smaller subdivisions that describe different aspects of these broad domains are variously referred to as trait facets, facet traits, facets, or subtraits. There also are dimensional approaches to PD diagnosis and assessment that are not essentially trait based, such as considering PD categories as dimensions rather than as dichotomous (present or absent) entities. In such an approach, a patient might be described as having, for example, no avoidant PD, avoidant PD subclinical features, avoidant PD-threshold level, or avoidant PD-extreme level. Our focus in this chapter is on trait-dimensional approaches, although we discuss other types of dimensional approaches when warranted.

Advantages of Dimensional Approaches to Personality Disorders

How Do Dimensional Approaches Correct Categorical Models' Failings? Comorbidity is addressed by identifying the traits that cross categorical boundaries, and by defining maladaptive personality using these trait spectra. Dimensional approaches can also replace the uninformative and commonly used PDNOS diagnosis with a dimensional trait profile, which describes patients' relative standing on clinically relevant traits. Lastly, the problem of diagnostic heterogeneity is obviated by this approach, because it does not group patients into categories on the basis of traits and other criteria that do not covary consistently.

Subclinical Cases and Characterizing Clinically Meaningful Aspects of Normal Personality   All types of dimensional approaches have the additional advantage of better capturing cases that fall short of diagnostic criteria but are nonetheless notably impaired, by allowing for a conceptualization of severity and impairment of functioning even in the absence of a supra-threshold PD. Specifically, with a trait-dimensional approach, when clients or patients do not have PD, the trait-specified method allows for the description of both normal and maladaptive traits that are likely to be clinically informative in terms of treatment conceptualization and diagnostic course. In the *DSM-IV*, the option to describe subclinical maladaptive personality traits and patterns was available to clinicians. This option reflected the perspective that personality was fundamental to the clinical picture, case conceptualization, treatment, and course. However, the *DSM-IV* did not provide a framework through which to interpret these traits in terms of how they might affect treatment, course, or prognosis, and so this option was seldom used by clinicians. Because trait-dimensional models allow for the assessment of both normal and abnormal personality, even in those who are not suspected of having a PD, it may encourage clinicians to assess personality dimensions as important predictors

of treatment response, outcome, and diagnostic course.

Advantages to Clinical Utility   One objection to the elimination of existing PD categories is that there is substantial diagnosis-specific research that identifies a method of treatment as specifically beneficial for a particular PD category. Widiger and Simonsen (2005) note, however, that any dimensional system that allows clinicians to represent *DSM-IV* or other PD categories would still be able to draw on this literature. Additionally, there is evidence to suggest that the existing diagnostic PD categories are far too broad and heterogeneous to help with these types of decisions. For example, there is little evidence that current diagnostic PD categories are able to assist professionals in determining whether to hospitalize or medicate a patient (Verheul, 2005). In contrast, personality dimensions have been shown to provide utility in important treatment considerations like choice of therapeutic model, duration of treatment, frequency of appointments, and medication selection (see Sanderson & Clarkin, 2002; Harkness & Lilienfeld, 1997; and Harkness, 2007, for examples).

Candidate Dimensional Models for Assessing Personality Disorder

There are many empirically derived and supported models and related measures of normal and maladaptive personality traits that might be considered as alternatives to the categorical diagnostic system. Widiger and Simonsen (2005) amassed and evaluated 18 alternative proposals for a dimensional classification system to consider for inclusion in *DSM-5*[2], and several more have appeared

---

2. Although Widiger and Simonsen (2005) listed 18 alternative proposals, two pairs of proposals were based on the same measurement instrument (the SWAP-200 and the PAS, respectively), and one was simply a reorganization of the *DSM* itself, thus reducing the number to 15. We discuss the Tyrer (2000) entry rather than Tyrer and Johnson (1996), because the latter is focused only on severity, not PD types, and we discuss the two SWAP-200 models together. Widiger and Simonsen also list two Millon instruments as the same model, but we consider them separately because one is focused on normal personality and one is on abnormal personality. Finally, Widiger and Simonsen consider the SNAP and MPQ together, and we do so as well. Thus, we consider 16 rather than 18 proposals.

subsequently. The models differ in their origins (e.g., from within psychology or psychiatry), purpose for development (e.g., to assess normal or pathological personality), degree of empirical support, and degrees of similarity versus difference from both the extant categorical PD system and established models of personality trait structure. However, a majority, as well as several new models, contain very similar higher order trait dimensions, although they differ somewhat at the level of lower order facets. These models are shown in Table 23.1, which we discuss subsequently. First, however, we review the non-trait-based dimensional models in Widiger and Simonsen (2005).

Non-Trait Models

Models that Use Personality Dimensions to Recreate Categorical Diagnoses Oldham and Skodol (2000) proposed a model similar to the *DSM-IV* system. This model retains the *DSM-IV* PD categorical diagnostic constructs by treating them as ordinal dimensions ranging from 0 symptoms endorsed to the total number of criteria for the respective PD. Similarly, the Millon Clinical Multiaxial Inventory-III (MCMI-III; Millon, Millon, Davis, & Grossman, 2009) contains 14 PD scales (Schizoid, Avoidant, Depressive, Dependent, Histrionic, Narcissistic, Antisocial, Sadistic, Compulsive, Negativistic, Masochistic, Schizotypal, Borderline, and Paranoid) that assess the PDs that were in either the body or an appendix of *DSM-III-R* and *DSM-IV*. Although these scales do not literally dimensionalize the *DSM* PDs as Oldham and Skodol proposed, they are intended to coordinate with *DSM-IV* Axis II disorders. These models have the advantage of preserving the *DSM-IV* PD categories, which might facilitate the transition from categorical to dimensional models of classification by retaining familiar diagnostic concepts that have some traction in the literature (e.g., borderline PD). However, they also retain diagnoses that have recruited little to no research or clinical attention (e.g., paranoid PD; Krueger & Eaton, 2010). Further, they do not incorporate traits that cut across diagnostic categories and, as a result, they cannot address the problem of PD diagnostic comorbidity. Thus, we do not consider them further.

A Prototype-Based Model of PD   The Shedler-Westen Assessment Procedure-200 (SWAP-200; Shedler &

Westen, 2004; Westen & Shedler, 2000) is a prototype-matching model that is quite different from the *DSM* system and other models. It was developed using Q-factor analysis, a method in which raters sort items depending on how well they describe a target, which may be a live patient or a prototype (an "ideal" form; e.g., the prototype of a bird includes that it has feathers, lays eggs, has wings, and can fly, etc.; thus robins are more prototypic birds than penguins). Shedler and Westen argue that normal personality models omit key constructs that the SWAP-200 assesses, without which the clinical complexity of PD is not well captured. Based on clinicians' item sortings with patients and various prototypes as targets, Westen and Shedler developed SWAP-200 profiles for (a) the *DSM-IV* PDs (Westen & Shedler, 1999a), (b) the domains of the five-factor model (FFM) of personality (Shedler & Westen, 2004), which we discuss further later in this chapter, and (c) several empirically derived prototype sets based on clinical patients. At least 45 different prototypes have been created using the SWAP-200 item set; however, exactly how they are interrelated has not been reported in the literature.

To derive a SWAP-200 "diagnosis," the SWAP-200's items are sorted into eight groups, each with a specific number of items, ranging from a group that contains only a few items that best describe the target to one containing many items that are not at all descriptive of or applicable to the target. Then, the similarity of a given patient's sorting is compared to that of one or more prototypes, each yielding a similarity score on a scale from –1.0 (completely opposite) to +1.0 (identical). Thus, a given patient could have 10 similarity scores—one each for how closely his or her SWAP-200 profile matched that of the 10 *DSM-IV* PD prototypes—and/or a set of 12 similarity scores based on a set of empirically derived prototypes (e.g., psychological health, psychopathy, hostility, narcissism, emotional dysregulation, dysphoria) which overlap—but certainly are not isomorphic—with the *DSM* PDs, and/or a set of seven similarity scores based on Westen and Shedler's (1999b) original analysis.

Thus, a strength of the SWAP-200 item set is that it can capture such diverse personality and PD systems as the *DSM-IV* and the FFM, and it does appear to provide clinically "useful, elaborated, and systematic descriptions of the PD space" (Clark, 2007, p. 233). A major problem with this approach, however, lies in the nature of the factor-analytic method that Shedler and Westen (2004) use to derive prototypes empirically, as Q-factor analysis and related approaches (e.g., various types of cluster analysis) are often sample dependent. That is, the prototypes that emerge in any given sample are often nonrobust and will vary, depending on the nature of the sample (see Eaton, Krueger, South, Simms, & Clark, 2011, for evidence and a discussion of this issue). Moreover, it is not clear how the absolute and relative validity of the various sets of potential prototypes might be established so as to determine whether one should use the set of 10 or 12 or all 45 prototype profiles identified to date or even others that have not yet been identified. Finally, even if the decision of which set of prototypes profiles could be made nonarbitrarily, it is not clear how one would use the diagnostic information contained in a set of 10 or 12—let alone 45—similarity scores clinically. Thus, again, we do not consider this model further.

Models that Integrate PD with Other Mental Disorders   Two other models, those of Siever and Davis (1991) and of Krueger (2002), also were rather different from both the *DSM-IV* PDs and the other models, because their focus is on integrating the PD domain with other types of mental disorder (e.g., mood and anxiety disorders, disorders of impulse control and addiction) using common dimensions or *clinical spectra* underlying the dysfunction to form a meta-structure of mental disorders. Siever and Davis (1991) posit that PD comprises characterological manifestations of clinical psychopathology and that PD shares genetic associations with clinical disorders with which they often overlap phenomenologically. For example, schizotypal PD relates to schizophrenia and avoidant PD to anxiety disorders. They posit four spectra that cross-cut common forms of psychopathology: anxiety-inhibition, impulsivity-aggression, affective instability, and cognitive-perceptual disorganization.

Siever and Davis were absolutely on the right track conceptually and, very broadly speaking, empirically as well. Subsequent research, including that of Krueger (2002) as well as many others (e.g., Acton & Zodda, 2005; Hettema, Neale, Myers, Prescott, & Kendler, 2006; Khan et al., 2005; Krueger & Markon, 2006; Markon, 2010), has refined and extended our understanding of the

spectra they proposed. However, this work is not directly in line with our focus on PD dimensional models, because it goes well beyond PD to encompass syndromal mental disorders as well, so we do not discuss it further here.

Trait-Based Models

The remaining 11 models in Widiger and Simonsen (2005) and, as mentioned earlier, several new models, all propose systems based on personality trait dimensions. They can be grouped on the basis of whether they were developed primarily to assess normal-range personality, personality pathology, or both. At first glance it may appear that there is great variety among these models, and that one must choose from among them to develop a PD trait-diagnostic system. However, upon further study, it becomes clear that these models generally can be encompassed within the "Big 5," or five factor model (FFM) of personality, which emerged in the last decades of the twentieth century as diverse research on normal-range personality structure converged empirically on a five-domain model. Moreover, a substantial body of work has shown further that pathological personality largely can be integrated within this model as well (e.g., O'Connor, 2002; Markon, Krueger, & Watson, 2005). Accordingly, we first review the FFM itself briefly, from the perspective of normal-range personality on which it was derived. We then provide brief explications of the 11 models and two others that have emerged recently, in relation to the FFM. We summarize these models, again using the FFM as a framework in Table 23.1, which draws from, integrates, and extends Widiger and Simonsen's (2005) Table 2 and Krueger et al.'s (2011) Table 1 (see also Tyrer, 2009, Table 2). For each model, we provide a key reference or two that documents the map between the models' factors and the FFM.

The Five-Factor Model (FFM)   The five factors, largely viewed as bipolar, are most commonly known as Negative Emotionality, also called Neuroticism (NE/N), Extraversion (E), Agreeableness (A), Conscientiousness (C), and Openness to Experience (O) (Costa & Widiger, 2001). In the terms that are used most often, emotional stability is the opposing pole of NE/N, introversion of E, antagonism of A, disinhibition of C, and being closed to new experiences the opposite of O. These factors have been validated extensively

Table 23.1 Placement of Domains and Some Facets of Models and Corresponding Instruments that Assess Normal-Range and Pathological Personality

Measures	Common Domains				Domains Needing Further Study	
	Negative Emotionality	Introversion	Antagonism	Disinhibition	Schizotypy/Openness	Compulsivity
NEO PI-R	Neuroticism	(low) Extraversion	(low) Agreeableness	(low) Conscientiousness	Openness	Conscientiousness?
EPQ	Neuroticism	(low) Extraversion	Psychoticism	Psychoticism		
Alternative Five	Emotionality	(low) Sociability/Activity	Aggressive Sensation Seeking	Impulsive Sensation Seeking		
MIPS	Maladaptation	(low) Surgency	Disagreeableness	(low) Conscientiousness	Closed mindedness	
HEXACO	Emotionality	(low) Extraversion	(low) Agreeableness/Honesty-Humility	(low) Conscientiousness		
PAS	Passive Dependence	Schizoid		Sociopathy	Eccentricity*	Anankastic
DAPP	Emotional Instability	Inhibitedness	Dissocial**	(low) Compulsivity*?	Cognitive Distortion*	Compulsivity*?
PSY-5 (via MMPI-2)	Negative Emotionality/Neuroticism	(low) Positive Emotionality/Introversion	Aggressiveness	Disconstraint	Psychoticism	
SNAP	Negative Emotionality	(low) Positive Emotionality	Aggression*, Manipulativeness*	Disinhibition	Eccentric Perceptions*	Workaholism*, Propriety*
MCMI†	Borderline/Dependent	Schizoid vs. Histrionic	Narcissistic, Sadistic	Antisocial vs. Compulsive		
TCI††	Harm Avoid. vs. Self-direct.	(low) Reward Seeking	(low) Cooperativeness	Novelty Seeking	Self-transcendence	Persistence
DIPSI	Emotional Instability	Introversion	Disagreeableness (Dominance-Egocentrism)	Disagreeableness (Impulsivity, Disorderliness)		Compulsivity
5DPT	Neuroticism	(low) Extraversion	Insensitivity	(low) Orderliness	Absorption	

Note: This table draws from, integrates, and extends and updates Widiger and Simonsen's (2005) Table 1 and Krueger et al.'s (2011) Table 1; see also Tyrer (2009), Table 2. Cell entries are domains labels unless otherwise indicated. Labels are the authors' own. Empty cells represent domains that do not emerge within data obtained from a specific assessment model and for which the model does not contain a lower order facet. Question marks indicate that there is debate or too little research to determine the correct placement of a scale or factor.

*A lower facet whose content fits well within a domain. Listed here typically when there is too little of the factor's content in the measure to form a factor, but the scale loads on the factor if analyzed with other measures.

**Some research suggests that the DAPP Dissocial factor encompasses both Antagonism and Disinhibition, similar to Eysenck's Psychoticism, PAS Sociopathy, and SNAP Disinhibition, when its scales are factored alone (when factored with FFM measures, the two factors are distinguished).

†Factors are based on the work of researchers other than the authors, who do not identify the measure as having factors. Cell entries are the primary scales loading on the factors.

††The TCI, having only seven scales, does not have factors per se. Thus, scale placement is based on analyses with other personality trait scales. See text for more details.

Measure abbreviations and sources for the table's data (not necessarily the reference for the instrument): NEO PI-R = NEO Personality Inventory-Revised (Krueger et al., 2011; Widiger & Simonsen, 2005); EPQ = Eysenck Personality Questionnaire (Markon et al., 2005); Alternative Five (Rossier et al., 2007); MIPS = Millon Inventory of Personality Style (Weiss, 1997); HEXACO = Honesty-Humility, Emotionality, eXtraversion, Agreeableness, Conscientiousness, Openness (to Experience) (Ashton & Lee, 2008; Gaughan, Miller, & Lynam, 2012; PAS = Personality Assessment Schedule (Tyrer, 2009; Tyrer & Alexander, 1979); DAPP = Dimensional Assessment of Personality Pathology (Livesley & Jackson, 2010); PSY-5 = Personality Psychopathology Five (via MMPI-2) (Harkness, Finn, McNulty, & Shields, 2012); SNAP = Schedule for Nonadaptive and Adaptive Personality (Clark, Simms, Wu, & Casillas (in press); MCMI = Millon Clinical Multiaxial Inventory (Aluja, Garcia, Cuevas, & Garcia, 2007); TCI = Temperament and Character Inventory (Clark & Ro, 2014; De Fruyt, Van De Wiele, & Van Heeringen, 2000); DIPSI = Dimensional Personality Symptom Itempool (De Clercq, De Fruyt, Van Leeuwen, & Mervielde, 2006); 5DPT = Five Dimensional Personality Test (van Kampen, 2009).

and shown to relate broadly to many other variables, including a wide range of real-life outcomes (McCrae & Costa, 2008) including, for example, "organizational citizenship" (Chiaburu, Oh, Berry, Li, & Gardner, 2011), academic performance (Poropat, 2009), social investment (Lodi-Smith & Roberts, 2007), satisfaction in close relationships (Malouff, Thorsteinsson, Schutte, Bhullar, & Rooke, 2010), and psychopathology (e.g., Kotov, Gamez, Schmidt, & Watson, 2010; Malouff, Thorsteinsson, Rooke, & Schutte, 2007; Ruiz, Pincus, & Schinka, 2008). The FFM carries substantial weight in the personality field because of its robustness and the extensive research that has established its stability and validity across samples and methods. For example, personality traits are stable across the life course in predictable ways (Roberts & DelVecchio, 2000; Roberts, Walton, & Viechtbauer, 2006), and relations between the FFM and job performance are even stronger for observer ratings (Oh, Wang, & Mount, 2011) than for self-report (Hurtz & Donovan, 2000).

It is important to emphasize that the FFM is a conceptual framework of traits that define personality, and extant measures assess different aspects of the FFM. Although each instrument samples at least part of the FFM model, each necessarily demarcates the space it surveys and as such cannot be said to assess the FFM model per se, but merely a portion of the full domain. For example, the Revised NEO Personality Inventory (NEO-PI-R; Costa & McCrae, 1992), arguably the best known and most widely used measure of the FFM, was created with exactly six facets for each domain. However, other FFM measures (e.g., see Watson, Stasik, Ro, & Clark, 2013) assess facets that the PI-R does not, such as "envy" or "frankness." Moreover, the NEO PI-R facets were not derived empirically from a psychopathological sample, and thus may not capture clinically significant forms of personality psychopathology that nevertheless can be integrated into a general FFM (e.g., dependency is a clinically important trait not assessed by the NEO PI-R that can be placed within the FFM; Morgan & Clark, 2010).

Models that Target Normal-Range Personality Dimensions Although *DSM* is meant to address abnormal psychological manifestations, Costa and McCrae (1990) and others have argued that abnormal and normal personality differ in severity, not in kind, and that description of normal personality is clinically informative in the context of other disorders. From this perspective, it is important to study normal-range personality models together with those that specifically target personality pathology.

The following models approach personality dysfunction from the perspective of normal personality. Hans Eysenck, a pioneer in the field of personality assessment and the developer of the Eysenck Personality Questionnaire (EPQ; Eysenck & Eysenck, 1975), proposed a three-factor model of biologically based temperament dimensions: E, NE/N, and Psychoticism (versus socialization), the last of which corresponds closely to the combined FFM domains of (low) A and C (see Markon et al., 2005). Zuckerman's (2002) five-factor model also emphasizes the biological-evolutionary basis of personality, citing biological markers, animal models, and trait heritability as evidence of the biological origins of personality. The five-factor Zuckerman-Kuhlman Personality Questionnaire (ZKPQ; Zuckerman, Kuhlman, Joireman, Teta, & Kraft, 1993) contains the domains of neuroticism-anxiety (NE/N), aggression-hostility (low A), impulsive sensation seeking (low C), and sociability and activity, which together correspond to E. The Millon Index of Personality Styles (MIPS; Millon, 2003) may be the most theoretically distant from the others in Widiger and Simonsen's (2005) review insofar as it uses the three polarities of pleasure versus pain, active versus passive, and self versus other to describe personality, and groups its scales under the labels of Motivating Aims, Cognitive Modes, and Interpersonal Behaviors. Nevertheless, when factored, it yields the familiar FFM (Weiss, 1997).

Recently, the HEXACO model of Lee and Ashton (2004) has gained considerable attention. Five of its six domains clearly map, with some variation, onto those of the FFM (e.g., Gaughan, Miller, & Lynam, 2012). The sixth—honesty/humility—is moderately related to A, and appears particularly relevant to certain types of personality pathology, including narcissism, psychopathy, egoism, and Machiavellianism (e.g., de Vries, de Vries, de Hoogh, & Feij, 2009; de Vries & van Kampen, 2010; Gaughan et al., 2012; Lee & Ashton, 2005), and materialistic tendencies and delinquency (Ashton & Lee, 2008). Further, it may provide incremental predictive power over FFM measures (e.g., Ashton & Lee, 2008; de Vries et al., 2009).

Models that Target Pathological Personality Dimensions Three personality models were developed specifically to assess personality pathology. Tyrer (2009; Tyrer & Alexander, 1979) factor analyzed the Personality Assessment Schedule (PAS), a set of 24 PD-relevant personality trait dimensions (e.g., vulnerability, aloofness, aggression, impulsiveness) and found four factors that he linked with four of the five FFM dimensions (Tyrer, 2009, Table 2). Interestingly, he used PD diagnostic labels for the factors, which may facilitate understanding of how personality traits are linked with PD categories: sociopathy he linked with antagonism (e.g., aggression), although it may be argued that it also has links with disinhibition (e.g., impulsivity), passive-dependent tapped negative affectivity (e.g., anxiousness), schizoid reflected low extraversion (e.g., aloofness), and anankastic tapped compulsivity (e.g. rigidity) and conscientiousness (e.g., conscientiousness).

The Dimensional Assessment of Personality Pathology (DAPP-BQ; Livesley, 2001; Livesley & Jackson, 2010) was constructed by modeling the empirical structure of psychopathological personality variants. The measure has 18 trait-facet dimensions that comprise four higher order personality domains: emotional dysregulation, dissocial behavior, inhibitedness, and compulsivity. In support of this model, a reanalysis of 33 previously published datasets investigating the empirical structure of PD variation yielded a model that closely resembled the DAPP's four-factor structure (O'Connor, 2005).

Harkness and McNulty (1994) developed the PSY-5, consisting of the five higher order factors of Aggressiveness, Psychoticism, Disconstraint, NE/N, and Introversion, along with scales from the Minnesota Multiphasic Personality Inventory-2 (MMPI-2) item pool to assess these domains (see Harkness, Finn, McNulty, & Shields, 2012, for a review). Unlike some of the other measures of pathological personality, the PSY-5 includes psychoticism, which emerges as a domain when maladaptive personality space is sampled to include wide coverage of psychotic or aberrant experiences. Measures that have some but not sufficiently broad coverage of this part of the maladaptive personality trait space (e.g., the DAPP) often have a facet rather than domain scale for psychotic experiences.

Earlier we described the MCMI-III as a model whose PD scales represent *DSM-IV* constructs as dimensions, but a number of factor analyses of the instrument also have revealed that the 14 PD scales form four factors. Aluja, Garcia, Cuevas, & Garcia (2007) showed that these factors align well with the FFM domains by replicating the frequently found structure and then jointly factoring the MCMI-III PD scales with two different FFM measures. Therefore, in Table 23.1, we include the MCMI-III and list the PD scales that most strongly mark each of the four common domains.

Models that Target Both Normal-Range and Maladaptive Personality Dimensions Tellegen and Waller (1987, cited in Almagor, Tellegen, & Waller, 1995) identified seven factors that spanned normal and abnormal personality. These factors were established by including more extreme evaluative terms (e.g., meticulous, impatient) that had been omitted from initial formulations of the FFM, which used the lexical approach (a method that uses trait terms such as *friendly* and *aggressive* to define the factors). Inclusion of these terms results in domains that are shifted in a more psychopathological direction (Simms, 2007; Simms, Yufik, & Gros, 2010) and yields two factors absent from the FFM: positive (e.g., *sophisticated, productive*) and negative (e.g., *narrow-minded, pretentious*) evaluation or valence.

Cloninger (2000) took issue with the development of models based on factor analysis of phenotypic, or surface/observable level, data. He argued that phenotypic variability is made up of genetic and environmental variance components, and it is potentially misleading to collapse across them to measure phenotypic variation. He initially proposed three (but later split one, yielding four) domains of temperament: Novelty Seeking, Harm Avoidance, Reward Dependence, and Persistence. Large-scale twin studies showed that each domain is genetically homogenous and independent of one another (Heath, Cloninger, & Martin, 1994; Stallings, Hewitt, Cloninger, Heath, & Eaves, 1996). He then expanded the model to include three character domains—self-directedness, cooperativeness, and self-transcendence—which he hypothesized were more environmentally and less genetically based, but results have not supported this putative etiological distinction (Ando et al., 2004). Rather, they have indicated that the scales fit well within an FFM framework without a temperament–character distinction.

Clark's (1993) model of personality, as measured by the Schedule for Nonadaptive and Adaptive

Personality (SNAP) and its second edition (SNAP-2; Clark, Simms, Wu, & Casillas, in press), integrates maladaptive personality variants extracted from the clinical and research PD literature with major domains of adult temperament variation researched by personality psychologists. The SNAP delineates three broad personality domains: negative emotionality (versus emotional stability), positive emotionality (versus detachment), and disinhibition (versus constraint), assessed with 15 lower order facets. When factored with FFM measures, the higher order scale of disinhibition and the facet scale of impulsivity load (negatively) on the FFM trait C, whereas aggression, mistrust, and manipulativeness form the opposite pole from A (Clark et al., in press; Ro & Clark, 2013). Included in this model are traits that capture trait-like manifestations of anxiety and mood disorders, intended to provide an empirical scaffolding for the substantial comorbidity observed between psychopathology of clinical syndromes and maladaptive personality.

The Dimensional Personality Symptom Item Pool (DIPSI; De Clercq, De Fruyt, Van Leeuwen, & Mervielde, 2006) was designed to capture both normal- and abnormal-range personality variation, by being supplemented with maladaptive items tapping *DSM-IV* PDs. The DIPSI's four factors again reflect the domains of disagreeableness (low A), emotional instability (NE/N), compulsivity (maladaptive C), and introversion (low E), and have been shown to combine into higher level internalizing and externalizing domains. Most recently, van Kampen (2009) developed the 5-Dimension Personality Test to extend Eysenck's three-factor model "to create a personality taxonomy of clinical relevance" (p. 9). Eysenck's NE/N and E factors were retained and Psychoticism was replaced by Insensitivity, which correlates with low A, Orderliness (correlated with C), and Absorption, which correlates with both O and measures of schizotypy (van Kampen, 2012). Moreover, the scales form a clear convergent/discriminant pattern with the HEXACO (van Kampen, 2012), and the first four scales form a clear convergent/discriminant pattern with Livesley's four DAPP-BQ dimensions (van Kampen, 2006).

Possible Pitfalls of FFM-Based Alternative Dimensional Models

Although the FFM was initially conceptualized as a descriptor of normal personality, it is clear that

four of the five FFM domains (the exception is openness) relate to the PD domain as well. Further, research indicates that normal and pathological personality differ primarily in degree, rather than in kind, meaning that it is trait severity that differentiates between those with and without personality pathology, not the presence or absence of the trait entirely (Krueger et al., 2011) or the way that different traits relate to each other, that is, trait structure (O'Connor, 2002). Nevertheless, there are several possible pitfalls in using measures that were developed to capture normal-range personality to assess dysfunctional personality. First, certain traits with pathological clinical relevance are absent from most measures of normal-range personality, including, for example, dependency and traits related to psychosis. Although some researchers argue that the latter are a form of extreme O (Gore & Widiger, 2013; Wiggins & Pincus, 1989), others have shown that they are distinct from O (e.g., Watson, Clark, & Chmielewski, 2008). DeYoung, Grazioplene, and Peterson (2012) have argued that these two views are reconciled by the fact that O combines facets related to schizotypy and intellect, and the various O measures assess these facets differentially. In any case, to assess PD comprehensively, some modification of normal-range personality measures is needed to address the issue of "missing" traits.

Second, the items of such measures may be too "mild" to capture the extremes of abnormal or maladaptive personality seen in PD. Consequently, personality differences between individuals with PD are not well captured by normal-range instruments. For example, Morey et al. (2002) used the NEO-PI-R to distinguish between personality-disordered patients and to differentiate personality-disordered patients from community norms. The results indicated that four of the PDs assessed (schizotypal, borderline, avoidant, obsessive-compulsive) could be distinguished from community norms on the measure, but were not easily distinguishable from each other because each shared the configuration of high Neuroticism, low Agreeableness, and low Conscientiousness. The authors interpreted this finding to mean that the *DSM-IV* PDs appeared to be variants of the same extreme configuration of traits and thus the FFM was not a viable way of describing PD. However, it is entirely possible that the FFM as a *model* is capable of encompassing and distinguishing between different PD configurations, but in this case was limited by an *instrument* designed to measure normal personality.

For example, Samuel, Riddell, Lynam, Miller, and Widiger (2012) showed that the FFM as a conceptual model can be augmented to include a more maladaptive set of traits that will still fit within the factor structure of normal-range personality. Specifically, they developed the Five-Factor Obsessive-Compulsive Inventory by augmenting the FFM traits assessed by measures of normal personality with traits relevant to obsessive-compulsive PD from the perspective of the FFM. The inventory sampled more extensively from maladaptive space (e.g., sampling perfectionism as a maladaptive variant of the FFM facet of competence) and demonstrated convergent validity with both the FFM and obsessive-compulsive PD, as assessed by other measures. Thus, the different assessment tools merely sample from different sections of the overall FFM configuration and, as such, measure different ranges of essentially the same constructs.

Similarities Across Alternative Dimensional Models

With the exceptions discussed in the brief model summaries, there are more commonalities than dissimilarities across the models that Widiger and Simonsen (2005) reviewed, plus the several others that have emerged since then. Those authors concluded that the solution to the question of which alternative dimensional model to use is to integrate the methods into a common hierarchical model, with Internalizing and Externalizing (Achenbach 1966; Krueger, 1999, 2002) as the highest order factors, with four or five broad personality trait domains underlying them. This is the level at which there is the most agreement across alternate models, as shown in Table 23.1, with all models sharing a similar factor structure even when they originate from different conceptual frameworks. At the next level below the broad domains would be personality trait facets, and below that, at the lowest level, could be "more behaviorally specific diagnostic criteria" (Widiger, Simonsen, Krueger, Livesley, & Verheul, 2005), which would correspond to items on a self-report measure or questions in an interview.

It is important to understand that trait structure is multilevel and hierarchical. For practical reasons, the term *domain* typically is used to designate traits at the highest levels of the hierarchy, and *facet* for those below that. Clarification of the trait hierarchy (Markon et al., 2005) not only facilitated the integration of diverse models of personality traits into a single model but also led to the insight that the various levels of the hierarchy were most useful for different purposes. Thus, for example, a higher level of the hierarchy may be best for PD diagnosis because it would facilitate recognition of a manageable number of broad trait patterns, whereas case formulation for treatment would be aided by using a lower level of the hierarchy that would describe an individual more precisely (Clark, 2012).

Broad Trait Domains

Although the various models generally conform to a similar factor structure, there are some differences between them at the trait domain level, some of which are semantic and others substantive. The semantic differences include terminological disagreement, that is, the optimal names for different traits, with some having historical or colloquial baggage (e.g., *extraversion* as a term meaning sociable in colloquial speech, or *neuroticism* having a different meaning within a Freudian context). There is also some more substantive disagreement regarding the optimal rotations of the traits in factor analysis, which can yield different interpretations of the traits' content. However, at the "big-picture" level, all models share a similar factor structure.

Extraversion in some form is ubiquitous across the models; it is variously described as sociability, activity, positive emotionality, and—when keyed in the opposite direction—inhibition, introversion, or withdrawal. Behaviors associated with extraversion are gregariousness, talkativeness, assertiveness, and activeness, whereas introverted behaviors are withdrawnness, isolation, and feeling a lack of pleasure.

All the models also include an NE/N factor, characterized by emotional dysregulation and frequently and intensely feeling anxious, depressed, angry, despondent, labile, helpless, self-conscious, and vulnerable, with the other pole being emotional stability, characterized by typically feeling self-assured, invulnerable, and calm. Disagreement remains as to whether extreme scores on this (low) end of the dimension reflect psychopathic glibness, shamelessness, and a sense of invincibility.

Antagonism is a trait in all models, although in three-factor models it is a "mid-to-high level facet" that, together with low constraint, forms a higher order factor of disinhibition. Antagonism reflects being suspicious, rejecting, exploitative, aggressive, antagonistic, callous, deceptive, and manipulative, whereas its other pole, agreeableness or compliance, describes the degree to which a person is trusting, modest, dependent, diffident, and empathic. Some measures define this trait more narrowly and pathologically, eschewing the normal personality aspects and focusing more on the maladaptive aspects of both ends of the trait.

Constraint is concerned with the control and regulation of behavior, including conscientiousness, with disinhibition or impulsivity at the other pole. In some models, this domain encompasses compulsivity, whereas in others, compulsivity is a distinct factor that is not the opposite of disinhibition/impulsivity. Reconciling these two views is an ongoing area of research inquiry (see Sharma, Markon, & Clark, 2014).

A minority of the models include a fifth trait that maps loosely onto the FFM domain of openness to experience. Openness has shown weak to no relationship to PD psychopathology, perhaps in part because of its "dual nature" mentioned earlier. The O facet that does have a pathological slant is unconventionality, schizotypy, or psychoticism on one pole, described as a tendency to experience illusions, misperceptions, and perceptual aberrations, and to have magical ideation, with "lucidity" on the opposite pole, whereas the "intellect" facet is marked by curiosity and broadmindedness, with its opposite end being "closedness to experience," lack of curiosity, and narrow-mindedness. Schizotypy/psychoticism has been shown to relate to schizotypal PD and is a clinically important construct to measure. Several models contain a lower order scale that taps this domain (see Table 23.1).

Developing and Implementing a Trait Approach to PD

DSM-5 and Development of the Alternative (Section III) Diagnostic Model

It was clear in approaching *DSM-5* that the *DSM*'s categorical PD system was deeply flawed. But there were obstacles to a smooth transition to a dimensional approach. Perhaps the most obvious problem facing a dimensional *DSM-5* PD model was what the dimension model should be. Work like that of Widiger and Simonsen (2005) was a crucial step toward integrating existing models and provided a broad framework from which to start. There also were practical and economic issues to address, such as copyright. Although not strictly scientific, such considerations were important to the APA, considering that the *DSM* is a publication it copyrights and sells, and many of the existing models are operationalized by inventories owned and sold for profit by various test publishers not affiliated with the APA. Finally, there were issues of continuity, such as linking a new system closely enough to the existing one that a smooth transition could be effected. After all, numerous clinicians and researchers had been trained on the *DSM* system since 1980, and although many of those were psychologists who were likely to be familiar with personality trait systems, many others—in fact, probably the majority—were not, and would be encountering a trait-based dimensional model for diagnosing PD for the first time. If the new model were too different from the old, it might be difficult for those in the field to grasp how it related to currently familiar PD constructs and might lead to its abandonment. We discuss this issue further below.

Therefore, the *DSM-5* Personality and Personality Disorders (P&PD) Work Group set out to develop a trait model and associated measure that would "belong to the APA" and bridge from the *DSM-IV* to *DSM-5*. The endeavor of creating this model began much the same way that most personality-trait model development begins, with a group of researchers and clinicians drawing on existing models to generate a list of traits that define their target constructs, in this case, the personality traits of PD patients. One goal was to include representations of the four domains well-established as common to almost all dimensional models of personality, as well as a fifth domain describing psychoticism, to capture the part of the broad personality domain covered by *DSM-IV* Schizotypal PD. An additional goal was to include facets within the domains that would permit the recreation of the *DSM-IV* categorical diagnoses, the bridge from the old system to the new. The resulting measure was then administered to several samples, including patients seeking mental health services, and was refined iteratively using modern psychometric techniques (see Krueger et al., 2011;

Krueger, Derringer, Markon, Watson, & Skodol, 2012, for more detail about the model and the measure, respectively). The result of this endeavor is that the APA now owns an empirically derived and supported trait-specified model of personality pathology, and an associated measure called the Personality Inventory for *DSM-5* (PID-5; Krueger et al., 2012).

Diagnosis of PD Using the *DSM-5* Section III Approach

There were enough practical obstacles, articulated earlier, to transitioning to a dimensional approach to PD in *DSM-5* that the APA elected to maintain the *DSM-IV* PD classification system in the Section II text of *DSM-5* (diagnostic criteria and codes) and to include the alternative dimensional approach to PD in Section III, "Emerging Models and Measures." The first part of diagnostic assessment in the new dimensional system is assessment of impairment in personality functioning. This assessment is necessary because simply exhibiting extreme personality traits is not necessarily pathological. That is, mental disorder, including PD, "reflects a dysfunction in the psychological, biological, or developmental processes underlying mental functioning" (*DSM-5*, p. 20). Because extremity on a personality trait may be simply the "tail" of a normal distribution, a certain level of dysfunction is needed to diagnose a PD. Thus, the first criterion for a *DSM-5* Section III PD is "moderate or greater impairment in personality (self/interpersonal) functioning," with self-functioning encompassing identity and self direction, and interpersonal functioning encompassing empathy and intimacy.

The Level of Personality Functioning scale was developed to operationalize this criterion, and it taps disturbances in each of the four subareas of self (identity, self-direction) and interpersonal (empathy, intimacy) functioning on continua ranging from 0 (healthy, adaptive functioning) to 4 (extreme impairment). These are then aggregated by the diagnostician into a single continuum, using the same 0–4 severity scale, with a moderate level (a rating of 2) or greater of personality impairment required for PD diagnosis. Even if the patient does not meet criteria for a PD, the rating of the level of personality functioning can be highly clinically informative (Skodol et al., 2011).

Patients who do have at least moderate impairment in personality functioning are then assessed on the traits. This may be done in one of at least two ways: (1) by focusing on the traits that comprise the six specific PD diagnoses that transitioned from *DSM-IV* (antisocial, avoidance, borderline, narcissistic, obsessive-compulsive, and schizotypal) or (2) by assessing trait domains (5) or facets (25). Each of the six specific PD diagnoses is defined by a particular configuration of impaired personality functioning and a set of pathological traits. The required trait sets in each case, assuming that the required configuration of impaired personality functioning is present, are as follows: Antisocial PD is diagnosed when there are elevations on any six of seven traits: manipulativeness, deceitfulness, callousness, hostility, irresponsibility, impulsivity, and risk taking. Avoidant PD is diagnosed when anxiousness is elevated, as well as at least two other trait facets from among withdrawal, anhedonia, and intimacy avoidance. Borderline PD is diagnosed when at least four of seven traits are present (emotional lability, anxiousness, separation insecurity, depressivity, impulsivity, risk taking, and hostility); one of these must be impulsivity, risk taking, or hostility. To be diagnosed with obsessive-compulsive PD, the trait of rigid perfectionism must be elevated, as well as at least two others from among perseveration, intimacy avoidance, and restricted affectivity. Narcissistic PD is diagnosed when there are elevations on both grandiosity and attention seeking. Schizotypal PD is diagnosed if at least four of the traits from among eccentricity, cognitive and perceptual dysregulation, unusual beliefs and experiences, restricted affectivity, withdrawal, and suspiciousness are present.

Patients who have at least moderate personality pathology as measured by the level of personality functioning dimension, but (1) do not meet the criteria for a specific PD, (2) meet the criteria for multiple PD types, so that their psychopathology is better defined globally than by several separate diagnoses, or (3) meet criteria for a specific PD but have additional pathological traits that are important to describe the clinical picture, would receive a diagnosis of PD-trait specified (PD-TS). In these cases, patients are described by a list of the pathological traits they manifest, selected from the hierarchical model composed of five higher order domains (negative affectivity, detachment, antagonism, disinhibition, and psychoticism), each of which is comprised of three to seven facets, totaling 25 specific trait facets. As noted earlier, these were developed initially from a review of existing models, chosen because of their clinical relevance, and then refined through iterative research on samples of persons, including those who sought mental health services. Importantly, 25 criterion traits is a substantial reduction from the 79 individual criteria that define the 10 PDs in *DSM-IV* and *DSM-5*, Section II.

Addressing Concerns Regarding the Alternate Dimensional Approach

A concern regarding implementation of a dimensional approach, as mentioned earlier, was how to minimize the disruption of transitioning from a categorical system, because the current PDs are familiar constructs to many in the field. A related concern was the loss of continuity with research literatures that pertained to specific diagnoses (although a counterargument was that research based in invalid diagnoses should not, in fact, be continued). The optimal solution would reflect the least disruptive way to deal with the fact that the empirically well-established broad domains of dimensional personality traits do not map neatly and cleanly onto the *DSM-IV* PD categories, at least in their current, specific, familiar particularities. It was out of these considerations that the hybrid model of *DSM-5* Section III was developed: to facilitate the transition to a dimensional diagnostic system, which was a rather dramatic departure from categorical conceptualization.

One way in which this was done was to develop the 25 trait facets so as to maximize linkage with the *DSM-IV* categorical system to the extent possible within the constraints of fidelity to the empirical data. A second way was to demonstrate that the model allows even the traditional categorical PD diagnoses to be represented using the trait-specified model. By the time the *DSM-5* had to go to print, however, the APA Board of Trustees (who had final responsibility for the *DSM-5*) took a conservative path of retaining the familiar *DSM-IV* criteria, instead of moving forward toward a more empirically based dimensional approach in Section II. Consequently, as mentioned earlier, the Board voted to retain the *DSM-IV* PD diagnoses in the main body of the manual, Section II, and to place the "alternative" dimensional model in Section III, "Emerging Measures and Models," to increase its familiarity to the field and facilitate the research needed to establish it more firmly.

Research on the PID-5

The American Psychiatric Association has made the PID-5 freely available online (at http://www.dsm5.org), which should facilitate research regarding the clinical utility of the *DSM-5* trait model. A 25-item short form of the PID-5 that assesses only the five domains, and an informant version of the PID-5 (Markon, Quilty, Bagby, & Krueger, 2013) are also available. The PID-5 has been shown to dovetail well with the Five Factor Model Rating Form (FFMRF; a very brief measure of the NEO PI-R facets; Thomas et al., 2013), the NEO-PI-3 (a revision of the NEO PI-R to make the instrument more appropriate for those with lower educational levels; De Fruyt et al., 2013; Quilty, Ayearst, Chmielewski, Pollock, & Bagby, 2013), and the MMPI-2 PSY-5 scales (Anderson et al., 2013). All of these conjoint analyses show the familiar five-factor structures one would anticipate, although they also reveal areas in which the PID-5 scales may fall outside the FFM space assessed by currently established measures. For example, 3 of the 25 PID-5 facets loaded <.40 on all factors when factored with the FFMRF; 10 of the 25 facets correlated <.40 and 3 correlated <.30 with all PSY-5 scales; and six correlated <.40 with all five NEO PI-R domain scores in a patient sample (Quilty et al., 2013). Two of these scales (Intimacy Avoidance and Risk Taking) had comparable results in a different patient sample (Watson et al., 2013), but only one, Risk Taking, did so in a university student sample (De Fruyt et al., 2013). However, Submissiveness had correlations <.40 in both the Watson et al. and the De Fruyt et al. samples. This underscores the important point that the PID-5 was not developed to replace or supersede any other widely used models, but rather to show that each time the maladaptive personality space is sampled broadly it results in a replicable five-factor structure, further establishing its robustness. In addition, work with the PID-5 reveals how there are new areas of the entire personality trait space that may not have been well sampled previously, and that no one instrument is completely comprehensive, and with good reason: Such an instrument might well be thousands of items in length.

Hopwood, Thomas, Markon, Wright, and Krueger (2012) investigated the PID-5's ability to capture *DSM-IV* PD constructs and found that the PID-5 not only explained substantial proportions of the variance in those PDs in a sample of undergraduates (2012) but also showed good convergence in terms of the traits associated with the diagnoses in *DSM-5*. For example, all seven traits used to diagnose antisocial PD in Section III of *DSM-5* correlated ≥.40 with the diagnosis as assessed by the Personality Disorder Questionnaire-IV+ (Hyler, 1994). More work is needed to verify this in other populations and to determine whether the current algorithms to assign diagnoses are optimal (see Samuel, Hopwood, Krueger, Thomas, & Ruggero, 2013, for a study that examined this issue). This finding highlights how the PID-5, and other similar measures of maladaptive personality, capture the same personality pathology as *DSM-IV* PDs, but in a way that more closely resembles the empirical structure of PD.

The Shifting of Continental Plates

Widiger and Trull (2007) commented that a shift as momentous as from a categorical to a dimensional model of personality pathology was equivalent to a shifting of continental plates. We concur, but we also note that this shift is long overdue. It is difficult at this point to claim that there is not enough evidence documenting that the *DSM-IV*'s PD diagnoses are flawed or that there is insufficient empirical research supporting the alternative dimensional approach, and it may be puzzling that a system with very little validity and questionable clinical utility (i.e., *DSM-IV*) is maintained and defended. However, it may be fair to say that there are not yet enough clinicians (particularly psychiatrists, and the *DSM* is published by the American *Psychiatric* Association) who are familiar with, let alone have used, a trait model to report on its subjective clinical utility. This is in contrast to most psychologists who have been trained—and therefore do—think dimensionally, for example, through the long use of MMPI-2 score profiles and other assessment tools that place patients along continua.

It may be helpful also to consider the challenging sociopolitical issues surrounding the existence of diagnostic categories. For instance, there are professionals whose research careers have centered on the study of a distinct diagnostic entity such as borderline or antisocial PD. Consideration must also be given to the perspective of patients who have been given a PD diagnosis and made sense of their difficulties—even, for better or worse,

developed an identity—through the lens of that diagnosis. Furthermore, there are funding agencies, private organizations, celebrity spokespeople, and patient advocacy groups that revolve around the idea of these disorders—or at least their particular disorder—being distinct "medical categories." It will take time for such individuals and groups to come to terms with the fact that there is a scientifically more valid way to understand personality and its pathology. Most likely the turning point will be when new understanding leads to more effective treatment.

Widiger et al. (2005) have given an account of key next steps in realizing the ability of dimensional models to improve clinical practice. They emphasize the need for work that investigates the alternate system's coverage, consistency with developmental and etiological models, consistency with models of course and change, user acceptability and accuracy, professional communication, interrater reliability, subtlety of diagnosis, and clinical decision-making. They also specifically highlight the importance of studies that address whether additional information provided by a dimensional classification system is actually helpful for clinical decisions, or whether it provides too much detail without utility.

What is clear is that the categorical diagnostic system is failing clinicians, researchers, and, most importantly, patients. A failure to adopt a new diagnostic system that cuts nature at its joints is a hindrance to the many avenues that researchers take to seek to understand psychopathology more fully, both as it is manifest in people's day-to-day lives and its processes within the brain. Research that accepts faulty diagnoses as its foundation is inherently problematic and ultimately doomed to failure. It is at best an inefficient use of resources, because any finding must surmount the noise resulting from the faulty categories to reach significance. At worst, false categories obscure findings entirely and lead to null results where there would have potential for scientific progress or patient benefit had the research been built on a better foundation. It is hopefully clear to the reader how important empirically valid classification approaches are to scientific research.

More so than its predecessors, *DSM-5* is intended to be a living document, with revisions along the way to its next iteration, so that it can better reflect our changing understanding of psychiatric constructs. Insofar as the Section III PD model moves us toward a hierarchically organized, dimensional model that cross-cuts current diagnostic categories to reflect the clinical reality better we will be moving in the right direction. The authors of this chapter hope that trainees in the field will take it upon themselves to work with the *DSM-5* Section III model and attempt to refine that model further.

References

Achenbach, T. M. (1966). The classification of children's psychiatric symptoms: A factor analytic study. *Psychological Monographs*, *80*(615).

Acton, G. S., & Zodda, J. J. (2005). Classification of psychopathology: Goals and methods in an empirical approach. *Theory & Psychology*, *15*, 373–99.

Almagor, M., Tellegen, A., & Waller, N. (1995). The Big Seven model: A cross-cultural replication and further exploration of the basic dimensions of natural language trait descriptors. *Journal of Personality and Social Psychology*, *69*, 300–307.

Aluja, A., Garcia, L. F., Cuevas, L., & Garcia, O. (2007). The MCMI-III personality disorders scores predicted by the NEO-FFI-R and the ZKPQ-50-CC: A comparative study. *Journal of Personality Disorders*, *21*(1), 58–71.

Anderson, J. L., Sellbom, M., Bagby, R. M., Quilty, L. C., Veltri, C. O., Markon, K. E., & Krueger, R. F. (2013). On the convergence between PSY-5 domains and PID-5 domains and facets: Implications for assessment of *DSM-5* personality traits. *Assessment*, *20*, 286–294.

Ando, J., Suzuki, A., Yamagata, S., Kijima, N., Maekawa, H., Ono, Y., & Jang, K. L. (2004). Genetic and environmental structure of Cloninger's temperament and character dimensions. *Journal of Personality Disorders*, *18*, 379–393.

Ashton, M. C., & Lee, K. (2008). The prediction of honesty-humility-related criteria by the HEXACO and five-factor models of personality. *Journal of Research in Personality*, *42*, 1216–1228.

Bernstein, D. P., Iscan, C., & Maser, J. (2007). Association for Research in Personality Disorders; International Society for the Study of Personality Disorders. Opinions of personality disorder experts regarding the *DSM-IV* personality disorders classification system. *Journal of Personality Disorders*, *21*, 536–551.

Blashfield, R. K. (1984). *The classification of psychopathology: Neo-Kraepelinian and quantitative approaches*. New York: Plenum Press.

Blashfield, R. K. (1998). Diagnostic models and systems. In A. S. Bellack, M. Herson, & Reynolds, C. R. (Eds.), *Clinical psychology: Assessment* (Vol. 4, pp. 57–79). New York: Elsevier Science.

Chiaburu, D. S., Oh, I., Berry, C. M., Li, N., & Gardner, R. G. (2011). The five-factor model of personality traits and organizational citizenship behaviors: A meta-analysis. *Journal of Applied Psychology*, *96*, 1140–1166.

Clark, L. A. (1993). *Schedule for Nonadaptive and Adaptive Personality (SNAP)*. Minneapolis, MN: University of Minnesota Press.

Clark, L. A. (2007). Assessment and diagnosis of personality disorders: Perennial issues and emerging conceptualization. *Annual Review of Psychology*, *58*, 227–258.

Clark, L. A. (2012, March). Trait diagnosis of personality disorder: Domains or facets? Master lecture presented at the 2012 Annual Meeting of the Society for Personality Assessment, Chicago, IL.

Clark, L. A., & Ro, E. (2014). Three-pronged assessment and diagnosis of personality disorder and its consequences: Personality functioning, pathological traits, and psychosocial disability. *Personality Disorder: Theory, Research, & Treatment*, *5*(1), 55–69.

Clark, L. A., Simms, L. J., Wu, K. D., & Casillas, A. (in press). *Manual for the schedule for nonadaptive and adaptive personality (SNAP-2)*. Minneapolis, MN: University of Minnesota Press.

Cloninger, C. R. (2000). A practical way to diagnosis personality disorders: A proposal. *Journal of Personality Disorders*, *14*, 99–108.

Coccaro, E. (2012). Personality disorder–not otherwise specified: Evidence of validity and consideration for DSM-5. *Comprehensive Psychiatry*, *53*, 907–914.

Costa, P. T., & McCrae, R. R. (1990). Personality disorders and the five-factor model of personality. *Journal of Personality Disorders*, *4*, 362–371.

Costa, P. T., & McCrae, R. R. (1992). *Revised NEO Personality Inventory (NEO-PI–R) and NEO Five-Factor Inventory (NEO–FFI) professional manual*. Odessa, FL: Psychological Assessment Resources.

Costa, P. T., & Widiger, T. A. (2001). *Personality disorders and the five-factor model of personality* (2nd ed.). Washington, DC: American Psychological Association.

De Clercq, B., De Fruyt, F., Van Leeuwen, K., & Mervielde, I. (2006). The structure of maladaptive personality traits in childhood: A step toward an integrative developmental perspective for *DSM-5*. *Journal of Abnormal Psychology, 115*, 639–657.

De Fruyt, F., De Clercq, B., Bolle, M., Wille, B., Markon, K., & Krueger, R. F. (2013). General and maladaptive traits in a five-factor framework for *DSM-5* in a university student sample. *Assessment, 20*, 295–307.

De Fruyt, F., Van De Wiele, L., & Van Heeringen, C. (2000). Cloninger's psychobiological model of temperament and character and the five-factor model of personality. *Personality and Individual Differences, 29*, 441–452.

de Vries, R. E., de Vries, A., de Hoogh, A., & Feij, J. (2009). More than the big five: Egoism and the HEXACO model of personality. *European Journal of Personality, 23*, 635–654.

de Vries, R. E., & van Kampen, D. (2010). The HEXACO and 5DPT models of personality: A comparison and their relationships with psychopathy, egoism, pretentiousness, immorality, and Machiavellianism. *Journal of Personality Disorders, 24*, 244–257.

DeYoung, C. G., Grazioplene, R. G., & Peterson, J. B. (2012). From madness to genius: The openness/intellect trait domain as a paradoxical simplex. *Journal of Research in Personality, 46*, 63–78.

Eaton, N. R., Krueger, R. F., South, S. C., Simms, L. J., & Clark, L. A. (2011). Contrasting prototypes and dimensions in the classification of personality pathology: Evidence that dimensions, but not prototypes, are robust. *Psychological Medicine, 41*, 1151–1163.

Eysenck, H. J., & Eysenck, S. B. G. (1975). *Manual of the Eysenck personality questionnaire*. London: Hodder and Stoughton.

Feighner, J. P., Robins, E., Guze, S. B., Woodruff, R. A., Jr., Winokur, G., & Munoz, R. (1972). Diagnostic criteria for use in psychiatric research. *Archives of General Psychiatry, 26*, 57–63.

First, M. B., Bell, C. B., Cuthbert, B., Krystal, J. H., Malison, R., Offord, D. R.,...Wisner, K. L. (2002). Personality disorders and relational disorders: A research agenda for addressing crucial gaps in *DSM*. In D. J. Kupfer, M. B. First, & D. A. Regier (Eds.), *A research agenda for DSM–V* (pp. 123–199). Washington, DC: American Psychiatric Association.

Gaughan, E. T., Miller, J. D., & Lynam, D. R. (2012). Examining the utility of general models of personality in the study of psychopathy: A comparison of the HEXACO-PI-R and NEO PI-R. *Journal of Personality Disorders, 26*, 513–523.

Gore, W. L., & Widiger, T. A. (2013). The DSM-5 dimensional trait model and five-factor models of general personality. *Journal of Abnormal Psychology, 122*(3), 816–821.

Grilo, C. M., Shea, M. T., Sanislow, C. A., Skodol, A. E., Stout, R. L., Gunderson, J.,...McGlashan, T. H. (2004). Two year stability and change in schizotypal, borderline, avoidant, and obsessive-compulsive personality disorders. *Journal of Consulting and Clinical Psychology, 72*, 767–775.

Grove, W. M., & Andreasen, N. (1989). Quantitative and qualitative distinctions between psychiatric disorders. In L. Robins & J. Barett (Eds.), *The validity of psychiatric diagnosis* (pp. 127–141). New York: Raven Press.

Harkness, A. R. (2007). Personality traits are essential for a complete clinical science. In S. O. Lilienfeld & W. T. O'Donohue (Eds.), *The great ideas of clinical science: 17 principles that every mental health professional should understand* (pp. 263–290). New York: Routledge/Taylor & Francis Group.

Harkness, A. R., Finn, J. A., McNulty, J. L., & Shields, S. M. (2012). The Personality Psychopathology—Five (PSY–5): Recent constructive replication and assessment literature review. *Psychological Assessment, 24*, 432–443

Harkness, A. R., & Lilienfeld, S. O. (1997). Individual differences science for treatment planning: Personality traits. *Psychological Assessment, 9*, 349–360.

Harkness, A. R., & McNulty, J. L. (1994). The Personality Psychopathology Five (PSY–5): Issue from the pages of a diagnostic manual instead of a dictionary. In S. Strack & M. Lorr (Eds.), *Differentiating normal and abnormal personality* (pp. 291–315). New York: Springer.

Heath, A. C., Cloninger, C. R., & Martin, N. G. (1994). Testing a model for the genetic structure of personality: A comparison of the personality systems of Cloninger and Eysenck. *Journal of Personality and Social Psychology, 66*, 762–775.

Hettema, J. M., Neale, M. C., Myers, J. M., Prescott, C. A., & Kendler, K. S. (2006). A population-based twin study of the relationship between neuroticism and internalizing disorders. *American Journal of Psychiatry, 163*, 857–864.

Hopwood, C. J., Thomas, K. M., Markon, K. E., Wright, A. G., & Krueger, R. F. (2012).

DSM-5 personality traits and DSM-IV personality disorders. *Journal of Abnormal Psychology*, 121, 424–432.

Hurtz, G. M., & Donovan, J. J. (2000). Personality and job performance: The Big Five revisited. *Journal of Applied Psychology*, 85, 869–879.

Hyler, S. E. (1994). *Personality Diagnostic Questionnaire, 4+*. New York: New York State Psychiatric Institute.

Kamphuis, J. H., & Noordhof, A. (2009). On categorical diagnoses in *DSM-V*: Cutting dimensions at useful points? *Psychological Assessment*, 21, 294–301.

Kendell, R., & Jablensky, A. (2003). Distinguishing between the validity and utility of psychiatric diagnoses. *American Journal of Psychiatry*, 160, 4–12.

Khan, A. A., Jacobson, K. C., Gardner, C. O., Prescott, C. A., & Kendler, K. S. (2005). Personality and comorbidity of common psychiatric disorders. *British Journal of Psychiatry*, 186, 190–96.

Kirk, S. A., & Kutchins, H. (1994). The myth of the reliability of *DSM* [Electronic Version]. *Journal of Mind and Behavior*, 15, 71–86.

Kotov, R., Gamez, W., Schmidt, F., & Watson, D. (2010). Linking "big" personality traits to anxiety, depressive, and substance use disorders: A meta-analysis. *Psychological Bulletin*, 136, 768–821.

Krueger, R. F. (1999). The structure of common mental disorders. *Archives of General Psychiatry*, 56, 921–926.

Krueger, R. F. (2002). Psychometric perspectives on comorbidity. In J. E. Helzer & J. J. Hudziak (Eds.), *Defining psychopathology in the 21st century: DSM-V and beyond* (pp. 41–54). Washington, DC: American Psychiatric Publishing.

Krueger, R. F., Derringer, J., Markon, K. E., Watson, D., & Skodol, A. E. (2012). Initial construction of a maladaptive personality trait model and inventory for *DSM-5*. *Psychological Medicine*, 42, 1879–1890.

Krueger, R. F., & Eaton, N. R. (2010). Personality traits and the classification of mental disorders: Toward a more complete integration in *DSM-5* and an empirical model of psychopathology. *Personality Disorders: Theory, Research, and Treatment*, 1, 97–118.

Krueger, R. F., Eaton, N. R., Clark, L. A., Watson, D., Markon, K. E., Derringer, J., Skodol, A., & Livesley, W. J. (2011). Deriving an empirical structure of personality pathology for *DSM-5*. *Journal of Personality Disorders*, 25, 170–191.

Krueger, R. F., & Markon, K. E. (2006). Reinterpreting comorbidity: A model-based approach to understanding and classifying psychopathology. *Annual Review of Clinical Psychology*, 2, 111–133.

Kupfer, D. J., First, M. B., & Regier, D. A. (Eds.). (2002). *A research agenda for DSM-V*. Washington, DC: American Psychiatric Association.

Lee, K., & Ashton, M. C. (2004). Psychometric properties of the HEXACO personality inventory. *Multivariate Behavioral Research*, 39, 329–358.

Lee, K., & Ashton, M. C. (2005). Psychopathy, Machiavellianism, and narcissism in the five-factor model and the HEXACO model of personality structure. *Personality and Individual Differences*, 38, 1571–1582.

Livesley, W. J. (2001). Conceptual and taxonomic issues. In W. J. Livesley (Ed.), *Handbook of personality disorders: Theory, research, and treatment* (pp. 3–38). New York: Guilford Press.

Livesley, W. J., & Jackson, D. (2010). *Dimensional assessment of personality pathology—Basic questionnaire*. Port Huron, MI: Sigma.

Lodi-Smith, J., & Roberts, B. W. (2007). Social investment and personality: A meta-analysis of the relationship of personality traits to investment in work, family, religion, and volunteerism. *Personality and Social Psychology Review*, 11, 1–19.

Malouff, J. M., Thorsteinsson, E. B., Rooke, S. E., & Schutte, N. S. (2007). Alcohol involvement and the five-factor model of personality: A meta-analysis. *Journal of Drug Education*, 37, 277–294.

Malouff, J. M., Thorsteinsson, E. B., Schutte, N. S., Bhullar, N., & Rooke, S. E. (2010). The five-factor model of personality and relationship satisfaction of intimate partners: A meta-analysis. *Journal of Research in Personality*, 44, 124–127.

Markon, K. E. (2010). Modeling psychopathology structure: A symptom-level analysis of axis I and II disorders. *Psychological Medicine*, 40, 273–288.

Markon, K. E., Krueger, R. F., & Watson, D. (2005). Delineating the structure of normal and abnormal personality: An integrative hierarchical approach. *Journal of Personality and Social Psychology*, 88, 139–157.

Markon, K. E., Quilty, L. C., Bagby, R. M., & Krueger, R. F. (2013). The development and psychometric properties of an informant-report form of the Personality Inventory for DSM-5 (PID-5). *Assessment*, 20(3), 370–383.

McCrae, R. R., & Costa, P. T., Jr. (2008). The five-factor theory of personality. In O. P. John, R. W. Robins, & L. A. Pervin (Eds.),

Handbook of personality: Theory and research (3rd ed.). New York: Guilford Press.

Millon, T. (2003). *Millon index of personality styles.* Minneapolis, MN: Pearson Education.

Millon, T., Millon, C., Davis, R., & Grossman, S. (2009). *MCMI-III manual* (4th ed.). Minneapolis, MN: Pearson Education.

Morey, L. C., Gunderson, J. G., Quigley, B. D., Shea, M. T., Skodol, A. E. . . . & Zanarini, M. (2002). The representation of borderline, avoidant, obsessive-compulsive, and schizotypal personality disorders by the five-factor model. *Journal of Personality Disorders, 16,* 215–234.

Morgan, T. A., & Clark, L. A. (2010). Passive-submissive and active-emotional trait dependency: Evidence for a two-factor model. *Journal of Personality, 78,* 1325–1352.

O'Connor, B. P. (2002). The search for dimensional structure differences between normality and abnormality: A statistical review of published data on personality and psychopathology. *Journal of Personality and Social Psychology, 83,* 962–982.

O'Connor, B. P. (2005). A search for consensus on the dimensional structure of personality disorders. *Journal of Clinical Psychology, 61,* 323–345.

Oh, I., Wang, G., & Mount, M. K. (2011). Validity of observer ratings of the five-factor model of personality traits: A meta-analysis. *Journal of Applied Psychology, 96,* 762–773.

Oldham, J. M., & Skodol, A. E. (2000). Charting the future of axis II. *Journal of Personality Disorders, 14,* 17–29.

Oldham, J. M., Skodol, A. E., Kellman, H. D., Hyler, S. E., Rosnick, L., & Davies, M. (1992). Diagnosis of *DSM-III-R* personality disorders by two structured interviews: Patterns of comorbidity. *American Journal of Psychiatry, 149,* 213–220.

Poropat, A. E. (2009). A meta-analysis of the five-factor model of personality and academic performance. *Psychological Bulletin, 135,* 322–338.

Quilty, L. C., Ayearst, L., Chmielewski, M., Pollock, B. G., & Bagby, R. M. (2013). The psychometric properties of the personality inventory for *DSM-5* in an APA *DSM-5* field trial sample. *Assessment 20*(3), 362–369.

Regier, D. A., Narrow, W. E., Kuhl, E. A., & Kupfer, D. J. (2009). The conceptual development of *DSM-V. American Journal of Psychiatry, 166,* 645–650.

Ro, E., & Clark, L. A. (2013). Interrelation between psychosocial functioning and adaptive- and maladaptive-range personality traits. *Journal of Abnormal Psychology, 122*(3), 822–835.

Roberts, B. W., & Del Vecchio, W. F. (2000). The rank-order consistency of personality traits from childhood to old age: A quantitative review of longitudinal studies. *Psychological Bulletin, 126,* 3–25.

Roberts, B. W., Walton, K. E., & Viechtbauer, W. (2006). Patterns of mean-level change in personality traits across the life course: A meta-analysis of longitudinal studies. *Psychological Bulletin, 132,* 1–25.

Robins, E., & Guze, S. B. (1970). Establishment of diagnostic validity in psychiatric illness: Its application to schizophrenia. *American Journal of Psychiatry, 126,* 983–987.

Rossier, J., Aluja, A., Garca, L. F., Angleitner, A., De Pascalis, V., Wang, W., Kuhlman, M., & Zuckerman, M. (2007). The cross-cultural generalizability of Zuckerman's alternative five-factor model of personality. *Journal of Personality Assessment, 89,* 188–196.

Rounsaville, B. J., Alarcon, R. D., Andrews, G., Jackson, J. S., Kendell, R. E., & Kendler, K. (2002). Basic nomenclature issues for *DSM-V.* In D. J. Kupfer, M. B. First, & D. E. Regier (Eds.), *A research agenda for DSM–V* (pp. 1–29). Washington, DC: American Psychiatric Association.

Ruiz, M. A., Pincus, A. L., & Schinka, J. A. (2008). Externalizing pathology and the five-factor model: A meta-analysis of personality traits associated with antisocial personality disorder, substance use disorder, and their co-occurrence. *Journal of Personality Disorders, 22,* 365–388.

Samuel, D. B., Hopwood, C. J., Ansell, E. B., Morey, L. C., Sanislow, C. A., Markowitz, J. C., ...Grilo, C. M. (2011). Comparing the temporal stability of self-report and interview assessed personality disorder. *Journal of Abnormal Psychology, 120,* 670–680.

Samuel, D. B., Hopwood, C. J., Krueger, R. F., Thomas, K. M., & Ruggero, C. (2013). Comparing methods for scoring personality disorder types using maladaptive traits in *DSM-5. Assessment, 20*(3), 353–361.

Samuel, D. B., Riddell, A. D., Lynam, D. R., Miller, J. D., & Widiger, T. A. (2012). A five-factor measure of obsessive-compulsive personality traits. *Journal of Personality Assessment, 94,* 456–65.

Sanderson, C. J., & Clarkin, J. F. (2002). Further use of the NEO PI-R personality dimensions in differential treatment planning. In P. T. Costa & T. A. Widiger (Eds.), *Personality disorders and the five–factor model of personality* (2nd ed., pp. 351–376). Washington, DC: American Psychological Association.

Sharma, L., Markon, K. E., & Clark, L. A. (2014). Toward a theory of distinct types of "impulsive" behaviors: A meta-analysis of self-report and behavioral measures. *Psychological Bulletin*, 140(2), 374–408.

Shedler, J., & Westen, D. (2004). Refining *DSM–IV* personality disorder diagnosis: Integrating science and practice. *American Journal of Psychiatry*, 161, 1350–1365.

Siever, L. J., & Davis, K. L. (1991). A psychobiological perspective on the personality disorders. *American Journal of Psychiatry*, 148, 1647–1658.

Simms, L. J. (2007). The big seven model of personality and its relevance to personality pathology. *Journal of Personality*, 75, 65–94.

Simms, L. J., Yufik, T., & Gros, D. F. (2010). Incremental validity of positive and negative valence in predicting personality disorder. *Personality Disorders: Theory, Research, and Treatment*, 1, 77–86.

Skodol, A. E., Grilo, C. M., Keyes, K., Geier, T., Grant, B. F., & Hasin, D. S. (2011). Relationship of personality disorders to the course of major depressive disorder in a nationally representative sample. *American Journal of Psychiatry*, 168, 257–264.

Skodol, A. E., Rosnick, L., Kellman, H. D., Oldham, J., & Hyler, S. E. (1988). Validating structures DSM-III-R personality disorder assessments with longitudinal data. *American Journal of Psychiatry*, 145, 1297–1299.

Spitzer, R. L., Endicott, J., & Robins, E. (1987). Research diagnostic criteria: Rationale and reliability. *Archives of General Psychiatry*, 35, 773–782.

Stallings, M. C., Hewitt, J. K., Cloninger, C. R., Heath, A. C., & Eaves, L. J. (1996). Genetic and environmental structure of the Tridimensional Personality Questionnaire: Three or four temperament dimensions? *Journal of Personality and Social Psychology*, 70, 127–140.

Thomas, K. M., Yalch, M. M., Krueger, R. F., Wright, A. G., Markon, K. E., & Hopwood, C. J. (2013). The convergent structure of *DSM-5* personality trait facets and five-factor model trait domains. *Assessment*, 20(3), 308–311.

Tyrer, P. (Ed.). (2000). *Personality disorder: Diagnosis, management, and course* (2nd ed.). London: Arnold.

Tyrer, P. (2009). Why borderline personality disorder is neither borderline nor a personality disorder. *Personality and Mental Health*, 3(2), 86–95.

Tyrer, P., & Alexander, J. (1979). Classification of personality disorder. *British Journal of Psychiatry*, 135, 163–167.

Tyrer, P., & Johnson, T. (1996). Establishing the severity of personality disorder. *American Journal of Psychiatry*, 153, 1593–1597.

van Kampen, D. (2006). The Dutch DAPP-BQ: Improvements, lower- and higher-order dimensions, and relationship with the 5DPT. *Journal of Personality Disorders*, 20, 81–101.

van Kampen, D. (2009). Personality and psychopathology: A theory-based revision of Eysenck's PEN model. *Clinical Practice and Epidemiology in Mental Health*, 5, 9–21.

van Kampen, D. (2012). The 5-dimensional personality test (5DPT): Relationships with two lexically based instruments and the validation of the absorption scale. *Journal of Personality Assessment*, 94, 92–101.

Verheul, R. (2005). Clinical utility for dimensional models for personality pathology. *Journal of Personality Disorders*, 19, 283–302.

Verhuel, R., & Widiger, T. A. (2007). Prevalence and construct validity of personality disorder not otherwise specified (PDNOS). *Journal of Personality Disorders*, 21(4), 359–370.

Watson, D., Clark, L. A., & Chmielewski, M. (2008). Structures of personality and their relevance to psychopathology: II. Further articulation of a comprehensive unified trait structure. *Journal of Personality*, 76(6), 1485–1522.

Watson, D., Stasik, S., Ro, E., & Clark, L. A. (2013). Integrating normal and pathological personality: Relating the *DSM-5* trait dimensional model to general traits of personality. *Assessment*, 20(3), 312–326.

Weiss, L. G. (1997). The MIPS: Gauging the dimensions of normality. In *The Millon inventories: Clinical and personality assessment* (pp. 498–522). New York: Guilford Press.

Westen, D., & Shedler, J. (1999a). Revising and assessing axis II, part I: Developing a clinically and empirically valid assessment method. *American Journal of Psychiatry*, 156(2), 258–272.

Westen, D., & Shedler, J. (1999b). Revising and assessing axis II, part II: Toward an empirically based and clinically useful classification of personality disorders. *American Journal of Psychiatry*, 156(2), 273–285.

Westen, D., & Shedler, J. (2000). A prototype matching approach to diagnosing personality disorders: Toward *DSM-V*. *Journal of Personality Disorders*, 14, 109–126.

Widiger, T. A., & Simonsen, E. (2005). Alternative dimensional models of personality disorder: Finding a common ground. *Journal of Personality Disorders*, 19, 110–130.

Widiger, T. A., Simonsen, E., Krueger, R., Livesley, J. W., & Verheul, R. (2005). Personality disorder research agenda for the *DSM-V*. *Journal of Personality Disorders, 19,* 315–338.

Widiger, T. A., & Trull, T. J. (2007). Plate tectonics in the classification of personality disorder: Shifting to a dimensional model. *American Psychologist, 62,* 71–83.

Wiggins, J., & Pincus, A. (1989). Conceptions of personality disorders and dimensions of personality. *Psychological Assessment, 1,* 305–316.

Zanarini, M., Frankenburg, F., Chauncey, D., & Gunderson, J. (1987). The Diagnostic Interview for Personality Disorders: Interrater and test-retest reliability. *Comprehensive Psychiatry, 28,* 467–480.

Zimmerman M., & Coryell W. H. (1990). *DSM-III* personality disorder dimensions. *Journal of Nervous and Mental Disease, 178,* 686–692.

Zuckerman, M. (2002). Zuckerman–Kuhlman Personality Questionnaire (ZKPQ): An alternative five–factorial model. In B. de Raad & M. Perugini (Eds.), *Big five assessment* (pp. 377–397). Kirkland, WA: Hogrefe & Huber.

Zuckerman, M., Kuhlman, D. M., Joireman, J., Teta, P., & Kraft, M. (1993). A comparison of three structural models for personality: The big three, the big five, and the alternative five. *Journal of Personality and Social Psychology, 65,* 757–768.

24

Schizoid and Avoidant Personality Disorders

DAVID P. BERNSTEIN,

ARNOUD ARNTZ,

AND LAURA TRAVAGLINI

Clinicians frequently fail to distinguish schizoid and avoidant personality disorders because these disorders are behaviorally similar diagnostic entities characterized by interpersonal detachment. Both types of personalities may appear socially isolated; such individuals have few or no close friendships, engage primarily in solitary and not social activities, and remain aloof or inhibited in social situations. Schizoids typically appear emotionally bland and unresponsive and often seem insensitive to the nuances of social interactions. Avoidants experience social interactions as aversive owing to their own propensity for self-criticism and may appear self-conscious in social situations.

A central distinction between these disorders lies in their motivation or capacity for attachment: Schizoid individuals lack the desire or ability to form social relationships, whereas avoidant individuals desire interpersonal contact but avoid it out of feelings of inferiority and an intense fear of rejection and humiliation. Millon (1981) described this difference as one of passive (schizoid) versus active (avoidant) detachment. The distinction between the schizoid's passive disinterest in interpersonal relationships and the avoidant's active avoidance of them is of central importance, for practical and theoretical reasons, because the differential diagnosis between the two disorders hinges on this distinction, as does the discriminant validity of the disorders themselves.

In fact, the classification of schizoid and avoidant personality disorders as separate diagnostic entities is a relatively recent development and remains the subject of much debate. The diagnostic label *schizoid personality*, introduced by Bleuler (1924), has a long history in the clinical and theoretical literature and has traditionally been used to describe individuals who are not psychotic yet exhibit interpersonal and emotional deficits such as social withdrawal, passivity and aimlessness, and flattened affect or anhedonia. Thus schizoids were seen as being schizophrenic in its attenuated form. The term *avoidant personality* was coined by Millon (1981) and was introduced into the *DSM-III* as part of its multiaxial reorganization, with a separate axis for personality disorders. Nevertheless, the *DSM-III* criteria for avoidant personality disorder were also based on an older clinical and theoretical literature that described individuals who were hypersensitive to rejection and highly self-critical, and simultaneously wished for closeness with others and were aversive to it (Fenichel, 1945; Kretschmer, 1925; MacKinnon & Michels, 1971; Rado, 1956). These individuals were sometimes labeled "schizoid," but were also referred to by a number of other diagnostic terms, such as the "phobic character" (Fenichel, 1945; Rado, 1956; MacKinnon & Michels, 1971).

The decision to include separate diagnostic categories in the *DSM-III* for schizoid and avoidant personality disorders has been criticized on a number of grounds. For example, several authors have noted that traditional descriptions of schizoid character often include the apparently contradictory qualities of superficial insensitivity and aloofness on the one hand, and underlying hypersensitivity on the other (Akhtar, 1987; Livesley & West, 1986). Kretschmer (1925) referred to these two poles of the schizoid character as "anesthetic" and "hyperaesthetic," respectively, a classification that informed the distinction between schizoid and avoidant personality disorders in the *DSM-III*. Nevertheless, the presence of these seemingly contradictory traits in the same individuals has raised questions about the justification for considering schizoid and avoidant personality disorders as truly separate diagnostic groups. An alternative conceptualization would be that of a spectrum of individuals who are socially isolated who vary in their capacity for attachment to others and underlying emotional sensitivity.

Similar questions have been raised about the diagnostic boundaries between schizoid and avoidant personality disorders and other psychiatric diagnoses. For example, the *DSM-III* introduced a new diagnostic category, schizotypal personality disorder, which shared many phenomenological features with the schizoid diagnosis. Although the *DSM-III* was ostensibly an atheoretical document, based on descriptive features rather than a theory of etiology, the raison d'être of schizotypal personality disorder was its presumed genetic relationship to schizophrenia. The classic Danish adoption studies (Kety, Rosenthal, Wender, & Schulsinger, 1971) found that relatives of individuals with schizophrenia often exhibited symptoms that were reminiscent of schizophrenia, such as peculiar ideas and odd, inappropriate affect, but without the frank breaks with reality that were seen in schizophrenia. In the older clinical descriptive literature, these individuals were often labeled "borderline," "latent schizophrenic," or "ambulatory schizophrenic" (Stone, 1980); in the *DSM-III*, the term *schizotypal* was adopted to denote individuals with a phenotypic resemblance to individuals with schizophrenia, presumably based on a shared underlying genotype (Meehl, 1990; Spitzer, Endicott, & Givvon, 1979). The *DSM* diagnostic criteria for schizoid and schizotypal individuals thus shared interpersonal and affective features, notably social isolation and odd or inappropriate affect, similar to the "negative"

(i.e., deficit) symptoms of schizophrenia. Although schizotypal individuals were presumed to exhibit psychotic-like disturbances of cognition and perception ("positive symptoms"), in practice, many individuals met criteria for both disorders, raising further questions about their independence (Kalus, Bernstein, & Siever, 1993). After the adoption of the *DSM-III*, many individuals who were formerly labeled "schizoid" were now classified as "schizotypal." In fact, it has been argued that most of the nosological "territory" formerly occupied by schizoid personality disorder has been claimed by the avoidant and schizotypal personality disorders, leaving a restricted version of the schizoid that applies to relatively few individuals. The very low prevalence of schizoid personality disorder in some studies (Kalus et al., 1993) has caused some to wonder whether schizoid personality disorder, in its present form, has been gerrymandered almost out of existence (Bernstein, 2005).

Similar concerns have been raised about the diagnostic boundaries between avoidant and dependent personality disorder. Dependent personality disorder is characterized by interpersonal submission, neediness, and fears of separation. Although superficially dissimilar from avoidant personality disorder—the individual who is avoidant shuns interpersonal intimacy, whereas the individual who is dependent seeks it—both share an underlying low self-esteem and lack of self-assertion (Reich, 1990; Trull, Widiger, & Frances, 1987). Moreover, as noted earlier, the individual who is avoidant may actually crave interpersonal contact but avoid it owing to fears of rejection. Thus, both avoidant and dependent traits may be present in the same individuals.

Likewise, avoidant personality disorder resembles social phobia, a condition marked by intense fear or avoidance of specific social or performance situations—for example, speaking in public (Herbert, Hope, & Bellack, 1992; Turner, Beidel, Dancee, & Keys, 1986). Although avoidant personality disorder reflects a pervasive avoidance of interpersonal interactions, owing to fear of criticism or rejection, social phobia represents a more circumscribed form of impairment. In clinical practice, however, this distinction often becomes blurred because many individuals who are avoidant also have specific social anxieties. Moreover, research has shown that discrete social phobias are less common than anxieties across a range of social or performance situations (Turner et al., 1986). As a result, *DSM-III-R* adopted a generalized subtype of social phobia, leading to a further blurring of the boundaries with avoidant personality.

In this chapter, we discuss the clinical presentation of schizoid and avoidant personality disorders, highlighting some of the diagnostic complexities that arise in differentiating these disorders from each other and from other related syndromes. A case history illustrating many of these diagnostic issues is presented. We then examine the epidemiology of schizoid and avoidant personality disorders and weigh the empirical evidence on the issue of their discriminant validity. Finally, we review the historical and contemporary theoretical literature on these disorders and evaluate the empirical status of various hypotheses concerning their etiology, development, and treatment.

Clinical Description

Schizoid individuals typically appear passive and detached, as if they were drifting aimlessly through life. They are emotionally bland, cold, unempathic, or unreactive, and seem insensitive to the nuances of social interaction, including praise and criticism. They are frequently experienced by others as dull or boring and are almost always socially isolated—not from social anxiety and an active avoidance of social situations but from an incapacity for meaningful social engagement. In fact, the incapacity for social relatedness can be considered the cardinal feature of the disorder (Millon, 1981). Closely connected with the lack of affective investment in social relationships is an inability to take pleasure in activities of either a social or a physical nature. Typically pleasurable activities such taking a walk on a beach, listening to a concert, going dancing, and playing sports are usually found wanting. Sex is seen as overrated. Activities that are pursued are usually solitary, involving interactions with inanimate objects rather than people. Occupations, such as computer programming or mail sorting, which involve a minimum of meaningful social interaction, are preferred. The world is experienced in shades of gray rather than in color.

In contrast to the schizoid's insensitivity to social and aesthetic surroundings, the avoidant can be considered overly sensitive, being acutely and painfully self-conscious in social situations, anticipating rejection and humiliation at every turn.

Even casual conversations can be excruciating experiences, as the seemingly innocuous remarks of others are scrutinized for hints of criticism or disapproval, and one's own interpersonal conduct is dissected for the embarrassing faux pas. In brief, avoidants are their own worst critics, constantly coming up short in their own estimation. As a result, they are usually diffident and inhibited in social situations or find them so aversive that they avoid them altogether. Occasionally, patients with avoidant personality disorder succeed in forming friendships, but this is usually only after they feel certain that potential friends are unlikely to criticize or reject them. Even in close friendships, these individuals are often reluctant to take risks or make intimate disclosures, for fear of embarrassment or betrayal.

As noted earlier, the differential diagnosis between schizoid and avoidant personality disorders can be difficult. Both are superficially socially inhibited or isolated. Accordingly, the distinction between them hinges on the incapacity for meaningful social relationships in the schizoid, and the desire for and conflict over them in the avoidant. In contrast to schizoids, avoidants are often distressed by their social isolation. They desire connections with others, and their inability to achieve this may leave them lonely and depressed. Some authors have observed that the superficial indifference to social relationships of the individual who is avoidant often masks a profound and intense wish for closeness (Fairbairn, 1952; Guntrip, 1969; Winnicott, 1991). Distinguishing between schizoid and avoidant personality disorders thus depends on an inference about the patient's subjective experience of interpersonal interactions.

In the initial diagnostic interview, this distinction may become clear if the patient acknowledges regret over social isolation or a propensity for self-criticism in social situations. Unfortunately, the awkwardness and inhibition of avoidants often make it difficult to obtain accurate information, particularly before the clinician has had the chance to build rapport. Moreover, the avoidant can be secretive during the interview to avoid feeling shameful. Conversations with relatives and friends may prove helpful if such informants are available. To further complicate matters, it has been noted that the clinical presentation of schizoid and avoidant patients may change over time. Livesley and West (1986) reported the case of a patient given an initial diagnosis of schizoid personality disorder who, over the course of treatment, began to exhibit more prominent avoidant features. Thus, extended observation sometimes may be required to clarify an otherwise confusing diagnostic picture.

These diagnostic issues are illustrated by the case of Mr. L., a patient who was seen by one of the authors (D.P.B.) in once-a-week group psychotherapy for approximately 3 years. Mr. L., a 45-year-old White, unemployed transit worker, presented for treatment of chronic alcohol addiction. At initial evaluation, he reported drinking steadily since age 15, interrupted only by military duty. Although he had worked for many years as a toll booth operator, he had recently lost his job and pension benefits owing to alcohol-related tardiness and absences, the precipitant for his seeking treatment. Mr. L. had never married. Instead, he lived with his mother and spent most of his free time alone in his room engaged in solitary hobbies such as stamp and coin collecting. Mr. L. reported having no close friends. Even as a child, he preferred to keep to himself because "people are a bother; I would rather be by myself." He denied that feelings of persecution were the basis for his isolation. Although he described a few brief sexual encounters, they ended as soon as they began to get serious, and he claimed they were not missed. Although sometimes annoyed by his mother's complaints and habits, he rarely expressed these feelings to her personally. In fact, he claimed to rarely experience intense feelings of any kind, either positive or negative. When questioned by the examiner, he was unable to think of any recreational activity or intellectual pursuit that got him excited. Mr. L. was passive and compliant throughout the interview, displaying an overly deferential attitude. He claimed no specific plans for the future, other than to achieve sobriety and eventually find a new job.

On the basis of this initial presentation, Mr. L. was given a diagnosis of schizoid personality disorder. He was socially isolated, lacked close friends or confidants (*DSM-IV*, Criterion 5), and preferred to keep to himself (Criterion 1). He seemed to have little interest in sexual experiences (Criterion 3). Most of his activities were solitary ones (Criterion 2) from which he derived little pleasure (Criterion 4). Mr. L. showed little emotional reactivity and claimed not to experience intense feelings (Criterion 7). Mr. L.'s social isolation appeared to reflect a fundamental lack of emotional investment in others, not paranoid ideation or anxiety about others' negative judgments. These disorders were thus ruled out. Although he exhibited a few of the negative or deficit schizotypal symptoms, such as constricted affect (Criterion 6) and lack of friends or confidants (Criterion 8), he did not display the more positive, psychotic-like, schizotypal features such as perceptual illusions, self-referential ideas, or odd beliefs. Therefore, schizotypal personality disorder also was ruled out. Although Mr. L.'s bland, passive, and constricted demeanor might be mistaken for dysthymia, his mood was better described as flat than as depressed. Moreover, he did not report associated dysthymic features such as appetite or sleep disturbance, poor concentration, or feelings of hopelessness. Nor did he report specific social phobias. In sum, he exhibited the passive, aimless, and disinterested approach to life characteristic of schizoid personality disorder.

Although a schizoid diagnosis seems appropriate for Mr. L., it also must be considered in relation to his chronic alcoholism. Untreated alcoholism usually exhibits a downward, deteriorating course. This can result in schizoid-like characteristics, including increasing abandonment of formerly important social, occupational, or recreational activities. For Mr. L., however, social isolation began in childhood, preceding the onset of drinking. Nor was alcoholism an attempt to overcome social inhibitions and become more comfortable in social situations, as is sometimes seen in individuals who are avoidant. Mr. L. usually drank alone. Social isolation was, therefore, a longstanding personality feature, not a consequence of a progressive deterioration in social functioning due to drinking.

During his first 2 years in treatment, Mr. L. attended daily therapy groups focused on maintaining sobriety and succeeded in abstaining from alcohol use. He was rarely an active participant in group, however, and formed no new friendships with other patients. Although he was in regular contact with treatment staff, almost nothing was known about his personal life or history. He was a benign, if innocuous presence, the kind of person who "faded into the woodwork." At the recommendation of his individual counselor, Mr. L. was invited to join a once-a-week process-oriented psychotherapy group led by one of the authors. This group was smaller and less structured than the other groups that Mr. L. had attended, and focused on interpersonal relationships, including interactions among the group members themselves.

643   Schizoid and Avoidant Personality Disorders

Over the next year, Mr. L. slowly began to disclose significant aspects of his personal history. His father had been an alcoholic who had died of liver disease. He remembered his father as a man who was prone to becoming verbally abusive when drunk but for the most part led a solitary existence, preferring to watch television alone in his bedroom than to be with his family. His mother was an ever-suffering woman, the "family martyr" who used guilt to control her children. Mr. L. suffered an extraordinary degree of social inhibition and self-contempt, describing himself as extremely uncomfortable and self-critical in social situations. He frequently censored himself for fear of appearing foolish. Although objectively pleasant looking, he was ashamed of his appearance and often admonished himself to dress more neatly. Hours were spent chastising himself for past failures, such as losing his transit job. He was convinced that his life would never amount to anything. Nevertheless, Mr. L. had also become more aware of own isolation and began to contemplate the possibility of forming friendships. However, when other members of the group invited him out for coffee or a movie, he always found reasons to decline.

A turning point in Mr. L.'s treatment occurred when his mother died after a brief illness. As her health deteriorated, he increasingly was called to care for her, becoming more and more exasperated by her rigid and controlling behavior. After being repeatedly confronted by the group, he finally admitted feeling angry toward her. This came almost as a revelation, his first recognition of any strong emotion. Shortly thereafter he talked about the absence of pleasure in his life, and the fact that absolutely nothing gave him enjoyment. When his mother finally died, he was unable to cry at her funeral. His incipient access to feelings was replaced by an emotional numbing. About a month after his mother's death, however, he came to a new realization: His mother was a mystery to him. Though he had lived with her nearly every day of his entire life, he knew almost nothing about her. He was thus free to begin the process of mourning and was able to experience sadness for the first time. His mother's death eventually provided an impetus for greater self-sufficiency. He formed a social relationship with several members of the group. These new friends described him as "a good listener" who rarely revealed much about himself. He now took pride in keeping his refrigerator stocked with food and took pleasure in his regular Sunday morning routine of coffee and the newspaper. With some trepidation he enrolled in a computer course and, despite some feelings of inadequacy, pursued it to completion. He also appeared to have gained a greater measure of self-acceptance, stating that perhaps he "wasn't so bad" after all.

Five years after his initial diagnosis of schizoid personality disorder, Mr. L. now appeared to meet many of the *DSM-IV* criteria for avoidant personality disorder. He felt unattractive to others (Criterion 6) and was tormented by self-criticism (Criterion 4). His feelings of inadequacy resulted in marked inhibition in social situations (Criterion 5). He was only willing to form friendships (for example, with the other group members) after being certain of approval (Criterion 2), but even then showed an undue degree of restraint in interpersonal relationships (Criterion 3). He typically avoided any new activities that carried the possibility of embarrassment or criticism (Criterion 1), and only embarked on such activities (e.g., the computer programming course) after overcoming considerable personal reluctance (Criterion 7).

Along with these avoidant features, Mr. L. continued to display many of the traits of schizoid personality disorder, though in somewhat attenuated form. For example, although his demeanor had become more animated—he was now capable of making occasional jokes—he was still emotionally flat and reported difficulties in identifying and expressing feelings. Similarly, his range of pleasurable activities, though increased, was still limited, with a need for solitude far in excess of the average person. Thus, Mr. L.'s clinical presentation now comprised a mixture of schizoid and avoidant personality features.

Interestingly, Mr. L.'s history also illustrated many of the risk factors theorized to contribute to the development of the schizoid and avoidant personalities. His father exhibited a marked tendency toward social avoidance and emotional aloofness, which raised the possibility that these schizoid traits were intergenerationally transmitted, through either hereditary or environmental mechanisms—a leading etiological hypothesis since the inception of the schizoid concept. The emotional distance within his family—a father who was grossly uncommunicative, a mother who was more subtly unavailable—is consistent with psychoanalytic theory on the role of emotional deprivation in the development of schizoid personality disorder. The rigid, controlling behavior displayed by his mother is consistent with recent speculation that parental overprotection—that is, excessive control combined with low parental warmth—contributes to the development of avoidant personality disorder. Finally, the verbally abusive behavior of his father is consistent with theory and research suggesting that emotional denigration contributes to low self-esteem, a cardinal feature of avoidant personality disorder. Thus, Mr. L.'s history largely converges with the major hypotheses about the etiology of schizoid and avoidant personality disorders.

The case of Mr. L. also illustrates the point that, although schizoid and avoidant individuals may be initially difficult to engage in treatment, group psychotherapy can be a powerful means of effecting change in these patients, by providing corrective feedback regarding their detached interpersonal styles and an opportunity to form attachments in a relatively safe environment. Of course, the schizoid or avoidant person's ability to make use of these experiences will depend on his or her latent capacity for interpersonal closeness and connectedness, which varies greatly across these individuals and may not be immediately apparent.

Prevalence

Although schizoid personality disorder is reputed to be a comparatively rare diagnosis, epidemiological data challenge this assumption. In a large, general population survey in Britain (Coid, Yang, Tyrer, Roberts, & Ullrich, 2006), the prevalence of *DSM-IV* schizoid personality was 0.8%—a prevalence that was comparable to that of several of the other *DSM-IV* personality disorders, including antisocial and borderline personality disorders, which are usually thought to be more common than schizoid personality disorder. An earlier epidemiological survey also using *DSM-IV* criteria (Samuels et al., 2002) found an almost identical prevalence for schizoid personality disorder, of 0.9%. Thus, schizoid personality disorder appears to be more prevalent in the general population than is typically believed. On the other hand, schizoid personality disorder appears to be one of the less frequently seen disorders in clinical populations. For example, in a large, representative study of psychiatric outpatients (Zimmerman, Rothschild, & Chelminski,

2005), schizoid personality disorder was one of the least frequently given *DSM-IV* personality disorder diagnoses, with a prevalence of 1.4%. Thus, the reputation of schizoid personality disorder as a rare diagnosis may stem from its relative infrequency in clinical settings.

However, schizoid personality disorder traits may be more common in forensic populations, for example, in prisons and forensic hospitals, where they may be comorbid with antisocial personality disorder and psychopathy. In one study, for example, psychopathy in prisoners in England and Wales was associated with higher levels of schizoid traits, along with traits of antisocial, narcissistic, and histrionic personality disorders (Coid et al., 2009). Thus, schizoid traits may be associated with the emotional callousness and detachment often seen in psychopathic and other criminal offenders.

The general population prevalence of avoidant personality disorder appears to be comparable to that of schizoid personality disorder, or perhaps higher. In the epidemiological surveys of Coid et al. (2006) and Samuels et al. (2002), the population prevalence of *DSM-IV* avoidant personality disorder was 0.8% and 1.8%, respectively. In a nationally representative mental health survey of over 43,000 adults in the United States, the lifetime prevalence of avoidant personality disorder was 2.4% (Cox, Pagura, Stein, & Sareen, 2009).

In contrast to schizoid personality disorder, however, avoidant personality disorder is typically one of the most prevalent personality disorders in clinical samples. For example, Zimmerman and colleagues (2005) found that avoidant personality disorder was the most common *DSM-IV* personality disorder in their representative sample of psychiatric outpatients, with a prevalence of 14.7%. Comparable findings were reported in earlier studies based on *DSM-III* or *DSM-III-R* criteria, which found low prevalences of schizoid personality disorder and high prevalences of avoidant personality disorder in clinical samples (Kalus et al., 1993; Millon & Martinez, 1991). Thus, individuals with avoidant personality disorder appear to seek treatment far more frequently than those with schizoid personality disorder—a difference that lends credibility to the notion that individuals with avoidant personality disorder are more disturbed by their interpersonal isolation and suffer more as a result of it. As a result, avoidant individuals may more often seek treatment, whereas schizoid individuals more often eschew it.

There appears to be no significant gender difference in the population prevalence of *DSM-IV* schizoid personality disorder (e.g., Coid et al., 2006), though some earlier studies reported that schizoid personality disorder is more common in males (Kass, Spitzer, & Williams, 1983). Avoidant personality disorder appears to be more prevalent in females (Cox et al., 2009; Zimmerman & Coryell, 1989). In the nationally representative survey cited earlier (Cox et al., 2009), significantly more females than males were diagnosed with lifetime avoidant personality disorder. The size of this gender difference was equivalent when considering avoidant personality disorder without comorbid generalized social phobia (62.1% versus 37.9%) and with comorbid generalized social phobia (59.4% versus 40.6%). Thus, the preponderance of avoidant personality disorder in females does not appear to be merely attributable to the greater prevalence of social phobia in women.

Diagnostic Comorbidity

An empirical review of studies using *DSM-III* or *DSM-III-R* criteria concluded that, despite considerable variation in rates of comorbidity across studies, schizoid frequently is associated with avoidant and schizotypal personality disorders (Kalus et al., 1993). A median of 53% of individuals who are avoidants also received a schizoid diagnosis, while 38% of schizotypals were also diagnosed as schizoid. Lesser degrees of comorbidity were shown with paranoid, antisocial, borderline, and passive–aggressive personality disorders. Avoidant personality disorder also overlapped extensively with dependent personality disorder (Reich, 1990; Trull et al., 1987). In one study of psychiatric inpatients, 71% of avoidants received a diagnosis of dependent personality, whereas 50% of dependents also received an avoidant diagnosis (Trull et al., 1987).

Not surprisingly, the high degree of diagnostic overlap between schizoid and avoidant personality disorders in studies using *DSM-III* or *DSM-III-R* criteria raised questions about their status as discrete disorders. Some authors raised the same issue on theoretical grounds, noting that the historical literature contains descriptions of "schizoid" individuals whose superficial indifference to social relations masks an underlying interpersonal hypersensitivity (Livesley & West, 1986).

The comorbidity between avoidant and schizoid personality disorders seems to have been reduced considerably with the introduction of the *DSM-IV*. A recent study in a large, mixed sample of patients and nonpatients ($N > 1700$) assessed with the Structured Clinical Interview for *DSM-IV-TR* Axis II Personality Disorders (SCID-II) interview found only 1.5% of avoidants receiving a diagnosis of schizoid personality disorder, but still 31% of the schizoid patients having avoidant personality disorder (Arntz, Broese, & Bernstein, 2013). Viewing personality disorders as dimensional constructs, a factor analysis gave good support for the independence of avoidant and schizoid factors, with a modest interfactor correlation of .30. Avoidant and dependent personality disorders were less independent, with an interfactor correlation of .66. Fifteen percent of the patients who were avoidant also had dependent personality disorder, and a remarkable 71% of the patients who were dependent had comorbid avoidant personality disorder. The overlap between schizoid and schizotypal personality disorder was also considerable, with an interfactor correlation of .75. Nineteen percent of the schizoid patients had a comorbid schizotypal personality disorder, and 33% of the schizotypal patients had a schizoid personality disorder (Arntz et al., 2013. In a much smaller sample, Fossati and colleagues (2000) found very similar associations. Thus, the change in criteria with the *DSM-IV* seems to have reduced overlap between avoidant and schizoid personality disorders, but there are still problems in the differentiation between avoidant and dependent personality disorders, and between schizoid and schizotypal personality disorders.

Schizoid and avoidant personality disorders also show comorbidity with several other disorders (Alnaes & Torgersen, 1988). The diagnostic comorbidity between avoidant personality disorder and social phobia is especially high, ranging from 21% to 89% (Ralevski et al., 2005), leading some authors to conclude that the *DSM-IV* avoidant personality disorder and social phobia criteria describe the same group of patients, rather than separate diagnostic groups (Ralevski et al., 2005).

Millon and Martinez (1991) contend that the distinction between avoidant personality disorder and social phobia is that "avoidant personality disorder is essentially a problem of relating to persons, whereas social phobia is largely a problem of performing in situations" (p. 222). In other words, the individual who is avoidant has a limited range of interpersonal contacts, owing to fear of social disapprobation; the individual who has social phobia may have normal friendships but has specific fears of performing in social settings—for example, speaking or eating in public. Although this distinction appears to be a theoretically meaningful one, the empirical overlap between the disorders has increased through successive editions of the *DSM* (Alden, Laposa, Taylor, & Ryder, 2002).

The introduction of the generalized social phobia subtype—which involves performance fears across a variety of situations—in the *DSM-III-R* blurred the distinction between avoidant personality disorder and social phobia, and increased the degree of comorbidity between them (Alden et al., 2002). In an attempt to resolve this confusion, the *DSM-IV* Committee on Personality Disorders modified the only avoidant personality disorder criterion that dealt with avoidance of nonsocial situations: *DSM-III-R* Criterion 7, "exaggerates the potential difficulties, physical dangers, or risks involved in doing something ordinary but outside his or her usual routine." In the *DSM-IV*, this criterion was rewritten to state that the exaggerated estimation of difficulties or risks of the patient with avoidant personality disorder was due to fears of embarrassment. This change was intended to focus the avoidant personality disorder criteria exclusively on avoidance due to social fears, as opposed to the performance-based fears that were emphasized by the social phobia diagnosis. Instead, this change appears to have only increased the comorbidity between the avoidant personality disorder and social phobia (Alden et al., 2002).

There is increasing evidence that the distinction between avoidant personality and generalized social phobia may be one of degree rather than kind, with avoidant personality disorder representing a more severe variant of generalized social phobia. Several studies have found that patients with generalized social phobia and comorbid avoidant personality disorder show more severe anxiety or depression, greater impairment, receive more frequent comorbid diagnoses, and have worse longitudinal outcomes than patients with social phobia alone (Cox et al., 2009; Cox, Turnbull, Robinson, Grant, & Stein, 2011; Feske, Perry, Chambless, Renneberg, & Goldstein, 1996; Herbert et al., 1992; Tran & Chambless, 1995; van Velzen, Emmelkamp, & Scholing, 2000). Moreover, a study of 1,427 female twin pairs

found that avoidant personality disorder and social phobia shared a substantial genetic component, while unique (i.e., unshared) environmental factors contributed separately to each disorder's etiology (Reichborn-Kjennerud et al., 2007). Thus, avoidant personality disorder and generalized social phobia may lie on a genetic spectrum with each other, with patients having both disorders representing a more severe subtype (Reichborn-Kjennerud et al., 2007). These findings have led to the recommendation that the avoidant personality disorder diagnosis be classified as a variant of social phobia.

A few studies, however, have failed to find differences between patients with social phobia with and without avoidant personality disorder (Boone et al., 1999; Brown, Heimberg, & Juster, 1995; Ralevski et al., 2005). Moreover, Arntz (1999) noted that nearly all studies of the comorbidity between avoidant personality disorder and social phobia have examined subgroups of patients selected for the presence of social phobia, rather than a broader range of patients including, for example, patients selected for avoidant personality disorder with and without comorbid social phobia (but see Ralevski et al., 2005, for an exception). When they included patients with different disorders, the overlap between generalized social phobia and avoidant personality disorder reduced considerably (Arntz, 1999; Jansen, Arntz, Merckelbach, & Mersch, 1994). In support of this view, only 36.4% of individuals with generalized social phobia were also diagnosed with comorbid avoidant personality disorder in a large, general population survey (Cox et al., 2009), which suggests that higher rates of overlap in some studies may be attributable to their exclusive use of patients with social phobia. On the other hand, in the same general population survey, rates of overlap were related to the extensiveness of social fears in the individuals with generalized social phobia (Cox et al., 2009). Among those individuals who reported the minimum number of feared social situations (i.e., seven) required for a diagnosis of generalized social phobia, only 16.1% were also diagnosed with avoidant personality disorder. However, among those reporting the maximum number of feared social situations (i.e., 13), the overlap with avoidant personality disorder was 57.3%. Thus, the number of feared social situations in generalized social phobia increases the likelihood of comorbid avoidant personality disorder. Studies have also found an association between depression and avoidant personality disorder, further questioning the claim that avoidant personality disorder is just an extreme position on a dimension of social anxiety (Alnaes & Torgersen, 1997). Whether avoidant personality disorder is merely a more severe variant of social phobia remains, therefore, a controversial but still unanswered question.

The degree of impairment in patients with avoidant personality disorder may be substantial. A study of 1,023 patients admitted to day treatment programs for personality disorders found that diagnoses of avoidant personality disorder and borderline personality disorder contributed most to dysfunction in this population (Wilberg, Karterud, Pedersen, & Urnes, 2009). Avoidant personality disorder was associated with lower levels of education, social support, and quality of life and with high degrees of interpersonal problems and psychiatric symptoms. This degree of impairment was comparable to that of borderline personality disorder, though the nature of the impairment in the two disorders was domain specific: patients with avoidant personality disorder were more socially isolated and had educational problems and poor quality of life, whereas those with borderline personality disorder had more legal problems, psychotic episodes, and hospitalizations (Wilberg et al., 2009). This study suggests that the impairment of patients with avoidant personality disorder is often underestimated, and that there is a subgroup of severely impaired patients who may require intensive treatment.

Arntz (1999) and Alden and colleagues (2002) have noted that historical descriptions of patients who are avoidant include the presence of social and nonsocial avoidance—thus, a more general avoidant syndrome. In addition to avoiding social situations where they fear rejection, these patients may also avoid situations involving novelty, risk, and strong emotions (positive and negative), including situations that are nonsocial in nature. For example, individuals with avoidant personality disorder may avoid going to an amusement park, traveling to new places, seeing a film about an emotional theme, or taking on new challenges. Instead, they prefer to stick to the routine, predictable, and familiar. In fact, these aspects of nonsocial avoidance were present in the original descriptions of avoidant personality disorder formulated by Millon (1981). Research by Alden and colleagues (Taylor, Laposa, & Alden, 2004) supports the notion that individuals who are avoidant (patients and nonpatients) avoid emotional and novel situations, including nonsocial situations. These authors (Taylor et al., 2004) contend that the *DSM-IV*'s narrow focus on the social aspects of avoidant personality disorder has decreased the validity of the diagnosis, while artificially increasing its comorbidity with social phobia. Whether a reformulated criteria set for avoidant personality disorder, including social and nonsocial avoidance, would increase the discriminant validity of this diagnosis with social phobia remains to be seen.

Historical Perspectives

The earliest descriptions of schizoid personality disorder can be traced to the European phenomenological psychiatrist Eugene Bleuler. Bleuler (1924) observed that schizoid and schizophrenic individuals shared an indifference to external reality and an overvaluation of internal life, and therefore viewed schizoid phenomena as forming a continuum with schizophrenia. Bleuler's observations were elaborated by Kretschmer (1925), who introduced the concept of *anesthetic* (i.e., insensitive) and *hyperaesthetic* (i.e., hypersensitive) personality traits, forming the basis for the later distinction between schizoid and avoidant personality disorders in *DSM-III*.

Psychoanalytic theorists of the British object relations school made major contributions to the elaboration of the schizoid concept. In her seminal writings, Melanie Klein (1996) speculated that the roots of schizoid personality organization could be found in the infant's difficulty integrating the nurturing and depriving aspects of caregiving figures, a phenomenon she referred to as "splitting." Although all infants passed through a "paranoid/schizoid" phase of psychosocial development, persistent difficulties in achieving a more integrated view of caregiving during this period could lead to lasting fears of persecution and psychological disintegration, along with a subjective sense of emptiness and an inability to experience emotions. Individuals with this developmental history typically appeared withdrawn, detached, and lacking in spontaneity, with a tenuous attachment to others.

Klein's views on schizoid phenomena were further refined by other adherents of the British school, including Fairbairn (1952), Winnicott

(1991), and Guntrip (1969). Although Klein did not explicitly link schizoid phenomena to the actual behavior of maternal figures, these later theorists viewed schizoid experience as the result of extreme maternal deprivation—that is, a catastrophic failure of maternal attuneness to the developing infant's needs. Fairbairn (1952) believed that to develop a healthy and spontaneous sense of self, a child needed to be loved unselfishly or unconditionally. When caregivers failed to meet this need, children came to fear that love itself was destructive, that loving would result in them or their love objects being left empty and depleted. Future schizoids, therefore, turned their affective investment inward, toward the world of ideas and away from human contact. Although they might wish to give and receive love, externally they shunned it. As a result, they often appeared remote, detached, and inhuman, "as if" they were playing a role, but had no real feelings.

Fairbairn's notion of the "as if" personality was further developed by Winnicott (1991), who introduced the concept of the *false self.* According to Winnicott, a degree of maternal attuneness to the needs of the infant is necessary to ensure the development of a healthy, spontaneous sense of self—that is, the "true self." The false self, by contrast, is the adaptive, compliant aspect of the personality that develops in response to inevitable failures of the caregiving environment. The false self serves the necessary and universal function of mediating between the developing person and external social reality. Under normal conditions, the false self serves this necessary protective function and allows the true self to grow and strengthen. When environmental failures are extreme, however, the false self comes to dominate the entire personality, whereas the true self remains hidden. The developing child thus becomes passive, compliant, and imitative, lacking in spontaneous emotional expression and genuine relatedness. As a result, when interacting with schizoid individuals, one often feels something essential to be missing. Subjectively these persons often feel incomplete and depersonalized.

Guntrip (1969) cogently described the experience of the schizoid: "Complaints of feeling cut off, shut off, out of touch, feeling apart or strange, of things being out of focus or unreal, of not feeling one with people, or of the point having gone out of life, interest flagging, things seeming futile

and meaningless" (pp. 16–17). He also noted that schizoid persons could appear either anxious and uncomfortable, or cold, reserved, and unfeeling, presaging the distinction between avoidant and schizoid personality disorders in the *DSM-III.* In essence, Guntrip saw schizoids as being starved for love, and as protecting themselves from this longing by denying their needs and withdrawing from relationships. This conflict between intense dependency needs and a powerful fear of them sometimes manifested itself in a flight in and out of relationships, careers, jobs, homes, and so forth.

Whereas the schizoid personality has a long tradition, avoidant personality disorder was introduced by Millon (1981) and first recognized in the *DSM-III.* Although Millon has acknowledged that the literature on the historical antecedents of avoidant personality disorder is sparse, he contends that the historical roots of this concept can be found in descriptions by Kretschmer (1925) of the "hyperaesthetic" temperament; writings on the schizoid personality by adherents of British object relations school (Fairbairn, 1952; Guntrip, 1969 Winnicott, 1991); and classic psychoanalytic writings on the "phobic character" (Fenichel, 1945; MacKinnon & Michels, 1971; Rado, 1956). As noted, Guntrip also described a subgroup of schizoid individuals who appeared anxious and uncomfortable in social situations and who, unlike schizoid persons who were outwardly cold and unfeeling, were aware of their needs for dependency. Several classical psychoanalytic theorists (Fenichel, 1945; MacKinnon & Michels, 1971; Rado, 1956) used the phrase *phobic character* or similar terms to describe individuals for whom avoidance was a predominant defensive mechanism. According to this formulation, avoidance was a means of managing the anxiety stemming from internal conflicts over unacceptable wishes. These individuals often employed elaborate precautions to avoid situations that were potentially anxiety arousing, but they were capable of forming interpersonal attachments.

Contemporary Views and Empirical Evidence

Contemporary psychoanalytic perspectives on the schizoid personality have stressed the use of primitive defense mechanisms, such as splitting, or the tendency to see others as either "all good" or "all bad." They have also stressed projective identification, or inducing one's own unacceptable feelings in others, that are shared in common with other forms of severe character pathology—for example, borderline personality disorder. Kernberg (1984) conceptualized the schizoid as a form of lower level ("borderline") character pathology in which impulsiveness predominates over the ability to delay gratification; primitive defenses such as splitting are employed rather than more adaptive means of coping; one's sense of personal identity is confused, fragmented, and diffuse; and moral values are poorly internalized. Similarly, Akhtar (1987) has emphasized the importance of distinguishing between the overt and covert manifestations of schizoid personality disorder. Thus, patients with schizoid and borderline personality disorder may be superficially dissimilar (e.g., the schizoid appears cold and unemotional, while the borderline shows exaggerated emotionality) but share an underlying lower level personality organization in which splitting and identity diffusion are central. In fact, for Akhtar (1987), the discrepancy between the inner and outer person is the defining characteristic of schizoid personality disorder. For example, though schizoids may appear overtly asexual, their sexual fantasy lives are often elaborate and perverse. Similarly, the schizoid person's apparent emotional indifference may hide an exquisite underlying sensitivity. For this reason, Ahktar and others (Livesley & West, 1986) have criticized the *DSM-III*'s description of schizoid personality disorder as an oversimplification that ignores the contradictions between superficial and "deeper" manifestations of the schizoid syndrome, as well as the *DSM-III*'s decision to categorize schizoid and avoidant personality disorders as separate diagnostic entities.

In contrast to the rich historical literature on schizoid personality disorder, little empirical research has been conducted on its pathogenesis. Although there continues to be a robust research literature on avoidant personality disorder, there have been few empirical studies of schizoid personality disorder since the publication of the second edition of this book (Blaney & Millon, 2009). A search of the psychology database *PsychInfo*, for the years 2009–2013, using the term "schizoid personality disorder," produced 93 hits, the vast majority of which were case studies, theoretical articles, and review articles, many of which were written from a psychoanalytic perspective. In contrast, the term "avoidant personality disorder," for the same period, produced 145 hits, many of which were empirical studies.

Earlier studies found little evidence that schizoid personality disorder is heritable or that it is genetically related to schizophrenia (Baron et al., 1985; Gunderson, Siever, & Spaulding, 1983; Torgersen, 1985). However, a more recent Norwegian study of 3,334 twin pairs found substantial heritability for schizoid personality disorders, with heritability estimates from 55% to 59% (Kendler, Myers, Torgersen, Neale, & Reichborn-Kjennerud, 2007). The remainder of the variance in schizoid personality disorder traits was due to measurement error and unshared environment. Thus, while there is evidence that schizoid personality disorder is heritable, its genetic relationship to schizophrenia remains unproven.

There is ample evidence that schizotypal personality disorder is genetically transmitted and that it is prevalent in the biological relatives of schizophrenics (Siever, Bernstein, & Silverman, 1991). As noted earlier, the major revision of the diagnostic nomenclature in the *DSM-III* created a new diagnostic category, schizotypal personality disorder, which encompassed some patients who would have formerly been considered "schizoid." These schizotypal individuals evinced emotional deficit (i.e., negative) symptoms similar to those seen in schizoid personality disorder, along with perceptual and ideational (i.e., positive) symptoms, such as perceptual illusions and ideas of reference. It seems plausible that some of the early clinical literature linking schizoid personality disorder to schizophrenia was based on observations of patients who would today be diagnosed as schizotypal. Further complicating this picture, one family study (Fogelson et al., 2007) reported a significantly elevated prevalence of avoidant personality disorder in the first-degree relatives of patients with schizophrenia, raising the possibility that some individuals with avoidant personality disorder may fall on a genetic spectrum with schizophrenia. These elevations remained when controlling for schizotypal and paranoid personality disorders. Further studies will be needed to definitively determine whether some individuals with a schizoid personality disorder or avoidant personality disorder lie on a "schizophrenia spectrum."

Millon (1981) speculated that schizoid individuals may be temperamentally placid and

underresponsive and therefore evoke little reciprocal attention, affection, and stimulation from caregivers. The result is a negative feedback loop that
reinforces the child's own innate tendency toward
emotional detachment. Millon (1981) also noted,
however, that extreme emotional deprivation may
lead to schizoid withdrawal, even in a child of
normal temperament. Quoting a case described
by Deutsch (1942), Millon (1981) noted that the
experiential histories of schizoid individuals are
often characterized by a virtual absence of parental warmth and affection.

More recently, Lenzenweger (2010) has
advanced the theory that schizoid personality
disorder arises from a developmental cascade
involving multiple pathways in childhood and
adolescence, including both environmental and
neurobiological inputs. In his view, diminished
proximal processes in childhood, such as lack of
opportunities for reciprocal interactions with parents or other caregivers (e.g., childhood neglect),
affect the child's developing temperament, particularly the temperamental dimension of sociability; this in turn undermines his or her developing
affiliation system which underlies the capacity for
adult attachment. These developmental processes
lead to schizoid phenomena in adulthood, namely,
a lack of desire or ability to form close relationships. Lenzenweger (2010) tested this model using
data from his multiwave longitudinal study of
personality disorders in college-aged young adults
(N = 250). Consistent with his predictions, measures of temperament and proximal processes in
childhood were positively associated with each
other, and with a measure of capacity for affiliation. These variables were negatively correlated
with traits of schizoid personality disorder at all
three waves of the study from ages 18 to 21 years.
This study used a retrospective measure of childhood proximal processes and inferred childhood
temperament from adult ratings. Nevertheless, it
is the only study that has tested a comprehensive
model of schizoid personality disorder, including
relationships between temperament, reciprocal
parent–child interactions, attachment, and longitudinal assessments of personality disorders in
young adulthood.

Little longitudinal research has been done
on the developmental course of schizoid personality disorder. In the only published study of its
kind, Wolff and Chick (1980) followed 20 schizoid children (mean age and equals; 10 years) and
20 matched controls from a child guidance clinic
into early adulthood. Nearly all of the schizoid
patients retained their initial diagnoses an average
of 10 years later, despite an average of 2 years of
psychotherapeutic treatment. In contrast, only one
of the matched controls developed a schizoid personality disorder. Although some of the schizoid
patients showed improvement in their educational
or occupational functioning over time—particularly those patients with higher intelligence—most
of them continued to display the same emotional
and interpersonal deficits at follow-up that were
seen during the initial evaluation. These findings
suggest that the symptoms of schizoid personality
disorder are relatively stable from childhood into
early adulthood, even after children receive intensive psychotherapy.

Recently, questions have been raised about the
relationship between schizoid personality and disorders of childhood marked by disturbed patterns
of reciprocal interaction. In certain respects, the
detachment of schizoid individuals resembles the
social and affective impairment of children with
autistic spectrum disorders such as Asperger's
syndrome and pervasive developmental disorder
not otherwise specified (PDDNOS) (Scheeringa,
2001). However, although these disorders share
in common a marked disinterest in social relationships, schizoid personality disorder lacks many of
the other symptoms of autistic spectrum disorders,
such as gaze aversion and stereotypic behaviors.
Historically, it seems likely that some patients with
autistic spectrum disorders were misdiagnosed as
schizoid. The resemblance between these disorders raises questions about whether in some cases
developmental disorders such as Asperger's or
PDDNOS may be precursors of schizoid personality disorder in adulthood. Schizoid personality
disorder also bears some resemblance to attachment disorders first described by Spitz (1945) and
Bowlby (1969), which are characterized by severe
emotional and social withdrawal in children who
experienced maternal loss or severe emotional
deprivation. The observation that some schizoid
individuals have histories of emotional deprivation raises questions about whether schizoid personality disorder is fundamentally a disorder of
impaired attachment (Bregman, 2011).

Theorizing on the origins of avoidant personality disorder has been directed toward the role of
innate temperament and early experience. Kagan
(1989) contends that shyness and inhibition in

unfamiliar situations can be traced to a temperamental style, "inhibited temperament," that is observable shortly after birth and has a genetic, physiological basis. His longitudinal research indicates that in the second year of life, approximately 15% of White children are timid, subdued, or fearful when they encounter unfamiliar adults or children. Moreover, this inhibition shows moderate stability from 2 to 7 years of age, with children who are very inhibited at first assessment being the most likely to maintain an inhibited style. About 75% of inhibited 7-year-olds in the study exhibited fears that were reminiscent of avoidant personality disorder or social phobia, such as speaking in class, attending summer camp, or going to bed alone at night. Kagan's research also suggests that children who are temperamentally inhibited have lower thresholds of limbic system reactivity, as indicated by increased heart rate, larger pupil diameters, greater motoric tension, and increased morning cortisol secretions. Kagan has suggested that his findings are more consistent with a qualitative rather than a quantitative distinction between inhibited and uninhibited temperamental types, implying that temperamental inhibition has a heritable basis that is analogous to a biological "strain." Nevertheless, because stability of inhibited temperament from infancy to childhood is only moderate, these heritable individual differences can be modified by experience.

Pilkonis (1995) argued that heritable temperamental vulnerability and early adverse experiences contribute to the development of avoidant personality disorder. Although some individuals may be temperamentally shy, others may develop social fears owing to early narcissistic injuries. For the latter group, early experiences of being scorned and shamed lead to damaged feelings of self-worth and engender an expectation of further humiliation. A similar view has been advanced by Stravynski, Elie, and Franche (1989), who posit that parental "overprotection" (i.e., a combination of low parental affection and high parental control) fosters feelings of insecurity, dependency, and inferiority—core characteristics of avoidant personality disorder. However, a comparison of patients with avoidant personality disorder and matched controls on retrospective measures of caregiving provided only partial support for the overprotection hypothesis. Patients with avoidant personality disorder reported less parental affection and more guilt-engendering and rejecting parental behavior

in childhood, but not more controlling behavior by parents (Stravynski et al., 1989).

Consistent with these findings, other retrospective studies have supported a link between feelings of low self-esteem and childhood emotional or verbal abuse (Briere & Runtz, 1988; Gross & Keller, 1992), and at least two studies found that symptoms of avoidant personality disorder were uniquely predicted by self-reported emotional abuse, when other co-occurring forms of maltreatment were statistically controlled for (i.e., partialed out) (Bernstein, Stein, & Handelsman, 1998; Lobbestael, Arntz, & Bernstein, 2010. One of these studies also found that self-reported emotional neglect (i.e., emotional deprivation), but not emotional abuse, was uniquely associated with the symptoms of schizoid personality disorder (Bernstein et al., 1998). The other study failed to confirm this relationship (Lobbestael et al., 2010). Thus, both of these retrospective studies suggest that parental emotional rejection (i.e., emotional abuse) plays a role in the development of avoidant personality disorder, while one of them supports the hypothesis that emotional deprivation (i.e., emotional neglect) plays a role in schizoid personality disorder. On the other hand, a longitudinal study of a community cohort (Johnson, Cohen, Chen, Kasen, & Brook, 2006) found that lack of parental affection or nurturing (i.e., emotional neglect) predicted the development of several *DSM-IV* personality disorders in adulthood, including schizoid and avoidant personality disorders. Thus, whether emotional neglect has a unique etiological relationship to schizoid personality disorder or has broader effects on personality pathology, including avoidant personality disorder, is still an open question.

In contrast to the paucity of empirical studies on schizoid personality disorder, there has been considerable research conducted on avoidant personality disorder, much of it sparked by the controversy over the relationship between avoidant personality disorder and social phobia. Authors of family history and longitudinal studies have attempted to clarify the etiological relationship between these disorders. For example, in a large, general population survey, Tillfors, Furmark, Ekselius, and Fredrikson (2001) found a two- to threefold increase in the risk of social anxiety in the relatives of probands with avoidant personality disorder or social phobia. The risk of familial social anxiety was not significantly different in probands with avoidant personality disorder alone, social phobia alone, or probands with both disorders. These findings raise the possibility that avoidant personality disorder and social phobia may share a common genetic diathesis. However, the study was limited by the use of questionnaires to measure avoidant personality disorder and social phobia, and a broad, nonspecific measure of familial social anxiety. As noted earlier, a large Norwegian twin study found a shared heritability for avoidant personality disorder and generalized social phobia, with heritability estimates of 37% and 39% for each disorder, respectively (Reichborn-Kjennerud et al., 2007). This shared genetic factor accounted entirely for the overlap between the two disorders. Furthermore, the probability that someone developed avoidant personality disorder or generalized social phobia depended entirely on environmental factors that were unique to each disorder, that is, involving different kinds of life events. Individuals experiencing both kinds of life events would be likely to develop both disorders (Reichborn-Kjennerud et al., 2007). Because the study did not assess environmental factors directly but only inferred them from twin-pair correlations, it is not known what these life events might be.

Data from the Collaborative Longitudinal Personality Disorders Study (CLPS) have shown that remission from avoidant personality disorder was related to remission from social phobia, and vice versa, supporting the notion that these may not be fully independent disorders (Shea et al., 2002). Remission rates for avoidant personality disorder in this study were surprisingly high: About one third of patients with avoidant personality disorder no longer had an avoidant diagnosis when retested after 6 months. Similar rates of remission were found for the other personality disorders examined in the study. These findings raise questions about whether some of the remission in avoidant personality disorder might be attributable to improvement in comorbid anxiety symptoms, for which many of the patients were being treated. The same study, however, found that there was considerable variability in the persistence of avoidant personality disorder features over a 2-year period (McGlashan et al., 2005). The most persistent features were feeling inadequate (62%), social ineptness (62%), and preoccupation with rejection (53%). The least persistent features were fears of ridicule and shame (38%) and avoiding

jobs involving contact with others (38%). Thus, it seems possible that the more enduring features of avoidant personality disorder, such as feeling inadequate and social ineptness, represent the core traits of the disorder, while other features are more "symptom-like" manifestations that fluctuate over time. Many patients who are avoidant appear to retain an underlying vulnerability for the disorder, even during periods of relatively better functional adaptation in which they are less symptomatic.

As noted previously, speculation about the nature of the underlying vulnerability in avoidant personality disorder has usually centered on an inherited propensity toward emotional or behavioral inhibition (e.g., Kagan, 1989). However, cognitive schemas may represent another enduring form of vulnerability. Beck et al. (2004) theorized that personality disorders coalesce around central schemas and that these schemas are disorder specific. For example, according to Beck et al. (2004), the central cognitive schemas in avoidant personality disorder concern the belief that if other people were to discover the real person behind the social facade, they wouldn't like the person, would see him or her as inferior, and reject the person. Other people are viewed as critical, demeaning, and rejecting. These patients view themselves as inferior and unattractive. Finally, they seem to believe that the best way to survive is to avoid social contact, intimacy, emotions, difficulties, challenges, and strong sensations.

Several studies have found evidence for the specificity of such beliefs for avoidant personality disorder (Arntz, Dreessen, Schouten, & Weertman, 2004; Arntz, Weertman, & Salet, 2011; Beck et al., 2001; Dreessen, Arntz, Hendriks, Keune, & van den Hout, 1999). Dreessen and colleagues (1999) conducted an experimental test of this cognitive hypothesis using a paradigm in which high- and low-avoidant students listened to ambiguous stories and made inferences about the causes of events. Consistent with the cognitive model, high-avoidant students endorsed more avoidant beliefs, and avoidant beliefs were associated with a schema-congruent information-processing bias. In a more recent study (Arntz, Weertman, & Salet, 2011), patients and nonpatients were asked to imagine themselves in 10 scenarios involving negative events and to note their feelings, thoughts, and behaviors. The results indicated interpretational biases that were specific to avoidant and dependent personality disorders as well as borderline personality disorder, but not to obsessive-compulsive personality disorder. The responses associated with avoidant and dependent personality disorders were characterized by less focus on solutions and more self-criticism, negative emotions, guilt, and fear of others' negative judgments (Arntz et al., 2011). Research also suggests that the information-processing styles of individuals with avoidant personality disorder traits may be inflexible and context unresponsive. In a study of undergraduate students, those with avoidant personality disorder traits made more negative appraisals of vignettes, even after exposure to a priming condition that was designed to create a feeling of attachment security (Bowles & Meyer, 2008). In contrast, those students without avoidant personality disorder features did not make negative appraisals of the vignettes unless they were negatively primed beforehand. These findings suggest that cognitive processes such as interpretational biases and a rigid, unresponsive information-processing style play an important role in avoidant personality disorder.

The success of cognitive-behavior therapies in treating anxiety disorders, including social phobia (Butler, Chapman, Forman, & Beck, 2006), has led to attempts to apply these treatments to patients with avoidant personality disorder. As noted earlier, patients with avoidant personality disorder appear to have core schemas that are similar to those in patients with anxiety disorders. Moreover, the conceptualization of avoidant personality disorder as a general avoidance syndrome (Alden et al., 2002) suggests that behavioral exposure may prove effective in counteracting the avoidant patient's pervasive social and nonsocial avoidance. One randomized clinical trial found that cognitive-behavior therapy was more effective in treating avoidant personality disorder than either brief psychodynamic psychotherapy or wait-list control (Emmelkamp et al., 2006). However, this study was limited by relatively small sample sizes per treatment condition and a short duration of treatment (20 weeks). In a multicenter randomized, clinical trial in the Netherlands, 323 outpatients with Cluster C, paranoid, histrionic, or narcissistic personality disorders received 50 sessions of either schema therapy (N = 147), an integrative form of cognitive-behavior therapy, client-centered therapy (N = 41), or treatment as usual (N = 135) (Bamelis, Evers, Spinhoven, & Arntz, 2014). Nearly two-thirds of these patients

(63.8%) had either a primary or secondary diagnosis of avoidant personality disorder. Outcomes were assessed at 3-year follow-up. Significantly more patients in the schema therapy condition (81.4%) recovered from their personality disorders, as determined by semi-structured interview, than those who received client-centered therapy (60%) or treatment as usual (51.8%). Schema therapy patients also had fewer dropouts, less depression, and better social and general functioning at follow-up. These findings suggest that schema therapy, which is an empirically supported treatment for borderline personality disorder (Giesen-Bloo et al., 2006), is also an effective treatment for patients with avoidant personality disorder, as well as for several other personality disorders. Other studies (e.g., Bartak et al., 2009) have also reported successful outcomes for many patients with avoidant personality disorder, as well as for those with other Cluster C personality disorders, suggesting a hopeful treatment prognosis for this population, despite the severe impairment seen in some of these cases.

Changes in the *DSM-5* and Beyond

Schizoid personality disorder was one of five personality disorders—the others being dependent, histrionic, narcissistic, and paranoid personality disorders—slated for deletion from the *DSM-5* (Skodol et al., 2011). However, schizoid personality disorder received a reprieve when the Board of Trustees of the American Psychiatric Association decided to copy all *DSM-IV* PD diagnostic criteria verbatim into the diagnostic criteria and codes section (Section II) of the *DSM-5*, placing a new, more dimensionally oriented system for PD classification into Section III (Emerging Measures and Models). Among the reasons behind the proposal to delete schizoid personality disorder was the lack of extant research supporting its validity (Skodol et al., 2011). However, as others have noted, a lack of *evidence* of validity because of insufficient research is not equivalent to a lack of validity (Shelder et al., 2010).

The research community appears to be ambivalent about the diagnosis of schizoid personality disorder. Mullins-Sweatt and colleagues (Mullins-Sweatt, Bernstein, & Widiger, 2012) surveyed the membership of two organizations representing experts in personality disorders, the

International Society for the Study of Personality Disorders (ISSPD) and the Association for Research on Personality Disorders (ARPD), regarding the validity and clinical utility of all 10 personality disorders in the *DSM-IV*. On the one hand, the majority of experts found that the diagnosis of schizoid personality disorder was somewhat or very valid (68.4%) and was important or very important for treatment (57.4%), and only 36.9% felt that it should be deleted from the *DSM-5*. On the other hand, it was the least frequently used of any of the personality disorder diagnoses in clinical practice (only 10.3% used it frequently or very frequently) and considered the least useful for the development of treatment or prevention programs (only 24.6% considered it useful or very useful for program development). One interpretation of these findings is that the experts were not ready to eliminate the schizoid personality disorder diagnosis, despite its infrequent use in clinical practice, because of the rich historical and theoretical literature supporting its validity and its importance for treatment in those cases where it appears. Thus, the diagnosis of schizoid personality disorder may be worth retaining over the long haul, if its validity can be supported by more empirical research and its clinical utility can be further justified.

Conclusions

It appears that with the advent of the *DSM-IV* (and now the *DSM-5*), the diagnostic overlap between schizoid and avoidant personality disorder has become less problematic. However, a fundamental question remains: Are these disorders truly separate, or do they represent apparently contradictory traits—that is, superficial insensitivity and underlying hypersensitivity—that can be present in the same individuals? Although there is some empirical evidence supporting the discriminant validity of schizoid and avoidant personality disorders (Arntz et al., 2013 Trull et al., 1987), only a few such studies have been conducted and further research is clearly needed. Anecdotal evidence (Livesley & West, 1986), including the case material presented in this chapter, suggests that schizoid and avoidant features can be discerned in the same individuals and that the manifestation of these disorders can change over time. At the very least, these case studies suggest the possibility of a mixed type in which schizoid and avoidant features co-occur,

and the need for extended observation in some cases to formulate an accurate diagnosis. Another related question is whether schizoid personality disorder represents a lower level form of character pathology and can be differentiated from avoidant personality disorder on the basis of more primitive defenses, greater ego impairment, identity diffusion, and so on (Akhtar, 1987; Kernberg, 1984). If this psychoanalytic formulation were correct, it would have clear prognostic implications, with schizoid patients expected to show poorer response to treatment. Unfortunately, no controlled studies comparing the treatment outcome of schizoid and avoidant patients have been conducted.

There are a number of other important, but still unresolved, issues concerning schizoid and avoidant personality disorders, including their high degree of comorbidity with other disorders (e.g., generalized social phobia, schizotypal personality disorder, dependent personality disorder), and the role of childhood experiences and genetic influence in their development. Any conclusion that schizoid personality and avoidant personality disorders have become expendable diagnoses seems premature. There is increasing evidence that schizoid personality disorder, though one of the less commonly occurring diagnoses in clinical samples, exists in the general population at prevalences comparable to those of many other personality disorders (Coid et al., 2006; Samuels et al., 2002). Similarly, although avoidant personality has shown a high degree of overlap with generalized social phobia in several studies, there is also evidence contradicting the notion that these are identical disorders (Alden et al., 2002; Arntz, 1999). Moreover, the presence of comorbid avoidant personality disorder in cases of generalized social phobia communicates important information about severity of impairment (Cox et al., 2009, 2011). There is increasing evidence for the dimensional nature of personality disorders, including both schizoid (Ahmed, Green, Buckley, & McFarland, 2012) and avoidant (Arntz et al., 2009) personality disorders. In another survey of personality disorders experts (Bernstein, Iscan, & Maser, 2007), the majority expressed dissatisfaction with the current categorical system and preference for dimensional approaches to personality disorder classification. While the *DSM-5* Section II continues to use a strictly categorical approach (by copying *DSM-IV* PD criteria over into *DSM-5*), an alternative dimensional system is now included in Section III to encourage further study of dimensional systems in clinical practice. It is conceivable that a dimensional model of personality disorders could help resolve some of the current ambiguity surrounding the diagnostic comorbidity of schizoid and avoidant personality disorders with each other, as well as with other diagnoses, such as schizotypal personality disorder and generalized social phobia (Roysamb et al., 2011; Samuel, Hopwood, Krueger, & Ruggero, 2013). The resolution of these and other issues will await the outcome of future studies of these two intriguing, but still not fully understood, personality disorders.

References

Ahmed, A., Green, B., Buckley, P., & McFarland, M. (2012). Taxometric analyses of paranoid and schizoid personality disorders. *Psychiatry Research*, 196, 123–132.

Akhtar, S. (1987). Schizoid personality disorder: A synthesis of developmental, dynamic, and descriptive features. *American Journal of Psychotherapy*, 41, 499–518.

Alden, L., Laposa, J., Taylor, C., & Ryder, A. (2002). Avoidant personality disorder: Current status and future directions. *Journal of Personality Disorders*, 16, 1–29.

Alnaes, R., & Torgersen, S. (1988). DSM-III symptom disorders (Axis I) and personal disorders (Axis II) in an outpatient population. *Acta Psychiatrica Scandanavica*, 78, 348–355.

Alnaes, R., & Torgersen, S. (1997). Personality and personality disorders predict development and relapses of major depression. *Acta Psychiatrica Scandanavica*, 95, 336–342.

Arntz, A. (1999). Do personality disorders exist? On the validity of the concept and its cognitive behavioural formulation and treatment. *Behaviour Research and Therapy*, 37, S97–S134.

Arntz, A., Bernstein, D., Gielen, D., van Nieuwenhuijzen, M., Penders, K., Haslam, N., & Ruscio, J. (2009). Cluster-C, paranoid, and borderline personality disorders are dimensional: Evidence from taxometric tests. *Journal of Personality Disorders*, 23, 606–628.

Arntz, A., Broese, S., & Bernstein, D. P. (2013). Factorial validity of the DSM-IV personality disorders. Manuscript in preparation.

Arntz, A., Dreessen, L., Schouten, E., & Weertman, A. (2004). Beliefs in personality disorders: A test with the Personality Disorder Belief Questionnaire. *Behaviour Research and Therapy*, 42(10), 1215–1225.

Arntz, A., Weertman, A., & Salet, S. (2011). Interpretation bias in Cluster-C and borderline personality disorders. *Behavior Research and Therapy*, 49, 472–481.

Bamelis, L., Evers, S., Spinhoven, P., & Arntz, A. (2014). Results of a multicentered randomized controlled trial on the clinical effectiveness of schema therapy for personality disorders. *American Journal of Psychiatry*, 171, 305–322.

Baron, M., Gruen, R., Rainer, J. D., Kane, J., Asnis, L., & Lork, S. (1985). A family study of schizophrenic and normal control probands: Implications for the spectrum concept of schizophrenia. *American Journal of Psychiatry*, 142, 447–454.

Bartak, A., Spreeuwenberg, M., Andrea, H., Holleman, L., Rijnierse, P., Rossum, B., et al. (2009). Effectiveness of different modalities of psychotherapeutic treatment for patients with cluster C personality disorders: Results of a large prospective multicenter study. *Psychotherapy and Psychosomatics*, 79, 20–30.

Beck, A. T., Butler, Brown, Dahlsgaard, Newman, & Beck, J. S. (2001). Dysfunctional beliefs discriminate personality disorders. *Behaviour Research and Therapy*, 39(10), 1213–1225.

Beck, A. T., Freeman, A., Davis, D. D., Pretzer, J., Fleming, B., Arntz, A., et al. (2004). *Cognitive therapy of personality disorders* (2nd ed.). New York: Guilford Press.

Bernstein, D. P. (2005). Have paranoid and schizoid personality disorders become dispensable diagnoses? A commentary on Parnas et al. In M. Maj (Ed.), *Evidence and experience in psychiatry—Volume 8. Personality disorders* (pp. 122–124). West Sussex, England: Wiley.

Bernstein, D. P., Iscan, C., & Maser, J. (2007). Opinions of personality disorder experts regarding the DSM-IV personality disorders classification system. *Journal of Personality Disorders*, 21, 536–551.

Bernstein, D. P., Stein, J., & Handelsman, L. (1998). Predicting personality pathology among adult patients with substance use disorders: Effects of childhood maltreatment. *Addictive Behavior: An International Journal*, 23, 855–868.

Blaney, P., & Millon, T. (2009). *Oxford textbook of psychopathology*. New York: Oxford University Press.

Bleuler, E. (1924). *Textbook of psychiatry* (Trans. A. A. Brill). New York: Macmillan.

Boone, M., McNeil, D., Masia, C., Turk, C., Carter, L., Ries, B., et al. (1999). Multimodal comparisons of social phobia subtypes and avoidant personality disorder. *Journal of Anxiety Disorders, 13,* 271–292.

Bowlby, J. (1969). *Attachment and loss, Volume I: Attachment* (2nd ed.). New York: Basic Books.

Bowles, D., & Meyer, B. (2008). Attachment priming and avoidant personality features as predictors of social-evaluation biases. *Journal of Personality Disorders, 22,* 72–88.

Bregman, J. (2011). Pervasive developmental disorder not otherwise specified. In E. Hollander, A. Kolevzon, & J. Coyle (Eds.), *Textbook of autism spectrum disorders* (pp. 89–98). Arlington, VA: American Psychiatric Publishing.

Briere, J., & Runtz, M. (1988). Multivariate correlates of childhood psychological and physical maltreatment among university women. *Child Abuse and Neglect, 12,* 331–341.

Brown, E., Heimberg, R., & Juster, H. (1995). Social phobia subtype and avoidant personality disorder: Effect on severity of social phobia, impairment, and outcome of cognitive behavioral treatment. *Behavior Therapy, 26,* 467–486.

Butler, A., Chapman, J., Forman, E., & Beck, A. (2006). The empirical status of cognitive-behavioral therapy: A review of meta-analyses. *Clinical Psychology Review, 26,* 17–31.

Coid, J., Yang, M., Tyrer, P., Roberts, A., & Ullrich, S. (2006). Prevalence and correlates of personality disorder in Great Britain. *British Journal of Psychiatry, 188,* 423–431.

Coid, J., Yang, M., Ullrich, S., Roberts, A., Moran, P., Bebbington, P., et al. (2009). Psychopathy among prisoners in England and Wales. *International Journal of Law and Psychiatry, 32,* 134–141.

Cox, B., Pagura, J., Stein, M., & Sareen, J. (2009). The relationship between generalized social phobia and avoidant personality disorder in a national mental health survey. *Depression and Anxiety, 26,* 354–362.

Cox, B., Turnbull, D., Robinson, J., Grant, B., & Stein, M. (2011). The effect of avoidant personality disorder on the persistence of generalized social anxiety disorder in the general population: Results from a longitudinal, nationally representative mental health survey. *Depression and Anxiety, 28,* 250–255.

Deutsch, H. (1942). Some forms of emotional disturbance and their relationship to schizophrenia. *Psychoanalytic Quarterly, 11,* 301–321.

Dreessen, L., Arntz, A., Hendriks, T., Keune, N., & van den Hout, M. (1999). Avoidant personality disorder and implicit schema-congruent information processing bias: A pilot study with a pragmatic inference task. *Behavior Research and Therapy, 37,* 619–632.

Emmelkamp, P., Benner, A., Kuipers, A., Feietag, G., Koster, H., & Apeldoorn, F. (2006). Comparison of brief dynamic and cognitive-behavioral therapies in avoidant personality disorder. *British Journal of Psychiatry, 189,* 60–64.

Fairbairn, W. R. D. (1952). *Psychoanalytic studies of the personality.* London: Routledge and Kegan Paul.

Fenichel, O. (1945). *The psychoanalytic theory of neurosis.* New York: W.W. Norton.

Feske, U., Perry, K., Chambless, D., Renneberg, B., & Goldstein, A. (1996). Avoidant personality disorder as predictor of treatment outcome among generalized social phobics. *Journal of Personality Disorders, 10,* 174–184.

Fogelson, D., Nuechterlein, K., Asarnow, R., Payne, D., Subotnik, K., Jacobson, K., et al. (2007). Avoidant personality disorder is a separable schizophrenia-spectrum personality disorder even when controlling for the presence of paranoid and schizotypal personality disorders. The UCLA Family Study. *Schizophrenia Research, 91,* 192–199.

Fossati, A., Maffeiu, C., Bagnato, M., Donati, D., Donini, M., Fiorilli, M., et al. (2000). Patterns of covariation of DSM-IV personality disorders in a mixed psychiatric sample. *Comprehensive Psychiatry, 41*(3), 206–215.

Giesen-Bloo, J., van Dyck, R., Spinhoven, P., van Tilburg, W., Dirksen, C., van Asselt, T., et al. (2006). Outpatient psychotherapy for borderline personality disorder: A randomized clinical trial of schema focused therapy versus transference focused psychotherapy. *Archives of General Psychiatry, 63,* 649–658.

Gross, A. B., & Keller, H. R. (1992). Long-term consequences of childhood physical and psychological maltreatment. *Aggressive Behavior, 18,* 171–185.

Gunderson, J. G., Siever, L. J., & Spaulding, E. (1983). The search for a schizotype: Crossing the border again. *Archives of General Psychiatry, 40,* 15–22.

Guntrip, H. (1969). *Schizoid phenomena, object-relations and the self.* New York: International Universities Press.

Herbert, J., Hope, D., & Bellack, A. (1992). Validity of the distinction between generalized social phobia and avoidant personality disorder. *Journal of Abnormal Psychology, 101,* 332–339.

Jansen, M. A., Arntz, A., Merckelback, H., & Mersch, P. P. A. (1994). Personality features and in social phobia and panic disorder. *Journal of Abnormal Psychology, 103,* 391–395.

Johnson, J., Cohen, P., Chen, H., Kasen, S., & Brook, J. (2006). Parenting behaviors associated with risk for offspring personality disorder during adulthood. *Archives of General Psychiatry, 63,* 579–587.

Kagan, J. (1989). Temperamental contributions to social behavior. *American Psychologist, 44,* 668–674.

Kalus, O., Bernstein, D., & Siever, L. (1993). Schizoid personality disorder: A review of current status and implications for DSM-IV. *Journal of Personality Disorders, 3,* 43–52.

Kass, F., Spitzer, R. L., & Williams, J. B. (1983). An empirical study of sex bias in the diagnostic criteria of DSM-III Axis II personality disorders. *American Psychologist, 38,* 799–801.

Kendler, K., Myers, J., Torgersen, S., Neale, M., & Reichborn-Kjennerud, T. (2007). The heritability of cluster A personality disorders assessed by both personal interview and questionnaire. *Psychological Medicine, 37,* 655–665.

Kernberg, O. (1984). *Severe personality disorders.* New Haven, CT: Yale University Press.

Kety, S. S., Rosenthal, D., Wender, P. H., & Schulsinger, F. (1971). Mental illness in the biological and adoptive families of adopted schizophrenics. *American Journal of Psychiatry, 128,* 302–306.

Klein, M. (1996). Notes on some schizoid mechanisms. *Journal of Psychotherapy Practice and Research, 5,* 164–179.

Kretschmer, E. (1925). *Physique and character.* New York: Harcourt Brace.

Lenzenweger, M. (2010). A source, a cascade, a schizoid: A heuristic proposal from the Longitudinal Study of Personality Disorders. *Development and Psychopathology, 22,* 867–881.

Livesley, J. W., & West, M. (1986). The DSM-III distinction between schizoid and avoidant personality disorders. *Canadian Journal of Psychiatry, 31,* 59–62.

Lobbestael, J., Arntz, A., & Bernstein, D.P. (2010). Disentangling the relationship between different types of childhood traumas and personality disorders. *Journal of Personality Disorders, 24,* 285–295.

MacKinnon, R. A., & Michels, R. (1971). *The psychiatric interview in clinical practice.* Philadelphia: W. B. Saunders.

McGlashan, T., Grilo, C., Sanislow, C., Morey, L., Gunderson, J., Skodol, A., et al. (2005). Two-year prevalence and stability of individual DSM-IV criteria for schizotypal, borderline, avoidant, and obsessive-compulsive personality disorders: Towards a hybrid model of Axis II disorders. *American Journal of Psychiatry, 162,* 883–889.

Meehl, P. (1990). Toward an integrated theory of schizotaxia, schizotypy, and schizophrenia. *Journal of Personality Disorders, 4,* 1–99.

Millon, T. (1981). *Disorders of personality: DSM-III, Axis II.* New York: Wiley-Interscience.

Millon, T., & Martinez, A. (1991). Avoidant personality disorder. *Journal of Personality Disorders, 5,* 353–362.

Mullins-Sweatt, S. N., Bernstein, D. P., & Widiger, T. (2012). Retention or deletion of personality disorder diagnoses in the DSM-5: A survey of expert opinion about validity and clinical utility. *Journal of Personality Disorders, 26,* 689–703.

Pilkonis, P. A. (1995). Commentary on avoidant personality disorder: Temperament, shame, or both? In J. Livesley (Ed.), *The DSM-IV personality disorders* (pp. 218–233). Washington, DC: American Psychiatric Association.

Rado, S. (1956). *Psychoanalysis of behavior: Collected papers.* New York: Grune and Stratton.

Ralevski, E., Sanislow, C., Grilo, C., Skodol, A., Gunderson, J., Shea, T., et al. (2005). Avoidant personality disorder and social phobia: Distinct enough to be separate disorders? *Acta Psychiatrica Scandanavica, 112,* 208–214.

Reich, J. (1990). The relationship between DSM-III avoidant and dependent personality disorders. *Psychiatry Research, 34,* 218–292.

Reichborn-Kjennerud, T., Czajkowski, N., Torgersen, S., Neale, M., Orstavik, R., Tambs, K., & Kendler, K. (2007). The relationship between avoidant personality disorder and social phobia: A population-based twin study. *American Journal of Psychiatry, 164,* 1722–1728.

Roysamb, E., Kendler, K. S., Tambs, K., Orstavik, R. E., Neale, M. C., Aggen, S. H., et al. (2011). The joint structure of DSM-IV Axis I and Axis II disorders. *Journal of Abnormal Psychology, 120,* 198–209.

Samuel, D., Hopwood, C., Krueger, R., & Ruggero, C. (2013). Comparing methods for scoring personality disorder types using maladaptive traits in DSM-5. *Assessment, 20,* 353–361.

Samuels, J., Eaton, W. W., Bienvenu, O. J., 3rd, Brown, C. H., Costa, P. T., Jr., & Nestadt, G.

(2002). Prevalence and correlates of personality disorders in a community sample. *British Journal of Psychiatry, 180,* 536–542.

Scheeringa, M. S. (2001). The differential diagnosis of impaired reciprocal social interaction in children: A review of disorders. *Child Psychiatry and Human Development, 32,* 71–89.

Shea, M. T., Stout, R., McGlashan, T., et al. (2002, May). Personality disorders and Axis I disorders: Longitudinal associations of course. Paper presented at the American Psychiatric Association, Annual Meeting, Philadelphia, PA.

Shelder, J., Beck, A., Fonagy, P., Gabbard, G., Gunderson, J., Kernberg, O., & Westen, D. (2010). Personality disorders in the DSM-5. *American Journal of Psychiatry, 167,* 1027–1028.

Siever, L., Bernstein, D., & Silverman, J. (1991). Schizoptypal personality disorder: A review of its current status. *Journal of Personality Disorders, 5,* 178–193.

Skodol, A., Clark, L. A., Bender, D., Kreuger, R., Livesley, W. J., Morey, L., et al. (2011). Proposed changes in personality and personality disorder assessment and diagnosis for DSM-5. Part I: Description and rationale. *Personality Disorders: Theory, Research, and Treatment, 2,* 4–22.

Spitz, R. (1945). Hospitalism: An inquiry into the genesis of psychiatric conditions in early childhood. *Psychoanalytic Study of the Child, 2,* 53–74.

Spitzer, R. L., Endicott, J., & Givvon, M. (1979). Crossing the border into borderline personality and borderline schizophrenia: The development of criteria. *Archives of General Psychiatry, 36,* 17–24.

Stone, M. (1980). *The borderline syndromes: Constitution, personality, and adaptation.* New York: McGraw-Hill.

Stravynski, A., Elie, R., & Franche, R. L. (1989). Perception of early parenting by patients diagnosed avoidant personality disorder: A test of the overprotection hypothesis. *Acta Psychiatrica Scandinavica, 80,* 415–420.

Taylor, C., Laposa, J., & Alden, L. (2004). Is avoidant personality disorder more than just social avoidance? *Journal of Personality Disorders, 18,* 571–594.

Tillfors, M., Furmark, T., Ekselius, L., & Fredrikson, M. (2001). Social phobia and avoidant personality disorder as related to parental history of social anxiety: A general population study. *Behaviour Research and Therapy, 39,* 289–298.

Torgersen, S. (1985). Relationship of schizoptypal personality disorder to schizophrenia: Genetics. *Schizophrenia Bulletin, 11,* 554–563.

Tran, G., & Chambless, D. (1995). Psychopathology of social phobia: Effects of subtype and avoidant personality disorder. *Journal of Anxiety Disorders, 9,* 489–501.

Trull, T. J., Widiger, T. A., & Frances, A. (1987). Covariation of criteria sets for avoidant, schizoid, and dependent personality disorder. *American Journal of Psychiatry, 144,* 767–772.

Turner, S. M., Beidel, D. C., Dancee, C. V., & Keys, D. J. (1986). Psychopathology of social phobia and comparison to avoidant personality disorder. *Journal of Abnormal Psychology, 95,* 389–394.

van Velzen, C., Emmelkamp, P., & Scholing, A. (2000). Generalized social phobia versus avoidant personality disorder: Differences in psychopathology, personality traits, and social and occupational functioning. *Journal of Anxiety Disorders, 14,* 395–411.

Wilberg, T., Karterud, S., Pedersen, G., & Urnes, O. (2009). The impact of avoidant personality disorder on psychosocial impairment is substantial. *Nordic Journal of Psychiatry, 63,* 390–396.

Winnicott, D. W. (1991). Psychotherapy of character disorders. In M. Kets de Vries & S. Perzow (Eds.), *Handbook of character studies: Psychoanalytic explorations* (pp. 461–475). Madison, CT: International Universities Press.

Wolff, S., & Chick, J. (1980). Schizoid personality in childhood: A controlled follow-up study. *Psychological Medicine, 10,* 85–100.

Zimmerman, M., & Coryell, W. (1989). DSM-III personality disorder diagnoses in a nonpatient sample. *Archives of General Psychiatry, 46,* 682–689.

Zimmerman, M., Rothschild, L., & Chelminski, I. (2005). The prevalence of DSM-IV personality disorders in psychiatric outpatients. *American Journal of Psychiatry, 162,* 1911–1918.

25

Dependent and Histrionic Personality Disorders

ROBERT F. BORNSTEIN,

CHRISTY A. DENCKLA,

AND WEI-JEAN CHUNG

Clinicians and researchers have long recognized that dependent personality disorder (DPD) and histrionic personality disorder (HPD) share at least one important feature: Both are rooted in exaggerated, inflexible dependency needs. Moreover, both DPD and HPD have a long psychoanalytic history. Beginning with Freud (1905, 1915, 1923) and continuing with the work of Abraham (1927), Fenichel (1945), and others (e.g., Kernberg, 1984; Kohut, 1971), theorists and researchers have devoted considerable effort to exploring the intrapsychic dynamics that underlie dependent and histrionic pathologies. In fact, DPD and HPD have received a great deal of attention from clinicians of various theoretical orientations, who have written extensively regarding therapeutic approaches that are most effective in treating these disorders (see Beck & Freeman, 1990; Bornstein, 2005; Millon, 2011).

This chapter reviews theory, research, and clinical data bearing on the dependent and histrionic personality disorders (PDs). Definitional and diagnostic issues are discussed, and the literature on epidemiology and comorbidity is reviewed. The most influential theoretical perspectives on each disorder are described, and research evidence related to these theoretical frameworks is assessed. Following overviews of the DPD and HPD literature the placement of both syndromes in future versions of the *DSM* is examined, and suggestions for further research are offered.

Dependent Personality Disorder

The empirical literature on trait dependency and DPD is extensive, with well over 1,000 published studies to date (Bornstein, 2011, 2012). A review of this literature suggests that *dependency* is best conceptualized as a personality style characterized by four primary components: (1) *motivational* (i.e., a marked need for guidance, approval, and support from others); (2) *cognitive* (i.e., a perception of oneself as powerless and ineffectual, along with the belief that others are comparatively powerful and potent); (3) *affective* (i.e., a tendency to become anxious when required to function independently, especially when one's efforts will be evaluated by others); and (4) *behavioral* (i.e., a tendency to seek help, support, guidance, and reassurance from others). The eight symptoms of DPD in the DSM-IV, which remain unchanged in *DSM-IV-TR*, and *DSM-5*, focus primarily on two of these four components: behavioral (symptoms 1, 2, 4, and 5), and affective (symptoms 3, 6, 7, and 8).

Although the clinical utility of the DPD construct is well established (Mullins-Sweatt, Bernstein, & Widiger, 2012), diagnosis of DPD is complicated by the fact that the behaviors exhibited by dependent patients vary markedly as a function of gender, ethnicity, and age. In general, men tend to express dependency-related symptoms and behaviors in a more indirect and disguised manner than women do (Bornstein, 2011; Ford & Widiger, 1989). As a result, men almost invariably obtain lower scores than women on dependency tests with high face validity (e.g., questionnaires like the Interpersonal Dependency Inventory), but women and men obtain comparable scores on dependency tests with low face validity such as the Rorschach Oral Dependency (ROD) scale (Bornstein, 1995; see also Bornstein, 1999, for a review of evidence regarding the behaviorally referenced validity of self-report and performance-based dependency tests).

Ethnicity complicates DPD diagnosis because there are profound cultural differences in attitudes on dependency and autonomy. In most Western societies individualistic attitudes predominate, and autonomy and self-reliance are valued more strongly than interdependence and connectedness; in more individualistic societies dependent behaviors connote immaturity and pathology (Cross, Bacon, & Morris, 2000). In cultures that have traditionally been more sociocentric, however—most notably Japan (Johnson, 1993) and India (Kaul, Mathur, & Murlidharan, 1982)—dependent behaviors in adults are not only tolerated but expected. The higher levels of normative dependency expressed by individuals from these cultures can lead to inappropriate, excessive DPD diagnoses in members of various cultural groups. In this context it is worth noting that as traditionally sociocentric cultures become increasingly Westernized, clinicians report increasing numbers of patients whose difficulties involve experienced conflict (both intra- and interpersonal) between strivings for autonomy and relatedness (Sato, 2001).

The DPD symptom picture also varies as a function of age, and some evidence suggests that DPD symptoms may diminish from middle to later adulthood (Gutierrez et al., 2012). Moreover, the support that dependent persons solicit from others is shaped by their vulnerabilities (e.g., instrumental, financial, medical), and as a result the expression of underlying dependency strivings varies across context (Fiori, Consedine, & Magai, 2008). For example, among individuals who experience health-related vulnerabilities, dependency is often expressed in terms of somatic complaints and exaggerated expressions of need for health-oriented support (O'Neill & Bornstein, 2001); among those with emotional vulnerabilities (e.g., anxiety, insecurity) dependency strivings may be manifest as more overt requests for guidance and reassurance (Murphy Meyer, & O'Leary, 1994).

Epidemiology and Comorbidity

Studies assessing the prevalence of DPD in different settings and populations have produced varying results. In what is considered to be the definitive contemporary epidemiological survey of PDs, Torgersen (2009) reported an overall DPD prevalence rate of 0.7% in American adults. Similar findings were obtained by Grant et al. (2004), who obtained an overall DPD prevalence rate of 0.4%. However, some investigations have found DPD prevalence rates in the range of 2% to 4% in community samples (Zimmerman & Coryell, 1989); others have reported frequencies as high at 10% (Samuel & Widiger, 2010). Taken together, studies suggest that DPD prevalence rates in most psychiatric inpatient and outpatient settings average between 5% and 15% (Jackson, Rudd, Gazis, & Edwards, 1991).

The DSM-IV assertion that "the sex ratio of [DPD] is not significantly different than the sex ratio of females within the respective clinical setting" (p. 667) was changed in the DSM-IV-TR, with the revised passage indicating that DPD "has been diagnosed more frequently in females, although some studies report similar prevalence rates among males and females" (p. 723). In fact, even this modified statement was incorrect: Studies consistently demonstrate that women receive DPD diagnoses at higher rates than men do, and those few studies that fail to detect significant gender differences generally have inadequate sample sizes (and inadequate statistical power) to contrast DPD prevalence rates in women and men (e.g., Reich, 1987). Women are far more likely than men to receive a DPD diagnosis, regardless of the setting in which diagnostic information is collected (Bornstein, 1997, 2005).

DPD shows substantial comorbidity with a variety of other mental disorders, including eating disorders (Bornstein, 2001), anxiety disorders (Alnaes & Torgersen, 1990), mood disorders (Maier, Lichtermann, Klingler, Heun, & Hallmayer, 1992), and somatization disorder

(Ng & Bornstein, 2005). Studies quantifying PD comorbidity in terms of odds ratios suggest that—like most PDs—DPD shows statistically significant comorbidity with most (sometimes all) PDs (e.g., Lenzenweger et al., 2007; Trull et al., 2010); comorbidity levels tend to be highest for DPD and schizoid, avoidant, borderline, and histrionic PDs (Bornstein, 2005; Millon, 2011).

Historical Perspectives

Neki (1976) pointed out that although some cultures condemn dependency while others embrace it, virtually every society has recognized and described highly dependent individuals. Modern thinking on the dependent personality can be traced to Kraepelin (1913) and Schneider (1923), who described precursors of what would eventually emerge as DPD in the *DSM* series. Although Kraepelin (1913) described the dependent person as "shiftless" while Schneider (1923) used the term "weak-willed," both theorists agreed that the dependent person was immature, gullible, and easily exploited by others.

Around the same time that Kraepelin (1913) and Schneider (1923) were describing the central features of pathological dependency, an independent stream of theoretical work was emerging in the psychoanalytic domain. First discussed by Freud (1905), and later elaborated by Abraham (1927), Fenichel (1945), and others, the psychoanalytic conceptualization of the "oral dependent" person bore a strong resemblance to contemporary viewpoints regarding dependency. Thus, Abraham (1927, p. 400) noted that dependent persons "are dominated by the belief that there will always be some kind person—a representative of the mother, of course—to care for them and give them everything they want." Neoanalytic theorists like Fromm (1947), Horney (1945), and Sullivan (1947) offered similar descriptions. For example, speculating on the parental roots of dependency, Sullivan (1947, p. 84) suggested that "these people have been obedient children of a dominating parent. They go through life needing a strong person to make decisions for them.... [They] learned their helplessness and clinging vine adaptation from parental example."

The influence of Sullivan's work is evident in the *DSM-I* precursor of DPD, the "passive-aggressive personality, passive-dependent type," which was characterized by "helplessness, indecisiveness, and

a tendency to cling to others as a dependent child to a supporting parent" (p. 37). When a full-fledged category of DPD was included for the first time in *DSM-III*, the syndrome was described in general terms and the central symptoms included: (1) an inability to function independently; (2) willingness to subordinate one's needs to those of others; and (3) lack of self-confidence. The *DSM-III-R*, *DSM-IV*, and *DSM-5* criteria for DPD were far more detailed, including an array of behavioral and affective symptoms (see Bornstein, 1997, 2005, for reviews).

Contemporary Theoretical Perspectives

Although a wide variety of theoretical frameworks have been offered (see Bornstein, 1992, 1993, 2005, 2012), three theoretical viewpoints have been particularly influential in the study of DPD during the past several decades. In the following sections we describe the psychoanalytic, biosocial-learning, and cognitive models of dependency, and review research testing each model.

The Psychoanalytic Perspective   In classical psychoanalytic theory, dependency is inextricably linked to the infantile oral stage of development (Freud, 1905). Frustration or overgratification during the oral stage is hypothesized to result in oral "fixation" and an inability to resolve the developmental issues that characterize this stage (i.e., conflicts regarding dependency and autonomy). Thus, classical psychoanalytic theory postulates that the orally fixated (or "oral dependent") person will (1) remain dependent on others for nurturance, guidance, and support; and (2) exhibit behaviors in adulthood that reflect the infantile oral stage (e.g., preoccupation with activities of the mouth, reliance on food and eating to cope with anxiety).

Early in his career Freud (1908, p. 167) discussed in general terms the links between "fixation" and the development of particular personality traits, noting that "one very often meets with a type of character in which certain traits are very strongly marked while at the same time one's attention is arrested by the behavior of these persons in regard to certain bodily functions." Subsequently, Freud (1938, p. 222) was more explicit in linking personality development to the feeding experience during infancy, arguing that "a child sucking at his mother's breast becomes the prototype of every relation of love." The evolution of Freud's thinking in this area paralleled what turned out to be, in retrospect, a pervasive trend in classical psychoanalytic theory, namely an ever-increasing emphasis on social rather than biological factors as key elements in personality development (Greenberg & Mitchell, 1983).

The object relations model of dependency extends the classical psychoanalytic model by emphasizing the internalization of mental representations of parents (and other significant figures) as critical developmental tasks of infancy and early childhood (Ainsworth, 1969; Bornstein, 1996). By focusing on mental representations that are formed during the first few years of life, object relations theory shifted the theoretical emphasis from the study of Oedipal dynamics to the phenomenon of infantile dependency as a key factor in normal and pathological personality development (Greenberg & Mitchell, 1983: Kernberg, 1975).

In object relations theory, social exchange between caregiver and infant is central to the development of dependent personality orientation. During the past several decades, Blatt's (1974) theoretical framework has been one of the most influential perspectives in this area. Blatt and his colleagues (e.g., Blatt & Shichman, 1983) have argued that dependent personality traits result from the internalization of a representation of the self as weak and ineffectual. Such a self-representation leads the individual to (1) look to others to provide protection, guidance, and support; (2) become preoccupied with fears of abandonment; and (3) behave in ways that strengthen ties to potential nurturers and caregivers (Blatt, Cornell, & Eshkol, 1993; Bornstein, 1992, 1993).

Studies testing the classical psychoanalytic model of dependency have generally produced weak results. There have been numerous investigations assessing the relationships of various feeding and weaning variables to dependency levels in childhood, adolescence, and adulthood, but these investigations failed to delineate any consistent connection between feeding or weaning experiences and later dependency (see, e.g., Heinstein, 1963). Along somewhat similar lines, a number of studies have assessed the relationship between dependency and various "oral" psychopathologies (e.g., eating disorders, alcoholism, tobacco addiction); these also produced mixed results. On the positive side, anorexic and bulimic individuals score higher than non-eating-disordered persons on self-report and performance-based measures of dependency (Narduzzi & Jackson, 2000) and

receive DPD diagnoses at higher rates than non-eating-disordered individuals (Bornstein, 2001). Beyond this, studies have found a link between dependency and risk for tobacco addiction, and prospective findings indicate that high levels of dependency actually predispose individuals to cigarette smoking rather than being a correlate or consequence of tobacco use (Vaillant, 1980).

Studies show that—in contrast to predictions made by the classical psychoanalytic model—increases in dependent traits, attitudes, and behaviors typically follow (rather than precede) the onset of alcoholism (Vaillant, 1980; see also Sprohge, Handler, Plant, & Wicker, 2002, for findings regarding increased oral-dependent Rorschach imagery following alcoholism onset). Despite numerous efforts to delineate a dependency-obesity link, there is no strong or consistent relationship between level of dependency and tendency to engage in pathological overeating during childhood, adolescence, or adulthood (Black, Goldstein, & Mason, 1992).

Bornstein, Galley, and Leone (1986) tested the object relations model of dependency using Blatt, Wein, Chevron, and Quinlan's (1979) Parental Representations Scale to assess qualities of participants' internalized mental representations of mother and father. Dependent participants described maternal introjects that were less nurturant, warm, and constructively involved than the maternal introjects of nondependent participants. However, the magnitudes of these relationships were small, and level of dependency was unrelated to qualities of the paternal introject. Similar findings were subsequently obtained by Sadeh, Rubin, and Berman (1993). Mongrain (1998) also showed results consistent with those of Bornstein et al. using a self-report (rather than open-ended) measure of parental perceptions. Findings from studies examining perceptions and memories of the parents in relation to level of dependency parallel those obtained in investigations where aspects of parental representations were assessed directly (Head, Baker, & Williamson, 1991).

Using a modified version of the Parental Representations Scale, Bornstein, Leone, and Galley (1988) assessed the relationship between level of dependency and qualities of the self-representation in a large mixed-sex sample of college students. Strong results were obtained, with dependent students' self-representations reflecting a view of the self as weak, submissive, and ineffectual. Other studies using different self-report and performance-based self-concept measures (e.g., Lee & Ashton, 2006; Weertman et al., 2006) produced results consistent with those of Bornstein et al. Moreover, studies indicate that activating the dependent person's "helpless self-concept" (e.g., via lexical priming procedures) leads to increases in dependency-related cognition, affective responding, and expressed behavior (Bornstein, 2007; Bornstein et al., 2005). Overall, research testing object relations models of dependency suggests that a representation of the self as helpless, ineffectual, and weak may be associated with exaggerated dependency needs in a variety of groups.

The Biosocial-Learning Perspective Millon's (1969, 1981, 1990) integrative, interdisciplinary biosocial-learning framework has roots in interpersonal theories of personality. As Wiggins and Pincus (1990) noted, interpersonal theories have a long history in psychology and psychiatry, with contemporary thinking in this area originating primarily in the work of Leary (1957). Many variants of the interpersonal approach have emerged since the late 1950s, including Benjamin's (1974) structural analysis of social behavior (SASB) model, Kiesler's (1982) interpersonal circle, and circumplex models of personality and personality pathology (Pincus, 2005). Some researchers have used a modified interpersonal framework to locate dependency (and DPD) along dimensions of the five-factor model, finding DPD to be associated with high levels of agreeableness and neuroticism and low levels of openness (Bornstein & Cecero, 2000; Gore, Presnall, Miller, Lynam, & Widiger, 2012; Lowe et al., 2009).

Despite their surface differences, interpersonal theories share at least two key assumptions: (1) that different personality types may be usefully conceptualized as styles of interacting with and relating to others, and (2) that different personality types can be reduced to some number of basic trait dimensions which, when combined, produce the major personality constellations identified by clinicians and researchers (Wiggins & Pincus, 1990). Beyond this, most interpersonal theories emphasize that personality traits are acquired and maintained through patterns of reward and punishment experienced in key relationships (see Benjamin, 1974; Kiesler, 1982). This is an important consideration in the dynamics of

dependency, insofar as interpersonal relationships are particularly salient for the dependent individual (Mongrain, Lubbers, & Struthers, 2004; Pincus & Gurtman, 1995).

Millon (1969, 1981) broadened interpersonal theory by emphasizing the interaction of organismic and environmental factors in the etiology and dynamics of personality traits and pathologies. Thus, biosocial-learning theory brings to the interpersonal framework a recognition that early learning and socialization experiences influence the strength and expression of motives that underlie various personality dimensions, and combine with biological factors (e.g., temperament variables) to produce particular constellations of traits, motivations, and behaviors (Millon & Grossman, 2005). Studies assessing the genetic underpinnings of DPD (e.g., Gjerde et al., 2012; Torgersen et al., 2000) suggest that between 30% and 60% of the variance in DPD symptoms may be attributable to genetic factors, providing indirect support for the hypothesized role of temperament variables in the etiology of DPD (see also South, Reichborn-Kjennerud, Eaton, & Krueger, 2012, for a review of research on the genetic underpinnings of PDs).

Millon (1990) undertook a major revision of his earlier model, linking personality traits and disorders to evolutionary theory. According to this view, personality traits evolved and are maintained through natural selection processes (Millon, 2003, 2011). Even those traits that represent exaggerations of adaptive behavior patterns have evolutionary roots (thus, strong dependency needs may be an extreme variant of normal affiliative strivings; see Baumeister & Leary, 1995).

Millon's (1990) interpersonal matrix combines four personality styles (*dependent, independent, ambivalent,* and *detached*) with two levels of activity (*active* versus *passive*). Dependency occupies the *dependent-passive* region and is characterized by

a search for relationships in which one can lean on others for affection, security, and leadership. [The dependent] personality's lack of both initiative and autonomy was considered to be a consequence largely of parental overprotection. As a function of these early experiences, these individuals simply learned the comforts of assuming a passive role in interpersonal relations, accepting whatever kindness and support they found, and willingly submitting to the wishes of others in order to maintain their affection (Millon & Davis, 1996, p. 68).

Research strongly supports Millon and Davis's (1996) contention that affection, security, and leadership seeking are central components of the dependent personality. Studies show that dependent people seek physical contact and comfort more readily than do nondependent people; prefer nurturant, protective romantic partners to those that encourage autonomy and independence; and subsume their needs to those of others (Birtchnell & Kennard, 1983; Mongrain, 1998). Other studies have shown that dependent individuals find comfort and reassurance in the presence of familiar people (Keinan & Hobfoll, 1989). Studies of infant–caregiver interactions and retrospective reports of parenting experiences confirm that the children of overprotective parents score high on a wide variety of dependency measures (Head et al., 1991); when parents exhibit both overprotectiveness and authoritarianism, high levels of dependency are particularly likely to result (Bornstein, 1993, 1996). Parental overprotectiveness and authoritarianism serve simultaneously to (1) reinforce dependent behavior; and (2) prevent the child from developing independent, autonomous behaviors (since the child is prevented from engaging in the kinds of trial-and-error learning that produce a sense of mastery and competence).

Research supports Millon's (1990, 2003) views regarding the relationships of the dependent person and the parenting characteristics that lead to high levels of dependency, but research does not support the notion that dependent individuals invariably "[assume] a passive role in interpersonal relations" (Millon & Davis, 1996, p. 68). As noted, studies show that the dependent person can be surprisingly assertive—even aggressive—in certain types of interpersonal transactions (e.g., when attempting to curry favor with a potential caregiver or preclude abandonment by a valued other; see Bornstein, 2006, 2007). Thus, the dependent individual is not as passive and compliant as psychologists once thought.

The Cognitive Perspective Cognitive models emphasize the role of the self-concept, beliefs regarding other people, and expectations of self–other interactions (sometimes referred to as "internal working models") in the etiology and

dynamics of normal and pathological personality traits. Cognitive theorists suggest that behavior can be understood and predicted with reference to an individual's core beliefs and interpersonal perceptions (see Mischel, 1973, 1979, 1984). Thus, Beck and Freeman (1990, p. 45) argued that the core belief of the dependent individual is "I am completely helpless," coupled with the sense that "I can function only if I have access to somebody competent." Beck and Freeman (1990, p. 290) went on to suggest that dependent persons ultimately "conclude that the solution to the dilemma of being inadequate in a frightening world is to try to find someone who seems able to handle life and who will protect and take care of them."

Bornstein (1993, 1996, 2011) extended traditional cognitive models of dependency by integrating into these models ideas and findings from object relations theory and developmental psychology. He contended that the etiology of DPD lies in two areas: overprotective, authoritarian parenting, and sex-role socialization. Consistent with Millon's (1969, 1981) biosocial-learning view, Bornstein (1993) argued that overprotective, authoritarian parenting fosters dependency by preventing the child from developing a sense of mastery following successful learning experiences. Consistent with Blatt's (1974) framework, Bornstein (1996) argued that parental overprotection and authoritarianism play a key role in the construction of a representation of the self as ineffectual and weak. Beyond this, sex-role socialization experiences further foster the development of a "dependent self-concept" in girls—and contribute to the higher rates of DPD diagnoses found in women relative to men—because traditional socialization practices encourage passivity and acquiescence in girls more strongly than in boys.

Cognitive structures formed in response to early experiences within the family affect the motivations, behaviors, and affective responses of the dependent person in predictable ways. A perception of the self as powerless and ineffectual will, first and foremost, have motivational effects: A person with such a self-concept is motivated to seek guidance, support, protection, and nurturance from other people. These motivations in turn produce particular patterns of dependent behavior: The person who is highly motivated to seek the guidance, protection, and support of others will behave in ways that maximize the probability that they will obtain the protection and support they desire. Finally, a representation of the self as powerless and ineffectual has important affective consequences (e.g., fear of abandonment, fear of negative evaluation).

Cognitive models of dependency differ from other theoretical frameworks in hypothesizing that while the dependent person's self-concept (and self-concept-based motives) remains stable, the dependent individual's behavior may vary considerably from situation to situation, depending on the demands, constraints, and risks of that situation (Bornstein, 2011, 2012). When behaving in a passive, submissive manner is likely to strengthen ties to potential nurturers and caregivers, the dependent person will behave passively and submissively. However, when active, assertive behavior seems more likely to strengthen important relationships, the dependent person becomes active and assertive. With this as context, Morgan and Clark (2010) delineated distinct active and passive expressions of underlying dependency that have noteworthy implications for social adjustment and risk for psychopathology (see also Bornstein, 2012, for a review of studies bearing on this issue).

Studies confirm that a view of the self as weak and ineffectual underlies a variety of dependency-related behaviors in DPD-diagnosed patients and nonclinical participants (Coyne & Whiffen, 1995; Overholser, 1996). Other studies suggest that dysfunctional beliefs about the self and other people play a role in the dynamics of dependency and help propagate dependency-related attitudes and responses (Lee & Ashton, 2006). Developmental investigations indicate that dependency-related cognitions are central to help, support, and reassurance seeking in children, adolescents, and adults (Birtchnell & Kennard, 1983). Recent laboratory investigations confirm that when the dependent person's helpless self-concept is activated or "primed" (i.e., brought into working memory), dependency-related thoughts, motives, and behaviors increase (Bornstein, 2007; Bornstein et al., 2005).

Along somewhat different lines, research offers strong support for the "interactionist" component of contemporary cognitive models of dependency. In a series of experiments, Bornstein, Riggs, Hill, and Calabrese (1996) pitted the dependent person's desire to please a figure of authority against his or her motivation to get along with a peer. Highly consistent results were obtained: When a dependent individual was led to believe that the

best way to strengthen ties to an important caregiver was to behave in a passive, compliant manner, the dependent person behaved passively and allowed a peer to outperform him or her on an intellectual task. Led to believe that the best way to strengthen ties to a nurturing, protecting figure was to become active and assertive, the dependent person behaved in an active—even aggressive—manner, competing quite vigorously with a peer on this same intellectual task. Simply put, when forced to choose between pleasing an authority figure and getting along with a peer, the dependent person almost invariably opted to please the authority figure—the person best able to provide help and support over the long term.

These results suggest that the behavior of the dependent person can be quite variable, but that underlying this variability is a fundamental cognitive consistency: a view of the self as weak, coupled with a belief that the best way to survive and thrive is to cultivate relationships with figures of authority. To predict the behavior of the dependent person one must focus first on dependency-related cognitions, then consider the effects of these cognitions on dependency-related motivations, behaviors, and emotional responses.

Histrionic Personality Disorder

There has been far less empirical research on HPD than DPD, and clinicians and researchers do not always agree on the characteristics that distinguish HPD from ostensibly similar forms of personality pathology (e.g., borderline PD; see Drapeau, Perry, & Korner, 2012). However, several common traits have emerged in recent descriptions of histrionic traits and tendencies. The "core" components of HPD include egocentricity, seductiveness, theatrical emotionality, denial of anger and hostility, and a diffuse (or global) cognitive style (Kellett, 2007; Pfohl, 1991, 1995). Among other traits frequently associated with HPD are impulsivity, gregariousness, manipulativeness, low frustration tolerance, pseudo-hypersexuality, suggestibility, and somatizing tendencies (Andrews & Moore, 1991; Kantor, 1992; Millon, 2011; Tomiatti, Gore, Lynam, Miller, & Widiger, 2012). The eight *DSM-IV/DSM-5* symptoms of HPD capture nicely these characteristics, and, in contrast to the *DSM* DPD criteria, which focus exclusively on behavior and affect, the HPD criteria capture the cognitive components of HPD (symptoms 5 and 8) in addition to its affective (symptoms 1 and 3) and behavioral features (symptoms 2, 4, 6, and 7).

HPD is unique among the 10 PDs in *DSM-IV* and *DSM-5* in at least one respect: It is the only disorder explicitly tied to physical characteristics of the individual. Several researchers have noted that HPD tends to appear primarily in women and men who are above average in physical attractiveness (Apt & Hurlbert, 1994; Char, 1985). In a sense this hypothesized link is not surprising. Clinicians and researchers agree that seductiveness is a key feature of the HPD individual's coping style, and physical appearance is an important feature of seductiveness. In this context, the *DSM-IV* noted that persons with HPD "consistently use physical appearance to draw attention to themselves are overly concerned with impressing others by their appearance and expend an excessive amount of time, energy, and money on clothes and grooming" (p. 655).

Although the existence of gender differences in HPD is well established, the processes that underlie these gender differences are not well understood. Research contrasting the expression of HPD symptoms in women and men has sought to disambiguate bias in diagnostic criteria from underlying gender differences in histrionic pathology (Hartung & Widiger, 1998). Some feminist perspectives suggest that inclusion of stereotypically feminine qualities within the diagnostic criteria for HPD reflects negative cultural attitudes toward traditionally feminine styles of interaction (Chodoff, 1982; Gould, 2011). In this context, findings point to gender differences in the expression of HPD symptoms, in at least two areas. First, clinicians agree that women more than men use overt sexual seductiveness to express histrionic needs in interpersonal relationships (Lilienfeld, Van Valkenburg, Larntz, & Akiskal, 1986; Stone, 1993). Second, researchers have argued that HPD in men often overlaps—or is subsumed completely by—antisocial traits and behaviors. It has even been suggested that histrionic and antisocial PDs are two sides of the same coin, and some epidemiological and family history data support that assertion (Blagov; Fowler, & Lilienfeld, 2007; Hamburger, Lilienfeld, & Hogben, 1996). According to this view, antisocial men tend to manipulate others through active intimidation while histrionic women achieve the same ends through seductive flirtation.

Consistent with these speculations, histrionic and antisocial symptoms show parallel associations with features of other *DSM-IV* PDs, suggesting that these disorders are linked by a shared predisposition toward impulsivity and behavioral disinhibition (Cale & Lilienfeld, 2002). Along somewhat different lines, findings indicate that people who behave in gender-consistent ways (i.e., highly masculine men and highly feminine women) exhibit more histrionic features than people who depart from traditional gender roles (Klonsky, Jane, Turkheimer, & Oltmanns, 2002).

Although few studies have assessed directly the relationships of ethnicity and cultural background to HPD symptoms and diagnoses (Makaremi, 1990), it appears that HPD is diagnosed more frequently in some cultural groups than others (Johnson, Cohen, Kasen, & Brook, 2006; Mullins-Sweatt, Wingate, & Lengel, 2012). Traditional socialization practices should lead to relatively low rates of HPD in many Asian cultures, where overt sexual seductiveness is often frowned upon (Johnson, 1993). Conversely, HPD should be diagnosed more frequently in those Hispanic and Latin American cultures where vivid, uninhibited emotionality is expected, especially among women (see Padilla, 1995). Grant et al. (2004) found that African American women are at significantly greater risk of HPD than Caucasian women.

As was true for DPD, HPD symptoms vary as a function of age. In children, histrionic tendencies are associated with manipulativeness, demandingness, and immaturity. The behavior of histrionic adolescents and adults is closer to HPD as described in *DSM-IV* and *DSM-5*, and is associated with seductiveness, theatricality, and pseudo-hypersexuality (i.e., overt sexual seductiveness coupled with an underlying fear and avoidance of sexuality; Crawford & Cohen, 2007). A prospective study of British patients showed a significant reduction in histrionic traits from early to middle adulthood (Seivewright, Tyrer, & Johnson, 2002), but—in contrast to DPD—HPD symptoms do not appear to diminish from middle to later adulthood (Gutierrez et al., 2012). It is likely that the expression of histrionicity evolves, however, as the flirtatiousness of early adulthood gives way to somatization and other indirect attention- and nurturance-seeking behaviors.

Epidemiology and Comorbidity

The prevalence of HPD varies from as low as 2% (Grant et al., 2004) to as high as 44% (Millon & Trignone 1989) or even 63% (Morey, 1988) in clinical and community samples. As is true of most PDs, HPD occurs more frequently in psychiatric patients than in community adults. A review of studies suggested that, despite some variation in base rates, the prevalence of HPD typically ranges from 0.2% to 2.9% in community samples (Lenzenweger, 2008).

Studies of gender differences in HPD prevalence rates have produced mixed results. Despite clinical lore, and the longstanding hypothesized association of HPD with femininity, several investigations have found no gender differences in HPD in psychiatric inpatients, outpatients, and nonclinical participants (Grant et al., 2004; Hamburger et al., 1996). However, other investigations using similar measures and methods have found that women receive HPD diagnoses more frequently than men do (Bakkevig, & Karterud, 2010; Schotte, de Doncker, Maes, Cluydts, & Cosyns, 1993).

Gender differences notwithstanding, it appears that gender stereotypes play an important role in predicting HPD diagnoses both among mental health professionals and for laypersons. For example, Sprock (2000) showed that clinical psychologists and psychiatrists rated masculine behavioral descriptions of HPD as being poorer examples of the HPD criteria than parallel feminine behavioral descriptions (see also Flanagan & Blashfield, 2003). In analog studies in which patient gender was varied across a common case description, community adults and university students assigned women 81% (Rubino, Saya, & Pezzarossa, 1992) and 100%, (Strangler & Printz, 1980) respectively, of all HPD diagnoses.

HPD shows substantial comorbidity with an array of psychological pathologies, including anxiety disorders (Blashfield & Davis, 1993), somatization disorder (Reich, 1987), dissociative disorders (Boon & Draijer, 1993), dysthymia (Pepper et al., 1995), and major depression (Dyck et al., 2001). HPD may also help determine the course of these disorders, with both positive and negative effects, depending on the population. For example, in one investigation patients with comorbid HPD and bipolar disorder had significantly more lifetime suicide attempts than bipolar patients without HPD (Garno, Goldberg, Ramirez, & Ritzler,

2005). However, in a Spanish sample of schizophrenics, the greater the number of histrionic traits the better the overall premorbid adjustment (Rodriguez-Solano & Gonzalez de Chavez, 2005).

As was true for DPD, studies quantifying PD comorbidity in terms of odds ratios suggest that HPD shows statistically significant comorbidity with most other PDs (e.g., Lenzenweger et al., 2007; Trull et al., 2010). Comorbidity levels tend to be highest for HPD and antisocial, narcissistic, borderline, and dependent PDs (Bakkevig, & Karterud, 2010; Drapeau et al., 2012; Flick, Roy-Byrne, Cowley, Shores, & Dunner, 1993). In a few studies HPD has also shown substantial comorbidity with paranoid, obsessive-compulsive, and avoidant PDs (Blashfield & Davis, 1993; Nestadt, Samuels, Romanoski, Folstein, & McHugh, 1994), but these are isolated findings that require replication before strong conclusions are drawn from such results.

Historical Perspectives

The history of HPD has been characterized by two major trends: (1) a gradual evolution from physical to psychological models, and (2) a parallel change in terminology from *hysterical* to *histrionic*. Both trends are ongoing, and both are incomplete. Most (but not all) theoretical speculation regarding the etiology and dynamics of HPD focuses on psychological rather than physical processes. Many (but not all) clinicians and researchers today use the term *histrionic* in lieu of the term *hysterical* to describe individuals who would fulfill the *DSM-IV/DSM-5* DPD criteria (Merskey, 1995).

Among the earliest writings in this area are those of Hippocrates and Plato (Ussher, 2003), who attributed hysterical traits in women to a "wandering womb" that moved too close to the brain and contaminated reason with emotion. Over time, such physical explanations were replaced with psychological theories, but the emphasis on emotionality remained. The eighteenth and nineteenth centuries saw a continued emphasis on sexuality in hysteria (a precursor of HPD), even prior to Freud's voluminous writings on this topic. Laycock (1840), Richer (1885), Janet (1907), and others helped solidify the link between "erotic passion" and hysterical traits and behaviors.

During the first decades of the twentieth century, theoretical writing on hysteria split into two independent streams, with psychoanalysts emphasizing the sexual origins of hysterical disorders, and descriptive psychiatrists like Kraepelin (1904) and Schneider (1923) focusing on the hysterical patient's immaturity and self-centeredness. Thus, while Freud (1931, p. 250) was asserting that "when persons of the erotic type fall ill they will develop hysteria," Kretschmer (1926, p. 26) was suggesting that hysterics show "a preference for what is loud and lively, a theatrical pathos, an inclination for brilliant roles...[and] a naïve, sulky egotism."

Oddly, neither the hysterical nor the histrionic personality appeared as a diagnostic category in *DSM-I*, although the *DSM-I* description of the "emotionally unstable personality" captured some of the qualities that would emerge in later *DSM* descriptions of HPD. In the *DSM-II*, hysterical and histrionic personality disorders became one: The formal diagnostic category "hysterical personality" was followed in parentheses by the term "histrionic personality disorder." The *DSM-II* symptoms of hysterical personality were much closer to modern conceptions of histrionicity than to contemporary models of hysteria (or the related construct of conversion disorder).

Not everyone favored the merging of hysteria and histrionicity in the *DSM-II* (see Gorton & Akhtar, 1990). Perhaps Kernberg (1984, 1986) has been the most vocal critic of this approach, arguing that these are distinct disorders that should be diagnosed independently and studied in relation to each other. Stone (1993) offered an opposing view as well, contending that hysteria represents the most profoundly disturbed, psychologically primitive manifestation of HPD.

A separate category of HPD emerged for the first time in *DSM-III*, and hysteria disappeared from the diagnostic nomenclature. In *DSM-III* the symptoms of HPD were divided into two broad, overlapping categories: (1) overly dramatic, intense behaviors (e.g., self-dramatization); and (2) characteristic disturbances in interpersonal relationships (e.g., being perceived by others as shallow). *DSM-III-R* and *DSM-IV* provided much more detailed (and precise) descriptions of HPD, but both continued to emphasize the emotionality, attention seeking, and shallow relationships that have long been associated with histrionic personality traits.

Contemporary Theoretical Perspectives

Only a small number of contemporary theoretical frameworks have been used to describe the etiology and dynamics of HPD—a far smaller number of models than has been used to conceptualize DPD in recent years (Beck & Freeman, 1990; Blacker & Tupin, 1991; Kantor, 1992). Similarly, while there has been a plethora of empirical studies of dependent personality traits since the early 1950s (Bornstein, 2005, 2012), there have been (at most) a few dozen empirical investigations testing hypotheses regarding the etiology and dynamics of histrionicity (Bakkevig & Karterud, 2010; Pfohl, 1991; Blagov & Westen, 2008). In the following sections we describe three of the most influential contemporary models of HPD: the psychoanalytic, cognitive-dynamic, and biosocial-learning models.

The Psychoanalytic Perspective   Although classical psychoanalytic theory got its start in Freud's treatment of hysterical patients (Breuer & Freud, 1895), early psychoanalytic theorists had little to say about hysterical personality traits, and even less to say about histrionicity. Freud's writings on this topic (and there were many) were limited almost entirely to speculation regarding hysterical conversion disorders (Kantor, 1992). It was Reich (1933, 1949) who provided the first detailed psychoanalytic description of the hysterical personality style, arguing that

> coquetry in gait, look or speech betrays, especially in women, the hysterical character type....We find fickleness of reactions...and...a strong suggestibility, which never appears alone but is coupled with a strong tendency to reactions of disappointment. An attitude of compliance is usually followed by its opposite, swift deprecation and groundless disparagement. (Reich, 1933, pp. 204–205)

A decade after Reich's initial work in this area, Fenichel (1945, pp. 527–528) linked hysterical and histrionic traits with pseudo-hypersexuality, noting that these individuals "are inclined to sexualize all nonsexual relations....The histrionic quality is a turning from reality to fantasy and probably also an attempt to master anxiety by 'acting' actively what otherwise might happen passively." Fenichel hinted at what psychodynamic theorists would later make explicit, namely that histrionicity is rooted in part in a rigid, maladaptive defensive style.

The assertive, attention-seeking behavior of the histrionic, coupled with his or her pseudo-hypersexuality, seemed to make the origins of histrionic personality traits obvious: Abraham (1927), Freud (1931), Reich (1933), and Fenichel (1945) quibbled about the details, but all agreed that hysterical traits stemmed from Oedipal fixation, penis envy (in women), and castration anxiety (in men). It was not until Marmor's classic (1953) paper on orality in the hysterical personality that the possibility was raised that histrionic traits might be rooted in oral rather than Oedipal needs. In Marmor's view, histrionic theatricality and pseudo-hypersexuality were not direct expressions of Oedipal wishes but served simultaneously as defenses and interpersonal coping strategies—defenses insofar as they kept underlying oral-dependent fantasies out of awareness, and coping strategies insofar as they enabled the histrionic person to maintain a network of gratifying, supportive relationships.

More recent psychoanalytic theorists have taken a compromise position regarding the oral-Oedipal dispute, suggesting that there exists a spectrum of histrionic personality configurations, ranging from those that are primarily oral in nature to those that are primarily Oedipal (Easser & Lesser, 1965; Kernberg, 1975; Stone, 1993). The "oral histrionic" appears to be functioning at a more primitive level than the "Oedipal histrionic," with less ego strength, poorer impulse control, weaker reality testing, and more primitive, maladaptive defenses (e.g., repression and denial rather than displacement and rationalization).

Factor-analytic investigations by Lazare, Klerman, and Armor (1966, 1970) offered indirect support for a hypothesized relationship between histrionicity and orality in that the "hysterical" personality factor that emerged in these studies included two oral traits (suggestibility and dependence) in addition to several histrionic traits (egocentricity, exhibitionism, emotionality, sexual provocativeness, and fear of sexuality). Subsequent factor analyses by Vandenberg and Helstone (1975) and Torgersen (1980) generally supported Lazare et al.'s findings, suggesting that certain oral traits tend to covary with histrionic traits and tendencies. Cogswell and Alloy (2006) demonstrated that neediness, a maladaptive component of dependency, is associated with histrionic features in college students; they concluded that HPD may be associated with explicit expressions of dependency. This conclusion contrasts with Bornstein's (1998) finding that HPD is correlated with increased implicit—but not

explicit—dependency, although this discrepancy may be in part a result of the two studies using different dependency scales.

Studies of the defensive style of the HPD individual offer some support for psychoanalytic writings in this area. When Von der Lippe and Torgersen (1984) assessed the relationship between hysterical traits and a performance-based measure of repression in a sample of pregnant women, they found a small but marginally significant relationship between these variables. Rubino et al. (1992) obtained similar results using Millon Clinical Multiaxial Inventory (MCMI) histrionicity scores and a behavioral index of repression in a heterogeneous sample of nonclinical participants.

Other studies of the histrionic person's defensive style used defense mechanism measures that did not include a separate repression index. Nonetheless, results of these investigations are generally consistent with psychoanalytic speculation in this area. Bornstein et al. (1990) found that Lazare-Klerman hysteria scores were positively correlated with scores on the Defense Mechanisms Inventory (DMI) *projection* and *turning-against-other* scales (Ihilevich & Gleser, 1986). Johnson, Bornstein, and Krukonis (1992) found that Personality Diagnostic Questionnaire–Revised (PDQ-R) HPD scores (Hyler et al., 1988) were positively correlated with maladaptive defense scores and negatively correlated with adaptive (mature) defense scores on the Defense Styles Questionnaire (DSQ; Bond et al., 1989). Johnson et al.'s results suggest that HPD symptoms are associated with reliance on more primitive defenses such as regression, and with an inability to use more mature defenses such as sublimation (see also Fernandez, 2010).

The Cognitive-Dynamic Perspective   The psychoanalytic hypothesis that histrionicity is associated with reliance on denial and repression has important implications for understanding the cognitive style of the histrionic person. This issue did not come completely to the fore until Shapiro (1965, pp. 111–112) argued that "hysterical cognition in general is global, relatively diffuse, and lacking in sharpness, particularly in sharp detail. In a word, it is impressionistic."

Subsequent theoretical analyses have tended to follow Shapiro's lead and emphasize the dysfunctional aspects of histrionic cognition. However, there were a few noteworthy exceptions to this trend. For example, Ortmeyer (1979) pointed out the links between a global cognitive style and creativity, while several theorists noted the relationship-facilitating functions of the histrionic person's inattention to detail (Andrews & Moore, 1991). As Andrews (1984, p. 217) wrote, the histrionic's "impressionistic approach facilitates the construction of conventionally idealized, oversimplified images of self and others…diverting attention away from displeasing realities, and [helping] maintain the pretense that everything in life is as 'nice' as it is supposed to be." This shift in emphasis from "histrionic cognition as deficit" to "histrionic cognition as both deficit and strength" parallels a similar shift (discussed earlier) in theorists' conceptualization of the interpersonal dynamics of dependency.

Horowitz (1991) altered the focus of the cognitive-dynamic perspective by considering the internal factors that bridge the gap between histrionic perception and histrionic behavior. In his view, a key component of HPD is an underlying information-processing bias that is reflected in the histrionic person's global perceptual style and manifested in other ways as well. As Horowitz noted, linking the various features of HPD is a mental representation of the self as "sexy star, wounded hero, worthy invalid, or appealing but neglected waif" (1991, p. 6). Histrionic behavior is choreographed by a *role-relationship model* (sometimes called an *internalized working model* or *script*), in which others play the supporting roles of "interested suitor, devoted rescuer, or rueful and now responsible caretaker" (p. 6).

A related approach to the conceptualization of HPD incorporates an interactionist perspective which contends that HPD-related responding is associated with activation of a maladaptive schema of the self in intimate interpersonal contexts (Rahamim, Meiran, Ostro, & Shahar, 2012). In two experiments participants with elevated HPD features exhibited increased automatic processing of hate/dislike information following a laboratory manipulation priming recall of intimacy. Rahamim et al.'s results are consistent with a conceptualization of histrionic behavior as being prompted in part by situational triggers such as perceived or imagined intimacy with a pseudo-parental figure.

Beck and Freeman (1990) have offered the most purely cognitive view of HPD, although they too acknowledge the psychodynamic roots of contemporary cognitive and cognitive-dynamic frameworks (see also Freeman & Leaf, 1989; Pfohl, 1991). Beck and Freeman (1990, p. 50) contend that

the core beliefs of the HPD person include, "Unless I captivate people I am nothing," "If I can't entertain people they will abandon me," and "If people don't respond to me they are rotten." This description echoes Beck and Freeman's conceptualization, with one important difference: To the naïve and succorant DPD person, relationships with nurturant caregivers are valued and cultivated, but to the more pessimistic HPD individual, potential caregivers are not to be trusted, so they must be manipulated instead. In fact, a study by Soygut, Nelson, and Safran (2001) supported this distinction, suggesting that HPD patients have a core belief that others will not take charge when needed.

Studies generally confirm that HPD is associated with a diffuse, impressionistic cognitive style. For example, McMullen and Rogers (1984) found that histrionic college students performed particularly well on intelligence and aptitude measures that tap global, impressionistic thinking, and relatively poorly on measures that assessed analytic thinking and attention to detail. Replicating and extending these results, Burgess (1992) found that HPD-diagnosed outpatients showed deficits on standardized tests of attention, memory, planning, and sequencing.

Along slightly different lines, Magaro, Smith, and Ashbrook (1983) found that histrionic female college students performed poorly on detailed visual search tasks involving focused attention and continuous tracking of stimuli. Studies indicating that histrionic individuals tend to show right-hemisphere dominance are also consistent with the hypothesis that histrionicity is associated with global, impressionistic thinking (Andrews, 1984; Burgess, 1992). A recent twin study suggested that HPD might be in part a manifestation of executive function deficits, as the two syndromes exhibit significant co-occurrence and may both be genetically correlated (Coolidge, Thede, & Jang, 2004). This finding sheds light on the neurocognitive basis for HPD-related impulsiveness, inability to delay gratification, and difficulty focusing on long-term goals.

The Biosocial-Learning Perspective Interpersonal and circumplex analyses of HPD emphasize its active, receptive, attention-seeking qualities (McLemore & Brokaw, 1987; Pincus, 2005), a conclusion confirmed empirically by five-factor model studies demonstrating that HPD patients are extraverted, open to experience, and low in agreeableness and conscientiousness (Furnam &

Crump, 2005; Tomiatti et al., 2012). Consistent with the interpersonal view, Millon and Davis (1996, p. 68) argued that the HPD person "shows an insatiable and indiscriminate search for stimulation and affection. This personality's sociable and capricious behaviors give the appearance of considerable independence of others, but beneath this guise lays a fear of autonomy and an intense need for signs of social approval and attention."

According to the biosocial-learning framework, HPD may arise in part from inconsistent patterns of reinforcement provided by parents and others (Millon, 2011). Like the infant whose caregivers do not respond until she screams at the top of her lungs, the histrionic child eventually learns that the way to get what she wants from others is to draw attention to herself through every means available—the more intrusive the better. Although the histrionic person's surface assertiveness belies an underlying insecurity and a tenuous, fragmented self-concept (Kernberg, 1984), over time the child who uses these attention- and nurturance-seeking strategies successfully may come to believe that she deserves special treatment, and that it will always be there if she continues to display attention-demanding behaviors.

Like the psychoanalytic and cognitive-dynamic theories, Millon's (1990) biosocial-learning model also emphasizes the seductive and stimulation-seeking qualities of the HPD person. Consequently, within Millon's framework HPD occupies the *active-dependent* region. Emphasizing affiliation over individuation and active modification of the environment over passive accommodation, the interpersonal style of the HPD person stands in marked contrast to the more solicitous, ingratiating style of DPD. Consistent with this framework, King and Terrance (2006) found that high MCMI-II histrionic scores were associated with ratings of close friendships as being high in self-affirmation and utilitarian value.

Millon and Davis's (1996) discussion of self-perpetuation processes in HPD expands upon the earlier work of Horowitz (1991) in making explicit the self-defeating nature of histrionic exploitation. While recognizing that histrionic seductiveness brings its share of rewards—both internal and external—Millon and Davis (1996, p. 386) also note that

one consequence of these fleeting and erratic relationships is that histrionics can never be sure of securing the affection and support they crave. By moving constantly and by devouring the affections of one person then another, they place themselves in jeopardy of having nothing to tide them over the times in between. They may be left high and dry, alone and abandoned with nothing to do and no excitement with which to be preoccupied.

If the central interpersonal risk of excessive dependency is abandonment and rejection, the central risk of histrionicity is alienation of others and a "sucking dry" of the surrounding interpersonal matrix—a histrionic "killing of the golden goose" (as it were) that can result from indiscriminate, unmodulated manipulation of others.

Several empirical findings offer indirect support for Millon's biosocial-learning model. For example, Baker, Capron, and Azorlosa (1996) found that the family dynamics of HPD individuals were characterized by a high degree of control but low cohesion—interaction patterns that would be expected to produce a histrionic self-presentation style later in life. Consistent with these results, Standage, Bilsbury, Jain, and Smith (1984) found that women with HPD showed impaired role- and perspective-taking skills and a lack of empathy: They had great difficulty assuming an objective, detached stance and seeing the world the way others might see it.

Along slightly different lines, studies offer some support for the notion that the HPD person's primary means of interpersonal influence is manipulation of others' needs and fears. Apt and Hurlbert (1994) found that HPD-diagnosed women showed overt sexual seductiveness in important interpersonal relationships, although underlying this pseudo-hypersexuality were powerful erotophobic feelings (see also Callaghan, Summers, & Weidman; 2003; Reise & Wright, 1996). Other investigations indicate that frustrated histrionics—like frustrated borderlines—are inclined to demand attention from others by making theatrical suicidal gestures directed toward therapists, friends, and romantic partners (see Fruensgaard & Hansen, 1988; Perry, 1989). Taken together, studies of family dynamics and interpersonal style confirm that HPD is rooted in inconsistent early reinforcement patterns, and that seductiveness and manipulativeness are central to the dynamics of HPD. It is also clear that HPD represents a particularly maladaptive expression of underlying dependency needs—more self-destructive in certain respects than the overt, unmodulated expression of dependency strivings characteristic of DPD.

Conclusion

Both DPD and HPD have a long history in psychology and psychiatry, but while research on DPD has reached maturity, research on HPD is still in its infancy. It is clear that a cognitive/interactionist model best accounts for the etiology and dynamics of DPD, but for HPD the picture is less clear. The psychoanalytic, cognitive-dynamic, and biosocial-learning approaches have all received some empirical support, but no theoretical framework has been tested definitively, and none has yet emerged as the most heuristic HPD model. One task for researchers during the coming years will be to assess empirically the many intriguing hypotheses regarding HPD that have been offered by clinicians and researchers.

Contrasting Dynamics in DPD and HPD

It is time to move beyond the longstanding distinction frequently applied to DPD and HPD—the notion that DPD represents "passive dependency" whereas HPD represents "active dependency." While it is true that, in general, the HPD individual tends to be more overtly assertive than the DPD individual, there is considerable flexibility in the behavior of DPD and HPD persons. Just as the HPD individual is capable of assuming a passive-receptive stance to seduce others, the DPD person is capable of being competitive and aggressive to obtain and maintain nurturant, supportive relationships. Studies are needed to ascertain which situations and circumstances elicit active behaviors in DPD and HPD individuals, and which situations and circumstances tend to elicit more passive behaviors.

A better way to contrast DPD and HPD is to focus on defenses and coping styles. Whereas DPD is associated with high levels of both implicit and self-attributed dependency needs, HPD is associated with high levels of implicit—but not self-attributed—dependency. Thus, while the DPD person expresses dependency needs directly, the HPD person displaces needs for support and reassurance from a valued other to the world at large. Finally, whereas the dependent person often recognizes anger and then directs it inward, the histrionic person relies more heavily on repression and denial to cope with unpleasant affect. Continued attention to the defenses and coping styles associated with DPD and HPD will allow clinicians and researchers to delineate additional distinctions between these two related disorders.

Extant research on DPD and HPD also points to several issues that warrant greater attention from clinicians and clinical researchers. For example, because studies did not support the *DSM-IV* assertion that women and men receive DPD diagnoses at equal rates, this passage was modified in *DSM-IV-TR*. Although there have been fewer studies of gender differences in HPD, extant data also suggest that women receive HPD diagnoses more often than men. Future investigations should address the sources of these gender differences more directly to determine whether they represent genuine differences in symptom patterns, self-report bias on the part of patients, problems with the diagnostic criteria, diagnostician bias, or some combination of these (and other) factors.

A second area for future research involves patienthood. Research indicates that DPD is associated with certain treatment-enhancing behaviors (e.g., conscientious adherence to medical and psychotherapeutic regimens) and with some treatment-interfering behaviors as well (e.g., overuse of health and mental health services). The same is true of HPD, which is associated with enhanced functioning in individuals with thought disorder, but diminished functioning in those with mood disorder. Given clinicians' increasing interest in understanding the links between personality pathology and treatment process and outcome, continued attention to the impact of DPD and HPD on patient-related responding is clearly needed.

DPD and HPD in DSM-5.1 *and Beyond*

Bornstein (1997, 2012) outlined an empirically supported set of DPD symptoms for future versions of the *DSM*; these may represent a useful starting point for revision of existing diagnostic criteria if DPD is included as a separate category in future versions of the manual. If DPD is not included as a unique PD category in *DSM-5.1* and beyond, and is instead replaced with a set of trait descriptors, preliminary studies suggest certain traits that may be useful in characterizing this syndrome. For example, when Hopwood et al. (2012) examined links between a broad array of higher and lower order traits and DPD symptoms in a large sample of undergraduates, they found that the higher order traits of negative affectivity, detachment, and psychoticism were most strongly related to DPD (among the lower order traits most strongly associated with DPD were separation insecurity, anxiousness, perseveration, depressivity, irresponsibility, distractability, and perceptual dysregulation). Using a modified version of the NEO Personality Inventory (NEO-PI) as their starting point, Gore et al. (2012) found separation insecurity, pessimism, helplessness, and ineptitude to be the trait descriptors most strongly predictive of pathological dependency as assessed by an array of established self-report scales.

Clearly, separation insecurity and pessimism/depressivity are among the core traits of excessive dependency in undergraduates; replication of these patterns in clinical populations is now needed. In addition, scrutiny of the diverse array of DPD-related traits obtained by Gore et al. (2012) and Hopwood et al. (2012) reaffirms that pathological dependency is more complex than clinicians initially believed, and is not characterized primarily by passivity and submissiveness as earlier DSM criteria had indicated (see Bornstein, 2012, for a discussion of this issue).

The picture is similarly complex for HPD, which—like DPD—will be included in *DSM-5*, with the *DSM-IV* symptoms retained. HPD might warrant inclusion as a distinct syndrome in *DSM-5.1*, or might instead be subsumed as a variant of DPD (akin to Morgan & Clark's [2010] active-emotional dependency), or as a high-functioning variant of borderline PD (with high emotional lability, impulsivity, and intimacy avoidance, but without the cognitive dysregulation and perceptual distortion characteristic of severe borderline pathology). Hopwood et al.'s (2012) undergraduate data suggest that the higher order traits most strongly linked with HPD are negative affectivity and antagonism (along with the lower order traits of emotional lability, and attention-seeking). Using the five-factor model as an overarching framework and NEO-PI as measure, Widiger, Lynam, Miller, and Oltmanns (2012) found emotionality, attention-seeking, suggestibility, vanity, and impressionistic thinking to be core features of histrionicity. As was the case for DPD, these preliminary trait-focused analyses, combined, suggest some common core traits characteristic of HPD across different samples and

measures (i.e., emotionality and attention-seeking), but—as with DPD—they also point to the complexity of histrionic pathology. In the absence of an empirically based set of symptom criteria for HPD in future versions of the *DSM*, the trait descriptions of Hopwood et al. (2012) and Widiger et al. (2012) represent a useful foundation for continued exploration of the intra- and interpersonal dynamics of histrionicity and HPD.

It is likely that the debate over dimensional versus category-based classification of DPD and HPD (as well as other PDs) will continue for some time; proponents of both positions have mustered compelling arguments. One possible pathway forward is to include both trait- and type-based diagnostic criteria in *DSM 5.1*, so that clinicians and clinical researchers can evaluate the relative merits of the two models and suggest ways of fine-tuning both. With this in mind, it is worth noting that Bornstein (2011; Bornstein & Huprich, 2011) and Hopwood et al. (2011) have offered integrative frameworks for PD diagnosis that combine elements of the type- and trait-focused approaches. Bornstein's (2011) model also includes a mechanism by which context-driven variability in PD responding can be included in the diagnostic record, as well as a procedure for noting the adaptive features of certain PD symptoms (e.g., the sensitivity to interpersonal cues often associated with exaggerated dependency, the relationship-facilitating theatricality sometimes found in high-functioning histrionics). Integrative perspectives like these may offer a useful mechanism for capturing the strengths of the categorical and dimensional diagnostic frameworks in future versions of the *DSM* and in other diagnostic systems as well.

References

Abraham, K. (1927). The influence of oral erotism on character formation. In C. A. D. Bryan & A. Strachey (Eds.), *Selected papers on psycho-analysis* (pp. 393–406). London: Hogarth.

Ainsworth, M. D. S. (1969). Object relations, dependency and attachment: A theoretical review of the infant-mother relationship. *Child Development, 40,* 969–1025.

Alnaes, R., & Torgersen, S. (1988). DSM-III symptom disorders and personality disorders in an outpatient population. *Acta Psychiatrica Scandinavica, 78,* 348–355.

Alnaes, R., & Torgersen, S. (1990). DSM-III personality disorders among patients with major depression, anxiety disorders and mixed conditions. *Journal of Nervous and Mental Disease, 178,* 693–698.

Andrews, J. D. (1984). Psychotherapy with the hysterical personality: An interpersonal approach. *Psychiatry, 47,* 211–232.

Andrews, J., & Moore, S. (1991). Social cognition in the histrionic/overconventional personality. In P. A. Magaro (Ed.), *Cognitive bases of mental disorders* (pp. 11–76). Newbury Park, CA: Sage.

Apt, C., & Hurlbert, D. F. (1994). The sexual attitudes, behavior and relationships of women with histrionic personality disorder. *Journal of Sex and Marital Therapy, 20,* 125–133.

Baker, J. D., Capron, E. W., & Azorlosa, J. (1996). Family environment characteristics of persons with histrionic and dependent personality disorders. *Journal of Personality Disorders, 10,* 82–87.

Bakkevig, J. F., & Karterud, S. (2010). Is the *Diagnostic and Statistical Manual of Mental Disorders, Fourth Edition,* histrionic personality disorder category a valid construct? *Comprehensive Psychiatry, 51,* 462–470.

Baumeister, R. F., & Leary, M. R. (1995). The need to belong: Desire for interpersonal attachment as a fundamental human motivation. *Psychological Bulletin, 117,* 479–529.

Beck, A. T., & Freeman, A. (1990). *Cognitive therapy of the personality disorders.* New York: Guilford Press.

Benjamin, L. S. (1974). A structural analysis of social behavior. *Psychological Review, 81,* 392–425.

Birtchnell, J., & Kennard, J. (1983). What does the MMPI dependency scale really measure? *Journal of Clinical Psychology, 39,* 532–543.

Black, D. W., Goldstein, R. B., & Mason, E. E. (1992). Prevalence of mental disorder in 88 morbidly obese bariatric clinic patients. *American Journal of Psychiatry, 149,* 227–234.

Blacker, K. H., & Tupin, J. P. (1991). Hysteria and hysterical structures: Developmental and social theories. In M. J. Horowitz (Ed.), *Hysterical personality style and the histrionic personality disorder* (pp. 17–66). Northvale, NJ: Jason Aronson.

Blagov, P. S., Fowler, K. A., & Lilienfeld, S. O. (2007). Histrionic personality disorder. In W. O'Donohue, K.A. Fowler, & S. O. Lilienfeld, (Eds.), *Personality disorders: Toward the DSM-V* (pp. 203–232). Thousand Oaks, CA: Sage.

Blagov, P. S., & Westen, D. (2008). Questioning the coherence of histrionic personality disorder: Borderline and hysterical personality subtypes in adults and adolescents. *Journal of Nervous and Mental Disease, 196,* 785–797.

Blashfield, R. K., & Davis, R. T. (1993). Dependent and histrionic personality disorders. In P. B. Sutker & H. E. Adams (Eds.), *Comprehensive handbook of psychopathology* (pp. 395–409). New York: Plenum Press.

Blatt, S. J. (1974). Levels of object representation in anaclitic and introjective depression. *Psychoanalytic Study of the Child, 29,* 107–157.

Blatt, S. J., Cornell, C. E., & Eshkol, E. (1993). Personality style, differential vulnerability, and clinical course in immunological and cardiovascular disease. *Clinical Psychology Review, 13,* 421–450.

Blatt, S. J., & Shichman, S. (1983). Two primary configurations of psychopathology. *Psychoanalysis and Contemporary Thought, 6,* 187–254.

Blatt, S. J., Wein, S. J., Chevron, E. S., & Quinlan, D. M. (1979). Parental representations and depression in normal young adults. *Journal of Abnormal Psychology, 88,* 388–397.

Bond, M., Perry, J. C., Gautier, M., Goldenberg, M., Openheimer, J., & Simand, J. (1989). Validating the self-report of defense styles. *Journal of Personality Disorders, 3,* 101–112.

Boon, S., & Draijer, N. (1993). The differentiation of patients with MPD or DDNOS from patients with a Cluster B personality disorder. *Dissociation, 6,* 126–135.

Bornstein, R. F. (1992). The dependent personality: Developmental, social and clinical perspectives. *Psychological Bulletin, 112,* 3–23.

Bornstein, R. F. (1993). *The dependent personality.* New York: Guilford Press.

Bornstein, R. F. (1995). Sex differences in objective and projective dependency tests: A meta-analytic review. *Assessment, 2,* 319–331.

Bornstein, R. F. (1996). Beyond orality: Toward an object relations/interactionist reconceptualization of the etiology and dynamics of dependency. *Psychoanalytic Psychology, 13,* 177–203.

Bornstein, R. F. (1997). Dependent personality disorder in the DSM-IV and beyond. *Clinical Psychology: Science and Practice, 4,* 175–187.

Bornstein, R. F. (1998). Implicit and self-attributed dependency strivings: Differential relationships to laboratory and field measures of help-seeking. *Journal of Personality and Social Psychology, 75,* 778–787.

Bornstein, R. F. (1999). Criterion validity of objective and projective dependency tests: A meta-analytic assessment of behavioral prediction. *Psychological Assessment, 11*, 48–57.

Bornstein, R. F. (2001). A meta-analysis of the dependency-eating disorders relationship: Strength, specificity, and temporal stability. *Journal of Psychopathology and Behavioral Assessment, 23*, 151–162.

Bornstein, R. F. (2005). *The dependent patient: A practitioner's guide.* Washington, DC: American Psychological Association.

Bornstein, R. F. (2006). The complex relationship between dependency and domestic violence: Converging psychological factors and social forces. *American Psychologist, 61*, 595–606.

Bornstein, R. F. (2007). Dependent personality disorder: Effective time-limited therapy. *Current Psychiatry, 6*, 37–45.

Bornstein, R. F. (2011). An interactionist perspective on interpersonal dependency. *Current Directions in Psychological Science, 20*, 124–128.

Bornstein, R. F. (2012). From dysfunction to adaptation: An interactionist model of dependency. *Annual Review of Clinical Psychology, 8*, 291–316.

Bornstein, R. F., & Cecero, J. J. (2000). Deconstructing dependency in a five-factor world: A meta-analytic review. *Journal of Personality Assessment, 74*, 324–343.

Bornstein, R. F., Galley, D. J., & Leone, D. R. (1986). Parental representations and orality. *Journal of Personality Assessment, 50*, 80–89.

Bornstein, R. F., Greenberg, R. P., Leone, D. R., & Galley, D. J. (1990). Defense mechanism correlates of orality. *Journal of the American Academy of Psychoanalysis, 18*, 654–666.

Bornstein, R. F., & Huprich, S. K. (2011). Beyond dysfunction and threshold-based classification: A multidimensional model of personality disorder diagnosis. *Journal of Personality Disorders, 25*, 331–337.

Bornstein, R. F., Leone, D. R., & Galley, D. J. (1988). Rorschach measures of oral dependence and the internalized self-representation in normal college students. *Journal of Personality Assessment, 52*, 648–657.

Bornstein, R. F., Ng, H. M., Gallagher, H. A., Kloss, D. M., & Regier, N. G. (2005). Contrasting effects of self-schema priming on lexical decisions and Interpersonal Stroop Task performance: Evidence for a cognitive/interactionist model of interpersonal dependency. *Journal of Personality, 73*, 731–761.

Bornstein, R. F., Riggs, J. M., Hill, E. L., & Calabrese, C. (1996). Activity, passivity, self-denigration, and self-promotion: Toward an interactionist model of interpersonal dependency. *Journal of Personality, 64*, 637–673.

Breuer, J., & Freud, S. (1895). *Studies on hysteria* (Standard Edition Vol. 2, pp. 1–307). London: Hogarth Press.

Burgess, W. J. (1992). Neurocognitive impairment in dramatic personalities: Histrionic, narcissistic, borderline and antisocial disorders. *Psychiatry Research, 42*, 283–290.

Cale, E. M. & Lilienfeld, S. O. (2002). Histrionic personality disorder and antisocial personality disorder: Sex-differentiated manifestations of psychopathy? *Journal of Personality Disorders, 16*, 52–72.

Callaghan, G. M., Summers, C. J., & Weidman, M. (2003). The treatment of histrionic and narcissistic personality disorder behaviors: A single-subject demonstration of clinical improvement using functional analytic psychotherapy. *Journal of Contemporary Psychotherapy, 33*, 321–339.

Char, W. F. (1985). The hysterical spouse. *Medical Aspects of Human Sexuality, 19*, 123–133.

Chodoff, P. (1982). Hysteria and women. *American Journal of Psychiatry, 139*, 545–551.

Cogswell, A., & Alloy, L. B. (2006) The relation of neediness and Axis II pathology. *Journal of Personality Disorders, 20*, 16–21.

Coolidge, F. L., Thede, L. L., & Jang, K. L. (2004). Are personality disorders manifestations of executive function deficits? Bivariate heritability evidence from a twin study. *Behavior Genetics, 34*, 75–84.

Coyne, J. C., & Whiffen, V. E. (1995). Issues in personality as diathesis for depression: The case of sociotropy-dependency and autonomy-self-criticism. *Psychological Bulletin, 118*, 358–378.

Crawford, T. N., & Cohen, P. R. (2007). Histrionic personality disorder. In A. Freeman & M. A. Reinecke (Eds.), *Personality disorders in childhood and adolescence* (pp. 495–532). Hoboken, NJ: John Wiley & Sons.

Cross, S. E., Bacon, P. L., & Morris, M. L. (2000). The relational-interdependent self-construal and relationships. *Journal of Personality and Social Psychology, 78*, 791–808.

Drapeau, M., Perry, J. C., & Korner, A. (2012). Interpersonal patterns in borderline personality disorder. *Journal of Personality Disorders, 26*, 583–592.

Dyck, I., Phillips, K., Warshaw, M., Dolan, R., Shea, M. T., Stout, R., Massion, A., Zlotnick, C. &

Keller, M. (2001). Patterns of personality pathology in patients with generalized anxiety disorder, panic disorder with and without agoraphobia, and social phobia. *Journal of Personality Disorders, 15*, 60–71.

Easser, R., & Lesser, S. (1965). Hysterical personality: A re-evaluation. *Psychoanalytic Quarterly, 34*, 390–402.

Fenichel, O. (1945). *The psychoanalytic theory of neurosis.* New York: Norton.

Fernandez, S. V. (2010). Complex case. Carmen: Histrionic personality disorder and psychotherapy. *Personality and Mental Health, 4*, 146–152.

Fiori, K., Consedine, N., & Magai, C. (2008). The adaptive and maladaptive faces of dependency in later life: Links to physical and psychological health outcomes. *Aging and Mental Health, 12*, 700–712.

Flanagan, E. H., & Blashfield, R. K. (2003). Gender bias in the diagnosis of personality disorders: The roles of base rates and social stereotypes. *Journal of Personality Disorders, 17*, 431–446.

Flick, S. N., Roy-Byrne, P. P., Cowley, D. S., Shores, M. M., & Dunner, D. L. (1993). DSM-III-R personality disorders in a mood and anxiety disorders clinic: Prevalence, comorbidity and clinical correlates. *Journal of Affective Disorders, 27*, 71–79.

Ford, M. R., & Widiger, T. A. (1989). Sex bias in the diagnosis of histrionic and antisocial personality disorders. *Journal of Consulting and Clinical Psychology, 57*, 301–305.

Freeman, A., & Leaf, R. C. (1989). Cognitive therapy applied to personality disorders. In A. Freeman, K. M. Simon, L. E. Beutler, & H. Arkowitz (Eds.), *Comprehensive handbook of cognitive therapy* (pp. 403–433). New York: Plenum Press.

Freud, S. (1905). *Three essays on the theory of sexuality* (Standard Edition Vol. 7, pp. 125–248). London: Hogarth Press.

Freud, S. (1908). *Character and anal erotism* (Standard Edition Vol. 9, pp. 167–176). London: Hogarth Press.

Freud, S. (1915). *Some character types met with in psycho-analytic work* (Standard Edition Vol. 14, pp. 310–333). London: Hogarth.

Freud, S. (1923). *The ego and the id* (Standard Edition Vol. 21, pp. 3–66). London: Hogarth Press.

Freud, S. (1931). *Libidinal types* (Standard Edition Vol. 22, pp. 310–333). London: Hogarth Press.

Freud, S. (1938). *An outline of psychoanalysis* (Standard Edition Vol. 23, pp. 125–248). London: Hogarth Press.

Fromm, E. (1947). *Man for himself.* New York: Rinehart.

Fruensgaard, K., & Hansen, H. F. (1988). Disease patterns seen in self-mutilating patients. *Nordisk Psykiatrisk Tidsskrift, 42*, 281–288.

Furnam, A., & Crump, J. (2005). Personality traits, types, and disorders: An examination of the relationship between three self-report measures. *European Journal of Personality 19*, 167–184.

Garno, J. L., Goldberg, J. F., Ramirez P. M., & Ritzler B. A. (2005) Bipolar disorder with comorbid Cluster B personality disorder features: Impact on suicidality. *Journal of Clinical Psychiatry, 66*, 339–345.

Gjerde, L. C., Czajkowski, N., Roysamb, E., Orstavik, R. E., Knudsen, G. P., Ostby, K., et al. (2012). The heritability of avoidant and dependent personality disorder assessed by personal interview and questionnaire. *Acta Psychiatrica Scandinavica, 126*, 448–457.

Gore, W. L., Presnall, J. R., Miller, J. D., Lynam, D. R., & Widiger, T. A. (2012). A five-factor measure of dependent personality traits. *Journal of Personality Assessment, 94*, 488–499.

Gorton, G., & Akhtar, S. (1990). The literature on personality disorders, 1985–1988: Trends, issues and controversies. *Hospital and Community Psychiatry, 41*, 39–51.

Gould, C. S. (2011). Why the histrionic personality disorder should not be in the DSM: A new taxonomic and moral analysis. *International Journal of Feminist Approaches to Bioethics, 4*, 26–40.

Grant, B. F., Hasin, D. S., Stinson, F. S., Dawson, D. A., Chou, S. P., Ruan, W. J., & Pickering, R. P. (2004). Prevalence, correlates, and disability of personality disorders in the U.S.: Results from the National Epidemiologic Survey on Alcohol and Related Conditions. *Journal of Clinical Psychiatry, 65*, 948–958.

Greenberg, J. R., & Mitchell, S. J. (1983). *Object relations in psychoanalytic theory.* Cambridge, MA: Harvard University Press.

Gutierrez, F., Vall, G., Peri, J. M., Bailles, E., Ferraz, L., Garriz, M., & Caseras, X. (2012). Personality disorders through the life course. *Journal of Personality Disorders, 26*, 763–774.

Hamburger, M. E., Lilienfeld, S. O., & Hogben, M. (1996). Psychopathy, gender and gender roles: Implications for antisocial and histrionic personality disorders. *Journal of Personality Disorders, 10*, 41–55.

Hartung, C. M., & Widiger, T. A. (1998). Gender differences in the diagnosis of mental disorders: conclusions and controversies of the DSM-IV. *Psychological Bulletin, 123*, 260–278.

Head, S. B., Baker, J. D., & Williamson, D. A. (1991). Family environment characteristics and dependent personality disorder. *Journal of Personality Disorders, 5*, 256–263.

Heinstein, M. L. (1963). Behavioral correlates of breast-bottle regiments under varying parent-infant relationships. *Monographs of the Society for Research in Child Development, 28*, 1–61.

Hopwood, C. J., Malone, J. C., Ansell, E. B., Sanislow, C. A., Grilo, C. M., McGlashan, T. H., et al. (2011). Personality assessment in DSM-5: Empirical support for rating severity, style, and traits. *Journal of Personality Disorders, 25*, 305–320.

Hopwood, C. J., Thomas, K. M., Markon, K. E., Wright, A. G. C., & Krueger, R. F. (2012). DSM-5 personality traits and DSM-IV personality disorders. *Journal of Abnormal Psychology, 121*, 424–432.

Horney, K. (1945). *Our inner conflicts.* New York: Norton.

Horowitz, M. J. (1991). *Hysterical personality disorder.* Northvale, NJ: Jason Aronson.

Hyler, S. E., Rieder, R. O., Williams, J. B. W., Spitzer, R. L., Hendler, J., & Lyons, M. (1988). The Personality Diagnostic Questionnaire: Development and preliminary results. *Journal of Personality Disorders, 2*, 229–237.

Ihilevich, D., & Gleser, G. C. (1986). *Defense mechanisms: Their classification, correlates and measurement with the Defense Mechanisms Inventory.* Owosso, MI: DMI Associates.

Jackson, H. J., Rudd, R., Gazis, J., & Edwards, J. (1991). Using the MCMI to diagnose personality disorders in inpatients: Axis I/Axis II associations and sex differences, *Australian Psychologist, 26*, 37–41.

Janet, P. (1907). *The mental state of hystericals: A study of mental stigmata and mental accidents.* New York: Putnam.

Johnson, F. A. (1993). *Dependency and Japanese socialization.* New York: New York University Press.

Johnson, J. G., Bornstein, R. F., & Krukonis, A. B. (1992). Defense styles as predictors of personality disorder symptomatology. *Journal of Personality Disorders, 6*, 408–416.

Johnson, J. G., Cohen, P., Kasen, S., & Brook, J. S. (2006). Personality disorders evident by early adulthood and risk for eating and weight problems during middle adulthood. *International Journal of Eating Disorders, 39*, 184–192.

Kantor, M. (1992). *Diagnosis and treatment of the personality disorders.* St. Louis: Ishiyaku Euroamerica.

Kaul, V., Mathur, P., & Murlidharan, R. (1982). Dependency and its antecedents: A review. *Indian Educational Review, 17*, 35–46.

Keinan, G., & Hobfoll, S. E. (1989). Stress, dependency and social support: Who benefits from husband's presence in delivery? *Journal of Social and Clinical Psychology, 8*, 32–44.

Kellett, S. (2007). A time series evaluation of the treatment of histrionic personality disorder with cognitive analytic therapy. *Psychology and Psychotherapy: Theory, Research and Practice, 80*, 389–405.

Kernberg, O. F. (1975). *Borderline conditions and pathological narcissism.* New York: Jason Aronson.

Kernberg, O. F. (1984). *Severe personality disorders.* New Haven, CT: Yale University Press.

Kernberg, O. F. (1986). Hysterical and histrionic personality disorders. In A. Cooper, A. Frances, & M. Sacks (Eds.), *Psychiatry, volume 1: The personality disorders and neuroses* (pp. 267–286). New York: Basic Books.

Kiesler, D. J. (1982). Interpersonal theory for personality and psychotherapy. In J. C. Anchinn & D. J. Kiesler (Eds.), *Handbook of interpersonal psychotherapy* (pp. 3–24). New York: Pergamon Press.

King, A. R., & Terrance, C. (2006). Relationships between personality disorder attributes and friendship qualities among college students. *Journal of Social and Personal Relationships, 23*, 5–20.

Klonsky, E. D., Jane, J. S., Turkheimer, E., & Oltmanns, T. F. (2002). Gender role and personality disorders. *Journal of Personality Disorders, 16*, 464–476.

Kohut, H. (1971). *The analysis of the self.* New York: International Universities Press.

Kraepelin, E. (1904). *Lectures on clinical psychiatry.* New York: Wood.

Kraepelin, E. (1913). *Psychiatrie: Ein Lehrbuch.* Leipzig: Barth.

Kretschmer, E. (1926). *Hysteria.* New York: Nervous and Mental Disease Publishers.

Laycock, T. (1840). *A treatise on the nervous disease of women.* London: Longmans, Orme, Brown, Green & Longmans.

Lazare, A., Klerman, G. L., & Armor, D. (1966). Oral, obsessive and hysterical personality patterns. *Archives of General Psychiatry, 14*, 624–630.

Lazare, A., Klerman, G. L., & Armor, D. (1970). Oral, obsessive and hysterical personality patterns: Replication of factor analysis in an independent sample. *Journal of Psychiatric Research, 7*, 275–290.

Leary, T. (1957). *Interpersonal diagnosis of personality*. New York: Ronald.

Lee, K., & Ashton, M. C. (2006). Further assessment of the HEXACO Personality Inventory: Two new facet scales and an observer report form. *Psychological Assessment, 18*, 182–191.

Lenzenweger, M. F. (2008). Epidemiology of personality disorders. *Psychiatric Clinics of North America, 31*, 395–403.

Lenzenweger, M. F., Lane, M. C., Loranger, A. W., & Kessler, R. C. (2007). DSM-IV personality disorders in the National Comorbidity Survey Replication. *Biological Psychiatry, 62*, 553–564.

Lilienfeld, S. O., Van Valkenburg, C., Larntz, K., & Akiskal, H. S. (1986). The relationship of histrionic personality disorder to antisocial personality and somatization disorders. *American Journal of Psychiatry, 143*, 718–722.

Lowe, J. R., Edmundsun, M., & Widiger, T. A. (2009). Assessment of dependency, agreeableness, and their relationship. *Psychological Assessment, 21*, 543–553.

Magaro, P., Smith, P., & Ashbrook, R. (1983). Personality style differences in visual search performance. *Psychiatry Research, 10*, 131–138.

Maier, W., Lichtermann, D., Klingler, T., Heun, R., & Hallmayer, J. (1992). Prevalences of personality disorders (DSM-III-R) in the community. *Journal of Personality Disorders, 6*, 187–196.

Makaremi, A. (1990). Histrionic disorder among Iranian high school and college students. *Psychological Reports, 66*, 835–838.

Marmor, J. (1953). Orality in the hysterical personality. *Journal of the American Psychoanalytic Association, 1*, 656–671.

McLemore, C. W., & Brokaw, D. W. (1987). Personality disorders as dysfunctional interpersonal behavior. *Journal of Personality Disorders, 1*, 270–285.

McMullen, L., & Rogers, D. (1984). WAIS characteristics of non-pathological obsessive and hysteric styles. *Journal of Clinical Psychology, 40*, 77–579.

Merskey, H. (1995). Commentary on histrionic personality disorder. In W. J. Livesley (Ed.), *The DSM-IV personality disorders* (pp. 193–200). New York: Guilford Press.

Millon, T. (1969). *Modern psychopathology: A biosocial approach to maladaptive learning and functioning*. Philadelphia: Saunders.

Millon, T. (1981). *Disorders of personality: DSM-III Axis 2*. New York: John Wiley & Sons.

Millon, T. (1990). *Toward a new personology: An evolutionary model*. New York: John Wiley & Sons.

Millon, T. (2003). Evolution: A generative source for conceptualizing the attributes of personality. In T. Millon & M. Lerner (Eds.), *Handbook of psychology: Personality and social psychology* (Vol. 5, pp. 3–30). New York: John Wiley & Sons.

Millon, T. (2011). *Disorders of personality: Introducing a DSM/ICD spectrum from normal to abnormal*. New York: John Wiley & Sons.

Millon, T., & Davis, R. D. (1996). *Disorders of personality: DSM-IV and beyond*. New York: John Wiley & Sons.

Millon, T., & Grossman, S. D. (2005). Personology: A theory based on evolutionary concepts. In M. F. Lenzenweger & J. F. Clarkin (Eds.), *Major theories of personality disorder* (2nd ed., pp. 332–390). New York: Guilford Press.

Millon, T., & Tringone, R. (1989). Co-occurrence and diagnostic efficiency statistics. Unpublished raw data.

Mischel, W. (1973). Toward a cognitive social learning reconceptualization of personality. *Psychological Review, 80*, 252–283.

Mischel, W. (1979). On the interface of cognition and personality: Beyond the person-situation debate. *American Psychologist, 34*, 740–754.

Mischel, W. (1984). Convergences and challenges in the search for consistency. *American Psychologist, 39*, 351–364.

Mongrain, M. (1998). Parental representations and support-seeking behaviors related to dependency and self-criticism. *Journal of Personality, 66*, 151–173.

Mongrain, M., Lubbers, R., & Struthers, W. (2004). The power of love: Mediation of rejection in roommate relationships of dependents and self-critics. *Personality and Social Psychology Bulletin, 30*, 94–105.

Morey, L. C. (1988). A psychometric analysis of the DSM-III-R personality disorder criteria. *Journal of Personality Disorders, 2*, 109–124.

Morgan, T. A., & Clark, L. A. (2010). Passive-submissive and active-emotional trait dependency: Evidence for a two-factor model. *Journal of Personality, 78*, 1325–1352.

Mullins-Sweatt, S. N., Bernstein, D. P., & Widiger, T. A. (2012). Retention or deletion of personality disorder diagnoses for DSM-5: An expert consensus approach. *Journal of Personality Disorders, 26*, 688–703.

Mullins-Sweatt, S. N., Wingate, L. R., & Lengel, G. J. (2012). Histrionic personality disorder: Diagnostic and treatment considerations. In P. K. Lundberg-Love, K. L. Nadal, & M. A. Paludi (Eds.) *Women and mental disorders* (pp. 57–73). Santa Barbara, CA: Praeger.

Murphy, C. M., Meyer, S. L., & O'Leary, K. D. (1994). Dependency characteristics of partner assaultive men. *Journal of Abnormal Psychology, 103,* 729–735.

Narduzzi, K. J., & Jackson, T. (2000). Personality differences between eating-disordered women and a nonclinical comparison sample. *Journal of Clinical Psychology, 56,* 699–710.

Neki, J. S. (1976). An examination of the cultural relativism of dependence as a dynamic of social and therapeutic relationships. *British Journal of Medical Psychology, 49,* 1–10.

Nestadt, G., Samuels, J. F., Romanoski, A. J., Folstein, M. F., & McHugh, P. R. (1994). Obsessions and compulsions in the community. *Acta Psychiatrica Scandinavica, 89,* 219–224.

Ng, H. M., & Bornstein, R. F. (2005). Comorbidity of dependent personality disorder and anxiety disorders: A meta-analytic review. *Clinical Psychology: Science and Practice, 12,* 395–406.

O'Neill, R. M., & Bornstein, R. F. (2001). The dependent patient in a psychiatric inpatient setting: Relationship of interpersonal dependency to consultation and medication frequencies. *Journal of Clinical Psychology, 57,* 289–298.

Ortmeyer, D. (1979). Interpersonal psychotherapy with the hysterical character. In G. Goldman & D. Millman (Eds.), *Parameters in psychoanalytic psychotherapy* (pp. 142–165). Dubuque, IA: Kendall/Hunt.

Overholser, J. C. (1996). The dependent personality and interpersonal problems. *Journal of Nervous and Mental Disease, 184,* 8–16.

Padilla, A. M. (1995). *Hispanic psychology: Critical issues in theory and research.* Newbury Pak, CA: Sage.

Pepper, C. M., Klein, D. N., Anderson, R. L., Riso, L. P., Ouimette, P. C., & Lizardi, H. (1995). DSM-III-R Axis II comorbidity in dysthymia and major depression. *American Journal of Psychiatry, 152,* 239–247.

Perry, J. C. (1989). Personality disorders, suicide and self-destructive behavior. In D. Jacobs & H. N. Brown (Eds.), *Suicide: Understanding and reporting* (pp. 157–169). Madison, CT: International Universities Press.

Pfohl, B. (1991). Histrionic personality disorder: A review of available data and recommendations for DSM-IV. *Journal of Personality Disorders, 5,* 150–166.

Pfohl B. (1995). Histrionic personality disorder. In W. J. Livesley (Ed.), *The DSM-IV personality disorders* (pp. 173–192). New York: Guilford Press.

Pincus, A. L. (2005). A contemporary integrative interpersonal theory of personality disorders. In M. F. Lenzenweger & J. F. Clarkin (Eds.), *Major theories of personality disorder* (2nd ed., pp. 282–331). New York: Guilford Press.

Pincus, A. L., & Gurtman, M. B. (1995). The three faces of interpersonal dependency: Structural analysis of self-report dependency measures. *Journal of Personality and Social Psychology, 69,* 744–758.

Rahamim, O., Meiran, N., Ostro, S., & Shahar, G. (2012). Individuals with histrionic personality disorder features categorize disliked persons as negative following intimacy induction: A state trait interaction analysis. *Personality and Individual Differences, 52,* 788–793.

Reich, J. (1987). Sex distribution of DSM-III personality disorders in psychiatric outpatients. *American Journal of Psychiatry, 144,* 181–187.

Reich, W. (1933). *Charakteranalyse.* Leipzig: Sexpol Verlag.

Reich, W. (1949). *Character analysis.* New York: Farrar, Straus and Giroux.

Reise, S. P. & Wright, T. M. (1996). Personality traits, Cluster B personality disorders, and sociosexuality. *Journal of Research in Personality, 30,* 128–136.

Richer, P. (1885). *Etudes cliniques sur la grande hysterie, ou hystero-epilepsie.* Paris: Adrien Delahaye et Emile LeCrosnier.

Rodriguez-Solano J. J., & Gonzalez de Chavez, M. (2005). Premorbid adjustment and previous personality in schizophrenic patients. *European Journal of Psychiatry, 19,* 243–254.

Rubino, I. A., Saya, A., & Pezzarossa, B. (1992). Percept-genetic signs of repression in histrionic personality disorder. *Perceptual and Motor Skills, 74,* 451–464.

Sadeh, A., Rubin, S. S., & Berman, E. (1993). Parental and relationship representations and experiences of depression in college students. *Journal of Personality Assessment, 60,* 192–204.

Samuel, D. B., & Widiger, T. A. (2010). A comparison of obsessive-compulsive personality disorder scales. *Journal of Personality Assessment, 92,* 232–240.

Sato, T. (2001). Autonomy and relatedness in psychopathology and treatment: A cross-cultural formulation. *Genetic, Social, and General Psychology Monographs, 127,* 89–127.

Schneider, K. (1923). *Psychopathic personalities.* London: Cassell.

Schotte, C., de Donker, D., Maes, M., Cluydts, R., & Cosyns, P. (1993). MMPI assessment of DSM-III-R histrionic personality disorder. *Journal of Personality Assessment, 60,* 500–510.

Seivewright, H., Tyrer, P., & Johnson T. (2002). Change in personality status in neurotic disorders. *Lancet, 359,* 9325.

Shapiro, D. (1965). *Neurotic styles.* New York: Basic Books.

South, S. C., Reichborn-Kjennerud, T., Eaton, N. R., & Krueger, R. F. (2012). Behavior and molecular genetics of personality disorders. In T. A. Widiger (Ed.), *Oxford handbook of personality disorders* (pp. 143–165). New York: Oxford University Press.

Soygut, G., Nelson, L., & Safran, J. D. (2001). The relationship between patient pretreatment interpersonal schemas and therapeutic alliance in short-term cognitive therapy. *Journal of Cognitive Psychotherapy, 15,* 59–66.

Sprock, J. (2000). Gender-typed behavioral examples of histrionic personality disorder. *Journal of Psychopathology and Behavioral Assessment, 22,* 107–122.

Sprohge, E., Handler, L., Plant, D. D., & Wicker, D. (2002). A Rorschach study of oral dependence in alcoholics and depressives. *Journal of Personality Assessment, 79,* 142–160.

Standage, L., Bilsbury, C., Jain, S., & Smith, D. (1984). An investigation of role-taking in histrionic personalities. *Canadian Journal of Psychiatry, 29,* 407–411.

Strangler, R. S., & Printz, A. M. (1980). DSM-III: Psychiatric diagnoses in a university population. *American Journal of Psychiatry, 137,* 937–940.

Stone, M. H. (1993). *Abnormalities of personality.* New York: Norton.

Sullivan, H. S. (1947). *Conceptions of modern psychiatry.* Washington, DC: William Alanson White Institute.

Tomiatti, M., Gore, W. L., Lynam, D. R., Miller, J. D., & Widiger, T. A. (2012). A five-factor measure of histrionic personality traits. In A. M. Columbus (Ed.), *Advances in psychology research* (pp. 113–138). Hauppauge, NY: Nova Science Publishers.

Torgersen, S. (1980). The oral obsessive and hysterical personality syndromes: A study of hereditary and environmental factors by means of the twin method. *Archives of General Psychiatry, 37,* 1272–1277.

Torgersen, S. (2009). The nature (and nurture) of personality disorders. *Scandinavian Journal of Psychology, 50,* 624–632.

Torgersen, S., Lygren, S., Oien, P. A., Skre, I., Onstad, S., & Edvardsen, J. (2000). A twin study of personality disorders. *Comprehensive Psychiatry, 41,* 416–425.

Trull, T. J., Jahng, S., Tomko, R. L., Wood, P. K., & Sher, K. J. (2010). Revised NESARC personality disorder diagnoses: Gender, prevalence, and comorbidity with substance dependence disorders. *Journal of Personality Disorders, 24,* 412–426.

Ussher, J. M. (2003). The role of premenstrual dysphoric disorder in the subjectification of women. *Journal of Medical Humanities, 24,* 131–146.

Vaillant, G. E. (1980). Natural history of male psychological health, VIII: Antecedents of alcoholism and orality. *American Journal of Psychiatry, 137,* 181–186.

Vandenberg, P., & Helstone, F. (1975). Oral, obsessive and hysterical personality factors: A Dutch replication. *Journal of Psychiatric Research, 12,* 319–327.

Von der Lippe, A., & Torgersen, S. (1984). Character and defense: Relationships between oral, obsessive and hysterical character traits and defense mechanisms. *Scandinavian Journal of Psychology, 25,* 258–264.

Weertman, A., Arntz, A., Schouten, E., & Dreessen, L. (2006). Dependent personality traits and information processing: Assessing the interpretation of ambiguous information using the Thematic Apperception Test. *British Journal of Clinical Psychology, 45,* 273–278.

Widiger, T. A., Lynam, D. R., Miller, J. D., & Oltmanns, T. F. (2012). Measures to assess maladaptive variants of the five-factor model. *Journal of Personality Assessment, 94,* 450–455.

Wiggins, J. S., & Pincus, A. L. (1990). Conceptions of personality disorders and dimensions of personality. *Psychological Assessment, 1,* 305–316.

Zimmerman, M., & Coryell, W. (1989). DSM-III personality disorder diagnoses in a nonpatient sample. *Archives of General Psychiatry, 46,* 682–689.

26

Antisocial Personality Disorder and Psychopathy

CHRISTOPHER J. PATRICK
AND LAURA E. DRISLANE

Among the various conditions classified as disorders of personality, antisocial personality disorder (ASPD) and the related condition of psychopathy have been of particular interest to researchers and practitioners because of the serious harm they cause to individuals and the high costs they pose to society more broadly. Our aim in this chapter is to provide an integrative summary of what is known about these conditions and how they have been represented in differing editions of the *DSM* up to the current fifth edition, which includes both categorical-diagnostic (Section II) and dimensional-trait (Section III) systems for characterizing personality pathology. In doing so, we highlight elements these clinical conditions have in common as well as important features that distinguish them. Additionally, we describe how these conditions relate to other forms of psychopathology and to constructs in the personality literature, and discuss models that have been proposed to account for these connections.

Following a brief summary of historical conceptions of ASPD and psychopathy, we describe how ASPD is represented in the *DSM-5* and summarize recent empirical findings pertaining to this condition. We consider ASPD in relation to the externalizing spectrum model (Krueger et al., 2002; Krueger, Markon, Patrick Benning, & Kramer, 2007), an empirically based conception that views adult antisocial behavior and other impulse control conditions (including conduct disorder, alcohol dependence, and drug dependence) as alternative phenotypic expressions of a common disinhibitory diathesis. We then turn to a description of differing instruments for assessing psychopathy and empirical findings pertaining to each, and discuss how the contrasting conceptions of psychopathy embodied in these differing instruments can be reconciled in terms of an integrative framework, the triarchic model of psychopathy (Patrick, Fowles, & Krueger, 2009), which interfaces with the externalizing spectrum model. We conclude by discussing how the new dimensional-trait system within *DSM-5* provides for improved coverage of psychopathy as defined in triarchic terms.

Historical Conceptions

The earliest accounts of the condition that came to be known as psychopathy (and later, ASPD) emphasized extreme behavioral deviance in the context of intact reasoning and communicative abilities. French physician Philippe Pinel (1801/1962) used the term *manie sans delire* ("insanity without delirium") to describe individuals who engaged repeatedly in impulsive acts injurious to themselves and others, despite ostensible awareness of the irrationality of such actions. An American contemporary of Pinel's, Benjamin Rush (1812), documented similar cases and postulated absence of guilt ("moral weakness") as the root cause. Rush's description placed emphasis on features of manipulativeness and deception. British physician J. C. Pritchard (1835) used a similar term, "moral insanity," but applied it to a much broader array of conditions including drug and alcohol addiction, sexual deviations, mood disorders, and conditions likely to be classified today as mental retardation or schizophrenia.

Some years later, German psychiatrist J. L. Koch (1891) introduced the term "psychopathic" to denote chronic forms of mental illness presumed to have an underlying organic (physical, brain-based) basis. Like Pritchard, Koch applied this term to a much wider array of conditions than would be recognizable today as ASPD or psychopathy. Operating from a similar perspective of biological causality, Kraepelin (1915) used the term "psychopathic personalities" for a narrower array of conditions that included sexual deviations, other impulse-related problems, and obsessional disorders—along with conditions he labeled "degenerative" personalities, which included "antisocial" (callous-destructive) and "quarrelsome" (hostile-alienated) subtypes that would be classifiable today as ASPD.

Countering this trend toward broad application of the term, Cleckley (1941/1976) argued that the diagnosis of "psychopathy" should be reserved for a highly specific condition marked by a distinct set of clinical features. The criteria that Cleckley proposed for the disorder included features of three types: (1) indications of psychological stability (social charm and good intelligence, absence of delusions or irrationality, absence of nervousness, and disinclination toward suicide); (2) tendencies toward emotional insensitivity and shallow or insincere relationships with others (self-centeredness and incapacity for love, lack of social reciprocity, deceitfulness, deficient affective reactivity, impaired insight); and (3) salient behavioral deviancy in the form of repeated antisocial acts (often without obvious motivation), irresponsibility, promiscuity, and absence of any clear life plan. According to Cleckley, the outward appearance of psychological stability in individuals of this type functioned as a convincing "mask of sanity," concealing the underlying interpersonal-affective deficits and deviant behavioral tendencies.

Origins of the ASPD Concept

In line with early conceptions of psychopathy that applied the term broadly, the first edition of the *DSM* included a category termed "sociopathic personality disturbance," encompassing a range of problems including sexual deviations, addictions, and a condition referred to as "sociopathic personality disturbance: antisocial reaction," marked by persistent aggression and criminal deviance. In *DSM-II*, the term "reaction" was eliminated as a descriptor, and sexual deviations, addictions, and delinquent personality types were grouped together under "Personality Disorders and Other Non-Psychotic Mental Disorders," which included an "antisocial personality" condition resembling the diagnosis of psychopathy as described by Cleckley (including features of undersocialization, selfishness, untrustworthiness, callousness, and absence of guilt).

However, a serious limitation of *DSM-II* (true also of *DSM-I*) was that diagnoses were assigned through reference to descriptions of prototype cases rather than on the basis of explicit behavioral criteria. As a result, the reliability of diagnostic decisions made using *DSM-II* was poor. This problem was addressed in *DSM-III* by establishing more specific, behaviorally oriented criteria for diagnoses. The criteria in *DSM-III* were influenced in particular by longitudinal research conducted by Lee Robins (1966, 1978) on the developmental course of "sociopathy" and variables predictive of persistent delinquency. Although the criteria for sociopathy initially proposed by Robins included items relating to lack of guilt, remorse, or shame, these items exhibited weak discrimination in her analyses (due in part to weak reliability) and thus were dropped. Following Robins' lead, the criteria for ASPD in *DSM-III* focused exclusively on symptoms of behavioral deviancy in childhood and adulthood, including truancy, stealing, vandalism, other delinquency acts, aggressiveness, impulsivity, irresponsibility, recklessness, and lying.

With this shift to explicit behavioral criteria, the diagnosis of ASPD within *DSM-III* proved highly reliable. However, concerns about the validity of the diagnosis were raised soon after its appearance (e.g., Frances, 1980; Hare, 1983), particularly in regard to its omission of many of the features identified by Cleckley as being essential to psychopathy, including superficial charm, lack of anxiety, absence of remorse or empathy, and general poverty of affect. Some effort was made to address these criticisms in the revised third edition (*DSM-III-R*) through the addition of lack of remorse (i.e., "feels justified in having hurt, mistreated, or stolen from another," p. 346) as an adult criterion for ASPD. Further changes along this line, directed at increasing coverage of interpersonal-affective features of psychopathy, were considered for *DSM-IV*, but ultimately rejected (Widiger et al., 1996). Consequently, the diagnostic criteria for ASPD in *DSM-IV* remained much the same as those in *DSM-III-R*. As discussed in the next section, a radically new dimensional-trait approach to the diagnosis of ASPD has been included in Section III of the *DSM-5*, as an alternative to the criterion-based version of the diagnosis within Section II— carried over without modification from *DSM-IV*.

ASPD: Current Conceptions and Empirical Findings

ASPD in DSM-5

The criteria for the categorical diagnosis of ASPD in the "Diagnostic Criteria and Codes" section (Section II) of *DSM-5* are identical to those specified in *DSM-IV*. The reason is that the Personality Disorders (PD) Work Group for *DSM-5* sought to establish a new trait-based system for characterizing personality pathology, rather than revise—and thereby perpetuate—an existing criterion-based approach that they and other scholars consider to be flawed and outdated. Despite endorsements of this new system by the *DSM-5*'s Scientific Review Committee and its main Task Force, the American Psychiatric Association's Board of Trustees opted to retain the existing *DSM-IV* system for PDs in Section II of *DSM-5*, and place the new trait-based system in Section III of the manual ("Emerging Measures and Models"). Over time and through continuing research efforts, it is expected that the new trait-based system will merge with, and ultimately supersede, the older criterion-based system. Given this expected transition, it is important to provide coverage here of both the old and new PD systems as used to define ASPD. We first consider some key points regarding the criterion-based approach to diagnosing ASPD, and then describe the alternative trait-based approach.

As with other disorders, the categorical diagnostic criteria for ASPD in *DSM-5* (carried over from *DSM-IV*) are polythetic. That is, only a portion of the criteria for the disorder at child and adult levels (see Table 26.1) need to be met, making it possible for individuals to achieve the diagnosis in many different ways. The child criteria for ASPD—which duplicate those for conduct disorder (CD)—include aggressive and destructive behaviors along with deceitfulness/theft and nonaggressive rule-breaking acts. Factor-analytic studies of these child criteria (e.g., Frick et al., 1991; Tackett, Krueger, Sawyer, & Graetz, 2003) have demonstrated that the aggressive and rule-breaking symptoms define separate, albeit correlated, subdimensions (factors). Tackett et al. (2003) reported that these two factors of CD showed differential relations with aggressive versus delinquent behavioral syndromes as defined by scores on the Child Behavior Checklist (Achenbach, 1991). This work dovetails with the distinction noted by Moffitt (1993) between adolescence-limited and life course–persistent delinquency, the former characterized by later onset and predominantly nonaggressive deviancy, and the latter by early onset of delinquency entailing both aggressive/destructive and rule-breaking behavior with continuation into adulthood. Moffitt postulated that the early-onset aggressive subtype had a stronger underlying neurobiological basis (see also Lynam, 1997).

Tackett, Krueger, Iacono, and McGue (2005) evaluated the possibility of differential etiological contributions to aggressive versus nonaggressive factors of CD in a male twin sample and found evidence for common as well as distinctive etiological underpinnings to these factors. Additive genetic and nonshared environment influences (i.e., experiences unique to the individual) contributed significantly to each, with the proportion of symptom variance attributable to genes somewhat higher for the aggressive than for the rule-breaking factor (35% versus 28%). A significant contribution of shared environment (i.e., influences common to siblings reared in the same household) was found for the rule-breaking but not the aggressive subdimension. More recently, Kendler, Aggen, and Patrick (2013) extended this work by presenting behavior-genetic evidence that (a) aggressive and rule-breaking subdimensions of conduct disorder reflect differing sources of genetic influence, and (b) the shared environmental contribution to the rule-breaking subdimension is concentrated in a subset of symptoms reflecting covert delinquent acts (e.g., stealing, telling lies).

The adult criteria for ASPD include one aggression-specific criterion (irritability/aggressiveness), three clearly nonaggressive criteria (deceitfulness, impulsivity, irresponsibility), and

Table 26.1 Criteria for Diagnosis of Antisocial Personality Disorder in *DSM-IV* and Section II of *DSM-5*

Criterion Category	Summary Description of Criterion Indicator(s)
A. Adult antisocial behavior (three or more of the following since age 15):	1. Repeated engagement in illegal acts 2. Lying 3. Impulsiveness or failure to make plans in advance 4. Irritability and aggressive behavior 5. Acts in ways that endanger self or others 6. Frequent irresponsible behavior 7. Absence of remorse
B. Age criterion	Current age at least 18
C. Child conduct disorder (three or more of the following before age 15, resulting in impaired social, academic or occupational function): *	*Aggression toward people or animals:* 1. Frequent threatening, intimidation, or bullying of others 2. Frequent initiation of fights 3. Use of weapons with potential to harm 4. Physical cruelty toward people 5. Physical cruelty toward animals 6. Theft involving confrontation of a victim 7. Forcible sexual behavior *Destroying property:* 8. Deliberate fire-setting with intent to cause damage 9. Willful destruction of property *Deceptiveness or stealing:* 10. Breaking/entering (vehicle, house, or building) 11. Frequent lying for gain or to avoid obligations 12. Serious theft without victim confrontation *Serious rule violations:* 13. Repetitive violations of parental curfew, beginning before age 13 14. Running away from home (two or more times) 15. Frequent truancy, beginning before age 13
D. Comorbidity criterion	Occurrence of antisocial behavior not limited to episodes of schizophrenia or mania

*The *DSM-IV/DSM-5* Section II criteria for conduct disorder require three or more of these behavioral symptoms before age 15. However, Criterion C for antisocial personality disorder (ASPD) is vague as to the number of symptoms needing to be met, specifying only "evidence of Conduct Disorder with onset before age 15 years." Some approaches to the assessment of ASPD, such as the Structured Clinical Interview for DSM-IV Axis II Personality Disorders (SCID-II; First et al., 1997), use a lower threshold for "evidence of" (i.e., occurrence of two as opposed to three child symptoms).

three nonspecific criteria (failure to conform to norms with respect to lawful behaviors, reckless disregard for safety of self or others, lacks remorse). As with the child (CD) criteria for the diagnosis, evidence exists for differing etiological influences underlying aggressive and nonaggressive antisocial behavior patterns in adulthood. In a study of adult twins, Kendler, Aggen, and Patrick (2012) reported the emergence of two distinct factors from a structural analysis of the adult symptoms for ASPD (as assessed by self-report), a *Disinhibition* factor entailing tendencies toward impulsivity, irresponsibility, and deceitfulness, and an *Aggressive-Disregard* factor entailing irritability or aggressiveness and behaviors indicative of recklessness and lack of concern for self and others. Paralleling the findings for distinct factors of CD (Kendler et al., 2013; Tackett et al., 2005), these authors reported that nonaggressive and aggressive facets of antisociality in adulthood were associated with differing sources of genetic influence.

This evidence for separable subdimensions underlying both the child and adult components of ASPD dovetails with two other key lines of research discussed in greater detail later in this chapter. One is the literature on psychopathic tendencies in youth, which has demonstrated the importance of callous-unemotional traits in distinguishing between more and less severe variants of conduct disorder (Frick & Marsee, 2006; Frick & White, 2008). This work served as the impetus for inclusion of a "limited prosocial emotions" specifier for CD in *DSM-5* (see subsection "Psychopathy in the *DSM-5*"). The other line of work consists of research on the structure of the externalizing psychopathology spectrum, encompassing child and adult facets of ASPD along with substance use disorders and disinhibitory personality traits (Krueger et al., 2007; see also Krueger et al., 2002). Working from a different database, this work has also provided evidence for separate Disinhibition and Callous-Aggression factors (along with a third Substance Abuse or Addiction factor) underlying this spectrum of problems and traits.

This key distinction between impulsive-disinhibitory and callous-aggressive tendencies is explicitly recognized in the alternative dimensional-trait approach to characterizing ASPD within Section III of *DSM-5*. As discussed in Chapter 23 of this volume, the characterization of personality pathology according to this approach entails two steps: (1) assessment for the presence of personality disturbance, as indicated by dysfunction in areas of self (identity, directedness) and social relations, and (2) designation of the specific nature of personality pathology, in terms of elevations on PD-relevant traits within five thematic domains. To facilitate linkages to (and transition from) the categorical system for PDs, the dimensional system in Section III includes criteria for identifying counterparts to six of the PDs specified in Section II—that is, ASPD, along with borderline, narcissistic, obsessive-compulsive, avoidant, and schizotypal PD. ASPD is defined by the presence of distinctive disturbances in self-concept and social relations, together with elevations on pertinent traits from two of five domains—Disinhibition and Antagonism (see Table 26.2). The inclusion of traits from these two distinct domains in the trait-based definition of ASPD provides for more balanced representation of impulsive-disinhibitory and callous-aggressive features in the diagnosis, allowing for potentially better convergence with conceptions of psychopathy that emphasize antagonistic (Lynam & Derefinko, 2006) or callous-unemotional tendencies (Frick & Marsee, 2006) as central to the condition. As discussed below, the trait-based conception of ASPD

Table 26.2 Criteria for Diagnosis of Antisocial Personality Disorder in Section III of *DSM-5*

Criterion Category	Summary Description of Criterion Indicator(s)
A. Significant impairments in personality functioning, manifested in two or more of the following areas:	1. *Identity* (egocentric; self-esteem derived from power or pleasure) 2. *Self-directedness* (lack of internalized prosocial values; goals based around hedonism or dominance) 3. *Empathy* (lacks concern for others; lacks remorse) 4. *Intimacy* (exploitative or controlling; lacks mutually intimate relationships)

B. Elevations on *six or all* of the following traits, from domains of:	1. *Antagonism*:
	  a. *Manipulativeness* (controls or exploits others through persuasion)
	  b. *Deceitfulness* (dishonest, distorts truth, misrepresents self)
	  c. *Callousness* (lacks concern for others; lacks guilt for harmful acts)
	  d. *Hostility* (frequently irritable or angry; sensitive to slights; vengeful)
	2. *Disinhibition*:
	  a. *Irresponsibility* (disregards or lacks respect for obligations and agreements)
	  b. *Impulsivity* (spontaneous; lacks planfulness; acts on immediate urges)
	  c. *Risk taking* (acts recklessly without considering consequences; disregards danger; easily bored)

C. Temporal stability criterion	Impairments in self or interpersonal functioning and expression of pathological traits persist across time and occur across situations.
D. Non-normativity criterion	Impairments in functioning and expression of pathological traits are atypical vis-à-vis developmental age and sociocultural milieu.
E. Physiological/medical criterion	Impairments in functioning and expression of pathological traits are not due to effects of substance use or a general medical condition.

in *DSM-5* also includes a psychopathic features specifier for designating a classically low-anxious/socially dominant ("primary psychopathic") variant of ASPD.

Prevalence

The estimated prevalence of ASPD in the general community as defined in *DSM-IV* (and Section II of *DSM-5*) is 2%, with the rate for men (3%) exceeding that for women (1%). This marked male/female difference has been the topic of much discussion, with one position being that gender role stereotypes and socialization pressures (i.e., expectations for men to be more aggressive and risk-taking) account for much of the difference, and another being that biologically based dispositional factors are mostly responsible. By contrast, rates of ASPD do not appear to differ as a function of race and ethnicity.

The prevalence of ASPD in clinical settings is generally much higher than in the community at large, with rates as high as 50%–80% reported in correctional and forensic settings (Hare, 2003). This high prevalence in forensic settings has contributed to claims that ASPD is simply a "wastebasket" diagnosis—an arbitrary entity without clinical or scientific utility. However, research on the externalizing spectrum of psychopathology, cited earlier and discussed further below, has in fact demonstrated the presence of a coherent dispositional liability contributing to child and adult symptoms of ASPD along with substance-related problems (Krueger et al., 2002, 2007). A key implication of this work is that a considerable portion of individuals who exhibit salient antisocial tendencies in childhood and later in life do so as an expression of this dispositional liability, with a smaller proportion exhibiting such problems mainly because of adverse environmental experiences (e.g., early abuse; deviant peers). Brain and other physiological response variables that operate as indicators of general externalizing proneness may provide a means for distinguishing between cases of these types.

Accounting for Comorbidity with other DSM *Disorders and Common Personality Correlates: The Externalizing Spectrum Model*

ASPD shows well-documented patterns of comorbidity with other disorders in the *DSM*, in particular substance use disorders (Grant et al., 2004;

Kessler & Walters, 2002; Koenigsberg, Kaplan, Gilmore, & Cooper, 1985; Lewis, Rice, & Helzer, 1983; Robins & Regier, 1991). Disorders of these types also show common personality correlates. Two personality traits that show consistent relations with both ASPD and alcohol and drug problems (Casillas & Clark, 2002; Krueger, 1999a; Lynam, Leukefeld, & Clayton, 2003; Sher & Trull, 1994) are (1) impulsiveness, represented in the five-factor model (FFM; cf. Digman, 1990) by Conscientiousness (reversed) and in Tellegen's (2003; Tellegen & Waller, 2008) Multidimensional Personality Questionnaire (MPQ) model by the higher order factor of Constraint (reversed), and (2) aggressiveness, represented in the FFM by Agreeableness (reversed) and in the MPQ by the lower order trait of aggression.

The finding of shared personality correlates along with diagnostic comorbidity raises the possibility that antisocial behavior and substance-related problems might represent expressions of a common dispositional liability of some type. Krueger et al. (2002) provided compelling evidence for this notion through structural modeling analyses of diagnostic symptom and personality trait data for a large sample consisting of male MZ and DZ twins. Results of these analyses revealed the best fit for a common pathway model that accounted for relations between child and adult symptoms of ASPD, alcohol and drug dependence, and disinhibitory personality traits (indexed by scores on the Constraint factor of the MPQ) in terms of a shared *Externalizing* factor. Evaluation of etiological sources of influence, made possible by the twin composition of the sample, revealed a strong heritable basis to this general Externalizing factor (i.e., ~80% of variance in scores was attributable to additive genetic influence; see also Kendler, Prescott, Myers, & Neale, 2003; Young, Stallings, Corley, Krauter, & Hewitt, 2000). The remaining variance in each disorder not accounted for by the general factor was attributable mainly to nonshared environmental influence—although for conduct disorder symptoms a significant contribution of shared environment was also found.

On the basis of these findings, Krueger et al. (2002) proposed that a broad dispositional liability contributes to the development of various disorders in this spectrum, with the precise symptomatic expression of this underlying liability determined by disorder-specific etiological influences. Krueger et al. (2007) extended these findings by undertaking a more comprehensive analysis of traits and problem behaviors in this domain. They targeted constructs embodied in the definitions of child and adult antisocial disorders and substance-related conditions within the *DSM*, along with additional constructs from the extant literature on disinhibitory problems and traits, and constructed self-report-based items to tap these constructs. Item- and scale-level analyses were used to refine the item set across multiple waves of data collection, resulting in a final 415-item instrument—the Externalizing Spectrum Inventory (ESI)—containing 23 facet scales that index constructs including impulsiveness, irresponsibility, theft, (dis)honesty and fraudulence, blame externalization, rebelliousness, excitement seeking, differing forms of aggression, (lack of) empathy, and alcohol, drug, and marijuana use or problems. Factor analyses of the ESI's 23 facet scales revealed the presence of a general factor (*Externalizing*, or *Disinhibition*) on which all scales loaded, along with two subordinate factors accounting for residual variance in specific subscales—a *Callous-Aggression* factor marked by subscales indexing aggression (all forms), low empathy, and excitement seeking, and a *Substance Abuse* factor marked by subscales indexing excessive use and problems with alcohol, marijuana, and other drugs.[1] The findings of this work provided additional support for the idea that problem behaviors and affiliated traits within this domain are indicators of a shared Dispositional factor,[2] and in addition revealed evidence for distinct aggressive and addictive expressions of this general factor.

Neurobiological Correlates

A variety of neurobiological correlates of ASPD have been identified. For example, antisocial individuals—in particular, those displaying impulsive aggressive behavior—show evidence of reduced

___

1. To facilitate use of the ESI as a screening tool and to allow for its inclusion in multimeasure protocols, an abbreviated 160-item version has been developed that yields scores on all 23 facet scales along with scores on the ESI's higher order factors (Patrick, Kramer, Krueger, & Markon, 2013).
2. Recent twin modeling research (Yancey, Venables, Hicks, & Patrick, 2013) has demonstrated appreciable heritability (estimated additive genetic contribution ~.6) for scores on the general Disinhibition factor of the ESI, computed as a manifest composite of items from subscales that loaded exclusively on this factor as reported by Krueger et al. (2007).

levels of the neurotransmitter serotonin in the brain (Minzenberg & Siever, 2006). Reduced serotonergic modulation of appetitive urges and negative emotional reactions (Davidson, Putnam, & Larson, 2000; Seo, Patrick, & Kennealy, 2008) may account in part for the lack of inhibitory control exhibited by high externalizing individuals. Other research documents low resting heart rate as a reliable correlate of antisocial deviance, with prospective studies showing reduced heart rate in childhood to be predictive of later antisocial behavior (Ortiz & Raine, 2004). This resting heart rate reduction, indicative of autonomic hypoarousal, has been interpreted as reflecting dispositional sensation-seeking tendencies in impulsive-antisocial individuals (Raine, 2002).

The best-established physiological indicator of proneness to externalizing problems more broadly is reduced amplitude of the P300 brain response— a positive cortical potential, maximal over parietal scalp regions, that follows the occurrence of infrequent attended targets in a stimulus sequence. Reduced P300 response has been observed in relation to various specific impulse control problems (Iacono, Carlson, Taylor, Elkins, & McGue, 1999; Iacono, Malone, & McGue, 2008) and is associated with risk for the development of such problems (Begleiter, Porjesz, Bihari, & Kissin, 1984; Iacono, Carlson, Malone, & McGue, 2002). Building on these observations, research examining effects for antisocial and substance-related disorders within the same participants has established that reduced P300 is in fact an indicator of the general Externalizing factor these disorders share (Hicks et al., 2007; Patrick, Bernat, et al., 2006). More recent work has demonstrated that scores on the general Disinhibition factor of the self-report-based ESI also predict reduced P300 response amplitude (Nelson, Patrick, & Bernat, 2011; Patrick, Durbin, & Moser, 2012; Patrick, Venables, et al., 2013), and that this association is attributable largely to heritable variance in ESI-Disinhibition scores that overlaps with *DSM*-defined externalizing disorders and the general factor they share (Yancey, Venables, Hicks, & Patrick, 2013).

Psychopathy: Current Conceptions and Empirical Findings

As discussed in detail already, ASPD as represented in *DSM-IV*, and in the main categorical diagnostic section of *DSM-5*, focuses predominantly on behavioral indicators of antisocial deviance with only limited coverage of interpersonal-affective symptoms emphasized by Cleckley and other historical writers. However, an extensive literature on psychopathy has accumulated separately from work on ASPD, using assessment instruments that are based directly or indirectly on Cleckley's classic conception as described in the initial historical section earlier in this chapter. In the discussion that follows, we review major approaches to the assessment of psychopathy in use today, highlighting ways in which they differ along with ways in which they converge, and then describe an integrative theoretical framework, the triarchic model (Patrick et al., 2009), for reconciling contrasting conceptions of psychopathy embodied in these differing assessment devices. We then use this model as a point of reference for discussing how psychopathy is represented within the new trait-based PD system of *DSM-5* (Section III) and discuss some new work that provides evidence for improved effectiveness of this new system for indexing psychopathy as classically described.

Psychopathy in Forensic Samples: Hare's Psychopathy Checklist-Revised (PCL-R)

Description The assessment instrument that has dominated contemporary research on psychopathy is Hare's (1991, 2003) Psychopathy Checklist-Revised (PCL-R), which was developed to identify the condition as described by Cleckley in incarcerated offenders. The PCL-R contains 20 items, each rated on a 0–2 scale (absent, equivocal, or present) using information derived from a semi-structured interview and institutional file records. Item scores are summed to yield a total psychopathy score, with scores of 30 or higher considered indicative of psychopathy (Hare, 2003).

The original 22-item version of the PCL (Hare, 1980) evolved out of a global (7-point) rating system that directly referenced Cleckley's diagnostic criteria. Items for the PCL were selected from a larger pool of candidate indicators on the basis of their effectiveness in discriminating between offender participants judged to be high versus low on the Cleckley global rating system. Two items were dropped in the subsequent revised version. Notably, the interpersonal-affective deficits and behavioral deviance features described by Cleckley are represented directly in the PCL-R, but the

positive adjustment features he emphasized (social efficacy and intelligence, absence of psychosis, lack of anxiety or neurotic symptoms, disinclination toward suicide) are not. Features of this type were likely excluded because items selected for the original PCL were required to correlate as a whole with one another, based on the implicit idea of psychopathy as a unitary condition (Patrick, 2006). Because the majority of Cleckley's criteria (12 of 16) reflect tendencies toward deviance, indicators of positive adjustment would have been excluded over the course of scale refinement because of their failure to coalesce with the larger contingent of (pathological) indicators.

The relations that overall scores on the PCL-R show with criterion measures of various types reinforce the notion that the PCL-R conception of psychopathy is more purely pathological than Cleckley's. PCL-R total scores correlate very highly with overall symptoms of ASPD (mean *r* reported by Hare [2003] across 10 offender studies = .67) and show robust positive associations with various behavioral indices of aggression (Hare, 2003) and scale measures of substance problems (Reardon, Lang, & Patrick, 2002). With respect to personality variables, PCL-R total scores exhibit especially robust relations with trait measures of impulsivity and aggression (Lynam & Derefinko, 2006; Verona, Patrick, & Joiner, 2001) and, in contrast with Cleckley's portrayal of psychopathic individuals as low-anxious, correlate either minimally or somewhat positively with measures of anxiety, neuroticism, and negative affectivity (Hare, 2003; Lynam & Derefinko, 2006; Hicks & Patrick, 2006). Also at odds with Cleckley's conception, PCL-R total scores show positive rather than negative associations with indices of suicidality (Verona et al., 2001; Verona, Hicks, & Patrick, 2005).

PCL-R Factors While developed to operationalize psychopathy as a unitary condition, structural analyses of the PCL-R's items have revealed distinctive subdimensions or factors that exhibit differential relations with criterion measures of various types. Initial work (Harpur, Hakstian, & Hare, 1988; Hare et al., 1990) indicated two correlated (*r* ~ .5) factors: an Interpersonal-Affective factor (Factor 1) marked by items indexing superficial charm, grandiosity, conning/deceptiveness, absence of remorse or empathy, shallow affect, and externalization of blame; and an Impulsive-Antisocial factor (Factor 2) encompassing early behavior problems, impulsivity, irresponsibility, boredom proneness, lack of long-term goals, and hot-tempered aggressiveness. Cooke and Michie (2001) proposed an alternative three-factor model in which Factor 1 was parsed into separate "Deficient Affect" and "Arrogant/Deceitful" factors, and items of Factor 2 considered most trait-like ($n = 5$) were included in a third "Impulsive-Irresponsible" factor. Subsequent to this, Hare (2003; Hare & Neumann, 2006) advanced an alternative four-facet model in which Factor 1 was parsed into Interpersonal and Affective facets mirroring Cooke and Michie's first two factors, and Factor 2 was partitioned into a "Lifestyle" facet mirroring Cooke & Michie's "Impulsive-Irresponsible" factor, and an "Antisocial" facet including the remaining antisocial behavior items from Factor 2 along with a "criminal versatility" item.

Most published work on subdimensions of the PCL-R has focused on the factors of the original two-factor model. These factors show differential relations with a variety of criterion measures, particularly when their shared variance is accounted for (e.g., through structural analysis, regression modeling, or partial correlation; Hare, 1991, 2003; Harpur, Hare, & Hakstian, 1989; Hicks & Patrick, 1994, 2006; Patrick, Hicks, Krueger, & Lang, 2005; Patrick, Hicks, Nichol, & Krueger, 2007; Verona et al., 2001, 2005). Variance unique to Factor 1 correlates negatively with measures of anxiousness and internalizing problems, and positively with measures of social dominance and (in some studies) positive affectivity and achievement, suggesting that the positive adjustment features of psychopathy specified by Cleckley are embodied to some extent in the variance of Factor 1 that is distinct from impulsive-antisocial tendencies. The interpersonal items of Factor 1 in particular account for its associations with indices of emotional stability and adjustment (Hall, Benning, & Patrick, 2004; Patrick et al., 2007). PCL-R Factor 1 also shows negative relations with scale measures of empathy, and positive relations with measures of narcissistic personality, Machivellianism, and proactive (instrumental) aggression. By contrast, variance unique to Factor 2 correlates *positively* with trait anxiety and internalizing problems, and is strongly predictive of both child and adult symptoms of ASPD as represented in *DSM-IV* (and Section II of *DSM-5*). Factor 2 also shows selective positive relations with scale measures of impulsivity, aggressiveness, general sensation seeking,

and substance dependence, and interview- or record-based indices of impulsive aggression (e.g., fighting, assault charges, partner abuse) and suicidal behavior.

These differential associations for Factors 1 and 2 of the PCL-R are notable for score variables considered as facets of a single higher order construct (e.g., Hare, 1991, 2003). Especially noteworthy are cases in which opposing relations of the two PCL-R factors with criterion measures become stronger once their covariance (overlap) is removed—a phenomenon known as *cooperative suppression* (Paulhus, Robins, Trzesniewski, & Tracy, 2004). As an example of this, Hicks and Patrick (2006) reported that correlations for each factor of the PCL-R with measures of negative affectivity (i.e., fearfulness, distress, and depression) increased, in opposite directions, when scores on the two factors were included together in a regression model. This result indicates that distinct opposing relations of the two PCL-R factors with indices of negative affectivity were partially concealed by the variance they share. A similar result was reported by Frick, Lilienfeld, Ellis, Loney, and Silverthorn (1999) for the two factors of the Antisocial Process Screening Device (Frick & Hare, 2001), an inventory for assessing psychopathy in children and adolescents that is patterned after the PCL-R (see next section). Effects of this type are conceptually important because they indicate that the items of the PCL-R, although intended to index a single underlying construct, are in fact indexing separate constructs. In particular, the finding of suppressor effects for the two PCL-R factors in relation to variables such as anxiety, depression, and suicidality appears consistent with Cleckley's view that psychopathy entails the convergence of contrasting dispositions toward psychological resiliency and behavioral deviancy.

Adaptations of the PCL-R Used with Young Clinical Samples The dominant inventories used for assessing psychopathy in child and adolescent clinical samples consist of adaptations of the PCL-R and include the youth version of the PCL-R (PCL:YV; Forth, Kosson, & Hare, 2003), the Antisocial Process Screening Device (APSD; Frick & Hare, 2001; Frick, O'Brien, Wooten, & McBurnett, 1994), and the Child Psychopathy Scale (CPS; Lynam, 1997; Lynam et al., 2005). The most widely used of these, the 20-item APSD, was devised for use with children aged 6–13 referred for treatment of behavioral problems and is rated by either parents or teachers. The APSD has two distinguishable factors—a Callous-Unemotional (CU) factor reflecting emotional insensitivity and exploitative disregard for others, and an Impulsive/Conduct Problems (I/CP) factor encompassing impulsive tendencies, reckless or delinquent behavior, and inflated sense of self-importance (Frick et al., 1994; Frick & Hare, 2001)—with some research (e.g., Frick, Boden, & Barry, 2000) suggesting distinguishable impulsive and narcissistic or attention-seeking components to the I/CP factor. Children who score high on the I/CP factor but not the CU factor exhibit lower levels of intellectual ability, higher anxiety and negative emotional reactivity, and greater proneness to angry-reactive (but not proactive-instrumental) aggression (Frick & Marsee, 2006; Frick & White, 2008). By contrast, children who score high on both factors of the APSD appear to have normal intellectual ability, exhibit lower levels of anxiety and neuroticism, are less reactive to distressing stimuli and learn less readily from punishment, and tend to be attracted to activities entailing novelty and risk. These children also show heightened levels of both proactive and reactive aggression and greater persistence of such behavior across time.

Prevalence of PCL-R-Defined Psychopathy The PCL-R was developed for use with male correctional and forensic samples, and thus prevalence estimates are available mainly for samples of this type. The estimated prevalence of PCL-R-defined psychopathy (total score of 30 or higher) in male correctional and forensic populations is 15%–25%, compared with 50%–80% for *DSM-IV*-defined ASPD (Hare, 2003, p. 92), with most of those who score as psychopathic also meeting criteria for ASPD. Because the PCL-R is designed for offender samples and limited efforts have been made to assess PCL-R psychopathy in community samples (for exceptions, see Ishikawa, Raine, Lencz, Bihrle, & Lacasse, 2001, and Gao, Raine, & Schug, 2011), the prevalence of PCL-R-defined psychopathy in community adults remains unknown. Based on median prevalence rates for male prisoners (20% for psychopathy and 65% for ASPD), and assuming a similar ratio of high PCL-R scorers among adults diagnosable as ASPD in the community, the estimated prevalence of PCL-R psychopathy among community men (3% of whom, as noted earlier, are expected to meet criteria for

ASPD) would be ~1% (i.e., 20/65 × 3%). Using an abbreviated, screening version of the PCL-R (the PCL:SV; Hart, Cox, & Hare, 1995), Farrington (2006) reported the prevalence of psychopathy to be around 2% (i.e., 8 cases out of 411) in a large sample of community boys followed up to age 48. Combining these figures, the prevalence of PCL-R psychopathy among men in the community is likely somewhere in the range of 1%–2%. However, this estimate does not include individuals who exhibit salient interpersonal-affective symptoms of psychopathy without sufficient overt behavioral deviancy to warrant a diagnosis of ASPD—cases that Cleckley referred to as "incomplete manifestations" of the condition. Because the field lacks accepted criteria for diagnosing psychopathy in noncriminal adults, population prevalence estimates for cases of this type are unknown.

Women are incarcerated at much lower rates than men and, as noted earlier, the prevalence of ASPD among women is only a third of that in men (*DSM-IV-TR*). Regarding PCL-R-defined psychopathy, some studies of incarcerated women have reported prevalence rates similar to those for incarcerated men, but others have reported lower rates (Verona & Vitale, 2006). Studies of psychopathy and related constructs in nonincarcerated samples have also demonstrated lower rates or levels in general for women than for men (Verona & Vitale, 2006). Given these findings, the prevalence of PCL-R-defined psychopathy among adult women in the community is likely no more than one-third the rate for community men (i.e., .3%–.7%) and probably lower. Again, this estimate omits individuals exhibiting interpersonal-affective features of psychopathy without salient antisocial behavior.

With regard to race and ethnicity, an initial study of incarcerated men by Kosson, Smith, and Newman (1990) yielded evidence that overall PCL-R scores were higher among African-American than European-American offenders. A recent meta-analysis of this and subsequent work (Skeem, Edens, Camp, & Colwell, 2004) revealed a small but significant effect size along this line. With regard to culture, there is evidence that American prison samples score higher in general on the PCL-R than do European prison samples (Sullivan & Kosson, 2006).

Comorbidity with *DSM* Disorders   The *DSM* disorder associated most closely with PCL-R-defined psychopathy is ASPD. However, the relationship between the two is asymmetric. Within offender samples, most individuals who meet the PCL-R criterion for psychopathy (total score ≥30) also meet criteria for *DSM-IV* ASPD, but the majority who meet criteria for ASPD fall below the PCL-R criterion for psychopathy. Additionally, the two PCL-R factors show differential relations with ASPD, with the association weaker for Factor 1 and largely attributable to its overlap with Factor 2 (Patrick et al., 2005). The reason is that the behaviorally based child and adult criteria for ASPD overlap substantially with the impulsive-antisocial features of psychopathy indexed by PCL-R Factor 2. By contrast, only 1 of the 15 child criteria for ASPD (lying) and only 2 of the 7 adult criteria (deceitfulness, lack of remorse) intersect with the interpersonal-affective features of psychopathy embodied in PCL-R Factor 1.

Factor 2 of the PCL-R also shows selective associations with measures of substance abuse and dependence (Reardon, Lang, & Patrick, 2002; Smith & Newman, 1990) and borderline personality symptoms (Shine & Hobson, 1997; Warren et al., 2003). By contrast, scores on Factor 1 relate more to measures of narcissistic and histrionic personality disorder (Harpur et al., 1989; Hart & Hare, 1989; Hildebrand & de Ruiter, 2004). Also, as noted earlier, the two factors of the PCL-R show opposing, mutually suppressive relations with measures of anxiety and depression (Hicks & Patrick, 2006). The fact that the unique variance in Factor 1 is negatively associated with anxiety and depression suggests that this component of the PCL-R (its Interpersonal facet, in particular; Hall et al., 2004) captures something of the positive adjustment and resiliency that Cleckley described as characteristic of psychopaths. The positive relations for Factor 2, on the other hand, coincide with data indicating that the *DSM* diagnosis of ASPD is associated with an increased prevalence of anxiety and mood disorders (*DSM-IV-TR*, p. 702; see also Krueger, 1999b).

Neurobiological Correlates Neurobiological correlates of psychopathy in adult offender samples have been studied mainly in relation to overall scores on the PCL-R or on the earlier Cleckley rating system that served as the referent for the PCL-R. Historically, one of the most consistent findings—beginning with Lykken's (1957) seminal multimethod investigation of anxiety and continuing with the autonomic reactivity studies of Hare

in the 1960s and 1970s (cf. Hare, 1978)—has been that individuals high in overall psychopathy show reduced skin conductance reactivity to stressors of various types, in particular cues signaling an upcoming aversive event (for reviews, see Arnett, 1997; Hare, 1978; Lorber, 2004; Siddle & Trasler, 1981). This finding has been interpreted as reflecting a basic deficiency in anxiety or fear (Fowles, 1980; Hare, 1978; Lykken, 1957).

Another reliable finding in the literature, also consistent with the idea of a negative emotional reactivity deficit, is that individuals diagnosed as psychopathic using the PCL-R fail to show normal augmentation of the startle blink reflex during viewing of aversive visual stimuli (e.g., Herpertz et al., 2001; Patrick, Bradley, & Lang, 1993; Sutton, Vitale, & Newman, 2002; Vanman, Mejia, Dawson, Schell, & Raine, 2003). This reactivity deficit has been tied specifically to elevations on the Interpersonal-Affective factor of the PCL-R (Patrick, 1994; Vanman et al., 2003; Vaidyanathan, Hall, Patrick, & Bernat, 2011). The selective association with PCL-R Factor 1 is notable because the startle reflex is a protective response known to increase with activation of the amygdala, a key structure in the brain's defensive (fear) system (Lang, Bradley, & Cuthbert, 1990). The lack of aversive startle potentiation therefore suggests a weakness in reactivity at this basic subcortical level among individuals exhibiting the core interpersonal-affective features of psychopathy. Consistent with this notion, participants with high PCL-R scores show deficits on behavioral tasks believed to be sensitive to amygdala function (Blair, 2006). Neuroimaging studies have demonstrated reduced amygdala activity during aversive conditioning and fear face processing, respectively, in high PCL-R–scoring adults (Birbaumer et al., 2005; Veit et al., 2002) and CD youth exhibiting callous-unemotional traits (Jones, Laurens, Herba, Barker, & Viding, 2009; Marsh et al., 2008).

Additionally, other lines of work, including cerebral asymmetry, brain potential, and neuroimaging studies (for reviews, see: Hare, 2003, pp. 124-126; Patrick, 2008; Patrick, Venables, & Skeem, 2012), have provided evidence for brain abnormalities in high PCL-R–scoring individuals. However, studies have not reliably demonstrated impairments on neuropsychological tests of frontal lobe function (for a review, see Rogers, 2006) or in P300 brain response (cf. Patrick, 2008). This contrasts with evidence that ASPD is reliably associated with deficits on tests of frontal lobe dysfunction (Morgan & Lilienfeld, 2000) and with reduced amplitude of P300 brain potential response (Bauer, O'Connor, & Hesselbrock, 1994; Patrick, Bernat, et al., 2006). Given that PCL-R Factor 2 is associated more strongly with ASPD and that Factor 1 (after controlling for overlap with Factor 2) shows positive relations with indices of psychological adjustment, it could be the case that the two factors of the PCL-R are differentially related to frontal lobe task performance and P300 brain response. Evidence in support of the latter of these possibilities was provided by a recent study demonstrating reductions in P300 response amplitude specifically in relation to Factor 2 of the PCL-R in a sample of male offenders (Venables & Patrick, 2014).

Psychopathy in Community Samples: Self-Report Based Operationalizations

Most research on psychopathy in noncriminal samples has utilized self-report assessment inventories. Whereas older inventories of this type emphasized measurement of the impulsive-antisocial (Factor 2) component of psychopathy, most akin to ASPD, newer measures such as the Psychopathic Personality Inventory (PPI; Lilienfeld & Andrews, 1996), Levenson et al.'s (Levenson, Kiehl, & Fitzpatrick, 1995) Self-Report Psychopathy Scale (LSRP), Hare's Self-Report Psychopathy Scale (HSRP; Paulhus, Hemphill, & Hare, in press; Williams, Paulhus, & Hare, 2007), the Youth Psychopathic Traits Inventory (YPI; Andershed, Kerr, Stattin, & Levander, 2002), the Elemental Psychopathy Assessment (EPA; Lynam et al., 2011), and the Triarchic Psychopathy Measure (TriPM; Patrick, 2010; Sellbom & Phillips, 2013) include coverage of interpersonal-affective (Factor 1) features as well as impulsive-antisocial features.

The LSRP, HSRP, and YPI were all patterned after the PCL-R and provide coverage of factors or facets specified by alternative structural models of the PCL-R. The LSRP includes "primary" and "secondary" subscales intended to parallel the factors of the original two-factor model (Hare et al., 1990; Harpur et al., 1989), the YPI contains subscales that align with Cooke and Michie's (2001) three-factor model, and the subscales of the HSRP align with Hare's (2003) four-facet model. In contrast with these PCL-R-based inventories, the EPA was developed as an extension of prior

work (Lynam & Widiger, 2007; Miller, Lynam, Widiger, & Leukefeld, 2001) undertaken to characterize psychopathy in terms of lower order traits of the NEO-PI five-factor inventory (Costa & McCrae, 1992). The EPA assesses maladaptive variants of the set of NEO-PI traits that appear most relevant to psychopathy. The EPA is quite new and thus evidence for its validity has begun to appear only recently (e.g., Miller et al., 2011). The TriPM, another new inventory developed to assess facet constructs specified by the triarchic model of psychopathy (Patrick et al., 2009), is described in a later section on this model.

The self-report inventory that has been used most widely in recent years is the PPI/PPI-R. The PPI was developed to index psychopathy in terms of dispositional tendencies (traits) considered relevant to psychopathy by historical writers (Lilienfeld & Andrews, 1996). Factor analyses of the PPI's eight subscales (e.g., Benning, Patrick, Hicks, Blonigen, & Krueger, 2003; Ross, Benning, Patrick, Thompson, & Thurston, 2009) have revealed distinguishable factors that exhibit relations with external criterion variables similar to those for the PCL-R factors (Poythress et al., 2010). Findings regarding these distinct factors of the PPI, along with those of the PCL-R and its affiliates, served as important referents for formulation of the triarchic model of psychopathy, described below. For these reasons, we focus the remainder of this section on research that has utilized the PPI to index psychopathy in community and offender samples.

The Psychopathic Personality Inventory and its Factors   The original PPI (Lilienfeld & Andrews, 1996), which has been used in most published work to date, consists of 187 items; a newer revised version (PPI-R; Lilienfeld & Widows, 2005) includes 154 items. The PPI's items are organized into eight scales that tap distinct dispositional constructs of relevance to psychopathy. In contrast with the PCL-R, the PPI includes specific coverage of nonanxiousness and low fear through its Stress Immunity and Fearlessness scales, along with coverage of interpersonal dominance (Social Potency scale), impulsivity (Carefree Nonplanfulness), oppositionality (Rebellious Nonconformity), alienation (Blame Externalization), aggressive exploitativeness (Machiavellian Egocentricity), and lack of empathic concern (Cold-heartedness).

As noted above, factor analyses of the PPI's subscales have revealed two higher order factors, the first defined by the Social Potency, Stress Immunity, and Fearlessness subscales, and the second by the Carefree Nonplanfulness, Rebellious Nonconformity, Blame Externalization, and Machiavellian Egocentricity scales. Benning, Patrick, Blonigen, Hicks, and Iacono (2005) labeled these two higher order factors *Fearless Dominance* and *Impulsive Antisociality*; Lilienfeld and Widows (2005) proposed *Self-Centered Impulsivity* as an alternative label for the latter of the two. The remaining PPI subscale, Cold-heartedness, does not load appreciably on either of these factors, indicating that it taps something distinct. In contrast with the interrelated factors of the PCL-R, the two higher order factors of the PPI are uncorrelated (Benning et al., 2003).

Psychological and Neurobiological Correlates of the PPI Factors   The two factors of the PPI show conceptually meaningful, and often diverging, patterns of relations with various criterion measures. Scores on the Fearless Dominance factor (PPI-FD) are associated with social efficacy and emotional stability (e.g., higher assertiveness and well-being; lower anxiousness and depression) as well as with narcissism, thrill seeking, and reduced emotional empathy (Benning, Patrick, Blonigen, et al., 2005; Blonigen, Hicks, Krueger, Patrick, & Iacono, 2005; Patrick, Edens, Poythress, Lilienfeld, & Benning, 2006; Ross et al., 2009). In contrast, scores on the Impulsive Antisociality or Self-Centered Impulsivity (SCI) factor are more uniformly associated with maladaptive tendencies, including impulsivity and aggressiveness, child and adult antisocial behavior, substance problems, high negative affect, and suicidal ideation and acts.

The two PPI factors also show differing neurobiological correlates. In a study of young men from the community, Benning, Patrick, and Iacono (2005) found that participants with very high scores on PPI-FD showed a deviant pattern of startle reactivity resembling that of offenders with high scores on PCL-R Factor 1 (i.e., lack of startle potentiation during viewing of aversive picture stimuli, indicating a lack of normal defensive mobilization). By contrast, participants scoring high on PPI-SCI (as compared to low) showed reduced electrodermal reactivity to picture stimuli in general (i.e., whether affective or neutral), suggesting reduced sympathetic arousability (cf. Raine, 1997). Extending the result for PPI-FD, Vaidyanathan, Patrick, and Bernat (2009) reported

a lack of aversive startle potentiation for participants low in dispositional fear as defined by scores on PPI-FD and other scale measures of fear and fearlessness (see also Kramer, Patrick, Krueger, & Gasperi, 2012). The finding of reduced electrodermal reactivity in high PPI-SCI–scoring participants has also been replicated (Verschuere, Crombez, de Clercq, & Koster, 2005). Additionally, mirroring the findings of reduced P300 brain response in relation to ASPD and externalizing proneness more broadly, Carlson, Thái, and McLaron (2009) found scores on PPI-SCI (but not PPI-FD) to be inversely associated with P300 response in a standard oddball task paradigm.

Other work has used functional magnetic resonance imaging (fMRI) to test for brain reactivity differences in relation to the two factors of the PPI. Gordon, Baird, and End (2004) reported reduced fMRI BOLD activation in the right amygdala and affiliated regions of frontal cortex during processing of affective faces in participants scoring high but not low on PPI-FD. By contrast, individuals scoring high as compared to low on PPI-SC showed *increased* amygdala activation when processing affective faces. Related to this latter finding, Buckholtz et al. (2010) reported enhanced bilateral activation in the nucleus accumbens for high versus low SCI–scoring individuals during anticipation of monetary rewards. These results may indicate a more immediate affect-driven response style in high SCI–score individuals. Another fMRI study by Harenski, Kim, and Hamann (2009) reported reduced activation in medial prefrontal cortex during viewing of scenes depicting moral violations in individuals scoring high on the PPI as a whole, with evidence of reduced amygdala activation for those scoring high on PPI Cold-heartedness specifically.

Reconciling Contrasting Conceptions of Psychopathy: The Triarchic Model

The triarchic model (Patrick et al., 2009) was formulated to reconcile alternative conceptions of psychopathy represented in historical writings and contemporary assessment instruments and to address persisting unresolved issues in the field. The model proposes that contrasting perspectives and apparent contradictions in the existing literature can be reconciled by conceiving of psychopathy as encompassing three distinct but intersecting phenotypic tendencies: disinhibition, boldness, and meanness. In contrast with other contemporary factor- or facet-oriented perspectives (e.g., Cooke & Michie, 2001; Frick & Hare, 2001; Hare & Neumann, 2006), the triarchic model is a construct-based framework not bound to any specific assessment instrument or approach—intended to serve as an organizing framework for reconciling differing instrument-based conceptions and integrating findings across them. Differing psychopathy inventories are viewed as indexing the triarchic constructs to varying degrees and in differing ways. Further, the three components of the triarchic model are not viewed as elements or indicators of a unitary higher order psychopathy construct but instead as distinguishable phenotypes that can be operationalized and investigated separately, as well as in relation to one another. In this respect, the constructs of the model can be viewed as building blocks for alternative conceptions of psychopathy and differing variants of the condition that have been described (e.g., psychiatric and criminological, primary and secondary, successful and unsuccessful, aggressive and non-aggressive, anxious and non-anxious). The next three subsections describe each of the triarchic constructs in turn.

Disinhibition   The term *"disinhibition"* refers to a general proneness toward impulse control problems, entailing lack of planfulness, a focus on immediate versus delayed gratification, difficulty in controlling emotions and urges, and weak behavioral restraint. Related concepts in the literature include disinhibitory psychopathology (Gorenstein & Newman, 1980; Sher & Trull, 1994), externalizing (Achenbach & Edelbrock, 1978; Krueger et al., 2002), and low inhibitory control (Kochanska, Murray, & Coy, 1997). In terms of basic personality traits, disinhibition represents the nexus of impulsivity and negative emotionality (Krueger, 1999a; Sher & Trull, 1994). Behaviorally, it is manifested by impatience, impulsive action leading to adverse consequences, irresponsibility, distrust and alienation, aggressive behavior (angry or reactive aggression, in particular), repetitive illegal and/or rule-breaking acts, and proclivities toward abuse of alcohol and other substances (Krueger et al., 2007).

Historical accounts of psychopathy have emphasized this disinhibitory facet to differing degrees, with some writers broadening the diagnosis to encompass alcohol and drug addiction and other non-normative tendencies ascribable to externalizing proneness (e.g., Prichard, 1835), and others characterizing psychopathy in terms that appear more characteristic of externalizing individuals (e.g., Arieti, 1963, 1967; Partridge, 1928a, 1928b) or describing psychopathic subtypes who might more aptly be considered high externalizers (e.g., Craft, 1966; Kraepelin, 1915). In particular, the traditional notion of the "symptomatic" or secondary psychopathy (Karpman, 1941; Lykken, 1957) appears consistent with the clinical presentation of the highly disinhibited-externalizing individual. Research has shown that variance unique to PCL-R Factor 2 reflects externalizing proneness to a large extent (Patrick et al., 2005), as do scores on the corresponding SCI factor of the PPI (Blonigen et al., 2005). Similarly, research on the factors of the APSD child psychopathy inventory indicates that the I/CP factor in particular indexes disinhibitory or externalizing tendencies.

Despite its importance to conceptions of psychopathy, however, investigators in the area would not equate disinhibition with psychopathy. In contrast with the condition as described by Cleckley, externalizing proneness is associated with higher rather than lower levels of negative affectivity (Krueger, 1999a), elevated rather than reduced rates of internalizing problems (Achenbach & Edelbrock, 1978; Krueger, 1999b), and heightened rather than diminished tendencies toward suicidal behavior (Verona & Patrick, 2000; Verona, Sachs-Ericsson, & Joiner, 2004). In contrast with the excessive, poorly regulated emotion that is characteristic of high-externalizing individuals, psychopathy is marked by salient "emotional detachment" (i.e., affective insensitivity and lack of social connectedness; Cleckley, 1976; Lykken, 1995; McCord & McCord, 1964; Patrick, 1994; Patrick et al., 1993). The triarchic model proposes that this distinguishing feature of psychopathy reflects the presence of boldness or meanness, or both. Stated another way, it is the occurrence of disinhibitory or externalizing tendencies in conjunction with high levels of dispositional boldness and/or meanness that signifies the presence of psychopathy.

Boldness   This term encompasses tendencies toward social assurance and self-confidence, calmness and poise in the face of stress or danger, rapid recovery from aversive experiences, and tolerance or preference for uncertainty and risk. Related terms include fearless temperament (Kochanska, 1997; Lykken, 1995), fearless dominance (Benning, Patrick, Blonigen, et al.,

2005), hardiness (Kobasa, 1979), and resiliency (Block & Block, 1980). In personality terms, boldness reflects the intersection of stress immunity, thrill-adventure seeking, and dominance (Benning et al., 2003, 2005; Kramer et al., 2012). Behavioral expressions include social assertiveness, persuasiveness, imperturbability, venturesomeness, and courageous action. As conceptualized in the triarchic model, boldness is not identical to fearlessness. Fearlessness is viewed as a biologically based (genotypic) disposition, entailing diminished sensitivity of the brain's defense-mobilization system to signals of danger or punishment (Fowles & Dindo, 2009; Kramer et al., 2012; Patrick, Durbin, et al., 2012). Boldness is one way in which genotypic fearlessness can be exhibited phenotypically, but as discussed next, this underlying disposition may also contribute to phenotypic meanness.

Cleckley's case histories and diagnostic criteria highlighted features of boldness in conjunction with disinhibitory (externalizing) tendencies. Boldness was represented directly in characteristic features of social charm, absence of anxiety or neurotic symptoms, lack of affective responsiveness, insensitivity to punishment ("failure to learn by experience"), and disinclination toward suicide. Other historical writers who focused on psychiatric patients as opposed to criminal offenders (e.g., Kraepelin, 1915; Schneider, 1934) also described bold-externalizing variants. Unresponsiveness to punishment and lack of fear were also emphasized in early psychophysiological research on psychopathy (cf. Hare, 1978) and in empirically based theories of psychopathy (Fowles, 1980; Lykken, 1995).

The Fearless Dominance (FD) factor of Lilienfeld's self-report based PPI, demarcated by Social Potency, Stress Immunity, and Fearlessness subscales, can be viewed as directly indexing boldness (Patrick et al., 2009). As mentioned earlier, scores on PPI-FD are uncorrelated with impulsive-antisocial tendencies tapped by PPI-SCI. Given this, boldness as operationalized by PPI-FD can be viewed as indexing a more adaptive expression of dispositional fearlessness—distinct from aggressive externalizing deviance—that is likely to be of importance for conceptualizing psychopathy in nonviolent, noncriminal samples (cf. Lykken, 1995). Boldness also appears to be tapped somewhat by Factor 1 of the PCL-R (Benning, Patrick, Blonigen, et al., 2005), in particular, by Interpersonal facet items of charm and glibness and a grandiose sense of self-worth (Patrick

et al., 2007). However, the Interpersonal facet of the PCL-R indexes boldness less directly and distinctively than PPI-FD, given its overlap with the PCL-R's Affective, Lifestyle, and Antisocial facets.

Meanness   The term *meanness* encompasses tendencies including deficient empathy, inability to bond with others, uncooperativeness, exploitativeness, and empowerment through cruelty and destructive acts. Related terms in the literature include callous-unemotionality (Frick & Marsee, 2006), antagonism (Lynam & Derefinko, 2006), and coldheartedness (Lilienfeld & Widows, 2005). From the standpoint of interpersonal traits (Leary, 1957; Wiggins, 1982), meanness entails high dominance in conjunction with low affiliation and nurturance (Blackburn, 2006; Harpur et al., 1989). Saucier (1992) documented a construct similar to meanness (represented by adjective descriptors such as tough, unemotional, and insensitive) entailing the conjunction of low affiliation, high dominance, and low neuroticism. From this standpoint, meanness can be viewed as disaffiliated agency—an orientation involving active pursuit of goals and resources without concern for and at the expense of others. Unlike social withdrawal, marked by passive disengagement ("moving away"; Horney, 1945) from people, meanness involves active exploitation of ("moving against"; Horney, 1945) people. Affiliated behavioral expressions include disdain toward others, arrogance, rebellious defiance, lack of close relationships, harsh competitiveness, exploitation of others for personal gain, proactive (predatory or instrumental) aggression, cruelty toward people or animals, and engagement in destructive acts for excitement.

Meanness is emphasized in historical accounts of psychopathy based on criminal and delinquent samples (McCord & McCord, 1964; Quay, 1964, 1986; Robins, 1966, 1978). The Affective facet of the PCL-R comprises items that capture McCord and McCord's lovelessness (item 7, "shallow affect," and item 8, "callous/lack of empathy") and guiltlessness (item 6, "lack of remorse or guilt," and item 16, "failure to accept responsibility for own actions"). The Interpersonal items of the PCL-R also include elements of meanness: Item 1 ("glibness and superficial charm") refers to excessive slickness and toughness; item 2 ("grandiose sense of self-worth") includes arrogance and a sense of superiority over others; item 4 ("pathological lying") refers to deceptiveness in social interactions and enjoyment in deceiving others; and item 5 ("conning/manipulative") entails active exploitation for gain without consideration of the effects on victims. The best-established psychopathy inventories for children and adolescents (PCL:YV, CPS, and APSD), patterned after the PCL-R, also emphasize meanness in their interpersonal-affective items.

Although psychopathy is frequently indexed through reference to aggressive and antisocial acts and attitudes that reflect tendencies toward disinhibition as well as meanness, research by Krueger et al. (2007) on the structure of externalizing problems and traits (described earlier) suggests that these facets of psychopathy can be indexed separately. The work of these investigators revealed a bifactor structure to scales comprising the ESI measure of this domain, with all scales loading on a superordinate Disinhibition factor, and certain scales loading also on subordinate factors of Callous-Aggression (meanness) and Substance Abuse. The scales that loaded most strongly and exclusively on the general Disinhibitory factor were scales indexing problematic impulsivity and irresponsibility. The best indicators of the Callous-Aggression subfactor were scales indexing presence versus absence of empathy and interpersonally oriented aggression.

The findings of this work indicate that tendencies toward meanness can be separated from tendencies toward disinhibition. Along with scales tapping empathic concern and interpersonal aggression, other scales that have helped to demarcate the Callous-Aggression subfactor include Excitement Seeking, Rebelliousness, and Dishonesty. Notably, these scale indicators of the ESI Callous-Aggression factor parallel the item content of the APSD's Callous-Unemotional (CU) factor, which reflects disregard for the feelings of others, shallowness and insincerity, lack of guilt, and lying and manipulativeness (Frick et al., 1994; Frick & Marsee, 2006). Also in line with the ESI findings, youth with CD who score high on the CU factor of the APSD show elevated rates of proactive aggression and enhanced excitement seeking in comparison to those low on the CU factor (Frick & Dickens, 2006; Frick & White, 2008). Additionally, high scores on the CU factor of the APSD predict lack of reactivity to affectively distressing or threatening stimuli, high tolerance for novelty and risk, and low scores on measures of neuroticism and anxiety, leading to proposals

that CU tendencies reflect dispositional fearlessness (e.g., Frick & Marsee, 2006; Frick & White, 2008). However, if this is true, then there must be additional factors (perhaps constitutional as well as experiential; Patrick et al., 2009) that shape the expression of fearlessness in this malignant direction, as opposed to the more benign direction of boldness.

Operationalizing Boldness, Meanness, and Disinhibition: The Triarchic Psychopathy Measure
The 58-item Triarchic Psychopathy Measure (TriPM; Patrick, 2010) indexes the disinhibition, meanness, and boldness facets of psychopathy as separate dimensions. Items comprising the TriPM Disinhibition and Meanness scales (20 and 19 items, respectively) are from the Externalizing Spectrum Inventory (ESI; Krueger et al., 2007), which, as noted earlier, provides for comprehensive assessment of disinhibitory problems and traits. The Disinhibition scale is composed of items from subscales of the ESI that exhibit strong, selective loadings on the inventory's general Disinhibition factor (i.e., Problematic Impulsivity, Irresponsibility, Boredom Proneness, Impatient Urgency, Alienation, Theft, Fraudulence, Dependability [-], Planful Control [-]). Scores on this scale correlate very strongly ($r > .9$) with regression-estimated scores on the general factor of the ESI (Patrick, Kramer, Krueger, & Markon, 2013). The TriPM Meanness scale consists of items from ESI scales that function as indicators of the inventory's Callous-Aggression subfactor (i.e., Empathy [-], Relational Aggression, Excitement Seeking, Destructive Aggression, Physical Aggression, Honesty [-]). Scores on this scale, after controlling for overlap ($r \sim .5$) with scores on the TriPM Disinhibition scale, correlate very highly ($r > .8$) with scores on the Callous-Aggression subfactor as estimated from the ESI bifactor model (Patrick, Kramer, et al., 2013). The 19-item TriPM Boldness scale consists of items that index fearless tendencies in the realms of interpersonal behavior (persuasiveness, social assurance, dominance), perceived emotional experience (resiliency, self-assurance, optimism), and venturesomeness (courage, thrill seeking, tolerance for uncertainty; cf. Kramer et al., 2012). Scores on this scale correlate very highly ($\sim .8$) with the FD factor of the PPI, but only modestly ($r \sim .2$) with the TriPM Meanness scale, and negligibly with the TriPM Disinhibition scale.

While the TriPM is relatively new, data regarding its validity in relation to established inventories of psychopathy and other relevant criteria measures are accumulating (e.g., Craig, Gray, & Snowdon, 2013; Drislane, Patrick, & Arsal, 2013; Marion et al., 2013; Sellbom & Phillips, 2013; Stanley, Wygant, & Sellbom, 2013). The inventory is freely available online, and a number of foreign-language translations (including Dutch, Finnish, German, Italian, Portuguese, Spanish, and Swedish) exist, making it likely that further validational evidence will accrue rapidly over time. Research has also been conducted to develop alternative scale measures of the triarchic model constructs (boldness, meanness, disinhibition) using items from other existing psychopathy inventories, including the PPI (Hall et al., 2014) and the YPI (Drislane et al., 2014).

Psychopathy in DSM-5

Provisions have been made in the fifth edition of the *DSM* to allow for more effective characterization of psychopathic tendencies at both the youth and adult levels. At the youth level, a "limited prosocial emotions" specifier for the diagnosis of conduct disorder is included (along with a three-level severity specifier) in Section II of *DSM-5*, to distinguish between variants of CD with and without CU traits as described in the youth psychopathy literature (Frick et al., 1994; Frick & Marsee, 2006). The specifier is applied in cases where individuals who meet criteria for CD also exhibit a persistent lack of concern for the feelings and welfare of others as indicated by clear expression of two or more symptoms from among a list of four (see Table 26.3, upper part) over a period of at least 12 months, across differing contexts. The instructions for the specifier state that multiple sources of information, including both self- and other-report, should be considered in assessing for these tendencies. To provide for this, formal protocols for the assessment of limited prosocial emotions as characterized in *DSM-5* are under development (e.g., Frick, 2013).

At the adult level, innovations along two lines have been made in Section III of *DSM-5* to provide for more effective representation of psychopathic tendencies. First, as noted earlier, the trait-based system for PDs characterizes ASPD in terms of traits from the domain of Antagonism (reflecting the meanness construct of the triarchic model) along with traits from the domain of Disinhibition (Table 26.2). Elevations on six of the seven designated traits are required for the trait-based diagnosis of ASPD. Since four of the relevant traits are from the domain of Antagonism, this ensures that individuals achieving the diagnosis will exhibit a

Table 26.3 Specifiers for Psychopathic Variants of Child Conduct Disorder (CD) and Adult Antisocial Personality Disorder (ASPD) in Sections II and III of *DSM-5*

Specifier	Summary Description of Criteria
CD: *Limited Prosocial Emotions Specifer* Persistent evidence of *two or more* of the following over at least 12 months, in two or more contexts:	1. *Lacks remorse or guilt* (does not express or exhibit regret for wrongdoing) 2. *Callous/unempathic* (lacks concern for feelings and welfare of others) 3. *Lacks concern about performance* (indifferent regarding underachievement or failure in key domains including school and work) 4. *Shallow affectivity* (limited, superficial or insincere expression of emotions)
ASPD: *Psychopathic Features Specifier* *Low* scores on the following two traits: AND *Elevated* score on the following trait:	1. *Anxiousness* (domain of negative affect) 2. *Withdrawal* (domain of detachment) 3. *Attention seeking* (domain of antagonism)

Note: The Limited Prosocial Emotions specifier is used to designate a "callous-unemotional" variant of conduct disorder as described in the child psychopathy literature (Frick et al., 1994; Frick & Marsee, 2006). The Psychopathic Features specifier is used to designate a classically low-anxious, socially assertive (i.e., "bold"; Patrick et al., 2009) variant of antisocial personality as described in the adult psychopathy literature (Cleckley, 1976; Karpman, 1941; Hicks et al., 2004), with high attention seeking and low withdrawal capturing the social assertiveness aspect.

balance of tendencies toward meanness and dis-inhibition—reflecting historical conceptions that have focused on criminal expressions of psychop-athy (cf. Patrick et al., 2009) and paralleling the revision to the diagnosis of CD, entailing speci-fication of a distinct callous-unemotional ("low prosocial") variant. This represents a shift from the criterion-based approach to the diagnosis of ASPD in Section II, which emphasizes disinhibi-tion more than meanness, particularly at the adult level (Kendler et al., 2012; Venables & Patrick, 2012). The second innovation consists of the inclu-sion of a psychopathic features specifier for the diagnosis of ASPD in *DSM-5*. The specifier, which entails extreme scores on three additional traits (one each from the domains of Negative Affect, Detachment, and Antagonism; see Table 26.3, lower part), provides for the designation of a clas-sically low-anxious, socially efficacious (i.e., bold) variant of ASPD (cf. Cleckley, 1976; Karpman, 1941; see also Hicks, Markon, Patrick, Krueger, & Newman, 2004; Skeem, Johansson, Andershed, Kerr, & Louden, 2007). This provision is particu-larly important in light of recent work demonstrat-ing the importance of boldness in distinguishing psychopathy as defined by the PCL-R from the criterion-based diagnosis of ASPD (Venables, Hall, & Patrick, 2014).

As described in Chapter 23 of this volume, a new inventory, the Personality Inventory for *DSM-5* (PID-5) has been developed to operationalize the new dimensional-trait system for PDs. In addition to the initial self-report-based PID-5 (Krueger, Derringer, Markon, Watosn, & Skodol, 2012), an informant rating form also exists (PID-IRF; Markon, Quilty, Bagby, & Krueger, 2013), and ini-tial work toward a clinician-rating version has been undertaken (Morey, Krueger, & Skodol, 2013). Evidence for convergent and discriminant validity of the self-report form has been reported in rela-tion to symptoms of categorical PDs as defined in *DSM-IV* and Section II of *DSM-5* (Hopwood, Thomas, Markon, Wright, & Krueger, 2012). Also, the development paper on the informant rating ver-sion (Markon et al., 2013) presented evidence for validity in relation to self-report PID-5 scores and observed ratings as well as self-report scores on NEO-PI five-factor domains. Two studies using the PID-5 have been conducted at this point to evalu-ate the effectiveness of the Section III trait-based approach to diagnosing ASPD in capturing facets of psychopathy as specified by the triarchic model. One

of these (Strickland, Drislane, Lucy, Krueger, & Patrick, 2013) used the TriPM in conjunction with the PID-5 in a mixed college and community adult sample; the other (Anderson, Sellbom, Wygant, Salekin, & Krueger, 2014) used the TriPM and PPI along with the PID-5 in separate samples of col-lege students and community adults, with the latter sample recruited in a manner designed to enhance representation of participants with increased psy-chopathic tendencies. Findings from these two studies converge in demonstrating highly effective coverage of the disinhibition and meanness facets of psychopathy (as indexed by the TriPM) through traits represented in the *DSM-5* Section III diagno-sis of ASPD (operationalized via the PID-5). Results from both studies also indicate markedly improved coverage of the boldness facet through use of traits included in the Section III psychopathy specifier.

Taken together, the findings of these studies pro-vide encouraging evidence that adult psychopathy as described in classic historical writings and inves-tigated empirically over the years can be indexed effectively using the new dimensional-trait system included in Section III of *DSM-5*. However, fur-ther work will be needed to address issues involv-ing mode of assessment (e.g., self-report versus interview assessment; cf. Blonigen et al., 2010) in evaluating relations between *DSM-5* trait-based operationalizations of ASPD—with and without psychopathic features—and other established measures of antisocial and psychopathic tenden-cies, including the PCL-R.

Acknowledgment

Preparation of this chapter was supported by grant MH089727 from the National Institute of Mental Health.

References

Achenbach, T. M. (1991). *Manual for the Child Behavior Checklist/4-18 and 1991 profile*. Burlington, VT: University of Vermont Department of Psychiatry.

Achenbach, T. M., & Edelbrock, C. S. (1978). The classification of child psychopathology: A review and analysis of empirical efforts. *Psychological Bulletin, 85*, 1275–1301.

Andershed, H., Kerr, M., Stattin, H., & Levander, S. (2002). Psychopathic traits in non-referred youths: A new assessment tool. In E. Blau & L. Sheridan (Eds.), *Psychopaths: Current international perspectives* (pp. 131–158). Amsterdam: Elsevier.

Anderson, J., Sellbom, M., Wygant, D. B., Salekin, R. T., & Krueger, R. F. (in press). Examining the associations between DSM-5 Section III antisocial personality disorder traits and psychopathy in community and university samples. *Journal of Personality Disorders*.

Arieti, S. (1963). Psychopathic personality: Some views on its psychopathology and psychodynamics. *Comprehensive Psychiatry, 4*, 301–312.

Arieti, S. (1967). *The intrapsychic self: Feeling, cognition, and creativity in health and mental illness*. New York: Basic Books.

Arnett, P. A. (1997). Autonomic responsivity in psychopaths: A critical review and theoretical proposal. *Clinical Psychology Review, 17*, 903–936.

Bauer, L. O., O'Connor, S. & Hesselbrock, V. M. (1994). Frontal P300 decrements in antisocial personality disorder. *Alcoholism: Clinical and Experimental Research, 18*, 1300–1305.

Begleiter, H., Porjesz, B., Bihari, B., & Kissin, B. (1984). Event-related brain potentials in boys at risk for alcoholism. *Science, 225*, 1493–1496

Benning, S. D., Patrick, C. J., Blonigen, D. M., Hicks, B. M., & Iacono, W. G. (2005). Estimating facets of psychopathy from normal personality traits: A step toward community-epidemiological investigations. *Assessment, 12*, 3–18.

Benning, S. D., Patrick, C. J., Hicks, B. M., Blonigen, D. M., & Krueger, R. F. (2003). Factor structure of the Psychopathic Personality Inventory: Validity and implications for clinical assessment. *Psychological Assessment, 15*, 340–350.

Benning, S. D., Patrick, C. J., & Iacono, W. G. (2005). Psychopathy, startle blink modulation, and electrodermal reactivity in twin men. *Psychophysiology, 42*, 753–762.

Birbaumer, N., Veit, R., Lotze, M., Erb, M., Hermann, C., Grodd, W., & Flor, H. (2005). Deficient fear conditioning in psychopathy: A functional magnetic resonance imaging study. *Archives of General Psychiatry, 62*, 799–805.

Blackburn, R. (2006). Other theoretical models of psychopathy. In C. J. Patrick (Ed.), *Handbook of psychopathy* (pp. 35–57). New York: Guilford Press.

Blair, R. J. R. (2006). Subcortical brain systems in psychopathy: The amygdala and associated structures. In C. J. Patrick (Ed.), *Handbook of psychopathy* (pp. 296–312). New York: Guilford Press.

Block, J. H., & Block, J. (1980). The role of ego-control and ego resiliency in the organization of behavior. In W. A. Collins (Ed.), *Development of cognition, affect, and social relations: The Minnesota symposium on child psychology* (Vol. 13, pp. 39–101). Hillsdale, NJ: Lawrence Erlbaum.

Blonigen, D. M., Hicks, B., Krueger, R., Patrick, C. J., & Iacono, W. (2005). Psychopathic personality traits: Heritability and genetic overlap with internalizing and externalizing pathology. *Psychological Medicine, 35*, 637–648.

Blonigen, D. M., Patrick, C. J., Douglas, K. S., Poythress, N. G., Skeem, J. L., Lilienfeld, S. O., et al., (2010). Multimethod assessment of psychopathy in relation to factors of internalizing and externalizing from the Personality Assessment Inventory: The impact of method variance and suppressor effects. *Psychological Assessment, 22*, 96–107.

Buckholtz, J. W., Treadway, M. T., Cowan, R. L., Woodward, N. D., Benning, S. D., Li R., et al. (2010). Mesolimbic dopamine reward system hypersensitivity in individuals with psychopathic traits. *Nature Neuroscience, 13*, 419–421.

Carlson, S. R., Thái, S., & McLaron, M. E. (2009). Visual P3 amplitude and self-reported psychopathic personality traits: Frontal reduction is associated with self-centered impulsivity. *Psychophysiology, 46*, 100–113.

Casillas, A., & Clark, L. A. (2002). Dependency, impulsivity, and self-harm: Traits hypothesized to underlie the association between Cluster B personality and substance use disorders. *Journal of Personality Disorders, 16*, 424–436.

Cleckley, H. (1976). *The mask of sanity* (5th ed.). St. Louis.: Mosby. (Original edition published in 1941)

Cooke, D. J., & Michie, C. (2001). Refining the construct of psychopathy: Towards a hierarchical model. *Psychological Assessment, 13*, 171–188.

Costa, P. T., & McCrae, R. R. (1992). *NEO PI-R professional manual*. Lutz, FL: Psychological Assessment Resources.

Craig, R. L., Gray, N. S., & Snowden, R. J. (2013). Recalled parent bonding, current attachment, and the triarchic conceptualization of psychopathy. *Personality and Individual Differences, 55*, 345–350.

Craft, M. (1966). *Psychopathic disorders and their assessment*. New York: Pergamon Press.

Davidson, R. J., Putnam, K. M., & Larson, C. L. (2000). Dysfunction in the neural circuitry of emotion regulation—A possible prelude to violence. *Science, 289*, 591–594.

Digman, J. M. (1990). Personality structure: Emergence of the five-factor model. *Annual Review of Psychology, 41*, 417–440.

Drislane, L. E., Brislin, S. J., Kendler, K. S., Andershed, H., Larsson, H., & Patrick, C. J. (in press). A triarchic model analysis of the Youth Psychopathic Traits Inventory. *Journal of Personality Disorders.*

Drislane, L. E., Patrick, C. J., & Arsal, G. (in press). Clarifying the content coverage of differing psychopathy inventories through reference to the Triarchic Psychopathy Measure. *Psychological Assessment.*

Farrington, D. (2006). Family background and psychopathy. In C. J. Patrick (Ed.), *Handbook of psychopathy* (pp. 229–250). New York: Guilford Press.

First, M. B., Gibbon, M., Spitzer, R. L., Williams, J. B. W., & Benjamin, L. S. (1997). *Structured Clinical Interview for DSM-IV axis II personality disorders, (SCID-II).* Washington, DC: American Psychiatric Press.

Forth, A. E., Kosson, D. S., & Hare, R. D. (2003). *The Psychopathy Checklist: Youth version manual.* Toronto, ON: Multi-Health Systems.

Fowles, D. C. (1980). The three arousal model: Implications of Gray's two-factor learning theory for heart rate, electrodermal activity, and psychopathy. *Psychophysiology, 17*, 87–104.

Fowles, D. C., & Dindo, L. (2009). Temperament and psychopathy: A dual-pathway model. *Current Directions in Psychological Science, 18*, 179–183.

Frances, A. J. (1980). The DSM-III personality disorders section: A commentary. *American Journal of Psychiatry, 137*, 1050–1054.

Frick, P. J. (2013). Clinical assessment of prosocial emotions. Unpublished preliminary manual. Available online at: http://psyc.uno.edu/Frick%20Lab/CAPE.html

Frick, P. J., Boden, D. S., & Barry, C. T. (2000). Psychopathic traits and conduct problems in community and clinic-referred samples of children: Further development of the Psychopathy Screening Device. *Psychological Assessment, 12*, 382–393.

Frick, P. J., & Dickens, C. (2006). Current perspectives on conduct disorder. *Current Psychiatry Reports, 8*, 59–72.

Frick, P. J., & Hare, R. D. (2001). *The Antisocial Process Screening Device (APSD).* Toronto: Multi-Health Systems.

Frick, P. J., Lahey, B. B., Loeber, R., Stouthamer-Loeber, M., Green, S., Hart, E. L., & Christ, M. A. G. (1991). Oppositional defiant disorder and conduct disorder in boys: Patterns of behavioral covariation. *Journal of Clinical Child Psychology, 20*, 202–208.

Frick, P. J., Lilienfeld, S. O., Ellis, M., Loney, B., & Silverthorn P. (1999). The association between anxiety and psychopathy dimensions in children. *Journal of Abnormal Child Psychology, 27*, 383–392.

Frick, P. J., & Marsee, M. A. (2006). Psychopathy and developmental pathways to antisocial behavior in youth. In C. J. Patrick (Ed.), *Handbook of psychopathy* (pp. 353–374). New York: Guilford Press.

Frick, P. J., O'Brien, B. S., Wooten, J. M., & McBurnett, K. (1994). Psychopathy and conduct problems in children. *Journal of Abnormal Psychology, 103*, 700–707.

Frick, P. J., & White, S. F. (2008). The importance of callous-unemotional traits for developmental models of aggressive and antisocial behavior. *Journal of Child Psychology and Psychiatry, 49*, 359–375.

Gao, Y., Raine, A., & Schug, R. A. (2011). P3 event-related potentials and childhood maltreatment in successful and unsuccessful psychopaths. *Brain and Cognition, 77*, 176–182.

Gordon, H. L., Baird, A. A., & End, A. (2004). Functional differences among those high and low on a trait measure of psychopathy. *Biological Psychiatry, 56*, 516–521.

Gorenstein, E. E., & Newman, J. P. (1980). Disinhibitory psychopathology: A new perspective and a model for research. *Psychological Review, 87*, 301–315.

Grant, B. F., Stinson, F. S., Dawson, D. A., Chou, S. P., Ruan, W. J., & Pickering, R. P. (2004). Co-occurrence of 12-month alcohol and drug use disorders and personality disorders in the United States. Results from the National Epidemiologic Survey on Alcohol and Related Conditions. *Archives of General Psychiatry, 61*, 361–368.

Hall, J., Benning, S. D., & Patrick, C. J. (2004). Criterion-related validity of the three-factor model of psychopathy: Personality, behavior, and adaptive functioning. *Assessment, 11*, 4–16.

Hall, J. R., Drislane, L. E., Patrick, C. J., Morano, M., Lilienfeld, S. O., & Poythress, N. G. (2014). Development and validation of Triarchic Construct Scales from the Psychopathic Personality Inventory. *Psychological Assessment, 26*, 447–461.

Hare, R. D. (1978). Electrodermal and cardiovascular correlates of psychopathy. In R. D. Hare & D. Schalling (Eds.), *Psychopathic behavior: Approaches to research* (pp. 107–143). Chichester, UK: Wiley.

Hare, R. D. (1980). A research scale for the assessment of psychopathy in criminal populations. *Personality and Individual Differences, 1*, 111–119.

Hare, R. D. (1983). Diagnosis of antisocial personality disorder in two prison populations. *American Journal of Psychiatry*, 140, 887–890.

Hare, R. D. (1991). *The Hare Psychopathy Checklist-Revised*. Toronto: Multi-Health Systems.

Hare, R. D. (2003). *The Hare Psychopathy Checklist—Revised*, 2nd ed. Toronto: Multi-Health Systems.

Hare, R. D., Harpur, T. J., Hakstian, A. R., Forth, A. E., Hart, S. D., & Newman, J. P. (1990). The Revised Psychopathy Checklist: Reliability and factor structure. *Psychological Assessment*, 2, 338–341.

Hare, R. D., & Neumann, C. S. (2006). The PCL-R assessment of psychopathy: Development, structural properties, and new directions. In C. J. Patrick (Ed.), *Handbook of psychopathy* (pp. 58–88). New York: Guilford Press.

Harenski, C. L., Kim, S., & Hamann, S. (2009). Neuroticism and psychopathic traits predict brain activity during moral and non-moral emotion regulation. *Cognitive, Affective, and Behavioral Neuroscience*, 9, 1–15.

Harpur, T. J., Hakstian, A. R., & Hare, R. D. (1988). Factor structure of the psychopathy checklist. *Journal of Consulting and Clinical Psychology*, 56, 741–747.

Harpur, T. J., Hare, R. D., & Hakstian, A. R. (1989). Two-factor conceptualization of psychopathy: Construct validity and assessment implications. *Psychological Assessment*, 1, 6–17.

Hart, S., Cox, D., & Hare, R. D. (1995). *Manual for the Psychopathy Checklist: Screening version (PCL:SV)*. Toronto: Multi-Health Systems.

Hart, S. D., & Hare, R. D. (1989). Discriminant validity of the Psychopathy Checklist in a forensic psychiatric population. *Psychological Assessment*, 1, 211–218.

Herpertz, S. C., Werth, U., Lukas, G., Qunaibi, M., Schuerkens, A., Kunert, H., Freese, R., et al. (2001). Emotion in criminal offenders with psychopathy and borderline personality disorder. *Archives of General Psychiatry*, 58, 737–744.

Hicks, B. M., Bernat, E. M., Malone, S. M., Iacono, W. G., Patrick, C. J., Krueger, R. F., & McGue, M. (2007). Genes mediate the association between P300 amplitude and externalizing psychopathology. *Psychophysiology*, 44, 98–105.

Hicks, B. M., Markon, K. E., Patrick, C. J., Krueger, R. F., & Newman, J. P. (2004). Identifying psychopathy subtypes on the basis of personality structure. *Psychological Assessment*, 16, 276–288.

Hicks, B. M., & Patrick, C. J. (2006). Psychopathy and negative affectivity: Analyses of suppressor effects reveal distinct relations with trait anxiety, depression, fearfulness, and anger-hostility. *Journal of Abnormal Psychology*, 115, 276–287.

Hildebrand, M., & de Ruiter, C. (2004). PCL-R psychopathy and its relation to DSM-IV Axis I and Axis II disorders in a sample of male forensic psychiatric patients in the Netherlands. *International Journal of Law and Psychiatry*, 24, 233–248.

Hopwood, C. J., Thomas, K. M., Markon, K., Wright, A. G. C., & Krueger, R. F. (2012). DSM-5 personality traits and DSM-IV personality disorders. *Journal of Abnormal Psychology*, 121, 424–432.

Horney, K. (1945). *Our inner conflicts*. New York: W. W. Norton.

Iacono, W. G., Carlson, S. R., Malone, S. M., & McGue, M. (2002). P3 event-related potential amplitude and risk for disinhibitory disorders in adolescent boys. *Archives of General Psychiatry*, 59, 750–757.

Iacono, W. G., Carlson, S. R., Taylor, J., Elkins, I. J., & McGue, M. (1999). Behavioral disinhibition and the development of substance-use disorders: Findings from the Minnesota Twin Family Study. *Development and Psychopathology*, 11, 869–900.

Iacono, W. G., Malone, S. M., & McGue, M. (2008). Behavioral disinhibition and the development of early-onset addiction: Common and specific influences. *Annual Review of Clinical Psychology*, 4, 325–348.

Ishikawa, S. S., Raine, A., Lencz, T., Bihrle, S., & Lacasse, L. (2001). Autonomic stress reactivity and executive functions in successful and unsuccessful criminal psychopaths from the community. *Journal of Abnormal Psychology*, 110, 423–432.

Jones, A. P., Laurens, K. R., Herba, C. M., Barker, G. J., & Viding, E. (2009). Amygdala hypoactivity to fearful faces in boys with conduct problems and callous-unemotional traits. *American Journal of Psychiatry*, 166, 95–102.

Karpman, B. (1941). On the need for separating psychopathy into two distinct clinical types: Symptomatic and idiopathic. *Journal of Criminology and Psychopathology*, 3, 112–137.

Kendler, K. S., Aggen, S. H., & Patrick, C. J. (2012). A multivariate twin study of the DSM-IV criteria for antisocial personality disorder. *Biological Psychiatry*, 71, 247–253.

Kendler, K. S., Aggen, S. H., & Patrick, C. J. (2013). Familial influences on conduct disorder criteria in males reflect two genetic factors and one shared environmental factor: A population-based twin study. *Journal of the American Medical Association Psychiatry, 70,* 78–86.

Kendler, K. S., Prescott, C. A., Myers, J., & Neale, M. C. (2003). The structure of genetic and environmental risk factors for common psychiatric and substance use disorders in men and women. *Archives of General Psychiatry, 60,* 929–937.

Kessler, R. C., & Walters, E. E. (2002). The National Comorbidity Survey. In M. T. Tsuang & M. Tohen (Eds.), *Textbook in psychiatric epidemiology* (2nd ed., pp. 343–362). New York: John Wiley & Sons.

Kobasa, C. S. (1979). Stressful life events, personality, and health: An inquiry into hardiness. *Journal of Personality and Social Psychology, 37,* 1–11.

Koch, J. L. (1891). *Die psychopathischen Minderwertigkeiten.* Ravensburg, Germany: Maier.

Kochanska, G. K. (1997). Multiple pathways to conscience for children with different temperaments: From toddlerhood to age 5. *Developmental Psychology, 33,* 228–240.

Kochanska, G., Murray, K., & Coy, K. C. (1997). Inhibitory control as a contributor to conscience in childhood: From toddler to early school age. *Child Development, 68,* 263–267.

Koenigsberg, H. W., Kaplan, R. D., Gilmore, M. M., & Cooper, A. M. (1985). The relation between syndrome and personality disorder in DSM III: Experience with 2,412 patients. *American Journal of Psychiatry, 142,* 207–212.

Kosson, D. S., Smith, S. S. & Newman, J. P. (1990). Evaluating the construct validity of psychopathy in African American and European American male inmates: Three preliminary studies. *Journal of Abnormal Psychology, 99,* 250–259.

Kraepelin, E. (1915). *Psychiatrie: Ein Lehrbuch* (8th ed.). Leipzig: Barth.

Kramer, M. D., Patrick, C. J., Krueger, R. F., & Gasperi, M. (2012). Delineating physiological defensive reactivity in the domain of self-report: Phenotypic and etiologic structure of dispositional fear. *Psychological Medicine, 42,* 1305–1320.

Krueger, R. F. (1999a). Personality traits in late adolescence predict mental disorders in early adulthood: A prospective-epidemiological study. *Journal of Personality, 67,* 39–65.

Krueger, R. F. (1999b). The structure of common mental disorders. *Archives of General Psychiatry, 56,* 921–926.

Krueger, R. F., Derringer, J., Markon, K. E., Watson, D., & Skodol, A. E. (2012). Initial construction of a maladaptive personality trait model and inventory for DSM-5. *Psychological Medicine, 42,* 1879–1890.

Krueger, R. F., Hicks, B., Patrick, C. J., Carlson, S., Iacono, W. G., & McGue, M. (2002). Etiologic connections among substance dependence, antisocial behavior, and personality: Modeling the externalizing spectrum. *Journal of Abnormal Psychology, 111,* 411–424.

Krueger, R. F., Markon, K. E., Patrick, C. J., Benning, S. D., & Kramer, M. (2007). Linking antisocial behavior, substance use, and personality: An integrative quantitative model of the adult externalizing spectrum. *Journal of Abnormal Psychology, 116,* 645–666.

Lang, P. J., Bradley, M. M., & Cuthbert, B. N. (1990). Emotion, attention, and the startle reflex. *Psychological Review, 97,* 377–398.

Leary, T. (1957). *Interpersonal diagnosis of personality.* New York: Ronald Press.

Levenson, M. R., Kiehl, K. A., & Fitzpatrick, C. M. (1995). Assessing psychopathic attributes in a noninstitutionalized population. *Journal of Personality and Social Psychology, 68,* 151–158.

Lewis, C. E., Rice, J., & Helzer, J. E. (1983). Diagnostic interactions: Alcoholism and antisocial personality. *Journal of Nervous and Mental Disease, 171,* 105–113.

Lilienfeld, S. O., & Andrews, B. P. (1996). Development and preliminary validation of a self report measure of psychopathic personality traits in noncriminal populations. *Journal of Personality Assessment, 66,* 488–524.

Lilienfeld, S. O., & Widows, M. R. (2005). *Psychopathic Personality Inventory—Revised (PPI-R) professional manual.* Odessa, FL: Psychological Assessment Resources.

Lorber, M. F. (2004). Psychophysiology of aggression, psychopathy, and conduct problems: A meta-analysis. *Psychological Bulletin, 130,* 531–552.

Lykken, D. T. (1957). A study of anxiety in the sociopathic personality. *Journal of Abnormal and Clinical Psychology, 55,* 6–10.

Lykken, D. T. (1995). *The antisocial personalities.* Hillsdale, NJ: Lawrence Erlbaum.

Lynam, D. R. (1997). Pursuing the psychopath: Capturing the fledgling psychopath in a nomological net. *Journal of Abnormal Psychology, 106,* 425–438.

Lynam, D. R., Caspi, A., Moffit, T. E., Raine, A., Loeber, R., & Stouthamer-Loeber, M. (2005). Adolescent psychopathy and the big five: Results from two samples. *Journal of Abnormal Child Psychology, 33,* 431–443.

Lynam, D. R., & Derefinko, K. J. (2006). Psychopathy and personality. In C. J. Patrick (Ed.), *Handbook of psychopathy* (pp. 133–155). New York: Guilford Press.

Lynam, D. R., Gaughan, E. T., Miller, J. D., Miller, D. J., Mullins-Sweatt, S., & Widiger, T. A. (2011). Assessing the basic traits associated with psychopathy: Development and validation of the Elemental Psychopathy Assessment. *Psychological Assessment, 18*, 106–114.

Lynam, D. R., Leukefeld, C., & Clayton, R. R. (2003). The contribution of personality to the overlap between antisocial behavior and substance use/misuse. *Aggressive Behavior, 29*, 316–331.

Lynam, D. R., & Widiger, T. A. (2007). Using a general model of personality to identify the basic elements of psychopathy. *Journal of Personality Disorders, 21*, 160–178.

Marion B. E., Sellbom, M., Salekin, R. T., Toomey, J. A., Kucharski, L. T., Duncan, S. (2013). An examination of the association between psychopathy and dissimulation using the MMPI-2-RF validity scales. *Law and Human Behavior, 37*, 219–230.

Markon, K. E., Quilty, L. C., Bagby, R. M., & Krueger, R. F. (2013). The development and psychometric properties of an informant-report form of the Personality Inventory for DSM-5 (PID-5). *Assessment, 20*, 370–383.

Marsh, A. A., Finger, E. C., Mitchell, D. G., Reid, M. E., Sims, C., Kosson, D. S., et al. (2008). Reduced amygdala response to fearful expressions in children and adolescents with callous-unemotional traits and disruptive behavior disorders. *American Journal of Psychiatry, 165*, 712–720.

McCord, W., & McCord, J. (1964). *The psychopath: An essay on the criminal mind*. Princeton, NJ: Van Nostrand.

Miller, J. D, Gaughan, E. T., Maples, J., Gentile, B., Lynam, D. R., & Widiger, T. A. (2011). Examining the construct validity of the elemental psychopathy assessment. *Assessment, 18*, 106–114.

Miller, J. D., Lynam, D. R., Widiger, T. A., & Leukefeld, C. (2001). Personality disorders as extreme variants of common personality dimensions: Can the five-factor model adequately represent psychopathy? *Journal of Personality, 69*, 253–276.

Minzenberg, M. J., & Siever, L. J. (2006). Neurochemistry and pharmacology of psychopathy and related disorders. In C. J. Patrick (Ed.), *Handbook of psychopathy* (pp. 251–277). New York: Guilford Press.

Moffitt, T. E. (1993). Adolescence-limited and life-course-persistent antisocial behavior: A developmental taxonomy. *Psychological Review, 100*, 674–701.

Morey, L. C., Krueger, R. F., & Skodol, R. E. (2013). The hierarchical structure of clinician ratings of DSM-5 pathological personality traits. *Journal of Abnormal Psychology, 122*, 836–841.

Morgan, A. B., & Lilienfeld, S. O. (2000). A meta-analytic review of the relation between antisocial behavior and neuropsychological measures of executive function. *Clinical Psychology Review, 20*, 113–136.

Nelson, L. D., Patrick, C. J., & Bernat, E. M. (2011). Operationalizing proneness to externalizing psychopathology as a multivariate psychophysiological phenotype. *Psychophysiology, 48*, 64–72.

Ortiz, J., & Raine, A. (2004). Heart rate level and antisocial behavior in children and adolescents: A meta-analysis. *Journal of the American Academy of Child & Adolescent Psychiatry, 43*, 154–162.

Partridge, G. E. (1928a). A study of 50 cases of psychopathic personality. *American Journal of Psychiatry, 7*, 953–973.

Partridge, G. E. (1928b). Psychopathic personalities among boys in a training school for delinquents. *American Journal of Psychiatry, 8*, 159–186.

Patrick, C. J. (1994). Emotion and psychopathy: Startling new insights. *Psychophysiology, 31*, 319–330.

Patrick, C. J. (2006). Back to the future: Cleckley as a guide to the next generation of psychopathy research. In C. J. Patrick (Ed.), *Handbook of psychopathy* (pp. 605–617). New York: Guilford Press.

Patrick, C. J. (2008). Psychophysiological correlates of aggression and violence: An integrative review. *Philosophical Transactions of the Royal Society B (Biological Sciences), 363*, 2543–2555.

Patrick, C. J. (2010). Operationalizing the triarchic conceptualization of psychopathy: Preliminary description of brief scales for assessment of boldness, meanness, and disinhibition. Unpublished test manual, Florida State University, Tallahassee, FL. Test is available online at: https://www.phenxtoolkit.org/index.php?pageLink=browse.protocoldetails&id= 121601

Patrick, C. J., Bernat, E., Malone, S. M., Iacono, W. G., Krueger, R. F., & McGue, M. K. (2006). P300 amplitude as an indicator of externalizing in adolescent males. *Psychophysiology, 43*, 84–92.

Patrick, C. J., Bradley, M. M., & Lang, P. J. (1993). Emotion in the criminal psychopath: Startle reflex modulation. *Journal of Abnormal Psychology*, *102*, 82–92.

Patrick, C. J., Durbin, C. E., & Moser, J. S. (2012). Conceptualizing proneness to antisocial deviance in neurobehavioral terms. *Development and Psychopathology*, *24*, 1047–1071.

Patrick, C. J., Edens, J. F., Poythress, N., Lilienfeld, S. O., & Benning, S. D. (2006). Construct validity of the PPI two-factor model with offenders. *Psychological Assessment*, *18*, 204–208.

Patrick, C. J., Fowles, D. C., & Krueger, R. F. (2009). Triarchic conceptualization of psychopathy: Developmental origins of disinhibition, boldness, and meanness. *Development and Psychopathology*, *21*, 913–938.

Patrick, C. J., Hicks, B. M., Krueger, R. F., & Lang, A. R. (2005). Relations between psychopathy facets and externalizing in a criminal offender sample. *Journal of Personality Disorders*, *19*, 339–356.

Patrick, C. J., Hicks, B. M., Nichol, P. E., & Krueger, R. F. (2007). A bifactor approach to modeling the structure of the Psychopathy Checklist-Revised. *Journal of Personality Disorders*, *21*, 118–141.

Patrick, C. J., Kramer, M. D., Krueger, R. F., & Markon, K.E. (2013). Optimizing efficiency of psychopathology assessment through quantitative modeling: Development of a brief form of the Externalizing Spectrum Inventory. *Psychological Assessment*, *2*, 1332–1348.

Patrick, C. J., Venables, N. C., & Skeem, J. L. (2012). Psychopathy and brain function: Empirical findings and legal implications. In: H. Häkkänen-Nyholm & J. Nyholm (Eds.), *Psychopathy and law: A practitioner's guide* (pp. 39–77). New York: John Wiley & Sons.

Patrick, C. J., Venables, N. C., Yancey, J. R., Hicks, B. M., Nelson, L. D., & Kramer, M. D. (2013). A construct-network approach to bridging diagnostic and physiological domains: Application to assessment of externalizing psychopathology. *Journal of Abnormal Psychology*, *122*, 902–916

Paulhus, D. L., Hemphill, J. F., & Hare, R. D. (in press). *Manual for the Self-Report Psychopathy scale*. Toronto: Multi-Health Systems.

Paulhus, D. L., Robins, R. W., Trzesniewski, K. H., & Tracy, J. L. (2004). Two replicable suppressor situations in personality research. *Multivariate Behavioral Research*, *39*, 303–328.

Pinel, P. (1962). *A treatise on insanity* (D. Davis, translator). New York: Hafner. (Original edition published in 1801)

Poythress, N. G., Lilienfeld, S. O., Skeem, J. L., Douglas, K. S., Edens, J. F., Epstein, M., & Patrick, C. J. (2010). Using the PCL-R to help estimate the validity of two self-report measures of psychopathy with offenders. *Assessment*, *17*, 206–219.

Pritchard, J. C. (1835). *A treatise on insanity and other disorders affecting the mind*. London: Sherwood, Gilbert & Piper.

Quay, H. C. (1964). Dimensions of personality in delinquent boys as inferred from the factor analysis of case history data. *Child Development*, *35*, 479–484.

Quay, H. C. (1986). Classification. In H. C. Quay & J. S. Werry (Eds.), *Psychopathological disorders of childhood* (3rd ed., pp. 1–42). New York: John Wiley & Sons.

Raine, A. (1997). Antisocial behavior and psychophysiology: A biosocial perspective and a prefrontal dysfunction hypothesis. In D. M. Stoff, J. Breiling, & J. D. Maser (Eds.), *Handbook of antisocial behavior* (pp. 289–303). New York: John Wiley & Sons.

Raine, A. (2002). Biosocial studies of antisocial and violent behavior in children and adults: A review. *Journal of Abnormal Child Psychology*, *30*, 311–326.

Reardon, M. L., Lang, A. R., & Patrick, C. J. (2002). Antisociality and alcohol problems: An evaluation of subtypes, drinking motives, and family history in incarcerated men. *Alcoholism: Clinical and Experimental Research*, *26*, 1188–1197.

Robins, L. N. (1966). *Deviant children grown up*. Baltimore, MD: Williams & Wilkins.

Robins, L. N. (1978). Sturdy predictors of adult antisocial behaviour: Replications from longitudinal studies. *Psychological Medicine*, *8*, 611–622.

Robins, L. N., & Regier, D. A. (1991). *Psychiatric disorders in America: The epidemiological catchment area study*. New York: Free Press.

Rogers, R. D. (2006). The functional architecture of the frontal lobes: Implications for research with psychopathic offenders. In C. J. Patrick (Ed.), *Handbook of psychopathy* (pp. 313–333). New York: Guilford Press.

Ross, S. R., Benning, S. D., Patrick, C. J., Thompson, A., & Thurston, A. (2009). Factors of the Psychopathic Personality Inventory: Criterion-related validity and relationship to the BIS/BAS and five-factor models of personality. *Assessment*, *16*, 71–87.

Rush, B. (1812). *Medical inquiries and observations upon the diseases of the mind*. Philadelphia: Kimber & Richardson.

Saucier, G. (1992). Benchmarks: Integrating affective and interpersonal circles with the Big-Five personality factors. *Journal of Personality and Social Psychology, 62,* 1025–1035.

Schneider, K. (1934). *Die psychopathischen Persönlichkeiten* (3rd ed.). Vienna: Deuticke.

Sellbom, M., & Phillips, T. R. (2013). An examination of the triarchic conceptualization of psychopathy in incarcerated and non-incarcerated samples. *Journal of Abnormal Psychology, 122,* 208–214.

Seo, D., Patrick, C. J., & Kennealy, P. J. (2008). Role of serotonin and dopamine system interactions in the neurobiology of impulsive aggression and its comorbidity with other clinical disorders. *Aggression and Violent Behavior, 13,* 383–395.

Sher, K. J., & Trull, T. (1994). Personality and disinhibitory psychopathology: Alcoholism and antisocial personality disorder. *Journal of Abnormal Psychology, 103,* 92–102.

Shine, J., & Hobson, J. (1997). Construct validity of the Hare Psychopathy Checklist Revised. *Journal of Forensic Psychiatry, 8,* 546–561.

Siddle, D.A.T., & Trasler, G.B. (1981). The psychophysiology of psychopathic behavior. In M. J. Christie & P. G. Mellett (Eds.), *Foundations of psychosomatics* (pp. 283–303). New York: John Wiley & Sons.

Skeem, J. L., Edens, J. F., Camp, J., & Colwell, L. H. (2004). Are there racial differences in levels of psychopathy? A meta-analysis. *Law and Human Behavior, 28,* 505–527.

Skeem, J. L., Johansson, P., Andershed, H., Kerr, M., & Louden, J. E. (2007). Two subtypes of psychopathic violent offenders that parallel primary and secondary variants. *Journal of Abnormal Psychology, 116,* 395–409.

Smith, S. S., & Newman, J. P. (1990). Alcohol and drug abuse-dependence disorders in psychopathic and nonpsychopathic criminal offenders. *Journal of Abnormal Psychology, 99,* 430–439.

Stanley, J. H., Wygant, D. B., Sellbom, M. (2013). Elaborating on the construct validity of the Triarchic Psychopathy Measure in a criminal offender sample. *Journal of Personality Assessment, 95,* 343–350.

Strickland, C. M., Drislane, L. E., Lucy, M. D., Krueger, R. F., & Patrick, C. J. (2013). Characterizing psychopathy using DSM-5 personality traits. *Assessment, 20,* 327–338.

Sullivan, E. A., & Kosson, D. S. (2006). Ethnic and cultural variations in psychopathy. In C. J. Patrick (Ed.), *Handbook of psychopathy* (pp. 437–458). New York: Guilford Press.

Sutton, S. K., Vitale, J. E., & Newman, J. P. (2002). Emotion among females with psychopathy during picture perception. *Journal of Abnormal Psychology, 111,* 610–619.

Tackett, J. L., Krueger, R. F., Iacono, W. G., & McGue, M. (2005). Symptom-based subfactors of DSM-defined conduct disorder: Evidence for etiologic distinctions. *Journal of Abnormal Psychology, 114,* 483–487.

Tackett, J. L., Krueger, R. F., Sawyer, M. G., & Graetz, B. W. (2003). Subfactors of DSM-IV conduct disorder: Evidence and connections with syndromes from the child behavior checklist. *Journal of Abnormal Child Psychology, 31,* 647–654.

Tellegen, A. (2003). *Multidimensional Personality Questionnaire-276, test booklet.* Minneapolis, MN: University of Minnesota Press.

Tellegen, A., & Waller, N. G. (2008). Exploring personality through test construction: Development of the Multidimensional Personality Questionnaire. In G. J. Boyle, G. Matthews, & D. H. Saklofske (Eds.), *Handbook of personality theory and testing: Personality measurement and assessment* (Vol. II, pp. 261–292). London: Sage.

Vaidyanathan, U., Hall, J. R., Patrick, C. J., & Bernat, E. M. (2011). Clarifying the role of defensive reactivity deficits in psychopathy and antisocial personality using startle reflex methodology. *Journal of Abnormal Psychology, 120,* 253–258.

Vaidyanathan, U., Patrick, C. J., & Bernat, E. M. (2009). Startle reflex potentiation during aversive picture viewing as an index of trait fear. *Psychophysiology, 46,* 75–85.

Vanman, E. J., Mejia, V. Y., Dawson, M. E., Schell, A. M., & Raine, A. (2003). Modification of the startle reflex in a community sample: Do one or two dimensions of psychopathy underlie emotional processing? *Personality and Individual Differences, 35,* 2007–2021.

Veit, R., Flor, H., Erb, M., Lotze, M., Grodd, W., & Birbaumer, N. (2002). Brain circuits involved in emotional learning in antisocial behavior and social phobia in humans. *Neuroscience Letters, 328,* 233–236.

Venables, N. C., Hall, J. R., & Patrick, C. J. (2014). Differentiating psychopathy from antisocial personality disorder: A triarchic model perspective. *Psychological Medicine, 44,* 1005–1013.

Venables, N. C., & Patrick, C. J. (2012). Validity of the Externalizing Spectrum Inventory in a criminal offender sample: Relations with disinhibitory psychopathology, personality, and psychopathic features. *Psychological Assessment, 24,* 88–100.

Venables, N. C., & Patrick, C. J. (2014). Reconciling discrepant findings for P3 brain response in criminal psychopathy through reference to the concept of externalizing proneness. *Psychophysiology, 51,* 427–436.

Verona, E., Hicks, B. M., & Patrick, C. J. (2005). Psychopathy and suicidal behavior in female offenders: Mediating influences of temperament and abuse history. *Journal of Consulting and Clinical Psychology, 73,* 1065–1073.

Verona, E., & Patrick, C. J. (2000). Suicide risk in externalizing syndromes: Temperamental and neurobiological underpinnings. In T. E. Joiner (Ed.), *Suicide science: Expanding the boundaries* (pp. 137–173). Boston: Kluwer Academic Publishers.

Verona, E., Patrick, C. J., & Joiner, T. E. (2001). Psychopathy, antisocial personality, and suicide risk. *Journal of Abnormal Psychology, 110,* 462–470.

Verona, E., Sachs-Ericsson, N., & Joiner, T. E. (2004). Suicide attempts associated with externalizing psychopathology in an epidemiological sample. *American Journal of Psychiatry, 161,* 444–451.

Verona, E., & Vitale, J. (2006). Psychopathy in women: Assessment, manifestations, and etiology. In C. J. Patrick (Ed.), *Handbook of psychopathy* (pp. 415–436). New York: Guilford Press.

Verschuere, B., Crombez, G., de Clercq, A., & Koster, E. H. W. (2005). Psychopathic traits and autonomic responding to concealed information in a prison sample. *Psychophysiology, 42,* 239–245.

Warren, J. I., Burnette, M. L., South, S. C., Preeti, C., Bale, R., Friend, R., & Van Patten, I. (2003). Psychopathy in women: Structural modeling and comorbidity. *International Journal of Law and Psychiatry, 26,* 223–242.

Widiger, T. A., Cadoret, R., Hare, R., Robins, L., Rutherford, M., Zanarini, M., et al. (1996). DSM-IV antisocial personality disorder field trial. *Journal of Abnormal Psychology, 105,* 3–16.

Wiggins, J. S. (1982). Circumplex models of interpersonal behavior in clinical psychology. In P. C. Kendall & J. N. Butcher (Eds.), *Handbook of research methods in clinical psychology* (pp. 183–221). New York: John Wiley & Sons.

Williams, K. M., Paulhus, D. L., & Hare, R. D. (2007). Capturing the four-factor structure of psychopathy in college students via self-report. *Journal of Personality Assessment, 88,* 205–219.

Yancey, J. R., Venables, N. C., Hicks, B. M., & Patrick, C. J. (2013). Evidence for a heritable brain basis to deviance-promoting deficits in self-control. *Journal of Criminal Justice, 41,* 309–317.

Young, S. E., Stallings, M. C., Corley, R. P., Krauter, K. S., & Hewitt, J. K. (2000). Genetic and environmental influences on behavioral disinhibition. *American Journal of Medical Genetics (Neuropsychiatric Genetics), 96,* 684–695.

27

Obsessive-Compulsive Personality Disorder

TED REICHBORN-KJENNERUD

AND GUN PEGGY KNUDSEN

Obsessive-compulsive personality disorder (OCPD) was one of the six specific personality disorders (PDs) proposed by the Personality and Personality Disorder Work Group for inclusion in *DSM-5*. The reason given for this was its high prevalence in the community and in clinical populations and its impact on the course and outcome of depression and anxiety disorders (Skodol et al., 2011). It was also noted that, although there appear to be low levels of impairment in patients with OCPD in the community, OCPD is associated with substantial clinical costs and, together with borderline PD, with the highest total economic burden in terms of direct medical costs and productivity losses compared to those of all other PDs (Soeteman, Hakkaart-van Roijen, Verheul, & Busschbach, 2008).

The current construct of OCPD has historical roots going back more than a century and has evolved through the various editions of the *DSM*. In this chapter we give a brief historical overview of the development of the diagnostic concepts leading up to the *DSM-IV-TR* conceptualization of OCPD, which is equivalent to the diagnosis of anakastic PD in the *ICD-10*. We also review research on OCPD, focusing mainly on studies using the *DSM-IV* criteria. Subsequently, we discuss diagnostic features and aspects of the validity of the construct. We then summarize the descriptive epidemiological findings, and discuss OCPD's co-occurrence with other PDs and clinical disorders (Axis I disorders in *DSM-IV*). Analytical epidemiological studies on risk factors are also presented, including work from quantitative and molecular genetics. Studies on temporal stability and functional impairment are reviewed, as well as results from studies of the relationship between OCPD and normal personality. Finally, we discuss changes made in the *DSM-5* classification.

Historical Review

The modern roots of OCPD go back to the early twentieth century. Janet (1904) described a "psychasthenic state" characterized by a need to do things perfectly which interfered with completing tasks, and by a strong focus on order, indecisiveness, and restricted emotional expression (Pitman, 1987). In 1908 Freud introduced the concept of "anal character." His hypothesis was that the core characteristics of orderliness, parsimony, and obstinacy tended to co-occur and were developed as a consequence of "anal-erotic" impulses in childhood (Freud, 1908). This construct was further developed theoretically by psychoanalysts like Ernest Jones and Karl Abraham (Oldham & Frosch, 1988), but there was no empirical evidence to support the hypothesized underlying etiology of this postulated character trait or personality type. Nevertheless, these authors' rich clinical descriptions inspired later generations of psychiatrists, and a similar construct called "compulsive personality" was included in *DSM-I* in 1952. In 1968 a diagnostic category called "obsessive-compulsive personality" was incorporated into the *DSM-II* and was characterized by rigidity, overinhibition, overconscientiousness, and excessive concern with conformity. In the *DSM-III* (1980) the description of the construct was expanded and the name changed to "compulsive personality disorder." It included five criteria, four of which were required for a diagnosis. In *DSM-III-R* (1987) the five criteria were kept, with minor changes made, and four more criteria were added. Five of nine criteria were required to make the diagnosis. The empirical research supporting the diagnosis was still limited. Changes made in *DSM-IV* (1994), however, were in part based on empirical evidence (Pfhol, 1994) and included changing the name to "obsessive-compulsive personality disorder" (OCPD), deleting two criteria (indecisiveness and restricted expression of affection) and adding one (rigidity and stubbornness). Four of eight criteria are required for a diagnosis of the disorder. (The criteria in *DSM-IV-TR* are the same as in *DSM-IV*.)

The *ICD-10* includes a diagnosis called "anankastic personality disorder," which is very similar to *DSM-IV*-defined OCPD. It includes, however, two criteria that do not appear in *DSM-IV*: feelings of excessive doubt and caution, and pedantry and adherence to social conventions. Likewise, two *DSM-IV* criteria, inability to discard objects and miserliness, are not included in *ICD-10*.

Diagnostic Features

The American Psychiatric Association Board of Trustees decided that the categorical model and criteria for the 10 PDs included in the *DSM-IV-TR* would be maintained in Section II of *DSM-5*. The essential feature of OCPD is defined as follows: "A pervasive pattern of preoccupation with orderliness, perfectionism and mental and interpersonal control at the expense of flexibility, openness and efficiency, beginning by early adulthood and present in a number of contexts" (p. 725). Individuals with OCPD try to maintain a sense of control through a preoccupation with details, rules, lists, order, organization, or schedules to the extent that they lose sight of the main point of the activity they are involved in (e.g., at work), which often prevents them from getting a task done. Task completion is also disturbed by a self-imposed perfectionism

with overly strict standards. For example, the completion of a scientific book chapter would be delayed by futile and time-consuming literature searches meant to ensure that all relevant research results were included, and deadlines would be missed in order to achieve this perfection. A person with OCPD is excessively devoted to work and productivity. This is again self-imposed and not driven by economic or other reasons. Such individuals feel that they do not have time for pleasurable activities and are often unable to take vacations. All activities, including hobbies, are regarded as serious tasks requiring perfection. This quality also interferes with relationships with other people, including friends and family. Collaboration, if it ever occurs, is characterized by the need for control. Individuals with OCPD insist that other people conform to their way of doing things. This results in a reluctance to delegate tasks or to work with others unless others submit completely to their way of doing things. Often this pattern will lead to the person with OCPD taking over others' responsibilities.

Individuals with OCPD are excessively conscientious, scrupulous, and inflexible about matters of morality, ethics, and values, regardless of the subculture the person belongs to. This stance will often lead to hash criticism of both self and others. Some individuals adopt a miserly spending style toward themselves and others. Money is viewed as something to be hoarded for future possible catastrophes and not to be spent on oneself or on others. Individuals with OCPD are often very reluctant to discard worn-out or worthless objects even when they have no sentimental value, which can lead to inconvenience of and criticism from people close to them.

Finally, OCPD is characterized by rigidity and stubbornness. These individuals are concerned with control and perfection and have trouble adapting to other people's ideas and suggestions, especially when it requires changing plans. They are wrapped up in their own perspective and have difficulty acknowledging the viewpoints of others; this often leads to problems with friends, family, and colleagues.

The *DSM-IV-TR/DSM-5* Section II classification system is polythetic in nature, which means that none of the criteria are essential or necessary for a diagnosis to be made. The only requirement for establishing a diagnosis is that four out of eight criteria be met. OCPD is thus a potentially heterogeneous disorder, and two individuals diagnosed with OCPD could, in theory, share no features in common. Obsessive-compulsive traits are probably widely disseminated in the population and can be understood as occurring on a continuum of severity from an adaptive coping style, particularly suitable for some aspects of modern life, to dysfunctional patterns of behavior interfering with social, occupational, or other important areas of functioning (Pollak, 1994). The point at which these traits stop being adaptive and start constituting psychopathological deviation is not clear.

Although the general criteria for personality disorders in *DSM-IV-TR/DSM-5* Section II require "clinically significant distress impairment in social, occupational, or other important areas of functioning," the apparent disagreement or lack of accordance between the low levels of impairment found in individuals with OCPD in community samples and the high medical costs and productivity loss in clinical samples may be due to the inclusion of a large proportion of less severe or, in some areas, adaptive cases of OCPD in general population samples compared to the more severely dysfunctional patients who seek treatment included in clinical samples (Skodol et al., 2011). Therefore, in the following sections we report results from clinical samples as well as those form population-based samples separately.

Empirical Studies

The degree to which criteria for a disorder are interrelated is called *internal consistency*. This is a measure reflecting the average correlation between the different criteria and is reflected in Cronbach's alpha. For OCPD, alpha was estimated to be .69 in the clinically based Collaborative Longitudinal Personality Disorders Study (CLPS), carried out in the United States (Grilo et al., 2001). This is close to what is usually considered acceptable (.7–.8). In the population-based AI/AII study (Reichborn-Kjennerud et al., 2007), by contrast, Cronbach's alpha was excellent (.9). Grilo et al. (2001) also investigated the degree to which OCPD criteria overlapped with criteria for other PDs (intercategory median intercriterion correlation) (Grilo et al., 2001). The results (range 0–.07) indicated that OCPD criteria are more related to each other than to those of other PD diagnoses.

In the CLPS, treatment-seeking individuals with PDs (schizotypal, antisocial, borderline,

avoidant, OCPD) were followed for more than 10 years (McGlashan et al., 2000). Using confirmatory factor analysis on the criteria to study the structure of the OCPD construct, Sanislow et al. (2002) found that "reluctance to delegate," "perfectionism," and "preoccupation with details, lists, rules" loaded most heavily on the latent OCPD factor, indicating that these three traits are most characteristic of OCPD. "Miserliness" loaded least strongly (Sanislow et al., 2002). Unpublished results from factor analyses based on data from a longitudinal population-based study of PDs and clinical disorders in young adult Norwegian twins (the AI/AII study) indicated that the same three criteria as those in the CLPS study—perfectionism, reluctance to delegate, and preoccupation with details, lists, rules—load most strongly on the latent OCPD factor. Also in this study, miserliness loaded least strongly. Both clinical and population-based studies thus seem to indicate that orderliness, perfectionism, and control may be the core features of the OCPD concept.

Although these analyses are consistent with OCPD as a unidimensional construct, to the best of our knowledge no studies have explored the structure of latent factors influencing the relationship between the criteria for OCPD (i.e., exploratory factor analyses or analyses of genetic and environmental influences) to investigate if a two- or three-factor solution would fit better.

The correspondence between *DSM-IV* OCPD and *ICD-10* anankastic PD has been shown to be excellent in community-based samples (Ekselius, Tillfors, Furmark, & Fredrikson, 2001) and very good in clinical samples (kappa .75–.79) (Ottosson, Ekselius, Grann, & Kullgren, 2002; Starcevic, Bogojevic, & Kelin, 1997).

Epidemiology

Prevalence of OCPD

According to the *DSM-5*, OCPD is one of the most prevalent PDs in the general population, with estimated prevalence ranging from 2.1% to 7.9%. In previous studies using *DSM-III, DSM-III-R,* and *DSM-IV* classifications, OCPD was found to be the most prevalent PD in the general population, with a median prevalence of 2.1% (Torgersen, 2009). The prevalence in clinical samples varies, depending on a number of factors, including comorbidity and type of psychiatric facility (i.e., outpatient versus inpatient), but OCPD is still among the most common PDs in treatment-seeking populations (Skodol et al., 2011).

Few population-based studies of prevalence that have used data derived from structured interview assessment of *DSM-IV* PDs have been published. Although estimates from such studies vary, most of them report that OCPD is the most prevalent PD. In a community sample from the United Kingdom assessed for PDs by structural interview, OCPD was the most prevalent *DSM-IV* PD, diagnosed in 1.9% of the sample (Coid, Yang, Tyrer, Roberts, & Ullrich, 2006). OCPD was also the most prevalent *DSM-IV* PD (2.5%) in the population-based AI/AII study from Norway (Reichborn-Kjennerud et al., 2007). In a huge representative study of the U.S. population, the National Epidemiologic Survey on Alcohol and Related Conditions (NESARC), OCPD was also found to be the most prevalent PD; the rate was considerably higher than that in the European studies, 7.9% of the population (B. F. Grant et al., 2004). Although the assessment in this study was done by interview, the overall rate of all the PDs included was substantially higher than that in other similar studies (Huang et al., 2009; Tyrer et al., 2010). In a revised version of the study, which required that each PD criterion be associated with significant distress or impairment in order to be counted toward a PD diagnosis, results demonstrated significant reductions in prevalence rates, a finding much more consistent with those of recent epidemiological studies. The revised prevalence of OCPD was 1.9% (Trull, Jahng, Tomko, Wood, & Sher, 2010). In another U.S. study, the National Comorbidity Survey Replication (NCS-R), which had a nationally representative sample from the United States, the prevalence of OCPD, based on the estimates in a small clinical reappraisal sample, was 2.4%. This estimate was suggested to be somewhat higher than that for the general population (Lenzenweger, Lane, Loranger, & Kessler, 2007).

Prevalence of OCPD Criteria

Few studies have estimated the prevalence of individual *DSM-IV* criteria for OCPD. In the clinically based CLPS study, McGlashan et al. (2005) found that reluctance to delegate, rigidity, and perfectionism were the three most prevalent criteria in

individuals with an OCPD diagnosis. Miserliness was the least frequent criterion (McGlashan et al., 2005). In the population-based AI/AII study, the most prevalent criterion was rigidity, endorsed by 21% of the sample, followed by excessively devoted to work (13%), reluctance to delegate (11%), and perfectionism (10%) (Reichborn-Kjennerud et al., unpublished results). As in the CLPS study, the least frequently reported criterion was miserliness, endorsed by 1% of the sample. Of the individuals in the sample who met criteria for an OCPD diagnosis (2.5%), 87% endorsed the rigidity criterion, 83% endorsed the criterion of reluctance to delegate, while perfectionism and excessively devoted to work both had a prevalence of 74%. Only 6% of the individuals with a full OCPD diagnosis endorsed the miserliness criterion. Taken together, these results indicate that the prevalence rates of the individual criteria are similar in clinical and community samples of individuals fulfilling criteria for OCPD.

Demographic Characteristics

With only a few exceptions, no significant gender differences in prevalence of OCPD have been reported in community samples. In both the Norwegian AI/AII study (Reichborn-Kjennerud et al., 2007) and the original NESARC study (B. F. Grant et al., 2004) OCPD rates were similar for males and females (2.5% and 2.4% respectively, and 7.9% and 7.9%). The prevalence of OCPD in the revised NESARC study was slightly, but significantly, higher in females (1.99%) compared to that for males (1.82%) (Trull et al., 2010). In the population-based study from the United Kingdom, however, prevalence was almost twofold higher among males than among females (2.6% vs. 1.3%) (Coid et al., 2006). The NCS-R PD prevalence rates were not associated with sex at the level of clusters or any PD, but specific estimates for OCPD were not available (Lenzenweger, 2008).

The relationship between age and OCPD varies according to the type of study design. Contrary to what is found for other PDs, higher prevalence of OCPD is usually found in older age groups in cross-sectional studies. In the NESARC study, the highest prevalence was found in the age group 45–65 years (8.97%) and the lowest in the 20- to 29-year group (5.25%) (J. E. Grant, Mooney, & Kushner, 2012). In a representative household population from the United Kingdom, Ullrich and Coid (2009) found a significant relationship between age and the number of OCPD traits, as well as a significantly higher prevalence among 41- to 50-year-olds than among 31- to 40-year-olds (Ullrich & Coid, 2009). Results from the longitudinal Children in the Community Study, from New York, in which the point prevalence of OCPD increased from 0.7% to 2.3% among individuals assessed at mean ages 22 and 33 (Johnson, Cohen, Kasen, Skodol, & Oldham, 2008), also support the suggestion that, contrary to other PDs, the prevalence of OCPD traits increases with age up to late adulthood.

In the sparse epidemiological literature, few associations between *DSM-IV* OCPD and other demographic characteristics have been reported. Marital status in OCPD has been studied but found to have an inconsistent link with OCPD. In the NESARC sample, no overall association between marital status and OCPD was found, but a possible sex difference was detected: females who were married were slightly more likely to have OCPD (J. E. Grant et al., 2012). Other studies have found no association of OCPD with marital status (Coid et al., 2006; Ullrich, Farrington, & Coid, 2007).

Co-occurrence

Comorbidity or co-occurrence between two or more disorders can be attributed to a number of factors, including direct causal relationships and common underlying etiological factors, that is, genetic and environmental factors significantly influencing several disorders (Krueger & Markon, 2006; Neale & Kendler, 1995). Understanding comorbidity is important not only for a deeper understanding of causal mechanisms but also for prevention, treatment, and classification. With regard to OCPD, a key discussion relating to classification is whether it should be placed in (a) the anxious/fearful Cluster C together with avoidant and dependent PD or (b) in a separate fourth cluster by itself, or whether (c) it should be regarded as part of an obsessive-compulsive spectrum together with obsessive-compulsive disorder (OCD).

Studies of comorbidity from clinical and population-based samples often give contrasting results. Because people seeking treatment are more likely to have more than one disorder, that is, treatment seeking is correlated with comorbidity, studies in clinical samples tend to find higher

co-occurrence rates, relative to community samples (Berkson's bias; Berkson, 1946). Comorbidity can also reflect the character of the clinical facility (e.g., inpatient versus outpatient) and not aspects of the disorders themselves.

Comorbidity with other Personality Disorders

OCPD and antisocial PD had the lowest co-occurrence rate with other PDs across a number of different studies (Trull, Sceiderer, & Tomko, 2012). In *DSM-IV*, OCPD is placed in Cluster C, anxious/fearful, together with avoidant and dependent PD. Contrary to expectations, however, higher co-occurrence rates have been reported for OCPD with PDs in Cluster A (odd/eccentric) and Cluster B (dramatic/emotional), than with Cluster C PDs in population-based samples (J. E. Grant et al., 2012; Roysamb et al., 2011) and in treatment-seeking populations (Rossi, Marinangeli, Butti, Kalyvoka, & Petruzzi, 2000; Sanislow et al., 2009).

In the original NESARC study (borderline PD was not assessed), OCPD was most strongly related to paranoid PD (OR = 4.1) and schizoid PD (3.7) in Cluster A and to histrionic PD (OR = 3.1) in Cluster B (J. E. Grant et al., 2012). Similar results from a factor-analytic study of all 10 *DSM-IV* PDs and 15 clinical disorders in the population-based AI/AII study of young Norwegian adult twins (Roysamb et al., 2011) showed that OCPD correlated highest with narcissistic PD from Cluster B (polychoric correlation = .41), followed by paranoid PD from Cluster A (.39). Substantial correlations were also seen with schizotypal PD from Cluster A (.34) and borderline and histrionic PD from Cluster B (.33 and .36, respectively). Correlations with PDs from Cluster C (avoidant and dependent) were more modest, at .23 and .24, respectively. In this study, the analytic strategy involved first applying exploratory factor analyses (EFAs) to develop a model of the underlying structure and then test this structure by confirmatory factor analyses (CFAs) in a second sample. The combination of EFAs and CFAs identified four latent liability factors that accounted for most of the co-occurrence between the 10 PDs and 15 clinical disorders. These factors were labeled Internalizing-I, Externalizing-I, Internalizing-II, and Externalizing-II. OCPD was located in the Externalizing II spectrum together with paranoid and schizotypal PD from Cluster A, and narcissistic, histrionic, and borderline PD from Cluster B. Several earlier phenotypic studies also indicated that OCPD stands apart from the other *DSM* Cluster C PDs (e.g., Hyler & Lyons, 1988; Sanislow et al., 2002).

Behavior-genetic studies suggest the same. In a twin study of genetic and environmental risk factors for Cluster C PDs (Reichborn-Kjennerud et al., 2007), etiological factors common to this cluster accounted for the majority of influences on avoidant and dependent PDs but explained only 11% of the variance in OCPD, indicating that OCPD is mostly etiologically distinct from the two other Cluster C PDs. This study also did not provide support for the validity of the *DSM-IV* Cluster C construct in its present form. A multivariate twin study including all 10 *DSM-IV* PDs from the same sample also showed that OCPD is only weakly etiologically related to the three traditional PD clusters (Kendler et al., 2008). This is in line with results from multivariate hierarchical studies of dimensional PD traits. According to Livesley and Jang (2008), this level of analysis has yielded perhaps the most robust finding in PD research: that four factors underlie PD constructs (Livesley & Jang, 2008). One of these factors has been labeled Anankastic/Compulsivity and resembles the OCPD diagnosis. It appears to be distinct from other PD traits both genetically and phenotypically (Livesley & Jang, 2008). Taken together, these results indicate that OCPD might represent a separate secondary PD domain distinct from the A, B, and C clusters.

Results from clinical samples also indicate that OCPD does not belong in Cluster C. In a study of 400 inpatients, OCPD was found to be most strongly related to cluster A PDs (Rossi et al., 2000). At baseline in the CLPS study, the percentage of co-occurrence with OCPD was highest for avoidant PD (27.5%), followed by borderline and paranoid PD (McGlashan et al., 2000). However, in a longitudinal follow-up (year 6 to year 10) of the CLPS sample (Sanislow et al., 2009), OCPD was more strongly related to STPD in Cluster A (correlation coefficient: .32, .41) and borderline PD in Cluster B (.33, .37) than to avoidant PD from Cluster C (.18 and .28). Antisocial and OCPD had a significantly negative association (McGlashan et al., 2000).

Comorbidity with Clinical Disorders

Co-occurrence between OCPD and specific clinical disorders has been postulated, and significant comorbidity with anxiety, mood, and eating disorders has been reported (Dolan-Sewell, Krueger, & Shea, 2004). But, in general, the results have been inconsistent, probably owing to the methodological problems (i.e., sample bias) mentioned earlier. The relationship between OCPD and OCD has been most frequently studied, as has the association with major depressive disorder (MDD) and with phenotypic eating disorders, especially anorexia nervosa has received attention. The main challenge in this field seems to be the lack of studies with scientifically acceptable designs from which sound conclusions can be drawn.

Few studies on the comorbidity between *DSM-IV* OCPD and clinical disorders in population-based studies have been published. In the NESARC study, associations remained significant between OCPD and all mood and anxiety disorders (OCD was not assessed) after controlling for sociodemographic variables and other comorbidities. The association was strongest with social phobia (OR = 2.3) and bipolar II disorder (OR = 2.1). Eating disorders were not included in the study (J. E. Grant et al., 2012).

In the Norwegian AI/AII study, phenotypic polychoric correlations between OCPD and 15 clinical disorders were, with a few exceptions, modest (–.6–.31). Highest correlations were found with the anxiety disorders posttraumatic stress disorder (PTSD;.31), agoraphobia (.25), and general anxiety disorder (GAD;.20). The association with MDD was modest (.19) and with anorexia nervosa low (.09). OCD was not included in the analyses (Roysamb et al., 2011).

In a 2-year follow-up of the CLPS sample focusing on specific PD and clinical disorder relationships it was found that schizotypal PD and OCPD showed little or no association with clinical disorders over time. Contrary to prediction, OCPD did not show associated changes with anxiety disorders (including OCD), thus failing to support a cross-cutting anxiety/inhibited dimension or underlying OCPD. The authors concluded that the findings suggest OCPD may not be well characterized as a disorder of the anxious cluster (Shea et al., 2004).

The relationship between OCPD and OCD has received substantial interest for over a century. While most of the studies have been done in clinical samples a few community studies have been published. In the British National Survey of Psychiatric Morbidity, the prevalence of *DSM-IV*

OCPD was found to be 29% among participants with OCD and 20% in those with other neurotic conditions (Torres et al., 2006). In previous studies using *DSM-III-R*, by contrast, OCPD was not particularly prevalent in participants with OCD (e.g., Rodrigues Torres & Del Porto, 1995). In clinical samples of patients with OCD, prevalence rates of *DSM-IV* OCPD have ranged from 23% to 34% (Albert, Maina, Forner, & Bogetto, 2004; Coles, Pinto, Mancebo, Rasmussen, & Eisen, 2008; Lochner et al., 2011; Pinto, Mancebo, Eisen, Pagano, & Rasmussen, 2006; Samuels et al., 2000). This is significantly higher than rates found in community samples (~2%, see earlier discussion). Although a substantial proportion of individuals with OCD have OCPD, most do not, and other PDs may be even more prevalent (Samuels & Costa, 2012).

Whether OCD with OCPD is a distinctive subtype of OCD or OCPD is merely a marker of severity in OCD has been discussed (Coles et al., 2008; Lochner et al., 2011). In a longitudinal study of patients with OCD, Coles and coworkers found that individuals with both OCPD and OCD had distinct clinical characteristics in terms of age at onset of symptoms, types of obsessions and compulsions, and psychiatric comorbidity. From these findings, together with results from a family study of OCD (*DSM-III-R*) in which OCPD was found in 32% of the case probands compared to 6% in the control probands and in 12% of relatives of cases compared to 6% of relatives of controls (Samuels et al., 2000), the authors concluded that OCD associated with OCPD may represent a specific subtype of OCD (Coles et al., 2008). In a more recent study of a large sample of OCD subjects with and without OCPD, Lochner et al. (2011) suggested that in OCD, patients with OCPD do not have a highly distinctive phenotypic or genetic profile; instead, OCPD represents a marker of severity (Lochner et al., 2011). Additional research is warranted before firm conclusions can be drawn.

Although previous studies have reported high co-occurrence between OCPD and MDD in treatment-seeking samples, stronger associations have been found for avoidant, borderline, and paranoid PD (McGlashan et al., 2000; Melartin et al., 2002). In the population-based AI/AII study, all *DSM-IV* PDs were significantly associated with MDD in bivariate analyses. However, after adjusting for the other PDs (because of high degree of comorbidity), only borderline, paranoid,

and avoidant PDs were significantly independently associated with MDD (Reichborn-Kjennerud et al., 2010). In the NESARC study, OCPD was significantly associated with MDD, but to a lesser degree than avoidant dependent, paranoid, and schizoid PDs (borderline PD was not assessed) (Hasin, Goodwin, Stinson, & Grant, 2005). Results from neither population-based nor clinical studies suggest a particularly strong relationship between OCPD and MDD. However, OCPD has been found to increase relapse rates of MDD (Grilo et al., 2010) and to be associated with increased rates of suicide attempts in depressed patients (Diaconu & Turecki, 2009). In the prospective CLPS study, OCPD was significantly associated with new onset of GAD, OCD, and agoraphobia over a 7-year period, and with relapse of GAD and PTSD (Ansell et al., 2011).

The relationship between anorexia nervosa (AN) and OCPD has received much theoretical investigation but empirical studies are scarce. In a review of studies using diagnostic interviews to asses prevalence of PDs in eating disorders, five small clinical studies (*n* = 16–48) and one small prospective community study (*n* = 51) were identified (Cassin & von Ranson, 2005); the results were inconclusive. In a follow-up of the longitudinal community study it was concluded that premorbid OCPD predicted poor outcome of AN (Wentz, Gillberg, Anckarsater, Gillberg, & Rastam, 2009). In a clinical study of patients with AN and bulimia nervosa no difference in the prevalence of OCPD and OCD was found across eating disorder subtypes (Halmi, 2005). In a principal component study from CLPS, Grilo et al. (2004) found that three of the OCPD criteria, rigidity, perfectionism, and miserliness, accounted for 65% of the variance in binge eating disorder (Grilo et al., 2004). Perfectionism has also been shown to be closely associated with OCPD and has been hypothesized to be a relevant core behavioral feature underlying eating disorders (Halmi et al., 2005). In a review of the limited family study research the authors concluded that OCPD and AN might share familial liability (Lilenfeld, Wonderlich, Riso, Crosby, & Mitchell, 2006).

Given the lack of relevant empirical data, it is difficult to conclude definitively regarding the degree of comorbidity between clinical disorders and OCPD. However, OCPD seems to predict an unfavorable outcome in OCD, MDD, and AN. Family studies and multivariate twin studies are needed to investigate the degree to which OCPD shares etiological factors with these disorders.

Etiology

PDs are etiologically complex disorders. A number of genetic and environmental factors are involved, but these are neither causally necessary nor sufficient. These contributors are thus often called risk factors, which increase the risk of disease without conferring a certain outcome. In epidemiology, associations between risk factors and the disease are estimated. Genetic epidemiology is an extension of this method where genetic factors are also included. Family studies are used to investigate whether a disorder aggregate in families. Higher prevalence rates among relatives of individuals with a disorder than those for relatives of normal controls indicate that genetic or environmental factors related to the family may be involved. To separate and quantify the relative contribution of genetic and environmental factors, twin or adoption studies are used. This approach is termed quantitative genetics and includes extended twin and family designs. Heritability is an estimate of how much of the *variability* of the disease (or trait) can be attributed to genetic variation. In order to identify specific genes or genetic variants involved, molecular genetic studies must be used.

Quantitative Genetics

Twin studies are the most commonly used quantitative genetic method. They can be understood as a natural experiment based on the fact that monozygotic (MZ) twins share 100% of their genes and dizygotic (DZ) twins share 50% of their genes (the same as other siblings). Both MZ and DZ twins share environmental factors that contribute to their similarity, and they are also influenced by environmental factors that are not shared and thus make them different. If the similarity (or correlation) for a disorder or trait is higher in MZ twins than in DZ twins, then some involvement of genetic factors is indicated. A correlation of less than 1.0 in MZ twins implies environmental factors unique to the individual twins (nonshared).

Advanced statistical twin analyses are used to estimate the proportion of the phenotypic variance that can be attributed to genetic, common environmental, and unique environmental factors,

respectively. The heritability estimate represents the proportion of genetic variance to the total variance. Measurement error will lead to differences in twins and will thus inflate estimates of nonshared environment and deflate estimates of genetic and shared environmental influences.

No family study of OCPD has been published. However, studies of OCD and the prevalence of OCPD in OCD relatives have indicated a familial aggregation of OCPD (e.g., Samuels et al., 2000). Two twin studies included OCPD and reported heritability estimates and the relative influence of genetic and environmental factors for OCPD. Taylor, Asmundson, and Jang (2011) found that 45% of phenotypic variance in scores on obsessive-compulsive personality traits was due to genetic factors and the remainder to nonshared environment. In the population-based Norwegian AI/AII twin study, the best-fitting model for OCPD included genetic and unique environmental factors only, and no difference in genetic and environmental influence between female and male subjects was found. Genetic effects accounted for 27% of the variance in OCPD (Reichborn-Kjennerud et al., 2007).

Compared to the heritability of other PDs, ranging from 21% to 38% (Kendler et al., 2006; Reichborn-Kjennerud et al., 2007; Torgersen et al., 2008), OCPD is moderately heritable. These heritability estimates are based on PDs assessed at interview. Subsequent studies that used both personal interviews and self-reported questionnaires to eliminate measurement error indicated that heritability might be substantially higher, with estimates ranging from 55% to 72% (Gjerde et al., 2012; Kendler, Myers, Torgersen, Neale, & Reichborn-Kjennerud, 2007; Torgersen et al., 2012). Unfortunately, the personality dysfunction items from the questionnaire captured OCPD too poorly to be used in these analyses (Gjerde et al., 2012), but the results from the other PDs indicate that the heritability of OCPD would be higher if measurement error were eliminated.

Twin studies can also be used to estimate the degree to which multiple disorders share etiological risk factors. In the population-based multivariate twin study mentioned earlier (Kendler et al., 2011), which included the 10 *DSM-IV* PDs and 12 clinical disorders, four correlated genetic factors were identified. OCPD had substantial loading on the factor Externalizing Axis II. The other PDs that were mainly influenced by this genetic factor were paranoid, histrionic, narcissistic, and borderline. The genetic influence on the other two Cluster C disorders, avoidant and dependent PD, came mainly from another factor, Internalizing Axis II.

Molecular Genetics

In recent years, molecular genetic studies have made much progress in their scope of study, moving from a candidate gene approach to genome-wide association studies (GWAS), in which a large number (millions) of common single-nucleotide polymorphisms (SNPs) are studied in a large number of individuals. Paralleling this, structural genomic variants, for example, copy number variation (CNV), have also been studied. Technological advances in DNA sequencing have led to a shift in the approaches to whole-genome or whole-exome sequencing, mainly to detect rare variants. These sequencing efforts require a large amount of computing power and storage capacity and are still in an early phase in their development.

Several genetic associations have been reported for psychiatric disorders, but generally for all such studies, replications of initially significant findings have proven difficult. Even for the few robust replicated findings, the effects are very small and explain only a fraction of the phenotypic and genetic variation in the disorders. Genetic association studies have thus failed to explain the heritability estimates, and missing heritability is often referred to. This failure might be explained by rare variants that have not yet been detected but that be uncovered by future sequencing efforts, by epigenetic variation interacting with environmental factors, and by gene–environment interactions.

In psychiatric genetics, the candidate gene approach has typically been to study genes directly associated with neurotransmitters. Several studies have focused on genes that code for synthesis or degradation of dopamine, serotonin, and other amines, while others have focused on genes associated with the regulation of activity of the neurotransmitters.

Although quantitative genetic studies of PDs have indicated substantial levels of heritability for psychiatric disorders in general and at least moderate heritability of PDs, very little molecular genetic research has been conducted on these disorders. Most of the molecular genetic analysis in this field has focused on more severe disorders with a clear-cut diagnostic threshold, such as schizophrenia, or on common disorders for which it is easier to collect larger samples, such as major depression. The genetics of *normal* personality have received far more attention than PDs, thus we will briefly mention the main results from these studies here.

Of the handful of molecular studies including measures of OCPD, two have investigated genetic variants in dopamine-related genes. In a study of 195 depressed patients, genetic variation in the dopamine D4 and D3 receptors (*DRD4* and *DRD3*) was explored in relation to symptoms and criterion counts for *DSM-III-R*-defined PDs (Joyce et al., 2003). The authors reported a significant association between variants in both *DRD4* and *DRD3* with OCPD traits. The association of *DRD3* with OCPD was later supported in a replication and meta-analytical study including two additional samples of depressed individuals, indicating that regulation of dopamine may have a role in the etiology of OCPD (Light et al., 2006). Given the nature of the samples studied, however, this could be specific for the group of individuals who had comorbid OCPD and depression and not for OCPD in general.

The most extensively investigated genetic variant in psychiatric genetics is the serotonin transporter linked polymorphic region (*5-HTTLPR*) in the gene that codes for the serotonin transporter. The 5-HTTLPR mainly exists in two variants: a short and a long allele. The short version generally seems to result in lower activity of the serotonin transporter. In a study of a patients with PDs (*DSM-IV*) compared with healthy controls, no difference in 5-HTTLPR genotype distribution was found between Cluster C PDs (OCPD grouped together with avoidant and dependent PD) and the controls (Jacob et al., 2004). The authors did find, however, that among patients with a Cluster C diagnosis, carriers of the 5-HTTLPR short allele had significantly higher scores for neuroticism and harm avoidance. This finding indicates that serotonin may be involved in some aspects of shaping the phenotypic variability of the Cluster C personality traits.

The gene linked to the monoamine oxidase A (MAOA) enzyme, involved in the degradation of amines like serotonin and dopamine, contains a functional polymorphic region, with a low-activity and a high-activity allelic variant. Several animal and human studies have suggested that *MAOA* is related to aggressive, impulsive, and addictive behavior. Inhibition of the MAOA enzyme is used as a treatment of clinical depression and anxiety. *MAOA* was studied in patients with PDs (*DSM-IV*), and a significant association was found between the low-activity variant for the Cluster B patients but not for the Cluster C patients (Jacob et al., 2005).

Studies of genetics of normal dimensional personality traits and domains greatly outnumber those of PDs, and several meta-analyses and reviews have been published. The main positive findings involve neurotransmitter-related genes, mainly through the candidate gene approach. Dopamine-related genes appear to be related to extraversion, serotonin-related genes to neuroticism, and *MAOA* to antisocial behavior (Ebstein, 2006). Several GWAS have also been done regarding personality; however, a meta-analysis concluded that while 15 samples comprising a total of 20,669 individuals had been studied, larger scale GWAS are required to confirm the association of the suggested novel genes (de Moor et al., 2012). Genome-wide significance ($p < 10^{-8}$) was found for SNPs near the *RASA1* gene for openness, and for an SNP in the *KATNAL2* gene for conscientiousness. Top SNPs for neuroticism, extraversion, and agreeableness did not reach genome-wide significance. The *RASA1* gene is involved in intracellular signaling and is highly expressed in the bone marrow and bone but only modestly in the brain. The *KATNAL2* gene is widely expressed in the central nervous system and may play a role in neurodevelopment (de Moor et al., 2012).

In summary, the existing genetic studies of PDs indicate that genes related to neurotransmitters such as serotonin and dopamine may be involved in the etiology of OCPD. However, the shortage of molecular genetic studies in this field is striking; no GWAS has been conducted for PDs. The complexity of these disorders, exemplified by the extensive comorbidity within the PDs and across clinical disorders, is challenging in terms of finding specific genetic effects. In addition, the interplay between genetic and environmental factors is likely to be of great importance for the development of PDs.

Environmental Risk Factors

While quantitative genetic approaches focus on the relative influence of genetic risk factors (the heritability estimates), another view of this approach is that it controls for the underlying genetics and estimates unconfounded environmental effects. For PDs, even though the estimated environmental proportion of explained variance includes measurement error, it is still evident that individual-specific environmental factors play an important role in the etiology.

Studies of specific environmental risk factors for PDs have mainly focused on childhood adversity, maltreatment, and traumatic events. In the community-based longitudinal Children in the Community Study study of youths, childhood physical abuse, sexual abuse, and neglect were all associated with elevated *DSM-IV* total PD symptoms (Johnson, Cohen, Brown, Smailes, & Bernstein, 1999). Different types of maltreatment during childhood were associated with specific PD symptoms during early adulthood. Cluster C PDs were significantly associated with childhood maltreatment, but this was mainly due to dependent PD. For OCPD symptoms, only a slight, nonsignificant increase in PD criteria was found among victims of physical abuse or neglect. When controlling for co-occurring PDs, only Cluster B PDs were independently associated with childhood abuse or neglect (Johnson et al., 1999).

In a study on treatment-seeking patients in the CLPS, presence of trauma or PTSD in association with borderline, schizotypal, or avoidant PD, OCPD, or MDD was investigated; no healthy control group was included in the study (Yen et al., 2002). The results showed that OCPD and avoidant PD had the lowest prevalence of trauma history, and among the patients with OCPD that reported a traumatic event, fewer had a PTSD diagnosis than did patients with other PDs. A later study from the same sample, but including a broader assessment of childhood experiences, showed similar results, with borderline PD overall being most strongly associated with childhood maltreatment. Females with OCPD had a higher rate of noncaretaker sexual abuse than females with other PDs (Battle et al., 2004). However, 40% of these females with OCPD also had a co-occurrence of borderline PD.

A small community-based study compared *DSM-IV* PD symptoms in 28 individuals with a reported history of abuse with 33 individuals with no history of abuse (Grover et al., 2007). Abused subjects had significantly more symptoms of personality disorders in all three clusters, as well as a higher symptom score of OCPD than that of the nonabused subjects. A slightly larger study of 105 individuals, 70 with a history of childhood mal-treatment and 35 without, showed that OCPD symptoms were significantly associated with emotional abuse or neglect and physical or sexual abuse (Tyrka, Wyche, Kelly, Price, & Carpenter, 2009).

In summary, the results of these studies indicate that there might be an association between history of childhood maltreatment and OCPD, but that this association is weaker than for that Cluster B PDs, especially borderline PD. It is also important to note that these studies only investigated the co-occurrence of childhood maltreatment and PD symptoms. They were not designed to clarify causal processes, thus it is still unknown if maltreatment causes PDs.

Temporal Stability in OCPD

Stability over time is a key feature in diagnostic definitions of PDs and is one of the main characteristics that has distinguished PDs from other mental disorders. Recent results from both clinical and community-based prospective longitudinal studies, however, challenge this conception.

The Children in the Community Study (CIC), which began in 1975, included 816 children aged 1–10 years at baseline. PD traits and clinical disorders were assessed at ages 14, 16, and 22 and DSM-IV assessment was done at age 33 (Cohen, Crawford, Johnson, & Kasen, 2005). Mean PD symptoms for all PDs except OCPD were consistently highest in early adolescence and decreased subsequently (Cohen et al., 2005; Crawford et al., 2005). For OCPD no decline in mean symptoms was found, and the stability levels were lower than those for other PDs. The authors suggest that this might be explained by a low prevalence of categorical OCPD in the sample (Johnson et al., 2000). Later, they reported that the point prevalence of categorical OCPD in fact increased from 0.7% at mean age 22 to 2.3% at mean age 33 (Johnson et al., 2008).

The Longitudinal Study of Personality Disorders (LSPD) began in 1990. After screening for DSM-III-R PD features, a total of 258 students were assigned to either a "no PD group" or a "possible PD group" and were included in the longitudinal study. They were subsequently reassessed for DSM-III-R PDs in their first, second and fourth years in college (Lenzenweger, 2006).

Results indicate that PD features have considerable variability across individuals over time, thus do not support the view that PDs are enduring and stable (Lenzenweger, Johnson, & Willett, 2004). Stability coefficients for OCPD were in the lower range compared with those for other PDs (Lenzenweger, 1999).

The Hopkins Epidemiology Study of Personality Disorders was designed to study the stability of PD criteria. Participants were 294 adults, mean age 47 years, who were recruited from 1993 on, from the general population in Baltimore, MD. DSM-III and DSM-IV criteria for PDs were assessed on two occasions approximately 12 to 18 years apart. Antisocial, borderline, histrionic, schizotypal, and avoidant PDs showed moderate stability with estimated intracorrelation coefficients (ICC) of .4 to .8. OCPD were less stable, with an estimated ICC of .2–.3. The remaining PD traits were excluded from the analyses because of low and inconsistent endorsement at the two time points. The authors also investigated the stability of the different traits within each PD. For OCPD, the prevalence of stubbornness decreased, while the prevalence of excessive work devotion increased. The traits emotional constriction and perfectionism were particularly stable (Nestadt et al., 2010).

The CLPS study began in 1996 and was designed to provide comprehensive data on subjects meeting criteria for DSM-IV categorical diagnoses of OCPD; schizotypal, borderline, or avoidant PDs; or major depression (Gunderson et al., 2000). The study included 668 treatment-seeking individuals aged 18 to 45 years. Several waves of follow-up data have been collected, after 6 months, 1, 2, 4, 6, and 10 years (Sanislow et al., 2009). Short-term follow-up of diagnostic stability over 12 months showed an overall decline in the number of endorsed DSM-IV criteria (Shea et al., 2002). Of the subjects initially diagnosed with OCPD, 42% remained at diagnostic threshold after 12 months. The mean number of endorsed criteria for OCPD for those with a full OCPD at baseline declined from 5.2 to 3.4 at 12 months.

Follow-up after 2 years showed a continuing significant decrease in the mean proportion of criteria met in each of the PD groups, suggesting consistent decreases in severity over time (Grilo et al., 2004). However, a high level of consistency was found when the relative stability of individual differences (rank order) was examined. The correlation between OCPD at baseline and after

2 years was .53 (Grilo et al., 2004). Of the subjects diagnosed with OCPD at baseline, 40% retained their diagnosis 2 years after. The mean number of endorsed criteria was 2.9 at 2 years of follow-up (Grilo et al., 2004). Investigating the criterion prevalence at 2 years follow-up, McGlashan et al. (2005) found that the eight OCPD criteria were variably represented at baseline, with a frequency of 31% to 83%. The rank order of prevalence over time nevertheless appeared to be stable. Rigidity, problems delegating, and perfectionism were the most prevalent and stable criteria. Miserliness was the least represented and most variable criterion.

The stability of the PDs was examined again at 10 years, this time by modeling latent factors and using a growth curve approach (Sanislow et al., 2009). The authors once again confirmed that OCPD had a pronounced drop in mean level of criteria in the first 2 years after baseline, but also that this was followed by a continuing steady decline. The latent construct changed during the first year, but an increased stability was observed in the later years. They argue that there is a reduction in pathology over time but support the theory of an enduring core aspect of personality pathology. One of the more recent papers from the CLPS study compared the stability of PD criteria count with the stability of personality traits and temperament (Hopwood et al., 2013). The PD 10-year stability ranged from .15 (Histrionic) to .60 (Antisocial). OCPD had a stability of .31. In comparison, the personality traits and temperament scales had stabilities of .43 to .73, with OCPD related traits like workaholism showing a stability of .53 and conscientiousness .63.

In summary, categorical measures of PDs have been shown to decline considerably over time (Grilo et al., 2004; Johnson et al., 2000; Lenzenweger, 2006; Zanarini, Frankenburg, Hennen, Reich, & Silk, 2006). Studies using dimensional measures have demonstrated modest decline in criteria fulfilled, but also a relatively high correlation between the proportion of PD criteria met (Grilo et al., 2004; Lenzenweger, 1999). Finally, latent variables underlying the PDs seem to reflect enduring properties with considerable ordinal stability (Sanislow et al., 2009; Warner et al., 2004). These results indicate that individuals may fluctuate above and below diagnostic thresholds but that interindividual differences in PD features are quite stable. The overall picture that emerges is that PD traits change, but the underlying factors that give

rise to manifest PD symptomatology are generally consistent (Krueger, 2005). OCPD seems to be one of the least stable PD, but individual traits like perfectionism appear to have a higher stability.

Functional Impairment

One of the main features of all personality disorders that distinguishes them from normal personality is the associated disability or dysfunction. Functional impairment is described by *DSM-IV-TR/DSM-5* Section II as "clinically significant distress or impairment in social, occupational, or other important areas of life," but it is not operationalized in the manual. From the literature on PDs and measured impairment, several scales have been made for capturing interviewer- or self-rated impairment of some sort, but they are often custom-made for each study. One exception is the Global Assessment of Functioning (GAF) scale, which reflects the evaluating clinician's judgment of a patient's ability to function in daily life. The 100-point scale measures psychological, social, and occupational functioning. GAF scores under 40 indicate severe impairment and danger of hurting self or other; scores of 41–50 indicate serious impairment; 51–60 indicates moderate impairment; 61–70, mild impairment; and above 70, good overall functioning. In addition to these scales, demographic measures such as income, education, employment status, and marital status are often used to evaluate functional impairment. Finally, examining the level of treatment seeking can give an objective measure of the impairments and the societal costs of a disorder.

Even though functional impairment is an essential part of the definition of the PDs, some variation in degree of severity exists. An assessment of self-rated levels of personality pathology in a clinical sample from the Netherlands indicated that patients with borderline and paranoid PD are more severely impaired, while individuals with OCPD are less severely affected (Morey et al., 2011). In the CLPS study, a comparison of four PDs and MDD showed that OCPD is associated with less functional impairment than is borderline and schizotypal PD (Skodol et al., 2002). The study included both self-reported and interviewer-rated measures, and the results were consistent regardless of mode of assessment.

A study from the NESARC sample showed that OCPD was inconsistently associated with disability scores. Only a mental component summary score was higher in OCPD patients; a social function score and a role emotional function score were not significantly elevated (B. F. Grant et al., 2004). This pattern was in contrast to that for other PDs (except histrionic PD). In a male community sample (*n* = 304), dimensionally measured OCPD was found to be positively associated with one indicator of life success, "status and wealth" (including social class, income, number of rooms in home, supervision of others at work, and home ownership), whereas no association with "successful intimate relationships" was found, thus for certain aspects of life OCPD may have a positive effect (Ullrich et al., 2007).

In a study from the CIC sample, mean GAF scores were lower in participants with a PD diagnosis (range 32–60) than in participants with no PD diagnosis (76) (Crawford et al., 2005). Participants with OCPD were in the upper range (GAF 60). The rank order was consistent with the findings from the CLPS study, but the mean values were slightly lower. Patients in the CLPS study with OCPD had a higher mean GAF score (64.7) than that of patients with other PDs or MDD (60.7). They were also more often employed and had more years of education than patients with borderline and schizotypal PD (Skodol et al., 2002). However, when the stability of functional impairment was investigated in the same population over 2 years, patients with OCPD showed no improvement in functioning overall (Skodol et al., 2002).

Socioeconomic status is one of the demographic correlates that is relevant for assessing functional impairment, but associations between OCPD and socioeconomic measures vary considerably across studies. OCPD has been associated with higher education in the NESARC study (B. F. Grant et al., 2004), whereas results from the British National Survey of Psychiatric Morbidity indicate no association (Coid et al., 2006). A more recent study from the NESARC reported an association between OCPD and lower education (J. E. Grant et al., 2012). Conceptually, individuals with OCPD have characteristics that should be positively associated with higher education (e.g., conscientiousness, preoccupied with details, rules, organization, or schedules; devoted to work and productivity). However, if these characteristics result in not being able to finish homework assignments, the opposite would be the result.

Most studies of PDs have included some measure related to work participation, such as income, economic active status, or employment status. Results from the British National Survey of Psychiatric Morbidity showed no individual association between Cluster C disorders and demographic characteristics apart from employment status, whereas Cluster C PDs were associated with economic inactivity (Coid et al., 2006). In a more recent study from the same sample, OCPD was found to be significantly associated with receiving disability benefits (Knudsen et al., 2012). Studies from the NESARC have reported no association between income and OCPD (B. F. Grant et al., 2004). However, there may be a sex difference in this regard, as females in the low-income group had a higher risk of OCPD, and males in the two middle-income strata had the highest risk of OCPD (J. E. Grant et al., 2012).

Analyses of the British National Survey of Psychiatric Morbidity sample showed that individuals with Cluster C PDs were more likely to have received psychotropic medication and counseling (Coid et al., 2006). OCPD seems to have a particularly high impact on social costs as patients with OCPD in the CLPS study were nearly three times as likely as depressed patients to have received individual psychotherapy, adjusting for age, gender, and race (Bender et al., 2001). In a treatment-seeking sample in the Netherlands, the economic burden of PDs was found to be considerably higher than that for depression and anxiety disorders and comparable to that for schizophrenia (Soeteman et al., 2008). Only borderline PD and OCPD were uniquely associated with increased mean total costs (Soeteman et al., 2008).

In summary, OCPD is associated with less functional impairment than are the other PDs, particularly in community-based studies but also to some degree in clinical samples. However, OCPD has been found to be associated with high treatment costs and is one of two PDs uniquely associated with increased economic burden to society.

Relation to Normal Personality

For many years the construct of normal personality was hotly debated. Since the early 1990s, the predominating model has been the five-factor model (FFM) (McCrae & John, 1992). This model includes five main factors: Extraversion, Agreeableness, Conscientiousness, Neuroticism, and Openness, with several underlying facets or definers. The link between the dimensional FFM normal personality constructs and PDs as an extreme form of these has been extensively investigated. Also, other models of normal personality have been proposed, containing three (Tellegen, 1985), six (Mullins-Sweatt & Widiger, 2007), or seven (Cloninger, 1994) factors, but the relationship between these and PDs have been investigated to a lesser degree and will not be discussed here. Several other models of pathological personality exist (Widiger & Simonsen, 2005); descriptions of these lie outside the scope of this chapter.

DSM-IV-defined OCPD, with its core elements of orderliness, perfectionism, and mental and interpersonal control, has been construed as the upper extreme of the Conscientiousness dimension (Samuels & Costa, 2012). Conscientiousness is defined by adjectives like efficient, organized, planful, reliable, responsible, and thorough (McCrae & John, 1992). Individuals with a high Conscientiousness score tend to be hard-working, self-disciplined, business-like, and punctual (Costa, 1992). Numerous studies of normal personality versus PDs have been performed, with a large variability in use of instruments for measuring normal personality, instruments and mode of assessment of PDs, and type of sample under study (clinical versus community-based). For OCPD, the findings have been less consistent than for other PDs. It has been suggested that the current assessment tools for conscientiousness traits are not capable of capturing sufficient psychopathology, thus there is low correlation between measured conscientiousness and OCPD. Haigler and Widiger demonstrated that by experimentally manipulating the FFM Conscientiousness items by adding terms like *excessively, too much*, and *preoccupied*, the correlation with three different OCPD scales increased dramatically (Haigler & Widiger, 2001).

In a more recent meta-analytic review of the relationship between the FFM and *DSM-IV* PDs, Samuel and Widiger (2008) reported that the six facets of the Conscientiousness factor were those that correlated strongest with OCPD, but the correlations were all of quite modest size, around .25. Several other facets of the other personality factors were statistically significantly associated, but with low correlations coefficients (.04–.16)

(Samuel & Widiger, 2008). Samuel and Widiger compared different instruments for assessing both the FFM and PDs and concluded that the variability in correlation between Conscientiousness and OCPD was probably largely due to the differences in the assessment of OCPD. In a study of 536 individuals that used multiple measures of self-reported conscientiousness-related personality traits, *DSM-IV* OCPD, and specific components of OCPD, similar variability of the relationship between the Conscientiousness traits measures and *DSM-IV* OCPD measures was found (Samuel & Widiger, 2011). The results from the study overall supported the view of OCPD as a maladaptive variant of conscientiousness.

Another community-based study of 898 adults, using both self-report and informant-report of FFM normal personality to predict interviewer-based *DSM-IV* PDs, showed that borderline, histrionic, narcissistic, and avoidant PD demonstrated good convergent validity, whereas OCPD was poorly predicted by the FFM prototype (Lawton, Shields, & Oltmanns, 2011). This study computed FFM prototypic scores based on Lynam and Widiger's (2001) FFM ratings for *DSM-IV* PDs. For OCPD this included six Conscientiousness items, four Openness items, two Neuroticism items, and one Extraversion item.

A new five-factor measure of obsessive-compulsive personality traits, designed to capture the maladaptive variants of FFM facets, has been proposed (Samuel, Riddell, Lynam, Miller, & Widiger, 2012). This measure, based on six Conscientiousness items, three Openness items, two Extraversion items, and one Neuroticism item, showed good convergent, discriminant, and incremental validity; interviewer-assessed OCPD was not a part of the study.

DSM-5

In addition to the categorical model and criteria for the 10 PDs included in the *DSM-IV-TR* and maintained in Section II of *DSM-5*, a new research model proposed by the *DSM-5* Personality and Personality Disorders Work Group is included in *DSM-5* Section III, which provides strategies to enhance clinical practice and new criteria to stimulate future research. In this alternative model, PDs are characterized by impairments in personality *functioning* (self and interpersonal) and by pathological personality *traits*, which include five broad domains: Negative Affectivity, Detachment, Antagonism, Disinhibition, and Psychoticism, and comprise 25 specific personality trait facets. The introduction of personality traits allows for a dimensional classification—that is, individuals can be located on a spectrum of trait dimensions, or different degrees of a trait, rather than whether it is absent or present. In clinical practice, the evaluation of these traits is facilitated by the use of formal psychometric instruments designed to measure domains and specific facets—for example, the Personality Inventory for *DSM-5* (PID-5; Krueger, Derringer, Markon, Watson & Skodol, 2012), which can be completed in self-report form. It can also be completed by informants (Markon, Quilty, Bagby, & Krueger, 2013) and clinicians (Morey, Krueger, & Skodol, 2013). The personality trait system also enables the exploration of a hierarchical structure of personality (Wright, Thomas, Hopwood, Markon, Krueger, 2012).

Six specific PD diagnoses including OCPD may be derived from this model. Characteristic impairment in functioning for OCPD (Criterion A) is apparent in *Identity* (e.g., sense of self derived predominantly from work or productivity), *Self-direction* (e.g., difficulties completing tasks and realizing goals, associated with rigid and unreasonably high standards of behavior), *Empathy* (e.g., difficulty understanding and appreciating the ideas, feelings, or behaviors of others), and *Intimacy* (e.g., relationships are seen as secondary to work and productivity). The maladaptive trait facet *Rigid Perfectionism* (e.g., rigid insistence in everything being flawless, perfect, and without errors or faults, including one's own and others' performance) in the Disinhibition domain must be present, in addition to two or three maladaptive trait facets in the domains of Negative Affectivity and/or Detachment: *Perseveration* (e.g., persistence at tasks long after the behavior has ceased to be functional or effective), *Intimacy Avoidance* (e.g., avoidance of close or romantic relationships, interpersonal attachments, and intimate sexual relationships), or *Restricted Affectivity* (e.g., little reaction to emotionally arousing situations) (Criterion B).

Few studies have investigated the relationship between *DSM-IV/DSM-5* Section II PDs and *DSM-5* personality traits (*DSM-5* Section III). In one study using a sample of university undergraduate students (*n* = 808), *DSM-5* traits, assessed with

PID-5, explained a substantial proportion of the variance in *DSM-IV* PDs, and traits were mostly specific to the individual PDs as measured by self-report measures of *DSM-IV/DSM-5* Section II. OCPD traits were most strongly related to the domain Negative Affectivity (correlation [*r*] = .43) and somewhat less to Detachment (*r* = .31). Of the lower order traits or facets, OCPD correlated highest (*r* = .54) with Rigid Perfectionism, a facet in the Disinhibition domain, and Perseveration (*r* = .46), a facet in the Negative Affectivity domain (Hopwood et al., 2013). Results from another study, also performed on undergraduates, suggest that the *DSM-5* Section III trait model can reproduce the *DSM-IV-TR* PD constructs (Samuel, Hopwood, Krueger, Thomas, & Ruggero, 2013). It has been shown that diagnostic rules can be derived that yield appreciable correspondence between *DSM-IV-TR* and Section III *DSM-5* diagnoses (Morey & Skodol, 2013). Further evaluation of the relationship between the *DSM-IV/DSM-5* Section II PDs and *DSM-5* Section III personality constructs is needed.

It may be of interest to note that OCD is no longer grouped with the anxiety disorders. Given the similarity across a range of validators, including symptoms, neurobiological substrates, familiarity, course of illness, and treatment response, OCD is now in a separate chapter on obsessive-compulsive and related disorders. These include body dysmorphic disorder, trichotillomania, hoarding disorder, and excoriation (skin-picking) disorder. In *DSM-5* Section II, hoarding disorder is listed as a differential diagnosis, which should be considered when hoarding is extreme (Criterion 5). When criteria for both diagnoses are met, both should be recorded. The relationship between OCPD and disorders in this group is unclear. Although data from the Johns Hopkins family study of OCD indicate that OCPD and OCD appear to coaggregate in families, this finding could to be related to an underlying vulnerability shared with neuroticism (Samuels et al., 2000). In latent class analyses of data from the same study identifying a four-class structure, OCPD was most strongly related to the class that included panic disorder, agoraphobia, and separation anxiety disorder and less strongly to the class including body dysmorphic disorder and pathological skin-picking (Nestadt et al., 2003). Additional studies, including behavioral genetic investigations, are needed to determine the extent to which OCPD share underlying genetic and neurobiological factors with the OCD and related disorders as defined by *DSM-5*.

A very different approach to the classification of personality disorders has been suggested by the *ICD-11* Working Group. They advise abolishing all individual diagnoses of PD. The main reason for this is the extensive overlap between the categories. Instead, this group proposes a system that includes a primary classification into four levels of personality pathology based on severity alone, thus allowing the dimensional element to be incorporated into the diagnosis. The second order of classification defines five domains, including Obsessional/Anankastic (Tyrer et al., 2011). Although there are similarities between the two systems, harmonizing them will probably not be easy if the removal of the individual disorder categories is approved for *ICD-11*.

Summary and Future Research

The concept of OCPD appears to be a valid construct with good internal consistency in population-based samples and can be used to discriminate a symptom pattern relatively distinct from other personality disorders. With a few exceptions it has retained its core features over more than a century, and the same criteria as those used in *DSM-IV* are now included in *DSM-5*, Section II. Despite this, there is a lack of empirical studies, and many aspects of OCPD still remain to be clarified. The *DSM-IV*-defined OCPD is the most common PD in the community. Contrary to other PDs, OCPD appears to be more common in older age groups. It has relatively low levels of comorbidity with other PDs and, based on results from both epidemiological and genetic epidemiological studies, appears to be more strongly related to PDs in the odd/eccentric and dramatic/emotional cluster than to those in the anxious/fearful cluster, where it is currently placed.

Although the data are limited and to some extent inconsistent, there do not appear to be clear indications of a specific relationship between OCPD and individual clinical disorders like OCD, MDD, and eating disorders. While there are very few genetic studies of *DSM-IV* OCPD, it appears to be significantly influenced by genetic factors with a modest heritability. So far, molecular genetic studies have not identified specific genetic variants associated with OCPD. The relationship between OCPD and environmental risk factors also remains to be clarified, but there are indications of an association with childhood maltreatment. Like other PDs, OCPD symptoms decrease over time, but individual traits appear to be more stable. Although individuals with OCPD show relatively low levels of impairment in the community, OCPD is associated with high costs to society, and it has a significantly negative impact on the course and treatment response of MDD and anxiety disorders. OCPD is moderately to strongly related to the normal personality trait conscientiousness, but also to neuroticism and extraversion.

More research is needed on all aspects of OCPD. Large prospective, population-based studies are necessary to clarify its course and outcome. Life-course genetic epidemiological studies in population-based samples (including twin studies, extended-family studies, and molecular genetic studies) are needed to address questions related to etiology. Such studies will also be useful for clarifying the role of common risk factors in comorbidity and classification of OCPD, especially in relation to the new obsessive-compulsive and related disorders group in the *DSM-5*. Information from studies of neurobiological substrates and treatment response will add additional relevant information.

References

Albert, U., Maina, G., Forner, F., & Bogetto, F. (2004). DSM-IV obsessive-compulsive personality disorder: Prevalence in patients with anxiety disorders and in healthy comparison subjects. *Comprehensive Psychiatry, 45*(5), 325–332.

Ansell, E. B., Pinto, A., Edelen, M. O., Markowitz, J. C., Sanislow, C. A., Yen, S.,…Grilo, C. M. (2011). The association of personality disorders with the prospective 7-year course of anxiety disorders. *Psychological Medicine, 41*(5), 1019–1028.

Battle, C. L., Shea, M. T., Johnson, D. M., Yen, S., Zlotnick, C., Zanarini, M. C.,…Morey, L. C. (2004). Childhood maltreatment associated with adult personality disorders: Findings from the Collaborative Longitudinal Personality Disorders Study. *Journal of Personality Disorders, 18*(2), 193–211.

Bender, D. S., Dolan, R. T., Skodol, A. E., Sanislow, C. A., Dyck, I. R., McGlashan, T. H.,…Gunderson, J. G. (2001). Treatment utilization by patients with personality disorders. *American Journal of Psychiatry, 158*(2), 295–302.

Berkson, J. (1946). Limitations of the application of fourfold table analysis to hospital data. *Biometrics*, 2(3), 47–53.

Cassin, S. E., & von Ranson, K. M. (2005). Personality and eating disorders: A decade in review. *Clinical Psychology Review*, 25(7), 895–916.

Cloninger, C. R. (1994). Temperament and personality. *Current Opinion in Neurobiology*, 4(2), 266–273.

Cohen, P., Crawford, T. N., Johnson, J. G., & Kasen, S. (2005). The Children in the Community Study of developmental course of personality disorder. *Journal of Personality Disorders*, 19(5), 466–486.

Coid, J., Yang, M., Tyrer, P., Roberts, A., & Ullrich, S. (2006). Prevalence and correlates of personality disorder in Great Britain. *British Journal of Psychiatry*, 188, 423–431.

Coles, M. E., Pinto, A., Mancebo, M. C., Rasmussen, S. A., & Eisen, J. L. (2008). OCD with comorbid OCPD: A subtype of OCD? *Journal of Psychiatric Research*, 42(4), 289–296.

Costa, P. T. M., R.R. (1992). *Revised NEO Personality Inventory (NEO-PI-R) and NEO Five-Factor Inventory (NEO-FFI) professional manual*. Odessa, FL: Psychological Assessment Resources.

Crawford, T. N., Cohen, P., Johnson, J. G., Kasen, S., First, M. B., Gordon, K., & Brook, J. S. (2005). Self-reported personality disorder in the children in the community sample: Convergent and prospective validity in late adolescence and adulthood. *Journal of Personality Disorders*, 19(1), 30–52.

de Moor, M. H., Costa, P. T., Terracciano, A., Krueger, R. F., de Geus, E. J., Toshiko, T.,…Boomsma, D. I. (2012). Meta-analysis of genome-wide association studies for personality. *Molecular Psychiatry*, 17(3), 337–349.

Diaconu, G., & Turecki, G. (2009). Obsessive-compulsive personality disorder and suicidal behavior: Evidence for a positive association in a sample of depressed patients. *Journal of Clinical Psychiatry*, 70(11), 1551–1556.

Dolan-Sewell, R. Krueger, R. F., & Shea, T. (2004). Co-occurence with syndrome disorders. In W. J. Livesley (Ed.), *Handbook of personality disorders* (pp. 84–104). New York: Guilford Press.

Ebstein, R. P. (2006). The molecular genetic architecture of human personality: Beyond self-report questionnaires. *Molecular Psychiatry*, 11(5), 427–445.

Ekselius, L., Tillfors, M., Furmark, T., & Fredrikson, M. (2001). Personality disorders in the general population: DSM-IV and ICD-10 defined prevalence as related to sociodemographic profile. *Personality and Individual Differences*, 30(2), 311–320.

Freud, S. (1908). Über infantile Sexualtheorien. In *Sexual-Probleme* (Vol. IV, pp. 763–779; G.W., Vol. VII, pp. 171–188). On the sexual theories of children (Standard Edition, Vol. 9, pp. 209–226).

Gjerde, L. C., Czajkowski, N., Roysamb, E., Orstavik, R. E., Knudsen, G. P., Ostby, K.,…Reichborn-Kjennerud, T. (2012). The heritability of avoidant and dependent personality disorder assessed by personal interview and questionnaire. *Acta Psychiatrica Scandinavica*, 126(6), 448–457.

Grant, B. F., Hasin, D. S., Stinson, F. S., Dawson, D. A., Chou, S. P., Ruan, W. J., & Pickering, R. P. (2004). Prevalence, correlates, and disability of personality disorders in the United States: Results from the National Epidemiologic Survey on Alcohol and Related Conditions. *Journal of Clinical Psychiatry*, 65(7), 948–958.

Grant, J. E., Mooney, M. E., & Kushner, M. G. (2012). Prevalence, correlates, and comorbidity of DSM-IV obsessive-compulsive personality disorder: Results from the National Epidemiologic Survey on Alcohol and Related Conditions. *Journal of Psychiatric Research*, 46(4), 469–475.

Grilo, C. M., McGlashan, T. H., Morey, L. C., Gunderson, J. G., Skodol, A. E., Shea, M. T.,…Stout, R. L. (2001). Internal consistency, intercriterion overlap and diagnostic efficiency of criteria sets for DSM-IV schizotypal, borderline, avoidant and obsessive-compulsive personality disorders. *Acta Psychiatrica Scandinavica*, 104(4), 264–272.

Grilo, C. M., Sanislow, C. A., Gunderson, J. G., Pagano, M. E., Yen, S., Zanarini, M. C.,…McGlashan, T. H. (2004). Two-year stability and change of schizotypal, borderline, avoidant, and obsessive-compulsive personality disorders. *Journal of Consulting and Clinical Psychology*, 72(5), 767–775.

Grilo, C. M., Stout, R. L., Markowitz, J. C., Sanislow, C. A., Ansell, E. B., Skodol, A. E.,…McGlashan, T. H. (2010). Personality disorders predict relapse after remission from an episode of major depressive disorder: A 6-year prospective study. *Journal of Clinical Psychiatry*, 71(12), 1629–1635.

Grover, K. E., Carpenter, L. L., Price, L. H., Gagne, G. G., Mello, A. F., Mello, M. F., & Tyrka, A. R. (2007). The relationship between childhood abuse and adult personality disorder symptoms. *Journal of Personality Disorders, 21*(4), 442–447.

Gunderson, J. G., Shea, M. T., Skodol, A. E., McGlashan, T. H., Morey, L. C., Stout, R. L.,…Keller, M. B. (2000). The Collaborative Longitudinal Personality Disorders Study: Development, aims, design, and sample characteristics. *Journal of Personality Disorders, 14*(4), 300–315.

Haigler, E. D., & Widiger, T. A. (2001). Experimental manipulation of NEO-PI-R items. *Journal of Personality Assessment, 77*(2), 339–358.

Halmi, K. A. (2005). Obsessive-compulsive personality disorder and eating disorders. *Eating Disorders, 13*(1), 85–92.

Halmi, K. A., Tozzi, F., Thornton, L. M., Crow, S., Fichter, M. M., Kaplan, A. S.,…Bulik, C. M. (2005). The relation among perfectionism, obsessive-compulsive personality disorder and obsessive-compulsive disorder in individuals with eating disorders. *International Journal of Eating Disorders, 38*(4), 371–374.

Hasin, D. S., Goodwin, R. D., Stinson, F. S., & Grant, B. F. (2005). Epidemiology of major depressive disorder: Results from the National Epidemiologic Survey on Alcoholism and Related Conditions. *Archives of General Psychiatry, 62*(10), 1097–1106.

Hopwood, C. J., Morey, L. C., Donnellan, M. B., Samuel, D. B., Grilo, C. M., McGlashan, T. H.,…Skodol, A. E. (2013). Ten-year rank-order stability of personality traits and disorders in a clinical sample. *Journal of Personality, 81*(3), 335–344.

Hopwood, C. J., Thomas, K. M., Markon, K. E., Wright, A. G. C., Krueger, R. F. (2012). DSM-5 personality traits and DSM-IV personality disorders. *Journal of Abnormal Psychology, 121*(2), 424–432.

Huang, Y., Kotov, R., de Girolamo, G., Preti, A., Angermeyer, M., Benjet, C.,…Kessler, R. C. (2009). DSM-IV personality disorders in the WHO World Mental Health Surveys. *British Journal of Psychiatry, 195*(1), 46–53.

Hyler, S. E., & Lyons, M. (1988). Factor analysis of the DSM-III personality disorder clusters: A replication. *Comprehensive Psychiatry, 29*(3), 304–308.

Jacob, C. P., Muller, J., Schmidt, M., Hohenberger, K., Gutknecht, L., Reif, A.,…Lesch, K. P. (2005). Cluster B personality disorders are associated with allelic variation of monoamine oxidase A activity. *Neuropsychopharmacology, 30*(9), 1711–1718.

Jacob, C. P., Strobel, A., Hohenberger, K., Ringel, T., Gutknecht, L., Reif, A.,…Lesch, K. P. (2004). Association between allelic variation

of serotonin transporter function and neuroticism in anxious Cluster C personality disorders. *American Journal of Psychiatry, 161*(3), 569–572.

Johnson, J. G., Cohen, P., Brown, J., Smailes, E. M., & Bernstein, D. P. (1999). Childhood maltreatment increases risk for personality disorders during early adulthood. *Archives of General Psychiatry, 56*(7), 600–606.

Johnson, J. G., Cohen, P., Kasen, S., Skodol, A. E., Hamagami, F., & Brook, J. S. (2000). Age-related change in personality disorder trait levels between early adolescence and adulthood: A community-based longitudinal investigation. *Acta Psychiatrica Scandinavica, 102*(4), 265–275.

Johnson, J. G., Cohen, P., Kasen, S., Skodol, A. E., & Oldham, J. M. (2008). Cumulative prevalence of personality disorders between adolescence and adulthood. *Acta Psychiatrica Scandinavica, 118*(5), 410–413.

Joyce, P. R., Rogers, G. R., Miller, A. L., Mulder, R. T., Luty, S. E., & Kennedy, M. A. (2003). Polymorphisms of DRD4 and DRD3 and risk of avoidant and obsessive personality traits and disorders. *Psychiatry Research, 119*(1–2), 1–10.

Kendler, K. S., Aggen, S. H., Czajkowski, N., Roysamb, E., Tambs, K., Torgersen, S.,…Reichborn-Kjennerud, T. (2008). The structure of genetic and environmental risk factors for DSM-IV personality disorders: A multivariate twin study. *Archives of General Psychiatry, 65*(12), 1438–1446.

Kendler, K. S., Aggen, S. H., Knudsen, G. P., Roysamb, E., Neale, M. C., & Reichborn-Kjennerud, T. (2011). The structure of genetic and environmental risk factors for syndromal and subsyndromal common DSM-IV Axis I and all Axis II disorders. *American Journal of Psychiatry, 168*(1), 29–39.

Kendler, K. S., Czajkowski, N., Tambs, K., Torgersen, S., Aggen, S. H., Neale, M. C., & Reichborn-Kjennerud, T. (2006). Dimensional representations of DSM-IV Cluster A personality disorders in a population-based sample of Norwegian twins: A multivariate study. *Psychological Medicine, 36*(11), 1583–1591.

Kendler, K. S., Myers, J., Torgersen, S., Neale, M. C., & Reichborn-Kjennerud, T. (2007). The heritability of Cluster A personality disorders assessed by both personal interview and questionnaire. *Psychological Medicine, 37*(5), 655–665.

Knudsen, A. K., Skogen, J. C., Harvey, S. B., Stewart, R., Hotopf, M., & Moran, P. (2012).

Personality disorders, common mental disorders and receipt of disability benefits: Evidence from the British National Survey of Psychiatric Morbidity. *Psychological Medicine, 42*(12), 2631–2640.

Krueger, R. F. (2005). Continuity of Axes I and II: Toward a unified model of personality, personality disorders, and clinical disorders. *Journal of Personality Disorders, 19*(3), 233–261.

Krueger, R. F., & Markon, K. E. (2006). Reinterpreting comorbidity: A model-based approach to understanding and classifying psychopathology. *Annual Review of Clinical Psychology, 2*, 111–133.

Krueger, R. F., Derringer, J., Markon, K. E., Watson, D., & Skodol, A. E. (2012). Initial construction of a maladaptive personality trait model and inventory for DSM-5. *Psychological Medicine, 42*(9), 1879–1890.

Lawton, E. M., Shields, A. J., & Oltmanns, T. F. (2011). Five-factor model personality disorder prototypes in a community sample: Self- and informant-reports predicting interview-based DSM diagnoses. *Personality Disorders, 2*(4), 279–292.

Lenzenweger, M. F. (1999). Stability and change in personality disorder features: The Longitudinal Study of Personality Disorders. *Archives of General Psychiatry, 56*(11), 1009–1015.

Lenzenweger, M. F. (2006). The Longitudinal Study of Personality Disorders: History, design considerations, and initial findings. *Journal of Personality Disorders, 20*(6), 645–670.

Lenzenweger, M. F. (2008). Epidemiology of personality disorders. *Psychiatric Clinics of North America, 31*(3), 395–403, vi.

Lenzenweger, M. F., Johnson, M. D., & Willett, J. B. (2004). Individual growth curve analysis illuminates stability and change in personality disorder features: The Longitudinal Study of Personality Disorders. *Archives of General Psychiatry, 61*(10), 1015–1024.

Lenzenweger, M. F., Lane, M. C., Loranger, A. W., & Kessler, R. C. (2007). DSM-IV personality disorders in the National Comorbidity Survey Replication. *Biological Psychiatry, 62*(6), 553–564.

Light, K. J., Joyce, P. R., Luty, S. E., Mulder, R. T., Frampton, C. M., Joyce, L. R.,…Kennedy, M. A. (2006). Preliminary evidence for an association between a dopamine D3 receptor gene variant and obsessive-compulsive personality disorder in patients with major depression. *American Journal of Medical Genetics B: Neuropsychiatric Genetics, 141B*(4), 409–413.

Lilenfeld, L. R., Wonderlich, S., Riso, L. P., Crosby, R., & Mitchell, J. (2006). Eating disorders and personality: A methodological and empirical review. *Clinical Psychology Review, 26*(3), 299–320.

Livesley, W. J., & Jang, K. L. (2008). The behavioral genetics of personality disorder. *Annual Review of Clinical Psychology, 4*, 247–274.

Lochner, C., Serebro, P., van der Merwe, L., Hemmings, S., Kinnear, C., Seedat, S., & Stein, D. J. (2011). Comorbid obsessive-compulsive personality disorder in obsessive-compulsive disorder (OCD): A marker of severity. *Progress in Neuropsychopharmacology and Biological Psychiatry, 35*(4), 1087–1092.

Lynam, D. R., & Widiger, T. A. (2001). Using the five-factor model to represent the DSM-IV personality disorders: An expert consensus approach. *Journal of Abnormal Psychology, 110*(3), 401–412.

Markon, K. E., Quilty, L. C., Bagby, R. M., & Krueger, R. F. (2013) The development and psychometric properties of an informant-report form of the Personality Inventory for DSM-5 (PID-5). *Assessment, 20*(3), 370–383.

McCrae, R. R., & John, O. P. (1992). An introduction to the five-factor model and its applications. *Journal of Personality, 60*(2), 175–215.

McGlashan, T. H., Grilo, C. M., Sanislow, C. A., Ralevski, E., Morey, L. C., Gunderson, J. G.,…Pagano, M. (2005). Two-year prevalence and stability of individual DSM-IV criteria for schizotypal, borderline, avoidant, and obsessive-compulsive personality disorders: Toward a hybrid model of Axis II disorders. *American Journal of Psychiatry, 162*(5), 883–889.

McGlashan, T. H., Grilo, C. M., Skodol, A. E., Gunderson, J. G., Shea, M. T., Morey, L. C.,…Stout, R. L. (2000). The Collaborative Longitudinal Personality Disorders Study: Baseline Axis I/II and II/II diagnostic co-occurrence. *Acta Psychiatrica Scandinavica, 102*(4), 256–264.

Melartin, T. K., Rytsala, H. J., Leskela, U. S., Lestela-Mielonen, P. S., Sokero, T. P., & Isometsa, E. T. (2002). Current comorbidity of psychiatric disorders among DSM-IV major depressive disorder patients in psychiatric care in the Vantaa Depression Study. *Journal of Clinical Psychiatry, 63*(2), 126–134.

Morey, L. C., Berghuis, H., Bender, D. S., Verheul, R., Krueger, R. F., & Skodol, A. E. (2011). Toward a model for assessing level of personality functioning in DSM-5, part II: Empirical articulation of a core dimension of personality pathology. *Journal of Personality Assessment, 93*(4), 347–353.

Morey, L. C., Krueger, R. F., & Skodol, A. E. (2013). The hierarchical structure of clinician ratings of proposed DSM-5 pathological personality traits. *Journal of Abnormal Psychology, 122*(3), 836–41.

Morey, L. C. & Skodol A. E. (2013). Convergence between DSM-IV-TR and DSM-5 diagnostic models for personality disorder: Evaluation of strategies for establishing diagnostic tresholds. *Journal of Psychiatric Practice 19*(3), 179–193.

Mullins-Sweatt, S. N., & Widiger, T. A. (2007). Millon's dimensional model of personality disorders: A comparative study. *Journal of Personality Disorders, 21*(1), 42–57.

Neale, M. C., & Kendler, K. S. (1995). Models of comorbidity for multifactorial disorders. *American Journal of Human Genetics, 57*(4), 935–953.

Nestadt, G., Addington, A., Samuels, J., Liang, K. Y., Bienvenu, O. J., Riddle, M.,...Cullen, B. (2003). The identification of OCD-related subgroups based on comorbidity. *Biological Psychiatry, 53*(10), 914–920.

Nestadt, G., Di, C., Samuels, J. F., Bienvenu, O. J., Reti, I. M., Costa, P.,...Bandeen-Roche, K. (2010). The stability of DSM personality disorders over twelve to eighteen years. *Journal of Psychiatric Research, 44*(1), 1–7.

Oldham, J. M., & Frosch, W. A. (1988). Compulsive personality disorder. In R. C. Michels, J. O. Cavenar, H. K. Brodie, A. M. Cooper, S. B. Guze, L. L. Judd, G. L. Klerman, & A. J. Solnit (Eds.), *Psychiatry*. Philadelphia: J.B. Lippincott.

Ottosson, H., Ekselius, L., Grann, M., & Kullgren, G. (2002). Cross-system concordance of personality disorder diagnoses of DSM-IV and diagnostic criteria for research of ICD-10. *Journal of Personality Disorders, 16*(3), 283–292.

Pfhol, B. B., N. (1994). Obsessive-compulsive personality disorder. In W. J. Livesley (Ed.), *The DSM-IV personality disorders* (pp. 261–277). New York: Guilford Press.

Pinto, A., Mancebo, M. C., Eisen, J. L., Pagano, M. E., & Rasmussen, S. A. (2006). The Brown Longitudinal Obsessive Compulsive Study: Clinical features and symptoms of the sample at intake. *Journal of Clinical Psychiatry, 67*(5), 703–711.

Pitman, R. K. (1987). Pierre Janet on obsessive-compulsive disorder (1903). Review and commentary. *Archives of General Psychiatry, 44*(3), 226–232.

Pollak, J. M. (1994). Commentary on obsessive-compulsive personality disorder. In W. J. Livesley (Ed.), *The DSM-IV personality disorders* (pp. 277–283). New York: Guilford Press.

Reichborn-Kjennerud, T., Czajkowski, N., Neale, M. C., Orstavik, R. E., Torgersen, S., Tambs, K.,...Kendler, K. S. (2007). Genetic and environmental influences on dimensional representations of DSM-IV Cluster C personality disorders: A population-based multivariate twin study. *Psychological Medicine, 37*(5), 645–653.

Reichborn-Kjennerud, T., Czajkowski, N., Roysamb, E., Orstavik, R. E., Neale, M. C., Torgersen, S., & Kendler, K. S. (2010). Major depression and dimensional representations of DSM-IV personality disorders: A population-based twin study. *Psychological Medicine, 40*(9), 1475–1484.

Rodrigues Torres, A., & Del Porto, J. A. (1995). Comorbidity of obsessive-compulsive disorder and personality disorders. A Brazilian controlled study. *Psychopathology, 28*(6), 322–329.

Rossi, A., Marinangeli, M. G., Butti, G., Kalyvoka, A., & Petruzzi, C. (2000). Pattern of comorbidity among anxious and odd personality disorders: The case of obsessive-compulsive personality disorder. *CNS Spectrum, 5*(9), 23–26.

Roysamb, E., Kendler, K. S., Tambs, K., Orstavik, R. E., Neale, M. C., Aggen, S. H.,...Reichborn-Kjennerud, T. (2011). The joint structure of DSM-IV Axis I and Axis II disorders. *Journal of Abnormal Psychology, 120*(1), 198–209.

Samuel, D. B., Hopwood, C. J., Krueger, R. F., Thomas, K. M., & Ruggero, C. J. (2013). Comparing methods for scoring personality disorder types using maladaptive traits in DSM-5. *Assessment, 20*(3), 353–361.

Samuel, D. B., Riddell, A. D., Lynam, D. R., Miller, J. D., & Widiger, T. A. (2012). A five-factor measure of obsessive-compulsive personality traits. *Journal of Personal Assessment, 94*(5), 456–465.

Samuel, D. B., & Widiger, T. A. (2008). A meta-analytic review of the relationships between the five-factor model and DSM-IV-TR personality disorders: A facet level analysis. *Clinical Psychology Review, 28*(8), 1326–1342.

Samuel, D. B., & Widiger, T. A. (2011). Conscientiousness and obsessive-compulsive personality disorder. *Personality Disorders, 2*(3), 161–174.

Samuels, J., & Costa, P. T. (2012). Obsessive-compulsive personality disorder.

In T. A. Widiger (Ed.), *The Oxford handbook of personality disorders*. New York: Oxford University Press.

Samuels, J., Nestadt, G., Bienvenu, O. J., Costa, P. T., Jr., Riddle, M. A., Liang, K. Y.,...Cullen, B. A. (2000). Personality disorders and normal personality dimensions in obsessive-compulsive disorder. *British Journal of Psychiatry, 177*, 457–462.

Sanislow, C. A., Little, T. D., Ansell, E. B., Grilo, C. M., Daversa, M., Markowitz, J. C.,...McGlashan, T. H. (2009). Ten-year stability and latent structure of the DSM-IV schizotypal, borderline, avoidant, and obsessive-compulsive personality disorders. *Journal of Abnormal Psychology, 118*(3), 507–519.

Sanislow, C. A., Morey, L. C., Grilo, C. M., Gunderson, J. G., Shea, M. T., Skodol, A. E.,...McGlashan, T. H. (2002). Confirmatory factor analysis of DSM-IV borderline, schizotypal, avoidant and obsessive-compulsive personality disorders: Findings from the Collaborative Longitudinal Personality Disorders Study. *Acta Psychiatrica Scandinavica, 105*(1), 28–36.

Shea, M. T., Stout, R., Gunderson, J., Morey, L. C., Grilo, C. M., McGlashan, T.,...Keller, M. B. (2002). Short-term diagnostic stability of schizotypal, borderline, avoidant, and obsessive-compulsive personality disorders. *American Journal of Psychiatry, 159*(12), 2036–2041.

Shea, M. T., Stout, R. L., Yen, S., Pagano, M. E., Skodol, A. E., Morey, L. C.,...Zanarini, M. C. (2004). Associations in the course of personality disorders and Axis I disorders over time. *Journal of Abnormal Psychology, 113*(4), 499–508.

Skodol, A. E., Bender, D. S., Morey, L. C., Clark, L. A., Oldham, J. M., Alarcon, R. D.,...Siever, L. J. (2011). Personality disorder types proposed for DSM-5. *Journal of Personality Disorders, 25*(2), 136–169.

Skodol, A. E., Gunderson, J. G., McGlashan, T. H., Dyck, I. R., Stout, R. L., Bender, D. S.,...Oldham, J. M. (2002). Functional impairment in patients with schizotypal, borderline, avoidant, or obsessive-compulsive personality disorder. *American Journal of Psychiatry, 159*(2), 276–283.

Soeteman, D. I., Hakkaart-van Roijen, L., Verheul, R., & Busschbach, J. J. (2008). The economic burden of personality disorders in mental health care. *Journal of Clinical Psychiatry, 69*(2), 259–265.

Starcevic, V., Bogojevic, G., & Kelin, K. (1997). Diagnostic agreement between the DSM-IV and ICD-10-DCR personality disorders. *Psychopathology, 30*(6), 328–334.

Taylor, S., Asmundson, G. J., & Jang, K. L. (2011). Etiology of obsessive-compulsive symptoms and obsessive-compulsive personality traits: Common genes, mostly different environments. *Depression & Anxiety, 28*(10), 863–869.

Tellegen, A. (1985). Structures of mood and personality and their relevance to assessing anxiety with an emphasis on self-report. In A. H. Tuma & J. D. Maser (Eds.), *Anxiety and the anxiety disorders* (pp. 681–706). Hillsdale, NJ: Lawrence Erlbaum.

Torgersen, S. (2009). The nature (and nurture) of personality disorders. *Scandinavian Journal of Psychology, 50*(6), 624–632.

Torgersen, S., Czajkowski, N., Jacobson, K., Reichborn-Kjennerud, T., Roysamb, E., Neale, M. C., & Kendler, K. S. (2008). Dimensional representations of DSM-IV Cluster B personality disorders in a population-based sample of Norwegian twins: A multivariate study. *Psychological Medicine, 38*(11), 1617–1625.

Torgersen, S., Myers, J., Reichborn-Kjennerud, T., Roysamb, E., Kubarych, T. S., & Kendler, K. S. (2012). The heritability of Cluster B personality disorders assessed both by personal interview and questionnaire. *Journal of Personality Disorders, 26*(6), 848–866.

Torres, A. R., Moran, P., Bebbington, P., Brugha, T., Bhugra, D., Coid, J. W.,...Prince, M. (2006). Obsessive-compulsive disorder and personality disorder: Evidence from the British National Survey of Psychiatric Morbidity 2000. *Society of Psychiatry and Psychiatric Epidemiology, 41*(11), 862–867.

Trull, T. J., Jahng, S., Tomko, R. L., Wood, P. K., & Sher, K. J. (2010). Revised NESARC personality disorder diagnoses: Gender, prevalence, and comorbidity with substance dependence disorders. *Journal of Personality Disorders, 24*(4), 412–426.

Trull, T. J., Sceiderer, E. M., & Tomko, R. L. (2012). Axis II comorbidity. In T. A. Widiger (Ed.), *The Oxford handbook of personality disorders*. New York: Oxford University Press.

Tyrer, P., Crawford, M., Mulder, R., & ICD-11 Working Group for the Revision of Classification of Personality Disorders (2011). Reclassifying personality disorders. *Lancet, 377*(9780), 1814–1815.

Tyrer, P., Mulder, R., Crawford, M., Newton-Howes, G., Simonsen, E., Ndetei, D.,...Barrett, B. (2010). Personality disorder: A new global perspective. *World Psychiatry, 9*(1), 56–60.

Tyrka, A. R., Wyche, M. C., Kelly, M. M., Price, L. H., & Carpenter, L. L. (2009). Childhood maltreatment and adult personality disorder symptoms: Influence of maltreatment type. *Psychiatry Research*, *165*(3), 281–287.

Ullrich, S., & Coid, J. (2009). The age distribution of self-reported personality disorder traits in a household population. *Journal of Personality Disorders*, *23*(2), 187–200.

Ullrich, S., Farrington, D. P., & Coid, J. W. (2007). Dimensions of DSM-IV personality disorders and life-success. *Journal of Personality Disorders*, *21*(6), 657–663.

Warner, M. B., Morey, L. C., Finch, J. F., Gunderson, J. G., Skodol, A. E., Sanislow, C. A.,…Grilo, C. M. (2004). The longitudinal relationship of personality traits and disorders. *Journal of Abnormal Psychology*, *113*(2), 217–227.

Wentz, E., Gillberg, I. C., Anckarsater, H., Gillberg, C., & Rastam, M. (2009). Adolescent-onset anorexia nervosa: 18-year outcome. *British Journal of Psychiatry*, *194*(2), 168–174.

Widiger, T. A., & Simonsen, E. (2005). Alternative dimensional models of personality disorder: Finding a common ground. *Journal of Personality Disorders*, *19*(2), 110–130.

Wright, A. G. C., Thomas, K. M., Hopwood, C. J., Markon, K. E., & Krueger, R. F. (2012). The hierarchical structure of DSM-5 pathological personality traits. *Journal of Abnormal Psychology*, *121*(2), 951–957.

Yen, S., Shea, M. T., Battle, C. L., Johnson, D. M., Zlotnick, C., Dolan-Sewell, R.,…McGlashan, T. H. (2002). Traumatic exposure and posttraumatic stress disorder in borderline, schizotypal, avoidant, and obsessive-compulsive personality disorders: Findings from the Collaborative Longitudinal Personality Disorders Study. *Journal of Nervous & Mental Disease*, *190*(8), 510–518.

Zanarini, M. C., Frankenburg, F. R., Hennen, J., Reich, D. B., & Silk, K. R. (2006). Prediction of the 10-year course of borderline personality disorder. *American Journal of Psychiatry*, *163*(5), 827–832.

28

Schizotypic Psychopathology
Theory, Evidence, and Future Directions

MARK F. LENZENWEGER

Schizotypic psychopathology has long intrigued researchers and clinicians for over 100 years. In short, schizotypic psychopathology represents a unique and rich window on schizophrenia liability Lenzenweger (1998, 2010), and therein lies the heuristic basis for much of the scientific activity in this area of psychopathology research. Beginning with early observations and speculations by Kraepelin and Bleuler in the early 1900s and continuing up through the most recent revision of the American Psychiatric Association's official diagnostic nomenclature (*DSM-5*) and the *International Classification of Diseases* (*ICD-10*), schizotypic psychopathology has posed to psychopathology a variety of challenges to classification, theory, and experimental approaches. In more recent years, schizotypic psychopathology has encompassed paranoid and schizotypal personality disorder as defined previously by the *DSM* nomenclatures, but, importantly, one must realize that definitions of *schizotypic psychopathology* are not solely reliant on the American Psychiatric Association's *DSM* nomenclature. Schizotypic psychopathology has been approached from a variety of theoretical and methodological vantage points, each offering useful insights into the fundamental nature of this class of psychopathology. The variation in these approaches has generated alternative units of analysis for schizotypic psychopathology that have not always conformed to prevailing diagnostic nomenclatures, thus yielding challenges to consistency, organization of findings, and other issues for the student of

schizotypic psychopathology. On the other hand, theory and research in schizotypic psychopathology enjoy a spirited level of debate and development that remains exceptional in psychopathology, especially among the personality disorders.

Although relatively rare even through the early 1980s, research on schizotypic psychopathology has grown in a meteoric fashion over the last 35 years and now represents one of the most active areas of inquiry in psychiatry, clinical psychology, and experimental psychopathology. For example, as of early 2014 there were 1,629 published reports (according to a *Web of Science—Science Citation Index* search) that included the words *schizotypal* or *schizotypy* just in their titles. Accordingly, this review must be necessarily selective and makes no claim to be comprehensive. The reader should be aware that there are topics or subareas that cannot be adequately detailed here because of space constraints.

The intention of this chapter's discussion is to introduce the reader to schizotypic psychopathology and to identify several central theoretical and research issues and how they are confronted in this area of psychopathology research. Several empirical and theoretical reviews on this topic are available (Chemerinski, Triebwasser, Roussos, & Siever, 2013; Lenzenweger, 2010, 2006b; Raine, 2006; Siever & Davis, 2004; Triebwasser, Chemerinski, Roussos, & Siever, 2013). A collection of papers on schizotypal personality that covers research and theory up through the early 1990s still remains well worth consulting (Raine, Lencz, & Mednick, 1995).

Current perspectives on schizophrenia spectrum disorders, which include schizotypic psychopathology, can be found in Ritsner's (2011) multivolume handbook. Although this chapter discusses research findings relevant to the *DSM*-defined schizotypal (SPD) and paranoid personality (PPD) disorders, it does *not* focus solely on these diagnostic entities as currently defined in the *DSM* system. Indeed, a central organizing theme here is that schizotypic psychopathology reflects underlying schizotypy, and the range phenotypic expression of schizotypy extends beyond SPD and PPD (Lenzenweger, 2010).

Schizotypic Psychopathology: Definitional Issues and Relevant Distinctions

It is important to explicate and clarify several relevant distinctions regarding the meaning of the term *schizotypic*. In this chapter, the terms *schizotypal* and *paranoid* are used to denote the personality disorders as defined by the *DSM* nomenclature. It is important to note that SPD and PPD are, by definition, merely sets of descriptors (signs and symptoms) that serve as diagnostic criteria; *DSM* systems (since 1980 and the *DSM-III*, continuing with the *DSM-5*) eschew any relationship to an explanatory framework for these disorders. Moreover, given their relatively high degree of comorbidity, shared phenomenologic features (e.g., suspiciousness), and relationship to clinical schizophrenia, SPD and PPD are often referred to as the "schizophrenia-related personality disorders" (SRPDs) and are viewed as falling within the realm of "schizophrenia spectrum disorders" (see Ritsner, 2011). In contrast, the term *schizotypic* can be used to describe signs and symptoms that are the phenotypic manifestation of schizotypy, or a latent personality organization that derives from a liability for schizophrenia as conceptualized in Meehl's classic model (1962, 1990; see Lenzenweger, 2010; e.g., Grant et al., 2013). The term *schizotypic* can also serve as a generic shorthand descriptor of attenuated "schizophrenia-like" phenomenology that is stable and enduring, but is fundamentally nonpsychotic, without necessarily referring to Meehl's model.

SPD and PPD can readily be conceived of as manifestations of schizotypy as well, but they are not isomorphic with the schizotypy construct. *Schizotypic psychopathology* serves as a generic term for this general class of mental disturbance. A *schizotype* is a person who evidences schizotypic psychopathology.

In this context, schizoid personality disorder is not considered to be a schizophrenia-related personality disorder in light of available evidence and, therefore, is not viewed as an example of schizotypic psychopathology in this discussion (see Triebwasser, Chemerinski, Roussos, & Siever, 2012; see also Chapter 24 in this textbook). The argument has been made that both schizoid personality disorders (SZD) and avoidant personality disorder (APD) could justifiably be included in the realm of schizotypic/schizophrenia spectrum pathology (Fogelson et al., 2007); however, SZD and APD are reviewed in detail elsewhere in this volume.

A Clinical Vignette

The following case vignette presents an example of a schizotypic person. Additional clinical vignettes of schizotypic cases can be found in Lenzenweger (2010). Consider the following:

Robin, a 24-year-old, single male graduate student in physics at a large midwestern research university, has a long history of exceedingly strong anxiety symptoms in response to social interactions. In fact, he describes his experience of social interaction as being similar to the feeling one has when one's "knuckles accidently scrape across a carrot grater." He has no interest in social interaction and leads a socially isolated life and does not seek out social contact; many see him as a "loner." He has but one friend with whom he has talks about only highly esoteric topics, and he refers to these discussions as "technicalizing." He frequently uses other words in a peculiar and vague manner. Aside from anxiety, he claims to feel no strong emotions such as joy or even sadness. He frequently thinks that neutral events have "special relevance" for him and often seems to misperceive aspects of his body (e.g., he misjudges the length of his arms or legs). Despite having adequate financial resources, Robin's attire is often best described as "odd" or "eccentric," though clearly not fashionably stylish.

Defining the Schizotype

Organization of Schizotypic Signs and Symptoms

As psychopathologists have come to learn that schizotypic psychopathology is likely to be related in a meaningful way to the liability for schizophrenia, some have sought to determine if the organization of schizotypic signs and symptoms bears any resemblance to what is known about the organization of schizophrenia phenomenology. In short, exploratory (see Andreasen, Arndt, Alliger, Miller, & Flaum, 1995) and confirmatory (Lenzenweger & Dworkin, 1996) factor analytic studies have suggested that schizophrenia symptoms are best organized into three factors: Negative Symptoms (flattened affect, avolition), Reality Distortion (hallucinations, delusions), and Disorganization (thought disorder), with a fourth possible factor consisting of premorbid social impairment (see Lenzenweger & Dworkin, 1996). Factor analytic studies of schizotypic signs and symptoms yield solutions or conform to models that are broadly consistent with the picture observed for schizophrenia. For example, Raine (1991) found a three-factor model, consisting of Cognitive/Perceptual, Interpersonal, and Disorganization components, that provided a good fit to observed data. And for the most part, results from factor and other latent structure analytic studies have been rather consistent (Vollema & Hoitjink, 2000; cf. Kwapil, Barrantes-Vidal, & Silvia, 2008). Thus, at the phenotypic level, schizotypic signs and symptoms appear not only as attenuated schizophrenia manifestations but also as being organized in a similar fashion at the latent level.

Methodological Approaches to Assessing Schizotypic Psychopathology

Schizotypic psychopathology can be defined in one of three ways: (1) clinically, (2) in terms of deviance on reliable dimensional laboratory measures, or (3) by virtue of having a first-degree biological relative affected with schizophrenia (Lenzenweger, 2010). The clinical approach implied in psychiatric diagnostic schemes involves, quite obviously, the use of explicit diagnostic criteria to identify either SPD or PPD (e.g., the *DSM* systems). Note that SPD and PPD, though highly associated with each other, constitute coherent and relatively separable syndromes; however, a recent review raises questions about the viability of PPD as a diagnosis given the minimal interest shown in it by researchers (Triebwasser et al., 2013).

A second approach involves the use of reliable and valid psychometric (or other laboratory) measures of schizotypy to detect schizotypic psychopathology as defined by quantitative deviance on

such measures. In this approach, psychometric scales designed to assess various schizotypic manifestations serve to define and measure the schizotypy construct; schizotypic status may be defined by deviance on one or more of such measures. The fundamentals of the psychometric high-risk approach have been discussed and reviewed extensively in other venues (Lenzenweger, 1994, 2010). The hypothetical relations among these alternative approaches in defining schizotypic psychopathology are depicted in Figure 28.1. Clearly, all cases of schizophrenia must be direct reflections of true schizotypy (discounting obvious and objectively classified phenocopies, e.g., PCP-induced psychosis). Schizotypy features assessed via psychometrics, as well as clinically assessed SPD and PPD, are not perfectly related to an underlying genuine schizotypy construct owing necessarily to imperfect measurement, thus they are considered fallible measures of true schizotypy. As depicted in Figure 28.1, SPD and PPD themselves overlap somewhat (see later discussion).

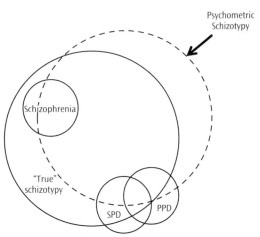

Figure 28.1 Hypothetical relations among schizotypy-related constructs. All cases of properly diagnosed schizophrenia (excluding phenocopies, such as drug-induced psychosis) are manifestations of "true schizotypy." *DSM* schizotypal (SPD) and paranoid (PPD) personality disorders, which themselves overlap, are fallible manifestations of "true schizotypy". Psychometrically assessed schizotypy is also fallible and, therefore, partially overlaps with a "true schizotypy" as well as observed manifestations such as schizophrenia, SPD, and PPD.

Finally, one can be concerned with the biological relatives of patients with schizophrenia and speak of "genotypic" schizotypes. Although many first-degree relatives of patients with schizophrenia will *not* evidence their underlying genetic predisposition to the illness through schizotypic symptomatology, they are, as a group, at increased statistical risk for schizophrenia and can be spoken of as schizotypes. Some relatives of patients with schizophrenia will, indeed, display schizotypic symptomatology (Kendler, 1985; Kendler et al., 1993; Maier, Falkai, & Wagner, 1999), and some will go on to develop clinical schizophrenia. Of course, some relatives can carry the liability for schizophrenia quietly, giving little indication of its presence (Gottesman & Bertelsen, 1989). Finally, it is essential to note that not every biological relative of a schizophrenia-affected person will harbor liability for the illness (Hanson, Gottesman, & Meehl, 1977); that is, it is possible to be a noncarrier.

Prevalence of Schizotypic Psychopathology

Epidemiology of Personality Pathology: General Considerations

Until relatively recently there existed no comprehensive, high-quality data regarding the population prevalence rates of personality disorders according to either *DSM* or *ICD* definitions. Weissman (1993) offered an impressionistic rough estimate for the overall lifetime rate for any Axis II disorder in the range of 10% to 13% (Weissman, 1993). However, the data on which this estimate was based were quite limited (i.e., few studies), and the studies from which the data derived suffered from various sampling defects or dubious methods of case ascertainment.

Whereas reliable structured interviews for Axis II personality pathology have existed since the late 1980s, such tools had not been used in epidemiological population-based studies of personality disorder prevalence. Such instruments typically required administration by clinically experienced diagnosticians and in many instances took several hours to complete, considerations that made the logistical requirements for their use in epidemiological study rather daunting. A related major obstacle to such epidemiological work was the cost of using experienced clinicians instead of lay interviewers to make personality disorder diagnoses. Lenzenweger, Loranger, Korfine, and Neff (1997) proposed that one way to curtail this expense might be to employ a two-stage design for case identification in which experienced clinicians would only interview screened positive cases and a random sample of negative ones drawn from a large sample screened with an effective self-report inventory. These investigators implemented this research strategy and reported on a personality disorder screen that is quite efficient, in that it generated no false negatives as indexed against criterial interview diagnoses in a large randomly ascertained nonclinical sample. Lenzenweger, Loranger, et al. (1997) estimated the point prevalence of diagnosed personality disorder to be approximately 11% (95% confidence interval [CI] = 7.57%–14.52%).

The two-stage procedure for case identification coupled with advanced estimation procedures was also used in the completed National Comorbidity Study-Replication (NCS-R) investigation (Lenzenweger, Lane, Loranger, & Kessler, 2007). In the NCS-R, which used well-trained screening personnel and experienced diagnosticians using the *International Personality Disorder Examination* (IPDE, Loranger et al., 1994), a population prevalence of 9.0% for "any personality disorder" was found for the U.S. general population. Importantly, several epidemiological studies that have relied on more traditional, door-to-door interviewing strategies have yielded broadly comparable estimates for personality disorder in community populations (see Lenzenweger, 2008, for review).

Epidemiology of Schizotypic Psychopathology

For most of the last century prevalence "estimates" for schizotypic psychopathology have been arrived at through indirect routes and considered at best to be educated guesses. The *DSM* systems have suggested prevalences for SPD of approximately 3% and for PPD 0.5% to 2.5% in the general population. Such "guesstimates" were derived from relatively large clinical (psychiatric patient) samples. For example, Loranger (1990) reported, in a large series of consecutive psychiatric admissions to a university teaching hospital, 2.1% for *DSM-III* SPD and 1.2% for PPD. On the basis of telephone interviews, Zimmerman and Coryell (1990) reported that SPD was found in 3.0% of their respondents and PPD in 0.4%. In a more recent series of 859 psychiatric outpatients (university hospital), prevalence rate of .6% for SPD and 4.2% for PPD were reported (Zimmerman, Rothschild, & Chelminski, 2005).

Since 1997, a number of community-based samples have been studied using epidemiological methods and state-of-the-art diagnostic interviews, and we now have reasonable estimates for SPD and PPD rates in the population. Lenzenweger (2008) has summarized the prevalence data for SPD and PPD from five community studies (four U.S. studies, two European studies) (see Table 28.1). For SPD, the prevalences ranged from 0.06% to 1.6% (median = 0.6%), whereas the prevalences for PPD ranged from 0.7% to 5.10% (median = 1.00%). In the NCS-R, Lenzenweger, Lane, et al. (2007) found a prevalence of 5.7% (SE = 1.6) for Cluster A disorders (which included schizoid personality disorder) for the U.S. population. The median prevalence value for "any Cluster A PD" (including schizoid PD) taken across the six epidemiological studies was 3.45%. Chemerinski et al. (2013) concluded that SPD remains best thought of as a relatively infrequent disorder, even in clinical settings.

One must remember that "schizotypic psychopathology" is a broader construct than the contemporary definitions of *DSM* SPD and PPD. Therefore, useful guidance on the epidemiology of this "broader construct" should be considered

as well. For example, Essen-Möller, Larsson, Uddenberg, and White (1956) reported from their landmark study of a rural Swedish population that schizoid personality, in the sense of "probably related to schizophrenia or to a schizophrenic taint" (*sic*) (p. 73), was found among 1.8% of women and 6.0% of men. Kety et al. (1994), in a report from their Danish Adoption Study of Schizophrenia, found that among the biological relatives of normal control adoptees, 0.8% were paranoid personality, 3.3% were schizoid personality, and 2.5% were "latent schizophrenia," a pre-*DSM-III* diagnostic designation roughly akin to SPD. In a secondary analysis of the Kety et al. (1994) data, Kendler, Gruenberg, and Kinney (1994) found that, according to *DSM-III* criteria, from 3.1% to 3.7% of the relatives of the normal control adoptees had either SPD or a "schizophrenia spectrum" diagnosis (or, schizotypic psychopathology more generally). Generalization from family-based data to population prevalences must be done with great caution, however, owing to various constraints inherent in family data (Carey, Gottesman, & Robins, 1980).

Finally, based on a consideration of familial risk rates, Meehl (1990) argued that approximately 10% of the population is genotypically schizotypic, though not all individuals manifest this

Table 28.1 Prevalence (Percentage) of Personality Disorders in Six Nonclinical Population/Community Studies Using Validated Structured Interviews

	Study					
	Lenzenweger, Loranger, et al. (1997)	Torgersen et al. (2001)	Samuels et al. (2002)	Crawford et al. (2005)	Coid et al. (2006)	Lenzenweger, Lane, et al. (2007)
Instrument	IPDE	SIDP-R	IPDE	SCID-II	SCID-II	IPDE
Nomenclature	*DSM-III-R*	*DSM-III-R*	*DSM-IV*	*DSM-IV*	*DSM-IV*	*DSM-IV*
Location	Ithaca, NY	Oslo, Norway	Baltimore, MD	Upstate New York	Great Britain (National)	United States (National)
Personality Disorder						
Paranoid	1.0	2.4	0.7	5.1	.7	—
Schizoid	1.0	1.7	0.9	1.7	.8	—
Schizotypal	1.6	0.6	0.6	1.1	.06	—
Cluster A	2.8	4.1	2.1	6.8	1.6	5.7

Note: Instruments indicate the structured clinical interview used: International Personality Disorder Examination (IPDE); Structured Interview for *DSM-III-R* Personality Disorders (SIDP-R); Structured Clinical Interview for *DSM-IV* Axis II Disorders (SCID-II). Dashes indicate not applicable. All prevalences reported are weighted prevalences. In this context another epidemiological study, the National Epidemiologic Study of Alcohol and Related Conditions (NESARC; Grant et al., 2004), generated prevalence estimates for *DSM-IV* Cluster A personality disorders that are strikingly higher than those reported in most of the studies contained in this table (Paranoid = 4.4%, Schizotypal = 3.9%, Schizoid = 3.13%). However, methodological limitations of the NESARC study (e.g., use of an unvalidated Axis II assessment instrument; use of census workers without clinical training to conduct Axis II assessments) urge substantial caution in any consideration of the NESARC prevalence data (thus, they are not included in this table).

predisposition in a highly visible manner. Meehl's conjecture is supported by empirical taxometric (Korfine & Lenzenweger, 1995; Lenzenweger & Korfine, 1992a; Linscott, 2007; Meyer & Keller, 2001) and mixture modeling results (Lenzenweger, McLachlan, & Rubin, 2007).

Comorbidity among *DSM*-Defined SPD and PPD

Comorbidity as an issue for schizotypic psychopathology is usually concerned with the presence of SPD and PPD diagnoses in the same individuals, as observed in clinical samples. The *DSM* systems have allowed (even encouraged) multiple diagnoses on Axis II of the multiaxial system. Therefore, this feature of the system complicates any discussion of comorbidity. Observed comorbidity may represent little more than an artifact of rules (or guidelines) of the prevailing diagnostic system. Therefore, as opposed to the implication that two diseases are actually present in the same person (genuine comorbidity), it may actually make greater sense to simply speak of "co-occurrence" of PD diagnoses within a *DSM* framework.

Available data indicate that PPD appears to be present in 0% to 60% of patients with SPD drawn from primarily clinical samples (Siever, Bernstein, & Silverman, 1991). SPD is present in 17% to 70% of patients diagnosed with PPD (Bernstein, Useda, & Siever, 1993). Zimmerman et al. (2005) found that PPD and SPD diagnoses co-occurred frequently in their outpatient clinical series, and Lenzenweger, Lane, et al. (2007) found substantial covariation between PPD and SPD features in the NCS-R sample. It is essential to note that PPD is, in fact, rarely found alone in patients, often occurring with SPD (Triebwasser et al., 2013). In this context "covariation" refers to associations or correlations among the personality disorders, where the unit of analysis is typically the number of diagnostic criteria met for each of the disorders, whereas "co-occurrence" refers to the rate at which two disorders appear together in the same person in a sample of individuals assessed for the presence or absence of different personality disorders.

These co-occurrence/covariation rates may reflect (1) a system that allows multiple diagnoses, (2) shared diagnostic criteria, (3) sampling bias (e.g., more individuals who are impaired tend to seek treatment), and/or (4) a common underlying

substrate (e.g., schizotypy as a latent liability for schizophrenia). Regarding shared diagnostic criteria, PPD and SPD share the features of suspiciousness and paranoia, but PPD lacks the cognitive and perceptual distortions included in the SPD criteria. The sampling bias issue is especially relevant here given that most individuals diagnosed with SPD or PPD probably never present for treatment, but when they do they are likely to be in crisis, be more impaired, or both (Lenzenweger & Korfine, 1992b).

Available data also reveal that 33% to 91% of individuals diagnosed with SPD tend to also receive the diagnosis of borderline personality disorder (BPD; Chemerinski et al., 2013), though fewer BPD-diagnosed cases have a co-occurring SPD diagnosis. Zimmerman et al. (2005) reported significant comorbidity between SPD and BPD as well as between PPD and BPD. Lenzenweger, Lane, et al. (2007) found a relatively strong association between PPD and BPD features, with a weaker association between SPD and BPD. This degree of co-occurrence/covariation may reflect, in part, the influence of the method used to derive the original SPD and BPD diagnostic criteria, as well as less specific psychotic-like features that occur in both disorders (Siever et al., 1991) and the sampling issue noted previously. The issue of comorbidity is not directly relevant to schizotypic psychopathology as assessed by psychometric measures, as these do not reflect a categorical approach to classification; measures of schizotypy, however, do tend to be intercorrelated (Kwapil et al., 2008) as one would expect of valid indices tapping a common underlying construct.

Longitudinal Course of Schizotypic Psychopathology

For many years, psychiatry and clinical psychology have assumed that personality pathology, including schizotypic psychopathology, was relatively stable over time. However, the data upon which such an assumption of continuity or stability has rested were relatively sparse, indeed, virtually nonexistent. Only within the last decade have the data from multiwave, prospective, longitudinal studies begun to emerge to address this question.

The Longitudinal Study of Personality Disorders (LSPD) (Lenzenweger, 1999a; 2006a) reported that SPD and PPD, while maintaining rank order stability over time, showed evidence for nontrivial declines in mean level feature counts over a 4-year study period. However, when the LSPD data were examined in finer detail using individual growth curve analysis, the amount of individual change observed in PPD over time was insignificant, whereas the amount of individual change in SPD over time was appreciable. Johnson et al. (2000) found evidence for substantial rank-order stability of PPD and SPD features through time as well as rather substantial and significant declines in the mean level of PPD and SPD feartures over time in a large, community-based longitudinal study. Finally, in a clinical sample of schizotypal patients followed longitudinally, Shea et al. (2002) reported a comparable set of results showing maintenance of individual difference (rank order) stability for SPD features over time, yet clear evidence of a decline in SPD features over time at the level of group means (see also Sanislow et al., 2009).

The overall picture, therefore, is consistent across studies, yet complex. PPD and SPD appear to maintain rank-order stability over time in the context of diminishing feature levels. The mechanisms and processes accounting for these changes have not been illuminated thus far.

Historical Overview of Schizotypic Psychopathology

Variants of psychopathology thought to be related to schizophrenia, or schizotypic pathology, have been identified in different ways across the years (see Kendler, 1985, for historical review; see also Planansky, 1972). The difficult methodological and conceptual issues attending research in this area have been carefully reviewed by Gottesman and colleagues (Gottesman, 1987; Shields, Heston, & Gottesman, 1975).

Kraepelin (1919/1971, p. 234) and Bleuler (1911/1950, p. 239) made note of what they termed "latent schizophrenia," a personality aberration regarded as a quantitatively less severe expression of schizophrenia. Interestingly, because Kraepelin and Bleuler believed that the signs and symptoms of the so-called latent schizophrenia were in fact continuous with the "principal malady" (Kraepelin, 1919/1971, p. 234) or "manifest types of the disease" (Bleuler, 1911/1950, p. 239), neither of these master phenomenologists provided extended clinical descriptions of such cases. Both suggested one merely envision schizotypic conditions as characterized by diminished schizophrenia signs and symptoms. In attending to schizotypic pathology, however, Kraepelin and Bleuler foreshadowed subsequent efforts to delineate the phenotypic boundaries of schizophrenia through exploration of the schizotypic states.

In reviewing the history of psychiatric developments that culminated in the diagnostic criteria for SPD in *DSM-III*, Kendler (1985) persuasively argued that much of the clinical literature dealing with schizotypic states can be organized along two major historical trends. The "familial" tradition emphasizes phenomenological descriptions of nonpsychotic, but aberrant, personality states that occur in the biological relatives of individuals suffering from clinical schizophrenia. The second tradition was termed "clinical," as it emphasizes the work of clinicians who describe the symptomatology of their patients presenting schizotypic, or schizophrenia-like, features. As detailed by Kendler (1985), workers within the familial tradition (e.g., Kraepelin, Bleuler, Kretschemer, Kallmann, Slater) frequently used terms such as "latent schizophrenia," "schizoid personality or character," or "schizoform abnormalities" to describe some family members of patients with schizophrenia. These early observers used terms like "eccentric-odd," "irritable-unreasonable," "socially isolated," "aloof/cold demeanor," and "suspiciousness" to describe the family members of schizophrenia patients (Kendler, 1985, p. 543, Table 1).

In contrast, researchers and clinicians working within the so-called clinical tradition (Kendler, 1985; e.g., Zilboorg, Deutsch, Hoch and Polatin, Rado, and Meehl) used terms such as "ambulatory schizophrenia," "as-if personality," "pseudoneurotic schizophrenia," and "schizotypal" to describe individuals who were severely affected but nonpsychotic. The patients described by these rubrics were observed to demonstrate "schizophrenia-like symptomatology" in their psychological and psychosocial functioning, and it was frequently hypothesized that a genuine schizophrenia-related process was driving the manifest pathology. Disordered ("primary process") thinking and the lack of deep interpersonal relations were the two features that occurred most frequently in the descriptions of schizotypic patients by clinical tradition workers (Kendler, 1985, p. 545, Table 2). Kendler (1985) noted apparent basic agreement in the descriptions of schizotypic individuals across the two traditions in terms of interpersonal functioning impairments as well as broad overlap in other areas (e.g., disordered thinking, anxiety, anger, hypersensitivity). However, Kendler (1985) concluded, "although the syndromes described by these two traditions share certain important symptoms, they are not fundamentally the same" (p. 546).

Early depictions of schizotypic psychopathology, with the exception of those discussions by Rado and Meehl, were primarily descriptive and lacked any detailed etiological or developmental consideration. Although there was speculation about an association with schizophrenia and a possible hereditary connection, the precise pathway leading from the underlying liability for schizophrenia or schizophrenia-related pathology to the phenotypic expression of a clinical disorder was absent. Only Meehl (1962, 1964, 1990, 2001) offered a complex developmental model, setting him apart from other clinical researchers. Meehl's views are discussed in detail later in the chapter.

Perhaps the most influential early evidence that helped to establish a link between schizotypic phenomenology and clinical schizophrenia came from the Danish Adoption Study of Schizophrenia (Kety, Rosenthal, Wender, & Schulsinger, 1968). Using a definition of "borderline schizophrenia" heavily influenced by the clinical tradition described here, Kety et al. (1968) found elevated rates of borderline or latent schizophrenia in the biological relatives of adoptees with schizophrenia. Kety et al. (1994) further confirmed these initial results through further study of adoptees from the entire Danish population. These early results provided compelling evidence derived from a rigorous adoption methodology for a genetically transmitted component underlying manifest schizophrenia and the less severe schizophrenia-like disorders. The hypothesized continuity between the conditions was thus not merely phenomenological but also genetic. The diagnostic framework used by Kety et al. (1968) to diagnose "borderline" schizophrenia was subsequently reexamined (Spitzer, Endicott, & Gibbon, 1979) for use in the Axis II section of the then newly developed DSM-III. However, Spitzer and colleagues were not attempting to distill from the Kety et al. framework only symptoms that identified biological relatives of individuals with schizophrenia, rather they sought to determine if there was a reliable parsing of Kety's criteria that might map more narrowly defined and identifiable disorders. Spitzer et al.

(1979) proposed the following eight symptoms and signs for SPD: magical thinking, ideas of reference, suspiciousness, recurrent illusions, social isolation, odd speech, undue social anxiety-hypersensitivity, and inadequate rapport (aloof/cold). These criteria were, in large part, adopted for use in the DSM-III. SPD was subsequently placed on Axis II, along with PPD and schizoid personality disorder, to constitute the so-called odd-eccentric personality disorders cluster. The DSM-III (and DSM-III-R) criteria for SPD remained essentially atheoretical in nature, reflecting merely a clustering of symptoms, denoting with no specification of etiology or development. The atheoretical nature of the DSM-III criteria for SPD stood in contrast to Meehl's model of schizotypy, a model that integrates etiological, developmental, and phenomenological considerations.

This overview provides a suggestion of the interest schizotypic conditions have enjoyed among clinical and research workers, especially since 1980. It is important to realize that with the advent of explicit diagnostic criteria for SPD in 1980 in the DSM-III and a simultaneous narrowing of the definition of schizophrenia, there was a marked decrease in the rate at which schizophrenia was diagnosed and a corresponding rise in diagnosis of Axis II schizophrenia-related personality disorders (Loranger, 1990). Such an effect generated by a shift in the nomenclature has surely facilitated the focus on schizotypic conditions. It is also reasonable to assume that interest in these conditions has been further augmented by the burgeoning of research work in personality disorders in general, which has been greatly facilitated by improvements in diagnostics (cf. Loranger, 1988, 1999). Clearly, this interest has been sustained through a rich descriptive tradition and supported by findings indicating that schizotypic pathology is related genetically to schizophrenia per se (see Torgersen, 1985, 1994, for reviews). Indeed, recent evidence, done in the form of genome-wide scans for loci relevant to schizophrenia and schizotypic psychopathology dimensions, confirms shared genetic substrates for the two forms of psychopathology (Fanous et al., 2007; see also Avramopoulos et al., 2002; Lin et al., 2005; Siever et al., 2011). Finally, nomenclature changes notwithstanding, a great deal of interest in the study of schizotypic pathology and schizophrenia has been generated by P. E. Meehl's genetic-developmental model of schizotypy and schizophrenia (Lenzenweger, 2006b).

Classic Model of Schizotypic Psychopathology: Meehl's Integrative Model of Schizotypy

As already noted, many of the early depictions of schizotypic pathology were primarily descriptive in nature. Although the peculiarities of the relatives of individuals with schizophrenia or the symptoms of outpatients with schizophrenic-like symptoms were noted and thought to be related to schizophrenia in some manner (Kendler, 1985), none of the early workers advanced a model that unambiguously posited a genetic diathesis for schizophrenia and traced its influence through developmental psychobiological and behavioral paths to a variety of clinical (and nonclinical) outcomes. Unlike his predecessors, Meehl (1962, 1990) proposed a model that was (and is) clearly developmental in nature.

The roots of Meehl's model can be found in the observations and psychodynamic formulations of Sandor Rado (1953, 1960). Working within the clinical tradition, Rado made initial strides toward an integrative model that sought to link genetic influences for schizophrenia and observed schizotypic personality functioning. In his two primary position papers on the topic, he argued from a psychodynamic position informed by an appreciation for genetics that schizotypal behavior derived from a fundamental liability to schizophrenia. Rado, in fact, coined the term *schizotype* to represent a condensation of "schizophrenic *pheno*type" (Rado, 1953, p. 410; Rado, 1960, p. 87). It is interesting to note that Rado did not suggest schizotype as a condensation of the terms *schizophrenia* and *genotype* (cf. Siever & Gunderson, 1983). Rado (1960) referred to the individual who possessed the schizophrenic phenotype as a schizotype, while the correlated traits deriving from this "type" were termed "schizotypal organization" and the overt behavioral manifestations of the schizotypal traits were termed "schizotypal behavior" (see p. 87).

For Rado, the causes of schizotypal "differentness" were to be found in two core psychodynamic features of such patients, both of which were thought to be driven by "mutated genes." The two core defects present in the schizotype's personality organization were (1) a diminished capacity for pleasure, or pleasure deficiency, speculated to have a neurochemical basis deriving from an inherited pleasure potential coded in the infant's genes (Rado, 1960, p. 88), and (2) a proprioceptive (kinesthetic) diathesis that resulted in an aberrant awareness of the body (a feature giving rise to schizotypic body-image distortions; Rado, 1960, see pp. 88 and 90). Rado (1960) believed the physiological nature of the proprioceptive diathesis was obscure and remained to be explored (p. 88). According to Rado, integration of the "action self," a necessity of psychodynamic/psychological health, was endangered by the diminished binding power of pleasure (p. 90) and the proprioceptive diathesis found in the schizotype. Consequently, Rado (1960) described the schizotype as struggling to retain a sense of personality integration through several compensatory mechanisms (see p. 90), such mechanisms frequently manifesting themselves as schizotypal traits and behaviors. An important feature of Rado's model concerned what he termed "developmental stages of schizotypal behavior," essentially a continuum view of clinical compensation (a view echoed later by Meehl, 1990, p. 25). Rado's continuum notion suggested that a common schizophrenia diathesis could lead to a variety of phenotypic outcomes ranging from compensated schizotypy to deteriorated schizophrenia; thus an etiological unity was proposed as underlying a diversity of clinical manifestations.

Influenced by Rado's (1953, 1960) hypotheses, Meehl's model of schizotypy was first articulated in a now-classic position paper, his 1962 presidential address to the American Psychological Association, titled "Schizotaxia, Schizotypy, Schizophrenia." In this paper, one that has been viewed as enormously transforming for schizophrenia research (Lenzenweger, 2010), Meehl laid out an integrative etiological framework for schizophrenia. The model not only encompassed genetic factors, social learning influences, and clinical symptomatology but also contained hypotheses about the precise nature of the fundamental defect underlying schizotypic functioning and its interactions with what he came to term "polygenic potentiators." Elaboration on and refinement of the original 1962 theory can be found in his later papers (e.g., Meehl, 1972, 1974, 1990, 2001). What follows is a distillation of the major points contained in Meehl's efforts to illuminate the development of schizophrenia. The reader is encouraged to consult Meehl's original position statement (Meehl, 1962), his 1990 treatise (Meehl, 1990), and additional refinements (Meehl, 2001, 2004; see also, Lenzenweger, 2010) to gain a full appreciation for his point of view.

In brief, Meehl's (1962, 1990) model holds that a single major gene (the schizogene) exerts its influence during brain development by coding for a specific "functional parametric aberration of the synaptic control system" in the central nervous system (CNS; 1990, pp. 14–15). The aberration, present at the neuronal level, is termed "hypokrisia" and suggests a neural integrative defect characterized by an "insufficiency of separation, differentiation, or discrimination" in neural transmission. Meehl (1990) argued that his conceptualization of schizotaxia should not be taken to represent a defect in basic sensory or information retrieval capacities (p. 14), nor a CNS inhibitory function deficit (p. 16). The defect in neural transmission amounts to the presence of "slippage" at the CNS synapse, and such slippage at the synapse has its behavioral counterparts (at the molar level) in the glaring clinical symptomatology of actual schizophrenia. In other words, just as the synaptic functioning in schizophrenia is characterized by slippage, so too are the symptoms of associative loosening and cognitive-affective aberrations observed in the patient with schizophrenia. Hypokrisia was hypothesized to characterize the neuronal functioning throughout the brain of the individual who was affected, thus producing what amounted to a rather ubiquitous CNS anomaly (Meehl, 1990, p. 14) termed "schizotaxia." It is particularly fascinating that even today (e.g., Owen, O'Donovan, & Harrison, 2005) models of synaptic dysfunction echo this conjecture about synaptic slippage. (In this context, it is important to note that many aspects of Meehl's model remain persuasive even in light of data indicating that multiple genes probably contribute to schizophrenia liability, or schizotypy [see Sullivan, Daly, & O'Donovan, 2012]).

Thus, according to the model, schizotaxia is the "genetically determined integrative defect, predisposing to schizophrenia and a sine qua non for that disorder" (Meehl, 1990, p. 35), and is conjectured to have a general population base rate of 10% (see Meehl, 1990, for derivation). Note that schizotaxia essentially describes an aberration in brain functioning characterized by pervasive neuronal slippage in the CNS; it is not a behavior or observable personality pattern. The schizotaxic brain, however, becomes the foundation that other factors will build upon, and interact aversively with, to possibly produce clinically diagnosable schizophrenia. The other factors that interact with the schizotaxic brain and influence individual development (as well as clinical status) are the social learning history of an individual as well as other genetic factors, termed "polygenic potentiators."

Meehl (1962, 1990, 2001) generally held that all (or nearly all) schizotaxic individuals develop schizotypy (i.e., a schizotypal personality organization) on essentially all existing social reinforcement schedules. Schizotypy, therefore, refers to the psychological and personality organization resulting from the schizotaxic individual interacting with and developing within the world of social learning influences. An individual who displays schizotypy is considered a schizotype. (Note that Meehl's "schizotypal personality organization" is not the same as the *DSM* personality disorder SPD.) Meehl (1990) considered the possibility that a schizotaxic individual might not develop schizotypy if reared in a sufficiently healthful environment, but he viewed this outcome as unlikely. In short, there are multiple possible observable or measureable manifestations of schizotypy, where schizotypy is the latent construct and the observables are thought of as indicators (e.g., schizophrenia, schizotypic pathology, laboratory measures) (see Figure 28.2).

The second major set of factors influencing the development of clinical schizophrenia in the schizotypic individual is a class of genetically determined factors (or dimensions) termed "polygenic potentiators." According to Meehl (1990), "a potentiator is any genetic factor which, given the presence of the schizogene *and therefore of the schizotypal personality organization* (italics in original), raises the probability of clinical decompensation" (p. 39). Potentiators include personality dimensions independent of schizotaxia, such as social introversion, anxiety proneness, aggressivity, and hypohedonia. Such potentiators do not modify (in the technical genetic sense of the term) the expression of the putative schizogene but rather interact with the established schizotypic personality organization and the social environment to facilitate (or, in some cases, "depotentiate") the development of decompensated schizotypy, namely schizophrenia. Meehl (1990) stated, "It's not as if the polygenes for introversion somehow 'get into the causal chain' between the schizogene in DNA and the parameters of social reinforcement" (p. 38), rather the potentiators push the schizotype toward psychosis. In this context it is interesting to note that Meehl's model encompasses the idea of a

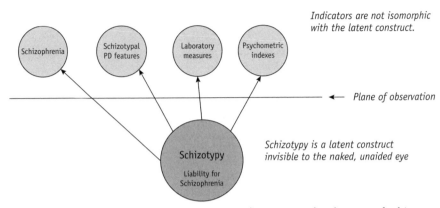

Figure 28.2 Relationship between the latent construct schizotypy and indicators of schizotypy, such as clinical, psychometric, and laboratory measures. One should not speak of observed indicators of the latent construct as schizotypy; for example, schizotypal personality disorder features should be described as a schizotypy indicator. See Cronbach and Meehl (1955) and McCorquodale and Meehl (1948) for extended discussion of these points. Copyright © 2010 by Mark F. Lenzenweger. Used with permission of the author.

"mixed" model of genetic influence, namely a single major gene (i.e., an autosomal diallelic locus) operating against a background due to an additive polygenic (or cultural) component (Morton & MacLean, 1974). Thus, reviewing briefly, according to Meehl (1962, 1990), the development of clinically diagnosable schizophrenia is the result of a complex interaction among several crucial factors: (1) a schizotaxic brain characterized by genetically determined hypokrisia at the synapse, (2) environmentally mediated social learning experiences (that bring about a schizotypal personality organization), and (3) the polygenic potentiators.

Although the modal schizotype does not decompensate into diagnosable schizophrenia, Meehl suggested that the latent diathesis is detectable through aberrant psychological and social functioning. This fundamental assumption has served as an organizing concept for decades of research on schizotypic psychopathology and schizophrenia (see Lenzenweger, 2010). Meehl (1962) described four fundamental signs and symptoms of schizotypy: cognitive slippage (or mild associative loosening), interpersonal aversiveness (social fear), anhedonia (pleasure capacity deficit), and ambivalence. Later, in 1964, he developed a clinical checklist for schizotypic signs that included rich clinical descriptions of not only these four signs or symptoms but also several

others that he suggested were valid schizotypy indicators. Basically, all aspects of the core clinical phenomenology and psychological functioning seen in the schizotype were hypothesized to derive fundamentally from aberrant CNS functioning (i.e., hypokrisia) as determined by the schizogene. For example, "primary cognitive slippage" gives rise to observable secondary cognitive slippage in thought, speech, affective integration, and behavior. He saw hypokrisia as the root cause of "soft" neurological signs as well as what he termed "soft" psychometric signs that could be detected among schizotypes. Finally, Meehl argued that hypokrisia also led to what he termed "primary aversive drift" or the steady developmental progression toward negative affective tone in personality functioning across the life span among schizotypes (see Meehl, 1990, Figure 1 in original, p. 27 in original). This primary aversive drift across the life span, according to Meehl, gave rise to social fear, ambivalence, and hypohedonia (Meehl, 2001). Figure 28.3 contains a depiction, inspired in large part by Meehl's thinking, of the relations between schizotaxia, schizotypy, schizophrenia, and related outcomes, including endophenotypes.

It is worth noting that the role anhedonia has played in Meehl's model has changed over the years. In the 1962 model, anhedonia was hypothesized to represent a fundamental and etiologically

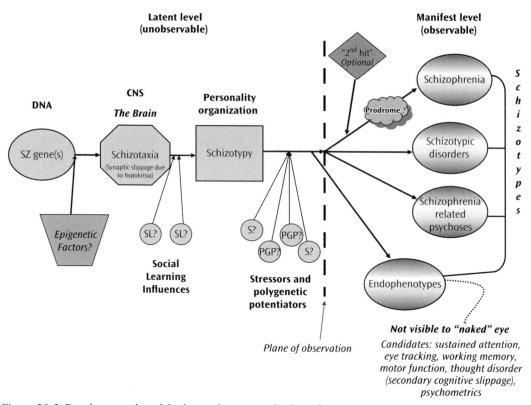

Figure 28.3 Developmental model relating the genetic diathesis for schizophrenia, schizotaxia, and schizotypy and implied levels of analysis (adapted from Meehl 1962, 1990), with modifications. Those factors to the left of the vertical broken line (i.e., plane of observation) are latent and therefore unobservable with the unaided naked eye, whereas those factors to the right of the plane of observation are manifest (or observable). A DNA-based (i.e., genetic) liability creates impaired CNS-based neural circuitry (schizotaxia) that eventuates in a personality organization (schizotypy) that harbors the liability for schizophrenia. Social learning schedules interact with schizotaxia to yield schizotypy. Psychosocial stressors and polygenic potentiators interact with schizotypy to yield manifest outcomes across a range of clinical compensation. Various possible manifest developmental outcomes are schizophrenia (assuming a "second hit," e.g., in utero exposure to maternal influenza), schizotypic psychopathology (e.g., schizotypal and/or paranoid personality disorders), or schizophrenia-related psychoses (e.g., delusional disorder). So-called prodromal features (withdrawal, reduced ideational richness, disorganized communication) may precede the onset of some (but *not* all) cases of schizophrenia. Endophenotypes (e.g., sustained attention deficits, eye-tracking dysfunction, working memory impairments, and/or psychometric deviance [PAS]; see Gottesman & Gould, 2003), which are invisible to the unaided, naked eye (but detectable with appropriate technologies), are found below the plane of observation. Epigenetic factors refer to nonmutational phenomena, such as DNA methylation and histone acetylation (modification), that alter the expression of the schizophrenia gene (or genes). Finally, all individuals represented across this range of manifest outcomes are considered schizotypes, which does not necessarily imply an *ICD* or *DSM* diagnosis. Copyright © 2010 Mark F. Lenzenweger. Used with permission of the author.

important factor in the development of schizotypy, actually falling somewhat "between" the genetic defect hypokrisia and the other schizotypic signs and symptoms of interpersonal aversiveness, cognitive slippage, and ambivalence. As of 1990, Meehl deemphasized anhedonia (then termed "hypohedonia"; but see also Meehl, 1964) as a fundamental etiological factor in the development of schizotypy and schizophrenia (see also Meehl, 1987). In the 1990 revision, Meehl strongly suggested that associative loosening and aversive drift are those psychological processes (deriving from hypokrisia) that genuinely determine the behavioral and psychological characteristics of the schizotype (see Meehl, 1990, p. 28). Hypohedonia was now viewed as playing an etiological role in the development of schizotypy by functioning as a dimensional polygenic potentiator (i.e., not deriving from the core genetically determined schizophrenia diathesis). The reconfiguration of hypohedonia's role in the 1990 model was major and was discussed further in Meehl (1993, 2001). In short, Meehl (1975, 1987, 1990) proposed that all persons displayed some level of hedonic capacity, which was conceived of as a normal-range, dimensional, individual differences construct, and it functioned as the potentiator noted previously. However, Meehl (2001) made it clear that a pathological variant of hypohedonia, determined perhaps by a genetic defect and similar to that proposed by Rado, could also exist in some people. However, the etiological basis of such a hedonic defect may or may not be directly attributable to a "schizogene." He did not see these two possibilities—a normal-range quantitative system and an anhedonic taxon or class—as mutually exclusive. Meehl (2001) discussed the challenges posed to interpretation of results from latent structure analyses of phenotypic indicators of hedonic capacity with reference to his model of schizotypy and the possible etiology of deviations in hedonic capacity. Meehl viewed this specific terrain (i.e., hedonic capacity) as ripe for continued exploration and saw it as consisting of open questions with respect to schizotypy (e.g., Strauss & Gold, 2012). Recent taxometric evidence focused on the hypohedonia and the distinction between hedonic capacity and experience and social withdrawal raises new doubts regarding the meaning of hypohedonia as a core process in schizotypy (Linscott, 2007).

A central, and perhaps the most important, assumption in Meehl's model is that schizotypy, as a personality organization reflective of a latent liability for schizophrenia, can manifest itself behaviorally and psychologically in various degrees of clinical compensation. Thus, following Rado (1960), Meehl (1962, 1990) argued that the schizotype may be highly compensated (showing minimal signs and symptoms of schizotypic functioning), or it may reveal transient failures in compensation, or it may be diagnosably schizophrenic. Schizotypes, therefore, can range clinically from apparent normality through to psychosis, yet all share the schizogene and resultant schizotypic personality organization.

A crucial implication of this assumption is that not all schizotypes develop diagnosable schizophrenia (i.e., one could genuinely be at risk yet never develop a psychotic illness); however, all schizotypes will display some evidence of their underlying liability in the form of aberrant psychobiological and/or psychological functioning. As noted, this particular implication of the model has guided nearly 45 years of research directed at developing methods for the valid and efficient detection of schizotypy endophenotypes (Gottesman & Gould, 2003; Lenzenweger, 1999c, 2013). Through clinical, psychometric, or other means the model has articulated the heart of the "diathesis-stressor" model or approach for psychopathology (Lenzenweger, 2010). In short, if valid schizotypy detection strategies could be developed, samples of "high-risk" individuals (i.e., schizotypes) could be assembled and examined in various efforts to better illuminate the nature and development of both schizophrenia and related schizotypic conditions.

Frequent Misunderstandings of Meehl's Model   In discussing Meehl's model of schizotypy, it is important to point out several misconceptions of the model and various misunderstandings (see Lenzenweger, 2010, for extensive details). There are five primary areas of misunderstanding:

(1) Meehl's schizotypy construct is *not* the same as *DSM*-defined SPD. Schizotypy is a latent construct, whereas SPD is an observable phenomenological entity (Figure 28.2).

(2) Schizotypy, as a latent construct, is *not* entirely genetic in origin. It reflects input from both genes (determining "schizotaxia") and environmental factors (e.g., social learning history) (Figure 28.3).

(3) The terms *schizotype* and *schizotypy* are not reserved only for those cases identified by *DSM*-defined SPD features. Thus, it makes no conceptual sense to reserve the term *schizotypy* for *interview-based* assessments of schizotypic features, whereas the term *psychometric schizotypy* is used for assessements of schizotypic features using psychometric methods. We do not speak of "structured interview depression" versus "psychometric depression" and we should not do so in schizotypy research.

(4) Not all schizotypes are expected to develop schizophrenia. Some schizotypes will develop (or convert to) schizophrenia,

some will show some continued nonpsychotic evidence of schizotypic features across the life span, and some schizotypes will remain quietly schizotypic (perhaps displaying evidence of their underlying personality organization on endophenotypic measures (Gottesman & Gould, 2003; Lenzenweger, 2013a, 2013b).

(5) Some observers (mis)believe that Meehl's entire developmental model hinges on the presence of a single, schizophrenia-specific gene (a "schizogene"). However, this is incorrect. Meehl did speculate on the possibility of a "schizogene" in his formulations and used it as starting point. However, the cascade of processes and outcomes in the model is entirely compatible with *multiple* genes contributing to the underlying schizotaxic pathology, which then plays itself out developmentally as noted in Figure 28.3.

What Determines Conversion to Schizophrenia from Nonpsychotic Schizotypy in Meehl's Model? There is increasing interest in determining what is termed the "conversion rate" for psychosis among those persons deemed to be in the "prodromal" stages of schizophrenia (with many prodromal cases appearing schizotypic in terms of phenomenology; Fusar-Poli et al., 2013). On a related note, Siever and Davis (2004) have speculated that the schizotypic individual who does not develop schizophrenia may have reduced striatal dopaminergic activity and increased frontal capacity, assets that spare him or her from the emergence of schizophrenia. However, recent evidence shows relations between genetic polymorphisms known be associated with both dopaminergic functioning and schizophrenia to also be associated with schizotypic features (Grant et al., 2013).

What is the precise recipe of polygenic potentiators, life stressors, and random events in interaction with the schizotaxic brain that might lead one to move from being a compensated schizotype to clinical schizophrenia? Simply stated, the answer is not known. Meehl articulated the rich matrix of components and developmental processes that he believed could eventually yield schizophrenia in some instances, but he was not able to identify those specific factors (genetic or otherwise) that propel one to transition from the nonpsychotic schizotype to clear-cut schizophrenia (i.e., psychosis). Clearly Meehl (1962, 1990) viewed the polygenic potentiators noted earlier as playing an important role in this

developmental process; however, he also stressed the importance of what he termed "unknown critical events" as well as the "random walk" (i.e., life histories may reflect divergent causality, rather than the impact solely of well-known systematic factors such as social class or birth order) in the determination of schizophrenia (Meehl, 1978; cf. Meehl, 1971, 1972). In this context it is worth noting that although Meehl saw the polygenic potentiators as important, he argued that the polygenic potentiators "do not *in the least* 'modify' the schizogene's *endo*phenotypic expression as schizotaxia, a CNS parametric aberration" [italics in original] (Meehl, 1972, p. 380), rather they simply alter the probability that a schizotype might move on to clinical schizophrenia. The precise manner whereby a schizotype moves on to schizophrenia, in those instances where it happens, remains an open issue and is ripe for life span developmental studies of schizotypy. Such research should also seek to understand those factors—polygenic potentiator or otherwise—that might buffer a schizotype from transitioning to schizophrenia.

Although various efforts have been made to expand upon and refine Meehl's basic framework (e.g., see examples in Lenzenweger & Dworkin, 1998), the core assumptions of contemporary liability models do not differ substantially from what he proposed in 1962. Contemporary neurocognitive (Andreasen, 1999), neuroscientific (e.g., Grace & Moore, 1998; Owen, O'Donovan, & Harrison, 2005; Phillips & Silverstein, 2003), and neurodevelopmental (Marenco & Weinberger, 2000; McGlashan & Hoffman, 2000; Weinberger, 1987) models for schizophrenia, albeit not wed to hypothetical processes such as hypokrisia, are nevertheless quite consistent with many of the major tenets of Meehl's framework for schizotypic psychopathology and schizophrenia proper. In short, nearly all major models of the underlying pathological processes in schizophrenia emphasize a neurobiologically driven dysregulation in neural transmission that impairs information processing and may lead to symptom formation, substantive views that echo Meehl's early conjectures (cf. Meehl, 1962).

The Claridge View of Schizotypy: A Necessary Scientific Excursus

As reviewed in Lenzenweger (2010), no discussion of contemporary views of schizotypic psychopathology and the schizotypy construct would be complete without an examination of the views of Gordon Claridge, a psychologist at Oxford University (England) (Claridge, 1997). The most distinctive features of his approach to schizotypy concern his propositions regarding (a) the putative existence of "healthy" manifestations of schizotypy, (b) schizotypy as part of normal personality, and (c) the proposal that the schizotypy construct has a dimensional (quantitative) structure at the latent level.

Unlike the views of Meehl (1962, 1990) or those advocated here and elsewhere (Lenzenweger, 1998, 2010), Claridge sees schizotypy as a *personality* trait varying by degree along a continuum. In adhering to the *methodological* view of his mentor, the British personality psychologist Hans J. Eysenck, as well as guided in part by the original content of the Eysenck's conceptualization of "psychoticism" as a personality trait, Claridge places his conceptualization of schizotypy squarely within the traditional dimensional view of normal personality. Indeed, Claridge's ideas regarding schizotypy have been introduced by his collaborators as consistent with those "writers who conceptualise the spectrum of schizophrenia-related characteristics as a continuous dimension, akin to other dimensions of personality," which represents a view "championed by writers such as Eysenck (Eysenck & Eysenck, 1976) (Rawlings, Williams, Haslam, & Claridge, 2008, p. 1641)." This view raises two questions: (1) Is schizotypy best thought of as a component of *normal personality*? (2) Does the available evidence support a dimensional view of schizotypy?

Schizotypy as Normal and "Healthy" Psychosis Is schizotypy best thought of as a component of normal personality? Unpacking this further, is schizotypy *normal*? Is schizotypy part of *personality*? These issues boil down to whether one views schizotypy as (a) the liability for schizophrenia (e.g., Meehl, Lenzenweger) or (b) a trait characterized by certain cognitive features and psychotic-like phenomena that are part of the general system of personality (Claridge, Bentall, Mason). As summarized recently by Rawlings et al. (2008), "Claridge and his colleagues have investigated schizotypy from many points of view. They have concluded that *psychotic traits constitute an essentially healthy dimension of personality*, which in adaptive form contributes to psychological variations as creativity, non-threatening hallucinations, and rewarding spiritual and mystical beliefs and experiences" (p. 1670, italics added).

As pursued elsewhere (Lenzenweger, 2010), one must ask, "What does it mean to argue that 'psychotic traits constitute an essentially healthy dimension of personality'?" In light of the observations of Kraepelin, Bleuler, Rado, Meehl, and many others, one must consider critically the views on schizotypy held by Claridge, particularly as regards the term *psychosis*. What does it mean to designate an individual or behavior "psychotic"? In traditional psychiatric usage, psychotic as a descriptive term has typically one of three potential meanings: (1) the *impairment of reality testing* as indicated by the presence of particular psychopathology signs and/or symptoms (hallucinations, delusions, thought disorder); (2) the *depth or severity* of an impairment (e.g., a psychotic depression, meaning a very deep or profound case of depression), and/or less frequently (3) a *degree of regression*, within a psychodynamic framework, to a developmentally primitive stage of psychological organization wherein thought and experience are characterized by *primary process* (i.e., not secondary process). In light of how the term *psychotic* is used, can we conceive of "psychotic traits" as being consistent with a "healthy dimensional of personality?" (Resorting to the locution "psychotic-like" does not get one out of this conceptual conundrum if one is serious about the notion that psychotic traits are representative of a healthy dimension of personality.) To do so, one must really confront the implication of this statement and consider the notion of "healthy psychosis." One impression of the implicit argument posed by this juxtaposition of terms is that it lacks an appreciation for the clinical and research basis supporting the notion of schizotypy as *schizophrenia liability*. In short, those who see patients in intensive diagnostic or therapeutic capacities may find an eerie unfamiliarity in a concept such as "healthy psychotic" traits. Can one realistically speak of "healthy" schizophrenia or schizophrenia as a healthy dimension of personality? Thus, from the standpoint of clinical relevance, Claridge's theoretical position seems distinctly ungrounded in the clinical realities of schizotypic pathology. Moreover, from the research standpoint, the literature by and large does *not* support a view of schizophrenia (the illness) as reflective of an extension of normal personality. Rather, schizophrenia reflects a complex *pathological* disease process, not a deviation in a normal personality process or dimension.

Schizotypy as a Fully Dimensional, Quantitative Construct   The second issue central to Claridge's view of schizotypy concerns the basic nature of the construct's (latent) structure. Is it quantitative in nature *at both the phenotypic level and the latent level*? This issue received considerable discussion during the 1993 NATO workshop on schizotypy (see Raine et al., 1995). At that time, although Claridge maintained a strong commitment to a dimensional view, there were *no* empirical data available to support a view that the schizotypy construct was quantitatively distributed—varying by degree (not kind)—at the latent level. All empirical evidence marshaled by Claridge and colleagues in support of the dimensional latent structure of schizotypy came from analytic techniques (i.e., factor analysis) that could *not* determine whether a latent entity was quantitatively (dimensionally) or qualitatively (taxonically) structured at a deeper level. *One can surely measure a psychopathological feature, symptom, or character in a quantitative manner, but that, in and of itself, does not ensure or mean that the construct measured is dimensional at the latent level.* For example, one could construct a quantitative measure of "maleness/femaleness" and acquire dimensional values on the "maleness/femaleness scale." However, the continuous variation in the scores on this scale would not mean that biological sex has a continuous (quantitative, "difference by degree") nature at the latent level.

The current empirical picture regarding the latent structure of schizotypy is one of *discontinuity*, which is either representative of a latent taxon (class, natural subgroup) or severe step-function (threshold) in the structure of the schizotypy construct. As discussed later in this chapter, there is an abundance of evidence drawing on taxometric and finite mixture modeling studies that are supportive of the discontinuous underlying nature of schizotypy. The corpus of evidence drawn from empirical data is *inconsistent* with a fully dimensional view of schizotypy such as that argued for by Claridge. Although Mason and Claridge (2006) state, "Suffice it to say that the evidence is strongly weighted in favour of the fully dimensional model" of schizotypy (p. 205), this is statement is simply incorrect. The bulk of the evidence that Claridge and colleagues interpret as supportive of

the dimensionality of schizotypy comes from (a) a methodological position committed to dimensionality *ala* Eysenck; (b) visual examination of the distributions of phenotypic psychometric values (recall that distributions of scores cannot resolve the latent structure question); (c) results of factor analyses of psychometric values (remember, factor analysis is a technique that always finds factors by organizing larger numbers of variables into a smaller number of large "factors"); and (d) a single taxometric investigation. Aside from evidence drawn from the one taxometric study (Rawlings et al., 2008), which suffered from marked methodological artifacts (Beauchaine, Lenzenweger, & Waller, 2008), the empirical picture painted overwhelmingly by results from latent structure analyses (taxometric, finite mixture modeling, latent class analysis) supports the existence of a discrete class of individuals harbored within large samples of persons who have completed schizotypy measures.

Eysenck, despite his preference for dimensional models and continuous measurement, stated that he "would not wish to dismiss the possibility or even the likelihood that in any random group of clinically diagnosed neurotics there would be found a small number of people who might 'constitute a group apart, different not in degree, but in kind, by reason of some specified biochemical error, which is highly predictable in terms of inheritance, and which operates in a manner quite different from anything observed' in the kinship relations of the remainder of that group" (Eysenck, 1958, p. 431). This view of Eyesenck is actually quite commensurate with what is known about schizotypy from modern empirical studies of latent structure.

Claridge's View of Meehl's Model as "Quasi-Dimensional"?   In this context one should also evaluate Claridge's view of Meehl's (1990) model of schizotypy as "quasi-dimensional," whereas he refers to his own model as "fully dimensional" as discussed above (Claridge, 1997). What is meant by the term *quasi-dimensional*? If one takes the word *quasi* to mean "having a likeness to, having some resemblance to," we would say *quasi-dimensional* would logically mean "having a likeness to or resembling a dimension." One would be hard pressed to find an indication in Meehl's writing that schizotaxia (or, by definition, schizotypy) is in any manner dimensional, quasi or otherwise. The term *quasi-dimensional* as a descriptor is really merely another way of saying "continuous latent liability with a threshold"—this *not* what Meehl proposed.

Meehl (1962, 1990) himself was quite clear as to the latent structure of schizotypy as reviewed earlier—he saw schizotypy as having a taxonic (qualitative) latent structure. As noted, he did speak of "polygenic potentiators," which could have a dimensional nature; however, schizotypy, according to his model, was taxonic. It may be the Claridge intended the notion of a "quasi-continuous" model of genetic influences, akin to a polygenic model with a distinct *threshold* effect, when describing Meehl's model as "quasi-dimensional." In fact, behavior geneticists distinguish between a polygenic model with continuous variation in a phenotype (e.g., height, IQ) and one where there is some form of discernible demarcation in the phenotype (e.g., cleft palate, diabetes) (see Falconer, 1989). However, Meehl's model does *not* encompass the polygenic perspective (without threshholds) that embraces fully continuous variation or quasi-continuous variation. His model, rather, represents a "mixed model," whereby a single major schizophrenia-relevant gene operates against a background of polygenic modifier effects (his so-called potentiators). To review, Meehl was clear on this issue—although not fully understood by some—in advocating for a *taxonic* view of schizotypy. In Meehl's view there is *no* gradation or quantitative variation insofar as schizotypy is concerned: *one is either a schizotype or not, there is no in-between place.* Claridge (1997), in contrast, advocates a fully dimensional view with continuous variation at the phenotypic level; his model is most consistent with a polygenic model (without a threshold) that reflects a continuous additive model of genetic influences.

Parting Thoughts on Claridge's Model of Schizotypy
In summary, Claridge has emphasized that his view of schizotypy differs from the construct of a broadly similar nature proposed by Eysenck, namely "psychoticism," which was an amalgam of aggression and impulsivity. (Psychoticism, incidentally, is a construct that has remarkably little to do with psychosis [see Chapman, 1994].) However, it may be that Claridge has actually been advocating a meaning of the term *psychotic* that is far more similar to that of Eysenck than Claridge himself maintains. The notion of "healthy psychosis" simply does not logically accord well with both clinical experience and the research literature on schizophrenia considered as a psychotic illness. Finally, the taxometric and finite mixture modeling results available across many studies support a taxonic view of schizotypy, in contrast to one study favoring a fully dimensional Claridgian conceptualization (see Beauchaine et al., 2008).

Classification and Diagnostic Technology

Assessment of Schizotypy and Schizotypal Phenomena

This section focuses on the assessment of schizotypy and schizotypic phenomena with a brief review of clinical interviews and psychometric inventories that have been developed for either clinical or research work. An evaluation of many psychometric measures conjectured to be putative schizotypy indicators developed before 1980 is available in Grove (1982); data bearing on psychometric measures through the early 1990s can be found in J. Chapman, Chapman, and Kwapil (1995). Not all of the assessment devices discussed here have been designed with Meehl's (1964) early effort in mind, though most have been influenced by his work. Some emerged from the increased interest in personality pathology that followed the introduction of *DSM-III* in 1980. All of the measures discussed here have been shown to have strong reliability and a reasonable degree of validity.

Clinical Interviews and Checklists for Schizotypic Psychopathology

Four interview-based procedures have been developed specifically to assess schizotypic phenomena. A competent extended review of interviews available for the assessment of schizotypy through the early 1990s can be found in Benishay and Lencz (1995); more recent reviews of interview methods have not been done in this area. In this context it should be noted that the following assessment devices are tailored specifically for the schizotypic psychopathology. One could, of course, use the relevant diagnostic modules for SPD and/or PPD from an established Axis II structured interview (e.g., International Personality Disorder Examination [IPDE]; Loranger, 1999) as an alternative to the specialized instruments.

Meehl's Checklist for Schizotypic Signs

Meehl's (1964) Checklist for Schizotypic signs is a treasure trove of clinical observation and phenomenological description for schizotypic psychopathology. The Checklist and the *Manual for Use with the Checklist for Schizotypic Signs* can be downloaded from Meehl's website (http://www.tc.umn.edu/~pemeehl/pubs.htm). Consisting of 25 clinical features that Meehl argued were of diagnostic importance to the recognition and diagnosis of schizotypic features, it represents the first genuine attempt to bring a structured diagnostic approach to the assessment and classification of schizotypic phenomenology. Although rarely used in actual research practice, the Checklist is worthy of careful study.

Symptom Schedule for the Diagnosis of Borderline Schizophrenia (SSDBS)

The Symptom Schedule for the Diagnosis of Borderline Schizophrenia (SSDBS) was developed by Khouri, Haier, Rieder, and Rosenthal (1980) to assess the symptoms of "borderline schizophrenia" as defined by Kety et al. (1968). The schedule was administered in an interview format, with eight symptoms rated on a three-point scale, including perceptual changes, body image aberrations, feelings of unreality, thought disturbances, ideas of reference, ideas of persecution, self-inflicted injuries, and preoccupation with perverse sexuality or violence. Interrater reliability for total scores was .83. Total scores of 2 or above appeared to accurately identify those individuals originally diagnosed "borderline schizophrenia" in the Danish Adoption Study sample (Khouri et al., 1980). The diagnostic criteria for "borderline schizophrenia" assessed by the SSDBS were influenced by the clinical tradition (cf. Kendler, 1985). The SSDBS has seen little use in the research literature in the last 20 years.

Schedule for Schizotypal Personalities (SSP)

Developed by Baron and associates (Baron, Asnis, & Gruen, 1981), the Schedule for Schizotypal Personalities (SSP) was designed to assess the diagnostic criteria for *DSM-III* SPD. The SSP assesses illusions, depersonalization/derealization, ideas of reference, suspiciousness, magical thinking, inadequate rapport, odd communication, social isolation, and social anxiety. The SSP also assesses delusions and hallucinations. Baron et al. (1981) reported generally excellent interrater and test–retest reliabilities for the SSP scales. The kappa coefficient for the diagnosis of SPD using the SSP was .88.

Structured Interview for Schizotypy (SIS)

Kendler and colleagues (Kendler, Lieberman, & Walsh, 1989) developed the Structured Interview for Schizotypy (SIS) to assess schizotypal signs and symptoms. The SIS consists of 19 sections, 18 to assess individual symptom dimensions and 1 to assess 36 separate schizotypal signs (Kendler et al., 1989). For example, the SIS includes social isolation, interpersonal sensitivity, social anxiety, ideas of reference, suspiciousness, and other schizotypal features. The SIS is intended to be given in conjunction with an Axis I assessment device. The interrater reliabilities associated with various aspects of the SIS are generally acceptable, with intraclass correlation coefficients typically above .70. Data based on the study of nonpsychotic relatives of patients with schizophrenia supported the criterion validity of the SIS as a measure of schizotypy (see Kendler et al., 1989). Additionally, results from the Roscommon Family Study of Schizophrenia (Kendler et al., 1993) provided additional validation of the SIS. Unlike the SSP, the SIS assesses a broader range of schizotypic signs, going considerably beyond *DSM* schizotypal personality disorder, including some aspects of Meehl's construct of schizotypy. The SIS is clearly one of the most heavily used interview methodologies for the assessment of schizotypic features, probably representing the specialized interview of choice for research work today.

Self-Report Psychometric Inventories for Schizotypy Detection

Chapman "Psychosis Proneness" Scales

Guided by Meehl's model of schizotypy and his rich clinical descriptions of schizotypic signs (Meehl, 1964) and in close accordance with construct validity principles (Cronbach & Meehl, 1955), L. J. Chapman and J. P. Chapman (1985, 1987) developed several objective self-report measures to assess traits reflective of a putative liability to psychosis, perhaps schizophrenia. For reviews of the early literature on these measures see J. P. Chapman,

Chapman, and Kwapil (1995) and Edell (1995). The corpus of research literature using these scales is immense and has not been reviewed recently; however, such a review is beyond the scope of this chapter.

Two of these scales, the Perceptual Aberration Scale (PAS; L. J. Chapman, Chapman, & Raulin, 1978) and the Magical Ideation Scale (MIS; Eckblad & Chapman, 1983), have been used extensively in recent research to detect schizotypy and assemble samples of respondents presumed to be at increased risk for psychosis from nonclinical populations. All of the Chapmans' psychosis proneness scales have been carefully constructed from the psychometric standpoint to minimize correlations with social desirability and acquiescence factors, while ensuring internal consistency, content validity, and construct validity (Cronbach & Meehl, 1955). The PAS is a 35-item true-false measure of disturbances and distortions in perceptions of the body as well as other objects. Internal consistency analyses of the PAS typically reveal coefficient alphas of around .90 with short-term test–retest stability of .75 (L. J. Chapman & Chapman, 1985). Regarding the MIS, L. J. Chapman and Chapman (1985) defined magical ideation as a "belief in forms of *causation* that, by conventional standards of our society, are not valid but magical" (p. 164, italics added). Coefficient alphas for the MIS run typically between .80 and .85. The PAS and MIS tend to be highly correlated (*r* at .68 to .70). As a result, both measures are often used in conjunction to select schizotypic patients from nonclinical populations. The PAS and MIS have been used extensively in schizotypy research and are associated with an impressive body of empirical literature supportive of their validity.

A third scale developed by the Chapmans, the Revised Social Anhedonia Scale (RSAS) (Mishlove & Chapman, 1985), has also been used with greater frequency because deviance on the scale was linked to later psychosis in the presence of elevated PAS/MIS scores (L. J. Chapman, Chapman, Kwapil, Eckblad, & Zinser, 1994). The extent to which the RSAS assesses "anhedonia" versus "social withdrawal" has become a focus of recent substantive discussion and empirical investigation (Linscott, 2007). Finally, abbreviated versions of the original Chapman scales (sometimes referred to as "Wisconsin Scales") have been published for research use (Winterstein et al., 2011).

Schizotypal Personality Questionnaire (SPQ)

The Schizotypal Personality Questionnaire (SPQ; Raine, 1991) is a 74-item true-false self-report questionnaire that assesses the features consistent with the symptoms for schizotypal personality disorder as defined by the *DSM-III-R*. The SPQ has excellent psychometric properties (Raine, 1991). The SPQ can also generate three general factors that correspond conceptually to the reality distortion, disorganization, and negative symptom components that are well known in the schizophrenia research literature (Lenzenweger & Dworkin, 1996). The SPQ has become one of the most heavily used psychometric assessment methods in the schizotypy/schizotypal personality research area and a revised short form was published in 2010 (Cohen, Matthews, Najolia, & Brown, 2010).

Other Psychometric Measures of Schizotypy

Several additional psychometric measures of schizotypy have been developed recently and should be mentioned. Unlike the PAS and MIS, these other measures have not yet been shown to be associated with a liability for schizophrenia (i.e., schizotypy) through systematic family, twin, or adoption studies; however, available validity data suggest that all are promising as schizotypy indicators. These measures include the Rust Inventory of Schizotypal Cognitions (RISC; Rust, 1988a, 1988b), the Referential Thinking Scale (Lenzenweger, Bennett, & Lilenfeld, 1997), the Social Fear Scale (Raulin & Wee, 1984), the Schizotypal Ambivalence Scale (Kwapil, Mann, & Raulin, 2002; Vaughn, Barrantes-Vidal, Raulin, & Kwapil, 2008), the Schizotypal Personality Scale (STA; Claridge & Broks, 1984) and its close cousin, the Oxford-Liverpool Inventory of Feelings and Experiences (O-LIFE, Mason, Claridge, & Jackson, 1995; see also Claridge, 1997; Grant et al., 2013), the Schizophrenism Scale (Venables, 1990), and the schizoid, schizotypal, and paranoid personality disorder scales derived from the Minnesota Multiphasic Personality Inventory (MMPI) (Morey, Waugh, & Blashfield, 1985). Finally, Harkness, McNulty, and Ben-Porath (1995) have developed a five-scale dimensional system (the Personality Pathology Five [PSY-5]), derived from MMPI-2 items, that can be used to describe personality and its disorders; one of the PSY-5 scales assesses psychoticism, a higher order construct of general relevance to schizotypy. Of these scales, Lenzenweger et al.'s Referential Thinking Scale, Kwapil et al.'s Schizotypal Ambivalence Scale, and Raulin and Wee's Social Fear Scale were designed specifically to assess aspects of Meehl's schizotypy construct.

Finally, a potentially promising new psychometric approach to the detection of schizophrenia liability (i.e., schizotypy) can be found in the Schizophrenia Proneness Scale (Bolinskey, Gottesman, & Nichols, 2003).

Etiology, Development, and Pathogenesis

There have been two major research thrusts in the area of schizotypic psychopathology research. First, many investigators have examined the correlates of schizotypic psychopathology, through the study of either clinically defined SPD and/or PPD, psychometrically defined schizotypic persons, or first-degree biological relatives of patients with schizophrenia. The second thrust, which is really more of a theme through much of the research in this area, has been directed at illuminating the relationship between schizotypic psychopathology and schizophrenia per se, as well as development of a latent liability construct.

Given that the theme of relating schizotypic pathology to schizophrenia is so prominent in this area and that one of the guiding assumptions in this work concerns the theoretical notion of latent liability, it seems appropriate to begin with a review of the need for such a construct. Following this discussion, empirical research related to schizotypic psychopathology is discussed from the vantage points of (1) family history, (2) laboratory findings, (3) clinical phenomenology, and (4) follow-up studies. This section is followed by a discussion of the delimitation of schizotypic psychopathology from other disorders at the latent (i.e., unobservable with the naked eye) level.

On the Need for a Latent Liability Construct Formulation

Much of the preceding discussion has assumed a common underlying liability for schizotypic psychopathology and schizophrenia (see 28.2 and 28.3). What is the empirical basis for such an assumption? As argued previously (Lenzenweger, 1998; Lenzenweger & Korfine, 1995), there is ample evidence in support of a latent liability

conceptualization in schizophrenia that includes schizotypic psychopathology, among other things. First, it was conjectured by Meehl (1962, 1990) and others that schizotypic psychopathology was linked, presumably via genetics (Torgersen, 1985), to schizophrenia (Kendler, 1985, Kendler et al., 1993) (see later discussion). Perhaps the most influential early evidence that helped to establish a link between schizotypic phenomenology and clinical schizophrenia came from the Danish Adoption Study of Schizophrenia (Kety et al., 1968), in which there were elevated rates of schizotypic psychopathology. These results provided compelling evidence for a genetically transmitted component underlying manifest schizophrenia and the less severe schizophrenia-like disorders. The hypothesized continuity between the conditions was thus not merely phenomenological but also genetic. Moreover, confirming the early Kety et al. findings, numerous family studies have found an excess of schizotypic disorders in the biological relatives of individuals with schizophrenia (see Kendler et al., 1993). As noted, genomic work (Avramopoulos et al., 2002; Fanous et al., 2007; Grant et al., 2013; Lin et al., 2005; Siever et al., 2011) has provided important confirming data linking schizotypic psychopathology indicators to genetic loci that have been implicated in schizophrenia. Clearly, the boundaries of the phenotypic expression of schizophrenia liability extend beyond manifest psychosis. Thus, liability manifestations are not isomorphic with expressed psychosis.

Second, the existence of a "clinically unexpressed" liability for schizophrenia has been confirmed (Gottesman & Bertelsen, 1989; Lenzenweger & Loranger, 1989a). Thus, liability can exist without obvious phenotypic, or symptomatic (i.e., psychotic), manifestations. Third, a well-established biobehavioral marker, namely eye-tracking dysfunction (Holzman et al., 1988; Levy, Holzman, Matthysse, & Mendell, 1993), which bears no immediately discernible phenotypic connection to overt schizophrenia, is known to be associated with a latent diathesis for the illness. Liability can thus manifest itself in an alternative phenotypic form (Lenzenweger, 1998, 2010). Finally, if the base rate of schizophrenia liability (or the schizotypy taxon) is in fact 10% as conjectured by Meehl (1990), then perhaps well over 50% of those carrying liability for schizophrenia may go clinically "undetected" across the life span (i.e., derived from the estimated combined prevalence of schizophrenia, SPD, and PPD of roughly 5%; cf. Loranger, 1990; see also Lenzenweger, Lane, et al., 2007). Taken together, theoretical and empirical considerations argue strongly for the plausibility of a complex latent liability construct in schizophrenia.

Given that most persons vulnerable to schizophrenia may never show flagrant psychosis or easily detectable signs and symptoms of schiztoypic personality functioning, researchers have sought ways to detect schizotypy using more sensitive laboratory and psychometric measures. Efforts have been made to discover valid objective indicators of schizotypy that function efficiently across a range of clinical compensation, as well as mental state, and are capable of detecting liability even in clinically unexpressed (nonsymptomatic) cases. Such indicators, psychometric and otherwise, are thought to assess an "endophenotype" (not visible to the unaided, naked eye; see Gottesman, 1991; Gottesman & Gould, 2003; Lenzenweger, 2013a, 2013b). Their inclusion in research investigations of the genetics and familiality of schizophrenia is likely to enhance those efforts, through increased power and precision, even when the putative indicators are only modestly correlated with the latent liability (Fanous & Kendler, 2005; Smith & Mendell, 1974).

Empirical Findings Relevant to Development and Pathogenesis

Family History of Schizophrenia Overall, it is now generally established that schizotypic psychopathology does indeed occur in the biological first-degree relatives of persons with schizophrenia at rates much higher than the population rate (for reviews see Kendler et al., 1993; Nigg & Goldsmith, 1994; Torgersen, 1994; Webb & Levinson, 1993). There is also evidence supportive of the familiality of schizophrenia and schizotypic psychopathology from studies that have found elevated rates of schizophrenia among the first-degree biological relatives of schizotypic patients (Battaglia, Bernardeschi, Franchini, Bellodi, & Smeraldi, 1995; Battaglia et al., 1991; Kendler & Walsh, 1995). The connection between schizotypic psychopathology and schizophrenia is now well established from the family study perspective (Chemerinski et al., 2013; Lenzenweger, 2010).

Three studies have reported a significant excess of PPD in the relatives of schizophrenia probands

(Baron et al., 1985; Kendler & Gruenberg, 1982; Kendler et al., 1993). However, PPD appears to be more prevalent in the first-degree relatives of those patients with Axis I delusional disorder, a psychotic illness (Kendler, 1985). One could argue that these data suggest a stronger link between PPD and the Axis I delusional disorder as opposed to schizophrenia, but more data would be required to resolve this issue.

From the "psychometric schizotypy" vantage point, Lenzenweger and Loranger (1989a) examined the lifetime expectancy (morbid risk) of treated schizophrenia, unipolar depression, and bipolar disorder in the biological first-degree relatives of 101 nonpsychotic psychiatric patients (probands) who were classified as either "schizotypy-positive" or "schizotypy-negative" according to the Perceptual Aberration Scale (PAS). The relatives of schizotypy-positive probands were significantly more likely to have been treated for schizophrenia than the relatives of schizotypy-negative probands; the morbid risk for treated unipolar depression or bipolar disorder among the relatives of the two proband groups did not differ. Berenbaum and McGrew (1993) also reported that PAS deviance is familial. Of related interest, Battaglia et al. (1991) found in a study of the relatives of schizotypal patients that recurrent illusions (akin to perceptual aberrations) were found in every patient with SPD with a positive family history of schizophrenia. Finally, Calkins, Curtis, Grove, and Iacono (2004) reported that the primary dimensions of psychometrically assessed schizotypal personality, particularly social-interpersonal deficits, derived from the Raine (1991) SPQ, can differentiate the first-degree relatives of patients with schizophrenia from controls.

Twin and Adoption Studies That schizophrenia, based on a long tradition of twin studies, is established as a complex genetically influenced phenotype represents a scientific statement of fact (Cardno & Gottesman, 2000; Gottesman, 1991; Sullivan, Kendler, & Neale, 2003). However, for years there had not been any extensive twin studies of clinically defined schizotypic psychopathology beyond an initial study conducted by Torgersen (1994), which supported a heritable component to SPD (subsequently confirmed in a later study by Torgersen et al., 2000). There were no known twin studies of PPD. Miller and Chapman (1993) demonstrated that the PAS has a substantial heritable component, and Kendler and Hewitt (1992) found that "positive trait schizotypy" (of which perceptual aberration, among other features, is a component) is substantially heritable. More recently, Jang, Woodward, Lang, Honer, and Livesley (2005) reported a twin study that used a psychometric dimensional assessment of schizotypic features and found all components to be subject to substantial genetic influences (i.e., heritable). Kendler, Myers, Torgersen, Neale, and Reichborn-Kjennerud (2007) reported on a twin study of dimensionalized representations of the Cluster A disorders (SPD, PPD, and schizoid personality disorder) and found evidence of heritability for all three disorders, with SPD showing the highest heritability.

In terms of adoption studies, the most relevant research comes from the Danish Adoption Study conducted by Kety and colleagues (Kety et al., 1968, 1994) and the subsequent secondary analyses of these data by Kendler and colleagues (e.g., Kendler et al., 1994). In short, whether working from the original data (Kety) or from secondary analyses (Kendler), schizotypic psychopathology is found at greater rates among the biological relatives of the adoptees with schizophrenia. These data are also consistent with the family and twin data supporting the familiality of schizotypic psychopathology and a heritable component to the pathology. There are no adoption studies of *DSM-III-R, DSM-IV, DSM-5* SPD or PPD.

Molecular Genetic Studies   The field of psychiatric genetics has clearly begun to move beyond the model-fitting research approach to assessing genetic effects in relation to schizotypy and schizophrenia. Some very exciting molecular genetic work has begun to appear, which as noted earlier provides tangible links between schizotypic psychopathology and schizophrenia. This pattern of results goes some distance in the direction of confirming the basic schizotypy model as developed by Meehl (1962, 1990). Avramopoulos et al. (2002) found that individuals who carried the high-activity catechol-O-methyltransferase (*COMT*) gene showed elevations on the PAS and SPQ. Lin et al. (2005) found that elevations in PAS scores were associated with a variant of the neuregulin-1 gene that is thought to be a susceptibility locus for schizophrenia. Fanous et al. (2007) reported the results of a genome-wide scan showing that a subset of schizophrenia susceptibility

genes are also related to schizotypy. Both Siever et al. (2011) and Grant et al. (2013) have reported findings linking SPD or deviations in schizotypy measures with genetic polymorphisms of considerable interest in schizophrenia.

This emerging body of research should prove powerfully transformative for schizotypy research in the coming decade. At the same time, despite the high heritability of schizophrenia ($h^2 = .80$ or higher), one must keep in mind that only about 14 genes have been shown to be consistently related to schizophrenic illness and they account for a tiny proportion of the likely overall genetic contribution to the illness (Sullivan et al., 2012). In short, there is much work to be done in terms of the molecular genetics of schizotypy and schizophrenia.

Laboratory Studies of Schizotypic Psychopathology

There have been a large number of laboratory studies of schizotypic psychopathology. These studies have examined either clinical schizotypes (e.g., SPD/PPD), psychometrically identified schizotypes, or the first-degree relatives of patients with schizophrenia. Only those findings related to the biobehavioral and neurocognitive processes that have received the greatest attention in the schizophrenia literature in recent years are reviewed here, namely sustained attention (Cornblatt & Keilp, 1994; Cornblatt & Malhotra, 2001), eye tracking (Levy, Holzman, Matthysse, & Mendell, 1994; Sponheim, Iacono, Thuras, Nugent, & Beiser, 2003), and various forms of executive functioning mediated by the prefrontal cortex (e.g., Gold & Harvey, 1993; Piskulic, Olver, Norman, & Maruff, 2007).

A deficit in sustained attention, a leading endophenotype for schizophrenia liability, has been found in clinically defined schizotypic individuals (e.g., SPD) (e.g., Condray & Steinhauer, 1992; Harvey et al., 1996). Similar deficits were found among psychometrically identified schizotypic individuals by Lenzenweger, Cornblatt, and Putnick (1991). Replication of the Lenzenweger et al. (1991) results, using the same measure of sustained attention, have been reported by Obiols, Garcia-Domingo, de Trincheria, and Domenech (1993) (see also Gooding, Matts, & Rollmann, 2006; Rawlings & Goldberg, 2001). Grove et al. (1991) have also reported a significant association between high PAS scores and poor sustained attention performance among the first-degree biological relatives of individuals with diagnosed schizophrenia (see also Chen et al., 1998). Finally, Cornblatt, Lenzenweger, Dworkin, and Erlenmeyer-Kimling (1992) found that attentional dysfunction that is detected in young children who are at risk for schizophrenia is correlated with schizotypic features in adulthood (assessed nearly 20 years later). There are no studies that have explicitly examined sustained attention in patients with PPD. Whereas many prior studies have examined the relationship between sustained attention deficits and schizotypy in carefully constructed samples (i.e., clinical SPD; psychometric high-risk schizotypyes), Bergida and Lenzenweger (2006) showed that schizotypic features are indeed related to deficits in sustained attention within a quasi-random, unselected population sample. The neural signature of sustained attention anomalies in relation to schizotypy has been studied by Sponheim, McGuire, and Stanwyck (2006). Clearly, sustained-attention deficit remains an endophenotype of great interest in the study of schizotypic psychopathology (Fusar-Poli et al., 2013; Snitz, MacDonald, & Carter, 2006). Moreover, careful consideration of the processes (e.g., working memory, context processing, vigilance) involved in alternative sustained tasks remains an area of open investigation (Lee & Park, 2005, 2006).

In terms of eye-tracking dysfunction (ETD) among individuals with schizotypic psychopathology, such deficits are clearly found among clinically defined schizotypes (e.g., Lencz et al., 1993; Siever et al., 1990; 1994; cf. Thaker, Cassady, Adami, & Moran, 1996) and psychometrically identified schizotypes (Gooding, Miller, & Kwapil, 2000; O'Driscoll, Lenzenweger, & Holzman, 1998; Simons & Katkin, 1985). ETD has also been found to aggregate in the biological family members of patients with schizophrenia across numerous studies (Levy et al., 1994; Sponheim et al., 2003). Finally, although most prior research on ETD was conducted on highly selected samples (which can exaggerate relations between ETD and criterial groups), Lenzenweger and O'Driscoll (2006) showed that an increased rate of catch-up saccades as well as impaired gain (poor pursuit) can be found in relatively unselected adult patients from the general population and that these deficits are indeed related to increased schizotypic features. It is important to note that, just as sustained attention and ETD do not occur

in all cases of schizophrenia, not all schizotypes evidence the dysfunctions (cf. Lenzenweger, 1998). Nonetheless, not only does the consistency in findings across patients with schizophrenia and individuals with schizotypic psychopathology inform us of the information-processing and psychophysiological deficits found in schizotypes, but these very deficits further link the schizotype to schizophrenia. To date, there are no reported studies of ETD or smooth pursuit performance specifically in patients with PPD.

Considerable attention has been focused on difficulties in abstract reasoning, executive functioning, and novel problem-solving in schizophrenia (Gold & Harvey, 1993), all processes that are hypothesized to be mediated by the prefrontal cortex. Moreover, early evidence was presented that suggested some schizophrenic symptoms might reflect a dysfunctional frontal system (e.g., Goldman-Rakic, 1991; Levin, 1984a, 1984b; Weinberger, Berman, & Zec, 1986). Much of this research employed the Wisconsin Card Sorting Test (WCST) as a measure of abstraction ability and executive functioning. Schizotypic patients, identified through either a clinical or psychometric approach, have been found to display deficits on the WCST (Gooding, Kwapil, & Tallent, 1999; Lenzenweger & Korfine, 1991, 1994; Park, Holzman, & Lenzenweger, 1995; Raine, Sheard, Reynolds, & Lencz, 1992) though not in all studies (Condray & Steinhauer, 1992). WCST findings for the biological relatives of schizophrenia-affected probands are mixed (Franke, Maier, Hardt, & Hain, 1993; Scarone, Abbruzzese, & Gambini, 1993; cf. Snitz et al., 2006). Clearly, the situation for WCST performance is somewhat inconsistent across mode of definition used in selecting patients, and the research corpus also shows some variability in the WCST performance variables on which deviance has been found (e.g., categories completed versus % perseverative errors versus failure to maintain set). Finally, in a more fine-grained assessment of the cognitive functions thought to be mediated frontally, Park et al. (1995) reported that psychometrically identified schizotypes revealed poorer "spatial working memory" performance, which is consistent with WCST deficits. Park, Holzman, and Levy (1993) have found that about half of the healthy relatives of patients with schizophrenia also displayed impaired spatial working memory. In general, it is safe to conclude that executive function and spatial working memory deficits are also of considerable interest in this area, both as clues to early pathological processes of schizophrenia as well as endophenotypes (Piskulic et al., 2007; Snitz et al., 2006) There are no reported studies of working memory performance in patients with PPD.

Other Endophenotypes of Interest

As this chapter is necessarily limited in scope, one cannot address all processes and factors studied in the domain of schizotypy research. The scope of inquiry in the field continues to expand and new processes are being studied (e.g., context processing, see Barch et al., 2004). In our laboratory, we have taken a focus on more basic processes, such as motor function (Lenzenweger & Maher, 2002) and somatosensory processing (Chang & Lenzenweger, 2001, 2005; Lenzenweger, 2000). There are two themes guiding this work: (1) simpler processes may be easier to dissect and understand genomically, and (2) we seek to "count" rather than "rate" the things we are interested in studying, thus avoiding the pitfalls associated with rating-based data. We also continue to study ecologically meaningful processes such as the impact of stress on spatial working memory (Smith & Lenzenweger, 2013) and social cognition (Miller & Lenzenweger, 2012). Finally, while much of the experimental psychopathology work on schizotypic psychopathology has emphasized neurocognitive processes, there is a resurgence of interest in hedonic capacity in schizophrenia and schizotypy (e.g., Strauss & Gold, 2012), which echos the early insights of Meehl (1962, 1974, 2001).

Schizophrenia-Related Deviance on Psychological Tests

Patients with SPD and PPD are by definition schizotypic at the level of phenomenology, and one would not necessarily anticipate using other measures of pathology to verify the presence of phenomenology already required by virtue of the *DSM* diagnostic criteria. However, psychometrically identified schizotypes that have been selected as a function of deviance on a schizotypy measure and other measures of psychopathology have been used to inform the validity of their schizotypic "status." For example, PAS-identified schizotypes reveal schizophrenia-related deviance on the MMPI (Lenzenweger, 1991), schizophrenia-related personality disorder features (Lenzenweger & Korfine, 1992b), and thought disorder (Coleman, Levy, Lenzenweger, & Holzman, 1996; Edell & Chapman, 1979). Lenzenweger, Miller, Maher, and Manschreck (2007) have found that PAS-identified schizotypes reveal hyperassociative language processing, consistent (albeit attenuated) with that seen in schizophrenia, and individual differences in hyperassociation are related to levels of reality distortion and disorganization. This study provides experimental evidence for mild thought disorder in schizotypes, thereby buttressing earlier findings based on ratings of thought disorder. See J. Chapman et al. (1995) for extensive reviews of the early studies that reported on the correlates of the Chapman psychosis-proneness scales.

Neuroimaging and Neurobiology of Schizotypic Psychopathology

In recent years, the corpus of neuroimaging studies of schizotypic psychopathology has expanded dramatically. In the mid-1990s, the literature was quite limited, and it was premature to highlight major trends in the area (see Flaum & Andreasen, 1995; Gur & Gur, 1995). Dickey, McCarley, and Shenton (2002), in their review of structural findings in schizotypal personality disorder (using either computed axial tomography or magnetic resonance imaging), revealed many areas of abnormality in SPD (see their Table 2, p. 11), and they note many areas of similarity between the SPD brain abnormalities and structural abnormalities found in patients with first-episode schizophrenia. Dickey et al. (2002) noted the relative absence of medial temporal lobe abnormalities in SPD (versus their presence in clinical schizophrenia) and they speculate, with caution, that the absence of such abnormalities in SPD might help to suppress psychosis in those with SPD. A particularly exciting new finding concerns reduction in gray matter volumes in SPD patients who have never been exposed to neuroleptics (Asami et al., 2013). Functional neuroimaging of schizotypic psychopathology still lags behind the structural neuroimaging work in quantity. With respect to functional neuroimaging studies, Siever and Davis (2004), in their review of SPD as a spectrum disorder, concluded that patients with SPD reveal many of the same disturbances in neural circuitry that are seen in clinical schizophrenia, albeit attenuated in severity (see also Lenzenweger & Korfine, 1994; Mohanty et al., 2005). Siever and Davis (2004) speculated that greater frontal capacity (along with somewhat reduced striatal reactivity) in the patients with SPD might spare them from psychosis.

The neurobiology of schizophrenia has undergone major revisions within the past 30 years in response to greater knowledge regarding basic neurobiology (see Grace, 1991; Grace & Moore, 1998; Guillin, Abi-Dargham, & Laruelle, 2007), developmental neurobiology (Breslin & Weinberger, 1990), and psychopharmacology (Davis, Kahn, Ko, & Davidson, 1991). A more contemporary view of the dopaminergic (DA) dysfunction in schizophrenia emphasizes multiple processes and their dysfunction (Davis et al., 1991; Goto & Grace, 2007; Guillin et al., 2007). For example, Weinberger (1987), among others, suggested that there is a two-process DA dysfunction in schizophrenia, with one process implicating the mesocortical DA pathway, underactivity in the prefrontal cortex, hypodopaminergia, and negative symptoms, and the other involving mesolimbic DA pathways, the striatum and related structures, hyperdopaminergia, and positive symptoms. Grace (1991; see also Goto & Grace, 2007) further refined this model of DA dysfunction in schizophrenia by suggesting that a glutamatergic dysfunction emanating from the prefrontal cortex affects "tonic" and "phasic" DA processes in the striatum. Additionally, though there is a continued focus on the role of DA in schizophrenia, there is a robust and developing interest in the role that serotonin (Abi-Dargham, 2007; Davis et al., 1991) and glutamate (Javitt, 2007) play in schizophrenia as well. Systematic efforts to determine the precise correspondence between the neurobiological models for schizophrenia and schizotypic psychopathology have been undertaken, and they are providing interesting clues as to the underlying neural circuitry and neurobiological dysfunction in schizotypes (Abi-Dargham et al., 2004; see also Siever & Davis, 2004). The fascinating results from Park's group (Woodward et al., 2011) point to amphetamine-induced dopamine release rate as a potential endophenotype for schizotypy, based on findings showing that dopamine release in the striatum was strongly associated with level of schizotypic features in nonpsychotic subjects (not unlike the findings of Howes et al. [2009] in the study of prodromal schizophrenia cases).

Clinical Phenomenology

Patients with SPD and PPD are by definition schizotypic at the level of phenomenology, and one would not necessarily anticipate using other measures of pathology to confirm the phenomenology of such patients. However, as noted previously, alternative methods of detecting schizotypes have been validated, in part, by examining the relations between schizotypic phenomenology as clinically assessed and psychometric measures of schizotypy. For example, Lenzenweger and Loranger (1989b) found that elevations on the PAS were most closely associated with schizotypal personality disorder symptoms and clinically assessed anxiety. Others have found that nonclinical patients, identified as schizotypic through application of the psychometric approach, also reveal schizotypic and "psychotic-like" phenomenology (cf. J. P. Chapman et al., 1995; L. J. Chapman, Edell, & Chapman, 1980; Kwapil, Chapman, & Chapman, 1999). Regarding first-degree biological relatives of patients with schizophrenia, Kendler et al. (1993) have shown that schizotypic features are found at higher levels among the relatives of schizophrenia cases than among the relatives of controls. However, it is important to note that not all psychometrically identified schizotypes or biological relatives of patients with schizophrenia will display levels of schizotypic phenomenology that would result in a diagnosis by *DSM-5* criteria for SPD or PPD.

Although it has long been known that there is no meaningful connection between autism and schizophrenia at the level of genetics (Gottesman, 1991; I. I. Gottesman, personal communication, May 19, 2007), correlations have been observed between self-report measures of schizotypy and Asperger's syndrome (a putative autism spectrum condition) (Hurst, Nelson-Gray, Mitchell, & Kwapil, 2007). The meaning of such cross-sectional correlations, however, remains obscure, and the trend in diagnosis and classification is to consider Asperger's disorder as separate from schizotypic psychopathology (including schizoid pathology) (Raja, 2006).

Finally, an area that has received increased attention in recent years concerns the nature of emotion and affective processing in schizotypes, particularly in light of Meehl's (1962, 1974) original conjectures regarding hedonic capacity (see also Meehl, 2001). Lenzenweger and Loranger (1989b) reported significant associations between measures of anxiety and depression with PAS scores. Berenbaum et al. (2006) reported that negative affect, not surprisingly, was related to interpersonal as well as cognitive schizotypic personality dimensions, whereas attention to emotion was less consistently related to schizotypic pathology (cf. Lewandowski et al., 2006). An important focus for this line of research in the future will be to find some way to resolve whether negative affect among schizotypes hails from the core schizotypy personality organization or whether it represents a secondary development, resulting from what Meehl (2001) has termed "aversive drift." The newly proposed Strauss and Gold (2012) model of hedonic capacity and anhedonia in schizophrenia may represent a new source of fruitful hypotheses for extension to the schizotypic realm in helping to address this and other questions.

Follow-up Studies of Schizotypic Psychopathology

There are few long-term follow-up data available on schizotypic samples that would help to determine how many schizotypes move on to clinical schizophrenia. Moreover, given the relative absence of large-scale longitudinal studies of personality disorders that involve multiple assessments, with the exception of the study being conducted by Lenzenweger's group, it is difficult to examine the stability of schizotypic features over time. Fenton and McGlashan (1989) conducted a follow-up study of patients that had been nonpsychotic at admission to the Chestnut Lodge Psychiatric Hospital, Rockville, MD. They found that 67% (12/18) of patients with a diagnosis of schizophrenia, located after a 15-year follow-up, were schizotypic (and nonpsychotic) at their initial admission. The L. J. Chapman et al. (1994) 10-year follow-up of their "psychosis-prone" (i.e., schizotypic) patients showed that high scorers on the PAS and MIS revealed greater levels of psychotic illness and schizotypic phenomenology at follow-up. Partial replication of the L. J. Chapman et al. (1994) findings was reported by Kwapil, Miller, Zinser, Chapman, and Chapman (1997). Interestingly, psychoticism, as a general schizotypy-relevant construct, does *not* predict heightened risk for psychosis (J. P. Chapman, 1994).

The new but maturing field of prodromal research, which owes much to the schizotypy research vector, is another arena in which conversion from schizotypic states to psychosis is being studied (Fusar-Poli et al., 2013; see also Nordentoft et al., 2006). The gist of the prodromal studies seeking to specify clinical and symptom feature predictors of conversion to psychosis is that they generally point to attenuated positive psychotic-like features, especially paranoia, suspiciousness, and thought disorganization (Fusar-Poli ete al., 2013; see also Barrantes-Vidal et al., 2013). However, given that prodromal studies of schizophrenia are focused on samples that are extremely enriched for likely psychosis, it is important to determine if psychotic-like symptoms, in previously nonpsychotic persons, in the population predict risk for nonaffective psychosis. Werbeloff et al. (2012) provide important data on this issue from a stratified full-probability population-based sample that show self-reported attenuated psychotic symptoms do in fact predict risk for nonaffective psychosis later in life. A common question in this area of research is: "How many schizotypes go on to develop full-blown schizophrenia and how many stay compensated (nonpsychotic) to one degree or another across the lifespan?" Meehl's model suggests that the modal schizotype never develops schizophrenia; this fascinating question awaits more empirical data from long-term follow-up study of schizotypic cases.

Another important contemporary question concerns the extent to which endophenotypes, assessed using laboratory procedures, predict psychotic outcome downstream in those initially identified as schizotypic. This approach has the benefit of using objective measures to define endophenotype status, thus being free of the difficulties associated with determining risk or prodromal status as a function of clinical ratings. At this time, only one prospective longitudinal study using this approach is underway, being conducted by Lenzenweger. Preliminary results from this study are promising and indicate considerable utility in using multiple endophenotypes (assessed at baseline) in the later prediction of psychosis, schizotypic psychopathology, psychosocial dysfunction, and other psychological characteristics suggestive of impaired functioning (Lenzenweger, 2010).

Delimitation from Other Disorders

Research on the delimitation of schizotypic psychopathology from other disorders has proceeded at phenotypic and latent levels. Phenotypic delimitation studies have typically taken the form of factor analytic studies and generally focused on data drawn from *DSM* Axis II symptoms. In short, Cluster A symptoms (i.e., schizotypal, paranoid, schizoid) typically hang together. The meaning and direction that can be extracted from such studies, however, is limited by the fact that method-related variance (e.g., structure of interviews) and overlapping definitions of the disorders are complicating factors. The issue of delimitation at the latent level is discussed here.

Assuming that schizotypy, as conceptualized by Meehl (1962, 1990, 1992, 2004), represents a latent liability construct and that current schizotypy indexes are valid, a basic question about the fundamental structure of schizotypy remains. Is it continuous (i.e., "dimensional") or is it truly discontinuous (or "qualitative") in nature? For example, at the level of the gene, Meehl's model (1962, 1990) and the latent trait model (Holzman et al., 1988; Matthysse, Holzman, & Lange, 1986) conjecture the existence of a qualitative discontinuity, whereas the polygenic multifactorial threshold model (Gottesman, 1991) predicts a continuous distribution of levels of liability. Clarification of the structure of schizotypy may help to resolve issues concerning appropriate genetic models for schizophrenia, and such information may aid in planning future studies in this area. Nearly all investigations of the structure of schizophrenia liability done to date have relied exclusively on fully expressed, diagnosable schizophrenia (see Gottesman, 1991), and the results of these studies have left the question of liability structure unresolved. Moreover, one surely cannot reason with confidence that a unimodal distribution of phenotypic schizotypic traits supports the existence of a continuum of liability (e.g., Kendler et al., 1991). In recent years, however, it has been proposed that a possible "expansion" of the schizophrenia phenotype to include other schizophrenia-related phenomena, such as ETD (Holzman et al., 1988), might be helpful in efforts to illuminate the latent structure of liability in schizophrenia. In my laboratory, we have pursued such an approach, complementary to the "expanded phenotype" proposal, through the psychometric detection of schizotypy (see Lenzenweger, 1993). Thus, we have undertaken over the past two decades a series of studies that begin to explore the latent structure of schizotypy. Our work has drawn extensively from the theoretical formulations of Rado and Meehl, and we have used a well-validated measure of schizotypy, the Chapmans' PAS, in these efforts.

We have explored the latent structure of schizotypy through application of Meehl's maximum covariance analysis (MAXCOV) (Meehl, 1973; Meehl & Yonce, 1996) procedure to the covariance structure of scores on the PAS. Our samples have been randomly ascertained from nonclinical university populations and they have been purged of invalid responders and those with suspect test-taking attitudes. Using the MAXCOV procedure, we (Korfine & Lenzenweger, 1995; Lenzenweger & Korfine, 1992a) have found evidence that suggests that the latent structure of schizotypy, as assessed by the PAS, is taxonic (i.e., qualitative) in nature. Moreover, the base rate of the schizotypy taxon is approximately 5% to 10%. The taxon base rate figure is relatively consistent with the conjecture by Meehl that schizotypes can be found in the general population at a rate of 10%. In our work we have also conducted a variety of control analyses that have served to check the MAXCOV procedure and ensure that the technique does not generate spurious evidence of taxonicity. We (Korfine & Lenzenweger, 1995) have demonstrated that (1) MAXCOV detects a latent continuum when one is hypothesized to exist, (2) MAXCOV results based on dichotomous data do not automatically generate "taxonic" results, and (3) item endorsement frequencies do not correspond to our taxon base rate estimates (i.e., our base rate estimates are not a reflection of endorsement frequencies). Finally, Lenzenweger (1999b) applied MAXCOV analysis to three continuous measures of schizotypy, and this revealed results that were highly consistent with our prior research in this area. Moreover, those individuals identified via taxometric analysis as putative taxon members display, as a group, higher levels of deviance on a psychometric measure known to be associated with schizophrenia liability. These data, taken in aggregate, though they do not unambiguously confirm that the structure of schizotypy is qualitative, are clearly consistent with such a conjecture. This suggests that schizotypic psychopathology is discontinuous in its latent structure and raises interesting possibilities for future genetic research in this area.

Most recently, latent structure work has moved from a consideration of psychometric values to analysis of actual laboratory measures of well-established endophenotypes, sustained attention and smooth pursuit eye movement, and the results, using taxometric analysis and state-of-the-art finite mixture modeling, support the existence of a qualitative discontinuity in the latent structure of such liability measures (Lenzenweger, McLachlan, et al., 2007). Although there has been some interest in the underlying structure of social anhedonia measures, recent taxometric work suggests that hedonic capacity, when measured using fine-grained assessments, appears to have a dimensional latent structure (Linscott, 2007). Issues worthy of careful consideration in the study of the latent structure of psychopathology and/or liability have been detailed recently and are recommended for review to avoid common pitfalls and errors in interpretation that have appeared in the literature (Lenzenweger, 2003, 2004; Meehl, 2004; Waller, Yonce, Grove, Faust, & Lenzenweger, 2006). As noted, aside from one taxometric study (Rawlings et al., 2008), which was marred by any number of methodological artifacts (see Beauchaine et al., 2008), the overwhelming picture from latent structure analyses (numerous studies across independent laboratories done with techniques that can discern between dimensional and categorical alternatives) supports the presence of some form of latent discontinuity in the distribution of schizotypy measures. This discontinuity is consistent with either a latent taxon (Meehl) or a severe step-function/threshold (Gottesman) harbored within schizotypy measure data.

Conclusions

In summary, as discussed in Lenzenweger (2010), the benefits of the schizotypy model approach in the search for the causes of schizophrenia are fivefold. First and foremost, the study of schizotypic psychopathology provides a "cleaner" window on underlying schizophrenia liability. A cleaner window means an opportunity to study, in the laboratory, genetically influenced, neurobiologically based processes (neurocognitive, affective, personality) that are uncontaminated by "third-variable" confounds, such as medication, deterioration, and institutionalization. Second, the schizotypy model approach to schizophrenia also provides a rich opportunity to discover *endophenotypes* for schizophrenia liability. Endophenotypes (Gottesman & Gould,

2003; Lenzenweger, 1999c; 2013a, 2013b) represent genetically influenced manifestations of the underlying liability for an illness that are invisible to the unassisted or naked eye. Third, incorporation of valid schizotypy indicators (e.g., schizotypic psychopathology) into genomic investigations directed at etiology and development of schizophrenia will enhance the power of such studies. Fourth, via longitudinal investigations, study of schizotypic psychopathology can elucidate *epigenetic* factors that might relate to the differences in outcome of schizotypes (i.e., stable schizotypal PD versus conversion to schizophrenia). Finally, the study of schizotypes provides an opportunity to home in on relatively specific deficits, should they exist, prior to the deterioration in schizophrenia that can give rise to generalized deficit, or the deficient functioning shown by many schizophrenia-affected patients. While generalized deficit remains an area of discussion in schizophrenia (Gold & Dickinson, 2013; Green, Horan, & Sugar, 2013), the schizotypy research model potentially represents a powerful methodological end run on generalized deficit.

Schizotypic psychopathology has long held the interest of researchers and clinicians alike, and it has been the subject of considerable theoretical discussion and empirical investigation. Continued study of this class of mental disturbance through the methods of experimental psychopathology, cognitive neuroscience, genetics, epidemiology, classification, and neurobiology will help to provide clues to the nature of schizophrenia, as well as to the schizotypic disorders themselves. In this context it is worth noting that future work in this area should find methods for embracing and resolving the heterogeneity in performance patterns, symptom features, and life history factors that are known to characterize schizotypy and schizophrenia (as well as hobble research in the area) (Lenzenweger, Jensen, & Rubin, 2003). Furthermore, as has long been advocated by Brendan Maher (1966, 2003), one should "count" rather than "rate" phenomena of interest in this area, thereby bringing greater precision to the research enterprise (see also Lenzenweger, 2010 for other "methodological morals"). The multiplicity of vantage points that have been brought to bear on schizotypic psychopathology has helped to move this area of inquiry further, and the continued existence of alternative vantage points in psychology and psychiatry in connection with these disorders will only serve to advance our knowledge.

References

Abi-Dargham, A. (2007). Alterations of serotonin transmission in schizophrenia. *International Review of Neurobiology*, 78, 133–164.

Abi-Dargham, A., Kegeles, L. S., Zea-Ponce, Y., Mawlawi, O., Martinez, D., Mitropoulou, V., et al. (2004). Striatal amphetamine-induced dopamine release in patients with schizotypal personality disorder studied with single photon emission computed tomography and [123I] iodobenzamide. *Biological Psychiatry*, 55, 1001–1006.

Andreasen, N. C. (1999). A unitary model of schizophrenia: Bleuler's "fragmented phrene" as shizencephaly. *Archives of General Psychiatry*, 56, 781–787.

Andreasen, N. C., Arndt, S., Alliger, R., Miller, D., & Flaum, M. (1995). Symptoms of schizophrenia: Methods, meanings, and mechanisms. *Archives of General Psychiatry*, 52, 341–351.

Asami, T., Whitford, T. J., Bouix, S., Dickey, C. C., Niznikiewicz, M., Shenton, M. E., Voglmaier, M. M., & McCarley, R. W. (2013). Globally and locally reduced MRI gray matter volumes in neuroleptic-naive men with schizotypal personality disorder: Association with negative symptoms. *Journal of the American Medical Association Psychiatry*, 70(4), 361–372.

Avramopoulos, D., Stefanis, N. C., Hantoumi, I., Smyrnis, N., Evdokimidis, I., & Stefanis C. N. (2002). Higher scores of self reported schizotypy in healthy young males carrying the *COMT* high activity allele. *Molecular Psychiatry*, 7, 706–711.

Barch, D. M., Mitropoulou, V., Harvey, P. D., New, A. S., Silverman, J. M., & Siever, L. J. (2004). Context-processing deficits in schizotypal personality disorder. *Journal of Abnormal Psychology*, 113, 556–568.

Baron, M., Asnis, L., & Gruen, R. (1981). The schedule for schizotypal personalities (SPP): A diagnostic interview for schizotypal features. *Psychiatry Research*, 4, 213–228.

Baron, M., Gruen, R., Rainer, J. D., Kanes, J., Asnis, L., & Lord, S. (1985). A family study of schizophrenic and normal control probands: Implications for the spectrum concept of schizophrenia. *American Journal of Psychiatry*, 142, 447–454.

Barrantes-Vidal, N., Gross, G. M., Sheinbaum, T., Mitjavila, M., Ballespi, S., & Kwapil, T. R. (2013). Positive and negative schizotypy are associated with prodromal and schizophrenia-spectrum symptoms. *Schizophrenia Research*, 145(1-3), 50–55.

Battaglia, M., Bernardeschi, L., Franchini, L., Bellodi, L., & Smeraldi, E. (1995). A family study of schizotypal disorder. *Schizophrenia Bulletin*, 21, 33–45.

Battaglia, M., Gasperini, M., Sciuto, G., Scherillo, P., Diaferia, G., & Bellodi, L. (1991). Psychiatric disorders in the families of schizotypal subjects. *Schizophrenia Bulletin*, 17, 659–668.

Beauchaine, T. P., Lenzenweger, M. F., & Waller, N. G. (2008). Schizotypy, taxometrics, and disconfirming theories in soft science comment on Rawlings, Williams, Haslam, and Claridge. *Personality and Individual Differences*, 44(8), 1652–1662.

Benishay, D. S., & Lencz, T. (1995). Semistructured interviews for the measurement of schizotypal personality. In A. Raine, T. Lencz, & S. Mednick (Eds.), *Schizotypal personality* (pp. 463–479). New York: Cambridge University Press.

Berenbaum, H., Boden, M. T., Baker, J. P., Dizen, M., Thompson, R. J., & Abramowitz, A. (2006). Emotional correlates of the different dimensions of schizotypal personality disorder. *Journal of Abnormal Psychology*, 115, 359–368.

Berenbaum, H., & McGrew, J. (1993). Familial resemblance of schizotypic traits. *Psychological Medicine*, 23, 327–333.

Bergida, H., & Lenzenweger, M. F. (2006). Schizotypy and sustained attention: Confirming evidence from an adult community sample. *Journal of Abnormal Psychology*, 115, 545–551.

Bernstein, D. P., Useda, D., & Siever, L. J. (1993). Paranoid personality disorder: Review of the literature and recommendations for DSM-IV. *Journal of Personality Disorders*, 7, 53–62.

Bleuler, E. (1950). *Dementia praecox or the group of schizophrenias* (J. Zinkin, Trans.). New York: International Universities Press. (Original work published 1911)

Bolinskey, P. K., Gottesman, I. I., & Nichols, D. S. (2003). The Schizophrenia Proneness (SzP) Scale: An MMPI-2 measure of schizophrenia liability. *Journal of Clinical Psychology*, 59, 1031–1044.

Breslin, N. A., & Weinberger, D. R. (1990). Schizophrenia and the normal functional development of the prefrontal cortex. *Development and Psychopathology*, 2, 409–424.

Calkins, M. E., Curtis, C. E., Grove, W. M., & Iacono, W. G. (2004). Multiple dimensions of schizotypy in first degree biological relatives of schizophrenia patients. *Schizophrenia Bulletin, 30*, 317–325.

Cardno, A. G., & Gottesman, I. I. (2000). Twin studies of schizophrenia: From bow-and-arrow concordances to Star Wars Mx and functional genomics. *American Journal of Medical Genetics, 97*, 12–17.

Carey, G., Gottesman, I., & Robins, E. (1980). Prevalence rates for the neuroses: Pitfalls in the evaluation of familiality. *Psychological Medicine, 10*, 437–443.

Chang, B. P., & Lenzenweger, M. F. (2001) Somatosensory processing in the biological relatives of schizophrenia patients: A signal detection analysis of two-point discrimination thresholds. *Journal of Abnormal Psychology, 110*, 433–442.

Chang, B. P., & Lenzenweger, M. F. (2005). Somatosensory processing and schizophrenia liability: Proprioception, exteroceptive sensitivity, and graphesthesia performance in the biological relatives of schizophrenia patients. *Journal of Abnormal Psychology, 114*, 85–95.

Chapman, J. P. (1994). Does the Eysenck Psychoticism Scale predict psychosis? A ten-year longitudinal study. *Personality and Individual Differences, 17*, 369–375.

Chapman, J. P., Chapman, L. J., & Kwapil, T. R. (1995). Scales for the measurement of schizotypy. In A. Raine, T. Lencz, & S. Mednick, (Eds.), *Schizotypal personality* (pp. 79–106). New York: Cambridge University Press.

Chapman, L. J., & Chapman, J. P. (1985). Psychosis proneness. In M. Alpert (Ed.), *Controversies in schizophrenia: Changes and constancies* (pp. 157–172). New York: Guilford Press.

Chapman, L. J., & Chapman, J. P. (1987). The search for symptoms predictive of schizophrenia. *Schizophrenia Bulletin, 13*, 497–503.

Chapman, L. J., Chapman, J. P., Kwapil, T. R., Eckblad, M., & Zinser, M. C. (1994). Putatively psychosis-prone subjects 10 years later. *Journal of Abnormal Psychology, 103*, 171–183.

Chapman, L. J., Chapman, J. P., & Raulin, M. L. (1978). Body-image aberration in schizophrenia. *Journal of Abnormal Psychology, 87*, 399–407.

Chapman, L. J., Edell, W. S., & Chapman, J. P. (1980). Physical anhedonia, perceptual aberration, and psychosis proneness. *Schizophrenia Bulletin, 6*, 639–653.

Chemerinski, E., Triebwasser, J., Roussos, P., & Siever, L. J. (2013). Schizotypal personality disorder. *Journal of Personality Disorders, 27*(5), 652–679.

Chen, W. J., Liu, S. K, Chang, C.-J., Lien, Y.-J., Chang, Y.-H., & Hwu, H.-G. (1998). Sustained attention deficit and schizotypal personality features in nonpsychotic relatives of schizophrenia patients. *American Journal of Psychiatry, 155*, 1214–1220.

Claridge, G. (Ed). (1997). *Schizotypy: Implications for illness and health*. Oxford, UK: Oxford University Press.

Claridge, G. S., & Broks, P. (1984). Schizotypy and hemisphere function: I. Theoretical considerations and the measurement of schizotypy. *Personality and Individual Differences, 5*, 633–648.

Cohen, A. S., Matthews, R. A., Najolia, G. M., & Brown, L. A. (2010). Toward a more psychometrically sound brief measure of schizotypal traits: Introducing the SPQ-Brief Revised. *Journal of Personality Disorders, 24*, 516–537.

Coid, J., Yang, M., Tyrer, P., Roberts, A., & Ullrich, S. (2006). Prevalence and correlates of personality disorder among adults aged 16 to 74 in Great Britain. *British Journal of Psychiatry, 188*, 423–431.

Coleman, M. J., Levy, D. L., Lenzenweger, M. F., & Holzman, P. S. (1996). Thought disorder, perceptual aberrations, and schizotypy. *Journal of Abnormal Psychology, 105*, 469–473.

Condray, R., & Steinhauer, S. R. (1992). Schizotypal personality disorder in individuals with and without schizophrenic relatives: Similarities and contrasts in neurocognitive and clinical functioning. *Schizophrenia Research, 7*, 33–41.

Cornblatt, B. A., & Keilp, J. G. (1994). Impaired attention, genetics, and the pathophysiology of schizophrenia. *Schizophrenia Bulletin, 20*, 31–46.

Cornblatt, B. A., Lenzenweger, M. F., Dworkin, R. H., & Erlenmeyer-Kimling, L. (1992). Childhood attentional dysfunction predicts social isolation in adults at risk for schizophrenia. *British Journal of Psychiatry, 161*(Suppl. 18), 59–68.

Cornblatt, B. A., & Malhotra, A. K. (2001). Impaired attention as an endophenotype for molecular genetic studies of schizophrenia. *American Journal of Medical Genetics (Neuropsychiatric Genetics), 105*, 11–15.

Crawford, T. N., Cohen, P., Johnson, J. G., Kasen, S., First, M. B., Gordon, K., Brook, J. S. (2005). Self-reported personality disorder in the Children in the Community Sample: Convergent and prospective validity in late adolescence and adulthood. *Journal of Personality Disorders, 19,* 30–52.

Cronbach, L. J., & Meehl, P. E. (1955). Construct validity in psychological tests. *Psychological Bulletin, 52,* 281–302.

Davis, K. L., Kahn, R. S., Ko, G., & Davidson, M. (1991). Dopamine in schizophrenia: A review and reconceptualization. *American Journal of Psychiatry, 148,* 1474–1486.

Dickey, C. C., McCarley, R. W., & Shenton, M. E. (2002). The brain in schizotypal personality disorder: A review of structural MRI and CT findings. *Harvard Review of Psychiatry, 10,* 1–15.

Eckblad, M., & Chapman, L. J. (1983). Magical ideation as an indicator of schizotypy. *Journal of Consulting and Clinical Psychology, 51,* 215–225.

Edell, W. S., & Chapman, L. J. (1979). Anhedonia, perceptual aberration, and the Rorschach. *Journal of Consulting and Clinical Psychology, 47,* 377–384.

Essen-Möller, E., Larsson, H., Uddenberg, C.-E., & White, G. (1956). Individual traits and morbidity in a Swedish rural population. *Acta Psychiatrica et Neurologica Scandinavica,* (Suppl. 100), 5–160.

Eysenck, H. J. (1958). The continuity of abnormal and normal behavior. *Psychological Bulletin, 55*(6), 429–432.

Eysenck, H. J., & Eysenck, S. B. G. (1976). *Psychoticism as a dimension of personality.* New York: Crane, Russak, & Co.

Falconer, D. S. (1989). *Introduction to quantitative genetics* (3rd ed.). New York: Longman.

Fanous, A. H., & Kendler, K. S. (2005). Genetic heterogeneity, modifier genes, and quantitative phenotypes in psychiatric illness: Searching for a framework. *Molecular Psychiatry, 10,* 6–13.

Fanous, A. H., Neale, M. C., Gardner, C. O., Webb, B. T., Straub, R. E., O'Neill, F. A., et al. (2007) Significant correlation in linkage signals from genome-wide scans of schizophrenia and schizotypy. *Molecular Psychiatry, 12,* 958–965.

Fenton, W. S., & McGlashan, T. H. (1989). Risk of schizophrenia in character disordered patients. *American Journal of Psychiatry, 146,* 1280–1284.

Flaum, M., & Andreasen, N. C. (1995). Brain morphology in schizotypal personality as assessed by magnetic resonance imaging. In A. Raine, T. Lencz, & S. Mednick (Eds.), *Schizotypal personality* (pp. 385–405). New York: Cambridge University Press.

Fogelson, D. L., Nuechterlein, K. H., Asarnow, R. A., Payne, D. L., Subotnik, K. L.,

Jacobson, K. C., et al. (2007). Avoidant personality disorder is a separable schizophrenia-spectrum personality disorder even when controlling for the presence of paranoid and schizotypal personality disorders: The UCLA family study. *Schizophrenia Research, 91,* 192–199.

Franke, P., Maier, W., Hardt, J., & Hain, C. (1993). Cognitive functioning and anhedonia in subjects at risk for schizophrenia. *Schizophrenia Research, 10,* 77–84.

Fusar-Poli, P., Borgwardt, S., Bechdolf, A., Addington, J., Riecher-Rössler, A., Schultze-Lutter, F., et al. (2013). The psychosis high-risk state: A comprehensive state-of-the-art review. *Journal of the American Medical Association Psychiatry, 70,* 107–120.

Gold, J. M., & Dickinson, D. (2013). "Generalized cognitive deficit" in schizophrenia: Overused or underappreciated? *Schizophrenia Bulletin, 39,* 263–265.

Gold, J. M., & Harvey, P. D. (1993). Cognitive deficits in schizophrenia. *Psychiatric Clinics of North America, 16,* 295–312.

Goldman-Rakic, P. S. (1991). Prefrontal cortical dysfunction in schizophrenia: The relevance of working memory. In B. Carroll (Ed.), *Psychopathology and the brain* (pp. 1–23). New York: Raven Press.

Gooding, D. C., Kwapil, T. R., & Tallent, K. A. (1999). Wisconsin Card Sorting Test deficits in schizotypic individuals. *Schizophrenia Research, 40,* 201–209.

Gooding, D. C., Matts, C. W., & Rollmann, E. A. (2006). Sustained attention deficits in relation to psychometrically identified schizotypy: Evaluating a potential endophenotypic marker. *Schizophrenia Research, 82,* 27–37.

Gooding, D. C., Miller, M. D., & Kwapil, T. R. (2000). Smooth pursuit eye tracking and visual fixation in psychosis-prone individuals. *Psychiatry Research, 93,* 41–54.

Goto, Y., & Grace, A. A. (2007). The dopamine system and the pathophysiology of schizophrenia: A basic science perspective. *International Review of Neurobiology, 78,* 41–68.

Gottesman, I. I. (1987). The psychotic hinterlands or the fringes of lunacy. *British Medical Bulletin, 43,* 557–569.

Gottesman, I. I. (1991). *Schizophrenia genesis: The origins of madness.* New York: W. H. Freeman.

Gottesman, I. I., & Bertelsen, A. (1989). Confirming unexpressed genotypes for schizophrenia: Risks in the offspring of Fischer's Danish identical and fraternal discordant twins. *Archives of General Psychiatry, 46,* 867–872.

Gottesman, I. I., & Gould, T. D. (2003). The endophenotype concept in psychiatry: Etymology and strategic intentions. *American Journal of Psychiatry, 160,* 636–645.

Grace, A. A. (1991). Phasic versus tonic dopamine release and the modulation of dopamine system responsivity: A hypothesis for the etiology of schizophrenia. *Neuroscience, 41,* 1–24.

Grace, A. A., & Moore, H. (1998). Regulation of information flow in the nucleus accumbens: A model for the pathophysiology of schizophrenia. In M. F. Lenzenweger & R. H. Dworkin (Eds.), *Origins and development of schizophrenia: Advances in experimental psychopathology* (pp. 123–157). Washington, DC: American Psychological Association.

Grant, B. F., Hasin, D. S., Stinson, F. S., Dawson, D. A., Chou, S. P., Ruan, W. J., & Pickering, R. P. (2004). Prevalence, correlates, and disability of personality disorders in the United States: Results from the National Epidemiologic Survey on Alcohol and Related Conditions. *Journal of Clinical Psychiatry, 65,* 948–958.

Grant, P., Kuepper, Y., Mueller, E. A., Wielpuetz, C., Mason, O., & Hennig, J. (2013). Dopaminergic foundations of schizotypy as measured by the German version of the Oxford-Liverpool Inventory of Feelings and Experiences (O-LIFE)—a suitable endophenotype of schizophrenia. *Frontiers of Human Neuroscience, 7,* 1–11.

Green, M. F., Horan, W. P., & Sugar, C. A. (2013). Has the generalilzed deficit become the generalized criticism? *Schizophrenia Bulletin, 39,* 257–262.

Grove, W. M. (1982). Psychometric detection of schizotypy. *Psychological Bulletin, 92,* 27–38.

Grove, W. M., Lebow, B. S., Clementz, B. A., Cerri, A., Medus, C., & Iacono, W. G. (1991). Familial prevalence and coaggregation of schizotypy indicators: A multitrait family study. *Journal of Abnormal Psychology, 100,* 115–121.

Guillin, O., Abi-Dargham, A., & Laruelle, M. (2007). Neurobiology of dopamine in schizophrenia. *International Review of Neurobiology, 78,* 1–39.

Gur, R. C., & Gur, R. E. (1995). The potential of physiological neuroimaging for the study of schizotypy: Experiences from applications to schizophrenia. In A. Raine, T. Lencz, & S. Mednick (Eds.), *Schizotypal personality* (pp. 406–425). New York: Cambridge University Press.

Hanson, D. R., Gottesman, I. I., & Meehl, P. E. (1977). Genetic theories and the validation of psychiatric diagnosis: Implications for the study of children of schizophrenics. *Journal of Abnormal Psychology, 86,* 575–588.

Harkness, A. R., McNulty, J. L., & Ben-Porath, Y. (1995). The personality pathology five (PSY-5): Constructs and MMPI-2 scales. *Psychological Assessment, 7,* 104–114.

Harvey, P. D., Keefe, R. S. E., Mitroupolou, V., DuPre, R., Roitman, S. L., Mohs, R., et al. (1996). Information-processing markers of vulnerability to schizophrenia: Performance of patients with schizotypal and nonschizotypal personality disorders. *Psychiatry Research, 60,* 49–56.

Holzman, P. S., Kringlen, E., Matthysse, S., Flanagan, S. D., Lipton, R. B., Cramer, G., et al. (1988). A single dominant gene can account for eye tracking dysfunctions and schizophrenia in offspring of discordant twins. *Archives of General Psychiatry, 45,* 641–647.

Howes, O. D., Montgomery, A. J., Asselin, M. C., Murray, R. M., Valli, I., Tabraham, P., et al. (2009). Elevated striatal dopamine function linked to prodromal signs of schizophrenia. *Archives of General Psychiatry, 66,* 13–20.

Hurst, R. M., Nelson-Gray, R. O., Mithcell, J. T., & Kwapil, T. R. (2007). The relationship of Asperger's characteristics and schizotypal personality traits in a non-clinical adult sample. *Journal of Autism and Developmental Disorders, 37,* 1711–1720.

Jang, K. L., Woodward, T. S., Lang, D., Honer, W. G., & Livesley, W. J. (2005). The genetic and environmental basis of the relationship between schizotypy and personality: A twin study. *Journal of Nervous and Mental Disease, 193,* 153–159.

Javitt, D. C. (2007). Glutamate and schizophrenia: Phencyclidine, N-methyl-d-aspartate receptors, and dopamine-glutamate interactions. *International Review of Neurobiology, 78,* 69–108.

Johnson, J. G., Cohen, P., Kasen, S., Skodol, A. E., Hamagan, F., & Brook J. S. (2000) Age-related change in personality disorder trait levels between early adolescence and adulthood: A community-based longitudinal investigation. *Acta Psychiatra Scandinavica, 102,* 265–275.

Kendler, K. S. (1985). Diagnostic approaches to schizotypal personality disorder: A historical perspective. *Schizophrenia Bulletin, 11,* 538–553.

Kendler, K., & Gruenberg, A. (1982). Genetic relationship between paranoid personality disorder and the "schizophrenic spectrum" disorders. *American Journal of Psychiatry*, *139*, 1185–1186.

Kendler, K. S., Gruenberg, A. M., & Kinney, D. K. (1994). Independent diagnoses of adoptees and relatives as defined by DSM-III in the provincial and national samples of the Danish Adoption Study of Schizophrenia. *Archives of General Psychiatry*, *51*, 456–468.

Kendler, K. S., & Hewitt, J. (1992). The structure of self-report schizotypy in twins. *Journal of Personality Disorders*, *6*, 1–17.

Kendler, K. S., Lieberman, J. A., & Walsh, D. (1989). The Structured Interview for Schizotypy (SIS): A preliminary report. *Schizophrenia Bulletin*, *15*, 559–571.

Kendler, K. S., McGuire, M., Gruenberg, A. M., O'Hare, A., Spellman, M., & Walsh, D. (1993). The Roscommon Family Study: III. Schizophrenia-related personality disorders in relatives. *Archives of General Psychiatry*, *50*, 781–788.

Kendler, K. S., Myers, J., Torgersen, S., Neale, M. C., & Reichborn-Kjennerud, T. (2007). The heritability of Cluster A personality disorders assessed by both personal interview and questionnaire. *Psychological Medicine*, *37*, 655–665.

Kendler, K. S., Ochs, A. L., Gorman, A. M., Hewitt, J. K., Ross, D. E., & Mirsky, A. F. (1991). The structure of schizotypy: A pilot multitrait twin study. *Psychiatry Research*, *36*, 19–36.

Kendler, K. S., & Walsh, D. (1995). Schizotypal personality disorder in parents and risk for schizophrenia in siblings. *Schizophrenia Bulletin*, *21*, 47–52.

Kety, S. S., Rosenthal, D., Wender, P. H., & Schulsinger, F. (1968). The types and prevalence of mental illness in the biological and adoptive families of adopted schizophrenics. *Journal of Psychiatric Research*, *6*, 345–362.

Kety, S. S., Wender, P. H., Jacobsen, B., Ingraham, L. J., Jansson, L., Faber, B., et al. (1994). Mental illness in the biological and adoptive relatives of schizophrenic adoptees: Replication of the Copenhagen Study in the rest of Denmark. *Archives of General Psychiatry*, *51*, 442–455.

Khouri, P. J., Haier, R. J., Rieder, R. O., & Rosenthal, D. (1980). A symptom schedule for the diagnosis of borderline schizophrenia: A first report. *British Journal of Psychiatry*, *137*, 140–147.

Korfine, L., & Lenzenweger, M. F. (1995). The taxonicity of schizotypy: A replication. *Journal of Abnormal Psychology*, *104*, 26–31.

Kraepelin, E. (1971). *Dementia praecox and paraphrenia* (R. M. Barclay, Trans., G. M. Robertson, Ed.). Huntington, NY: Krieger. (Original work published 1919).

Kwapil, T. R., Barrantes-Vidal, N., & Silvia, P. J. (2008). The dimensional structure of the Wisconsin schizotypy scales: Factor identification and construct validity. *Schizophrenia Bulletin*, *34*, 444–457.

Kwapil, T. R., Chapman, L. J., Chapman, J. P. (1999). Validity and usefulness of the Wisconsin manual for assessing psychotic-like experiences. *Schizophrenia Bulletin*, *25*, 363–375.

Kwapil, T. R., Mann, M. C., & Raulin, M. L. (2002). Psychometric properties and concurrent validity of the schizotypal ambivalence scale. *Journal of Nervous and Mental Disease*, *190*, 290–295.

Kwapil, T. R., Miller, M. B., Zinser, M. C., Chapman, J. P., & Chapman L. J. (1997). Magical ideation and social anhedonia as predictors of psychosis proneness: A partial replication. *Journal of Abnormal Psychology*, *106*, 491–495.

Lee, J., & Park, S. (2005). Working memory impairments in schizophrenia: A meta-analysis. *Journal of Abnormal Psychology*, *114*, 599–611.

Lee, J., & Park, S. (2006). The role of stimulus salience in CPT-AX performance of schizophrenia patients. *Schizophrenia Research*, *81*, 191–197.

Lencz, T., Raine, A., Scerbo, A., Redmon, M., Brodish, S., Holt, L., et al. (1993). Impaired eye tracking in undergraduates with schizotypal personality disorder. *American Journal of Psychiatry*, *150*, 152–154.

Lenzenweger, M. F. (1991). Confirming schizotypic personality configurations in hypothetically psychosis-prone university students. *Psychiatry Research*, *37*, 81–96.

Lenzenweger, M. F. (1993). Explorations in schizotypy and the psychometric high-risk paradigm. In L. J. Chapman, J. P. Chapman, & D. Fowles (Eds.), *Progress in experimental personality and psychopathology research, #16* (pp. 66–116). New York: Springer.

Lenzenweger, M. F. (1994). The psychometric high-risk paradigm, perceptual aberrations, and schizotypy: An update. *Schizophrenia Bulletin*, *20*, 121–135.

Lenzenweger, M. F. (1998). Schizotypy and schizotypic psychopathology: Mapping an alternative expression of schizophrenia liability. In M. F. Lenzenweger & R. H. Dworkin (Eds.), *Origins and development of schizophrenia: Advances in experimental psychopathology* (pp. 93–121). Washington, DC: American Psychological Association.

Lenzenweger, M. F. (1999a). Stability and change in personality disorder features: The Longitudinal Study of Personality Disorders. *Archives of General Psychiatry, 56,* 1009–1015.

Lenzenweger, M. F. (1999b). Deeper into the schizotypy taxon: On the robust nature of maximum covariance (MAXCOV) analysis. *Journal of Abnormal Psychology, 108,* 182–187.

Lenzenweger, M. F. (1999c). Schizophrenia: Refining the phenotype, resolving endophenotypes [Invited Essay]. *Behaviour Research and Therapy, 37,* 281–295.

Lenzenweger, M. F. (2000). Two-point discrimination thresholds and schizotypy: Illuminating a somatosensory dysfunction. *Schizophrenia Research, 42,* 111–124.

Lenzenweger, M. F. (2003). On thinking clearly about taxometrics, schizotypy, and genetic influences: Correction to Widiger (2001). *Clinical Psychology: Science & Practice, 10,* 367–369.

Lenzenweger, M. F. (2004). Consideration of the challenges, complications, and pitfalls of taxometric analysis. *Journal of Abnormal Psychology, 113,* 10–23.

Lenzenweger, M. F. (2006a). The Longitudinal Study of Personality Disorders: History, design, and initial findings [Special Essay]. *Journal of Personality Disorders, 6,* 645–670.

Lenzenweger, M. F. (2006b). Schizotaxia, schizotypy and schizophrenia: Paul E. Meehl's blueprint for experimental psychopathology and the genetics of schizophrenia. *Journal of Abnormal Psychology, 115,* 195–200.

Lenzenweger, M. F. (2008). Epidemiology of personality disorders. *Psychiatric Clinics of North America, 31,* 395–403.

Lenzenweger, M. F. (2010). *Schizotypy and schizophrenia: The view from experimental psychopathology.* New York: Guilford Press.

Lenzenweger, M. F. (2013a). Endophenotype, intermediate phenotype, biomarker: Definitions, concept comparisons, clarifications. *Depression and Anxiety, 30,* 185–189.

Lenzenweger, M. F. (2013b). Thinking clearly about the endophenotype–intermediate phenotype–biomarker distinctions in developmental psychopathology research. *Development & Psychopathology, 25,* 1347–1357.

Lenzenweger, M. F., Bennett, M. E., & Lilenfeld, L. R. (1997). The referential thinking scale as a measure of schizotypy: Scale development and initial construct validation. *Psychological Assessment, 9,* 452–463.

Lenzenweger, M. F., Cornblatt, B. A., & Putnick, M. E. (1991). Schizotypy and sustained attention. *Journal of Abnormal Psychology, 100,* 84–89.

Lenzenweger, M. F., & Dworkin, R. H. (1996). The dimensions of schizophrenia phenomenology? Not one or not two, at least three, perhaps four. *British Journal of Psychiatry, 168,* 432–440.

Lenzenweger, M. F., & Dworkin, R. H. (Eds.). (1998). *Origins and development of schizophrenia: Advances in experimental psychopathology.* Washington, DC: American Psychological Association.

Lenzenweger, M. F., Jensen, S., & Rubin, D. B. (2003). Finding the "genuine" schizotype: A model and method for resolving heterogeneity in performance on laboratory measures in experimental psychopathology research. *Journal of Abnormal Psychology, 112,* 457–468.

Lenzenweger, M. F., & Korfine, L. (1991, December). *Schizotypy and Wisconsin Card Sorting Test performance.* Paper presented at the sixth annual meeting of the Society for Research in Psychopathology, Harvard University, Cambridge, MA.

Lenzenweger, M. F., & Korfine, L. (1992a). Confirming the latent structure and base rate of schizotypy: A taxometric analysis. *Journal of Abnormal Psychology, 101,* 567–571.

Lenzenweger, M. F., & Korfine, L. (1992b). Identifying schizophrenia-related personality disorder features in a nonclinical population using a psychometric approach. *Journal of Personality Disorders, 6,* 264–274.

Lenzenweger, M. F., & Korfine, L. (1994). Perceptual aberrations, schizotypy and the Wisconsin Card Sorting Test. *Schizophrenia Bulletin, 20,* 345–357.

Lenzenweger, M. F., & Korfine, L. (1995). Tracking the taxon: On the latent structure and base rate of schizotypy. In A. Raine, T. Lencz, & S. A. Mednick (Eds.), *Schizotypal personality* (pp. 135–167). New York: Cambridge University Press.

Lenzenweger, M. F., Lane, M., Loranger, A. W., & Kessler, R. C. (2007). *DSM-IV* personality disorders in the National Comorbidity Survey Replication (NCS-R). *Biological Psychiatry, 62,* 553–564.

Lenzenweger, M. F., & Loranger, A. W. (1989a). Detection of familial schizophrenia using a psychometric measure of schizotypy. *Archives of General Psychiatry, 46,* 902–907.

Lenzenweger, M. F., & Loranger, A. W. (1989b). Psychosis proneness and clinical psychopathology: Examination of the correlates of schizotypy. *Journal of Abnormal Psychology, 98,* 3–8.

Lenzenweger, M. F., Loranger, A. W., Korfine, L., & Neff, C. (1997). Detecting personality disorders in a nonclinical population: Application of a two-stage procedure for case identification. *Archives of General Psychiatry, 54,* 345–351.

Lenzenweger, M. F., & Maher, B. A. (2002). Psychometric schizotypy and motor performance. *Journal of Abnormal Psychology, 111,* 546–555.

Lenzenweger, M. F., McLachlan, G., & Rubin, D. B. (2007). Resolving the latent structure of schizophrenia endophenotypes using expectation-maximization-based finite mixture modeling. *Journal of Abnormal Psychology, 116,* 16–29.

Lenzenweger, M. F., Miller, A. B., Maher, B. A., & Manschreck, T. C. (2007). Schizotypy and individual differences in the frequency of normal associations in verbal utterances. *Schizophrenia Research, 95,* 96–102.

Lenzenweger, M. F., & O'Driscoll, G. A. (2006). Smooth pursuit eye movement dysfunction and schizotypy in an adult community sample. *Journal of Abnormal Psychology, 4,* 779–786.

Levin, S. (1984a). Frontal lobe dysfunctions in schizophrenia—I. Eye movement impairments. *Journal of Psychiatric Research, 18,* 27–55.

Levin, S. (1984b). Frontal lobe dysfunctions in schizophrenia—II. Impairments of psychological brain functions. *Journal of Psychiatric Research, 18,* 57–72.

Levy, D. L., Holzman, P. S., Matthysse, S., & Mendell, R. (1993). Eye tracking dysfunction and schizophrenia: A critical perspective. *Schizophrenia Bulletin, 19,* 461–536.

Levy, D. L., Holzman, P. S., Matthysse, S., & Mendell, N. R. (1994). Eye tracking and schizophrenia: A selective review. *Schizophrenia Bulletin, 20,* 47–62.

Lewandowski, K. B., Barrantes, V. N., Nelson, G. R., Clancy, C., Kepley, H. O., & Kwapil, T. R. (2006). Anxiety and depression symptoms in psychometrically identified schizotypy. *Schizophrenia Research, 83,* 225–235.

Lin, H.-S., Liu, Y.-L., Liu, C.-M., Hung, S.-I., Hwu, H.-G., & Chen, W. J. (2005).

Neuregulin 1 gene and variations in perceptual aberration of schizotypal personality in adolescents. *Psychological Medicine, 35,* 1589–1598.

Linscott, R. J. (2007). The latent structure and coincidence of hypohedonia and schizotypy and their validity as indices of psychometric risk for schizophrenia. *Journal of Personality Disorders, 21,* 225–242.

Loranger, A. (1988). *The Personality Disorder Examination (PDE) manual.* Yonkers, NY: DV Communications.

Loranger, A. (1990). The impact of DSM-III on diagnostic practice in a university hospital: A comparison of DSM-II and DSM-III in 10,914 patients. *Archives of General Psychiatry, 47,* 672–675.

Loranger, A. W. (1999). *International personality disorder examination: DSM-IV and ICD-10 interviews.* Odessa, FL: Psychological Assessment Resources.

Loranger, A. W., Sartorius, N., Andreoli, A., Berger, P., Channabasavanna, S. M., Coid, B., et al. (1994). The International Personality Disorder Examination (IPDE): The World Health Organization/Alcohol, Drug Abuse, and Mental Health Administration International Pilot Study of Personality Disorders. *Archives of General Psychiatry, 51,* 215–224.

Maher, B. A. (1966). *Principles of psychopathology: An experimental approach.* Oxford, UK: McGraw-Hill.

Maher, B. A. (2003). Psychopathology and delusions: Reflections on methods and models. In M. F. Lenzenweger & J. M. Hooley (Eds.), *Principles of experimental psychopathology: Essays in honor of Brendan A. Maher* (pp. 9–28). Washington, DC: American Psychological Association.

Maier, W., Falkai, P., & Wagner, M. (1999). Schizophrenia-spectrum disorders. In M. Maj (Ed.), *World Psychiatric Association Series: Evidence and experience in psychiatry. Schizophrenia* (Vol. 2, pp. 311–371). Chichester, UK: Wiley.

Marenco, S., & Weinberger, D. R. (2000). The neurodevelopmental hypothesis of schizophrenia: Following a trail of evidence from cradle to grave. *Development and Psychopathology (Special Issue: Reflecting on the Past and Planning for the Future of Developmental Psychopathology), 12,* 501–527.

Mason, O., Claridge, G., & Jackson, M. (1995). New scales for the assessment of schizotypy. *Personality and Individual Differences, 18,* 7–13.

Mason, O., & Claridge, G. (2006). The Oxford-Liverpool inventory of feelings and experiences (O-LIFE): Further description and extended norms. *Schizophrenia Research*, 82(2–3), 203–211.

Matthysse, S., Holzman, P. S., & Lange, K. (1986). The genetic transmission of schizophrenia: Application of Mendelian latent structure analysis to eye tracking dysfunctions in schizophrenia and affective disorder. *Journal of Psychiatric Research*, 20, 57–67.

McGlashan, T. H., & Hoffman, R. E. (2000). Schizophrenia as a disorder of developmentally reduced synaptic connectivity. *Archives of General Psychiatry*, 57, 637–648.

Meehl, P. E. (1962). Schizotaxia, schizotypy, schizophrenia. *American Psychologist*, 17, 827–838.

Meehl, P. E. (1964). Manual for use with Checklist of Schizotypic Signs. Minneapolis: University of Minnesota. Available at http://www.tc.umn.edu/~pemeehl/pubs.htm

Meehl, P. E. (1971). High school yearbooks: A reply to Schwarz. *Journal of Abnormal Psychology*, 77, 143–148.

Meehl, P. E. (1972). Specific genetic etiology, psychodynamics, and therapeutic nihilism. *International Journal of Mental Health*, 1, 10–27.

Meehl, P. E. (1973). MAXCOV-HITMAX: A taxonomic search method for loose genetic syndromes. In P. E. Meehl, *Psychodiagnosis: Selected papers* (pp. 200–224). Minneapolis: University of Minnesota Press.

Meehl, P. E. (1974). Hedonic capacity: Some conjectures. *Bulletin of the Menninger Clinic*, 39, 295–307.

Meehl, P. E. (1978). Theoretical risks and tabular asterisks: Sir Karl, Sir Ronald, and the slow progress of soft psychology. *Journal of Consulting and Clinical Psychology*, 46, 806–834.

Meehl, P. E. (1987). "Hedonic capacity" ten years later: Some clarifications. In D. C. Clark & J. Fawcett (Eds.), *Anhedonia and affect deficit states* (pp. 47–50). New York: PMA Publishing.

Meehl, P. E. (1990). Toward an integrated theory of schizotaxia, schizotypy, and schizophrenia. *Journal of Personality Disorders*, 4, 1–99.

Meehl, P. E. (1992). Factors and taxa, traits and types, differences of degree and differences in kind. *Journal of Personality*, 60, 117–174.

Meehl, P. E. (1993) The origins of some of my conjectures concerning schizophrenia. In L. J. Chapman, J. P. Chapman, & D. C. Fowles (Eds.), *Progress in experimental personality and psychopathology research* (pp. 1–10). New York: Springer.

Meehl, P. E. (2001). Primary and secondary hypohedonia. *Journal of Abnormal Psychology*, 110, 188–193.

Meehl, P. E. (2004). What's in a taxon? *Journal of Abnormal Psychology*, 113, 39–43.

Meehl, P. E., & Yonce, L. J. (1996). Taxometric analysis: II. Detecting taxonicity using covariance of two quantitative indicators in successive intervals of a third indicator (MAXCOV procedure). *Psychological Reports* (Monograph Suppl. 1-V78).

Meyer, T. D., & Keller, F. (2001). Exploring the latent structure of the perceptual aberration, magical ideation, and physical anhedonia scales in a German sample. *Journal of Personality Disorders*, 15, 521–535.

Miller, A. B., & Lenzenweger, M. F. (2012). Schizotypy, social cognition, and interpersonal sensitivity. *Personality Disorders: Theory, Research, & Treatment*, 3, 379–392.

Miller, M. B., & Chapman, J. P. (1993, October 7–10). A twin study of schizotypy in college-age males. Presented at the eighth annual meeting of the Society for Research in Psychopathology, Chicago, IL.

Mishlove, M., & Chapman, L. J. (1985). Social anhedonia in the prediction of psychosis proneness. *Journal of Abnormal Psychology*, 94, 384–396.

Mohanty, A., Herrington, J. D., Koven, N. S., Fisher, J. E., Wenzel, E. A., Webb, A. G., et al. (2005). Neural mechanisms of affective interference in schizotypy. *Journal of Abnormal Psychology*, 114, 16–27.

Morey, L. C., Waugh, M. H., & Blashfield, R. K. (1985). MMPI scales for DSM-III personality disorders: Their derivation and correlates. *Journal of Personality Assessment*, 49, 245–251.

Morton, N. E., & MacLean, C. J. (1974). Analysis of family resemblance. III. Complex segregation of quantitative traits. *American Journal of Human Genetics*, 26, 489–503.

Nigg, J., & Goldsmith, H. (1994). Genetics of personality disorders: Perspectives from psychology and psychopathology research. *Psychological Bulletin*, 115, 346–380.

Nordentoft, M., Thorup, A., Petersen, L., Ohlenschlaeger, J., Melau, M., Christensen, T. O., et al. (2006). Transition rates from schizotypal disorder to psychotic disorder for first-contact patients included in the OPUS trial. A randomized clinical trial of integrated treatment and standard treatment. *Schizophrenia Research*, 83, 29–40.

Obiols, J. E., Garcia-Domingo, M., de Trincheria, I., & Domenech, E. (1993). Psychometric schizotypy and sustained attention in young males. *Personality and Individual Differences*, *14*, 381–384.

O'Driscoll, G., Lenzenweger, M. F., & Holzman, P. S. (1998). Antisaccades and smooth pursuit eye tracking performance and schizotypy. *Archives of General Psychiatry*, *55*, 837–843.

Owen, M. J., O'Donovan, M. C., & Harrison, P. J. (2005). Schizophrenia: A genetic disorder of the synapse? Glutamatergic synapses might be the primary site of abnormalities. *British Medical Journal*, *330*, 158–159.

Park, S., Holzman, P. S., & Lenzenweger, M. F. (1995). Individual differences in working memory in relation to schizotypy. *Journal of Abnormal Psychology*, *104*, 355–363.

Park, S., Holzman, P. S., & Levy, D. L. (1993). Spatial working memory deficit in the relatives of schizophrenic patients is associated with their smooth pursuit eye tracking performance. *Schizophrenia Research*, *9*, 185.

Phillips, W. A., & Silverstein, S. M. (2003). Convergence of biological and psychological perspectives on cognitive coordination in schizophrenia. *Behavioral and Brain Sciences*, *26*, 65–82.

Piskulic, D., Olver, J. S., Norman, T. R., & Maruff, P. (2007). Behavioural studies of spatial working memory dysfunction in schizophrenia: A quantitative literature review. *Psychiatry Research*, *150*, 111–121.

Planansky, K. (1972). Phenotypic boundaries and genetic specificity in schizophrenia. In A. R. Kaplan (Ed.), *Genetic factors in "schizophrenia"* (pp. 141–172). Springfield, IL: Charles C. Thomas.

Rado, S. (1953). Dynamics and classification of disordered behavior. *American Journal of Psychiatry*, *110*, 406–416.

Rado, S. (1960). Theory and therapy: The theory of schizotypal organization and its application to the treatment of decompensated schizotypal behavior. In S. C. Scher & H. R. Davis (Eds.), *The outpatient treatment of schizophrenia* (pp. 87–101). New York: Grune and Stratton.

Raine, A. (1991). The SPQ: A scale for the assessment of schizotypal personality disorder based on DSM-III-R criteria. *Schizophrenia Bulletin*, *17*, 555–564.

Raine, A. (2006). Schizotypal personality: Neurodevelopmental and psychosocial trajectories. *Annual Review of Clinical Psychology*, *2*, 291–326.

Raine, A., Lencz, T., & Mednick, S. (1995). *Schizotypal personality.* New York: Cambridge University Press.

Raine, A., Sheard, C., Reynolds, G., & Lencz, T. (1992). Pre-frontal structural and functional deficits associated with individual differences in schizotypal personality. *Schizophrenia Research*, *7*, 237–247.

Raja, M. (2006). The diagnosis of Asperger's syndrome. *Directions in Psychiatry*, *26*, 89–104.

Raulin, M. L., & Wee, J. L. (1984). The development and initial validation of a scale to measure social fear. *Journal of Clinical Psychology*, *40*, 780–784.

Rawlings, D., & Goldberg, M. (2001). Correlating a measure of sustained attention with a multidimensional measure of schizotypal traits. *Personality & Individual Differences*, *31*, 421–431.

Rawlings, D., Williams, B., Haslam, N., & Claridge, G. (2008). Taxometric analysis supports a dimensional latent structure for schizotypy. *Personality and Individual Differences*, *44*(8), 1640–1651.

Ritsner, M. S. (2011). *Handbook of schizophrenia spectrum disorders: Volume 1. Conceptual and neurobiological advances.* New York: Springer.

Rust, J. (1988a). *The handbook of the Rust Inventory of Schizotypal Cognitions (RISC).* London: Psychological Corporation.

Rust, J. (1988b). The Rust Inventory of Schizotypal Cognitions (RISC). *Schizophrenia Bulletin*, *14*, 317–322.

Sanislow, C. A., Little, T. D., Ansell, E. B., Grilo, C. M., Daversa, M., Markowitz, J. C., et al. (2009). Ten-year stability and latent structure of the DSM-IV schizotypal, borderline, avoidant, and obsessive-compulsive personality disorders. *Journal of Abnormal Psychology*, *118*, 507–519.

Scarone, S., Abbruzzese, M., & Gambini, O. (1993). The Wisconsin Card Sorting Test discriminates schizophrenic patients and their siblings. *Schizophrenia Research*, *10*, 103–107.

Shea, M., Stout, R., Gunderson, J., Morey, L., Grilo, C., McGlashan, T., et al. (2002). Short-term diagnostic stability of schizotypal, borderline, avoidant, and obsessive-compulsive personality disorders. *American Journal of Psychiatry*, *159*, 2036–2041.

Shields, J., Heston, L. I., & Gottesman, I. I. (1975). Schizophrenia and the schizoid: The problem for genetic analysis. In R. R. Fieve, D. Rosenthal, & H. Brill (Eds.), *Genetic research in psychiatry* (pp. 167–197). Baltimore: Johns Hopkins University Press.

Siever, L. J., Bernstein, D. P., & Silverman, J. M. (1991). Schizotypal personality disorder: A review of its current status. *Journal of Personality Disorders*, *5*, 178–193.

Siever, J. L., & Davis, K. L. (2004). The pathophysiology of schizophrenia disorders: Perspectives from the spectrum. *American Journal of Psychiatry, 161*, 398–413.

Siever, L. J., Friedman, L., Moskowitz, J., Mitropoulou, V., Keefe, R., Roitman, S. L., et al. (1994). Eye movement impairment and schizotypal psychopathology. *American Journal of Psychiatry, 151*, 1209–1215.

Siever, L. J., & Gunderson, J. G. (1983). The search for a schizotypal personality: Historical origins and current status. *Comprehensive Psychiatry, 24*, 199–212.

Siever, L. J., Keefe, R., Bernstein, D. P., Coccaro, E. F., Klar, H. M., Zemishlany, Z., et al. (1990). Eye tracking impairment in clinically identified patients with schizotypal personality disorder. *American Journal of Psychiatry, 147*, 740–745.

Siever, L. J., Roussos, P., Greenwood, T., et al. (2011). Genetic association and pathway analysis of 94 candidate genes in schizotypal personality disorder. *Schizophrenia Bulletin, 37*(Suppl. 1), 90.

Simons, R. F., & Katkin, W. (1985). Smooth pursuit eye movements in subjects reporting physical anhedonia and perceptual aberrations. *Psychiatry Research, 14*, 275–289.

Smith, C., & Mendell, N. R. (1974). Recurrence risks from family history and metric traits. *Annuals of Human Genetics, 37*, 275–286.

Smith, N. T., & Lenzenweger, M. F. (2013). Increased stress responsivity in schizotypy leads to diminished spatial working memory performance. *Personality Disorders, 4*(4), 324–331.

Snitz, B. E., MacDonald, A. W., & Carter, C. S. (2006). Cognitive deficits in unaffected first-degree relatives of schizophrenia patients: A meta-analytic review of putative endophenotypes. *Schizophrenia Bulletin, 32*, 179–194.

Spitzer, R. L., Endicott, J., & Gibbon, M. (1979). Crossing the border into borderline personality and borderline schizophrenia: The development of criteria. *Archives of General Psychiatry, 36*, 17–24.

Sponheim, S. R., Iacono, W. G., Thuras, P. D., Nugent, S. M., & Beiser, M. (2003). Sensitivity and specificity of select biological indices in characterizing psychotic patients and their relatives. *Schizophrenia Research, 63*, 27–38.

Sponheim, S. R., McGuire, K. A., & Stanwyck, J. J. (2006). Neural anomalies during sustained attention in first-degree biological relatives of schizophrenia patients. *Biological Psychiatry, 60*, 242–252.

Strauss, G. P., & Gold, J. M. (2012). A new perspective on anhedonia in schizophrenia. *American Journal of Psychiatry, 169*, 364–373.

Sullivan, P. F., Daly, M. J., & O'Donovan, M. (2012). Genetic architectures of psychiatric disorders: The emerging picture and its implications. *Nature Reviews (Genetics), 13*, 537–551.

Sullivan, P. F., Kendler, K. S., & Neale, M. C. (2003). Schizophrenia as a complex trait: Evidence from a meta-analysis of twin studies. *Archives of General Psychiatry, 60*, 1187–1192.

Thaker, G. K., Cassady, S., Adami, H., & Moran, M. (1996). Eye movements in spectrum personality disorder: Comparison of community subjects and relatives of schizophrenic patients. *American Journal of Psychiatry, 153*, 362–368.

Torgersen, S. (1985). Relationship of schizotypal personality disorder to schizophrenia: Genetics. *Schizophrenia Bulletin, 11*, 554–563.

Torgersen, S. (1994). Personality deviations within the schizophrenia spectrum. *Acta Psychiatrica Scandinavica, 90*(Suppl. 384), 40–44.

Torgersen, S., Lygren, S., Oien, P. A., Skre, I., Onstad, S., Edvardsen, J., et al. (2000). A twin study of personality disorders. *Comprehensive Psychiatry, 41*, 416–425.

Triebwasser, J., Chemerinski, E., Roussos, P., & Siever, L. J. (2012). Schizoid personality disorder. *Journal of Personality Disorders, 26*, 919–926.

Triebwasser, J., Chemerinski, E., Roussos, P., & Siever, L. J. (2013). Paranoid personality disorder. *Journal of Personality Disorders, 27*(6), 795–805.

Vaughn, M. C., Barrantes-Vidal, A. G., Raulin, M. L., & Kwapil, T. R. (2008). The schizotypal ambivalence scale as a marker of schizotypy. *Journal of Nervous and Mental Disease, 196*, 399–404.

Venables, P. H. (1990). The measurement of schizotypy in Mauritius. *Personality and Individual Differences, 11*, 965–971.

Vollema, M. G., & Hoijtink, H. (2000). The multidimensionality of self-report schizotypy in a psychiatric population: An analysis using multidimensional Rasch models. *Schizophrenia Bulletin, 26*, 565–575.

Waller, N. G., Yonce, L. J., Grove, W. M., Faust, D. A., & Lenzenweger, M. F. (2006). *A Paul Meehl reader: Essays on the practice of scientific psychology.* Mahwah, NJ: Lawrence Erlbaum.

Webb, C. T., & Levinson, D. F. (1993). Schizotypal and paranoid personality disorder in the relative of patients with schizophrenia and affective disorders: A review. *Schizophrenia Research*, *11*, 81–92.

Weinberger, D. R. (1987). Implications of normal brain development for the pathogenesis of schizophrenia. *Archives of General Psychiatry*, *44*, 660–669.

Weinberger, D. R., Berman, K. F., & Zec, R. F. (1986). Physiologic dysfunction of dorsolateral prefrontal cortex in schizophrenics I. Regional cerebral blood flow evidence. *Archives of General Psychiatry*, *43*, 114–124.

Weissman, M. (1993). The epidemiology of personality disorders: A 1990 update. *Journal of Personality Disorders*, *7*(Suppl. Spring), 44–62.

Werbeloff, N., Drukker, M., Dohrenwend, B. P., Levav, I., Yoffe, R., van Os, J., Davidson, M., & Weiser, M. (2012). Self-reported attenuated psychotic symptoms are forerunners of severe mental disorders later in life. *Archives of General Psychiatry*, *69*, 467–475.

Winterstein, B. P., Silvia, P. J., Kwapil, T. R., Kaufman, J. C., Reiter-Palmon, R., & Wigert, B. (2011). Brief assessment of schizotypy: Developing short forms of the Wisconsin schizotypy scales. *Personality and Individual Differences*, *51*, 920–924.

Zimmerman, M., & Coryell, W. (1990). Diagnosing personality disorders in the community: A comparison of self-report and interview measures. *Archives of General Psychiatry*, *47*, 527–531.

Zimmerman, M., Rothschild, L., & Chelminski, I. (2005). The prevalence of DSM-IV personality disorders in psychiatric outpatients. *American Journal of Psychiatry*, *162*, 1911–1918.

29

Borderline Personality Disorder
Contemporary Approaches to Conceptualization and Etiology

TIMOTHY J. TRULL

In this chapter, the general features and correlates of one of the more vexing and challenging forms of psychopathology, borderline personality disorder (BPD), are discussed. After presenting a historical overview of this disorder, the clinical features of modern conceptualizations of BPD are detailed. Next, the comorbidity of BPD with both Axis I and other Axis II disorders is discussed, and the sociodemographic features associated with BPD are outlined. In this chapter, I focus primarily on putative genetic causes of BPD, given the increased interest in this area of study. This focus leads to several important questions and issues about how best to define the BPD phenotype. The chapter closes with a discussion of the future of the BPD diagnosis.

At the outset, it is also important to note what is not discussed in this chapter: treatments for BPD and assessment of BPD. The interested reader is referred to several excellent reviews of evidence-based treatments for BPD (e.g., Lieb, Völlm, Rücker, Timmer, & Stoffers, 2010; Paris, 2009; Stoffers et al., 2012) and evidence-based assessment of BPD (e.g., Widiger & Samuel, 2005).

Historical Overview

BPD is a severe mental disorder associated with extreme emotional, behavioral, and interpersonal dysfunction (*DSM-IV-TR*). In a recent essay, Gunderson (2009) reviewed the ontogeny of the BPD diagnosis. Most scholars credit Adolph Stern

(1938) and Robert Knight (1953) for introducing the term *borderline* to the psychiatric nomenclature to designate a condition that was believed to share a boundary with schizophrenia but was seen as more temporary and more likely to occur in the context of unstructured clinical situations. Later, Otto Kernberg's (1967) designation of "borderline personality organization" was applied to a group of patients who on the one hand showed features of psychotic personality organization (e.g., primitive defenses, fragmented sense of self) but on the other hand showed reality testing that was generally intact. As for the earliest empirical approach to the definition and characterization of borderline personality, Roy Grinker (Grinker, Werble, & Drye, 1968) is credited with providing discriminating features of four subtypes of borderline personality and identifying four common features of the "borderline syndrome:" anger, impaired intimate relationships, identity problems, and depressive loneliness. These contributions, as well as that by John Gunderson in further delimiting borderline personality from other psychiatric conditions (e.g., Gunderson & Singer, 1975), have served as the basis for what we now know to be the BPD diagnosis.

Following the introduction of the formal BPD diagnosis in *DSM-III* in 1980, debates about the boundaries of BPD continued. For example, instead of schizophrenia, critics argued that BPD was a variant of affective disorder (especially depression or bipolar disorder; Akiskal, 1981) or of posttraumatic stress disorder (PTSD; Herman,

1992). Complicating the debates and investigations into these boundary issues was the fact that BPD frequently co-occurred with mood disorders, PTSD, and other disorders characterized by emotional dysregulation and impulsivity. In addition, among more biologically oriented researchers, no specific biological etiology (e.g., a biomarker) was found for BPD that would distinguish BPD from other disorders. However, despite these questions, the validity of the BPD diagnosis is well recognized by the general psychiatric and psychological communities. The diagnosis itself remains one of the most prevalent diagnoses in mental health settings, it continues to be associated with great impairment and increased mortality, and BPD is increasingly recognized as a major public health problem.

Clinical Description

Since the publication of *DSM-III* in 1980, the diagnostic criteria for BPD have remained relatively consistent, with the one exception being the addition in *DSM-IV* of a criterion for temporary, stress-dependent, quasi-psychotic experiences. Individuals with BPD have a maladaptive personality style that is present in a variety of contexts, emerges by early adulthood, and leads to distinct patterns of dysfunction in behavior and relationships (*DSM-IV-TR* and *DSM-V*). Those diagnosed with BPD frequently experience strong, intense negative emotions and are prone to suicidal threats, gestures, or attempts. They are unsure of their self-image as well as their own views of other people. They harbor intense abandonment fears and feelings of emptiness. Stressful situations may invoke transient paranoid ideation or dissociation. Associated features include a propensity for engaging in self-defeating behavior (e.g., making a bad decision that destroys a good relationship), high rates of mood or substance use disorders, and premature death from suicide. Concerning the latter, it is estimated that approximately 3%–10% of individuals with BPD will have committed suicide by the age of 30 (Gunderson, 2001).

Table 29.1 presents the nine individual criteria for BPD as defined by both *DSM-IV-TR* and *DSM-5*, in Section II. To receive a BPD diagnosis, at least five of the nine criteria must be present and the symptoms must result in significant distress or impairment. A calculation of unique combinations of five or more items from nine total items

Table 29.1 Nine *DSM-IV* Criteria for Borderline Personality Disorder

- Extreme attempts to avoid real or imagined abandonment
- Intense and unstable interpersonal relationships
- Lack of a sense of self, or unstable self-image
- Impulsivity that is potentially self-damaging (e.g., excessive spending, substance abuse, binge eating)
- Recurrent suicidal behavior (i.e., threats, gestures) or self-mutilating behavior
- Affective instability
- Chronic feeling of emptiness
- Anger control problems
- Dissociation (e.g., depersonalization or derealization) or paranoid thoughts that occur in response to stress

reveals that there are 256 possible ways to meet *DSM-IV-TR* and *DSM-5* criteria for BPD! In the case of BPD, this heterogeneity in diagnosis has been recognized for some time and has proved challenging for both etiological and treatment research.

Epidemiology

BPD affects 1%–3% of the general population, and it is the most common personality disorder in clinical settings, representing 10% of the patients in outpatient settings, 15%–20% of the patients in inpatients settings, and 30%–60% of the patients diagnosed with personality disorders (Gunderson, 2001; Lenzenweger, Lane, Loranger, & Kessler, 2007; Paris, 2009; Tomko, Trull, Wood, & Sher, in press; Trull, Jahng, Tomko, Wood, & Sher, 2010; Widiger & Weissman, 1991; Widiger & Trull, 1993). It is believed that significantly more women than men meet the criteria for BPD, but this belief is based primarily on clinical studies. It is important to distinguish BPD symptoms, which are more chronic and pervasive, from emotional and impulsive behaviors that may be exhibited for short periods of time in adolescence. Studies that have followed children and adolescents who initially received a BPD diagnosis typically find that only a small percentage retain a BPD diagnosis years later. This finding raises the possibility that BPD may be overdiagnosed in children and adolescents, and a more conservative approach to diagnosis in this age group is necessary. A set of longitudinal findings on adult BPD patients followed over 10 years suggests that while the symptoms of BPD may remit, the level of impairment and dysfunction in social and occupational spheres appears to continue (e.g., Gunderson, Stout, et al., 2011).

Although BPD has been studied extensively in clinical and treatment samples, less is known about demographic features associated with BPD in the general population. Recently, one of the largest epidemiological studies assessing mental illness and its correlates, the National Epidemiologic Survey on Alcohol and Related Conditions (NESARC), was completed in the United States. The NESARC is a nationally representative, face-to-face survey that evaluated mental health in the civilian, noninstitutionalized population of the United States (Grant, Kaplan, Shepard, & Moore, 2003). BPD symptoms were assessed in Wave 2 of this survey (2004-2005). Initial reports from the NESARC indicated very high prevalence rates for the personality disorders (Grant, Stinson, et al., 2004). However, these estimates were likely inflated because the original NESARC investigators only required the endorsement of extreme distress, impairment, or dysfunction for one (but not all) of the requisite endorsed personality disorder items in order for a diagnosis to be assigned (Grant, Hasin, Chou, Stinson, & Dawson, 2004; Trull et al., 2010). Trull et al. (2010) presented an alternative method for diagnosing personality disorders from the NESARC data, which resulted in prevalence rates much more in line with those from other, recent epidemiological studies.

A reanalysis of the BPD NESARC data (Tomko et al., in press), taking into account distress and impairment for each requisite symptom, resulted in a weighted prevalence rate for BPD overall of 2.7% (instead of the original estimate of 5.9%; Grant et al., 2008), and the rate was only slightly higher among women than among men (3.0% and 2.4%, respectively) (see Table 29.2). Elevated risk for BPD was also suggested for individuals with a family income of less than $20,000 per year (4.8%), people younger than 30 (4.3%), and individuals who are separated, divorced, or widowed (4.5%). Racial and ethnic differences were evident, with Native Americans (5.0%) and Blacks (3.5%) reporting higher rates of the disorder, on average, than Whites (2.7%) or Hispanics (2.5%), and Asian Americans having a significantly lower rate (1.2%). Individuals with less than a high school education also showed slightly elevated rates of BPD (3.3%) compared to those with at least a high school degree. Urban and rural respondents showed similar rates of the disorder. Regional differences were also minimal, and there were no significant region × sex differences.

Table 29.2 Lifetime Prevalence of *DSM-IV* Borderline Personality Disorder and Sociodemographic Characteristics by Sex

Characteristic	Total %	Men %	Women %
Total	2.7		
Sex			
Men	2.4		
Women	3.0		
Age			
20–29 years	4.3	3.8	4.8
30–44 years	3.4	2.6	4.3
45–64 years	2.6	2.5	2.7
65 and up	0.6	0.7	0.5
Race-ethnicity			
White	2.7	2.3	3.1
Black	3.5	3.2	3.7
Native American	5.0	5.2	4.8
Asian	1.2	1.7	0.7
Hispanic	2.5	2.4	2.5
Family income			
< $20,000	4.8	5.4	4.4
$20,000–$34,999	3.1	2.7	3.4
$35,000–$69,999	2.5	2.1	2.8
≥ $70,000	1.4	1.1	1.8
Marital Status			
Married/cohabiting	1.9	1.5	2.4
Separated/divorced/ widowed	4.5	5.9	3.8
Never married	3.8	3.5	4.2
Education			
Less than high school	3.3	3.3	3.4
High school	3.1	2.7	3.4
Some college or higher	2.4	2.1	2.7

Comorbidity

BPD is frequently comorbid with Axis I disorders and with other personality disorders. This comorbidity is associated with poorer outcome (Skodol, Gunderson, McGlashan, et al., 2002).

BPD–Axis I Comorbidity

BPD is highly comorbid with a number of Axis I disorders in both clinical and community samples (Coid, Yang, Tyrer, Roberts, & Ullrich, 2006; Lenzenweger et al., 2007; Skodol, Gunderson, Pfohl, et al., 2002). Unlike many conditions, BPD is unique in that it has commonalities with *both* internalizing and externalizing disorders (e.g., Eaton et al., 2011). Concerning internalizing disorders, features of BPD such as affective instability, emptiness, and interpersonal difficulties may be driving the high rates of comorbidity between BPD and mood or anxiety disorders. Concerning externalizing disorders, previous research has established a strong link between BPD and substance use disorders (SUDs) (e.g., Sher & Trull, 2002; Trull, Sher, Minks-Brown, Durbin, & Burr, 2000). To the extent that BPD is related to impulse control disorders, we might expect that BPD also shares genetic risk with both antisocial personality disorder (ASPD) and SUD and falls on an externalizing factor of psychopathology. However, BPD is not generally considered to be solely an externalizing disorder (Eaton et al., 2011). Thus, the BPD-SUD co-occurrence may be explained by a combination of impulsivity and negative emotionality (Sher & Trull, 2002; Trull et al., 2000).

High rates of comorbidity are the rule not the exception in clinical samples. Therefore, it is also of interest to investigate BPD comorbidity rates in the general population. Referring again to the NESARC study of the general U.S. population, Table 29.3 presents the odds ratios for the association between BPD and a range of other psychiatric disorders (Tomko et al., in press). BPD is significantly associated with almost every Axis

Table 29.3 Odds Ratios for Lifetime Borderline Personality Disorder and Other Lifetime Psychiatric Disorders Associations

Psychiatric Disorder	Total		Men		Women	
	OR	(99% CI)	OR	(99% CI)	OR	(99% CI)
Any Substance Use Disorder	4.50	(3.57– 5.71)	4.42	(2.80– 6.99)	5.41	4.10– 7.14)
Substance abuse	0.58	(0.42– 0.81)	0.46	(0.28– 0.75)	0.83	0.53– 1.30)
Substance dependence	5.29	(4.27– 6.54)	5.21	(3.62– 7.52)	5.92	4.55– 7.69)
Any Alcohol Use Disorder	3.36	(2.73– 4.12)	4.29	(2.90– 6.33)	3.80	2.93– 4.93)
Alcohol abuse*	0.77	(0.59– 1.01)	0.60	(0.41– 0.89)	1.14	0.78– 1.65)
Alcohol dependence	5.38	(4.37– 6.58)	6.25	(4.52– 8.62)	5.92	4.46– 7.81)
Nicotine dependence	4.07	(3.32– 4.98)	3.75	(2.71–5.18)	4.57	3.51– 5.92)
Any Drug Use Disorder	5.78	(4.67– 7.14)	6.06	(4.39– 8.33)	6.54	4.90– 8.77)
Drug abuse	2.63	(2.03– 3.41)	2.55	(1.76– 3.70)	3.08	2.14– 4.42)
Drug dependence	10.10	(7.69–13.33)	9.52	(6.41–14.08)	12.20	8.26–17.86)
Any Mood Episode	14.93	(11.63–19.61)	13.51	(9.35–19.61)	17.54	12.20–25.64)
Major depressive episode	11.76	(9.35–14.93)	11.36	(8.13–15.87)	13.16	9.52–17.86)
Dysthymia	8.33	(6.62–10.53)	7.25	(4.76–10.99)	8.85	6.67–11.76)
Manic episode	16.39	(13.33–20.41)	16.95	(11.90–24.39)	16.13	12.20–21.28)
Hypomanic episode	3.70	(2.71– 5.05)	2.62	(1.49– 4.63)	4.69	3.22– 6.80)
Any Anxiety Disorder	14.29	(10.87–18.87)	15.15	(10.20–22.22)	14.71	10.00–21.72)
Panic disorder with agoraphobia	13.89	(10.20–18.87)	13.33	(7.19–25.00)	13.70	9.71–19.61)
Panic disorder without agoraphobia*	5.29	(4.12– 6.85)	7.52	(4.88–11.49)	4.22	3.09–5.78)
Social phobia	9.17	(7.41–11.49)	7.87	(5.49–11.24)	10.10	7.63–13.33)
Specific phobia	5.03	(4.08– 6.17)	5.08	(3.61– 7.09)	5.03	3.86– 6.49)
Generalized anxiety disorder	11.11	(9.01–13.70)	11.36	(8.00–16.39)	11.11	8.55–14.49)
Posttraumatic stress disorder	10.42	(8.47–12.82)	11.76	(8.40–16.67)	10.00	7.63–12.99)
Any Other Personality Disorder	15.87	(12.82–19.61)	14.93	(10.64–20.83)	18.18	13.70–23.81)
Any Cluster A PD	20.83	(16.13–27.03)	21.74	(14.71–33.33)	20.00	14.29–27.78)
Paranoid	12.20	(8.93–16.39)	10.87	(6.49–18.18)	12.66	8.70–18.52)
Schizoid	14.29	(8.40–24.39)	11.90	(5.46–25.64)	17.24	8.40–34.48)
Schizotypal	111.11	(66.67–200.00)	125.00	(55.56–250.00)	100.00	50.00–200.00)
Any other Cluster B PD	13.16	(10.42–16.39)	13.89	(9.80–19.23)	16.67	11.90–23.26)
Histrionic	14.49	(6.85–31.25)	14.29	(4.18–50.00)	14.93	5.95–37.04)
Narcissistic	55.56	(40.00–83.33)	62.50	(40.00–100.00)	55.56	33.33–90.91)
Antisocial	6.33	(4.76– 8.40)	6.33	(4.31– 9.35)	8.47	5.46–13.16)
Any Cluster C PD	9.52	(7.19–12.66)	7.63	(4.72–12.35)	10.87	7.63–15.38)
Avoidant	11.63	(7.87–17.24)	7.81	(3.47–17.54)	13.70	8.70–21.74)
Dependent	20.41	(9.71–41.67)	12.82	(3.03–55.56)	23.26	10.20–52.63)
Obsessive-compulsive	7.75	(5.65–10.64)	6.94	(4.15–11.63)	8.40	5.56–12.66)

Note: *Signifies significant gender differences in the odds ratios for this disorder (p < .01).

I diagnosis, including all forms of anxiety, mood, and drug use disorder.

BPD–Axis II Comorbidity

In addition to extensive Axis I comorbidity, BPD is highly comorbid with other Axis II disorders (Cohen, Chen, Crawford, Brook, & Gordon, 2007; Lenzenweger et al., 2007; McGlashan, Grilo, & Skodol, 2000). For example, Lenzenweger and colleagues (2007) found BPD to have an average correlation of .56 with Cluster A PDs and .55 with Cluster C PDs. Although there were no instances of histrionic or narcissistic PD in this sample, the correlation with the remaining Cluster B PD, ASPD, was the highest at .64.

Trull, Scheiderer, and Tomko (2012) evaluated the results from four large studies (at least 200 participants) that used structured diagnostic interviews to establish *DSM-IV-TR* PD diagnoses. This included comorbidity data from two major epidemiological studies, the NESARC and the National Comorbidity Survey Replication (NCS-R), as well as large clinical investigations of personality disorder comorbidity.

Despite different methods and sampling strategies, it is clear that a BPD diagnosis is significantly associated with the full range of other Axis II but especially the other Cluster B diagnoses of antisocial, narcissistic, and histrionic personality disorder (Trull et al., 2012). However, the comorbidity patterns in this study did vary to some degree depending on the sample. Thus proclamations about specific BPD-other PDs comorbidity patterns should be offered with some caveats; these patterns do seem to be sample-specific.

General Functioning and Mental Health Treatment Utilization in BPD

BPD is not only associated with more impairment than many psychiatric disorders (Ansell, Sanislow, McGlashan, & Grilo, 2007), but this impairment appears to be more stable over time (Skodol et al., 2005). Specifically, individuals with BPD show impaired functioning in social relationships, occupation, and leisure activities (Ansell et al., 2007; Skodol et al., 2005). They are also more likely to have legal problems and financial difficulties (Coid et al., 2009). Consistent with BPD being a severely debilitating condition, individuals with

the disorder frequent mental health treatment settings more than individuals with mood, anxiety, or other personality disorders (Ansell et al., 2007). For example, a large epidemiological study in Great Britain estimated that 56.3% of individuals with BPD had sought help from a professional for mental health concerns in the past year (Coid et al., 2009).

Several longitudinal studies assessing the course of BPD over time have provided some provocative findings, some of which run counter to prevailing notions about the long-term stability of the BPD diagnosis (Morey & Hopwood, 2013). For example, Gunderson, Stout, et al. (2011) reported on the course and functioning of 175 individuals over a 10-year period who had originally met criteria for BPD. Using a 12-month definition of remission, the authors found that 85% of those originally diagnosed with BPD no longer met diagnostic criteria for the disorder 10 years later. Compared to other diagnostic groups (major depression; Cluster C personality disorders), the rate of remission for BPD was slower over 10 years. Among those with BPD that did remit, the relapse rate was low (11%) and tended to occur in the first 4 years before leveling off. Interestingly, although there was improvement in functioning over time, the average overall level of functioning of the BPD patients at the end of the 10-year follow-up was relatively low and suggested continuing problems in both social and occupational functioning despite significant symptom remission.

Similarly, Zanarini, Frankenburg, Reich, and Fitzmaurice (2012) reported high rates of sustained remission (2–8 years) over a 16-year follow-up of 290 patients with BPD, although at slower rates than those for individuals with other personality disorders. Furthermore, relapse among those that remitted was relatively infrequent (e.g., only 10% among those with an 8-year remission). Finally, consistent with the Gunderson, Stout, et al. (2011) findings, symptomatic recovery was not always accompanied by clinically significant improvement in functioning. In particular, many of these patients continued to experience significant vocational problems (including unemployment).

Impaired functioning of those with BPD is also observed in the general population (Tomko et al., in press). Results from the NESARC study indicate those with BPD were significantly more likely to have reported separation or divorce over the preceding 12 months, having significant trouble with one's boss or employer, and having serious problems with neighbors, friends, or relatives. Among those endorsing depression or low mood, a BPD diagnosis was also significantly associated with attempted suicide, presence of suicidal ideation, wanting to die, and thinking a lot about one's own death over the previous 3 years. Individuals with BPD also showed significant impairment in functioning on self-reported scales, even after controlling for the presence of other personality disorders, current Axis I disorders, sociodemographic risk factors (e.g., age, ethnicity or race, family income), and medical conditions (where relevant). BPD was a significant predictor of impaired social functioning, role emotional functioning, mental health, bodily pain, poorer general health, and decreased vitality (Tomko et al., in press).

Treatment Utilization

It is generally believed that those with BPD often seek out (perhaps excessively) health services, including emergency room (ER) services, while in crisis. ER visits for those with BPD are often precipitated by suicidal behavior, self-harm behaviors, or substance overdoses. Recent large scale studies also provide some additional information regarding the specific types of mental health services those with BPD seek out and receive. For example, Hörz et al. (Hörz, Zanarinini, Frankenburg, Reich, & Fitzmaurice, 2010) reported on the use of treatment modalities among 290 BPD patients and 72 patients with other personality disorders followed over a 10-year period. All were originally inpatients and between the ages of 18 and 35. There were five follow-up assessments, separated by 24 months. Overall, the percentage of those in individual therapy, taking regular medication, and being hospitalized decreased significantly over the follow-up period. Comparing those with BPD to those with other personality disorders, a significantly higher percentage of BPD patients reported taking medications regularly and being hospitalized over the 10-year follow-up period. Furthermore, of those with BPD that terminated outpatient treatment at some point during the follow-up period, 85% of them later resumed treatment at a later date. In contrast, rehospitalization was much less frequent and more sporadic.

Even in the general population, individuals with BPD report high rates of lifetime mental health treatment utilization (Tomko et al., in press). For example, in the NESARC study, individuals with BPD were highly likely to seek mental health services at some point in their lifetime, with 74.9% presenting to a physician, therapist, counselor, or other mental health professional for diagnosable mental health concerns. In addition, 63.1% of individuals diagnosed with BPD were prescribed medication for mental health issues.

Etiology

The etiology of BPD has been investigated and debated since the advent of the diagnosis itself. Almost all practitioners now agree that the causes of and contributors to the disorder are multifactorial and complex. There are studies that indicate a genetic disposition to BPD (Distel, Trull, et al., 2008; Kendler, Aggen et al., 2011), but research has also suggested a genetic association with mood and impulse disorders (Kendler, Aggen, et al., 2011). There is also empirical support for BPD patients having a childhood history of physical abuse, sexual abuse, or both, as well as parental conflict, loss, and neglect (Gunderson, 2001; Johnson, Cohen, Brown, Smailes, & Bernstein, 1999; Paris, 2009; Zanarini, 2000). It appears that past traumatic events are important in many if not most cases of BPD, contributing to the development of malevolent perceptions of others (Ornduff, 2000) as well as comorbidity with PTSD and mood and dissociative disorders. BPD may involve the interaction of a genetic disposition for lack of mood and impulse control with an evolving series of intense and unstable relationships. Linehan (1993) hypothesizes that persons with a BPD failed to learn important and useful skills for regulating emotional arousal and tolerating emotional distress; they learned instead that drug abuse, promiscuity, and self-injurious behavior produce temporary relief from stress.

There are numerous theories regarding the pathogenic mechanisms of BPD; most concern expectations of abandonment, separation, exploitative abuse, or any combination of these (Gunderson, 2001). Persons with BPD have usually had quite intense, disturbed, or abusive relationships with the significant persons of their lives, including their parents. They continue to expect and may even recreate unstable and intense relationships throughout their adult lives. Other views emphasize biological foundations for the core

BPD features of affective instability and impulsive aggression (e.g., Siever & Weinstein, 2009).

Genetic Perspectives

Although an increasing amount of attention has been paid to the disorder in recent years, its specific etiology and development remain uncertain. Currently, most new work on the etiology of BPD focuses on genetic influences on the expression of the disorder. This will be the focus in this chapter. As will become clear in the following discussion, a genetic predisposition seems to play a role in the development of BPD, but the specific genes responsible for this have not yet been identified.

Family and Twin Studies   Several studies support the idea that BPD and BPD-related traits are familial (e.g., Gunderson, Zanarini, et al., 2011). However, family studies cannot be used to disentangle the effects of genes from the effects of environment shared by family members. In contrast, twin studies can illuminate the effects of common environment and genes by modeling the different genetic relatedness of monozygotic (MZ) and dizygotic (DZ) twins. To date, eight twin studies have provided data on the heritability of BPD diagnoses and features. Torgersen (1984) reported a MZ concordance rate of 0.0% and a DZ concordance rate of 11.1% for BPD, which suggests that shared environmental factors influence the variance in BPD. However, the low number of twin pairs ($N = 25$) limits any conclusions that can be drawn. In a later study, Torgersen et al. (2000) assessed 221 twin pairs with a structured Axis II interview. Results suggested a heritability of 69%, though this estimate must be considered approximate because of the small number of twins, the ascertainment method (sampling those who were treated for mental disorder), and the fact that the zygosity and diagnostic status of co-twins was not hidden from the interviewers. More recently, in another Norwegian sample, Torgersen et al. (2008) assessed personality disorder traits in 1,386 twin pairs between the ages of 19 and 35 years using a structured PD interview. The prevalence rate for BPD (0.4%) was too low to analyze the data categorically, so a dimensional representation based on subclinical criteria was used to study the degree to which genetic and environmental factors influence PDs. The heritability of BPD was estimated at 35%, with the remaining variance explained by unique environmental factors.

Using a quantitative scale of BPD features, Distel, Trull, et al. (2008) assessed 5,496 twins (1,852 complete pairs) between the ages of 18 and 86 years from the Netherlands, Belgium, and Australia. Results indicated that genetic influences explained 42% of the variation in BPD features in both men and women. Interestingly, this heritability estimate was equal between the three countries, suggesting no interaction between genotype and country. The MZ correlation was more than twice as high as the DZ correlation in all three countries, indicating that nonadditive genetic effects may explain part of the variation in BPD features.

Kendler, Myers, and Reichborn-Kjennerud (2011a) used a Web-based Internet survey to collect questionnaire data on four BPD feature subscales (cognitive distortion, identity problems, insecure attachment, and affect instability) from 44,112 adult twins (including 542 twin pairs). Results for the best-fitting genetic model suggested a heritability index of .60 for BPD traits and .40 for specific environmental influences on liability.

In a Norwegian sample, Kendler, Aggen, et al. (2011b) used structured diagnostic interviews to assess *DSM-IV* BPD criteria in 2,111 twins (669 MZ pairs and 377 DZ pairs) from the Norwegian Institute of Public Health Twin Panel (NIPHTP) to estimate the heritability of BPD liability. Because too few individuals met *DSM-IV* cutoff scores for a BPD diagnosis, the authors analyzed a dimensional count of level of BPD symptoms endorsed. Specifically, a score of "subthreshold" or above was used as a cutoff for the presence of each BPD criterion, and five categories of endorsement were used in the analyses. Results indicated a heritability estimate of .49 for BPD liability, and, in the context of multivariate genetic analyses of a range of Axis I and Axis II disorders, BPD liability was associated with genetic risk for both Axis I and Axis II externalizing disorders as well as with environmental risk for Axis II disorders and Axis I internalizing disorders.

In a U.S. sample, Belsky et al. (2012) estimated the heritability of BPD features in a sample of over 1,000 same-sex twin pairs at age 12. Caregivers were asked to rate each child on 15 features believed to be related to borderline personality. Results indicated a MZ twin correlation of .66, a DZ twin correlation of .29, and a heritability estimate of .66 (95% CI = .62–.70) for these features.

Finally, in a series of studies, Bornovalova and colleagues (Bornovalova, Hicks, Iacono, & McGue,

2013; Bornovalova, Huibregtse, et al., 2013) conducted biometric analyses of questionnaire items judged to be relevant to BPD in 640 twin pairs at age 14 and age 18, as well as 1,382 twin pairs at age 24 (all part of the same longitudinal study). Heritability for BPD traits was estimated to be .25 at age 14, .48 at age 18, and .35 at age 24.

Twin Family Studies   The combination of data from twins and other family members, their parents, spouses, siblings, and/or offspring offers a powerful approach to study several mechanisms that cannot be assessed in twin or family data alone (Boomsma, Busjahn, & Peltonen, 2002), including cultural transmission of features from parents to offspring, passive G × E correlation or covariance, social homogamy, phenotypic assortment, and social interaction. Concerning the latter, twin methods assume that the social interaction between MZ and DZ twins is approximately equivalent. Twin family studies, because of their extended sampling of family members, can test this assumption. In a study by Distel, Trull, et al. (2008), a maximum likelihood test of variance differences between MZ and DZ twins indicated no differences in variances between MZ and DZ twins and, thus, given the large sample size, did not suggest that social interaction between twin siblings is of significant importance.

Distel, Rebollo-Mesa, et al. (2009) examined the genetic and environmental influences on individual differences in BPD features using an extended twin-family design. Data were collected on BPD features in twins (N = 5,017), their spouses (N = 939), siblings (N = 1,266), and parents (N = 3,064). Additive and nonadditive genetic effects, individual specific environmental influences, and assortment and cultural transmission were tested. Results indicated that resemblance among biological relatives could be attributed completely to genetic effects. Variation in borderline personality features was explained by additive genetic (21%) and dominant genetic (24%) factors, while environmental influences (55%) explained the remaining variance. *Additive genetic variance* refers to variance attributed to the additive effects of alleles segregating in the population, whereas *dominant genetic variance* refers to that attributed to nonadditive effects such that an allele can mask the effect of other allele at the same locus. In Distel, Rebollo-Mesa, et al.'s (2009) study, significant resemblance between spouses was observed,

best explained by phenotypic assortative mating, but it had only a small effect on the genetic variance (1% of the total variance). There was no effect of cultural transmission from parents to offspring.

Multivariate Twin Family Studies   Multivariate twin family studies, in which more than one phenotype per person is analyzed, can shed light on the genetic and environmental causes of association between traits, comorbidity between disorders, or overlap between traits and disorder. Distel et al. (2010) investigated the extent to which the covariance among four important components of BPD (affective instability, identity problems, negative relationships, and self-harm) could be explained by common genes. The phenotypic correlations among the scales ranged from .21 to .56 and were best explained by a genetic common pathway model, in which a single latent factor influenced all four components. Results indicated that a single genetic factor underlies most of the genetic variance in BPD, but each contributing component to BPD was also influenced by specific genetic factors, which do not overlap with each other.

Another multivariate twin family study from this group examined the genetic etiology of the relationship between BPD features and the five-factor model (FFM) of personality (Distel, Trull, et al., 2009). Data were available for 4,403 MZ twins, 4,425 DZ twins, and 1,661 siblings from 6,140 Dutch, Belgian, and Australian families. Heritability estimates for neuroticism, agreeableness, conscientiousness, extraversion, openness to experience, and borderline personality were 43%, 36%, 43%, 47%, 54%, and 45%, respectively. The phenotypic correlations between borderline personality and the FFM personality traits ranged from .06 for openness to experience to .68 for neuroticism. Results from multiple regression analyses revealed that a combination of high neuroticism and low agreeableness best predicted borderline personality. Multivariate genetic analyses showed that the genetic factors that influence individual differences in neuroticism, agreeableness, conscientiousness, and extraversion account for all genetic liability to borderline personality. Unique environmental effects on borderline personality, however, were not completely shared with those for the FFM traits (33% was unique to borderline personality).

Linkage Studies   To date, only one linkage study has been conducted to identify the genomic region(s) that may contain the quantitative trait loci (QTLs) that influence the manifestation of BPD features. Distel, Hottenga, Trull, and Boomsma (2008) conducted a family-based linkage study with 711 sibling pairs with phenotype and genotype data, and 561 additional parents with genotype data. BPD features were assessed on a quantitative scale. Evidence for linkage was found on chromosomes 1, 4, 9, and 18. The highest linkage peak was found on chromosome 9p at marker D9S286 with a LOD score of 3.548 (empirical P-value = .0001). Results suggest that these regions may harbor risk variants, but more empirical work is needed to provide greater resolution at these regions.

Candidate Gene Studies   The introduction of the National Institute of Mental Health's (NIMH's) Research Domain Criteria (RDoC) approach (Insel et al., 2010), as well as the revision of the *DSM* (i.e., *DSM-5*), which incorporates to some extent a dimensional approach to psychiatric classification, highlights the promise of transitioning from pure categorical diagnostic approaches to a more continuous, dimensional approach. For example, the RDoC approach (Insel et al., 2010) offers a promising avenue by which to study etiological factors that may be common to a number of diagnostic phenotypes. By defining and focusing on underlying dimensions of psychopathology and their biological and genetic underpinning (instead of studying heterogeneous phenotypes included in traditional diagnostic classifications), it may be possible to attain more specific and useful information that can inform description, treatment, and prevention.

This transition to a more dimensional, endophenotypic perspective has spurred many theorists and researchers to focus on common dimensions of dysfunction that may underlie many existing diagnostic categories. This is particularly relevant to personality disorders, including BPD (Regier, 2007). This transition has been reinforced by a methodological shift in the study of the genetics of BPD to more emphasis on the identification of endophenotypes related to this disorder (Siever, Torgersen, Gunderson, Livesley, & Kendler, 2002). Although most examinations of BPD's genetic underpinnings have utilized categorical and diagnostic approaches, we now see more studies examining the heritability of individual borderline personality traits and not the diagnosis per se, based on the rationale that this approach may improve understanding of component phenotypes (McCloskey et al., 2009; Siever et al., 2002).

Several candidate gene association studies have been conducted for BPD or for correlated personality traits; however, findings thus far remain unreplicated or inconsistent (Joyce et al., 2006; Maurex, Zaboli, Ohman, Asberg, & Leopardi, 2010; McCloskey et al., 2009; Nemoda et al., 2010; Ni et al., 2006; Pascual et al., 2008; Perez-Rodriguez et al., 2010; Siever et al., 2002; Stoltenberg, Christ, & Highland, 2012; Wilson et al., 2009). Presented here is a brief review of some of the recent major studies that have examined the association between several gene polymorphisms and the BPD diagnosis, BPD features, or major dimensions believed to underlie the BPD phenotype.

Regarding related BPD traits, altered serotonergic function in anger (Giegling, Hartmann, Möller, & Rujescu, 2006), aggression (Bortolato et al., 2013; Siever, 2008), suicidal behavior (Bah et al., 2008; Bortolato et al., 2013; Mann et al., 2009; Zaboli et al., 2006), emotion regulation (Canli, Ferri, & Duman, 2009), emotional lability (Hoefgen et al., 2005), and impulsivity (New et al., 1998; Passamonti et al., 2008) suggests several serotonergic candidate genes for BPD. The tryptophan hydroxylase genes (*TPH1* and *TPH2*) and the serotonin transporter gene (*SLC64A; 5-HTT*) are the most frequently studied candidate genes. TPH plays a role in the biosynthesis of serotonin (5-HT) and is thus expected to be related to dysfunction of the 5-HT system (Bortolato et al., 2013). For example, Zaboli et al. (2006) conducted a case–control study to determine whether specific TPH1 single nucleotide polymorphism (SNP)-based haplotypes were associated with BPD in 95 suicidal female BPD patients. They found that several haplotypes were associated with BPD but no individual SNP was associated with BPD. 5-HTT transports serotonin from synaptic spaces into presynaptic neurons. Ni, Chan, et al. (2006) examined associations between *SLC64A* and BPD in 89 BPD patients and 269 healthy controls at three polymorphisms: 5-HTTLPR (the SLC6A4-linked polymorphic region), VNTR (variable number of tandem repeat) in intron 2, and an SNP within the LPR region (A/G; rs25531). Significant associations between BPD and the 10 repeat allele of the intron 2 VNTR as well as a haplotype containing this allele and the short allele of the 5-HTTLPR were reported. Subsequent studies, including those investigating other serotonergic pathway genes (e.g., *HTR1A, HTR1B, HTR1D, HTR3A,* and *TPH2*), have yielded a mix of positive and negative results (Maurex et al., 2010; Ni et al., 2009; Pascual et al., 2008; Perez-Rodriguez et al., 2010). Notably, the largest study among these consisted of a comparison group of 300 patients with mood disorders (Wilson et al., 2009, 2012), making it difficult to draw strong conclusions about the involvement of serotonergic genes in the development of BPD.

In addition to serotonergic dysfunction, there is some evidence that dopamine (DA) dysfunction may be associated with BPD. DA dysfunction is associated with emotional dysregulation, impulsivity and cognitive-perceptual impairment (Friedel, 2004), three important dimensions of BPD. For example, there have been positive associations reported between the dopamine transporter gene (*SLC6A3; DAT1*), the dopamine D4 receptor gene (*DRD4*), and the dopamine D2 receptor gene (*DRD2*) and BPD (Joyce et al., 2006; Nemoda et al., 2010), but negative results have also been reported (Schmahl et al., 2012).

The gene that encodes monoamine oxidase-A (*MAOA*), which degrades 5-HTT and DA, is suggested to be involved in BPD because it has been shown to be associated with aggression (Buckholtz & Meyer-Lindenberg 2008), impulsivity (Manuck, Flory, Ferrell, Mann, & Muldoon, 2000), and mood lability (Furlong et al., 1999). To test whether *MAOA* is also associated with the BPD diagnosis Ni et al. (2007) genotyped two *MAOA* polymorphisms (promoter VNTR and rs6323) in 111 BPD patients and 289 control subjects. A high frequency of the high-activity VNTR alleles, which result in reduced monoamine levels, was found in patients with BPD. This finding suggests that *MAOA* may play a role in the etiological development of BPD; however, this result has not been replicated.

Most recently, Panagopoulos et al. (2013) examined the association between BPD phenotypes and *NRXN3* gene polymorphisms in a study of heroin-dependent adults and matched controls form similar neighborhoods. *NRXN3* polymorphisms have been previously reported to be associated with substance dependence disorders (Docampo et al., 2012; Hishimoto et al., 2007; Lachman et al., 2007; Liu et al., 2005; Stoltenberg et al., 2011). Genotypic and BPD phenotypic data were available for 1,439 cases and 507 controls. One or more *NRXN3* SNPs were nominally associated with all BPD phenotypes; however, none met the conservative significance threshold employed to correct for multiple testing. The most strongly

associated SNPs included rs10144398 with identity disturbance and rs10151731 with affective instability. The strongest association with screening positive for BPD was found for the *NRXN3* SNP, rs10083466. Neither the correlation of BPD phenotypes nor the linkage disequilibrium relationships of the SNPs account for the number of observed associations involving *NRXN3* SNPs.

Summary of Genetically Informative Studies of BPD

Existing twin data make a strong case for the heritability of the BPD phenotype. However, to date, the results of candidate gene studies have been somewhat inconsistent, and few replications of specific polymorphisms and BPD phenotypes have been reported. These inconsistencies are likely due to multiple factors but especially to very small sample sizes and to great variation in the nature of the target samples (e.g., psychiatric patients versus general population, patients with comorbid conditions) and the control samples (e.g., clinical controls, healthy controls). Therefore, the task for the next generation of studies is to conduct larger scale molecular genetic investigations or to form major collaborations in order to obtain large pools of genetic data that will provide enough statistical power to detect what are likely to be small effects of genes on the BPD phenotype. However, the success of such investigations will be contingent on identifying and using reliable measures of the phenotype. In particular, it can be questioned whether adopting the *DSM-IV-TR* and *DSM-5* definition of the phenotype and using the resulting categorical diagnosis will be optimal (because there are 256 ways to obtain a BPD diagnosis). I now turn to a discussion of the evidence supporting different conceptualizations of the BPD phenotype, some of which are not tethered to the *DSM-IV* and current *DSM-5* Section II BPD definition.

What Is the Best Way to Conceptualize and Define the BPD Phenotype?

From the beginning (see Historical Review earlier in this chapter), there have been disagreements and debates about how best to define and characterize BPD. Although, to some extent, the definition of BPD has been standardized by the series of diagnostic manuals, starting with *DSM-III*, many investigators still question whether these diagnostic criteria best operationalize this personality disorder. Furthermore, previous diagnostic manuals have adopted a categorical approach to the diagnosis, and many believe this is not supported by existing research on personality disorders in general and BPD in particular (Trull & Durrett, 2005; Widiger & Trull, 2007). In this last section of the chapter, several issues about the BPD phenotype are discussed, whose resolution will have a great impact on the future description and study of BPD.

Is BPD Categorical or Dimensional?

In order to determine whether BPD is best conceptualized as a categorical or dimensional construct, several researchers have used taxometric analyses to address the nature of the construct itself. Taxometric analyses help address whether a diagnostic construct is best conceptualized as a latent class (to which individuals either do or do not belong; a categorical variable) or as a dimension of pathology (representing a continuum of severity or degree). To date, published taxometric analyses of BPD criteria have all arrived at the same conclusion: BPD, as defined by *DSM*-based measures, appears best conceptualized as a dimensional variable (Arntz et al., 2009; Edens, Marcus, & Ruiz, 2008; Rothschild, Cleland, Haslam, & Zimmerman, 2003; Trull, Widiger, & Guthrie, 1990).

For example, two relatively recent studies arrived independently at this conclusion. Arntz et al. (2009) used Axis II BPD structured diagnostic interview data from women and men in mental health and forensic institutes as well as data from nonpatients. Overall, the results of these analyses supported a latent dimensional structure for the BPD criteria. Taxometric analyses have not focused exclusively on *DSM* BPD criteria. Using a popular questionnaire measure of BPD *features*, Edens et al. (2008) investigated the latent structure of BPD in an incarcerated sample of men and women. The same taxometric analyses used by Arntz et al. (2009) were performed on these data, and findings supported a dimensional construal of BPD for both the full and the female samples.

Is BPD Uni- or Multidimensional?

Given that evidence suggests that both BPD and borderline pathology are best viewed as dimensional constructs, the question becomes: How many dimensions of psychopathology appear to underlie the symptoms and features of BPD? Taxometric analyses do not, in and of themselves, speak to the uni- versus multidimensionality of constructs. To address this question, a number of studies have examined the factor structure of the *DSM* BPD criteria over the last 20 years. Results have suggested both unitary and multiple latent factors underlying the BPD criteria. For example, Sanislow, Grilo, and McGlashan (2000) used confirmatory factor analyses to test a factor model developed previously using *DSM-III-R* BPD criteria. A later study used *DSM-IV* BPD criteria and a much larger sample of clinical and treatment-seeking participants (Sanislow et al., 2002). Sanislow et al. (2002) reported results supporting both the original three-factor solution (Disturbed Relatedness, Behavioral Dysregulation, and Affective Dysregulation) and a one-factor solution; the two models produced comparable fit indices. However, the factors from the three-factor model solution were so highly correlated (range = .84 to .90) as to question the utility of this model over a one-factor model. Nevertheless, this 2002 study is often cited as evidence for a three-factor model of BPD symptoms.

Adopting a somewhat broader view of BPD pathology, Giesen-Bloo, Wachters, Schouten, and Arntz (2010) used data obtained from a semi-structured interview based on *DSM-IV-TR* BPD criteria and associated features. In this study of personality-disordered and Axis I patients as well as nonpatients, the authors compared the model fit between previously proposed models of BPD pathology and both a one- and "all-factor" solution (nine factors). The all-factor solution reflected the nine subscales of their own measure, each of which targets one of the nine *DSM-IV* criteria for BPD. In each case, the fit of the all-factor models was better than that for previously proposed models. However, because the items of this measure were written and developed specifically to assess each respective BPD criterion and this factor structure had been validated previously in the development of their measure, these results are perhaps not surprising. The competing models were derived from other measures and indices of BPD symptoms.

Are There Subtypes of BPD?

Latent class analyses (LCAs) are used to identify classes or groups of *individuals*, based on their scores on a range of categorical indicators. Fossati et al. (1999) conducted an LCA on BPD interview data from consecutively admitted patients. A three-class model fit the data best; the three latent classes identified (a) an asymptomatic group; (b) a group characterized by high endorsement of all BPD symptoms; and (c) a group characterized by low endorsement rates for all BPD symptoms except impulsivity and inappropriate anger. Because a confirmatory analysis of the BPD criteria in this sample supported a one-factor model, the authors interpreted the LCA findings as further evidence for a unitary dimension of BPD pathology.

Thatcher, Cornelius, and Clark, (2005) conducted an LCA using *DSM* BPD structured interview data from young adults (recruited originally from treatment facilities and from the community) that endorsed at least one BPD criterion. A three-class solution fit the data best: (a) a severe class–high endorsement rate across all items, (b) a moderate class, and (c) an impulsivity class–high endorsement rate on the impulsivity and inappropriate anger criteria.

Clifton and Pilkonis (2007) reported on an LCA of *DSM-III-R* BPD criteria in a mixed clinical and nonclinical sample of adults. Results suggested two latent classes: a borderline class with high to moderate endorsement rates of criteria across the board and a nonborderline class populated by those with low rates of endorsement of BPD criteria. Clifton and Pilkonis interpreted their results as being most consistent with a single dimension of BPD pathology.

Personality Traits and BPD

Up to this point, our discussion has focused on studies that have largely adopted the *DSM-IV-TR* definition of BPD. However, there is reason to question whether the nine *DSM-IV-TR* BPD criteria are necessarily the best way to conceptualize the BPD phenotype. In particular, much is known about the universality, and genetic and biological bases of major personality traits, and there is a clear conceptual and empirical connection between major personality traits and personality disorders (Widiger & Trull, 2007). Indeed, over the last 20 years, researchers have examined the correspondence between major personality traits and both symptoms and diagnoses of the *DSM*

personality disorders (Widiger & Trull, 2007; Trull & Widiger, 2008). By far, the personality model that has received the most attention is the five-factor model (FFM) of personality (Costa & McCrae, 1992). The five broad FFM domains include Neuroticism (versus emotional stability), Extraversion (or surgency), Agreeableness (versus antagonism), Conscientiousness (or constraint), and Openness (or intellect, imagination, or unconventionality).

A description of each of the 10 *DSM-IV* personality disorders in terms of the 30 facets of the FFM was developed by Lynam and Widiger (2001) on the basis of a survey of personality disorder researchers; these descriptions were then replicated by Samuel and Widiger (2004) in a subsequent survey of clinicians. The FFM description of BPD (Lynam & Widiger, 2001; see Table 29.4) includes high levels of Neuroticism (high anxiousness, angry hostility, depressiveness, impulsiveness, and vulnerability), high levels of Openness (high openness to feelings and to actions), low levels of Agreeableness (low compliance), and low levels of Conscientiousness (low deliberation).

Lynam and Widiger's (2001) FFM account of BPD has received empirical support both at the domain and facet level (Samuel & Widiger, 2008; Saulsman & Page, 2004). For example, a meta-analysis of 16 empirical articles that examined the relations between FFM traits and

Table 29.4 Five Factor Model of Personality-Borderline Personality Disorder (FFM-BPD) Traits and *DSM-5* Section III Borderline Personality Disorder Elevated Personality Traits

---

FFM-BPD traits[1]

 Neuroticism: anxiousness; angry hostility; depressiveness; impulsiveness; vulnerability
 Agreeableness: low compliance
 Conscientiousness: low deliberation
 Openness: feelings; actions

DSM-5 borderline traits

 Negative Emotionality: emotional lability; separation insecurity; anxiousness; depressivity
 Antagonism: hostility
 Disinhibition: impulsivity; risk taking

Note: [1]FFM-BPD predicted relations based on Lynam and Widiger (2001). Note that the FFM is a model. There are many measures available to assess the FFM traits in this particular model. We use the facet names of the NEO-PI-R (Costa & McCrae, 1992).

BPD indicated a moderate, positive correlation between Neuroticism scores and BPD (.54), and negative correlations with Agreeableness (–.24) and Conscientious (–.29) scores, respectively (Samuel & Widiger, 2008). In addition, BPD was positively related to all Neuroticism facet scores (i.e., anxiousness, angry hostility, depressiveness, self-consciousness, impulsiveness, and vulnerability) and negatively related to a range of Extraversion, Agreeableness, and Conscientiousness scores (i.e., warmth, positive emotions, trust, straightforwardness, compliance, competence, dutifulness, self-discipline, and deliberation). In general, these findings corresponded highly with predictions based on BPD pathology and personality styles (e.g., Lynam & Widiger, 2001; Widiger et al., 2002). Other, more recent studies have also supported these FFM trait predictions for BPD diagnosis and features (Bagby, Sellbom, Costa, & Widiger, 2008; Davenport, Bore, & Campbell, 2010).

Major Dimensions of Psychopathology Underlying BPD

Another approach to defining and understanding BPD is to focus on major dimensions of psychopathology that underlie the construct. Although this approach overlaps to some extent with a personality trait description of BPD, identifying major dimensions of psychopathology that presumably have biological underpinnings is perhaps more directly relevant to the NIMH's RDoC approach to psychopathology research (Sanislow et al., 2010).

In this spirit, we can review and discuss what many believe to be the three major dimensions of psychopathology that account for the symptoms of BPD: *emotional dysregulation, impulsivity*, and *interpersonal hypersensitivity*. Although there is some debate over the predominance of one or two of these over the other(s) (as well as the names of these dimensions), most researchers agree that these three dimensions capture the essence of the disorder.

Emotional Dysregulation

Emotional dysregulation is a core and perhaps the central feature of BPD (Linehan, 1993). Despite the prevalent use of the term, there is much confusion about the construct, and it seems best to conceptualize emotional dysregulation as a multicomponent process that includes but is not synonymous with the BPD symptom affective instability (Carpenter & Trull, 2013). *Affective instability* refers to the highly reactive moods of borderline individuals. Those with BPD typically shift between different varieties (e.g., anger, depression, anxiety) and degrees (e.g., moderate to extreme) of negative affect. Therefore, in the context of BPD, a more accurate description of the process that includes affective instability might be *negative emotional dysregulation*. The contextualization of affective instability within the negative emotional dysregulation process distinguishes BPD from disorders such as bipolar disorder, in which a person may shift between both positive and negative affect (e.g., from depression to elation). Also, affective instability in BPD is unique in that the affect shifts occur in response to external stimuli in the person's environment. These extreme shifts in negative mood typically last a few hours to a few days, and may occur as a result of factors such as interpersonal stressors, perceived rejections, or events prompting identity crises. This pattern differentiates BPD from major depression, for example, in which the shifts in affect may result more from internal cues (e.g., self-critical thinking, pessimism about the future).

Specific BPD criteria that appear to arise directly from negative emotion dysregulation include *affective instability, extreme anger, and emptiness*. In addition, negative emotion dysregulation may be the driving force behind many additional behaviors seen in the disorder (Carpenter & Trull, 2013). For example, Linehan (1993) has postulated that, in BPD, emotional vulnerability and the inability to regulate emotions lead to maladaptive attempts to regulate the intense affective states or control the problematic outcomes associated with these affective states. Impulsive behavior (including suicidal behavior) may be seen as a maladaptive solution to painful negative affect. Identity disturbance may result from a lack of emotional consistency and predictability. And disturbed interpersonal relationships may be the product of the difficulty in regulating emotional states and impulses as well as the inability to tolerate painful stimuli. As another example, it has been proposed that those with BPD may be especially vulnerable to developing substance use disorders because alcohol or drugs may be used to cope with negative affective states. Therefore, this feature can be quite dysfunctional in its own right and may well contribute to other symptoms and features of BPD.

Impulsivity and Behavioral Dysregulation

A second dimension of psychopathology that underlies BPD features is that of impulsivity or behavioral dysregulation. Individuals with BPD frequently engage in potentially harmful behaviors, such as substance abuse, promiscuity, excessive spending, gambling, binge eating, reckless driving, or shoplifting. In the *DSM-IV-TR* and *DSM-5* Section II, the major impulsivity criterion of BPD is defined as "impulsivity in at least two areas that are potentially self-damaging." Some argue that impulsivity is the single best defining feature of the disorder (Bornovalova, Fishman, Strong, Kruglanski, & Lejuez, 2008; Links, Heslegrave, & van Reekum, 1999). Furthermore, this criterion is one of the most commonly occurring symptoms among BPD patients (McGlashan et al., 2005). Crowell, Beauchaine, and Linehan (2009) suggest that impulsivity is one of the earliest detectable features of the disorder, and they note that genetic and family studies show a significant increase in the rate of impulse control disorders among family members of individuals with BPD. In addition, some initial research suggested that impulsivity is the most stable BPD symptom and the strongest predictor of overall BPD pathology (Links et al., 1999). More recent research, however, has found that impulsivity generally decreases with age among BPD patients (Morey & Hopwood, 2013; Stepp & Pilkonis, 2008).

The impulsivity diagnostic criterion of BPD highlights overt, maladaptive, impulsive behaviors. However, the etiology of these behaviors is not well understood. A biological predisposition toward disinhibition is one potential mechanism underlying the impulsivity associated with BPD. From this viewpoint, impulsive behaviors are seen as manifestations of underlying personality characteristics. Others have suggested that impulsive behaviors may be maladaptive attempts to regulate negative emotions (e.g., Brown, Comtois, & Linehan, 2002; Kruedelbach, McCormick, Schulz, & Grueneich, 1990). From this perspective, impulsivity in BPD is secondary to affective instability and intense negative emotionality. More research is needed to examine how impulsivity and emotion dysregulation may interact to produce behaviors and actions characterizing BPD.

Interpersonal Hypersensitivity

In addition to difficulties in regulating both emotions and behaviors, BPD is associated with many interpersonal difficulties, including interpersonal conflict, catastrophizing of interpersonal problems, termination of relationships, and distrust of central members in interpersonal networks (Bray, Barrowclough, & Lobban, 2007; Clifton, Pilkonis, & McCarty, 2007). Three BPD diagnostic criteria reflect the interpersonal difficulties associated with the disorder. First, *frantic efforts to avoid abandonment* relates to a general intolerance of being alone; the individual may react with fear or even anger at a time-limited separation or possible termination of a relationship. This criterion suggests that someone suffering from BPD may feel a strong desire to keep others close, yet engage in aversive and at times destructive behaviors in order to maintain this closeness. The second interpersonal criterion for BPD, *patterns of unstable and intense interpersonal relationships*, reflects an initial strong idealization of another that may abruptly change to equally extreme devaluation of the same person. Finally, *transient, stress-related paranoid ideation or dissociation* is believed to occur primarily in the context of real or imagined abandonment by others.

Gunderson and Lyons-Ruth (2008) present a developmental model that argues there is a factor of *interpersonal hypersensitivity* of similar importance to BPD as affective instability and impulsivity. Their view suggests that negative interpersonal experiences combined with a biological disposition to be emotionally reactive may lead to an attribution bias toward perceived abandonment and rejection, resulting in excessive bids for attention and proximity seeking, which the recipient may find aversive. Clinical observation and empirical data suggest that rejection and abandonment experiences (or even perceptions of rejection or abandonment) seem to be central to interpersonal dysfunction in BPD. Those with BPD report rejection experiences from childhood as well as thought patterns or schemas that touch on the theme of rejection by others (Linehan, 1993; Meyer, Ajchenbrenner, & Bowles, 2005). These thought patterns appear to be a major source of daily interpersonal distress that is characteristic of the lives of those with BPD.

BPD-related interpersonal problems have also been described within a framework of *rejection sensitivity*. Rejection sensitivity is a cognitive-affective trait that causes individuals to anxiously expect, readily perceive, and overreact to rejection cues in the environment (Berenson et al., 2009; Downey & Feldman, 1996). Those who are high in rejection sensitivity automatically perceive rejection-relevant stimuli information as threatening, especially in ambiguous situations (Berenson et al., 2009; Downey, Mougios, Ayduk, London, & Shoda, 2004). However, they seek to maintain social ties while avoiding potential rejection (Downey & Feldman, 1996). This cognitive and affective style has significant interpersonal consequences, including early termination of relationships, attributing negative intentions to partners, and avoiding relationship-threatening stimuli (Berenson et al., 2009).

There is some evidence that impulsivity may moderate the relationship between rejection sensitivity and the interpersonal dysfunction seen in BPD (Ayduk et al., 2008). Not all those who are high in rejection sensitivity have BPD, nor do they all experience significant interpersonal dysfunction; however, effective self-regulation may moderate the relationship between rejection sensitivity styles and interpersonal dysfunction. The ability to inhibit one's impulses, thus, may be an explanatory factor in the relation between rejection sensitivity and borderline pathology.

Rejection sensitivity also appears to be related to negative emotionality. Experimental manipulations that induce feelings of rejection also elicit increased negative facial expressions among those high in rejection sensitivity (e.g., Downey & Feldman, 1996). Further, Ayduk, Mischel, and Downey (2002) found that if participants were instructed to focus on the physiological and emotional aspects of a personal rejection experience, they felt more hostile than if they were told to focus either on the setting of the experience or if they were given no specific instructions. In a study of reactions to teasing scenarios, Tragesser, Lippman, Trull, and Barrett (2008) found that those high in BPD features expected to feel increased levels of anger and sadness in response to teasing by a friend, even in benign contexts. Even when self-reported levels of anger were controlled for, those higher in BPD features more often endorsed that they would want to *behave* angrily toward the teaser (e.g., glaring at, retaliating). These results suggest that behaviors and emotions characteristic of those with BPD may be linked to a hypersensitivity to real or imagined rejection from others. Thus, when faced with possible signs of rejection, a person with BPD may be likely to experience heightened negative affect that, when accompanied by difficulties in regulating that affect, triggers reactive behaviors that his or her companion finds harmful or aversive.

As for mechanisms of interpersonal sensitivity in BPD, of major relevance are studies of social cognition, or the exchange of social signals between individuals (Roepke, Vater, Preibler, Heekeren, & Dziobek, 2013). Those with BPD pathology seem to have significant difficulty taking others' perspective and correctly identifying the mental states of others, especially in situations that involve more complex and more ecologically valid situations (i.e., not simply static pictures of faces). Furthermore, when in the context of rejection and exclusion, those with BPD pathology appear to have a bias toward more negative and malevolent interpretations of the intentions and motivations of others. Regarding the emotional states of others, those with BPD pathology show significant deficiencies in being able to empathize with others' distress, and this is exacerbated under high-arousal situations. Finally, others have difficulty recognizing emotions in the facial expressions of those with BPD pathology, which appears to be due to limited facial expressions and more mixed facial expressions. In summary, there appear to be several documented tendencies and deficits among those with BPD pathology that can lead to confusing or misinterpreted social interactions, and these seem exacerbated by stress or high arousal.

The Future of the BPD Diagnosis

Our review of the various issues related to the best way to define the BPD phenotype begs the question: How is BPD likely to be conceptualized and defined in the future?

The American Psychiatric Association Board of Trustees decided to maintain the same criteria and diagnostic rules outlined in *DSM-IV* for the PDs (including BPD) in Section II of the new *DSM-5*. This decision was made in order to preserve continuity with current clinical practice. The decision was based on an evaluation that there was not sufficient empirical evidence to justify a new trait-based approach to the personality disorders. Furthermore, many personality disorder scholars and researchers decried the proposed changes and expressed concern that much of what we know about the PDs, based on a relatively stable set of diagnostic criteria, may not be applicable to these proposed newly defined PDs. Despite these concerns, *DSM-5* Section III presents an alternative model for personality disorders in order to introduce an approach that seeks to address many of the shortcomings of previous categorical approaches to the diagnosis of personality disorders.

Specifically, the *DSM-5* Personality Disorders Workgroup proposal for a BPD diagnosis requires (1) significant impairment in personality functioning (i.e., the domains of self-functioning and of interpersonal functioning); (2) elevated personality traits in negative affectivity, disinhibition, and antagonism; (3) stability and pervasiveness across situations; (4) these impairments and trait expressions to not be normative or part of the person's culture; and (5) these impairments and trait expressions to not be due to the effects of substances or medications.

Here, I focus only on the first two components of the Workgroup's proposed BPD diagnosis (assessing impairment in personality functioning and assessing pathological personality traits associated with BPD), with special emphasis on the trait ratings that are included in this BPD conceptualization.

The first step in assessing an individual for a Section III *DSM-5* BPD diagnosis involves rating a patient's *level of personality functioning*—specifically, the level of self- and interpersonal functioning for each individual assessed. *Self-functioning* is defined in two areas (identity integration; self-directedness), as is *interpersonal functioning* (empathy and intimacy). A five-point scale is used to rate overall level of personality functioning for this purpose (0 = no impairment; 1 = some impairment; 2 = moderate impairment; 3 = severe impairment; and 4 = extreme impairment); examples for the ratings are provided (*DSM-5*, pp. 775–778). A moderate level of impairment of personality functioning in two or more of these four areas is required for a diagnosis of BPD. The clinician is reminded that the ratings must reflect functioning that is of multiple years in duration, and must reflect patterns of functioning that are relatively inflexible and pervasive across a wide range of personal and social situations, not due solely to another mental disorder, physical condition, or effect of a substance, and not a norm within a person's cultural background.

The second step involves evaluating personality trait elevations in the individual. Section III *DSM-5* BPD personality traits include those

tapping *negative affectivity* (emotional lability, anxiousness, separation insecurity, and depressivity), *disinhibition* (impulsivity, risk taking), and *antagonism* (hostility) (see Table 29.4). Section III calls on diagnosticians to decide whether these seven traits are elevated in the individual; this judgment can be made on the basis of clinical interview or questionnaire scores. It is required that an individual show elevations on at least four of these seven pathological personality traits, and at least one of these elevations must be on impulsivity, risk taking, or hostility.

The new alternative *DSM-5* model for personality disorders in Section III clearly represents an attempt to provide a more dimensional perspective on personality pathology in general, and on BPD in particular. Further, this trait-focused system is more consistent with the large body of research supporting the reliability and validity of using the framework of major dimensions of personality and personality pathology to conceptualize, describe, and study personality disorders (Widiger & Trull, 2007). However, a major challenge is convincing clinicians that such a framework is clinically useful, can be applied reliably, and can preserve what we have learned about BPD in the past using a traditional categorical system of symptom lists.

Conclusion

It is very clear that clinicians and researchers deem BPD to be a syndrome that is quite important given its prevalence in both clinical and nonclinical samples, its association with impairment and dysfunction, and its relationship to increased risk for suicidal behavior, interpersonal conflict, substance dependence, and early mortality. Despite the attention given to BPD by clinicians and researchers alike, its specific etiology remains largely uncharted. The causes of BPD are multifactorial and complex, involving some interplay between social, environmental, and genetic factors. However, the widely accepted *DSM* definition of BPD breeds great heterogeneity, and this will likely limit advances in uncovering etiological factors and in designing more effective treatments for BPD. It is recommended that scholars and researchers focus on the dimensions underlying BPD symptoms in order to identify the essence of the disorder, investigate both biological and environmental influences on these core dimensions, and ultimately develop better treatments.

References

Akiskal, H. S. (1981). Subaffective disorders: Dysthymic, cyclothymic, and bipolar II disorders in the "borderline" realm. *Psychiatric Clinics of North America, 4*, 25–46.

Ansell, E. B., Sanislow, C. A., McGlashan, T. H., & Grilo, C. M. (2007). Psychosocial impairment and treatment utilization by patients with borderline personality disorder, other personality disorders, mood and anxiety disorders, and a healthy comparison group. *Comprehensive Psychiatry, 28*, 329–336.

Arntz, A., Bernstein, D., Gielen, D., van Nieuwenhuyzen, M., Penders, K., Haslam, N., & Ruscio, J. (2009). Taxometric evidence for the dimensional structure of Cluster C, paranoid, and borderline personality disorders. *Journal of Personality Disorders, 23*(6), 606–628.

Ayduk, O., Mischel, W., & Downey, G. (2002). Attentional mechanisms linking rejection to hostile reactivity: The role of "hot" versus "cool" focus. *Psychological Science, 13*, 443–448.

Ayduk, O., Zayas, V., Downey, G., Cole, A. B., Shoda, Y., & Mischel, W. (2008). Rejection sensitivity and executive control: Joint predictors of borderline personality features. *Journal of Research in Personality, 42*, 151–168.

Bagby, R. M., Sellbom, M., Costa, P. T., & Widiger, T. A. (2008). Predicting *Diagnostic and Statistical Manual of Mental Disorders-IV* personality disorders with the five-factor model of personality and the personality psychopathology five. *Personality and Mental Health, 2*, 55–69.

Bah, J., Lindström, M., Westberg, L., Manneräs, L., Ryding, E., Henningsson, S.,...Eriksson, E. (2008). Serotonin transporter gene polymorphisms: Effect on serotonin transporter availability in the brain of suicide attempters. *Psychiatry Research: Neuroimaging, 162*(3), 221–229.

Belsky, D. W., Caspi, A., Arseneault, L., Bleidorn, W., Fonagy, P., Goodman, M., Houts, R., & Moffitt, T. E. (2012). Etiological features of borderline personality related characteristics in a birth cohort of 12-year-old children. *Development and Psychopathology, 24*, 251–265.

Berenson, K. R., Gyurak, A., Adyuk, O., Downey, G., Garner, M. J., Mogg, K., et al. (2009). Rejection sensitivity and disruption of attention by social threat cues. *Journal of Research in Personality, 43*, 1064–1072.

Boomsma, D. I., Busjahn, A., & Peltonen, L. (2002). Classical twin studies and beyond. *Nature Reviews Genetics, 3*, 872–882.

Bornovalova, M. A., Fishman, S., Strong, D. R., Kruglanski, A. W., & Lejuez, C. W. (2008). Borderline personality disorder in the context of self-regulation: Understanding symptoms and hallmark features as deficits in locomotion and assessment. *Personality and Individual Differences, 44*, 22–31.

Bornovalova, M. A., Hicks, B. M., Iacono, W. G., & McGue, M. (2013). Longitudinal twin study of borderline personality disorder traits and substance use in adolescence: Developmental change, reciprocal effects, and genetic and environmental influences. *Personality Disorders: Theory, Research, and Treatment, 4*(1), 23–32.

Bornovalova, M. A., Huibregtse, B. M., Hicks, B. M., Keyes, M., McGue, M., & Iacono, W. (2013). Tests of a direct effect of childhood abuse on adult borderline personality disorder traits: A longitudinal discordant twin design. *Journal of Abnormal Psychology, 122*(1), 180–194.

Bortolato, M., Pivac, N., Seler, D. M., Perkovic, M. N., Pessia, M., & Giovanni, G. D. (2013). The role of the serotonergic system at the interface of aggression and suicide. *Neuroscience, 236*, 160–185.

Bray, S., Barrowclough, C., & Lobban, F. (2007). The social problem-solving abilities of people with borderline personality disorder. *Behaviour Research and Therapy, 45*, 1409–1417.

Brown, M. Z., Comtois, K. A., & Linehan, M. M. (2002). Reasons for suicide attempts and nonsuicidal self-injury in women with borderline personality disorder. *Journal of Abnormal Psychology, 111*, 198–202.

Buckholtz, J. W., & Meyer-Lindenberg, A. (2008). MAOA and the neurogenetic architecture of human aggression. *Trends in Neurosciences, 31*(3), 120–129.

Canli, T., Ferri, J., & Duman, E. A. (2009). Genetics of emotion regulation. *Neuroscience, 164*, 43–54.

Carpenter, R. W., & Trull, T. J. (2013). Components of emotion dysregulation in borderline personality disorder: A review. *Current Psychiatry Reports, 15*, 1–8.

Clifton, A., & Pilkonis, P. A. (2007). Evidence for a single latent class of Diagnostic and Statistical Manual of Mental Disorders borderline personality pathology. *Comprehensive Psychiatry, 48*(1), 70–78.

Clifton, A., Pilkonis, P. A., & McCarty, C. (2007). Social networks in borderline personality disorder. *Journal of Personality Disorders, 21,* 434–441.

Cohen, P., Chen, H., Crawford, T. N., Brook, J. S., & Gordon, K. (2007). Personality disorders in early adolescence and the development of later substance use disorders in the general population. *Drug and Alcohol Dependence, 88S,* S71–S84.

Coid, J., Yang, M., Bebbington, P., Moran, P., Brugha, T., Jenkins, R., et al. (2009). Borderline personality disorder: Health service use and social functioning among a national household population. *Psychological Medicine, 39,* 1721–1731.

Coid, J., Yang, M., Tyrer, P., Roberts, A., & Ullrich, S. (2006). Prevalence and correlates of personality disorder among adults aged 16 to 74 in Great Britain. *British Journal of Psychiatry, 188,* 423–431.

Costa, P. T., & McCrae, R. R. (1992). *Revised NEO Personality Inventory (NEO PI-R) and NEO Five-Factor Inventory (NEO-FFI) professional manual.* Odessa, FL: Psychological Assessment Resources.

Crowell, S. E., Beauchaine, T. P., & Linehan, M. M. (2009). A biosocial developmental model of borderline personality disorder: Elaborating and extending Linehan's theory. *Psychological Bulletin, 135,* 495–510.

Davenport, J., Bore, M., & Campbell, J. (2010). Changes in personality in pre- and post-dialectical behaviour therapy borderline personality disorder groups: A question of self-control. *Australian Psychologist, 45,* 59–66.

Distel, M. A., Hottenga, J. J., Trull, T. J., & Boomsma, D. I. (2008). Chromosome 9: Linkage for borderline personality disorder features. *Psychiatric Genetics, 18,* 302–307.

Distel, M. A., Rebollo-Mesa, I., Willemsen, G., Derom, C. A., Trull, T. J., & Boomsma, D. I. (2009). Familial resemblance of borderline personality disorder features: Genetic or cultural transmission? *PloS ONE, 4*(4), 1–8.

Distel, M. A., Trull, T. J., Vink, J. M., Willemsen, G., Derom, C. A., Lynskey, M., Martin, N. G., & Boomsma, D. I. (2009). The five factor model of personality and borderline personality disorder: A genetic analysis of comorbidity. *Biological Psychiatry, 66,* 1131–1138.

Distel, M. A., Trull, T. J., Willemsen, G., Derom, C., Thiery, E., Grimmer, M., Martin, N. G., & Boomsma, D. I. (2008). Heritability of borderline personality features is similar across three countries. *Psychological Medicine, 38,* 1219–1229.

Distel, M. A., Willemsen, G., Ligthart, L., Derom, C., Martin, N. G., Neale, M. C., Trull, T. J., & Boomsma, D. I. (2010). Genetic covariance structure of the four main features of borderline personality disorder. *Journal of Personality Disorders, 24,* 427–444.

Docampo, E., Ribasés, M., Gratacòs, M., Bruguera, E., Cabezas, C., Sánchez-Mora, C.,...Estivill, X. (2012). Association of neurexin 3 polymorphisms with smoking behavior. *Genes, Brain and Behavior, 11*(6), 704–711.

Downey, G., & Feldman, S. I. (1996). Implications of rejection sensitivity for intimate relationships. *Journal of Personality and Social Psychology, 70,* 1327–1343.

Downey, G., Mougios, V., Ayduk, O., London, B. E., & Shoda, Y. (2004). Rejection sensitivity and the defensive motivational system. *Psychological Science, 15,* 668–673.

Eaton, N. R., Krueger, R. F., Keyes, K. M., Skodol, A. E., Markon, K.E., Grant, B. F., & Hasin, D. S. (2011). Borderline personality disorder comorbidity: Relationship to the internalizing-externalizing structure of common mental disorders. *Psychological Medicine, 41,* 1041–1050.

Edens, J. F., Marcus, D. K., & Ruiz, M. A. (2008). Taxometric analyses of borderline personality features in a large-scale male and female offender sample. *Journal of Abnormal Psychology, 117*(3), 705.

Fossati, A., Maffei, C., Bagnato, M., Donati, D., Namia, C., & Novella, L. (1999). Latent structure analysis of DSM-IV borderline personality disorder criteria. *Comprehensive Psychiatry, 40*(1), 72–79.

Friedel, R. O. (2004). Dopamine dysfunction in borderline personality disorder: A hypothesis. *Neuropsychopharmacology, 29*(6), 1029–1039.

Furlong, R. A., Ho, L., Rubinsztein, J. S., Walsh, C., Paykel, E. S., & Rubinsztein, D. C. (1999). Analysis of the monoamine oxidase A (MAOA) gene in bipolar affective disorder by association studies, meta-analyses, and sequencing of the promoter. *American Journal of Medical Genetics, 88*(4), 398–406.

Giegling, I., Hartmann, A. M., Möller, H. J., & Rujescu, D. (2006). Anger- and aggression-related traits are associated with polymorphisms in the 5-HT-2A gene. *Journal of Affective Disorders, 96*(1), 75–81.

Giesen-Bloo, J. H., Wachters, L. M., Schouten, E., & Arntz, A. (2010). The Borderline Personality Disorder Severity Index-IV: Psychometric evaluation and dimensional structure. *Personality and Individual Differences*, 49(2), 136–141.

Grant, B. F., Chou, S. P., Goldstein, R. B., Huang, B., Stinson, F. S., Saha, T. D.,…Ruan, W. J. (2008). Prevalence, correlates, disability, and comorbidity of DSM-IV borderline personality disorder: Results from the Wave 2 National Epidemiologic Survey on Alcohol and Related Conditions. *Journal of Clinical Psychiatry*, 69(4), 533–545.

Grant, B. F., Hasin, D. S., Chou, S. P., Stinson, F. S., & Dawson, D. A. (2004). Nicotine dependence and psychiatric disorders in the United States. *Archives of General Psychiatry*, 61, 1107–1115.

Grant B. F., Kaplan, K., Shepard, J., & Moore, T. (2003). *Source and accuracy statement for wave 1 of the 2001–2002 National Epidemiologic Survey on Alcohol and Related Conditions*. Bethesda, MD: National Institute on Alcohol Abuse and Alcoholism.

Grant, B. F., Stinson, F. S., Dawson, D. A., Chou, S. P., Ruan, W. J., & Pickering, R. P. (2004). Co-occurrence of 12-month alcohol and drug use disorders and personality disorders in the United States. *Archives of General Psychiatry*, 61, 361–368.

Grinker, R., Werble, B., & Drye, R. (1968). *The borderline syndrome: A behavioral study of ego functions*. New York: Basic Books.

Gunderson, J. (2001). *Borderline personality disorder: A clinical guide*. Washington, DC: American Psychiatric Publishing.

Gunderson, J. (2009). Borderline personality disorder: Ontogeny of a diagnosis. *American Journal of Psychiatry*, 166, 530–539.

Gunderson, J., & Lyons-Ruth, K. (2008). BPD's interpersonal hypersensitivity phenotype: A gene-environment-developmental model. *Journal of Personality Disorders*, 22, 22–41.

Gunderson, J., & Singer, M. T. (1975). Defining borderline patients: An overview. *American Journal of Psychiatry*, 132, 1–10.

Gunderson, J., Stout, R. L., McGlashan, T. H., Shea, T., Morey, L. C., Grilo, C. M.,…Skodol, A. E. (2011). Ten-year course of borderline personality disorder: Psychopathology and function from the collaborative longitudinal personality disorders study. *Archives of General Psychiatry*, 68, 827–837.

Gunderson, J., Zanarini, M. C., Choi-Kain, L. W., Mitchell, K. S., Jang, K. L., & Hudson, J. I. (2011). Family study of borderline personality disorder and its sectors of psychopathology. *Archives of General Psychiatry*, 68, 753–762.

Herman, J. (1992). *Trauma and Recovery*. New York, Basic Books.

Hishimoto, A., Liu, Q. R., Drgon, T., Pletnikova, O., Walther, D., Zhu, X. G.,…Uhl, G. R. (2007). Neurexin 3 polymorphisms are associated with alcohol dependence and altered expression of specific isoforms. *Human Molecular Genetics*, 16(23), 2880–2891.

Hoefgen, B., Schulze, T. G., Ohlraun, S., von Widdern, O., Höfels, S., Gross, M.,…Rietschel, M. (2005). The power of sample size and homogenous sampling: Association between the 5-HTTLPR serotonin transporter polymorphism and major depressive disorder. *Biological Psychiatry*, 57(3), 247–251.

Hörz, S., Zanarinini, M. C., Frankenburg, F. R., Reich, D. B., & Fitzmaurice, G. (2010). Ten-year use of mental health services by patients with borderline personality disorder and with other Axis II disorders. *Psychiatric Services*, 61, 612–616.

Insel, T. R., Cuthbert, B. N., Garvey, M. A., Heinssen, R. K., Pine, D. S., Quinn, K. J.,…Wang, P. S. (2010). Research domain criteria (RDoC): Toward a new classification framework for research on mental disorders. *American Journal of Psychiatry*, 167, 748–751.

Johnson, J. G., Cohen, P., Brown, J., Smailes, E. M., & Bernstein, D. P. (1999). Childhood maltreatment increases risk for personality disorders during early adulthood. *American Journal of Psychiatry*, 56, 600–606.

Joyce, P. R., McHugh, P. C., McKenzie, J. M., Sullivan, P. F., Mulder, R. T., Luty, S. E.,…Kennedy, M. A. (2006). A dopamine transporter polymorphism is a risk factor for borderline personality disorder in depressed patients. *Psychological Medicine*, 36, 807–814.

Kendler, K. S., Aggen, S. H., Knudsen, G. P., Røysamb, E., Neale, M. C., & Reichborn-Kjennerud, T. (2011). The structure of genetic and environmental risk factors for syndromal and subsyndromal common DSM-IV Axis I and all Axis II disorders. *American Journal of Psychiatry*, 168, 29–39.

Kendler, K. S., Myers, J., & Reichborn-Kjennerud, T. (2011). Borderline personality disorder traits and their relationship with dimensions of normative personality: A web-based cohort and twin study. *Acta Psychiatrica Scandinavica*, 123(5), 349–359.

Kernberg, O. (1967). Borderline personality organization. *Journal of the American Psychoanalytic Association*, 15, 641–685.

Knight, R. (1953). Borderline states. *Bulletin of the Menninger Clinic*, 17, 1–12.

Kruedelbach, N., McCormick, R. A., Schulz, S. C., & Grueneich, R. (1990). Impulsivity, coping styles, and triggers for craving in substance abusers with borderline personality disorder. *Journal of Personality Disorders, 7*, 214–222.

Lachman, H. M., Fann, C. S., Bartzis, M., Evgrafov, O. V., Rosenthal, R. N., Nunes, E. V.,…Knowles, J. A. (2007). Genomewide suggestive linkage of opioid dependence to chromosome 14q. *Human Molecular Genetics, 16*(11), 1327–1334.

Lenzenweger, M. F., Lane, M. C., Loranger, A. W., & Kessler, R. C. (2007). DSM-IV personality disorders in the National Comorbidity Survey Replication. *Biological Psychiatry, 62*, 553–564.

Lieb, K., Völlm, B., Rücker, G., Timmer, A., & Stoffers, J. M. (2010). Psychopharmacotherapy for borderline personality disorder: Cochrane systematic review of randomized trials. *British Journal of Psychiatry, 196*, 4–12.

Linehan, M. M. (1993). *Cognitive–behavioral treatment of borderline personality disorder.* New York: Guilford Press.

Links, P. S., Heslegrave, R., & van Reekum, R. (1999). Impulsivity: Core aspect of borderline personality disorder. *Journal of Personality Disorders, 13*, 1–9.

Liu, Q. R., Drgon, T., Walther, D., Johnson, C., Poleskaya, O., Hess, J., & Uhl, G. R. (2005). Pooled association genome scanning: Validation and use to identify addiction vulnerability loci in two samples. *Proceedings of the National Academy of Sciences of the United States of America, 102*(33), 11864–11869.

Lynam, D. R., & Widiger, T. A. (2001). Using the five factor model to represent the DSM-IV personality disorders: An expert consensus approach. *Journal of Abnormal Psychology, 110*, 401–412.

Mann, J. J., Arango, V. A., Avenevoli, S., Brent, D. A., Champagne, F. A., Clayton, P.,…& Wenzel, A. (2009). Candidate endophenotypes for genetic studies of suicidal behavior. *Biological Psychiatry, 65*(7), 556–563.

Manuck, S. B., Flory, J. D., Ferrell, R. E., Mann, J. J., & Muldoon, M. F. (2000). A regulatory polymorphism of the monoamine oxidase-A gene may be associated with variability in aggression, impulsivity, and central nervous system serotonergic responsivity. *Psychiatry Research, 95*, 9–23.

Maurex, L., Zaboli, G., Ohman, A., Asberg, M., & Leopardi, R. (2010). The serotonin transporter gene polymorphism (5-HTTLPR) and affective symptoms among women diagnosed with borderline personality disorder. *European Psychiatry, 25*, 19–25.

McCloskey, M. S., New, A. S., Siever, L. J., Goodman, M., Koenigsberg, H. W., Flory, J. D., & Coccaro, E. F. (2009). Evaluation of behavioral impulsivity and aggression tasks as endophenotypes for borderline personality disorder. *Journal of Psychiatric Research, 43*, 1036.

McGlashan, T. H., Grilo, C. M., Sanislow, C. A., Ralevski, E., Morey, L. C., Gunderson, J. G., et al. (2005). Two-year prevalence and stability of individual DSM-IV criteria for schizotypal, borderline, avoidant, and obsessive-compulsive personality disorders: Toward a hybrid model of axis II disorders. *American Journal of Psychiatry, 162*, 883–889.

McGlashan, T. H., Grilo, C. M., & Skodol, A. E. (2000). The Collaborative Longitudinal Personality Disorders Study: Baseline Axis I/II and II/II diagnostic co-occurrence. *Acta Psychiatrica Scandinavia, 102*, 256–264.

Meyer, B., Ajchenbrenner, M., & Bowles, D. P. (2005). Sensory sensitivity, attachment experiences, and rejection responses among adults with borderline and avoidant features. *Journal of Personality Disorders, 19*, 641–658.

Morey, L. C., & Hopwood, C. J. (2013). Stability and change in personality disorders. *Annual Review of Clinical Psychology, 9*, 499–528.

Nemoda, Z., Lyons-Ruth, K., Szekely, A., Bertha, E., Faludi, G., & Sasvari-Szekely, M. (2010). Association between dopaminergic polymorphisms and borderline personality traits among at-risk young adults and psychiatric inpatients. *Behavioral and Brain Functions, 6*(4), 1–11.

New, A. S., Gelernter, J., Yovell, Y., Trestman, R. L., Nielsen, D. A., Silverman, J.,…Siever, L. J. (1998). Tryptophan hydroxylase genotype is associated with impulsive aggression measures: a preliminary study. *American Journal of Medical Genetics, 81*(1), 13–17.

Ni, X., Bismil, R., Chan, K., Sicard, T., Bulgin, N., McMain, S., & Kennedy, J. L. (2006). Serotonin 2A receptor gene is associated with personality traits, but not to disorder, in patients with borderline personality disorder. *Neuroscience Letters, 408*, 214–219.

Ni, X., Chan, K., Bulgin, N., Sicard, T., Bismil, R., McMain, S., & Kennedy, J. L. (2006). Association between serotonin transporter gene and borderline personality disorder. *Journal of Psychiatric Research, 40*, 448–453.

Ni, X., Chan, D., Chan, K., McMain, S., & Kennedy, J. L. (2009). Serotonin genes and gene–gene interactions in borderline personality disorder in a matched case-control study. *Progress in Neuro-Psychopharmacology and Biological Psychiatry*, *33*(1), 128–133.

Ni, X., Sicard, T., Bulgin, N., Bismil, R., Chan, K., McMain, S., & Kennedy, J. L. (2007). Monoamine oxidase a gene is associated with borderline personality disorder. *Psychiatric Genetics*, *17*(3), 153–157.

Ornduff, S. R. (2000). Childhood maltreatment and malevolence: Quantitative research findings. *Clinical Psychology Review*, *20*, 991–1018.

Panagopoulos, V. N., Trull, T. J., Glowinski, A. L., Lynskey, M. T., Heath, A. C., Agrawal, A.,…Nelson, E. C. (2013). Examining the association of *NRXN3* SNPs with borderline personality disorder phenotypes in heroin dependent cases and socioeconomically disadvantaged controls. *Drug and Alcohol Dependence*, *128*, 187–193.

Paris, J. (2009). The treatment of borderline personality disorder: Implications of research on diagnosis, etiology, and outcome. *Annual Review of Clinical Psychology*, *5*, 277–290.

Pascual, J. C., Soler, J., Barrachina, J., Campins, M. J., Alvarez, E., Perez, V., Cortes, A., & Baiget, M. (2008). Failure to detect an association between the serotonin transporter gene and borderline personality disorder. *Journal of Psychiatric Research*, *42*, 87–88.

Passamonti, L., Cerasa, A., Gioia, M. C., Magariello, A., Muglia, M., Quattrone, A., & Fera, F. (2008). Genetically dependent modulation of serotonergic inactivation in the human prefrontal cortex. *Neuroimage*, *40*(3), 1264–1273.

Perez-Rodriguez, M. M., Weinstein, S., New, A. S., Bevilacqua, L., Yuan, Q., Zhou, Z.,…Siever, L. J. (2010). Tryptophan-hydroxylase 2 haplotype association with borderline personality disorder and aggression in a sample of patients with personality disorders and healthy controls. *Journal of Psychiatric Research*, *44*, 1075–1081.

Regier, D. A. (2007). Dimensional approaches to psychiatric classification: refining the research agenda for DSM-V: An introduction. *International Journal of Methods in Psychiatric Research*, *16*(S1), S1–S5.

Roepke, S., Vater, A., Preibler, S. Heekeren, H. R., & Dziobek, I. (2013). Social cognition in borderline personality disorder. *Frontiers in Neuroscience*, *6*, 1–12.

Rothschild, L., Cleland, C., Haslam, N., & Zimmerman, M. (2003). A taxometric study of borderline personality disorder. *Journal of Abnormal Psychology*, *112*(4), 657.

Samuel, D., & Widiger, T. A. (2004). Clinicians' descriptions of prototypic personality disorders. *Journal of Personality Disorders*, *18*, 286–308.

Samuel, D., & Widiger, T. (2008). A meta-analytic review of the relationships between the five-factor model and DSM-IV-TR personality disorder: A facet level analysis. *Clinical Psychology Review*, *28*, 1326–1342.

Sanislow, C. A., Grilo, C. M., & McGlashan, T. H. (2000). Factor analysis of the DSM-III-R borderline personality disorder criteria in psychiatric inpatients. *American Journal of Psychiatry*, *157*(10), 1629–1633.

Sanislow, C. A., Grilo, C. M., Morey, L. C., Bender, D. S., Skodol, A. E., Gunderson, J. G.,…McGlashan, T. H. (2002). Confirmatory factor analysis of the DSM-IV criteria for borderline personality disorder: Findings from the collaborative longitudinal personality disorders study. *American Journal of Psychiatry*, *159*(2), 284–290.

Sanislow, C. A., Pine, D. S., Quinn, K. J., Kozak, M. J., Garvey, M. A., Heinssen, R. K., Wang, P. S., & Cuthbert, B. N. (2010). Developing constructs for psychopathology research: Research domain criteria. *Journal of Abnormal Psychology*, *119*, 631–639.

Saulsman, L. M., & Page, A. C. (2004). The five-factor model and personality disorder empirical literature: A meta-analytic review. *Clinical Psychology Review*, *23*, 1055–1085.

Schmahl, C., Ludäscher, P., Greffrath, W., Kraus, A., Valerius, G., Schulze, T. G.,…Bohus, M. (2012). COMT val158met polymorphism and neural pain processing. *PloS one*, *7*(1), e23658.

Sher, K. J., & Trull, T. J. (2002). Substance use disorder and personality disorder. *Current Psychiatry Reports*, *4*, 25–29.

Siever, L. (2008). Neurobiology of aggression and violence. *American Journal of Psychiatry*, *165*(4), 429–442.

Siever, L. J., Torgersen, S., Gunderson, J. G., Livesley, W. J., & Kendler, K. S. (2002). The borderline diagnosis III: Identifying endophenotypes for genetic studies. *Biological Psychiatry*, *51*, 964–968.

Siever, L. J., & Weinstein, L. N. (2009). The neurobiology of personality disorders: Implications for psychoanalysis. *Journal of the American Psychoanalytic Association*, *57*, 361–398.

Skodol, A. E., Gunderson, J. G., McGlashan, T. H., Dyck, I. R., Stout, R. L., Bender, D. S.,...Oldham, J. M. (2002). Functional impairment in patients with schizotypal, borderline, avoidant, and obsessive-compulsive personality disorder. *American Journal of Psychiatry, 159*(2), 276–283.

Skodol, A. E., Gunderson, J. G., Pfohl, B., Widiger, T. A., Livesley, W. J., & Siever, L. J. (2002). The borderline diagnosis I: Psychopathology, comorbidity, and personality structure. *Biological Psychiatry, 51*, 936–950.

Skodol, A. E., Pagano, M. E., Bender, D. S., Shea, M. T., Gunderson, J. G., Yen, S.,...McGlashan, T. H. (2005). Stability of functional impairment in patients with schizotypal, borderline, avoidant, or obsessive compulsive personality disorder over two years. *Psychological Medicine, 35*(3), 443–451.

Stepp, S. D., & Pilkonis, P. A. (2008). Age-related differences in individual DSM criteria for borderline personality disorder. *Journal of Personality Disorders, 22*, 427–432.

Stern, A. (1938). Psychoanalytic investigation and therapy in the borderline group of neuroses. *Psychoanalytic Quarterly, 7*, 467–489.

Stoffers, J. M., Völlm, B. A., Rücker, G., Timmer, A., Huband, N., & Lieb, K. (2012). Psychological therapies for people with borderline personality disorder. *Cochrane Database of Systematic Reviews, 8*, CD005652.

Stoltenberg, S. F., Christ, C. C., & Highland, K. B. (2012). Serotonin system gene polymorphisms are associated with impulsivity in a context dependent manner. *Progress in Neuro-Psychopharmacology and Biological Psychiatry, 39*, 182–191.

Stoltenberg, S. F., Lehmann, M. K., Christ, C. C., Hersrud, S. L., & Davies, G. E. (2011). Associations among types of impulsivity, substance use problems and Neurexin-3 polymorphisms. *Drug and Alcohol Dependence, 119*(3), e31–e38.

Thatcher, D. L., Cornelius, J. R., & Clark, D. B. (2005). Adolescent alcohol use disorders predict adult borderline personality. *Addictive Behaviors, 30*(9), 1709–1724.

Tomko, R. L., Trull, T. J., Wood, P. K., & Sher, K. J. (in press). Characteristics of borderline personality disorder in a community sample: Comorbidity, treatment utilization, and general functioning. *Journal of Personality Disorders*.

Torgersen, S. (1984). Genetic and nosological aspects of schizotypal and borderline personality disorders: A twin study. *Archives of General Psychiatry, 41*(6), 546–554.

Torgersen, S., Czajkowski, N., Jacobson, K., Reichborn-Kjennerud, T., Roysamb, E., Neale, M. C., & Kendeler, K. S. (2008). Dimensional representations of DSM-IV cluster B personality disorders in a population-based sample of Norwegian twins: A multivariate study. *Psychological Medicine, 38*, 1617–1625.

Torgersen, S., Lygren, S., Øien, P. A., Skre, I., Onstad, S., Edvardsen, J.,...Kringlen, E. (2000). A twin study of personality disorders. *Comprehensive Psychiatry, 41*(6), 416–425.

Tragesser, S. L., Lippman, L. G., Trull, T. J., & Barrett, K. C. (2008). Borderline personality disorder features and cognitive, emotional, and predicted behavioral reactions to teasing. *Journal of Research in Personality, 42*, 1512–1523.

Trull, T. J., & Durrett, C. A. (2005). Categorical and dimensional models of personality disorder. *Annual Review of Clinical Psychology, 1*, 355–380.

Trull, T. J., Jahng, S., Tomko, R. L., Wood, P. K., & Sher, K. J. (2010). Revised NESARC personality disorder diagnoses: Gender, prevalence, and comorbidity with substance dependence disorders. *Journal of Personality Disorders, 21*, 412–426.

Trull, T. J., Scheiderer, E., & Tomko, R. L. (2012). Axis II comorbidity. In T. A. Widiger (Ed.), *The Oxford handbook of personality disorders* (pp. 219–236). New York: Oxford University Press.

Trull, T. J., Sher, K. J., Minks-Brown, C., Durbin, J., & Burr, R., (2000). Borderline personality disorder and substance use disorders: A review and integration. *Clinical Psychology Review, 20*, 235–253.

Trull, T. J., & Widiger, T. A. (2008). Geology 102: More thoughts on a shift to a dimensional model of personality disorders. *Social and Personality Psychology Compass, 2*, 949–967.

Trull, T. J., Widiger, T. A., & Guthrie, P. (1990). Categorical versus dimensional status of borderline personality disorder. *Journal of Abnormal Psychology, 99*(1), 40–48.

Widiger, T. A., & Samuel, D. B. (2005). Evidence-based assessment of personality disorders. *Psychological Assessment, 17*, 278–287.

Widiger, T. A., & Trull, T. J. (1993). Borderline and narcissistic personality disorders. In H. Adams & P. Sutker (Eds.), *Comprehensive handbook of psychopathology* (2nd ed., pp. 371–394). New York: Plenum Press.

Widiger, T. A., & Trull, T. J. (2007). Plate tectonics in the classification of personality disorder: Shifting to a dimensional model. *American Psychologist, 62,* 71–83.

Widiger, T. A., Trull, T. J., Clarkin, J. F., Sanderson, C. J., & Costa, P. T., Jr. (2002). A description of the DSM-IV personality disorders with the five factor model of personality. In P. T. Costa, Jr., & T. A. Widiger (Eds.), *Personality disorders and the five-factor model of personality* (2nd ed., pp. 89–99). Washington, DC: American Psychological Association.

Widiger, T. A., & Weissman, M. M. (1991). Epidemiology of borderline personality disorder. *Hospital and Community Psychiatry, 42,* 1015–1021.

Wilson, S. T., Stanley, B., Brent, D. A., Oquendo, M. A., Huang, Y., Haghighi, F., Hodgkinson, C. A., & Mann, J. J. (2012). Interaction between tryptophan hydroxylase I polymorphisms and childhood abuse is associated with increased risk for borderline personality disorder in adulthood. *Psychiatric Genetics, 22*(1), 15–24.

Wilson, S. T., Stanley, B., Brent, D. A., Oquendo, M. A., Huang, Y. Y., & Mann, J. J. (2009). The tryptophan hydroxylase-1 A218C polymorphism is associated with diagnosis, but not suicidal behavior, in borderline personality disorder. *American Journal of Medical Genetics Part B: Neuropsychiatric Genetics, 150*(2), 202–208.

Zaboli, G., Gizatullin, R., Nilsonne, A., Wilczek, A., Jonsson, E. G., Anhemark, E., Asberg, M., & Leopardi, R. (2006). Tryptophan hydroxylase-1 gene variants associate with a group of suicidal women. *Neuropsychopharmacology, 31,* 1982–1990.

Zanarini, M. C. (2000). Childhood experiences associated with the development of borderline personality disorder. *Psychiatric Clinics of North America, 23,* 89–101.

Zanarini, M. C., Frankenburg, F. R., Reich, D. B., & Fitzmaurice, G. (2012). Attainment and stability of sustained symptomatic remission and recovery among patients with borderline personality disorder and Axis II comparison subjects: A 16-year prospective follow-up study. *American Journal of Psychiatry, 169,* 476–483.

30

Narcissistic Personality Disorder and Pathological Narcissism

AARON L. PINCUS,

MICHAEL J. ROCHE,

AND EVAN W. GOOD

The concept of narcissism can be traced to the Greek myth of Narcissus and its retelling in Homeric hymns. Psychology has considered narcissism a characteristic of personality pathology for over 100 years. Clinicians have been writing about narcissistic pathology and its treatment since Freud's (1914) initial discussion of narcissism through contemporary clinical models (Campbell & Miller, 2011; Ogrodniczuk, 2013). Psychiatry scholars classified pathological narcissism as narcissistic personality disorder (NPD) in *DSM-III*, and criteria for this diagnosis appear in all subsequent revisions, including *DSM-5*.

Yet in spite of more than a century of attention, the conceptualization, classification, and assessment of narcissistic personality pathology are in a state of significant flux (Bender, 2012). Recent reviews recognize that the literature across disciplines is splintered, reflecting different approaches to conceptualizing and assessing narcissism (Cain, Pincus, & Ansell, 2008, Miller & Campbell, 2008). Pincus and Lukowitsky (2010) concluded that "despite narcissism's longevity as a construct in psychology and psychiatry, action must be taken to resolve disjunctions and integrate findings in future conceptualizations of pathological narcissism; otherwise continuing disparate efforts will impede progress towards a more sophisticated understanding of this complex clinical construct" (p. 422).

This chapter is organized in sections articulating the two main clinical perspectives on how to best conceptualize narcissistic personality pathology. First, we present the conceptualization of pathological narcissism as extreme expressions of grandiosity, reflected in *DSM*-defined NPD. Next, we present a contemporary clinical conceptualization of pathological narcissism as states of grandiosity and vulnerability based on self-regulation theory (Morf & Rhodewalt, 2001). We then review important associated clinical features of NPD and pathological narcissism. The chapter concludes with a consideration of future theoretical, clinical, and empirical issues for research.

DSM NPD: Pathological Narcissism as Extreme Grandiosity

The *DSM-5* NPD diagnosis exemplifies the conceptualization of pathological narcissism as excessive or extreme grandiosity.

Criteria for NPD in DSM-III, DSM-III-R, DSM-IV, *and* DSM-5

The introduction of NPD in *DSM-III* was based on a review of the pathological narcissism literature published prior to 1980. Most of the criteria reflected grandiose attitudes and behaviors, including a grandiose sense of self-importance or uniqueness; preoccupation with fantasies of unlimited success, power, brilliance, beauty, or ideal love; exhibitionism; entitlement; exploitativeness; and a lack of empathy. A minority of criteria reflected impairments in self and emotion regulation, including "a reaction to criticism characterized by rage, shame or humiliation" and "alternating states of idealized and devalued views of self and others." Beyond the diagnostic criteria, the discussion and examples included dysregulated and vulnerable aspects of narcissism, noting that the grandiose sense of self-importance frequently alternates with feelings of unworthiness, and self-esteem is often fragile and contingent on successful achievements and receiving recognition and admiration from others. The implementation of *DSM-III* NPD diagnostic criteria assumed that grandiose behaviors, beliefs, and expectations existed in tandem with dysregulated, vulnerable states marked by low self-esteem and negative affectivity.

In an effort to improve the reliability and reduce the overlap among *DSM* PD criteria sets, notable changes to the NPD diagnosis from *DSM-III* to *DSM-5* included adding a number of criteria explicitly emphasizing grandiosity (e.g., arrogant, haughty behaviors and/or attitudes; frequently infers others are envious of him or her) and eliminating criteria and text describing dysregulation and vulnerability (e.g., shameful reactivity or humiliation in response to narcissistic injury, alternating states of idealization and devaluation) (Gunderson, Ronningstam, & Smith, 1995). Although a major revision of the PD diagnostic system was proposed for *DSM-5* (Skodol, 2012), it was rejected by the publication review committees and placed in Section III of *DSM-5* describing emerging measures and models. Therefore, *DSM-5* retains the *DSM-IV* PD criteria sets unchanged, moving them from a separate diagnostic axis to 1 of 20 chapters describing all diagnoses.

DSM-5 criteria for NPD describe the following symptoms: the person with NPD has an inflated sense of self-worth; is preoccupied with fantasies of unlimited influence, achievement, intelligence, attractiveness, or romance; believes that he or she is extraordinary or distinctive and can only be understood by, and should only associate with, other unusual or elite status people or institutions; requires excessive respect, appreciation, and praise; has a sense of privilege and due; is willing to use and take advantage of others for personal gain; lacks compassion; is often jealous of others or believes that others are jealous of him or her; and exhibits conceited, self-aggrandizing behaviors and attitudes. A confirmatory factor analysis of these NPD criteria supported a one-factor solution (Miller, Hoffman, Campbell, & Pilkonis, 2008). The *DSM-5* diagnosis of NPD reflects chronic expressions of excessive or extreme grandiosity. Self-esteem vulnerability and emotional dysregulation are only mentioned in the "Associated Features Supporting Diagnosis" section, where clinicians are also cautioned that patients with NPD may not outwardly exhibit vulnerable characteristics.

Case Example: Mr. A

Mr. A was a single male in his late 30s who lived alone, met criteria for *DSM* NPD, and presented at a community mental health clinic twice for treatment within a 2-year period. He saw two different therapists and unilaterally terminated both therapies after 7 sessions and 18 sessions, respectively. He was a disabled veteran who reported feeling angry toward and envious of the Veterans Administration, neighbors, women, and society as a whole. He also reported feeling very mistreated and disrespected by most other people and institutions. In therapy he regularly belittled, mocked, and challenged therapists, "I know I'm narcissistic and there's nothing you can do about it," "You can do your empathy thing, but it will have no effect on me," "You're just a trainee, you don't know enough to help me," and "I'm only here to get medication because the VA requires too much paperwork and makes me wait too long." In addition to deriding his therapists, Mr. A. regularly threatened people he found parked in his apartment's assigned parking space and fantasized to his therapist about buying a gun and shooting the next person who parked there. A clinically relevant fact to note is that Mr. A did not drive or even own a car.

In treatment Mr. A reported that he felt his parents were cold and aloof, emphasizing that they had not helped him resolve highly competitive feelings he developed toward his older brothers. He recalled being treated frequently with strong allergy medicines that left him foggy and detached from others. As an adult Mr. A's contingent self-esteem and unresolved competitive needs appeared compensated for by a distorted self-view that he was far more capable, powerful, and deserving than reality suggested. Mr. A exhibited chronic grandiosity and entitlement throughout his two therapies and never acknowledged receiving anything beneficial from them before unilaterally terminating treatment. In fact, it may very well be that Mr. A's main motivation for seeking help from the clinic was to bypass whatever he found intolerable about receiving treatment from the Veteran's Administration. This is a cycle that might repeat itself with numerous treatment providers.

Prevalence

The *DSM-IV* Task Force found that the identification of NPD as a primary clinical diagnosis is relatively unusual in both outpatient and inpatient settings, ranking it as the least commonly diagnosed PD (Gunderson, Ronningstam, & Smith, 1994). Fourteen community studies (e.g., Torgersen, Kringlen & Cramer, 2001) investigating the prevalence of *DSM-III, DSM-III-R*, and *DSM-IV* NPD found rates ranging from 0% to 5.7% with a median rate of 0.2%. Four nationally representative epidemiological studies of PD prevalence (e.g., Lenzenweger, Lane, Loranger, & Kessler, 2007; Stinson et al., 2008) found rates of NPD ranging from 0% to 6.2% with a median rate of 1.45%. Finally, five studies in clinical populations (e.g., Zimmerman, Rothschild & Chelminski, 2005) found rates ranging from 0% to 22% with a median rate 2.3%.

Stability

Examination of the temporal stability of NPD varies depending on whether NPD is assessed by clinical interview or self-report. Ronningstam, Gunderson, and Lyons (1995) employed the Diagnostic Interview for Narcissism (DIN; Gunderson, Ronningstam, & Bodkin, 1990) on 20 patients diagnosed with NPD over a 3-year period. They found only modest diagnostic stability, with only 33% of the patients continuing to meet the DIN criteria for NPD at follow up. The 3-year stability of *DSM-III-R* diagnoses (50%) and *DSM-IV* diagnoses (46%) was slightly higher. Lenzenweger, Johnson, and Willett (2004) conducted individual growth curve analyses of interviewer-rated PD features over a 4-year period in a sample of 250 participants. Results revealed significant variability in PD features, including NPD features, over time. Nestadt and colleagues (2010) interviewed 294 participants on two occasions, 12 to 18 years apart, and found that NPD had among the lowest temporal stability levels (ICC = .10), and NPD traits at baseline did not significantly predict those same traits at follow-up.

Self-reported NPD symptoms yielded a higher level of stability. Ball, Rounseville, Tennen, and Kranzler (2001) reported a 1-year temporal stability coefficient of .42 for the self-reported *DSM-III-R* NPD features in a clinical sample of 182 substance abusing inpatients. Samuel and colleagues (2011) examined the 2-year rank order and mean level stability of PDs using self-report and interview-based assessments. They found the rank-order stability for NPD was higher for self-report than for interview ratings, and the mean level decrease in symptoms over time was smaller for the self-report than for the interview ratings. Even with self-report measures, the temporal stability of NPD remained quite modest.

Discriminant Validity of NPD Criteria

The discriminant validity of *DSM-III* and *DSM-III-R* NPD criteria was generally weak (Gunderson et al., 1995). Morey (1988a, 1988b) found that NPD criteria appeared scattered across other symptom clusters, unlike most other *DSM* PDs, whose features largely clustered together. For example, *DSM-III-R* diagnostic features for NPD overlapped 53.1% with histrionic PD, 46.9% with borderline PD, and 35.9% with paranoid and antisocial PDs (see also Morey & Jones, 1998). Unfortunately, the revisions to NPD for *DSM-IV* (retained in *DSM-5*) did not substantially improve discriminant validity for the NPD diagnosis. Although discriminant validity was generally poor for all *DSM* PD diagnoses, Blais and Norman (1997) noted that NPD was among the worst performers. In a study of Cluster B PDs, Holdwick, Hilsenroth, Castlebury, and Blais (1998) retrospectively examined the charts of outpatients meeting *DSM-IV* criteria for NPD, antisocial PD, and borderline PD. They found exploitativeness and lack of empathy did not discriminate NPD patients from antisocial PD patients. Fantasies of unlimited success, exploitativeness, and feelings of envy did not discriminate NPD patients from borderline PD patients.

Studies using the DIPD-IV found mixed results in establishing the discriminant validity of NPD criteria. In a large clinical sample, Grilo et al.

(2001) correlated all the between-category criterion pairs to obtain a baseline for how intercorrelated symptoms from distinct PD categories were. They then calculated the intercorrelations for NPD criteria and found this median intercorrelation value was higher than the median baseline intercorrelation, suggesting modest support for discriminant validity. However, using a similar method in a sample of patients with binge eating disorder, Grilo and McGlashan (2000) found that NPD was among the three PD criteria sets that did not exhibit evidence of discriminate validity.

In a large community sample, Lawton, Shields and Oltmanns (2011) investigated whether self- and informant-reported PD prototypes demonstrated convergent and discriminant validity with interview-rated PD symptoms. The study correlated the narcissistic prototype with interview-rated PD symptoms and found that the narcissistic prototype (both self- and informant-reported) evidenced its strongest correlation to the interview-based NPD ratings, providing evidence for convergent validity. However, these results also revealed that the interview-based NPD score correlated as strongly with the antisocial PD prototype as it did for the narcissistic prototype (in both self and informant ratings), indicating that the interview-based ratings of NPD could not discriminate between NPD and antisocial PD. In contrast, Fossati et al. (2005) reported that *DSM-IV* NPD exhibited adequate discriminant validity in their sample of 641 outpatients who were administered the Structured Clinical Interview for *DSM-IV* Personality Disorders (SCID-II; First, Spitzer, Gibbon, Williams, & Benjamin, 1994) and the SCID-II Personality Questionnaire.

Comorbidity

Across a number of studies examining diagnostic comorbidity among *DSM* PDs, NPD consistently exhibits the highest rates of comorbidity with antisocial and histrionic PDs (Widiger, 2011). NPD also has significant comorbidity with symptom syndromes (Simonsen & Simonsen, 2011). Stinson et al. (2008) used 34,653 participants enrolled in an epidemiological study to examine the comorbidity of NPD with Axis I psychiatric disorders. They calculated the odds ratios (i.e., the increase or decrease in likelihood of meeting NPD diagnosis given the presence of another 12-month or lifetime non-PD psychiatric diagnosis), controlling

for demographic variables. They found that almost every psychiatric disorder was significantly related to having an NPD diagnosis. After controlling for other psychiatric disorders, many associations became smaller but remained significant. The diagnoses in the past 12 months that most strongly predicted comorbid NPD diagnosis were bipolar I disorder (2.3 times more likely to have an NPD diagnosis), anxiety disorders (2.0 times more likely to have an NPD diagnosis), drug dependence (1.9 times more likely to have an NPD diagnosis), posttraumatic stress disorder (PTSD) (1.7 times more likely to have an NPD diagnosis), mood disorders (1.5 times more likely to have an NPD diagnosis), and substance use disorders (1.5 times more likely to have an NPD diagnosis). Comorbidity with lifetime diagnosis of psychiatric disorders yielded similar results, with the strongest predictors being a lifetime diagnosis of bipolar I disorder (1.9 times more likely to have an NPD diagnosis) and PTSD (1.9 times more likely to have an NPD diagnosis). These findings are consistent with clinical samples of NPD that cite the most frequent comorbid diagnoses as major depression or dysthymia (41% to 50%), substance abuse (24% to 50%), and bipolar disorder (5% to 18%) (Clemence, Perry, & Plakun, 2009; Ronningstam, 1996). Oulis, Lykouras, Hatzimanolis and Tomaras (1997) found that among 102 recovered schizophrenic patients, 15% met criteria for NPD, and a clinical epidemiological study of 32 first-episode psychotic patients indicated that 16% met criteria for NPD (Simonsen et al., 2008).

NPD Research

In part because of the low prevalence of NPD, substantive research on even modest samples of patients diagnosed with NPD is extremely rare. Most of the work has focused on examining empathy deficits and self-esteem in NPD. The best research of this nature involves a well-diagnosed sample of NPD patients in Germany. The investigators (Ritter et al., 2011) used both self-report and experimental methods to assess empathy and found that, compared to controls and patients with borderline PD, patients with NPD exhibited deficits in emotional empathy (i.e., an observer's emotional response to another person's emotional state) but not cognitive empathy (i.e., the ability to take another person's perspective and to represent others' mental states). This distinction could explain the NPD patient's tendency to successfully exploit others.

In another study of these NPD patients (Schulze et al., 2013), the investigators used brain imaging techniques and found that, relative to controls, NPD patients had smaller gray matter volume in the left anterior insula. Importantly, gray matter volume in the left anterior insula is positively correlated with self-reported emotional empathy. Complementary whole-brain analyses yielded smaller gray matter volume in frontoparalimbic brain regions comprising the rostral and median cingulate cortex as well as dorsolateral and medial parts of the prefrontal cortex, all of which are implicated in empathic functioning.

Consistent with these findings, another group of investigators (Marissen, Deen, & Franklen, 2012), using an independent small clinical sample of NPD patients, found that the patients generally performed worse on a facial emotion recognition task than did controls. In addition to this general deficit in emotion recognition, patients with NPD showed a specific deficit for emotions representing fear and disgust. Empirical studies of self-esteem in NPD patients converge in concluding that, despite the grandiosity emphasized in the diagnostic criteria, NPD patients have lower explicit self-esteem than that of controls (Vater, Ritter, et al., 2013; Vater, Schröder-Abé, et al., 2013). This makes sense, considering that NPD is commonly comorbid with anxiety disorders, mood disorders, and PTSD.

Research on treatment of NPD is limited to case studies. There are no published randomized clinical psychotherapy trials, naturalistic studies of psychotherapy, or empirical evaluations of community-based interventions for NPD (Dhawan, Kunik, Oldham, & Coverdale, 2010; Levy, Reynoso, Wasserman, & Clarkin, 2007). Thus, there are no empirically validated treatments for NPD.

Critiques of NPD

The lack of research on patients diagnosed with NPD renders the validity and clinical utility of the diagnosis questionable, and this was the primary reason NPD was initially recommended for deletion in the proposed PD revisions for *DSM-5* (Skodol et al., 2011). Currently, it is unclear whether the *DSM* NPD diagnosis serves its central purpose, that is, to facilitate the accurate diagnosis of patients exhibiting pathological narcissism. Unlike what is seen with other PD diagnoses, the low prevalence rates of NPD reported in large-scale epidemiological studies (often 0%) are notably lower than the rates of narcissistic pathology being treated in psychotherapy that are based on surveys of practicing clinicians (Doidge et al., 2002; Morey & Ochoa, 1989; Ogrodniczuk, 2013; Ronningstam & Gunderson, 1990; Westen, 1997). This indicates a possible limitation of the *DSM* criteria to identify patients whom clinicians consider to be exhibiting pathological narcissism (Pincus et al., 2009; Pincus & Lukowitsky, 2010; Ronningstam, 2009). The relatively low prevalence of NPD diagnoses in all populations could be due, in part, to the narrow range of content of the diagnostic criteria. NPD emphasizes grandiose attitudes and behaviors and lacks assessment of self-esteem vulnerability and impaired self- and emotion regulation found in clinical descriptions of pathological narcissism. It may be that many narcissistic patients seek therapists and encounter diagnosticians when they are in a vulnerable self-state with increased mood and anxiety symptoms and lower self-esteem (Kealy & Ogrodniczuk, 2012; Kealy & Rasmussen, 2012). In such instances, relying solely on *DSM* NPD diagnostic criteria may impede clinical recognition of pathological narcissism. The lack of sufficient NPD criteria assessing self-esteem vulnerability and impaired regulation is a common criticism in the recent literature (Cain et al., 2008, Gabbard, 2009, Levy et al., 2007, Miller, Widiger, & Campbell, 2010; Pincus, 2011, Ronningstam, 2009).

In response to the initial proposal to eliminate NPD as a diagnosis in *DSM-5*, Pincus (2011) noted that the *DSM* is merely an imperfect operationalization of clinical knowledge, not the benchmark for evaluating it (Regier, Narrow, Kuhl, & Kupfer, 2009), and he argued that the performance of the *DSM* NPD criteria set should not be the sole or even primary basis for considering the ontological status of NPD. Problematic comorbidity, stability, and particularly validity may be a function of construct definition problems (e.g., Acton, 1998) with *DSM* NPD criteria themselves and criterion problems (McGrath, 2005) with *DSM* NPD research rather than an indication that pathological narcissism does not exist. The narrow-construct definition of *DSM* NPD creates a fundamental criterion problem for research on the validity and clinical utility of the diagnosis (Pincus & Lukowitsky, 2010), as "the disparity between the diagnostic nomenclature and actual psychiatric phenomena is largely ignored, and extensive research is conducted to understand the psychosocial and treatment implications of the existing diagnostic categories" (McGrath, 2005, p. 114). In contrast to the limitations of *DSM* NPD criteria, a contemporary clinical model encompassing narcissistic grandiosity and narcissistic vulnerability is supported by an emergent, and more clinically informed, empirical research base that we discuss in the next section.

Clinical Theory and Research: Pathological Narcissism as Grandiosity and Vulnerability

In contrast to the emphasis on extreme grandiosity in *DSM* NPD, clinical theory and observation have always included states of negative affectivity (e.g., shame, rage), fragile and contingent self-esteem, and behavioral dysregulation (e.g., suicidality, aggression, withdrawal) in the clinical portrait of pathological narcissism (Cain et al., 2008). The comorbidity of NPD with mood and anxiety disorders suggests there could be a more comprehensive conceptualization that moves beyond grandiosity and includes impairments in self- and emotion regulation that could better account for why individuals with a pathologically inflated self-image commonly enter psychotherapy reporting low self-esteem, depressed mood, and anxiety (Pincus, Cain, & Wright, 2014).

Clinical Theory and Observation: Origins and Early Conceptualizations

Clinical conceptualizations of pathological narcissism have deep roots in psychodynamic theories of personality spanning a century of clinical observation and treatment (Freud, 1914; Kernberg, 2010). Here we briefly review the most influential of these perspectives and then describe a contemporary clinical model of pathological narcissism emerging from a synthesis of clinical theory and research.

The myth of Narcissus (Ovid, 8/1958) describes a handsome man who becomes so enamored with his own reflection that he neglects all else and eventually wastes away to death. Commonly understood as a story reflecting the perils of self-absorption, British sexologist-physician Havlock Ellis (1898) used this myth as a metaphor for patients with an autoerotic condition in which their sexual emotions were lost in the service of self-admiration.

This work introduced narcissism as a personality characteristic, and later Otto Rank (1911) published the first psychoanalytic paper on narcissism, describing different aspects of self-love. Freud (1914) addressed the topic most extensively in the paper "On Narcissism: An Introduction," where he introduced definitions of primary and secondary narcissism, identified narcissistic object-choice, highlighted the self-protective strategy inherent in the narcissistic character, and articulated methods of studying narcissism through examinations of organic disease, hypochondria, and human erotic life. Freud's work was influential in shaping future clinical theories of narcissism (Levy, Ellison, & Reynoso, 2011; Ronningstam, 2011d).

Object Relations and Self Psychology

Narcissism as a psychodynamic construct evolved from the theorizing of Rank and Freud, through the important reformulations of Otto Kernberg (1984, 1988) and Heinz Kohut (1971, 1977). These reformulations stimulated worldwide interest in how narcissism should be conceptualized and treated (Levy et al., 2011).

Object relations theories recognize that humans are social beings who experience much of life relating to others. These theories emphasize the importance of understanding how people's mental representations of self and others positively or negatively impact their identity, emotions, and relationships. Early in development, a child is unable to attribute good and bad experiences to the same person, so she or he experiences the other as "all bad" or "all good." Similarly, the self is experienced as "all good," and any information to the contrary is pushed out of awareness (denial) or located in another person (projection). Over time, the child learns to integrate good and bad experiences into a complex and integrated view of self and others (Clarkin, Yeomans, & Kernberg, 2006).

Kernberg's (1984, 1988) conceptualization of narcissism is embedded within this object relations model. Parental figures (some of the earliest "objects" one can relate to) are experienced as cold and harsh, and they may concurrently hold high (yet superficial) expectations for their child in hopes of vicarious fulfillment of their own failed ambition. These conditions lead to good and bad experiences remaining un-integrated in the form of idealized and devalued views of self and others. The narcissistic individual libidinally invests in a distorted self-structure, based on immature real and ideal self-representations, as well as ideal object-representations. Devalued or aggressively determined self- and object-representations are split off or projected. A pathological grandiose self is constructed by combining all of the positive and idealized characteristics of the self and others, leading to an unrealistic self-image that is hard to maintain. This grandiosity functions as an acquired defense against experiencing an enraged and empty self that is hungry for authentic recognition (Kernberg, 1970).

In contrast, Kohut (1971, 1977) defined narcissism as a normal stage of development. A primary narcissistic structure first exists where the self and other are both idealized (e.g., grandiosity). Through receipt of healthy support and empathic mirroring from parental figures, this structure is reinforced and leads the child to experience the world as secure and consistent. Parental figures will occasionally not support or gratify the child's needs, but such frustration is tolerable, not traumatic, and allows the child an opportunity to regulate their own needs. These experiences of support and opportunities for self- and emotion regulation coalesce into a new healthier self-structure that is better equipped to navigate disappointments. This in turn transforms immature grandiosity into realistic ambition that energizes the individual to use his or her skills and talents to pursue realistic goals that validate an authentic positive self-concept (Kohut, 1977). Narcissistic pathology results when parental figures do not provide appropriate support or mirroring, or when parental support is excessive (e.g. overinvolved and enmeshed). Neither condition affords the child an opportunity to experience the appropriate and tolerable empathic failures needed to develop mature regulatory strategies and form a realistic view of the self and the world. Millon (1981) and Benjamin (1996) noted that excessive parental indulgence and admiration that is unrealistic can also result in narcissistic pathology through social learning mechanisms, as the parental figures teach the child that success and admiration are not contingent upon effort.

A Contemporary Clinical Model

Of course, clinical theories of pathological narcissism and descriptions of its phenotypic expression extend well beyond the psychodynamic literature. Recent efforts to synthesize the corpus of description, theory, and research on pathological narcissism across the disciplines of clinical psychology, psychiatry, and social-personality psychology[1] generated a contemporary model that conceptualizes pathological narcissism as a combination of maladaptive self-enhancement motivation (Grandiosity) and impaired self- and emotion regulation in response to self-enhancement failures and lack of recognition and admiration from others (Vulnerability) (Pincus, 2013; Roche, Pincus, Lukowitsky, Ménard, & Conroy, 2013).

Self-Enhancement and Regulation   *Narcissism* can be defined as an individual's tendency to employ a variety of self-regulation, affect-regulation, and interpersonal processes in order to maintain a relatively positive self-image. Thus, it is necessarily a complex personality construct involving (a) needs for recognition and admiration, (b) motivations to overtly and covertly seek out self-enhancement experiences from the social environment, (c) strategies to satisfy these needs and motives, and (d) abilities to manage disappointments and self-enhancement failures (Morf, Horvath, & Torchetti, 2011; Morf, Torchetti, & Schürch, 2011). Generally, such needs and motives are normal aspects of personality, but they become pathological when they are extreme and coupled with impaired regulatory capacities. It is normal for individuals to strive to see themselves in a positive light and to seek experiences of self-enhancement (Hepper, Gramzow, & Sedikides, 2010) such as successful achievements and competitive victories (Conroy, Elliot, & Thrash, 2009). Most individuals manage these needs effectively, seek out their gratification in culturally and socially acceptable ways and contexts, and regulate self-esteem, negative emotions, and interpersonal behavior when disappointments are experienced. In basing the definition of narcissism on the individual's needs, motives, and regulatory capacities, we can explicitly distinguish between what pathological narcissism is (i.e., impairments in motivation, psychological structures, and regulatory capacities and processes) and how the symptoms present in

---

1. This chapter focuses mainly on the clinical psychology and psychiatry literature. Social-personality psychology research supporting the contemporary clinical model is reviewed in several sources (e.g., Cain et al., 2008; Miller et al., 2010; Pincus & Lukowitsky, 2010; Pincus & Roche, 2011).

thought, feeling, and behavior (i.e., its phenotypic expression).

Pathological narcissism involves impairment in the ability to regulate the self, emotions, and behavior in seeking to satisfy needs for recognition and admiration. Put another way, narcissistic individuals have notable difficulties transforming narcissistic needs (recognition and admiration) and impulses (self-enhancement motivation) into mature and socially appropriate ambitions and conduct (Kohut, 1977, Stone, 1998). Morf and colleagues have provided a compelling argument for conceptualizing pathological narcissism through regulatory mechanisms in their dynamic self-regulatory processing model (Morf & Rhodewalt, 2001; Morf, Torchetti, et al., 2011). They suggested that early empathic failures by parental figures (see also Kohut, 1971) leave the child ill-equipped to regulate the self, and instead self-regulation is played out in the social arena (Dickinson & Pincus, 2003; Kernberg, 2010). However, the early negative parenting experience also leaves the self with a mistrust and disdain for others, resulting in a tragic paradox in which other people are needed for the narcissist to self-enhance, but the devalued and skeptical view of others limits the narcissist's ability to experience others' admiration, praise, and validation as self-enhancing. This leads to lingering self-doubt and increased vulnerability, re-energizing the self to continue seeking these self-enhancement experiences in increasingly maladaptive ways and inappropriate contexts (Morf, 2006; Morf & Rhodewalt, 2001). Thus, the fundamental dysfunction associated with pathological narcissism involves chronically unsatisfied needs for recognition and admiration that lead to an equally chronic preoccupation with the social status of the self and an unremitting prioritization of self-enhancement motivation. This heightens narcissistic individuals' sensitivity to the daily ups and downs of life and relationships (e.g., Besser & Priel, 2010; Zeigler-Hill & Besser, 2013) and impairs their regulation of self-esteem, emotion, and behavior (Roche, Pincus, Lukowitsky, et al., 2013). Importantly, conceptualizing narcissism from a regulatory perspective, unlike *DSM* NPD, accounts for both narcissistic grandiosity and narcissistic vulnerability.

Narcissistic Grandiosity and Narcissistic Vulnerability
To the layperson, narcissism is most often associated with conceited, arrogant, and domineering attitudes and behaviors (Buss & Chiodo 1991), which are captured by the term *narcissistic grandiosity*. This accurately identifies some common expressions of maladaptive self-enhancement associated with pathological narcissism. However, our definition of narcissism combines maladaptive self-enhancement (e.g. grandiosity) with self, emotional, and behavioral dysregulation in response to ego threats or self-enhancement failures (e.g., vulnerability). This *narcissistic vulnerability* is reflected in experiences of anger, envy, aggression, helplessness, emptiness, low self-esteem, shame, avoidance of interpersonal relationships, and even suicidality (Kohut & Wolf, 1978; Krizan & Johar, 2012; Pincus & Roche, 2011; Ronningstam, 2005b). A comprehensive hierarchical model of pathological narcissism is presented in Figure 30.1. In recent years, recognition of both grandiose and vulnerable themes of narcissistic pathology has increasingly become the norm (e.g., Kealy & Rasmussen, 2012; Levy, 2012; Miller et al., 2011).

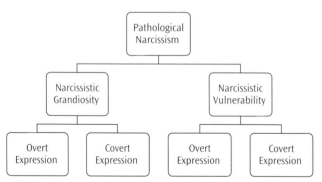

Figure 30.1 The hierarchical structure of pathological narcissism. Reprinted with the author's permission, from Pincus, A. L., & Lukowitsky, M. R. (2010). Pathological narcissism and narcissistic personality disorder. *Annual Review of Clinical Psychology, 6,* p. 431.

Reviews of clinical literature on narcissism and narcissistic personality pathology over the past 45 years have identified more than 50 distinct labels describing variability in the expression of pathological narcissism (Cain et al., 2008; Pincus & Lukowitsky, 2010). The authors concluded that two broad themes of narcissistic pathology, labeled *narcissistic grandiosity* and *narcissistic vulnerability*, could be synthesized across the literature with varying degrees of emphasis. Clinical theorists have employed these themes to describe the core aspects of narcissistic dysfunction through defects in self-structure (Kernberg 1998, Kohut 1977), difficulties in the therapeutic relationship (Gabbard 2009, Kernberg, 2007), and maladaptive coping and defensive strategies used in response to stressors (Masterson, 1993). We highlight some of the most recent work next.

Ronningstam (2005a) identified subtypes of narcissistic personality based on similarities and differences in self-esteem dysregulation, affect dysregulation, and difficulties in interpersonal relationships. Grandiose themes are emphasized in descriptions of the arrogant narcissist and the psychopathic narcissist. The former copes with self-esteem dysregulation by creating an exaggerated sense of superiority and uniqueness as well as by engaging in grandiose fantasies. These individuals exhibit entitlement, exploitativeness, and a lack of empathy, and they experience intense envy and aggression as a result of their affect dysregulation. The psychopathic narcissist copes with self-esteem dysregulation by engaging in antisocial behaviors to protect or enhance their inflated self-image. Such individuals will commit violent criminal acts to gain admiration from others, display extreme rage reactions to criticism, and are sadistic without experiencing remorse or empathy. Consistent with Akhtar's (2003) and Dickinson and Pincus's (2003) description of narcissistic vulnerability, Ronningstam's shy narcissist deals with self-esteem dysregulation by engaging in grandiose fantasy while also feeling intense shame regarding their needs and ambition. The dominant affect problem for the shy narcissist is shame rather than aggression, and they avoid interpersonal relationships because of hypersensitivity to ego threats and self-enhancement failures.

The *Psychodynamic Diagnostic Manual* (*PDM*; PDM Task Force, 2006) subdivided narcissistic personality disturbance into an arrogant/entitled (grandiose) subtype and a depressed/depleted (vulnerable) subtype. This is consistent with results of a Q-factor analysis of NPD patients' Shedler-Westen Assessment System (SWAP-II) profiles that also described two pathological subtypes (Russ, Shedler, Bradley, & Westen, 2008). The grandiose/malignant subtype is characterized by seething anger, manipulativeness, pursuit of interpersonal power and control, lack of remorse, exaggerated self-importance, and feelings of privilege. These individuals tend to be externalizing and have little insight into their behavior. In contrast, the fragile subtype fails to consistently maintain a grandiose sense of self such that when their defenses fail, narcissistic injury evokes shame, anxiety, depression, and feelings of inadequacy.

Research on Narcissistic Grandiosity and Narcissistic Vulnerability   Pincus and colleagues developed the Pathological Narcissism Inventory (PNI; Pincus et al., 2009) with three scales assessing narcissistic grandiosity (Exploitativeness, Grandiose Fantasies, Self-sacrificing Self-enhancement) and four scales assessing narcissistic vulnerability (Contingent Self-esteem; Entitlement Rage, Hiding the Self, Devaluing). Confirmatory factor analysis indicated an oblique two-factor hierarchical structure (Grandiosity, Vulnerability) fit the data well (Wright, Lukowitsky, Pincus, & Conroy, 2010), consistent with the structure in Figure 30.1. Importantly, the Grandiosity and Vulnerability facets of the PNI correlate about .5, indicating they are interrelated. Although they are positively intercorrelated, in clinical and nonclinical samples, Grandiosity and Vulnerability exhibit convergent and divergent patterns of relationships across important clinical domains, including personality traits, psychopathology and externalizing problems, emotions and self-esteem, attachment, recalled parenting, early maladaptive schemas, and psychotherapy (Pincus, 2013).

Grandiosity and Vulnerability exhibit distinct and substantively meaningful patterns of correlations across narcissistic and impulsive traits, and omnibus models of general personality. Grandiosity exhibits modest positive correlations with the Narcissistic Personality Inventory (NPI; Raskin & Hall, 1981) total score, all NPI subscales, and other measures of psychological entitlement. In contrast, Vulnerability is only positively correlated with measures of psychological entitlement (Ackerman et al., 2011; Pincus et al., 2009). Regarding impulsivity, Grandiosity correlated positively with "positive urgency" (positive affect-based impulsivity) and "sensation seeking" while Vulnerability was positively correlated with both "positive urgency" and "negative urgency" (negative affect-based impulsivity) (Miller, Dir, et al., 2010). With regard to the five-factor model, Grandiosity is negatively correlated with Neuroticism and Agreeableness and positively correlated with Extraversion (N–, A–, E+), and Vulnerability is similarly negatively correlated with Agreeableness but is positively correlated with Neuroticism and negatively correlated with Extraversion (N+, A–, E–) (Miller, Dir, et al., 2010). Similar patterns are found in relation to the HEXACO personality model with the notable addition that both Grandiosity and Vulnerability are related to low Honesty-Humility (Bresin & Gordon, 2011). These varied trait associations suggest that pathological narcissists are not merely "disagreeable extraverts" (Miller, Gaughan, Pryor, Kamen, & Campbell, 2009; Paulhus, 2001).

Grandiosity and Vulnerability exhibit distinct and substantively meaningful patterns of correlations across measures of psychopathological symptoms in both normal and clinical samples. In a study of psychotherapy outpatients (Ellison, Levy, Cain, Ansell, & Pincus, 2013), scores on Grandiosity significantly predicted presenting patients' initial scores for mania and violence, and scores on Vulnerability significantly predicted presenting patients' initial scores for depression, psychosis, and sleep disturbance. In a student sample, Miller, Dir, et al. (2010) found that Vulnerability exhibited significant correlations with anxiety, depression, hostility, interpersonal sensitivity, paranoid ideation, and global distress. In contrast, Grandiosity only exhibited a significant negative correlation with interpersonal sensitivity. Using a sample of undergraduates, Tritt, Ryder, Ring, and Pincus (2010) found that Vulnerability was positively related to depressive and anxious temperaments and negatively related to the extraverted, energetic hyperthymic temperament. In contrast, Grandiosity was strongly positively correlated with hyperthymic temperament. In clinical samples, both Grandiosity and Vulnerability were related to depressive tendencies (Kealy, Tsai, & Ogrodniczuk, 2012; Marčinko et al., 2014). Grandiosity and Vulnerability were also both associated with borderline personality pathology in student samples (Miller, Dir, et al., 2010; Pincus et al., 2009). In a clinical sample, both Grandiosity

and Vulnerability predicted suicide attempts (Pincus et al., 2009), but, consistent with Miller, Dir, et al.'s (2010) findings, only Vulnerability predicted parasuicidal behaviors. Finally, only Grandiosity significantly predicted criminal behavior and gambling (Miller, Dir, et al., 2010), and Vulnerability uniquely interacted with child sexual abuse to predict perpetration of overt and cyberstalking by men (Ménard & Pincus, 2012).

Narcissistic grandiosity and vulnerability exhibit distinct associations with measures of self-esteem, self-conscious emotions, and core affect. Vulnerability is negatively associated with self-esteem whereas Grandiosity is positively associated with self-esteem (Maxwell, Donnellan, Hopwood, & Ackerman, 2011; Miller et al., 2010; Pincus et al., 2009). Vulnerability is positively correlated with shame and hubris, negatively correlated with authentic pride, and unrelated to guilt. In contrast, Grandiosity is positively related to guilt and unrelated to pride and shame (Pincus, Conroy, Hyde, & Ram, 2010). Vulnerability is positively correlated with negative affectivity and envy, and negatively correlated with positive affectivity, while Grandiosity is only positively correlated with positive affectivity (Krizan & Johar, 2012; Miller, Dir et al., 2010). Finally, high scores on the PNI predicted strong experimental effects for the implicit priming of self-importance (Fetterman & Robinson, 2010).

Miller, Dir and colleagues (2010) found that Vulnerability was associated with attachment anxiety and avoidance, recalling parents as cold and psychologically intrusive, and reporting a history of emotional, verbal, physical, and sexual abuse. Grandiosity was unrelated to these variables. Zeigler-Hill, Green, Arnau, Sisemore, and Myers (2011) examined the distinctions between Grandiosity and Vulnerability regarding early maladaptive schemas. They found that both Grandiosity and Vulnerability correlated positively with the Mistrust and Abandonment schema domains, reflecting beliefs that others will abuse, manipulate, or leave them. Grandiosity was also correlated positively with the Entitlement schema domain and negatively correlated with the Defectiveness schema domain, reflecting belief that the self is perfect and should be able to do or have whatever it wants. Vulnerability was positively correlated with the Subjugation, Unrelenting Standards, and Emotional Inhibition, and negatively correlated with the Dependence schema domains, reflecting beliefs in unrealistically high standards in a world of important others where emotional expression and interpersonal dependency have negative consequences.

PNI Grandiosity scales were associated with hostile, domineering, and intrusive interpersonal problems (Pincus et al., 2009), replicating findings for psychiatric day hospital patients high in NPD symptoms (Ogrodniczuk, Piper, Joyce, Steinberg, & Duggal, 2009). In addition, PNI Vulnerability scales exhibited unique associations with exploitable and avoidant interpersonal problems. Similarly, PNI subscales were meaningfully associated with a variety of interpersonal sensitivities (i.e., being bothered by others' warm and submissive behaviors; Hopwood et al., 2011). In a series of studies examining pathological narcissism and response to ego threat (Besser & Priel, 2010; Besser & Zeigler-Hill, 2010), Grandiosity was associated with significant increases in anger and negative affect in response to achievement failures but not in response to interpersonal rejection. In contrast, Vulnerability was associated with significant increases in anger and negative affect mainly in response to interpersonal rejection. Additionally, these effects were further impacted by their public or private status, with Grandiosity particularly associated with public threats and Vulnerability particularly associated with private threats.

A study examining the PNI and psychotherapy (Ellison et al., 2013) found that Grandiosity was negatively correlated with treatment utilization (telephone-based crisis services, partial hospitalizations, inpatient admissions, taking medications) and positively correlated with outpatient therapy no-shows. Vulnerability was positively correlated with use of telephone-based crisis services, inpatient admissions, and outpatient therapy sessions attended and cancelled. Results indicating that narcissistic vulnerability is positively associated with treatment utilization support the view that narcissistic patients are likely to present for services when they are in a vulnerable self-state (Pincus et al., 2014). Finally, both novice and expert clinicians were able to predict a priori PNI associations with established indices of normal personality traits, psychopathology, clinical concerns, and pathological personality traits (Thomas, Wright, Lukowitsky, Donnellan, & Hopwood, 2012). The authors concluded there was substantial evidence for the criterion validity and clinical utility of the PNI.

Week-long daily-diary studies have indicated that narcissistic grandiosity and narcissistic vulnerability were related to individuals' behavior in social interactions in daily life and fluctuations in daily self-esteem. Specifically, narcissistic grandiosity was associated with responding to perceiving others as behaving dominantly with reciprocal dominant behavior (Roche, Pincus, Conroy, Hyde, & Ram, 2013). The authors concluded that narcissistic individuals my view the dominant behavior of others as a threat to their status and respond in ways to self-enhance and reassert their superiority. In another daily-diary study, Zeigler-Hill and Besser (2013) found that Vulnerability was uniquely associated with day-to-day fluctuations in feelings of self-worth.

Summary   In contrast to the emphasis on extreme grandiosity reflected in *DSM* NPD, clinical theory and empirical evidence supporting the contemporary clinical model suggest that a person's grandiose self-states may oscillate with vulnerable self-states marked by low self-esteem and emotional and behavioral dysregulation. Ronningstam (2009) noted, "The narcissistic individual may fluctuate between assertive grandiosity and vulnerability" (p. 113). Similarly, Kernberg (2009) indicated that narcissistic personalities endure "bouts of insecurity disrupting their sense of grandiosity or specialness" (p. 106). Horowitz (2009) suggested that as narcissistic pathology negatively impacts relationships, creativity, and occupational adjustment, grandiosity cannot be maintained and narcissists are "more vulnerable to shame, panic, helplessness, or depression as life progresses" (p. 126). Such emerging views are consistent with the conceptualization of narcissistic grandiosity and narcissistic vulnerability as interrelated dimensions of pathological narcissism (Wright et al., 2010) and with the assertion that narcissistic patients are best differentiated from each other on the basis of *relative* levels of grandiosity and vulnerability rather than making categorical distinctions based on grandiose or vulnerable subtypes (Pincus & Lukowitsky, 2010).

Case Example: Mr. B

Mr. B is a patient we diagnosed as suffering from pathological narcissism but who may not meet *DSM* NPD criteria because of his pronounced vulnerability. We present his vulnerable characteristics first, and then follow this with his grandiose features. We chose this approach because narcissistic patients who seek outpatient treatment in community mental health centers typically present in dysregulated states in which more vulnerable symptoms are prominent and grandiosity is only detectable later in treatment after patient stabilization (Pincus et al., 2014).

Vulnerability   Mr. B was a 40-year-old single, college-educated male living with his parents after discharge from his most recent hospitalization. He presented for therapy as socially isolated with impaired intimacy. He had no friends or relationships except with his parents, had difficulty maintaining employment as a dishwasher, and expressed pessimism about his ability to improve his life. He wished to pursue permanent disability status and was interested in moving to a residential facility for the mentally ill. His most pronounced symptom was an empty depression characterized by agitation and anhedonia but an absence of sadness or melancholia. Mr. B was chronically suicidal and described waking up each day feeling "horrified" he was still alive. Early in treatment, he would commonly respond to therapist questions with long latencies where he lowered his head into his hands and repeatedly rubbed his head in anguish before responding with one or two words or "I don't know." Mr. B tried many different antidepressants with minimal effects and was admitted to the hospital three times in a 12-month period, one of which included a long course of ECT that was similarly ineffective. Clearly Mr. B's initial presentation was one of a vulnerable and anguished patient, and a diagnostician might reasonably consider a diagnosis of a mood disorder. Mr. B would not meet criteria for *DSM* NPD.

Grandiosity   Over the course of psychotherapy, the therapist learned about several other features of Mr. B's thoughts, feelings, and behaviors that suggest narcissistic grandiosity. But unlike the first case, these expressions were at first subtle or unacknowledged by the patient and they oscillated with more depressive states. Mr. B was a skilled keyboard player with a sizable home recording studio setup. But the instruments lay untouched, and he reported no intrinsic pleasure in playing them. He reported that he only enjoyed it when people paid to hear him play. He tried playing with a few local bands, but none were "serious enough" or

"talented enough" and he even devalued his own musical interests as too "flawed and disappointing" to pursue. Mr. B also used to be an avid bicyclist. However, after excitedly purchasing a new and high-quality model, Mr. B became obsessed with the various noises the bicycle made while riding it. He was unhappy and felt it was too noisy. He tried to stop the offending noises without success. With the encouragement of his therapist, Mr. B tried for some time to ride the bike despite his disappointment over its imperfections. However, like playing music, he eventually lost interest in riding his bike and felt depressed about that as well.

Mr. B also felt that daily responsibilities like buying groceries, finding a job, balancing his checkbook, filling out forms, and paying taxes were a "hassle" and he should not have to do them. In fact, he continued to rely on his parents to do most of these things for him. When he was living in his own apartment, he lived off of a trust fund and his mother still balanced his checkbook and took him on a weekly shopping trip. When the trust fund ran out, he strategically took an overdose to ensure his mother would find him when she arrived for their weekly grocery shopping. Despite all of his parents' help (for better or worse), in therapy he expressed resentment toward them for aging and having decreasing resources. For example, he complained bitterly that his mother took much longer to balance his checkbook than she used to and he was disappointed when they could not immediately buy him a car. The therapist learned the main reason Mr. B could not hold a job was because he resented the lack of control over his schedule. He would angrily quit jobs when asked to change his schedule to accommodate other employees' vacations or even his employers' changing needs. He had no friends because he saw relationships as meaningless and insisted he "can't tolerate listening to other people's shit." Ultimately, his grandiose expectations of self and others contributed to virtually all of his social, occupational, and recreational activities becoming disappointing and flawed.

Mr. B was very depressed at times, but recognition that it was due to his personality pathology improved his treatment. He was told explicitly that the therapist did not expect medication or ECT to improve his depression and recommended transference-focused psychotherapy (Stern, Yeomans, Diamond, & Kernberg, 2013) for his narcissistic personality. A long-term psychotherapy helped Mr. B remain out of the hospital, improve his relationship with his parents, get off disability, resume work and playing music, and seek independent living arrangements. Treatments that did not take the patient's pathological narcissism into account were not effective.

A Note on Overt and Covert Narcissism

We wish to alert students that they will occasionally come across the terms *overt* and *covert narcissism* when reading narcissism literature. Unfortunately, many incorrectly associate overt expressions of narcissism exclusively with grandiosity and covert expressions of narcissism exclusively with vulnerability. There is no empirical support for these linkages, nor is there empirical support for the view that overt and covert narcissism are distinct subtypes of narcissism. In fact, there are no existing interviews or self-report measures of overt and covert narcissism. *DSM* NPD criteria as well as items on various self-reports, interviews, and rating instruments assessing pathological narcissism include a mix of overt elements (behaviors, expressed attitudes, and emotions) and covert experiences (cognitions, private feelings, motives, needs) (e.g., McGlashan et al., 2005). Our clinical experience with narcissistic patients indicates they virtually always exhibit both covert and overt grandiosity and covert and overt vulnerability. In Figure 30.1, the distinction between overt and covert expressions of narcissism is secondary to phenotypic variation in grandiosity and vulnerability.

Clinically Important Associated Features of NPD and Pathological Narcissism

Research on the associated features of NPD and pathological narcissism typically examines correlational associations between relevant constructs and NPD symptom counts, scores on self-report measures of narcissism, or informant ratings. Research using the NPD diagnosis, NPD symptom counts, or scales based on *DSM* NPD effectively assesses grandiosity but not vulnerability. In other research, pathological narcissism is assessed through interviews or scales that can include vulnerable content. It is notable that both NPD and the broader conceptualization of pathological narcissism are associated with the three associated clinical features we review next.

Suicidality

Pathological narcissism and NPD are clinically and empirically recognized as significant risk factors for suicidal ideation and behavior in adolescent, adult, and geriatric populations. It has been estimated that 4.7%–23% of suicide completers exhibit elevated NPD symptom counts (Apter et al., 1993; Brent et al., 1994) and that the presence of comorbid depression may accrue even greater risk of suicide in patients with NPD (Heisel, Links, Conn, van Reekum, & Flett, 2007). Although all Cluster B personality disorders are associated with risk for suicide, individuals with NPD exhibit more deliberate and lethal forms of suicidal behavior than do individuals with histrionic, antisocial or borderline personality disorders (Blasco-Fontecilla et al., 2009).

Experiencing difficult life stressors increases suicide risk (e.g. Orbach, 1997), and certain stressors are particularly impactful for narcissistic individuals. In a sample of 375 suicide attempters, domestic stressors (e.g., arguing more with spouse) and significant life changes, including employment termination, house foreclosure, and personal injury or illness, preceded attempted suicide in individuals with NPD (Blasco-Fontecilla et al., 2010; see also Marttunen, Aro, & Lönngvist, 1993). Additionally, narcissistic personality was associated with increased suicide risk among depressed older (65+ years) adults, highlighting their difficulties with age-related life changes and transitions (Conner et al., 2001; Heisel et al., 2007).

Research on pathological narcissism demonstrates that an increased suicide risk is related to both narcissistic grandiosity and narcissistic vulnerability. Pincus and colleagues (2009) conducted a chart review of 25 patients and found that the report and number of suicide attempts was positively associated with both grandiose and vulnerable facets of the PNI. In contrast, the frequency of parasuicidal behaviors was uniquely predicted by narcissistic vulnerability. Grandiosity may catalyze suicidality by promoting a view of the self as indestructible, a preoccupation with one's physical appearance, and a detachment from one's emotional and physical self. In such cases, suicide may function as a means of complying with fantasies of invincibility or eliminating perceived imperfections of the body (Ronningstam & Weinberg, 2009). It may also serve an aggressive function to punish others or to bolster an illusion of control over one's life and relationships with others (Kernberg, 1984; Ronningstam &

Maltsberger, 1998). This would be consistent with suicidality following domestic arguments, for example. Vulnerability may catalyze suicidality by promoting the experience of narcissistic injury, leading to the deflation of grandiose self-views and the experience of shame in recognizing imperfections, personal weaknesses, and defeat (Pincus et al., 2009; Ronningstam & Weinberg, 2009). It may also serve an aggressive function to punish the self in response to experiencing disappointments of entitled expectations and self-enhancement failures (Pincus, 2013). This is also consistent with the increased risk of suicidality in response to age-related life transitions, as one is confronted with their increasing physical and socioeconomic limitations (see also Horowitz, 2009).

Narcissism confers a serious risk for suicidality in part because it may be difficult to detect. Usually suicidality will present with depression, but case studies suggest narcissistic individuals have an increased risk for suicide, even when not in a depressed state (Ronningstam & Maltsberger, 1998; Ronningstam & Weinberg, 2009). Similarly, Cross, Westen, and Bradley (2011) identified a narcissistic subtype of suicide attempters in an adolescent sample who were not characterized by mood or anxiety problems. Furthermore, the life stressors identified for narcissistic individuals remained significantly associated with suicide when controlling for Axis I disorders including depression (Blasco-Fontecilla et al., 2010). Information from case studies also suggests that suicide attempters with narcissistic features may be more likely to deny intent, minimize the risk of suicidal gestures, and ignore obvious identifiable stressors that ultimately trigger such events (Ronningstam & Maltsberger, 1998; Ronningstam & Weinberg, 2009). Together, this means the clinician may have a harder time detecting and treating narcissistic suicidality.

Depressive Experiences

Although mood disorders including depression and bipolar disorder are common comorbid diagnoses with NPD, the phenomenology of depression in narcissistic patients may vary considerably. In a sample of 117 psychiatric outpatients, Kealy, Tsai, and Ogrodniczuk (2012) found that anaclitic/dependent themes of depression were positively associated with PNI Grandiosity, while introjective/self-critical themes of depression were positively associated with PNI Vulnerability. The authors suggested that patients with grandiose features may be

more likely to suffer depressive states in the context of violated expectations of external validation, whereas patients with vulnerable features may be more likely to experience depressive exacerbations of their chronic sense of deficit.

A similar study with 234 clinical outpatients (Marčinko et al., 2014) found that the relationship between PNI Vulnerability and depressive symptoms was partially mediated by dysfunctional perfectionistic attitudes. These findings suggest that self-criticism and perfectionism commonly seen in depressed patients may involve deeper narcissistic issues (Ronningstam, 2011b, 2012), potentially fuelling further depressive episodes. Recognition of this can allow for treatment and relapse-prevention protocols that target shame and hypersensitivity. The link between vulnerability and depression has been replicated in student samples where narcissistic vulnerability was positively associated with depression and depressive temperament (Miller et al., 2011; Thomas et al., 2012; Tritt et al., 2010; Weikel, Avara, Hanson & Kater, 2010). Narcissistic individuals may be susceptible to depression because their self-worth is dependent on external affirmations from the social world, and their psychic cohesion can become threatened if these needs for recognition and admiration are not met (Kohut & Wolf, 1978; Morf, Horvath, et al., 2011; Morf, Torchetti, et al., 2011).

Aggression

Several methodologies converge in confirming a link between grandiose narcissistic traits and aggression in children. Thomaes, Bushman, Stegge and Olthof (2008) conducted a laboratory-based study in which 163 adolescents lost a competitive task and shame-inducing feedback was manipulated. The participant's response was measured using an aggression paradigm, in which the participant was given the opportunity to punish their competitor with a noise blast. They found that grandiose children were more aggressive than others only after the shame condition.

Other studies have examined informant reports from parents, teachers, and peers and have reported that ratings of grandiose narcissistic traits are positively associated with both reactive aggression (in response to a perceived threat) and proactive aggression (aggression for personal gain) (Barry et al., 2007; Bukowski, Schwartzman, Santo, Bagwell, & Adams, 2009). Similar effects for proactive and reactive aggression were also observed in self-reported data from 698 Asian adolescents (Seah & Ang, 2008). In addition to these objective methods, performance-based or "projective" methods also confirm the link between narcissism and aggression in children. Weise and Tuber (2004) employed a clinical sample of 32 elementary school–aged children referred for psychological assessment. Sixteen met criteria for NPD using *DSM-IV* criteria, and the other 16 served as a clinical control group. The authors evaluated responses to the Thematic Apperception Test (Murray, 1943) using the Social Cognition and Object Relations Scale (SCORS; Westen, 1995), finding that narcissistic children gave responses that suggested greater difficulty managing aggressive impulses.

Similar associations have been found in adult student samples, where grandiose narcissistic traits predict aggressive responses in laboratory settings, particularly when following shame-inducing feedback (Bushman & Baumeister, 1998; Ferriday, Vartanian, & Mandel, 2011; Reidy, Zeichner, Foster & Martinez, 2008; Twenge & Campbell, 2003). This result replicates with the use of self-report questionnaires (e.g. Donellan et al., 2005; Maples et al., 2010; Miller et al., 2011; Pincus et al., 2009) and real-world aggression measures (Bushman & Baumeister, 2002). The association between grandiose narcissistic symptoms and aggression is also evident in clinical settings as assessed through self-report (Pincus et al., 2009), in documented aggressive acts on an inpatient unit (Goldberg et al., 2007), and in the endorsement of violence by outpatients seeking psychotherapy (Ellison et al., 2013). The association between grandiosity and aggression also extends to incidents of sexual aggression (Mouilso & Calhoun 2012; Widman & McNulty, 2010), as well as to the use of arguments, pressure, and position of authority to force women into unwanted sexual activity (Kosson, Kelly, & White, 1997). In contrast, narcissistic vulnerability (when combined with early childhood trauma) is associated with overt and covert stalking behaviors in college students (Ménard & Pincus, 2012).

Narcissistic grandiosity and vulnerability exhibit distinct associations with forms of aggression. In a sample of 262 Japanese students (Okada, 2010), narcissistic vulnerability predicted aggressive feelings (hostility and anger), but not aggressive acts (physical or verbal aggression). In contrast, narcissistic grandiosity predicted direct displays of aggression (physical and verbal aggression) along with feelings of anger. Similar results were found in a sample of

1,715 American students after controlling for gender and childhood maltreatment (Ménard & Pincus, 2011), where narcissistic vulnerability was positively associated with aggressive feelings (anger and hostility) and both grandiosity and vulnerability were positively associated aggressive acts (physical or verbal aggression). Grandiosity and vulnerability may also sensitize individuals to different triggers for anger. Grandiosity is associated with increased anger following an achievement threat, while vulnerability is associated with increased anger following an interpersonal threat (Besser & Priel, 2010). When combined with findings on depression (Kealy et al., 2012), this research suggests that narcissistic grandiosity may contribute to anger in response to achievement failures and depression in response to relational difficulties, whereas narcissistic vulnerability may contribute to anger in response to relational difficulties and depression in response to achievement failures. Therefore, pathologically narcissistic individuals are at risk for both aggression and depression when coping with social disappointments and self-enhancement setbacks.

The Future of NPD and Pathological Narcissism

Further theory and research on how to best integrate NPD and pathological narcissism are needed. Three areas of focus are noted next.

Diagnosis

Three suggestions for revising the diagnosis of NPD have appeared in the literature. One suggestion is to revise the *DSM* criteria to include features reflecting narcissistic vulnerability (e.g., Ronningstam, 2009, 2011c). An alternative proposal is to consider narcissistic vulnerability a specifier for NPD diagnoses (e.g., NPD with vulnerable features) similar to specifiers used for other diagnoses (Miller, Gentile, Wilson, & Campbell, 2013). A third alternative is to consider pathological narcissism a facet of general personality pathology, representing a core feature of all PDs rather than a specific PD diagnosis (Morey, 2005; Morey & Stagner, 2012).

Mechanisms and Processes

DSM-5 continues to diagnose NPD on the basis of criteria emphasizing extreme grandiosity. Although

NPD lacks criteria assessing vulnerable characteristics that clinicians have long identified as important for understanding and treating narcissism, research shows that NPD is associated with mood and anxiety disorders, suicidality, and aggression. A contemporary clinical model includes narcissistic vulnerability (i.e., self- and emotional dysregulation triggered by self-enhancement failures and disappointment of entitled expectations) in order to better capture characteristics of narcissistic patients presenting for treatment (Pincus et al., 2014; Ronningstam, 2011a, 2011b). Research shows that grandiosity and vulnerability are related to each other and have divergent and convergent clinical correlates. Importantly, like grandiosity, narcissistic vulnerability also is associated with suicidality, depression, and aggression. It may be that these two facets of pathological narcissism will be most helpful in focusing future research on the psychological mechanisms and social processes that give rise to narcissistic symptoms and associated dysfunction. Clearly, more research is necessary to understand these complex associations.

Within-Person Dynamics of Grandiosity and Vulnerability

Although the contemporary clinical understanding of pathological narcissism recognizes its grandiose and vulnerable expressions, one area for further research involves clarifying the within-person dynamics of grandiosity and vulnerability. Clinical theory and observation suggest states of grandiosity and vulnerability as dynamically patterned, oscillating in ascension in relation to the outcomes of self-enhancement efforts and the receipt of social supplies of recognition and admiration. Future research should explore the temporal patterning of shifts in grandiosity and vulnerability or markers such as self-esteem. Do shifts in grandiose and vulnerable self states occur rapidly or over long time periods? How are they related to important associated features like suicidality, depression, and aggression? How do they impact patient presentation, diagnosis, and treatment?

Conclusions

Narcissism remains a relevant and important form of personality pathology in psychology and psychiatry. However, clinical conceptualization of narcissistic personality pathology is in flux and a consensus is not immediately apparent (e.g., Alarcón & Sarabia, 2012; Paris, 2014; Wright, 2014). The lack of theoretical and research integration across clinical psychology, psychiatry, and social-personality psychology contributed to the perception that the NPD diagnosis lacked empirical support for its validity and clinical utility, and was slated for deletion in the initial *DSM-5* PD proposal. Recognition of the splintered state of the literature and the shock of the possible deletion from *DSM-5* have initiated renewed efforts to examine the construct validity and clinical utility of NPD and pathological narcissism. Combined with advances in neuroscience, experience sampling, longitudinal, and statistical methods, future research has great potential to improve our understanding of one of the first recognized, yet most complex, expressions of personality pathology.

References

Ackerman, R. A., Witt, E. A., Donnellan, M. B., Trzesniewski, K. H., Robins, R. W., & Kashy, D. A. (2011).What does the Narcissistic Personality Inventory really measure? *Assessment, 18*, 67–87.

Acton, G. S. (1998). Classification of psychopathology: The nature of language. *Journal of Mind and Behavior, 19*, 243–256.

Akhtar, S. (2003). *New clinical realms.* London: Jason Aronson.

Alarcón, R. D., & Sarabia, S. (2012). Debates on the narcissism conundrum: Trait, domain, dimension, type, or disorder? *Journal of Nervous and Mental Disease, 200*, 16–25.

Apter, A., Bleich, A., King, R. A., Kron, S., Fluch, A., Kotler, M., & Cohen, D. J. (1993). Death without warning? A clinical postmortem study of suicide in 43 Israeli adolescent males. *Archives of General Psychiatry, 50*, 138–142.

Ball, S. A., Rounsaville, B. J., Tennen, H., & Kranzler, H. R. (2001). Reliability of personality disorder symptoms and personality traits in substance-dependent inpatients. *Journal of Abnormal Psychology, 110*, 341–352.

Barry, T. D., Thompson, A., Barry, C. T., Lochman, J. E., Adler, K., & Hill, K. (2007). The importance of narcissism in predicting proactive and reactive aggression in moderately to highly aggressive children. *Aggressive Behavior, 33*, 185–197.

Bender, D. S. (2012). Mirror, mirror on the wall: Reflecting on narcissism. *Journal of Clinical Psychology, 68*, 877–885.

Benjamin, L. S. (1996). *Interpersonal diagnosis and treatment of personality disorders* (2nd Ed.). New York: Guilford Press.

Besser, A., & Priel, B. (2010). Emotional responses to a romantic partner's imaginary rejection: The roles of attachment anxiety, covert narcissism and self evaluation. *Journal of Personality*, 77, 287–325.

Besser, A., & Zeigler-Hill, V. (2010). The influence of pathological narcissism on emotional and motivational responses to negative events: The roles of visibility and concern about humiliation. *Journal of Research in Personality*, 44, 520–534.

Blais, M. A., & Norman, D. K. (1997). A psychometric evaluation of the DSM-IV personality disorder criteria. *Journal of Personality Disorders*, 11, 168–176.

Blasco-Fontecilla, H., Baca-Garcia, E., Dervic, K., Perez-Rodriguez, M. M., Lopez-Castroman, J., Saiz-Ruiz, J., & Oquendo, M. A. (2009). Specific features of suicidal behavior in patients with narcissistic personality disorder. *Journal of Clinical Psychiatry*, 70, 1583–1587.

Blasco-Fontecilla, H., Baca-Garcia, E., Duberstein, P., Perez-Rodriguez, M. M., Dervic, K., Saiz-Ruiz, J.,…Oquendo, M. A. (2010). An exploratory study of the relationship between diverse life events and specific personality disorders in a sample of suicide attempters. *Journal of Personality Disorders*, 24, 773–784.

Brent, D. A., Johnson, B. A., Perper, J., Connolly, J., Bridge, J., Bartle, S., & Rather, C. (1994). Personality disorder, personality traits, impulsive violence, and completed suicide in adolescents. *Journal of the American Academy of Child & Adolescent Psychiatry*, 33, 1080–1086.

Bresin, K., & Gordon, K. H. (2011). Characterizing pathological narcissism in terms of the HEXACO model of personality. *Journal of Psychopathology and Behavioral Assessment*, 33, 228–235.

Bukowski, W. M., Schwartzman, A., Santo, J., Bagwell, C., & Adams, R. (2009). Reactivity and distortions in the self: Narcissism, types of aggression, and the functioning of the hypothalamic-pituitary-adrenal axis during early adolescence. *Development and Psychopathology*, 21, 1249–1262.

Bushman, B. J., & Baumeister, R. F. (1998). Threatened egotism, narcissism, self-esteem, and direct and displaced aggression: Does self-love or self-hate lead to violence? *Journal of Personality and Social Psychology*, 75, 219–229.

Bushman, B. J., & Baumeister, R. F. (2002). Does self-love or self-hate lead to violence? *Journal of Research in Personality*, 36, 543–545.

Buss, D. M., & Chiodo, L. M. (1991). Narcissistic acts in everyday life. *Journal of Personality*, 59, 179–215.

Cain, N. M., Pincus, A. L., & Ansell, E. B. (2008). Narcissism at the crossroads: Phenotypic description of pathological narcissism across clinical theory, social/personality psychology, and psychiatric diagnosis. *Clinical Psychology Review*, 28, 638–656.

Campbell, W. K., & Miller, J. D. (2011). *Handbook of narcissism and narcissistic personality disorder: Theoretical approaches, empirical findings, and treatment*. Hoboken, NJ: John Wiley & Sons.

Clarkin, J. F., Yeomans, F. E., & Kernberg, O. F. (2006). *Psychotherapy for borderline personality: Focusing on object relations*. Washington, DC: American Psychiatric Publishing.

Clemence, A. J., Perry, J. C., & Plakun, E. M. (2009). Narcissistic and borderline personality disorders in a sample of treatment refractory patients. *Psychiatric Annals*, 39, 175–184.

Conner, K. R., Cox, C., Duberstein, P. R., Tian, L., Niset, P., & Conwell, Y. (2001). Violence, alcohol, and completed suicide: A case-control study. *American Journal of Psychiatry*, 158, 1701–1705.

Conroy, D. E., Elliot, A. J., & Thrash, T. M. (2009). Achievement motivation. In M. R. Leary & R. H. Hoyle (Eds.), *Handbook of individual differences in social behavior* (pp. 382–399). New York: Guilford Press.

Cross, D., Westen, D., & Bradley, B. (2011). Personality subtypes of adolescents who attempt suicide. *Journal of Nervous and Mental Disease*, 199, 750–756.

Dhawan, N., Kunik, M. E., Oldham, J., & Coverdale, J. (2010). Prevalence and treatment of narcissistic personality disorder in the community: A systematic review. *Comprehensive Psychiatry*, 51, 333–339.

Dickinson, K. A., & Pincus, A. L. (2003). Interpersonal analysis of grandiose and vulnerable narcissism. *Journal of Personality Disorders*, 17, 188–207.

Doidge, N., Simon, B., Brauer, L., Grant, D., First, M., Brunshaw, J.,…Mosher, P. (2002). Psychoanalytic patients in the U.S., Canada, and Australia: I. DSM-III-R disorders, indications, previous treatment, medications, and length of treatment. *Journal of the American Psychoanalytic Association*, 50, 575–614.

Donellan, M. B., Trzesniewski, K. H., Robins, R. W., Moffitt, T. E., & Caspi, A. (2005). Low self-esteem is related to aggression, antisocial behavior, and delinquency. *Psychological Science, 16,* 328–335.

Ellis, H. (1898). Auto-eroticism: A psychological study. *Alienest Neurology, 19,* 260–299.

Ellison, W. D., Levy, K. N., Cain, N. M., Ansell, E. B., & Pincus, A. L. (2013). The impact of pathological narcissism on psychotherapy utilization, initial symptom severity, and early-treatment symptom change: A naturalistic investigation. *Journal of Personality Assessment, 95,* 291–300.

Ferriday, C., Vartanian, O., & Mandel, D. R. (2011). Public but not private ego threat triggers aggression in narcissists. *European Journal of Social Psychology, 41,* 564–568.

Fetterman, A. K., & Robinson, M. D. (2010). Contingent self-importance among pathological narcissists: Evidence from an implicit task. *Journal of Research in Personality, 44,* 691–697.

First, M. B., Spitzer, R. L., Gibbon, M., Williams, J. B. W., & Benjamin, L. (1994). *Structured Clinical Interview for DSM-IV Axis II Personality Disorders (SCID-II).* New York: Biometric Research Department.

Fossati, A., Beauchaine, T. P., Grazioli, F., Carretta, I., Cortinovis, F., & Maffai, C. (2005). A latent structure analysis of *Diagnostic and Statistical Manual of Mental Disorders, Fourth Edition,* narcissistic disorder criteria. *Comprehensive Psychiatry, 46,* 361–367.

Freud, S. (1914). On narcissism. In J. Strachey (Ed., Trans.), *The standard edition of the complete psychological works of Sigmund Freud* (Vol. XIV, pp. 66–102). London: Hogarth Press.

Gabbard, G. O. (2009). Transference and countertransference: Developments in the treatment of narcissistic personality disorder. *Psychiatric Annals, 39,* 129–136.

Goldberg, B. R., Serper, M. R., Sheets, M., Beech, D., Dill, C., & Duffy, K. G. (2007). Predictors of aggression on the psychiatric inpatient service: Self-esteem, narcissism, and theory of mind deficits. *Journal of Nervous and Mental Disease, 195,* 436–442.

Grilo, C. M., & McGlashan, T. H. (2000). Convergent and discriminant validity DSM-IV Axis II personality disorder criteria in adult outpatients with binge eating disorder. *Comprehensive Psychiatry, 41,* 163–166.

Grilo, C. M., McGlashan, T. H., Morey, L. C., Gunderson, J. G., Skodol, A. E., Shea, M. T.,…Stout, R. L. (2001). Internal consistency, intercriterion overlap, and diagnostic efficiency of criteria sets DSM-IV schizotypal, borderline, avoidant, and obsessive-compulsive personality disorders. *Acta Psychiatrica Scandinavica, 104,* 264–272.

Gunderson, J., Ronningstam, E., & Bodkin, A. (1990). The diagnostic interview for narcissistic patients. *Archives of General Psychiatry, 47,* 676–680.

Gunderson, J., Ronningstam, E., & Smith, L. E. (1994). Narcissistic personality disorder. In T. A. Widiger (Ed.), *DSM-IV sourcebook* (Vol. 1, pp. 745–756). Washington, DC: American Psychiatric Press.

Gunderson, J., Ronningstam, E., & Smith, L. E. (1995). Narcissistic personality disorder. In J. Livesley (Ed.), *The DSM-IV personality disorder diagnoses* (pp. 201–212). New York: Guilford Press.

Heisel, M. J., Links, P. S., Conn, D., van Reekum, R., & Flett, G. L. (2007). Narcissistic personality and vulnerability to late-life suicidality. *American Journal of Geriatric Psychiatry, 15,* 734–741.

Hepper, E. G., Gramzow, R. H., & Sedikides, C. (2010). Individual differences in self-enhancement and self-protection strategies: An integrative analysis. *Journal of Personality, 78,* 781–814.

Holdwick, D. J., Hilsenroth, M. J., Castlebury, F. D., & Blais, M. A. (1998). Identifying the unique and common characteristics among the DSM-IV antisocial, borderline, and narcissistic personality disorders. *Comprehensive Psychiatry, 39,* 277–286.

Hopwood, C. J., Ansell, E. A., Pincus, A. L., Wright, A. G. C., Lukowitsky, M. R., & Roche, M. J. (2011). The circumplex structure of interpersonal sensitivities. *Journal of Personality, 79,* 707–740.

Horowitz, M. (2009). Clinical phenomenology of narcissistic pathology. *Psychiatric Annals, 39,* 124–128.

Kealy, D., & Ogrodniczuk, J. S. (2012). Pathological narcissism: A front-line guide. *Practice: Social Work in Action, 24,* 161–174.

Kealy, D., & Rasmussen, B. (2012). Veiled and vulnerable: The other side of grandiose narcissism. *Clinical Social Work Journal, 40,* 356–366.

Kealy, D., Tsai, M., & Ogrodniczuk, J. S. (2012). Depressive tendencies and pathological narcissism among psychiatric outpatients. *Psychiatry Research, 196,* 157–159.

Kernberg, O. F. (1970). Factors in the psychoanalytic treatment of narcissistic personalities. *Journal of the American Psychoanalytic Association, 18,* 51–85.

Kernberg, O. F. (1984). *Severe personality disorders: Psychotherapeutic strategies.* New Haven, CT: Yale University Press.

Kernberg, O. F. (1988). Object relations theory in clinical practice. *Psychoanalytic Quarterly, 57,* 481–504.

Kernberg, O. F. (1998). Pathological narcissism and narcissistic personality disorder: Theoretical background and diagnostic classification. In E. Ronningstam (Ed.), *Disorders of narcissism: Diagnostic, clinical, and empirical implications* (pp. 29–51). Washington DC: American Psychiatric Press.

Kernberg, O. F. (2007). The almost untreatable narcissistic patient. *Journal of the American Psychoanalytic Association, 55,* 503–539.

Kernberg, O. F. (2009). Narcissistic personality disorders: Part 1. *Psychiatric Annuals, 39,* 105–107, 110, 164–167.

Kernberg, O.F. (2010). Narcissistic personality disorder. In J. F. Clarkin, P. Fonagy, & G. O. Gabbard (Eds.), *Psychodynamic psychotherapy for personality disorders: A clinical handbook* (pp. 257–287). Washington DC: American Psychiatric Press.

Kohut, H. (1971). *The analysis of the self.* New York: International Universities Press.

Kohut, H. (1977). *The restoration of the self.* New York: International Universities Press.

Kohut, H., & Wolf, E. (1978). The disorders of the self and their treatment: An outline. *International Journal of Psychoanalysis, 59,* 413–425.

Kosson, D. S., Kelly, J. C., & White, J. W. (1997). Psychopathy-related traits predict self-reported sexual aggression among college men. *Journal of Interpersonal Violence, 12,* 241–254.

Krizan, Z., & Johar, O. (2012). Envy divides the two faces of narcissism. *Journal of Personality, 80,* 1415–1451.

Lawton, E. M., Shields, A. J., & Oltmanns, T. F. (2011). Five-factor model personality disorder prototypes in a community sample: Self- and informant-reports predicting interview-based DSM diagnoses. *Personality Disorders: Theory, Research, and Treatment, 2,* 279–292.

Lenzenweger, M. F., Johnson, M. D., & Willett, J. (2004). Individual growth curve analysis illuminates stability and change in personality disorder features: The longitudinal study of personality disorders. *Archives of General Psychiatry, 61,* 1015–1024.

Lenzenweger, M. F., Lane, M. C., Loranger, A. W., & Kessler, R. C. (2007). DSM-IV personality disorders in the National Comorbidity Survey Replication. *Biological Psychiatry, 15,* 553–564.

Levy, K. N. (2012). Subtypes, dimensions, levels and mental states in narcissism and narcissistic personality disorder. *Journal of Clinical Psychology, 68,* 886–897.

Levy, K. N., Ellison, W. D., & Reynoso, J. S. (2011). A historical review of narcissism and narcissistic personality. In W. K. Campbell & J. D. Miller (Eds.), *Handbook of narcissism and narcissistic personality disorder: Theoretical approaches, empirical findings, and treatment* (pp. 3–13). Hoboken, NJ: John Wiley & Sons.

Levy, K. N., Reynoso, J. S., Wasserman, R. H., & Clarkin, J. F. (2007). Narcissistic personality disorder. In W. O'Donohue, K. A. Fowler, & S. O. Lilienfeld (Eds.), *Personality disorders: Toward the DSM-V* (pp. 233–277). Thousand Oaks, CA: Sage.

Maples, J. L., Miller, J. D., Wilson, L. F., Seibert, L. A., Few, L. R., & Zeichner, A. (2010). Narcissistic personality disorder and self-esteem: An examination of differential relations with self-report and laboratory-based aggression. *Journal of Research in Personality, 44,* 559–563.

Marčinko, D., Jakšić, N., Ivezić, E., Skočić, M., Suranyi, Z., Lončar, M., & Jakovljević, M. (2014). Pathological narcissism and depressive symptoms in psychiatric outpatients: Mediating role of dysfunctional attitudes. *Journal of Clinical Psychology, 70,* 341–352.

Marissen, M. A. E., Deen, M. L., & Franken, I. H. A. (2012). Disturbed emotion recognition in patients with narcissistic personality disorder. *Psychiatry Research, 198,* 269–273.

Marttunen, M. J., Aro, H. M., & Lönnqvist, J. K. (1993). Precipitant stressors in adolescent suicide. *Journal of the American Academy of Child & Adolescent Psychiatry, 32,* 1178–1183.

Masterson, J. F. (1993). *The emerging self: A developmental, self, and object relations approach to the treatment of the closet narcissistic disorder of the self.* New York: Brunner/Mazel.

Maxwell, K., Donnellan, M. B., Hopwood, C. J., & Ackerman, R. A. (2011). The two faces of Narcissus? An empirical comparison of the Narcissistic Personality Inventory and the Pathological Narcissism Inventory. *Personality and Individual Differences, 50,* 577–582.

McGlashan, T. H., Grilo, C., Sanislow, C. A., Ralevski, E., Morey, L. C., Gunderson, J. G.,…Pagano, M. E. (2005). Two-year prevalence and stability of individual DSM-IV criteria for schizotypal, borderline, avoidant, and obsessive–compulsive personality disorders: Toward a hybrid model of Axis II disorders. *American Journal of Psychiatry, 165,* 883–889.

McGrath, R. E. (2005). Conceptual complexity and construct validity. *Journal of Personality Assessment, 85,* 112–124.

Ménard, K. S., & Pincus, A. L. (2011, June). Predicting interpersonal aggression: Childhood trauma, psychological symptoms, and pathological narcissism. Paper presented at the Society for Interpersonal Theory and Research annual meeting, Zurich, Switzerland.

Ménard, K. S., & Pincus, A. L. (2012). Predicting overt and cyber stalking perpetration by male and female college students. *Journal of Interpersonal Violence, 27*, 2183–2207.

Miller, J. D., & Campbell, W. K. (2008). Comparing clinical and social-personality conceptualizations of narcissism. *Journal of Personality, 76*, 449–476.

Miller, J. D., Dir, A., Gentile, B. Wilson, L., Pryor, L. R., & Campbell, W. K. (2010). Searching for a vulnerable dark triad: Comparing factor 2 psychopathy, vulnerable narcissism, and borderline personality disorder. *Journal of Personality, 78*, 1529–1564.

Miller, J. D., Gaughan, E. T., Pryor, L. R., Kamen, C., & Campbell, W. K. (2009). Is research using the NPI relevant for understanding narcissistic personality disorder? *Journal of Research in Personality, 43*, 482–488.

Miller, J. D., Gentile, B., Wilson, L., & Campbell, W. K. (2013). Grandiose and vulnerable narcissism and the DSM–5 pathological personality trait model. *Journal of Personality Assessment, 95*, 284–290.

Miller, J. D., Hoffman, B., Campbell, W. K., & Pilkonis, P. A. (2008). An examination of the factor structure of DSM-IV narcissistic personality disorder criteria: One or two factors? *Comprehensive Psychiatry, 49*, 141–145.

Miller, J. D., Hoffman, B. J., Gaughan, E. T., Gentile, B., Maples, J., & Campbell, W. K. (2011). Grandiose and vulnerable narcissism: A nomological network analysis. *Journal of Personality, 79*, 1013–1042.

Miller, J. D., Widiger, T. A., & Campbell, W. K. (2010). Narcissistic personality disorder and the DSM-V. *Journal of Abnormal Psychology, 119*, 640–649.

Millon, T. (1981). *Disorders of personality. DSM-III: Axis II.* New York: John Wiley & Sons.

Morey, L. C. (1988a). A psychometric analysis of the DSM-III-R personality disorder criteria. *Journal of Personality Disorders, 2*, 109–124.

Morey, L. C. (1988b). Personality disorders in DSM-III and DSM-III-R: Convergence, coverage, and internal consistency. *American Journal of Psychiatry, 145*, 573–577.

Morey, L. C. (2005). Personality pathology as pathological narcissism. In M. Maj, H. S. Akiskal, J. E. Mezzich, & A. Okasha (Eds.), *Evidence and experience in psychiatry, volume 8: Personality disorders* (pp. 328–331). New York: John Wiley & Sons.

Morey, L. C., & Jones, J. K. (1998). Empirical studies of the construct validity of narcissistic personality disorder. In E. Ronningstam (Ed.), *Disorders of narcissism: Diagnostic, clinical, and empirical implications* (pp. 351–373). Washington DC: American Psychiatric Press.

Morey, L. C., & Ochoa, E. S. (1989). An investigation of adherence to diagnostic criteria: Clinical diagnosis of the DSM-III personality disorders. *Journal of Personality Disorders, 3*, 180–192.

Morey, L. C., & Stagner, B. H. (2012). Narcissistic pathology as core personality dysfunction: Comparing the DSM-IV and DSM-5 proposal for narcissistic personality disorder. *Journal of Clinical Psychology, 68*, 908–921.

Morf, C. C. (2006). Personality reflected in a coherent idiosyncratic interplay of intra- and interpersonal self-regulatory processes. *Journal of Personality, 76*, 1527–1556.

Morf, C. C., Horvath, S., & Torchetti, T. (2011). Narcissistic self-enhancement: Tales of (successful?) self-portrayal. In M. D. Alicke & C. Sedikides (Eds.), *Handbook of self-enhancement and self-protection* (pp. 399–424). New York: Guilford Press.

Morf, C., & Rhodewalt, F. (2001). Unraveling the paradoxes of narcissism: A dynamic self-regulatory processing model. *Psychological Inquiry, 12*, 177–196.

Morf, C. C., Torchetti, T., & Schürch, E. (2011). Narcissism from the perspective of the dynamic self-regulatory processing model. In W. K. Campbell & J. D. Miller (Eds.), *The handbook of narcissism and narcissistic personality disorder: Theoretical approaches, empirical findings, and treatment* (pp. 56–70). Hoboken, NJ: John Wiley & Sons.

Mouilso, E. R., & Calhoun, K. S. (2012). A mediation model of role of sociosexuality in associations between narcissism, psychopathy, and sexual aggression. *Psychology of Violence, 2*, 16–27.

Murray, H. A. (1943). *Thematic Apperception Test.* Cambridge, MA: Harvard University Press.

Nestadt, G., Di, C., Samuels, J. F., Bienvenu, O. J., Reti, I. M., Costa, P., Eaton, W. W., & Bandeen-Roche, K. (2010). The stability of DSM personality disorders over twelve to eighteen years. *Journal of Psychiatric Research, 44*, 1–7.

Ogrodniczuk, J. S. (2013). *Understanding and treating pathological narcissism.* Washington, DC: American Psychological Association.

Ogrodniczuk, J. S., Piper, W. E., Joyce, A. S., Steinberg, P. I., & Duggal, S. (2009). Interpersonal problems associated with narcissism among psychiatric outpatients. *Journal of Psychiatric Research*, 43, 837–842.

Okada, R. (2010). The relationship between vulnerable narcissism and aggression in Japanese undergraduate students. *Personality and Individual Differences*, 49, 113–118.

Orbach, I. (1997). A taxonomy of factors related to suicidal behavior. *Clinical Psychology: Theory and Research*, 4, 208–224.

Oulis, P., Lykouras, L., Hatzimanolis, J., & Tomaras, V. (1997). Comorbidity of DSM-III-R personality disorders in schizophrenic and unipolar mood disorders: A comparative study. *European Psychiatry*, 12, 316–318.

Ovid. (1958). *The metamorphoses* (H. Gregory, Trans.). New York: Viking Press. (Original work published in 8 C.E.)

Paris, J. (2014). Modernity and narcissistic personality disorder. *Personality Disorders: Theory, Research, and Treatment*, 5, 220–226.

Paulhus, D. L. (2001). Normal narcissism: Two minimalist accounts. *Psychological Inquiry*, 12, 228–230.

PDM Task Force. (2006). *Psychodynamic diagnostic manual*. Silver Spring, MD: Alliance of Psychoanalytic Organizations.

Pincus, A. L. (2011). Some comments on nomology, diagnostic process, and narcissistic personality disorder in DSM-5 proposal for personality and personality disorders. *Personality Disorders: Theory, Research, and Treatment*, 2, 41–53.

Pincus, A.L. (2013). The Pathological Narcissism Inventory. In J. S. Ogrodniczuk (Ed.), *Understanding and treating pathological narcissism* (pp. 93–110). Washington, DC: American Psychological Association.

Pincus, A. L., Ansell, E. B., Pimentel, C. A., Cain, N. M., Wright, A. G. C., & Levy, K. N. (2009). Initial construction and validation of the Pathological Narcissism Inventory. *Psychological Assessment*, 21, 365–379.

Pincus, A. L., Cain, N. M., & Wright, A. G. C. (2014). Narcissistic grandiosity and narcissistic vulnerability in psychotherapy. *Personality Disorders: Theory, Research, and Treatment*. Available online in advance of publication, doi:10.1037/per0000031.

Pincus, A. L., Conroy, D. E., Hyde, A. L., & Ram, N. (2010, May). Pathological narcissism and the dynamics of self-conscious emotions. Paper presented at the Association for Psychological Science annual meeting, Boston, MA.

Pincus, A. L., & Lukowitsky, M. R. (2010). Pathological narcissism and narcissistic personality disorder. *Annual Review of Clinical Psychology*, 6, 421–446.

Pincus, A. L., & Roche, M. J. (2011). Narcissistic grandiosity and narcissistic vulnerability. In W. K. Campbell & J. D. Miller (Eds.), *Handbook of narcissism and narcissistic personality disorder: Theoretical approaches, empirical findings, and treatment* (pp. 31–40). Hoboken, NJ: John Wiley & Sons.

Rank, O. (1911). A contribution to narcissism. *Jahrbuch für Psychoanalytische und Psychopathologische Forschungen*, 3, 401–426.

Raskin, R. N., & Hall, C. S. (1981). The Narcissistic Personality Inventory: Alternate form reliability and further evidence of construct validity. *Journal of Personality Assessment*, 45, 159–162.

Regier, D. A., Narrow, W. E., Kuhl, E. A., & Kupfer, D. J. (2009). The conceptual development of DSM-V. *American Journal of Psychiatry*, 166, 645–650.

Reidy, D. E., Zeichner, A., Foster, J. D., & Martinez, M. A. (2008). Effects of narcissistic entitlement and exploitativenedd on human physical aggression. *Personality and Individual Differences*, 44, 865–875.

Ritter, K., Dziobek, I., Preissler, S., Ruter, A., Vater, A., Fydrich T.,…Roepke, S. (2011). Lack of empathy in patients with Narcissistic Personality Disorder. *Psychiatry Research*, 187, 241–247.

Roche, M. J., Pincus, A. P., Conroy, D. E., Hyde, A. L., & Ram, N. (2013). Pathological narcissism and interpersonal behavior in daily life. *Personality Disorders: Theory, Research, and Treatment*, 4, 315–323.

Roche, M. J., Pincus, A. L., Lukowitsky, M. R., Ménard, K. S., & Conroy, D. E. (2013). An integrative approach to the assessment of narcissism. *Journal of Personality Assessment*, 95, 237–248.

Ronningstam, E. (1996). Pathological narcissism and narcissistic personality disorder in Axis I disorders. *Harvard Review of Psychiatry*, 39, 326–340.

Ronningstam, E. (2005a). *Identifying and understanding narcissistic personality*. New York: Oxford University Press.

Ronningstam, E. (2005b). Narcissistic personality disorder: A review. In M. Maj, H. S. Akiskal, J. E. Mezzich, & A. Okasha (Eds.), *Evidence and experience in psychiatry, volume 8: Personality disorders* (pp. 277–327). New York: John Wiley & Sons.

Ronningstam, E. (2009). Narcissistic personality disorder: Facing DSM-V. *Psychiatric Annals*, 39, 111–121.

Ronningstam, E. (2011a). Narcissistic personality disorder. *Personality and Mental Health*, 5, 222–227.

Ronningstam, E. (2011b). Narcissistic personality disorder: A clinical perspective. *Journal of Psychiatric Practice*, 17, 89–99.

Ronningstam, E. (2011c). Narcissistic personality disorder in DSM-V: In support of retaining a significant diagnosis. *Journal of Personality Disorders*, 25, 248–259.

Ronningstam, E. (2011d). Psychoanalytic theories on narcissism and narcissistic personality. In W. K. Campbell & J. D. Miller (Eds.), *Handbook of narcissism and narcissistic personality disorder: Theoretical approaches, empirical findings, and treatment* (pp. 41–55). Hoboken, NJ: John Wiley & Sons.

Ronningstam, E. (2012). Alliance building and narcissistic personality disorder. *Journal of Clinical Psychology*, 68, 943–953.

Ronningstam, E., & Gunderson, J. (1990). Identifying criteria for NPD. *American Journal of Psychiatry*, 147, 918–922.

Ronningstam, E., Gunderson, J., & Lyons, M. (1995). Changes in pathological narcissism. *American Journal of Psychiatry*, 152, 253–257.

Ronningstam, E., & Maltsberger, J. T. (1998). Pathological narcissism and sudden suicide related collapse. *Suicide and Life Threatening Behavior*, 28, 261–271.

Ronningstam, E., & Weinberg, I. (2009) Contributing factors to suicide in narcissistic personalities. *Directions in Psychiatry*, 29, 317–329.

Russ, E., Shedler, J., Bradley, R., & Westen, D. (2008). Refining the construct of narcissistic personality disorder: Diagnostic criteria and subtypes. *American Journal of Psychiatry*, 165, 1473–1481.

Samuel, D. B., Hopwood, C. J., Ansell, E. B., Morey, L. C., Sanislow, C. A., Markowitz, J. C.,...Grilo, C. M. (2011). Comparing the temporal stability of self-report and interview assessed personality disorder. *Journal of Abnormal Psychology*, 120, 670–680.

Schulze, L., Dziobek, I., Vater, A., Heekeren, H.R., Bajbouh, M., Renneberg, B.,...Roepke, S. (2013). Gray matter abnormalities in patients with narcissistic personality disorder. *Journal of Psychiatric Research*, 47, 1363–1369.

Seah, S. L., & Ang., R. P. (2008). Differential correlates of reactive and proactive aggression in Asian adolescents: Relations to narcissism, anxiety, schizotypal traits, and peer relations. *Aggressive Behavior*, 34, 553–562.

Simonsen, E., Haahr, U., Mortensen, E. L., Friis, S., Johannessen, J. O., Larsen, T. K.,...Vaglum, P. (2008). Personality disorders in first episode psychosis. *Personality and Mental Health*, 2, 230–239.

Simonsen, S., & Simonsen, E. (2011). Comorbidity between narcissistic personality disorder and Axis I diagnoses. In W. K. Campbell & J. D. Miller (Eds.), *The handbook of narcissism and narcissistic personality disorder: Theoretical approaches, empirical findings, and treatments* (pp. 239–247). Hoboken, NJ: John Wiley & Sons.

Skodol, A. E. (2012). Personality disorders in DSM-5. *Annual Review of Clinical Psychology*, 8, 317–344.

Skodol, A. E., Bender, D. S., Morey, L. C., Clark, L. A., Oldham, J. M., Alarcon, R. D.,...Siever, L. J. (2011). Personality disorder types proposed for DSM-5. *Journal of Personality Disorders*, 25, 136–169.

Stern, B. L., Yeomans, F., Diamond, D., & Kernberg, O. F. (2013). Transference-focused psychotherapy for narcissistic personality. In J. S. Ogrodniczuk (Ed.), *Understanding and treating pathological narcissism* (pp. 235–252). Washington DC: American Psychological Association.

Stinson, F. S., Dawson, D. A., Goldstein, R. B., Chou, S. P., Huang, B., Smith, S. M.,...Grant, B. F. (2008). Prevalence, correlates, disability, and comorbidity of DSM-IV narcissistic personality disorder: Results from the Wave 2 National Epidemiologic Survey on Alcohol and Related Conditions. *Journal of Clinical Psychiatry*, 69, 1033–1045.

Stone, M. H. (1998). Normal narcissism: An etiological and ethological perspective. In E. Ronningstam (Ed.), *Disorders of narcissism: Diagnostic, clinical, and empirical implications* (pp. 7–28). Washington, DC: American Psychiatric Publishing.

Thomaes, S., Bushman, B. J., Stegge, H., & Olthof, T. (2008). Trumping shame by blasts of noise: Narcissism, self-esteem, shame, and aggression in young adolescents. *Child Development*, 79, 1792–1801.

Thomas, K. M., Wright, A. G. C., Lukowitsky, M. R., Donnellan, M. B., & Hopwood, C. J. (2012). Evidence for the criterion validity and clinical utility of the pathological narcissism inventory. *Assessment*, 19, 135–145.

Torgersen, S., Kringlen, E., & Cramer, V. (2001). The prevalence of personality disorders in a community sample. *Archives of General Psychiatry*, 58, 590–596.

Tritt, S. M., Ryder, A. G., Ring, A. J., & Pincus, A. L. (2010) Pathological narcissism and the depressive temperament. *Journal of Affective Disorders*. 122, 280–284.

Twenge, J. M., & Campbell, W. K. (2003). "Isn't it fun to get the respect we're going to deserve?" Narcissism, social rejection, and aggression. *Personality and Social Psychology Bulletin, 29,* 261–272.

Vater, A., Ritter, K., Schröder-Abé, M., Schutz, A., Lammers, C. H., Bosson, J. K., & Roepke, S. (2013). When grandiosity and vulnerability collide: Implicit and explicit self-esteem in patients with narcissistic personality disorder. *Journal of Behavior Therapy and Experimental Psychiatry, 44,* 37–47.

Vater, A., Schröder-Abé, M., Ritter, K., Renneberg, B., Schulze, L., Bosson, J.K., & Roepke, S. (2013). The Narcissistic Personality Inventory: A useful tool for assessing pathological narcissism? Evidence from patients with narcissistic personality disorder. *Journal of Personality Assessment, 95,* 301–308.

Weikel, K. A., Avara, R. M., Hanson, C.A., & Kater, H. (2010). College adjustment difficulties and overt and covert forms of narcissism. *Journal of College Counseling, 13,* 100–110.

Weise, K. L., & Tuber, S. (2004) The self and object representations of narcissistically disturbed children. *Psychoanalytic Psychology, 21,* 244–258.

Westen, D. (1995). SCORS-Q for projective stories, Addendum. Unpublished manuscript, Harvard Medical School at Cambridge, MA.

Westen, D. (1997). Divergences between clinical and research methods for assessing personality disorders: Implications for research and the evolution of Axis II. *American Journal of Psychiatry, 154,* 895–903.

Widiger, T. A. (2011). The comorbidity of narcissistic personality disorder with other DSM-IV personality disorders. In W. K. Campbell & J. D. Miller (Eds.), *Handbook of narcissism and narcissistic personality disorder: Theoretical approaches, empirical findings, and treatment* (pp. 248–260). Hoboken, NJ: John Wiley & Sons.

Widman, L., & McNulty, J. K. (2010). Sexual narcissism and the perpetration of sexual aggression. *Archives of Sexual Behavior, 39,* 926–939.

Wright, A.G.C. (2014). Narcissism and its discontents. *Personality Disorders: Theory, Research, and Treatment, 5,* 232–233.

Wright, A. G. C., Lukowitsky, M. R., Pincus, A. L., & Conroy, D. E. (2010). The higher-order factor structure and gender invariance of the pathological narcissism inventory. *Assessment, 17,* 467–483.

Zeigler-Hill, V., & Besser, A. (2013). A glimpse behind the mask: Facets of narcissism and feelings of self-worth. *Journal of Personality Assessment, 95,* 249–260.

Zeigler-Hill, V., Green, B. A., Arnau, R. C., Sisemore, T. B., & Meyers, E. M. (2011). Trouble ahead, trouble behind: Narcissism and early maladaptive schemas. *Journal of Behavior Therapy and Experimental Psychiatry, 42,* 96–103.

Zimmerman, M., Rothschild, L., & Chelminski, I. (2005). The prevalence of DSM-IV personality disorders in psychiatric outpatients. *American Journal of Psychiatry, 162,* 1911–1918.

Index

NOTE: Page numbers in *italics* indicate figures.